Asset Valuation and Equity

CFA® PROGRAM CURRICULUM • VOLUME 4

LEVEL II
2008

Printed in the United States of America

10 9 8 7 6 5 4 3 2

ISBN 0-536-34238-5

2006160832

AG/JS

Please visit our web site at *www.pearsoncustom.com*

PEARSON CUSTOM PUBLISHING
501 Boylston Street, Suite 900, Boston, MA 02116
A Pearson Education Company

CONTENTS

www.cfainstitute.org/toolkit—Your online preparation resource

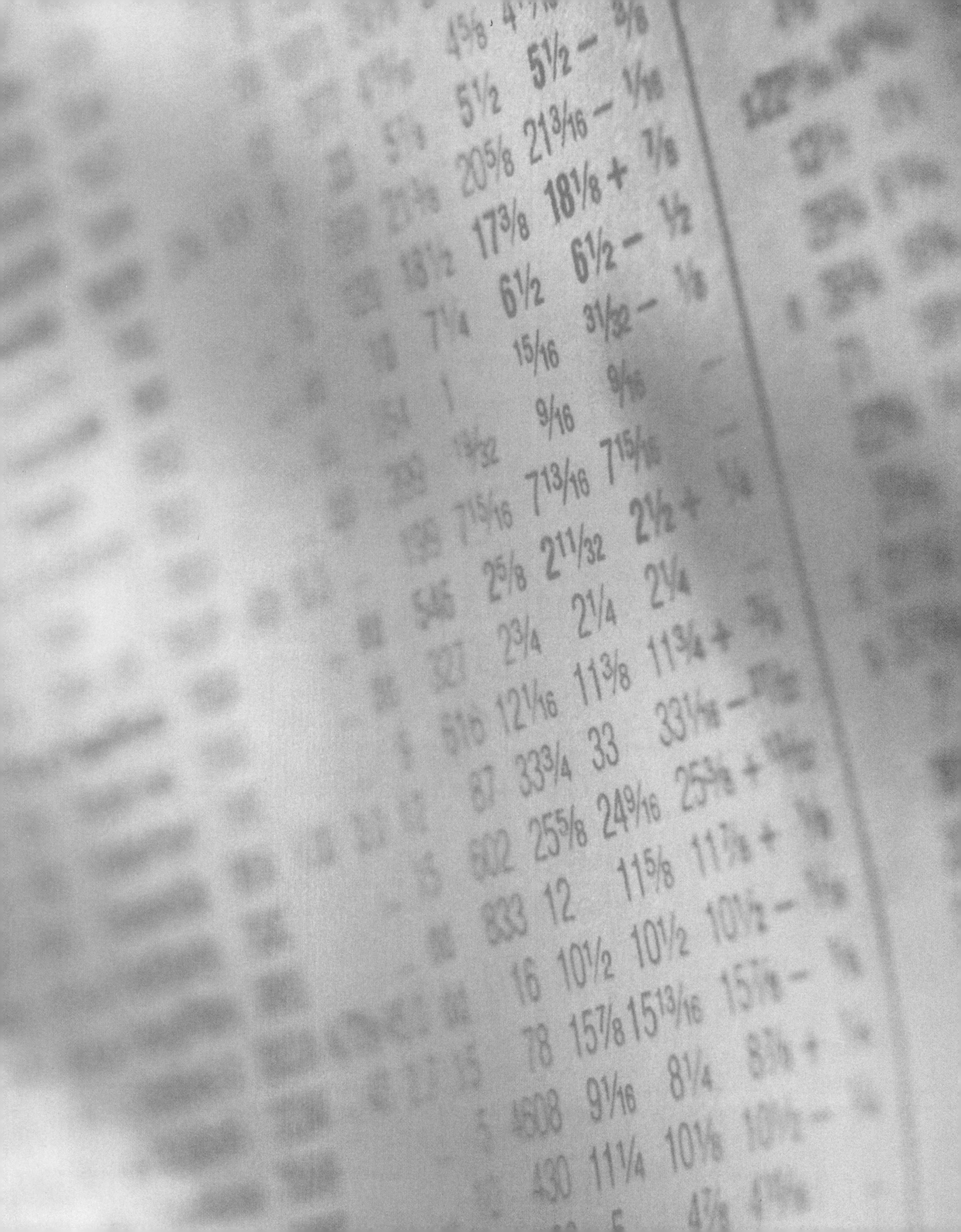

4⅝ 4⅛ · ³⁄₈

5½ 5½ — ⅜

20⅝ 21³⁄₁₆ — ⅛

17⅜ **18⅛ +** ⅞

6½ **6½ —**

7¼ 3¹⁄₃₂ — ⅛

15⁄16

9⁄16 9⅝

7¹⁵⁄₁₆ 7¹³⁄₁₆ 7¹⁵⁄₁₆

2⅝ 2¹¹⁄₃₂ **2½ +**

2¾ 2¼ 2¼

12¹⁄₁₆ 11⅜ 11¾ +

33¾ 33 33¼ —

25⅝ 24⁹⁄₁₆ 25⅜ +

12 11⅝ 11⅞ +

10½ 10½ 10½ —

15⅞ 15¹³⁄₁₆ 15⅞ —

9¹⁄₁₆ 8¼ 8⅝ +

11¼ 10⅛

HOW TO USE THE CFA PROGRAM CURRICULUM

Congratulations on passing Level I of the Chartered Financial Analyst (CFA®) Program. This exciting and rewarding program of study reflects your desire to become a serious investment professional. You are participating in a program noted for its requirement of ethics and breadth of knowledge, skills, and abilities.

The credential you seek is respected around the world as a mark of accomplishment and dedication. Each level of the program represents a distinct achievement in professional development. Successful completion of the program is rewarded with membership in a prestigious global community of investment professionals. CFA charterholders are dedicated to life-long learning and maintaining currency with the ever-changing dynamics of a challenging profession.

The CFA examination measures your degree of mastery of the assigned CFA Program curriculum. Effective study and preparation based on that curriculum are keys to your success on the examination.

Curriculum Development

The CFA Program curriculum is grounded in the practice of the investment profession. CFA Institute regularly conducts a practice analysis survey of investment professionals around the world to determine the knowledge, skills, and abilities that are relevant to the profession. The survey results define the Candidate Body of Knowledge (CBOK™), an inventory of knowledge and responsibilities expected of the investment management professional at the level of a new CFA charterholder. The survey also determines how much emphasis each of the major topic areas receives on the CFA examinations.

A committee made up of practicing charterholders, in conjunction with CFA Institute staff, designs the CFA Program curriculum to deliver the CBOK to candidates. The examinations, also written by practicing charterholders, are designed to allow you to demonstrate your mastery of the CBOK as set forth in the CFA Program curriculum. As you structure your personal study program, you should emphasize mastery of the CBOK and the practical application of that knowledge. For more information on the practice analysis, CBOK, and development of the CFA Program curriculum, please visit www.cfainstitute.org/toolkit.

Organization

The Level II CFA Program curriculum is organized into 10 topic areas. Each topic area begins with a brief statement of the material and the depth of knowledge expected.

Each topic area is then divided into one or more study sessions. These study sessions—18 sessions in the Level II curriculum—should form the basic structure of your reading and preparation.

Each study session includes a statement of its structure and objective, and is further divided into specific reading assignments. The outline on the inside front cover of each volume illustrates the organization of these 18 study sessions.

The reading assignments are the basis for all examination questions, and are selected or developed specifically to teach the CBOK. These readings are drawn from textbook chapters, professional journal articles, research analyst reports, CFA Program-commissioned content, and cases. Many readings include problems and solutions as well as appendices to help you learn.

xiii

Reading-specific Learning Outcome Statements (LOS) are listed in the pages introducing each study session as well as at the beginning of each reading. These LOS indicate what you should be able to accomplish after studying the reading. We encourage you to review how to properly use LOS, and the descriptions of commonly used LOS "command words," at www.cfainstitute.org/toolkit. The command words signal the depth of learning you are expected to achieve from the reading. You should use the LOS to guide and focus your study, as each examination question is based on an assigned reading and one or more LOS. However, the readings provide context for the LOS and enable you to apply a principle or concept in a variety of scenarios. It is important to study the whole of a required reading.

Features of the Curriculum

▶ **Required vs. Optional Segments** - You should read all of the pages for an assigned reading. In some cases, however, we have reprinted an entire chapter or article and marked those parts of the reading that are not required as "optional." The CFA examination is based only on the required segments, and the optional segments are included only when they might help you to better understand the required segments (by seeing the required material in its full context). When an optional segment begins, you will see an icon and a solid vertical bar in the outside margin that will continue until the optional segment ends, accompanied by another icon. *Unless the material is specifically marked as optional, you should assume it is required.* Keep in mind that the optional material is provided strictly for your convenience and will not be tested. You should rely on the required segments and the reading-specific LOS in preparing for the examination.

▶ **Problems/Solutions** - *All questions and problems in the readings as well as their solutions (which are provided in an appendix at the end of each volume) are required material.* When appropriate, we have included problems after the readings to demonstrate practical application and reinforce your understanding of the concepts presented. The questions and problems are designed to help you learn these concepts. Many of the questions are in the same style and format as the actual CFA examination and will give you test-taking experience in that format. Examination questions that come from a past CFA examination are marked with the CFA logo in the margin.

▶ **Margins** - The wide margins in each volume provide space for your note-taking.

▶ **Two-color Format** - To enrich the visual appeal and clarity of the exhibits, tables, and text, the curriculum is printed in a two-color format.

▶ **Six-volume Structure** - For portability of the curriculum, the material is spread over six volumes.

▶ **Glossary and Index** - For your convenience, we have printed a comprehensive glossary and index in each volume. Throughout the curriculum, a **bolded blue** word in a reading denotes a term defined in the glossary.

Designing Your Personal Study Program

Create a Schedule - An orderly, systematic approach to examination preparation is critical. You should dedicate a consistent block of time every week to reading and studying. Complete all reading assignments and the associated problems

and solutions in each study session. Review the LOS both before and after you study each reading to ensure that you have mastered the applicable content and can demonstrate the knowledge, skill, or ability described by the LOS and the assigned reading.

CFA Institute estimates that you will need to devote a minimum of 10–15 hours per week for 18 weeks to study the assigned readings. Allow a minimum of one week for each study session, and plan to complete them all at least 30–45 days prior to the examination. This schedule will allow you to spend the final four to six weeks before the examination reviewing the assigned material and taking multiple online sample examinations.

At CFA Institute, we believe that candidates need to commit to a *minimum* of 250 hours reading and reviewing the curriculum, and taking online sample examinations, to master the material. This recommendation, however, may substantially underestimate the hours needed for appropriate examination preparation depending on your individual circumstances, relevant experience, and academic background.

You will undoubtedly adjust your study time to conform to your own strengths and weaknesses, and your educational and professional background. You will probably spend more time on some study sessions than on others. You should allow ample time for both in-depth study of all topic areas and additional concentration on those topic areas for which you feel least prepared.

Candidate Preparation Toolkit - We have created the online toolkit to provide a single comprehensive location for resources and guidance for candidate preparation. In addition to in-depth information on study program planning, the CFA Program curriculum, and the online sample examinations, the toolkit also contains curriculum errata, printable study session outlines, sample examination questions, and more. Errata identified in the curriculum are corrected and listed periodically in the errata listing in the toolkit. We encourage you to use the toolkit as your central preparation resource during your tenure as a candidate. Visit the toolkit at www.cfainstitute.org/toolkit.

Online Sample Examinations - After completing your study of the assigned curriculum, use the CFA Institute online sample examinations to measure your knowledge of the topics and to improve your examination-taking skills. After each question, you will receive immediate feedback noting the correct response and indicating the assigned reading for further study. The sample examinations are designed by the same people who create the actual CFA examinations, and reflect the question formats, topics, and level of difficulty of the actual CFA examinations, in a timed environment. Aggregate data indicate that the CFA examination pass rate was higher among candidates who took one or more online sample examinations than among candidates who did not take the online sample examinations. For more information on the online sample examinations, please visit www.cfainstitute.org/toolkit.

Preparatory Providers - After you enroll in the CFA Program, you may receive numerous solicitations for preparatory courses and review materials. Although preparatory courses and notes may be helpful to some candidates, you should view these resources as *supplements* to the assigned CFA Program curriculum. The CFA examinations reference only the CFA Institute assigned curriculum—no preparatory course or review course materials are consulted or referenced.

Before you decide on a supplementary prep course, do some research. Determine the experience and expertise of the instructors, the accuracy and currency of their content, the delivery method for their materials, and the provider's claims of success. Most importantly, make sure the provider is in compliance with the CFA Institute Prep Provider Guidelines Program. Three years of prep course products can be a significant investment, so make sure you're getting a sufficient return. Just remember, there are no shortcuts to success on the CFA examinations. Prep products can enhance your learning experience, but the CFA curriculum is the key to success. For more information on the Prep Provider Guidelines Program, visit www.cfainstitute.org/cfaprog/resources/prepcourse.html.

SUMMARY

Every question on the CFA examination is based on specific pages in the required readings and on one or more LOS. Frequently, an examination question is also tied to a specific example highlighted within a reading or to a specific end-of-reading question/problem and its solution. To make effective use of the curriculum, please remember these key points:

1. All pages printed in the Custom Curriculum are required reading for the examination except for occasional sections marked as optional. You may read optional pages as background, but you will not be tested on them.

2. All questions/problems printed at the end of readings and their solutions in the appendix to each volume are required study material for the examination.

3. Make appropriate use of the CFA Candidate Toolkit, the online sample examinations, and preparatory courses and review materials.

4. Commit sufficient study time to cover the 18 study sessions, review the materials, and take sample examinations.

Feedback

At CFA Institute, we are committed to delivering a comprehensive and rigorous curriculum for the development of competent, ethically grounded investment professionals. We rely on candidate and member feedback as we work to incorporate content, design, and packaging improvements. You can be assured that we will continue to listen to your suggestions. Please send any comments or feedback to curriculum@cfainstitute.org. Ongoing improvements in the curriculum will help you prepare for success on the upcoming examinations, and for a lifetime of learning as a serious investment professional.

ASSET VALUATION

STUDY SESSION

Study Session 10   Valuation Concepts

STUDY SESSION 10
ASSET VALUATION:
Valuation Concepts

This study session examines the well-established methodologies of security valuation, the process an analyst uses in applying these models, and the limitations of each. The reading on markets and instruments compares the characteristics of markets around the world.

READING ASSIGNMENTS

Reading 36   A Note on Asset Valuation
Reading 37   The Equity Valuation Process
Reading 38   Equity: Markets and Instruments
Reading 39   Capital Markets and the Economy

LEARNING OUTCOMES

Reading 36: A Note on Asset Valuation

The candidate should be able to explain how the classic works on asset valuation by Graham and Dodd and John Burr Williams are reflected in modern techniques of equity and fixed income valuation.

Reading 37: The Equity Valuation Process

The candidate should be able to:

a. define valuation and discuss the uses of valuation models;

b. contrast quantitative and qualitative factors in valuation;

c. discuss the importance of quality of inputs in valuation;

d. discuss the importance of the interpretation of footnotes to accounting statements and other disclosures;

e. calculate alpha;

f. contrast the going-concern and non-going-concern assumptions in valuation;

g. contrast absolute valuation models to relative valuation models;

h. discuss the role of ownership perspective in valuation.

3

Reading 38: Equity: Markets and Instruments
The candidate should be able to:

a. explain the origins of different national market organizations;

b. differentiate between an order-driven market and a price-driven market, and explain the risks and advantages of each;

c. calculate the impact of different national taxes on the return of an international investment;

d. discuss the various components of execution costs (i.e., commissions and fees, market impact, and opportunity cost) and explain ways to reduce execution costs, and discuss the advantages and disadvantages of each;

e. describe an American Depositary Receipt (ADR), and differentiate among the various forms of ADRs in terms of trading and information supplied by the listed company;

f. explain why firms choose to be listed abroad and calculate the cost tradeoff between buying shares listed abroad and buying ADRs;

g. state the determinants of the value of a closed-end country fund;

h. discuss the advantages of exchange traded funds (ETFs) and explain the pricing of international ETFs in relation to their net asset value (NAV);

i. discuss the advantages and disadvantages of the various alternatives to direct international investing.

Reading 39: Capital Markets and the Economy
The candidate should be able to:

a. describe how the innovations of Mortgage Backed Securities (MBS) and inter-state banking have improved capital market efficiency and how that impacts economic growth;

b. explain how legal, regulatory, and structural issues affect MBS optionality, regulatory restrictions on credit quality, and index-based investing;

c. review the changes in capital markets that have led to a shift from corporate credit spreads based on Treasuries to credit spreads linked to swaps.

A NOTE ON ASSET VALUATION

by George H. Troughton

LEARNING OUTCOME

The candidate should be able to explain how the classic works on asset valuation by Graham and Dodd and John Burr Williams are reflected in modern techniques of equity and fixed income valuation.

In the 1940s, Benjamin Graham, often called the dean of security analysis, began championing the idea of a professional rating for security analysts. In the premier issue of the *Analysts Journal* (now the *Financial Analysts Journal*) in January 1945, Graham summarized the issue as follows: "The crux of the question is whether security analysis as a calling has enough of the professional attribute to justify the requirement that its practitioners present to the public evidence of fitness for their work."[1] It took almost two decades to decide that question in the affirmative, but in June of 1963, some 300 security analysts sat for the examination that would earn them the designation of Chartered Financial Analyst.

In the first decade of the CFA Study Program, the primary valuation text for Level II candidates was the fourth edition of the (by then) classic *Security Analysis*, co-authored by Benjamin Graham and his Columbia Business School colleague David Dodd. That epic work stressed a philosophy of investing centered on the concept of "intrinsic value."

In their early readings, Graham and Dodd discussed the common elements of analysis that applied to various asset classes. The following discussions present some of Graham and Dodd's philosophy to today's candidate. In their view, distinguishing investment from speculation is essential:

> . . . investment is grounded on the past whereas speculation looks primarily to the future. But this statement is far from complete. Both investment and speculation

---

[1] Nancy Regan, *The Institute of Chartered Financial Analysts: A Twenty-Five Year History* (Charlottesville, VA: The Institute of Chartered Financial Analysts, 1987), p. 5.

5

must meet the test of the future; they are subject to its vicissitudes and are judged by its verdict. But what we have said about the analyst and the future applies equally well to the concept of investment. For investment, the future is something to be guarded against rather than to be profited from. If the future brings improvement, so much the better; but investment as such cannot be founded in any important degree upon the expectation of improvement. Speculation, on the other hand, may always properly—and often soundly—derive its basis and its justi-fication from prospective developments that differ from past performance.[2]

Graham and Dodd stipulated that investing, as opposed to speculating, requires the purchase of leading issues, such as growth stocks, at prices within a range of their intrinsic value or the purchase of secondary issues, such as **cyclical stocks** and medium quality bonds, at bargain prices. Intrinsic value is to be determined independently of market price. The most important factor in deter-mining a security's intrinsic value is a forecast of "earning power."

An additional criterion that distinguished investment from speculation was that the investment asset's earning power should provide a margin of safety. When analyzing bonds and preferred stock, the analyst was to determine whether the securities had a sufficient earning power in excess of interest and preferred **stock dividend** requirements. When analyzing common stocks, the analyst was to forecast earning power and multiply that prediction by an appropriate capitaliza-tion factor. Earning power was the *unifying* factor in determining the attractive-ness of all securities from the highest-grade bond down to the secondary common stocks that were considered investment opportunities because their prices were well below indicated minimum intrinsic values. In investing, diversification was counted on to offset the recognized risk of individual securities.

Graham and Dodd applied their philosophy to the leading asset classes at that time—common stocks, preferred stocks, high-grade fixed-income securities, sen-ior securities of questionable quality, and warrants. In the decades that followed the publication of the last revision of Graham and Dodd's *Security Analysis* in 1962, asset classes expanded rapidly and the Level II CFA curriculum changed to reflect a wide array of assets. The asset valuation curriculum now includes readings from several sources rather than one primary text. Equity analysis, which traditionally centered on common stocks, now includes such securities as real estate, venture capital, and closely held securities. In addition, whereas the analysis of fixed-income securities once centered on credit analysis, much of the fixed-income curriculum now focuses on structured securities such as asset-backed securities. Derivative securities—options, futures, forwards, and swaps—are used for both speculation and to modify the risk and return characteristics of both debt and equity securities.

In the twenty-first century, candidates naturally tend to regard the invest-ment valuation process as segmented, with peculiar terminology and techniques associated with particular assets. In the study sessions that follow, the candidate should realize that certain general principles underlie the **valuation process** regardless of asset class. The readings in corporate finance, for example, take an "inside the company" look at corporate financial performance, with emphasis on capital budgeting, leverage, cost of capital, dividend policy, and mergers and restructurings. The Porter and Hooke readings focus on industry and company factors. All of these methodologies are related to Graham and Dodd's estimate of earning power.

[2] Benjamin Graham, David L. Dodd, and Sidney Cottle, *Security Analysis*, 4th edition (New York McGraw-Hill, 1962), p 52.

The Fabozzi fixed income valuation readings supplement Graham and Dodd's emphasis on credit analysis with a valuation framework that includes **term structure**, interest rate volatility, and embedded options.

The Stowe, Robinson, Pinto, and McLeavey readings on equity valuation and the Fabozzi readings on fixed income valuation reinforce Graham and Dodd's philosophy by emphasizing the common elements in determining the value of various asset classes. These readings emphasize that valuation models are universal, not country specific, and as such they are also applicable to markets outside the United States. Although Stowe, et al. sometimes use different terminology (such as free cash flow to firm and free cash flow to equity) in the valuation process, their methodology is consistent with Graham and Dodd's approach of determining whether earning power is sufficient to provide a margin of safety. In their reading on **price multiples**, Stowe et al. revive Graham and Dodd's justifiable multiple approach.

Another work, John Burr Williams' *The Theory of Investment Value*,[3] used a financial technique called discounting that was incorporated in the CFA Program within its first decade. Williams proposed that a share of common stock had an intrinsic value that could be estimated by calculating the present value of all future dividends per share. Candidates will find that Stowe et al. refine the discounted cash flow technique.

Taken together, Graham and Dodd, and John Burr Williams provided the core of the equity valuation study sessions in the early CFA Candidate Program. This work, sometimes called "blocking and tackling" is continued and updated in the readings currently assigned in the Program.

To some extent, then, as the CFA candidate curriculum approaches its sixth decade, things have come full circle.

---

[3] John Burr Williams, *The Theory of Investment Value* (Cambridge: Harvard University Press, c1938).

4⅛ +

5½ 5½ −

5½ 20⅝ 21³/₁₆ − ¹/₁₆

17⅜ 18⅛ + ⅞

6½ 6½ 6½ − ½

7¼ 31/32 − ¹/₁₆

15/16

1 9/16 9/16

5/32 9/16

7¹¹/₁₆ 7¹³/₁₆ 7¹⁵/₁₆

2⅝ 2¹¹/₃₂ 2½ +

2¾ 2¼ 2¼

6⅛ 12¹/₁₆ 11⅜ 11¾ +

33¾ 33 33¹/₁₆ −

25⅝ 24⁹/₁₆ 25⅜ +

12 11⅝ 11⅞ +

16 10½ 10½ 10½ −

78 15⅞ 15¹³/₁₆ 15⅞ −

508 9¹/₁₆ 8¼ 8⅛ +

430 11¼ 10⅛ 10⅛

5 4⅞

THE EQUITY VALUATION PROCESS

by John D. Stowe, Thomas R. Robinson, Jerald E. Pinto, and
Dennis W. McLeavey

LEARNING OUTCOMES

The candidate should be able to:

a. define valuation and discuss the uses of valuation models;

b. contrast quantitative and qualitative factors in valuation;

c. discuss the importance of quality of inputs in valuation;

d. discuss the importance of the interpretation of footnotes to accounting statements and other disclosures;

e. calculate alpha;

f. contrast the going-concern and non-going-concern assumptions in valuation;

g. contrast absolute valuation models to relative valuation models;

h. discuss the role of ownership perspective in valuation.

INTRODUCTION 1

Every day thousands of participants in the investment profession—investors, portfolio managers, regulators, researchers—face a common and often perplexing question: What is the value of a particular asset? The answers to this question usually determine success or failure in achieving investment objectives. For one group of those participants—equity analysts—the question and its potential answers are particularly critical, for determining the value of an ownership stake is at the heart of their professional activities and decisions. To determine value received for money paid, to determine relative value—the prospective differences in risk-adjusted return offered by different stocks at current market prices—the

Jan R. Squires, CFA, provided invaluable comments and suggestions for this reading.

Analysis of Equity Investments: Valuation, by John D. Stowe, Thomas R. Robinson, Jerald E. Pinto, and Dennis W. McLeavey. Copyright © 2002 by AIMR. Reprinted with permission.

9

analyst must engage in valuation. **Valuation** is the estimation of an asset's value based either on variables perceived to be related to future investment returns or on comparisons with similar assets. Skill in valuation is one very important element of success in investing.

Benjamin Graham and David L. Dodd's *Security Analysis* (1934) represented the first major attempt to organize knowledge in this area for the investment profession. Its first sentence reads: "This book is intended for all those who have a serious interest in security values." *Analysis of Equity Investments: Valuation* addresses candidates in the Chartered Financial Analyst (CFA®) Program of the Association for Investment Management and Research (AIMR); all readers, however, with a "serious interest in security values" should find the book useful. Drawing on knowledge of current professional practice as well as both academic and investment industry research in finance and accounting, this book presents the major concepts and tools that analysts use in conducting valuations and communicating the results of their analysis to clients.

In this reading we address some basic questions: "What is equity valuation?" "Who performs equity valuation?" "What is the importance of industry knowledge?" and "How can the analyst effectively communicate his analysis?"

The reading is organized as follows: Section 2 surveys the scope of equity valuation within the overall context of the portfolio management process. In various places in this book, we will discuss how to select an appropriate valuation approach given a security's characteristics. In Section 3, we address valuation concepts and models and examine the first three steps in the valuation process— understanding the company, forecasting company performance, and selecting the appropriate valuation model. Section 4 discusses the analyst's role and responsibilities in researching and recommending a security for purchase or sale. Section 5 discusses the content and format of an effective research report—the analyst's work in valuation is generally not complete until he communicates the results of his analysis—and highlights the analyst's responsibilities in preparing research reports. We close with a summary of the reading.

2   THE SCOPE OF EQUITY VALUATION

Investment analysts work in a wide variety of organizations and positions; as a result, they find themselves applying the tools of equity valuation to address a range of practical problems. In particular, analysts use valuation concepts and models to accomplish the following:

> ▶ *Selecting stocks.* Stock selection is the primary use of the tools presented in this book. Equity analysts must continually address the same question for every common stock[1] that is either a current or prospective portfolio

---

[1] In the United Kingdom, *ordinary share* is the term corresponding to *common stock* (for short, *share* or *stock*)—the ownership interest in a corporation that represents the residual claim on the corporation's assets and earnings.

holding, or for every stock that he or she is professionally assigned to analyze: Is this a security my clients should purchase, sell, or continue to own?
Equity analysts attempt to identify securities as fairly valued, overvalued, or
undervalued, relative to either their own market price or the prices of comparable securities.

► *Inferring (extracting) market expectations.* Market prices reflect the expectations
  of investors about the future prospects of companies. Analysts may ask, what
  expectations about a company's future performance are consistent with the
  current market price for that company's stock? This question may concern
  the analyst for several reasons:

  ► There are historical and economic reasons that certain values for earn-
    ings growth rates and other company fundamentals may or may not be
    reasonable. (**Fundamentals** are characteristics of a company related to
    profitability, financial strength, or risk.)

  ► The extracted expectation for a fundamental characteristic may be use-
    ful as a benchmark or comparison value of the same characteristic for
    another company.[2]

► *Evaluating corporate events.* Investment bankers, corporate analysts, and
  investment analysts use valuation tools to assess the impact of corporate
  events such as mergers, acquisitions, divestitures, spin-offs, **management
  buyouts (MBOs)**, and leveraged recapitalizations.[3] Each of these events may
  affect a company's future cash flows and so the value of equity. Furthermore, in mergers and acquisitions, the company's own common stock is
  often used as currency for the purchase; investors then want to know
  whether the stock is fairly valued.

► *Rendering fairness opinions.* The parties to a merger may be required to seek
  a fairness opinion on the terms of the merger from a third party such as an
  investment bank. Valuation is at the center of such opinions.

► *Evaluating business strategies and models.* Companies concerned with maximizing shareholder value must evaluate the impact of alternative strategies on
  share value.

► *Communicating with analysts and shareholders.* Valuation concepts facilitate
  communication and discussion among company management, shareholders, and analysts on a range of corporate issues affecting company value.

► *Appraising private businesses.* Although we focus on publicly traded companies, another important use of the tools we present is to value the common
  stock of private companies. The stock of private companies by definition
  does not trade publicly; consequently, we cannot compare an estimate of the
  stock's value with a market price. For this and other reasons, the valuation of

---

[2] To extract or reverse-engineer a market expectation, the analyst must specify a model that relates
market price to expectations about fundamentals, and calculate or assume values for all fundamentals except the one of interest. Then the analyst calculates the value of the remaining fundamental
that calibrates the model value to market price (makes the model value equal market price)—this
value is the extracted market expectation for the variable. Of course, the model that the analyst uses
must be appropriate for the characteristics of the stock.

[3] A **merger** is the combination of two corporations. An **acquisition** is also a combination of two
corporations, usually with the connotation that the combination is not one of equals. In a **divestiture**,
a corporation sells some major component of its business. In a **spin-off**, the corporation separates
off and separately capitalizes a component business, which is then transferred to the corporation's
common stockholders. In an **MBO**, management repurchases all outstanding stock, usually using
the proceeds of debt issuance; in a **leveraged recapitalization**, some stock remains in the hands of
the public.

private companies has special characteristics. The analyst encounters these challenges in evaluating initial public offerings (IPOs), for example.[4]

EXAMPLE 1

Inferring Market Expectations

On 21 September 2000, Intel Corporation (Nasdaq NMS: INTC)[5] issued a press release containing information about its expected revenue growth for the third quarter of 2000. The announced growth fell short of the company's own prior prediction by 2 to 4 percentage points and short of analysts' projections by 3 to 7 percentage points. In response to the announcement, Intel's stock price fell nearly 30 percent during the following five days.

Was the information in Intel's announcement sufficient to explain a loss of value of that magnitude? Cornell (2001) examined this question using a valuation approach that models the value of a company's equity as the present value of expected future cash flows from operations minus the expenditures needed to maintain the company's growth. What future revenue growth rates were consistent with Intel's stock price of $61.50 just prior to the press release, and $43.31 only five days later?

Using a conservatively low discount rate, Cornell estimated that the price of $61.50 was consistent with a growth rate of 20 percent a year for the subsequent 10 years (and then 6 percent per year thereafter). The price of $43.31 was consistent with a decline of the 10-year growth rate to well under 15 percent per year. In the final year of the forecast horizon (2009), projected revenues with the lower growth rate would be $50 billion below the projected revenues based on the pre-announcement price. Because the press release did not obviously point to any changes in Intel's fundamental long-run business conditions (Intel attributed the quarterly revenue growth shortfall to a cyclical slowing of demand in Europe), Cornell's detailed analysis left him skeptical that the stock market's reaction could be explained in terms of fundamentals.

Was investors' reaction to the press release therefore irrational? That was one possible interpretation. Cornell also concluded, however, that Intel's stock was overvalued prior to the press release. For example, the 20 percent revenue growth rate consistent with the pre-announcement stock price was much higher than Intel's growth rate averaged over the previous five years when the company was much smaller. Cornell viewed the press release as "a kind of catalyst which caused movement toward a

---

[4] An **initial public offering** is the initial issuance of common stock registered for public trading by a formerly private corporation. Later in this reading, we mention one issue related to valuing private companies, marketability discounts.

[5] In this reading, the shares of real companies are identified by an abbreviation for the stock exchange or electronic marketplace where the shares of the company are traded, followed by a ticker symbol or formal acronym for the shares. For example, Nasdaq NMS stands for "Nasdaq National Market System," an electronic marketplace in the United States managed by the National Association of Securities Dealers, Inc., and INTC is the ticker symbol for Intel Corporation on the Nasdaq NMS. (Many stocks are traded on a number of exchanges worldwide, and some stocks may have more than one formal acronym; we usually state just one marketplace and one ticker symbol.) For fictional companies we do not give the marketplace, but we often give the stock an acronym by which we can refer to it.

more rational price, even though the release itself did not contain sufficient long-run valuation information to justify that movement."[6] Analysts can perform the same type of analysis as Cornell did. Exercises of
this type are very useful for forming a judgment on the reasonableness
of market prices. It is also noteworthy that Cornell found much lacking
in the valuation discussions in the 28 contemporaneous analysts' reports
on Intel that he examined. Although all reports made buy or sell recommendations, he characterized their discussions of fundamental value
as "typically vague and nebulous."[7] To the extent Cornell's assessment
was accurate, the reports would not meet the criteria for an effective
research report that we present later in this reading.

2.1 Valuation and Portfolio Management

Although valuation can take place without reference to a portfolio, the analysis
of equity investments is conducted within the context of managing a portfolio.
We can better appreciate the scope of valuation when we recognize valuation as
a part of the overall portfolio management process. An investor's most basic concern is generally not the characteristics of a single security but the risk and
return prospects of his or her total investment position. How does valuation,
focused on a single security, fit into this process?

From a portfolio perspective, the investment process has three steps: *planning, execution,* and *feedback* (which includes *evaluating* whether objectives have
been achieved, and *monitoring and rebalancing* of positions). Valuation, including equity valuation, is most closely associated with the planning and execution
steps.

▶ *Planning.* In the planning step, the investor identifies and specifies **investment objectives** (desired investment outcomes relating to both risk and
return) and constraints (internal or external limitations on investment
actions). An important part of planning is the concrete elaboration of an
investment strategy, or approach to investment analysis and security selection, with the goal of organizing and clarifying investment decisions.

Not all investment strategies involve making valuation judgments about individual securities. For example, in indexing strategies, the investor seeks only to
replicate the returns of an externally specified index—such as the Financial
Times Stock Exchange (FTSE) Eurotop 300, which is an index of Europe's 300
largest companies. Such an investor could simply buy and hold those 300 stocks
in index proportions, without the need to analyze individual stocks.

Valuation, however, is relevant, and critical, to active investment strategies.
To understand **active management**, it is useful to introduce the concept of a
benchmark—the comparison portfolio used to evaluate performance—which
for an index manager is the index itself. **Active investment managers** hold portfolios that differ from the benchmark in an attempt to produce superior risk-
adjusted returns. Securities held in different-from-benchmark weights reflect

---

[6] Cornell (2001, p. 134).
[7] Cornell (2001, p. 131).

expectations that differ from consensus expectations (**differential expectations**). The manager must also translate expectations into value estimates, so that securities can be ranked from relatively most attractive to relatively least attractive. This step requires valuation models. In the planning phase, the active investor may specify quite narrowly the kinds of active strategies to be used and also specify in detail valuation models and/or criteria.

► *Execution.* In the execution step, the manager integrates investment strategies with expectations to select a portfolio (the **portfolio selection/ composition problem**), and portfolio decisions are implemented by trading desks (the **portfolio implementation problem**).

3   VALUATION CONCEPTS AND MODELS

In Section 3, we turn our attention to the valuation process. This process includes understanding the company to be valued, forecasting the company's performance, and selecting the appropriate valuation model for a given valuation task.

3.1 The Valuation Process

We have seen that the valuation of a particular company is a task within the context of the portfolio management process. Each individual valuation that an analyst undertakes can be viewed as a process with the following five steps:

1. *Understanding the business.* This involves evaluating industry prospects, competitive position, and corporate strategies. Analysts use this information together with financial statement analysis to forecast performance.
2. *Forecasting company performance.* Forecasts of sales, earnings, and financial position (pro forma analysis) are the immediate inputs to estimating value.
3. *Selecting the appropriate valuation model.*
4. *Converting forecasts to a valuation.*
5. *Making the investment decision (recommendation).*

The fourth and fifth steps are addressed in detail in succeeding readings of this book. Here we focus on the first three steps. Because common stock represents the ownership interest in a company, analysts must carefully research the company before making a recommendation about the company's stock.

An in-depth understanding of the business and an ability to forecast the performance of a company help determine the quality of an analyst's valuation efforts.

3.2 Understanding the Business

Understanding a company's economic and industry context and management's strategic responses are the first tasks in understanding that company. Because similar economic and technological factors typically affect all companies in an industry, industry knowledge helps analysts understand the basic characteristics of the markets served by a company and the economics of the company. An airline industry analyst will know that jet fuel costs are the second biggest expense for airlines behind labor expenses, and that in many markets airlines have difficulty passing through higher fuel prices by raising ticket prices. Using this knowledge, the analyst may inquire about the degree to which different airlines hedge the commodity price risk inherent in jet fuel costs. With such information in hand, the analyst is better able to evaluate risk and forecast future cash flows. Hooke (1998) discussed a broad framework for industry analysis.

An analyst conducting an industry analysis must also judge management's strategic choices to better understand a company's prospects for success in competition with other companies in the industry or industries in which that company operates. Porter (1998) may lead analysts to focus on the following questions:

1. *How attractive are the industries in which the company operates, in terms of offering prospects for sustained profitability?* Inherent industry profitability is one important factor in determining a company's profitability. Analysts should try to understand **industry structure**—the industry's underlying economic and technical characteristics—and the trends affecting that structure. Analysts must also stay current on facts and news concerning all the industries in which the company operates, including the following:

   ▶ industry size and growth over time;

   ▶ recent developments (management, technological, financial) in the industry;

   ▶ overall **supply** and **demand** balance;

   ▶ subsector strength/softness in the demand–supply balance; and

   ▶ qualitative factors, including the legal and regulatory environment.

2. *What is the company's relative competitive position within its industry?* Among factors to consider are the level and trend of the company's market share in the markets in which it operates.

3. *What is the company's **competitive strategy**?* Three general corporate strategies for achieving above-average performance are:

   ▶ **cost leadership**—being the lowest cost producer while offering products comparable to those of other companies, so that products can be priced at or near the industry average;

   ▶ **differentiation**—offering unique products or services along some dimensions that are widely valued by buyers so that the company can command premium prices; and

   ▶ **focus**—seeking a competitive advantage within a target segment or segments of the industry, based on either cost leadership (cost focus) or differentiation (differentiation focus).

   The analyst can assess whether a company's apparent strategy is logical or faulty only in the context of thorough knowledge of the company's industry or industries.

4. *How well is the company executing its strategy?* Competitive success requires not only appropriate strategic choices, but also competent execution.

One perspective on the above issues often comes from the companies themselves in regulatory filings, which analysts can compare with their own independent research.[8]

---

[8] For example, companies filing Form 10-Ks with the U.S. Securities and Exchange Commission identify legal and regulatory issues and competitive factors and risks.

EXAMPLE 2

Competitive Analysis

Veritas DGC Inc. (NYSE: VTS) is a provider of seismic data—two- or three-dimensional views of the earth's subsurface—and related geophysical services to the natural gas and crude oil (petroleum) industry. Oil and gas drillers purchase such information to increase drilling success rates and so lower overall exploration costs.

According to Standard & Poor's Corporation, VTS's peer group is "Oil & Gas-Geophysical Data Technologies" in Oil & Gas Equipment and Services. Competitors include WesternGeco, a joint venture of Schlumberger Ltd. (NYSE: SLB) and Baker Hughes Inc. (NYSE: BHI); Petroleum Geo-Services (NYSE: PGO) which in late 2001 announced plans to merge with VTS; Dawson Geophysical (Nasdaq NMS: DWSN); Compagnie Générale de Géophysique (NYSE: GGY); and Seitel, Inc. (NYSE: SEI).

1. Discuss the economic factors that may affect demand for the services provided by VTS and its competitors, and explain a logical framework for analyzing and forecasting revenue for these companies.

2. Explain how comparing the level and trend in profit margin (net income/sales) and revenue per employee for the above companies may help in evaluating whether one of these companies is the cost leader in the peer group.

Solution to 1: Because VTS provides services related to oil and gas exploration, the level of exploration activities by oil and gas producers is probably the major factor determining the demand for VTS's services. In turn, the prices of natural gas and crude oil are critical in determining the level of exploration activities. Therefore, among other economic factors, an analyst should research those relating to supply and demand for natural gas and crude oil.

► Supply factors in natural gas. Factors include natural gas inventory levels. Energy analysts should be familiar with sources for researching this information, such as the American Gas Association (AGA) for gas inventory levels in the United States.

► Demand factors in natural gas. These factors include household and commercial use of natural gas and the amount of new power generation equipment being fired by natural gas.

► Supply factors in crude oil. Factors include capacity constraints and production levels in OPEC and other oil-producing countries. Analysts should be familiar with sources such as the American Petroleum Institute for researching these factors.

► Demand factors in crude oil. Factors include household and commercial use of oil and the amount of new power generation equipment using oil products as its primary fuel.

For both crude oil and natural gas, projected economic growth rates could be examined as a demand factor and depletion rates as a supply side factor.

Solution to 2: Profit margin reflects cost structure; in interpreting profit margin, however, analysts should evaluate any differences in companies' abilities to affect profit margin through power over price. A successfully executed cost leadership strategy will lower costs and raise profit margins. All else equal, we would also expect a cost leader to have relatively high sales per employee, reflecting efficient use of human resources.

3.3 Forecasting Company Performance

The second step in the valuation process—forecasting company performance—can be viewed from two perspectives: the economic environment in which the company operates and the company's own financial characteristics.

3.3.1 Economic Forecasting

Industry analysis and competitive analysis take place within the larger context of macroeconomic analysis. As an approach to forecasting, moving from the international and national macroeconomic forecasts to industry forecasts and then to individual company and asset forecasts is known as a **top-down forecasting approach**. For example, Benninga and Sarig (1997) illustrated how, starting with forecasts of the level of macroeconomic activity, an analyst might project overall industry sales and the market share of a company within the industry to arrive at revenue forecasts for the company.[9] It is also possible to aggregate individual company forecasts of analysts (possibly arrived at using various methodologies) into industry forecasts, and finally into macroeconomic forecasts; doing so is called a **bottom-up forecasting approach**. Figure 1 illustrates the two approaches.

A bottom-up forecasting approach is subject to the problem of inconsistent assumptions. For example, different analysts may assume different inflationary environments, and this may compromise the comparability of resulting individual stock valuations. In a **top-down** approach, an organization can ensure that all analysts use the same inflation assumption.[10]

3.3.2 Financial Forecasting

The analyst integrates the analysis of industry prospects and competitive and corporate strategy with financial statement analysis to formulate specific numerical forecasts of such items as sales and earnings. Techniques of financial forecasting are presented in detail in later readings of this book, and also in White, Sondhi,

[9] Benninga and Sarig (1997, Chapter 5). See also Chapter 19 of Reilly and Brown (2000).

[10] A related but distinct concept is **top-down investing** versus **bottom-up investing** as one broad description of types of active investment styles. For example, a top-down investor, based on a forecast that an economy is about to transition out of an economic recession, might increase exposure to shares in the Basic Materials sector, because profits in that economic sector are typically sensitive to changes in macroeconomic growth rates; at the same time exposure to recession-resistant sectors such as Consumer Non-Durables might be reduced. (The preceding would describe a **sector rotation strategy**, an investment strategy that overweights **economic sectors** that are anticipated to outperform or lead the overall market.) In contrast, an investor following a bottom-up approach might decide that a security is undervalued based on some valuation indicator, for example, without making an explicit judgment on the overall economy or the relative value of different sectors. Note that some forecasting and investing approaches mix top-down and bottom-up elements.

FIGURE 1   The Top-Down and Bottom-Up Approaches to Equity Analysis

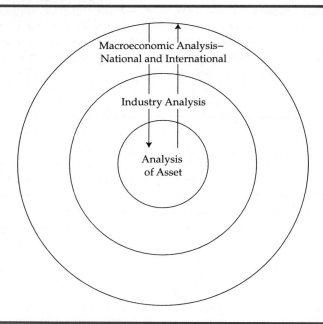

and Fried (1998), Higgins (2001), Reilly and Brown (2000), and Benninga and Sarig (1997), which are useful complementary readings.

Analysts may consider qualitative as well as quantitative factors in financial forecasting and valuation. For example, some analysts may modify their overall valuation judgments and recommendations based on qualitative factors. These may include the analyst's viewpoint on the business acumen and integrity of management as well as the transparency and quality of a company's accounting practices. Although analysts may attempt to reflect the expected direction of such considerations in their financial forecasts or to otherwise quantify such factors, no formal valuation expression can fully capture these factors.[11] We caution that qualitative adjustments to valuation opinions are necessarily subjective.

3.3.2.1 Using Accounting Information

In working with quantitative forecasting tools, the analyst must attempt to use the most appropriate and reliable information available. A key source of such information is a company's accounting information and financial disclosures. Equity analysts study financial results and disclosures for information bearing on the company's current and future ability to create economic value. Reports to shareholders can differ substantially, however, with respect to the *accuracy* of reported accounting results as reflections of economic performance and the *detail* in which results are disclosed.

The investigation of issues relating to accuracy is often broadly referred to as **quality of earnings analysis**. The term broadly includes the scrutiny of *all* financial statements, including the balance sheet; that is, quality of earnings analysis includes scrutiny of balance sheet management as well as earnings management. With respect to detail, more detail is almost always superior to less, particularly in

---

[11] For example, management will react to future opportunities and risks that the analyst cannot anticipate at the time of the valuation.

those areas of accounting practice (e.g., pensions, mergers and acquisitions, currency translation) where cursory examination seldom proves useful.

Equity analysts will generally benefit by developing their ability to assess a company's quality of earnings. An analyst who can skillfully analyze a company's financial statements can more accurately value a security than peer analysts with only a superficial understanding of the numbers. Also, extensive research suggests that analysts can generally expect stock prices to reflect quality of earnings considerations.[12] Skill in quality of earnings analysis, however, comes only with a thorough knowledge of financial statement analysis as well as practical experience.[13] Careful scrutiny and interpretation of footnotes to accounting statements, and of all other relevant disclosures, is essential to a quality of earnings analysis. Examples of only a few of the many available indicators of possible problems with a company's quality of earnings are provided in Table 1.

Various examples throughout this book will touch on analyst adjustments to reported financial results. Both the importance of accounting practices in influencing reported financial results and the judgment that analysts need to exercise in using those results in any valuation model are illustrated in Example 3.

EXAMPLE 3

Quality of Earnings Warning Signs

Livent, Inc., was a publicly traded theatrical production company that staged a number of smash hits such as Tony-award winning productions of *Showboat* and *Fosse*. Livent capitalized preproduction costs including expenses for pre-opening advertising, publicity and promotion, set construction, props, costumes, and salaries and fees paid to the cast and crew musicians during rehearsals. The company then amortized these capitalized costs over the expected life of the theatrical production based on anticipated revenues.

1. State the effect of Livent's accounting for preproduction costs on its reported earnings per share.

In Reading 47 and elsewhere we will encounter the popular concept of EBITDA: earnings before interest, taxes, depreciation, and amortization (interest, taxes, depreciation, and amortization are added back to earnings). Some analysts use ratios such as EBITDA/interest expense and debt/EBITDA to assess one aspect of a company's financial strength, debt-paying ability.

---

[12] The literature is vast, but see in particular Fairfield and Whisenant (2000) and the references therein. Studies have also documented the *Briloff effect* showing that when a company's accounting games are exposed in *Barron's*, its stock price declines rapidly (Abraham Briloff is an accounting professor at Baruch College, City University of New York, who has explored the subject extensively). Other literature shows that bond market participants see through attempts at smoothing earnings and in some cases (the institutional bond market) penalize it (see Robinson and Grant 1997 and Robinson, Grant, Kauer, and Woodlock 1998).

[13] Sources for our discussion on quality of earnings analysis and accounting risk factors include Hawkins (1998), Levitt (1998), Schilit (2002), and White, Sondhi, and Fried (1998), as well as American Institute of Certified Public Accountants *Consideration of Fraud in a Financial Statement Audit* (28 February 2002) and International Federation of Accountants, International Standards on Auditing 240, *The Auditor's Responsibility to Consider Fraud and Error in an Audit of Financial Statements* (March 2001).

TABLE 1	Selected Quality of Earnings Indicators	
Category	**Observation**	**Potential Interpretation**
Revenues and gains	Recognizing revenue early, for example: ▶ bill-and-hold sales ▶ lessor use of **capital lease** classification ▶ recording sales of equipment or software prior to installation and acceptance by customer	Acceleration in the recognition of revenue boosts reported income masking a decline in operating performance.
	Classification of nonoperating income or gains as part of operations.	Income or gains may be nonrecurring and may not relate to true operating performance, in fact perhaps masking a decline in operating performance.
Expenses and losses	Deferral of expenses by capitalizing expenditures as an asset. For example: ▶ customer acquisition costs ▶ product development costs	May boost current income at the expense of future income. May mask problems with underlying business performance.
	Use of nonconservative estimates and assumptions, such as: ▶ long depreciable lives ▶ long periods of amortization ▶ high pension discount rate ▶ low assumed rate of compensation growth for pensions ▶ high expected return on assets for pension	Nonconservative estimates may indicate actions taken to boost current reported income. Changes in assumptions may indicate an attempt to mask problems with underlying performance in the current period.
Balance sheet issues (may also affect earnings)	Use of special purpose entities (SPEs).[14]	Assets and/or liabilities may not be properly reflected on the balance sheet. Income may also be overstated by sales to the special purpose entity or a decline in the value of assets transferred to the SPE.

[14] A **special purpose entity** is a nonoperating entity created to carry out a specified purpose, such as leasing assets or securitizing receivables. The use of SPEs is frequently related to off-balance-sheet financing (financing that does not currently appear on the balance sheet).

2. If an analyst calculated EBITDA/interest expense and debt/EBITDA based on Livent's accounting for preproduction costs without adjustment, how might the analyst be misled in assessing Livent's financial strength?

Solution to 1: Livent's accounting for preproduction costs immediately increased reported earnings per share because it deferred expenses. Instead of immediately expensing costs. Livent reported them on its balance sheet as an asset. The warning signal—the deferral of expenses—indicates very aggressive accounting; preproduction costs should have been expensed immediately because of the tremendous uncertainty about revenues from theatrical productions. There was no assurance that there would be revenues against which expenses could be matched.

Solution to 2: Livent did not deduct preproduction costs from earnings as expenses. If the amortization of capitalized preproduction costs were then added back to earnings, the EBITDA/interest and debt/EBITDA ratios would not reflect in any way the cash outflows associated with items such as paying pre-opening salaries; but cash outflows reduce funds available to meet debt obligations. The analyst who mechanically added back amortization of preproduction costs to calculate EBITDA would be misled into overestimating Livent's financial strength. Based on a closer look at the company's accounting, we would properly not add back amortization of preproduction expenses in computing EBITDA. If preproduction expenses are not added back, a very different picture of Livent's financial health would emerge. In 1996, Livent's reported debt/EBITDA ratio was 1.7, but the ratio without adding back amortization for preproduction costs was 5.5. In 1997, debt/EBITDA was 3.7 based on positive EBITDA of $58.3 million, but EBITDA without the add-back was *negative* $52.6 million.[15] In November 1998, Livent declared bankruptcy and it is now defunct.

Analysts recognize a variety of risk factors that may signal possible future negative surprises. A working selection of these risk factors would include the following (AICPA, 2002):

► Poor quality of accounting disclosures, such as segment information, acquisitions, accounting policies and assumptions, and a lack of discussion of negative factors.

► Existence of related-party transactions.

► Existence of excessive officer, employee, or director loans.

► High management or director turnover.

► Excessive pressure on company personnel to make revenue or earnings targets, particularly when combined with a dominant, aggressive management team or individual.

► Material non-audit services performed by audit firm.

---

[15] Moody's Investor Services (2000). The discussion of this example is indebted to that report.

► Reported (via regulatory filings) disputes with and/or changes in auditors.

► Management and or directors' compensation tied to profitability or stock price (through ownership or compensation plans). Although such arrangements are desirable, they can indicate a risk of aggressive reporting as well.

► Economic, industry, or company-specific pressures on profitability, such as loss of market share or declining margins.

► Management pressure to meet debt covenants or earnings expectations.

► A history of securities law violations, reporting violations, or persistent late filings.

EXAMPLE 4

Benjamin Graham on Accounting

In a manuscript from 1936 (reprinted in Ellis 1991), Benjamin Graham pictures the chair of a major corporation outlining how his company will return to profitability in the middle of the Great Depression of the 20th century:

"Contrary to expectations, no changes will be made in the company's manufacturing or selling policies. Instead, the bookkeeping system is to be entirely revamped. By adopting and further improving a number of modern accounting and financial devices the corporation's earning power will be amazingly transformed."

The top item on the chair's list gives a flavor of the progress that will be made: "Accordingly, the Board has decided to extend the write-down policy initiated in the 1935 report, and to mark down the Fixed Assets from $1,338,552,858.96 to a round *Minus* $1,000,000,000 . . . As the plant wears out, the liability becomes correspondingly reduced. Hence, instead of the present depreciation charge of some $47,000,000 yearly there will be an annual *appreciation credit* of 5 percent, or $50,000,000. This will increase earnings by no less than $97,000,000 per annum." Summing up, the chair shares the foresight of the Board: ". . . [T]he Board is not unmindful of the possibility that some of our competitors may seek to offset our new advantages by adopting similar accounting improvements . . . Should necessity arise, moreover, we believe we shall be able to maintain our deserved superiority by introducing still more advanced bookkeeping methods, which are even now under development in our Experimental Accounting Laboratory."

3.4 Selecting the Appropriate Valuation Model

Skill in selecting, applying, and interpreting valuation models is important in investment analysis and valuation.[16] In this section, we discuss the third step in the valuation process—selecting the appropriate model for the valuation task at hand. First we address alternative value perspectives, then we present absolute and relative valuation models, and we close with a discussion of issues in model selection.

---

[16] The remaining readings of this volume will discuss these issues in detail for the valuation approaches presented.

3.4.1 Value Perspectives

Several value perspectives serve as the foundation for the variety of valuation models available to the equity analyst; intrinsic value is the necessary starting point, but other concepts of value—going-concern value, liquidation value, and fair value—are also important.

3.4.1.1 Intrinsic Value The quality of the analyst's forecasts, in particular the expectational inputs used in valuation models, is a key element in determining investment success. *For an active strategy to be consistently successful, the manager's expectations must differ from consensus expectations and be, on average, correct as well.* Only when accurate forecasts are combined with an appropriate valuation model will the analyst obtain a useful estimate of intrinsic value. The **intrinsic value** of an asset is the value of the asset given a hypothetically complete understanding of the asset's investment characteristics.

Valuation is an inherent part of the active manager's attempt to produce positive excess risk-adjusted return. An excess risk-adjusted return is also called an **abnormal return** or **alpha**. The manager hopes to capture a positive alpha as a result of his efforts to estimate intrinsic value. Any departure of market price from the manager's estimate of intrinsic value is a perceived **mispricing** (calculated as the difference between the estimated intrinsic value and the market price of an asset). Any perceived mispricing becomes part of the manager's expected holding-period return estimate, which is the manager's forecast of the total return on the asset for some holding period.[17] An expected holding-period return is the sum of expected capital appreciation and investment income, both stated as a proportion of purchase price. Naturally, expected capital appreciation incorporates the investor's perspective on the convergence of market price to intrinsic value. In a forward-looking (*ex ante*) sense, an asset's **alpha** is the manager's expected **holding-period return** minus the fair (or equilibrium) return on the asset given its risk, using some model relating an asset's average returns to its risk characteristics. The fair return on an asset given its risk is also known as its required rate of return.

> *Ex ante* alpha = **Expected holding-period return**
>   − Required return   **(37-1)**

In a backward-looking (*ex post*) sense, alpha is actual return minus the contemporaneous required return. Contemporaneous required return is what investments of similar risk actually earned during the same period.

> *Ex post* alpha = Actual holding-period return
>   − Contemporaneous required return   **(37-2)**

To illustrate these concepts, assume that an investor's expected holding-period return for a stock for the next 12 months is 12 percent, and the stock's required return, given its risk, is 10 percent. The *ex ante* alpha is $12 - 10 = 2$ percent. Assume that a year passes, and the stock has a return of −5 percent. The *ex post* alpha depends on the contemporaneous required return. If the contemporaneous required return was −8 percent, the stock would have an *ex post* alpha of $-5 - (-8) = 3$ percent.

---

[17] For brevity, we sometimes use *return* for *rate of return* in this discussion.

EXAMPLE 5

Intrinsic Value and Return Concepts (1)

As an automotive industry analyst, you are researching Fiat S.p.A. (Milan Stock Exchange: FIA.MI), a leading Italian-headquartered automobile manufacturer. You have assembled the following information and assumptions as of late March 2002:

▶ The current share price of FIA.MI is €15.895 (based on the closing price on 22 March 2002).

▶ Your estimate of FIA.MI's intrinsic value is €17.26.

▶ Over the course of one year, you expect the mispricing of FIA.MI shares, equal to €17.26 − €15.895 = €1.365, to be fully corrected. In addition to the correction of mispricing, you forecast additional price appreciation of €1.22 per share over the course of the year as well as the payment of a cash dividend of €0.61.

▶ You estimate that the required rate of return on FIA.MI shares is 10.6 percent a year.

Using the above information:

1. State whether FIA.MI shares are overvalued, fairly valued, or undervalued, based on your forecasts.

2. Calculate the expected one-year holding-period return on FIA.MI stock.

3. Determine the expected alpha for FIA.MI stock.

Solution to 1: Because FIA.MI's intrinsic value of €17.26 is greater than its current market price €15.895, FIA.MI appears to be undervalued, based on your forecasts.

Solution to 2: The expected holding-period return is the sum of expected price appreciation plus the expected return from dividends. To calculate the expected price appreciation, we add €1.365 (from the convergence of price to intrinsic value) plus €1.22 (from the additional forecasted price appreciation) and obtain €2.585. The expected dividend is €0.61. The sum of expected price appreciation plus expected dividends is €3.195. The expected holding-period return for one year is €3.195/€15.895 = 0.201 or 20.1 percent.

Solution to 3: The expected holding-period return of 20.1 percent minus the required rate of return of 10.6 percent gives a positive expected excess risk-adjusted return or positive expected alpha of 9.5 percent.

The equity analyst recognizes that, no matter how hard he or she works to identify mispriced securities, uncertainty is associated with realizing a positive expected alpha, however accurate the forecasts and whatever the valuation approach used. Even if the analyst is highly confident about the accuracy of forecasts and risk adjustments, there is no means of ensuring the ability to capture the benefits of any perceived mispricing without risk. Convergence of the market price to perceived intrinsic value may not happen within the investor's investment horizon, if at all.[18] One uncertainty in applying any valuation methodology concerns whether the analyst has accounted for all sources of risk reflected in an asset's price. Because competing equity risk models will always exist, there is no possible final resolution to this dilemma. Differences in valuation judgments resulting from applying alternative models of equity risk are illustrated in Example 6.

EXAMPLE 6

Intrinsic Value and Return Concepts (2)

As an active investor, you have developed forecasts of returns for three securities and translated those forecasts into expected rate of return estimates. You have also estimated the securities' required rates of return using two models that we will discuss in Reading 46: the capital asset pricing model (CAPM) and the Fama–French (FF) three-factor model. As a next step, you intend to rank the securities by alpha.

TABLE 2   Rates of Return

	Expected Rate of Return	CAPM Required Rate of Return	FF Required Rate of Return
Security 1	0.15	0.10	0.12
Security 2	0.07	0.12	0.07
Security 3	0.09	0.10	0.10

Based on the information in Table 2:

1. Calculate the *ex ante* alphas of each security.
2. Rank the securities by relative attractiveness using the CAPM, and state whether each security is overvalued, fairly valued, or undervalued.

Solution to 1: The analyst can develop two sets of estimates of alpha, because the securities have different required rates of return depending on whether risk is modeled using the CAPM or FF models.

---

[18] Related to this uncertainty is the concept of a catalyst. Besides evidence of mispricing, some active investors look for the presence of a particular market or corporate event (catalyst) that will cause the marketplace to re-evaluate a company's prospects.

CAPM

Alpha of Security 1 = 0.15 − 0.10 = 0.05 or 5 percent
Alpha of Security 2 = 0.07 − 0.12 = −0.05 or −5 percent
Alpha of Security 3 = 0.09 − 0.10 = −0.01 or −1 percent

Fama–French

Alpha of Security 1 = 0.15 − 0.12 = 0.03 or 3 percent
Alpha of Security 2 = 0.07 − 0.07 = 0.00 or 0 percent
Alpha of Security 3 = 0.09 − 0.10 = −0.01 or −1 percent

Solution to 2: With an alpha of 5 percent, using the CAPM, Security 1 is the only security with a positive expected risk-adjusted return and is relatively most attractive. Security 3 ranks second with an alpha of −1 percent, and Security 2 is last with an alpha of −5 percent. Both Security 3 and 2 appear to be overvalued, however, because they have negative alphas.

We distinguish between market price, *P*, and intrinsic value (value for short), *V*. We accept the possibility of mispricing, which raises the question of the relationship between the analyst's efforts and the concept of market efficiency. **Market efficiency** is a finance perspective on capital markets that asserts, in the **traditional efficient markets formulation**, that an asset's market price is the best available estimate of its intrinsic value. A more modern formulation, the **rational efficient markets formulation** (Grossman and Stiglitz 1980), recognizes that no investor will rationally incur the expenses of gathering information unless he or she expects to be rewarded by higher gross returns compared with the free alternative of accepting the market price. Furthermore, modern theorists recognize that when intrinsic value is hard to ascertain (as is the case for common stock) and when trading costs exist, there is even further room for price to diverge from value.[19]

Thus the perspective of this reading is consistent with some concepts of market efficiency. Many analysts often view market prices both with respect and with skepticism. They seek to identify mispricing. At the same time, they often rely on price eventually converging to intrinsic value. They also recognize distinctions between the levels of market efficiency in different markets or tiers of markets (for example, stocks heavily followed by analysts and stocks neglected by analysts).

3.4.1.2 Other Value Measures A company generally has one value if it is immediately dissolved, and another value if it continues in operation. The **going-concern assumption** is the assumption that the company will maintain its business activities into the foreseeable future. The **going-concern value** of a company is its value under a going-concern assumption. Once established as publicly traded, most companies have relatively long lives. Models of going-concern value are the focus of this reading.

In addition to going-concern value, however, the marketplace considers other values. A company's **liquidation value** is its value if it were dissolved and its

---

[19] See Lee, Myers, and Swaminathan (1999).

assets sold individually.[20] For many companies, the value added by assets working together and by human capital applied to managing those assets makes estimated going-concern value greater than liquidation value. A persistently unprofitable business, however, may be worth more "dead" than "alive." The higher of going-concern value or liquidation value is the company's fair value. If the marketplace has confidence that the company's management is acting in the owners' best interests, market prices should on average reflect fair value. **Fair value** is the price at which an asset (or liability) would change hands between a willing buyer and a willing seller when the former is not under any compulsion to buy and the latter is not under any compulsion to sell.

3.4.2 Absolute Valuation Models

The two broad types of going-concern models of valuation are absolute valuation models and relative valuation models. An **absolute valuation model** is a model that specifies an asset's intrinsic value. Such models can supply a point estimate of value that can be compared with the asset's market price. Present value models, the most important type of absolute equity valuation model, are regarded in academic finance theory as the fundamental approach to equity valuation. The logic of such models is that the value of an asset to an investor must be related to the returns that investor expects to receive from holding that asset. Loosely speaking, we can refer to those returns as the asset's cash flows, and such models are also referred to as dicounted cash flow models.

A **present value model** or **discounted cash flow model** of equity valuation views the value of common stock as being the present or discounted value of its expected future cash flows. For common stock, one familiar type of cash flow is dividends, which are discretionary distributions to shareholders authorized by a corporation's board of directors. Dividends represent cash flows at the shareholder level in the sense that they are paid directly to shareholders. Present value models based on dividends are called **dividend discount models**. Rather than defining cash flows as dividends, analysts frequently define cash flows at the company level. Common shareholders in principle have an equity ownership claim on the balance of the cash flows generated by a company after payments have been made to claimants senior to common equity, such as bondholders and preferred stockholders (and the government as well, which takes taxes), whether or not such flows are distributed in the form of dividends.

The two main company-level definitions of cash flow in current use are free cash flow and residual income.[21] Free cash flow is based on cash flow from operations but takes into account the reinvestment in fixed assets and working capital necessary for a going concern; we will define free cash flow with more precision in later readings. Present value models based on a free cash flow concept include models known as the **free cash flow to equity model** and the **free cash flow to the firm model**. **Residual income models** are present value models of equity valuation based on accrual **accounting earnings** in excess of the opportunity cost of generating those earnings.

As discussed, an important group of equity valuation models is present value models. The present value approach is the familiar technique for valuing bonds,

---

[20] Liquidation value should be distinguished from what is sometimes called the **breakup value** or **private market value** of a company, which is the sum of the expected value of the company's parts if the parts were independent entities. In contrast to liquidation value, breakup value is a going-concern concept of value because in estimating a company's break-up value, the company's parts are usually valued individually as going concerns.

[21] To reiterate, we are using *cash flow* in a broad rather than technical accounting sense in this discussion.

and models such as the dividend discount model are often presented as straight-forward applications of the bond valuation model to common stock. In practice, however, the application of present value models to common stock typically involves greater uncertainty than is the case with bonds; that uncertainty centers on two critical inputs for present value models—the cash flows and the discount rate(s). Bond valuation addresses a stream of cash payments specified in number and amount in a legal contract (the **bond indenture**). In contrast, in valuing a stock, an analyst must define the specific cash flow stream to be valued—dividends or free cash flow, for example. No cash flow stream is contractually owed to common stockholders. Evaluating business, financial, technological, and other risks, the analyst must then forecast the amounts of the chosen flows without reference to contractual targets. Substantial uncertainty often surrounds such forecasts. Furthermore, the forecasts must extend into the indefinite future because common stock has no maturity date. Establishing the appropriate discount rate or rates in equity valuation is also subject to greater uncertainty for a stock than for an option-free bond of an issuer with no credit risk (e.g., a U.S. government security) or a corporate issuer of high investment grade quality. The widespread availability, use, and acceptance of bond ratings—coupled with the more certain nature of cash flows described above for such bonds—mean that appropriate discount rates for different levels of risk can be at least inferred if not observed directly from yields in the bond market. No such ratings or certain cash flows exist for stocks, so the analyst is faced with a much more subjective and uncertain assessment of the appropriate discount rate for a given stock. (For some bonds, however, such as mortgage-backed securities, asset-backed securities, and **structured notes,** the appropriate discount rate as well as the bond's cash flows can pose challenges in estimation comparable to those for equity.) Finally, in addition to the uncertainty associated with cash flows and discount rates, the equity analyst may need to address other issues, such as the value of corporate control or the value of unutilized assets.

The present value approach applied to stock valuation, therefore, presents a high order of complexity. Present value models are ambitious in what they attempt—an estimate of intrinsic value—and offer concomitant challenges. Graham and Dodd (1934) suggested that the analyst consider stating a range of intrinsic values. To that end, in later readings we discuss the usefulness of sensitivity analysis in discounted cash flow valuation.

Although we present many of the equity valuation tools in wide professional use today, we cannot explore every specialist valuation tool the analyst may encounter. For example, a company may be valued on the basis of the market value of the assets or resources it controls. This approach is sometimes called **asset-based valuation** and also qualifies as a type of absolute valuation model. For appropriate companies, asset-based valuation can provide an independent estimate of value, and experienced analysts are always interested in alternative, independent estimates of value.

EXAMPLE 7

Asset-Based Valuation

Analysts often apply asset-based valuation to natural resource companies. For example, a crude oil producer such as Petrobras (NYSE: PBR) might be valued on the basis of the market value of its current proven reserves in barrels of oil, minus a discount for estimated extraction costs. A forest industry company such as Weyerhauser (NYSE: WY) might be valued on the basis of the board meters (or board feet) of timber it controls. Today, however, fewer companies than in the past are involved only in natural resources extraction or production. For example, Occidental Petroleum (NYSE: OXY) features petroleum in its name but also has substantial chemical manufacturing operations. For such cases, the total company might be valued as the sum of its divisions, with the natural resource division valued on the basis of its proven resources.

3.4.3 Relative Valuation Models

Relative valuation models constitute the second chief type of going-concern valuation models. **Relative valuation models** specify an asset's value relative to that of another asset. The idea underlying relative valuation is that similar assets should sell at similar prices, and relative valuation is typically implemented using price multiples.

Perhaps the most familiar price multiple, reported in most newspaper stock quotation listings, is the **price–earnings multiple** (P/E), which is the ratio of a stock's market price to the company's earnings per share. A stock selling at a P/E that is low relative to the P/E of another closely comparable stock (in terms of anticipated earnings growth rates and risk, for example) is *relatively undervalued* (a good buy) relative to the comparison stock. For brevity, we might state simply *undervalued*, but we must realize that if the comparison stock is overvalued (in an absolute sense, in relation to intrinsic value), so might be the stock we are calling undervalued. Therefore, it is useful to maintain the verbal distinction between *undervalued* and *relatively undervalued*.[22] Frequently, relative valuation involves a group of comparison assets, such as an industry group, rather than a single comparison asset, and the comparison value of the P/E might be the mean or median value of the P/E for the group of assets. The approach of relative valuation as applied to equity valuation is often called the **method of comparables** (or just comparables).

EXAMPLE 8

Relative Valuation Models

While researching Smithson Genomics, Inc. (STHI),[23] in the Healthcare Information Services industry, you encounter a difference of opinions. One analyst's report claims that STHI is at least 15 percent *overvalued*, based on a comparison of its P/E with the median P/E of peer companies

---

[22] Only **expectational arbitrage**—investing on the basis of differential expectations—is possible whether a stock is absolutely or relatively mispriced. When two stocks are relatively mispriced, an investor might use the expectational arbitrage strategy known as pairs arbitrage to attempt to exploit the mispricing. **Pairs arbitrage** is a trade in two closely related stocks that involves buying the relatively undervalued stock and selling short the relatively overvalued stock.

[23] This company is fictional; as such, we do not identify a stock exchange or other marketplace before stating the (fictional) ticker symbol or acronym.

in the Healthcare Information Services industry and taking account of company and peer group fundamentals. A second analyst asserts that Smithson is *undervalued* by 10 percent, based on a comparison of STHI's P/E with the median P/E of the **Russell 3000 Index**, a broad-based U.S. equity index. Both analyzes appear to be carefully executed and reported. Can both analysts be right?

Yes. The assertions of both analysts concern *relative* valuations. The first analyst claims that STHI is *relatively* overvalued compared with its peers (in the sense of the purchase cost of a unit of earnings, P/E). Suppose that the entire Healthcare Information Services industry is substantially undervalued in relation to the overall market as represented by the Russell 3000. STHI could then also be relatively undervalued relative to the Russell 3000. Both analysts can be right because they are making relative valuations. Analysts ultimately care about the investment implications of their information. If the second analyst believes that the market price of the Russell 3000 fairly represents that index's intrinsic value, then she might expect a positive alpha from investing in STHI, even if some other peer group companies possibly command higher expected alphas. In practice, the analyst may consider other factors such as market liquidity in relation to the intended position size. On the other hand, if the analyst thought that the overall market valuation was high, the analyst might anticipate a negative alpha from investing in STHI. Relative valuation is tied to relative performance. The analyst in many cases may want to supplement such information with estimates of intrinsic value.

The method of comparables is characterized by a wide range of possible implementation choices. Practitioners will often examine a number of price multiples for the complementary information they may provide. In summary, the method of comparables does not specify intrinsic value without making the further assumption that the comparison asset is fairly valued. The method of comparables has the advantages of being simple, related to market prices, and grounded in a sound economic principle (that similar assets should sell at similar prices). Price multiples are widely recognized by investors, and analysts can restate an absolute valuation in terms of a price multiple to communicate their analysis in a way that will be widely understood.

3.4.4 Issues in Model Selection and Interpretation

How do we select a valuation model? The broad criteria for model selection are that the valuation model be:

▶ consistent with the characteristics of the company being valued;
▶ appropriate given the availability and quality of data; and
▶ consistent with the purpose of valuation, including the analyst's ownership perspective.

We have argued that understanding the business is the first step in the valuation process. When we understand the company, we understand the nature of its assets and also how it uses those assets to create value. For example, a bank is composed largely of marketable or potentially marketable assets and securities, and a relative valuation based on assets (as recognized in accounting) has more relevance than a similar exercise for a service company with few marketable assets.

The availability and quality of data are limiting factors in making forecasts and sometimes in using specific financial performance measures. As a result, data availability and quality also bear on our choice of valuation model. Discounted cash flow models make intensive use of forecasts. As we shall see, the dividend discount model is the simplest such model, but if we do not have a record of dividends or other information to accurately assess a company's dividend policy, we may have more confidence applying an apparently more complex present value model. Similar considerations also apply in selecting a specific relative valuation approach. As an example, meaningful comparisons using **P/E ratios** may be hard to make for a company with highly volatile or persistently negative earnings.

The purpose or perspective of the analyst—for example, the ownership perspective—can also influence the choice of valuation approach. This point will become more apparent as we study concepts such as free cash flow and enterprise value later in this book. Related to purpose, the analyst is frequently a consumer as well as a producer of valuations and research reports. Analysts must consider potential biases when reading reports prepared by others: Why was this particular valuation method chosen? Are the valuation model and its inputs reasonable? Does the adopted approach make the security look better (or worse) than another standard valuation approach?

In addition to the preceding broad considerations in model selection, three other specific issues may affect the analyst's use and interpretation of valuation models: control premiums, marketability discounts, and liquidity discounts. A controlling ownership position in a company (e.g., more than 50 percent of outstanding shares) carries with it control of the board of directors and the valuable option of redeploying the company's assets. When control is at issue, the price of that company's stock will generally reflcet a **control premium**. Most quantitative valuation expressions do not explicitly model such premiums. As we shall discuss later, however, certain models are more likely than others to yield valuations consistent with a control position. A second consideration generally not explicitly modeled is that investors require an extra return to compensate for lack of a public market or lack of marketability. The price of non-publicly traded stocks then generally reflects a **marketability discount**. There is also evidence that among publicly traded stocks, the price of shares with less depth to their markets (less liquidity) reflects a **liquidity discount**.[24]

As a final note to this introduction of model selection, it is important to recognize that professionals frequently use multiple valuation models or factors in common stock selection. According to the *Merrill Lynch Institutional Factor Survey* (2001), respondent institutional investors report using an average of approximately eight valuation factors in selecting stocks.[25] There are a variety of ways in which multiple factors can be used in stock selection. For example, analysts may rank each security in a given investment universe by relative attractiveness according to a particular valuation factor. They could then combine the rankings for a security into a single composite ranking by assigning weights to the individual factors. Analysts may use a quantitative model to assign those weights.

---

[24] See, for example, Amihud and Mendelson (1986).

[25] *Factors* include valuation models as well as variables such as return on equity; these surveys included 23 such factors and covered the period 1989–2001.

4

PERFORMING VALUATIONS: THE ANALYST'S ROLE AND RESPONSIBILITIES

Whatever the setting in which they work, investment analysts are involved either directly or indirectly in valuation. Their activities are varied:

► Although sometimes focusing on organizing and analyzing corporate information, the publicly distributed research reports and services of independent vendors of financial information almost invariably offer valuation information and opinions.

► In investment management firms, trusts and bank trust departments, and similar institutions, an analyst may report valuation judgments to a portfolio manager or to an investment committee.[26] The analyst's valuation expertise is important not only in investment disciplines involving security selection based on detailed company analysis, but also in highly quantitative investment disciplines; quantitative analysts work in developing, testing, and updating security selection methodologies.[27]

► Analysts at corporations may perform some valuation tasks similar to those of analysts at money management firms (e.g., when the corporation manages in-house a sponsored pension plan). Both corporate analysts and investment bank analysts may also identify and value companies that could become acquisition targets.

► Analysts associated with investment firms' brokerage operations are perhaps the most visible group of analysts offering valuation judgments—their research reports are widely distributed to current and prospective retail and institutional brokerage clients.

In conducting their valuation activities, investment analysts play a critical role in collecting, organizing, analyzing, and communicating corporate information, and in recommending appropriate investment actions based on sound analysis. When they do those tasks well, analysts:

► help their clients achieve their investment objectives by enabling those clients to make better buy and sell decisions;

► contribute to the efficient functioning of capital markets. In providing analysis that leads to informed buy and sell decisions, analysts help make asset prices better reflections of underlying values. When asset prices accurately reflect underlying values, capital flows more easily to its highest-value uses; and

► benefit the suppliers of capital, including shareholders, by monitoring management's performance. Monitoring managers may inhibit those managers from exploiting corporate resources for their own benefit.[28]

---

[26] Such analysts are widely known as **buy-side analysts**, in contrast to analysts who work at brokerages, who are known as **sell-side analysts**. Brokerages provide or sell services to institutions such as investment management firms, explaining this terminology. **Brokerage** is the business of acting as agents for buyers or sellers, usually in return for commissions.

[27] Ranking stocks by some measure(s) of relative attractiveness (subject to a risk control discipline), as we will discuss in more detail later, forms one key part of quantitative equity investment disciplines.

[28] See Jensen and Meckling (1976) for a classic analysis of the costs of stockholder–manager conflicts.

EXAMPLE 9

What Are Analysts Expected to Do?

When analysts at brokerage firms recommend a stock to the public that later performs very poorly, or when they fail to uncover negative corporate activities, they can sometimes come under public scrutiny. Industry leaders may then be asked to respond to such criticism and to comment on expectations about the role and responsibilities of analysts. One such instance occurred in the United States as a consequence of the late 2001 collapse of Enron Corporation, an energy trading company. In testimony before the U. S. Senate (excerpted below), the President and CEO of AIMR offered a summary of the working conditions and responsibilities of brokerage analysts. In the following passage, **due diligence** refers to investigation and analysis in support of a recommendation; the failure to exercise due diligence may sometimes result in liability according to various securities laws. "Wall Street analysts" refers to analysts working in the U.S. brokerage industry (sell-side analysts).

What are Wall Street analysts expected to do? These analysts are assigned companies and industries to follow, are expected to research fully these companies and the industries in which they operate, and to forecast their future prospects. Based on this analysis, and using appropriate valuation models, they must then determine an appropriate fair price for the company's securities. After comparing this fair price to the current market price, the analyst is able to make a recommendation. If the analyst's "fair price" is significantly above the current market price, it would be expected that the stock be rated a "buy" or "market outperform."

How do Wall Street analysts get their information? Through hard work and due diligence. They must study and try to comprehend the information in numerous public disclosure documents, such as the annual report to shareholders and regulatory filings . . . and gather the necessary quantitative and qualitative inputs to their valuation models.

This due diligence isn't simply reading and analyzing annual reports. It also involves talking to company management, other company employees, competitors, and others, to get answers to questions that arise from their review of public documents. Talking to management must go beyond participation in regular conference calls. Not all questions can be voiced in those calls because of time constraints, for example, and because analysts, like journalists, rightly might not wish to "show their cards," and reveal the insights they have gotten through their hard work, by asking a particularly probing question in the presence of their competitors.

Wall Street analysts are also expected to understand the dynamics of the industry and general economic conditions before finalizing a research report and making a recommendation. Therefore, in order for their firm to justify their continued employment, Wall Street analysts must issue research reports on their assigned companies and must make recommendations based on their reports to clients who purchase their firm's research.[29]

---

[29] Thomas A. Bowman, CFA. Testimony to the Committee on Governmental Affairs (excerpted) U. S. Senate, 27 February 2002.

From the beginnings of the movement to organize financial analysis as a profession rather than as a commercial trade, one guiding principle has been that the analyst must hold himself accountable to both standards of competence and standards of conduct.[30]

Competence in investment analysis requires a high degree of training, experience, and discipline.[31] Additionally, the investment professional is in a position of trust, requiring ethical conduct towards the public, clients, prospects, employers, employees, and fellow analysts. For AIMR members, this position of trust is reflected in the Code of Ethics and Standards of Professional Conduct to which AIMR members subscribe, as well as in the Professional Conduct Statement that they submit annually. The Code and Standards guide the analyst to independent, well-researched, and well-documented analysis. Valuation is closely associated with analyst recommendations that often form the basis for investment action; ensuring that work product is consistent with the Code and Standards is therefore an overriding priority.

5 COMMUNICATING VALUATION RESULTS: THE RESEARCH REPORT

Writing is an important part of an analyst's job. Whether a research report is for review by an investment committee or a portfolio manager in an investment management firm, or for distribution to the retail or institutional clients of a brokerage firm, research reports share several common elements. In this section we discuss the content of an effective research report, one adaptable format for writing such a report, and the analyst's responsibilities in preparing a research report.

5.1 Contents of a Research Report

To understand what a research report should include, we need to ask what readers seek to gain from reading the report. One key focus is the investment recommendation. In evaluating how much attention and weight to give to a recommendation, the reader will look for persuasive supporting arguments. The relevance to this book, of course, is that a key element supporting a recommendation is the valuation of the security. Understanding the business is the first step in valuation. Therefore, the reader will want to understand the prospects for both the industry and the company. The quality of this industry and company analysis bears heavily on the quality of the valuation and recommendation. Some readers of research reports are also interested in background information, and some reports contain detailed historical descriptive statistics about the industry and company. To summarize, most research reports cover the following three broad areas:

► description (presentation of facts). This brings the reader up to date on the company's sales, earnings, new products, and the macroeconomic and industry contexts in which the company operates;

---

[30] See the Articles of Incorporation (1959) of the Institute of Chartered Financial Analysts, a predecessor organization of AIMR, as well as Hayes (1962) and Graham (1963).

[31] Competence in this sense is reflected in the examination and work experience requirements that are prerequisites for obtaining the CFA designation.

▶ analysis and forecasts for the industry and company; and

▶ valuation and recommendation.

How well the analyst executes the above tasks determines the usefulness of the report. Writing an effective research report is a challenging task. An effective research report:

▶ contains timely information;

▶ is written in clear, incisive language;

▶ is unbiased, objective, and well researched;

▶ contains analysis, forecasts, valuation, and a recommendation that are internally consistent;

▶ presents sufficient information that the reader can critique the valuation;

▶ states the risk factors present for an investment in the company; and

▶ discloses any potential conflicts of interests faced by the analyst.

Analysts, whose goal is to produce research of distinguished quality and usefulness, should keep the above points in mind when writing a research report.

Because our subject is valuation, we focus our remaining comments on the valuation information in research reports. Observers have sometimes criticized the **valuation analysis** in many research reports.[32] The analyst needs to maintain a conceptual distinction between a *good company* and a *good investment.* The expected alpha on a common stock purchase depends on the price paid for the stock, whatever the business prospects of the issuing company. The analyst who is overly enthusiastic about a company's prospects sometimes may be tempted to state a positive recommendation without substantial effort at valuation. Such a report might offer interesting background industry information, but the analysis would not be thorough.

The analyst can state his or her specific forecasts, convert those forecasts into an estimate of intrinsic value (describing the model), and compare intrinsic value with market price (or make a similarly careful relative valuation). Qualitative factors and other considerations may affect a recommendation and merit discussion. Superior research reports also contain a section on risk factors that objectively addresses the uncertainty associated with investing in the security. Research reports often state a target price for a stock. Readers can make little use of a target price for a stock unless the report describes the basis for computing the target, supplies a time frame for reaching the target, and conveys information on the uncertainty of reaching the target.

EXAMPLE 10

Research Reports

The following two passages are closely based on the valuation discussions of actual companies in two short research notes (for Passage A, a two-page report dated March 2002; for B, a single-page report issued July 2001). The company names used in the passages, however, are fictional.

---

[32] Cornell (2001) is one example, and comments in the financial press have appeared from time to time.

A. At a recent multiple of 6.5, our earnings per share multiple for 2002, the shares were at a discount to our projection of 14 percent growth for the period . . . MXI has two operating segments . . . In valuing the segments separately, employing relative acquisition multiples and peer mean values, we found fair value to be above recent market value. In addition, the shares trade at a discount to book value (0.76). Based on the value indicated by these two valuation metrics, we view the shares as worth holding. However, in light of a weaker economy over the near term, dampening demand for MXI's services, our enthusiasm is tempered. [*Elsewhere in the report, MXI receives the firm's highest numerical quantitative outlook evaluation.*]

B. Although TXI outperformed the overall stock market by 20 percent since the start of the year, it definitely looks undervalued as shown by its low multiples . . . [*the values of the P/E and another multiple are stated*]. According to our dividend discount model valuation, we get to a valuation of €3.08 implying an upside potential of 36.8 percent based on current prices. The market outperform recommendation is reiterated. [*In a parenthetical expression, the current dividend, assumed dividend growth rates and their time horizons are given. The analyst also briefly explains and calculates the discount rate. Elsewhere in the report the current price of TXI is given as €2.25.*]

Although some of the concepts mentioned in the two passages may not yet be familiar, we can begin to assess the above two reporting efforts.

Passage A communicates the analysis awkwardly. The meaning of "the shares were at a discount to our projection of 14 percent growth for the period" is not completely clear. Presumably the analyst is projecting the earnings growth rate for 2002 and stating that the P/E is low in relation to that expected growth rate. The analyst next discusses valuing MXI as the sum of its divisions. In describing the method as "employing relative acquisition multiples and peer mean values," the analyst does not convey a clear picture of what was done. It is probable that companies similar to each of MXI's divisions were identified; then the mean or average value of some unidentified multiple for those comparison companies was calculated and used as the basis for valuing MXI. The writer is vague, however, on the extent of MXI's undervaluation. The analyst states that MXI's price is below its book value (an accounting measure of shareholders' investment) but draws no comparison with the average price-to-book value ratio for stocks similar to MXI, for example. Finally, the verbal summation is feeble and hedged. Although filled with technical verbiage, Passage A does not communicate a coherent valuation of MXI.

In the second sentence of Passage B, by contrast, the analyst gives an explicit valuation of TXI and the information needed to critique it. The reader can also see that €3.08, which is elsewhere stated in the research note as the target price for TXI, implies the stated price appreciation potential for TXI (€3.08/€2.25 − 1, approximately 37 percent). In the first sentence in Passage B, the analyst gives information that might support the conclusion that TXI is undervalued, although the statement lacks strength because the analyst does not explain why the P/E is "low." The verbal summary is clear. Using much less space than the analyst in Passage A, the analyst in Passage B has done a superior job of communicating the results of his valuation.

5.2 Format of a Research Report

Equity research reports may be logically presented in several ways. The firm in which the analyst works sometimes specifies a fixed format for consistency and quality control purposes. Without claiming superiority to other ways to organize a report, we offer Table 3 as an adaptable format by which the analyst can communicate research and valuation findings in detail. (Shorter research reports and research notes obviously may employ a more compact format.)

TABLE 3   A Format for Research Reports

Section	Purpose	Content	Comments
Table of contents	▶ Show report's organization	▶ Consistent with narrative in sequence and language	This is typically used in very long research reports only.
Summary and investment conclusion	▶ Communicate the large picture ▶ Communicate major specific conclusions of the analysis ▶ Recommend an investment course of action	▶ Capsule description of the company ▶ Major recent developments ▶ Earnings projections ▶ Other major conclusions ▶ Valuation summary ▶ Investment action	An executive summary; may be called simply "Summary."
Business summary	▶ Present the company in more detail ▶ Communicate a detailed understanding of the company's economics and current situation ▶ Provide and explain specific forecasts	▶ Company description to the divisional level ▶ Industry analysis ▶ Competitive analysis ▶ Historical performance ▶ Financial forecasts	Reflects the first and second steps of the valuation process. Financial forecasts should be explained adequately and reflect quality of earnings analysis.
Risks	▶ Alert readers to the risk factors in investing in the security	▶ Possible negative industry developments ▶ Possible negative regulatory and legal developments ▶ Possible negative company developments ▶ Risks in the forecasts ▶ Other risks	Readers should have enough information to determine how the analyst is defining and assessing the risks specific to investing in the security.
Valuation	▶ Communicate a clear and careful valuation	▶ Description of model(s) used ▶ Recapitulation of inputs ▶ Statement of conclusions	Readers should have enough information to critique the analysis.
Historical and pro forma tables	▶ Organize and present data to support the analysis in the Business Summary		This is generally a separate section in longer research reports only. Many reports fold all or some of this information into the Business Summary section.

5.3 Research Reporting Responsibilities

All analysts have an obligation to provide substantive and meaningful content in a clear and comprehensive report format. Analysts who are AIMR members, however, have an additional and overriding responsibility to adhere to the Code of Ethics and the Standards of Professional Conduct in all activities pertaining to their research reports.[33] The AIMR Code of Ethics states:

> Members of the Association for Investment Management and Research shall use reasonable care and exercise independent professional judgment.

Going beyond this general statement of responsibility, some specific Standards of Professional Conduct particularly relevant to an analyst writing a research report are shown in Table 4.

TABLE 4	Selected AIMR Standards of Professional Conduct Pertaining to Research Reports
Standard of Professional Conduct	**Responsibility**
II(C)	Members shall not copy or use, in substantially the same form as the original, material prepared by another without acknowledging and identifying the name of the author, publisher, or source of such material. Members may use, without acknowledgment, factual information published by recognized financial and statistical reporting services or similar sources.
IV(A)1(a)	Members shall exercise diligence and thoroughness in making investment recommendations or in taking investment actions.
IV(A)1(b)	Members shall have a reasonable and adequate basis, supported by appropriate research and investigation, for such recommendations or actions.
IV(A)1(c)	Members shall make reasonable and diligent efforts to avoid any material misrepresentation in any research report or investment recommendation.
IV(A)1(d)	Members shall maintain appropriate records to support the reasonableness of such recommendations or actions.
IV(A)2(a)	Members shall use reasonable judgment regarding the inclusion or exclusion of relevant factors in research reports.
IV(A)2(b)	Members shall distinguish between facts and opinions in research reports.
IV(A)2(c)	Members shall indicate the basic characteristics of the investment involved when preparing for public distribution a research report that is not directly related to a specific portfolio or client.
IV(A)3	Members shall use reasonable care and judgment to achieve and maintain independence and objectivity in making investment recommendations or taking investment action.

---

[33] AIMR changed its name to CFA Institute in 2004. The current Code and Standards are contained in Study Session 1.

SUMMARY

In this reading, we have discussed the scope of equity valuation, outlined the valuation process, introduced valuation concepts and models, discussed the analyst's role and responsibilities in conducting valuation, and described the elements of an effective research report in which analysts communicate their valuation analysis.

▶ Valuation is the estimation of an asset's value based on variables perceived to be related to future investment returns, or based on comparisons with closely similar assets.

▶ Valuation is used for:
  ▶ stock selection;
  ▶ inferring (extracting) market expectations;
  ▶ evaluating corporate events;
  ▶ fairness opinions;
  ▶ evaluating business strategies and models;
  ▶ communication among management, shareholders, and analysts; and
  ▶ appraisal of private businesses.

▶ The three steps in the portfolio management process are planning, execution, and feedback. Valuation is most closely associated with the planning and execution steps.
  ▶ For active investment managers, plans concerning valuation models and criteria are part of the elaboration of an investment strategy.
  ▶ Skill in valuation plays a key role in the execution step (in selecting a portfolio, in particular).

▶ The valuation process has five steps:
  1. Understanding the business.
  2. Forecasting company performance.
  3. Selecting the appropriate valuation model.
  4. Converting forecasts to a valuation.
  5. Making the investment decision (recommendation).

▶ The tasks within "understanding the business" include evaluating industry prospects, competitive position, and corporate strategies. Because similar economic and technological factors typically affect all companies in an industry, and because companies compete with each other for sales, both industry knowledge and competitive analysis help analysts understand a company's economics and its environment. The analyst can then make more accurate forecasts.

▶ Two approaches to economic forecasting are top-down forecasting and bottom-up forecasting. In top-down forecasting, analysts use macroeconomic forecasts to develop industry forecasts and then make individual company and asset forecasts consistent with the industry forecasts. In bottom-up forecasting, individual company forecasts are aggregated to industry forecasts, which in turn may be aggregated to macroeconomic forecasts.

▶ Careful scrutiny and interpretation of financial statements, footnotes to financial statements, and other accounting disclosures are essential to a quality of earnings analysis. Quality of earnings analysis concerns the scrutiny of possible earnings management and balance sheet management.

► The intrinsic value of an asset is its value given a hypothetically complete understanding of the asset's investment characteristics.

► Alpha is an asset's excess risk-adjusted return. *Ex ante* alpha is expected holding-period return minus required return given risk. Historical alpha is actual holding-period return minus the contemporaneous required return.

► Active investing is consistent with rational efficient markets and the existence of trading costs and assets whose intrinsic value is difficult to determine.

► The going-concern assumption is the assumption that a company will continue operating for the foreseeable future. A company's going-concern value is its value under the going-concern assumption and is the general objective of most valuation models. In contrast, liquidation value is the company's value if it were dissolved and its assets sold individually.

► Fair value is the price at which an asset would change hands if neither buyer nor seller were under compulsion to buy/sell.

► Absolute valuation models specify an asset's intrinsic value, supplying a point estimate of value that can be compared with market price. Present value models of common stock (also called discounted cash flow models) are the most important type of absolute valuation model.

► Relative valuation models specify an asset's value relative to the value of another asset. As applied to equity valuation, relative valuation is known as the method of comparables: In applying the method of comparables, analysts compare a stock's price multiple to the price multiple of a similar stock or the average or median price multiple of some group of stocks.

► Relative equity valuation models do not address intrinsic value without the further assumption that the price of the comparison value accurately reflects its intrinsic value.

► The broad criteria for selecting a valuation approach are that the valuation approach be:
  ► consistent with the characteristics of the company being valued;
  ► appropriate given the availability and quality of the data; and
  ► consistent with the analyst's valuation purpose and perspective.

► Valuation may be affected by control premiums (premiums for a controlling interest in the company), marketability discounts (discounts reflecting the lack of a public market for the company's shares), and liquidity discounts (discounts reflecting the lack of a liquid market for the company's shares).

► Investment analysts play a critical role in collecting, organizing, analyzing, and communicating corporate information, as well as in recommending appropriate investment actions based on their analysis. In fulfilling this role, they help clients achieve their investment objectives and contribute to the efficient functioning of capital markets. Analysts can contribute to the welfare of shareholders through monitoring the actions of management.

► In performing valuations, analysts need to hold themselves accountable to both standards of competence and standards of conduct.

► An effective research report:
  ► contains timely information;
  ► is written in clear, incisive language;
  ► is unbiased, objective, and well researched;
  ► contains analysis, forecasts, valuation, and a recommendation that are internally consistent;

► presents sufficient information that the reader can critique the valuation;

► states the risk factors for an investment in the company; and

► discloses any potential conflicts of interests faced by the analyst.

► Analysts have an obligation to provide substantive and meaningful content. AIMR members have an additional overriding responsibility to adhere to the AIMR Code of Ethics and relevant specific Standards of Professional Conduct.

PRACTICE PROBLEMS FOR READING 37

1. **A.** State four uses or purposes of valuation models.

   B. Which use of valuation models may be the most important to a working equity portfolio manager?

   C. Which uses would be particularly relevant to a corporate officer?

2. In Example 1 based on Cornell's (2001) study of Intel Corporation, in which Cornell valued Intel using a present value model of stock value, we wrote:

   "What future revenue growth rates were consistent with Intel's stock price of $61.50 just prior to the release, and $43.31 only five days later? Using a conservatively low discount rate, Cornell estimated that the price of $61.50 was consistent with a growth rate of 20 percent a year for the subsequent 10 years (and then 6 percent per year thereafter)."

   A. If Cornell had assumed a higher discount rate, would the resulting revenue growth rate estimate consistent with a price of $61.50 be higher or lower than 20 percent a year?

   B. Explain your answer to Part A.

3. **A.** Explain the role of valuation in the planning step of the portfolio management process.

   B. Explain the role of valuation in the execution step of the portfolio management process.

4. Explain why valuation models are important to active investors but not to investors trying to replicate a stock market index.

5. An analyst has been following Kerr-McGee Corporation (NYSE: KMG) for several years. He has consistently felt that the stock is undervalued and has always recommended a strong buy. Another analyst who has been following Nucor Corporation (NYSE: NUE) has been similarly bullish. The tables below summarize the prices, dividends, total returns, and estimates of the contemporaneous required returns for KMG and NUE from 1998 to 2001.

Data for KMG

Year	Price at Year-End	Dividends	Total Annual Return	Contemporaneous Required Return
1997	$54.22			
1998	33.97	$1.80	−34.0%	26.6%
1999	54.38	1.80	65.4	19.6
2000	63.96	1.80	20.9	−8.5
2001	53.93	1.80	−12.9	−11.0

Data for NUE				
Year	Price at Year-End	Dividends	Total Annual Return	Contemporaneous Required Return
1997	$45.66			
1998	41.31	$0.48	−8.5%	29.2%
1999	52.93	0.52	29.4	21.5
2000	38.96	0.60	−25.3	−9.3
2001	52.80	0.68	37.3	−12.1

The total return is the price appreciation and dividends for the year divided by the price at the end of the previous year. The contemporaneous required return is the average actual return for the year realized by stocks that were of the same risk as KMG or NUE, respectively.

A. Without reference to any numerical data, what can be said about each analyst's *ex ante* alpha for KMG and NUE, respectively?

B. Calculate the *ex post* alphas for each year 1998 through 2001 for KMG and for NUE.

6. On the last trading day of 2000 (29 December 2000), an analyst is reviewing his valuation of Wal-Mart Stores (NYSE: WMT). The analyst has the following information and assumptions:

▶ The current price is $53.12.

▶ The analyst's estimate of WMT's intrinsic value is $56.00.

▶ In addition to the full correction of the difference between WMT's current price and its intrinsic value, the analyst forecasts additional price appreciation of $4.87 and a cash dividend of $0.28 over the next year.

▶ The required rate of return for Wal-Mart is 9.2 percent.

A. What is the analyst's expected holding-period return on WMT?

B. What is WMT's *ex ante* alpha?

C. Calculate *ex post* alpha, given the following additional information:

▶ Over the next year, 29 December 2000 through 31 December 2001, Wal-Mart's actual rate of return was 8.9 percent.

▶ In 2001, the realized rate of return for stocks of similar risk was −10.4 percent.

7. The table below gives information on the expected and required rates of return based on the CAPM for three securities an analyst is valuing:

	Expected Rate	CAPM Required Rate
Security 1	0.20	0.21
Security 2	0.18	0.08
Security 3	0.11	0.10

   A. Define *ex ante* alpha.

   B. Calculate the expected alpha of Securities 1, 2, and 3 and rank them from most attractive to least attractive.

   C. Based on your answer to Part B, what risks attach to selecting among Securities 1, 2, and 3?

8. Benjamin Graham (1963) wrote that "[t]here is . . . a double function of the Financial Analyst, related in part to securities and in part to people."

   A. Explain the analyst's function related to people.

   B. How does the analyst's work contribute to the functioning of capital markets?

9. In a research note on the ordinary shares of the Mariella Burani Fashion Group (Milan Stock Exchange: MBFG.MI) dated early July 2001 when a recent price was €7.73 and projected annual dividends were €0.05, an analyst stated a target price of €9.20. The research note did not discuss how the target price was obtained or how it should be interpreted. Assume the target price represents the expected price of MBFG.MI. What further specific pieces of information would you need to form an opinion on whether MBFG.MI was fairly valued, overvalued, or undervalued?

10. You are researching XMI Corporation (XMI). XMI has shown steady earnings per share growth (18 percent a year during the last seven years) and trades at a very high multiple to earnings (its P/E ratio is currently 40 percent above the average P/E ratio for a group of the most comparable stocks). XMI has generally grown through acquisition, by using XMI stock to purchase other companies. These companies usually trade at lower P/E ratios than XMI.

   In investigating the financial disclosures of these acquired companies and in talking to industry contacts, you conclude that XMI has been forcing the companies it acquires to accelerate the payment of expenses before the acquisition deals are closed. Such acceleration drives down the acquired companies' last reported cash flow and earnings per share numbers. As one example, XMI asks acquired companies to immediately pay all pending accounts payable, whether or not they are due. Subsequent to the acquisition, XMI reinstitutes normal expense payment patterns. After it acquires a company, XMI appears to have a pattern of speeding up revenue recognition as well. For example, one overseas telecommunications subsidiary changed its accounting to recognize up front the expected revenue from sales of network capacity that spanned decades. The above policies and accounting facts do not appear to be have been adequately disclosed in XMI's shareholder communications.

   A. Characterize the effect of the XMI expensing policies with respect to acquisitions on XMI's post-acquisition earnings per share growth rate.

   B. Characterize the quality of XMI earnings based on its expensing and revenue-recognition policies with respect to acquisitions.

   C. In discussing the current price of XMI, the question states that XMI's "P/E ratio is currently 40 percent above the average P/E ratio for a group of the most comparable stocks." Characterize the type of valuation model implicit in such a statement.

   D. State two *risk factors* in investing in XMI, in the sense in which that term was used in the discussion of quality of earnings.

EQUITY: MARKETS AND INSTRUMENTS

by Bruno Solnik and Dennis McLeavey

LEARNING OUTCOMES

The candidate should be able to:

a. explain the origins of different national market organizations;

b. differentiate between an order-driven market and a price-driven market, and explain the risks and advantages of each;

c. calculate the impact of different national taxes on the return of an international investment;

d. discuss the various components of execution costs (i.e., commissions and fees, market impact, and opportunity cost) and explain ways to reduce execution costs, and discuss the advantages and disadvantages of each;

e. describe an American Depositary Receipt (ADR), and differentiate among the various forms of ADRs in terms of trading and information supplied by the listed company;

f. explain why firms choose to be listed abroad and calculate the cost tradeoff between buying shares listed abroad and buying ADRs;

g. state the determinants of the value of a closed-end country fund;

h. discuss the advantages of exchange traded funds (ETFs) and explain the pricing of international ETFs in relation to their net asset value (NAV);

i. discuss the advantages and disadvantages of the various alternatives to direct international investing.

INTRODUCTION   1

This reading discusses equity markets worldwide, and also presents facts and concepts relevant to executing trades in those markets.[1] The financial specialist is often struck by the differences among stock market organizations across the

---

[1] Jan R. Squires, CFA, and Philip J. Young, CFA, provided important suggestions for this reading.

International Investments, Fifth Edition, by Bruno Solnik and Dennis McLeavey. Copyright © 2004 by Pearson Education. Reprinted with permission of Pearson Education, publishing as Pearson Addison Wesley.

world. Traditionally, national stock markets have not only different legal and physical organizations but also different transaction methodologies. The international investor must have a minimal familiarity with these technical differences because they influence the execution costs of every transaction. After reviewing some statistics on the market size, liquidity, and concentration, we discuss some practical aspects of international investing. These include taxes, market indexes, and the availability of information. A major practical aspect of international investing is the estimation of execution costs in each market. Understanding the determinants and magnitude of overall transaction costs is very important when implementing a global investment strategy. Getting best execution does not reduce to minimizing commissions and fees; **market impact** must also be estimated. Investment performance depends on the overall execution costs incurred in implementing a strategy. This reading concludes with a review of alternatives to direct international investing, which involve the purchase of foreign shares listed at home. These alternatives include American Depositary Receipts (ADRs), closed-end country funds, and **open-end funds**, especially exchange traded funds (ETFs). Each of these investment vehicles has advantages and disadvantages relative to directly investing on foreign markets.

2 MARKET DIFFERENCES: A HISTORICAL PERSPECTIVE

Financial paper, in the form of debt obligations, has long been traded in Europe, whereas trading in company shares is relatively recent. The Amsterdam Bourse is usually considered the oldest stock market. The first common stock to be publicly traded in the Netherlands was the famous East Indies Trading Company (Verenigde Oost-Indische Compagnie) in the 17th century. But organized stock markets really started in the mid to late 18th century. In Paris, a stock market was started on a bridge (Pont au Change). In London, the stock market originated in a tavern; churches and open-air markets were also used as stock markets on the Continent. For example, the Amsterdam Bourse spent some time in the Oude-Kerk (Old Church) and later in the Nieuwe-Kerk (New Church). Most of these European exchanges became recognized as separate markets and were regulated around 1800. The same holds for the United States. However, **stock exchanges** in Japan and other countries in Asia and most of the Americas are more recent creations.

Historical and cultural differences explain most of the significant differences in stock-trading practices around the world. Rather than engage in a detailed analysis of each national market, this section looks at the major differences in terms of market structures and trading procedures. Many of these differences are being eliminated, but some historical perspective helps gain a better understanding of the current working of those stock markets.

Historical Differences in Market Organization

Each stock exchange (bourse) has its own unique characteristics and legal organization, but broadly speaking, all exchanges have evolved from one of three market organization types.

Private Bourses Private stock exchange corporations are founded by private individuals and entities for the purpose of securities trading. Several private stock exchanges may compete within the same country, as in the United States, Japan, and Canada. In other countries, one leading exchange has emerged through either attrition or absorption of its competitors. Although these bourses are private, they are not free of public regulation, but the mix of self-regulation and government supervision is oriented more toward self-regulation than in the public bourses. Historically, these private bourses developed in the British sphere of influence.

Public Bourses The public bourse market structure has its origin in the legislative work of Napoleon I, the French emperor. He designed the bourse to be a public institution, with brokers appointed by the government and enjoying a monopoly over all transactions. Commissions are fixed by the state. Brokerage firms are private, but their number is fixed and new brokers are proposed to the state for nomination by the brokers' association. The Paris Bourse followed this model until 1990. Stock exchanges organized under the authority of the state were found in the sphere of influence of Napoleon I: Belgium, France, Spain, Italy, Greece, and some Latin American countries. Most have moved toward a private bourse model.

Bankers' Bourses In some countries, banks are the major, or even the only, securities traders. In Germany, the Banking Act granted a brokerage monopoly to banks. Bankers' bourses were found in the German sphere of influence: Austria, Switzerland, Scandinavia, and the Netherlands. Bankers' bourses may be either private or semipublic organizations, but their chief function is to provide a convenient place for banks to meet. Sometimes trading takes place directly between banks without involving the official bourse at all. Government regulation is imposed both on the bourse itself and directly on the banks. Bankers' bourses suffered from potential conflicts of interests, and more trading transparency was required by international investors. Most bankers' bourses moved to a private bourse model in the 1990s to allow foreign financial intermediaries to become brokers.

Historical Differences in Trading Procedures

Apart from legal structure, numerous other historical differences are found in the operation of national stock markets. The most important differences are in the trading procedures.

Cash versus Forward Markets In most markets, stocks are traded on a cash basis, and transactions must be settled within a few days (typically three business days after the transaction). To allow more leveraged investment, margin trading is available on most cash markets. In margin trading, the investor borrows money (or shares) from a broker to finance a transaction. This is still a cash market transaction, and trade settlement takes place in three days; however, a third party steps in to lend money (shares) to the buyer (seller) to honor a cash transaction commitment.

In contrast, some stock markets were organized as a forward market. This was the case for London and Paris, as well as some markets in Latin America and Asia. In Paris, the settlement date was the end of the month for all transactions made during the month (London settled accounts every two weeks). To simplify the clearing operations, all transactions were settled at the end of the month on the settlement day. This is a periodic settlement system. Of course, a deposit is required to guarantee a position, as on most forward markets. Moreover, the transaction price is fixed at the time of the transaction and remains at this value even if the market price has changed substantially by the settlement time. Settling all accounts once a month greatly simplifies the security clearing system, but it also opens the door to short-term speculation and to frequent misconceptions on the part of foreign investors who are unfamiliar with the technique. Although most forward markets have moved to a cash market, they usually have institutionalized procedures to allow investors to trade forward, if desired.

Price-Driven versus Order-Driven Markets   U.S. investors are accustomed to a *continuous* market, whereby transactions take place all day and *market makers* (also called *dealers*) ensure market liquidity at virtually any point in time. The market maker quotes both a *bid* price (the price at which the dealer offers to buy the security) and an *ask* price (the price at which the dealer offers to sell the security). The ask price is sometimes called the *offer* price. These quotes are firm commitments by the market maker to transact at those prices for a specified transaction size. The customer will turn to the market maker who provides the best quote. Of course, market makers adjust their quotes continuously to reflect supply and demand for the security as well as their own inventory. This type of market is often referred to as a *dealer market*. It is also known as a *price-driven* market (or *quote-driven* market), because market makers publicly post their bid–ask prices to induce orders. For example, Nasdaq is a dealer market.[2]

In many other markets and countries, however, active market makers do not exist, and the supply and demand for securities are matched directly in an ***auction market***. Because the quantities demanded and supplied are a function of the transaction price, a price will exist that equilibrates demand and supply. In a traditional auction market, liquidity requires that an asset be traded only once or a few times per day. This is known as a *call* or ***fixing*** procedure, whereby orders are batched together in an order book until the auction when they are executed at a single price that equilibrates demand and supply. This auction price maximizes trade volume. In the past, many stock markets used an open *criée* (outcry) system in which brokers would negotiate loudly until a price was found that would equilibrate buy and sell orders (quietness is restored). All these stock markets have moved to computerized trading systems in which buy-and-sell orders are entered on the computer trading system, which matches them directly. An auction market is also known as an ***order-driven*** market because all traders publicly post their orders, and the transaction price is the result of the equilibrium of supply and demand. Although a single call auction provides excellent liquidity at one point in time, it makes trading at other times difficult. Hence, the market-making function is being developed on all ***call auction*** markets, (e.g., Paris, Tokyo, or Frankfurt) to allow the possibility of trading throughout the day.

Automation on the Major Stock Exchanges

Trading on a floor where participants noisily meet is increasingly being replaced by computerized trading. Automation allows more efficient handling of orders, especially a large number of small orders. Competition across national stock exchanges and the increased volume of trading hastened the adoption of computerized systems, including price quotation, order routing, and automatic

---

[2] The New York Stock Exchange (NYSE) has a unique system where each stock is allocated to one specialist who acts both as a dealer and as an auctioneer. As a dealer, a specialist posts bid and ask quotes and uses its own capital to buy or sell securities (under strict regulations). As an auctioneer, a specialist maintains the order book of all orders that are submitted.

order matching. The design of the automated systems reflects the historical and cultural heritage of the national market. Automated trading systems have followed two different paths, depending on whether the traditional market organization was dominated by dealers making the market or by brokers acting as agents in an auction system.

Price-Driven and Order-Driven Systems   The U.S. Nasdaq is a typical *price-driven* system. The automated system posts firm quotes by market makers. There is no centralized book of limit orders. When posting a quote, the market maker does not know what trades it will generate. In a price-driven system, a market maker is placing the equivalent of limit orders: a buy limit order representing his bid and a sell limit order representing his ask.

At the other extreme, *auction markets,* such as Paris, Frankfurt, or Tokyo (and most other markets), have put in place electronic order-driven systems. The computer stores all orders, which become public knowledge. All limit orders that have not been executed are stored in a central *order book.* A new order is immediately matched with the book of orders previously submitted. The central limit order book is the hub of these automated systems. Viewing all standing orders, a trader knows exactly what trades will be executed if she enters a new order. Market makers provide liquidity by entering limit buy-and-sell orders in the order book. The highest limit bid and the lowest limit offer act as the bid and ask prices in a **price-driven market**.

EXAMPLE 1

Order-Driven Market

LVMH (Moët Hennesy Louis Vuitton) is a French firm listed on the Paris Bourse. You can access the central limit order book directly on the Internet and find the following information (the limit prices for sell orders are ask prices and those for buy orders are bid prices):

Sell Orders		Buy Orders	
Quantity	Limit	Limit	Quantity
1,000	58	49	2,000
3,000	54	48	500
1,000	52	47	1,000
1,000	51	46	2,000
500	50	44	10,000

You wish to buy 1,000 shares and enter a market order to buy those shares. A market order will be executed against the best matching order. At what price will you buy the shares?

Solution: Unless a new sell order is entered at a price below 51 before your order is executed, you will buy 500 shares at 50 and 500 shares at 51.

To improve liquidity, most order-driven markets have retained periodic call auctions. There is a fixing at the opening of the market, where all orders that arrived before opening are stored and the opening price is set through a call auction.[3] In Frankfurt, call auctions take place periodically throughout the day, at prespecified times other than opening and closing. At the time of the call auction, the continuous trading of the stock on XETRA is interrupted. (XETRA is a trading platform that includes all stocks on the Deutsche Boerse.) In a *pretrading* phase, traders can submit limit and **market orders**, which are accumulated in the order book. At auction time, orders are automatically crossed (matched) at a price that maximizes the volume of trading. In Tokyo, a call auction system, called *itayose,* is used to establish prices at the start of the morning and afternoon sessions (the market closes for lunch). During the sessions, a continuous auction is used for new orders. This auction system, called *zaraba,* is an order-matching method and does not require the intervention of a market maker.

The NYSE combines price-driven and order-driven systems. Specialists maintain limit order books and shares may also trade in auctions.

Advantages and Risks of Each System   Automation brings many improvements in the speed and costs of trading. An order-driven system requires little human intervention and is therefore less costly to run. Cost considerations have pushed all markets in this direction. Only American stock markets have retained a price-driven model. Markets with lesser transaction volumes have found it more efficient to adopt order-driven electronic trading systems. For example, London had a price-driven market with competitive market makers. Cost-efficiency considerations caused it to move to an automated order-driven system called SETS (*Stock Exchange Electronic Trading Service*) at the end of the 20th century.[4] Market makers enter their bid-and-ask quotes directly in the order book in the form of limit orders. Most emerging stock markets have adopted an order-driven electronic trading system.

The cost of running the trading system, however, is only one component of the transaction cost borne by investors. Investors try to get the best execution price for each trade. This raises the question: Which market structure provides the best liquidity and lowest execution costs? Theoretical and experimental research suggests that the market design affects trader behavior, transaction prices, and market efficiency. In real life, the answer depends on the market environment, and there is no clear-cut conclusion. An electronic auction market is cheaper to operate, but that could be at the expense of liquidity—hence, trading could be more costly because of overall execution costs, including price impact.[5] Domowitz (2001) suggests that the public dissemination of the electronic order book in order-driven markets allows traders to monitor liquidity and provide liquidity at a lower cost than in price-driven markets.

A drawback of electronic order-driven systems is their inability to execute large trades. In the absence of active market makers, trading a block (a large transaction) on an automated order-driven system is difficult. Because of the lack of depth in the market, it may take a long time before the block is traded. This will leave the trader who discloses the block on the system fully exposed to the

---

[3] On the New York Stock Exchange, the opening price is determined through a call auction.

[4] Smaller companies and foreign companies, however, are still traded in a traditional nonautomated price-driven model (SEAQ and SEAQ International).

[5] Conrad, Johnson and Wahal (forthcoming) find some evidence that realized execution costs are lower on electronic trading systems for U.S. stocks. Using data up to 2000, Huang (2002) finds that electronic communication network quoted spreads are smaller than dealer spreads for Nasdaq stocks. However, the period of study was prior to the U.S. adoption of decimal quotations, which reduced spreads markedly.

risk that new information might hurt him unless he continuously updates the limit on the block order. This is the risk of being "picked off"; that is, having an order accepted at a price no longer desired by the trader at the time of the transaction. Blocks are generally traded away from the automated system. This is often called *upstairs* trading. Order-driven systems have developed in part because they are much cheaper to operate than traditional dealers' markets. However, market makers are still needed for trading large blocks.

Another drawback of a continuous order-driven system, in the absence of developed market making, is the danger in placing market orders (i.e., orders with no **price limits**). In the absence of **competitive market** makers providing liquidity, a sell market order will be immediately crossed with the highest "buy" **limit order**, which could be very far from the lowest "sell" limit order. The Tokyo Stock Exchange has a special procedure to limit this risk. Other markets are trying to implement rules protecting market orders. This is typically true for less active stocks, in which market making would help provide liquidity.

Any automated trading system exposes one party to transparency risk. It forces one side of the transaction to expose itself first and, therefore, run the risk of being "picked off." In all cases, a limit order gives a free trading option to other market participants. In an order-driven market, the trader who submits the order implicitly gives the free option to the rest of the market. In a price-driven market, it is the dealer posting a firm quote who gives this free option, as shown in Example 2. Of course, the option holder depends on the dealer to deliver in a non-automated system, and "backing away" (reneging) can be a problem.

EXAMPLE 2

Exposition Risk in Two Types of Markets

LVMH is traded on the Paris Bourse, and the last transaction was at 50 euros per share. An investor entered on the French electronic trading system NSC *(Nouveau Système Cotation)* a limit order to sell LVMH shares at 51 euros while the market price was 50.

LVMH is also traded as an ADR on Nasdaq. One ADR represents one-fifth of an LVMH French share (so 5 ADRs equal one LVMH share). The exchange rate is one dollar per euro, and the ADR price is quoted by a market maker at 10–10.20. Assume that the exchange rate remains constant over time.

Suppose that favorable information suddenly arrives that justifies a higher price for LVMH—say, 55 euros. Who are the parties exposed to losses on the Paris Bourse and on Nasdaq if they do not react immediately?

Solutions:

▶ On the Paris Bourse, informed market participants have an option worth four euros per share, and the investor who has a standing order in the electronic order book gets "picked off" (the informed participant can buy at 51 euros a share now worth 55 euros).

▶ On Nasdaq, the market maker posts a firm bid–ask quote for LVMH of 10–10.20 for the dollar ADR, which is equivalent for the French share of LVMH quoted in euros to a quote of 50–51. Under the same scenario, informed market participants suddenly get a free option worth 0.8 dollar per ADR or four euros per French

> share (they can buy at 10.2 dollars from the market maker a share now worth 11 dollars). In a price-driven market, dealers run the risk of being "picked off."
>
> The danger of automation is that market liquidity may be reduced, because dealers (in a price-driven system) or public investors (in an order-driven system) may be less willing to publicly place limit orders.

Electronic Communication Networks and Electronic Crossing Networks (ECNs)
Some electronic trading systems have developed alongside official exchanges. They tend to be privately owned and offer trading on stocks of one market or of a region. Electronic communication networks and electronic crossing networks are both often called ECNs, although they are quite different.

Electronic communication networks are order-driven systems, in which the limit order book plays a central role as previously described. Many of them coexist in the United States. (Instinet-Island, Tradebook, Archipelago, Nasdaq SuperMontage, and others). Virt-x is a pan-European ECN specialized in **blue chips**.

Electronic crossing networks are different systems. These crossing systems anonymously match the buy and sell orders of a pool of participants, generally institutional investors and broker-dealers. Participants enter market orders,[6] which are crossed at prespecified times (once or a few times every day) at prices determined in the primary market for the security. The trade price is the mid-market quote, the midpoint between the bid and the ask, observed on the primary market at the prespecified time. POSIT® is a major crossing network in the United States; Instinet also provides some crossing at the close of the NYSE and Nasdaq. In Europe, E-Crossnet and POSIT provide crossing for European stocks.

EXAMPLE 3

Crossing

Market orders for LVMH have been entered on a crossing network for European shares. There is one order from Participant A to buy 100,000 shares, one order from Participant B to sell 50,000 shares, and one order from Participant C to sell 70,000 shares. Assume that orders were entered in that chronological order and that the network gives priority to the oldest orders. At the time specified for the crossing session, LVMH transacts at 51 euros on the Paris Bourse, its primary market.

1. What trades would take place on the crossing network?
2. Assume now that all the orders are AON (all or nothing), meaning that the whole block has to be traded at the same price. What trades would take place?

---

[6] Participants also can specify various constraints on their orders.

Solutions:

1. One hundred thousand shares would be exchanged at 51 euros. Participant A would buy 100,000. Participants B and C would sell 50,000. Participant B's order has priority, so Participant C's order would not be executed entirely (20,000 shares remain unsold).
2. There is no way that the AON condition could be achieved for the three orders; so, no trade would take place.

Crossing networks present two advantages for large orders of institutional investors:

▶ *Low transaction costs.* The trade is executed at mid-market prices, so there is no market impact or bid–ask spread, even for large trades.

▶ *Anonymity.* The identity of the buyers and sellers, and the magnitude of their order is not revealed, so there is little exposure risk.

On the other hand, crossing networks have a distinct disadvantage:

▶ *No trading immediacy.* The trader must wait until the crossing session time to execute a trade, and the trade takes place only if there are offsetting orders entered by other participants. Only a small proportion of orders are executed at each crossing session. The order has to wait in the system, or needs to be worked through other market mechanisms.

Basically, crossing networks allow a substantial reduction in execution cost for large trades at the detriment of immediacy.

Cross-Border Alliances of Stock Exchanges Fragmentation of national stock markets, especially the smaller ones, is a hindrance to international investors who often think in terms of regions rather than individual countries. Periodically, plans for cross-border mergers of national stock exchanges are drafted. But most of these projects collapse, in part because of the cultural heritage of different trading, legal, and regulatory systems, which makes it very difficult to harmonize trading systems. The canceled merger between the *London Stock Exchange* and the *Deutsche Boerse* is a vivid example. As of 2002, *Euronext* is the only successful merger. Paris, Amsterdam, Brussels, and Lisbon merged their trading platform using the French NSC electronic trading system. As we shall see later, stock markets also internationalize by listing shares of foreign companies. This is the route followed by U.S. stock exchanges (discussed in the next section).

A related hindrance is the fragmentation of settlement systems. The multiplicity of national settlement systems adds to the cost of international investing. But a consolidation of settlement systems is taking place, especially in Europe. A common depository and **counterparty** platform has been developed around Euronext and Euroclear, the international securities clearing house. So, trades in several European stock markets, as well as international securities such as **Eurobonds**, use the same system, Clearnet. Another platform, Clearstream, has been created around the Deutsche Boerse and the other international securities clearing house, Cedel.

SOME STATISTICS

Market Size

Relative national market capitalizations give some indication of the importance of each country for global investors. Market-capitalization weights are used in the commonly used global benchmarks; hence, market sizes guide global investment strategies.

Developed and emerging markets are usually classified in two different asset classes. Although they are somewhat arbitrary, and some countries have been moved from the status of emerging to developed in the recent past, these classifications are still widely used by investors.

Developed Markets   The U.S. stock exchanges are the largest exchanges in the world. It is worth noting that the U.S. capital market is very large compared with the U.S. economy. The U.S. stock market capitalization (cap) is much larger than the annual U.S. gross domestic product (GDP). Britain also has a market cap almost double its GDP, but the corresponding figure for France or Germany is below 80%. This difference between the United States and continental Europe has several explanations. Most U.S. firms prefer to go public, whereas in France, as well as in the rest of Europe, tradition calls for maintaining private ownership as much as possible. In many European countries, corporations are undercapitalized and rely heavily on bank financing. Germany is a typical example because banks finance corporations extensively, thereby reducing the need for outside equity capital. In Europe, banks tend to provide corporations with all financial services, assisting them in both their commercial needs and their long-term debt and equity financing. In contrast to banks in the United States, it is common for European banks to own shares of their client companies. U.S. companies, especially small- and medium-sized ones, tend to go public and raise capital in the marketplace, thereby increasing the public stock market cap. In other countries, many large firms are nationalized and, therefore, not listed on the capital markets. In France, for example, large portions of telecommunication, arms manufacturing, automobile, banking, and transportation industries are partly owned by the government. If countries like France, Italy, and Germany evolve along the U.S. model, their weights in a global index are likely to rise.

The market values of developed stock markets are given in Exhibit 1. Japan and the United Kingdom have the largest markets outside of the United States. The size of the world stock market grew steadily in the 1970s and 1980s and neared the $30 trillion mark at the end of 2000. It has multiplied by approximately 30 since the end of 1974. Currency movements induce changes in the total size and geographical breakdown of the world market. A drop in the value of the dollar reduces the market share of U.S. stocks; the dollar value of non-U.S. stocks increases by the amount of the dollar depreciation, assuming that the stocks' values in domestic currency do not change and that the dollar value of U.S. stocks stays constant. The share of U.S. markets has decreased from almost two-thirds of the world market cap in 1972 to only one-third by the early 1990s. It moved back up to over 50 percent in the early 2000s, partly because of a big drop in Asian markets. Meanwhile, the share of European markets grew from roughly 20 to 30 percent. Asia's importance increased dramatically from the 1980s through the mid 1990s. However, the lingering economic crisis in Japan, compounded by the 1997 crisis in southeastern Asia, drastically reduced Asia's importance in the world market cap.

The figure for Japan is somewhat inflated by the practice of cross-holding of stocks among publicly traded Japanese companies and financial institutions

EXHIBIT 1	Market Sizes of Developed Markets

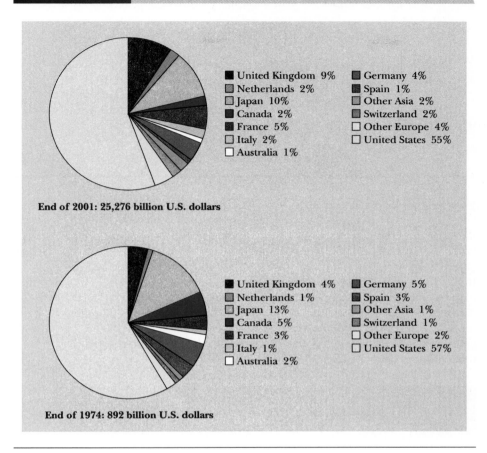

End of 2001: 25,276 billion U.S. dollars

Legend (top chart):
- United Kingdom 9%
- Netherlands 2%
- Japan 10%
- Canada 2%
- France 5%
- Italy 2%
- Australia 1%
- Germany 4%
- Spain 1%
- Other Asia 2%
- Switzerland 2%
- Other Europe 4%
- United States 55%

End of 1974: 892 billion U.S. dollars

Legend (bottom chart):
- United Kingdom 4%
- Netherlands 1%
- Japan 13%
- Canada 5%
- France 3%
- Italy 1%
- Australia 2%
- Germany 5%
- Spain 3%
- Other Asia 1%
- Switzerland 1%
- Other Europe 2%
- United States 57%

Source: Morgan Stanley Capital International.

(*Mochiai*). A similar feature can be found in South Korea, where companies within large conglomerates (*chaebols*) are linked with extensive equity cross-holding. Index providers are trying to adjust the market cap weights used in the index. This is part of the so-called free-float adjustment, which attempts to eliminate the effects of cross-holdings, as illustrated in Example 4.

EXAMPLE 4

Example of Adjustment for Cross-Holding

Three companies belong to a group and are listed on the stock exchange:

► Company A owns 30 percent of Company B.

► Company B owns 20 percent of Company C.

► Company C owns 10 percent of Company A.

Each company has a total market cap of 100 million.

> You wish to adjust for cross-holding to reflect the weights of these companies in a market cap–weighted index. What adjustment would you make to reflect the free float?
>
> **Solution:** The apparent market cap of these three companies taken together is 300 million. But because of their cross-holding, there is some double counting. The usual free-float adjustment would be to retain only the portion that is not owned by other companies within the group. Hence, the adjusted market capitalization is:
>
> 90 + 70 + 80 = 240 million

Emerging Markets   The 1980s saw the emergence and rapid growth of stock markets in many developing countries. In Africa, stock markets opened in Egypt, Morocco, and the Ivory Coast, but with limited growth. Growth has been somewhat faster in Latin America, especially in Brazil and Mexico. The most spectacular change, however, has been witnessed in Asia. Stock markets have grown rapidly in India, Indonesia, Malaysia, Thailand, South Korea, and Taiwan. The emerging market crisis of 1997 stopped that growth, but growth picked up again in 2002. Nevertheless, we see in Exhibit 2 that the total capitalization of emerging markets represents less than 10 percent of the world stock market cap. Taken together, all emerging markets have a market size somewhere between that of Great Britain and that of France or Germany.

EXHIBIT 2	Market Sizes of Emerging Markets (as a % of the total value of US$1,790 billion, year-end 2001)		
Europe	5%	Taiwan	12%
Malaysia	7%	Thailand	2%
Mexico	8%	Peru	1%
Middle East	6%	South Korea	11%
India	6%	Indonesia	1%
Chile	3%	China	8%
Africa	10%	Brazil	11%
Philippines	3%	Other	5%
Argentina	1%		

Source: Morgan Stanley Capital International.

Liquidity

Transaction volume gives indications on the liquidity of each market. In a liquid market, investors can be more active and design various arbitrage strategies. Some markets are large via their market cap, and hence their weight in a global index, but with little turnover. Illiquidity tends to imply higher transaction costs. Investors measuring performance relative to a global benchmark will tend to be more passive on such illiquid markets.

Exhibit 3 gives the turnover ratio of major markets computed as the ratio of the annual transaction volume to the market cap at year-end. This is a simple indicator of the liquidity on each market. Depending on market activity, these figures can vary widely from one year to the next, but it is apparent that some national markets are more active than others. The ranking of countries based on the volume of transactions differs slightly from that based on market cap. European markets tend to be more active than indicated by their relative market size, resulting in a higher turnover ratio.

EXHIBIT 3	Annual Turnover Ratio on Major Stock Exchanges

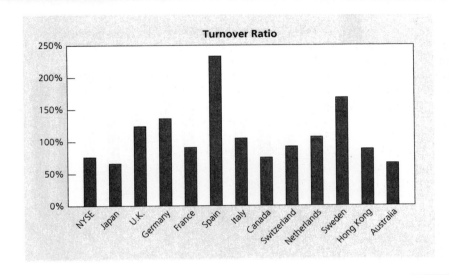

Source: Morgan Stanley Capital International 2002.

In fact, the turnover ratio varies significantly over time. For example, the transaction volume in Japan soared in the late 1980s to surpass that of the NYSE, and the Japanese turnover ratio became a multiple of the U.S. ratio, but it dropped dramatically in the 1990s. Therefore, comparison of national market liquidity based on this variable could lead to different conclusions, depending on the years observed.

In addition, the transaction volume on some emerging markets is very large relative to their size. Transaction volumes in South Korea or Taiwan are sometimes larger than that of any developed market except the United States. But this is not the case for many other emerging markets that are quite illiquid.

Concentration

Another informative statistic is the degree of concentration of the market cap found in the major markets. It is important that investors know whether a national market is made up of a diversity of firms or concentrated in a few large firms. Institutional investors are reluctant to invest in small firms, fearing that they offer poor liquidity. Also, it is easier for the investor to track the performance of a market index, which is usually market cap weighted, if it is dominated by a few large issues. On the other hand, a market dominated by a few large firms provides fewer opportunities for risk diversification and **active portfolio** strategies.

As shown in Exhibit 4 the U.S. stock exchange is a diverse market in which the top 10 firms represent less than 20 percent of total market cap. In the United States, the largest firm represents less than 3 percent of the capitalization for the NYSE. At the other end of the spectrum, the top 10 Swiss multinational firms account for more than 70 percent of the Swiss stock exchange. Nokia is larger than the sum of all other Finnish firms.

EXHIBIT 4	Share of the 10 Largest Listed Companies in the National Market Capitalization

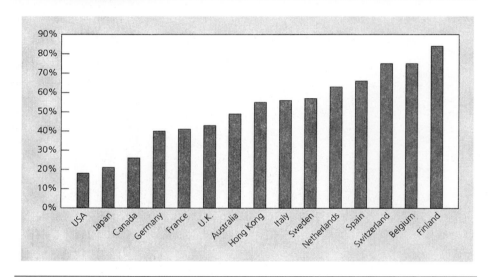

Source: Morgan Stanley Capital International, March 2002.

4   SOME PRACTICAL ASPECTS

A few practical aspects must be taken into account when investing abroad.

Tax Aspects

Taxes can add to the cost of international investment. Foreign investments may be taxed in two locations: the investor's country and the investment's country. Taxes are applied in any of three areas: transactions, capital gains, and income (dividends, etc.).

Some countries impose a tax on transactions. The United Kingdom has retained a stamp tax of 0.5 percent on purchases of domestic securities (but not on sales). Most countries have eliminated, or drastically reduced, such transaction taxes. In countries where brokers charge a commission rather than trade on net prices, a tax proportional to the commission is sometimes charged. For example, France levies a 19.6 percent VAT (value-added tax) on commissions (not on the transaction value), just as on any service. Market makers are usually exempted from these taxes when they trade for their own accounts.

Capital gains are normally taxed where the investor resides, regardless of the national origin of the investment. In other words, domestic and international investments are taxed the same way.

Income on foreign stocks is paid from the legal entity of one country to a resident of another country. This transaction often poses a conflict of jurisdiction, because both countries may want to impose a tax on that income. The international convention on taxing income is to make certain that taxes are paid by the investor in at least one country, which is why withholding taxes are levied on dividend payments. Because many investors are also taxed on income received in their country of residence, double taxation can result from this practice but is avoided through a network of international tax treaties. An investor receives a dividend net of withholding tax plus a tax credit from the foreign government. The investor's country of residence imposes its tax on the gross foreign dividends, but the amount of this tax is reduced by the **withholding tax** credit. In other words, the foreign tax credit is applied against the home taxes. Tax rules change frequently, but the typical with-holding tax rate is 15 percent of dividends.

To a tax-free investor, such as a pension fund, this tax credit is worthless, because the investor does not pay taxes at home. In this case, the investor can reclaim the tax withheld in the foreign country. Reclaiming a withholding tax is often a lengthy process requiring at least a few months and even up to a couple of years. In a few countries, part of the withholding tax is kept by the country of origin. In other countries, tax-free foreign investors, especially public pension funds, can apply for a direct exemption from tax withholding.

EXAMPLE 5

Example of Tax Adjustments

To illustrate these fiscal aspects, let's consider a U.S. investor who buys 100 shares of Heineken listed in Amsterdam for 40 euros. She goes through a U.S. broker, and the current exchange rate is one euro = 1.1 U.S. dollars. Her total cost is $4,400, or $44 per share of Heineken (40 times 1.1 $/€). Three months later, a gross dividend of €2 is paid (15 percent withholding tax), and she decides to sell the Heineken shares. Each share is now worth 38 euros, and the current exchange rate is $/€ = 1.2, because the euro has sharply risen against the dollar. The same exchange rate applied on the dividend payment date. What are the cash flows received in U.S. dollars?

Solution: The cash flows are as follows:

Dividend Payment minus Withholding Tax ($/€ = 1.2)

	Net Dividend	Tax Credit
In euros per share	1.70	0.30
In dollars per share	2.04	0.36
Net in dollars (100 shares)	204	36

(continued on next page . . .)

Sale of Heineken Shares ($/€ = 1.2)

In euros per share	38
In dollars per share	45.6
Net in dollars (100 shares)	4560

Our investor has made a capital gain of $160 ($4,560 − $4,400), which will be taxed in the United States at the U.S. capital gains tax rate. She will also declare a total gross dividend of $240 as income, which will be taxed at her income tax rate. She can deduct from her income tax a tax credit of $36, however, thanks to the United States–Netherlands tax treaty.

Stock Market Indexes

Stock market indexes allow one to measure the average performance of a national market. One or several market indexes may track a national market at any given time. Historically, country stock indexes were computed by the local stock market, but global organizations have started to provide indexes for national markets around the world, as well as a series of global indexes.

Domestic Stock Indexes   Domestic investors usually prefer indexes that are calculated and published locally. Most of these are broadly based, market value–weighted indexes. Each company is assigned an index weight proportional to its market cap. Market value–weighted indexes are true market portfolio indexes in the sense that when the index portfolio is held by an investor, it truly represents movements in the market. This is not true of equal-weighted indexes, such as the U.S. Dow Jones 30 Industrial Average (DJIA) or the Japanese Nikkei 225 Stock Average. The DJIA adds up the stock price of 30 corporations. Each company is assigned an index weight proportional to its market price, when computing the index percentage price movement. For example, the return on a share with a price of $100 will have ten times more importance than the return on a share with a price of $10. So the weighting method is quite artificial. Not only is the DJIA narrowly based, but also its composition is somewhat arbitrary; for example, IBM was removed from the index in the 1970s because its price was too high compared with the other 29 corporations. Many stock exchanges have introduced indexes based on a small number of large stocks. There are two reasons for this trend toward narrow-based indexes. First, investors like to get instantaneous information and market movements by accessing Internet or information providers such as Reuters or Bloomberg. Meaningful market indicators must be computed using the most actively traded stocks, not those that trade infrequently. Second, exchanges have introduced derivatives (futures, options) on these stock indexes. Dealers in those derivative markets prefer to have an index that is based on a small number of actively traded stocks, because it makes it much easier to hedge their derivatives exposure in the cash stock market. Most stock indexes published do not include dividends, although some countries also report dividend-adjusted indexes.

Because some stocks are listed on several exchanges, some companies appear in different national indexes. For example, the S&P 500 used to include some very large non-U.S. companies.

Global Stock Indexes[7] Morgan Stanley Capital International (MSCI) has published international market cap weighted indexes since 1970. They now publish country indexes for all developed as well as numerous emerging markets. They also publish a variety of regional and global indexes. The World index includes only developed markets, while the All Country World index includes both developed and emerging markets. Their index of non-U.S. stock markets has been extensively used as a benchmark of foreign equity portfolios by U.S. investors; it is called EAFE (Europe/Australasia/Far East). Besides market cap–weighted indexes, MSCI also publishes indexes with various weighting schemes (e.g., GDP weights) and with full currency hedging. Global industry indexes are also available.

FTSE, created as a joint venture of the *Financial Times* and the London Stock Exchange, has published international indexes since 1987. The most important international indexes are the World index, the Europe index, the Pacific Basin index, and the Europe and Pacific index. Country indexes are provided for developed and emerging markets, as well as numerous industrial and regional indexes. Global industry indexes are available.

Other series of global indexes are also available. Salomon Smith Barney publishes a series of global indexes that cover developed and emerging markets. There are country, region, and industry indexes. In 2000, Dow Jones started to publish a series of global indexes called the DJGI that covers developed and emerging markets. S&P publishes an S&P Global 1200 index of developed markets, as well as various subindexes, including the S&P 350 Europe index, intended to be the European counterpart of the S&P 500.

The introduction of the euro has created intensive competition among index suppliers. They all try to provide a European index that will be used as benchmark by global money managers. Besides, the well-established indexes of MSCI and FTSE, Dow Jones has launched a series of European indexes in collaboration with the French, German, and Swiss stock exchanges, which are named DJ Stoxx.

Emerging market indexes are available from the index providers mentioned previously. In the past the International Finance Corporation (IFC) of the World Bank published popular emerging market indexes. Standard and Poor's acquired its emerging market database and now performs the calculation of

CONCEPTS IN ACTION

S&P Goes All-American

Standard & Poor's said it will remove all seven non-U.S. companies from the large-cap S&P 500, the world's most widely benchmarked index, at the end of trading on July 19. It will replace them with seven U.S. corporations. On the out list: Royal Dutch/Shell, Unilever, Nortel, Alcan, Inco, Barrick Gold, and Placer Dome. S&P said foreign companies often cause **tracking errors** between the index and the markets they intend to track. . . . The newcomers are UPS, Goldman Sachs, Prudential, Principal Financial, as well as three tech companies—SunGard Data, Electronic Arts, and eBay. S&P, like *Business Week,* is owned by McGraw-Hill.

Sources: Robin Ajello, "S&P Goes All-American," reprinted from July 22, 2002 issue of *Business Week* by special permission, copyright 2002 by the McGraw-Hill Companies, Inc.

---

[7] Up-to-date information can be found on the websites of the index providers: www.msci.com, www.ftse.com, www.spglobal.com, www.ssbgei.com, indexes.dowjones.com, and www.stoxx.com.

various S&P/IFC indexes. The Global index series (S&P/IFCG) is the broadest possible indicator of market movements, and the coverage exceeds 75 percent of local market capitalizations. Weights are adjusted for government and cross-holdings. The Investable index series (S&P/IFCI) is designed to represent the market that is legally and practically available to foreign investors. The Frontier index series tracks small and illiquid markets.

All these global indexes are widely used by international money managers for **asset allocation decisions** and performance measurements (benchmarks). They differ in terms of coverage and weights. Hence, these global indexes can have significant differences in performance. Besides deciding on which company and country should be included in the respective indexes, the provider must decide on the market-cap weights to be used. Because of cross-holding, government ownership, and/or regulations applying to foreign investors, the amount of market value available to foreign investors (the free float) can differ significantly from the market cap that can be obtained by multiplying the number of shares issued by their market price. Most indexes now perform an adjustment so that the weight of each security represents its free float.

Not all indexes are intended as investable benchmarks tracking an overall market. Specific European indexes have been launched, on which derivatives can be traded. They must comprise a small number of highly liquid stocks, so that market makers in the derivatives can easily hedge their exposure on the stock markets. The DJ Euro Stoxx 50 (50 leading Eurozone stocks) and the FTSE Eurotop 100 (100 leading European stocks) are European indexes on which futures, options, and ETFs are traded.

Which Index to Use?   Local indexes are widely used by domestic investors. Private investors often prefer these indexes over country indexes of international providers, such as MSCI or FTSE, for several reasons:

► In most cases, the local indexes have been used for several decades.
► Local indexes are used for derivative contracts (futures, options) traded in that country.
► Local indexes are calculated immediately and are available at the same time as stock market quotations on all electronic price services.
► Local indexes are available every morning in all the newspapers throughout the world.
► The risk of error in prices and capital adjustment is possibly minimized in local indexes by the fact that all calculations are done locally, with excellent information available on the spot.

Institutional investors, on the other hand, prefer to use the MSCI, FTSE, or other international indexes for the following reasons:

► The pension funds do not need up-to-the-minute indexes.
► The indexes on all stock markets are available in a central location, whereas local indexes must be drawn from several locations.
► All international indexes are calculated in a single consistent manner, allowing for direct comparisons between markets.
► MSCI and FTSE provide global or regional indexes (World, Europe, EAFE), which international money managers need to measure overall performance.
► They also provide indexes cum-dividends.

The choice of index is important. In any given year, the performance between two indexes for the same stock market can differ by as much as several percentage points.

Information

The information available from different countries and companies varies in quality. Accounting standards differ across countries, but most developed countries are now enforcing accounting standards of increased quality. Under the pressure of international investors, companies are learning that they must report accurate information on their accounts and prospects in a timely fashion. The situation can be worse for smaller firms in countries where there is less tradition of information transparency, and it can become worrisome in some emerging markets.

In some emerging countries, the earnings forecasts announced by companies that become publicly listed are totally unverifiable. A notable case is China. The rapid move from a centrally planned economy to a partly capitalistic system means that the notion of accounting at the firm level is a new concept. State-owned companies have been listed on Chinese or foreign stock exchanges but have no tradition of having separate accounts, and therefore have problems trying to identify earnings to shareholders during a given time period. It is equally difficult to assess who is the legal owner of some of the assets of a Chinese firm; the state, the province, and the municipality all lay some claim on existing firms' assets, and legal property titles do not exist historically. Shanghai Petrochemical Co., for example, was the largest company to be introduced on the NYSE in 1993. Its value is clearly a function of its properties and equipment. A letter from America Appraisal Hong Kong Ltd., included in the 1993 listing prospectus, illustrates that reliable information on companies from emerging markets is sometimes difficult to get:

> We have relied to a considerable extent on information provided by you. . . . As all the properties are situated in the People's Republic of China, we have not searched the original documents to verify ownership. . . . All dimensions, measurements and areas are approximate. We have inspected the exterior and, when possible, the interior of all the properties valued. However, no structural survey has been made and we are therefore unable to report as to whether the properties are or not free of rot, infestation or any other structural defects.

Given the uncertainty about a company's information, it is not surprising that its valuation is a matter of highly subjective judgment. The uncertainty surrounding companies' information is damaging. Most emerging markets trade at low price–earnings ratios compared with developed markets with similar or lesser growth potential. Local authorities and the management of listed firms have come to realize that stricter standards must be applied to the timely release of reliable information. Many countries are adopting accounting standards that conform to the International Accounting Standards or U.S. generally accepted accounting principles (GAAP), but progress in their implementation can only be slow.

EXECUTION COSTS   5

The importance of execution costs, also referred to as *transaction costs,* is sometimes overlooked in portfolio management. These costs should be taken into account in active global investment strategies because execution costs vary among countries. Execution costs can reduce the expected return and diversification benefits of an international strategy. The difference in return between a paper portfolio and a managed portfolio can be significant. In theory, forecasted costs should be subtracted from expected return before implementing any active strategies. This is all the more important when investing in high-cost countries such as emerging countries. Portfolio managers must gain a good understanding of the determinants of execution costs and should develop some ability to measure them for trades worldwide.

A manager should try to get the best execution for each trade. *Best execution* refers to executing client transactions so that total cost is most favorable to the client under the particular circumstances at the time. Best execution is an objective even though it is difficult to quantify. Execution costs take many forms: some explicit and easily measurable, others implicit and more difficult to measure.

Components of Execution Costs

Costs can be listed in decreasing reliability of estimation, as described in the following three sections.

Commissions, Fees, and Taxes   Commissions paid to brokers are generally negotiated. They depend on the characteristics of the trade (market, liquidity of the stock, size of the order, etc.) and of the market mechanism used (see next section).

Some additional fees are generally paid to compensate for various services, including post-trade settlement costs. As discussed, some taxes are also levied in various countries.

The payment of commissions to brokers often allows access to the broker's research and other services. Therefore, some of the cost is an indirect way to obtain various services beyond direct trading execution. In theory, one should separate the direct dealing cost component and the cost of other services provided ("soft dollars").

All these costs are explicit and easily measurable, but getting the best execution is not equivalent to minimizing commissions and fees.

Market Impact   Executing a transaction will generally have an impact on the price of the security traded. Market impact can be defined as the difference between the actual execution price and the market price that would have prevailed had the manager not sought to trade the security. For example, an order to buy that is large relative to the normal transaction volume in that security will move the price up, at least temporarily. So, one must estimate the market impact of any trade.

In a price-driven system, the bid–ask spread is a major component of the market impact.[8] However, a bid–ask spread is generally quoted for a maximum number of shares that the market maker is willing to trade and is adjusted upward for large transactions; so, a large order will move quoted prices. When investing directly on an order-driven market, there is no bid–ask quote and the market impact has to be estimated from market data. Measuring the overall price impact is a difficult exercise because the price that would have prevailed if the transaction had not taken place, the benchmark price, is not observable. A traditional method

---

[8] This is also the case when transacting on an order-driven market but asking the broker for a firm bid–ask quotation.

to estimate this benchmark price is to compute the volume-weighted average price (VWAP) on the day of the transaction. The idea is that an average of the prices before and after the transaction is an unbiased estimate of the benchmark price. The VWAP method is further discussed below. Market impact is measured as the percentage difference between the execution price and this benchmark price. It must be stressed that the market impact is highly dependent on the order size, market liquidity for the security traded, and the speed of execution desired by the investor. Institutional investors often trade securities in order sizes which are a significant percentage, and even multiple, of the typical daily trading volume for that security. Hence, the market impact for institutional trades can be high, especially if the investor requires immediacy of trading.

Opportunity Cost   The costs mentioned in the preceding section are incurred on an executed trade. But there is also an opportunity cost in case of nonexecution. This opportunity cost can be defined as the loss (or gain) incurred as the result of delay in completion of, or failure to complete in full, a transaction following an initial decision to trade. Opportunity costs can be significant for investors using crossing networks or order-driven systems, in which the risk of nonexecution or partial execution is significant. On any market, it could take hours or days to execute a large trade, and the opportunity cost can be significant in case of an adverse market movement over that period, (for example a price rise in the case of a buy order). Because of this opportunity cost, an active manager is reluctant to complete a trade over a long time period. The information on which the manager bases his trading decision could be quickly reflected in market prices; that is, before the trade is completed. Furthermore there is a risk of information leakage, whereby the progressive price movement caused by the large order reveals that some trader possesses useful information; this can even be more pronounced if the trader's anonymity is not preserved. Anonymity is very important for large active fund managers. If it becomes known that a large active asset manager starts buying or selling some specific shares, other participants will immediately imitate on the assumption that the manager has some superior analysis or information or that the manager will continue buying or selling. The slower an order is completed, the higher the potential opportunity cost. But trading a large order with immediacy induces high market impact. So there is a trade-off between market impact and opportunity cost.

Estimation and Uses of Execution Costs

Deregulation and increased globalization of all stock markets has led to a global trend toward negotiated commissions. Market impact has also been reduced because of the improvement in trading mechanisms and liquidity on most markets. This does not alleviate the need for measurement of execution costs. Some surveys provide estimates of the average cost of a trade in various markets. Other methods, reviewed below, attempt to measure **ex-post** execution costs on a trade by trade basis. All these measures allow us to derive estimates of expected execution costs that can affect investment strategies.

Global Surveys   Several global surveys of execution costs are available. These give market averages for a typical trade in each country. Various studies come up with different estimates. Exhibit 5 reports some cost estimates for trading in the shares on major developed and emerging stock markets obtained from Barclays Global Investors. Market impact is measured at half the bid–ask spread plus price impact for a typical small transaction; the impact would be larger for a large

EXHIBIT 5	Execution Costs in Basis Points

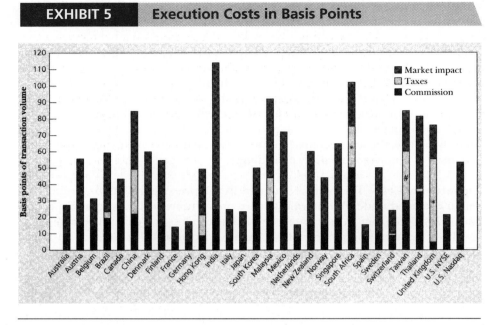

* Tax on puchases only.
# Tax on sales only.

Source: Barclays Global Investors, 2002.

transaction. Trading in non-U.S. securities tends to be somewhat more expensive than trading in U.S. securities. But trading in some European markets, notably France, the Netherlands, Spain, and Germany, tends to be cheaper than in the United States. The execution cost on U.K. securities is large on the buy side (0.76 percent) because of the stamp tax levied on purchases; it is much lower on sales (0.26 percent). Trading on emerging markets incurs large execution costs, often close to 1 percent; these costs can significantly affect the return on a portfolio invested in emerging markets.

Of course, the total execution cost is a function of the size of the transaction and the market depth. The average execution costs for buying a $10 million slice of an EAFE portfolio is estimated to be 0.36 percent by Barclays Global Investors (0.25 percent to sell). The same cost is 0.63 percent for a $1 billion slice (0.53 percent to sell). Execution costs for a large trade in a single stock can be considerably higher than the figures reported here for a diversified EAFE basket of stocks, for which the magnitude of a trade in each stock is rather small.

Detailed Measures: VWAP As mentioned above, a traditional method to estimate the ex-post execution costs for a trade is to compute the volume-weighted average price (VWAP) on the day of the transaction. The difference between the actual trade price and this benchmark price is an indication of execution costs. The idea is that an average of the prices before and after the transaction is an unbiased estimate of the benchmark price.

Unfortunately, this method tends to understate the true market price impact of a trade that represents a significant proportion of the day's trading volume. Another criticism is that this method fails to reflect another hidden cost, namely opportunity cost. For example, suppose that a manager wishes to buy 100,000 shares of a stock upon the belief that its price will rise in the near future. An immediate purchase will result in a transaction price that will be significantly higher than the daily VWAP. Spreading the trade over ten days would result in daily transaction prices which will be closer to their daily VWAP. However if the expected price appreciation takes place very quickly, the manager will miss taking full advantage of the initial prediction. The opportunity cost is large and not reflected by the VWAP methodology.

The daily VWAP method has been adapted to measure the VWAP over longer time intervals to better reflect the impact of opportunity costs.

Detailed Measures: Implementation Shortfall   A somewhat different approach to measure ex-post costs is the *implementation shortfall.* The implementation shortfall is the difference between the value of the executed portfolio (or share position) and the value of the same portfolio at the time the trading decision was made. This analysis does not require the use of market data on transaction prices and volumes over the period surrounding the executed transaction. The implementation shortfall measures the impact of the trade as well as the impact of intervening market events until the transaction is completed. While opportunity cost is captured, general market movements caused by other factors are also captured. This shortfall can be adjusted for general market movements by subtracting the return on some broad market index over the measurement period.

Using Expected Execution Costs   Estimates of ex-post execution costs can be used to judge whether best execution has been achieved. They also allow us to formulate expectations for execution costs on various types of prospective trades. Indeed, some sophisticated execution cost models have been developed.

Active international strategies should factor forecasted execution costs into their expected return estimates. For example, a manager who desires to sell German stocks and replace them with French stocks should estimate whether the expected return overweighs the execution costs incurred in the buy-and-sell transactions. More generally, execution costs are a drag on returns. To see how execution costs should be taken into account to calculate net expected returns, let's consider a strategy in which:

- ▶ $E(R)$ is the annual expected return on a strategy before execution costs;
- ▶ execution costs are measured (in percentage) as the average cost of a round trip trade (purchase and sale) on the portfolio; and
- ▶ the annual turnover ratio is the percentage of the portfolio that is traded during the year; it is commonly measured as the lesser of purchases or sales for a year divided by the average market value of the portfolio during that year.

Then the annual expected return net of execution costs is measured as

$$\text{Net expected return} = E(R) - \text{Turnover ratio} \times \text{Execution costs}$$

EXAMPLE 6

Example of the Impact of Execution Costs

An asset manager follows an active international asset allocation strategy. The average execution cost for a buy or a sell order is forecasted at 0.5 percent. On average, the manager turns the portfolio over 1.5 times a year. The annual expected return before transaction costs is 10%. What is the annual expected return net of execution costs?

Solution: On the average, the portfolio is turned over 1.5 times. The average execution cost for a simultaneous purchase and sale of securities is 1 percent (0.5 percent for a buy and 0.5 percent for a sale). Hence, the net expected return is equal to

$$E(R) - \text{Turnover ratio} \times \text{Execution costs} = 10\% - 1.5 \times 1\% = 8.5\%$$

Clearly, the impact of execution costs on returns depends on the level of activity of the account and the markets in which the account is invested.

Some Approaches to Reducing Execution Costs

International investment strategies can be costly, especially for large portfolios. Several approaches can be used to reduce execution costs. Let's take the example of a **tactical asset allocation** approach, whereby a fund manager decides to reduce the exposure to a country or a region. This would require the sale of a large number of stocks from that region. Rather than trading stock by stock, the manager could engage in *program trading*, in which the manager offers simultaneously a basket of securities for sale. The manager would require a quote from the broker for the whole basket. For the other counterparty, such large trades are often deemed as less risky than a large trade for a single stock because it is clear that they are not motivated by useful information on a specific company; hence, the bid–ask spread quoted could be smaller. There is less risk for the counterparty making a firm quote.

When engaging in a large trade—that is, a trade size that is beyond the normal trade size for which dealers give a standard bid–ask spread, or one that will result in significant market impact—a manager can try to get the best execution through a variety of trading techniques:

▶ *Internal crossing.* The manager will attempt to cross the order with an opposite order for another client of the firm.

  ▶ The *advantage* is that this is the trading method that minimizes costs.

  ▶ The *disadvantage* is that few managers can use this technique because having offsetting orders among clients is rare. There is also a problem in setting the transaction price. One must be sure to determine the price that would have been obtained in the marketplace and not privilege one client at the expense of another. Internal crossing is mostly applied by very large asset management firms specialized in passive strategies, such as index funds. For example, it could be the case that one client wants to reduce its exposure to European stocks, while another is in the process of building a global portfolio, including European stocks. Active managers would have a difficult time justifying selling shares of one company for a client, based on some forecast or model, and at the same time buying shares of the same company for another client.

▶ *External crossing.* The manager sends the order to an electronic crossing network, as described above.

  ▶ The *advantage* is that execution costs are very low and anonymity is assured.

  ▶ The *disadvantage* is that it can take a very long time before an opposite order is entered on the crossing network and the trade is executed. Often orders have to be redirected to another trading venue. A large block is less likely to be swiftly crossed than a small order, as it is unlikely that another party will happen to be interested in an opposite transaction of that magnitude. The speed of execution is a clear disadvantage of this technique which is exposed to opportunity cost.

▶ *Principal trade.* The manager trades through a dealer who guarantees full execution at a specified discount/premium to the prevailing price. The dealer acts as a principal because he commits to taking the opposite side of the order at a firm price.

  ▶ The *advantage* is that trading immediacy is assured and opportunity cost minimized.

  ▶ The *disadvantage* is the overall execution costs can be quite large. The principal broker commits some of its capital to complete the trade, often buying or selling shares on its own account. A principal dealer must maintain, and finance, an inventory of shares. Hence the dealer has to charge a "rent" for its capital, which increases execution costs. Anonymity cannot be assured, but this is not important as the trade is executed in full and immediately.

▶ *Agency trade.* The fund manager negotiates a competitive commission rate and selects a broker on the basis of his ability to reduce total execution costs. In turn the broker will "work" the order to try to get the best price for the manager. In a way, the search for best execution is delegated to the broker. The broker acts as an agent because he does not act as the counterparty on its own account but executes the order with another client.

  ▶ The *advantage* is that the fund manager expects to achieve best execution by relying on the quality of the broker who is compensated by a commission. This often leads to a compromise between opportunity cost and market impact.

  ▶ The potential *disadvantage* is that the commission paid could be too large for the quality of service provided. Also anonymity cannot be assured.

▶ *Use of dealer "indications of interest" (IOI).* Some other party might have a wish to engage in an opposite trade for a stock or basket of stocks. Polling IOIs from various dealers helps to identify possible pools of liquidity.

  ▶ The *advantage* is that the fund manager can hope to achieve low execution costs by finding some opposite trading interest.

  ▶ The *disadvantage* is that this search for liquidity among numerous dealers reveals publicly an interest in the security. Even if the anonymity of the investor is preserved, the trading interest is not.[9] It also slows trading speed. This technique is best suited for informationless trading by passive managers.

---

[9] Investors can ask for intentions of interest on a basket of securities to hide their interest in a specific security.

► *Use of futures.* There is an opportunity cost associated with the delay in execution of a large trade. The fund manager could use futures to monitor the position while the trade is progressively executed. For example, a manager whose tactical asset allocation decision is to reduce the French exposure on a large portfolio, because of the fear of a sudden drop in the French stock market, could immediately sell futures on the CAC, the French stock index. The manager will progressively sell the French stocks in the portfolio with low execution costs, while simultaneously reducing his position in futures.

   ► An *advantage* is the reduction in the opportunity cost component of execution costs.

   ► A *disadvantage* is the additional source of risk if the price of the security traded is not strongly correlated to that of the **futures contract**. Use of futures is well suited for building positions in diversified portfolios of stocks, with a high correlation between the price of the futures contract and that of the portfolio traded. But it is not well suited for trading in a single security, where the correlation with a stock index futures contract is not so large. So adding a futures position does little to eliminate the opportunity cost for that specific security while adding a new source of risk (the **futures price** volatility).

Several services, and asset management firms, provide models of expected execution costs. These can also be used as a benchmark when executing a trade. Looking at deviations from the forecasted cost model over a number of trades allows one to review the quality of execution of a broker and of various trading techniques. Choosing a venue to get best execution is basically searching for liquidity. It is a difficult task that depends on the type of trade and implies **tradeoffs** that depend on several parameters such as:

► *Desire for confidentiality.* An active manager looking for alphas (i.e., betting on the misvaluation of some securities) will be very sensitive to the confidentiality of trades, while a passive manager will be less sensitive.

► *Desire for urgency.* An active manager looking for alphas (i.e., betting on the misvaluation of some securities) will be very sensitive to the speed of transaction, while a passive manager will be a bit less sensitive.

► *Size of transaction.* The larger the transaction relative to the typical daily transaction volume, the higher the market impact.

Finally, fund managers often pay commissions to get additional services such as broker or third-party research (soft dollars). A detailed analysis of execution costs should unbundle these additional services, so that a broker charging a commission is not unduly penalized relative to other trading venues.

In the United Kingdom, the Myners report has prompted managers to focus on minimizing execution costs. A similar focus can be found in the United States. The need to invest in a sophisticated cost-reduction program[10] depends on the type of portfolio strategy followed. Passive index-linked strategies tend to incur lower execution costs than active stock-picking strategies because they trade on diversified baskets of securities. But execution cost is an important component of the performance of a manager attempting to closely track an index.[11]

---

[10] Such a program is quite costly in terms of human resources, data management, and modeling.

[11] This is not only true for a purely indexed strategy, but also for any strategy that promises a small alpha while closely tracking a preassigned index (enhanced indexing).

Saving a few basis points in execution costs is worth the effort, given the typical size of a **passive portfolio**. Also, index-linked basket trades are typically repetitive and more easily modeled.

On the other hand, in an active stock-picking strategy, trades are generally not repetitive. A pairwise trade, for example, buying an undervalued French oil company and selling an overvalued British one has unique characteristics. Such trades are not repetitive, and their costs are difficult to model *ex ante*. A focus on execution costs will usually mean finding the broker offering the best execution for this type of trade.

INVESTING IN FOREIGN SHARES LISTED AT HOME

6

Investors need not go abroad to diversify internationally. We shall discuss several ways to accomplish this.

Global Shares and American Depositary Receipts

Some companies are listed on several stock markets around the world. Multinational firms, such as Royal Dutch/Shell or BP, are traded on more than a dozen markets.

Motivation for Multiple Listing   Foreign companies have a variety of reasons for being listed on several national stock markets, in spite of the additional costs involved:

▶ Multiple listing gives them more access to foreign ownership, allowing a better diversification of their capital and access to a larger amount of funds than is available from smaller domestic equity markets. For example, numerous firms combine an initial listing on the NYSE with a public offering of new shares in their home market.

▶ Diversified ownership in turn reduces the risk of a domestic takeover.

▶ Also, foreign listing raises the profile of a firm in foreign markets, which enables it to raise financing more easily both on the national level and abroad, and is good advertising for its product brands.

▶ Some companies from emerging countries, especially from remote countries, find multiple listing particularly attractive. Listing abroad allows access to a wider capital base and increases the business visibility of the firm. Chinese companies provide a good illustration of this opportunity. Foreign listing is the way to raise new capital abroad. The advantage for non-Chinese investors is that it is easier, and sometimes cheaper, to buy shares on a well-known, developed market. The currency of quotation for shares listed in the United States is the dollar, dividends are paid in dollars, and information in English is provided.

A danger of foreign listing may be the increased volatility of the firm's stock due to a stronger response in foreign versus domestic markets to domestic economic news. Bad political and economic (domestic) news in the Scandinavian countries, for example, has frequently been followed by an immediate negative impact from shares cross-listed on foreign markets. Scandinavian shareholders display less volatile behavior than foreign investors for two reasons: They are not as shaken by bad domestic news, and they tend to keep their capital invested at home anyhow (home bias).

Foreign Listing and ADRs   The procedure for admitting foreign stocks to a local market varies; in some markets, the regulations are quite lenient. For example, in 1986 the Quebec Securities Act allowed a foreign company to list in Montreal simply by meeting the same regulatory requirements as those in the foreign company's jurisdiction. In other markets, foreign companies must abide by the same rules as domestic companies. For instance, non-U.S. companies wanting to be listed on U.S. stock exchanges must satisfy the requirements of both the exchange and the U.S. Securities and Exchange Commission. Although this SEC regulation offers some protection to the U.S. investor, it imposes substantial dual-listing costs on non-U.S. companies, which must produce frequent reports in English.

In the United States and a few other countries, trading takes place in negotiable certificates representing ownership of shares of the foreign company. In the U.S., trading is in American Depositary Receipts (ADRs). Under this arrangement foreign shares are deposited with a U.S. bank, which in turn issues ADRs in the name of the foreign company. To avoid unusual share prices, ADRs may represent a combination of several foreign shares. For example, Japanese shares are often priced at only a few yen per share. They are therefore combined into lots of 100 or more so that their value is more like that of a typical U.S. share. Conversely, some ADRs represent a fraction of the original share. For example, the NASDAQ ADR of LVMH, the French luxury-goods firm, represents one-fifth of a French share.

The United States is the country of preference for foreign listing, with some 450 foreign companies traded on the NYSE and a similar number on the NASDAQ. The total turnover of foreign companies represents over 10% of the NYSE transaction volume. Foreign companies can be traded in several different ways in the United States.

An ADR program created without the company's involvement is usually called an *unsponsored* ADR. These **over-the-counter (OTC)** shares are traded through *pink sheets,* electronic bulletin boards, or an electronic trading system called PORTAL. An ADR program created with the assistance of the foreign company is called a *sponsored* ADR. Sponsored ADRs are often classified at three levels:

▶ *Level I:* The company does not comply with SEC registration and reporting requirements, and the shares can be traded only on the OTC market (but not NASDAQ).

▶ *Level II:* The company registers with the SEC and complies with its reporting requirements. The shares can be listed on an official U.S. stock exchange (NYSE, ASE) or NASDAQ.

▶ *Level III:* The company's ADRs are traded on a U.S. stock exchange or NASDAQ and the company may raise capital in the United States through a public offering of the ADRs.

A nonregistered (Level I) company can also raise capital in the United States, but it must be done through a private placement under **rule 144A**. A drawback of this type of private placement is that only certain private investors and **qualified institutional buyers (QIBs)** can participate. The retail sector is excluded. Furthermore, liquidity of ADRs on the OTC market is not good. The cost of being registered with the SEC (Levels II and III) is the public reporting that must be performed. The foreign company must file a Form 20-F annually. If domestic statements using national accounting standards are presented as primary statements on Form 20-F, the company must provide a reconciliation of earnings and shareholder equity under domestic and U.S. GAAP. This implies that the company must supply all information necessary to comply with U.S. GAAP. Furthermore the stock exchanges require timely disclosure of various information, including quarterly accounting statements. Some national accounting practices can very easily be reconciled with U.S. practices. For example, the SEC considers that Canadian accounting practices are similar to U.S. practices and accepts Canadian statements: Canadian firms are not required to go through an ADR program; they can simply list their shares on a U.S. stock exchange. Many companies from Bermuda, the Cayman Islands, the Netherlands Antilles, Hong Kong, or Israel simply use the U.S. GAAP statements as their primary financial statements, so they do not even need to provide reconciliation data. At the other extreme, German and Swiss firms have been very reluctant to list shares in the United States because of the difficulty of reconciling U.S. and German or Swiss accounting practices and the detailed information that these firms are not accustomed to disclosing. German and Swiss have tended to smooth reported earnings by using various hidden reserves.

Some firms have issued Global Depositary Receipts (GDRs) that are simultaneously listed on several national markets. These GDRs give the firms access to a larger base to raise new capital. Several Japanese and Chinese firms have seized this opportunity.

When Daimler Benz merged with Chrysler, it decided to become listed on both the Deutsche Bourse and the NYSE. The *same* DaimlerChrysler share is traded on both exchanges, in euros in Frankfurt and in dollars in New York. This is exactly the same share, often called a "global share," that is traded on both exchanges (not an ADR), so an investor can buy shares in Frankfurt and sell them in New York. This would not be possible with an ADR that must go through a difficult conversion process. To make this dual trading possible, several legal and regulatory constraints have to be overcome, besides the accounting harmonization discussed previously. The NYSE has an ambitious program of listing the regular shares of many other foreign companies.

London is another market with trading of depositary receipts as well as very active trading of foreign stocks (SEAQ International). Foreign companies can list their shares and the listings can be in all major currencies. The motivation for trading in London is to reduce transaction costs by avoiding some taxes or high commissions charged on the home market and to benefit from the liquidity provided by highly professional market makers based in London. The reduction in cost brought by the automation of non-U.K. markets has reduced the attraction of London.

Valuation of ADRs   Multiple listing implies that the share values of a company are linked on several exchanges. One company should sell at the same share price all over the world, once adjustments for exchange rates and transactions costs have been made. Arbitrage among markets ensures that this is so. An important question is: What is the dominant force affecting the stock price of a multiple-listed company? In a dominant–satellite market relationship the home market is the dominant force, and the price in the foreign market (the satellite) simply adjusts to the home market price. This is clearly the case for many dual-listed stocks of which only a very small proportion of capitalization is traded abroad. For most ADRs, the price quoted by market makers is simply the home price of the share adjusted by the exchange rate. But, because the ADR market is less liquid, a large bid–ask spread is added. A fairly large discrepancy in prices between the home and foreign market can be observed because the arbitrage costs between the ADR and the original share can be sizable. The answer is less obvious, however, for a few large European companies that have a very active market in other countries (especially the United States). The volume of trading of a few European multinationals is sometimes bigger in New York and London than on their home market. This also applies to a few Latin American firms and to many of the GDRs.

The influence of time zones should also be noted. Because stock trading takes place at different times around the world, U.S. stocks listed on the Paris Bourse are traded before the opening of the U.S. markets. Their French prices reflect not only the previous close in New York and the current exchange rate, but also anticipation about the current day's new price, based on new information released following the U.S. close.

Advantages/Disadvantages   ADRs allow an easy and direct investment in some foreign firms. Although buying ADRs is an attractive alternative for retail investors, it is usually more costly than a direct purchase abroad for a large investor. On the other hand, some ADRs issued by companies from emerging countries tend to have larger trading volumes in New York than in their home markets, and the execution costs are lower in New York. Whereas the small investor may find it more convenient to trade in foreign shares listed on the home market, the large investor may often find the primary market of overseas companies to be more liquid and cheaper. In all cases, price levels, transaction costs, taxes, and administrative costs should be major determinants of whichever market the investor chooses.

Another disadvantage of ADRs is that only a limited number of companies have issued ADRs, and they represent only a small proportion of foreign market capitalization. They tend to be large companies in each country, so they do not offer full international diversification benefits.

EXAMPLE 7

Example of Price Arbitrage

DaimlerChrysler shares are listed in Frankfurt (XETRA) and on the NYSE. You are a German investor with a large portfolio of German and international stocks. You just bought 10,000 shares in Frankfurt at 51 euros per share. In addition, your broker charges a 0.25 percent commission. At the same time, a U.S. broker quotes DaimlerChrysler traded on the NYSE at 44.70–44.90 dollars, net of commissions. The exchange rate quoted in dollar per euro is 0.8800–0.8820 net. So you can buy one euro for 0.8820 dollar and sell one euro for 0.8800 dollar. Would it have been better to buy the shares in New York rather than in Frankfurt, knowing that these are the same global shares?

Solution: Let's compute the euro purchase price of one share listed on the NYSE. You would buy the shares from the broker at 44.90 dollars. To pay for this purchase, you would need to exchange euros for dollars (sell euros, buy dollars) at the rate of 0.8800 dollar per euro. The net purchase cost per share in euros is

$$44.90/0.88 = 51.0227 \text{ euros}$$

> The cost of purchasing shares directly in Frankfurt is the purchase price plus the 0.25 percent commission:
>
> 51 × 1.0025 = 51.1275 euros
>
> You would have saved 0.1048 euro per share, or 1,048 euros for the 10,000 shares. Of course, you would end up with shares delivered in New York, but they could be held in custody with the rest of your U.S. stock portfolio.

Closed-End Country Funds

Closed-end country funds have been created for many countries, especially emerging countries.

Definition and Motivation   A **closed-end fund** is an investment vehicle that buys stocks in the market; in turn, shares of the closed-end fund are traded in the stock market at a price determined by supply and demand for that fund. The number of shares of the fund usually remains fixed and shares cannot be redeemed but are only traded in the stock market. The fund's market price can differ from the value of the assets held in its portfolio, which is called the *net asset value* (NAV). The *premium* on the fund is the difference between the fund market price and its NAV:

Fund market price = NAV + Premium

The premium is often expressed as a *percentage of the NAV* and is usually called a discount when negative. The situation is quite different for a portfolio directly entrusted to a portfolio manager or for an open-end fund, such as a mutual fund. There, the value of the portfolio or fund is, by definition, equal to the market value of the invested assets (the NAV). The advantage of a closed-end fund for the investment manager is that she does not have to worry about redemptions; once a closed-end fund is initially subscribed, the investment manager keeps the money under management. This vehicle is well suited to investing in emerging markets, because the manager does not face redemption demands and so the manager can invest it in the long term without liquidity concerns. The disadvantage for the closed-end shareholder is the uncertainty in the premium, as will be discussed later.

A *country fund* (e.g., the Korea Fund) is a closed-end fund whose assets consist primarily of stocks of the country for which the fund is named (e.g., stocks of Korean companies). Numerous country funds are listed in the United States, the United Kingdom, and major stock markets.

The motivation for investing in those country funds is twofold. First, they offer a simple way to access the local market and benefit from international diversification. For example, country funds invested in Italy, Spain, Australia, the United Kingdom, or Germany can be purchased in the United States. These funds invested in developed markets are of interest primarily to private investors, who find an easy way to hold a diversified portfolio of that country. Country funds are simply managed portfolios specializing in stocks of a specific country. The case for country funds investing in emerging markets is more compelling, because the alternative of investing directly in emerging markets is a more difficult process. Furthermore, some countries (e.g., Brazil, India, Korea, and Taiwan) traditionally restricted foreign investment. Country funds, approved by the local government, are a way to overcome foreign investment restrictions. So, foreign investment restriction is a second motivation for the creation and use of some of

EXAMPLE 8

Example of Movements in Premium

Paf is an emerging country with severe foreign investment restrictions but an active stock market open mostly to local investors. The exchange rate of the pif, the local currency, with the U.S. dollar remains fixed at 1 Pif/$. A closed-end country fund, called *Paf Country Fund,* has been approved by Paf. Its net asset value is 100 dollars. It trades in New York with a premium of 30 percent.

1. Give some intuitive explanations for this positive premium.
2. Paf unexpectedly announces that it will lift all foreign investment restrictions, which has two effects. First, stock prices in Paf go up by 20 percent because of the expectation of massive foreign investment attracted by the growth opportunities in Paf. Second, the premium on the Paf Country Fund drops to zero. Is this scenario reasonable? What would be your total gain (loss) on the shares of Paf Country Fund?

Solutions:

1. There is no alternative to investing in the closed-end fund for foreign investors. Foreign investors may find Paf shares attractive from a risk–return viewpoint so that they compete and bid up the price.
2. The scenario is reasonable. The net result can be calculated for 100 of original NAV. Before the lifting of restrictions, the fund was worth 130 for 100 of NAV. After the lifting of restrictions, the NAV moves up to 120 and the fund is now worth its NAV, or 120. The rate of return for the foreign investor is

$$\frac{120 - 130}{130} = -7.7\%$$

these country funds. The International Finance Corporation (IFC) of the World Bank has been instrumental in the launching of country funds in small emerging markets.

The Pricing of Country Funds   The price of a country fund is seldom equal to its NAV. Some funds trade at a substantial premium or discount from their NAV, which poses problems for investors. The change in market price of a country fund is equal to the change in NAV plus the change in the premium (discount). If the premium decreases or the discount widens, the return on the fund will be less than the return on underlying assets making up the portfolio.

Some country funds provide a unique way to invest in emerging countries with foreign investment restrictions. When these foreign investment restrictions are binding, one would expect the country fund to sell at a premium over its NAV; see Bonser-Neal et al. (1990) or Eun, Janakiramanan, and Senbet (1995). The premium should be equal to the amount that investors are willing to pay to circumvent the restriction. Indeed, funds invested in India, Korea, Taiwan, or

Brazil have generally sold at a steep but volatile premium. Emerging countries are progressively liberalizing foreign access to their financial markets. When the lifting of a foreign investment restriction is announced, the premium on a local-country fund should drop, as local shares will be more widely available to foreign investors. This drop in premium is a risk associated with investing in these country funds. It can only be hoped that the local market will respond favorably to the prospect of attracting more foreign investors and that a rise in NAV will compensate for a drop in the fund's premium. The liberalization in Brazil and Korea has indeed led to large drops in the premium of closed-end funds invested in those countries.

The volatility in the value of the premium can add volatility to that of the underlying assets. Historically, premiums on country funds have been very volatile. Johnson, Schneeweiss, and Dinning (1993) studied a sample of country funds listed in the United States and invested either in developed markets or in emerging markets. They measured the U.S. dollar volatilities of the fund, the fund's NAV, and the local underlying stock index (e.g., the Korean index for the Korean Fund). For emerging-country funds, the volatility of the fund was about 30 percent more than that of its NAV, and 10 percent more than that of the local stock index. This additional volatility might be a necessary cost to bear when few other alternatives are open. Because these markets are becoming much more accessible, the attraction of country funds is reduced. For developed-country funds, Johnson et al. (1993) found that the volatility of the fund was almost twice as large as that of its NAV or of the local stock index. To avoid the additional volatility of closed-end country funds invested in developed markets investors can buy open-end funds or buy a portfolio directly on the foreign market. These portfolios will always be valued at their NAV, without premium or discount. It can be argued that the large discount observed on many developed-country funds simply reflects large management fees[12] and the lack of liquidity of the market for the fund's shares.

Another interesting feature of the pricing of country closed-end funds listed in the United States is the fact that a fund's value is often strongly correlated with the U.S. stock market and reacts only slowly to changes in the fundamentals (i.e., changes in the NAV). Both phenomena are inconsistent with market efficiency. For example, a Korean fund is a portfolio of Korean stocks; its value should not be affected by movements in the U.S. stock market (beyond the normal correlation between Korea and the United States). Many **behavioral finance** explanations are provided, including over- and underreaction to news, investor demand, and investor "sentiment." Klibanoff, Lamont, and Wizman (1998) provide an interesting study that focuses on the "salience" of news. They show that, although the elasticity of the fund's price to news is less than one, it is much higher when the news appears on the front page of the *New York Times*. So, investors will react quickly only to salient news.

Advantages/Disadvantages   Closed-end funds allow investors access to a portfolio invested in some foreign region. The portfolio is generally better diversified than a collection of a few ADRs of that region.

The previous discussion of costs and volatility suggests, however, that buying closed-end funds is an inferior substitute for direct investment in foreign stock markets, even for most emerging markets.

---

[12] Indeed, Bekaert and Urias (1999) suggest that closed-end funds are not an attractive substitute for direct investment in foreign stock markets, even for most emerging markets.

Open-End Funds

An open-end mutual fund is publicly offered and its shares can be purchased and redeemed at the NAV of the assets owned by the fund. Although an open-end fund is attractive from the shareholders' viewpoint, it would be risky for the fund manager if investors could redeem shares at a known NAV (which the manager might not be able to realize if he needs to liquidate assets to meet redemptions). Typically investors must announce their decision to buy/redeem their shares before the NAV is calculated. For example, investors must notify their decision before noon, and the NAV is calculated the end of the day. For open-end funds invested in foreign shares, the lag between notification and determination of the NAV that will be used to execute the transaction can be a couple of days. A large bid-ask spread on the fund's price can also be imposed. The efficiency improvements in many emerging markets have allowed managers to offer open-end funds on the most liquid markets. Open-end funds are now offered not only for individual countries but also for regions or international industries. Many of these funds take the form of index funds tracking an international index of developed or emerging market. Most new international open-end funds now take the form of ETFs.

Exchange Traded Funds

ETFs are funds that trade on a stock market like shares of any individual company. They can be traded at any time during market hours, and can be sold short or margined. But ETFs are shares of a portfolio, not of an individual company. ETFs are generally designed to closely track the performance of a specific index. ETFs on the indexes of several individual, developed stock markets, as well as on many international indexes, are listed on all major stock markets. ETFs on some emerging markets, or international emerging indexes, are also offered. So, they can be used for international diversification strategies. ETFs have been an exceptional commercial success in the early 2000s. ETFs are offered by the large asset management firms that specialize in indexing. Other financial institutions offer ETFs under their name by subcontracting with these specialists.

Definition and Motivation   An ETF is an open-end fund with special characteristics (see Gastineau, 2001). ETFs have a management cost advantage over traditional mutual funds because there is no shareholder accounting at the fund level. ETFs are traded like common stocks. A major feature is the redemption in-kind process. Creation/redemption units are created in large multiples of individual ETF shares, for example 50,000 shares. These units are available to exchange specialists (*authorized participants*) who will generally act as market makers for the individual shares. If an authorized participant decides to redeem ETF shares, it will do so by exchanging the redemption unit for a portfolio of stocks held by the fund and used to track the index. The fund publishes the portfolio that it is willing to accept for in-kind transactions. As opposed to traditional open-end funds, the in-kind redemption means that no capital gain will be realized in the fund's portfolio on redemption. If the redemption is in cash, a traditional fund may have to sell stocks held in the fund's portfolio. If their price has appreciated, the fund will realize a capital gain and the tax burden will have to be passed to all existing fund shareholders. This is not the case with ETFs. As in any open-end fund, though, individual ETF shareholders[13] can

---

[13] But authorized participants commit to redeem only in kind.

require in-cash redemption based on the NAV. Redemption in cash by individual ETF shareholders is discouraged in two ways:

► Redemption is based on the NAV computed one or a couple of days after the shareholder commits to redemption. So, the redemption value is unknown when the investor decides to redeem.

► A large fee is assessed on in-cash redemptions.

It is more advantageous for individual ETF shareholders to sell their shares on the market than to redeem them in cash. The sale can take place immediately based on observed share prices at a low cost. Arbitrage by authorized participants ensures that the listed price is close to the fund's NAV.[14] Authorized participants maintain a market in the ETF share by posting bid and ask prices with a narrow spread, or by entering buy-and-sell limit orders in an electronic order book. The transaction costs of ETFs can be estimated as the sum of the commission charged by the broker plus half this bid–ask spread.

International ETFs have distinguishing features. An ETF indexed on some less-liquid emerging market is bound to have high bid–ask spreads. Managing an ETF on a broad international index, such as EAFE, means holding stock from numerous countries with different custodial arrangements and time zones. Again, the bid–ask spreads are likely to be larger than for **plain-vanilla** ETFs. But the size of the ETF is an important factor influencing costs. The effect of non-overlapping time zones should be taken into account when comparing the ETF price with its NAV. Consider the example of an ETF on a Japanese stock index, traded in New York. During Wall Street opening hours, the Tokyo stock market is closed. The NAV available in the morning in the United States is based on the closing prices in Tokyo several hours before New York opens. Except for currency fluctuations, the NAV will remain unchanged as Tokyo is closed throughout the New York trading session. However, the ETF price will be affected by expectations about future stock prices in Tokyo, so it could differ significantly from the official NAV. This is not an inefficiency and there are no arbitrage opportunities, because the NAV is stale and does not correspond to current market pricing.

EXAMPLE 9

ETF Pricing

An ETF is indexed on a Japanese stock index and is listed in New York. Its NAV is computed based on closing prices in Tokyo. When it is 9 A.M. in New York, it is already 11 P.M. in Tokyo, on the same day. The NAV based on Tokyo closing prices is 10,000 yen. The exchange rate at 9 A.M. EST is 1 dollar = 100 yen.

1. What is the dollar NAV of this ETF at the opening of trading in New York?

2. When New York closes at 4 P.M. EST, Tokyo is still closed (6 A.M. local time), but the exchange rate is now 99 yen per dollar. What is the dollar NAV at closing time?

---

[14] The fund publishes an indicative intraday NAV every 15 seconds; it is available on major data providers, such as Bloomberg, Reuters, or Telekurs.

3. Bad international news hit after the Tokyo closing. European and U.S. stock markets dropped by 5 percent. Should the ETF price have remained at its NAV? Assuming that the Tokyo market is strongly correlated with the U.S. market (at least for this type of international news), give an estimate of the ETF price at the New York closing.

Solutions:

1. The dollar NAV is $100 (= 10,000/100).
2. The closing dollar NAV is $101.01 (= 10,000/99)
3. The price of the ETF should reflect expectations that the Tokyo stock index will drop in reaction to the news, so its price should be below the NAV computed on past closing prices in Tokyo. If the markets are strongly correlated, we could estimate that Tokyo will also drop by 5 percent. Hence, we should have an estimated market value for the dollar NAV equal to

$$10,000 \times (1 - 0.05)/99 = \$95.96$$

This is an estimate of the current price of the ETF. It will trade at a 5 percent discount from its "official" NAV.

Advantages/Disadvantages   ETFs are attractive to individual investors because they offer the benefits of international diversification with excellent liquidity at a low cost. They are also designed to be tax efficient. ETFs are useful in an international portfolio strategy. They can be purchased in the home market while offering a diversified play on a foreign market or region. They are well designed to be used in active asset allocation. On the other hand, they usually are designed to match a benchmark and will not provide active return above that benchmark. To add **active return**, investors can combine them with the direct purchase of specific companies or ADRs.

For large institutional investors, the alternative is to invest directly in an indexed, or actively managed, international portfolio; the cost structure could be less and the tax situation equivalent or better.

SUMMARY

▶ Stock exchanges throughout the world evolved from three models: private bourses, public bourses, and bankers' bourses.

▶ Trading procedures differ in an order-driven market and in a price-driven market. In a price-driven market, there are market makers who stand ready to buy or sell at posted prices (bid and ask prices). In an order-driven market, all buy-and-sell orders are entered in a central order book and a new order is immediately matched with the book of limit orders previously submitted. Each system presents advantages and risks for traders and customers.

▶ Electronic communication and crossing networks (ECNs) have developed alongside official stock exchanges. Electronic crossing networks match anonymously buy-and-sell orders submitted by institutional investors and broker-dealers at prespecified times and at prices determined in the primary market for the security. The trade is made at the midpoint between the bid and the ask prices of the primary market, so there is no market impact or bid–ask spread even for large orders. But there is also no trading immediacy.

▶ The relative market capitalization of national equity markets has changed dramatically over time. The share of the U.S. equity markets moved from two-thirds of the world market in 1972 to only one-third by the early 1990s, when Japan had about the same market size as the United States. In 2002, the U.S. equity market represented some 50 percent of the world market cap, followed by Europe (around 30 percent) and Japan (around 10 percent).

▶ Numerous stock indexes are available to track country and regional markets and measure performance. They can be domestic stock indexes computed locally, such as the U.S. **Dow Jones Industrial Average** or the Japanese Nikkei 225 stocks average. They can be global stock indexes computed by a global organization, such as MSCI, FTSE, DJ, or S&P.

▶ Many practical aspects must be taken into account in global equity investing: market concentration, liquidity, tax aspects, and transaction costs.

▶ Asset managers should try to get the best execution for each trade. Execution costs include several components: commissions and fees, market impact, and opportunity cost. Although commissions and fees are easy to measure, this is less true for market impact and opportunity cost. A transaction has an impact on the price of the security traded, so market impact can be a significant component of execution cost.

▶ To optimize global asset management, one should forecast the execution cost of trading in the various markets. Several global surveys of execution costs are available, but the actual cost depends on the transaction size and the market depth for the specific trade. Various trading techniques allow reduction of execution costs.

▶ It is possible to get some of the benefits of international diversification by investing solely in securities or funds listed at home:

  ▶ Some companies have their shares traded on foreign exchanges; these are called ADRs in the United States. Unfortunately, the number of foreign-listed companies is small, and the price of these ADRs is sometimes unattractive. A few companies offer global shares listed and traded simultaneously in several stock markets.

► Some closed-end funds specialize in investing in foreign stock markets. The market price of these country funds often differs from their net asset value by a large premium (or discount). The uncertainty concerning this premium adds to investment risk.

► Exchange traded funds (ETFs) are special open-end funds that trade on a stock market like shares of individual companies. Their design has made them very successful. The most popular ETFs track some country or regional stock indexes.

PRACTICE PROBLEMS FOR READING 38

1. Which of the following statements about stock markets is not true?

   I. Many of the stock markets are organized as private bourses.

   II. On most markets, stocks are traded on a cash basis, and transactions are settled within a two- to five-day period.

   III. The central electronic limit order book is the hub of those automated markets that are price-driven.

   IV. An auction market, such as the Paris Bourse, is also known as an order-driven market.

2. The central limit order book of Air Liquide, a French firm that trades on the Paris Bourse, is currently as follows:

Sell Orders		Buy Orders	
Quantity	Limit	Limit	Quantity
500	151	145	500
2,000	150	143	2,000
1,000	149	142	1,000
500	147	141	2,000
500	146	140	1,000

   A. Vincent Jacquet wishes to buy 1,500 shares and enters a market order to buy those shares. At what price will Jacquet buy the shares?

   B. Suppose Vincent Jacquet had instead wanted to sell 1,000 shares of Air Liquide that he already had in his investment portfolio. At what price will he sell those shares?

3. *Business Objects* trades on the Paris Bourse as ordinary shares and on the Nasdaq as American Depositary Receipts (ADRs). One ADR of *Business Objects* corresponds to one share on the Paris Bourse. Suppose the last transaction of *Business Objects* on the Paris Bourse was at €25. An investor then entered on the French electronic trading system a limit order to purchase *Business Objects* shares at €24. The ADR price quoted by a Nasdaq dealer is $23.90–24.45. The exchange rate is $0.96/€. Suppose that some unfavorable information suddenly arrives that suggests that a lower price of *Business Objects* shares at €21 would be fair. Assuming that the exchange rate has not changed, discuss which parties stand to lose on the Paris Bourse and on NASDAQ.

4. It is often argued that automated order-driven trading systems must provide special arrangements for small trades (which are often market orders), as well as for block trades. Advance some explanations for this argument.

5. Which of the following statements about electronic communication and crossing networks (ECNs) is/are true?

   I. Electronic communication networks are order-driven systems, in which the limit order book plays a central role.

   II. Electronic crossing networks anonymously match buy-and-sell orders by a pool of participants, generally institutional investors and broker-dealers.

III. In an ECN, a trade takes place only during a crossing session time and only if there are offsetting orders entered by other participants.

6. Consider a European electronic crossing network that runs six crosses daily, that is, the orders are matched six times a day. This network allows a participant to specify several constraints, such as price and minimum fill. Suppose that all the orders submitted to this network for the shares of Christian Dior are Good for Day (GFD); that is, any unfulfilled part of an order is automatically resubmitted to subsequent crossing sessions during the day.

A. The following orders are on the network for the shares of Christian Dior at the time of the first crossing session of the day. The most recent trading price of Christian Dior at the Paris Bourse is €37.

▶ Participant A: a market order to buy 100,000 shares

▶ Participant B: a market order to sell 50,000 shares

▶ Participant C: a market order to sell 150,000 shares, with a minimum fill of 125,000 shares

▶ Participant D: an order to buy 20,000 shares at €36

Discuss what trades would take place on the crossing network and what orders would remain unfulfilled.

B. The following new orders are submitted to the next crossing session. The most recent trading price of Christian Dior at the Paris Bourse is €38.

▶ Participant E: a market order to buy 150,000 shares

▶ Participant F: a market order to sell 50,000 shares

Discuss what trades would take place on the crossing network in this crossing session and what orders would remain unfulfilled.

7. The U.S. stock market capitalization is larger relative to U.S. GDP than is the case in most European countries for all the following reasons *except*

A. A greater proportion of firms in Europe is nationalized.

B. European banks cannot own shares of stock of their client firms.

C. Many European companies rely heavily on bank financing.

D. Privately held companies are a tradition in Europe.

8. Standard & Poor's (S&P) announced in 2001 that it was considering integrating free-float adjustments to its existing practices for the S&P Australian index. It said that it would use a measure called Investable Weight Factor (IWF) to reflect a company's free float. A full free-floated company will have an IWF of 100 percent. For others, the IWF will be adjusted downward by subtracting the percentage of shares that are not freely available for trade. Now consider three Australian manufacturing companies: Alpha, Beta, and Gamma. Alpha owns 5 percent each of Beta and Gamma. Gamma owns 15 percent of Beta. Taking into account the cross-holdings, what will be the IWF of each company?

9. Four companies belong to a group and are listed on a stock exchange. The cross-holdings of these companies are as follows:

▶ Company A owns 20 percent of Company B and 10 percent of Company C.

▶ Company B owns 15 percent of Company C.

▶ Company C owns 10 percent of Company A, 10 percent of Company B, and 5 percent of Company D.

▶ Company D has no ownership in any of the other three companies.

Each company has a market capitalization of $50 million. You wish to adjust for crossholding in determining the weights of these companies in a free-float market capitalization–weighted index.

   A. What are the market capitalizations of each company after adjustment to reflect free float?

   B. What would be the total adjusted market cap of the four companies?

10. The shares of Volkswagen trade on the Frankfurt stock exchange. A U.S. investor purchased 1,000 shares of Volkswagen at €56.91 each, when the exchange rate was $/€ = 0.9790–0.9795. Three months later, the investor received a dividend of €0.50 per share, and the investor decided to sell the shares at the then prevailing price of €61.10 per share. The exchange rate was $/€ = 0.9810–0.9815. The dividend withholding tax rate in Germany is 15% and there is a tax treaty between the United States and Germany to avoid double taxation.

   A. How much did the U.S. investor receive in dividends in dollars, net of tax?

   B. What were the capital gains from the purchase and sale of Volkswagen shares?

   C. How would the dividend income be declared by the investor on a U.S. tax return, and what tax credit would he receive?

11. The shares of Microsoft were trading on Nasdaq on January 1 at $41. A Swedish investor purchased 100 shares of Microsoft at that price. The Swedish kroner to dollar exchange rate then was Skr/$ = 9.4173–9.4188. One year later, the investor received a dividend of $2 per share, and the investor then sold the shares at a price of $51 per share. The exchange rate at that time was Skr/$ = 9.8710–9.8750. The dividend withholding tax rate in the United States is 15 percent and there is a tax treaty between the United States and Sweden that allows the U.S. withholding tax to be used as a tax credit in Sweden. Suppose the Swedish investor is taxed at 50 percent on income and 15 percent on capital gains, and ignore any commissions on purchase and sale of shares.

   A. What is the gross rate of return on the investment, in dollars?

   B. What is the gross rate of return on the investment, in kroners?

   C. What is the rate of return on the investment, in kroners, net of taxes?

12. Which of the following statements best characterizes the taxation of returns on international investments in an investor's country and the country where the investment is made?

   A. Capital gains normally are taxed only by the country where the investment is made.

   B. Tax-exempt investors normally must pay taxes to the country where the investment is made.

   C. Investors in domestic common stock normally avoid double taxation on dividend income by receiving a tax credit for taxes paid to the country where the investment is made.

   D. The investor's country normally withholds taxes on dividends payments.

13. A U.S. institutional investor would like to purchase 10,000 shares of Lafarge. Lafarge is a French firm that trades on the Paris Bourse, the London stock exchange, and the NYSE as an ADR. At the NYSE, one depositary receipt is equivalent to one-fourth of a Lafarge share. The U.S. investor asks its brokers to quote net prices, without any commissions, in the three trading venues. There is no stamp tax in London on foreign shares listed there. The stock quotes are as follows:

New York $24.07–24.37
London   £66.31–67.17
Paris   €99.40–100.30

The exchange rate quotes from banks are as follows:

$/£ = 1.4575–1.4580
$/€ = 0.9691–0.9695

Compare the dollar costs of purchasing 10,000 shares, or its equivalent, in New York, London, and Paris.

14. The chief financial executive of a German firm is considering raising capital in the United States by cross-listing her firm on the NYSE as an ADR and having a public offering. However, the executive has some concerns about this. Discuss what you think some of these concerns might be.

15. A U.S. institutional investor would like to buy 10,000 shares of British polythene industries. This U.K. firm trades on the London stock exchange, but not on the NYSE or NASDAQ. A U.K.-based broker of the investor quotes the price as £3.45–3.60, with a commission of 0.10 percent of the transaction value. There is a 0.50 percent U.K. securities transaction tax on purchase. The exchange rate quoted by a bank is $/£ = 1.5005–1.5010. What would be the total cost in dollars?

16. A French institutional investor wishes to decrease its exposure to Taiwan. It is interested in selling 20,000 shares of a particular Taiwanese firm that is currently in its portfolio. This firm trades on the Taiwan Stock Exchange. A Taiwan-based broker quotes the Taiwan dollar (TW$) price of the shares of this firm as 150.35–150.75, with a commission of 0.10 percent of the transaction value. The Taiwan Stock Exchange charges a tax of 0.30 percent of the value traded from the seller. A bank is quoting the TW$ to € exchange rate as 32.8675–32.8800. How many euros will the French institutional investor receive on selling the shares?

17. Which of the following statements is/are true about stock indexes?

   I. Compared with the equal-weighted indexes, market value–weighted indexes are better representative of movements in the market.

   II. Many of the global indexes, such as those provided by MSCI (Morgan Stanley Capital International) and Standard and Poor's (S&P), are widely used by international money managers for asset allocation decisions and performance measurements.

   III. It is possible that, in any given year, the performance between two indexes for the same stock market can differ significantly, by as much as several percentage points.

18. In 1996, a group of securities called the World Equity Benchmark Shares (WEBS) started trading on the American Stock Exchange. WEBS for a country is a passively managed ETF indexed on the MSCI country benchmark index for that country. All else equal, what do you think would be the effect of the launch of WEBS for a country on the premium or discount of the closed-end country fund for that country?

19. Consider a closed-end country fund that trades in the United States. Suppose that country decides to impose restrictions on investments by foreigners in that country. All other things constant, what do you think would be the effect of these international investment restrictions on the price–net asset value ratio of the closed-end fund for that country?

20. A U.S. institutional investor with a large portfolio of U.S. and international stocks wants to add 20,000 shares of DaimlerChrysler to its portfolio. DaimlerChrysler trades as the same global share on several exchanges in the world. A U.S. broker quotes the NYSE price of DaimlerChrysler as $43.45–43.65, net of commissions. The institutional investor is also considering purchasing shares in Germany, where the offer price quoted for DaimlerChrysler's shares on the Frankfurt stock exchange (XETRA) is €44.95, with a 0.10 percent commission to be paid on the transaction value. Which of the two alternatives is better for the investor? How much would be the total saving by using the better of the two alternatives? The exchange rate is $/€ 0.9705–0.9710.

21. Consider a U.K. index fund that trades on a U.S. exchange. This fund is indexed on a British stock index based on several stocks that trade on the London stock exchange. The different time zones of the U.K. and the U.S. markets result in four distinct time periods in a 24-hour period: one, a six-hour time period prior to the U.S. open, when the market in London is open but the market in the United States is not. Two, a two-hour period between 9:30 A.M. and 11:30 A.M. in New York when both London and New York markets are open. Three, a 4.5 hour time period between 11:30 A.M. and 4:00 P.M. in New York when the New York market is open but the London market is not. And, four, the subsequent period when both markets are closed. For each of these time periods, discuss how British pound NAV and the U.S. dollar price of the fund would fluctuate.

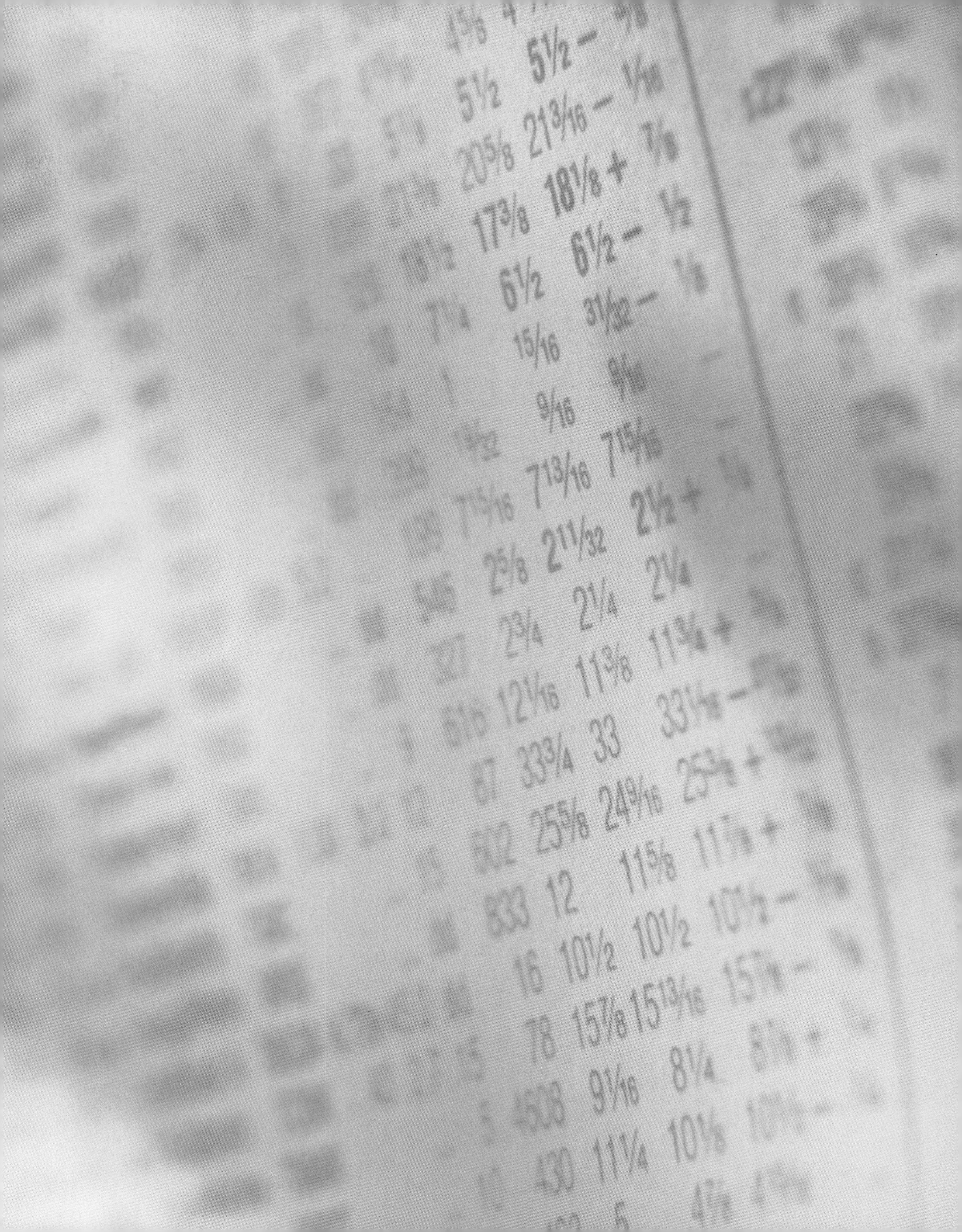

4⅝ 4

5½ 5½ − ⅛

20⅝ 21¹³⁄₁₆ − ⅛

17⅜ 18⅛ + ⅞

6½ 6½ − ½

6½ 31⁄32 − ⅛

15⁄16

9⁄16 9⁄16

7⁵⁄₁₆ 7¹³⁄₁₆ 7¹⁵⁄₁₆

2⅝ 2¹¹⁄₃₂ 2½ +

2¾ 2¼ 2¼

6½ 12¹⁄₁₆ 11⅜ 11⅜ +

87 33¾ 33 33⅛ −

602 25⅝ 24⁹⁄₁₆ 25⅜ +

833 12 11⅝ 11⅞ +

16 10½ 10½ 10⅛ −

78 15⅝ 15¹³⁄₁₆ 15⅞ +

4508 9¹⁄₁₆ 8¼ 8⅛ +

430 11¼ 10⅛ 10⅛ −

CAPITAL MARKETS AND THE ECONOMY

by David P. Goldman

LEARNING OUTCOMES

The candidate should be able to:

a. describe how the innovations of Mortgage Backed Securities (MBS) and inter-state banking have improved capital market efficiency and how that impacts economic growth;

b. explain how legal, regulatory, and structural issues affect MBS optionality, regulatory restrictions on credit quality, and index-based investing;

c. review the changes in capital markets that have led to a shift from corporate credit spreads based on Treasuries to credit spreads linked to swaps.

Capital market innovations during the past two decades improved market efficiency, reduced the cost of capital, and contributed to economic growth. This coin has a flip side, however. Capital market inefficiencies have led to significant market disruptions, with deleterious consequences for economic growth. This reading calls attention to several examples of how capital market behavior affects the broader economy.

Capital markets are an expression of the human life cycle: Old people lend money to young people. At the global level, countries with aging populations lend money to countries with young populations, except when the risk associated with young populations discourages such lending. Milton Friedman's permanent-income hypothesis of 1957, the basis of his 1976 Nobel Prize in Economics, provided the first crack in the edifice of the **Keynesian** school: If individuals adjust their spending according to life-cycle needs rather than momentary changes in their income, Keynesian policy tools would not have the predicted effect. By putting long-term expectations at the center of economics, Friedman's work placed

Flying on One Engine: The Bloomberg Book of Master Market Economists, edited by Thomas R. Keene. Copyright © 2005 by Bloomberg L.P. Reprinted with permission of Bloomberg L.P.

89

capital markets at the center of attention. Monetary economics as well as the "**rational expectations**" hypothesis of Robert Lucas both have their origin in Friedman's 1957 challenge to Keynes.

Another challenge to Keynes, namely **supply-side economics**, proceeded directly from consideration of the role of capital markets in the economy. In 1965, Robert Mundell observed that future household income flows were more uncertain and therefore more difficult to discount in present markets than corporate income flows. For that reason, he argued, an increase in the outstanding volume of government debt might contribute to economic efficiency, because government debt discounts into present markets the future tax receipts from households. Such an increase in efficiency would occur, Mundell argued, in the event that a reduction in tax rates contributed to higher economic growth. Overall tax receipts would decline, but if the increase in tax receipts due to higher growth exceeded the interest cost of the additional debt issued by the government to cover the revenue shortfall, the result would be an increase in efficiency and **economic welfare**.

Mundell's observation provides a sort of Rosetta Stone between the abstract world of economics and the workaday world of capital markets. Rather than assuming fixed expectations and efficient markets, Mundell's hypothesis assumes that capital markets are imperfectly efficient. The interesting question then becomes: What innovations or policy changes would make capital markets more efficient or less efficient? That has enormous repercussions for economic growth.

1 INNOVATIONS THAT IMPROVED CAPITAL MARKET EFFICIENCY

The absence of a banking system in many developing countries, for example, leaves savers with little choice but to bury gold coins in their gardens or the equivalent. If a village has many old people and few young people, the coins will stay buried; if a neighboring village has many young people, they will languish for lack of capital. Something like this characterized the state of the American banking system in the early 1980s, when the rapidly expanding, youthful population of the Sunbelt developed a huge appetite for capital, while the aging savers of the northern Rustbelt lacked local opportunities for investment. Two great innovations matched the income requirements of aging savers with the capital requirements of young families in different regions. They were, of course, the invention of the mortgage-backed securities (MBS) market and the development of interstate banking. Prior to the advent of the MBS market, 14,000 thrift institutions funded local mortgages with local deposits. The thrifts had limited access to sources of capital outside their own local deposit base, for example, by issuing certificates of deposit nationally, but the lending system ultimately depended upon local market knowledge of the lenders and local funding.

Securitization of mortgages solved several problems at once. By pooling thousands of mortgages into a **pass-through security** under the aegis of the two government-sponsored enterprises, the Federal National Mortgage Corporation and the Federal Home Loan Mortgage Corporation, the MBS market allowed mortgage investors to spread their risk across a geographically diverse portfolio. Second, thrifts with excess loan demand could write mortgages and sell them into a liquid market, for purchase by thrifts with excess deposits. Third, and most important, the existence of a liquid MBS market drew in new classes of investors, including overseas lenders. Not only the excess deposits of the Rustbelt or Florida retirees were available but also (for example) the resources of Japanese banks, who bought a substantial portion of the floating-rate **tranches** of **collateralized mortgage obligations** during the late 1980s and early 1990s.

Interstate branch banking, meanwhile, allowed regions with excess savings (such as Florida) to fund loans in regions with rising capital requirements, such as Atlanta. Hugh McColl Jr. of National Bank of North Carolina (later Nationsbank and Bank of America) hailed from Bennettsville, South Carolina, where his family owned the town's sole bank until the Great Depression. No capital flowed through the capillary system from the great national banks or even the regional banks of the South down to towns like Bennettsville. Local economies cannot do without branch banking. Although the MBS market could diversify away the idiosyncratic risk associated with individual borrowers or regions, business loans are a far more heterogeneous entity. Local lending expertise is required to drive business lending. McColl and others broke down the barriers to interstate branch banking during the 1980s and 1990s, allowing deposits to flow to where they were needed.

WITH INNOVATIONS, NEW PROBLEMS   2

Along with the creation of the high-yield bond market, mortgage-backed securities and interstate branch banking made up the trio of debt capital market innovations that underpinned the great U.S. economic expansion of 1982–2000. Every solution, however, generates its own set of problems. Mobilizing capital from new sources through liquid markets stimulates economic growth. But it also makes the economy dependent on the efficiency of capital markets. Legal, regulatory, and structural issues create fragilities in capital markets, which in turn affect economic performance.

Four characteristics of capital markets deserve attention in the broader economic context:

1. **The optionality of mortgage-backed securities.** Almost alone in the world, American mortgages may be prepaid, or called, at the borrowers' whim. Sharp movements in interest rates can destabilize the MBS market.

2. **Regulatory restrictions on credit quality.** Pension funds and life insurance companies must maintain the vast majority of their fixed-income holdings in investment-grade instruments. Unexpected credit migration toward speculative-grade ratings can create perverse effects.

3. **The migration of the pricing standard for fixed income away from the Treasury curve to the swaps curve.** Volatility in the spread between swaps and Treasuries can translate into credit market instability.

4. **Index-based investing.** When investors gauge their returns against an aggregate benchmark index in fixed income, the results are quite different than in the equities market. The broad equity indices reflect the market's valuation of expected future income streams, because equity prices adjust continuously to market expectations. The composition of the fixed-income market has more to do with regulation, tax effects, and custom than the

expected composition of output. Index-based investing can set at odds the **economic risk** of bond portfolios and the business risk of the investors who manage these portfolios.

3

THE MBS MARKET

On two occasions in the past decade, sharp swings in the duration of MBS portfolios led to undesirable economic consequences. The first occurred in 1994, when several leading hedge funds (most prominently Granite Capital) collapsed in the wake of Federal Reserve tightening. The second occurred in 1998, when a decline in the value of MBS contributed to the failure of Long-Term Capital Management (LTCM), producing a temporary panic in capital markets.

As financial market participants well know, American law gives homeowners the right to call their mortgages at will without penalty. When interest rates decline, homeowners prepay their mortgages and take out new loans at lower interest rates. Conversely, when interest rates rise, the rate of prepayment slows and the duration of MBS extends. Like Schrödinger's Cat, who dwelt in a superposed condition of being alive and dead, mortgages live in a superposed condition of being a bond and a checking account. There is a small "natural" market for bonds paying extra yield in exchange for an embedded short call position in an option on interest rates, but it is quite limited. Traditional purchasers of bonds, such as pension funds and life insurance companies, require well-defined cash flows in order to meet a well-defined stream of liabilities, namely future pension or insurance payouts.

Mortgage pass-through securities do not satisfy the requirements of traditional bondholders. The financial industry offered a partial remedy to this problem starting in 1984, with the invention of collateralized mortgage obligations, or CMOs. **CMOs** split a pool of mortgages into tranches offering less duration volatility and more duration volatility, respectively. Up to a given threshold, for example, all prepayments will be assigned to a more volatile "companion" tranche, whose purpose is to reduce prepayments to a less volatile planned amortization class (PAC) tranche. The industry sold PACs to insurance companies and pension funds, and sold the companions to whoever would take on additional prepayment risk.

With the advent of complex models to predict the change in the duration and average life of MBS under a variety of interest-rate scenarios (**option-adjusted spread** modeling), the financial industry found a wider market for the asset class. Thrift institutions, insurance companies, and other investors employed these systems to create MBS portfolios to match liabilities. The models, the investors believed, would help control average life and duration volatility of MBS portfolios that offered more yield than the alternative, namely corporate bonds.

No natural buyer existed for the enormous embedded optionality in the MBS universe, however. For that reason, Wall Street sought unnatural buyers. In part it solved the problem by selling the companion tranches, whose average life is extremely volatile, in the form of floating-rate instruments, on the theory that the value of such an instrument would deviate widely from par only in extreme scenarios. Japanese banks became major investors in such instruments during the early 1990s. Insurance companies bought companion "**inverse floaters**" (whose performance resembles that of a levered position in a fixed-rate companion bond) in order to add to yield, and to enhance duration in a falling interest-rate environment. In addition, the most option-laden tranches of the MBS universe (popularly qualified as "toxic waste") became the specialized province of MBS hedge funds, of which the largest was Granite Capital.

In other words, regulation led to a market inefficiency (namely, the excess offering of interest rate call options); inefficiency led to an innovative solution (the creation of the CMO); and the solution led to a new set of problems. These erupted in the spring of 1994 when the Federal Reserve raised interest rates after a prolonged period of low short-term rates. Granite Capital failed, along with some smaller MBS hedge funds, and a number of institutional investors incurred painful losses, notably Piper Jaffrey. Several insurance companies faced uncomfortably large losses in their holdings of CMOs, especially inverse floaters. CMO production shut down for the better part of a year. Complex CMO tranches traded at a deep discount to fair value. A salesperson would call a customer in late 1994 explaining that a certain inverse floater could be had at 40 percent below fair value, and the customer would respond, "Yes, I know that bond. My boss got fired for buying it."

An entire generation of MBS investors left the business. **Market failures** occur when existing market participants cannot buy the existing float, and are resolved when new market participants enter the market in order to take advantage of distressed prices. A new generation of MBS investors appeared in the form of hedge funds managed by former Wall Street MBS traders, attracting investment on the strength of their expertise in hedging the volatile securities. Again, the solution created the conditions for a new crisis. When the Federal Reserve again tightened interest rates during the spring of 1998, hedge funds heavily invested in MBS suffered distress. Disorder in the MBS market was aggravated by the Russian default in August 1998, leading to the celebrated failure of Long-Term Capital Management, which had invested heavily in both MBS and emerging market securities.

Once again, the composition of ownership of MBS changed. This time the government-sponsored enterprises (GSEs), namely the Federal National Mortgage Corporation ("Freddie Mac") and the Federal Home Loan Mortgage Corporation ("Fannie Mae") increased their holdings, along with large commercial bank treasury departments. At this writing just over half of the total universe of MBS securities is held by the GSEs and the commercial banks. Unlike traditional bond investors, the GSEs and the banks hedge the duration exposure of MBS using a variety of tools, mainly interest-rate swaps and options on swaps ("**swaptions**"). Federal regulators as well as private commentators have expressed concern about the potential exposure of the GSEs to violent swings in MBS valuation. I believe that the likelihood is quite remote that MBS volatility would exceed the management capacity of the GSEs, but we shall have to wait for another interest rate cycle with the shock value of a 1994 to know that for sure.

REGULATORY RESTRICTIONS ON CREDIT QUALITY AND INDEX-BASED INVESTING

4

During 2002, more than 3 percent of the nominal value of the U.S. investment-grade debt universe defaulted—the worst number since the Great Depression (see Figure 1). Enron, WorldCom, and a handful of merchant power issuers accounted for most of that quotient. Associated with the high default rate for investment-grade debt was the first true market failure in the investment-grade credit market in two generations. Like all market failures I have observed, this one stemmed directly from a market inefficiency brought about by regulation, namely the requirement that pension funds and life insurance companies hold 95 percent of their debt portfolio in names of investment grade. From the vantage point of financial theory this restriction is senseless. If it were

**FIGURE 1   Dollar-Weighted Investment-Grade
             Corporate Bond Default Rate**

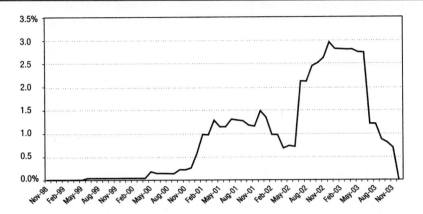

Source: Moody's Investor Services.

not, why should the same pension funds not have a requirement to own large-capitalization rather than small-capitalization equities, or for that matter, equities of firms that also enjoy an investment-grade debt rating? There is no evidence that speculative-grade debt offers worse performance over the long time horizon of pension-fund investors than does investment-grade debt. Nonetheless, that is the rule, and it is unlikely to change in the foreseeable future.

Although Enron and WorldCom were special cases, they expressed in a somewhat more extreme fashion a governance problem that became rampant during the late 1990s and the early part of this decade. During the boom years of the equity market, corporate managers paid themselves in options. In consequence they had a **long position** in volatility, which is to say that they had much more to gain from the potential success of risky business strategies than they had to lose in the event of failure. In consequence, corporate America levered up its balance sheet in order to double down on its debts, while it placed bets on whatever fad seemed likely to attract the attention of shareholders—broadband, Internet content, and so forth. In fact, the majority of all corporate bond issuance between 1996 and 2002 was used to buy back equity, that is, to increase balance sheet leverage (see Figure 2).

Why did investors agree to finance the buildup in leverage? Neither lack of intellect nor lack of information explains investor behavior in this regard; I am quite sure that this is the case due to personal observation. Instead, the practice of measuring fixed-income portfolio returns against an aggregate bond market index introduced a conflict between investors' long-term economic risk and their short-term business risk. As long as the ultimate beneficiaries of investment managers—that is, corporate pension funds—measure performance on the basis of a **Sharpe ratio** calculated monthly, a decision to deviate from index weightings presents risk to the investment-management business. Corporate pension fund sponsors are highly risk averse; they tend to reward managers with additional funds for a slight degree of outperformance, and punish them drastically for underperformance.

The behavior of plan sponsors jars with the nature of corporate bond excess returns. If a manager exhibits superior credit judgment, her excess returns necessarily will be bunched into the small number of months in which credit events actually occur. Telecom bonds, for example, were the single best-

FIGURE 2 More than Half of All Net Corporate Issuance since 1995 Funded Share Repurchases

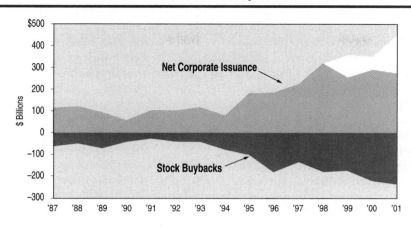

Source: Trimtabs.

performing sector in the investment-grade market during 2001, and WorldCom, whose fraudulent accounting had not yet been detected, was among the best performers. Consequently, it was a most popular name at the outset of 2002 among investment-grade managers. A manager who knew in late 2000 that WorldCom would fail, but did not know quite when, would have underperformed miserably during 2001, and lost funds under management to other managers.

Because the ratings process is backward-looking and tends to lag events, investment-grade managers accumulate names during a deteriorating credit cycle that later become subject to downgrade. The business risk of the money manager under the present regime of performance management causes managers to stick fairly close to index weightings. When the telephone sector flooded the market with new issues during 2001 and 2002, most managers simply bought according to index weightings, despite widespread skepticism about the sector.

FIGURE 3 Higher Leverage Led to Increased Volatility

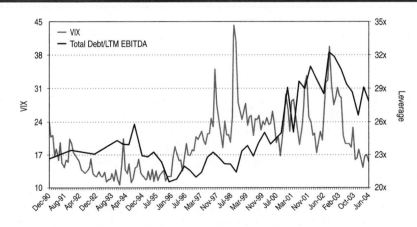

By the time that the credit cycle reaches the point at which substantial portions of the universe are downgraded to speculative grade, it is too late.

Under the circumstances it is no surprise that the volatility of prospective business outcomes reached levels hitherto unknown (see Figure 3). The **implied volatility** of options on the S&P 500 equity index (the VIX index) reflected the underlying volatility of prospective earnings. VIX had traded in the low teens during the halcyon days of the mid-1990s, but averaged somewhere in the mid-20s during 1999–2002, spiking above the 40 percent range on several occasions (see Figure 4). A volatile business, by the same token, is more likely to suffer a ratings downgrade. In the wake of the WorldCom failure and the downgrade to speculative grade of most of the merchant power sector, corporate bond investors froze. By the summer of 2002, viable investment-grade companies had lost access to the capital markets. Because investment-grade managers must sell a name in their portfolio in the event that it descends to speculative grade, they will not buy a name in danger of a downgrade.

During the first week of August 2002, for example, Sprint bonds traded at 43 cents on the dollar, despite the fact that Sprint maintained a respectable investment-grade rating and was in no financial difficulty. Instead, investors feared a repetition of the mass reduction to speculative grade that had occurred earlier in the merchant power sector and backed away from the market.

Once again, a new class of investors resolved the market failure, in this case the commercial banks. It had become an article of faith in the financial industry that the banks had been disintermediated out of the investment-grade market. Why would investment-grade borrowers tolerate loans with inconvenient covenants, as well as bank supervision, when the public market would lend them money with virtually no conditions? The patience of the public market gave out, of course, and the banks came back in. During the second week of August 2002, a bank consortium provided for Sprint's liquidity needs, and within a day or two of the announcement of a syndicated loan for the beleaguered issuer, its bonds once again were trading in the mid-70s.

Between October 2002 and the end of April 2003, the average spread to **LIBOR (London interbank offered rate)** of five-year U.S. investment-grade debt shrank from 180 basis points to only 110 basis points—the fastest rate of spread compression of which I am aware. By the same token, the average implied volatility

FIGURE 4   VIX Index of Equity-Implied Volatility versus BBB Credit Spreads

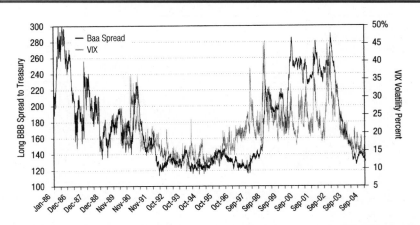

of options on the equities of investment-grade issuers fell from a frightening 60 percent in mid-October 2002 to the low 30 percent range at the end of April 2003. Once the banks resolved the market failure by reentering the investment-grade market, public market investors considered the governance crisis at an end.

There appears to be little doubt that the corporate credit crisis of 2002–2003 contributed to the onset of recession as well as to the languid pace of recovery. Corporations invested too much during 1998–2001, saturating the economy with broadband and other technology. They required a pause in which to work off the excess capital stock, in real terms, and to rebuild their balance sheets, in financial terms. Credit cycles of this sort are long. Not since the early 1990s, when the real-estate market nearly brought some major commercial banks to their knees, had the U.S. economy suffered credit difficulties of this kind. In fact, there is a close parallel between the 1991 and 2001 recessions as well as the pattern of recovery afterwards.

THE SHIFT TO A SWAP-BASED BENCHMARK FOR CREDIT

5

During the spring of 2000, the spread between the ten-year U.S. **Treasury note** and the ten-year **interest rate swap** rate spiked to more than 140 basis points, from fewer than 70 basis points at the end of 1999 (see Figure 5). Corporate investors who typically measure their returns against a benchmark index composed of Treasuries as well as corporates found that corporate spreads to Treasuries widened sharply along with **swap spreads**. The emergence of swaps rather than Treasuries as a benchmark for corporate debt threw a monkey wrench into the works of traditional corporate bond management.

According to the textbook, the market for intermediate- and long-term corporate debt should mediate savings and investment over the same time horizon. Individuals who wish to retire in thirty years lend money to corporates who wish to acquire assets that depreciate over thirty years. In the remote past of, say, 1996, this model applied quite well. Life insurance companies and pension funds bought most new corporate debt issues. During 1999, however, the balance of

FIGURE 5 Yield Curve Flattening of 2000 versus Swap Spreads Weekly Observations 1/1/98 to 11/5/04

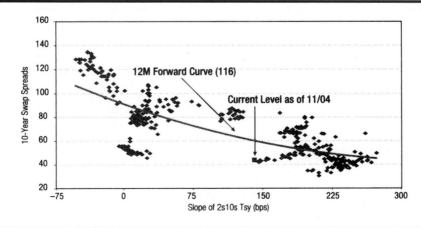

Source: Bloomberg.

power on capital markets swung toward levered credit buyers: commercial banks, bank-sponsored securities arbitrage conduits, semi-official agencies (such as German and Austrian *Landesbanken*), central banks, and so forth. Hedge funds emerged as a major factor in corporate bond markets during 2002.

This is quite different from the old maturity mismatch game, of course. Once upon a time, American **thrift institutions** borrowed from the public in the form of passbook savings accounts and lent the money in the form of thirty-year mortgages. The elimination of federal restrictions on short-term deposit interest at the outset of the 1980s coincided with a spike in short-term interest rates. The thrifts found themselves paying higher interest on their liabilities than they could earn on their assets, and the entire sector became insolvent. Today's financial institutions use the swap market to match floating-rate liabilities to floating-rate assets. In other words, they wish to pay fixed (sell swaps) to offset the fixed-rate payments they receive from corporate issuers, and receive floating in order to pay their own floating-rate liabilities. As more and more leverage is applied to spread product, it is the swap market that bears all the pressure, and it is in the swap market that little crises of adjustment break out with unpleasant regularity.

Crises break out when supply and demand fall into imbalance and too many market participants wish to pay fixed. In August 1998 and August 1999, payers of fixed lined up at the swaps window out of fear (of systemic failure in the first case and of Y2K in the second case). At the end of January 2000, they wished to pay fixed because the relative income advantage for receiving fixed as opposed to floating had disappeared with the flattening of the yield curve.

With the best of intentions, the three principal official influences on capital markets—**monetary policy**, fiscal policy, and bank regulation—have conspired together to bring about the worst of all possible outcomes:

1. Monetary policy was attempting to exorcise the ghost of inflation, leading market participants to weight their bets in favor of falling future interest rates, thereby inverting the yield curve.

2. Fiscal policy was removing Treasuries from circulation, and the U.S. Treasury has led the market to believe that it will remove the longest-term debt from circulation fastest.

FIGURE 6   Foreign Corporate Bond Purchases Made Higher Issuance Possible

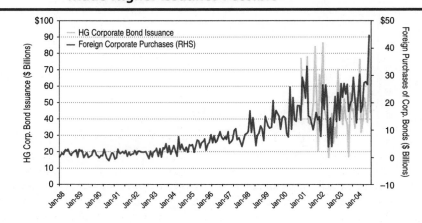

Source: Trimtabs; Federal Reserve Board.

3. Regulatory policy required dealers to calculate their capital according to a **Value-at-Risk** model that compels them to reduce exposure in periods of market volatility. In short, dealers could not provide sufficient liquidity to make swaps an efficient benchmark.

The following sequence of events caused the spring 2000 distress in the swaps market:

1. The **yield curve** inverted in anticipation of Fed tightening, starting from the yield differential between maturities of from ten to thirty years and moving toward the front.

2. As the long end of the **coupon** curve rallied, the inversion began working its way through to the yield differential between 2- and 10-year Treasuries.

3. Swaps market participants began selling 10-year swaps—that is, trying to pay fixed (or reversing receive-fixed positions) as the curve flattened— eliminating the economic incentive for receiving fixed in the first place.

4. Faced with a long line of customers seeking to pay fixed, dealers scrambled to obtain on-the-run Treasuries with which to hedge swap positions in the longer swap maturities.

5. On-the-run Treasury prices gapped relative to off-the-run prices, while the repo rate for on-the-run ten-year notes fell to a zero handle.

6. Dealers aggressively widened their bid for 10-year swaps, pushing the ten-year swap spread out to a late-April level of +146 basis points (at which level, to be sure, little execution took place).

The derivative market outguns the Treasury market. It is becoming hard to tell whether disarray in the derivatives markets whipsawed the Treasury market or vice versa. The Treasury's confusion about potential buyback programs was a lit match, to be sure, but the match had the misfortune to land on a gasoline spill.

Multiple choice: In the future, corporate spreads will be bench-marked against:

1. on-the-run Treasuries

2. off-the-run Treasuries

3. swaps

4. agencies

5. other corporate debt

6. all of the above

7. none of the above

As far as I can tell, both (6) and (7) are full credit answers. There really is no benchmark for credit markets, and enduring confusion over how to price corporate debt will make the credit markets susceptible to the kind of turbulence the markets endured in the spring of 2000. Swaps rather than Treasuries have become the "benchmark" for corporate debt, in the same way that Lucky Strikes became a currency in Germany after April 1945. Lucky Strikes, of course, never were intended to be a currency, did a poor job of acting like a currency, and ceased to be a currency as soon as circumstances changed. Nonetheless, American cigarettes were for a time the closest things to a currency that Germany possessed. Lucky Strikes became the German currency because American troops occupied Germany and could provide liquidity in the form of cigarettes. Swaps have become the benchmark for credit markets because LIBOR-based credit buyers set prices at the margin for liquid, higher-rated corporate product.

U.S. agencies buy mortgage-backed securities, that is, sell convexity in the form of embedded call options. They repurchase the **convexity** they sell in the MBS market by purchasing swaptions (options to enter into swap agreements). Whether the agencies swap proceeds of their bullet bond issues into floating, or buy swaptions giving them the option to do so at a later date, agency supply has a direct influence upon swap spreads.

What makes swaps problematic as a benchmark is the market's attempt to use them as a universal hedging instrument. As spreads themselves become more volatile, dealers, investors, and issuers increasingly use swaps as the preferred hedging vehicle. This phenomenon was also reinforced after the LTCM crisis in the fall of 1998, as many levered speculators in the swap market were driven out. When the swap market itself becomes volatile, it becomes difficult to hedge with swaps. In this situation, we expect swap dealers to quote higher swap spreads to compensate for the additional risk they are taking. In other words, in a swap market dominated by hedging activities, swap spread and swap volatility should be positively correlated.

ANALYSIS OF EQUITY INVESTMENTS

TOPIC LEVEL LEARNING OUTCOME

The candidate should be able to apply fundamental analysis to investment valuation, including global applications, and use various equity valuation models to estimate equity risk and return.

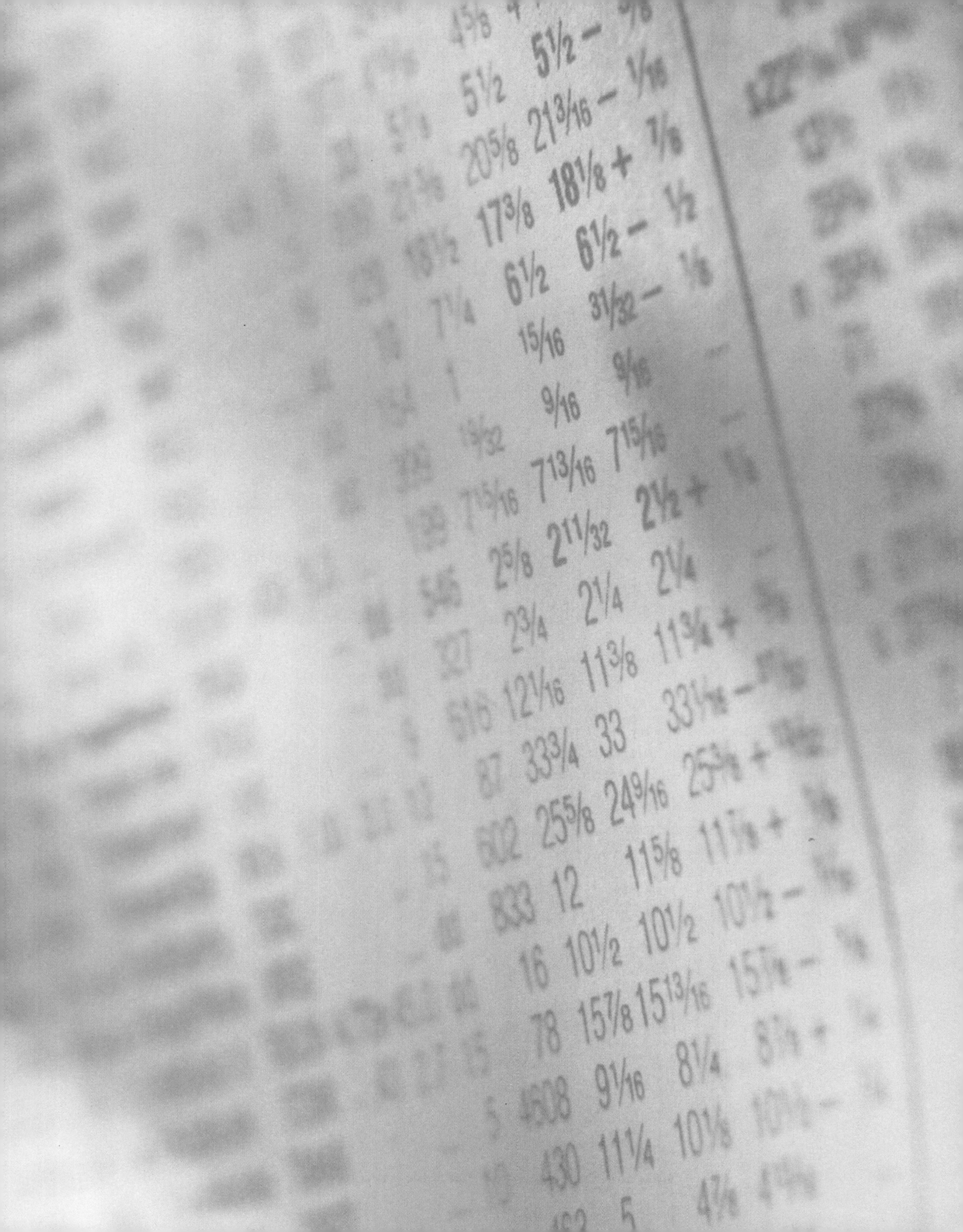

STUDY SESSION 11
EQUITY INVESTMENTS:
Industry and Company Analysis in a Global Context

This study session provides insights on issues that affect security valuation internationally. Differences in accounting standards are described to aid in making reasonable comparisons among companies based in different countries. Analyzing industries in a global context and evaluating competitive forces that will affect returns provide a foundation for security valuation decisions.

READING ASSIGNMENTS

Reading 40   Equity: Concepts and Techniques
Reading 41   Competitive Strategy: The Core Concepts
Reading 42   Industry Analysis
Reading 43   Valuation in Emerging Markets
Reading 44   Company Analysis and Stock Valuation
Reading 45   U.S. Portfolio Strategy: Seeking Value—Anatomy of Valuation

LEARNING OUTCOMES

Reading 40: Equity: Concepts and Techniques

The candidate should be able to:

a. discuss the most important issues, such as the information problem, that arise when investing internationally;

b. contrast the major differences among national accounting standards and international accounting standards (IAS);

c. demonstrate the various steps involved in global industry analysis, including country analysis;

d. discuss the concepts of business cycle synchronization and growth theory;

e. distinguish between country analysis and industry analysis and compare and evaluate key concepts of industry analysis such as demand analysis, industry life cycle analysis, and competition structure analysis as well as risk elements inherent in industry analysis;

f. demonstrate how to conduct a global industry analysis by analyzing the return potential and risk characteristics of a prospective investment in a global context;

Note:
See Reading 44, Company Analysis and Stock Valuation, for more on the franchise factor.

g. evaluate two common approaches of equity analysis (ratio analysis and discounted cash flow models including the franchise value model) and demonstrate how to find attractively priced stocks by using either of these methods;

h. analyze the effects of inflation on asset valuation;

i. discuss multi factor models as applied in the global context.

Reading 41: Competitive Strategy: The Core Concepts
The candidate should be able to:

a. analyze the competitive advantage and competitive strategy of a company and the competitive forces that affect the profitability of a company and discuss the two fundamental questions determining the choice of competitive strategy;

b. explain how competitive forces determine industry profitability;

c. analyze basic types of competitive advantage that a company can possess and the generic strategies for achieving a competitive advantage, the risks associated with each of the generic strategies, the difficulties and risks of simultaneously using more than one of the generic strategies, and the difficulties in sustaining a competitive advantage with any generic strategy;

d. explain the role of a generic strategy in the strategic planning process.

Reading 42: Industry Analysis
The candidate should be able to:

a. discuss the key components that should be included in an industry analysis model;

b. illustrate the life cycle of a typical industry;

c. analyze the effects of business cycles on industry classification (i.e., growth, defensive, cyclical);

d. analyze the impact of external factors (e.g., technology, government, foreign influences, demography, and social changes) on industries;

e. illustrate the inputs and methods used in preparing an industry demand-and-supply analysis;

f. explain factors that affect industry pricing practices.

Reading 43: Valuation in Emerging Markets
The candidate should be able to:

a. describe how inflation affects the estimation of cash flows for a company domiciled in an emerging market;

b. calculate nominal and real-term financial projections in order to prepare a discounted cash flow valuation of an emerging market company;

c. discuss the arrangements for adjusting cash flows, rather than adjusting the discount rate, to account for emerging market risks (e.g., inflation, macroeconomic volatility, capital control, and political risk) in a scenario analysis;

d. estimate the cost of capital for emerging market companies, and calculate and interpret a country risk premium.

Reading 44: Company Analysis and Stock Valuation
The candidate should be able to:

a. describe the elements of a franchise P/E;

b. describe how an analyst can use the growth duration model to determine whether a firm's P/E ratio is justified and describe the factors to consider when using the growth duration technique to infer a company's P/E.

Reading 45: U.S. Portfolio Strategy: Seeking Value—Anatomy of Valuation
The candidate should be able to:

a. explain why an analyst would use a ten-year moving average as a benchmark in the valuation process;

b. determine the importance of correlation analysis when using a multi-matrix valuation approach;

c. illustrate why the PEG valuation technique must be used with care;

d. indicate the impact of discount rate sensitivity in valuation models.

Note:
The Goldman Sachs research report should be studied for the generic features of security analysis rather than for specific characteristics of a company, industry, or country. Candidates are not expected to know details of the companies, industries, or countries, but rather to understand how the analytical techniques can be applied.

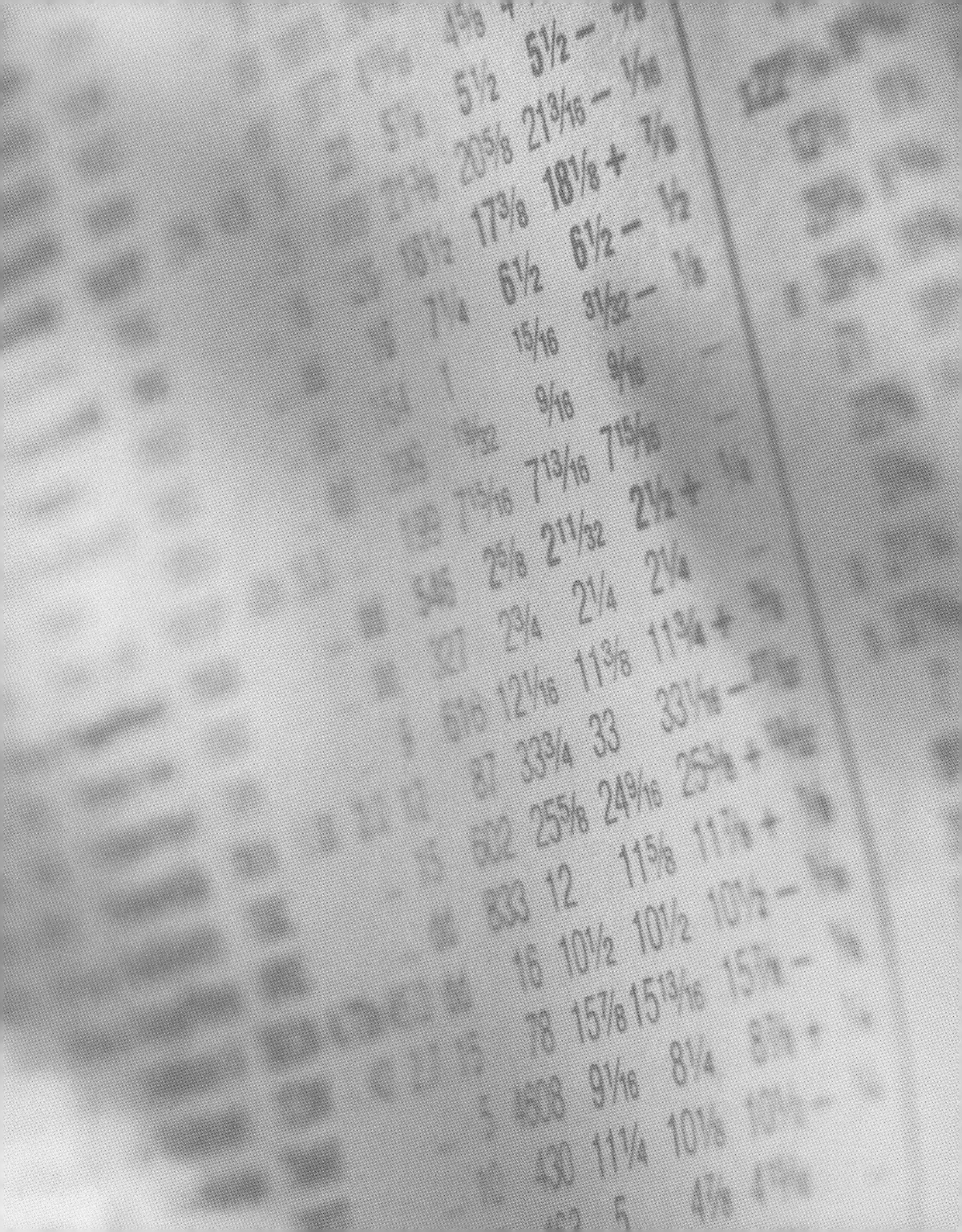

4⅝ + ⁷⁄

5½ **5½** – ⁷⁄₈

5⅛ 5½ **5½** – ¹⁄₁₆

20⅝ 21³⁄₁₆ – ¹⁄₁₆

17⅜ **18⅛** + ⁷⁄₈

18½ 6½ **6½** – ½

7¼ **6½** 6½ –

15⁄16 31⁄32 – ⅛

1 9⁄16 9⁄16

9⁄16 9⁄16

¹⁹⁄₃₂

7¹⁵⁄₁₆ 7¹³⁄₁₆ 7¹⁵⁄₁₆

2½ +

546 2⅝ 2¹¹⁄₃₂ **2½** +

527 2¾ 2¼ 2¼

6⅛ 12¹⁄₁₆ 11⅜ 11¾ +

87 33¾ 33 33¼₆ –

602 25⅝ 24⁹⁄₁₆ 25⅜ +

833 12 11⅝ 11⅜ +

16 10½ 10½ 10½ –

78 15⅝ 15¹³⁄₁₆ 15⅞ –

4608 9¹⁄₁₆ 8¼ 8⅞

430 11¼ 10⅛ 10⅛

5 4⅞ 4⅞

EQUITY: CONCEPTS AND TECHNIQUES

by Bruno Solnik and Dennis McLeavey

LEARNING OUTCOMES

The candidate should be able to:

a. discuss the most important issues, such as the information problem, that arise when investing internationally;

b. contrast the major differences among national accounting standards and international accounting standards (IAS);

c. demonstrate the various steps involved in global industry analysis, including country analysis;

d. discuss the concepts of business cycle synchronization and growth theory;

e. distinguish between country analysis and industry analysis and compare and evaluate key concepts of industry analysis such as demand analysis, industry life cycle analysis, and competition structure analysis as well as risk elements inherent in industry analysis;

f. demonstrate how to conduct a global industry analysis by analyzing the return potential and risk characteristics of a prospective investment in a global context;

g. evaluate two common approaches of equity analysis (ratio analysis and discounted cash flow models including the franchise value model) and demonstrate how to find attractively priced stocks by using either of these methods;

h. analyze the effects of inflation on asset valuation;

i. discuss multi factor models as applied in the global context.

Note:
See Reading 44, Company Analysis and Stock Valuation, for more on the franchise factor.

INTRODUCTION 1

Investing in foreign stocks poses at least two types of problems: First, the portfolio manager must gain sufficient familiarity with the operations, trading

Thomas R. Robinson, CPA, CFA, made significant contributions to the accounting material in this reading.

International Investments, Fifth Edition, by Bruno Solnik and Dennis McLeavey. Copyright © 2004 by Pearson Education. Reprinted with permission of Pearson Education, publishing as Pearson Addison Wesley.

107

mechanisms, costs, and constraints of foreign markets. Second, the portfolio manager's investment approach must be global; that is, his method of analyzing and selecting stocks should be part of an optimal worldwide investment strategy. The conceptual and technical aspects of this analysis are discussed in this reading.

To structure their analysis of expected return and risk of stocks, investors must start from a view of the world. What are the worldwide factors affecting stock prices? In an open-economy world, companies should be valued relative to their global competitors; hence, global industry analysis is of primary importance. Before conducting such an analysis, it is important to understand the differences in national accounting standards that affect the raw information used. Then the important aspects of global industry analysis can be studied with data adjusted for comparability across countries. Global industry analysis of expected returns and risks leads naturally to a discussion of risk factor models used to structure global portfolios and manage their risk.

2   APPROACHING INTERNATIONAL ANALYSIS

There is nothing unique to financial analysis in an international context. Analysts must already take foreign variables into account in evaluating domestic firms. After all, product markets in which many domestic industrial companies compete are international.

CONCEPTS IN ACTION

Toyota Eclipses Its U.S. Rivals
Japanese Carmaker Delivers Record Half-Year Results with a 90% Surge in Profits

Toyota Motor yesterday reinforced the Japanese car industry's ranking as the most profitable in the world when it produced record half-year results.

The 90 percent jump in consolidated net profits to ¥553bn ($4.5bn) put it on track to top Ford's profits of $7.2bn in 1999, the record by any carmaker excluding one-off gains.

In the six months to September the world's third-biggest carmaker made more than the combined profits of its U.S. rivals, General Motors, Ford and Chrysler, part of the German-U.S. group DaimlerChrysler. Its automotive operating margins of 10.1 percent were more than five times the average of Detroit's big three.

The ability of Toyota and domestic competitors Nissan Motor and Honda Motor to make record profits while America's big three are struggling with restructuring plans reflects the popularity of their vehicles in the U.S., which has driven strong growth in sales.

"The biggest reason why Japanese have suddenly started to make supernormal profits is not what is going on in their domestic market but what is happening in their export markets," said Mark Little, motor industry analyst at Deutsche Bank.

American carmakers blame their loss of market share on the weakness of the yen against the dollar. Bill Ford, chairman of Ford, told shareholders this week: "It really, competitively, puts us at a disadvantage."

Even Europe's BMW, which operates exclusively in the high-margin luxury sector, cannot match the operating margins of the Japanese.

Unlike their U.S. counterparts, Japan's leading manufacturers have implemented cost-cutting measures while simultaneously increasing sales in their core markets—especially the U.S. . . .

All three carmakers have drawn attention to the fact that they increased sales without relying on discounts.

Toyota also reported rising sales in its three remaining markets. In Europe, where Toyota has struggled in the past, sales rose 21 percent to ¥746.2bn, while sales in Japan where it has a dominant market share of 42 percent, were up 9.5 percent at ¥5,388bn. Sales to the rest of the world rose 61.9 percent to ¥823bn.

It announced an interim dividend of ¥16 per share, an increase of ¥3 per share on the same period last year.

Source: Financial Times, October 31, 2002, p. 1.

Large domestic firms tend to export extensively and head a network of foreign subsidiaries. These companies must be analyzed as global firms, not purely domestic ones. In many sectors, the competition is fully global. The methods and data required to analyze international manufacturers are quite similar. In brief, research on a company should produce two pieces of information:

► *Expected return.* The expected return on an investment can be measured by a rate of return, including potential price appreciation, over some time period, or by some other quantified form of buy-or-sell recommendation.

► *Risk exposure.* Risk sensitivity, or risk exposure, measures how much a company's value responds to certain key factors, such as economic activity, energy costs, interest rates, currency volatility, and general market conditions. Risk analysis enables a manager or investment policy committee to simulate the performance of an investment in different scenarios. It also helps the manager to design more diversified portfolios.

The overall purpose of analysis is to find securities with superior expected returns, given current (or foreseeable) domestic and international risks.

Quantifying the analysis facilitates a consistent global approach to international investment. This is all the more desirable when the parameters that must be considered are numerous and their interrelationships are complex. Although qualitative analysis seems easier to conduct in some institutions than in others, it must be carefully structured so that it is consistent for every security, and provides an estimation of the reaction of security prices to various risk factors.

The Information Problem

Information on foreign firms is often difficult to obtain; once obtained, it is often difficult to interpret and analyze using domestic methods. It is no wonder, then, that comparisons of similar figures for foreign firms are often misleading.

In the United States, companies publish their quarterly earnings, which are publicly available within just a couple of weeks after the close of the quarter. The 10-K reports are particularly useful for trend analysis and intercompany comparisons. Moreover, these reports are available on computerized databases. In contrast, certain European and Far Eastern firms publish their earnings only once a year and with a considerable reporting time lag. French companies, for example, follow this pattern and don't actually publish their official earnings until two to six months after the end of their fiscal years. As a result, official earnings figures are outdated before they become public. To remedy this lack of information, most corporations with significant foreign ownership have begun announcing quarterly or semiannual earnings estimates a short time after the close of the quarter. This is true worldwide for large international corporations. These corporations also follow the American practice of issuing "warnings" as soon as some bad news is likely to affect earnings. The format and reliability of these announcements vary from firm to firm, but overall, they help investors to get better financial information more quickly. As do U.S. firms, British firms publish detailed financial information frequently. Similarly, Japanese firms have begun publishing U.S.-style financial statements, though sometimes only once a year.

Other problems arise from the language and presentation of the financial reports. Many reports are available only in a company's domestic language. Whereas multinational firms tend to publish both in their domestic language and in English, many smaller but nevertheless attractive firms do not. In general, financial reports vary widely from country to country in format, degree of detail, and reliability of the information disclosed. Therefore, additional information must sometimes be obtained directly from the company. Differences in national accounting standards are discussed later in this reading.

As international investment has grown, brokers, banks, and information services have, fortunately, started to provide more financial data to meet investors' needs. In fact, today, many large international brokerage houses and banks provide analysts' guides covering companies from a large number of countries. The guides include information ranging from summary balance sheet and income statement information to growth forecasts, expected returns on equity investments, and risk measures, such as betas, which are discussed later. The reports are usually available in both the domestic language and English. Similarly, several data services, such as Bloomberg, Reuters, Thomson Financial, Factset, and Moody's, are extending their international coverage on companies and currently feature summary financial information on an increasing number of international corporations. Some financial firms, such as Thomson First Call, have specialized in collecting earnings forecasts from financial analysts worldwide. They provide a service giving the individual analyst's forecast for most large companies listed on the major stock exchanges of the world. They also calculate a consensus forecast, as well as various other global statistics.

Despite these developments, to get the most timely information possible, financial analysts may have to visit international corporations. This, of course, is a time-consuming and expensive process. Moreover, the information obtained is often not homogeneous across companies and countries. The next section reviews differences in international accounting standards.

A Vision of the World

A major challenge faced by all investment organizations is structuring their international research efforts. Their choice of method depends on what they believe are the major factors influencing stock returns. The objective of security analysis is to detect relative misvaluation, that is, investments that are preferable to other *comparable* investments. That is why sectoral analysis is so important. A financial analyst should be assigned the study of securities that belong to the same sector, that is, that are influenced by the *same* common factors and that can therefore be directly compared. The first task, though, is defining these sectors, or common factors. For example, one can reasonably claim that all dollar

Eurobonds with fixed coupons belong to the same sector. Another sector would be French common stocks, which are all influenced by national factors. An alternative would be all high-technology companies across the world, which should be influenced by similar worldwide industrial factors. In a homogeneous sector, research should detect securities that are underpriced or overpriced relative to the others.

A first step for an organization to structure its global equity investment requires that it adhere to some vision of the world regarding the dominant factors affecting stock returns. Traditionally, investment organizations use one of three major approaches to international research, depending on their vision of the world:

▶ If a portfolio manager believes that the value of companies worldwide is affected primarily by global industrial factors, her research effort should be structured according to industrial sectors. This means that companies are valued relative to others within the same industry, for example, the chemical industry. Naturally, financial analysts who use this approach are specialists in particular industrial sectors.

▶ If a portfolio manager believes that all securities in a national stock market are influenced primarily by domestic factors, her research effort should be structured on a country-by-country basis. The most important investment decision in this approach is how to allocate assets among countries. Thereafter, securities are given a relative valuation within each national market.

▶ If a portfolio manager believes that some particular attributes of firms are valued worldwide, she will engage in *style* investing. For example, *value stocks* (corporations with a low stock market price compared with their book value) could be preferred to *growth stocks* (corporations with a high stock market price compared with their book value).

In general, an organization must structure its investment process based on some vision of the major common factors influencing stock returns worldwide.

DIFFERENCES IN NATIONAL ACCOUNTING STANDARDS   3

In this reading, we develop a top-down approach to global equity investing. We examine country and industry analysis before moving to **equity security** analysis. Global industry financial analysis examines each company in the industry against the industry average. Plots of one financial ratio against another can show the relative location of individual companies within the industry. To carry out such analysis, we must first know something about the differences in national accounting standards so that we can adjust ratios to make them comparable. For example, discounted cash flow analysis (DCF) and compound annual growth rates (CAGR) in cash flows must be based on comparable data to be meaningful.

In global industry financial analysis, the pattern is to contrast the financial ratios of individual firms against the same ratios for industry averages. The analyst will encounter and possibly need to adjust such ratios as: enterprise value (EV) to earnings before interest, taxes, depreciation, and amortization (EBIDTA), return on equity (ROE), and the book value multiple of price to book value per share (BV). In practice, one also sees such ratios as price to net asset value (NAV), EV to capital employed (CE), return on capital employed

(ROCE), and value added margin. *Capital employed* is usually defined[1] as equity plus long-term debt. *Net asset value* is usually defined on a per-share basis as equity minus goodwill. *Value added margin* is ROCE minus the weighted average cost of capital (WACC).

With an understanding of differences in national accounting standards, the analyst will be prepared to evaluate companies from around the world within the context of global industry. After discussing these differences, we will return to global industry analysis.

Today all companies compete globally. Capital markets of developed countries are well integrated, and international capital flows react quickly to any perceived mispricing. Hence, companies tend to be priced relative to their global competitors, and it is for this reason that this reading focuses on global industry analysis.

Companies and investors have become more global. Mergers and acquisitions often occur on a global basis. Further, it is not unusual for a company to have its shares listed on multiple exchanges. Similarly, investors often seek to diversify their holdings and take advantage of opportunities across national borders. This globalization of financial markets creates challenges for investors, creditors, and other users of financial statements. Comparing financial statements of companies located in different countries is a difficult task. Different countries may employ different accounting principles, and even where the same accounting methods are used, currency, cultural, institutional, political, and tax differences can make between-country comparisons of accounting numbers hazardous and misleading.

For example, the treatment of depreciation and extraordinary items varies greatly among countries, such that net income of a company located in one country might be half that of a similarly performing company located in another country, even after adjustment for differences in currency. This disparity is partly the result of different national tax incentives and the creation of "secret" reserves (provisions) in certain countries. German and Swiss firms (among others), for example, have been known to stretch the definition of a liability; that is, they tend to overestimate contingent liabilities and future uncertainties when compared with other firms. The provisions for these liabilities reduce income in the current year, but increase income in later years when the provisions are reduced. This can have a smoothing impact on earnings and mask the underlying variability or riskiness of business operations.

Similarly, German and Swiss firms allow goodwill resulting from acquisitions to be deducted from equity immediately, bypassing the income statement and resulting in reporting the balance sheet based on book value, not on actual transaction prices. Similar idiosyncrasies often make comparisons of Japanese and U.S. earnings figures or accounting ratios meaningless. As a result, many large Japanese companies publish secondary financial statements in English that conform to the U.S. generally accepted accounting principles (GAAP). But even when we examine these statements, we find that financial ratios differ markedly between the two countries. For example, financial leverage is high in Japan compared with the United States, and coverage ratios are poor. But this does not necessarily mean that Japanese firms are more risky than their U.S. counterparts, only that the relationship between banks and their client corporations is different than in the United States.

With increasing globalization there has been a movement toward convergence of accounting standards internationally. In spite of this movement, there are still substantial differences in existing accounting standards that must be considered by investors.

---

[1] See Temple (2002) for definitions.

Historical Setting

Each country follows a set of accounting principles that are usually prepared by the accounting profession and the national authorities. These sets of accounting principles are sometimes called national GAAP. Two distinct models can describe the preparation of these national accounting principles:

▶ In the Anglo-American model, accounting rules have historically been set in standards prepared by a well-established, influential accounting profession.

▶ In the Continental model, used by countries in Continental Europe and Japan, accounting rules have been set in a codified law system; governmental bodies write the law, and the accounting profession is less influential than in the Anglo-American model.

Anglo-American countries typically report financial statements intended to give a true and fair view of the firm's financial position. Hence, there can be large differences between accounting statements, the intent of which is to give a fair representation of the firm's financial position, and tax statements, the intent of which is to reflect the various tax provisions used to calculate the amount of income tax owed. Many other countries (France, Germany, Italy, and Japan, for example) have a tradition that the reported financial statements and earnings conform to the method used to determine taxable income. This implies that financial statements are geared to satisfy legal and tax provisions and may not give a true and fair view of the firm. This confusion between tax and book accounting is slowly disappearing under the pressure of international harmonization, as noted in the next section.

International Harmonization of Accounting Practices

Investors, creditors, and other users of financial statements have exerted pressure to harmonize national accounting principles. The *International Accounting Standards Committee* (*IASC*) was set up in 1973 by leading professional accounting organizations in nine countries: Australia, Canada, France, Germany, Japan, Mexico, the Netherlands, the United Kingdom and Ireland, and the United States. Over time, additional countries became members of the IASC. The IASC issued its first international accounting standard (IAS) in 1974, entitled Disclosure of Accounting Policies. In 2001, the IASC was renamed the *International Accounting Standards Board* (*IASB*), and we will use this name hereafter.

Although the IASB is able to propose international accounting standards, it does not have the authority to require companies to follow these standards. Without a mechanism to compel companies to use IAS and enforce the standards, harmonization is not easily achievable. In 1995, the *International Organization of Securities Commissions* (*IOSCO*) stated that it would consider adopting the international accounting standards once the IASB had prepared a comprehensive set of standards covering all the major areas of importance to general business. IOSCO is an important organization whose members are the agencies regulating securities markets in all countries.[2] IOSCO's objectives are to promote high standards of regulation in order to maintain just, efficient, and sound markets. IOSCO has two important committees: The Emerging Markets Committee endeavors to promote the development and improvement of efficiency of emerging securities and futures markets. The Technical Committee is made up of

---

[2] One hundred seventy members as of 31 December 2001, according to IOSCO Annual Report 2001.

sixteen agencies that currently regulate the world's larger, more developed and internationalized markets in fourteen countries: Australia, France, Germany, Hong Kong, Italy, Japan, Mexico, the Netherlands, Canada, Spain, Sweden, Switzerland, the United Kingdom, and the United States.

"Multinational disclosure and accounting" is a major subject before this committee, and has led to the cooperation with the IASB. At the start of 1999, the IASB prepared a core set of standards and submitted them to IOSCO for review and endorsement. After deliberation, in May 2000 the Technical Committee of IOSCO recommended that IOSCO members use 30 selected IASB standards for cross-border listings and offerings by multinational companies. These 30 selected standards, referred to as IASB 2000 Standards by IOSCO, are listed in Exhibit 1. Due to concerns with some standards, the Technical Committee recommends that **supplemental information** be required for some standards in the form of reconciliations to national standards, additional disclosure, or specification of which alternative treatment in IAS must be used.

EXHIBIT 1	IOSCO Selected Standards for Cross-Border Listings

IAS	Description
IAS 1	Presentation of Financial Statements (revised 1997)
IAS 2	Inventories (revised 1993)
IAS 4	Depreciation Accounting (reformatted 1994)
IAS 7	Cash Flow Statements (revised 1992)
IAS 8	Net Profit or Loss for the Period, Fundamental Errors and Changes in Accounting Policies (revised 1993)
IAS 10	Events after the Balance Sheet Date (revised 1999)
IAS 11	Construction Contracts (revised 1993)
IAS 12	Income Taxes (revised 1996)
IAS 14	Segment Reporting (revised 1997)
IAS 16	Property, Plant and Equipment (revised 1998)
IAS 17	Leases (revised 1997)
IAS 18	Revenue (revised 1993)
IAS 19	Employee Benefits (revised 1998)
IAS 20	Accounting for Government Grants and Disclosure of Governmental Assistance (reformatted 1994)
IAS 21	The Effects of Changes in Foreign Exchange Rates (revised 1993)
IAS 22	Business Combinations (revised 1998)
IAS 23	Borrowing Costs (revised 1993)
IAS 24	Related Party Disclosures (reformatted 1994)
IAS 27	Consolidated Financial Statements and Accounting for Investments in Subsidiaries (reformatted 1994)
IAS 28	Accounting for Investments in Associates (revised 1998)
IAS 29	Financial Reporting in Hyperinflationary Economies (reformatted 1994)
IAS 31	Financial Reporting of Interests in Joint Ventures (revised 1998)

(Exhibit continued on next page . . .)

| EXHIBIT 1 | (continued) |

IAS 32   Financial Instruments: Disclosure and Presentation (revised 1998)

IAS 33   Earnings Per Share (1997)

IAS 34   Interim Financial Reporting (1998)

IAS 35   Discontinuing Operations (1998)

IAS 36   Impairment of Assets (1998)

IAS 37   Provisions, Contingent Liabilities and Contingent Assets (1998)

IAS 38   Intangible Assets (1998)

IAS 39   Financial Instruments: Recognition and Measurement (1998)

Source: IASB Standards—Assessment Report, Report of the Technical Committee of the International Organization of Securities Commissions, May 2000.

These two international organizations, one representative of the accounting profession (private sector) and the other of government regulators, play an important role in moving toward global harmonization of disclosure requirements and accounting practices. This is all the more important for multinational corporations that wish to raise capital globally. They need to be able to present their accounts in a single format, wherever they want to be listed or raise capital. Of particular importance is the attitude of the United States toward IAS. Convergence of the U.S. GAAP and IAS is a desirable but difficult goal. A topic under discussion is to allow foreign firms listed on a U.S. stock exchange to publish accounts according to IAS, rather than asking them to provide earnings statements calculated according to the U.S. GAAP.

The IASB also received the support of the *World Bank*. A large number of emerging countries, as well as Hong Kong, have adopted the IAS as a basis for their accounting standards. Corporations from many developed countries also use the IAS in their financial reporting. For example, most of the leading industrial companies in Switzerland voluntarily report their accounts according to international accounting standards.

In countries where accounting rules are governed by law, specific legislation is required to allow for the use of other accounting standards. The European Union (EU) is supporting the use of IAS. The harmonization of European accounting principles has come mostly through *Directives* published by the EU. These EU Directives are drafted by the EU Commission, and member states' parliaments must adapt the national law to conform to these Directives. The EU also issues *Regulations,* which have the force of law without requiring formal transposition into national legislation. In 2002, the EU issued a Regulation requiring listed companies to prepare their consolidated financial statements in accordance with IAS from 2005 onward.[3] The road to global cooperation is never easy, and it will be a long time before full harmonization of financial reporting is achieved.

Differences in Global Standards

A complete presentation of International Accounting Standards is beyond our present scope. The full text of standards can be obtained from the International

---

[3] Regulation (EC) No. 1606/2002 of the European Parliament and of the Council of the European Union on the application of international accounting standards, 19 July 2002.

Accounting Standards Board (www.iasb.org.uk).[4] We focus here on areas of differences among IAS and various national GAAP. A group of international accounting firms prepared a comparison of IAS and national GAAP for 62 countries.[5] The study found that there remains a lack of convergence globally particularly with regard to the following:

► The recognition and measurement of:
  ► financial assets and derivative financial instruments
  ► impairment losses
  ► provisions
  ► employee benefit liabilities
  ► income taxes
► Accounting for business combinations
► Disclosure of:
  ► related party transactions
  ► segment information

Several inconsistencies in accounting standards require that the analyst take particular care in making cross-border comparisons. For example, one question to ask is whether all assets and/or liabilities are properly reflected on the balance sheet. If not, these off-balance-sheet assets and liabilities must be analyzed and appropriate adjustments made in any valuation exercise.

Business Combinations   Under IAS 22 the *purchase method* of accounting is generally used (recording acquired assets and liabilities at fair value at the acquisition date), although the *uniting of interest method* (recording acquired assets and liabilities at historical book value) is used when the acquirer cannot be identified (i.e., which one is the acquirer?). Until recently, the United States permitted use of the *pooling method* (substantially equivalent to uniting of interest) for many acquisitions. Now all new acquisitions in the United States must be accounted for by using the purchase method. Previous acquisitions under the pooling method continue to be reported by using the pooling method. Australia prohibits the pooling/uniting of interest method. In France, Germany, and Italy (at least until 2005), there is a more liberal use of uniting of interests than under IAS. Japan and Switzerland do not have specific rules related to the classification of business combinations.

Consolidation   In most countries, corporations publish financial statements that consolidate, to some extent, the accounts of their subsidiaries and affiliates. A full range of consolidation practices exists. In all countries, majority interests in domestic subsidiaries are typically consolidated. This is not always the case when dealing with foreign subsidiaries or with minority interests. In Italy and Japan, certain dissimilar subsidiaries can be excluded. In France, there is considerable leeway in the method used for consolidation. Japanese companies, like many German firms, tend to publish separately the (nonconsolidated) financial statements of the various companies belonging to the same group. This can be

---

[4] Various summaries of IAS are also available. For example, *IAS In Your Pocket*, Deloitte Touche Tohmatsu, April 2002, and *GAAP Differences in Your Pocket: IAS and US GAAP*, Deloitte Touche Tohmatsu. Both are available at www.iasplus.com.

[5] *GAAP 2001: A Survey of National Accounting Rules Benchmarked against International Accounting Standards*, Anderson, BDO, Deloitte Touche Tohmatsu, Ernst & Young, Grant Thornton, KPMG, Pricewaterhouse-Coopers: Editor, Christopher W. Nobes. Available at www.ifad.net.

CONCEPTS IN ACTION

Rules Set for Big Change

Millions of Dollars of Debt Could Be Brought back on to Companies' Balance Sheets

Among the many consequences of the collapse of Enron has been a new focus by regulators on how companies account for off-balance-sheet transactions.

Enron's swift demise raised questions over its complex web of off-balance-sheet transactions, leading the U.S.'s Financial Standards Accounting Board to consider new rules governing special purpose entities (SPEs). The changes could result in millions of dollars of debt being brought back on to corporate balance sheets, and represent a significant challenge for the rapidly developing structured finance market. SPEs are used for a wide range of financial transactions because they isolate assets from the financial fortunes of companies that own them.

SPEs can be organized in a variety of forms, such as trusts or corporations, but usually have no full-time employees or operating business. They can be used for different activities, including acquiring financial assets, property or equipment, and as a vehicle for raising funds from investors by issuing stock or other securities.

Depending on the type of SPE, its assets and liabilities may not appear in the financial statements of the entity that created it. . . .

Source: Jenny Wiggins, "Special Purpose Entities," *Financial Times,* October 7, 2002, p. 4.

---

partly explained by the extent of cross-holdings in these countries. The perimeter of consolidation is often difficult to establish in Japan because of the extent of cross-holding. The practice of publishing (partly) nonconsolidated statements renders the valuation of a company a difficult exercise. IAS 27 imposes consolidation for all subsidiaries with uniform accounting policies. In addition to subsidiaries, there is also the question of nonoperating entities created to carry out a special purpose, such as leasing assets or securitizing receivables.

Under IAS 27, special purpose entities (SPEs) are consolidated if controlled. This is also the case in the United Kingdom. In the United States, SPEs are consolidated if certain criteria are met (or not met); this leaves considerable leeway. Germany, Spain, and Switzerland have no requirement regarding SPEs. France requires holding at least one share of an SPE to consolidate. The ability of firms to avoid consolidation of SPEs has often enabled them to keep large amounts of liabilities off the balance sheet to the detriment of investors and creditors alike. National standards setters, such as the U.S. **Financial Accounting Standards Board**, are reconsidering standards in this area.

Joint Ventures   Joint ventures are increasingly used in international business. Most European countries consolidate joint ventures using *proportional consolidation,* as provided under IAS. In this method, assets, liabilities, and earnings are consolidated line by line, proportional to the percentage of ownership in the subsidiary. U.K. and U.S. corporations use the *equity method.* A share of the subsidiary profits is consolidated on a one-line basis, proportional to the share of equity owned by the parent. The value of the investment in the subsidiary is adjusted to reflect the change in the subsidiary's equity. The two methods lead to marked differences in the corporation's balance sheet. IAS 31 states that the benchmark treatment should be proportional consolidation, although jointly controlled entities can alternatively be accounted for by using equity consolidation.

CONCEPTS IN ACTION

Enron Collapse Is IAS Weapon

Enron's multibillion dollar collapse is set to become the weapon the global accounting standard-setter has been looking for in its battle to convince the U.S. to adopt international accounting rules.

Sir David Tweedie, International Accounting Standards Board chairman, and Allan Cook, U.K. Accounting Standards Board technical director, have indicated Enron's collapse could not have happened under existing U.K. or global rules. U.K. standards are the closest in the world to international rules.

Tweedie is now likely to reapply pressure to U.S. watchdog the Securities and Exchange Commission to allow American companies to use global rules. Both U.K. and global rules on off-balance sheet reporting, which brought Enron to its knees, are much tougher.

But FASB, the U.S. standard setter, has consistently resisted attempts to push through an updated standard. Highlighting Enron's off-balance sheet reporting, Cook said: 'The IASB would probably have got it on the balance sheet. It's very tough.'

As if to show the U.S. its determination, the IASB could issue an even tougher rule on off-balance-sheet reporting, or derecognition, as early as next year.

The ASB is compiling research into off-balance-sheet reporting to submit to the IASB in January.

Sir David Tweedie, IASB chairman, said: 'This wakes people up to the fact that accounting matters. They are looking across at us. The U.K. is well ahead of the rest of the world on this.'

A letter to the *Wall Street Journal* last week by Joe Berardino, chief executive of Andersen, Enron's auditor, also showed him in favor of a change in rules.

Source: Michelle Perry, "Enron Collapse Is IAS Weapon," *Financial Director*, December 13, 2001.

Goodwill   Goodwill can appear in various ways. Most commonly, goodwill is created when a company engages in an acquisition or merger at a market value different from the book value. Under IAS, goodwill is capitalized and amortized, usually over 20 years or less, and is subject to an impairment ("loss of value") test. In Switzerland and Germany, goodwill can be written off against equity immediately and does not affect the income statement. In the United Kingdom, goodwill need not be amortized. In the United States, until recently goodwill was capitalized as an asset and amortized. Now in the United States, goodwill and other intangibles without a determinable useful life are no longer amortized, but are subject to impairment tests.

Financial Leases   Financial leases are an indirect way to own an asset and provide the financing for it. In some countries, they are simply carried as off-balance-sheet items. In other countries, these leases are capitalized both as assets and liabilities. This was not common in countries in which accounting systems are driven by tax considerations (e.g., France, Germany, and Italy), but it is progressively implemented in most countries. IAS 17 requires capitalization of financial leases.

Asset Revaluation   Revaluation of assets is generally not permitted except when the market value declines, with the exception of financial assets discussed below. Investment properties can be revalued in Switzerland and Sweden. In Japan, land can be revalued. In Switzerland, Canada, and France, there is no requirement for recognizing impairment. Special laws have permitted periodic revaluation in France, Italy, and Spain in order to compensate for inflation, but the tax implications of these revaluations have sometimes been negative, making revaluation unpopular. Countries with higher inflation, such as Brazil, tend to have systems for automatic inflation indexing.

Provisions   A provision is an estimate of a likely future loss or expense. It appears as a liability on the balance sheet and is deducted from current reported earnings when initially taken. In many countries, such as the United States, United Kingdom, Italy, and Spain, provisions can be taken only for specific and likely future events. In Germany and Switzerland, generous provisions can be taken for all types of general risks. In the Netherlands, certain provisions can be made where there may not be a current obligation. In good times, German firms will build provisions to reduce earnings growth; in bad times, they will draw on these provisions to boost reported earnings. These provisions are called "hidden reserves" because they do not appear as equity reserves on the balance sheet, but rather as general liability (debt). However, they can be used to boost profits in bad times. IAS 37 supports a strong limitation on the creation of provisions, and when created, requires discounting. In the United States, provisions are not discounted.

Pensions   The accounting for pensions and retirement liabilities differs widely across countries, in part because of the national differences in pension systems. One difference is whether pension liabilities are accrued, that is, whether there is an actuarial evaluation of future pension expenses (and on what basis). Another difference is whether the pensions are funded off-balance sheets or whether pension assets and liabilities remain on a company's balance sheet. Some countries, for example, France and Italy, have primarily a national pay-as-you-go pension system, whereby current workers pay for the pensions of retired workers; companies contribute to pensions, but future pension liabilities are neither accrued nor funded, and current pension costs are expensed as incurred. In the United States, the Netherlands, Switzerland, the United Kingdom, and, to some extent, Japan, pensions are accrued and funded off-balance sheets; a separate entity, called a "pension fund," manages the pension assets and liabilities. In Germany or Spain, pensions are accrued but not funded, so pension liabilities do not appear on the company's balance sheet. The assumptions used to estimate accrued pension liabilities also vary among countries and firms.

Financial Assets and Derivatives   Under IAS and U.S. standards, trading and available-for-sale securities are recorded at fair value. Similarly, derivatives are reported at fair value, except certain hedging activities. In Switzerland, the United Kingdom, Spain, Canada, and Germany, trading securities, available-for-sale securities, and derivatives are not reported at fair value. Similarly, trading and derivative liabilities are not reported at fair value, and hedging treatment is applied more liberally.

Employee Stock Options   Employee stock options represent potential earnings dilution to existing shareholders. As a form of employee compensation, these stock options should be treated as expenses from an economic perspective. The fair value of this compensation paid to employees is treated as an expense, a deduction to pretax earnings recorded at the time the options are granted. The fair value is computed by using a standard option pricing model.

Currently IAS, as well as most national GAAP including the U.S. GAAP, does not require that an expense be recorded for the value of options granted to employees. In the United States, footnote disclosures are required, but recording

EXAMPLE 1

Employee Stock Options

A company has 100,000 shares outstanding at $100 per share. To its senior management, the company granted employee stock options on 5,000 shares. The options can be exercised at a price of $105 any time during the next five years. For five years, the employees thus have the right but not the obligation to purchase shares at the $105 price, regardless of the prevailing market price of the stock. Using price volatility estimates for the stock, a standard Black–Scholes valuation model gives an estimated value of $20 per share option. Without expensing the options, the company's pretax earnings per share are reported as $1 million/ 100,000 = $10 per share. What would they have been if they had been expensed?

Solution: The expense is $5000 \times \$20 = \$100,000$. The pretax income per share would be ($1,000,000 − $100,000)/100,000 = $9 per share.

of an expense is optional for most stock options. IAS requires some disclosures regarding options. In July 2000, the IASB in conjunction with some national standard-setters, issued a discussion paper proposing, among other things, that share based payments be expensed. The IASB added this project to their agenda and issued an exposure draft in November 2002. This matter is getting wide attention, and some U.S. firms have recently decided to voluntarily begin recording an expense for such stock options allocation.

CONCEPTS IN ACTION

So Many Options

Have Accounting Regulators Chosen the Best Way of Expensing Share Options?

Several features of the wild bull market of the 1990s have since been branded as evil. Perhaps none more so than the billions of dollars of share options awarded to bosses and other employees. Once praised for their incentivizing power, share options are now blamed for encouraging bosses to do all manner of bad things to prop up their company's share price and so keep their lucrative options packages **in the money**, as the jargon has it. In this, it is now generally agreed, executives have been abetted by accounting standards that did not require the cost of awarding options to be treated as compensation and lopped off a company's reported profits.

This week, to right this wrong, the International Accounting Standards Board (IASB) unveiled proposals for expensing options, i.e., deducting their cost from a company's profits. In doing so, however, not only was the IASB declaring war on some powerful political opponents of expensing. It also took sides in a lively economic dispute.

Among economists, the debate is largely about how to value options and when to expense them, not about whether they should be expensed at all. (Only a few "renegades" disagree with expensing, declares Robert Merton, who won a Nobel prize in economics for his work on options pricing.) Economists mostly agree that options should be expensed using a so-called fair value method, one that broadly reflects what the options would cost to buy in the market, were they available.

In this, the economists agree with the IASB, which has chosen fair value accounting of options, ruling out several other methods. These include, for instance, intrinsic value: the difference between the market price of the underlying shares that the option confers the right to buy and the exercise price at which the underlying shares may be bought. If, when an option is issued, the exercise price equals the market price (and it often does), the intrinsic value is zero—which is nonsensical. Also ruled out is the minimum-value method, which is what somebody would willingly pay for an option if they knew that the firm's share price would be fixed for the life of the option. This ignores a big part of an option's value, namely the ability to cash in should the share price rise.

The IASB does not, though, specify exactly which method of fair value option pricing should be used. And here academics dispute vigorously. Mr. Merton helped to devise the Black–Scholes model for pricing options, named after Myron Scholes (who shared Mr. Merton's Nobel prize) and Fisher Black (who would have done, had he lived a little longer). The main alternative is what is called the binomial pricing model, developed by John Cox, Stephen Ross and Mark Rubinstein.

Both models were devised to price simple options traded on an exchange. So, as the IASB acknowledges, each needs to be modified to reflect several peculiarities of employee share options—such as longer lifespan or term (a typical executive option lasts ten years, against a few months to two years for an exchange-traded option), restrictions on when options may be exercised, and even the fact that they may not be sold. How these adjustments are made—and the IASB allows wide discretion—can make a big difference to the size of the expense.

The binomial method is much more complex than Black–Scholes, but if done properly, the price it produces is likely to be accurate more often. Of course, the very complexity may make it easier for the price to be manipulated by a company wanting to massage its profits. On the other hand, plenty of scope for creativity exists with the Black–Scholes method, even given the few simple assumptions that are used. These assumptions, in essence, are expected volatility (how much a share price is likely to fluctuate), term, the expected dividend yield, the risk-free interest rate, and the exercise price.

Some critics reckon that these vagaries of valuation undermine the entire case for expensing. Few economists agree, however. Whatever uncertainties there are in fair value option pricing, goes the argument, they are smaller than the uncertainty in the value of other items already routinely expensed, such as depreciation and pension fund gains or losses.

Ask Not Whether, but When

The biggest philosophical dispute among economists concerns when options should be expensed. The IASB wants it done once and for all from the date they are awarded to employees (in other words, the grant date). Mr. Scholes, the Nobel laureate, agrees. But others, such as Mr. Rubinstein, one of the creators of binomial pricing, do not. He argues for full expensing at the time options are exercised, i.e., when the holder trades in the options for underlying shares. Under this approach, options would still initially be expensed on the grant date; but in subsequent public filings this estimate would be adjusted to take into account changes in their value. Upon exercise, the company would take a final extraordinary gain or loss to match up with the option's actual value when exercised. Mr. Rubinstein argues that, under this method, there would be less incentive to manipulate option valuations, because any divergence from an option's final true value would, in the end, result in an extraordinary charge.

The issue boils down to this: is the granting of an option a once-only expense for the company, the equivalent of paying the employee in cash? Or is it a contingent liability, the potential cost of which to shareholders changes with the market price of the company's shares, and with the true cost becoming clear only when the option is either exercised or it expires? A once-only expense or a contingent liability: these are matters over which reasonable people can agree to differ. What is important is that share options are to be expensed at all.

The Effects of Accounting Principles on Earnings and Stock Prices

The same company using different national accounting standards could report different earnings. Some accounting standards are more conservative than others, in the sense that they lead to smaller reported earnings. Several comparative studies have attempted to measure the relative conservativeness of national standards. For example, Radebaugh and Gray (1997) conclude that U.S. accounting principles are significantly more conservative than U.K. accounting principles but significantly less conservative than Japanese and Continental European accounting principles. If the United States' earnings are arbitrarily scaled at 100, Japanese earnings would scale at 66, German earnings at 87, French earnings at 97, and British earnings at 125. Various studies come up with somewhat different adjustments, so these figures should be interpreted with some caution. Also, recent changes, particularly in the United States and Europe, will impact this assessment in the future.

These national accounting principles also affect the reported book value of equity. Speidell and Bavishi (1992) report the adjustment that should be made to the book value of foreign shareholders' equity if the U.S. GAAP were used. They find that the book value of equity would be increased by 41 percent in Germany and 14 percent in Japan, and would be reduced by 14 percent in the United Kingdom and 28 percent in France.

Price–earnings (P/E) ratios are of great interest to international investors, who tend to compare the P/E ratios of companies in the same industrial sector across the world. The P/E ratio divides the market price of a share by its current or estimated annual earnings. As of November 30, 1998, P/E ratios in the markets ranged from a low of 18.1 in Hong Kong to a high of 191.0 in Japan (at this time, the U.S. market P/E was 28.5).[6] Japanese companies have traditionally traded at very high P/E ratios in comparison with those of U.S. companies. For comparison purposes, these P/E ratios should be adjusted because of the accounting differences in reporting earnings. They also should be adjusted to reflect the fact that Japanese firms tend to report nonconsolidated statements despite the extent of cross-holding. For example, if Company A owns 20 percent of the shares of Company B, it will include in its own earnings only the dividend paid by Company B, not a proportion of Company B's earnings. In the P/E ratio

---

[6] Schieneman (2000).

of Company A, the stock price reflects the value of the holding of shares of Company B, but the earnings do not reflect the earnings of Company B. For all these reasons, French and Poterba (1991) claim that the average 1989 Japanese P/E ratio should be adjusted from 53.7 to 32.6. Other authors come up with an even bigger reduction in Japanese P/E ratios.

The Information Content of International Differences in GAAP

Investors request that companies disclose accurate information on a timely basis. The national GAAP dictates the format in which the information is disclosed. Investors would like companies to use accounting principles that provide the most informative presentation of the accounting numbers. It is difficult to tell whether an optimal accounting standard exists that would apply equally to all nations. The U.S. Securities and Exchange Commission (SEC) requests that all foreign firms listed on a public stock exchange in the United States, including Nasdaq, provide financial reports according to the U.S. GAAP (Form 10-K) or provide all necessary reconciliation information (Form 20-F). This is a controversial policy, as many foreign firms, especially medium-sized ones, do not wish to carry the burden and costs of presenting all their financial statements under two different accounting standards.

A major question for investors is determining which GAAP provides the best information. This is a difficult question to answer. Some insights can be gained by looking at the reaction of stock prices to earnings reported according to different national standards. Studies have focused on foreign firms that are dual-listed in the United States, which must also provide earnings statements calculated according to the U.S. GAAP. If the U.S. GAAP provides incremental information relative to the foreign GAAP, stock prices should show some reaction to the difference between the two reported earnings. Preliminary evidence seems to suggest that "the GAAP earnings adjustments add marginally to the ability of earnings to explain returns" (Pope and Rees, 1992, p. 190).

Another approach has been to survey international money managers to see whether they find added value in obtaining financial statements under different national GAAP. Choi and Levich (1991) surveyed a variety of capital market participants (institutional investment managers, corporate issuers, and regulators) and found that roughly half of them feel that their capital market decisions are affected by accounting diversity. However, most of them find ways to cope with this diversity. Some translate all financial statements to a common, more familiar accounting framework; others have become familiarized with foreign accounting practices and adopt a local perspective when analyzing foreign statements; others simply do not use accounting numbers in their investment decisions. Bhushan and Lessard (1992) surveyed 49 U.S.-based international money managers. All of them regard accounting harmonization as a good thing but do not find that providing reconciled accounting information is crucial; they tend to focus on valuing firms within their own markets and stress the importance of the quality and timeliness of the information disclosed.

Indeed the quality and speed of information disclosure are of paramount importance to investors. Restating the same information in a different accounting standard does not address the issue of the quality of the information disclosed or the firm's future prospects. Investment managers deciding to include a specific stock in a portfolio need to do more than simply look at past accounting data.

4   GLOBAL INDUSTRY ANALYSIS

The valuation of a common stock is usually conducted in several steps. A company belongs to a global industry and is based in a country. Hence, country and industry analysis is necessary. Companies compete against global players within their industry. Studying a company within its global industry is the primary approach to stock valuation.

With the knowledge that financial ratios from different international companies are difficult to compare, the analyst still faces the task of looking forward. What conditions in the industry prevail, and how are companies likely to compete in the future?

Within the framework of industrial organization, this section outlines the most important elements that should be looked at when conducting a company analysis in a global setting. Because a company is based in a country, we begin with a general introduction to country analysis to provide a starting point for the analysis of the company and industry.

Country Analysis

Companies tend to favor some countries in their business activities. They target some countries for their sales and base their production in only a few countries. Hence, country analysis is of importance in studying a company. In each country, economists try to monitor a large number of economic, social, and political variables, such as:

▶ anticipated real growth;

▶ monetary policy;

▶ fiscal policy (including fiscal incentives for investments);

▶ wage and employment rigidities;

▶ competitiveness;

▶ social and political situations; and

▶ investment climate.

In the long run, real economic growth is probably the major influence on a national stock market. Economists focus on economic growth at two horizons:

▶ business cycle

▶ long-term sustainable growth

What are favorable country conditions for equity investment? There can be favorable business cycle conditions as well as favorable long-term sustainable growth conditions. If the favorable conditions are a consensus view, however, they will already be priced in the equity markets. The analyst must find a way of discerning these conditions before others do.

A high long-term sustainable growth rate in gross domestic product (GDP) is favorable, because this translates into high long-term profits and stock returns. In creating GDP and productivity growth rate expectations, the analyst will undoubtedly examine the country's savings rate, investment rate, and total factor productivity (TFP). TFP measures the efficiency with which the economy converts capital and labor into goods and services. Increased investment rates due to technical progress will increase rates of return; but the savings and investment rates themselves must be closely analyzed. A country's investments reflect replacement and capacity expansion, and influences future productivity gains. If the ratio of investment to GDP is low, then the investments are largely replacement investments; whereas a high rate suggests that capacity expansion is under way.[7] Further, a positive correlation between investment rates and subsequent GDP growth rates cannot be taken for granted, because there are other factors to consider.

The main factors that interact with the country's investment rate to affect GDP growth are the rate of growth in employment, work hours, educational levels, technological improvement, business climate, political stability, and the public or private nature of the investment. A higher long-term growth in the work force will lead to higher GDP growth just as a reduction in work hours will lead to less GDP growth. Increasing skills in the work force complement technological advances as they will both lead to higher GDP growth. A business climate of more privatization and reduced regulation is conducive to more investment. Attractive investment opportunities will also lead to more investment, although an increased propensity to invest can depress rates of return. Political stability will reduce the risk and hence increase the attractiveness of investments. Finally, private investments are more likely to be made with maximal return-on-invested capital as the objective and hence lead to higher GDP growth.

In the short term, business cycle conditions can be favorable for investments, but business cycle turning points are so difficult to predict that such predictions should only cause the analyst to make investment recommendations to slightly adjust portfolio. Business cycles represent a complex control system with many causes and interacting private and governmental decisions. For example, companies invest in plant and equipment and build inventories based on expected demand but face the reality that actual demand does not continuously meet expectations. Although an investor would benefit from buying stocks at the **trough** of a business cycle and bonds at the peak, such perfect market timing is virtually impossible, and one might better take the approach of ignoring the country's business cycle and concentrate rather on its long-term sustainable growth rate in GDP. Nevertheless, even limited prescient ability can lead to informed adjustments to portfolio holdings. Calverley (2003, pp. 15–19) classifies the business cycle stages and attractive investment opportunities as:

▶ *Recovery.* The economy picks up from its slowdown or recession. Good investments to have are the country's cyclical stocks and commodities, followed by riskier assets as the recovery takes hold.

▶ *Early upswing.* Confidence is up and the economy is gaining some momentum. Good investments to have are the country's stocks and also commercial and residential property.

▶ *Late upswing.* Boom mentality has taken hold. This is not usually a good time to buy the country's stocks. The country's commodity and property prices will also be peaking. This is the time to purchase the country's bonds (yields are high) and interest rate sensitive stocks.

▶ *Economy slows or goes into recession.* The economy is declining. Good investments to have are the country's bonds, which will rally (because of a drop in market interest rates), and its interest rate sensitive stocks.

▶ *Recession.* Monetary policy will be eased but there will be a lag before recovery. Particularly toward the end of the recession, good investments to make are the country's stocks and commodities.

---

[7] See Calverley (2003, p. 11).

Inflation is generally associated with the late upswing, and deflation is possible in a recession. Inflation effects on equity valuation are analyzed later in this reading.

Business Cycle Synchronization   Stock market performance is clearly related to the business cycle and economic growth.[8] National business cycles are not fully synchronized. This lack of synchronization makes country analysis all the more important. For example, the United States witnessed a strong economic recovery in 1992, Britain started to enjoy strong economic growth in 1993, and the European continent only started to recover in 1995, but Japan's economy was still stagnant.

However, economies are becoming increasingly integrated. Growth of major economies is, in part, exported abroad. For example, growth in the United States can sustain the activity of an exporting European firm even if demand by

---

CONCEPTS IN ACTION

Irish Central Bank Sees Uncertainty, Modest Growth Ahead

The Central Bank of Ireland said Thursday that a high degree of uncertainty and modest growth lie ahead for the Irish economy next year.

In its quarterly bulletin for autumn 2002, the bank sees gross national product growth of about 3.0% this year and 4.25% in 2003, which depends on whether the international economy picks up.

"This growth would be good by international standards and would be close to the medium-term sustainable rate for the economy," it said.

But, both the U.S. and U.K. economies, which take about four-fifths of Irish exports, are registering growth around 1.0%.

It is unlikely, therefore, that there will be an appreciable increase in Irish export demand in the short-run, the central bank said.

It said foreign direct investment is also likely to be adversely affected by the decline in stock markets and uncertainty regarding the true profitability of major multinationals.

The bank also cautioned the Irish government to ensure that the country's heady rate of inflation falls back as quickly as possible in-line with the rest of the euro zone.

Irish inflation, currently forecast at about 4.75% this year, continues to run above the European Central Bank's upper limit of 2.0% for euro-zone countries.

This, plus a stronger euro, has reduced Ireland's competitiveness and will subsequently impede employment growth in the future, the bank warned.

The European Union harmonized index of consumer prices, or HICP, forecasts Irish consumer price inflation to average about 4.25% next year owing to lower mortgage rates.

Adding more gloom to the central bank's report, Wednesday's data on third-quarter exchequer returns showed the Irish budget is back in the red for the first time since 1997.

The Irish government said it will now face a 2002 deficit of EUR750 million, compared with the EUR170 million surplus forecast nearly a year ago.

Many analysts, however, predict matters are even worse. Bloxham Stockbrokers forecasts a 2002 deficit of closer to EUR800 million, citing 20% annual growth in day-to-day spending in September.

Similarly, IIB Bank expects the government 2002 deficit to hit more than EUR1.0 billion owing to the government's high day-to-day spending.

Source: Quentin Fottrel, Dow Jones Newswires, October 3, 2002.

---

[8] See Canova and De Nicolo (1995). An analysis of the business cycle is provided in Reilly and Brown (2003).

European consumers is stagnant. But rigidities in a national economy can prevent it from quickly joining growth in a world business cycle. Studies of rigidities are important here.

What are the business cycle synchronization implications for equity valuation? Although national economies are becoming increasingly integrated with a world economy, there are so many economic variables involved that the chances of full synchronization are extremely remote. For example, within the European Union, tensions arise because governments are not free to pursue domestic and fiscal economic policies to deal with their own domestic business cycles. The experience of the 1990s and early 2000s is that the economies of Continental Europe, Japan, the United Kingdom, and the United States had markedly different GDP growth rates and entered various stages of the business cycle at different times. Recalling that any correlation less than unity supports diversification benefits, the lack of perfect business cycle synchronization is an a priori argument in favor of international diversification. If long-term GDP growth and business cycles were perfectly synchronized among countries, then one would expect a high degree of correlation between markets, especially in periods of crisis. In making investment asset-allocation decisions, one must always consider long-term expected returns, variances, and correlations. In the long term, international diversification will always be advantageous until national economies are expected to be perfectly synchronized around the world. It is difficult to imagine such a possibility. Expected returns and expected standard deviations will differ among countries with unsynchronized short-term business cycles and long-term GDP growth rates, even though investors may follow the crowd in their short term reactions to crises.

Further considerations in the divergence between countries come from a consideration of growth clubs. Baumol (1986) examined three convergence growth clubs (clubs converging to a similar steady state in terms of income per capita): western industrialized countries, centrally planned economies, and less developed countries. Regardless of the number of growth clubs, one can expect within-group convergence but inter-group divergence in TFP and income **per capita**. The degree of business cycle synchronicity also varies over time depending on the pattern of regional shocks and changes in economies' propagation mechanisms.

Growth Theory   Growth theory is a branch of economics that examines the role of countries in value creation. The output of a country is measured by gross domestic product (GDP), and growth theory attempts to explain the rate of GDP growth in different countries. For two countries with equal risk, portfolio managers will want to overweight the country with sustainable expected long-term GDP growth. The inputs considered are labor, capital, and productivity. In addition to labor and capital, there are also human capital and natural resources. Increases in educational levels can lead to an increase in labor skills, and discoveries of natural resources can lead to resource-based growth. Two competing economic theories attempt to shed light on the sustainable long-term growth rate of a nation.

Neoclassical growth theory assumes that the marginal productivity of capital declines as more capital is added. This is the traditional case in economics with **diminishing marginal returns** to input factors. *Endogenous growth theory* assumes that the marginal productivity of capital does not necessarily decline as capital is added. Technological advances and improved education of the **labor force** can lead to efficiency gains. Any one firm faces diminishing returns, but endogenous growth theory assumes that externalities arise when a firm develops a new technology. Thus, one firm's technical breakthrough, begets another's breakthrough, perhaps through imitation. In this case, the **marginal product** of capital does not decline with increasing capital per capita.

In growth theory, *steady state* is defined as the condition of no change in capital per capita. This comes about when the savings rate times GDP per capita just matches the investment required to maintain the amount of capital per capita. The rate of growth in the population plus the yearly depreciation in equipment gives a replacement rate to be multiplied by the amount of capital per capita, and this multiplication yields the investment required to maintain the amount of capital per capita.

Neoclassical growth theory predicts that the long-term level of GDP depends on the country's savings rate, but the long-term growth rate in GDP does not depend on the savings rate. This is because a steady state is reached, and this steady state is reached, because additions to the capital stock provide smaller and smaller increases to GDP and consequently to savings (the savings rate times GDP). In the context of endogenous growth theory, steady state may never be reached, because the ability to avoid a decline in the marginal product of capital means there is no necessary decline in savings as capital is increased. Thus, endogenous growth theory predicts that the long-term growth rate in GDP depends on the savings rate.

Equity valuation implications are different for countries experiencing neoclassical versus endogenous growth. If a country is experiencing neoclassical growth and its savings rate increases, there would be an increase in dividends as the new level of GDP is reached, but not an increase in the dividend growth rate. For a country experiencing endogenous growth with cascading breakthroughs, however, there would be an increase in both dividends and the dividend growth rate.

In an open world economy, it is important to ascertain whether growth is caused by an increased mobilization of inputs or by efficiency gains. Input-driven growth is necessarily limited. For example, many developing countries have witnessed high growth rates because of capital flows from abroad, but face diminishing returns in the absence of productivity gains. National sustainable growth rates require careful examination.

CONCEPTS IN ACTION

Nearly 30 Transnational Corporations Richer than Many Nations, UN Study Finds

Twenty-nine of the world's 100 largest economic entities are transnational corporations, according to a new list produced by the United Nations Conference on Trade and Development (UNCTAD) ranking both states and corporations.

Exxon Mobile, with a "value added" worth of $63 billion, is bigger in economic size than Pakistan, while General Motors, worth $56 billion, outpaces both Peru and New Zealand, according to the list.

UNCTAD also reports that Ford Motor and DaimlerChrysler, with value added of over $42 billion, are both larger than Nigeria, which is worth just $41 billion. Kuwait, at $38 billion, is outranked by General Electric. And Honda, Nissan and Toshiba all have more value than Syria.

The rising importance of transnational corporations in the global economy is revealed in other statistics compiled by UNCTAD. The agency reports that the 100 largest companies accounted for 3.5 percent of global gross domestic product in 1990—a figure that jumped to 4.3 percent in 2000. There were 24 corporations in the 1990 combined top 100 list of companies and countries, compared with 29 in 2000.

Source: UN News Centre, August 13, 2002.

The Limitation of the Country Concept in Financial Analysis The distinction between countries and companies is misleading in some respects. Both types of economic entities produce and market a portfolio of products. Indeed, some companies are bigger in economic size than some countries.

Many companies compete globally. The national location of their headquarters is not a determinant variable. Many multinational corporations realize most of their sales and profits in foreign countries. So, an analysis of the economic situation of the country of their headquarters is not of great importance. Many national stock markets are dominated by a few multinationals. For example, Nokia market capitalization is larger than the sum of that of all other Finnish firms. The top ten Swiss multinational firms account for more than 70 percent of the Swiss stock exchange. But these companies do most of their business outside of their home country, so their valuation should be based on the global competition they face in their industry, not on the state of their home economy.

Industry Analysis: Return Expectation Elements

To achieve excess equity returns on a risk-adjusted basis, an investor must find companies that can earn return on equity (ROE) above the required rate of return and do this on a sustained basis. For this reason, global industry analysis centers on an examination of sources of growth and sustainability of competitive advantage. Growth must be distinguished from level. A high profit level may yield high current cash flows for valuation purposes, but there is also the question of how these cash flows will grow. Continued reinvestment opportunities in positive net present value investment opportunities will create growth. Curtailment of research and development expenditures may yield high current cash flows at the expense of future growth.

An analyst valuing a company within its global industry should study several key elements. Following are some important conceptual issues.

Demand Analysis Value analysis begins with an examination of demand conditions. The concepts of complements and substitutes help, but demand analysis is quite complex. Usually, surveys of demand as well as explanatory regressions are used to try to estimate demand. Demand is the target for all capacity, location, inventory, and production decisions. Often, the analyst tries to find a leading indicator to help give some forecast of demand.

In the global context, *demand* means *worldwide demand*. One cannot simply define the automobile market as a domestic market. A starting point, then, is a set of forecasts of global and country-specific GDP figures. The analyst will want to estimate the sensitivity of sales to global and national GDP changes.

Country analysis is important for demand analysis, because most companies tend to focus on specific regions. Most European car manufacturers tend to sell and produce outside of Europe, but the European car market is their primary market. An increase in demand for cars in Europe will affect them more than it will affect Japanese car producers.

Value Creation Sources of value come from using inputs to produce outputs in the value chain. The *value chain* is the set of transformations in moving from raw materials to product or service delivery. This chain can involve many companies and countries, some providing raw materials, some producing intermediate goods, some producing finished consumer goods, and some delivering finished goods to the consumer. From the point of view of an **intermediate goods** producer, basic raw materials are considered to be *upstream* in the value chain, and transformations closer to the consumer are considered *downstream*.

Within the value chain, each transformation adds value. **Value chain** analysis can be used to determine how much value is added at each step. Indeed, some countries have a value-added tax. The value added at each transformation stage is partly a function of four major factors:

► *The learning (experience) curve.* As companies produce more output, they gain experience, so that the cost per unit produced declines.

► *Economies of scale.* As a company expands, its fixed costs may be spread over a larger output, and average costs decline over a range of output.

► ***Economies of scope***. As a company produces related products, experience and reputation with one product may spill over to another product.

► *Network externalities.* Some products and services gain value as more consumers use them, so that they are able to share something popular.

Equity valuation implications come from an analysis of the industry's value chain and each company's strategy to exploit current and future profit opportunities within the chain. For company managers, Christensen, Raynor, and Verlinden (2001) recommend a strategy of predicting profit migration within the industry's value chain. For example they break the computer industry down into value chain stages: equipment, materials, components, product design, assembly, operating system, application software, sales and distribution, and field service. In the early days of the computer industry, vertically integrated manufacturers delivered the entire value chain. The advent of the personal computer led to specialization within each stage and profits migrated to stages such as components and operating systems. For the analyst also, the strategy of predicting dividends and dividend growth rates must be based on profit migration in the value chain. The risk can be gauged from the degree of competition within the stage—the more the competition, the more the risk. The ability of companies to compete at each stage will be enhanced by their learning curve progress, economies of scale or scope, and network externalities.

Christensen et al. also point out that industries often evolve from vertical integration to disintegration. If an industry becomes too fragmented, however, consolidation pressures will come from resource bottlenecks as well as the continuing search for economies of scale. During the industry's life cycle, tension between disintegration and consolidation will require the company and the analyst to constantly monitor company positions in the profit migration cycle.

Industry Life Cycle   Traditionally, the industry life cycle is broken down into stages from pioneering development to decline. Of course, one must be careful in industry definition. If railroads were defined as an *industry*, we would see a global industry life cycle. Defining the industry as transportation provides a different picture. In any case, industry life cycles are normally categorized by rates of growth in sales. The stages of growth can clearly vary in length.

1. Pioneering development is the first stage and has a low but slowly increasing industry sales growth rate. Substantial development costs and acceptance by only early adopters can lead to low profit margins.

2. Rapid accelerating growth is the second stage, and the industry sales growth rate is still modest but is rapidly increasing. High profit margins are possible because firms from outside the new industry may face barriers to entering the newly established markets.

3. Mature growth is the third stage and has a high but more modestly increasing industry sales growth rate. The entry of competitors lowers profit margins, but the return on equity is high.

One would expect that somewhere in stage 2 or 3 the industry sales growth rate would move above the GDP growth rate in the economy.

4. Stabilization and market maturity is the fourth stage and has a high but only slowly increasing sales growth rate. The sales growth rate has not yet begun to decline, but increasing capacity and competition may cause returns on equity to decline to the level of average returns on equity in the economy.

5. Deceleration of growth and decline is the fifth stage with a decreasing sales growth rate. At this stage, the industry may experience overcapacity, and profit margins may be completely eroded.

One would expect that somewhere in stage 5, the industry sales growth rate would fall back to the GDP growth rate and then decline below it. (This cannot happen in stage 4 where the sales growth is still increasing.) The position of an industry in its life cycle should be judged on a global basis.

Competition Structure   One of the first steps in analyzing an industry is the determination of the amount of industry concentration. If the industry is fragmented, many firms compete, and the theories of competition and product differentiation are most applicable. With more concentration and fewer firms in the industry, oligopolistic competition and game theories become more important. Finally, the case of one firm is the case in which the theory of monopoly applies.

In analyzing industry concentration, two methods are normally used. One method is the N firm **concentration ratio**: the combined market share of the largest N firms in the industry. For example, a market in which the three largest firms have a combined share of 80 percent would indicate largely oligopolistic competition. A related but more precise measure is the **Herfindahl index**, the sum of the squared market shares of the firms in the industry. Letting M_i be the market share of an individual firm, the index is $H = M_1^2 + M_2^2 + \ldots + M_N^2$.

If two firms have a 15 percent market share each and one has a 70 percent market share, $H = 0.15^2 + 0.15^2 + 0.7^2 = 0.535$.

The Herfindahl index has a value that is always smaller than one. A small index indicates a competitive industry with no dominant players. If all firms have an equal share, $H = N(1/N^2) = 1/N$, and the reciprocal of the index shows the number of firms in the industry. When the firms have unequal shares, the reciprocal of the index indicates the "equivalent" number of firms in the industry. Using our example above, we find that the market structure is equivalent to having 1.87 firms of the same size:

$$\frac{1}{H} = \frac{1}{(0.15^2 + 0.15^2 + 0.70^2)} = \frac{1}{0.535} = 1.87$$

One can classify the competition structure of the industry according to this ratio.

In practice, the equity analyst will see both the N firm concentration ratio and the Herfindahl index. The analyst is searching for indicators of the likely degree of cooperation versus competition within the industry. Although the balance between cooperation and competition is dynamic and changing, the higher the N firm concentration ratio and the higher the Herfindahl index, the less likely it is that there is cut-throat competition and the more likely it is that companies will cooperate.

The advantage of the N firm concentration ratio is that it provides an intuitive sense of industry competition. If the analyst knows that the seven largest firms have a combined share of less than 15%, he or she immediately knows that the industry is extremely fragmented and thus more risky because of competitive pressures and the likely lack of cooperation.

The Hefindahl index (*H*) has the advantage of greater discrimination because it reflects all firms in the industry and it gives greater weight to the companies with larger market shares. An *H* below 0.1 indicates an unconcentrated industry, an *H* of 0.1 to 0.18 indicates moderate concentration, and an *H* above 0.18 indicates high concentration. A high Herfindahl index can also indicate the presence of a market leader with a higher share than others, another indication of likely coordination as the leader might impose discipline on the industry.

Suppose the analyst is comparing two industries:

Market Shares in Industry A	Market Shares in Industry B
One firm has 45%	Four firms have 15% each
Three firms have 5% each	Four firms have 10% each
Ten firms have 4% each	
Four firm concentration ratio is 60%	Four firm concentration ratio is 60%
Herfindahl index is 0.23	Herfindahl index is 0.13

Even though the four firm concentration ratios are the same for both industries, the Herfindahl index indicates that industry A is highly concentrated, but industry B is only moderately concentrated.

Competitive Advantage   In his book, *The Competitive Advantage of Nations*,[9] Michael Porter used the notions of economic geography that different locations have different competitive advantages. National factors that can lead to a competitive advantage are:

▶ factor conditions such as human capital, perhaps measured by years of schooling;

▶ demand conditions such as the size and growth of the domestic market;

▶ related supplier and support industries such as the computer software industry to support the hardware industry; and

▶ strategy, structure, and rivalry such as the corporate governance, management practices, and the financial climate.

Competitive Strategies   A competitive strategy is a set of actions that a firm is taking to optimize its future competitive position. In *Competitive Advantage*,[10] Porter distinguishes three generic competitive strategies:

▶ *Cost leadership*. The firm seeks to be the low-cost producer in its industry.

▶ *Differentiation*. The firm seeks to provide product benefits that other firms do not provide.

▶ *Focus*. The firm targets a niche with either a cost or a benefit (differentiation) focus.

[9] Porter (1990).
[10] Porter (1985).

Equity valuation analysis in large part is analysis of the probability of success of company strategies. Analysts will consider the company's commitment to a strategy as well as the likely responses of its competitors. Is the company a tough competitor that is likely to survive a war of attrition? Is it likely that a **Nash equilibrium** will hold, in which each company adopts a strategy to leave itself with the best outcome regardless of the competitor's strategy and, by doing this, causes a reduction in the size of the total reward to both?

Co-opetition and the Value Net   *Co-opetition* refers to cooperation along the value chain and is an application of **game theory**. Brandenberger and Nalebuff[11] developed the concept of the value net as the set of participants involved in producing value along the value chain: the suppliers, customers, competitors, and firms producing complementary goods and services. Although these participants compete with each other, they can also cooperate to produce mutually beneficial outcomes. In this respect, co-opetition is an application of cooperative game theory.

In the context of equity valuation, co-opetition analysis is an important element of risk analysis. Cooperating participants in a good economy may become staunch competitors in a poor economy. If a company's abnormal profits depend on co-opetition, those profits are riskier than if they are the result of a purely competitive environment. In a good economy, a company may outsource some of its production to cooperating value net participants who may build capabilities based on lucrative long-term contracts. In a poor economy, however, no new contracts may be forthcoming.

Sector Rotation   Many commercial providers sell reports on the relative performance of industries or sectors over the business cycle, and sector rotation is a popular investment-timing strategy. Some investors put more weight on industries entering a profitable portion of their role in the business cycle. Certainly industries behave differently over the business cycle. Because consumer cyclical industries (durables and nondurables) correlate highly with the economy as a whole, these industries do well in the early and middle growth portion of the business cycle. Defensive consumer staples (necessities) maintain their profitability during recessions. Nevertheless, a successful sector rotation strategy depends on an intensive analysis of the industry and faces many pitfalls. An upturn in the economy and the demand for industry products do not automatically mean an increase in profits, because factors such as the status of industry capacity, the competitive structure, the lead time to increase capacity, and the general supply/demand conditions in the industry also have an impact on profits.

Indicators of the various stages of the business cycle are complex. We have already seen that different sectors, for example cyclical sectors, will do well at various stages of the business cycle and that the five stages are:

▶ *Recovery.* The economy picks up from its slowdown or recession.

▶ *Early upswing.* Confidence is up and the economy is gaining some momentum.

▶ *Late upswing.* Boom mentality has taken hold.

▶ *Economy slows or goes into recession.* The economy is declining.

▶ *Recession.* Monetary policy will be eased but there will be a lag before recovery.

---

[11] Brandenberger and Nalebuff (1996).

Industry Analysis: Risk Elements

To achieve excess equity returns on a risk-adjusted basis, investors must be able to distinguish sources of risk in the investments they make. For example, an increase in ROE may be attributable solely to an increase in leverage (**gearing**). This increased leverage raises the financial risk and hence the required rate of return; the increased ROE then does not yield an excess risk-adjusted return. Although return expectations can be established by evaluating firm strategies within the industry, the analyst must always examine the risk that the strategy may be flawed or that assumptions about competition and co-opetition may hold only in a good economic environment. What seems to be an attractive strategy in good times, can turn into a very dangerous one in bad times. The risks can differ widely, not only between firms in the same industry, but also across industries. Some industries are more sensitive to technological change and the business cycle than are others. So, the outlined growth factors that affect return expectations should also be taken into account to assess industry risk.

Ultimately, firms that follow high-risk strategies in an industry that is also risky will have a higher ex ante stock market risk, and this should be incorporated in expected risk measures. Ex post, this stock market risk will eventually be measured by looking at volatility and covariance measures.

Market Competition   Microeconomics[12] examines the various types of competition in markets. The question is always to look at price versus average cost. Particularly with oligopolies and monopolies, game theory helps to discern the likely success or failure of corporate strategies. Preservation of competitive position and competitive advantage often involves entry-deterring or exit-promoting strategies. *Limit pricing* is pricing below average cost to deter entry. Similarly, *holding excess capacity* can deter entry. *Predatory pricing* is pricing below average cost to drive others out of the industry. Any valuation of an individual company must examine the strategy contest in which companies in the industry are engaged. Risks are always present that the company's strategy will not sustain its competitive advantage.

Value Chain Competition   In producing goods and services of value, companies compete not just in markets, but also along the value chain. Suppliers can choose to compete rather than simply cooperate with the intermediate company. Labor, for example, may want some of the profit that a company is earning. In lean times, labor may make concessions, but in good times labor may want a larger share of the profits. Buyers may organize to wrest some of the profit from the company.

A major issue in value chain analysis is whether labor is unionized. Japanese automobile companies producing in the United States face lower production costs because of their ability to employ non-unionized workers. Union relations are a major factor in valuing airline companies worldwide.

Suppliers of commodity raw materials have less ability to squeeze profits out of a downstream company than do suppliers of differentiated intermediate products. Companies may manage their value chain competition by vertically integrating (buying upstream or downstream) or, for example, by including labor in their ownership structure.

Co-opetition risks are presented by the possibility that the company's supply may be held up or that its distributors may find other sources of products and services. Suppose a firm acts as a broker between producers and distributors and outsources its distribution services by selling long-term distribution contracts to producers, thus also keeping distributors happy. Because of the low

---

[12] See Besanko, Dranove, and Shanley (2000).

fixed costs involved in brokering, this business strategy should make the firm less sensitive to recession than a distribution company with heavy fixed costs. But what if producers are unwilling to enter long-term distribution contracts during a recession?

In his book, Porter (1985) discussed five industry forces, as well as the generic competitive strategies mentioned earlier. Porter's so-called five forces analysis can be seen as an examination of the risks involved in the value chain. Oster (1999) provides a useful analysis of the five forces, and we show her insights as bulleted points below. In some cases, we slightly modify or extend them.

Rivalry Intensity   This is the degree of competition among companies in the industry. For example, airline competition is more intense now with more carriers and open skies agreements between countries than in the days of heavier regulation with fewer carriers limited to domestic companies. Coordination can make rivalry much less intense. The analyst must be alert for possible changes in coordination and rivalry intensity that are not yet reflected in equity prices.

► Intense rivalry among firms in an industry reduces average profitability.

► In an industry in which coordination yields excess profits (prices exceed marginal costs), there are market share incentives for individual companies to shade (slightly cut) prices as they weigh the benefits and costs of coordination versus shading.

► Large numbers of companies in a market reduce coordination opportunities.

► Rivalry is generally more intense when the major companies are all similarly sized, and no one large company can impose discipline on the industry.

► Generally, coordination is easier if companies in the market are similar. All gravitate to a mutually agreeable focal point, the solution that similar companies will naturally discern.

► Industries which have substantial specific (cannot be used for other purposes) assets exhibit high barriers to exit and intensified rivalry.

► Variability in demand creates more rivalry within an industry. For example, high fixed costs and cyclical demand creates capacity mismatches and price cutting from excess capacity.

Substitutes   This is the threat of products or services that are substitutes for the products or services of the industry. For example, teleconferencing is a substitute for travel. The analyst must be alert for possible changes in substitutes that are not yet reflected in equity prices.

► Substitute products constrain the ability of firms in the industry to raise their prices substantially.

► Industries without excess capacity or intense rivalry can present attractive investment opportunities; but substitute products can reduce the attraction by constraining the ability of firms in the industry to substantially raise their prices.

Buyer Power   This is the bargaining power of buyers of the producer's products or services. For example, car rental agencies have more bargaining power with automobile manufacturers than have individual consumers. The analyst must be alert for possible changes in buyer power that are not yet reflected in equity prices.

► The larger the number of buyers and the smaller their individual purchases, the less the bargaining power.

► Standardization of products increases buyer power because consumers can easily switch between suppliers.

► If buyers can integrate backwards, this increases their bargaining power because they would cut out the supplier if they choose to integrate.

► Greater buyer power makes an equity investment in the producer less attractive because of lower profit margins.

Supplier Power   This is the bargaining power of suppliers to the producers. For example, traditional aircraft manufacturers lost supplier power when niche players entered the market and began producing short-haul jets. The analyst must be alert for possible changes in supplier power that are not yet reflected in equity prices.

► The more suppliers there are for the industry, the less is the supplier power.

► Standardized raw materials (commodities) reduce supplier power because the supplier has no differentiation or quality advantage.

► If buyers can integrate backwards, this reduces supplier power because the buyer would cut out the supplier if it chooses to integrate.

► Greater supplier power makes an equity investment in the producer less attractive because of the possibility of a **squeeze** on profits.

New Entrants   This is the threat of new entrants into the industry. For example, a European consortium entered the aircraft manufacturing industry and has become a major company now competing globally. In addition, a Brazilian and a Canadian company have entered the short-haul aircraft market. The analyst must be alert for possible changes in new entrant threats that are not yet reflected in equity prices.

► The higher the **payoffs** the more likely will be the entry, all else equal.

► Barriers to entry are industry characteristics which reduce the rate of entry below that needed to remove excess profits.

► Expectations of incumbent reactions influence entry.

► Exit costs influence the rate of entry.

► All else equal, the larger the volume needed to reach minimal unit costs, the greater the difference between pre- and post-entry price (the increase in industry capacity would drive down prices), and thus the less likely entry is to occur.

► The steeper the cost curve, the less likely is entry at a smaller volume than the minimal unit cost volume.

► Long-term survival at a smaller than minimal unit cost volume requires an offsetting factor to permit a company to charge a price premium. **Product differentiation** and a monopoly in location are two possible offsets.

► Excess capacity deters entry by increasing the credibility of price cutting as an entry response by incumbents.

► Occasional actions that are unprofitable in the short run can increase a company's credibility for price cutting to deter entry, giving an entry deterring reputation as a tough incumbent.

► An incumbent contract to meet the price of any responsible rival can deter entry.

▶ Patents and licenses can prevent free entry from eliminating excess profits in an industry. They deter entry.

▶ Learning curve effects can deter entry unless new entrants can appropriate the experience of the incumbents. For example, Boeing learned about metal fatigue from the British experience of accidents with the Comet, the first commercial jet airliner.

▶ Pioneering brands can dominate the industry and deter entry when network externalities exist and when consumers find it costly to make product mistakes.

▶ High exit costs discourage entry. A primary determinant of high exit costs is asset specificity and the irreversibility of capital investments.

After presenting the insights above, Oster follows up with an excellent presentation of many related topics: strategic groups within industries, competition in global markets, issues of organizational structure and design, competitive advantage, corporate diversification, and the effect of rival behavior. Indeed, industry analysis is a complex subject as the analyst attempts to deduce the valuation implications of corporate strategies.

Government Participation   Government subsidies to companies can seed companies in the **early stages** and can also give companies an unfair advantage in steady state. There is extra uncertainty for a company competing head to head with one subsidized by its home country. Governments also participate by supporting their domestic country stock prices in one way or another. This creates uncertainty about future policy in addition to the normal risk associated with cash flows.

Governments participate indirectly by their involvement in the social contract. In the United States, automobile companies bear the costs of defined benefit pension funds. Japanese automobile companies do not bear these costs because of government-sponsored pension schemes. Some European governments dealt with the possibility of increased unemployment by shortening the work week to keep employment spread out. Such government policy may make a European company less competitive.

Governments control competition. Open-skies laws allow foreign airlines to operate between domestic cities. Closed-skies laws in the past prevented Canadian carriers from operating between U.S. cities. Closed-skies laws have also been a factor in the Eurozone. Risks are presented by the uncertainty involved in trying to predict government policy.

Risks and Covariance   Investors care about stock market risk, that is, the uncertainty about future stock prices. Risk is usually viewed at two levels. The total risk of a company or an industry is the first level of risk, and it is usually measured by the standard deviation of stock returns of that company or industry. But part of this risk can be diversified away in a portfolio. So, the second level of risk is measured by the covariance with the aggregate economy, which tells how the returns of a company vary with global market indexes. Although this risk is usually measured by the beta from regressions of company returns against market returns, it is useful to note those beta changes over time as a function of business cycle conditions and shifting competition within the industry.

When analyzing an industry, the analyst is faced with a continuing challenge of determining diversifiable versus **nondiversifiable risk**. Because future cash flow and return covariance must be predicted in order to estimate the firm and industry's beta, simple reliance on past regressions is not sufficient. Part of the risk from a strategy failure or a change from co-opetition to competition may be firm-specific and diversifiable. At the same time, part of the risk may be nondiversifiable, because it involves fundamental shifts in industry structure.

In order to manage a global equity portfolio, the risk of a company is usually summarized by its exposure to various risk factors. The last section of this reading is devoted to global risk factor models.

Global Industry Analysis in Practice: An Example

In the following analysis of the transportation and logistics industry, several global industry analysis factors are considered. Indeed, such analyses usually include a discussion of the competitive structure of the industry, the strategies of the players, and a comparative ratio analysis of companies within the industry.

CONCEPTS IN ACTION

Transportation and Logistics

Logistics remains a growth market. . . . the Asian logistics market should be a growth driver. For the individual logistics segments, we expect the following compound annual growth rates for the period 2002 to 2010: air freight: +5.9%; sea freight: +5.6%; overland transport: +3.3%; and value-added services/logistics outsourcing: 11%–12%.

Average 2003e price/earnings ratios of just below 10 and a price/book ratio of around 1.2 indicate attractive valuation levels for the sector. DCF and an economic profit analysis support this thesis. Higher valuation levels are strongly dependent on macroeconomic expectations. We will see ongoing dynamic changes in industry structures that are driven by positioning and repositioning questions. Related to this is the continuing consolidation process in the highly fragmented logistics market.

Attractive Sector Growth
Air Freight: Business Is Expected to Grow until 2010 by 5.9% (CAGR)

In the period between 1981 and 2001, transport traffic in cross-border air freight increased at an average multiple of 2.5 times global GDP growth. In the last five years, the average multiple was much lower at 1.2 (3.4% p.a.[13]), because there were two slumps in a short period with the economic crisis in Asia and the terrorist attacks in the U.S. It is noticeable that the growth trend has been slowing since the mid-1980s and that the top peaks have declined steadily since 1985.

For the period 2002 to 2010, 5.9% compound annual growth amounts to a multiple of 2.1. This is lower than the 1981–2001 average multiple. The declining growth trend in air freight traffic is extrapolated in the long-term projection and growth dips were perpetuated with a weaker annual growth dynamic. In the event of economic crisis and open hostilities, the multiples are expected to be sharply lower in the corresponding years.

Sea Freight: Expect a Volume Growth of 5.6% (CAGR)

That translates into an average multiple of 2.0 times global GDP. In the past, the growth of container handling has significantly exceeded GDP growth. This outperformance is due, on the one hand, to a rising use of containers in total sea freight tonnage—in eight years it has doubled from 5% to 10%—and, on the other, to more frequent turnover per container.

---

[13] The abbreviation p.a. means per annum, or annually.

Land Transport: Up to 2010 Overland Transport in Europe Is Expected to Increase by 3.3% p.a.

The reluctance of many companies to penetrate this market is understandable given the competitive pressure and especially the resources needed to create a Europe-wide network. Compared with sea and air freight as well as value-added services, historical growth is more modest: between 1970 and 1998, ton kilometers transported by road (in the EU) increased by an average of 4% per year with a falling trend.

Continental Europe Still Has Ground to Make up on Outsourcing

In the field of value-added services (VAS), we expect further potential to catch up in outsourcing value-added services in Continental Europe. A comparison of the different outsourcing levels in the UK (currently 37%) and the states of Continental Europe (29%) suggests that the latter has a lot of ground to make up. We expect the overall European outsourcing ratio to come close to approaching the UK level by 2005. For the UK market, we project no significant increase in the outsourcing ratio.

Consolidation Momentum Driven by an Extremely Fragmented Market

The logistics market is one of the most fragmented markets and the structure of the market will change over the coming years. Besides the search for economies of scale, resource bottlenecks are resulting in acquisition pressure. This relates to management, employees, warehousing capacities and other operating structures. In air freight, the 10 largest forwarding companies have a combined share of less than 40%. The seafreight market is even more fragmented: the seven largest transportation companies have a combined market share of less than 15%.

The most fragmented market is European overland transport. Danzas and Schenker are the leading providers, each with a market share of 2.2%. Apart from the French company Geodis (1.5%) and the unlisted Dachser (1.0%), the market shares of the other providers are less than one-tenth of a percent. In a market undergoing dynamic change, the big players and the innovative niche players are expected to win additional market share. The companies "stuck in the middle" will run into problems.

Furthermore, state-owned or formerly state-owned companies (Deutsche Post, TPG, SNCF, La Poste, Deutsche Bahn, etc.) are driving the consolidation process. They are looking into portfolio changes in order to improve their core business. We assume the sale of Stinnes will rekindle the consolidation pressure.

Trend Toward Consolidation Accompanied by Difficult Questions of Positioning

The consolidation trend and the following market pressure force companies to continuously monitor their positioning. Within the European sample, we think Exel is the strategy leader. But the UK company cannot rest on its laurels because some competitors are in close pursuit. When looking at the positioning of companies, there are four major issues:

▶ the high-volume players are attempting to achieve the optimal mix by filling in the network gaps and upgrading their portfolio of services;

▶ the outsourcing-driven business models are expanding their range of services in order to become more deeply involved in the customer's value chain within the framework of outsourcing;

▶ companies caught between these areas must take care not to be backed into a corner; and

▶ regional providers have little prospect of closing the gap to the big players; because they lack the financial strength to close the gap, they must rely on cooperation agreements or they will be purchased.

Valuation Multiples in Line with Economic Projections

The performance of logistics stocks hinges to a great extent on the market's expectations for the economy. Such a statement is underpinned by correlating the performance of our HVB logistics index (excluding postal service companies), HVB-Logidexx, with the economic indicator provided by the price of copper, which trades every day. The susceptibility of the individual companies to cyclical fluctuation should be assessed on the basis of their cost and contract-business structures, outsourcing focus, the cyclical resistance of the sector in general, as well as their diversification by segment, customer and regional breakdown.

A look at these parameters indicates that Tibbett & Britten and Kuehne & Nagel have defensive capabilities within this pan-European sampling, while UK-based Exel is highly susceptible to cyclical fluctuation because of its exposure to the high tech and U.S. markets. We believe that a recovery by Exel is for the most part already factored into the price of its stock. We favor the stock of Tibbett & Britten and Kuehne & Nagel at present, both of which are likely to show more gains in market share.

A turnaround in the relative performance of the HVB-Logidexx and the Euro STOXX 50 index set in after September 11. Sentiment turned around: multiples of asset value—enterprise value/capital employed and price/book ratio—in some cases of well over one were exaggerated and did not correspond to either medium-term projections of earnings or forecast added-value margins. Upbeat guidance issued by Kuehne & Nagel, T&B and Stinnes, among others, resulted in the Logidexx's outperformance of the Euro STOXX.

Opinions differ at present over the logistics business. We still expect to see a macroeconomic turnaround in the second half of the year. The uptrend in cargo volume in both Asia and Europe, which has been gathering speed since April, underpins this view. The risk lies in the fact that the brightening picture in terms of cargo volume, driven partly by companies restocking, might be a mere flash in the pan.

First Up in the Clouds, Then Down in the Dumps

D.Logistics and Thiel, Europe's former high flyers, have seen both their operating profits and stock prices plunge. This has had a negative impact on sentiment vis-à-vis the sector. The capital market is increasingly coming to the realization that the majority of their problems are specific to these companies. They proved incapable of adjusting their internal structures to the pace of acquisition. The assumption that their business models, which are focused on logistics outsourcing are resistant to cyclical fluctuation proved to be erroneous. What emerged was rather that customers are not prepared in tough times to enter into major contracts to outsource.

Adding Value: Looking at the Margin Alone Is Being Too Short-Sighted

When looking at the returns on capital employed (2003), we find significant differences within the industry. Comparing Exel and Kuehne & Nagel makes it clear that looking at the margin alone does not provide guidance, because capital turnover can vary substantially due to the different business models. Kuehne & Nagel, for example, leads the ocean freight market but does not own a single vessel.

Compared with Exel, K&N's proportion of brokerage business is much greater, meaning that capital turnover on a low base of capital employed is substantially higher. A higher ROCE in particular reflects this. We think that Exel will grow at a stronger pace in the future and that it will boost its value driver of capital employed—without diluting its value-added margin—more quickly than K&N.

An Attractive Sector Valuation

In our opinion, the European logistics stocks are favorably valued in fundamental terms. We would like to focus on the NAV multiples. We think Stinnes will be acquired without a valuation premium; one indication of this is the 2003 price/book ratio of

1.2x. On the basis of EV/capital employed, including goodwill, we calculate a multiple of 0.7x for the sample; even if all of the goodwill is subtracted, this value comes to 1.0x. A value of 1.0x means that the company will not create value in the future (value-added margin equals zero). But in fact, the value-added margins (ROCE minus WACC) are on average roughly three percentage points above the capital costs.

Things Will Remain Exciting

Additional expected IPOs, such as that of Panalpina's, Deutsche Bahn's potential either full or partial access to the capital market, UPS' full war chest and Kuehne & Nagel's major scope for investment will keep the sector on the edge. Deregulation of postal markets, moreover, will provide a further source of conjecture, change and speculative appeal. A favorably priced growth market is just waiting for the economy to turn up.

Source: Markus Hesse and Christian Cohrs, *The Euromoney: International Equity Capital Markets Handbook* (Adrian Hornbrook: Colchester, Essex, U.K.), 2003, pp. 15–21. (For further information about *Euromoney Handbooks,* visit www.euromoney-yearbooks.com.)

EQUITY ANALYSIS   5

Because it should be forward looking, equity analysis needs to be carried out within the context of the country and the industry. Reasonable prediction of cash flows and risk is required to provide useful inputs to the valuation process.

Industry Valuation or Country Valuation   A frequently asked question is whether a company should primarily be valued relative to the global industry to which it belongs or relative to other national companies listed on its home stock market. Indeed, many corporations are now very active abroad and, even at home, face worldwide competition. So, there are really two aspects to this question:

▶ Should the *financial analysis* of a company be conducted within its global industry?

▶ Do the stock prices of companies within the same global industry move together worldwide, so that the *relative valuation* of a company's equity should be conducted within the global industry rather than within its home stock market?

The answer to the first question is a clear yes. Prospective earnings of a company should be estimated taking into account the competition it is facing. In most cases, this competition is international as well as domestic. Most large corporations derive a significant amount of their cash flows from foreign sales and operations, so their competition is truly global.

The answer to the second question raised is less obvious. At a given point in time, different industries face different growth prospects, and that is true worldwide. Furthermore, different industries exhibit different sensitivities to unexpected changes in worldwide economic conditions. This implies that the stock market valuation should differ across industries. Some industries, such as "electronic components" or "health and personal care," have large P/E and P/BV ratios while other industries, such as "energy" and "materials," have low P/E and P/BV ratios. The major question related to the importance of industry factors in stock prices, however, is whether a company has more in common with other companies in the same global industry than with other companies in the same country. By "more in common," we mean that its stock price tends to move together with that of other companies, and to be influenced by similar events. Before presenting some empirical evidence on the relative importance of country and industry factor in stock pricing, let's stress some caveats:

▶ Any industry classification is open to questions. MSCI, S&P, FTSE, and Dow Jones produce global industry indexes with different industry classification systems. The number of industry groups identified differs. It is not easy to assign each company to a single industry group. Some industry activities are clearly identified (e.g., producing automobiles), but others are not so clear-cut. It is not unusual to see the same company assigned to different industry groups by different classification systems. Some large corporations have diversified activities that cut across industry groups. Standard and Poor's and Morgan Stanley Capital International have recently designed a common Global Industry Classification Standard (GICS). The GICS system consists of four levels of detail: 10 sectors, 23 industry groupings, 59 industries, and 122 subindustries. At the most specific level of detail, an individual company is assigned to a single GICS subindustry, according to the definition of its principal business activity determined by S&P and MSCI. The hierarchical nature of the GICS structure will automatically assign the company's industry, industry group, and sector. There are currently over 25,000 companies globally that have been classified.

▶ The answer could be industry-specific. Some industries are truly global (e.g., oil companies), while others are less so (e.g., leisure and tourism). However, competition is becoming global in most, if not all, industries. For example, travel agencies have become regional, if not global, through a wave of mergers and acquisitions. Supermarket chains now cover many continents, and many retailers capitalize on their brand names globally.

▶ The answer could be period-specific. There could be periods in which global industry factors dominate, and other periods in which national factors are more important (desynchronized business cycles).

▶ The answer could be company-specific. Some companies in an industry group have truly international activities with extensive global competition, while others are mostly domestic in all respects. Small Swiss commercial banks with offices located only in one province (canton) of Switzerland have little in common with large global banks (even Crédit Suisse or UBS).

▶ Even if industry factors dominate, two opposing forces could be at play.[14] A worldwide growth in the demand for goods produced could benefit all players within the industry. However, competition also means that if one major player is highly successful, it will be at the expense of other major players in the industry. For example, Japanese car manufacturers could grow by extensively exporting to the United States, but it will be at the expense of U.S. car manufacturers. The stock price of Nissan would therefore be negatively correlated with that of GM or Ford.

Despite these caveats, all empirical studies find that industry factors have grown in importance in stock price valuation.[15] Global industry factors tend now to dominate country factors, but country factors are still of significant importance.

---

[14] See Griffin and Stulz (2001).

[15] See, for example, Cavaglia, Brightman, and Aked (2000) and Hopkins and Miller (2001).

Companies should be valued relative to their industry, but country factors should not be neglected, particularly when conducting a risk analysis.

Two industry valuation approaches are traditionally used: ratio analysis and discounted cash flow models.

Global Financial Ratio Analysis   As already mentioned, global industry financial analysis examines each company in the industry against the industry average. One well-accepted approach to this type of analysis is the DuPont model. (It may be better to think of this as an *approach* of decomposing return ratios, but this approach is usually called the DuPont model.) The basic technique of the DuPont model is to explain ROE or return on assets (ROA) in terms of its contributing elements. For example, we will see that ROA can be explained in terms of net profit margin and **asset turnover**. The analysis begins with five contributing elements, and these elements appear in several variations, depending on what most interests the analyst. The five elements reflect the financial and operating portions of the income statement as linked to the assets on the balance sheet and the equity supporting those assets. In the analysis here, past performance is being examined. Because income is a flow earned over a period of time, but the balance sheet reflects a balance (stock) at only one point in time, economists would calculate the flow (e.g., net income) over an average (e.g., the average of beginning and ending assets). The typical decomposition of ROE is given by:

$$\frac{NI}{EBT} \times \frac{EBT}{EBIT} \times \frac{EBIT}{Sales} \times \frac{Sales}{Assets} \times \frac{Assets}{Equity} = \frac{NI}{Equity}$$

where

NI	is net income
EBT	is earnings before taxes
NI/EBT	is one minus the tax rate, or the tax retention rate with a maximum value of 1.0 if there were no taxes (lower values imply higher tax burden)
EBIT	is earnings before interest and taxes, or operating income
EBT/EBIT	is interest burden, with a maximum value of 1.0 if there are no interest payments (lower values imply greater debt burden)
EBIT/Sales	is operating margin
Sales/Assets	is asset turnover ratio (a measure of efficiency in the use of assets)
Assets/Equity	is leverage (higher values imply greater use of debt)
NI/Equity	is return on equity (ROE)

The analyst would then compare each firm ratio with the comparable ratio for the industry. Does the firm have a higher operating margin than the industry's? If the company has a higher ROE than the industry ROE, is this higher-than-average ROE due to leverage, or is it due to more operations management-oriented ratios, such as operating margin or asset turnover?

Depending on the analyst's focus, the ratios can be combined in different ways. What is essential in DuPont analysis is the specification of the question of interest rather than the question of whether the model has five, three, or two factors.

One can collapse the first three ratios into the net profit margin (NI/sales) to leave

$$\text{ROE} = \text{Net profit margin} \times \text{Asset turnover} \times \text{Leverage}$$

One could also combine the first three ratios and include the fourth ratio to yield a return on assets breakdown:

$$\text{ROA} = \frac{\text{NI}}{\text{Assets}} = \text{Net profit margin} \times \text{Asset turnover}$$

Without combining the first three ratios, one could also have a four ratio ROA breakdown (tax retention rate × interest burden × operating margin × asset turnover). Also, one could explore a two-ratio ROE explanation by using ROA × leverage.

In all of this analysis, a global comparison of ratios of different companies in the same industry should take into account national valuation specificities. Due to national accounting differences detailed previously, earnings figures should sometimes be reconciled to make comparisons meaningful.

In global financial analysis, the methods of debt analysis can inform and supplement those of equity analysis. The following Concepts in Action feature provides a look at capital structure and industry analysis concerns resulting from debt burden and production capacity analysis.

The Role of Market Efficiency in Individual Stock Valuation   The notion of an efficient market is central to finance theory and is important for valuing securities. Generally, the question in company analysis is whether a security is priced correctly, and if it is not, for how long will it be mispriced. In an efficient market, any new information would be immediately and fully reflected in prices. Because all current information is already impounded in the asset price, only news (unanticipated information) could cause a change in price in the future.

EXAMPLE 2

DuPont Analysis of General Motors and Toyota

A comparison of Toyota Motor Corporation (NYSE: TM) with General Motors Corporation (NYSE: GM) reveals Toyota's superior net profit margin but inferior ROE as of late 2002. Is this a recent development? Has an ROE comparison been in General Motors' favor, historically, and how have differences in operating margin and other factors explained differences in ROE? In making an international comparison, differences in accounting must be considered. Toyota prepares its original financials according to Japanese GAAP. However, because Toyota trades on the NYSE as ADRs, Toyota also reports financial results according to U.S. GAAP, the basis for General Motors' accounting. Thus, the analyst's task is eased. Exhibit 2 presents a side-by-side DuPont analysis for General Motors and Toyota using Toyota's U.S. GAAP prepared financial results.

EXHIBIT 2	DuPont Analysis of ROE

GM and Toyota

	FY 1998		FY1999		FY 2000		FY 2001		Average	
	GM	TM	GM	TM	GM	TM	GM	TM	GM	TM
(1) NI/EBT	0.682	0.514	0.655	0.520	0.666	0.527	0.494	0.525	0.624	0.522
(2) EBT/EBIT	0.209	0.536	0.279	0.609	0.221	0.806	0.047	0.903	0.189	0.714
(3) EBIT/Sales	0.161	0.127	0.175	0.120	0.163	0.120	0.130	0.097	0.157	0.116
(4) Net profit margin = (1) × (2) × (3)	0.023	0.035	0.032	0.038	0.024	0.051	0.003	0.046	0.019	0.043
(5) Sales/Assets	0.627	0.805	0.643	0.773	0.609	0.772	0.547	0.742	0.607	0.773
(6) Assets/Equity	17.18	2.380	13.31	2.379	10.04	2.405	16.44	2.658	14.24	2.456
(7) ROE = (4) × (5) × (6)	0.248	0.067	0.274	0.070	0.147	0.095	0.027	0.091	0.164	0.082

Note: Fiscal year end is 31 March (of the following calendar year) for Toyota, and 31 December for General Motors.

Source: Company reports, Thomson Financial, *The Value Line Investments Survey*, September 2002.

Exhibit 2 shows that in each year from 1998 through 2001, General Motors has had a higher operating margin than Toyota: Toyota's operating margin averaged 11.6 percent compared with 15.7 percent for General Motors, and was lower in each individual year. Despite General Motors' advantages in operating margin and generally lower tax rates, Toyota's much lower interest burden translated into a consistent advantage in net profit margin. Nevertheless, a raw comparison of ROE is dramatically in General Motors' favor. GM's average ROE was 16.4 percent, compared with 8.2 percent for Toyota. Toyota held the advantage in net profit margin and efficiency in the use of assets (as shown by a higher asset turnover ratio) but had consistently lower ROE. However, General Motors' highly levered its operating results using debt, while Toyota employed a conservative level of debt. General Motors' average assets–equity ratio was about 14.2 versus only about 2.5 for Toyota. Because of its leverage, the stream of returns to GM shareholders as reflected by ROE was much more volatile than for Toyota. What does this mean in practice? ROE must be evaluated in relation to risk. According to valuation theory, the benchmark for risk in evaluating a company's ROE would be the required rate of return on its equity. If the analyst were pursuing the implications of the differences in ROE on valuation, a next step would be to estimate these required rates of return.

CONCEPTS IN ACTION

Ford and GM's Bonds Looking Less Roadworthy
Gyrations of the Carmakers' Securities Cause Concern
Corporate bond investors once thought of Ford and General Motors as bulletproof. Their strong balance sheets and well-established positions in the automotive industry

CONCEPTS IN ACTION

meant that their paper was eagerly snapped up by investors looking for safe, liquid investments. They were also active issuers of debt, making them easy credits to buy and sell.

But times have changed. Wearied by the unprecedented numbers of bond defaults and shocked by how quickly corporate creditworthiness can deteriorate, investors are re-evaluating how much they are prepared to invest in any one company.

"It used to be that a 2 percent position in Ford was fine," said Lee Crabbe, head of the corporate bond group at Credit Suisse Asset Management.

"Now a 2 percent position in any name isn't fine."

Meanwhile, concern has grown over the U.S. manufacturers' ability to compete with European rivals and to fund their pension liabilities.

More recently, worries have surfaced over the continuing strength of U.S. consumer demand. In July, Ford Credit's 10-year bonds started to diverge from those of similarly rated mid-investment grade companies. They have since widened some 300 basis points to trade at 570 basis points over U.S. Treasuries—in other words, like "junk" bonds.

General Motors Acceptance Corp's 10-year bonds have also widened and now trade at 455 basis points over Treasuries. Both companies recently had their long-term debt ratings lowered one notch by Standard & Poor's.

The widening in spreads does not reflect fears that the vehicle makers will go bankrupt—most investors say they believe Ford's fundamentals are sound. However, it does show that investors are no longer prepared simply to follow the index.

The vehicle manufacturers are among the largest issuers of debt in the U.S. corporate bond market, with Ford, GM and Daimler-Chrysler accounting for 6.5 percent of Lehman's Credit Index, or some $128bn in debt.

Ford, with $61bn in debt outstanding, has the biggest weighting in the index, accounting for 3 percent.

The group has issued an increasing amount of debt over the past decade to fund the growing activities of Ford Motor Credit, its financial services business. In 1992 it sold about $12bn of debt in the U.S., but last year sold more than $40bn, according to Thomson Financial.

As the amount of debt Ford has issued has risen, so has its weight in market indices, which in turn has encouraged investors to buy its securities, because most investment funds gauge their performance against market indices.

This, however, leaves funds with a conundrum. Those that hold the bonds as spreads widen may take losses if the securities do not recover. Many investors were burnt earlier this year on investments in energy and telecommunications companies.

"Anything that smacks of excess capacity and a high debt burden has been a disaster this year," says Steven Zamsky, corporate bond strategist at Morgan Stanley.

However, funds that sell the vehicle makers' securities run the risk of missing a rally if the bonds tighten, and having their performance look bad in comparison with their peers.

Ford and GM's bonds have been extraordinarily volatile this year—in part because of increased activity by short sellers and hedge funds—so any rally could be quite substantial.

"When investors get nervous, they sell at any price," says Mark Kiesel, portfolio manager at bond fund Pimco. "But if the market bounces, they've lost both ways."

Source: Jenny Wiggins. "Ford and GM's Bonds Looking Less Roadworthy," *Financial Times,* Thursday, October 31, 2002, p. 15.

An efficient financial market quickly, if not instantaneously, discounts all available information. Any new information will immediately be used by some privileged investors, who will take positions to capitalize on it, thereby making the asset price adjust (almost) instantaneously to this piece of information. For example, a new balance of payments statistic would immediately be used by foreign exchange traders to buy or sell a currency until the foreign exchange rate reached a level considered consistent with the new information. Similarly, investors might use surprise information about a company, such as a new contract or changes in forecasted income, to reap a profit until the stock price reached a level consistent with the news. The adjustment in price would be so rapid it would not pay to buy information that has already been available to other investors. Hundreds of thousands of expert financial analysts and professional investors throughout the world search for information and make the world markets close to fully efficient.

In a perfectly efficient market, the typical investor could consider an asset price to reflect its true *fundamental value* at all times. The notion of fundamental value is somewhat philosophical; it means that at each point in time, each asset has an intrinsic value that all investors try to discover. Nevertheless, the analyst tries to find mispriced securities by choosing from a variety of valuation models and by carefully researching the inputs for the model. In this research, forecasting cash flows and risk is critical.

Valuation Models   Investors often rely on some form of a discounted cash flow analysis (DCF) for estimating the "intrinsic" value of a stock investment. This is simply a "present value" model, where the intrinsic value of an asset at time zero, P_0, is determined by the stream of cash flows it generates for the investor. This price is also called the "justified" price because it is the value that is "justified" by the forecasted cash flows. In a **dividend discount model (DDM)**, the stock market price is set equal to the stream of forecasted dividends, D, discounted at the required rate of return, r

$$P_0 = \frac{D_1}{1 + r} + \frac{D_2}{(1 + r)^2} + \frac{D_3}{(1 + r)^3} \cdots \qquad \textbf{(40-1)}$$

Financial analysts take great care in forecasting future earnings, and hence, dividends.

A simple version of the DDM assumes that dividends will grow indefinitely at a constant compounded annual growth rate (CAGR), g. Hence, Equation 40-1 becomes

$$P_0 = \frac{D_1}{1 + r} + \frac{D_1(1 + g)}{(1 + r)^2} + \frac{D_1(1 + g)^2}{(1 + r)^3} \cdots$$

or

$$P_0 = \frac{D_1}{r - g} \qquad \textbf{(40-2)}$$

Analysts forecast earnings, and a payout ratio is applied to transform earnings into dividends. Under the assumption of a constant earnings payout ratio, we find

$$P_0 = \frac{E_1(1 - b)}{r - g} \qquad \textbf{(40-3)}$$

where

P_0 is the justified or intrinsic price at time 0 (now)
E_1 is next year's earnings
b is the earnings retention ratio
$1 - b$ is the earnings payout ratio
r is the required rate of return on the stock
g is the growth rate of earnings

Note that Equation 40-3 requires that the growth rate g remain constant infinitely and that it must be less than the required rate of return r. Take the example of a German corporation whose next annual earnings are expected to be €20 per share, with a constant growth rate of 5 percent per year, and with a 50 percent payout ratio. Hence, the next-year dividend is expected to be €10. Let's further assume that the required rate of return for an investment in such a corporation is 10 percent, which can be decomposed into a 6 percent risk-free rate plus a 4 percent risk premium. Then the firm's value is equal to

$$P_0 = \frac{10}{0.10 - 0.05} = €200$$

The intrinsic price-to-earnings ratio (P/E) is defined as P_0/E_1. The intrinsic P/E of this corporation, using prospective earnings, is equal to

$$P/E = \frac{1 - b}{r - g} = \frac{0.50}{0.10 - 0.05} = 10$$

A drop in the risk-free interest rate would lead to an increase in the P/E and in the stock price. For example, if the risk-free rate drops to 5 percent, and everything else remains unchanged, a direct application of the formula indicates that the P/E will move up to 12.5 and the stock price to €250.

A more realistic DDM approach is to decompose the future in three phases. In the near future (e.g., the next two years), earnings are forecasted individually. In the second phase (e.g., years 3 to 5), a general growth rate of the company's earnings is estimated. In the final stage, the growth rate in earnings is assumed to revert to some sustainable growth rate.[16]

A final step required by this approach is to estimate the **normal rate of return** required on such an investment. This rate is equal to the risk-free interest rate plus a risk premium that reflects the relevant risks of this investment. Relevant risks refer to risks that should be priced by the market.

Franchise Value and the Growth Process   Given the risk of the company's forecasted cash flows, the other key determinant of value is the growth rate in cash flows. The growth rate depends on relevant country GDP growth rates, industry growth rates, and the company's sustainable competitive advantage within the industry. Regardless of the valuation model used, some analysis of the growth-rate input is useful. Using the DDM as a representative model, Leibowitz and Kogelman (2000) developed the *franchise value* method and separated the intrinsic P/E value of a corporation into a tangible P/E value (the no-growth or zero-earnings retention P/E value of existing business) and the franchise P/E value (derived from prospective new investments). The franchise P/E value is related to the *present value of growth opportunities* (PVGO) in the traditional breakdown

---

[16] A detailed analysis of the use of DDM in companies' valuation is provided in Stowe et al. (2002).

of intrinsic value into the no-growth value per share and the present value of growth opportunities. In that breakdown, the no-growth value per share is the value of the company if it were to distribute all its earnings in dividends, creating a perpetuity valued at E_1/r, where E_1 is next year's earnings and r is the required rate of return on the company's equity. Using the DDM and the company's actual payout ratio to generate an intrinsic value per share, P_0, the present value of growth opportunities must be the difference between intrinsic value and the **no-growth value per share**, $P_0 - E_1/r$.

The franchise value approach focuses on the intrinsic P/E rather than on the intrinsic value P_0; thus, the franchise value P/E is $\boldsymbol{PVGO}/E_1$. In the franchise value approach, however, the franchise value P/E is further broken down into the *franchise factor* and the *growth factor*. The growth factor captures the present value of the opportunities for productive new investments, and the franchise factor is meant to capture the return levels associated with those new investments. The *Sales-Driven Franchise Value* has been developed to deal with multinational corporations that do business globally (see Leibowitz, 1997, 1998).

The separation of franchise P/E value into a franchise factor and a growth factor permits a direct examination of the response of the intrinsic P/E to ROE.[17] This factor helps an investor determine the response of the P/E to the ROE expected to be achieved by the company. It focuses on the sustainable growth rate of earnings per share. Earnings per share will grow from one period to the next because reinvested earnings will earn the rate of ROE. So the company's sustainable growth rate is equal to the retention rate (b) multiplied by ROE: $g = b \times \text{ROE}$. Substituting into Equation 40-3 the sustainable growth rate calculation for g, we get the intrinsic price:

$$P_0 = \frac{E_1(1-b)}{r - b \times \text{ROE}}$$

and converting to an intrinsic P/E ratio,

$$\frac{P_0}{E_1} = \frac{(1-b)}{r - b \times \text{ROE}}$$

Now, multiplying through by r/r yields

$$\frac{P_0}{E_1} = \frac{1}{r}\left[\frac{r(1-b)}{r - b \times \text{ROE}}\right]$$

$$= \frac{1}{r}\left[\frac{r - r \times b}{r - \text{ROE} \times b}\right]$$

and arbitrarily adding and subtracting $\text{ROE} \times b$ in the numerator,

$$\frac{P_0}{E_1} = \frac{1}{r}\left[\frac{r - r \times b + \text{ROE} \times b - \text{ROE} \times b}{r - \text{ROE} \times b}\right]$$

$$= \frac{1}{r}\left[\frac{r - \text{ROE} \times b + \text{ROE} \times b - r \times b}{r - \text{ROE} \times b}\right]$$

[17] The model is derived here under the assumptions of a constant growth rate g, a constant earnings retention rate b, and a constant ROE. It can accommodate more complex assumptions about the pattern of growth.

or

$$\frac{P_0}{E_1} = \frac{1}{r}\left[1 + \frac{b(\text{ROE} - r)}{r - \text{ROE} \times b}\right] \qquad \textbf{(40-4)}$$

This P_0/E_1 equation is extremely useful because one can use it to examine the effects of different values of b and of the difference between ROE and r; that is, ROE $-$ r. Two interesting results can be found. First, if ROE $=$ r, the intrinsic P_0/E_1 equals $1/r$ regardless of b, the **earnings retention ratio**. Second, if $b = 0$, the intrinsic P_0/E_1 equals $1/r$ regardless of whether ROE is greater than r. These two results have an intuitive explanation.

▶ When the return on equity is exactly equal to the required rate of return (ROE $=$ r), there is no *added* value in retaining earnings for additional investments, rather than distributing them to shareholders. A company with ROE $=$ r has no franchise value potential because its return on equity is just what the market requires, but no more.

▶ An earnings retention ratio of zero ($b = 0$) means that the company distributes all its earnings. So equity per share stays constant. There is no growth of equity and the stream of future earnings will be a perpetuity because the rate of return on equity (ROE) remains constant. The value of a share is given by discounting a perpetuity of E_1 at a rate r, hence the $P_0/E_1 = 1/r$ result. Of course, the total equity of the company could grow by issuing new shares, but there will be no growth of earnings per existing share. There is potential franchise value in the company with ROE $>$ r, but because the company does not reinvest earnings at this superior rate of return, existing shareholders do not capture this potential.

In general, there is a franchise value created for existing shareholders, if the company can reinvest past earnings ($b > 0$) at a rate of return (ROE) higher than the market-required rate (r).

Examining Equation 40-4 further, we return to the intrinsic value version of the equation. We can transform 40-4 by multiplying and dividing by ROE and replacing $b \times$ ROE by g:

$$\frac{P_0}{E_1} = \frac{1}{r}\left[1 + \frac{\text{ROE} \times b \times (\text{ROE} - r)}{\text{ROE} \times (r - \text{ROE} \times b)}\right] = \frac{1}{r} + \frac{g \times (\text{ROE} - r)}{r \times \text{ROE} \times (r - g)}$$

and simplify it as

$$\frac{P_0}{E_1} = \frac{1}{r} + \left(\frac{\text{ROE} - r}{\text{ROE} \times r}\right)\left(\frac{g}{r - g}\right)$$

$$\frac{P_0}{E_1} = \frac{1}{r} + \text{FF} \times \text{G} \qquad \textbf{(40-5)}$$

where the franchise factor is FF $=$ $(\text{ROE} - r)/(\text{ROE} \times r)$ or $1/r - 1/\text{ROE}$, and the growth factor is G $=$ $g/(r - g)$.

The growth factor is the ratio of the present value of future increases in the book value (BV) of equity to the current BV of equity. If the current BV of equity is B_0, then next year's increment to BV is gB_0. With a constant growth rate in BV increments, these increments can be treated as a growing perpetuity with a present value of $gB_0/(r - g)$. Because the present value of the BV increments is to be given as a ratio to the most recent BV, the growth factor is then given as $g/(r - g)$.

The **franchise factor** stems from the fact that a firm has a competitive advantage allowing it to generate a rate of return (ROE) greater than the rate of return normally required by investors for this type of risk (r). If the franchise factor is positive, it gives the rate of response of the intrinsic P_0/E_1 ratio to in the growth factor. The growth factor G will be high if the firm can sustain a growth rate that is high relative to r.

Consider a pharmaceutical firm with some attractive new drugs with large commercial interest. Its ROE will be high relative to the rate of return required by investors for pharmaceutical stocks. Hence, it has a large positive franchise factor FF. If it continues to make productive new investments (G positive), such a firm can continue to generate a return on equity well above the rate of return required by the stock market, and thus has a large positive franchise value. On the other hand, if the pharmaceutical company's sustainable growth rate is small because of a low earnings retention rate b, then G will be small and so will the franchise value, even though the franchise factor is large. For a firm with less franchise potential and ROE possibilities only equal to the company's required rate of return ($r =$ ROE) the franchise factor is zero and the intrinsic P_0/E_1 is simply $1/r$, regardless of the earnings retention ratio.

The Effects of Inflation on Stock Prices   Because inflation rates vary around the world and over time, it is important to consider the effects of inflation on stock prices. To do this, we begin at the obvious place—earnings. After examining the effects of inflation on reported earnings, we discuss an inflation flow-through model.[18]

Because historical costs are used in accounting, inflation has a distorting effect on reported earnings. These effects show up primarily in replacement,

---

EXAMPLE 3

Franchise Value

A company can generate an ROE of 15 percent and has an earnings retention ratio of 0.60. Next year's earnings are projected at $100 million. If the required rate of return for the company is 12 percent, what is the company's tangible P/E value, franchise factor, growth factor, and franchise P/E value?

Solution: The company's tangible P/E value is $1/r = 1/0.12 = 8.33$. The company's franchise factor is $1/r - 1/\text{ROE} = 1/0.12 - 1/0.15 = 1.67$.

Because the company's sustainable growth rate is $0.6 \times 0.15 = 0.09$, the company's growth factor is $g/(r - g) = 0.09/(0.12 - 0.09) = 3$.

The company's franchise P/E value is the franchise factor times the growth factor, $1.67 \times 3 = 5.01$.

Because its tangible P/E value is 8.33 and its franchise P/E value is 5.01, the company's intrinsic P/E is 13.34. Note that the intrinsic P/E calculated directly is $P/E = (1 - b)/(r - g) = 0.4/(0.12 - 0.09) = 13.33$. Thus, the franchise value method breaks this P/E into its basic components.

---

[18] For example, see Leibowitz and Kogelman (2000).

inventories, and borrowing costs. Replacement must be made at inflated costs, but depreciation is recorded at historical cost—hence, reported earnings based on depreciation as an estimate of replacement costs gives an overstatement of earnings. Similarly, a first-in, first-out inventory accounting system leads to an understatement of inventory costs and an overstatement of reported earnings. Unlike replacement and inventory distortions, borrowing costs at historical rates cause an understatement of reported earnings. Inflation causes borrowing costs to increase, but nominal interest costs do not reflect the increase. Finally, capital gains taxes reflect an inflation tax, because the base for the capital gains tax is historical cost.

To analyze the effects of inflation on the valuation process, analysts try to determine what part of inflation flows through to a firm's earnings. A full-flow-through firm has earnings that fully reflect inflation. Thus, any inflation cost increases must be getting passed along to consumers.

In an inflationary environment, consider a firm that would otherwise have no growth in earnings, a zero earnings retention ratio and full-inflation flow-through. So, earnings only grow because of the inflation rate I, assumed constant over time. For example, we have

$$E_1 = E_0 \times (1 + I)$$

By discounting this stream of inflation-growing earnings at the required rate r, we find that the intrinsic value of such a firm would then be

$$P_0 = \frac{E_1}{r - I} = E_0 \left(\frac{1 + I}{r - I} \right) \qquad \textbf{(40-6)}$$

where

  P_0 is the intrinsic value
  E_0 is the initial earnings level
  I is the annual inflation rate
  r is the nominal required rate of return

Let's now consider a company with a partial inflation flow-through of λ percent, so that earnings are only inflated at a rate λI:

$$E_1 = E_0(1 + \lambda I)$$

By discounting this stream of earnings at the nominal required rate r, we find

$$P_0 = E_0 \times \frac{1 + \lambda I}{r - \lambda I} \qquad \textbf{(40-7)}$$

If we introduce the real required rate of return $\rho = r - I$, we get

$$P_0 = E_0 \times \frac{1 + \lambda I}{\rho + (1 - \lambda)I} = \frac{E_1}{\rho + (1 - \lambda)I}$$

The intrinsic P/E using prospective earnings is now equal to

$$P_0/E_1 = \frac{1}{\rho + (1 - \lambda)I} \qquad \textbf{(40-8)}$$

From Equation 40-8 we can see that the higher the inflation flow-through rate, the higher the price of the company. Indeed, a company that cannot pass inflation through its earnings is penalized. Thus, the P/E ratio ranges from a high of $1/\rho$ to a low of $1/r$. For example, assume a real required rate of return of 6 percent and an inflation rate of 4 percent. Exhibit 3 shows the P/E of the company with different flow-through rates. With a full-flow-through rate ($\lambda = 100$ percent), the P/E is equal to P/E $= 1/\rho = 1/0.06 = 16.67$. The ratio drops to 12.5 if the company can only pass 50 percent of inflation through its earnings. If the company cannot pass through any inflation ($\lambda = 0$), its earnings remain constant, and the P/E ratio is equal to P/E $= 1/(\rho + I) = 1/r = 10$. The higher the inflation rate, the more negative the influence on the stock price if full inflation pass-through cannot be achieved.

This observation is important if we compare similar companies in different countries experiencing different inflation rates. A company operating in a high-inflation environment will be penalized if it cannot pass through inflation.

The Inflation-like Effects of Currency Movements on Stock Prices   A currency movement is a monetary variable that affects stock valuation in a fashion similar to the inflation variable. Just as some companies cannot fully pass inflation through their earnings, they cannot fully pass exchange rate movements either. Consider an importing firm faced with a sudden depreciation of the home currency. The products it imports suddenly become more expensive in terms of the home currency. If this price increase can be passed through to customers, earnings will not suffer from the currency adjustment. But this is often not the

---

EXHIBIT 3	Inflation Effects on P/E

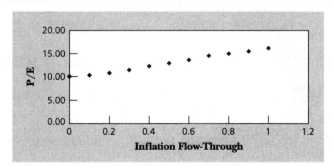

EXAMPLE 4

Inflation

Consider two companies in the same line of business, but with mostly domestic operations. Company A is based in a country with no inflation. Company B is based in a country with a 4 percent inflation rate. There is no real growth in earnings for both companies. The real rate of return required by global investors for this type of stock investment is 6 percent.

Company B can only pass 80 percent of inflation through its earnings. What should be the P/E of the two companies?

Solution: The nominal required rate of return for Company A is equal to the real rate because there is no inflation: $r = \rho = 6\%$. Earnings are constant and the P/E is equal to

$$P/E(A) = 1/\rho = 1/0.06 = 16.67$$

There is a 4 percent inflation rate in the country of Company B. Its earnings will only be inflated at a rate of $\lambda I = 80\% \times 4\% = 3.2\%$. The P/E of company B will be

$$P/E(B) = \frac{1}{6\% + (20\%) \times 4\%} = \frac{1}{6.8\%} = 14.71$$

In the inflationary environment, Company B's earnings cannot grow as fast as inflation. Penalized by inflation and its inability to pass along inflation, Company B's P/E ratio is below that of Company A.

case. First, the price increase will tend to reduce demand for these imported products. Second, locally produced goods will become more attractive than imported goods, and some substitution will take place.

Currency exposure depends on such factors as each particular company's production cycle, the competitive structure of its product market, and the company's financing structure.

6   GLOBAL RISK FACTORS IN SECURITY RETURNS

The analysis of an individual company can require a detailed review of various strategic risk elements that are difficult to quantify precisely. However, a portfolio manager needs to summarize the information on a large number of securities into a few statistics that help construct a portfolio and manage its risk. To structure a portfolio properly, a manager must have a clear understanding of the main factors influencing the return on a security and of the risk exposures of each security.

The risk premium of a security should be proportional to the covariance (or beta) of the security's return with the world market return; this is the world market risk of a security. The world market risk of a security is the result of the exposure to many sources of risk that can be detailed in factor models. Factor models allow a better understanding of the risks that affect stock returns in the short run and allow the risk management of a portfolio.

Risk-Factor Model: Industry and Country Factors

A factor model, where R is the rate of return on the security, may be written mathematically as

$$R = \alpha + \beta_1 f_1 + \beta_2 f_2 + \ldots + \beta_k f_k + \varepsilon \tag{40-9}$$

where

R is the rate of return on a security

α is a constant

$f_1 \ldots f_k$ are the k factors common to all securities

$\beta_1 \ldots \beta_k$ represent the sensitivity, or risk exposure, of this security to each factor

ε is a random term specific to this security

The ε is the source of idiosyncratic or **diversifiable risk** for the security, and $\beta_1 \ldots \beta_k$ represent the risk exposure of this security to each factor. The betas vary among securities. Some stocks may be highly sensitive to certain factors and much less sensitive to others, and vice versa.

A global risk-factor model would use industry and country as factors. The degree of granularity can be adapted; for example, one could use global sector factors, global industry factors, or regional industry factors. The geographical factors could be a list of regions (e.g., Europe) or of individual countries.

The factors are measured as the return on some index portfolio representative of the factor ("mimicking portfolios"). For example, the oil industry factor could be proxied by the return on a global stock index of oil firms. Various statistical techniques can be used to optimize the factor structure.

The determination of the risk-factor exposures can follow one of two techniques or a combination of the two:

► The exposure can be assessed a priori by using information on the company studied. This usually leads to a 0/1 exposure. For example, TotalFinaElf would have a unitary exposure to the oil industry factor and zero exposures to all other industry factors, because it is an oil company.

► The exposure can be estimated using a multiple regression approach. The exposures would then be the estimated betas in a time-series regression.

The question of currency should be addressed. A global risk-factor model can be written in some arbitrary currency (e.g., the U.S. dollar). It also can be written in currency-hedged terms. If companies are reacting differently to currency movements, currencies could be added as risk factors. For example, an exporting firm could be influenced negatively by an appreciation of its currency, while the reverse would be true for an importing firm. These currency exposures could be cancelled if the company adopts a currency-hedging policy in its business operations.

Other Risk Factors: Styles

Other factors influence the stock price behavior of companies worldwide. As mentioned, many researchers believe that the future performance of a stock also depends on other attributes of a company that have not been discussed so far. Among many others, three attributes have been researched extensively:

► *Value* stocks do not behave like *growth* stocks. A value stock is a company whose stock price is "cheap" in relation to its book value, or in relation to the cash flows it generates (low stock price compared with its earnings, cash flows, or dividends). A growth stock has the opposite attribute, implying that the stock price capitalizes growth in future earnings. This is known as the *value effect*.

▶ *Small* firms do not exhibit the same stock price behavior as *large* firms. The size of a firm is measured by its stock market capitalization. This is known as the *size effect*.

▶ In the short run, winners tend to repeat. In other words, stocks that have performed well (or badly) in the recent past, say in the past six months, will tend to be winners (or losers) in the next six months. This is known as the *momentum, success,* or *relative strength effect*.

The observation of these effects, or factors, has led to the development of *style investing*, in which portfolios are structured to favor some of these attributes (e.g., value stocks).

Risk-factor models often incorporate style factors in which the factors are proxied by some mimicking portfolio (e.g., long in value stocks and short in growth stocks). A security's exposure is either measured *a priori* by using some information on the company or by a regression technique, or by a combination of the two techniques.

Although this style approach has been extensively used in the United States, there is some practical difficulty in applying it in a global setting. This is best illustrated by looking at the size factor. An Austrian company that is regarded as "large" in Austria would be regarded as "medium-sized" in Europe and probably as "small" according to U.S. standards. To construct a global size factor, one must make assumptions on how to measure relative size. Different risk-factor models use different criteria.

Other Risk Factors: Macroeconomic

Factors are postulated *a priori* as sources of risk that are common to all companies. This clearly leads us to some macroeconomic variables that affect the economics of all firms, as well as the behavior of stock market participants who price those firms.

Selecting a set of *macroeconomic factors* is as much an art as a science. These factors must be logical choices, easy to interpret, robust over time, and able to explain a significant percentage of variation in stock returns. Some macroeconomic variables are logical candidates as factors but suffer from serious measurement error or long publication lags. For example, the evolution in industrial production is a logical candidate, but it is difficult to get timely, good-quality, reliable data. The technique is to use as factor proxies the returns on mimicking portfolios that are most strongly correlated with the economic variable.

Burmeister, Roll, and Ross (1994) propose a set of five factors.[19] These five factors, listed here, apply to domestic U.S. stocks:

▶ *Confidence factor* (f_1). This factor is measured by the difference in return on risky corporate bonds and on government bonds. The default-risk premium

---

[19] Earlier, Chen, Roll, and Ross (1986) had identified four factors for the U.S. equity market as (1) growth rate in industrial production, (2) unexpected inflation, (3) slope of the yield curve (the difference between long- and short-term interest rates), and (4) changes in the attitude toward risk as proxied by changes in the pricing of **default risk** implicit in the difference between yields on Aaa and Baa corporate bonds.

required by the market to compensate for the risk of default on corporate bonds is measured as the spread between the yields on risky corporate bonds and government bonds. A decrease in the default-risk spread will give a higher return on corporate bonds and implies an improvement in the investors' confidence level. Hence, confidence risk focuses on the willingness of investors to undertake risky investments. Most stocks have a positive exposure to the confidence factor ($\beta_1 > 0$), so their prices tend to rise when the confidence factor is positive ($f_1 > 0$). The underlying idea is that in periods when investors are becoming more sensitive to risks (less confident with $f_1 < 0$), they require a higher premium on risky corporate bonds, compared with government bonds. They also require a higher risk premium on risky stocks and will bid their prices down, inducing a negative stock-price movement.

▶ *Time horizon factor* (f_2). This factor is measured as the difference between the return on a 20-year government bond and a 1-month Treasury bill. A positive difference in return is caused by a decrease in the term spread (long minus **short interest rates**). This is a signal that investors require a lesser premium to hold long-term investments. Growth stocks are more exposed (higher β_2) to time horizon risk than **income stocks**. The underlying idea is to view the stock price as the discounted stream of its future cash flows. The present value of growth stocks is determined by the long-term prospects of growing earnings while current earnings are relatively weak (high P/E ratio). An increase in the market-required discount rate will penalize the price of growth stocks more than the price of value stocks.

▶ *Inflation factor* (f_3). This factor is measured as the difference between the actual inflation for a month and its expected value, computed the month before, using an econometric inflation model. An unexpected increase in inflation tends to be bad for most stocks ($\beta_3 < 0$), so they have a negative exposure to this inflation surprise ($f_3 > 0$). Luxury goods stocks tend to be most sensitive to inflation risk, whereas firms in the sectors of foods, cosmetics, or tires are less sensitive to inflation risk. Real estate holdings typically benefit from increased inflation.

▶ *Business-cycle factor* (f_4). This factor is measured by the monthly variation in a business activity index. Business-cycle risk comes from unanticipated changes in the level of real activity. The business-cycle factor is positive ($f_4 > 0$) when the expected real growth rate of the economy has increased. Most firms have a positive exposure to business-cycle risk ($\beta_4 > 0$). Retail stores are more exposed to business-cycle risk than are utility companies, because their business activity (sales) is much more sensitive to recession or expansion.

▶ *Market-timing factor* (f_5). This factor is measured by the part of the S&P 500 total return that is not explained by the first four factors. It captures the global movements in the market that are not explained by the four macroeconomic factors. The inclusion of this market-timing factor makes the capital asset pricing model (CAPM) a special case of this approach. If all relevant macroeconomic factors had been included, it would not be necessary to add this market-timing factor.

A common criticism of this approach is that the risk exposures (betas) have to be estimated statistically from past data and may not be stable over time. Even the factor proxies (mimicking portfolios) have to be constructed using statistical optimization, and the procedure could yield unstable proxies.

Practical Use of Factor Models

Risk-factor models are used in risk management and in selecting stocks. A major application is the analysis of the risk profile of portfolios. The exposure of the portfolio to the various factors is the weighted average of the exposures of the stocks making up the portfolio. A manager can estimate the risks taken and the exposure of the portfolio to the various sources of risk. If some specific stock index is assigned as a benchmark to measure performance, the manager can analyze the risks of deviations from the benchmark. This helps the manager identify and quantify the bets and risks that are taken in the portfolio.

Managers can also use factor models to tilt the portfolio along some factor bets. Assume, for example, that a manager believes that the economy is going to grow at a faster rate than generally forecasted, leading to some inflationary pressure. The manager will tend to increase the portfolio exposure to business risk but reduce its exposure to inflation risk. This could also lead the manager to take some industry bets and invest in small companies.

SUMMARY

▶ The major differences in accounting standards around the world appear in the treatment of business combinations, consolidation of subsidiary and affiliate information, goodwill, **financial leases**, asset revaluation, provisions for likely future losses or expenses, pensions, financial assets and derivatives, and employee stock options.

▶ Off-balance-sheet assets and liabilities are those assets and liabilities not properly reflected in the balance sheet. Examples are special purpose entities and financial leases.

▶ From an economic perspective, employee stock option compensation should be treated as an expense, with the options valued by an option-pricing model.

▶ Neoclassical growth theory predicts that the long-term level of GDP depends on the country's savings rate, but the long-term growth rate in GDP does not depend on the savings rate. Endogenous growth theory predicts that the long-term growth rate in GDP depends on the savings rate.

▶ A global industry analysis should examine return potential evidenced by demand analysis, value creation, industry life cycle, competition structure, competitive advantage, competitive strategies, co-opetition and the value net, and **sector rotation**. The analysis also should examine risk elements evidenced by market competition, value chain competition, government participation, and cash flow covariance.

▶ Global financial analysis involves comparing company ratios with global industry averages. In this context, DuPont analysis uses various combinations of the tax retention, debt burden, operating margin, asset turnover, and leverage ratios.

▶ The role of market efficiency in individual asset valuation is to equate fundamental value with asset valuation so that the analyst searches for mispricing or market inefficiency.

▶ Franchise value is the present value of growth opportunities divided by next year's earnings. The intrinsic P_0/E_1 ratio equals $1/r$ plus the franchise value, where r is the nominal required return on the stock. The franchise value is further divided into a franchise factor (FF) and a growth factor (G) to give $P_0/E_1 = 1/r + \text{FF} \times \text{G}$.

▶ To analyze the effects of inflation for valuation purposes, the analyst must recognize the distorting effects of historical inventory and borrowing costs on reported earnings, as well as recognize the inflation tax reflected in capital gains taxes. Further, the analyst must estimate the degree of inflation flow-through, λ.

▶ With earnings that are constant except for inflation, I as the inflation rate, r as the required nominal return on the stock, and ρ as the required real return on the stock, the P/E ratio can be estimated as $P_0/E_1 = 1/(\rho + (1 - \lambda)I)$.

▶ Multifactor models can be used in the analysis of the risk profile of portfolios. The exposure of a portfolio to the various factors is the weighted average of the exposures of the stocks making up the portfolio.

PRACTICE PROBLEMS FOR READING 40

1. Explain why a corporation can have a stock market price well above its accounting book value.

2. The accounting and fiscal standards of many countries allow corporations to build general provisions (or "hidden reserves") in anticipation of foreseen or unpredictable expenses. How would this practice affect the book value of a corporation and its ratio of market price to book value?

3. Discuss some of the reasons why the earnings of German firms tend to be understated, compared with the earnings of U.S. firms.

4. Consider a firm that has given stock options on 20,000 shares to its senior executives. These call options can be exercised at a price of $22 anytime during the next three years. The firm has a total of 500,000 shares outstanding, and the current price is $20 per share. The firm's net income before taxes is $2 million.

   A. What would be the firm's pretax earnings per share if the options are not expensed?

   B. Under certain assumptions, the Black–Scholes model valued the options given by the firm to its executives at $4 per share option. What would be the firm's pretax earnings per share if the options are expensed accordingly?

   C. Under somewhat different assumptions, the Black–Scholes model valued the options at $5.25 per share option. What would be the firm's pretax earnings per share if the options are expensed based on this valuation?

5. Japanese companies tend to belong to groups (*keiretsu*) and to hold shares of one another. Because these cross-holdings are minority interest, they tend not to be consolidated in published financial statements. To study the impact of this tradition on published earnings, consider the following simplified example:

   Company A owns 10 percent of Company B; the initial investment was 10 million yen. Company B owns 20 percent of Company A; the initial investment was also 10 million yen. Both companies value their minority interests at historical cost. The annual net income of Company A was 10 million yen. The annual net income of Company B was 30 million yen. Assume that the two companies do not pay any dividends. The current stock market values are 200 million yen for Company A and 450 million yen for Company B.

   A. Restate the earnings of the two companies, using the equity method of consolidation. Remember that the share of the minority-interest earning is consolidated on a one-line basis, proportionate to the share of equity owned by the parent.

   B. Calculate the P/E ratios, based on nonconsolidated and consolidated earnings. How does the nonconsolidation of earnings affect the P/E ratios?

6. The annual revenues (in billion dollars) in financial year 2001 for the top five players in the global media and entertainment industry are given in the following table. The top five corporations in this industry include three U.S.-based corporations (AOL Time Warner, Walt Disney, and Viacom), one French corporation (Vivendi Universal), and one Australian corporation (News Corporation). The revenue indicated for Vivendi Universal does not include the revenue from its environmental

business. Assume that the total worldwide revenue of all firms in this industry was $250 billion.

Company	Revenue
AOL Time Warner	38
Walt Disney	25
Vivendi Universal	25
Viacom	23
News Corporation	13

A. Compute the three-firm and five-firm concentration ratios.

B. Compute the three-firm and five-firm Herfindahl indexes.

C. Make a simplistic assumption that in addition to the five corporations mentioned in the table, there are 40 other companies in this industry with an equal share of the remaining market. Compute the Herfindahl index for the overall industry.

D. Suppose there were not 40, but only 10 other companies in the industry with an equal share of the remaining market. Compute the Herfindahl index for the overall industry.

E. Interpret your answers to Parts C and D in terms of the competition structure of the industry.

7. News Corporation is headquartered in Australia, and its main activities include television entertainment, films, cable, and publishing.

A. Collect any relevant information that you may need and discuss whether an analyst should do the valuation of News Corporation primarily relative to the global media and entertainment industry or relative to other companies based in Australia.

B. One of the competitors of News Corporation is Vivendi Universal, a firm headquartered in France. Should an analyst be concerned in comparing financial ratios of News Corporation with those of Vivendi Universal?

8. You are given the following data about Walt Disney and News Corporation, two of the major corporations in the media and entertainment industry. The data are for the end of the financial year 1999, and are in US$ millions. Though News Corporation is based in Australia, it also trades on the NYSE and its data in the following table, like those for Walt Disney, is according to the U.S. GAAP.

	Walt Disney	**News Corporation**
Sales	23,402	14,395
EBIT	3,035	1,819
EBT	2,314	1,212
NI	1,300	719
Assets	43,679	35,681
Equity	20,975	16,374

    A. Compute the ROE for Walt Disney and News Corporation.

    B. Use the DuPont model to analyze the difference in ROE between the two companies, by identifying the elements that primarily cause this difference.

9. In the past 20 years, the best-performing stock markets have been found in countries with the highest economic growth rates. Should the current growth rate guide you in choosing stock markets if the world capital market is efficient?

10. Consider a French company that pays out 70 percent of its earnings. Its next annual earnings are expected to be €4 per share. The required return for the company is 12 percent. In the past, the company's compound annual growth rate (CAGR) has been 1.25 times the world's GDP growth rate. It is expected that the world's GDP growth rate will be 2.8 percent p.a. in the future. Assuming that the firm's earnings will continue to grow forever at 1.25 times the world's projected growth rate, compute the intrinsic value of the company's stock and its intrinsic P/E ratio.

11. Consider a company that pays out all its earnings. The required return for the firm is 13 percent.

    A. Compute the intrinsic P/E value of the company if its ROE is 15 percent.

    B. Compute the intrinsic P/E value of the company if its ROE is 20 percent.

    C. Discuss why your answers to parts (A) and (B) differ or do not differ from one another.

    D. Suppose that the company's ROE is 13 percent. Compute its intrinsic P/E value.

    E. Would the answer to part (D) change if the company retained half of its earnings instead of paying all of them out? Discuss why or why not.

12. Consider a firm with a ROE of 12 percent. The earnings next year are projected at $50 million, and the firm's earnings retention ratio is 0.70. The required return for the firm is 10 percent. Compute the following for the firm:

    i. franchise factor

    ii. growth factor

    iii. franchise P/E value

    iv. tangible P/E value

    v. intrinsic P/E value

13. Consider a firm for which the nominal required rate of return is 8 percent. The rate of inflation is 3 percent. Compute the P/E ratio of the firm under the following situations:

    i. The firm has a full inflation flow-through.

    ii. The firm can pass only 40 percent of inflation through its earnings.

    iii. The firm cannot pass any inflation through its earnings.

    What pattern do you observe from your answers to items (i) through (iii)?

14. Company B and Company U are in the same line of business. Company B is based in Brazil, where inflation during the past few years has averaged about 9 percent. Company U is based in the United States, where the inflation during the past few years has averaged about 2.5 percent. The real rate of return required by global investors for investing in stocks such as B and U is 8 percent. Neither B nor U has any real growth in earnings, and both of them can only pass 60 percent of inflation through their earnings. What should be the P/E of the two companies? What can you say based on a comparison of the P/E for the two companies?

15. Omega, Inc., is based in Brazil, and most of its operations are domestic. During the period 1995–99, the firm has not had any real growth in earnings. The annual inflation in Brazil during this period is given in the following table:

Year	Inflation (%)
1995	22.0
1996	9.1
1997	4.3
1998	2.5
1999	8.4

Source: International Monetary Fund.

The real rate of return required by global investors for investing in stocks such as Omega, Inc., is 7 percent.

A. Compute the P/E for Omega in each of the years if it can completely pass inflation through its earnings.

B. Compute the P/E for Omega in each of the years if it can only pass 50 percent of inflation through its earnings.

C. What conclusion can you draw about the effect of inflation on the stock price?

16. Consider a French company that exports French goods to the United States. What effect will a sudden appreciation of the euro relative to the dollar have on the P/E ratio of the French company? Discuss the effect under both the possibilities—the company being able to completely pass through the euro appreciation to its customers and the company being unable to completely pass through the euro appreciation to its customers.

17. Using the five macroeconomic factors described in the reading, you outline the factor exposures of two stocks as follows:

Factor	Stock A	Stock B
Confidence	0.2	0.6
Time horizon	0.6	0.8
Inflation	−0.1	−0.5
Business cycle	4.0	2.0
Market timing	1.0	0.7

[handwritten note: take avg of two exposures for each factor]

A. What would be the factor exposures of a portfolio invested half in Stock A and half in Stock B?

B. Contrary to general forecasts, you expect strong economic growth with a slight increase in inflation. Which stock should you overweigh in your portfolio?

18. Here is some return information on firms of various sizes and their price-to-book (value) ratios. Based on this information, what can you tell about the *size* and *value* style factors?

Stock	Size	P/BV	Return (%)
A	Huge	High	4
B	Huge	Low	6
C	Medium	High	9
D	Medium	Low	12
E	Small	High	13
F	Small	Low	15

19. You are analyzing whether the difference in returns on stocks of a particular country can be explained by two common factors, with a linear-factor model. Your candidates for the two factors are changes in interest rates and changes in the approval rating of the country's president, as measured by polls. The following table gives the interest rate, the percentage of people approving the president's performance, and the prices of three stocks (A, B, and C) for the past 10 periods.

Period	Interest Rate (%)	Approval (%)	Price of Stock A	B	C
1	7.3	47	22.57	24.43	25.02
2	5.2	52	19.90	12.53	13.81
3	5.5	51	15.46	17.42	19.17
4	7.2	49	21.62	24.70	23.24
5	5.4	68	14.51	16.43	18.79
6	5.2	49	12.16	11.56	14.66
7	7.5	72	25.54	24.73	28.68
8	7.6	45	25.83	28.12	21.47
9	5.3	47	13.04	14.71	16.43
10	5.1	67	11.18	12.44	12.50

Try to assess whether the two factors have an influence on stock returns. To do so, estimate the factor exposures for each of the three stocks by doing a time series regression for the return on each stock against the changes in the two factors.

20. You are a U.S. investor considering investing in Switzerland. The world market risk premium is estimated at 5 percent, the Swiss franc offers a 1 percent risk premium, and the current risk-free rates are equal to 4 percent in dollars and 3 percent in francs. In other words, you expect the Swiss franc to appreciate against the dollar by an amount equal to the interest rate differential plus the currency risk premium, or a total of 2 percent. You believe that the following equilibrium model (ICAPM) is appropriate for your investment analysis.

$$E(R_i) = R_f + \beta_1 \times RP_w + \beta_2 \times RP_{SFr}$$

where all returns are measured in dollars, RP_w is the risk premium on the world index, and RP_{SFr} is the risk premium on the Swiss franc. Your broker provides you with the following estimates and forecasted returns.

	Stock A	Stock B	Stock C	Stock D
Forecasted return (in francs)	0.08	0.09	0.11	0.07
World beta (β_1)	1	1	1.2	1.4
Dollar currency exposure (β_2)	1	0	0.5	−0.5

A. What should be the expected dollar returns on the four stocks, according to the ICAPM?

B. Which stocks would you recommend buying or selling?

[handwritten annotations:]

5 %
risk Premium

Swiss = 1%

4%

make sure to add 2% risk premium

$E_r(A) = 0.04 + 1 \times 0.05 + 1 \times 0.01$

$= 0.04 + .05 + .01$

10%

$E_r(B) = 0.04 + 0.05 + = 9\%$

$E_r(C) = 0.04 + 1.2(0.05) = 10.5\%$ +0.05

$E_r(D) = 1.1 - 0.5 \times (0.01)$

$= 10.5\%$

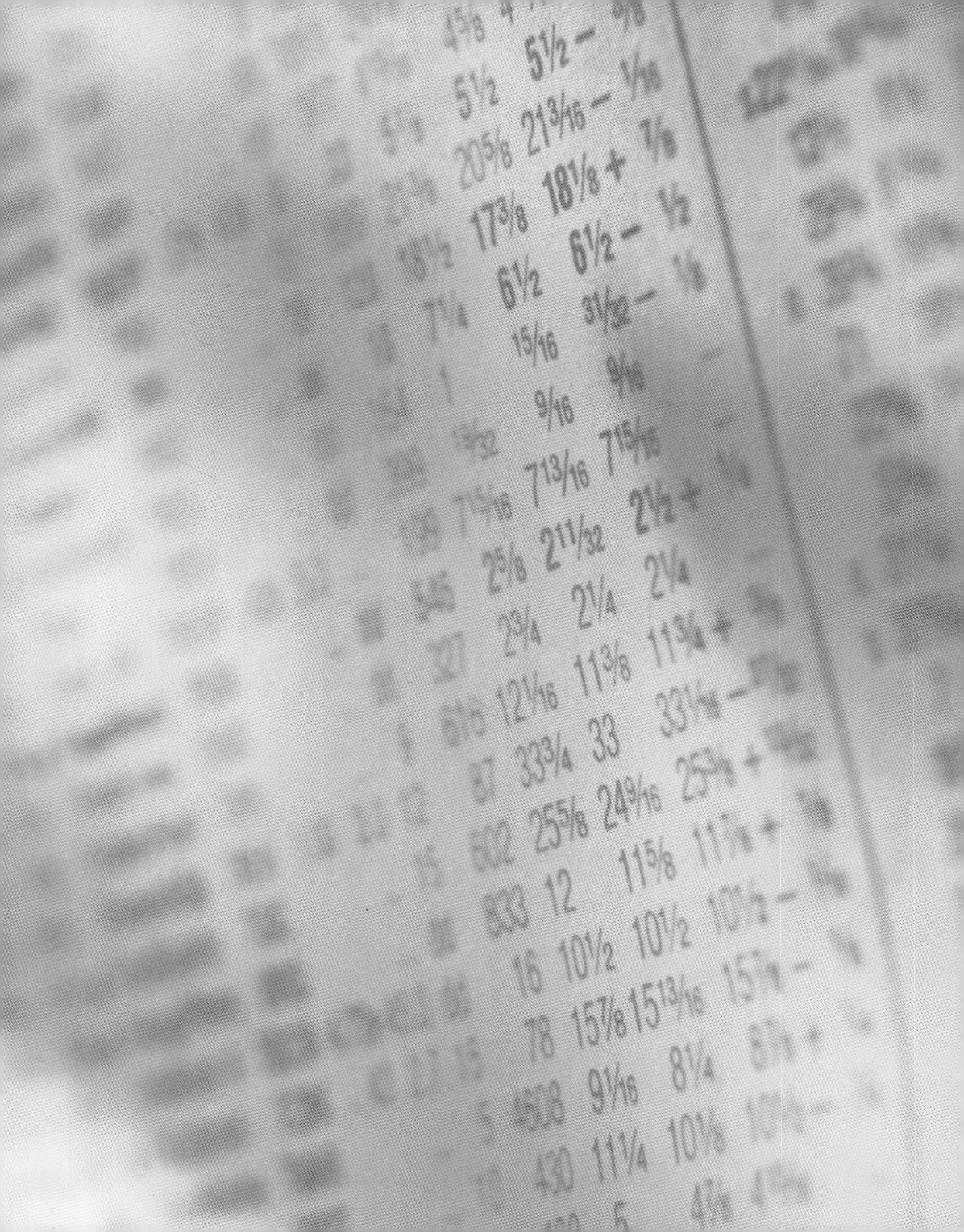

COMPETITIVE STRATEGY: THE CORE CONCEPTS

by Michael E. Porter

LEARNING OUTCOMES

The candidate should be able to:

a. analyze the competitive advantage and competitive strategy of a company and the competitive forces that affect the profitability of a company and discuss the two fundamental questions determining the choice of competitive strategy;

b. explain how competitive forces determine industry profitability;

c. analyze basic types of competitive advantage that a company can possess and the generic strategies for achieving a competitive advantage, the risks associated with each of the generic strategies, the difficulties and risks of simultaneously using more than one of the generic strategies, and the difficulties in sustaining a competitive advantage with any generic strategy;

d. explain the role of a generic strategy in the strategic planning process.

Competition is at the core of the success or failure of firms. Competition determines the appropriateness of a firm's activities that can contribute to its performance, such as innovations, a cohesive culture, or good implementation. Competitive strategy is the search for a favorable competitive position in an industry, the fundamental arena in which competition occurs. Competitive strategy aims to establish a profitable and sustainable position against the forces that determine industry competition.

Two central questions underlie the choice of competitive strategy. The first is the attractiveness of industries for long-term profitability and the factors that determine it. Not all industries offer equal opportunities for sustained profitability, and the inherent profitability of its industry is one essential ingredient in determining the profitability of a firm. The second central question in competitive strategy

Competitive Advantage: Creating and Sustaining Superior Performance, by Michael E. Porter. Copyright © 1985, 1998 by Michael E. Porter. Reprinted with permission of The Free Press, a division of Simon & Schuster Adult Publishing Group.

is the determinants of relative competitive position within an industry. In most industries, some firms are much more profitable than others, regardless of what the average profitability of the industry may be.

Neither question is sufficient by itself to guide the choice of competitive strategy. A firm in a very attractive industry may still not earn attractive profits if it has chosen a poor competitive position. Conversely, a firm in an excellent competitive position may be in such a poor industry that it is not very profitable, and further efforts to enhance its position will be of little benefit.[1] Both questions are dynamic; industry attractiveness and competitive position change. Industries become more or less attractive over time, and competitive position reflects an unending battle among competitors. Even long periods of stability can be abruptly ended by competitive moves.

Both industry attractiveness and competitive position can be shaped by a firm, and this is what makes the choice of competitive strategy both challenging and exciting. While industry attractiveness is partly a reflection of factors over which a firm has little influence, competitive strategy has considerable power to make an industry more or less attractive. At the same time, a firm can clearly improve or erode its position within an industry through its choice of strategy. Competitive strategy, then, not only responds to the environment but also attempts to shape that environment in a firm's favor.

These two central questions in competitive strategy have been at the core of my research. My book *Competitive Strategy: Techniques for Analyzing Industries and Competitors* presents an analytical framework for understanding industries and competitors, and formulating an overall competitive strategy. It describes the five competitive forces that determine the attractiveness of an industry and their underlying causes, as well as how these forces change over time and can be influenced through strategy. It identifies three broad generic strategies for achieving competitive advantage. It also shows how to analyze competitors and to predict and influence their behavior, and how to map competitors into strategic groups and assess the most attractive positions in an industry. It then goes on to apply the framework to a range of important types of industry environments that I term *structural settings*, including fragmented industries, emerging industries, industries undergoing a transition to maturity, declining industries, and global industries. Finally, the book examines the important strategic decisions that occur in the context of an industry, including vertical integration, capacity expansion, and entry.

––––––––––––––

[1] Many strategic planning concepts have ignored industry attractiveness and stressed the pursuit of market share, often a recipe for pyrrhic victories. The winner in a fight for share in an unattractive industry may not be profitable, and the fight itself may make industry structure worse or erode the winner's profitability. Other planning concepts associate stalemates, or inability to get ahead of competitors, with unattractive profits. In fact, stalemates can be quite profitable in attractive industries.

My aim is to build a bridge between strategy and implementation, rather than treat these two subjects independently or consider implementation scarcely at all as has been characteristic of much previous research in the field.

Competitive advantage grows fundamentally out of value a firm is able to create for its buyers that exceeds the firm's cost of creating it. Value is what buyers are willing to pay, and superior value stems from offering lower prices than competitors for equivalent benefits or providing unique benefits that more than offset a higher price. There are two basic types of competitive advantage: cost leadership and differentiation. Competitive advantage in one industry can be strongly enhanced by interrelationships with business units competing in related industries, if these interrelationships can actually be achieved. Interrelationships among business units are the principal means by which a diversified firm creates value, and thus provide the underpinnings for corporate strategy.

This reading assumes an understanding of industry structure and competitor behavior, and is preoccupied with how to translate that understanding into a competitive advantage. Actions to create competitive advantage often have important consequences for industry structure and competitive reaction.

In this reading, I will describe and elaborate on some core concepts. In the process, I will address some of the most important questions that arise in applying the core concepts in practice. Thus even readers familiar with my earlier book may find the review of interest.

THE STRUCTURAL ANALYSIS OF INDUSTRIES   1

The first fundamental determinant of a firm's profitability is industry attractiveness. Competitive strategy must grow out of a sophisticated understanding of the rules of competition that determine an industry's attractiveness. The ultimate aim of competitive strategy is to cope with and, ideally, to change those rules in the firm's favor. In any industry, whether it is domestic or international or produces a product or a service,[2] the rules of competition are embodied in five competitive forces: the entry of new competitors, the threat of substitutes, the bargaining power of buyers, the bargaining power of suppliers, and the rivalry among the existing competitors (see Figure 1).

The collective strength of these five competitive forces determines the ability of firms in an industry to earn, on average, rates of return on investment in excess of the cost of capital. The strength of the five forces varies from industry to industry, and can change as an industry evolves. The result is that all industries are not alike from the standpoint of inherent profitability. In industries where the five forces are favorable, such as pharmaceuticals, soft drinks, and data base publishing, many competitors earn attractive returns. But in industries where pressure

---

[2] These concepts apply equally to products and services. I will use the term "product" in the generic sense throughout this reading to refer to both product and service industries.

**FIGURE 1   The Five Competitive Forces that
Determine Industry Profitability**

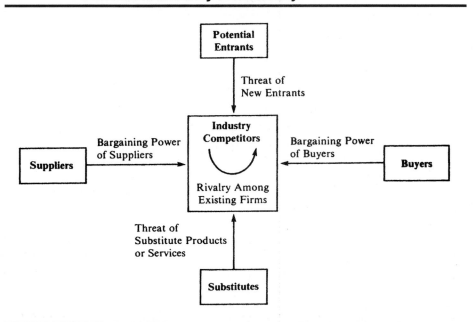

from one or more of the forces is intense, such as rubber, steel, and video games, few firms command attractive returns despite the best efforts of management. Industry profitability is not a function of what the product looks like or whether it embodies high or low technology, but of industry structure. Some very mundane industries such as postage meters and grain trading are extremely profitable, while some more glamorous, high-technology industries such as personal computers and cable television are not profitable for many participants.

The five forces determine industry profitability because they influence the prices, costs, and required investment of firms in an industry—the elements of return on investment. Buyer power influences the prices that firms can charge, for example, as does the threat of substitution. The power of buyers can also influence cost and investment, because powerful buyers demand costly service. The bargaining power of suppliers determines the costs of raw materials and other inputs. The intensity of rivalry influences prices as well as the costs of competing in areas such as plant, product development, advertising, and sales force. The threat of entry places a limit on prices, and shapes the investment required to deter entrants.

The strength of each of the five competitive forces is a function of *industry structure*, or the underlying economic and technical characteristics of an industry. Its important elements are shown in Figure 2. Industry structure is relatively stable, but can change over time as an industry evolves. **Structural change** shifts the overall and relative strength of the competitive forces, and can thus positively or negatively influence industry profitability. The industry trends that are the most important for strategy are those that affect industry structure.

If the five competitive forces and their structural determinants were solely a function of intrinsic industry characteristics, then competitive strategy would rest heavily on picking the right industry and understanding the five forces better than competitors. But while these are surely important tasks for any firm, and are the essence of competitive strategy in some industries, a firm is usually not a

FIGURE 2   Elements of Industry Structure

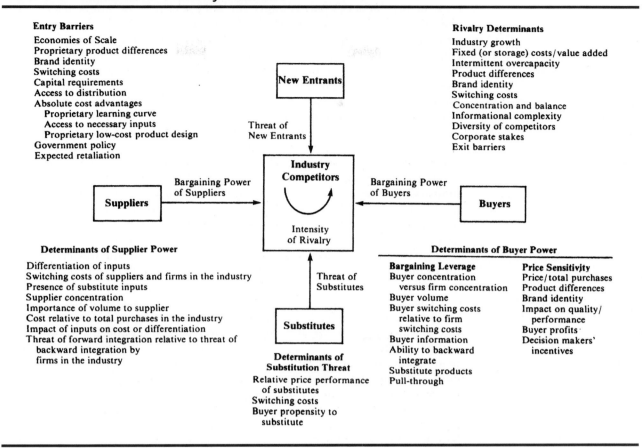

Entry Barriers

Economies of Scale
Proprietary product differences
Brand identity
Switching costs
Capital requirements
Access to distribution
Absolute cost advantages
   Proprietary learning curve
   Access to necessary inputs
   Proprietary low-cost product design
Government policy
Expected retaliation

Rivalry Determinants

Industry growth
Fixed (or storage) costs/value added
Intermittent overcapacity
Product differences
Brand identity
Switching costs
Concentration and balance
Informational complexity
Diversity of competitors
Corporate stakes
Exit barriers

New Entrants

Threat of
New Entrants

Bargaining Power
of Suppliers

Suppliers

**Industry
Competitors**

Intensity
of Rivalry

Bargaining Power
of Buyers

Buyers

Determinants of Supplier Power

Differentiation of inputs
Switching costs of suppliers and firms in the industry
Presence of substitute inputs
Supplier concentration
Importance of volume to supplier
Cost relative to total purchases in the industry
Impact of inputs on cost or differentiation
Threat of forward integration relative to threat of
   backward integration by
   firms in the industry

Threat of
Substitutes

Substitutes

**Determinants of
Substitution Threat**

Relative price performance
  of substitutes
Switching costs
Buyer propensity to
  substitute

Determinants of Buyer Power

Bargaining Leverage	**Price Sensitivity**
Buyer concentration versus firm concentration	Price/total purchases
Buyer volume	Product differences
Buyer switching costs relative to firm switching costs	Brand identity
Buyer information	Impact on quality/performance
Ability to backward integrate	Buyer profits
Substitute products	Decision makers' incentives
Pull-through	

prisoner of its industry's structure. Firms, through their strategies, can influence the five forces. If a firm can shape structure, it can fundamentally change an industry's attractiveness for better or for worse. Many successful strategies have shifted the rules of competition in this way.

Figure 2 highlights all the elements of industry structure that may drive competition in an industry. In any particular industry, not all of the five forces will be equally important and the particular structural factors that are important will differ. Every industry is unique and has its own unique structure. The five-forces framework allows a firm to see through the complexity and pinpoint those factors that are critical to competition in its industry, as well as to identify those strategic innovations that would most improve the industry's—and its own—profitability. The five-forces framework does not eliminate the need for creativity in finding new ways of competing in an industry. Instead, it directs managers' creative energies toward those aspects of industry structure that are most important to long-run profitability. The framework aims, in the process, to raise the odds of discovering a desirable strategic innovation.

Strategies that change industry structure can be a double-edged sword, because a firm can destroy industry structure and profitability as readily as it can improve it. A new product design that undercuts entry barriers or increases the volatility of rivalry, for example, may undermine the long-run profitability of an industry, though the initiator may enjoy higher profits temporarily. Or a sustained period of price cutting can undermine differentiation. In the tobacco industry, for example, generic cigarettes are a potentially serious threat to industry structure. Generics may enhance the price sensitivity of buyers, trigger price competition, and erode the high advertising barriers that have kept out new entrants.[3] Joint ventures entered into by major aluminum producers to spread risk and lower capital cost may have similarly undermined industry structure. The majors invited a number of potentially dangerous new competitors into the industry and helped them overcome the significant entry barriers to doing so. Joint ventures also can raise exit barriers because all the participants in a plant must agree before it can be closed down.

Often firms make strategic choices without considering the long-term consequences for industry structure. They see a gain in their competitive position if a move is successful, but they fail to anticipate the consequences of competitive reaction. If imitation of a move by major competitors has the effect of wrecking industry structure, then everyone is worse off. Such industry "destroyers" are usually second-tier firms that are searching for ways to overcome major competitive disadvantages, firms that have encountered serious problems and are desperately seeking solutions, or "dumb" competitors that do not know their costs or have unrealistic assumptions about the future. In the tobacco industry, for example, the Liggett Group (a distant follower) has encouraged the trend toward generics.

The ability of firms to shape industry structure places a particular burden on industry leaders. Leaders' actions can have a disproportionate impact on structure, because of their size and influence over buyers, suppliers, and other competitors. At the same time, leaders' large market shares guarantee that anything that changes overall industry structure will affect them as well. A leader, then, must constantly balance its own competitive position against the health of the industry as a whole. Often leaders are better off taking actions to improve or protect industry structure rather than seeking greater competitive advantage for themselves. Such industry leaders as Coca-Cola and Campbell's Soup appear to have followed this principle.

Industry Structure and Buyer Needs

It has often been said that satisfying buyer needs is at the core of success in business endeavor. How does this relate to the concept of industry structural analysis? Satisfying buyer needs is indeed a prerequisite to the viability of an industry and the firms within it. Buyers must be willing to pay a price for a product that exceeds its cost of production, or an industry will not survive in the long run. A firm can differentiate itself by satisfying buyer needs better than its competitors.

Satisfying buyer needs may be a prerequisite for industry profitability, but in itself is not sufficient. The crucial question in determining profitability is whether firms can capture the value they create for buyers, or whether this value is competed away to others. Industry structure determines who captures the value. The threat of entry determines the likelihood that new firms will enter an industry and compete away the value, either passing it on to buyers in the form of lower prices or dissipating it by raising the costs of competing. The power of buyers determines the extent to which they retain most of the value created for themselves, leaving firms in an industry only modest returns. The threat of substitutes determines the extent to which some other product can meet the same buyer needs, and thus places a ceiling on the amount a buyer is willing to pay for

---

[3] Generic products pose the same risks to many consumer good industries.

an industry's product. The power of suppliers determines the extent to which value created for buyers will be appropriated by suppliers rather than by firms in an industry. Finally, the intensity of rivalry acts similarly to the threat of entry. It determines the extent to which firms already in an industry will compete away the value they create for buyers among themselves, passing it on to buyers in lower prices or dissipating it in higher costs of competing.

Industry structure, then, determines who keeps what proportion of the value a product creates for buyers. If an industry's product does not create much value for its buyers, there is little value to be captured by firms regardless of the other elements of structure. If the product creates a lot of value, structure becomes crucial. In some industries such as automobiles and heavy trucks, firms create enormous value for their buyers but, on average, capture very little of it for themselves through profits. In other industries such as bond rating services, medical equipment, and oil field services and equipment, firms also create high value for their buyers but have historically captured a good proportion of it. In oil field services and equipment, for example, many products can significantly reduce the cost of drilling. Because industry structure has been favorable, many firms in the oil field service and equipment sector have been able to retain a share of these savings in the form of high returns. Recently, however, the structural attractiveness of many industries in the oil field services and equipment sector has eroded as a result of falling demand, new entrants, eroding product differentiation, and greater buyer price sensitivity. Despite the fact that products offered still create enormous value for the buyer, both firm and industry profits have fallen significantly.

Industry Structure and the Supply/Demand Balance

Another commonly held view about industry profitability is that profits are a function of the balance between supply and demand. If demand is greater than supply, this leads to high profitability. Yet, the long-term supply/demand balance is strongly influenced by industry structure, as are the consequences of a supply/demand imbalance for profitability. Hence, even though short-term fluctuations in supply and demand can affect short-term profitability, industry structure underlies long-term profitability.

Supply and demand change constantly, adjusting to each other. Industry structure determines how rapidly competitors add new supply. The height of entry barriers underpins the likelihood that new entrants will enter an industry and bid down prices. The intensity of rivalry plays a major role in determining whether existing firms will expand capacity aggressively or choose to maintain profitability. Industry structure also determines how rapidly competitors will retire excess supply. Exit barriers keep firms from leaving an industry when there is too much capacity, and prolong periods of excess capacity. In oil tanker shipping, for example, the exit barriers are very high because of the specialization of assets. This has translated into short peaks and long troughs of prices. Thus industry structure shapes the supply/demand balance and the duration of imbalances.

The consequences of an imbalance between supply and demand for industry profitability also differs widely depending on industry structure. In some industries, a small amount of excess capacity triggers **price wars** and low profitability. These are industries where there are structural pressures for intense rivalry or powerful buyers. In other industries, periods of excess capacity have relatively little impact on profitability because of favorable structure. In oil tools, ball valves, and many other oil field equipment products, for example, there has been intense price cutting during the recent sharp downturn. In drill bits, however, there has been relatively little discounting. Hughes Tool, Smith International, and Baker International are good competitors operating in a favorable industry structure. Industry structure also determines the profitability of excess demand. In a boom, for example, favorable structure allows firms to reap extraordinary profits, while a poor structure restricts the ability to capitalize on it. The presence of powerful suppliers or the presence of substitutes, for example, can mean that the fruits of a boom pass to others. Thus industry structure is fundamental to both the speed of adjustment of supply to demand and the relationship between capacity utilization and profitability.

2   GENERIC COMPETITIVE STRATEGIES

The second central question in competitive strategy is a firm's relative position within its industry. Positioning determines whether a firm's profitability is above or below the industry average. A firm that can position itself well may earn high rates of return even though industry structure is unfavorable and the average profitability of the industry is therefore modest.

The fundamental basis of above-average performance in the long run is *sustainable competitive advantage.*[4] Though a firm can have a myriad of strengths and weaknesses vis-à-vis its competitors, there are two basic types of competitive advantage a firm can possess: low cost or differentiation. The significance of any strength or weakness a firm possesses is ultimately a function of its impact on relative cost or differentiation. Cost advantage and differentiation in turn stem from industry structure. They result from a firm's ability to cope with the five forces better than its rivals.

The two basic types of competitive advantage combined with the scope of activities for which a firm seeks to achieve them lead to three *generic strategies* for achieving above-average performance in an industry: cost leadership, differentiation, and focus. The focus strategy has two variants, cost focus and differentiation focus. The generic strategies are shown in Figure 3.

Each of the generic strategies involves a fundamentally different route to competitive advantage, combining a choice about the type of competitive advantage sought with the scope of the strategic target in which competitive advantage is to be achieved. The cost leadership and differentiation strategies seek competitive advantage in a broad range of industry segments, while focus strategies aim at cost advantage (cost focus) or differentiation (differentiation focus) in a narrow segment. The specific actions required to implement each generic strategy vary widely from industry to industry, as do the feasible generic strategies in a particular industry. While selecting and implementing a generic strategy is far from simple, however, they are the logical routes to competitive advantage that must be probed in any industry.

The notion underlying the concept of generic strategies is that competitive advantage is at the heart of any strategy, and achieving competitive advantage requires a firm to make a choice—if a firm is to attain a competitive advantage, it must make a choice about the type of competitive advantage it seeks to attain and the scope within which it will attain it. Being "all things to all people" is a recipe for strategic mediocrity and below-average performance, because it often means that a firm has no competitive advantage at all.

---

[4] Without a sustainable competitive advantage, above-average performance is usually a sign of harvesting.

FIGURE 3   Three Generic Strategies

COMPETITIVE ADVANTAGE

	Lower Cost	Differentiation
Broad Target	1. Cost Leadership	2. Differentiation
Narrow Target	3A. Cost Focus	3B. Differentiation Focus

COMPETITIVE SCOPE

Cost Leadership

Cost leadership is perhaps the clearest of the three generic strategies. In it, a firm sets out to become *the* low-cost producer in its industry. The firm has a broad scope and serves many industry segments, and may even operate in related industries—the firm's breadth is often important to its cost advantage. The sources of cost advantage are varied and depend on the structure of the industry. They may include the pursuit of economies of scale, proprietary technology, preferential access to raw materials, and other factors. In TV sets, for example, cost leadership requires efficient size picture tube facilities, a low-cost design, automated assembly, and global scale over which to amortize R&D. In security guard services, cost advantage requires extremely low overhead, a plentiful source of low-cost labor, and efficient training procedures because of high turnover. Low-cost producer status involves more than just going down the learning curve. A low-cost producer must find and exploit all sources of cost advantage. Low-cost producers typically sell a standard, or no-frills, product and place considerable emphasis on reaping scale or absolute cost advantages from all sources.

If a firm can achieve and sustain overall cost leadership, then it will be an above-average performer in its industry provided it can command prices at or near the industry average. At equivalent or lower prices than its rivals, a cost leader's low-cost position translates into higher returns. A cost leader, however, cannot ignore the bases of differentiation. If its product is not perceived as comparable or acceptable by buyers, a cost leader will be forced to discount prices well below competitors' to gain sales. This may nullify the benefits of its favorable cost position. Texas Instruments (in watches) and Northwest Airlines (in air transportation) are two low-cost firms that fell into this trap. Texas Instruments could not overcome its disadvantage in differentiation and exited the watch industry. Northwest Airlines recognized its problem in time, and has instituted efforts to improve marketing, passenger service, and service to travel agents to make its product more comparable to those of its competitors.

A cost leader must achieve *parity* or *proximity* in the bases of differentiation relative to its competitors to be an above-average performer, even though it relies on cost leadership for its competitive advantage. Parity in the bases of differentiation allows a cost leader to translate its cost advantage directly into higher profits than competitors'.[5] Proximity in differentiation means that the price discount necessary to achieve an acceptable market share does not offset a cost leader's cost advantage and hence the cost leader earns above-average returns.

The strategic logic of cost leadership usually requires that a firm be *the* cost leader, not one of several firms vying for this position.[6] Many firms have made serious strategic errors by failing to recognize this. When there is more than one aspiring cost leader, rivalry among them is usually fierce because every point of market share is viewed as crucial. Unless one firm can gain a cost lead and "persuade" others to abandon their strategies, the consequences for profitability (and long-run industry structure) can be disastrous, as has been the case in a number of petrochemical industries. Thus cost leadership is a strategy particularly dependent on preemption, unless major technological change allows a firm to radically change its cost position.

Differentiation

The second generic strategy is differentiation. In a differentiation strategy, a firm seeks to be unique in its industry along some dimensions that are widely valued by buyers. It selects one or more attributes that many buyers in an industry perceive as important, and uniquely positions itself to meet those needs. It is rewarded for its uniqueness with a premium price.

The means for differentiation are peculiar to each industry. Differentiation can be based on the product itself, the delivery system by which it is sold, the marketing approach, and a broad range of other factors. In construction equipment, for example, Caterpillar Tractor's differentiation is based on product durability, service, spare parts availability, and an excellent dealer network. In cosmetics, differentiation tends to be based more on product image and the positioning of counters in the stores.

A firm that can achieve and sustain differentiation will be an above-average performer in its industry if its price premium exceeds the extra costs incurred in being unique. A differentiator, therefore, must always seek ways of differentiating that lead to a price premium greater than the cost of differentiating. A differentiator cannot ignore its cost position, because its premium prices will be nullified by a markedly inferior cost position. A differentiator thus aims at cost *parity* or *proximity* relative to its competitors, by reducing cost in all areas that do not affect differentiation.

The logic of the differentiation strategy requires that a firm choose attributes in which to differentiate itself that are *different* from its rivals'. A firm must truly be unique at something or be perceived as unique if it is to expect a premium price. In contrast to cost leadership, however, there can be more than one successful differentiation strategy in an industry if there are a number of attributes that are widely valued by buyers.

---

[5] Parity implies either an identical product offering to competitors, or a different combination of product attributes that is equally preferred by buyers.

[6] While the cost leader will be the most profitable, it is not necessary to be the cost leader to sustain above-average returns in commodity industries where there are limited opportunities to build efficient capacity. A firm that is in the lowest quartile of costs though not the cost leader will usually still be an above-average performer. Such a situation exists in the aluminum industry, where the ability to add low-cost capacity is limited by access to low-cost power, bauxite, and infrastructure.

Focus

The third generic strategy is focus. This strategy is quite different from the others because it rests on the choice of a narrow competitive scope within an industry. The focuser selects a segment or group of segments in the industry and tailors its strategy to serving them to the exclusion of others. By optimizing its strategy for the target segments, the focuser seeks to achieve a competitive advantage in its target segments even though it does not possess a competitive advantage overall.

The focus strategy has two variants. In *cost focus* a firm seeks a cost advantage in its target segment, while in *differentiation focus* a firm seeks differentiation in its target segment. Both variants of the focus strategy rest on *differences* between a focuser's target segments and other segments in the industry. The target segments must either have buyers with unusual needs or else the production and delivery system that best serves the target segment must differ from that of other industry segments. Cost focus exploits differences in cost behavior in some segments, while differentiation focus exploits the special needs of buyers in certain segments. Such differences imply that the segments are poorly served by broadly-targeted competitors who serve them at the same time as they serve others. The focuser can thus achieve competitive advantage by dedicating itself to the segments exclusively. Breadth of target is clearly a matter of degree, but the essence of focus is the exploitation of a narrow target's differences from the balance of the industry.[7] Narrow focus in and of itself is not sufficient for above-average performance.

A good example of a focuser who has exploited differences in the production process that best serves different segments is Hammermill Paper. Hammermill has increasingly been moving toward relatively low-volume, high-quality specialty papers, where the larger paper companies with higher volume machines face a stiff cost penalty for short production runs. Hammermill's equipment is more suited to shorter runs with frequent setups.

A focuser takes advantage of suboptimization in either direction by broadly-targeted competitors. Competitors may be *underperforming* in meeting the needs of a particular segment, which opens the possibility for differentiation focus. Broadly-targeted competitors may also be *overperforming* in meeting the needs of a segment, which means that they are bearing higher than necessary cost in serving it. An opportunity for cost focus may be present in just meeting the needs of such a segment and no more.

If a focuser's target segment is not different from other segments, then the focus strategy will not succeed. In soft drinks, for example, Royal Crown has focused on cola drinks, while Coca-Cola and Pepsi have broad product lines with many flavored drinks. Royal Crown's segment, however, can be well served by Coke and Pepsi at the same time they are serving other segments. Hence Coke and Pepsi enjoy competitive advantages over Royal Crown in the cola segment due to the economies of having a broader line.

If a firm can achieve sustainable cost leadership (cost focus) or differentiation (differentiation focus) in its segment and the segment is structurally attractive, then the focuser will be an above-average performer in its industry. Segment structural attractiveness is a necessary condition because some segments in an industry are much less profitable than others. There is often room for several sustainable focus strategies in an industry, provided that focusers

---

[7] Overall differentiation and differentiation focus are perhaps the most often confused strategies in practice. The difference is that the overall differentiator bases its strategy on widely valued attributes (e.g., IBM in computers), while the differentiation focuser looks for segments with special needs and meets them better (e.g., Cray Research in computers).

choose different target segments. Most industries have a variety of segments, and each one that involves a different buyer need or a different optimal production or delivery system is a candidate for a focus strategy.

Stuck in the Middle

A firm that engages in each generic strategy but fails to achieve any of them is "stuck in the middle." It possesses no competitive advantage. This strategic position is usually a recipe for below-average performance. A firm that is stuck in the middle will compete at a disadvantage because the cost leader, differentiators, or focusers will be better positioned to compete in any segment. If a firm that is stuck in the middle is lucky enough to discover a profitable product or buyer, competitors with a sustainable competitive advantage will quickly eliminate the spoils. In most industries, quite a few competitors are stuck in the middle.

A firm that is stuck in the middle will earn attractive profits only if the structure of its industry is highly favorable, or if the firm is fortunate enough to have competitors that are also stuck in the middle. Usually, however, such a firm will be much less profitable than rivals achieving one of the generic strategies. Industry maturity tends to widen the performance differences between firms with a generic strategy and those that are stuck in the middle, because it exposes ill-conceived strategies that have been carried along by rapid growth.

Becoming stuck in the middle is often a manifestation of a firm's unwillingness to make *choices* about how to compete. It tries for competitive advantage through every means and achieves none, because achieving different types of competitive advantage usually requires inconsistent actions. Becoming stuck in the middle also afflicts successful firms, who compromise their generic strategy for the sake of growth or prestige. A classic example is Laker Airways, which began with a clear cost-focus strategy based on no-frills operation in the North Atlantic market, aimed at a particular segment of the traveling public that was extremely price-sensitive. Over time, however, Laker began adding frills, new services, and new routes. It blurred its image, and suboptimized its service and delivery system. The consequences were disastrous, and Laker eventually went bankrupt.

The temptation to blur a generic strategy, and therefore become stuck in the middle, is particularly great for a focuser once it has dominated its target segments. Focus involves deliberately limiting potential sales volume. Success can lead a focuser to lose sight of the reasons for its success and compromise its focus strategy for growth's sake. Rather than compromise its generic strategy, a firm is usually better off finding new industries in which to grow where it can use its generic strategy again or exploit interrelationships.

Pursuit of More than One Generic Strategy

Each generic strategy is a fundamentally different approach to creating and sustaining a competitive advantage, combining the type of competitive advantage a firm seeks and the scope of its strategic target. Usually a firm must make a choice among them, or it will become stuck in the middle. The benefits of optimizing the firm's strategy for a particular target segment (focus) cannot be gained if a firm is simultaneously serving a broad range of segments (cost leadership or differentiation). Sometimes a firm may be able to create two largely separate business units within the same corporate entity, each with a different generic strategy. A good example is the British hotel firm Trusthouse Forte, which operates five separate hotel chains each targeted at a different segment. However, unless a firm strictly separates the units pursuing different generic strategies, it may compromise the ability of any of them to achieve its competitive advantage. A suboptimized approach to competing, made likely by the spillover among units of corporate policies and culture, will lead to becoming stuck in the middle.

Achieving cost leadership and differentiation are also usually inconsistent, because differentiation is usually costly. To be unique and command a price premium, a differentiator deliberately elevates costs, as Caterpillar has done in construction equipment. Conversely, cost leadership often requires a firm to forego some differentiation by standardizing its product, reducing marketing overhead, and the like.

Reducing cost does not always involve a sacrifice in differentiation. Many firms have discovered ways to reduce cost not only without hurting their differentiation but while actually raising it, by using practices that are both more efficient and effective or employing a different technology. Sometimes dramatic cost savings can be achieved with no impact on differentiation at all if a firm has not concentrated on cost reduction previously. However, cost reduction is not the same as achieving a cost advantage. When faced with capable competitors also striving for cost leadership, a firm will ultimately reach the point where further cost reduction requires a sacrifice in differentiation. It is at this point that the generic strategies become inconsistent and a firm must make a choice.

If a firm can achieve cost leadership and differentiation simultaneously, the rewards are great because the benefits are additive—differentiation leads to premium prices at the same time that cost leadership implies lower costs. An example of a firm that has achieved both a cost advantage and differentiation in its segments is Crown Cork and Seal in the metal container industry. Crown has targeted the so-called "hard to hold" uses of cans in the beer, soft drink, and aerosol industries. It manufactures only steel cans rather than both steel and aluminum. In its target segments, Crown has differentiated itself based on service, technological assistance, and offering a full line of steel cans, crowns, and canning machinery. Differentiation of this type would be much more difficult to achieve in other industry segments which have different needs. At the same time, Crown has dedicated its facilities to producing only the types of cans demanded by buyers in its chosen segments and has aggressively invested in modern two-piece steel canning technology. As a result, Crown has probably also achieved low-cost producer status in its segments.

There are three conditions under which a firm can simultaneously achieve both cost leadership and differentiation:

Competitors are stuck in the middle. Where competitors are stuck in the middle, none is well enough positioned to force a firm to the point where cost and differentiation become inconsistent. This was the case with Crown Cork. Its major competitors were not investing in low-cost steel can production technology, so Crown achieved cost leadership without having to sacrifice differentiation in the process. Were its competitors pursuing an aggressive cost leadership strategy, however, an attempt by Crown to be both low-cost and differentiated might have doomed it to becoming stuck in the middle. Cost reduction opportunities that did not sacrifice differentiation would have already been adopted by Crown's competitors.

While stuck-in-the-middle competitors can allow a firm to achieve both differentiation and low cost, this state of affairs is often temporary. Eventually a competitor will choose a generic strategy and begin to implement it well, exposing the tradeoffs between cost and differentiation. Thus a firm must choose the type of competitive advantage it intends to preserve in the long run. The danger in facing weak competitors is that a firm will begin to compromise its cost position or differentiation to achieve both and leave itself vulnerable to the emergence of a capable competitor.

Cost is strongly affected by share or interrelationships. Cost leadership and differentiation may also be achieved simultaneously where cost position is heavily determined by market share, rather than by product design, level of technology, service provided, or other factors. If one firm can open up a big market share advantage, the cost advantages of share in some activities allow the firm to incur added costs elsewhere and still maintain net cost leadership, or share reduces the cost of differentiating relative to competitors. In a related situation, cost leadership and differentiation can be achieved at the same time when there are important interrelationships between industries that one competitor can exploit and others cannot. Unmatched interrelationships can lower the cost of differentiation or offset the higher cost of differentiation. Nonetheless, simultaneous pursuit of cost leadership and differentiation is always vulnerable to capable competitors who make a choice and invest aggressively to implement it, matching the share or interrelationship.

A firm pioneers a major innovation. Introducing a significant technological innovation can allow a firm to lower cost and enhance differentiation at the same time, and perhaps achieve both strategies. Introducing new automated manufacturing technologies can have this effect, as can the introduction of new information system technology to manage logistics or design products on the computer. Innovative new practices unconnected to technology can also have this effect. Forging cooperative relations with suppliers can lower input costs and improve input quality, for example.

The ability to be both low cost and differentiated is a function of being the *only* firm with the new innovation, however. Once competitors also introduce the innovation, the firm is again in the position of having to make a tradeoff. Will its information system be designed to emphasize cost or differentiation, for example, compared to the competitor's information system? The pioneer may be at a disadvantage if, in the pursuit of both low cost and differentiation, its innovation has not recognized the possibility of imitation. It may then be neither low cost nor differentiated once the innovation is matched by competitors who pick one generic strategy.

A firm should always aggressively pursue all cost reduction opportunities that do not sacrifice differentiation. A firm should also pursue all differentiation opportunities that are not costly. Beyond this point, however, a firm should be prepared to choose what its ultimate competitive advantage will be and resolve the tradeoffs accordingly.

Sustainability

A generic strategy does not lead to above-average performance unless it is sustainable vis-à-vis competitors, though actions that improve industry structure may improve industrywide profitability even if they are imitated. The sustainability of the three generic strategies demands that a firm's competitive advantage resists erosion by competitor behavior or industry evolution. Each generic strategy involves different risks which are shown in Table 1.

The sustainability of a generic strategy requires that a firm possess some barriers that make imitation of the strategy difficult. Since barriers to imitation are never insurmountable, however, it is usually necessary for a firm to offer a moving target to its competitors by investing in order to continually improve its position. Each generic strategy is also a potential threat to the others—as Table 1 shows, for example, focusers must worry about broadly-targeted competitors and vice versa.

TABLE 1   Risks of the Generic Strategies

Risks of Cost Leadership	Risks of Differentiation	Risks of Focus
Cost leadership is not sustained ▶ competitors imitate ▶ technology changes ▶ other bases for cost leadership erode	Differentiation is not sustained ▶ competitors imitate ▶ bases for differentiation become less important to buyers	The focus strategy is imitated The target segment becomes structurally unattractive ▶ structure erodes ▶ demand disappears
Proximity in differentiation is lost	Cost proximity is lost	Broadly-targeted competitors overwhelm the segment ▶ the segment's differences from other segments narrow ▶ the advantages of a broad line increase
Cost focusers achieve even lower cost in segments	Differentiation focusers achieve even greater differentiation in segments	New focusers sub-segment the industry

Table 1 can be used to analyze how to attack a competitor that employs any of the generic strategies. A firm pursuing overall differentiation, for example, can be attacked by firms who open up a large cost gap, narrow the extent of differentiation, shift the differentiation desired by buyers to other dimensions, or focus. Each generic strategy is vulnerable to different types of attacks.

In some industries, industry structure or the strategies of competitors eliminate the possibility of achieving one or more of the generic strategies. Occasionally no feasible way for one firm to gain a significant cost advantage exists, for example, because several firms are equally placed with respect to scale economies, access to raw materials, or other cost drivers. Similarly, an industry with few segments or only minor differences among segments, such as low-density polyethylene, may offer few opportunities for focus. Thus the mix of generic strategies will vary from industry to industry.

In many industries, however, the three generic strategies can profitably coexist as long as firms pursue different ones or select different bases for differentiation or focus. Industries in which several strong firms are pursuing differentiation strategies based on different sources of buyer value are often particulary profitable. This tends to improve industry structure and lead to stable industry competition. If two or more firms choose to pursue the same generic strategy on the same basis, however, the result can be a protracted and unprofitable battle. The worst situation is where several firms are vying for overall cost leadership. The past and present choice of generic strategies by competitors, then, has an impact on the choices available to a firm and the cost of changing its position.

The concept of generic strategies is based on the premise that there are a number of ways in which competitive advantage can be achieved, depending on industry structure. If all firms in an industry followed the principles of competitive strategy, each would pick different bases for competitive advantage. While not all would succeed, the generic strategies provide alternate routes to superior performance. Some strategic planning concepts have been narrowly based on only one route to competitive advantage, most notably cost. Such concepts not only fail to explain the success of many firms, but they can also lead all firms in an industry to pursue the same type of competitive advantage in the same way—with predictably disastrous results.

Generic Strategies and Industry Evolution

Changes in industry structure can affect the bases on which generic strategies are built and thus alter the balance among them. For example, the advent of electronic controls and new image developing systems has greatly eroded the importance of service as a basis for differentiation in copiers. Structural change creates many of the risks shown in Table 1.[8]

Structural change can shift the relative balance among the generic strategies in an industry, since it can alter the sustainability of a generic strategy or the size of the competitive advantage that results from it. The automobile industry provides a good example. Early in its history, leading automobile firms followed differentiation strategies in the production of expensive touring cars. Technological and market changes created the potential for Henry Ford to change the rules of competition by adopting a classic overall cost leadership strategy, based on low-cost production of a standard model sold at low prices. Ford rapidly dominated the industry worldwide. By the late 1920s, however, economic growth, growing familiarity with the automobile, and technological change had created the potential for General Motors to change the rules once more—it employed a differentiation strategy based on a wide line, features, and premium prices. Throughout this evolution, focused competitors also continued to succeed.

Another long-term battle among generic strategies has occurred in general merchandising. K Mart and other discounters entered with cost leadership strategies against Sears and conventional department stores, featuring low overhead and nationally branded merchandise. K Mart, however, now faces competition from more differentiated discounters who sell fashion-oriented merchandise, such as Wal-Mart. At the same time, focused discounters have entered and are selling such products as sporting goods (Herman's), health and beauty aids (CVS), and books (Barnes and Noble). Catalog showrooms have also focused on appliances and jewelry, employing low-cost strategies in those segments. Thus the bases for K Mart's competitive advantage have been compromised and it is having difficulty outperforming the industry average.

Another more recent example of the jockeying among generic strategies has occurred in vodka. Smirnoff has long been the differentiated producer in the industry, based on early positioning as a highclass brand and heavy supporting advertising. As growth has slowed and the industry has become more competitive, however, private label vodkas and low price brands are undermining Smirnoff's position. At the same time, PepsiCo's Stolichnaya vodka has established an even more differentiated position than Smirnoff through focus. Smirnoff is caught in a squeeze that is threatening its long-standing superior performance. In response, it has introduced several new brands, including a premium brand positioned against Stolichnaya.

Generic Strategies and Organizational Structure

Each generic strategy implies different skills and requirements for success, which commonly translate into differences in organizational structure and culture. Cost leadership usually implies tight control systems, overhead minimization,

---

[8] Michael E. Porter, *Competitive Strategy*, (1998), Chapter 8, describes the processes that drive industry structural change.

pursuit of scale economies, and dedication to the learning curve; these could be counterproductive for a firm attempting to differentiate itself through a constant stream of creative new products.[9]

The organizational differences commonly implied by each generic strategy carry a number of implications. Just as there are often economic inconsistencies in achieving more than one generic strategy, a firm does not want its organizational structure to be suboptimal because it combines inconsistent practices. It has become fashionable to tie executive selection and motivation to the "mission" of a business unit, usually expressed in terms of building, holding, or harvesting market share. It is equally—if not more—important to match executive selection and motivation to the generic strategy being followed.

The concept of generic strategies also has implications for the role of culture in competitive success. Culture, that difficult to define set of norms and attitudes that help shape an organization, has come to be viewed as an important element of a successful firm. However, different cultures are implied by different generic strategies. Differentiation may be facilitated by a culture encouraging innovation, individuality, and risk-taking (Hewlett-Packard), while cost leadership may be facilitated by frugality, discipline, and attention to detail (Emerson Electric). Culture can powerfully reinforce the competitive advantage a generic strategy seeks to achieve, if the culture is an appropriate one. There is no such thing as a good or bad culture per se. Culture is a means of achieving competitive advantage, not an end in itself.

The link between generic strategy and organization also has implications for the diversified firm. There is a tendency for diversified firms to pursue the same generic strategy in many of their business units, because skills and confidence are developed for pursuing a particular approach to competitive advantage. Moreover, senior management often gains experience in overseeing a particular type of strategy. Emerson Electric is well known for its pursuit of cost leadership in many of its business units, for example, as is H. J. Heinz.

Competing with the same generic strategy in many business units is one way in which a diversified firm can add value to those units. However, employing a common generic strategy entails some risks that should be highlighted. One obvious risk is that a diversified firm will impose a particular generic strategy on a business unit whose industry (or initial position) will not support it. Another, more subtle risk is that a business unit will be misunderstood because of circumstances in its industry that are *not* consistent with the prevailing generic strategy. Worse yet, such business units may have their strategies undermined by senior management. Since each generic strategy often implies a different pattern of investments and different types of executives and cultures, there is a risk that a business unit that is "odd man out" will be forced to live with inappropriate corporate policies and targets. For example, an across-the-board cost reduction goal or firmwide personnel policies can be disadvantageous to a business unit attempting to differentiate itself on quality and service, just as policies toward overhead appropriate for differentiation can undermine a business unit attempting to be the low-cost producer.

Generic Strategies and the Strategic Planning Process

Given the pivotal role of competitive advantage in superior performance, the centerpiece of a firm's strategic plan should be its generic strategy. The generic strategy specifies the fundamental approach to competitive advantage a firm is

---

[9] A more detailed review of the differing skills required by each generic strategy is given in Michael E. Porter, *Competitive Strategy*, (1998), Chapter 2, pp. 40–41.

pursuing, and provides the context for the actions to be taken in each functional area. In practice, however, many strategic plans are lists of action steps without a clear articulation of what competitive advantage the firm has or seeks to achieve and how. Such plans are likely to have overlooked the fundamental purpose of competitive strategy in the process of going through the mechanics of planning. Similarly, many plans are built on projections of future prices and costs that are almost invariably wrong, rather than on a fundamental understanding of industry structure and competitive advantage that will determine profitability no matter what the actual prices and costs turn out to be.

As part of their strategic planning processes, many diversified firms categorize business units by using a system such as build, hold, or harvest. These categorizations are often used to describe or summarize the strategy of business units. While such categorizations may be useful in thinking about resource allocation in a diversified firm, it is very misleading to mistake them for strategies. A business unit's strategy is the route to competitive advantage that will determine its performance. Build, hold, and harvest are the results of a generic strategy, or recognition of the inability to achieve any generic strategy and hence of the need to harvest. Similarly, acquisition and vertical integration are not strategies but means of achieving them.

Another common practice in strategic planning is to use market share to describe a business unit's competitive position. Some firms go so far as to set the goal that all their business units should be leaders (number one or number two) in their industries. This approach to strategy is as dangerous as it is deceptively clear. While market share is certainly relevant to competitive position (due to scale economies, for example), industry leadership is *not a cause but an effect of competitive advantage*. Market share per se is not important competitively; competitive advantage is. The strategic mandate to business units should be to achieve competitive advantage. Pursuit of leadership for its own sake may guarantee that a firm never achieves a competitive advantage or that it loses the one it has. A goal of leadership per se also embroils managers in endless debates over how an industry should be defined to calculate shares, obscuring once more the search for competitive advantage that is the heart of strategy.

In some industries, market leaders do not enjoy the best performance because industry structure does not reward leadership. A recent example is Continental Illinois Bank, which adopted the explicit goal of market leadership in wholesale lending. It succeeded in achieving this goal, but leadership did not translate into competitive advantage. Instead, the drive for leadership led to making loans that other banks would not, and to escalating costs. Leadership also meant that Continental Illinois had to deal with large corporations that are extremely powerful and price-sensitive buyers of loans. Continental Illinois will be paying the price of leadership for some years. In many other firms, such as Burlington Industries in fabrics and Texas Instruments in electronics, the pursuit of leadership for its own sake seems to have sometimes diverted attention from achieving and maintaining competitive advantage.

PRACTICE PROBLEMS FOR READING 41

Duvalier Securities
Maxim Duvalier, CFA

International/Switzerland
Manufacturers
6 March 2006

JQC Industries (JQC)

Price–Local/ADR:	CHF36.05/$27.87
12-Month Price Target:	CHF42.50/$32.90

Only Time Will Tell?   **Accumulate**

Overview

We are upgrading our rating on JQC to "Accumulate" from "Hold" and increasing our price target to CHF42.50/$32.90 from CHF39.10/$30.25. JQC is a manufacturer of fine watches headquartered in Geneva, Switzerland. Our change in rating is based on four factors: JQC's development of a new product line, its expansion into China and India, strong growth in exports of Swiss watches, and consolidation occurring within the Swiss watch making industry. We estimate a long-term EPS growth rate of 10 percent annually. This reflects our expectation of 4 to 7 percent unit growth and operating margin improvement of 40–60 basis points.

Swiss Watch Industry

Swiss watchmakers' most serious competitors are Chinese and Hong Kong producers. The Swiss enjoy a worldwide reputation for quality and style. Although 80 percent of the approximately 500 million watches sold worldwide are made in China and Hong Kong, more than 50 percent of the sales value is generated by the Swiss watch industry.

In 2005, the watch industry was Switzerland's third largest exporter after the machine and chemical industries. Swiss watch exports are distributed mainly in three continents: Asia (43 percent), Europe (34 percent), and North America (21 percent). Sales and earnings have followed the overall economic growth of these primary export markets. Industry profits benefit from economic upturns but suffer in downturns. Assuming a 3.5 percent average real GDP growth and an inflation rate of 2.5 percent in their primary export markets, Duvalier Securities forecasts that sales will grow by 6 percent in 2006 in the industry's three primary export markets.

Based on an analysis of the underlying economic and technical characteristics of the Swiss watch making industry, we believe the primary determinant of industry profitability is high barriers to entry. In 1992, Switzerland passed a law regulating the use of the term "Swiss made" for watches. This law requires that the assembly work on the watch and its movement, as well as the final testing of the movement, be carried out in Switzerland. It also requires that at least 50 percent of the components of the movement be manufactured in Switzerland. As a result, the

"Swiss made" designation enjoys a solid reputation throughout the world and globalization of trade has not diminished its importance.

JQC's Industry Position

Three years ago, JQC hired renowned designer Luigi Gastón to be its president and chief executive officer because of his successful career in fashion design and extensive marketing experience. Gastón has implemented a differentiation strategy and concentrated the company's manufacturing and marketing efforts. At the same time, he has expanded and rejuvenated JQC's product line. Gastón's philosophy is that "a watch has to be more than just technically brilliant to sell; it has to be desirable, modern, and glamorous." As a result, he has launched fashionable new lines for both men and women. Both lines consist of watches targeted at the high-end, standard, and entry-level segments of the market.

---

1. Based on Duvalier's description, the Swiss watch making industry can *best* be described in terms of its industrial life cycle and business cycle reaction, respectively, as

	Industrial Life Cycle	Business Cycle Reaction
A.	Growth	Defensive
B.	Growth	Cyclical
C.	Mature	Defensive
D.	Mature	Cyclical

2. Duvalier's conclusion about the primary determinant of industry profitability in the Swiss watch making industry is *least likely* to be based on

A. brand identity.

B. switching costs.

C. expected retaliation.

D. supplier concentration.

3. The *most* appropriate conclusion is that the value implied by the premium prices of Swiss watches is likely to be

A. appropriated by suppliers.

B. dissipated by competition among Swiss watch makers.

C. dissipated by competition with non-Swiss watch makers.

D. kept by companies in the industry in the form of higher profits.

4. The structure of the Swiss watch industry could *most likely* influence the industry's balance between supply and demand by

A. reducing the likelihood of new entrants and lower prices.

B. increasing the likelihood that existing companies will expand capacity.

C. reducing the likelihood of prolonged periods of excess capacity as a result of companies leaving the industry.

D. increasing the likelihood that a small amount of excess capacity will trigger price wars and result in reduced profitability.

5. A risk that is *most likely* associated with JQC's competitive strategy is that

   A. cost proximity is lost.

   B. segmentation declines.

   C. switching costs increase.

   D. proximity in differentiation is lost.

6. The factors that have contributed *most* to the Swiss watch industry's profitability are

   A. government intervention and product segmentation.

   B. technological developments and product segmentation.

   C. government intervention and a high degree of industry concentration.

   D. technological developments and a high degree of industry concentration.

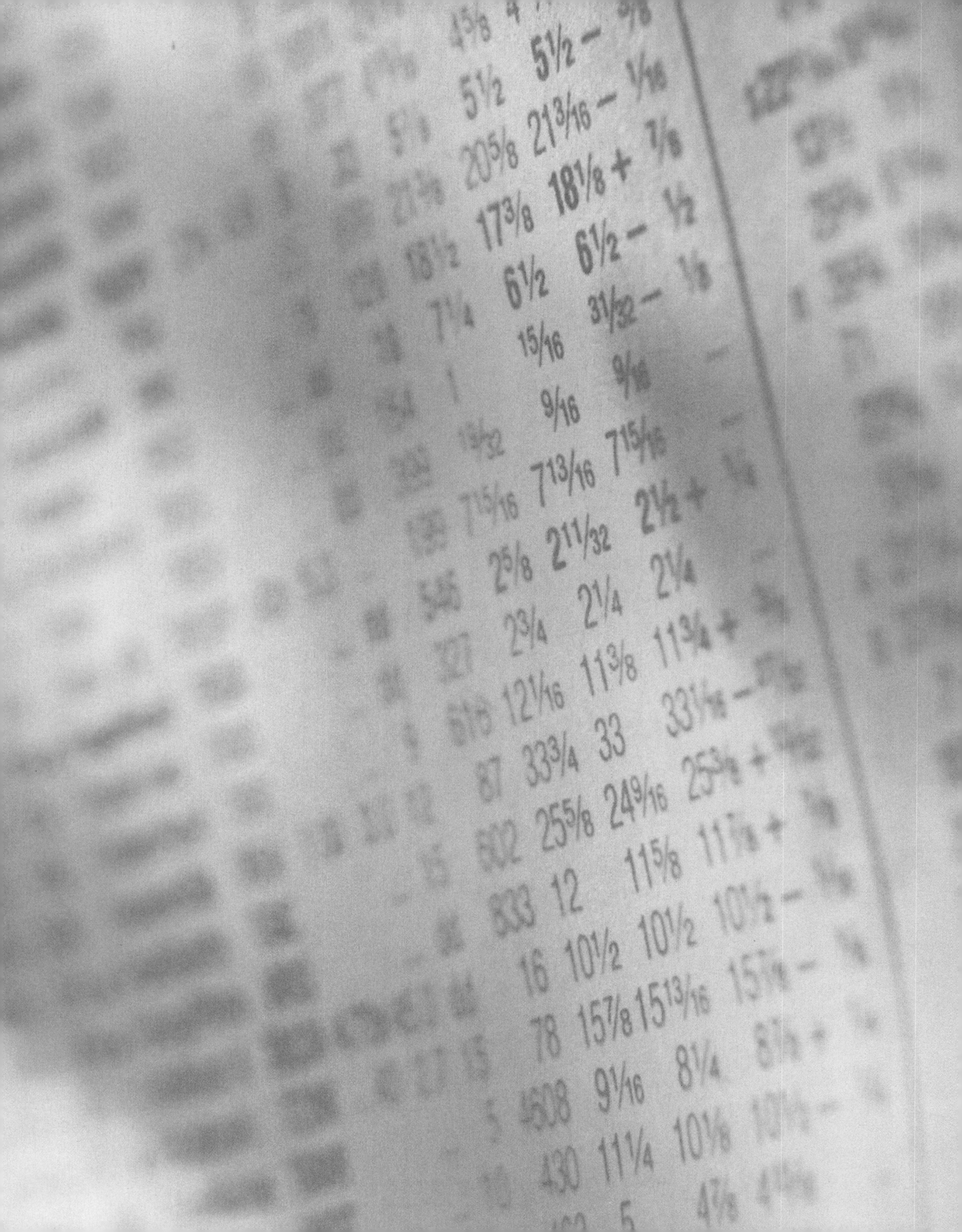

INDUSTRY ANALYSIS

by Jeffrey C. Hooke

LEARNING OUTCOMES

The candidate should be able to:

a. discuss the key components that should be included in an industry analysis model;

b. illustrate the life cycle of a typical industry;

c. analyze the effects of business cycles on industry classification (i.e., growth, defensive, cyclical);

d. analyze the impact of external factors (e.g., technology, government, foreign influences, demography, and social changes) on industries;

e. illustrate the inputs and methods used in preparing an industry demand-and-supply analysis;

f. explain factors that affect industry pricing practices.

The industry analysis is an important part of the research report. The proper organization of this analysis, the five principal themes of such a study and the common pitfalls of an industry evaluation are discussed herein.

In developing investment recommendations, the typical analyst begins serious research at the industry level. The analyst receives "top-down" economic and capital market forecasts from others. The initial responsibility is tying these macro parameters into an industry outlook, thus laying the groundwork for judging the prospects of selected participants. The fortunes of an individual company are closely intertwined with those of the industry in which it operates. An in-depth industry study is thus a prerequisite for a proper security analysis. A thorough understanding of the industry facilitates the evaluation process, and for this reason, many practitioners limit themselves to one or two industries. This reading

---

EXHIBIT 1	Model Research Report

1. Introduction

2. Macroeconomic Review

3. Relevant Stock Market Prospects

4. Review of the Company and Its Business ✔
    Industry Analysis ✔

5. Financial Analysis

6. Financial Projections

7. Application of Valuation Methodologies

8. Recommendation

---

reviews preparing an industry analysis, which is covered under Section 4 of the model research report (Exhibit 1).

1 BACKGROUND

Whatever outlook an analyst develops for a particular industry, not all companies have prospects mirroring the broader view. Some perform better than the general expectation; others worse. Consider the waste disposal industry in December 1996. The principal companies were mired in the industry's image of operating problems, poor economics in **recycling**, and a glut of landfill space. As a result, their P/E ratios suffered. Meanwhile, three young enterprises carried premium P/E ratios, as the market showed interest in their strong acquisition programs (see Exhibit 2).

The dual track status of waste disposal firms is duplicated in other industries. Wal-Mart, for example, has enjoyed far higher valuation ratios than other general merchandise retailers, such as Sears, although many of these competitors make money. The big difference has been Wal-Mart's higher growth rate.

EXHIBIT 2	Snapshot of the Waste Disposal Industry

Established Companies	P/E Ratio
Laidlaw	23
WMX Technologies	25
Browning-Ferris	18

New Acquisitive Players	
Allied Waste	56
USA Waste Services	26
Republic Industries	72

As a general rule, institutional investors want analysts to stick to industries with a positive outlook. Even the best buggy whip manufacturer was a poor bet at the turn of the 20th century. Similarly, the most attractive CB radio producer turned out to be a loser in the 1980s. The chosen industries don't have to be stellar performers; they just require a reasonable justification for investment.

Broad Industry Trends

While the competent analyst has a broad knowledge of the industry he covers, his research reports have a narrow focus, limiting reviews of industry trends to those that affect a specific company's future performance. Contributing to the reader's understanding of the industry requires comparisons. For example, analysts covering the early years of the VCR compared it with the introduction of the television. Original themes are important. Rehashing widely available data is of little use to the reader, unless it sets the stage for company-specific projections. These forecasts appear toward the end of the research report, after a groundwork has been laid.

As the subject company grows larger, the industry analysis becomes complicated. Major corporations today have multiple lines, many of which are not comparable. General Electric has 13 separate divisions producing products as dissimilar as gas turbines and home appliances. For those firms with disparate businesses, the industry analysis evolves into an *industries* analysis, as each distinct segment is valued separately as a part of a larger whole.

Contrary Opinions

Of particular interest to investors are contrarian opinions. Research analysts are reluctant to stick their necks out. They follow the herd, and as a result, their reports are disappointingly similar. For the most part, analysts work around the edges of the consensus view on an industry's prospects and a company's forecasts. When a practitioner reaches a strikingly different conclusion from that of everyone else, he tends to couch it in vague terms. Then, if he ends up wrong, his error is less obvious. The depressing outcome of this environment is that many analysts, particularly those on the sell side, are reduced to arguing about a company's next quarterly earnings report. Will earnings be 46 cents per share or 45 cents? When a respected analyst goes against the grain and replies that earnings will be 15 cents instead of 45 cents, institutional investors sit up and take notice.

Few analysts predict reversals of trends that have been long accepted on Wall Street, despite the frequency of such occurrences, so a fresh look at the status quo is real news. One important industry reversal happened in June 1996. After years of raising prices for their brand-name products, Kellogg Co., General Mills, and Ralcorp.—the three principal U.S. cereal makers—cut prices by 20 percent in response to declining demand for their products. In a few days, cereal prices dropped to the levels of the late 1980s. Some observers had noticed increasing consumer resistance to high cereal prices, but few analysts predicted this change, which caused cereal company share prices to decline as earnings projections fell.

ORGANIZING AN INDUSTRY ANALYSIS   2

An industry analysis can take various forms, but the outline set forth in Exhibit 3 is customary. The industry analysis begins with positioning the specific industry within its life cycle. Defining a sector in this way is important on Wall Street. Investors place

EXHIBIT 3	Model of an Industry Analysis

Industry classification
  Life cycle position
  Business cycle

External factors
  Technology
  Government
  Social
  Demographic
  Foreign

Demand analysis
  End users
  Real and nominal growth
  Trends and cyclical variation around trends

Supply analysis
  Degree of concentration
  Ease of entry
  Industry capacity

Profitability
  Supply/demand analysis
  Cost factors
  Pricing

International competition and markets

Source: Association for Investment Management and Research. Note how the industry analysis is broken down into its key components.

---

a premium on simple investment themes. Thus, the faster the analyst pigeonholes an industry into the "life cycle" chart, the better.

3   INDUSTRY CLASSIFICATION

Classification by Industrial Life Cycle

In general conversation, industries are described by the product they produce or the service they provide. Hospital chains, HMOs, and physician health groups are "medical service" industries. Newspaper firms, magazine publishers, and book companies fall in the "publishing" category. Sporting goods manufacturers, recorded music distributors, and toy producers are lumped into the "recreation" sector. Security analysis uses these descriptions, while further classifying industries by certain economic characteristics.

   The most popular segmentation tool is the industrial life cycle, which reflects the vitality of an industry over time. A staple of business textbooks and management consulting firms, the life cycle theory outlines four phases that

EXHIBIT 4	Industry Classification: The Industrial Life Cycle

Life Cycle Phase	Description
Pioneer	Product acceptance is questionable and implementation of business strategy is unclear. There is high risk and many failures.
Growth	Product acceptance is established. Roll-out begins and growth accelerates in sales and earnings. Proper execution of strategy remains an issue.
Mature	Industry trend line corresponds to the general economy. Participants compete for share in a stable industry.
Decline	Shifting tastes or technologies have overtaken the industry, and demand for its products steadily decreases.

mark the beginning to end of an industry: the *pioneer, growth, mature,* and *decline* phases (see Exhibit 4).

As its name implies, the pioneer phase is the riskiest point of corporate life. The industry is struggling to establish a market for its products. Cash needs for working capital and fixed assets are substantial, yet the industry is losing money or is marginally profitable. Its potential for success attracts equity investors, who are prepared to take a total loss on their investment and know that. Seven out of 10 start-up businesses fail to survive. During overheated stock markets, speculative ventures often go public and become fodder for the security analyst community.

The second stage is the **growth phase**. Here, practitioners acknowledge the industry's product acceptance and have a brief historical framework for estimating future demand. The big questions are: How far, and how fast? So-called growth industries occupy a large amount of analysts' time, because they sometimes provide excellent returns. Of particular interest to analysts is identifying a growth industry at the ground floor, before everyone jumps on the bandwagon and boosts the stock price.

A classic growth industry spurs demand for a product that the consumer (or the industrial client) didn't know he needed. The best example is a new technology; cellular advances, for example, sparked a demand for car phones, which few people realized they needed beforehand. Another growth story is the better mousetrap. Before Office Depot, few people realized they needed an office supply superstore; most shopped at local stationers and department stores for these items. The total market for office supplies is stagnant, but office superstores represent a legitimate growth industry within the larger market. Growth companies prosper independent of the business cycle.

Besides experiencing rapidly increasing sales, growth industries frequently enjoy fat profit margins. This happy situation continues until new competitors, attracted to the high returns, enter the industry. As competition stabilizes and market penetration reaches practical limits, the industry progresses to the *mature phase*.

If growth industries have above-average increases in sales and earnings, mature industries produce "average" results. Unit sales gains follow economic growth. Thus, if the economy improves by 3 percent in one year, an analyst expects a mature industry's unit sales to rise by 3 percent. Adding a 5 percent inflation factor means the industry's sales increase by 8 percent annually. Mature industries usually provide a staple product or service. Examples include the food, auto, and furniture industries.

Within a mature industry may be one or more *growth companies.* Typically, such firms achieve above-average growth in one of two ways. First, they gain market share by offering an improved quality or service (i.e., the better mousetrap). American Greetings' market share in the mature greeting card industry has increased from 33 to 35 percent over the past five years. Consumers like its products better than those of the competition. Alternatively, a company grows in a mature industry by gobbling up others. Since 1991, Service Corporation International has increased its market share in the funeral business from 5 to 10 percent, by acquiring over 200 competitors. Sales in its industry advanced 8 percent annually over that time, but Service Corporation's gains averaged 31 percent each year.

The last stage in the life cycle is the decline phase. Demand for the industry's products decreases and the remaining participants fight over shares of a smaller market. With no new capacity needs and diminished profit margins, the industry attracts little capital and established firms begin to exit the sector. As demand dries up, companies fail and the remaining participants consolidate. The better-managed survivors anticipate this fate and avoid it by using cash flow to diversify into promising industries. Westinghouse's takeover of CBS exemplified such diversification.

Classification by Business Cycle Reaction

In addition to the industry life cycle, Wall Street characterizes industries by the way in which they react to the business cycle. Market economies do not grow in a straight line. They expand, go into a recession where growth slows or stops, and then enter a recovery, which leads into the next expansion (see Exhibit 5). The duration of a U.S. business cycle can be 5 to 10 years. Certain industries

EXHIBIT 5	U.S. Business Cycles 1976 to 1996

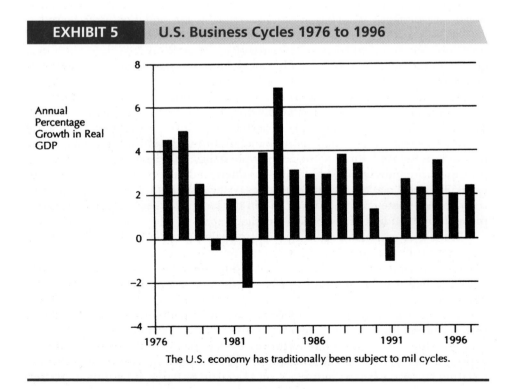

The U.S. economy has traditionally been subject to mil cycles.

EXHIBIT 6	Industry Classification by Business Cycle Behavior

Behavior Pattern	Description
Growth	Above-normal expansion in sales and profits occurs independent of the business cycle.
Defensive	Stable performance during both ups and downs of business cycle.
Cyclical	Profitability tracks the business cycle, often in an exaggerated manner.

prosper more than others during different phases of the business cycle. Industry's behavior places it into one of three categories: *growth, defensive,* or *cyclical* (see Exhibit 6).

A growth industry achieves an above-normal rate of expansion, independent of the business cycle. Even if the economy is in a recession, the growth industry's sales and earnings rise. New technology and products are the hallmarks of a growth industry. The computer software industry sailed through the 1990–1991 recession with higher revenues.

Defensive industries exhibit stable performance through the business cycle. Sales and earnings proceed in an upward direction. Strong growth is apparent during an economic upturn, but there is a slight dip in profitability during recession years. **Defensive industries** usually fall into the mature category. Examples include (1) electric and gas utilities since people require heat and light in their homes regardless of economic conditions; (2) food, cigarette, and beer companies since demand for their products remains inelastic (although consumers may shift to lower-priced brands); and (3) government contractors since governments tend to spend whether or not the economy expands.

Cyclical industries are those whose earnings track the cycle. Their profits benefit from economic upturns, but suffer in a downturn. The earnings movement is exaggerated. Boom times are followed by "bust times." Thus, when economic growth rates only move a few percentage points, **cyclicals** go from substantial losses to huge profits. General Motors' operating loss in 1991 was $2.8 billion; its 1996 operating profit topped $4 billion, representing a huge swing in profitability.

Classic cyclical businesses produce discretionary products, the consumption of which is dependent on economic optimism. The auto industry is cyclical, because consumers defer large purchases until they are confident of the economy's positive direction. Heavy equipment and machine tool producers are **cyclical businesses**. Their customers, capital-intensive concerns, defer investment during recessions and increase spending during recoveries.

Exhibits 7 and 8 provide examples of three firms and how their earnings changed over the preceding business cycle.

Certain cyclical firms experience earnings patterns that do not correlate well against the general economy, but trend against other economic variables. Brokerage firms, for example, show cyclicality based on stock prices. Agricultural firms exhibit earnings tied to the crop price cycle. These firms are lumped into the cyclical category.

The characterization of an industry through the life cycle or business cycle techniques colors the follow-up analysis. Practitioners compare those industries with similar designations and draw inferences about future revenue, earnings

EXHIBIT 7	Business Cycle Earnings Comparison Gross National Product (GNP) versus Earnings per Share (EPS)

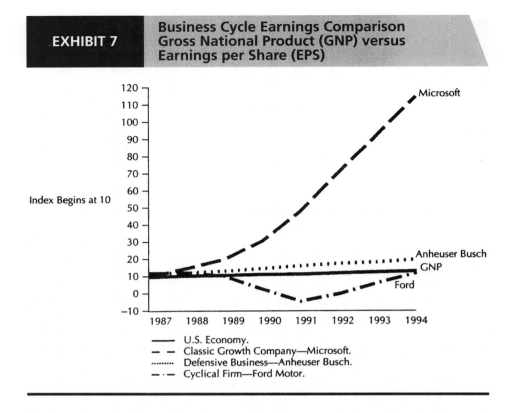

Index Begins at 10

- U.S. Economy.
- Classic Growth Company—Microsoft.
- Defensive Business—Anheuser Busch.
- Cyclical Firm—Ford Motor.

EXHIBIT 8	Business Cycle Earnings Comparison GNP Changes versus EPS Changes

		1987	1988	1989	1990	1991	1992	1993	1994
Real GDP	% Chg	2.9	3.8	3.4	1.3	−1.0	2.7	2.3	3.5
Growth company— Microsoft	EPS	0.16	0.25	0.34	0.52	0.82	1.21	1.58	1.98
	% Chg	77.8	56.3	36.0	52.9	57.7	47.6	30.6	25.3
Defensive business— Anheuser Busch	EPS	1.02	1.23	1.34	1.48	1.63	1.73	1.78	1.94
	% Chg	20.0	20.6	8.9	10.4	10.1	6.1	2.9	9.0
Cyclical firm— Ford Motor	EPS	4.53	5.48	4.57	0.93	−2.40	−0.73	2.28	4.97
	% Chg	47.1	21.0	−16.6	−79.6	Neg.	Neg.	—	218.0

Note: The recession began in 1990 and extended through 1991. The cyclical behavior of Ford Motor is evident.

performance, and valuation. In such side-by-side evaluations, industry-specific nuances are ignored in favor of the broader theme.

A second problem associated with industry classification is self-deception. Once an analyst labels an industry as a growth industry, he (and his audience) is tempted to place subsequent facts that come to light within the growth framework. Pigeonholing an industry helps in telling the investment story, but the experienced analyst doesn't let labels prejudge developments that don't fit the model.

As one illustration, consider the Internet service industry in 1996. Many early investors compared this industry with cable TV in the late 1970s. Both Internet and cable TV were hooked into the home by wire and both required monthly subscription charges. As analysts monitored the Internet services industry more closely, however, they noticed a significant difference. Internet service was not a quasi monopoly like cable TV, and customers switched suppliers more frequently than cable TV subscribers. The Internet industry fell into the growth classification, but practitioners needed a fresh look at its economics. Internet stock prices dropped accordingly in late 1996.

Likewise, the bagel chain industry attracts comparisons with the formerly fast food business. Dennis Lombardi, who heads a restaurant consulting practice, repeated a familiar premise, "There's an awful lot of room for more bagel shops. All you have to do is contrast it to the hamburger chains." With 11,000 restaurants, McDonald's has several times the total number of bagel shops, but the differences are compelling. Hamburgers are viewed as all-American lunch and dinner food. In contrast, bagels occupy the breakfast segment and have an ethnic tradition.

A common error with industry classification occurs when the analyst paints all industry participants with the same brush. Inevitably, not all companies in a *mature* industry are *mature* companies. Beer brewing is a mature industry, yet small microbrewers are considered growth companies. Steel is a cyclical industry, but Nucor's stability defies this classification.

The process of placing an industry into its life cycle and business cycle categories involves performing the work outlined in Exhibit 3. By studying the industry's external influences, demand trends, supply factors, profitability and competition, an analyst forms opinions about its prospects and suitability for investment.

EXTERNAL FACTORS   4

No industry operates in a vacuum. Each is subject to numerous outside influences that significantly impact sales and earnings. The first stage of the top-down analysis considers the economic variables that affect industry performance, and the life cycle and business cycle techniques provide direction in this regard. As the industry study unfolds, however, the practitioner examines external factors that aren't purely economic (see Exhibit 9).

External issues fall into five broad categories: technology, government, social changes, demographics, and foreign influences. For each of these categories, there are "big picture" themes that affect a particular industry, and the analyst's job is twofold. One, he avoids the temptation to fall into the role of futuristic visionary. Instead, he concentrates on trends that can demonstrably affect the industry over a three- to five-year period. Two, he addresses the impact of these trends in quantifiable form. It is not enough to say "advances in satellite technology and capacity will fuel the global pager business"; investors want to know the percentage gains in industry sales from these factors. A numerical forecast is better than a vague pronouncement.

EXHIBIT 9	Industry Analysis—External Factors Affecting Sales and Profitability
Technology	For established industries, the question is: Does the industry face obsolescence from competing technologies? (Typewriters were quickly replaced by word processors in the early 1980s). Infant industries introducing new technologies pose a different question: Will the market accept innovation?
Government	Government plays a large role in many industries. New regulations, or changes to old laws, can impact an industry's sales and earnings. In certain cases, government policies create new industries (e.g., the automobile protective safety bag industry).
Social changes	Changes in lifestyle spark many industries. The rise of two-earner families fueled growth in the convenience food and restaurant industries. Concern over animal rights hurt the fur retailing industry.
Demographics	Demographic shifts are watched by analysts. The "greying" of America supports nursing home stocks. It is also a factor in the rebound of the golf equipment industry, as baby boomers reduce strenuous activity in their later years.
Foreign influences	The United States is the largest economy, but its industries are subject to foreign influences. Overseas textile firms decimated the U.S. textile industry. Higher income levels in developing nations, meanwhile, contributed to huge overseas demand for U.S. movies and musical recordings.

In the majority of research reports, the basic assumption regarding the industry's external environment is that history will repeat itself. Past trends continue into the future, and thus, most industry sales projections are based on time series analysis. Projecting the sales of new industries is more tricky, but 99 percent of public companies are beyond the **start-up stage**, so analysts extrapolate brief historical results into a forecast. Unless there is a firm basis for a contrary opinion, this rearview-mirror approach is reasonable. As noted earlier, this method encourages complacency, and the analyst relying on it can miss important reversals. Nonetheless, a historical grounding in an industry is a prerequisite for an evaluation of external influences. Exhibit 10 provides an example of the effects of external factors on an industry.

Technology

The initial analysis of technology focuses on *survival*. Will the industry's product offerings fend off perceived substitutes derived from newer technology?

EXHIBIT 10	Sample External Factors Affecting Health Care Industry Sales

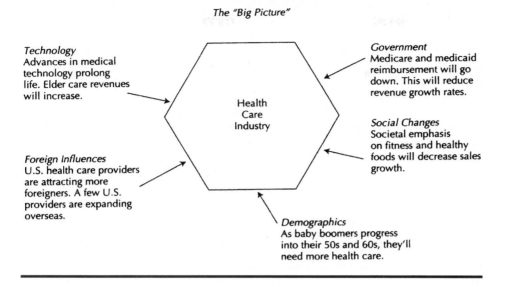

The "Big Picture"

Technology
Advances in medical technology prolong life. Elder care revenues will increase.

Government
Medicare and medicaid reimbursement will go down. This will reduce revenue growth rates.

Health Care Industry

Social Changes
Societal emphasis on fitness and healthy foods will decrease sales growth.

Foreign Influences
U.S. health care providers are attracting more foreigners. A few U.S. providers are expanding overseas.

Demographics
As baby boomers progress into their 50s and 60s, they'll need more health care.

The eyeglass industry, for example, has prospered for years against several contact lens technologies. The record player industry, in contrast, became obsolete with the introduction of the CD player.

In many cases, an outside technological idea enhances an industry. Gains in the biotechnology area were eventually transferred to the agricultural industry, where they contributed to higher crop yields. Improvements in civil aviation technology led directly to a travel boom, which lifted tourist industry revenues. VCRs represented 100 percent of electric appliance sales growth in the mid-1980s. Current pundits believe digital technology will spur growth in digital TV sales.

Sometimes, a new technology is a blessing and a curse. Nuclear power originated in the defense industry. Transferred to electric utilities, nuclear power was quickly accepted in the 1970s because its variable costs were lower than conventional technologies, such as coal and oil generation. Unforeseen problems in safety and the environment tainted nuclear power in the 1980s, and the related expenses crippled many utilities.

In the case of a new competing technology, the established industry usually has several years to prepare a defense. A common strategic response is either:

1. Copy the competition, as Wal-Mart did in the wholesale club industry with Sam's Wholesale Club (a virtual clone of Price Club).

2. Buy the competition, as IBM's software division did when it acquired Lotus Development Corporation.

Competent managements recognize technological trends and adjust their companies accordingly.

Government

Government taxes, laws, and regulations impact every industry in the United States. That's one reason Washington, DC, has over 50,000 registered lobbyists.

The federal tax code serves a legitimate revenue raising function, but it's loaded with loopholes designed to serve special interests. For example, the oil exploration industry has depreciation allowances that are far more favorable than those available to the average manufacturing industry. Federal quotas on imported goods provide certain industries with extra benefits. For example, the quota levied on Japanese auto imports protects the sales and earnings of domestic producers. A negative shift in the political fortunes of either the oil exploration industry or the auto industry could result in unfavorable government actions, leading to lower earnings. The analyst's projections would be modified accordingly.

Business organizations complain about regulation, but regulations play a valuable role in promoting worker safety, consumer protection, and fair play. Government influence cuts both ways. Some government agencies practice regulatory overkill that harms industry unnecessarily, but it is a fact that multiple businesses were founded on new government initiatives or rely on government regulation to prosper. If you're a business, what better way to avoid risk than to have the government require a minimum price for your products, set up barriers to foreign imports, or allow you to merge with the competition? Regulation "creep" has continued in Republican and Democratic administrations, and the analysts of the 1990s monitor government developments much more closely than did their 1960s' counterparts.

A recent example of a negative external influence is the government assault on the tobacco industry. By declaring tobacco a drug and placing it under FDA jurisdiction, the government clearly seeks to diminish the industry's prospects. Alternatively, the federal emphasis on environment enforcement is a boon to the environmental services sector. One relatively new industry that received a huge leg up from the government was the cellular phone industry. Rather than sell cellular monopolies to the highest bidder, the government gave the rights away via lottery in the 1980s, saving the operators billions of dollars. State deregulation is sweeping through the electric utilities, and this turning point means dramatic changes for this staid industry.

Consider Paxson Communications Corp., a network of 46 UHF stations that run half-hour informercials most of the day. Faced with limited capacity, many cable TV systems declined to carry these broadcasts, but in March 1997 the U.S. Supreme Court upheld the government's "must carry" rules, requiring cable companies to show any and all local broadcast channels, even Paxson's low-rent UHF programs. On the day of the ruling, the company's share price jumped 30 percent, illustrating the effect of government.

Federal, state, and local government spending accounts for 35 percent of gross national product. Any shifts in the spending patterns of these organizations influence the affected industries. Declines in the defense budget during the 1990s prompted a wave of consolidations among defense contractors. At the local level, the privatization of municipal waste services contributed to revenue gains among waste management firms. Imagine the shift in dollars if the government privatized just a small portion of the public education system!

External factors relating to government play a significant role in the analysis of foreign stocks. Most countries have more restrictive trade regimes than the United States, and local producers get complacent after years of protection. A dramatic liberalization in tariff policy can destroy a local industry that is uncompetitive with the global multinationals. Similarly, nations set up artificial barriers to protect favored industries (and companies) from outside threats. Japan, for example, has a maze of bizarre regulations that limit U.S. agricultural imports, thereby assisting Japanese farmers. Brazil's "local content" rules forestall the importation of cars and ensure the survival of the inefficient local auto industry. Argentina has a special tax on cola drinks, designed to punish Coke and Pepsi bottlers in favor of local fruit drink producers.

Social Changes

Social factors boil down to lifestyle and fashion changes. In either case, the analyst is ready to evaluate their impacts on the relevant industry.

Of the two social influences, fashion is the more unpredictable, and this complicates the job of researching fashion-oriented industries. The women's fashion cycle, for example, is quite short, and a hot clothing item may only have a shelf life of one, maybe two years, before it is replaced by another style. Baseline sales for the industry trend upward, but fashion changes impact short-term projections. Similar phenomena occur in the toy, recreation, and film industries.

Analysts can mistake a short-term fashion cycle for a long-term trend. In one of my financings, an analyst projected a steady upward move in leather coat sales, despite evidence that demand for such garments historically went through up and down cycles. Three years after the transaction, leather coat sales had dropped by over 20 percent.

Lifestyle changes, in contrast, take place over long periods of time. An increase in health consciousness, for example, resulted in a per capita decline in hard liquor consumption. Given fair warning, several spirits producers, such as Seagram's, responded by diversifying into the production of wine, which increased in popularity over the same time span. The gradual shift of women into the workforce, from 41 percent in 1965 to 58 percent in 1995, and the increasing suburbanization of society, acutely affected the auto industry. Besides spawning a need for two cars per family, these changes prompted the minivan boom, as suburban parents juggled responsibilities for ferrying children to after-school activities.

Demographics

Demography is the science that studies the vital statistics of population, such as distribution, age, and income. By observing trends in these statistics, analysts develop investment themes regarding various industries. In the United States for example, the age shift of the baby boomers into their 40s and 50s has sparked a strong interest in retirement planning. The result has been higher revenues for money management firms as the boomers put savings into stocks and bonds. In Malaysia, about 50 percent of the population is under the age of 21, and analysts tout local brewing stocks, in anticipation of a large increase in the beer-drinking population. In Indonesia, rising per capita incomes push a demand for electric appliances, giving analysts reason to be optimistic about the future growth of local utilities.

Demographic trends unfold over long periods of time, and they are thus easier to identify and track than other external factors. This circumstance doesn't lead to absolute certainty. Analysts frequently agree on the existence of a trend (e.g., the rising percentage of single-parent families) but disagreement occurs in sizing up its impact on relevant industries.

Foreign Influences

As global trade expands, industries become sensitive to foreign influences. For example, the U.S. economy's health is heavily dependent on imported oil. Overseas disruptions in the supply/demand dynamic of this resource ripple through several industries, including the oil, chemical, and leisure sectors. Other U.S. industries are under assault from foreign competitors: automobile parts, apparel, and electronics are three of the more popular targets. At the same time, U.S. exports have never been stronger, reflecting the economic liberalization of nations previously keeping out U.S. products.

Reflecting this liberalization theme, analysts evaluate selected industries on a global basis. Demand projections are aggregated by country, and the external influences referred to herein are considered from a global perspective. This approach is appropriate for worldwide commodity businesses such as oil, metals, and agricultural products, although it is applied at times to categories such as defense, semiconductors, and airlines.

Keeping Your Focus

Big-picture trends are interesting to study, but undisciplined research does little to advance an equity evaluation. Isolating the critical elements in an external analysis is difficult and most research reports fail in this regard. The reports often present outside factors that resemble a jumble of competing influences, and the identifiable opportunities for an industry seem canceled out by the emerging threats. The end result: analysts extrapolate the past into the future, and fail to uncover compelling changes that can move an industry's sales off historical trends. As noted earlier, this rearview-mirror method is appropriate for many industries, but an incisive effort is required either to unlock an industry's potential or to spot its incumbent weakness.

Two external reviews are set forth in the following case studies.

CASE STUDY

Cable TV Industry

The cable TV industry is a latter stage growth business. It is a defensive industry in terms of the business cycle, with growth aspects. Most U.S. homes have been wired for cable TV, but the industry is still grabbing advertising dollars away from the broadcast networks. Cable TV is fundamentally a regulated monopoly, and regulators generally allow monthly subscriber charges to track inflation.

December 1996 research reports emphasized the influence of technology and government in the industry's future, as shown in Exhibit 11.

The external factors were largely positive in 1996, and analysts concluded that the cable TV industry's above-average revenue growth rate would continue. Higher pay-TV revenues and increased channel availability would enable the industry to garner a growing share of ad revenues, while docile regulators would rubber-stamp inflation-driven subscriber rates. Direct broadcast satellite service, an obvious cable TV substitute was a minor threat. It had just a 3 percent market share in TV homes and its premium service (and rates) were acceptable to only high-end consumers.

| EXHIBIT 11 | Cable TV Industry External Factors and Related Threats |

Technology

Opportunities

Improved pay TV technology increases revenues.

More compression means more channels *and* more revenues.

New technology permits phone service over cable lines.

Threats

Improved technology enhances the direct broadcast satellite (DBS) industry's ability to attract customers.

Technology may be available for phone companies to send TV programming through telephone wires.

Government

Opportunities

There is no political will to cut the industry's monthly subscriber rates.

Liberal regulatory policies expand cable merger options to phone companies and software providers.

After new telecommunications law passed, U.S. West (5th largest telephone company) agreed to merge with Continental Cablevision (third largest cable TV company).

Threats

Regulators can change their minds on subscriber fees.

New law allows phone companies to compete in cable TV. These companies are larger and have more resources than most cable firms.

Social Changes

Opportunities

No significant opportunities were gleaned from existing social trends.

Threats

American television viewing on a per capita basis is up 5% from 1990 to 1995, but it may be reaching a saturation point at 4.3 hours per day.

Demographics

No significant opportunities or threats are apparent from underlying demographic changes.

Foreign Influences

The industry's customers and principal suppliers are located in the United States. Foreign influences are practically nil.

CASE STUDY

Trucking Industry

The trucking industry is divided into two sectors, the long-haul business, whereby a full truckload is shipped long distances over several days; and the short-haul business, which consists primarily of less than full loads shipped within a 200-mile radius. Trucking is a cyclical industry, and its volumes are directly correlated to industrial production. The industry also follows a capacity cycle. The industry over-expands during good times, and new trucks may be running half empty when the economy is prospering. Labor costs are 60 percent of sales and qualified drivers are hard to find. This capacity problem and labor issue can lead to rate cuts in good economic times and lower profits. The primary competitors are railroads in the long-haul segment and air freight companies in the short-haul business. Exhibit 12 lists external factors affecting the trucking industry.

No external factors threaten the industry's survival. Trucking is going to be with us for a long time, but serious issues involve new competition and a driver shortage, with few counterbalancing opportunities. External factors contribute to the consensus belief that trucking industry revenues will grow slower than the general economy. Future profitability will be below average.

EXHIBIT 12	Trucking Industry External Factors and Related Threats

Technology

Opportunities	Threats
Growing use of on-board computers and satellite tracking improve delivery times for truckers. **Just-in-time**-inventory acceptance is helping truckers vis-à-vis railroads.	Railroads' introduction of *Roadrailer* (a trailer equipped with highway and rail wheels) and the *Iron Highway* (a flexible train that facilitates truck trailer hauling) brings new competitive threats to the short-haul market.

Government

Opportunities	Threats
No significance.	The federal government is permitting large railroad mergers, which will increase pressure on the long-haul segment. New safety regulations tighten the driver licensing process, acerbating a shortage of drivers. Government is cutting back its loan program to truck driving schools, thus contributing to the driver shortage.

(Exhibit continued on next page . . .)

> ### EXHIBIT 12   (continued)
>
> **Social Changes**
>
> *Opportunities*
> Increasing acceptance of women and minorities as truck drivers could relieve driver shortage.
>
> *Threats*
> Desire to spend more time at home reduces pool of applicants, as people choose alternative professions.
>
> **Demographics**
>
> *Opportunities*
> No special issues.
>
> *Threats*
> Truck driving is a younger person's profession. The baby boom years (1946–1964) were followed by a birth decline, so there's a smaller pool of eligible drivers.
>
> **Foreign Influences**
>
> The trucking industry's customers and principal suppliers are located in the United States, except for oil, which is 50% imported. Gasoline costs account for 15% to 20% of revenues, but gas prices are reasonably stable.

DEMAND ANALYSIS   5

The ultimate purpose of preparing an economic analysis, industry life cycle placement, and external factor review is an assessment of future demand for the industry's products. Applying such study to numerical forecasts is accomplished differently, as discussed below:

1. *Top-down economic analysis.* We look for specific macroeconomic variables that affect an industry's sales. An ideal situation is when revenues correlate strongly to one economic statistic, thus reducing the need for multiple forecast inputs. Cement demand growth in Mexico, for example, is historically $1.7 \times$ GNP growth. Analysts, as a result, rely on GNP forecasts to project cement unit volume.

2. *Industry life cycle.* Categorizing the industry within its life cycle position (or its business cycle sensitivity) provides a framework for demand forecasts. The U.S. food industry is "mature," so unit sales should track GNP and population growth. The Internet industry is "growing," and this characterization provides a guide to above-normal sales increases.

3. *External factors.* Many outside factors are fairly stable, and their impact on an industry are easily predictable. Others are highly variable, and thus bring an element of uncertainty into the analysis. Including these, items into a sales forecast is a qualitative exercise, requiring judgment.

By considering the preceding three major themes, the analyst establishes a future sales line for the industry. Most times, this sales trend turns out to be an extrapolation of past history, as suggested by the trend line for the established industry in Exhibit 13, but not always. Sometimes, careful study reveals the likelihood of a turning point that affects the industry's fortunes dramatically. Even an extrapolation result provides useful insights. For example, the water service industry has shown a 7 percent growth rate. Suppose your analysis indicates a continuation of the trend, but only at 5 percent. The 2 percent difference leads you to believe the industry's prospects are overblown, and you sell your shareholdings while prices are still high. In Exhibit 13, a mild decrease in the growth rate produces 10 percent lower sales in the future.

Once a trend has been forecast, the analyst's next step is studying the industry's customers. Where does the demand originate? Who's buying and why?

Customer Study

A forecast of aggregate demand is helpful, but a full understanding of what drives an industry's revenue is achieved through learning the customers. Since a typical industry serves thousands of clients, evaluating them individually is impossible. Segmenting the customers into submarkets, on the other hand, enables the analyst to study a smaller number of factors that contribute to demand. As he sequentially studies each submarket, he builds an **aggregate demand** profile, submarket by submarket.

For example, the demand forecast for the Mexican cement market relied heavily on GNP trends. As a backup to this methodology, I subdivided the market into five segments and considered demand in each segment to verify the accu-

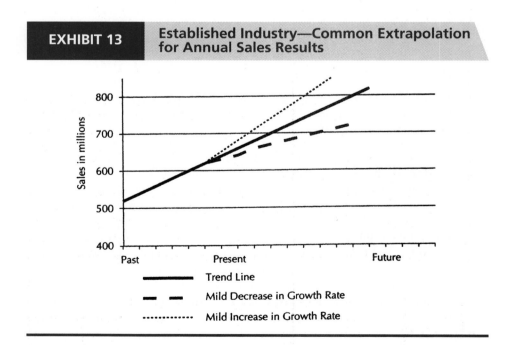

| EXHIBIT 13 | Established Industry—Common Extrapolation for Annual Sales Results |

Submarket	Estimated Demand (MM Tons)
EXHIBIT 14 — Mexican Cement Market—Building Aggregate Demand by Submarket	
Residential	10.5
Commercial	8.2
Infrastructure	7.3
Transformers[a]	2.2
Export	3.0
Total Submarket Demand	31.2
GNP-Based Demand	30.4

[a] Manufacturing of concrete block, concrete pipe, and so on.

racy of the GNP **multiplier**. Both methods revealed a likely demand around 31 million tons, including exports (see Exhibit 14).

In Exhibit 14, I categorized the submarkets by usage: homebuilding, infrastructure projects, and commercial construction. But demand segments can be classified by different definitions. David Aaker, a noted business strategist, divides segments between customer characteristics and product-related approaches. Exhibit 15 shows samples from the U.S. market.

A careful analyst studies demand on the basis of several submarket classifications. Following Dr. Aaker's advice, I examined Mexican cement forecasts on a geographic basis. I divided Mexico into five regions and looked at individual market need (see Exhibit 16). In this instance, the GNP, usage, and geographic methods delivered aggregate forecasts that were highly correlated. Utilizing multiple approaches is a good double check for any sales forecast.

Established Industries　For established industries, the analyst should contact long-time customers to figure what drives demand in each submarket. What guides the customer's buying decisions? How does it differ by submarket? What changes are occurring in the customer's motivation? What implication will they have on industry revenues? Discussions with customers and a study of buying habits indicate whether prior trends continue.

For example, VCRs captured 70 percent of the U.S. housing market after ten years. Unit growth dropped in the 1990s. Personal computers represent a newer appliance. They appear in 32 percent of U.S. homes but are concentrated in the higher income households. This low penetration (relative to VCRs) promotes a high growth rate until computer saturation occurs in all income segments (see Exhibit 17).

Growth Industries　A growth industry has yet to penetrate all its future submarkets. In addition to researching the existing customer base, the analyst considers new outlets for the industry's products. The pager business, for example, was

| EXHIBIT 15 | Approaches to Defining Demand Segments |

Customer Characteristics	Demand Segment
Geographic	Southern region as a market for trendy clothing versus the West Coast
Type of business	Computer needs of restaurants versus manufacturing firms versus banks versus retailers
Size of firm	Large hospital versus midsize versus small
Lifestyle	Tendency of Jaguar buyers to be more adventurous, less conservative than buyers of Mercedes-Benz
Sex	The Virginia Slims cigarettes for women
Age	Cereals for children versus adults
Occupation	The paper copier needs of lawyers versus dentists

Product-Related Approaches	Demand Segment
User type	Appliance buyer—home builder, homeowner, small business
Usage	The heavy potato users—the fast-food outlets
Benefits sought	Dessert eaters—those who are calorie-conscious versus those who are more concerned with convenience
Price sensitivity	Price-sensitive Honda Civic buyer versus the luxury Mercedes-Benz buyer
Competitor	Those computer users now committed to IBM
Application	Professional users of chain saws versus the homeowner
Brand loyalty	Those committed to IBM versus others

Source: Developing Business Strategies by David Aaker (New York: John Wiley & Sons, Inc., 1995).

---

confined to businesspeople. In recent years, it has expanded to personal use. Fast-food chains were selling to the lunch and dinner market. In the 1980s, they attracted the breakfast segment. Identifying a new use or user group is important to confirming a growth industry's upward movement.

Untested Industries   Some publicly-traded companies furnish a truly new product or service. Given a minimal level of product acceptance, these firms have little or no track record from which the analyst can build a sales forecast. Although the risk profile of these stocks is higher than most, the decision process is not entirely speculative.

EXHIBIT 16	Mexican Cement Market Building Aggregate Demand by Submarket Geographic Basis

Geographic Market	Estimated Demand (MM Tons)
Central Mexico	11.2
Northern Gulf	5.9
South Mexico	5.2
Central Pacific	3.2
North Pacific	2.2
Export	3.0
Total Geographic Market Demand	**30.7**
Submarket Based Demand	31.2
GNP-Based Demand	30.4

A first step is determining whether the new industry fulfills a need that (1) exists, and (2) isn't being met by another industry. The managed care industry was founded in response to the urgent need of corporations to cut employee medical costs. Assuming a need is verified, analysts typically forecast new industry sales based on the experience of a similar industry.

One illustration is the office products superstore industry, as typified by Office Depot and Staples. No sooner did these two companies go public than analysts settled into a comparison with discount warehouse clubs, such as Price Club and Costco. Market share and saturation levels for Office Depot and Staples were calculated on models similar to the warehouse club experience. For every 250,000 people in a metropolitan market, for example, analysts figured one warehouse club could succeed. After some observation, they used similar logic in quantifying 25,000 white collar workers and 100,000 people per office products superstore.

EXHIBIT 17	Comparable Household Penetration Two Electronic Products

	1980	1985	1990
VCR	2%	37%	70%
	1985	**1990**	**1995**
Personal computers	10%	23%	32%

EXHIBIT 18	Demand Analysis Model for the Hotel Furniture Market

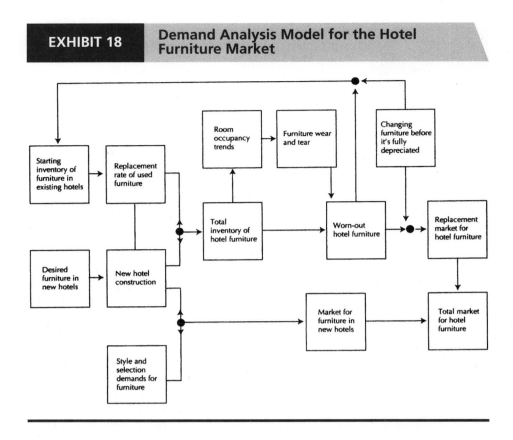

Input/Output and Industry Demand Forecasts

Input-output analysis observes the flow of goods and services through the production process, including intermediate steps as the goods proceed raw-material to finished product. A rising consumption of the finished product boosts demand for industries supplying the intermediate steps. For example, the personal computer boom elevates the demand for the semiconductor, an important PC component.

If one industry is a major customer of another, an analyst uses input-output analysis to derive partial demand for the latter's products. Alternatively, the higher consumption of one industry's offerings sparks demand for complementary products. The wide-scale introduction of the VCR boosted the video rental business. In the 1980s, analysts calculated video demand through algebraic formulas based on VCR purchases. A typical formula was that one VCR purchase meant three video rentals per month. The demand models can be complex and contain many variables. Exhibit 18 shows one rendition for the hotel furniture market.

6   SUPPLY ANALYSIS IN THE INDUSTRY STUDY

In reviewing industries, analysts spend most of their time studying *demand* trends. They usually assume the supply side of the equation takes care of itself. If industry revenues are rising, more investment pours in. If revenues are declining, existing capacity services the falling demand. This model is valid in the long term, but its applicability over the short to intermediate term varies by industry.

The temporary help industry fits the classic model well. With its emphasis on low-skilled workers, the industry can find new employees quickly, thus ramping up capacity in a short time. In contrast, supply that is dependent on capital intensive producers is a different story. Steel and packaging require three- to five-year periods to build plants that add capacity. Industries that use highly skilled workers, such as software, can face short-term capacity constraints as they wait for training programs to provide new employees.

Projecting Supply Availability

Supply is a function of unused capacity and the ability to bring on new capacity. Interpreting these variables well enough to make a reasonable forecast is complicated. That's why few analysts attempt the job. Ideally, a supply forecast dovetails with a demand forecast, and the analyst has an idea about future market equilibrium. If future supply and demand are out of balance, prices for the industry's products will be affected unless the suppliers change their behavior in time. The ideal research report has a supply/demand graph like the one shown in Exhibit 19. In this case, the graph predicts a future capacity problem.

The supply projection is easiest when the industry has only a few competitors, generating output at a discrete number of sizable facilities. It also helps if the industry's economics make imports prohibitively expensive, so the analyst can ignore foreign capacity. The cement industry is a good example of this model. First, only large plants, with long construction lead times, make cement. Second, the low value per ton makes transportation uneconomical beyond a 250-mile radius from the plant. Thus, it's a simple matter to forecast available supply: An analyst counts nearby capacity and adds expansions planned for the next three to five years.

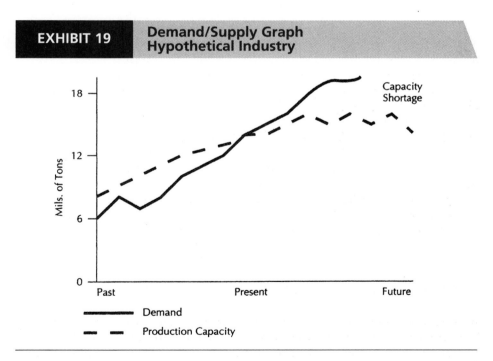

| EXHIBIT 19 | Demand/Supply Graph Hypothetical Industry |

Note: There's a capacity shortage in the future. This could mean higher product prices.

EXHIBIT 20	1996 Mexican Cement Market Availability of Supply Calculation (millions of tons per year)			
	1996	**1997**	**1998**	**1999**
1996 capacity	36.0	36.0	36.0	36.0
1997 additions, net	—	1.0	1.0	1.0
1998 additions, net	—	—	3.7	3.7
1999 additions, net	—	—	—	1.3
Total estimated capacity	36.0	37.0	40.7	42.0

Note: Additions are net of closures.

EXHIBIT 21	1996 Supply/Demand Forecast Mexican Cement Industry			
	1996	**1997**	**1998**	**1999**
Available capacity	36.0	37.0	40.7	42.0
Expected demand	31.0	33.0	35.5	38.0
Capacity utilization	86%	89%	87%	90.5%

In Mexico, for example, this process is straightforward. The cement market is dominated by two companies operating just 29 plants, and their expansion plans are public knowledge. All plants have ample reserves of raw materials. An illustrative calculation for supply appears in Exhibit 20.

The forecast demand for cement is matched against the supply trend, as shown in Exhibit 21. The chart shows capacity utilization rates exceeding 88 percent from 1996 to 1999, which is considered *high* for the industry. The projection suggests that additional capacity be initiated.

7   PROFITABILITY, PRICING, AND THE INDUSTRY STUDY

A security analyst wants to select profitable industries. What's the point of investing in growth industries if sales go up, but profits go down? A supply/demand forecast gives an indication of future profitability. If supply appears to be in line with demand, industry earnings will probably stay on their trend line. Indeed, profitability is vital for industries to make the investment needed to increase supply. A projected oversupply will retard investment since it augurs lower prices. A 1997 study by Lehman Brothers predicted sharply lower prices for copper (from 110¢/lb. to 60¢/lb.), resulting from prospective increases in mining capacity.

Factors contributing to *pricing* include:

► Product segmentation.
► Degree of industry concentration.
► Ease of industry entry.
► Price changes in key supply inputs.

To begin, most industries effectively segment their product offerings by brand name, reputation, or service, even when the products are quite similar. Over-the-counter medicines are one example. The ingredients of the store brand and the name-brand are typically identical, yet the name-brand product has a 40 percent price premium.

An industry with a high degree of concentration inhibits price movements. Assuming that demand and supply are in reasonable balance, the major players have an incentive to engage in monopolistic behavior. Artificially high prices can be sustained by price signaling, confidential agreements, and other means. Outsiders have problems breaking into the inner circle to learn what's going on. In Mexico's cement market, for example, the two major producers control 85 percent of the market, and they barely hide the fact that collusion exists. In several U.S. industries, similar behavior occurs, but it's kept behind closed doors.

Monopolies promote artificial pricing, and an industry's ease of entry is a key variable in holding prices to the free **market model**. Semiconductor production poses an obvious problem; the entry ticket—a new plant—costs $1 billion. The specialty retailing industry, in contrast, is wide-open. An entrepreneur can rent store space, lease fixtures, and stock inventory for less than $75,000.

Certain industries rely heavily on one or two inputs. Price changes in these inputs affect products costs and profitability. Sometimes, the industry can pass through increased costs in the form of higher prices. At other times, competitive pressures stand in the way. In 1996, for example, the price of corn, a key chicken feed, reached historical highs. Poultry producers, such as Tyson Foods and WLR Corp., were unable to raise prices enough to compensate and their profitability fell.

Industry Profitability Is Important

Supply/demand analysis, cost factors, and pricing flexibility are critical elements in determining future industry profitability. Without earnings, an industry can't finance the commitment to personnel, plant, and research and development that is needed to prosper. An industry with a poor profit outlook is an unlikely investment candidate indeed.

INTERNATIONAL COMPETITION AND MARKETS   8

Competition

Competitive analysis is the topic of many books. Michael Porter of the Harvard Business School, is a leader in the field, and approaches competition from multiple directions, as set forth in Exhibit 22. Security analysis synthesizes the work of experts like Dr. Porter, and this section provides a brief treatment of the subject.

EXHIBIT 22	Five Competitive Forces that Determine Industry Profitability

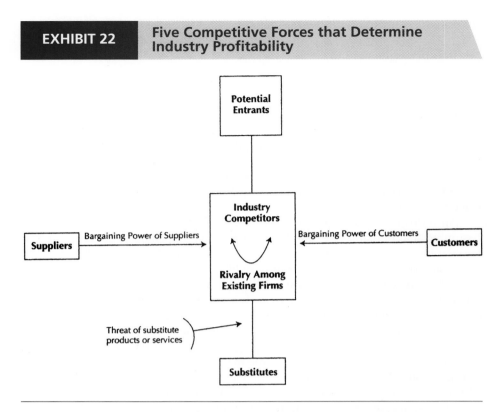

Source: Competitive Advantage by Michael E. Porter (New York: The Free Press, 1985).

A first step in the competitive analysis is defining the industry. While this task was discussed earlier, it is helpful to remember that some analysts cover the chemical industry; some follow the chemical fertilizer industry; and still others research the specialty chemical industry. Industries are segmented into smaller industries. *Institutional Investor* magazine divides the computer industry into seven subindustries: computer services, data networking, the Internet, PC hardware, PC software, server and enterprise hardware, and server and enterprise software. Placing your company into its subindustry and identifying its competitors becomes the second step in your competitive analysis.

For each competitor, the analyst develops an appreciation of its business strategy and its effects on the company under study. For example, in the managed care business, Aetna pursues a national program. Physician Health Services focuses on the Southeast region. Managed Care Solutions sticks to Medicaid managed care. If Aetna shifted to Medicaid contracts, it would harm Managed Care Solutions' prospects.

Finally, the analyst is advised to outline the strengths and weaknesses of industry participants. Exhibit 23 illustrates many of the items considered in such an outline. Financial track record and balance sheet strength are priorities for analysts, but a review of other factors reveals whether better results can be achieved by the competition, perhaps at the expense of the subject company. Similarly, if the subject company's strengths dominate areas where the competition is weak, a higher degree of confidence is gained for your forecasts.

Each industry has a few dominant success factors that can be drawn from Exhibit 23. Analysts (and corporate strategists) inventory these items and the relative positions of competitors. Exhibit 24 presents this comparative analysis in tabular form.

| EXHIBIT 23 | Competitive Analysis: Analysis of Strengths and Weaknesses of Each Industry Participant |

Innovation

Technical product or service superiority
New product capability
Research & development
Technologies
Patents

Management

Quality of top and middle management
Knowledge of business
Culture
Strategic goals and plans
Entrepreneurial thrust
Planning/operation system
Loyalty—turnover
Quality of strategic decision making

Manufacturing

Cost structure
Flexible production operations
Equipment
Access to raw material
Vertical integration
Workforce attitude and motivation
Capacity

Marketing

Product quality reputation
Product characteristics/differentiation
Brand-name recognition
Breadth of product line—systems capability
Customer orientation
Segmentation/focus
Distribution
Retailer relationship
Advertising/promotion skills
Sales force
Customer service/product support

Finance—Access to Capital

From operations
From cash on hand
Ability to use debt and equity financing

Customer Base

Size and loyalty
Market share
Growth of segments served

Source: Developing Business Strategies by David Aaker (New York: John Wiley & Sons, Inc., 1995).

A firm's ability to sustain its sales and earnings is highly dependent on the status of the competition. Does the subject company have the ability to be aggressive—take the offense? Or, does it have to protect market share and husband financial resources—play defense? The competitor profile facilitates **game theory** for the practitioner.

International Competition

The world is becoming a smaller place and industries increasingly reflect a globalization theme. This characterization is most advanced with commodity industries such as oil, metals, and basic foodstuffs, but it also dominates intermediate

EXHIBIT 24	Sample Competitor Analysis for a Research Report			

	Major Competitors			
Competition Indicators	A	B	C	D
Market position	Vulnerable	Prevalent	Strong	Vulnerable
Profitability	Low	Average	Average	Average
Financial strength	Low	High	Unknown	Low
Product mix	Narrow	Broad	Narrow	Narrow
Technological capability	Average	Strong	Average	Weak
Product quality	Minimum	Good	Satisfactory	Minimum

Source: Management Policy, Strategy and Plans by Milton Leontiades (New York: Little, Brown & Company, 1982).

sectors such as textiles, semiconductors, and chemicals. Indeed, about 40 percent of the S&P 500's earnings are connected to international activities.

The United States is the leading economy, has the greatest number of publicly traded securities, and operates the most developed financial markets. For these reasons, the security analysis profession has made great strides here. The downside of this situation has been a nearsightedness on the part of many United States practitioners. Even though industries extend globally, Wall Street research often stops at the U.S. border, and analysts frequently give short shrift to corporate foreign operations and international trends. As institutions emphasize global research, more work will be dedicated to this important area.

SUMMARY

The industry analysis is a continuation of the top-down approach. By studying the industry, its external environment, demand and supply balance, likely profitability and competitive situation, the security analyst confirms whether the industry is appropriate for investment. The written research report only presents a limited amount of information and practitioners highlight a few key factors in reviewing an industry. Frequently, their audience prefers a one-word summary in the industry review, such as *growth, mature,* or *decline*. With a knowledge of the industry terrain, the analyst proceeds to a specific stock selection. Which of the participants are the winners? Which are the losers?

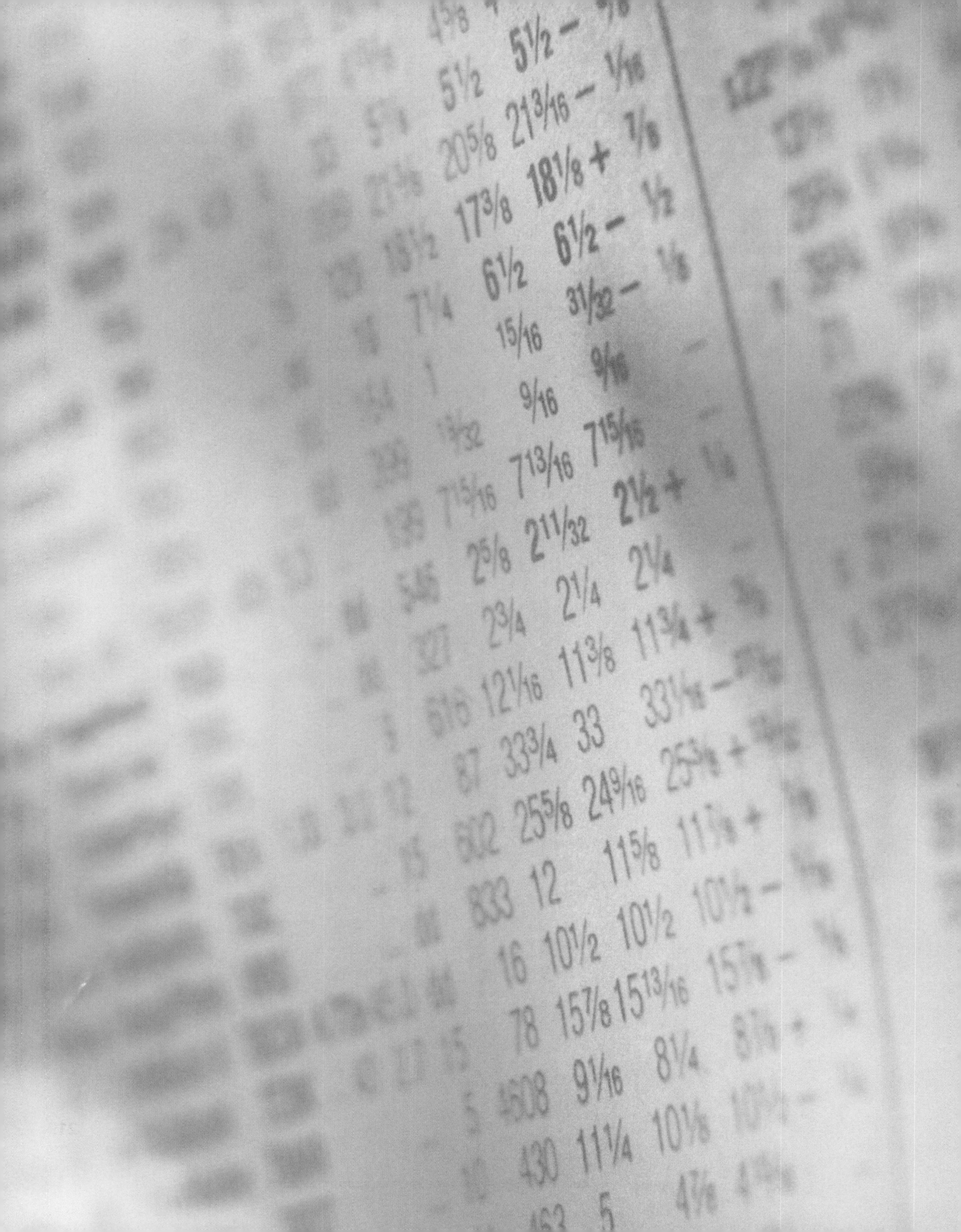

5½   5½ − ⅜

5½   21³⁄₁₆ − ⅛

20⅝   18⅛ + ⅞

17⅜   6½ − ½

15½   6½   31⁄32 − ⅛

7¼   15⁄16

1   9⁄16   9⁄16

1⁄32

7⁵⁄₁₆   7¹³⁄₁₆   7¹⁵⁄₁₆

2⅝   2¹¹⁄₃₂   2½ +

2¾   2¼   2¼

6⅛   12¹⁄₁₆   11⅜   11¾ +

87   33¾   33   33¹⁄₁₆ −

602   25⅝   24⁹⁄₁₆   25⁷⁄₈ +

833   12   11⅝   11⅞ +

16   10½   10½   10⅛ −

78   15⅞   15¹³⁄₁₆   15⅞ −

608   9¹⁄₁₆   8¼   8⅛

430   11¼   10⅛   10⅛

463   5   4⅝   4⅝

VALUATION IN EMERGING MARKETS

by Tim Koller, Marc Goedhart, and David Wessels

LEARNING OUTCOMES

The candidate should be able to:

a. describe how inflation affects the estimation of cash flows for a company domiciled in an emerging market;

b. calculate nominal and real-term financial projections in order to prepare a discounted cash flow valuation of an emerging market company;

c. discuss the arrangements for adjusting cash flows, rather than adjusting the discount rate, to account for emerging market risks (e.g., inflation, macroeconomic volatility, capital control, and political risk) in a scenario analysis;

d. estimate the cost of capital for emerging market companies, and calculate and interpret a country risk premium.

The emerging economies in Asia and South America will experience strong growth over the next decades; many analysts see China and India moving into the ranks of the world's largest economies.[1] This sometimes spectacular economic development will produce many situations requiring sound analysis and valuation. In the rising number of privatizations, joint ventures, mergers and acquisitions, local financial parties such as banks and capital markets will display growing sophistication. Institutional investors will also continue to diversify their portfolios, adding international holdings in emerging-market stocks.

In this reading we focus on issues that arise in financial analysis and valuation of businesses in emerging markets. Valuation is much more difficult in these

---

Special thanks to our colleagues William Jones and Gustavo Wigman, who contributed to this reading.

[1] See, for example, D. Wilson and R. Purushothaman, "Dreaming with BRICs: The Path to 2050" (Global Economics paper no. 99, Goldman Sachs & Co., October 2003).

219

environments because of risks and obstacles to businesses, including great macro-economic uncertainty, illiquid capital markets, controls on the flow of capital into and out of the country, less-rigorous accounting standards and disclosure levels, and high levels of political risk. Academics, investment bankers, and industry practitioners have yet to agree on how to address these challenges. Methods vary considerably and practitioners often make arbitrary adjustments based on intuition and limited empirical evidence.

With agreement lacking and emerging-market valuations so complex, we recommend a triangulation approach—comparing estimates of the value from three methods. First, we use discounted cash flows with probability-weighted scenarios that explicitly model the risks the business faces. Then we compare the value obtained from this approach with the results of two secondary approaches: a DCF approach with a country risk premium built into the cost of capital, and a valuation based on comparable trading and transaction multiples.

The basics of estimating a DCF value are the same in emerging markets as elsewhere. Therefore, we focus on complications specific to emerging-market valuations:

▶ handling foreign exchange rates, inflation, and interest rate gaps with developed markets consistently when making financial projections
▶ factoring inflation into historical financial analysis and cash flow projections
▶ incorporating special emerging-market risks consistently in the valuation
▶ estimating the cost of capital in emerging markets
▶ using market-based references such as trading multiples and transaction multiples when interpreting and calibrating valuation results

We will apply our valuation approach in this reading to ConsuCo, a leading Brazilian manufacturer of consumer goods.[2]

1   EXCHANGE RATES, INFLATION, AND INTEREST RATE GAPS

Because exchange rates, inflation, and interest rates can fluctuate wildly from year to year in emerging markets, assumptions underlying estimates of future financial results in domestic or foreign currency and cost of capital must be consistent. Some fundamental monetary assumptions should be defined consistently to avoid any biases in the valuation results. This becomes even more important when you value companies in emerging markets.

The components of the cash flows of emerging-market companies are often denominated in several currencies. Consider an oil exporter. Its revenues are determined by the dollar price of oil, while many of its costs (labor and domestic

---

[2] This case illustration is a disguised example.

purchases) are determined by the domestic currency. If foreign-exchange rates would perfectly reflect inflation differentials—so that purchasing power parity would hold—the company's operating margins and cash flows in real terms would be unaffected. In that case, changes in exchange rates would be irrelevant for valuation purposes.

However, at least in the short run, this does not always hold, because in emerging markets, exchange rates move far and fast. For example, in Argentina at the end of 2001, the exchange rate rose from 1.0 peso per U.S. dollar to nearly 1.9 pesos per U.S. dollar in 15 days, and to 3.1 in less than 4 months. During a period of just a couple of weeks in 1999, Brazil's currency, the Real, weakened by more than 50 percent relative to the U.S. dollar.

When estimating the impact of exchange rate movements on cash flow forecasts, keep in mind that evidence shows that, over the long run, purchasing power parity does hold,[3] even between emerging and developed economies. In other words, exchange rates ultimately do adjust for differences in inflation between countries. For example, if you held $100 million of Brazilian currency in 1964, by 2004 it would have been practically worthless in U.S. dollars. Yet, if we adjust for purchasing power, the value of the currency didn't change very much, as Exhibit 1 shows. In other words, suppose that, instead of holding $100 million of Brazilian currency, you held $100 million of assets in Brazil whose value increased with inflation. In 2004, your assets would have been worth about $90 million (in real terms). Therefore, when you perform valuations, your best assumption is that purchasing power parity holds in the long term; any other approach implies taking a bet on future real exchange rate movements.

Nevertheless, as Exhibit 1 also shows, exchange rates can deviate from purchasing power parity (PPP) by as much as 20 percent to 30 percent for several years (keeping in mind that PPP-adjusted exchange rates are difficult to

EXHIBIT 1	Brazilian PPP-Adjusted Dollar Exchange Rates

Reais per U.S. dollar index, 1964 = 100

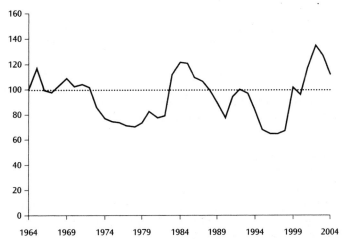

Source: MCM Consultants, IMF International Financial Statistics.

_____

[3] For a recent overview, see Alan M. Taylor and Mark Peter Taylor, "The Purchasing Power Parity Debate" (CEPR discussion paper no. 4495, 2004).

estimate). Therefore, before making financial projections, assess whether the current exchange rate is over- or undervalued on a PPP basis and, if so, by how much. Then model the convergence of currency rates to purchasing power parity, and reflect its impact on the company's profitability in your long-term financial projections. Because it is hard to predict how long the current PPP deviation will persist, you could conduct a sensitivity analysis to assess the valuation impact of the timing of the return to purchasing power parity. As you develop your forecasts, remember your overall perspective about the economics of the business. The long-term sustainable operating profit margin and ROIC should not be affected by any short-term deviations from PPP. Relying on a set of fundamental monetary assumptions keeps your projections consistent with your cost of capital whether you project in domestic, foreign, real, or nominal currency.

Regardless of any short- or long-term economic exposure to varying exchange rates, your valuation results should be independent of the currency or mix of currencies in which you forecast the company's cash flows. Use actual or synthetic forward exchange rates to convert any future cash flow into another currency. In many emerging economies, the forward-exchange market is nonexistent or illiquid, so actual forward rates provide little guidance on likely future exchange rate movements or inflation differentials. In that case, estimate a synthetic forward rate from your assumptions about future inflation and interest rates for the currencies concerned.

2   FACTORING INFLATION INTO HISTORICAL ANALYSIS AND FORECASTS

Even with consistent assumptions about inflation, interest rates, and foreign exchange rates, sound analysis and forecasting of the financial performance of emerging-market companies remains challenging. Inflation distorts the financial statements, so it is hard to make year-to-year historical comparisons, perform ratio analysis, or forecast performance.

For companies operating in high-inflation environments, historical analysis and forecasting should be carried out in both nominal and real (constant currency) terms whenever possible. As we will explain, nominal indicators are sometimes not meaningful (e.g., for capital turnover), and in other cases, real indicators are problematic (e.g., to determine corporate income taxes). Proper valuation requires insights from both nominal- and real-terms historical analyses. Financial projections can be made in real or nominal terms or both; properly done projections should yield an identical value.

Historical Analysis

Accounting conventions in emerging markets often differ substantially from those of developed markets, so a company's economics may be difficult to understand. Furthermore, in many countries, complicated tax credits and adjustments make cash taxes harder to estimate than in developed markets. For example, Brazil has made large and frequent changes to its tax code. Brazil eliminated inflation accounting and reduced the corporate tax rate to 30.5 percent in 1996, and in 1997 disallowed the deductibility of the social contribution tax, effectively increasing the tax rate to 33 percent. To make up for the loss of the tax shields that inflation accounting had generated, Brazil's government allowed companies to deduct deemed interest on equity net of a withholding tax of 15 percent.

Large accounting and tax differences are frequently eliminated when the income statement and the balance sheet are brought together in the cash flow calculation. Still, before starting a valuation, you need to understand these differences. Unfortunately, the differences across emerging markets are too complex and varied for a detailed discussion in this reading. Instead, we highlight the most common issues involving the impact of high inflation on your historical analysis.

In countries experiencing extreme inflation (more than 25 percent per year), companies often report in year-end currency. In the income statement, items such as revenues and costs that were booked throughout the year are restated at year-end purchasing power. Otherwise, the addition of these items would not be meaningful. The balance sheet usually has adjustments to fixed assets, inventory, and equity; the accounts payable and receivable are already in year-end terms.

In most countries, however, financial statements are not adjusted to reflect the effects of inflation. If inflation is high, this leads to distortions in the balance sheet and income statement. In the balance sheet, so-called nonmonetary assets, such as inventories and property, plant, and equipment, are shown at values far below current replacement value if they are long-lived assets. In the income statement, depreciation charges are too low relative to current replacement costs. Sales and costs in December and January of the same year are typically added as if they represent the same purchasing power.

As a result, many financial indicators typically used in historical analyses can be distorted when calculated directly from the financial statements. In emerging markets, companies often index their internal management accounts to overcome these issues. If they do not, or if you are doing an outside-in analysis, at least correct for the following distortions:

► Growth is overstated in times of inflation, so restate it in real terms by deflating with an annual inflation index if sales are evenly spread across the year. If sales are not spread evenly, use quarterly or monthly inflation indexes to deflate the sales in each corresponding interval.

► Capital turnover is typically overstated because operating assets are carried at historical costs. You can approximate the current costs of long-lived assets by adjusting their reported value with an inflation index for their estimated average lifetime. Or consider developing ratios of real sales relative to physical capacity indicators appropriate for the sector—for example, sales per square meter in consumer retail. Inventory levels also need restating if turnover is low and inflation is very high.

► Operating margins (operating profit over sales) can be overstated because of too-low depreciation and large holding gains on slow-moving inventories. Corrections for depreciation charges follow from adjustments to property, plant, and equipment. You can estimate cash operating expenses at current-cost basis by inflating the reported costs for the average time held in inventory. Alternatively, use historical EBITDA-to-sales ratios to assess the company's performance relative to peers; these ratios at least do not suffer from any depreciation-induced bias.

► Use caution in interpreting credit ratios and other indicators of capital structure health. Distortions are especially significant in solvency ratios such as debt to equity or total assets, because long-lived assets are understated relative to replacement costs, and floating-rate debt is at current currency units. Use coverage ratios such as EBITDA to interest expense.[4] These are

---

[4] Distortions occur in the ratio of EBITA to interest coverage if operating profit is overstated due to low depreciation charges and low costs of procured materials.

less exposed to accounting distortions because depreciation has no impact and debt financing in emerging markets is mostly at floating interest rates or in foreign currency.

Financial Projections in Real and Nominal Terms

When you make financial projections of income statements and balance sheets under high inflation for a valuation, keep in mind that accounting adjustments cannot affect free cash flow. Thus, for valuation purposes, we project financial statements without any accounting adjustments for inflation. The projections can be made in nominal or real terms. Exhibit 2 summarizes the major advantages and shortcomings of each approach.

Neither approach is perfect, so use elements of both to prepare consistent financial projections. Specifically, when projecting in real terms, it is often difficult to calculate taxes correctly, as taxes are often calculated based on nominal financial statements. Furthermore, you need to explicitly project the cash flow effects of working capital changes because these do not automatically follow from the annual change in working capital. The main downside of using nominal cash flows is that future capital expenditures are difficult to project because the typically stable relationship between revenues and fixed assets does not hold under high inflation. As a result, depreciation charges and EBITA also are difficult to project.

EXHIBIT 2	Combining Real and Nominal Approaches to Financial Modeling

Estimates	Modeling approach		Preferred application
	Real	Nominal	
Operational performance			
Sales	✓	✓	
EBITDA	✓	✓	
EBITA	✓	–	
Capital expenditures	✓	–	
Investments in working capital	✓ [a]	✓	
Income taxes	–	✓	
Financial statements	✓ [b]	✓	
Continuing value	✓ [a]	✓	

[a] If inflation impact on investments in working capital is explicitly included.
[b] If inflation corrections are separately modeled and included in income statement and balance sheet.

Five-Step Approach to Combined Nominal and Real-Terms Financial Projections

We illustrate below how to combine both nominal and real forecasts in a DCF valuation. In this example, the company's revenues grow at 2 percent in real terms, and the annual inflation rate is 20 percent in the first forecasted year and 10 percent thereafter (see Exhibit 3). To simplify, we assumed that all cash flows

EXHIBIT 3	DCF under Inflation: Key Assumptions

		Forecasts					
Operations	Year 1	2	3	4	5		25
Real growth rate (percent)	2	2	2	2	2		
Real revenues	1,000	1,020	1,040	1,061	1,082		1,608
Real EBITDA	300	306	312	318	325		483
Net working capital/revenues (percent)	20	20	20	20	20		20
Real net PPE/real revenues (percent)	40	40	40	40	40		40
Lifetime of net PPE	5						
Other							
Inflation rate (percent)		20	10	10	10		10
Inflation index	1.00	1.20	1.32	1.45	1.60		10.75
Tax rate (percent)	35	35	35	35	35		35
Real WACC (percent)		8.0	8.0	8.0	8.0		8.0
Nominal WACC (percent)		29.6	18.8	18.8	18.8		18.8

Note: Adjusted formula for real-terms continuing value.

occur at the end of the year. Under extreme inflation levels, this assumption could distort financial projections because the cash flows that accumulate throughout the year are subject to different inflation rates. In that case, split the year into quarterly or even monthly intervals, project cash flows for each interval, and discount the cash flows at the appropriate discount rate for that interval.

In practice, many more issues around financial projections arise in emerging-market valuations than in this simplified example. Nevertheless, it shows how to address some key issues when developing a cash flow forecast under high inflation, by means of the following step-by-step approach, leading to the real and nominal valuation results shown in Exhibit 4.

Step 1: Forecast Operating Performance in Real Terms To the extent possible, convert historical nominal balance sheets and income statements into real terms (usually at the current year's currency value). At a minimum, make a real-terms approximation of the historical development of the key value drivers: growth and return on capital and the underlying capital turnover and EBITA margin, so you can understand the true economics of the business. With these approximations, forecast the operating performance of the business in real terms:

▶ Project future revenues and cash expenses to obtain EBITDA forecasts.[5]

▶ Estimate property, plant, and equipment (PPE) and capital expenditures from your assumptions on real-terms capital turnover.

▶ Working capital follows from projected revenues and assumptions on days of working capital required.

▶ From projected net PPE and assumptions on the lifetime of the assets, derive the annual depreciation to estimate real-terms EBITA.

---

[5] This step assumes that all expenses included in EBITDA are cash costs.

EXHIBIT 4   DCF under Inflation: Real and Nominal Models

	Real projections						Nominal projections					
NOPLAT	**Year 1**	**2**	**3**	**4**	**5**	**25**	**Year 1**	**2**	**3**	**4**	**5**	**25**
Revenues	1,000	1,020	1,040	1,061	1,082	1,608	1,000	1,224	1,373	1,541	1,729	17,283
EBITDA	300	306	312	318	325	483	300	367	412	462	519	5,185
Depreciation	(80)	(80)	(82)	(83)	(85)	(126)	(80)	(80)	(85)	(92)	(100)	(926)
EBITA	220	226	231	235	240	356	220	287	327	370	419	4,259
Taxes	(77)	(84)	(87)	(89)	(92)	(139)	(77)	(101)	(114)	(130)	(147)	(1,491)
NOPLAT	143	142	144	146	148	218	143	187	212	241	272	2,768
Free cash flow												
NOPLAT	143	142	144	146	148	218	143	187	212	241	272	2,768
Depreciation	80	80	82	83	85	126	80	80	85	92	100	926
Capital expenditures	(80)	(88)	(90)	(92)	(93)	(139)	(80)	(106)	(118)	(133)	(149)	(1,491)
Investment in net working capital		(37)	(23)	(23)	(24)	(35)		(45)	(30)	(34)	(38)	(376)
Free cash flow	143	97	113	114	116	170	143	116	149	166	185	1,827
Invested capital												
Net PPE (beginning of year)	400	400	408	416	424	631	400	400	426	459	500	4,631
Depreciation	(80)	(80)	(82)	(83)	(85)	(126)	(80)	(80)	(85)	(92)	(100)	(926)
Capital expenditures	80	88	90	92	93	139	80	106	118	133	149	1,491
Net PPE (end of year)	400	408	416	424	433	643	400	426	459	500	549	5,196
Net working capital	200	204	208	212	216	322	200	245	275	308	346	3,457
Invested capital	600	612	624	637	649	965	600	670	734	808	895	8,653
Ratios (percent)												
Net PPE/revenues	40	40	40	40	40	40		35	33	32	32	30
Net working capital/revenues	20	20	20	20	20	20		20	20	20	20	20
ROIC	24	24	24	23	23	23		31	32	33	34	36
Free cash flow growth rate			17	1	1	2			28	11	12	12
DCF valuation												
Free cash flow		97	113	114	116	170		116	149	166	185	1,827
Continuing value (value driver formula)[a]						2,891						31,063
Continuing value (cash flow perpetuity formula)						2,891						31,064
Present value factor	0.93	0.86	0.79	0.74		0.16	0.77	0.65	0.55	0.46		0.01
DCF value	1,795						1,795					

[a] Adjusted formula for real-terms continuing value.

Step 2: Build Financial Statements in Nominal Terms   Nominal projections can be readily derived by converting the real operating projections into nominal terms (note that these projections do not include any monetary adjustments as under, for example, inflation accounting):

► Project nominal revenues, cash expenses, EBITDA, and capital expenditures by multiplying their real-terms equivalents by the inflation index for the year.

► Estimate net property, plant, and equipment on a year-by-year basis from the prior-year balance plus nominal capital expenditures minus nominal depreciation (which is estimated as a percentage of net PPE according to the estimated lifetime).

► Working capital follows from revenues and days of working capital required.

► Subtract the depreciation charges from EBITDA to obtain nominal EBITA.

► Calculate income taxes on nominal EBITA without inflation corrections. (Always check the local tax rules for the reasonableness of this assumption.)

In contrast to the real-terms projections, the capital turnover is now increasing over time because nominal net PPE grows slower than revenues in a high-inflation environment. In this example, we did not build a complete balance sheet and income statement. That would require the following additional steps:

► Forecast interest expense and other nonoperating income statement items in nominal terms (based on the prior year's balance sheet).

► Equity should equal last year's equity plus earnings, less dividends, plus or minus any share issues or repurchases.

► Finally, balance the balance sheet with debt or marketable securities.[6]

Step 3: Build Financial Statements in Real Terms   Most of the operating items for the real-terms income statement and balance sheet were already estimated in step 1. Now also include the real-terms taxes on EBITA by deflating the nominal taxes as estimated in step 2. For full financial statements, use the inflation index to convert debt, marketable securities, interest expense, income taxes, and nonoperating terms from the nominal statements into real terms. The real-terms equity account is a plug to balance the balance sheet. To make sure you have done this correctly, be sure the real equity account equals last year's equity plus earnings, less dividends, plus or minus share issues or repurchases, and plus or minus inflationary gains or losses on the monetary assets (such as cash, receivables, payables, and debt).

Step 4: Forecast the Future Free Cash Flows in Real and Nominal Terms from the Projected Income Statements and Balance Sheets   The real-terms investment

---

[6] As noted, these projections are made for valuation purposes and not necessarily in accordance with local or international accounting standards prescribing any inflation or monetary corrections for particular groups of assets and liabilities. Free cash flows are not affected by such adjustments.

in net working capital (NWC^R) is equal to the increase in working capital plus a monetary loss due to inflation:[7]

$$\text{Investment in NWC}_t = \text{Increase in NWC}_t^R + \text{NWC}_{t-1}^R \left[1 - \frac{\text{IX}_{t-1}}{\text{IX}_t} \right]$$

where IX_t is the inflation index for the year t.

To check for consistency, use the inflation index to convert the free cash flows from the nominal projections to real terms. These should equal the free cash flows from the real-terms projections in each year.

Step 5:   Estimate DCF Value in Real and Nominal Terms   When discounting real and nominal cash flows under high inflation, you must address three key issues:

1. Ensure that the WACC estimates in real terms ($WACC^R$) and nominal terms ($WACC^N$) are defined consistently with the inflation assumptions in each year:

$$(1 + WACC_t^N) = (1 + \text{WACC}_t^R) \times (1 + \text{Inflation}_t)$$

Later in this reading, we will discuss how to estimate WACC for companies in emerging markets.

2. The value-driver formula should be adjusted when estimating continuing value in real terms. The returns on capital in real-terms projections overestimate the economic returns in the case of positive net working capital. The free cash flow in real terms differs from the cash flow implied by the value driver formula by an amount equal to the annual monetary loss on net working capital:

$$FCF_t^R = \left(1 - \frac{g_t^R}{\text{ROIC}_t^R} \right) \times \text{NOPLAT}_t^R - \text{NWC}_{t-1}^R \left(1 - \frac{\text{IX}_{t-1}}{\text{IX}_t} \right)$$

The real-terms value driver formula is adjusted for this monetary loss, reflecting the perpetuity assumptions for inflation (i) and the ratio of net working capital to invested capital (NWC^R/IC^R):

$$CV^R = \frac{\left(1 - \frac{G^R}{\text{ROIC}^R} \right) \text{NOPLAT}^R}{\text{WACC}^R - g^R}$$

where

$$G^R = g^R - \left[\frac{\text{NWC}^R}{\text{IC}^R} \times \left(\frac{i}{1+i} \right) \right]$$

---

[7] Even for assets held at constant levels in real-terms balance sheets, replacement investments are required at increasing prices in an inflationary environment. These replacement investments represent a cash outflow, also in real terms, but do not show up from real-terms balance sheet differences from year to year. In contrast, the nominal investment cash flow does follow from the nominal balance sheet differences from year to year.

The resulting continuing-value estimate is the same as that obtained from a free cash flow perpetuity formula. After indexing for inflation, it also equals the continuing-value estimates derived from nominal projections.

3. When using the continuing-value formulas, make sure the explicit forecast period is long enough for the model to reach a steady state with constant growth rates of free cash flow. Because of the way inflation affects capital expenditures and depreciation, you need a much longer horizon than for valuations with no or low inflation.

ConsuCo Case Example: Inflation Adjustments

Let's explore how to handle inflation and accounting issues in the financial analysis and valuation of ConsuCo.

Historical Analysis　In analyzing ConsuCo's historical financial statements, we made adjustments in two areas. First, we rearranged the balance sheet and the income statements to get the statements for NOPLAT, invested capital, and free cash flow. The ConsuCo statements follow Brazilian GAAP, so we had to make some additional adjustments. Most of these were relatively minor. The largest involved the consolidation of a securitization vehicle, for which only the net asset position is shown under Brazilian GAAP.

Second, we estimated some key financial ratios on an approximate real-terms basis. Although annual inflation in Brazil has been moderate since 1997 at levels between 5 and 10 percent, ratios such as operating margin and capital turnover are likely to be biased when directly calculated from the financial statements. Therefore, we looked at trends in cash operating margins (EBITDA over sales). In addition, we estimated the sales revenues in real terms per unit of production capacity over time to better understand the development of real-terms capital turnover.

The results are reflected in Exhibit 5. Between 1998 and 2003, ConsuCo's sales grew significantly in real terms at around 15 percent per year, largely driven by acquisitions. But growth has slowed considerably since 2000. Cash operating margins improved significantly, from 5.7 percent in 1998 to 9.2 percent in 2003. In real terms, annual sales per unit of production capacity have been fairly stable

EXHIBIT 5	ConsuCo: Key Historical Financial Indicators

percent

Nominal indicators	1998	1999	2000	2001	2002	2003
Sales growth	41	32	31	6	17	14
Adjusted EBITA/sales	3.5	4.6	5.7	5.3	5.3	6.9
NOPLAT/sales	2.9	3.3	4.8	4.5	3.9	5.3
Invested capital (excluding goodwill)/sales	35.2	34.8	57.0	64.9	62.4	64.5
Invested capital (including goodwill)/sales	42.3	40.3	61.9	74.7	71.7	72.9
ROIC (excluding goodwill)	8.3	9.5	8.4	6.9	6.2	8.2
ROIC (including goodwill)	6.9	8.2	7.7	6.0	5.4	7.3
Approximate real indicators						
Sales growth (inflation-adjusted)	32	24	23	(2)	9	5
EBITDA/sales	5.7	6.7	7.2	7.6	7.5	9.2
Sales/capacity[a]	8.7	7.9	7.0	6.4	6.3	6.2

[a]In inflation-adjusted Reais million per capacity unit.

since 2000 at around 6.0 to 6.5 million Reais, as have nominal turnover levels for invested capital (excluding goodwill).

Financial projections   Based on the findings from the historical analysis and analyst consensus forecasts as of July 2004, we made the operating and financial forecasts summarized in Exhibit 6 in real and nominal terms. We assumed that no major economic crisis will materialize in Brazil.

ConsuCo is investing heavily for future growth. Real-terms sales growth is projected to peak at 8 percent in 2005 and then gradually decline over the next four years to around 3 percent, close to Brazil's long-term expected real GDP growth. Cash margins will continue to rise to 9.7 percent in 2005 and stay at that level in perpetuity. Tougher competition will create downward pressure on margins, but the company's improvements in selling, general and administrative expenses compensate for this.

Capacity requirements are derived from sales forecasts in real terms, assuming sales productivity of 6.2 million Reais per unit of capacity. Capital expenditures for maintenance are estimated in real terms as a percentage of projected total capacity and expenditures for capacity expansion are projected at around 2.3 million Reais per unit. The future development of net PPE in real terms is derived from the capital expenditure projections.

The resulting ROIC (excluding goodwill) in real terms for ConsuCo decreases from its current value of around 7.6 percent to around 6.6 percent in the continuing value period. In contrast, the ROIC in nominal terms increases from 8.4 to around 10.1 percent because of the inflation impact on capital turnover.

EXHIBIT 6	ConsuCo: Summary Financial Projections, Base Case

Reais million, percent

	2004	2005	2006	2007	2008	2009	2014	2019
Operating projections								
Sales growth (real, percent)	7.0	8.0	7.0	6.0	5.0	3.0	3.0	3.0
EBITDA/sales (percent)	9.5	9.7	9.7	9.7	9.7	9.7	9.7	9.7
EBITDA (real terms, percent)	2,201	2,427	2,597	2,753	2,890	2,977	3,451	4,001
Sales/capacity[a]	6.2	6.2	6.2	6.2	6.2	6.2	6.2	6.2
Capacity units	3,757	4,058	4,342	4,602	4,832	4,977	5,770	6,689
Capital expenditures (expansion)[b]	558	682	645	591	522	329	382	442
Capital expenditures (maintenance)[b]	663	709	766	819	869	912	1,057	1,226
Real projections								
Sales	23,126	24,976	26,724	28,327	29,744	30,636	35,516	41,172
Adjusted EBITA/sales (percent)	7.2	7.4	7.5	7.5	7.6	7.6	7.7	7.8
NOPLAT/sales (percent)	4.8	4.8	4.7	4.6	4.5	4.4	4.2	4.1
Invested capital (excluding goodwill)/ sales (percent)	70.2	69.3	68.6	68.0	67.6	67.2	65.9	65.0
ROIC (excluding goodwill, percent)	7.6	7.6	7.4	7.3	7.2	7.0	6.7	6.6
Nominal projections								
Sales	24,778	28,258	31,721	35,164	38,558	41,474	59,717	85,984
Adjusted EBITA/sales (percent)	6.9	7.0	7.0	7.0	6.9	6.9	6.8	6.8
NOPLAT/sales (percent)	5.0	5.2	5.2	5.2	5.2	5.1	5.1	5.1
Invested capital (excluding goodwill)/ sales (percent)	60.0	58.3	57.2	56.3	55.5	54.7	52.2	51.0
ROIC (excluding goodwill, percent)	8.4	8.9	9.0	9.2	9.3	9.3	9.8	10.1

[a] In inflation-adjusted Reais million per capacity unit.
[b] In inflation-adjusted Reais million.

INCORPORATING EMERGING-MARKET RISKS IN THE VALUATION

The major distinction between valuing companies in developed markets and emerging markets is the increased level of risk. Not only must you account for risks related to the company's strategy, market position, and industry dynamics, as you would in a developed market, you must also deal with the risks caused by greater volatility in the capital markets and in the macroeconomic and political environments.

There is no consensus on how to reflect this higher level of risk in a DCF valuation. The most common approach is to add a country risk premium to the discount rate. The alternative is to model risks explicitly in the cash flow projections in what we call the *scenario DCF approach*. Both methodologies, if correctly and consistently applied, lead to the same result. We show this in the following example of an investment in two identical production plants, one in Europe and the other in an emerging economy (see Exhibit 7). However, the scenario DCF approach is analytically more robust and better shows the impact of emerging-market risks on value.

Scenario DCF Approach

The scenario DCF approach simulates alternative trajectories for future cash flows. At a minimum, model two scenarios: One should assume that cash flow develops according to conditions reflecting business as usual (i.e., without major economic distress). The second should reflect cash flows assuming that any emerging-market risks materialize.

In the example, the cash flows for the European plant grow steadily at 3 percent per year into perpetuity. For the plant in the emerging market, the cash flow growth is the same under a business-as-usual scenario, but there is a 25 percent probability of economic distress resulting in a cash flow that is 55 percent lower into perpetuity. The emerging-market risk is taken into account, not in the cost of capital, but in the lower expected value of future cash flows from weighting both scenarios at the assumed probabilities. The resulting value of the emerging-market plant (€1,917) is clearly below the value of its European sister plant (€2,222), using a WACC of 7.5 percent.

We assumed for simplicity that if adverse economic conditions develop in the emerging market, they will do so in the first year of the plant's operation. In reality, of course, the investment will face a probability of domestic economic distress in each year of its lifetime. Modeling risk over time would require more complex calculations yet would not change the basic results. We also assumed that in a local crisis, the emerging-market business would face significantly lower cash flows but not wind up entirely worthless.

Country Risk Premium DCF Approach

The second approach is to add a country risk premium to the cost of capital for comparable investments in developed markets. We then apply the resulting discount rate to the cash flow projections following a business-as-usual scenario. The key drawback is that there is no objective way to establish the country risk premium. For our two-plant example, we can derive in hind-sight what the premium should be to obtain the same result as under the scenario DCF approach. For us to arrive at a value of €1,917 for the emerging-market plant, the

EXHIBIT 7   Scenario DCF versus Country Risk Premium DCF

Net present value for identical facilities in ...

Scenario approach

... a European market

Probability	Cash flows in perpetuity[a]				
		Year 1	2	3	4...
100%	"As usual"	100	103	106	109
0%	"Distressed"				
	Expected cash flows	100	103	106	109
					7.5%
	Cost of capital				
	Net present value	2,222			

... an emerging market

Probability	Cash flows in perpetuity[b]				
		Year 1	2	3	4...
75%	"As usual"	100	103	106	109
25%	"Distressed"	45	46	48	49
	Expected cash flows	86	89	92	94
					7.5%
	Cost of capital				
	Net present value	1,917			86% of European NPV

Country risk premium approach

... a European market

Cash flows in perpetuity[a]				
	Year 1	2	3	4...
"As usual"	100	103	106	109
				7.5%
Cost of capital				
Net present value	2,222			

... an emerging market

Cash flows in perpetuity[b]				
	Year 1	2	3	4...
"As usual"	100	103	106	109
Cost of capital				7.5%
Country risk premium				0.7%
Adjusted cost of capital				8.2%
Net present value	1,917			86% of European NPV

[a] Assuming perpetuity cash flow growth of 3%.
[b] Assuming perpetuity cash flow growth of 3% and recovery under distress of 45% of cash flows "as usual."

discount rate for the business-as-usual projections would have to be 8.2 percent, which translates to a country risk premium of 0.7 percent.

On occasion, practitioners make the mistake of adding the country risk premium to the cost of capital to discount the *expected* value of future cash flows rather than to the "promised" cash flows of a business-as-usual scenario. The resulting value is too low because the probability of a crisis is accounted for twice.[8]

Scenario DCF as Prime Valuation Approach

Some surveys show that managers generally adjust for emerging-market risks by adding a risk premium to the discount rate.[9] Nonetheless, we recommend the scenario DCF approach. It provides a more solid analytical foundation and a more robust understanding of the value than incorporating country risks in the discount rate.

One reason is that most country risks, including expropriation, devaluation, and war, are largely diversifiable (though not entirely, as the economic crisis in 1998 demonstrated). Consider the international consumer goods player illustrated in Exhibit 8. Its returns on capital were highly volatile for individual emerging markets, but taken together, these markets were hardly more volatile than developed markets; the corporate portfolio diversified away most of the risks. Finance theory clearly indicates that the cost of capital should not reflect risk that can be diversified. This does not mean that diversifiable risk is irrelevant for a valuation: the possibility of adverse future events will affect the level of

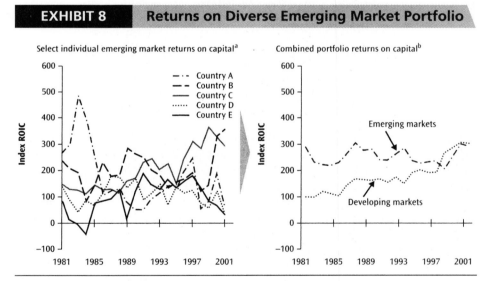

EXHIBIT 8   Returns on Diverse Emerging Market Portfolio

Select individual emerging market returns on capital[a]

Combined portfolio returns on capital[b]

[a] In stable currency and adjusted for local accounting differences.
[b] Combined portfolio included additional countries not reflected here.

Source: Company information.

---

[8] This is analogous to the error made by discounting the expected coupon and principal payments on a corporate bond at the promised yield (i.e., the yield to maturity) instead of the expected yield (i.e., the cost of debt).

[9] T. Keck, E. Levengood, and A. Longfield, "Using Discounted Cash Flow Analysis in an International Setting: A Survey of Issues in Modeling the Cost of Capital," *Journal of Applied Corporate Finance*, 11(3) (1998).

expected cash flows, as in the example in Exhibit 7. But once this has been incorporated in the forecast for cash flows, there is no need for an additional markup of the cost of capital if the risk is diversifiable.

Another argument against a country risk premium is that many country risks apply unequally to companies in a given country. For example, banks are more likely to be affected than retailers. Some companies (raw-materials exporters) might benefit from a currency devaluation, while others (raw-materials importers) will be damaged. For the consumer goods company in Exhibit 8, economic crises had only a short-term impact on sales and profit as measured in stable currency. In most cases, after a year or two, sales and profits roughly regained their original growth trajectories. Applying the same risk premium to all companies in an emerging market could overstate the risk for some businesses and understate it for others.

Furthermore, there is no systematic method to calculate a country risk premium. In our example, we could reengineer this premium because the true value of the plant was already known from the scenario approach. In practice, the country risk premium is sometimes set at the spread of the local government debt rate[10] denominated in U.S. dollars and a U.S. government bond of similar maturity. However, that is reasonable only if the returns on local government debt are highly correlated with returns on corporate investments.

Finally, when managers have to discuss emerging-market risks and their effect on cash flow in scenarios, they gain more insights than they would get from a "black box" addition to the discount rate. By identifying specific factors with a large impact on value, managers can plan to mitigate these risks. Furthermore, managers easily underestimate the impact of even a small country risk premium in the discount rate: In the example of Exhibit 8, setting a country risk premium to 3 percent would be equivalent to assuming a 70 percent probability of economic distress.

Constructing Cash Flow Scenarios and Probabilities

To use the scenario DCF approach, construct at least two scenarios. The base case, or business-as-usual scenario, describes how the business will perform if no major crises occur. The downside scenario describes the financial results if a major crisis does occur.

For both scenarios, start by projecting the macroeconomic environment because this influences industry and company performance. The major macroeconomic variables to forecast are GDP growth, inflation rates, foreign-exchange rates, and interest rates. These items must be linked in a way that reflects economic realities and should be included in the basic set of monetary assumptions underlying your valuation. For instance, when constructing a downside scenario with high inflation, make sure that the same inflation rates underlie the financial projections and cost of capital estimates for the company to be valued. Foreign exchange rates should also reflect this inflation in the long run because of purchasing power parity.

Given the assumptions for macroeconomic performance, construct the industry scenarios basically in the same way as in developed markets. The major difference is in the greater uncertainty involved in modeling outcomes under severe crises for which there may be no precedent.

---

[10] This is also a promised yield rather than an expected yield on government bonds, further underlining the point that the cost of capital based on country risk premium should not be applied to expected cash flows, but to "promised" cash flows (those following a business-as-usual scenario in which no country risk materializes).

While estimating probabilities for the cash flow scenarios is ultimately a matter of management judgment, there are indicators of reasonable probabilities. Historical data on previous crises can give some indication of frequency and severity of country risk and the time required for recovery. Analyzing the changes in GDP of 20 emerging economies over the past 20 years, we found that these economies had experienced economic distress about once every five years (a real-terms GDP decline of more than 5 percent). This would suggest a 20 percent probability for a downside scenario.

Another source of information for estimating probabilities is prospective data from current government bond prices.[11] Recent academic research suggests that government default probabilities five years into the future in emerging markets such as Argentina, were around 30 percent in nondistress years.[12]

ConsuCo Case Example: Cash Flow Scenarios and Probabilities

Returning to the ConsuCo example, we already constructed a business-as-usual scenario in the previous section. For a downward scenario, we analyzed ConsuCo's performance under more adverse economic conditions in the past. Brazil has experienced several severe economic and monetary downturns, including an inflation rate that surpassed 2,000 percent in 1993. Judging by its key financial indicators, such as EBITDA to sales and real-terms sales growth, the impact on ConsuCo's business performance was significant. ConsuCo's cash operating margin was negative for four years, at around -10 to -5 percent, and then recovered to its normal levels. In the same period, sales in real terms declined by 10 to 15 percent per year but grew sharply after the crisis. For the downside scenario projections, we assumed similar negative cash margins and real-terms sales decline for up to five years, followed by a gradual return to the long-term margins and growth assumed under the business-as-usual scenario. Exhibit 9 compares the nominal and real returns on invested capital under both scenarios: In the downside scenario, the returns plummet and then increase as the recovery starts. After 2010, the nominal returns even surpass those in the base case as the extreme inflation levels push up the capital turnovers. Of course, the nominal returns are artificially high, as a comparison with the real returns shows. The DCF value under the downside scenario will turn out to be only half of the base-case value. We estimated the probability of this downside scenario at 25 to 35 percent.

ESTIMATING COST OF CAPITAL IN EMERGING MARKETS

4

Calculating the cost of capital in any country can be challenging, but for emerging markets, the challenge is an order of magnitude higher. In this section, we provide our fundamental assumptions, background on the important issues, and a practical way to estimate the components of the cost of capital.

---

[11] See, for example, D. Duffie and K. Singleton, "Modeling Term Structures of Defaultable Bonds," *Review of Financial Studies* 12 (1999): 687–720; and R. Merton, "On the Pricing of Corporate Debt: The Risk Structure of Interest Rates," *Journal of Finance*, 29(2) (1974): 449–470.

[12] See J. Merrick, "Crisis Dynamics of Implied Default Recovery Ratios: Evidence from Russia and Argentina," *Journal of Banking and Finance*, 25(10) (2001): 1921–1939.

EXHIBIT 9	ConsuCo: ROIC in Downside Scenario versus Base Case

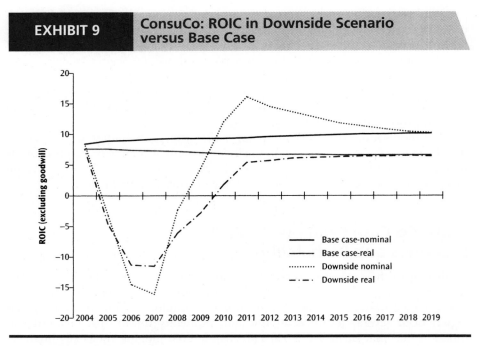

Fundamental Assumptions

Our analysis adopts the perspective of a global investor—either a multinational company or an international investor with a diversified portfolio. Of course, many emerging markets are not well integrated with the global market, and local investors may face barriers to investing outside their home market. As a result, local investors cannot always hold **well-diversified portfolios**, and their cost of capital may be considerably different from that of a global investor. Unfortunately, there is no established framework for estimating the capital cost for local investors. Furthermore, as long as international investors have access to local investment opportunities, local prices will be based on an international cost of capital. Finally, according to empirical research, emerging markets have become increasingly integrated into global capital markets.[13] We believe that this trend will continue and that most countries will gradually reduce foreign-investment restrictions for local investors in the long run.

Another assumption is that most country risks are diversifiable from the perspective of the global investor. We therefore need no additional risk premiums in the cost of capital for the risks encountered in emerging markets when discounting expected cash flows. Of course, if you choose to discount the cash flow from the business-as-usual scenario only, you should add a country risk premium.

Given these assumptions, the cost of capital in emerging markets should generally be close to a global cost of capital adjusted for local inflation and capital structure. It is also useful to keep some general guidelines in mind:

► *Use the CAPM to estimate the cost of equity in emerging markets.* The CAPM may be a less robust model for the less-integrated emerging markets, but there is no better alternative model today. Furthermore, we believe it will become a better predictor of equity returns world-wide as markets continue to become more integrated.

---

[13] See, for example, C. Harvey, "The Drivers of Expected Returns in International Markets," *Emerging Markets Quarterly* (Fall 2000): 1–17.

▶ *There is no one "right" answer, so be pragmatic.* In emerging markets, there are often significant information and data gaps (e.g., for estimating betas or the risk-free rate in local currency). Be flexible as you assemble the available information piece by piece to build the cost of capital, and triangulate your results with country risk premium approaches and multiples.

▶ *Be sure monetary assumptions are consistent.* Ground your model in a common set of monetary assumptions to ensure that the cash flow forecasts and discount rate are consistent. If you are using local nominal cash flows, the cost of capital must reflect the local inflation rate that is embedded in the cash flows. For real-terms cash flows, subtract inflation from the nominal cost of capital.

▶ *Allow for changes in cost of capital.* The cost of capital in an emerging-market valuation may change, based on evolving inflation expectations, changes in a company's capital structure and cost of debt, or foreseeable reforms in the tax system. For example, for valuations in Argentina during the economic and monetary crisis of 2002, the short-term inflation rate of 30 percent could not be considered a reasonable basis for a long-term cost of capital estimate because such a crisis could not be expected to last forever.[14] In such cases, estimate the cost of capital on a year-by-year basis, following the underlying set of basic monetary assumptions.

▶ *Don't mix approaches.* Use the cost of capital to discount the cash flows in a probability-weighted scenario approach. Do not add any risk premium, because you would be double-counting risk. If you are discounting only future cash flows in a business-as-usual scenario, add a risk premium to the discount rate.

Estimating the Cost of Equity

To estimate the components of the cost of equity, use the standard CAPM model.

Risk-free Rate   In emerging markets, the risk-free rate is harder to estimate from government bonds than in developed markets. Three main problems arise. First, most of the government debt in emerging markets is not, in fact, risk free: The ratings on much of this debt are often well below investment grade. Second, it is difficult to find long-term government bonds that are actively traded with sufficient liquidity. Finally, the long-term debt that is traded is often in U.S. dollars, a European currency, or the Japanese yen, so it is not appropriate for discounting local nominal cash flows.

Our recommendation is to follow a very straightforward approach. Start with a risk-free rate based on the 10-year U.S. government bond yield, as in developed markets. Add to this the projected difference over time between U.S. and local inflation to develop a nominal risk-free rate in local currency.[15] Sometimes you can derive this inflation differential from the spread between local government bond yields denominated in local currency versus U.S. dollars.[16]

Beta   Sometimes practitioners calculate beta relative to the local market index. This is not only inconsistent from the perspective of a global investor, but also potentially distorted by the fact that the index in an emerging market will rarely

---

[14] Annual consumer price inflation came down to around 5 percent in Argentina in 2004.

[15] In this way, we do not model the U.S. **term structure of interest rates**. Technically, this should be included as well, but it will not make a large difference in the valuation.

[16] Technically, this is correct only if the emerging-market bonds are relatively low risk, as for example for Chile and South Korea.

be representative of a diversified economy. Instead, estimate industry betas relative to a well-diversified or global market index as recommended in Reading 58. Since equity markets in emerging economies are often small, with liquidity concentrated in a few stocks, it may be hard to find a representative sample of publicly traded local companies to estimate an industry beta. In that case, derive an industry beta from international comparables that operate in the same or a similar sector. The implicit assumption is that the fundamental drivers of systematic risk will be similar in emerging and developed markets.

For ConsuCo, we used three sources for estimates of beta in an international peer group: Bloomberg betas calculated against the FT World Index, Barra betas, and betas adjusted for the high-tech boom. Note that the unlevered beta estimates are similar for industry peers, with some exceptions, as shown in Exhibit 10. Overall, our estimate for the unlevered industry beta is 0.55, translating into an equity beta for ConsuCo of 0.8 (given a debt-to-capital target weight of 0.3, as discussed later).

Market Risk Premium Excess returns of local equity markets over local bond returns are not a good proxy for the market risk premium. This holds even more so for emerging markets given the lack of diversification in the local equity market. Furthermore, the quality and length of available data on equity and bond market returns are usually unsuitable for making long-term estimates. To use a market risk premium that is consistent with the perspective of a global investor, use a global estimate of 4.5 to 5.5 percent.

In Exhibit 11, we summarize the nominal cost of equity calculation for ConsuCo. In the base case, we have assumed a decreasing rate of inflation for the Brazilian economy from 7.1 percent in 2004 to 4.4 percent in 2008 and beyond. This is also reflected in the cost of capital estimates going forward. For the downside scenario, inflation projections follow a different trajectory, and the cost of capital for this scenario is adjusted accordingly.

EXHIBIT 10	**ConsuCo: Estimating Beta**

| | Unlevered betas | | | |
Peers	Bloomberg[a]	Barra	Adjusted[b]	Average
ConsuCo	0.733	1.343	0.748	1.038
PeerCo 1	0.664	0.712	0.782	0.688
PeerCo 2	0.589	0.407	0.846	0.498
PeerCo 3	0.795	0.693	1.232	0.744
PeerCo 4	0.492	0.236	0.346	0.364
PeerCo 5	0.475	0.749	0.439	0.612
PeerCo 6	0.480	0.231	0.381	0.356
PeerCo 7	0.294	0.198	0.271	0.246
PeerCo 8	0.278	0.361	0.386	0.319
PeerCo 9	0.418	0.384	0.641	0.401
PeerCo 10	0.820	0.635	0.803	0.728
PeerCo 11	0.649	0.688	0.625	0.669
Average	**0.557**	**0.553**	**0.625**	**0.555**
Median	**0.541**	**0.521**	**0.633**	**0.531**

[a] Against FT World Index on a weekly basis over past two years.
[b] Adjusted for the high-tech boom.
Source: Bloomberg, Barra, Datastream, McKinsey analysis.

		EXHIBIT 11		ConsuCo: Estimating the Nominal Cost of Equity					

	2004	2005	2006	2007	2008	2009	2014	2019
United States								
Inflation (percent)	2.0	2.0	2.0	2.0	2.0	2.0	2.0	2.0
Risk-free interest rate (percent)	4.6	4.6	4.6	4.6	4.6	4.6	4.6	4.6
Brazil								
Inflation (IPCA, percent)	7.1	5.6	4.9	4.6	4.4	4.4	4.4	4.4
Risk-free interest rate (percent)[a]	9.8	8.2	7.5	7.2	7.0	7.0	7.0	7.0
Relevered beta	0.8	0.8	0.8	0.8	0.8	0.8	0.8	0.8
Market risk premium (percent)	5.0	5.0	5.0	5.0	5.0	5.0	5.0	5.0
Cost of equity (percent)	14.0	12.4	11.7	11.3	11.1	11.1	11.1	11.1

[a] Brazilian risk-free rate estimated as: $(1 + \text{U.S. risk free rate}) \times (1 + \text{Brazilian inflation}) \div (1 + \text{U.S. inflation}) - 1$.

Source: Banco Central do Brasil, Bloomberg, EIU Viewswire, McKinsey analysis.

Estimating the After-Tax Cost of Debt

In most emerging economies, there are no liquid markets for corporate bonds, so little or no market information is available to estimate the cost of debt. However, from an international investor's perspective, the cost of debt in local currency should simply equal the sum of the dollar (or euro) risk-free rate, the systematic part of the credit spread, and the inflation differential between local currency and dollars (or euros). Most of the country risk can be diversified away in a global bond portfolio. Therefore, the systematic part of the default risk is probably no larger than that of companies in international markets, and the cost of debt should not include a separate country risk premium. This explains why the funding costs of multinationals with extensive emerging-market portfolios, companies including Coca-Cola and Colgate-Palmolive, have a cost of debt no higher than their mainly U.S.-focused competitors.

Returning to the ConsuCo example, we calculated the cost of debt in Brazilian Reais. ConsuCo does not have its own credit rating, but based on its EBITDA coverage ratios versus rated peers, we estimated that ConsuCo would probably have a B to B+ rating. ConsuCo's cost of debt can be estimated as the sum of the risk-free rate in Brazilian Reais plus the systematic credit spread for a U.S. corporate bond rated B+ versus the U.S. government bond yield as shown in Exhibit 12. Of course, the inflation assumptions underlying the estimates for cost of debt should be consistent with those for the base-case and downside scenarios.

Remember that ConsuCo's cost of debt is significantly lower than the interest rate it is currently paying because the latter represents the promised yield, not the expected yield.

The marginal tax rate in emerging markets can be very different from the effective tax rate, which often includes investment tax credits, export tax credits, taxes, equity or dividend credits, and operating loss credits. Many of these do not provide a tax shield on interest expense. Only taxes that apply to interest expense should be used in the WACC estimate. Other taxes or credits should be modeled directly in the cash flows. For ConsuCo, we used the Brazilian corporate income tax rate of 25 percent plus social contribution tax of 9 percent.

| EXHIBIT 12 | ConsuCo: Estimating the Nominal Cost of Debt |

percent

	2004	2005	2006	2007	2008	2009	2014	2019
Risk-free interest rate	9.8	8.2	7.5	7.2	7.0	7.0	7.0	7.0
BBB credit spread	1.2	1.2	1.2	1.2	1.2	1.2	1.2	1.2
Systematic credit spread for B+	0.5	0.5	0.5	0.5	0.5	0.5	0.5	0.5
Cost of debt	11.5	9.9	9.2	8.9	8.8	8.8	8.8	8.8
Tax rate	34	34	34	34	34	34	34	34
After-tax cost of debt	7.6	6.6	6.1	5.9	5.8	5.8	5.8	5.8

Source: Standard & Poor's, McKinsey analysis.

Estimating WACC

Given the estimates for cost of equity and after-tax cost of debt, we need debt and equity weights to derive an estimate of the weighted average cost of capital. In emerging markets, many companies have unusual capital structures compared with their international peers. One reason is, of course, the country risk. The possibility of macroeconomic distress makes companies more conservative in setting their leverage. Another reason could be anomalies in the local debt or equity markets. In the long run, when the **anomalies** are corrected, the companies should expect to converge to a capital structure similar to that of their global competitors. You could forecast explicitly how the company evolves to a capital structure that is more similar to global standards. In that case, you should consider using the APV approach.

For the ConsuCo case, we kept the capital structure going forward at its long-term historical levels, with leverage somewhat below the peer group average at a ratio of debt to enterprise value of 0.3. Exhibit 13 summarizes the WACC estimates for both the base case and downside scenario in nominal terms. Note how the extreme inflation assumption underlying the downside scenario leads to a radically higher cost of capital in the crisis years until 2009.

Estimating the Country Risk Premium

If you are discounting business-as-usual cash flows instead of expected cash flows, you should add a country risk premium to the WACC. There is no agreed-upon approach to estimating this premium, but we have some advice.

Do Not Simply Use the Sovereign Risk Premium   The long-term **sovereign risk premium** equals the difference between a long-term (e.g., 10-year) U.S. government bond yield and a dollar-denominated local bond's stripped yield[17] with the same maturity. This difference will reasonably approximate the country risk premium only if the cash flows of the corporation being valued move closely in line with the payments on government bonds. This is not necessarily the case. In the consumer goods or raw-materials sector, for example, cash flows have low correlation with local government bond payments and lower volatility.

---

[17] Some emerging markets' country debt is partially guaranteed by international institutions or backed by U.S. Treasury bonds. For these bonds, you need to estimate the yield on the nonguaranteed part of the bond, the "stripped" yield. Stripped yields are available from bond data suppliers.

EXHIBIT 13	ConsuCo: Estimating Nominal WACC for ConsuCo							
	2004	**2005**	**2006**	**2007**	**2008**	**2009**	**2014**	**2019**
Base case								
After-tax cost of debt (percent)	7.6	6.6	6.1	5.9	5.8	5.8	5.8	5.8
Cost of equity (percent)	14.0	12.4	11.7	11.3	11.1	11.1	11.1	11.1
Debt/enterprise value	0.3	0.3	0.3	0.3	0.3	0.3	0.3	0.3
WACC (percent)	12.0	10.5	9.9	9.5	9.4	9.4	9.4	9.4
Downside								
After-tax cost of debt (percent)	7.6	37.1	105.9	37.1	19.9	6.2	5.8	5.8
Cost of equity (percent)	14.0	59.6	166.0	59.6	33.0	11.7	11.1	11.1
Debt/enterprise value	0.3	0.3	0.3	0.3	0.3	0.3	0.3	0.3
WACC (percent)	12.0	52.3	146.5	52.3	28.8	9.9	9.4	9.4

Understand Estimates from Different Sources   Estimates for country risk premiums from different sources usually fall in a very wide range because analysts use different methods.[18] But they frequently compensate for high estimates of country risk premiums by making aggressive estimates for growth and return forecasts.

An example is the valuation of a large Brazilian chemicals company that we undertook in 2002. Using a local WACC of 10 percent, we reached an enterprise value of 4.0 to 4.5 times EBITDA. A second advisor was also asked to value the company and came to a very similar valuation result—an EBITDA multiple of around 4.5—in spite of using a very high country risk premium of 11 percent on top of the WACC. The result was similar because the second advisor made performance assumptions that were extremely aggressive: real sales growth of almost 10 percent per year and a ROIC increasing to 46 percent in the long term. Such long-term performance assumptions are unrealistic for a commodity-based, competitive industry such as chemicals.

Be Careful to Avoid Setting the Country Risk Premium Too High   Make sure you understand the economic implications of a high country risk premium. We believe that a country risk premium for Brazil is far below the premiums of 5 percent and higher that analysts typically use.

One reason is that current valuations in the stock market do not support the discount rates implied by higher risk premiums. We estimated the trading multiples of enterprise value to the 2004 forecasted EBITA for the 30 largest Brazilian companies in terms of market capitalization. The median value for the multiple was 7.4 in October 2004. We estimated the implied WACC by means of a DCF valuation. We set the future long-term return on invested capital at 11 percent, approximately equal to the median historical ROIC for these companies over the past five or six years (a period after Brazil brought inflation under control, so it is indicative of a business-as-usual scenario). Assuming future long-term inflation at 4.4 percent and real growth at 3.0 percent for the Brazilian economy as a whole, the WACC for the Brazilian market implied by the EBITA multiple of 7.4 is around 10.3 percent. The WACC estimated with the CAPM method previously described is around 9.8 percent.[19] This would imply a country risk

---

[18] For an overview, see, for example, L. Pereiro, *Valuation of Companies in Emerging Markets: A Practical Approach* (New York: Wiley, 2002), 118.

[19] Based on a real risk-free rate of 2 percent, long-term inflation of 4.4 percent, a market risk premium of 5.0 percent, cost of debt of 7.6 percent, and a debt-to-capital ratio of 0.25.

premium for Brazil of around 0.5 percent. Of course, this is not a precise estimate; as the Brazilian market goes up and down, the implied WACC and country risk premium would change as well. But it does suggest a country risk premium that is far below the 5 percent that many analysts currently use.

The other reason for such a low country risk premium is that historical returns in the Brazilian stock market do not support a high premium. The average real-terms return on the Brazilian stock market over the past 10 years is 3.8 percent per year. Let's take this period as a proxy for a business-as-usual scenario: real GPD grew by around 2 percent per year on average, and inflation was moderate at around 9 percent annually. At a country risk premium of 5 percent, the expected return on a stock with a beta equal to one under a business-as-usual scenario should be around 12 percent in real terms,[20] which is far above these historical returns.

5 CALCULATING AND INTERPRETING RESULTS

Given the estimates for cash flow and the cost of capital, we can discount the free cash flows for ConsuCo under the base-case and downside scenarios. The resulting present values of operations are shown in Exhibit 14. Under each scenario, the valuation results are exactly the same for the nominal and real projections. The next step is to weight the valuation results by the scenario probabilities and derive the present value of operations. Finally, add the market value of the nonoperating assets and subtract the financial claims to get at the estimated equity value. The estimated value obtained for ConsuCo is 188 to 206 Reais per share, given a probability of economic distress of 25 to 35 percent.

ConsuCo's share price, like the Brazilian stock market in general, has been extremely volatile over recent years, as shown in Exhibit 15 on page 244. Thus, you need to be careful in comparing the valuation outcome of 188 to 206 Reais per share with the current (December 2004) share price of 230 Reais. Just four months earlier, the price was 150 Reais. At the beginning of that year it traded for 270 Reais.

Of course, in emerging markets share prices are not always reliable references for intrinsic value, for several reasons. First, free float is often limited, with large equity stakes in the hands of a small group of owners, leaving public shareholders with little or no influence. As a result, the share price in the market could well be below intrinsic value, as estimated from a DCF analysis. Also, liquidity in emerging-markets stocks is often much lower than in developed markets. Share prices may not fully reflect intrinsic value because not all information is incorporated in the market value. Finally, share prices in emerging markets are often much more volatile than in developed markets. The share price on any particular day could therefore be off from intrinsic value.

ConsuCo has a primary listing on the Brazilian stock exchange. Turnover in the stock, as measured by the number of days to trade the free float, is around 130 days, not too far above typical levels of around 100 days in the United States and Europe. Still, because of the share price volatility, triangulation of the DCF results with multiples and a country risk premium approach is important.

---

[20] Assuming a real risk-free rate of 2 percent and a market risk premium of 5 percent.

EXHIBIT 14   ConsuCo: Scenario DCF Valuation

Reais million, percent

		2004	2005	2006	2007	2008	2009	2014	2019
Base case									
Nominal projections									
Free cash flow		331	(161)	(14)	166	379	833	1,065	1,491
WACC (percent)		12.0	10.5	9.9	9.5	9.4	9.4	9.4	9.4
Real projections									
Free cash flow		309	(143)	(12)	134	293	615	633	714
WACC (percent)		4.5	4.6	4.7	4.7	4.7	4.7	4.7	4.7
Downside									
Nominal projections									
Free cash flow		135	(2,817)	(11,192)	(11,205)	(10,491)	(4,039)	(3,851)	8,004
WACC (percent)		12.0	52.3	146.5	52.3	28.8	9.9	9.4	9.4
Real projections									
Free cash flow		126	(1,753)	(2,786)	(1,859)	(1,392)	(511)	(392)	656
WACC (percent)		4.5	1.5	(1.4)	1.5	3.0	4.7	4.7	4.7

1 – p[a] = 75%
(65%)

DCF value	**24,459**
Nonoperating assets	3,010
Debt and debt equivalents	(11,097)
Equity value	**16,372**
Value per share (Reais)	**253**

**Value
per
share
(Reais)**

206
(188)

p[a] = 25%
(35%)

DCF value	**12,427**
Nonoperating assets	3,010
Debt and debt equivalents	(11,097)
Equity value	**4,340**
Value per share (Reais)	**67**

[a] p = probability of economic distress.

| EXHIBIT 15 | ConsuCo: Historical Share Price Development |

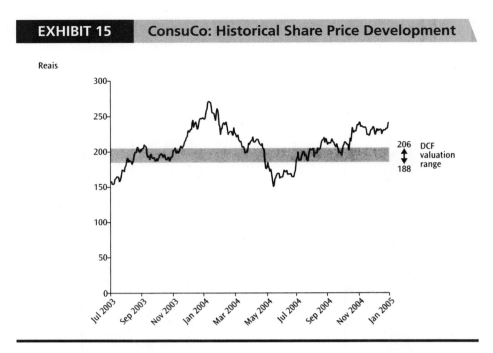

Triangulating with Multiples and Country Risk Premium Approach

For triangulation with multiples, do a best-practice multiples analysis to check valuation results. For the ConsuCo example, we compared the implied multiples of enterprise value over EBITDA with those of peer companies across the world. All multiples are forward-looking multiples over EBITDA as expected for 2005, based on analyst consensus forecasts. As Exhibit 16 illustrates, the implied multiple from our ConsuCo valuation is quite similar to most of its peers, at around seven times EBITDA. Apparently, the fact that ConsuCo is domiciled in Brazil does not matter much for the relative pricing of its stock. This is another indication that any country risk premium for ConsuCo should be very small. Using the average multiple for the peer group of 8.3, the value of ConsuCo would end up at 228 Reais, as shown in Exhibit 17. Note that this is probably an aggressive estimate, given that there are some outliers in the peer group with extremely high multiples. Using the median multiple of 7.1 would lead to a valuation estimate of 176 Reais per share.

The last part of the triangulation consists of a valuation of ConsuCo using a country risk premium approach. We estimated the country risk premium for Brazil at around 0.5 percent earlier in this reading. Discounting the business-as-usual scenario at the cost of capital plus this country risk premium leads to a value per share of 167 Reais, below the result obtained in the scenario DCF approach.

Note that a risk premium of 5 percent (as typically used in Brazil) would either result in unrealistically low valuations relative to current share price and peer group multiples, or require an unrealistic, bullish forecast of future performance with returns on capital of at least 15 percent and real growth rates of at least 6 percent for many years. Given long-term returns and growth in its industry and the historical performance of ConsuCo, even taking just the good years into account, such forecasts are unreasonable.

EXHIBIT 16	ConsuCo: Multiples Analysis versus Peers

EV/EBITDA 05

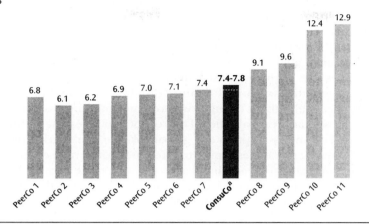

[a] Multiple of EV/EBITDA implied by DCF valuation range.

EXHIBIT 17	ConsuCo: Valuation Summary

Reais, million

	Scenario DCF valuation[a] low	Scenario DCF valuation[a] high	Average multiple valuation	Median multiple valuation	Country risk premium DCF valuation
EBITDA multiple			8.3	7.1	
EBITDA 2005			2,746	2,746	
DCF value	20,248	21,451	22,841	19,496	18,933
Nonoperating assets	3,010	3,010	3,010	3,010	3,010
Debt and debt equivalents	(11,097)	(11,097)	(11,097)	(11,097)	(11,097)
Equity value	12,161	13,364	14,754	11,409	10,846
Number of shares (million)	65	65	65	65	65
Value per share	188	206	228	176	167

[a] Shown are the probability-weighted values.

Given the inherent uncertainty in valuing emerging-market companies, it is best to use an explicit value range instead of a point estimate. For ConsuCo, we summarize the valuation findings in Exhibit 17. Based on the DCF valuation and multiples comparison, we end up with a range of about 175 to 205 Reais per share, depending on the exact scenario and probability assumptions, compared with a 12-month share price range of 150 to 270 Reais per share.

SUMMARY

To value companies in emerging markets, we use concepts similar to the ones applied to developed markets. However, the application of these concepts can be somewhat different. Inflation, which is often high in emerging markets, is factored into the cash flow projections by combining insights from both real and nominal financial analyses. Emerging market risks such as macroeconomic or political crises can be incorporated following the scenario DCF approach by developing alternative scenarios for future cash flows, discounting the cash flows at the cost of capital without country risk premium, and then weighting the DCF values by the scenario probabilities. The cost of capital estimates for emerging markets build on the assumption of a global risk-free rate, market risk premium and beta, following guidelines similar to those used for developed markets. Since the value of companies in emerging markets is often more volatile than in developed markets, we recommend triangulating the scenario DCF results with a country risk premium DCF and a multiples-based valuation.

COMPANY ANALYSIS AND STOCK VALUATION
by Frank K. Reilly and Keith C. Brown

LEARNING OUTCOMES

The candidate should be able to:

a. describe the elements of a franchise P/E;

b. describe how an analyst can use the growth duration model to determine whether a firm's P/E ratio is justified and describe the factors to consider when using the growth duration technique to infer a company's P/E.

THE FRANCHISE FACTOR   1

The franchise factor concept is similar to EVA since it recognizes that, to add value to a firm, it is necessary to invest in projects that provide excess NPV—that is, the firm must generate rates of return above its WACC. This technique is directly related to the valuation approach we have been using since the franchise value approach breaks a firm's observed P/E ratio down into two components: (1) the P/E that is based on the company's ongoing business (its base P/E), plus (2) a franchise P/E that the market assigns to *the expected value of new and profitable business opportunities.* This can be visualized as:

$$\text{Franchise } P/E = \text{Observed } P/E - \text{Base } P/E \qquad \text{(44-1)}$$

The base P/E is the reciprocal of the market discount rate k (it is $1/k$). For example, if the stock's market discount rate is 8 percent, the base P/E would be about 12.5 times.

What determines the franchise P/E? Not surprising, it is a function of the relative rate of return on new business opportunities compared to the firm's cost

The authors acknowledge comments and suggestions on this reading by Professor Edgar Norton of Illinois State University.

Investment Analysis and Portfolio Management, Eighth Edition, by Frank K. Reilly and Keith C. Brown. Copyright © 2005 by Thomson South-Western. Reprinted with permission of South-Western, a division of Thomson Learning.

247

of equity (the franchise factor) and the size of the superior return opportunities (the growth factor).

$$\text{Incremental Franchise } P/E = \text{Franchise Factor} \times \text{Growth Factor}$$
$$= \frac{R - k}{rk} \times G \qquad \text{(44-2)}$$

where

> R = the expected return on the new opportunities
> k = the current cost of equity
> r = the current ROE on investment
> G = the present value of the new growth projects relative to the current value of the firm

The critical factors determining the franchise P/E are the difference between R and k and the size of these growth opportunities relative to the firm's current size (i.e., G).[1]

2   GROWTH DURATION MODEL

The purpose of the growth duration model is to help you *evaluate* the high P/E ratio for the stock of a **growth company** by relating its P/E ratio to the firm's *rate* of growth and *duration* of growth. A stock's P/E ratio is a function of (1) the firm's expected rate of growth of earnings per share, (2) the stock's required rate of return, and (3) the firm's dividend-payout ratio. Assuming equal risk and no significant difference in the payout ratio for different firms, the principal variable affecting differences in the earnings multiple for two firms *is the difference in expected growth*. The growth estimate must consider both the *rate* of growth and how long this growth rate can be sustained—that is, the *duration* of expected growth. No company can grow indefinitely at a rate substantially above normal. For example, Wal-Mart cannot continue to grow at 20 percent a year for an extended period, or it will eventually become the entire economy. In fact, Wal-Mart or any similar growth firm will eventually run out of excess profit investment projects. Recall that continued growth at a constant rate requires that larger amounts of money be invested in high-return projects because it requires that you invest a constant percentage of current earnings. Eventually, competition will encroach on these high-return investments and the firm's growth rate will decline to a rate consistent with the rate for the overall economy. Therefore, a reasonable and accurate estimate of the implied duration of a firm's high-growth period becomes significant.

Computation of Growth Duration

The growth duration concept was suggested by Holt (1962), who showed that if you assume equal risk between a given security and a market security, such as the S&P Industrials (i.e., a beta close to one), you can concentrate on the differential expected growth rates for the market and the growth firm as a factor causing the

---

[1] For further detail and examples of the application, see Leibowitz and Kogelman (1994).

alternative *P/E* ratios. This allows you to compute the market's *implied growth duration* for the growth firm.

If $E'(0)$ is the firm's current earnings per share, then $E'(t)$ is earnings in Period *t* according to the expression

$$E'(t) = E'(0)(1 + G)^t \qquad \text{(44-3)}$$

where *G* is the expected annual percentage growth rate for earnings. To adjust for dividend payments, it was assumed that all such payments are used to purchase further shares of the stock. This means the number of shares (*N*) will grow at the dividend rate (*D*). Therefore

$$N(t) = N(0)(1 + D)^t \qquad \text{(44-4)}$$

To derive the total earnings for a firm, $E(t)$, the growth rate in per-share earnings and the growth rate in shares are combined as follows:

$$E(t) = E'(t)N(t) = E'(0)\big[(1 + G)(1 + D)\big]^t \qquad \text{(44-5)}$$

Because *G* and *D* are small, this expression can be approximated by

$$E(t) \simeq E'(0)(1 + G + D)^t \qquad \text{(44-6)}$$

Assuming the growth stock (*g*) and the nongrowth stock (*a*) have similar risk and payout, the market should value the two stocks in direct proportion to their earnings in year *T* (i.e., they will have the same *P/E* ratio), where *T* is the time when the growth company will begin to grow at the same rate as the market (i.e., the non-growth stock). Put another way, *T* is the number of years the growth stock is expected to grow at the high rate. In other words, *current prices should be in direct proportion to the expected future earnings ratio that will prevail in year T*. This relationship can be stated

$$\left(\frac{P_g(0)}{P_a(0)}\right) \simeq \left(\frac{E_g(0)(1 + G_g + D_g)^T}{E_a(0)(1 + G_a + D_a)^T}\right) \qquad \text{(44-7)}$$

or

$$\left(\frac{P_g(0)/E_g(0)}{P_a(0)/E_a(0)}\right) \simeq \left(\frac{1 + G_g + D_g}{1 + G_a + D_a}\right)^T \qquad \text{(44-8)}$$

As a result, *the P/E ratios of the two stocks are in direct proportion to the ratio of composite growth rates raised to the Tth power.* You can solve for *T* by taking the log of both sides as follows:

$$\ln\left(\frac{P_g(0)/E_g(0)}{P_a(0)/E_a(0)}\right) \simeq T\ln\left(\frac{1 + G_g + D_g}{1 + G_a + D_a}\right) \qquad \text{(44-9)}$$

The growth duration model answers the question: How long must the earnings of the growth stock grow at this expected high rate, relative to the nongrowth stock, to justify its prevailing above-average *P/E* ratio? You must then determine whether this *implied* growth duration estimate is reasonable in terms of the company's potential.

Consider the following example. The stock of Walgreens is selling for $42 a share with expected per-share earnings of $1.50 (its future earnings multiple is 28.0 times). The expected EPS growth rate for Walgreens is estimated to be 13 percent a year, and its dividend yield has been 1 percent and is expected to remain at this level. In contrast, the S&P Industrials Index has a future P/E ratio of about 18, an average dividend yield of 2 percent, and an expected growth rate of 6 percent. Therefore, the comparison is as follows:

	S&P Industrials	Walgreens
P/E ratio	18.00	28.00
Expected growth rate	0.06	0.13
Dividend yield	0.02	0.01

Inserting these values into Equation 44-9 yields the following:

Note:
The reading uses log base 10.

Using log base e:

$T = \ln(1.56) / \ln(1.055)$

$T = 0.4447 / 0.0535$

$T = 8.31$ years

$$\ln\left(\frac{28.00}{18.00}\right) = T\ln\left(\frac{1 + 0.13 + 0.01}{1 + 0.06 + 0.02}\right)$$

$$\ln(1.56) = T\ln\left(\frac{1.14}{1.08}\right)$$

$$\ln(1.56) = T\ln(1.055)$$

$$T = \ln(1.56)/\ln(1.055)(\text{log base 10})$$

$$= 0.1931/0.02325$$

$$= 8.31 \text{ Years}$$

These results indicate the market is implicitly assuming that Walgreens can continue to grow at this composite rate (14 percent) for about 8 more years, after which it is assumed Walgreens will grow at the same total rate (8 percent) as the aggregate market (i.e., the S&P Industrials). You must now ask, can this superior growth rate be sustained by Walgreens for at least this period? If the implied growth duration is greater than you believe is reasonable, you would advise against buying Walgreens stock. If the implied duration is below your expectations, you would recommend buying the stock.

Intraindustry Analysis

Besides comparing a company to a market series, you can directly compare two firms. For an intercompany analysis, you should compare firms in the same industry because the equal risk assumptions of this model are probably more reasonable.

Consider the following example from the computer software industry:

	Company A	Company B
P/E ratios	31.00	25.00
Expected annual growth rate	0.1700	0.1200
Dividend yield	0.0100	0.0150
Growth rate plus dividend yield	0.1800	0.1350
Estimate of T[a]		5.53 years

[a] Readers should check to see that they get the same answer.

These results imply that the market expects Company A to grow at an annual total rate of 18 percent for about 5.5 years, after which it will grow at Company B's rate of 13.5 percent. If you believe the implied duration for growth at 18 percent is too long, you will prefer Company B; if you believe it is reasonable or low, you will recommend Company A.

An Alternative Use of *T*

Instead of solving for *T* and then deciding whether the figure derived is reasonable, you can use this formulation to compute a reasonable *P/E* ratio for a security relative to the aggregate market (or another stock) if the implicit assumptions are reasonable for the stock involved. Again, using Walgreens as an example, you estimate its expected composite growth to be 14 percent a year compared to the expected total market growth of 8 percent. Further, you believe that Walgreens can continue to grow at this above-normal rate for about five years. Using Equation 44-9, this becomes

$$\ln(X) = 5 \times \ln \frac{1.14}{1.08}$$
$$= 5 \times \ln(1.055)$$
$$= 5 \times (0.02325)$$
$$= 0.11625$$

> **Note:**
> Using log base e:
> $\ln(X) = 5 \times \ln(1.055)$
> $\ln(X) = 5 \times 0.05354$
> $\ln(X) = 0.2677$
> The antilog is:
> $e^{0.2677} = 1.3069$

To determine what the *P/E* ratio should be given these assumptions, you must derive the antilog of 0.11625, which is approximately 1.3069. Therefore, assuming the market multiple is 18, the earnings multiple for Walgreens should be about 1.3069 times the market *P/E* ratio, or about 24.

Alternatively, if you estimate that Walgreens can maintain a lower growth rate of .12 for a long time period of 10 years, you would derive the antilog for 1.5794 (10 × 0.01579). The answer is 1.4386, which implies a *P/E* ratio of about 26 times for Walgreen Co.'s stock. Notably, both of these estimates are below the current forward *P/E* for Walgreens of 28 times.

> **Note:**
> Using log base e:
> $\ln(X) = 10 \times \ln(1.12/1.08)$
> $\ln(X) = 10 \times \ln(1.0370)$
> $\ln(X) = 10 \times (0.3637)$
> $\ln(X) = 0.3637$
> The antilog is:
> $e^{0.3637} = 1.4386$

Factors to Consider

When using the growth duration technique, remember the following factors: First, the technique assumes equal risk, which may be acceptable when comparing two large, well-established firms in the same industry (e.g., Merck and Pfizer) to each other. It is also reasonable for a large conglomerate, like General Electric, with a beta close to one. In the case of Walgreens, which has a beta of about 0.90, the result is conservative, meaning that the duration would be lower than the estimated 8 years. It is probably *not* a valid assumption when comparing a small firm with a beta of 1.50 to the aggregate market. In this case, the duration generated would be an underestimate of what should be required.

Second, which growth estimate should be used? We prefer to use the *expected* rate of growth based on the factors that affect *g* (i.e., the retention rate and the components of *ROE*).

Third, the growth duration technique assumes that stocks with higher *P/E* ratios have the higher growth rates. However, there are cases in which the stock with the higher *P/E* ratio does not have a higher expected growth rate or the stock with a higher expected growth rate has a lower *P/E* ratio. Either of the cases generates a useless negative growth duration value. Inconsistency between the expected growth and the *P/E* ratio could be attributed to one of four factors:

1. A major difference in the risk involved.

2. Inaccurate growth rate estimates. You may want to reexamine your growth rate estimate for the firm with the higher *P/E* ratio—that is, could it be higher or should the growth estimate for the low *P/E* stock be lower?

3. The stock with a low *P/E* ratio relative to its expected growth rate is undervalued. (Before you accept this possibility, consider the first two factors.)

4. The stock with a high *P/E* and a low expected growth rate is overvalued. (Before this is accepted, consider both its risk and your estimated growth rate.)

The growth duration concept is valid, *given the assumptions made,* and can help you evaluate growth investments. It is not universally valid, though, because its answers are only as good as the data inputs (expected growth rates) and the applicability of the assumptions. The answer must be evaluated based on the analyst's knowledge.

The technique probably is most useful for helping spot overvalued growth companies with very high multiples. In such a case, the technique will highlight that the company must continue to grow at some very high rate for an extended period of time to justify its high *P/E* ratio (e.g., 15 to 20 years). Also, it can help you decide between two growth companies in the same industry by comparing each to the market, the industry, or directly to each other. Such a comparison has provided interesting insights wherein the new firms in an industry were growing faster than the large competitor, but their *P/E* ratios were *substantially* higher and implied that these new firms had to maintain this large growth rate superiority for over *10 years* to justify the much higher *P/E* ratio.

U.S. PORTFOLIO STRATEGY: SEEKING VALUE—ANATOMY OF VALUATION

by David J. Kostin, Jessica Binder, Robert Koyfman, and Caesar Maasry

READING
45

LEARNING OUTCOMES

The candidate should be able to:

a. explain why an analyst would use a ten-year moving average as a benchmark in the valuation process;

b. determine the importance of correlation analysis when using a multi-matrix valuation approach;

c. illustrate why the PEG valuation technique must be used with care;

d. indicate the impact of discount rate sensitivity in valuation models.

INTRODUCTION 1

We dissect the S&P 500 and identify the least and most expensive stocks across the market and within sectors. We highlight a "super-value" portfolio of 50 stocks to buy that trade at low valuations on seven metrics and an "anti-value" portfolio of 50 expensive stocks to sell.

The S&P 500 is Undervalued on All Metrics from a Bottom-Up Perspective On a bottom-up basis, the S&P 500 trades one standard deviation below its 10-year average on EV/Sales, EV/EBITDA, Price/Book, Free Cash Flow Yield, P/E, PEG & Implied Growth. Larger-caps are more undervalued than smaller-caps, particularly in Consumer Discretionary.

Information Technology and Health Care Are the Most Undervalued Sectors Information Technology and Health Care are the ONLY sectors that are inexpensive today on ALL seven metrics relative to how they have been valued during the past ten-years. Utilities and Financials are the most overvalued sectors.

Note:
The Goldman Sachs research report should be studied for the generic features of security analysis rather than for specific characteristics of a company, industry, or country. Candidates are not expected to know details of the companies, industries, or countries, but rather to understand how the analytical techniques can be applied.

S&P 500 on a Bottom-Up Basis Is Inexpensive Relative to History

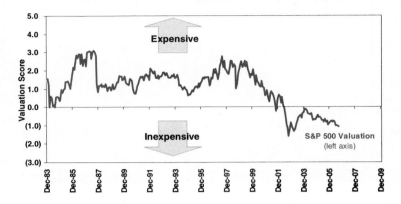

Sources: Compustat and Goldman Sachs Research.

Weatherford International, Stryker and Apollo Are Least Expensive Stocks
Within the S&P 500, Weatherford International (WFT, Buy), Stryker Corp. (SYK, Buy) and Apollo Group (APOL, NC) are the three most undervalued stocks ranked on seven metrics.

Introducing Our "Super-Value" and "Anti-Value" Portfolios

We dissect the S&P 500 and identify the least and most expensive stocks across the market and within sectors. We highlight a "super-value" portfolio of 50 stocks to buy that trade at low valuations on seven metrics and an "anti-value" portfolio of 50 expensive stocks to sell.

"What Looks Cheap in the Market Now?"

We have noticed a significant increase in the number of clients who call to ask the question: "What looks cheap in the market now?" Clients have always asked variations on this theme, such as "what do you like in the market?" but more than the usual suspects are now probing around the topic of valuation. Market participants recognize that the U.S. economy is in transition, and the outlook is less certain now than it was just several months ago. Attractive valuation offers portfolio managers some comfort when selecting stocks in an uncertain market.

How One Portfolio Strategist Responds

We characterize a stock as "undervalued" if it trades at a discount to its historical average valuation relative to the market on a variety of financial measures. We use a combination of seven metrics to identify an "undervalued" equity security:

- ► enterprise value/sales (EV/Sales);
- ► enterprise value/EBITDA (EV/EBITDA);
- ► price/book;
- ► free cash flow yield (FCF);

► price/earnings (P/E);

► P/E-to-long-term growth (PEG); and

► implied growth (computed by reversing the dividend discount model.

Obviously, investors use many different techniques to classify a stock as attractively valued. An entire library of academic books has been written on the subject of how to value a stock. We prefer to use several valuation measures to facilitate comparison across sectors. The correlation between the individual metrics ranges from 0.2 to 0.9.

Just How "Cheap" Is "Cheap"?

We often view the world through the prism of a distribution. In seeking to identify "cheap" stocks, we focused on companies trading at extreme undervaluation across the seven metrics. In fact, on a bottom-up basis, the S&P 500 is trading at roughly one standard deviation below its 10-year average on nearly every one of the seven metrics (see Exhibits 2 and 3). One drawback to this approach is that "broken growth" stocks screen as attractively valued today based on the lofty valuations assigned to them when their growth prospects were much brighter.

Introducing Our "Super-Value" and "Anti-Value" Portfolios

We have created a 50-stock sector-neutral portfolio of the most "undervalued" stocks in the S&P 500 (see Bloomberg ticker <GSTHSVLU> on <GSSU5>). We created a similar 50-stock sector-neutral basket of "overvalued" stocks in the S&P 500 (see Bloomberg <GSTHAVLU>).

Taking a Comprehensive Look at Valuation

A Comprehensive View of Valuation that Incorporates Seven Metrics and History

This report expands our view of stock valuation to incorporate seven different valuation metrics and also examines how individual stocks are currently valued on these measures relative to how they have been valued over the past decade.

High Relative P/E Stocks Continue to Underperform

In a report published earlier in 2006 we focused exclusively on P/E as a measure of valuation and looked solely at current relative valuation within a sector. Our February 2006 report entitled *High P/E means high expectations but low returns* noted that high relative P/E stocks have consistently underperformed both low relative P/E stocks and the S&P 500 for most of the past 15 years. In 2006 YTD, a sector-neutral basket of low-relative P/E stocks has beat a high-relative P/E basket by 540 basis points.

History of Buying "Super-Value" Portfolio and Selling "Anti-Value" Appears Positive

We back-tested our more comprehensive valuation framework by tracking the performance of stocks we would have identified as "Super-value" against stocks we would have identified as "Anti-value." Our analysis shows a positive average return for holdings periods of one, three, six and 12 months (see Exhibit 1).

EXHIBIT 1	Return Summary of "Super-Value" versus "Anti-Value" Trade since 1995 as of September 8, 2006

Invest. Horizon:	1M	3M	6M	12M
Observations:	139	137	134	128
10 +	2 %	9 %	12 %	21 %
5 to 10	6	8	13	8
2 to 5	17	15	7	8
1 to 2	11	9	5	1
0 to 1	12	9	7	2
(1) to 0	20	8	7	2
(2) to (1)	13	7	5	6
(5) to (2)	13	20	16	9
(10) to (5)	6	11	19	21
(10) -	0	4	10	21
Total	100 %	100 %	100 %	100 %
Positive	48	50	43	40
Negative	52	50	57	60
Total	100 %	100 %	100 %	100 %

Probability of Return (%) (vertical axis label)

Return Summary				
Invest. Horizon:	1M	3M	6M	12M
Max	18 %	25 %	33 %	46 %
75th %tile	2	4	4	8
Average	0.5 %	0.7 %	0.4 %	1.3 %
25th %tile	(2)	(3)	(6)	(10)
Min	(9)	(21)	(21)	(28)

Average return of long "Super-value" and short "Anti-value" trade is positive for all holding periods shown.

Sources: Compustat and Goldman Sachs Research.

Our back-tested portfolios were created employing the same methodology we use to construct the current "Super-value" and "Anti-value" portfolios. We constructed the portfolios sector-neutral to the S&P 500 to reduce the influence of thematic trends and to capture valuation-driven returns. We believe money managers will focus increased attention on valuation in the coming months.

2   GOLDMAN SACHS U.S. VALUATION MONITOR

On a bottom-up basis the S&P 500 currently trades approximately one standard deviation below the ten-year average on all seven financial metrics we analyzed. In fact, the market is about as inexpensive as at any time over the past 23 years, with the exception of late 2002/early 2003 before the current bull market began (see Exhibit 2).

From a sector perspective, Information Technology and Health Care are notably undervalued relative to how these sectors have traded versus the market over the past ten years (see Exhibit 2). Utilities and Financials are even more dramatically overvalued, trading two standard deviations above their long-term averages.

EXHIBIT 2	S&P 500 on a Bottom-Up Basis Is Inexpensive Relative to History as of September 8, 2006

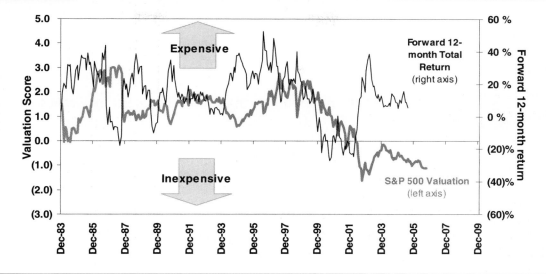

Sources: Compustat and Goldman Sachs Research.

EXHIBIT 3	Information Technology and Health Care Are the Most Attractively Valued Sectors as of September 8, 2006

Goldman Sachs US Valuation Monitor

	EV/ Sales	EV/ EBITDA	Price/ Book	FCF Yield	P/E	PEG Ratio	Implied Growth	Average	
S&P 500	(1.4)	(1.9)	(1.0)	(0.7)	(1.3)	(0.9)	(0.6)	(1.1)	
Information Technology	(0.4)	(0.9)	(0.5)	(1.9)	(0.9)	(0.6)	(4.3)	(1.3)	INEXPENSIVE
Health Care	(1.3)	(0.8)	(1.1)	(1.6)	(0.1)	0.3	(0.8)	(0.8)	
Energy	(0.6)	(1.1)	1.6	(0.5)	(1.2)	(1.6)	0.1	(0.5)	
Telecommunication Services	(0.7)	1.3	0.2	(0.5)	0.0	0.4	1.4	0.3	
Materials	1.1	0.5	1.3	0.9	(0.4)	(1.7)	1.0	0.4	
Industrials	1.3	0.7	0.5	(0.5)	0.9	0.3	0.7	0.6	
Consumer Staples	1.0	0.4	(1.5)	0.3	1.3	2.5	0.2	0.6	
Consumer Discretionary	1.5	0.7	0.1	1.7	1.0	0.9	1.1	1.0	
Utilities		2.2	2.4	0.8	2.0	(0.0)	4.4	2.0	
Financials			0.2		1.5	1.3	4.9	2.0	EXPENSIVE

Note: S&P valuation calculated on an absolute basis, sector valuations calculated relative to S&P 500. Valuation score calculated as the average number of standard deviations seven valuation metrics differ from 10-year averages: EV/Sales, EV/EBITDA, P/B, FCF yield, P/E, PEG, and Implied Growth.

Sources: Compustat and Goldman Sachs Research.

Bottom-Up Valuation of the S&P 500: A Look at Seven Metrics

On an absolute basis the S&P 500 appears most undervalued on an EV/ EBITDA, trading almost two standard deviations below the average of the past decade. The S&P 500 appears least undervalued in terms of implied 5-year EPS growth that we compute by reversing the dividend discount model.

The Exhibits on the left side provide the absolute level of the seven metrics since 1983. Valuation scores on the right side show the standard deviations from the 10-year average.

EXHIBIT 4	S&P 500 Bottom-Up Valuation on Seven Key Financial Metrics as of September 8, 2006

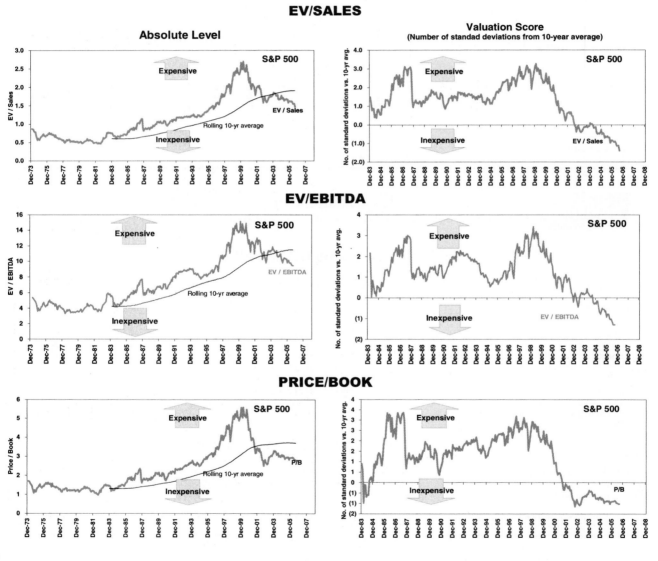

(Exhibit continued on next page . . .)

EXHIBIT 4 (continued)

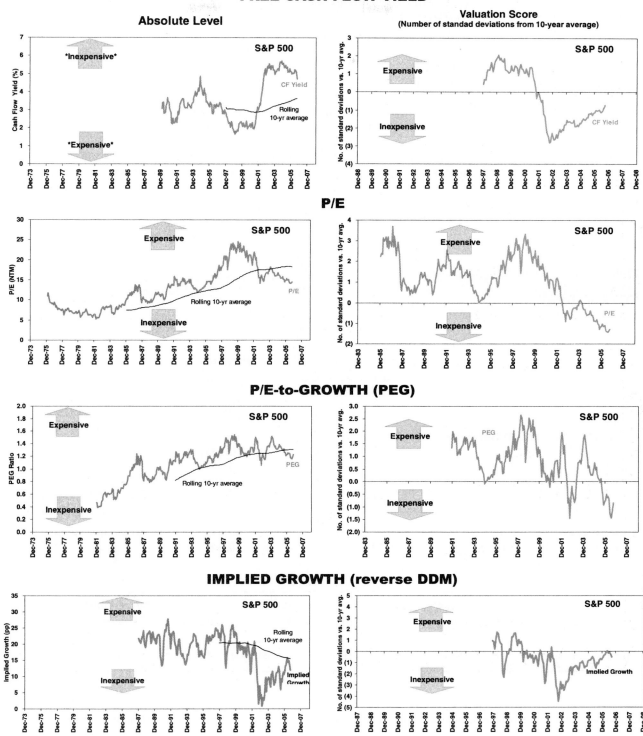

FREE CASH FLOW YIELD

Absolute Level

Valuation Score
(Number of standad deviations from 10-year average)

P/E

P/E-to-GROWTH (PEG)

IMPLIED GROWTH (reverse DDM)

Sources: Compustat and Goldman Sachs Research.

Mean versus Median (Larger-Cap Stocks Are More Undervalued)

Within the S&P 500, the magnitude of the current undervaluation of larger-cap stocks relative to their history appears greater than the degree of undervaluation of the smaller-cap stocks in the index relative to their history (see Exhibit 1).

The equal-weighted average of company valuation scores is greater than the market-cap weighted average in every sector, suggesting that the smaller-cap stocks are more expensive vs. larger-cap stocks across the S&P.

Note that the overall S&P 500 on a bottom-up basis is more undervalued (less expensive) than small-cap stocks in the Russell 2000 Index.

The larger-cap stocks appear valued most similarly to smaller-cap stocks in Utilities, where the difference appears negligible.

Within Consumer Discretionary and Health Care, the equal-weighted average of valuation scores suggests stocks are slightly expensive compared with history. But the market-cap weighted average suggests stocks are inexpensive. This disparity indicates that the larger-cap names in these two sectors are undervalued (see Exhibit 5).

EXHIBIT 5	Number of Standard Deviations from 10-Year Average: Market-Cap Weighted versus Equal-Weighted Average as of September 8, 2006

	Average Valuation		
	Mkt Cap. Weighted	Equal Weighted	Difference
S&P 500	0.1	0.3	(0.20)
Utilities	1.6	1.6	(0.00)
Financials	0.6	0.7	(0.08)
Telecommunication Services	0.6	0.7	(0.11)
Energy	(0.4)	(0.3)	(0.11)
Materials	0.4	0.6	(0.14)
Consumer Staples	0.5	0.7	(0.16)
Industrials	0.1	0.3	(0.18)
Information Technology	(0.7)	(0.4)	(0.22)
Health Care	(0.1)	0.2	(0.31)
Consumer Discretionary	(0.2)	0.1	(0.34)

Larger-caps INEXPENSIVE vs. Smaller-caps

Positive equal weighted average suggests that stocks are slightly expensive relative to history, but negative market-cap weighted averages suggest stocks are inexpensive.

Larger-cap stocks appear relatively undervalued vs. smaller-cap stocks.

Note: S&P valuation calculated on an absolute basis, sector valuations calculated relative to S&P 500. Valuation score calculated as the average number of standard deviations seven valuation metrics differ from 10-year averages: EV/Sales, EV/EBITDA, P/B, FCF yield, P/E, PEG, and Implied Growth.

Sources: Compustat and Goldman Sachs Research.

THE GOLDMAN SACHS "SUPER-VALUE" AND "ANTI-VALUE" PORTFOLIOS

3

We ranked the individual stocks in the S&P 500 based on the difference between current and historical valuations using the seven financial metrics discussed previously. Taking the current sector composition of the S&P 500 Index, we created two 50-stock sector-neutral portfolios comprised of the least and most expensive stocks in each sector. The stocks and their historical relative valuation scores appear in Exhibits 8 and 10 respectively, and the current valuation ratios appear in Exhibits 9 and 11, respectively.

Exhibit 6 shows the performance of the Goldman Sachs "Super-value" and "Anti-value" portfolios and the S&P 500 over the past 10 years.

EXHIBIT 6	Goldman Sachs "Super-Value" and "Anti-Value" Portfolios and S&P 500 Total Returns, 1995–2006 YTD as of September 8, 2006

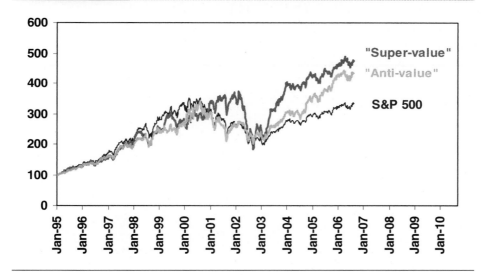

Sources: Compustat and Goldman Sachs Research.

Appendix A contains a list of the 25 least and more expensive stocks in the S&P 500.

Appendix B contains the 50 largest stocks in the S&P 500 ranked by valuation scores.

EXHIBIT 7	Valuation of "Super-Value" and "Anti-Value" Portfolios as of September 8, 2006

	Historical Relative Valuation							Valuation Score
	EV/ Sales	EV/ EBITDA	Price/ Book	FCF Yield	P/E (NTM)	PEG Ratio	Implied Growth	8-Sep-06
"Super-value" portfolio	(1.2)	(1.0)	(0.7)	(1.3)	(1.1)	(0.8)	(1.5)	(1.0)
"Anti-value" portfolio	1.4	1.3	1.2	0.6	1.6	1.3	2.4	1.5
S&P 500 (median)	0.0	(0.0)	0.1	(0.0)	0.4	0.0	1.1	0.3

	Current Valuation Metrics						
	EV/ Sales	EV/ EBITDA	Price/ Book	FCF Yield	P/E (NTM)	PEG Ratio	Implied Growth
"Super-value" portfolio	2.7	9.6	3.4	4.7 %	16.3	1.2	(6.6) pp
"Anti-value" portfolio	2.3	10.3	3.4	4.2	17.1	1.7	11.2
S&P 500 (median)	1.7	9.1	2.8	4.7	16.1	1.4	3.7

Sources: Compustat and Goldman Sachs Research.

The Goldman Sachs "Super-Value" Portfolio

EXHIBIT 8	Our Sector-Neutral Portfolio of the 50 Most Undervalued Stocks in the S&P 500 as of September 8, 2006

Weight (%)	Company	Ticker	Rating	Sub-Sector	Equity Cap ($ bill)	Total Return YTD	Valuation Score 8-Sep-06
10%	**Consumer Discretionary**						
2	Apollo Group	APOL	NC	Education Services	8	(21)%	(2.0)
2	Home Depot	HD	Buy	Home Improvement Retail	71	(14)	(1.8)
2	News Corporation	NWS.A	Neutral	Movies & Entertainment	60	22	(1.5)
2	Bed Bath & Beyond	BBBY	Neutral	Homefurnishing Retail	10	(6)	(1.5)
2	Gap, Inc.	GPS	Neutral	Apparel Retail	14	(3)	(1.5)
10%	**Consumer Staples**						
2	Wal-Mart Stores	WMT	Buy	Hypermarkets & Super Centers	195	1%	(1.8)
2	Coca-Cola Co.	KO	Neutral	Soft Drinks	105	12	(0.9)
2	Wrigley (Wm) Jr.	WWY	NC	Packaged Foods & Meats	13	(12)	(0.7)
2	Coca-Cola Enterprises	CCE	Neutral	Soft Drinks	10	13	(0.4)
2	Walgreen Co.	WAG	Buy	Drug Retail	51	16	(0.4)
10%	**Energy**						
2	Weatherford International Ltd.	WFT	Buy	Oil & Gas Equipment & Services	14	13%	(2.7)
2	National Oilwell Varco	NOV	Buy	Oil & Gas Equipment & Services	11	(1)	(1.4)
2	BJ Services	BJS	Neutral	Oil & Gas Equipment & Services	10	(12)	(1.2)
2	Nabors Industries Ltd.	NBR	Neutral	Oil & Gas Drilling	10	(17)	(0.9)
2	Rowan Cos.	RDC	Neutral	Oil & Gas Drilling	4	(5)	(0.8)
22%	**Financials**						
2	American Int'l. Group	AIG	Buy	Multi-line Insurance	167	(5)%	(1.2)
2	Simon Property Group, Inc	SPG	Buy	Retail REITs	19	16	(0.9)
2	Fifth Third Bancorp	FITB	Neutral	Regional Banks	22	6	(0.8)
2	Charles Schwab	SCHW	Neutral	Investment Banking & Brokerage	21	12	(0.8)
2	Synovus Financial	SNV	NC	Regional Banks	9	8	(0.5)
2	Capital One Financial	COF	Buy	Consumer Finance	22	(16)	(0.4)
2	Northern Trust Corp.	NTRS	Neutral	Asset Management & Custody Banks	12	10	(0.4)
2	CIT Group	CIT	NC	Specialized Finance	9	(12)	(0.4)
2	ProLogis	PLD	Buy	Industrial REITs	14	24	(0.3)
2	E*Trade Financial Corp.	ET	Neutral	Investment Banking & Brokerage	10	8	(0.3)
2	Prudential Financial	PRU	Neutral	Life & Health Insurance	35	(2)	(0.2)
12%	**Health Care**						
2	Stryker Corp.	SYK	Buy	Health Care Equipment	20	10%	(2.2)
2	Medtronic Inc.	MDT	Neutral	Health Care Equipment	56	(18)	(1.5)
2	Zimmer Holdings	ZMH	NC	Health Care Equipment	17	(0)	(1.3)
2	BIOGEN IDEC Inc.	BIIB	Neutral	Biotechnology	15	(3)	(1.0)
2	Amgen	AMGN	Buy	Biotechnology	80	(14)	(1.0)
2	Genzyme Corp.	GENZ	Neutral	Biotechnology	17	(7)	(0.9)
10%	**Industrials**						
2	Cintas Corporation	CTAS	NC	Diversified Commercial & Professional Services	6	(8)%	(1.8)
2	United Parcel Service	UPS	NC	Air Freight & Logistics	75	(6)	(1.5)
2	L-3 Communications Holdings	LLL	Buy	Aerospace & Defense	9	2	(1.2)
2	Robert Half International	RHI	Neutral	Human Resource & Employment Services	5	(19)	(1.1)
2	Southwest Airlines	LUV	NC	Airlines	13	0	(0.8)
16%	**Information Technology**						
2	eBay Inc.	EBAY	Buy	Internet Software & Services	40	(34)%	(1.9)
2	Linear Technology Corp.	LLTC	Buy	Semiconductors	10	(8)	(1.6)
2	Xilinx, Inc	XLNX	Neutral	Semiconductors	7	(16)	(1.5)
2	Maxim Integrated Prod	MXIM	Neutral	Semiconductors	9	(20)	(1.5)
2	Microsoft Corp.	MSFT	Buy	Systems Software	261	(1)	(1.4)
2	Altera Corp.	ALTR	Neutral	Semiconductors	7	4	(1.3)
2	Analog Devices	ADI	Neutral	Semiconductors	11	(16)	(1.3)
2	Jabil Circuit	JBL	Buy	Electronic Manufacturing Services	6	(28)	(1.2)
2%	**Materials**						
2	Newmont Mining Corp. (Hldg. Co.)	NEM	Neutral	Gold	22	(9)%	(0.6)
4%	**Telecommunication Services**						
2	AT & T Inc.	T	Not Rated	Integrated Telecommunication Services	122	33%	0.0
2	Sprint Nextel Corp.	S	Buy	Wireless Telecommunication Services	49	(22)	0.1
4%	**Utilities**						
2	AES Corp.	AES	NC	Independent Power Producers & Energy Traders	13	29%	0.4
2	DTE Energy Co.	DTE	NC	Multi-Utilities	7	(2)	0.7
100%	**Total**						
	"Super-value" portfolio (average)					(2.4)%	(1.0)
	S&P 500					5.4%	(1.2)

Note: S&P valuation calculated on an absolute basis, sector valuations calculated relative to S&P 500. Valuation score calculated as the average number of standard deviations seven valuation metrics differ from 10-year averages: EV/Sales, EV/EBITDA, P/B, FCF yield, P/E, PEG, and Implied Growth.

Sources: Compustat, Lionshare via FactSet, and Goldman Sachs Research.

| EXHIBIT 9 | Current Valuation Data for Our Sector-Neutral Portfolio of 50 Most Undervalued Stocks in the S&P 500 as of September 8, 2006 |

Weight (%)	Company	Ticker	Rating	Price 8-Sep-06	EV/ Sales	EV/ EBITDA	Price/ Book	FCF Yield	P/E (NTM)	PEG Ratio	Implied Growth
10%	**Consumer Discretionary**										
2	Apollo Group	APOL	NC	$47.87	2.9	7.7	10.7	9.6%	16.7	1.1	(10.3) pp
2	Home Depot	HD	Buy	34.28	0.8	6.2	2.7	4.5	10.8	0.8	(16.6)
2	News Corporation	NWS.A	Neutral	18.87	2.5	8.5	1.5	5.1	18.0	1.0	(4.0)
2	Bed Bath & Beyond	BBBY	Neutral	34.11	1.3	8.6	4.1	4.0	15.2	1.0	(11.3)
2	Gap, Inc.	GPS	Neutral	16.90	0.7	3.4	1.7	13.2	14.1	1.2	(7.1)
10%	**Consumer Staples**										
2	Wal-Mart Stores	WMT	Buy	46.72	0.7	6.0	2.2	3.0	15.3	1.2	(8.0)
2	Coca-Cola Co.	KO	Neutral	44.60	4.3	11.4	5.5	4.9	18.4	2.3	(8.3)
2	Wrigley (Wm) Jr.	WWY	NC	46.05	2.9	11.1	4.4	2.6	22.4	2.0	0.2
2	Coca-Cola Enterprises	CCE	Neutral	21.46	1.3	6.8	1.1	7.6	15.7	1.9	(1.6)
2	Walgreen Co.	WAG	Buy	50.91	1.0	NM	5.6	2.4	26.4	1.7	4.8
10%	**Energy**										
2	Weatherford International Ltd.	WFT	Buy	41.01	2.1	10.8	3.0	0.6	13.6	0.5	(7.0)
2	National Oilwell Varco	NOV	Buy	62.16	1.4	12.4	2.5	2.9	14.7	0.5	(9.6)
2	BJ Services	BJS	Neutral	32.26	1.9	8.1	4.2	3.8	10.3	0.5	(16.7)
2	Nabors Industries Ltd.	NBR	Neutral	31.61	2.1	6.7	3.1	(0.6)	7.0	0.2	(21.9)
2	Rowan Cos.	RDC	Neutral	33.53	2.0	6.5	2.3	(0.6)	7.2	0.2	(21.3)
22%	**Financials**										
2	American Int'l. Group	AIG	Buy	64.24	NM	NM	1.9	NM	10.9	0.8	(8.1)
2	Simon Property Group, Inc	SPG	Buy	86.62	NM	NM	4.9	NM	15.8	2.0	(13.9)
2	Fifth Third Bancorp	FITB	Neutral	39.05	NM	NM	2.3	NM	13.9	1.4	(5.0)
2	Charles Schwab	SCHW	Neutral	16.28	NM	NM	3.8	NM	18.9	1.3	(3.6)
2	Synovus Financial	SNV	NC	28.87	NM	NM	3.0	NM	15.2	1.2	(1.1)
2	Capital One Financial	COF	Buy	72.46	NM	NM	1.7	NM	9.8	0.8	(3.7)
2	Northern Trust Corp.	NTRS	Neutral	56.49	NM	NM	2.9	NM	17.5	1.5	0.4
2	CIT Group	CIT	NC	44.90	NM	NM	1.3	NM	9.1	1.1	(6.1)
2	ProLogis	PLD	Buy	56.57	NM	NM	3.4	NM	17.9	4.0	(2.0)
2	E*Trade Financial Corp.	ET	Neutral	22.61	NM	NM	3.1	NM	14.0	1.0	(1.8)
2	Prudential Financial	PRU	Neutral	72.00	NM	NM	1.6	NM	11.8	0.8	NM
12%	**Health Care**										
2	Stryker Corp.	SYK	Buy	48.82	3.3	9.8	4.2	4.2	22.2	1.1	(2.0)
2	Medtronic Inc.	MDT	Neutral	46.66	4.6	13.3	5.5	4.2	19.3	1.3	(7.4)
2	Zimmer Holdings	ZMH	NC	67.37	4.5	12.6	3.6	4.5	18.4	1.1	(1.2)
2	BIOGEN IDEC Inc.	BIIB	Neutral	43.98	5.1	11.2	2.2	3.6	20.3	1.4	(5.7)
2	Amgen	AMGN	Buy	67.93	5.5	13.4	4.4	5.3	17.5	1.2	(6.5)
2	Genzyme Corp.	GENZ	Neutral	65.79	5.4	17.0	3.3	2.9	21.4	1.2	(0.7)
10%	**Industrials**										
2	Cintas Corporation	CTAS	NC	37.53	1.8	7.7	2.5	5.9	17.2	1.2	(6.2)
2	United Parcel Service	UPS	NC	69.56	1.5	9.1	4.5	4.1	17.2	1.4	(4.4)
2	L-3 Communications Holdings	LLL	Buy	75.26	1.0	9.0	2.0	8.9	14.1	1.2	(0.3)
2	Robert Half International	RHI	Neutral	30.42	1.1	9.6	5.4	5.1	17.7	0.9	(21.2)
2	Southwest Airlines	LUV	NC	16.48	1.3	6.2	1.8	9.5	18.5	1.2	7.3
16%	**Information Technology**										
2	eBay Inc.	EBAY	Buy	28.51	5.5	15.1	3.5	5.1	25.2	1.2	(7.7)
2	Linear Technology Corp.	LLTC	Buy	32.59	6.4	12.1	4.8	4.5	20.4	1.0	(15.1)
2	Xilinx, Inc	XLNX	Neutral	21.07	3.1	11.4	2.7	5.9	19.3	1.3	(16.8)
2	Maxim Integrated Prod	MXIM	Neutral	28.56	3.5	11.3	3.5	4.5	17.5	1.0	(19.6)
2	Microsoft Corp.	MSFT	Buy	25.60	4.4	9.3	5.1	5.7	17.7	1.5	(12.5)
2	Altera Corp.	ALTR	Neutral	19.33	4.2	14.9	5.3	5.6	19.5	1.0	(13.7)
2	Analog Devices	ADI	Neutral	29.63	2.9	9.2	2.9	5.1	16.1	0.8	(20.8)
2	Jabil Circuit	JBL	Buy	26.46	0.4	7.8	2.1	3.5	15.5	0.6	(12.0)
2%	**Materials**										
2	Newmont Mining Corp. (Hldg. Co.)	NEM	Neutral	48.19	3.6	11.0	2.6	0.4	22.2	0.6	(5.7)
4%	**Telecommunication Services**										
2	AT & T Inc.	T	Not Rated	31.35	1.8	8.1	2.5	6.4	13.6	1.4	(2.6)
2	Sprint Nextel Corp.	S	Buy	16.51	1.5	4.7	1.4	10.3	12.6	0.9	14.3
4%	**Utilities**										
2	AES Corp.	AES	NC	20.45	NM	8.1	7.3	7.9	22.5	1.4	13.6
2	DTE Energy Co.	DTE	NC	41.17	NM	8.6	1.3	(0.9)	10.6	2.4	8.3
100%	**Total**										
	"Super-value" portfolio (average)				2.7	9.6	3.4	4.7%	16.3	1.2	(6.6) pp
	S&P 500				1.5	8.4	2.8	4.7%	14.3	1.2	

Sources: Compustat, Lionshare via FactSet, and Goldman Sachs Research.

The Goldman Sachs "Anti-value" Portfolio

EXHIBIT 10	Our Sector-Neutral Portfolio of the 50 Most Overvalued Stocks in the S&P 500 as of September 8, 2006

Weight (%)	Company	Ticker	Rating	Sub-Sector	Equity Cap ($ bill)	Total Return YTD	Valuation Score 8-Sep-06
10%	**Consumer Discretionary**						
2	Wendy's International	WEN	Neutral	Restaurants	7	16 %	2.1
2	McGraw-Hill	MHP	Neutral	Publishing	20	11	1.7
2	Snap-On Inc.	SNA	NC	Household Appliances	3	18	1.6
2	Federated Dept. Stores	FD	Buy	Department Stores	22	20	1.6
2	V.F. Corp.	VFC	NC	Apparel Accessories & Luxury Goods	8	32	1.5
10%	**Consumer Staples**						
2	Altria Group, Inc.	MO	Neutral	Tobacco	173	14%	2.2
2	UST Inc.	UST	Sell	Tobacco	9	36	1.9
2	Sara Lee Corp.	SLE	NC	Packaged Foods & Meats	11	(8)	1.7
2	Archer-Daniels-Midland	ADM	NC	Agricultural Products	26	62	1.7
2	Constellation Brands	STZ	Buy	Distillers & Vintners	6	6	1.4
10%	**Energy**						
2	Murphy Oil	MUR	Buy	Integrated Oil & Gas	9	(12)%	1.0
2	Occidental Petroleum	OXY	Neutral	Integrated Oil & Gas	40	19	0.7
2	El Paso Corp.	EP	NC	Oil & Gas Storage & Transportation	10	16	0.7
2	Devon Energy Corp.	DVN	Neutral	Oil & Gas Exploration & Production	30	8	0.5
2	Sunoco., Inc.	SUN	Neutral	Oil & Gas Refining & Marketing	9	(16)	0.3
22%	**Financials**						
2	Chubb Corp.	CB	Neutral	Property & Casualty Insurance	21	4%	2.1
2	AmSouth Bancorporation	ASO	Not Rated	Regional Banks	10	12	2.0
2	T. Rowe Price Group	TROW	Neutral	Asset Management & Custody Banks	12	23	2.0
2	Mellon Bank Corp.	MEL	Neutral	Asset Management & Custody Banks	16	12	2.0
2	Aon Corp.	AOC	NC	Insurance Brokers	11	(4)	1.8
2	Loews Corp.	LTR	Neutral	Multi-line Insurance	21	21	1.8
2	PNC Bank Corp.	PNC	Neutral	Regional Banks	21	19	1.8
2	KeyCorp	KEY	Neutral	Regional Banks	15	14	1.8
2	First Horizon National	FHN	Sell	Regional Banks	5	1	1.7
2	Principal Financial Group	PFG	Sell	Life & Health Insurance	15	12	1.6
2	Huntington Bancshares	HBAN	Sell	Regional Banks	6	3	1.6
12%	**Health Care**						
2	Becton, Dickinson	BDX	Neutral	Health Care Equipment	17	15%	2.0
2	Bard (C.R.) Inc.	BCR	NC	Health Care Equipment	8	15	1.9
2	Laboratory Corp. of America Holt	LH	NC	Health Care Services	8	24	1.8
2	Manor Care Inc.	HCR	NC	Health Care Facilities	4	32	1.7
2	Humana Inc.	HUM	Buy	Managed Health Care	10	13	1.6
2	Thermo Electron	TMO	NC	Life Sciences Tools & Services	6	30	1.2
10%	**Industrials**						
2	United Technologies	UTX	Buy	Aerospace & Defense	64	15%	1.9
2	CSX Corp.	CSX	NC	Railroads	13	20	1.8
2	General Dynamics	GD	Buy	Aerospace & Defense	28	23	1.5
2	Allied Waste Industries	AW	NC	Environmental & Facilities Services	4	17	1.4
2	Cooper Industries, Ltd.	CBE	Neutral	Electrical Components & Equipment	7	13	1.3
16%	**Information Technology**						
2	Electronic Arts	ERTS	NC	Home Entertainment Software	16	0%	1.1
2	Autodesk, Inc.	ADSK	Neutral	Application Software	8	(22)	0.9
2	Apple Computer	AAPL	Buy	Computer Hardware	62	1	0.7
2	Freescale Semiconductor Inc.	FSL.B	Neutral	Semiconductors	13	23	0.6
2	Unisys Corp.	UIS	Neutral	IT Consulting & Other Services	2	(8)	0.6
2	Convergys Corp.	CVG	Sell	Data Processing & Outsourced Services	3	30	0.5
2	Intuit, Inc.	INTU	NC	Application Software	11	17	0.5
2	NVIDIA Corp.	NVDA	Neutral	Semiconductors	10	52	0.5
2%	**Materials**						
2	Pactiv Corp.	PTV	NC	Metal & Glass Containers	4	21%	1.8
4%	**Telecommunication Services**						
2	ALLTEL Corp.	AT	Neutral	Wireless Telecommunication Services	21	9%	1.2
2	BellSouth	BLS	Not Rated	Integrated Telecommunication Services	75	56	1.0
4%	**Utilities**						
2	Entergy Corp.	ETR	Buy	Electric Utilities	16	16%	2.2
2	Keyspan Energy	KSE	NC	Multi-Utilities	7	20	2.2
100%	**Total**						
	"Anti-value" portfolio (average)					15.5%	1.5
	S&P 500					5.4%	(1.2)

Note: S&P valuation calculated on an absolute basis, sector valuations calculated relative to S&P 500. Valuation score calculated as the average number of standard deviations seven valuation metrics differ from 10-year averages: EV/Sales, EV/EBITDA, P/B, FCF yield, P/E, PEG, and Implied Growth.

Sources: Compustat and Goldman Sachs Research.

EXHIBIT 11	Current Valuation Data for Our Sector-Neutral Portfolio of 50 Most Overvalued Stocks in the S&P 500 as of September 8, 2006

					Current Valuation Metrics						
Weight (%)	Company	Ticker	Rating	Price 8-Sep-06	EV/ Sales	EV/ EBITDA	Price/ Book	FCF Yield	P/E (NTM)	PEG Ratio	Implied Growth
10%	**Consumer Discretionary**										
2	Wendy's International	WEN	Neutral	$63.59	1.9	12.8	3.4	0.5%	25.5	2.1	24.4 pp
2	McGraw-Hill	MHP	Neutral	56.55	3.1	11.2	8.1	7.5	22.8	1.8	10.0
2	Snap-On Inc.	SNA	NC	43.36	1.1	10.3	2.5	8.1	21.2	1.8	19.4
2	Federated Dept. Stores	FD	Buy	39.58	1.0	7.9	2.2	22.9	15.7	1.3	15.5
2	V.F. Corp.	VFC	NC	71.42	1.2	7.1	2.3	6.2	13.8	1.4	11.4
10%	**Consumer Staples**										
2	Altria Group, Inc.	MO	Neutral	82.97	2.7	10.2	4.7	6.3	15.1	1.9	15.4
2	UST Inc.	UST	Sell	54.05	5.0	10.1	NM	6.2	16.9	2.4	19.5
2	Sara Lee Corp.	SLE	NC	14.50	1.3	10.7	3.7	4.9	18.4	2.4	12.5
2	Archer-Daniels-Midland	ADM	NC	39.59	0.8	9.8	2.8	2.4	16.0	1.8	12.0
2	Constellation Brands	STZ	Buy	27.74	1.8	8.9	1.9	4.3	15.3	1.2	4.4
10%	**Energy**										
2	Murphy Oil	MUR	Buy	47.34	4.5	4.4	2.3	(4.1)	11.8	1.2	2.9
2	Occidental Petroleum	OXY	Neutral	46.79	2.4	4.3	2.6	8.7	8.4	0.8	1.6
2	El Paso Corp.	EP	NC	14.01	4.6	10.8	2.9	(14.9)	12.5	1.6	5.0
2	Devon Energy Corp.	DVN	Neutral	67.56	3.0	4.7	2.0	(2.6)	9.4	1.2	6.1
2	Sunoco., Inc.	SUN	Neutral	65.50	0.3	4.2	4.2	10.8	7.6	0.8	1.8
22%	**Financials**										
2	Chubb Corp.	CB	Neutral	50.41	NM	NM	1.8	NM	10.2	1.0	2.2
2	AmSouth Bancorporation	ASO	Not Rated	28.86	NM	NM	2.8	NM	13.1	1.7	10.6
2	T. Rowe Price Group	TROW	Neutral	44.15	NM	NM	5.9	NM	22.2	1.8	11.0
2	Mellon Bank Corp.	MEL	Neutral	37.55	NM	NM	3.7	NM	16.7	1.6	7.6
2	Aon Corp.	AOC	NC	34.04	NM	NM	2.0	NM	13.3	1.9	8.7
2	Loews Corp.	LTR	Neutral	38.05	NM	NM	1.1	NM	10.5	1.3	9.8
2	PNC Bank Corp.	PNC	Neutral	71.72	NM	NM	2.5	NM	13.6	1.5	9.5
2	KeyCorp	KEY	Neutral	36.62	NM	NM	2.0	NM	12.5	1.6	9.6
2	First Horizon National	FHN	Sell	38.10	NM	NM	2.0	NM	13.7	1.7	5.5
2	Principal Financial Group	PFG	Sell	53.07	NM	NM	2.0	NM	15.4	1.3	8.1
2	Huntington Bancshares	HBAN	Sell	23.90	NM	NM	2.1	NM	13.0	1.9	7.0
12%	**Health Care**										
2	Becton, Dickinson	BDX	Neutral	68.60	2.8	11.0	5.0	4.2	19.5	1.6	10.2
2	Bard (C.R.) Inc.	BCR	NC	75.44	3.6	13.3	4.9	3.5	21.9	1.6	14.4
2	Laboratory Corp. of America Holdings	LH	NC	67.01	2.5	10.5	4.0	6.6	19.8	1.5	6.7
2	Manor Care Inc.	HCR	NC	51.96	1.2	9.9	4.8	5.6	20.5	1.4	14.3
2	Humana Inc.	HUM	Buy	61.46	0.3	10.3	4.1	16.9	19.5	1.2	18.3
2	Thermo Electron	TMO	NC	39.29	2.3	14.2	2.4	3.6	21.2	1.4	10.0
10%	**Industrials**										
2	United Technologies	UTX	Buy	63.34	1.5	10.5	3.8	4.8	16.4	1.5	6.9
2	CSX Corp.	CSX	NC	30.30	1.9	7.0	1.7	0.0	13.2	0.8	10.9
2	General Dynamics	GD	Buy	69.37	1.2	10.7	3.4	7.1	15.7	1.6	9.4
2	Allied Waste Industries	AW	NC	10.26	2.5	6.7	0.9	(0.7)	20.3	1.7	20.8
2	Cooper Industries, Ltd.	CBE	Neutral	81.15	1.6	11.3	3.2	6.4	16.2	1.5	14.2
16%	**Information Technology**										
2	Electronic Arts	ERTS	NC	52.51	4.5	26.2	4.9	2.9	NM	NM	47.3
2	Autodesk, Inc.	ADSK	Neutral	33.49	3.8	16.2	10.0	5.4	21.1	1.3	26.8
2	Apple Computer	AAPL	Buy	72.52	2.5	21.0	7.6	1.5	29.6	1.7	8.9
2	Freescale Semiconductor Inc.	FSLB	Neutral	30.94	1.8	7.4	2.8	7.4	15.7	1.6	(6.7)
2	Unisys Corp.	UIS	Neutral	5.39	0.4	7.9	1.4	(3.2)	30.8	3.4	28.3
2	Convergys Corp.	CVG	Sell	20.59	1.1	7.4	2.1	6.1	17.6	1.5	8.1
2	Intuit, Inc.	INTU	NC	31.16	3.7	13.0	6.2	5.0	22.2	1.5	(2.3)
2	NVIDIA Corp.	NVDA	Neutral	27.70	3.0	17.8	6.9	3.3	20.7	1.1	(4.2)
2%	**Materials**										
2	Pactiv Corp.	PTV	NC	26.70	1.6	8.6	4.2	3.4	17.6	1.7	15.8
4%	**Telecommunication Services**										
2	ALLTEL Corp.	AT	Neutral	55.24	2.8	6.1	1.9	7.3	20.7	3.4	14.2
2	BellSouth	BLS	Not Rated	41.19	2.5	9.9	3.1	3.4	17.2	2.6	9.2
4%	**Utilities**										
2	Entergy Corp.	ETR	Buy	78.11	NM	8.1	2.0	(2.6)	17.0	2.3	16.6
2	Keyspan Energy	KSE	NC	41.28	NM	8.7	1.6	(1.9)	17.0	4.5	9.7
100%	**Total**										
	"Anti-value" portfolio (average)				2.3	10.3	3.4	4.2%	17.1	1.7	11.2 pp
	S&P 500				1.5	8.4	2.8	4.7%	14.3	1.2	

Sources: Compustat and Goldman Sachs Research.

APPENDIX 45A

| EXHIBIT A-1 | Correlation of Valuation Metrics as of September 8, 2006 |

S&P 500	P/E	PEG	EV/ Sales	EV/ EBITDA	Cash Flow Yield	P/B	Growth	Valuation Score
P/E		0.7	0.6	0.6	0.5	0.3	0.7	**0.9**
PEG	0.7		0.4	0.3	0.2	0.1	0.4	**0.6**
EV/Sales	0.6	0.4		0.5	0.3	0.5	0.5	**0.7**
EV/EBITDA	0.6	0.3	0.5		0.4	0.5	0.5	**0.8**
Cash Flow Yield	0.5	0.2	0.3	0.4		0.4	0.3	**0.6**
P/B	0.3	0.1	0.5	0.5	0.4		0.2	**0.6**
Growth	0.7	0.4	0.5	0.5	0.3	0.2		**0.8**
Valuation Score	**0.9**	**0.6**	**0.7**	**0.8**	**0.6**	**0.6**	**0.8**	

Sources: Compustat and Goldman Sachs Research.

APPENDIX 45B

EXHIBIT B-1	The 25 Least and Most Expensive Stocks in the S&P 500 as of September 8, 2006

25 Least Expensive Stocks

Company	Ticker	Rating	Price 8-Sep	MktCap ($ bill)	YTD Return	EV/ Sales	EV/ EBITDA	Price/ Book	FCF Yield	P/E	PEG Ratio	Implied Growth	Average
Weatherford International Ltd.	WFT	Buy	$41.01	14	13	NM	NM	NM	NM	(3.8)	(2.2)	(2.2)	(2.7)
Stryker Corp.	SYK	Buy	48.82	14	10	(1.0)	(3.3)	(2.5)	(3.8)	(1.4)	(1.5)	NM	(2.2)
Apollo Group	APOL	NC	47.87	7	(21)	(2.0)	(2.3)	(1.2)	NM	(1.8)	0.8	(3.7)	(2.0)
eBay Inc.	EBAY	Buy	28.51	33	(34)	(2.1)	(2.3)	(2.2)	(1.2)	(2.3)	(1.2)	NM	(1.9)
Cintas Corporation	CTAS	NC	37.53	5	(8)	(1.5)	(2.0)	(1.7)	(2.1)	(1.6)	(1.9)	NM	(1.8)
Wal-Mart Stores	WMT	Buy	46.72	117	1	(1.2)	(3.1)	(2.4)	(0.1)	(1.6)	(1.4)	(2.6)	(1.8)
Home Depot	HD	Buy	34.28	71	(14)	(1.6)	(1.4)	(1.5)	(1.5)	(1.7)	(1.6)	(3.0)	(1.8)
Linear Technology Corp.	LLTC	Buy	32.59	10	(8)	(1.8)	(1.3)	(1.3)	(2.5)	(1.2)	(1.2)	NM	(1.6)
Xilinx, Inc.	XLNX	Neutral	21.07	7	(16)	(1.4)	(1.4)	(1.2)	(3.2)	(1.5)	(0.5)	NM	(1.5)
News Corporation	NWS.A	Neutral	18.87	45	22	1.7	(3.1)	(2.1)	(3.4)	(1.1)	(1.2)	NM	(1.5)
Bed Bath & Beyond	BBBY	Neutral	34.11	10	(6)	(1.8)	(1.4)	(1.4)	(1.7)	(1.8)	(1.0)	NM	(1.5)
United Parcel Service	UPS	NC	69.56	75	(6)	(0.3)	(1.2)	(1.5)	(0.7)	(1.9)	(1.1)	(3.8)	(1.5)
Maxim Integrated Prod	MXIM	Neutral	28.56	9	(20)	(2.2)	(0.6)	(1.7)	(2.1)	(1.5)	(0.9)	NM	(1.5)
Medtronic Inc.	MDT	Neutral	46.66	56	(18)	(2.2)	(0.6)	(1.7)	(1.1)	(2.0)	(1.3)	NM	(1.5)
Gap, Inc.	GPS	Neutral	16.90	9	(3)	(1.1)	(1.7)	(1.3)	(3.7)	(0.7)	(0.4)	(1.3)	(1.5)
Coach, Inc.	COH	Buy	31.88	12	(4)	(1.7)	(0.4)	(0.1)	(1.2)	(2.0)	(1.9)	(2.8)	(1.4)
Microsoft Corp.	MSFT	Buy	25.60	225	(1)	(1.4)	(1.6)	(0.7)	(0.7)	(1.1)	(1.3)	(3.1)	(1.4)
National Oilwell Varco	NOV	Buy	62.16	11	(1)	NM	(1.7)	0.1	NM	(3.2)	(0.7)	NM	(1.4)
Sears Holding Corp.	SHLD	NC	151.50	15	31	(0.1)	(1.2)	(2.8)	NM	(1.1)	(1.6)	NM	(1.4)
Altera Corp.	ALTR	Neutral	19.33	7	4	(1.0)	(0.6)	(0.4)	(1.7)	(1.2)	(0.9)	(3.7)	(1.3)
Analog Devices	ADI	Neutral	29.63	11	(16)	(1.4)	(1.3)	(1.1)	(1.2)	(1.4)	(1.5)	NM	(1.3)
Zimmer Holdings	ZMH	NC	67.37	17	(0)	(0.8)	(0.6)	(0.7)	(1.9)	(1.4)	(1.3)	(2.5)	(1.3)
American Int'l. Group	AIG	Buy	64.24	167	(5)	NM	NM	(1.1)	NM	(1.5)	(1.1)	(1.3)	(1.2)
Jabil Circuit	JBL	Buy	26.46	5	(28)	(2.4)	(0.8)	(1.4)	0.6	(1.5)	(1.9)	NM	(1.2)
Paychex Inc.	PAYX	Neutral	35.22	12	(6)	(1.2)	(1.1)	(1.4)	(1.2)	(1.4)	(0.7)	NM	(1.2)
S&P 500				11751	5	(1.4)	(2.0)	(1.0)	(0.7)	(1.3)	(0.9)	(1.0)	(1.2)
(median)				11	4	0.0	(0.0)	0.1	(0.0)	0.4	0.0	1.1	0.3
PNC Bank Corp.	PNC	Neutral	71.72	21	19	NM	NM	2.1	NM	2.0	1.3	NM	1.8
American Electric Power	AEP	Sell	35.91	14	(0)	NM	1.6	1.1	3.9	1.2	(0.0)	3.1	1.8
Peoples Energy	PGL	NC	41.05	2	21	NM	2.7	1.5	1.0	2.6	1.3	NM	1.8
Loews Corp.	LTR	Neutral	38.05	15	21	NM	NM	1.0	NM	2.2	2.3	NM	1.8
Aon Corp.	AOC	NC	34.04	11	(4)	NM	NM	0.3	NM	0.8	2.4	3.8	1.8
Constellation Energy Group	CEG	NC	59.62	11	6	NM	2.4	2.8	2.4	1.2	(1.3)	3.6	1.8
Pinnacle West Capital	PNW	NC	44.89	4	13	NM	2.2	1.1	2.8	1.5	0.3	3.3	1.9
Bard (C.R.) Inc.	BCR	NC	75.44	8	15	2.0	2.4	1.5	1.1	2.0	1.3	2.7	1.9
Consolidated Edison	ED	Sell	45.29	11	2	NM	2.4	1.2	NM	1.7	0.4	3.8	1.9
UST Inc.	UST	Sell	54.05	9	36	2.2	0.1	NM	0.3	2.8	2.2	3.8	1.9
FPL Group	FPL	NC	44.25	18	9	NM	2.2	1.6	3.0	1.4	(0.4)	3.7	1.9
PPL Corp.	PPL	NC	33.57	13	17	NM	2.5	1.1	2.5	2.2	(0.4)	3.6	1.9
United Technologies	UTX	Buy	63.34	64	15	2.0	3.2	1.0	1.1	1.9	1.8	2.6	1.9
Mellon Bank Corp.	MEL	Neutral	37.55	16	12	NM	NM	1.3	NM	2.1	1.4	3.1	2.0
T. Rowe Price Group	TROW	Neutral	44.15	12	23	NM	NM	2.6	NM	1.9	2.0	1.3	2.0
Becton, Dickinson	BDX	Neutral	68.60	17	15	2.1	2.6	2.2	1.8	1.6	1.2	2.4	2.0
Southern Co.	SO	NC	34.05	25	2	NM	2.8	1.2	NM	1.5	0.6	4.0	2.0
Public Serv. Enterprise Inc.	PEG	NC	67.46	17	7	NM	1.9	2.0	3.0	2.9	0.3	NM	2.0
AmSouth Bancorporation	ASO	Not Rated	28.86	10	12	NM	NM	1.3	NM	1.5	1.8	3.5	2.0
Xcel Energy Inc.	XEL	NC	20.29	8	13	NM	1.3	1.2	2.0	2.6	1.5	3.8	2.1
Wendy's International	WEN	Neutral	63.59	7	16	2.7	NM	1.8	0.4	2.8	2.8	NM	2.1
Chubb Corp.	CB	Neutral	50.41	21	4	NM	NM	1.5	NM	1.7	1.9	3.3	2.1
Keyspan Energy	KSE	NC	41.28	7	20	NM	2.8	(0.1)	2.9	2.1	1.7	3.6	2.2
Entergy Corp.	ETR	Buy	78.11	16	16	NM	2.1	2.2	3.5	2.8	0.3	NM	2.2
Altria Group, Inc.	MO	Neutral	82.97	173	14	2.4	2.9	0.5	0.8	2.3	3.1	3.6	2.2

25 Most Expensive Stocks

Note: S&P valuation calculated on an absolute basis, sector valuations calculated relative to S&P 500. Valuation score calculated as the average number of standard deviations seven valuation metrics differ from 10-year averages: EV/Sales, EV/EBITDA, P/B, FCF yield, P/E, PEG, and Implied Growth.

Sources: Compustat and Goldman Sachs Research.

APPENDIX 45C

| EXHIBIT C-1 | Valuation of Largest 50 Stocks in S&P 500 as of September 8, 2006 |

Company	Ticker	Rating	Price 8-Sep-06	Mkt Cap ($ bill)	YTD Return	EV/ Sales	EV/ EBITDA	Price/ Book	FCF Yield	P/E	PEG Ratio	Implied Growth	Average
Wal-Mart Stores	WMT	Buy	46.72	195	1	(1.2)	(3.1)	(2.4)	(0.1)	(1.6)	(1.4)	(2.6)	**(1.8)**
Home Depot	HD	Buy	34.28	71	(14)	(1.6)	(1.4)	(1.5)	(1.5)	(1.7)	(1.6)	(3.0)	**(1.8)**
News Corporation	NWS.A	Neutral	18.87	60	22	1.7	(3.1)	(2.1)	(3.4)	(1.1)	(1.2)	NM	**(1.5)**
United Parcel Service	UPS	NC	69.56	75	(6)	(0.3)	(1.2)	(1.5)	(0.7)	(1.9)	(1.1)	(3.8)	**(1.5)**
Medtronic Inc.	MDT	Neutral	46.66	56	(18)	(2.2)	(0.6)	(1.7)	(1.1)	(2.0)	(1.3)	NM	**(1.5)**
Microsoft Corp.	MSFT	Buy	25.60	261	(1)	(1.4)	(1.6)	(0.7)	(0.7)	(1.1)	(1.3)	(3.1)	**(1.4)**
American Int'l. Group	AIG	Buy	64.24	167	(5)	NM	NM	(1.1)	NM	(1.5)	(1.1)	(1.3)	**(1.2)**
Cisco Systems	CSCO	Buy	21.75	133	27	(0.9)	(0.6)	(0.5)	(1.0)	(1.0)	(0.6)	(3.3)	**(1.1)**
QUALCOMM Inc.	QCOM	Buy	36.54	61	(15)	(0.3)	(0.8)	(0.5)	(2.0)	(1.8)	(1.0)	NM	**(1.1)**
Amgen	AMGN	Buy	67.93	80	(14)	(1.0)	(0.5)	(0.9)	(1.0)	(0.9)	(0.8)	(1.9)	**(1.0)**
Oracle Corp.	ORCL	Neutral	15.91	85	30	(0.1)	(0.6)	(1.1)	(1.7)	(0.8)	(0.3)	(2.2)	**(1.0)**
Coca-Cola Co.	KO	Neutral	44.60	105	12	(0.8)	(0.7)	(1.2)	(1.1)	(1.0)	0.4	(2.2)	**(0.9)**
Walt Disney Co.	DIS	Buy	29.58	65	23	0.2	(0.0)	0.4	(1.3)	(1.4)	(0.7)	(3.2)	**(0.8)**
International Bus. Machines	IBM	Neutral	80.66	125	(1)	0.2	(0.7)	(0.8)	(2.3)	(0.6)	(1.2)	(0.2)	**(0.8)**
Time Warner Inc.	TWX	Neutral	16.87	69	(2)	(0.7)	(0.5)	(0.6)	0.6	(0.4)	(0.5)	(2.7)	**(0.7)**
Exxon Mobil Corp.	XOM	Buy	66.81	404	21	(1.0)	(0.7)	1.8	(1.3)	(1.9)	(1.6)	0.2	**(0.6)**
Lilly (Eli) & Co.	LLY	Buy	55.26	62	(0)	(1.2)	(0.9)	(1.2)	1.5	(1.0)	(0.4)	(1.4)	**(0.6)**
Pfizer, Inc.	PFE	Not Rated	27.59	202	22	(0.7)	(0.9)	(1.4)	(2.2)	(1.0)	3.1	(1.2)	**(0.6)**
Chevron Corp.	CVX	Neutral	64.22	142	16	(1.0)	(0.9)	0.6	(0.7)	(1.3)	(1.7)	0.8	**(0.6)**
Intel Corp.	INTC	Buy	19.45	113	(21)	(1.1)	(0.9)	(1.2)	(0.0)	0.2	0.2	(0.9)	**(0.6)**
General Electric	GE	Buy	34.01	354	(2)	1.5	(0.3)	(1.5)	0.3	(0.9)	(0.4)	(1.8)	**(0.4)**
Comcast Corp.	CMCSA	Neutral	34.90	74	35	(0.5)	(0.3)	(0.6)	0.5	(0.8)	(0.7)	NM	**(0.4)**
Johnson & Johnson	JNJ	Not Rated	63.59	188	8	(0.0)	0.0	(0.7)	(0.5)	(0.7)	0.1	(0.8)	**(0.4)**
Wyeth	WYE	Neutral	$48.25	65	6	(0.4)	(0.9)	(0.5)	(0.5)	(0.5)	0.0	0.4	**(0.3)**
Motorola Inc.	MOT	Neutral	23.70	59	5	0.2	0.1	1.9	(1.0)	(0.9)	(0.2)	(1.9)	**(0.2)**
Hewlett-Packard	HPQ	Buy	36.17	101	27	0.1	(0.3)	0.5	(1.0)	0.2	(0.4)	0.6	**(0.0)**
Schlumberger Ltd.	SLB	Buy	57.95	68	20	0.8	(0.0)	2.1	(0.2)	0.4	(0.8)	(2.3)	**0.0**
ConocoPhillips	COP	Buy	60.34	100	5	(0.6)	(0.8)	(0.4)	0.6	0.1	(0.3)	1.7	**0.0**
AT & T Inc.	T	Not Rated	31.35	122	33	(1.4)	2.9	(0.7)	(0.0)	0.2	(0.7)	0.1	**0.0**
Morgan Stanley	MS	Buy	66.69	71	19	NM	NM	0.2	NM	NM	NM	NM	**0.2**
Merck & Co.	MRK	Sell	41.06	90	33	0.7	(0.7)	(1.0)	(0.9)	0.8	1.9	0.8	**0.3**
Abbott Labs	ABT	Neutral	48.90	75	27	(0.1)	0.5	(0.9)	(1.1)	1.0	0.9	1.7	**0.3**
Merrill Lynch	MER	Neutral	72.71	67	8	NM	NM	0.7	NM	(0.2)	(1.2)	1.9	**0.3**
Citigroup Inc.	C	Neutral	48.72	242	4	NM	NM	(0.8)	NM	0.0	0.6	1.9	**0.4**
PepsiCo Inc.	PEP	Neutral	64.73	107	11	1.4	(0.2)	0.7	0.7	1.0	0.6	(0.9)	**0.5**
Boeing Company	BA	Neutral	72.80	58	5	1.1	0.3	2.2	(0.4)	0.5	(0.1)	1.2	**0.7**
Apple Computer	AAPL	Buy	72.52	62	1	2.0	0.7	2.5	0.5	0.1	(0.5)	(0.4)	**0.7**
Procter & Gamble	PG	Neutral	61.14	201	7	1.7	2.4	(0.9)	0.9	0.7	(0.5)	0.6	**0.7**
United Health Group Inc.	UNH	Sell	50.90	69	(18)	0.2	1.1	0.4	(0.1)	1.4	1.3	0.9	**0.7**
American Express	AXP	NC	52.62	65	3	NM	NM	1.7	NM	1.0	(0.3)	1.1	**0.9**
Verizon Communications	VZ	Neutral	35.40	103	22	(0.3)	1.0	(1.1)	(0.4)	1.4	2.8	2.8	**0.9**
Wachovia Corp.	WB	Buy	54.34	87	6	NM	NM	0.1	NM	0.9	0.0	2.7	**0.9**
JPMorgan Chase & Co.	JPM	Neutral	45.26	157	17	NM	NM	(0.5)	NM	1.8	1.5	NM	**1.0**
BellSouth	BLS	Not Rated	41.19	75	56	(0.1)	NM	0.7	1.2	2.2	1.1	NM	**1.0**
U.S. Bancorp	USB	Buy	32.19	57	10	NM	NM	0.7	NM	0.7	0.9	3.3	**1.4**
Bank of America Corp.	BAC	Buy	51.66	236	16	NM	NM	0.6	NM	0.9	1.2	3.5	**1.5**
United Technologies	UTX	Buy	63.34	64	15	2.0	3.2	1.0	1.1	1.9	1.8	2.6	**1.9**
Altria Group, Inc.	MO	Neutral	82.97	173	14	2.4	2.9	0.5	0.8	2.3	3.1	3.6	**2.2**
Wells Fargo	WFC	Buy	34.98	118	14	NM	NM	0.7	NM	NM	NM	3.9	**2.3**
Google Inc.	GOOG	Buy	377.85	115	(9)	NM	NM	NM	NM	NM	NM	NM	**NM**

Note: S&P valuation calculated on an absolute basis, sector valuations calculated relative to S&P 500. Valuation score calculated as the average number of standard deviations seven valuation metrics differ from 10-year averages: EV/Sales, EV/EBITDA, P/B, FCF yield, P/E, PEG, and Implied Growth.

Sources: Compustat and Goldman Sachs Research.

The Equities Division of the firm has previously introduced a basket of securities discussed in this report. The Equity Analyst may have been consulted as to the composition of the basket prior to its launch. However, the views expressed in this research and its timing were not shared with the Equities Division.

$4\frac{5}{8}$ 4

$5\frac{1}{2}$ $5\frac{1}{2}$ — $\frac{5}{8}$

$5\frac{1}{2}$ $21\frac{3}{16}$ — $\frac{1}{16}$

$20\frac{5}{8}$ $21\frac{3}{16}$ — $\frac{7}{8}$

$17\frac{3}{8}$ **$18\frac{1}{8}$** + $\frac{1}{2}$

$6\frac{1}{2}$ **$6\frac{1}{2}$** — $\frac{1}{2}$

$7\frac{1}{4}$ $31\frac{1}{32}$ — $\frac{1}{8}$

$\frac{15}{16}$ $\frac{9}{16}$

1 $\frac{9}{16}$

$\frac{9}{16}$

$1\frac{7}{32}$

$7\frac{15}{16}$ $7\frac{13}{16}$ $7\frac{15}{16}$

$2\frac{5}{8}$ $2\frac{11}{32}$ $2\frac{1}{2}$ +

$2\frac{3}{4}$ $2\frac{1}{4}$ $2\frac{1}{4}$

$6\frac{1}{8}$ $12\frac{1}{16}$ $11\frac{3}{8}$ $11\frac{3}{4}$ +

87 $33\frac{3}{4}$ 33 $33\frac{1}{16}$ —

602 $25\frac{5}{8}$ $24\frac{9}{16}$ $25\frac{3}{8}$ +

833 12 $11\frac{5}{8}$ $11\frac{7}{8}$ +

16 $10\frac{1}{2}$ $10\frac{1}{2}$ $10\frac{1}{4}$ —

78 $15\frac{7}{8}$ $15\frac{13}{16}$ $15\frac{7}{8}$ —

4508 $9\frac{1}{16}$ $8\frac{1}{4}$ $8\frac{7}{8}$

430 $11\frac{1}{4}$ $10\frac{1}{8}$

STUDY SESSION 12
EQUITY INVESTMENTS:
Valuation Models

This study session addresses the valuation methodologies that, in many cases, may provide a good estimate of a firm's real value. The dividend discount model remains a baseline model. The free cash flow approach to valuation is an important alternative to the dividend discount model when dividends are not the best representation of a company's value. Price multiples are among the most familiar and widely used valuation measures because of their simplicity and the ease with which they can be used and communicated.

READING ASSIGNMENTS

Reading 46   Discounted Dividend Valuation
Reading 47   Free Cash Flow Valuation
Reading 48   Market-Based Valuation: Price Multiples

LEARNING OUTCOMES

Reading 46: Discounted Dividend Valuation

The candidate should be able to:

a. discuss the advantages and disadvantages of dividends, free cash flow, and residual income as measures of cash flow in discounted cash flow valuation, and identify the investment situation for which each measure is suitable;

b. determine the circumstances in which a dividend discount model (DDM) is appropriate for valuing a stock;

c. explain the capital asset pricing model (CAPM), arbitrage pricing theory (APT), and bond yield plus risk premium approaches for estimating the required rate of return for an equity investment, and calculate the required rate of return using each approach;

d. estimate the Gordon growth model equity risk premium;

e. discuss the limitations of using the CAPM and APT to estimate the required return on equity;

f. calculate the expected holding-period return on a stock, given its current price, expected next-period price, and expected next-period dividend and contrast the expected holding-period return to the required rate of return;

271

g. discuss the effect on expected return of the convergence of price to value, given that price does not equal value;

h. calculate the value of a common stock using the DDM for one-, two-, and multiple-period holding periods;

i. calculate the value of a common stock using the Gordon growth model, and explain the underlying assumptions;

j. calculate justified leading and trailing price-to-earnings (P/E) ratios based on fundamentals, using the Gordon growth model;

k. calculate the value of fixed-rate perpetual preferred stock, given the stock's annual dividend and the discount rate;

l. calculate the present value of growth opportunities (PVGO), given current earnings per share, the required rate of return, and the value of the stock;

m. explain the strengths and limitations of the Gordon growth model, and justify the selection of the Gordon growth model to value a company, given the characteristics of the company being valued;

n. explain the assumptions and justify the selection of the two-stage DDM, the H-model, the three-stage DDM, or spreadsheet modeling;

o. explain the growth phase, transitional phase, and maturity phase of a business;

p. explain terminal value and discuss alternative approaches to determining the terminal value in a discounted dividend model;

q. calculate the value of a common stock using the two-stage DDM, the H-model, and the three-stage DDM;

r. explain how to estimate the implied expected rate of return for any DDM, including the two-stage DDM, the H-model, the three-stage DDM, and the spreadsheet model, and calculate the implied expected rate of return for the H-model and a general two-stage model;

s. explain the strengths and limitations of the two-stage DDM, the H-model, the three-stage DDM, and the spreadsheet model;

t. define sustainable growth rate and explain the underlying assumptions and calculate and interpret the sustainable growth rate for a company;

u. estimate, using the DuPont model, a forecast for return on equity that can be used to estimate a company's sustainable growth rate.

Reading 47: Free Cash Flow Valuation

The candidate should be able to:

a. define and interpret free cash flow to the firm (FCFF) and free cash flow to equity (FCFE);

b. describe the FCFF and FCFE approaches to valuation, and contrast the appropriate discount rates for each model and explain the strengths and limitations of the FCFE model;

c. contrast the ownership perspective implicit in the FCFE approach to the ownership perspective implicit in the dividend discount approach;

d. discuss the appropriate adjustments to net income, earnings before interest and taxes (EBIT), earnings before interest, taxes, depreciation, and amortization (EBITDA), or cash flow from operations (CFO) to calculate FCFF and FCFE;

e. calculate FCFF and FCFE given a company's financial statements prepared according to U.S. GAAP or International Accounting Standards;

f. discuss approaches for forecasting FCFF and FCFE;

g. contrast the recognition of value in the FCFE model to the recognition of value in dividend discount models;

h. explain how dividends, share repurchases, share issues, and changes in leverage may affect FCFF and FCFE;

i. critique the use of net income and EBITDA as proxies for cash flow in valuation;

j. discuss the single-stage (stable-growth), two-stage, and three-stage FCFF and FCFE models (including assumptions), and explain the company characteristics that would justify the use of each model;

k. calculate the value of a company using the single-stage, two-stage, and three-stage FCFF and FCFE models;

l. explain how sensitivity analysis can be used in FCFF and FCFE valuations;

m. discuss the approaches for calculating the terminal value in a multi-stage valuation model;

n. describe the characteristics of companies for which the FCFF model is preferred to the FCFE model.

Reading 48: Market-Based Valuation: Price Multiples

The candidate should be able to:

a. distinguish between the method of comparables and the method based on forecasted fundamentals as approaches to using price multiples in valuation, and discuss the economic rationales for each approach;

b. define a justified price multiple;

c. discuss rationales for using each price multiple and dividend yield in valuation, discuss possible drawbacks to the use of each price multiple and dividend yield, and calculate each price multiple and dividend yield;

d. calculate underlying earnings given earnings per share (EPS) and nonrecurring items in the income statement and discuss the methods of normalizing EPS, and calculate normalized EPS by each method;

e. explain and justify the use of earnings yield (E/P);

f. discuss the fundamental factors that influence each price multiple and dividend yield;

g. calculate the justified price-to-earnings ratio (P/E), price-to-book ratio (P/B), and price-to-sales ratio (P/S) for a stock, based on forecasted fundamentals;

h. calculate a predicted P/E, given a cross-sectional regression on fundamentals, and explain limitations to the cross-sectional regression methodology;

i. define the benchmark value of a multiple;

j. evaluate a stock by the method of comparables using each of the price multiples and explain the importance of fundamentals in using the method of comparables;

k. calculate the P/E-to-growth ratio (PEG), and explain its use in relative valuation;

l. calculate and explain the use of price multiples in determining terminal value in a multi-stage discounted cash flow (DCF) model;

m. discuss alternative definitions of cash flow used in price multiples, and explain the limitations of each definition;

n. discuss the sources of differences in cross-border valuation comparisons;

o. describe the main types of momentum indicators and their use in valuation.

4⅛ 4

5½ 5½ − ⅜

20⅝ 21³⁄₁₆ − ⅛

17⅜ 18⅛ + ⅞

18½ 6½ 6½ − ½

7¼ 31½₂ − ⅛
15/16

9/16 9/16

19/32 7¹³⁄₁₆ 7¹⁵⁄₁₆

7¹⁵⁄₁₆ 2¹¹⁄₃₂ 2½ +

2⅝ 2¼ 2¼

2¾ 2¼ 2¼

6⅛ 12¹⁄₁₆ 11⅜ 11¾ +

87 33¾ 33 33⅛ −

602 25⅝ 24⁹⁄₁₆ 25¾ +

833 12 11⅝ 11⅞ +

16 10½ 10½ 10½ −

78 15⅞ 15¹³⁄₁₆ 15⅞ −

508 9¹⁄₁₆ 8¼ 8⅛ +

430 11¼ 10⅛ 10⅛

DISCOUNTED DIVIDEND VALUATION

by John D. Stowe, Thomas R. Robinson, Jerald E. Pinto,
and Dennis W. McLeavey

LEARNING OUTCOMES

The candidate should be able to:

a. discuss the advantages and disadvantages of dividends, free cash flow, and residual income as measures of cash flow in discounted cash flow valuation, and identify the investment situation for which each measure is suitable;

b. determine the circumstances in which a dividend discount model (DDM) is appropriate for valuing a stock;

c. explain the capital asset pricing model (CAPM), arbitrage pricing theory (APT), and bond yield plus risk premium approaches for estimating the required rate of return for an equity investment, and calculate the required rate of return using each approach;

d. estimate the Gordon growth model equity risk premium;

e. discuss the limitations of using the CAPM and APT to estimate the required return on equity;

f. calculate the expected holding-period return on a stock, given its current price, expected next-period price, and expected next-period dividend and contrast the expected holding-period return to the required rate of return;

g. discuss the effect on expected return of the convergence of price to value, given that price does not equal value;

h. calculate the value of a common stock using the DDM for one-, two-, and multiple-period holding periods;

i. calculate the value of a common stock using the Gordon growth model, and explain the underlying assumptions;

j. calculate justified leading and trailing price-to-earnings (P/E) ratios based on fundamentals, using the Gordon growth model;

k. calculate the value of fixed-rate perpetual preferred stock, given the stock's annual dividend and the discount rate;

l. calculate the present value of growth opportunities (PVGO), given current earnings per share, the required rate of return, and the value of the stock;

Analysis of Equity Investments: Valuation, by John D. Stowe, Thomas R. Robinson, Jerald E. Pinto, and Dennis W. McLeavey. Copyright © 2002 by AIMR. Reprinted with permission.

m. explain the strengths and limitations of the Gordon growth model, and justify the selection of the Gordon growth model to value a company, given the characteristics of the company being valued;

n. explain the assumptions and justify the selection of the two-stage DDM, the H-model, the three-stage DDM, or spreadsheet modeling;

o. explain the growth phase, transitional phase, and maturity phase of a business;

p. explain terminal value and discuss alternative approaches to determining the terminal value in a discounted dividend model;

q. calculate the value of a common stock using the two-stage DDM, the H-model, and the three-stage DDM;

r. explain how to estimate the implied expected rate of return for any DDM, including the two-stage DDM, the H-model, the three-stage DDM, and the spreadsheet model, and calculate the implied expected rate of return for the H-model and a general two-stage model;

s. explain the strengths and limitations of the two-stage DDM, the H-model, the three-stage DDM, and the spreadsheet model;

t. define sustainable growth rate and explain the underlying assumptions and calculate and interpret the sustainable growth rate for a company;

u. estimate, using the DuPont model, a forecast for return on equity that can be used to estimate a company's sustainable growth rate.

1   INTRODUCTION

Common stock represents an ownership interest in a business. A business in its operations generates a stream of cash flows, and as owners of the business, common stockholders have an equity ownership claim on those future cash flows. Beginning with John Burr Williams (1938), analysts have developed this insight into a group of valuation models known as **discounted cash flow (DCF)** valuation models. DCF models—which view the intrinsic value of common stock as the present value of its expected future cash flows—are a fundamental tool in both investment management and investment research. This reading is the first of three readings that describe DCF models and address how to apply those models in practice.

What tasks do we face in approaching common stock valuation as a present value problem? We can distinguish two broad challenges.

The first challenge is to define exactly what we mean by *future cash flows* and, what is practically the heart of valuation, forecast what they will be in the future. In this reading, we take the perspective that dividends—distributions to shareholders authorized by a corporation's board of directors—are an appropriate definition of cash flows. The class of models based on this idea is called dividend discount models, or DDMs. The basic objective of using a DDM is to value a stock. Among the questions we will address in this reading that will help us apply DDMs are:

► What implementation of the dividend discount model is suitable for a specific company?

► How do we forecast dividends?

► How can we use a dividend discount model to infer the market's estimate of the earnings growth rate or to infer a stock's expected rate of return?

► How are dividend discount models used in security selection?

Our second challenge is to estimate the appropriate rate of return to use for discounting cash flows back to the present, the discount rate. Our definitions of discount rate and cash flow must be coordinated, but the main alternative approaches to estimating discount rates are common to all present value models, so we shall also discuss discount rates in this reading.

The reading is organized as follows: Section 2 provides an overview of present value models. A general statement of the dividend discount model follows in Section 3. Forecasting dividends, individually and in detail, into the indefinite future is not generally practicable, so we usually simplify the dividend-forecasting problem. One approach is to assign dividends to a stylized growth pattern. The simplest pattern—dividends growing at a constant rate forever—is the constant growth (or Gordon growth) model, discussed in Section 4. For some companies, it is more appropriate to view earnings and dividends as having multiple stages of growth; we present multistage dividend discount models in Section 5. An alternative approach is to forecast dividends individually up to some date and then apply a simplifying assumption to estimate the terminal stock price. This approach is conveniently handled with the use of spreadsheets. We present spreadsheet modeling in Section 5 as well. Finally, Section 6 lays out the determinants of dividend growth rates and the use of DDMs in investment management.

PRESENT VALUE MODELS   2

The end product of the equity analysis process for individual securities is an investment recommendation. In the valuation part of the process, we estimate whether an asset is fairly valued, overvalued, or undervalued in the marketplace. Present value models are important tools for reaching such judgments. In this section, we discuss the economic rationale for valuing an asset as the present value of its expected future cash flows. We also discuss alternative definitions of cash flows and present the major alternative methods for estimating the discount rate.

2.1 Valuation Based on the Present Value of Future Cash Flows

The value of an asset must be related to the benefits or returns we expect to receive from holding it. We call those returns the asset's future cash flows (we will define *cash flow* more concretely and technically later). We also need to recognize that a given amount of money received in the future is worth less than the same amount of money received today. Money received today gives us the option of immediately spending and consuming it. So money has a time value. When valuing an asset, before adding up the estimated future cash flows, we must **discount** each cash flow back to the present: We reduce the cash flow's value with respect to how far away it is in time. The two elements of discounted cash flow valuation—estimating the cash flows, and discounting the cash flows to account for the time value of money—provide the economic rationale for discounted cash flow valuation. Additional intuition comes from the observation that in the baseline case, in which the timing and amounts of future cash flows are known with certainty, if we invest an amount equal to the present value of future cash flows at the given discount rate, that investment will replicate all of the asset's cash flows (with no money left over).

For some assets, such as government debt, cash flows may be essentially known with certainty—that is, they are risk-free. The appropriate discount rate for a risk-free cash flow is a risk-free rate of interest. For example, if an asset has a single, certain cash flow of \$100 to be received in two years, and the risk-free interest rate is 5 percent a year, the value of the asset is the present value of \$100 discounted at the risk-free rate, $\$100/(1.05)^2 = \$90.70$.

In contrast to risk-free debt, future cash flows for equity investments are not known with certainty—they are risky. Introducing risk makes applying the present value approach much more challenging. The most common approach to dealing with risky cash flows involves two adjustments relative to the risk-free case. First, we discount the *expected* value of the cash flows, viewing the cash flows as random variables.[1] Second, we adjust the discount rate to reflect the risk of the cash flows.

The following equation expresses the concept that an asset's value is the present value of its (expected) future cash flows:

$$V_0 = \sum_{t=1}^{\infty} \frac{CF_t}{(1+r)^t} \qquad \textbf{(46-1)}$$

where

V_0 = the value of the asset at time $t = 0$ (today)
CF_t = the cash flow (or the expected cash flow, for risky cash flows) at time t
r = the discount rate or required rate of return

For simplicity, we represent the discount rate in Equation 46-1 as the same for all time periods, a flat term structure of discount rates. The analyst has the latitude in this model, however, to apply different discount rates to different cash flows.[2]

Equation 46-1 gives an asset's value from the perspective of today ($t = 0$). Likewise, an asset's value at some point in the future equals the value of all subsequent cash flows discounted back to that point in time. Example 1 illustrates these points.

---

[1] The expected value of a random quantity is the mean or average value of its possible outcomes, in which each outcome's weight in the average is its probability of occurrence. See DeFusco, McLeavey, Pinto, and Runkle (2001) for all statistical concepts used in this reading.

[2] Different discount rates could reflect different degrees of cash flow riskiness or different risk-free rates at different time horizons. Differences in cash flow riskiness may be caused by differences in business risk, operating risk (use of fixed assets in production), or financial risk or leverage (use of debt in the capital structure). The simple expression given is adequate for the discussion, however.

Although the principles behind discounted cash flow valuation are simple, applying the theory to equity valuation can be challenging. Four broad steps in applying DCF analysis to equity valuation are:

- ▶ choosing the class of DCF model—equivalently, selecting a specific definition of cash flow;
- ▶ forecasting the cash flows;
- ▶ choosing a discount rate methodology; and
- ▶ estimating the discount rate.

EXAMPLE 1

Value as the Present Value of Future Cash Flows

We expect an asset to generate cash flows of \$100 in one year, \$150 in two years, and \$200 in three years. The value of this asset today, using a 10 percent discount rate, is

$$V_0 = \frac{100}{(1.10)^1} + \frac{150}{(1.10)^2} + \frac{200}{(1.10)^3}$$

$$= 90.909 + 123.967 + 150.263 = \$365.14$$

The value at $t = 0$ is \$365.14. We use this same logic to value an asset at a future date. The value of the asset at $t = 1$ is the present value, discounted back to $t = 1$, of all cash flows after this point. This value, V_1, is

$$V_1 = \frac{150}{(1.10)^1} + \frac{200}{(1.10)^2}$$

$$= 136.364 + 165.289 = \$301.65$$

At any point in time, the asset's value is the value of future cash flows (CF) discounted back to that point. Because V_1 represents the value of CF_2 and CF_3 at $t = 1$, the value of the asset at $t = 0$ is also the present value of CF_1 and V_1:

$$V_0 = \frac{100}{(1.10)^1} + \frac{301.653}{(1.10)^1}$$

$$= 90.909 + 274.23 = \$365.14$$

Finding V_0 as the present value of CF_1, CF_2, and CF_3 is logically equivalent to finding V_0 as the present value of CF1 and V_1.

In the next section, we present an overview of three alternative definitions of cash flow. The selected cash flow concept defines the type of DCF model we can use: the dividend discount model, the free cash flow model, or the residual income model. The next section also broadly characterizes the types of valuation problems for which analysts often choose a particular model. (We supply further details when each model is discussed individually.) Then, in Section 2.3, we discuss choosing a discount rate methodology and estimating the discount rate. We leave the discussion of cash flow forecasting to the readings on each alternative DCF model.

2.2 Streams of Expected Cash Flows

In present value models of stock valuation, the three most widely used definitions of returns are dividends, free cash flow, and residual income. We discuss each definition in turn.

The dividend discount model defines cash flows as dividends. The basic argument for using this definition of cash flow is that an investor who buys and holds a share of stock generally receives cash returns only in the form of dividends.[3] In practice, analysts usually view investment value as driven by earnings. Does the definition of cash flow as dividends ignore earnings not distributed to shareholders as dividends? Reinvested earnings should provide the basis for increased future dividends. Therefore, the DDM accounts for reinvested earnings when it takes all future dividends into account. Because dividends are less volatile than earnings and other return concepts, the relative stability of dividends may make DDM values less sensitive to short-run fluctuations in underlying value than alternative DCF models. Analysts often view DDM values as reflecting long-run intrinsic value.

A stock either pays dividends or does not pay dividends. A company might not pay dividends on its stock because the company is not profitable and has no cash to distribute. Also, a company might not pay dividends for the opposite reason: because it is very profitable. For example, a company may reinvest all earnings—paying no dividends—to take advantage of profitable growth opportunities. As that company matures and faces fewer attractive investment opportunities, it may initiate dividends.

There are international differences in dividend policy. As one contrast, more than 90 percent of the FTSE Eurotop 300 stocks pay dividends, compared with approximately 70 percent of the stocks in the S&P 500 as of the beginning of 2002.[4] Nevertheless, in the United States, the majority of all companies with publicly traded shares do not pay dividends, and the fraction of dividend-paying companies has been declining. According to Fama and French (2001), 20.8 percent of U.S. stocks paid dividends in 1999, compared with 66.5 percent in 1978. This decline was caused by a reduced propensity to pay dividends over time as well as an increase in the population of smaller publicly traded companies with low profitability and large growth opportunities.[5] Can we apply the DDM to non-dividend paying companies? In theory we can, as we will illustrate later, but in practice we generally do not.

Predicting the timing of dividend initiation and the magnitude of future dividends without any prior dividend data or specifics about dividend policy to guide the analysis is generally not practical. For a non-dividend-paying company, analysts usually prefer a model that defines returns at the company level (as free cash flow or residual income—we define these concepts shortly), rather than at the stockholder level (as dividends). Another consideration in the choice of models relates to ownership perspective. An investor purchasing a small ownership share does not have the ability to meaningfully influence the timing or magnitude of the distribution of the company's cash to shareholders. That perspective is the one taken in applying a dividend discount model. The only access to the company's value is through the receipt of dividends, and dividend policy is taken as a given. If dividends do not bear an understandable relation to value creation in the company, applying the DDM to value the stock is prone to error.

---

[3] Corporations can also effectively distribute cash to stockholders through stock repurchases (also called buybacks). This fact does not affect the argument, however.

[4] *Financial Times of London,* January 28, 2002.

[5] Even controlling for profitability and growth opportunities, the propensity of companies to pay dividends has been declining in the U.S. markets, according to Fama and French (2000).

Generally, the definition of returns as dividends, and the DDM, is most suitable when:

▶ the company is dividend-paying (i.e., the analyst has a dividend record to analyze);

▶ the board of directors has established a dividend policy that bears an understandable and consistent relationship to the company's profitability; and

▶ the investor takes a non-control perspective.

Often, companies with established dividends are seasoned companies, profitable but operating outside the economy's fastest-growing subsectors. Professional analysts often apply a dividend discount model to value the common stock of such companies.

EXAMPLE 2

Occidental Petroleum and Hormel Foods: Is the DDM an Appropriate Choice?

As director of equity research at a brokerage, you have final responsibility in the choice of valuation models. Two analysts have approached you on the use of a dividend discount model: an oil industry analyst examining Occidental Petroleum Corporation (NYSE: OXY) and a food industry analyst examining Hormel Foods (NYSE: HRL). Table 1 gives the most recent 10 years of data. (In the table, EPS is earnings per share. DPS is dividends per share, and payout ratio is DPS divided by EPS. "E$4.92" means that $4.92 is an estimated value.)

TABLE 1   OXY and HRL: The Earnings and Dividends Record

	1992	1993	1994	1995	1996	1997	1998	1999	2000	2001
OXY										
EPS	$0.41	$0.12	−$0.36	$1.31	$1.86	$0.39	$0.88	$1.58	$4.26	E$4.92
DPS	$1.00	$1.00	$1.00	$1.00	$1.00	$1.00	$1.00	$1.00	$1.00	$1.00
Payout Ratio	244%	833%	NM[a]	76%	54%	256%	114%	63%	23%	E20%
HRL										
EPS	$0.62	$0.66	$0.77	$0.79	$0.52	$0.72	$0.93	$1.11	$1.20	$1.30
DPS	$0.18	$0.22	$0.25	$0.29	$0.30	$0.39	$0.32	$0.33	$0.35	$0.37
Payout Ratio	29%	33%	32%	37%	58%	54%	34%	30%	29%	28%

[a] NM = Not meaningful.
Source: Standard & Poor's Stock Reports.

Answer the following questions based on the information in Table 1:

1. State whether a dividend discount model is an appropriate choice for valuing OXY. Explain your answer.

2. State whether a dividend discount model is an appropriate choice for valuing HRL. Explain your answer.

Solution to 1: Based only on the data given in Table 1, a DDM does not appear to be an appropriate choice for OXY. Although OXY is dividend-paying, OXY's dividends do not bear an understandable and consistent relationship to earnings. Dividend payout ratios have varied from 833 percent to 20 percent when earnings have been positive. Dividends have been constant at $1.00 a share throughout the period, and earnings have been very volatile. If the volatility reflected only random, transitory effects on profitability, the analyst might consider a DDM. However, earnings since 1998 appear to be at a consistently higher level than in 1992–94. Expected EPS of $4.92 in 2001 represents a 12-fold increase from $0.41 in 1992. Because dividends do not appear to adjust to reflect changes in value, applying a DDM to OXY is probably inappropriate. Valuing OXY on another basis, such as company-level definition of cash flows, is more appropriate.

Solution to 2: The historical earnings of HRL show a long-term upward trend, with the exception of 1996 and 1997. Although you might want to research those divergent payout ratios, HRL's dividends have generally followed its growth in earnings. Dividends per share of $0.37 in 2001 were roughly twice the level of $0.18 in 1992, and earnings per share have also doubled over that period. In summary, because HRL is dividend-paying and dividends bear an understandable and consistent relationship to earnings, using a DDM to value HRL is appropriate.

Valuation is a forward-looking exercise. In practice, the analyst would check for public disclosures concerning changes in dividend policy going forward. We will return to discuss the valuation of Hormel stock in Example 22.

A second definition of returns is free cash flow. The term *cash flow* has been given many meanings in different contexts. Above, we have used the term informally, referring to returns to ownership (equity). We now want to give it a more technical meaning, related to accounting usage. Over a given period of time, a company can add to cash (or use up cash) by selling goods and services. This money is cash flow from operations (for that time period). Cash flow from operations is the critical cash flow concept addressing a business's underlying economics. Companies can also generate (or use up) cash in two other ways. First, a company affects cash through buying and selling assets, including investment and disinvestment in plant and equipment. Second, a company can add to or reduce cash through its financing activities. Financing includes debt and equity. For example, issuing bonds increases cash, and buying back stock decreases cash (all else equal).[6]

---

[6] Internationally, accounting definitions may not be fully consistent with the above concepts in distinguishing between types of sources and uses of cash. Although the implementation details are not the focus here, an example can be given. U.S. generally accepted accounting principles (GAAP) include a financing item, net interest payments, in *cash flow from operating activities*, so careful analysts working with U.S. accounting data often add back after-tax net interest payments to cash flow from operating activities when calculating cash flow from operations. Under International Accounting Standards, companies may or may not include interest exposed as an operating cash flow.

Assets supporting current sales may need replacement because of obsolescence or wear and tear, and the company may need new assets to take advantage of profitable growth opportunities. The concept of free cash flow responds to the reality that, for a going concern, some of the cash flow from operations is not "free" but rather needs to be committed to reinvestment and new investment in assets. **Free cash flow to the firm** (FCFF) is cash flow from operations minus capital expenditures. Capital expenditures—reinvestment in new assets, including working capital—are needed to maintain the company as a going concern, so only that part of cash flow from operations remaining after such reinvestment is "free." (This definition is conceptual.) FCFF is the part of the cash flow generated by the company's operations that can be withdrawn by bondholders and stockholders without economically impairing the company. Conceptually, the value of common equity is the present value of expected future FCFF—the total value of the company—minus the market value of outstanding debt.

Another approach to valuing equity works with free cash flow to equity. **Free cash flow to equity** (FCFE) is cash flow from operations minus capital expenditures, or FCFF, from which we net all payments to debtholders (interest and principal repayments net of new debt issues). Debt has a claim on the cash of the company that must be satisfied before any money can be paid to stockholders, so money paid on debt is not available to common stockholders. Conceptually, common equity can be valued as the present value of expected FCFE. FCFF is a pre-debt free cash flow concept; FCFE is a post-debt free cash flow concept. The FCFE model is the baseline free cash flow valuation model for equity, but the FCFF model may be easier to apply in several cases, such as when the company's leverage (debt in its capital structure) is expected to change significantly over time, as we will discuss in more detail in the reading on free cash flow valuation.

Valuation using a free cash flow concept is popular in current investment practice. We can calculate free cash flow (FCFF or FCFE) for any company. We can always examine the record of free cash flows, in contrast to dividends. FCFE can be viewed as measuring what a company can afford to pay out in dividends. Even for dividend-paying companies, a free cash flow model valuation may be preferred when dividends exceed or fall short of FCFE by significant amounts.[7] FCFE also represents cash flow that can be redeployed outside the company without affecting the company's capital investments. A controlling equity interest can effect such a redeployment. As a result, free cash flow valuation is appropriate for investors who want to take a control perspective. (Even a small shareholder may want to take such a perspective when there is potential for the company to be acquired, because stock price should reflect the price an acquirer would pay.)

Just as there are cases in which an analyst would find it impractical to apply the DDM, applying the free cash flow approach is a problem in some cases. Some companies have intense capital demands and, as a result, have negative expected free cash flows far into the future. As one example, a retailer may be constantly constructing new outlets and be far from saturating even its domestic market. Even if the retailer is currently very profitable, free cash flow may be negative indefinitely because of the level of capital expenditures. The present value of a series of negative free cash flows is a negative number: The use of a free cash flow model may entail a long forecast horizon to capture the point at which expected free cash flow turns positive. The uncertainty associated with distant forecasts may be considerable. In such cases, the analyst may have more confidence using another approach, such as residual income valuation.

---

[7] In theory, when period-by-period dividends equal FCFE, the DDM and FCFE models should value stock identically, if all other assumptions are consistent. See Miller and Modigliani (1961), a classic reference for the mathematics and theory of present value models of stock value.

Generally, defining returns as free cash flow and using the FCFE (and FCFF) models are most suitable when:

► the company is not dividend-paying;

► the company is dividend-paying but dividends significantly exceed or fall short of free cash flow to equity;

► the company's free cash flows align with the company's profitability within a forecast horizon with which the analyst is comfortable; and

► the investor takes a control perspective.

The third and final definition of returns that we will discuss in this overview is residual income. Conceptually, **residual income** for a given time period is the earnings for that period in excess of the investors' required return on beginning-of-period investment (common stockholders' equity). Suppose shareholders' initial investment is $200 million, and the required rate of return on the stock is 8 percent. The required rate of return is investors' **opportunity cost** for investing in the stock: the alternative return that investors forgo when investing in the stock. The company earns $18 million in the course of a year. How much value has the company added for shareholders? A return of $0.08 \times \$200$ million = $16 million just meets the amount investors could have earned in an equivalent-risk investment (by the definition of opportunity cost). Only the residual or excess amount of $18 million − $16 million = $2 million represents value added, or an economic gain, to shareholders. So, $2 million is the company's residual income for the period. The residual income approach attempts to match profits to the time period in which they are earned (but not necessarily realized as cash); in contrast to accounting net income (which has the same goal in principle), how-ever, residual income attempts to measure the value added in excess of opportunity costs.

The residual income model states that a stock's value is book value per share plus the present value of expected future residual earnings. (Book value per share is common stock-holders' equity divided by the number of common shares outstanding.) In contrast to the dividend and free cash flow models, the residual income model introduces a stock concept, book value per share, into the present value expression. Nevertheless, the residual income model can be viewed as a restatement of the dividend discount model, using a company-level return concept. Dividends are paid out of earnings and are related to earnings and book value through a simple expression.[8] The residual income model is a useful addition to an analyst's toolbox. Because we can always calculate the record of residual income, we may use a residual income model for both dividend-paying and non-dividend-paying stocks. Analysts may choose a residual income approach for companies with negative expected free cash flows within their comfortable forecast horizon. In such cases, a residual income valuation often brings the recognition of value closer to the present as compared with a free cash flow valuation, producing higher value estimates.

---

[8] Book value of equity at t = (Book value of equity at $t − 1$) + (Earnings over $t − 1$ to t) − (Dividends paid at t), so long as anything that goes through the balance sheet (affecting book value) first goes through the income statement (reflected in earnings), apart from ownership transactions. The condition that all changes in the book value of equity other than transactions with owners are reflected in income is known as **clean surplus accounting**. U.S. and international accounting standards do not always follow clean surplus accounting; the analyst, therefore, in using this expression, must critically evaluate whether accounting-based results conform to clean surplus accounting and, if they do not, adjust them appropriately.

The residual income model has an attractive focus on profitability in relation to opportunity costs.[9] Knowledgeable application of the residual income model requires a detailed knowledge of accrual accounting; consequently, in cases for which the dividend discount model is suitable, analysts may prefer it as the simpler choice. Management sometimes exercises its discretion within allowable accounting practices to distort the accuracy of its financials as a reflection of economic performance. If the quality of accounting disclosure is good, the analyst may be able to calculate residual income by making appropriate adjustments (to reported net income and book value, in particular). In some cases, the degree of distortion and the quality of accounting disclosure can be such that the application of the residual income model is error-prone.

Generally, the definition of returns as residual income, and the residual income model, is most suitable when:

▶ the company is not dividend-paying, as an alternative to a free cash flow model; or

▶ the company's expected free cash flows are negative within the analyst's comfortable forecast horizon.

In summary, the three most widely used definitions of returns to investors are dividends, free cash flow, and residual income. Although claims are often made that one cash flow definition is inherently superior to the rest—often following changing fashions in investment practice—a more flexible viewpoint is practical. The analyst may find that one model is more suitable to a particular valuation problem. The analyst may also develop more expertise in applying one type of model. In practice, skill in application—in particular, the quality of forecasts—is frequently decisive for the usefulness of the analyst's work.

In the next section, we discuss a task that we face no matter which DCF model we apply: the determination of the discount rate. We will then present the dividend discount model in detail.

2.3 Discount Rate Determination

In a previous section, we stated that two of the tasks in applying DCF analysis to equity valuation are choosing a discount rate methodology and estimating the discount rate. In this section, we present and illustrate the major alternative methods available for determining the discount rate. (**Discount rate** is a general term for any rate used in finding the present value of a future cash flow.)

In choosing a discount rate, we want it to reflect both the time value of money and the riskiness of the stock. The risk-free rate represents the time value of money. A **risk premium** represents compensation for risk, measured relative to the risk-free rate. The risk premium is an expected return in excess of the risk-free rate that is related to risk. When we decide on a discount rate that reflects both the time value of money and an asset's risk, as we perceive it, we have determined our required rate of return. A **required rate of return** is the minimum rate of return required by an investor to invest in an asset, given the asset's riskiness. Sometimes we refer to *the* required rate of return for an asset. This is a required rate of return on an asset that we infer using market data, which should represent a type of consensus perspective on the asset's risk. Generally, we use such required rates of return in DCF valuation. In this book, we use the notation

---

[9] Executive compensation schemes are sometimes based on a residual income concept, including branded variations such as Economic Value Added (EVA®) from Stern Stewart & Co.

r for the required rate of return on the asset we are discussing. The required rate of return on common stock is also known as the **cost of equity**.

Whether we define cash flow as dividends, free cash flow to equity, or residual income, we use a cost-of-equity concept of the required rate of return, because each of those return concepts is a post-debt flow to equity. If we use a FCFF valuation model, we are defining cash flows as the cash flows available to bondholders, common stockholders, and preferred stockholders, if any. Consequently, in FCFF valuation, we use the cost of capital (taking into account all sources of financing) as the required rate of return. To use the precise term, we use the **weighted-average cost of capital**—the weighted average of the cost of equity, the after-tax cost of debt,[10] and the cost of preferred stock. The weight on each cost component is the fraction of total long-term financing (common stock, debt, preferred stock) that each financing source represents, at market values, in the company's desired or target capital structure. No matter what cash flow concept we use, we need to calculate the cost of equity. The cost of equity is the most challenging element in discount-rate determination and will be our focus in this discussion.

We present two major approaches to determining the cost of equity:

▶ an equilibrium model method, based on either the capital asset pricing model (CAPM) or arbitrage pricing theory (APT); and

▶ the bond **yield** plus risk premium method.

Equilibrium methods are based on formal economic models. (**Equilibrium** describes a condition in which supply equals demand.) These models address in particular the structure of the risk premium that we add to the risk-free rate. The bond yield plus risk premium method is based on empirical relationships.

The CAPM states that the expected return on an asset is related to its risk as measured by beta:

$$E(R_i) = R_F + \beta_i[E(R_M) - R_F]$$ **(46-2)**

where

$E(R_i)$ = the expected return on asset *i* given its beta
R_F = the risk − free rate of return
$E(R_M)$ = the expected return on the market portfolio
β_i = the asset's sensitivity to returns on the market portfolio, equal to Cov (R_i, R_M)/Var (R_M)

The term in square brackets is the **market risk premium**, the expected return on the market minus the risk-free rate. The CAPM thus states that the expected return on an asset, given its beta, is the risk-free rate plus a risk premium equal to beta times the market risk premium. In practice, we always estimate beta with respect to an equity market index when using the CAPM to estimate the cost of equity. So in practice, discussing equity, we are concerned specifically with the **equity risk premium** (defining the market as the equity market).

We can use the CAPM-based expected rate of return for a common stock as the cost of equity in a DCF valuation. That rate is $E(R_i) = r$, the required rate of return on equity. Given that the CAPM describes equilibrium, so that all risk is captured by beta, investors make risk adjustments based on beta. We must clearly

---

[10] In some countries, including the United States, interest on debt is tax deductible, which reduces its cost. Common and preferred stock dividends are not tax deductible, so an after-tax/before-tax distinction is not made for those components of the cost of capital.

distinguish between the expected return given by a model, which is an equilib-rium expected return (an estimate of the fair return) based on a model, and an individual's expected return on an asset based on current market prices (which may differ from intrinsic value). The CAPM can be used in any national market.

EXAMPLE 3

Calculating the Cost of Equity Using the CAPM

You are valuing J.C. Penney Company (NYSE: JCP), a major consumer goods retailer, as of the end of 2001. As one step, you need to estimate the required rate of return on JCP stock. Based on its beta of 0.55, a historical risk premium of 5.7 percent, and a risk-free rate of 5.7 percent, the required rate of return on JCP according to the CAPM is $R_F + \beta_i[E(R_M) - R_F] = 0.057 + (0.55 \times 0.057) = 0.08835$, or 8.8 percent. (In this case, the risk-free rate and the risk premium happen to be the same.)

To use the CAPM, we need to answer two questions:

▶ What proxy for risk-free rate of return do we adopt?[11]
▶ How do we define and estimate the equity risk premium?

The definition of the risk-free rate should be coordinated with how the equity risk premium is calculated.

The choices for the risk-free rate are a short-term government debt rate, such as a 30-day T-bill rate, or a long-term government bond yield to maturity. Common stock has no maturity date. As a consequence, common stock is a long-duration asset (Fabozzi [2000] discusses duration as a measure of the futurity of an asset's cash flows). Because it is logical to match the duration of the risk-free measure to the duration of the asset being valued, this book uses the **current yield** to maturity on a liquid long-term government bond as the risk-free rate. The available maturi-ties of government bonds change over time and differ among national markets. If a 20-year maturity is available and trades in a liquid market, however, its yield is a reasonable choice as an estimate of the risk-free rate for equity valuation.[12] In many international markets, only bonds of shorter maturity are available or have a liquid market. A 10-year government bond yield is another common choice.

We need to address estimation of the equity risk premium to have a workable method. Clearly, to be consistent, the equity risk premium should be relative to a long-term government bond yield. So we define the equity risk premium as the expected return on a broad equity index in excess of the long-term government bond yield to maturing (or yield). The CAPM estimate of the cost of equity is then

CAPM cost of equity = Current long-term government bond yield + Stock's beta × Estimated equity risk premium relative to the long-term yield **(46-3)**

[11] In this context, a proxy is something used to represent a concept.

[12] The Ibbotson U.S. long-term government bond yield is based on a portfolio of 20-year average maturity T-bonds. We use that series in the suggested historical estimate of the U.S. equity risk premium.

Two broad approaches exist for estimating the equity risk premium, one based on historical average differences between equity market returns and government debt returns, the other based on expectational data (for example, expected earnings on the equity index). When reliable, long-term records of equity return are available, the **historical method** is the most familiar and popular choice. An expectational method is consistent with the forward-looking nature of valuation; it may be the only available alternative for an emerging stock market.

In taking a historical approach, we face a choice between using the arithmetic mean return (typically, the average of one-year rates of return) and using the geometric mean return (the compound rate of growth of the index over the study period). The arithmetic mean more accurately measures average one-period returns; the geometric mean more accurately measures multiperiod growth. The dilemma is that the CAPM (as well as the APT) is a single-period model, suggesting the use of the arithmetic mean; but common stock investment often has a long time horizon, and valuation involves discounting cash flows over many periods, suggesting the use of the geometric mean. Estimates of risk premiums using **geometric means** are consistently smaller than estimates using **arithmetic means**, and the differences can be significant. We can illustrate this concept for U.S. markets using data from *Stocks, Bonds, Bills, and Inflation,* published annually by Ibbotson Associates, given in Table 2.

Using long-term government bond returns as a proxy for the risk-free rate of return and geometric means, the historical estimate of the U.S. equity risk premium is 5.7 percent (11.0 percent minus 5.3 percent).[13] Using arithmetic means, we arrive at an estimate of 7.3 percent (13.0 percent minus 5.7 percent). Although the debate is inconclusive, this book uses geometric means, not only for the previously given reasons but also because geometric means produce estimates of the equity risk premium that are more consistent with the predictions of economic theory.[14] To summarize, we can calculate the historical estimate of the market risk premium as the historical geometric mean return on a representative equity index minus the historical geometric mean return on long-term government bonds in the same country's markets.

Table 3 shows historical estimates of the equity risk premium for 12 major markets over the period 1900–2000.

Historical estimates of the equity premiums have limitations. **Survivorship bias,** which results when poorly performing companies are removed from membership in an index, tends to inflate historical estimates of the equity risk premium (the data in Table 3 reflect a correction for survivorship bias, however).[15] Because of the great volatility in equity returns, a long data series is needed to estimate the premium with any precision, even assuming the target (the underlying value) is fixed. However, there is evidence from a number of markets that the equity risk premium varies over time. Data from distant periods may be questionably relevant for the future, our concern in valuation. To address this concern, we can use an estimator of the equity risk premium based

---

[13] Calculating the geometric mean of the difference of two series as the difference in geometric means involves an approximation with a negligible error.

[14] See Mehra and Prescott (1985). The relatively large size of the historical U.S. equity premium relative to that predicted by theory, given estimates of investors' risk aversion, is known as the "equity premium puzzle." The geometric mean was also the choice of Dimson, Marsh, and Staunton (2000) in their authoritative survey of world equity markets.

[15] Copeland, Koller, and Murrin (2000) recommend a downward adjustment of 1.5 percent to 2.0 percent for survivorship bias in the S&P 500 Index, using arithmetic mean estimates. In their development of the Millennium Book series, Dimson et al. took great care to correct for survivorship data.

TABLE 2   U.S. Annual Total Returns: 1926–2000

Series	Geometric Mean (%)	Arithmetic Mean (%)	Standard Deviation (%)
Common stocks	11.0	13.0	20.2
Small company stocks	12.4	17.3	33.4
Long-term corporate bonds	5.7	6.0	8.7
Long-term government bonds	5.3	5.7	9.4
Intermediate-term government bonds	5.3	5.5	5.8
Treasury bills	3.8	3.9	3.2
Inflation	3.1	3.2	4.4

Source: Ibbotson Associates.

explicitly on expectational data. Probably the most frequently encountered estimate of this type (that is, based on expectational data) is the Gordon growth model (GGM) equity risk premium estimate:[16]

GGM equity risk premium estimate = (Dividend yield on the index based on year-ahead forecasted dividends + Consensus long-term earnings growth rate) − Current long-term government bond yield   **(46-4)**

As of the end of 2001, the consensus future five-year earnings growth rate on the S&P 500 Index was 7.0 percent, according to First Call/Thomson Financial (compared with a 12.15 percent earnings growth rate over the previous five years). Based on consensus forecasts of the next year's earnings and an S&P 500 level of 1145, the forecasted dividend yield was 1.2 percent. The 20-year U.S. government bond yield was 5.8 percent. Therefore, according to Equation 46-4, the Gordon growth model estimate of the U.S. equity risk premium was 0.012 + 0.070 − 0.058 = 0.024, or 2.4 percent. As with any approach to estimating the risk premium, the Gordon growth model has possible limitations. The fact that different approaches may lead to different premium estimates and possibly different actions is part of the challenge of valuation.[17]

The CAPM is an established method of estimating the cost of equity. Its strengths are simplicity and familiarity. Beta is easily obtained from a variety of sources. The balance of evidence, however, shows that the CAPM beta describes risk incompletely. In practice, coefficients of determination (*R*-squared)

---

[16] Recent examples of the application of this model (to U.S. markets) are Jagannathan, McGrattan, and Scherbina (2000) and Fama and French (2001). The Gordon growth model estimate has also been used in institutional research for international markets (Stux 1994). Most analysts forecast the earnings growth rate rather than the dividend growth rate, which is technically specified in theory, so we use the earnings growth rate in the above expression. Given a constant dividend payout ratio, a reasonable approximation for broad equity indexes, the two growth rates should be equal. We present the Gordon growth model later in this reading.

[17] Fama and French (2001) found that prior to 1950, the historical and Gordon growth model estimates for the U.S. equity risk premium agree, but from 1950–99, the Gordon growth model estimate averages less than half the historical estimate. They attribute the difference to the effect of positive earnings surprises relative to expectations on realized returns.

TABLE 3	Historical Equity Risk Premiums around the World: 1900–2000	
Country	Equity Risk Premium (based on long bond rate)	Equity Risk Premium (based on T-bill rate)
Australia	5.9%	7.1%
Canada	4.6	4.6
Denmark (from 1915)	2.5	2.8
France	5.0	7.7
Germany (98 years ex-1923/4)	6.9	5.1
Italy	5.0	7.1
Japan	6.4	7.5
Netherlands	4.8	5.2
Sweden	5.8	6.1
Switzerland (from 1911)	2.8	4.3
United Kingdom	5.3	4.9
United States	4.6	5.8
Average	5.0	5.7

Source: Dimson, Marsh, and Staunton (2000).

for individual stocks' beta regressions may range from 2 percent to 40 percent, with many under 10 percent. For many markets, evidence suggests that multiple factors drive returns. At the cost of greater complexity and expense, the analyst can consider using an equilibrium model based on multiple factors. Such models are known as arbitrage pricing theory (APT) models. Whereas the CAPM adds a single risk premium to the risk-free rate, APT models add a set of risk premiums. APT models have the form

$$E(R_i) = R_F + (\text{Risk premium})_1 + (\text{Risk premium})_2 + \cdots + (\text{Risk premium})_K \tag{46-5}$$

where $(\text{Risk premium})_i = (\text{Factor sensitivity})_i \times (\text{Factor risk premium})_i$. **Factor sensitivity** is the asset's sensitivity to a particular factor (holding all other factors constant). The **factor risk premium** is the factor's expected return in excess of the risk-free rate.[18]

One type of APT model incorporates company-specific attributes. An example of such models is the Fama–French (1993) three-factor model. This model's factors are:

► RMRF, the return on a value-weighted equity index in excess of the one-month T-bill rate.

[18] For a slightly more technical statement of the APT, see Chapter 11 of DeFusco, McLeavey, Pinto, and Runkle (2001).

► SMB (small minus big), a size (market capitalization) factor. SMB is the average return on three small-cap portfolios minus the average return on three large-cap portfolios.

► HML (high minus low), the average return on two high book-to-market portfolios minus the average return on two low book-to-market portfolios.[19]

A second type of APT model employs macroeconomic factors. For example, the Burmeister, Roll, and Ross (1994) or BIRR model is based on five macroeconomic factors that affect the average returns of U.S. stocks. The five factors are the following:

► Confidence risk, the unanticipated change in the return difference between 20-year corporate and 20-year government bonds. (When investors' confidence is high, investors should be willing to accept a smaller reward for bearing this risk, hence the name.)

► Time horizon risk, the unanticipated change in the return difference between 20-year government bonds and 30-day Treasury bills. This factor reflects willingness to invest for the long term.

► Inflation risk, the unexpected change in the inflation rate. Nearly all stocks have negative sensitivity to this factor, as their returns decline with positive surprises in inflation.

► Business-cycle risk, the unexpected change in the level of real business activity.

► Market-timing risk, the portion of the S&P 500 total return that is not explained by the first four risk factors. Almost all stocks have positive sensitivity to this factor.

Each of the five BIRR factors can be interpreted as affecting the numerator or the denominator of Equation 46-1, the DCF valuation equation. Equation 46-6 is the equation for the BIRR model for the United States, using factor risk premium values in Burmeister et al; that study estimated risk premiums relative to the T-bill rate.

$$
\begin{aligned}
E(R_i) = \text{T-bill rate} + &(\text{Sensitivity to confidence risk} \times 2.59\%) \\
- &(\text{Sensitivity to time horizon risk} \times 0.66\%) \\
- &(\text{Sensitivity to inflation risk} \times 4.32\%) \\
+ &(\text{Sensitivity to business-cycle risk} \times 1.49\%) \\
+ &(\text{Sensitivity to market-timing risk} \times 3.61\%)
\end{aligned}
$$

(46-6)

EXAMPLE 4

Calculating the Cost of Equity Using an APT Model

You have estimated the factor sensitivities of Johnson & Johnson, Inc. common stock (NYSE: JNJ) on BIRR factors. These are given in Table 4, with the factor sensitivities of the S&P 500 for comparison.

---

[19] See http://mba.tuck.dartmouth.edu/pages/faculty/ken.french/ for more information on the Fama–French model and factor data information.

TABLE 4   Factor Sensitivities in the BIRR Model

Risk Factor	JNJ Factor Sensitivity	S&P 500 Factor Sensitivities
Confidence risk	0.17	0.27
Time horizon risk	0.74	0.56
Inflation risk	−0.15	−0.37
Business-cycle risk	1.16	1.71
Market-timing risk	0.72	1.00

Using the factor risk premiums estimated by Burmeister et al. and with a T-bill rate of 5 percent, calculate the required rate of return for JNJ using the multifactor model.

The required rate of return for JNJ is

$$r = 5.00\% + (0.17 \times 2.59\%) - (0.74 \times 0.66\%) - (-0.15 \times 4.32\%) + (1.16 \times 1.49\%) + (0.72 \times 3.61\%) = 9.93\%$$

Using the CAPM or APT, at least three possible sources of error exist in our cost-of-equity estimates: model uncertainty (concerning whether the model is correct), input uncertainty (for example, are the equity risk premium and risk-free rate used in the CAPM correct?), and uncertainty about the true current value of the stock's beta or factor sensitivity or sensitivities. (When we obtain beta by conducting the needed regression of stock returns on an equity index's returns ourselves, we should check the *t*-statistic of beta and note the regression's *R*-squared as indicators of the usefulness of CAPM for explaining returns on the stock.)[20] Having an alternative to the CAPM and APT is useful. For companies with publicly traded debt, the **bond yield plus risk premium method** provides a quick estimate of the cost of equity.[21] The estimate is

BYPRP cost of equity = YTM on the company's long-term debt + Risk premium   (46-7)

The yield to maturity (YTM) on the company's long-term debt incorporates the time value of money and default risk, which is related to the business's profitability and leverage. The risk premium compensates for the additional risk of equity compared with debt (debt has a prior claim on the cash flows of the company). In U.S. markets, the typical risk premium added is 3–4 percent, based on experience.

---

[20] See DeFusco et al. (2001) for definitions of these terms and a discussion of issues surrounding estimating beta.

[21] Although simple, the method has been used in serious contexts. For example, the Board of Regents of the University of California in a retirement plan asset/liability study (July 2000) used the 20-year T-bond rate plus 3.3 percent as the single estimate of the equity risk premium.

EXAMPLE 5

The Cost of Equity of IBM from Two Perspectives

You are valuing the stock of International Business Machines Corporation (NYSE: IBM) as of December 21, 2001, and you have gathered the following information:

20-year T-bond yield to maturity	5.8%
IBM 8.375s of 2019 yield to maturity	6.238%

The IBM bonds, you note, are investment grade (rated A1 by Standard & Poor's and A+ by Moody's Investors Service). The beta on IBM stock is 1.24.

1. Calculate the cost of equity using the CAPM. Assume that the equity risk premium is 5.7 percent.

2. Calculate the cost of equity using the bond yield plus risk premium approach, with a risk premium of 3 percent.

3. Suppose you found that IBM stock, which closed at 121.45 on December 21, 2001, was slightly undervalued based on a DCF valuation using the CAPM cost of equity from Question 1. Does the alternative estimate of the cost of equity from Question 2 support the conclusion based on Question 1?

Solution to 1: $E(R_i) = 0.058 + 0.057\beta_i = 0.058 + 0.057 \times 1.24 = 0.058 + 0.0706 = 0.1286$, or 12.9%.

Solution to 2: We add 3 percent to the IBM bond YTM: 6.238% + 3% = 9.238%, or 9.2%. Note that the difference between the IBM and T-bond YTM is 0.438 percent, or 44 basis points. This amount plus 3 percent is the total risk premium versus Treasury debt.

Solution to 3: Undervalued means that the value of a security is greater than market price. All else equal, the smaller the discount rate, the higher the estimate of value. The **inverse relationship** between discount rate and value, holding all else constant, is a basic relationship in valuation. If IBM appears to be undervalued using the CAPM cost of equity estimate of 12.9 percent, it will appear to be even more undervalued using a 9.2 percent cost of equity based on the bond yield plus risk premium method.

How can we estimate the cost of equity for a privately held company? In contrast to publicly traded shares, we will not have a record of market prices for a private company's stock and cannot calculate beta or factor sensitivities of the shares directly. The cost of equity using either the CAPM or APT is the sum of the risk-free rate and one or more risk premiums. Business valuators of privately held businesses often determine a discount rate by a **build-up method**. The cost of equity using a build-up method is the sum of risk premiums, in which one or more of the risk premiums is typically subjective rather than grounded in a formal model such as the CAPM or APT. For example, the cost of equity may be calculated as the sum of the current risk-free rate and an equity risk premium, plus or minus a subjective company-specific risk adjustment.[22]

The bond yield plus risk premium method is, in fact, a build-up method applying to companies with publicly traded debt. A build-up method other than the bond yield plus risk premium method can sometimes be useful when valuing publicly traded stock as well (as Example 10 later will show). The CAPM's reliability for estimating the cost of equity, as judged by R-squared or beta's t-statistic, may be suspect in a particular case. The company may have no publicly traded debt so that the bond yield plus risk premium method is not feasible. Using an APT estimate of the cost of equity is one alternative; using an estimate that is the sum of the risk-free rate, an equity risk premium, and a company-specific risk adjustment is another.

In the next section, we present the general form of the dividend discount model as a prelude to discussing the particular implementations of the model that are suitable for different sets of attributes of the company being valued.

3   THE DIVIDEND DISCOUNT MODEL

Investment analysts use a wide range of models and techniques to estimate the value of common stock, including present value models. In Section 2.2, we discussed three common definitions of returns for use in present value analysis: dividends, free cash flow, and residual income. In this section, we develop the most general form of the dividend discount model.

The DDM is the simplest and oldest present value approach to valuing stock. In a survey of AIMR members by Block (1999), 42 percent of respondents viewed the DDM as "very important" or "moderately important" for determining the value of individual stocks. Beginning in 1989, the *Merrill Lynch Institutional Factor Survey* has assessed the popularity of 23 valuation factors and methods among a group of institutional investors. From 1989 to 2000, the DDM has ranked as high as fifth in popularity. Besides its continuing significant position in practice, the DDM has an important place in both academic and practitioner equity research. The DDM is, for all these reasons, a basic tool in equity valuation.

3.1 The Expression for a Single Holding Period

From the perspective of a shareholder who buys and holds a share of stock, the cash flows he or she will obtain are the dividends paid on it and the market price of the share when he or she sells it. The future selling price should in turn reflect expectations about dividends subsequent to the sale. In this section, we will see how this argument leads to the most general form of the dividend discount model. In addition, the general expression we develop for a finite holding period corresponds to one practical approach to DDM valuation; in that approach, the analyst forecasts dividends over a finite horizon, as well as the terminal sales price.

If an investor wishes to buy a share of stock and hold it for one year, the value of that share of stock today is the present value of the expected dividend to be received on the stock plus the present value of the expected selling price in one year:

$$V_0 = \frac{D_1}{(1+r)^1} + \frac{P_1}{(1+r)^1} = \frac{D_1 + P_1}{(1+r)^1} \qquad \textbf{(46-8)}$$

---

[22] See Hawkins and Paschall (2000) for more information on private company valuation, including the determination of the discount rate in private market valuations.

where

V_0 = the value of a share of stock today, at $t = 0$
P_1 = the expected price per share at $t = 1$
D_1 = the expected dividend per share for Year 1, assumed to be paid at
     the end of the year at $t = 1$
r = the required rate of return on the stock

Equation 46-8 applies to a single holding period the principle that an asset's value is the present value of its future cash flows. In this case, the expected cash flows are the dividend in one year (for simplicity, assumed to be received as one payment at the end of the year)[23] and the price of the stock in one year.

EXAMPLE 6

DDM Value with a Single Holding Period

Suppose that you expect General Motors Corporation (NYSE: GM) to pay a $2.00 dividend next year and that you expect the price of GM stock to be $58.00 in one year. The required rate of return for GM stock is 10 percent. What is your estimate of the value of GM stock?

Discounting the expected dividend of $2.00 and the expected sales price of $58.00 at the cost of equity of 0.10, we obtain

$$V_0 = \frac{D_1 + P_1}{(1 + r)^1} = \frac{\$2.00 + \$58.00}{(1 + 0.10)^1} = \frac{\$60.00}{1.10} = \$54.55$$

Using Equation 46-8, we can explore an important point concerning return concepts. Supposing V_0 is equal to today's market price, P_0, solve Equation 46-8 for r

$$r = \frac{D_1 + P_1}{P_0} - 1 = \frac{D_1}{P_0} + \frac{P_1 - P_0}{P_0}$$

(46-9)

This sum of the expected dividend yield (D_1/P_0) and the expected price appreciation ($[P_1 - P_0]/P_0$) is the **expected holding-period return,** or simply expected return, on the stock. We must clarify that we have equated value to price in Equation 46-9; however, we typically use the DDM to try to identify securities for which price differs from value. We use some method independent of the DDM to obtain the required rate of return for use in a DDM valuation. Although *expected return* and *required rate of return* are often used interchangeably on an informal basis, the two are different concepts that should not be confused. Specifically, an expected return based on a calculation such as Equation 46-9 and the required rate of return (whether based on the CAPM or another model) differ when price does not exactly reflect value.[24] When current price equals value, we can interpret the required rate of return as an expected holding period return.

The difference between the expected rate of return based on market prices and the required rate of return is the expected abnormal return or alpha. As active investors, we seek positive alphas: returns in excess of returns that simply

---

[23] Throughout the discussion of the DDM, we assume that dividends for a period are paid in one sum at the end of the period.

[24] The expected return based on the CAPM is a distinct concept from the expected (holding-period) return.

compensate for risk. Only with efficient prices (prices equal to intrinsic values) does expected return equal required return (and the difference between expected return and required return, alpha, equals zero).

EXAMPLE 7

The Expected Holding-Period Return on DaimlerChrysler Stock

The current stock price of DaimlerChrysler AG ADR (NYSE: DCX) is $44.70. You expect a dividend of $2.08 in one year. You forecast the stock price to be $49.00 in one year. If you purchase DCX at the current market price, what return do you expect to earn over one year?

You use Equation 46-9 to find that the expected one-year return on DCX is

$$r = \frac{D_1 + P_1}{P_0} - 1 = \frac{2.08 + 49.00}{44.70} - 1$$

$$= \frac{51.08}{44.70} - 1$$

$$= 1.1427 - 1$$

$$= 0.1427 = 14.27\%$$

The expected return of 14.27 percent is the sum of the expected dividend yield of $D_1/P_0 = 2.08/44.70 = 4.65$ percent and the expected capital appreciation of $(P_1 - P_0)/P_0 = (49.00 - 44.70)/44.70 = 9.62$ percent.

3.2 The Expression for Multiple Holding Periods

If an investor plans to hold a stock for two years, the value of the stock is the present value of the expected dividend in Year 1, plus the present value of the expected dividend in Year 2, plus the present value of the expected selling price at the end of Year 2.

$$V_0 = \frac{D_1}{(1+r)^1} + \frac{D_2}{(1+r)^2} + \frac{P_2}{(1+r)^2} = \frac{D_1}{(1+r)^1} + \frac{D_2 + P_2}{(1+r)^2} \quad \textbf{(46-10)}$$

The expression for the DDM value of a share of stock for any finite holding period is a straightforward extension of the expressions for one-year and two-year holding periods. For an n-period model, the value of a stock is the present value of the expected dividends for the n periods plus the present value of the expected price in n periods (at $t = n$).

$$V_0 = \frac{D_1}{(1+r)^1} + \cdots + \frac{D_n}{(1+r)^n} + \frac{P_n}{(1+r)^n} \quad \textbf{(46-11)}$$

If we use summation notation to represent the present value of the first n expected dividends, the general expression for an n-period holding period or investment horizon can be written as

$$V_0 = \sum_{t=1}^{n} \frac{D_t}{(1+r)^t} + \frac{P_n}{(1+r)^n} \quad \textbf{(46-12)}$$

Equation 46-12 is significant in DDM application, because analysts may make individual forecasts of dividends over some finite horizon (often two to five years), then estimate the terminal price, P_n, based on one of a number of approaches. We will discuss valuation using a finite forecasting horizon later, under the heading of spreadsheet modeling. Example 8 reviews the mechanics of this calculation.

EXAMPLE 8

Finding the Stock Price for a Five-Year Forecast Horizon

For the next five years, the annual dividends of a stock are expected to be $2.00, $2.10, $2.20, $3.50, and $3.75. In addition, the stock price is expected to be $40.00 in five years. If the cost of equity is 10 percent, what is the value of this stock?

The present values of the expected future cash flows can be written out as

$$V_0 = \frac{2.00}{(1.10)^1} + \frac{2.10}{(1.10)^2} + \frac{2.20}{(1.10)^3} + \frac{3.50}{(1.10)^4} + \frac{3.75}{(1.10)^5} + \frac{40.00}{(1.10)^5}$$

Calculating and summing these present values gives a stock value of $V_0 =$ 1.818 + 1.736 + 1.653 + 2.391 + 2.328 + 24.837 = $34.76.

The five dividends have a total present value of $9.926 and the terminal stock value has a present value of $24.837, for a total stock value of $34.76.

With a finite holding period, whether one, two, five, or some other number of years, the dividend discount model finds the value of stock as the sum of (1) the present values of the expected dividends over the holding period, and (2) the present value of the expected stock price at the end of the holding period. As we increase the holding period by one year, we have an extra expected dividend term. In the limit (i.e., if we let the holding period extend into the indefinite future), the stock's value is the present value of all expected future dividends.

$$V_0 = \frac{D_1}{(1+r)_1} + \cdots + \frac{D_n}{(1+r)^n} + \cdots \qquad \text{(46-13)}$$

This value can be expressed with summation notation as

$$V_0 = \sum_{t=1}^{\infty} \frac{D_t}{(1+r)^t} \qquad \text{(46-14)}$$

Equation 46-14 is the general form of the dividend discount model, first presented by John Burr Williams (1938). Even from the perspective of an investor with a finite investment horizon, the value of stock depends on all future dividends. For that investor, stock value today depends *directly* on the dividends the investor expects to receive before the stock is sold and *indirectly* on the expected dividends after the stock is sold, because those future dividends determine the expected selling price.

Equation 46-14, expressing the value of stock as the present value of expected dividends into the indefinite future, presents a daunting forecasting challenge. In practice, of course, we cannot make detailed, individual forecasts of an infinite number of dividends. To use the DDM, we must simplify the forecasting problem. There are two broad approaches, each of which has several variations:

1. We can forecast future dividends by assigning the stream of future dividends to one of several stylized growth patterns. The most commonly used patterns are:

▶ constant growth forever (the Gordon growth model);

▶ two distinct stages of growth (the two-stage growth model and the H-model); and

▶ three distinct stages of growth (the three-stage growth model).

The DDM value of the stock is then found by discounting the dividend streams back to the present. We present the Gordon growth model in Section 4. We present the two-stage, H-model, and three-stage growth models in Section 5.

2. We can forecast a finite number of dividends individually up to a terminal point, using pro forma financial statement analysis, for example. The horizon selected reflects the **visibility** of the companies' operations—the extent to which they are predictable with substantial confidence—and will differ for different companies; analysts' detailed forecasts often extend two to five years into the future. We can then forecast either:

▶ the remaining dividends from the terminal point forward by assigning those dividends to a stylized growth pattern; or

▶ the share price at the terminal point of our dividend forecasts (**terminal share price**), using some method (such as taking a multiple of forecasted book value or earnings per share as of that point, based on one of several methods for estimating such multiples).

The stock's DDM value is then found by discounting the dividends (and forecasted price, if any) back to the present. Because a spreadsheet is a convenient way to implement this approach, we call this method **spreadsheet modeling**. We address spreadsheet modeling in Section 5.

Whether we are using dividends or some other definition of cash flow, we generally use one of the above forecasting approaches when we value stock. The challenge in practice is to choose an appropriate model for a stock's future dividends and to develop quality inputs to that model.

THE GORDON GROWTH MODEL

The Gordon growth model, developed by Gordon and Shapiro (1956) and Gordon (1962), assumes that dividends grow indefinitely at a constant rate. This assumption, applied to the general dividend discount model (Equation 46-14), leads to a simple and elegant valuation formula that has been influential in investment practice. This section explores the development of the GGM, illustrates its uses, and discusses its strengths and limitations.

4.1 The Gordon Growth Model Equation

The simplest pattern we can assume in forecasting future dividends is growth at a constant rate. In mathematical terms, we can state this assumption as

$$D_t = D_{t-1}(1 + g)$$

where g is the expected constant growth rate in dividends and D_t is the expected dividend payable at time t. Suppose, for example, that the most recent dividend, D_0, was €10. Then, if we forecast a 5 percent dividend growth rate, we have for the expected dividend at $t = 1$, $D_1 = D_0(1 + g) = €10 \times 1.05 = €10.5$. For any time t, D_t also equals the $t = 0$ dividend, compounded at g for t periods:

$$D_t = D_0(1 + g)^t \qquad \text{(46-15)}$$

To continue the example, at the end of five years the expected dividend is $D_5 = D_0(1 + g)^5 = €10 \times (1.05)^5 = €10 \times 1.276282 = €12.76$. If $D_0(1 + g)^t$ is substituted into Equation 46-14 for D_t, we obtain the Gordon growth model. If all of the terms are written out, they are

$$V_0 = \frac{D_0(1 + g)}{(1 + r)} + \frac{D_0(1 + g)^2}{(1 + r)^2} + \cdots + \frac{D_0(1 + g)^n}{(1 + r)^n} + \cdots \qquad \text{(46-16)}$$

Equation 46-16 is a geometric series; that is, each term in the expression is equal to the previous term times a constant, which in this case is $(1 + g)/(1 + r)$. This equation has a large number of terms that can be simplified algebraically into a much more compact equation:

$$V_0 = \frac{D_0(1 + g)}{r - g}, \text{ or } V_0 = \frac{D_1}{r - g} \qquad \text{(46-17)}$$

Both equations are equivalent because $D_1 = D_0(1 + g)$. In Equation 46-17 we must specify that the cost of equity must be greater than the expected growth rate: $r > g$. If $r = g$ or $r < g$, Equation 46-17 as a compact formula for value assuming constant growth is not valid. If $r = g$, dividends grow at the same rate at which they are discounted, so the value of the stock (as the undiscounted sum of all expected future dividends) is infinite. If $r < g$, dividends grow faster than they are discounted, so the value of the stock is infinite. Of course, infinite values do not make economic sense; so constant growth with $r = g$ or $r < g$ does not make sense.

To illustrate the calculation, suppose that an annual dividend of €5 has just been paid ($D_0 = €5$). The expected long-term growth rate is 5 percent and the cost of equity is 8 percent. The Gordon growth model value per share is $D_0(1 + g)/(r - g) = (€5 \times 1.05)/(0.08 - 0.05) = €5.25/0.03 = €175$. When calculating the model value, be careful to use D_1 and not D_0 in the numerator.

The Gordon growth model (Equation 46-17) is one of the most widely recognized equations in the field of security analysis. Because the model is based on indefinitely extending future dividends, the model's required rate of return and growth rate should reflect long-term expectations. Further, model values are very sensitive to both the required rate of return, r, and the expected dividend growth rate, g. In this and other valuation models, it is helpful to perform a sensitivity analysis on the inputs, particularly when we are not confident about the proper values.

Earlier we stated that analysts typically apply DDMs to dividend-paying stocks when dividends bear an understandable and consistent relation to the company's profitability. The same qualifications hold for the Gordon growth model. In addition, the Gordon growth model form of the DDM is most appropriate for companies with earnings expected to grow at a rate comparable to or lower than the economy's nominal growth rate. Businesses growing at much higher rates than the economy often grow at lower rates in maturity, and our horizon in using the Gordon growth model is the entire future stream of dividends.

To determine whether the company's growth rate qualifies it as a candidate for the Gordon growth model, we need an estimate of the economy's nominal growth rate. We can estimate this rate as the sum of the estimated **real gross domestic product** (GDP) growth rate plus the expected long-run inflation rate. (GDP is a

	Real GDP Growth Rate	
TABLE 5 Average Annual Real GDP Growth Rates: 1980–2000		
Country	**1980–1990**	**1990–2000**
Australia	3.5%	4.1%
Canada	3.3	2.9
Denmark	2.0	2.4
France	2.4	1.7
Germany	N/A	1.5
Italy	2.4	1.5
Japan	4.0	1.3
Netherlands	2.3	2.9
Sweden	2.3	1.8
Switzerland	2.0	0.7
United Kingdom	3.2	2.5
United States	3.6	3.4

N/A = not available.
Source: World Bank.

money measure of the goods and services produced within a country's borders.) National government agencies as well as the World Bank (www.worldbank.org) publish GDP data. Table 5 shows the recent real GDP growth record for the countries listed in Table 3. For example, an estimate of the underlying real growth rate of the Canadian economy is 3 percent as of late 2001. With expected inflation of 3 percent, an estimate of the Canadian economy's nominal annual growth rate is 6 percent. When forecasting an earnings growth rate far above the economy's nominal growth rate, analysts should use a multistage DDM in which the final-stage growth rate reflects a growth rate that is more plausible relative to the economy's nominal growth rate, rather than using the Gordon growth model.

EXAMPLE 9

Valuation Using the Gordon Growth Model (1)

In Example 3, you estimated a required rate of return on J.C. Penney (NYSE: JCP) stock as 8.8 percent using the CAPM. On examination, you believe stable growth at a rate of 6 percent is a good description of the long-term prospects of JCP. JCP's current dividend is $0.50.

1. Calculate the Gordon growth model value for JCP stock.
2. The current market price of JCP stock is $25. Using your answer to Question 1, state whether JCP stock is fairly valued, undervalued, or overvalued.

Solution to 1: Using Equation 46-17,

$$V_0 = \frac{D_0(1 + g)}{r - g} = \frac{\$0.50 \times 1.06}{0.088 - 0.06} = \frac{\$0.53}{0.028} = \$18.93$$

Solution to 2: Because the Gordon growth model indicates an intrinsic value for JCP ($18.93) that is less than its market price ($25), you conclude that JCP stock is overvalued according to the Gordon growth model.

The next example illustrates a Gordon growth model valuation introducing some problems the analyst might face in practice.

EXAMPLE 10

Valuation Using the Gordon Growth Model (2)

As an analyst for a U.S. domestic equity–income mutual fund, you are evaluating Connecticut Water Service, Inc. (Nasdaq NMS: CTWS) for possible inclusion in the approved list of investments.

Not all countries have traded water utility stocks. In the United States, about 85 percent of the population gets its water from government entities. A group of investor-owned water utilities, however, also supplies water to the public. CTWS is the parent company of three regulated water utility companies serving Connecticut and Massachusetts.

Because CTWS operates in a regulated industry providing an important staple to a stable population, you are confident that its future earnings growth should follow its stable historical growth record. CTWS's return on equity has consistently come in close to the historical median ROE for U.S. businesses of 12.2 percent, reflecting the regulated prices for its product.

Estimated FY2001 and FY2002 EPS are $1.27 and $1.33 according to First Call/Thomson Financial, reflecting 4.7 percent growth. CTWS has a current dividend rate of $0.81. Although CTWS's dividend payout ratio has been relatively stable (73 percent in 2000, 77 percent in 1999, 75 percent in 1998, 77 percent in 1997, and 78 percent in 1996), you conclude that CTWS has not followed an exact fixed-payout dividend policy. CTWS has been conservative in reflecting earnings growth in increased dividends. Your forecast of dividends for FY2002 is $0.83 your nominal annual GDP growth estimate is 4 percent.

Compared with a mean dividend payout ratio of 76 percent from 1996–2000, you expect a long-term average dividend payout ratio of 70 percent going forward. You anticipate a 3.7 percent long-term dividend growth rate. A recent price for CTWS is $30.00. You estimate CTWS's cost of equity at 6.2 percent.

1. Calculate the Gordon growth model estimate of value for CTWS stock.
2. State whether CTWS appears to be overvalued, fairly valued, or undervalued based on the Gordon growth model estimate of value.

3. Justify the selection of the Gordon growth model for valuing CTWS.

4. CTWS's beta is −0.16. Calculate the CAPM estimate of the cost of equity for CTWS. (Assume an equity risk premium of 5.7 percent. The risk-free rate based on the long-term T-bond was also 5.7 percent as of the price quotation date.)

5. Calculate the Gordon growth estimate of value using the cost of equity from your answer to Question 4. Assuming that a price-earnings ratio (P/E) of 24 based on estimated FY2002 EPS is an approximate guide to value, evaluate whether this Gordon growth estimate is plausible.

6. How does uncertainty in CTWS's cost of equity affect your confidence in your answer to Question 2?

Solution to 1: From Equation 46-17,

$$V_0 = \frac{D_1}{r - g} = \frac{\$0.83}{0.062 - 0.037} = \frac{\$0.83}{0.025} = \$33.20$$

Solution to 2: Because the Gordon growth model estimate of $33.20 is $3.20 higher than the market price of $30.00, CTWS appears to be slightly undervalued.

Solution to 3: Stable dividend growth is a realistic model for CTWS for the following reasons:

▶ CTWS profitability is stable as reflected in its return on equity. This reflects predictable demand and regulated prices for its product, water.

▶ Dividends bear an understandable and consistent relationship to earnings, as evidenced here by a stable dividend payout ratio.

▶ Earnings growth, at 3.7 percent a year, is less than nominal annual GDP growth for the United States and is plausibly sustainable long term.

Solution to 4: The cost of equity as given by the CAPM is $R_F + \beta_i[E(R_M) - R_F] = 0.057 + (-0.16 \times 0.057) = 0.04788$, or 4.8 percent. As noted above, both R_F and $[E(R_M) - R_F]$ equal the same rate, here 5.7 percent.

Solution to 5: The Gordon growth value of CTWS using a cost of equity of 4.8 percent is

$$V_0 = \frac{D_1}{r - g} = \frac{\$0.83}{0.048 - 0.037} = \frac{\$0.83}{0.011} = \$75.45$$

$75.45 is an implausible estimate for the value of CTWS judged by a P/E of 24. The $75.45 estimated value represents a P/E of 57 on FY2002 earnings, calculated as $75.45/$1.33 = 56.7 or 57. (The number 24 is taken from peer-group comparisons.) The CAPM estimate of the cost of equity does not appear to be reliable for this stock. In fact, the *R*-squared for the regression for beta for CTWS is about 2 percent, and the CAPM does not do a good job of explaining the returns on this stock.

Note that Problem 1 used a more plausible cost of equity figure, given as 6.2 percent. CTWS does not have publicly traded debt, so the bond yield plus risk premium method was not available. The cost of equity estimate of 0.062 stated in the problem comes from a build-up approximation. As of year-end 2001, based on the Gordon growth model applied to the S&P 500, the cost of equity for an average U.S. stock was estimated as 8.2 percent. (An average stock has a beta of 1 and should earn the S&P 500 return, on average.) Because CTWS has below-average risk (its earnings have above-average stability and its beta is less than 1.0), we subtracted a subjective company-specific risk adjustment of 2 percent. We should note that an APT estimate of the cost of equity is another possibility to consider.

Solution to 6: Because of the uncertainty in the cost-of-equity estimate, one has less confidence that CTWS is undervalued. In particular, the analyst may view CTWS as approximately fairly valued.

As mentioned earlier, we need to be aware that Gordon growth model values can be very sensitive to small changes in the values of the required rate of return and expected dividend growth rate. Example 11 illustrates a format for a sensitivity analysis.

EXAMPLE 11

Valuation Using the Gordon Growth Model (3)

In Example 10, the Gordon growth model value for CTWS was estimated as $33.20 based on an expected dividend growth rate of 3.7 percent, a cost of equity of 6.2 percent, and an expected year-ahead dividend of $0.83. What if our estimates of r and g can each vary by 25 basis points? How sensitive is the model value to perturbations in our estimates of r and g? Table 6 provides information on this sensitivity.

TABLE 6 Estimated Price Given Uncertain Inputs

	$g = 3.45\%$	$g = 3.70\%$	$g = 3.95\%$
$r = 5.95\%$	$33.20	$36.89	$41.50
$r = \mathbf{6.20\%}$	$30.18	**$33.20**	$36.89
$r = 6.45\%$	$27.67	$30.18	$33.20

A point of interest following from the mathematics of the Gordon growth model is that when the spread between r and g is widest ($r = 6.45$ percent and $g = 3.45$ percent) the Gordon growth model value is smallest ($27.67), and when the spread is narrowest ($r = 5.95$ percent and $g = 3.95$ percent) the model value is largest ($41.50). As the spread goes to zero, in fact, the model value increases without bound. The largest value in Table 6, $41.50, is 50 percent larger than the smallest value,

> $27.67. The range of values includes one entry, $27.67, which implies that CTWS is overvalued at its current market price of $30. In summary, our best estimate of the value of CTWS given our assumptions is $33.20, bolded in Table 6, but the estimate is quite sensitive to rather small changes in inputs.

Examples 10 and 11 illustrate the application of the Gordon growth model to a utility, a traditional source for such illustrations. Before applying any valuation model, however, we need to know much more about a company than industry membership. Many utility holding companies in the U.S., for example, now have major, non-regulated business subsidiaries that have fundamentally changed their business characteristics.

In addition to individual stocks, analysts have often used the Gordon growth model to value broad equity market indexes, particularly in developed markets. Such indexes by their nature reflect average economic growth rates.

We can also use the Gordon growth model to value a traditional form of preferred stock, **fixed-rate perpetual preferred stock** (stock with a specified dividend rate that has a claim on earnings senior to the claim of common stock, and no maturity date).[25] If the dividend on the preferred stock is D and payments extend into the indefinite future, we have a **perpetuity** (a stream of level payments extending to infinity) in the constant amount of D. With $g = 0$, which is true because dividends are fixed for such preferred stock, the Gordon growth model becomes

$$V_0 = \frac{D}{r} \qquad\qquad (46\text{-}18)$$

The discount rate, r, capitalizes the amount D, and for that reason is often called a **capitalization rate** in this and any other expression for the value of a perpetuity.

EXAMPLE 12

Valuing Perpetual Preferred Stock

The Royal Bank of Scotland Preferred J (NYSE: RBS-J) stock pays an annual dividend of $2.36 and has a required return of 9.06 percent. What is the value of this preferred stock?

According to the model in Equation 46-18, RBS-J preferred stock is worth $D/r = 2.36/0.0906 = 26.05.

A perpetual preferred stock has a level dividend. Another case is a declining dividend (a negative growth rate). The Gordon growth model also accommodates this possibility, as illustrated in Example 13.

---

[25] With respect to **tenor** or maturity, perpetual preferred stock has no fixed maturity date; term or retractable preferred stock has a fixed maturity date set at issue.

EXAMPLE 13

Gordon Growth Model with Negative Growth

Afton Mines is a profitable company that is expected to pay a $4.25 dividend next year. Because it is depleting its mining properties, the best estimate is that dividends will decline forever at a 10 percent rate. The required rate of return on Afton stock is 12 percent. What is the value of Afton shares?

For Afton, the value of the stock is

$$V_0 = \frac{4.25}{0.12 - (-0.10)}$$

$$= \frac{4.25}{0.22} = \$19.32$$

The negative growth results in a $19.32 valuation for the stock.

4.2 The Implied Dividend Growth Rate

Because the dividend growth rate affects the estimated value of a stock using the Gordon growth model, differences between estimated values of a stock and its actual market value might be explained by different growth rate assumptions. Given price, the expected next-period dividend, and an estimate of the required rate of return, we can infer the dividend growth rate reflected in price assuming the Gordon growth model. (Actually, it is possible to infer the market-price-implied dividend growth based on other DDMs as well.) An analyst can then judge whether the implied dividend growth rate is reasonable, high, or low, based on what he or she knows about the company. In effect, the calculation of the implied dividend growth rate provides an alternative perspective on the valuation of the stock (fairly valued, overvalued, or undervalued). Example 14 shows how the Gordon growth model can be used to infer the market's implied growth rate for a stock.

EXAMPLE 14

The Growth Rate Implied by the Current Stock Price

Suppose a company has a beta of 1.1. The risk-free rate is 5.6 percent and the market risk premium is 6 percent. The current dividend of $2.00 is expected to grow at 5 percent indefinitely. What is the value of the company's stock? The price of the stock is $40; what dividend growth rate would be required to justify a $40 price?

The required rate of return is $r = R_F + \beta_i[E(R_M) - R_F] = 0.056 + (1.1 \times 0.06) = 0.122$ or 12.2%. The value of one share, using the Gordon growth model, is

$$V_0 = \frac{D_1}{r - g}$$

$$= \frac{2.00(1.05)}{0.122 - 0.05}$$

$$= \frac{2.10}{0.072} = \$29.17$$

The valuation estimate of the model ($29.17) is less than the market value of $40.00. Assuming that the model and the other assumptions (D_0 = $2.00 and r = 12.2 percent) are reasonable, the growth rate in dividends required to justify the $40 stock price can be calculated by substituting all known values into the Gordon growth model equation except for g:

$$40 = \frac{2.00(1 + g)}{0.122 - g} \text{ which simplifies to } 4.88 - 40g = 2 + 2g$$

$$42g = 2.88$$
$$g = 0.0686, \text{ or } g = 6.86\%$$

An expected dividend growth rate of 6.86 percent is required for the stock price to be properly valued at $40.

4.3 Estimating the Expected Rate of Return with the Gordon Growth Model

Under the assumption of efficient prices, the Gordon growth model is frequently used to estimate a stock's expected rate of return given the stock's price and expected growth rate. When the Gordon growth model is solved for r, the expected rate of return is

$$r = \frac{D_0(1 + g)}{P_0} + g = \frac{D_1}{P_0} + g \qquad \textbf{(46-19)}$$

The expected rate of return is composed of two parts; the dividend yield (D_1/P_0) and the capital gains (or appreciation) yield (g).

This expected rate of return is similar to the internal rate of return in capital budgeting: The IRR is the discount rate that makes the present value of an investment project's future cash flows equal the investment in the project. Likewise, it is the same concept as the yield to maturity on a bond: The yield to maturity is the discount rate that makes the present value of the bond's coupons and principal repayment equal the bond's market price. The discount rate that makes the present value of future dividends equal the current stock price is the stock's required rate of return.

EXAMPLE 15

Finding the Expected Rate of Return with the Gordon Growth Model

Bob Inguigiatto, CFA, has been given the task of developing mean return estimates for a list of stocks as preparation for a portfolio optimization. On his list is FPL Group, Inc. (NYSE: FPL). On analysis, he decides that it is appropriate to model FPL using the Gordon growth model, and he takes prices as reflecting value. The company paid dividends of $2.24 during the past year, and the current stock price is $56.60. The growth rates of dividends and earnings per share have been 4.01 percent and 5.30 percent, respectively, for the past five years. Analysts' consensus estimate of the five-year earnings growth rate is 7.0 percent. Based on his own analysis, Inguigiatto has decided to use 5.50 percent as his best estimate of the long-term earnings and dividend growth rate. Next year's projected dividend, D_1, should be $2.24 (1.055) = $2.363. Using the Gordon growth model, FPL's expected rate of return should be

$$r = \frac{D_1}{P_0} + g$$

$$= \frac{2.363}{56.60} + 0.055$$
$$= 0.0417 + 0.055$$
$$= 0.0967 = 9.67\%$$

FPL's expected rate of return is 9.67 percent. The total return can be broken into two components, the dividend yield ($D_1/P_0 = 4.17$ percent) and the capital gains yield ($g = 5.50$ percent).

The Gordon growth model implies a set of relationships about the growth rates of dividends, earnings, and stock value. Stock value will also grow at constant rate g. The current stock price is $V_0 = D_1/(r - g)$. Multiplying both sides by $(1 + g)$, we have $V_0 (1 + g) = D_1 (1 + g)/(r - g)$, which is $V_1 = D_2/(r - g)$: Both dividends and value have grown at a rate of g (holding r constant). Given a constant payout ratio—a constant, proportional relationship between earnings and dividends—dividends and earnings grow at g.

To summarize, g in the Gordon growth model is the rate of value or capital appreciation (sometimes also called the capital gains yield). Some textbooks state that g is the rate of price appreciation. If prices are efficient (price equals value), price will indeed grow at a rate of g. If there is mispricing, however (i.e., price is different from value), the actual rate of capital appreciation depends on the nature of the mispricing and how fast it is corrected, if at all. For example, if a stock's current price (P_0) is $50 and intrinsic value ($V_0$) is $50.50, the stock is undervalued by $0.50. Suppose that g is 5 percent and we expect the mispricing to correct in one year. We expect additional capital appreciation of $0.50/$50 = 0.01 = 1 percent over and above 5 percent, for total capital gains of 6 percent. As another example, if we expected the mispricing to correct gradually over five years, we would expect an additional capital appreciation of ($0.50/5)$50 = 0.002, or 20 basis points a year over and above 5 percent, for total capital gains of 5.2 percent.[26]

---

[26] Another issue related to using a DDM to estimate expected return concerns the effects of common stock repurchases. Companies can distribute free cash flow to shareholders in the form of stock repurchases as well as dividends. Dividends and stock repurchases together may better reflect value creation in the company than dividends alone, as a consequence. The DDM can be adapted to explicitly include both dividends and share repurchases. Value and expected return estimates from a DDM should be consistent with such estimates from a discounted dividends and repurchases model.

Another characteristic of the model is that the components of total return (dividend yield and capital gains yield) will also stay constant over time, given that price tracks value exactly. The dividend yield, which is D_1/P_0 at $t = 0$, will stay unchanged because both the dividend and the price grow at the same rate, leaving the dividend yield unchanged over time. The capital gains yield, $(V_{t+1} - V_t)/V_t$, will stay constant at g.[27] In the FPL Group example above, the current stock price of \$56.60 will grow at 5.50 percent annually. The dividend yield of 4.17 percent, the capital gains yield of 5.50 percent, and the total return of 9.67 percent will be the same at $t = 0$ and at any time in the future.

4.4 The Present Value of Growth Opportunities

The **present value of growth opportunities** is the part of a stock's total value that comes from profitable future growth opportunities, in contrast to the stock's value associated with assets already in place. In this section, we present an expression for analyzing the total value of a stock into these two components.

Earnings growth can occur under several scenarios, including when a company retains earnings (increasing its capital base) and earns a constant positive return on equity, even if that return is low. Increases in shareholder wealth, however, occur only when reinvested earnings are directed to investments that earn more than the opportunity cost of the funds needed to undertake them (positive net present value projects).[28] Thus, investors actively assess whether and to what degree companies will have the opportunity to invest in profitable projects in the future. In principle, companies without any positive NPV projects should distribute most or all of earnings to shareholders as dividends so the shareholders can redirect capital to more attractive areas. (If earnings are defined as earnings in excess of expenditures needed to preserve the economic value as assets depreciate, theoretically all earnings should be distributed as dividends for such companies.)

We define a company without positive expected NPV projects as a **no-growth company**. When a company distributes all its earnings in dividends (appropriate for a no-growth company), earnings (E) will be flat in perpetuity, assuming a constant return on equity. This flatness occurs because $E = \text{ROE} \times \text{Equity}$, and equity is constant because retained earnings are not added to it. The present value of a perpetuity of E is E/r. We define the **no-growth value per share** as E/r. For any company, the difference between the actual value per share and the no-growth value per share must be the **present value of growth opportunities** (PVGO)—also known as the value of growth.

$$V_0 = \frac{E}{r} + \text{PVGO} \qquad \textbf{(46-20)}$$

If prices reflect value ($P_0 = V_0$), PVGO gives the market's estimate of the value of the company's growth. In Example 10, for instance, with current earnings of \$1.27 for CTWS and a current price of \$30, we have \$30 = (\$1.27/0.062)

---

[27] The fact that the capital gains yield is equal to g is easy to demonstrate:

$$\frac{V_{t+1} - V_t}{V_t} = \frac{D_{t+2}/(r - g) - D_{t+1}/(r - g)}{D_{t+1}/(r - g)} = \frac{D_{t+2} - D_{t+1}}{D_{t+1}} = 1 + g - 1 = g$$

[28] We can interpret this condition of profitability as ROE $> r$ with ROE calculated with the *market* value of equity (rather than the book value of equity) in the denominator. Book value based on historical cost accounting can present a distorted picture of the value of shareholders' investment in the company.

+ PVGO, \$30 = \$20.48 + PVGO, so PVGO = \$30 − \$20.48 = \$9.52. The market assigns 32 percent of the company's value to the value of growth (\$9.52/\$30 = 0.317). As analysts, we may be interested in this assignment because the value of growth and the value in hand (no-growth value, based on existing assets) may have different risk characteristics. Whenever we calculate a stock's value, V_0, whether using the Gordon growth or any other valuation model, we can calculate the value of growth, based on the value estimate, using the above equation.

4.5 Gordon Growth Model and the Price–Earnings Ratio

The price–earnings ratio (P/E), which we discuss in detail in Reading 48, is perhaps the most widely recognized valuation indicator, familiar to readers of both newspaper financial tables and institutional research reports. Using the Gordon growth model, we can develop an expression for P/E in terms of the fundamentals. This expression has two uses:

▶ When used with forecasts of the inputs to the model, the analyst obtains a **justified** (**fundamental**) **P/E**—the P/E that is fair, warranted, or justified on the basis of fundamentals (given that the valuation model is appropriate). The analyst can then state his or her view of value in terms not of the Gordon growth model value but of the justified P/E. Because P/E is so widely recognized, this method may be an effective way to communicate the analysis.

▶ The analyst may also use the expression for P/E to weigh whether the forecasts of earnings growth built into the current stock price are reasonable. What expected earnings growth rate is implied by the actual market P/E? Is that growth rate plausible?

We can state the expression for P/E in terms of the current (or trailing) P/E (today's market price per share divided by trailing 12 months' earnings per share) or in terms of the leading (or forward) P/E (today's market price per share divided by a forecast of the next 12 months' earnings per share, or sometimes the next fiscal year's earnings per share).

Leading and trailing justified P/E expressions can be developed from the Gordon growth model. Assuming that the model can be applied for a particular stock's valuation, the dividend payout ratio is considered fixed. Define b as the retention rate, the fraction of earnings reinvested in the company rather than paid out in dividends. The dividend payout ratio is then, by definition, $(1 - b) =$ Dividend per share/Earnings per share $= D_t/E_t$. If we divide $P_0 = D_1/(r - g)$ by next year's earnings per share, E_1, we have

$$\frac{P_0}{E_1} = \frac{D_1/E_1}{r - g} = \frac{1 - b}{r - g} \tag{46-21}$$

This represents a leading P/E, current price divided by next year's earnings. Alternatively, if we divide $P_0 = D_0(1 + g)/(r - g)$ by the current year's earnings per share, E_0, we have

$$\frac{P_0}{E_0} = \frac{D_0(1 + g)/E_0}{r - g} = \frac{(1 - b)(1 + g)}{r - g} \tag{46-22}$$

This is a trailing P/E, current price divided by trailing (current-year) earnings.

EXAMPLE 16

The Expected P/E Found with the Gordon Growth Model

Harry Trice wants to use the Gordon growth model to find a justified P/E for the French company Carrefour SA (Euronext: CA), a global food retailer specializing in hypermarkets and supermarkets. Trice has assembled the following information:

- ▶ current stock price = €56.94
- ▶ estimated earnings per share for the current year = €1.837
- ▶ dividends for the current year = €0.575
- ▶ dividend growth rate = 8.18%
- ▶ risk-free rate = 5.34%
- ▶ equity risk premium = 5.32%
- ▶ beta versus the CAC index = 0.83

1. What are the justified trailing and leading P/Es based on the Gordon growth model?
2. Based on the justified trailing P/E and the actual P/E, is CA fairly valued, overvalued, or undervalued?

Solution to 1: For CA, the required rate of return using the CAPM is

$$
\begin{aligned}
E(R_i) &= R_F + \beta_i[E(R_M) - R_F] \\
&= 5.34\% + 0.83(5.32\%) \\
&= 9.76\%
\end{aligned}
$$

The dividend payout ratio is

$$
\begin{aligned}
(1 - b) &= D_0/E_0 \\
&= 0.575/1.837 \\
&= 0.313
\end{aligned}
$$

The justified leading P/E (based on next year's earnings) is

$$
\frac{P_0}{E_1} = \frac{1 - b}{r - g} = \frac{0.313}{0.0976 - 0.0818} = 19.8
$$

The justified trailing P/E (based on current-year earnings) is

$$
\frac{P_0}{E_0} = \frac{(1 - b)(1 + g)}{r - g} = \frac{0.313(1.0818)}{0.0976 - 0.0818} = 21.4
$$

Solution to 2: Based on a current price of €56.94 and trailing earnings of €1.837, the trailing P/E is €56.94/€1.837 = 31.0. Because the actual P/E of 31.0 is greater than the justified trailing P/E of 21.4, we conclude that CA appears to be overvalued. We can also express the apparent mispricing in terms of the Gordon growth model. Using Trice's assumptions, the Gordon growth model assigns a value of 0.575(1.0818)/(0.0976 − 0.0818) = €39.37, which is below the current market value of €56.94. The Gordon growth model approach gives a lower stock value than the market price and a lower P/E than the current market P/E.

Later in the reading, we will present multistage DDMs. We can also develop expressions for the P/E in terms of the variables of multistage DDMs, but the usefulness of these expressions is not commensurate with their complexity. For multistage models, the simple way to calculate a justified leading P/E is to divide the model value directly by the first year's expected earnings. In all cases, the P/E is explained in terms of the cost of equity, expected dividend growth rate(s), and the dividend payout ratio(s). All else equal, higher prices are associated with higher anticipated dividend growth rates.

4.6 Strengths and Weaknesses of the Gordon Growth Model

In Section 2.2, we presented general characteristics of companies for which dividend discount models are appropriate. For the Gordon growth model implementation to be appropriate, as stated earlier, additional qualifications should be met. The basic question is always whether a model is suitable for the company being valued. Each model has some characteristic strengths and weaknesses. Here we list those of the Gordon growth model, recapping comments on suitability.

Strengths

▶ The Gordon growth model is often useful for valuing stable-growth, dividend-paying companies.

▶ It is often useful for valuing broad-based equity indexes.

▶ The model features simplicity and clarity; it is useful for understanding the relationships among value and growth, required rate of return, and payout ratio.

▶ It provides an approach to estimating the expected rate of return given efficient prices (for stable-growth, dividend-paying companies). As we show in the next section, the Gordon growth model can readily be used as a component of more-complex DDMs, particularly to model the final stage of growth.

Weaknesses

▶ Calculated values are very sensitive to the assumed growth rate and required rate of return.

▶ The model is not applicable, in a practical sense, to non-dividend-paying stocks.

▶ The model is also inapplicable to unstable-growth, dividend-paying stocks.

MULTISTAGE DIVIDEND DISCOUNT MODELS   5

Earlier, we noted that the basic expression for the DDM (Equation 46-14) is too general for investment analysts to use in practice, as one cannot forecast individually more than a relatively small number of dividends. The strongest simplifying assumption—a stable dividend growth rate from now into the indefinite future, leading to the Gordon growth model—is not realistic for many or even most companies. For many publicly traded companies, practitioners assume growth falls into three stages [see Sharpe, Alexander, and Baily (1999)]:

▶ **Growth phase**. A company in its growth phase typically enjoys rapidly expanding markets, high profit margins, and an abnormally high growth rate in earnings per share (**supernormal growth**). Companies in this phase often have negative free cash flow to equity, because the company invests heavily in expanding operations. Given high prospective returns on equity, the dividend payout ratios of growth-phase companies are often low, or even zero. As the company's markets mature or as unusual growth opportunities attract competitors, earnings growth rates eventually decline.

▶ **Transition phase**. In this phase, which is a transition to maturity, earnings growth slows as competition puts pressure on prices and profit margins, or as sales growth slows because of market saturation. In this phase, earnings growth rates may be above average but declining towards the growth rate for the overall economy. Capital requirements typically decline in this phase, often resulting in positive free cash flow and increasing dividend payout ratios (or the initiation of dividends).

▶ **Mature phase**. In maturity, the company reaches an equilibrium in which investment opportunities on average just earn their opportunity cost of capital. Return on equity approaches the cost of equity, and earnings growth, the dividend payout ratio, and the return on equity stabilize at levels that can be sustained long term. We call the dividend and earnings growth rate of this phase the **mature growth rate**. This phase, in fact, reflects the stage in which a company can properly be valued using the Gordon growth model, and that model is one tool for valuing this phase of a currently high-growth company's future.

A company may attempt to restart the growth phase by changing its strategic focuses and business mix. Technological advances may alter a company's growth prospects for better or worse with surprising rapidity. Nevertheless, this growth-phase picture of a company is a useful approximation. The growth-phase concept provides the intuition for multistage DCF models of all types, including multistage dividend discount models. Multistage models are a staple valuation discipline of investment management companies using DCF valuation models. In this section, we present three popular multistage DDMs: the two-stage DDM, the H-model (a type of two-stage model), and the three-stage DDM. Keep in mind that all these models represent stylized patterns of growth; we are attempting to identify the pattern that most accurately approximates our view of the company's future growth.

5.1 Two-Stage Dividend Discount Model

Two common versions of the two-stage DDM exist. The first model assumes a constant growth rate in each stage, such as 15 percent in Stage 1 and 7 percent in Stage 2. The second model assumes a declining dividend growth rate in Stage 1 followed by a fixed growth rate in Stage 2. For example, the growth rate could begin at 15 percent and decline continuously in Stage 1 until it reaches 7 percent. Then it grows forever at 7 percent in Stage 2. This second model, called the H-model, will be presented after the model with fixed growth rates in each stage.

The first two-stage DDM provides for two dividend growth rates: a high growth rate for the initial period, followed by a sustainable and usually lower growth rate thereafter. The two-stage DDM is based on the multiple-period model

$$V_0 = \sum_{t=1}^{n} \frac{D_t}{(1 + r)^t} + \frac{V_n}{(1 + r)^n} \tag{46-23}$$

where we use V_n as an estimate of P_n. The two-stage model assumes that the first n dividends grow at an extraordinary short-term rate, g_S:

$$D_t = D_0(1 + g_S)^t \tag{46-24}$$

After time n, the annual dividend growth rate changes to a normal long-term rate, g_L. The dividend at time $n + 1$ is $D_{n+1} = D_n(1 + g_L) = D_0(1 + g_S)^n(1 + g_L)$, and this dividend continues to grow at g_L. Using D_{n+1}, we can use the Gordon growth model to find V_n:

$$V_n = \frac{D_0(1 + g_S)^n(1 + g_L)}{r - g_L} \tag{46-25}$$

To find the value at $t = 0$, V_0, we simply find the present value of the first n dividends and the present value of the projected value at time n

$$V_0 = \sum_{t=1}^{n} \frac{D_0(1 + g_S)^t}{(1 + r)^t} + \frac{D_0(1 + g_S)^n(1 + g_L)}{(1 + r)^n(r - g_L)} \tag{46-26}$$

EXAMPLE 17

Valuing a Stock Using the Two-Stage Dividend Discount Model

General Mills (NYSE: GIS) is a large manufacturer and distributor of packaged consumer food products. Benoit Gagnon, a buy-side analyst covering General Mills, has studied the historical growth rates in sales, earnings, and dividends for GIS, and also has made projections of future growth rates. Gagnon expects the current dividend of $1.10 to grow at 11 percent for the next five years, and that the growth rate will decline to 8 percent and remain at that level thereafter.

Gagnon feels that his estimate of GIS's beta is unreliable, so he is using the bond yield plus risk premium method to estimate the required rate of return on the stock. The yield to maturity of GIS's long-term bond (6.27s of 2019) is 6.67 percent. Adding a 4.0 percent risk premium to the yield-to-maturity gives a required return of 10.67 percent, which Gagnon rounds to 10.7 percent.

Table 7 shows the calculations of the first five dividends and their present values discounted at 10.7 percent. The terminal stock value at $t = 5$ is

$$V_5 = \frac{D_0(1 + g_S)^n(1 + g_L)}{r - g_L}$$

$$= \frac{1.10(1.11)^5(1.08)}{0.107 - 0.08}$$

$$= 74.143$$

The terminal stock value and its present value are also given in the table.

TABLE 7 General Mills Dividend Calculation

Time	Value	Calculation	D_t or V_t	Present Values $D_t/(1.107)^t$ or $V_t/(1.107)^t$
1	D_1	$1.10(1.11)$	1.221	1.103
2	D_2	$1.10(1.11)^2$	1.355	1.106
3	D_3	$1.10(1.11)^3$	1.504	1.109
4	D_4	$1.10(1.11)^4$	1.670	1.112
5	D_5	$1.10(1.11)^5$	1.854	1.115
5	V_5	$1.10(1.11)^5(1.08)/(0.107 - 0.08)$	74.143	44.5997
Total				50.1447

In this two-stage model, we are forecasting the five individual dividends during the first stage and then calculating their present values. We use the Gordon growth model to derive the terminal value (the value of the dividends in the second stage at the beginning of Stage 2). As shown above, the terminal value is $V_5 = D_6/(r - g_L)$. The Period 6 dividend is \$2.002 ($= D_5 \times 1.08 = \$1.854 \times 1.08$). Using the standard Gordon growth model, $V_5 = \$74.14 = 2.002/(0.107 - 0.08)$. The present value of the terminal value is \$44.60 $= 74.14/1.107^5$. The total estimated value of GIS is \$50.14 using this model. Notice that almost 90 percent of this value, \$44.60, is the present value of V_5, and the balance, \$50.14 − \$44.60 = \$5.54, is the present value of the first five dividends. Recalling our discussion of the sensitivity of the Gordon growth model to changes in the inputs, we might calculate an interval for the intrinsic value of GIS by varying the mature growth rate over the range of plausible values.

The two-stage DDM is very useful because many scenarios exist in which a company can achieve a supernormal growth rate for a few years, after which time the growth rate falls to a more sustainable level. For example, a company may achieve supernormal growth through possession of a patent, first-mover advantage, or another factor that provides a temporary lead in a specific marketplace. Subsequently, earnings must descend to a level that is more consistent with competition and the growth in the overall economy. Accordingly, that is why in the two-stage model, extraordinary growth is often forecast for a few years, and then normal growth is forecast thereafter. The accurate estimation of V_n, the **terminal value of the stock**,[29] is an important part of correct use of DDMs. In practice, analysts estimate the terminal value either by applying a multiple to a projected terminal value of a fundamental, such as earnings per share or book value per share, or they estimate V_n using the Gordon growth model. In the reading on market multiples, we will discuss using price–earnings multiples in this context.

---

[29] The terminal value of a stock has also been called the stock's continuing value.

In our examples, we use a single discount rate, r, for all phases, reflecting both a desire for simplicity and lack of a clear objective basis for adjusting the discount rate for different phases. Some analysts, however, use different discount rates for different phases.

The following example values E.I. DuPont de Nemours and Company by combining the dividend discount model and a P/E valuation model.

EXAMPLE 18

Combining a DDM and P/E Model to Value a Stock

In the past year, DuPont (NYSE: DD) paid a $1.40 dividend that an analyst expects to grow at 9.3 percent annually for the next four years. At the end of Year 4, the analyst expects the dividend to equal 40 percent of earnings per share and the trailing P/E for DD to be 11. If the required return on DD common stock is 11.5 percent, calculate the per-share value of DD common stock.

Table 8 summarizes the relevant calculations. When the dividends are growing at 9.3 percent, the expected dividends and the present value of each (discounted at 11.5 percent) are shown. The terminal stock price, V_4, deserves some explanation. As shown in the table, the Year 4 dividend is $1.40(1.093)^4 = 1.9981$. Because dividends at that time are assumed to be 40 percent of earnings, the EPS projection for Year 4 is $\text{EPS}_4 = D_4/0.40 = 1.9981/0.40 = 4.9952$. With a trailing P/E of 11.0, the value of DD at the end of Year 4 should be $11.0(4.9952) = \$54.95$. Discounted at 11.5 percent for four years, the present value of V_4 is $35.55.

TABLE 8   Value of DuPont Common Stock

Time	Value	Calculation	D_t or V_t	Present Values $D_t/(1.115)^t$ or $V_t/(1.115)^t$
1	D_1	$1.40(1.093)^1$	1.5302	1.3724
2	D_2	$1.40(1.093)^2$	1.6725	1.3453
3	D_3	$1.40(1.093)^3$	1.8281	1.3188
4	D_4	$1.40(1.093)^4$	1.9981	1.2927
4	V_4	$11 \times [1.40(1.093)^4/0.40]$ $= 11 \times [1.9981/0.40]$ $= 11 \times 4.9952$	54.9472	35.5505
Total				40.88

The present values of the dividends for Years 1 through 4 sum to $5.33. The present value of the terminal value of $54.95 is $35.55. The estimated total value of DD is the sum of these, or $40.88 per share.

5.2 Valuing a Non-Dividend-Paying Company (First-Stage Dividend = 0)

The fact that a stock is currently paying no dividends does not mean that the principles of the dividend discount model do not apply. Even though D_0 and/or D_1 may be zero, and the company may not begin paying dividends for some time, the present value of future dividends may still capture the value of the company. Of course, if a company pays no dividends and will never be able to distribute cash to shareholders, the stock is worthless.

If a company is not paying a dividend but is very profitable, an analyst might be willing to forecast its future dividends. Of course, for non-dividend-paying, unprofitable companies, such a forecast would be very difficult. Furthermore, as discussed in Section 2.2 (Streams of Expected Cash Flows), it is usually difficult for the analyst to estimate the timing of the initiation of dividends and the dividend policy that will then be established by the company. Thus the analyst may prefer a free cash flow or residual income model for valuing such companies.

EXAMPLE 19

Valuing a Non-Dividend-Paying Stock

Assume that a company is currently paying no dividend and will not pay one for several years. If the company begins paying a dividend of $1.00 five years from now, and the dividend is expected to grow at 5 percent thereafter, we can discount this future dividend stream back to find the value of the company. This company's required rate of return is 11 percent. Because the expression

$$V_n = \frac{D_{n+1}}{r - g}$$

values a stock at period n using the next period's dividend, the $t = 5$ dividend is used to find the value at $t = 4$:

$$V_4 = \frac{D_5}{r - g} = \frac{1.00}{0.11 - 0.05} = \$16.67$$

To find the value of the stock today, we simply discount V_4 back for four years:

$$V_0 = \frac{V_4}{(1 + r)^4} = \frac{16.67}{(1.11)^4} = \$10.98$$

The value of this stock, even though it will not pay a dividend until Year 5, is $10.98.

5.3 The H-Model

The basic two-stage model assumes a constant, extraordinary rate for the supernormal growth period that is followed by a constant, normal growth rate thereafter. In Example 17, the growth rate for General Mills was 11 percent annually for 5 years, followed by a precipitous drop to 8 percent growth in Year 6 and thereafter. Fuller and Hsia (1984) developed a variant of the two-stage model in which growth begins at a high rate and declines linearly throughout the supernormal growth period until it reaches a normal rate at the end. The value of the dividend stream in the H-model is

$$V_0 = \frac{D_0(1 + g_L)}{r - g_L} + \frac{D_0 H(g_S - g_L)}{r - g_L}$$

(46-27)

or

$$V_0 = \frac{D_0(1 + g_L) + D_0 H(g_S - g_L)}{r - g_L}$$

where

V_0 = value per share at $t = 0$
D_0 = current dividend
r = required rate of return on equity
H = half-life in years of the high-growth period
  (i.e., high-growth period = $2H$ years)
g_S = initial short-term dividend growth rate
g_L = normal long-term dividend growth rate after Year $2H$

The first term on the right-hand side of Equation 46-27 is the present value of the company's dividend stream if it were to grow at g_L forever. The second term is an approximation to the extra value (assuming $g_S > g_L$) accruing to the stock because of its supernormal growth for Years 1 through $2H$ (see Fuller and Hsia for technical details).[30] Logically, the longer the supernormal growth period (i.e., the larger the value of H, which is one-half the length of the supernormal growth period) and the larger the extra growth rate in the supernormal growth period (measured by g_S minus g_L), the higher the share value, all else equal.

EXAMPLE 20

Valuing a Stock with the H-Model

You are valuing Siemens AG (Frankfurt: SIE) with the H-model approach. The relevant inputs to your valuation are as follows:

- ▶ Current dividend is €1.00.
- ▶ The dividend growth rate is 29.28 percent, declining linearly over a 16-year period to a final and perpetual growth rate of 7.26 percent.
- ▶ The risk-free rate is 5.34 percent, the market risk premium is 5.32 percent, and SIE's beta, estimated against the DAX, is 1.37.

The required rate of return for SIE is

$$R_F + \beta_i[E(R_M) - R_F] = 0.0534 + (1.37 \times 0.0532) = 0.1263,$$
$$\text{or } 12.63\%$$

---

[30] We can provide some intuition on the expression, however. On average, the expected excess growth rate in the supernormal period will be $(g_S - g_L)/2$. Over $2H$ periods, we expect a total excess amount of dividends (compared with the level given g_L) of $2HD_0(g_S - g_L)/2 = D_0 H(g_S - g_L)$. This term is the H-model upward adjustment to the first dividend term, reflecting the extra expected dividends as growth declines from g_S to g_L over the first period. Note, however, that the timing of the individual dividends in the first period is not reflected by individually discounting them; the expression is thus an approximation.

Using the H-model, the per-share value estimate of the company is

$$V_0 = \frac{D_0(1 + g_L)}{r - g_L} + \frac{D_0 H(g_S - g_L)}{r - g_L}$$

$$= \frac{1.00(1.0726)}{0.1263 - 0.0726} + \frac{1.00(8)(0.2928 - 0.0726)}{0.1263 - 0.0726}$$

$$= 19.97 + 32.80 = €52.77$$

If SIE experienced normal growth starting now, its value would be €19.97. The extraordinary growth adds €32.80 to its value, which results in an SIE share being worth an estimated total of €52.77.

The H-model is an approximation model, which estimates the valuation that would result from discounting all of the future dividends individually. In many circumstances, this approximation is very close. For a long extraordinary growth period (a high H) or for a large difference in growth rates (the difference between g_S and g_L), however, the analyst might abandon the approximation model for the more exact model. Fortunately, the many tedious calculations of the exact model are made fairly easy using a spreadsheet program.

5.4 Three-Stage Dividend Discount Models

There are two popular versions of the three-stage DDM. In the first version, the company is assumed to have a constant dividend growth rate in each of the three stages. For example, Stage 1 could assume 20 percent growth for three years, Stage 2 could have 10 percent growth for four years, and Stage 3 could have 5 percent growth thereafter. In the second version, in the middle (second) period, the growth rate is assumed to decline linearly. The example below shows how the first type of three-stage model can be used to value a stock, in this case IBM.

A second version of the three-stage DDM has a middle stage similar to the first stage in the H-model. In the first stage, dividends grow at a high, constant (supernormal) rate for the whole period. In the second stage, dividends decline linearly as they do in the H-model. Finally, in Stage 3, dividends grow at a sustainable, constant growth rate. The process of using this model is illustrated in Example 22, valuing Hormel Foods.

EXAMPLE 21

The Three-Stage DDM with Three Distinct Stages

IBM currently pays a dividend of $0.55 per year. We estimate the current required rate of return at 12 percent. Assume we believe that dividends will grow at 7.5 percent for the next two years, 13.5 percent for the following four years, and 11.25 percent into perpetuity. What is the current estimated value of IBM using a three-stage approach? We show our calculations in Table 9.

TABLE 9   Estimated Value of IBM

Time	Value	Calculation	D_t or V_t	Present Values $D_t/(1.12)^t$ or $V_t/(1.12)^t$
1	D_1	$0.55(1.075)$	0.5913	0.5279
2	D_2	$0.55(1.075)^2$	0.6356	0.5067
3	D_3	$0.55(1.075)^2(1.135)$	0.7214	0.5135
4	D_4	$0.55(1.075)^2(1.135)^2$	0.8188	0.5204
5	D_5	$0.55(1.075)^2(1.135)^3$	0.9293	0.5273
6	D_6	$0.55(1.075)^2(1.135)^4$	1.0548	0.5344
6	V_6	$0.55(1.075)^2(1.135)^4(1.1125)/(0.12 - 0.1125)$	156.4595	79.2673
Total				82.3975

Given these assumptions, the three-stage model indicates that a fair price should be $82.40. Nevertheless, an analyst might well question whether an 11.25 percent long-term growth rate is plausible.

EXAMPLE 22

The Three-Stage DDM with Declining Growth Rates in Stage 2

Elaine Bouvier is evaluating HRL (addressed earlier in Example 2). She wishes to value HRL using the three-stage dividend growth model with a linearly declining dividend growth rate in Stage 2. After considerable study, Bouvier has decided to use the following information in her valuation (as of beginning of 2003):

► The current dividend is $0.39.

► Bouvier estimates the required rate of return on HRL stock at 8.72 percent.

► In Stage 1, the dividend will grow at 11.3 percent annually for the next five years.

► In Stage 2, which will last 10 years, the dividend growth rate will decline linearly, starting at the Stage 1 rate and ending at the Stage 3 rate.

► The equilibrium long-term dividend growth rate (in Stage 3) will be 5.7 percent.

Bouvier values HRL by computing the five dividends in Stage 1 and finding their present values at 8.72 percent. The dividends in Stages 2 and 3 can be valued with the H-model, which estimates their value at the beginning of Stage 2. This value is then discounted back to find the dividends' present value at $t = 0$.

The calculation of the five dividends in Stage 1 and their present values are given in Table 10. The H-model for calculating the value of the Stage 2 and Stage 3 dividends at the beginning of Stage 2 ($t = 5$) would be

$$V_5 = \frac{D_5(1 + g_L)}{r - g_L} + \frac{D_5 H(g_S - g_L)}{r - g_L}$$

where

$D_5 = D_0(1 + g_S)^5 = 0.39(1.113)^5 = \$0.6661$
$g_S = 11.3\%$
$g_L = 5.7\%$
$r = 8.72\%$
$H = 5$ (the second stage lasts $2H = 10$ years)

Substituting these values into the equation for the H-model gives us V_5:

$$V_5 = \frac{0.6661(1.057)}{0.0872 - 0.057} + \frac{0.6661(5)(0.113 - 0.057)}{0.0872 - 0.057}$$

$$= 23.3135 + 6.1758$$
$$= \$29.4893$$

The present value of V_5 is $\$29.4893/(1.0872)^5 = \$19.4141$.

TABLE 10   Hormel Foods Corp.

Time	D_t or V_t	Value of D_t or V_t	PV at 8.72%	Explanation of D_t or V_t
1	D_1	0.4341	0.3993	$0.39(1.113)^1$
2	D_2	0.4831	0.4087	$0.39(1.113)^2$
3	D_3	0.5377	0.4184	$0.39(1.113)^3$
4	D_4	0.5985	0.4284	$0.39(1.113)^4$
5	D_5	0.6661	0.4385	$0.39(1.113)^5$
5	V_5	29.4893	19.4141	H-model explained above
Total			21.5074	

According to this three-stage DDM model, the total value of HRL is $21.51. The dividends in Stages 2 and 3 have a total present value of $19.41, and the five dividends in Stage 1 have a total present value of about $2.10 ($21.51 − $19.41).

The three-stage DDM with declining growth in Stage 2 has been widely used among companies using a DDM approach to valuation. An example is the DDM adopted by Bloomberg L.P., a financial services company that provides "Bloomberg terminals" to professional investors and analysts. The Bloomberg DDM is a model that provides an estimated value for any stock that the user selects. The DDM is a three-stage model with declining growth in Stage 2. The model uses fundamentals about the company for assumed Stage 1 and Stage 3 growth rates, and then assumes that the Stage 2 rate is a linearly declining rate between the Stage 1 and Stage 3 rates. The model also makes estimates of the lengths of the three stages and the required rate of return. Because the Bloomberg DDM value is just a mouse click away, the analyst can easily compare the Bloomberg value to the analyst's own model value or to the stock's current market price.

5.5 Spreadsheet Modeling

DDMs such as the Gordon growth model and the multistage models presented earlier assume stylized patterns of dividend growth. With the computational power of personal computers, calculators, and personal digital assistants, however, *any* assumed dividend pattern is easily valued.

Spreadsheets allow the analyst to build complicated models that would be very cumbersome to describe using algebra. Furthermore, built-in spreadsheet functions (such as those to find rates of return) use algorithms to get a numerical answer when a mathematical solution would be impossible or extremely challenging. Because of spreadsheets' widespread use, several analysts can work together or exchange information through the sharing of their spreadsheet models. Example 23 presents the results of using a spreadsheet to value a stock with dividends changing substantially through time.

EXAMPLE 23

Finding the Value of a Stock Using a Spreadsheet Model

Yang Co. is expected to pay a $21.00 dividend next year. The dividend will decline by 10 percent annually for the following three years. In Year 5, Yang will sell off assets worth $100 per share. The Year 5 dividend, which includes a distribution of some of the proceeds of the asset sale, is expected to be $60. In Year 6, we expect the dividend to decrease to $40. We expect that this dividend will be maintained at $40 for one additional year. It is then expected to grow by 5 percent annually thereafter. If the required rate of return is 12 percent, what is the value of one share of Yang?

The value is shown in Table 11. Each dividend, its present value discounted at 12 percent, and an explanation are included in the table. The final row treats the dividends from $t = 8$ forward as a Gordon growth model because after Year 7, the dividend grows at a constant 5 percent annually. V_7 is the value of these dividends at $t = 7$.

		Value of	Present Value	
Year	D_t or V_t	D_t or V_t	at 12%	Explanation of D_t or V_t
1	D_1	21.00	18.75	Dividend set at $21
2	D_2	18.90	15.07	Previous dividend × 0.90
3	D_3	17.01	12.11	Previous dividend × 0.90
4	D_4	15.31	9.73	Previous dividend × 0.90
5	D_5	60.00	34.05	Set at $60
6	D_6	40.00	20.27	Set at $40
7	D_7	40.00	18.09	Set at $40
7	V_7	600.00	271.41	$V_7 = D_8/(r - g)$
				$V_7 = (40.00 \times 1.05)/(0.12 - 0.05)$
Total			399.48	

TABLE 11   Value of Yang Co. Stock

As the table shows, the total present value of Yang Co.'s dividends is $399.48. In this example, the terminal value of the company (V_n) at the end of the first stage was found using the Gordon growth model using a mature growth rate of 5 percent. Several alternative approaches to estimating g are available in this context:

▶ Use the formula $g = (b$ in the mature phase$) \times$ (ROE in the mature phase). We will discuss the expression $g = b \times$ ROE in Section 6. We have several ways to estimate ROE. We can use the DuPont expression for ROE, also presented in Section 6. Some analysts assume that ROE = r, the required rate of return on equity, in the mature phase. An alternative assumption is that ROE in the mature phase equals the median industry ROE. The earnings retention ratio, b, may be empirically based. For example, Bloomberg assumes that $b = 0.55$ in the mature phase, equivalent to a dividend payout ratio of 45 percent, a long-run average payout ratio for mature dividend-paying companies in the United States. In addition, sometimes analysts project the dividend payout ratio for the company individually.

▶ The analyst may estimate the growth rate g with other models relating the mature growth rate to macroeconomic, including industry, growth projections.

5.6 Finding Rates of Return for Any DDM

This reading has focused on finding the value of a security using assumptions for dividends, required rates of return, and expected growth rates. The models are also useful for other purposes. Given the current price as shown in Section 4.3, we can calculate the implied expected rate of return as an input to security selection. For example, given a current stock price, dividend estimates, and forecasts of growth, we can derive the implied expected rate of return. Finding value and finding expected rates of return are two sides of the same coin. If you know what is on one side, you can deduce what is on the other. In the following discussion, keep in mind that if price does not equal intrinsic value, the expected return will need to be adjusted to reflect the additional component of return that accrues when the mispricing is corrected, as discussed in Section 4.3.

In some cases, it is very easy to find the expected rate of return. With a one-period investment horizon, the expected return was simply $r = (D_1 + P_1)/P_0 - 1$. This calculation requires a forecast of next year's stock price (P_1) in addition to knowledge of the current price (P_0).

In the Gordon growth model, $r = D_1/P_0 + g$. The expected rate of return is the dividend yield plus the expected growth rate. For a security with a current price of $10, an expected dividend of $0.50, and expected growth of 8 percent, the expected rate of return would be 13 percent.

For the H-model, the expected rate of return can be derived as[31]

$$r = \left(\frac{D_0}{P_0}\right)\left[(1 + g_L) + H(g_S - g_L)\right] + g_L \qquad \textbf{(46-28)}$$

When the short- and long-term growth rates are the same, this model reduces to the Gordon growth model. For a security with a current dividend of $1, a current price of $20, and an expected short-term growth rate of 10 percent declining over 10 years ($H = 5$) to 6 percent, the expected rate of return would be

$$r = \left(\frac{\$1}{\$20}\right)\left[(1 + 0.06) + 5(0.10 - 0.06)\right] + 0.06 = 12.3\%$$

For multistage models and spreadsheet models, it can be more difficult to find a single equation for the rate of return. The process generally used is similar to that of finding the internal rate of return for a series of varying cash flows. Using a computer or trial and error, the analyst must find the rate of return such that the present value of future expected dividends equals the current stock price.

5.7 Strengths and Weaknesses of Multistage DDMs

The multistage dividend discount models have several strengths and weaknesses.

Strengths

▶ The multistage DDMs can accommodate a variety of patterns of future streams of expected dividends.

▶ Even though the multistage DDMs may use stylized assumptions about growth, they can provide useful approximations.

▶ In addition to valuing dividend streams with a DDM, the expected rates of return can be imputed by finding the discount rate that equates the present value of the dividend stream to the current stock price. These expected return values can be adjusted to reflect the expected market correction of mispricing.

▶ Because of the variety of DDMs available, the analyst is both enabled and compelled to carefully evaluate the assumptions about the stock under examination. The valuation model should fit the assumptions (because the analyst is not forced to accept a set of assumptions that fit a specific model).

▶ Spreadsheets are widely available, allowing the analyst to construct and examine an almost limitless number of models.

▶ Using a model forces the analyst to specify assumptions, rather than simply using subjective assessments. Analysts can thus use common assumptions, understand the reasons for differing valuations when they occur, and react to changing market conditions in a systematic manner.

---

[31] Fuller and Hsia (1984).

EXAMPLE 24

Finding the Expected Rate of Return for Varying Expected Dividends

An analyst expects JNJ's (Johnson & Johnson, from Example 4) current dividend of $0.70 to grow by 14.5 percent for six years and then grow by 8 percent into perpetuity. JNJ's current price is $53.28. What is the expected return on an investment in JNJ's stock?

In performing trial and error with the two-stage model to estimate the expected rate of return, it is important to have a good initial guess. We can use the expected rate of return formula from the Gordon growth model and JNJ's long-term growth rate to find a first approximation: $r = (\$0.70 \times 1.08)/\$53.28 + 0.08 = 9.42\%$. Because we know that the growth rate in the first six years is more than 8 percent, the **estimated rate of return** must be above 9.42 percent. Using 9.42 percent and 10.0 percent, we calculate the implied price in Table 12.

TABLE 12   Johnson & Johnson

Time	D_t	Present Value of D_t and V_6 at $r = 9.42\%$	Present Value of D_t and V_6 at $r = 10.0\%$
1	$0.8015	$0.7325	$0.7286
2	$0.9177	$0.7665	$0.7584
3	$1.0508	$0.8021	$0.7895
4	$1.2032	$0.8394	$0.8218
5	$1.3776	$0.8783	$0.8554
6	$1.5774	$0.9191	$0.8904
7	$1.7035		
6		$69.90	$48.0805
Total		$74.84	$52.9246
Market Price		$53.28	$53.28

The present value of the terminal value is $V_6/(1 + r)^6 = [D_7/(r - g)]/(1 + r)^6$. For $r = 9.42$ percent, the present value is $[1.7035/(0.0942 - 0.08)]/(1.0942)^6 = \$69.90$. The present value for other values of r is found similarly. Apparently, the expected rate of return is slightly less than 10 percent, assuming efficient prices.

Weaknesses

► Garbage in, garbage out. If the inputs are not economically meaningful and appropriate for the company being valued, the outputs from the model will not be useful.

► Analysts sometimes employ models that they do not understand fully. For example, the H-model is an approximation model. An analyst may think it is exact and misuse it.

► As a sensitivity analysis usually shows, valuations are very sensitive to the models' inputs.

► Programming and data errors in spreadsheet models are very common. Spreadsheet models should be checked thoroughly.

THE FINANCIAL DETERMINANTS OF GROWTH RATES

In a number of examples earlier in this reading, we have implicitly used the relationship that the dividend growth rate (g) equals the earning retention ratio (b) times the return on equity (ROE). In this section, we explain this relationship and show how we can combine it with a method of analyzing return on equity, called DuPont analysis, as a simple tool for forecasting dividend growth rates.

6.1 Sustainable Growth Rate

We define the **sustainable growth rate** as the rate of dividend (and earnings) growth that can be sustained for a given level of return on equity, keeping the capital structure constant over time and without issuing additional common stock. The reason to study this concept is that it can help us estimate the stable growth rate in a Gordon growth model valuation, or the mature growth rate in a multistage DDM in which we use the Gordon growth formula for the terminal value of the stock.

The expression to calculate the sustainable growth rate is

$$g = b \times \text{ROE} \tag{46-29}$$

where

g = dividend growth rate
b = earnings retention rate ($1 - $ Dividend payout ratio)
ROE = return on equity.

Example 25 is an illustration of the fact that growth in shareholders' equity is driven by reinvested earnings alone (no new issues of equity, and debt growing at the rate g).[32] Equation 46-29 implies that the higher the return on equity, the higher the dividend growth rate, all else constant. The expression also implies that the higher the earnings retention ratio, the higher the growth rate in dividends, holding all else constant.[33]

A practical logic for defining *sustainable* in terms of growth through internally generated funds (retained earnings) is that external equity (secondary issues of stock) is considerably more costly than internal equity (reinvested earnings), because of investment banker fees. Continuous issuance of new stock is

---

[32] With debt growing at the rate g, the capital structure is constant. If the capital structure is not constant, ROE would not be constant in general because ROE depends on leverage.

[33] ROE is a variable that reflects underlying profitability as well as the use of leverage or debt. The retention ratio or dividend policy, in contrast, is not a fundamental variable in the same sense as ROE. A higher dividend growth rate through a higher retention ratio (lower dividend payout ratio) is neutral for share value in and of itself. Holding investment policy (capital projects) constant, the positive effect on value from an increase in g will just be offset by the negative effect from a decrease in dividend payouts in the expression for the value of the stock in any DDM. Sharpe, Alexander, and Bailey (1999) discuss this concept in more detail.

> ## EXAMPLE 25
>
> ### Example Showing $g = b \times$ ROE
>
> In the year just ended, a company began with shareholders' equity of $1,000,000, earned $250,000 net income, and paid dividends of $100,000. Its ROE is 25 percent and its retention rate is 60 percent. The company begins the next year with $1,150,000 of shareholders' equity because it retained $150,000. There are no additions to equity from an increase in shares outstanding.
>
> If the company again earns 25 percent on equity in the next year, net income will be $287,500, which is a 15 percent increase. The increase in earnings is $287,500 − $250,000 = $37,500. This is 15 percent above the previous year's earnings of $250,000. The company retains 60 percent of earnings (60% × $287,500 = $172,500) and pays out the other 40 percent (40% × $287,500 = $115,000) as dividends.
>
> The formula for the dividend growth rate is $g = b \times$ ROE, which is $g = 0.60 \times 25\% = 15\%$. Notice that dividends for the company grew from $100,000 to $115,000, which is exactly a 15 percent growth rate.

not a practical funding alternative for companies, in general.[34] Growth of capital through issuance of new debt can sometimes be sustained for considerable periods, however. Further, if a company manages its capital structure to a target percentage of debt to total capital (debt and common stock), it will need to issue debt to maintain that percentage as equity grows through reinvested earnings. (This approach is one of a variety of observed capital structure policies.) In addition, the earnings retention ratio nearly always shows year-to-year variation in actual companies. For example, earnings may have transitory components that management does not want to reflect in dividends. The analyst may thus observe actual dividend growth rates straying from the growth rates predicted by Equation 46-29 because of these effects, even when his input estimates are unbiased. Nevertheless, the equation can be useful as a simple expression for approximating the average rate at which dividends can grow over a long horizon.

6.2 Dividend Growth Rate, Retention Rate, and ROE Analysis

Thus far we have seen that a company's sustainable growth, as defined above, is a function of its ability to generate return on equity (which depends on investment opportunities) and its retention rate. We now expand this model by examining what drives ROE. Remember that ROE is the return (net income) generated on the equity invested in the company:

---

[34] As a long-term average, about 2 percent of U.S. publicly traded companies issue new equity in a given year, which corresponds to a secondary equity issue once every 50 years, on average. Businesses may be rationed in their access to secondary issues of equity because of the costs associated with informational asymmetries between management and the public. Because management has more information on the future cash flows of the company than the general public, and equity is an ownership claim to those cash flows, the public may react to additional equity issuance as possibly motivated by an intent to "share (future) misery" rather than "share (future) wealth."

$$ROE = \frac{\text{Net income}}{\text{Stockholders' equity}} \qquad \textbf{(46-30)}$$

If a company has a ROE of 15 percent, it generates $15 of net income for every $100 invested in stockholders' equity. For purposes of analyzing ROE, we can relate it to several other financial ratios. For example, ROE can be seen as related to return on assets (ROA) and the extent of financial leverage (equity multiplier):

$$ROE = \frac{\text{Net income}}{\text{Total assets}} \times \frac{\text{Total assets}}{\text{Stockholders' equity}} \qquad \textbf{(46-31)}$$

Therefore, a company can increase its ROE either by increasing ROA or the use of leverage (assuming the company can borrow at a rate lower than that it earns on its assets).

We can further expand this model by breaking ROA into two components, profit margin and turnover (efficiency):

$$ROE = \frac{\text{Net income}}{\text{Sales}} \times \frac{\text{Sales}}{\text{Total assets}}$$
$$\times \frac{\text{Average total assests}}{\text{Stockholders' equity}} \qquad \textbf{(46-32)}$$

The first term is the company's profit margin. A higher profit margin will result in a higher ROE. The second term measures total asset turnover, which is the company's efficiency. A turnover of 1 indicates that a company generates $1 in sales for every $1 invested in assets. A higher turnover will result in higher ROE. The last term is the equity multiplier, which measures the extent of leverage, as noted earlier. This relationship is widely known as the DuPont model or analysis of ROE. Although ROE can be analyzed further using a five-way analysis, the three-way analysis will provide us with insight into the determinants of ROE that are pertinent to our understanding of the growth rate. Combining Equations 46-29 and 46-32, we find that the dividend growth rate is equal to the retention rate multiplied by ROE:[35]

$$g = \frac{\text{Net income} - \text{Dividends}}{\text{Net income}} \times \frac{\text{Net income}}{\text{Sales}} \times \frac{\text{Sales}}{\text{Assets}}$$
$$\times \frac{\text{Assets}}{\text{Shareholders' equity}} \qquad \textbf{(46-33)}$$

The model is also useful to the analyst in analyzing the factors that can affect the sustainable growth rate. Higgins (2001) explains this model and calls it the PRAT model (although we have altered the notation and calculations slightly to use averages in the ratios above). Growth is a function of profit margin (P), retention rate (R), asset turnover (A), and financial leverage (T). Two of these factors determine ROA—the profit margin and the asset turnover. The other two factors are based on a company's financial policies—the retention rate and financial leverage. So, the growth rate in dividends can be viewed as determined by the company's ROA and financial policies. The example below illustrates the logic behind this equation.

---

[35] Strictly speaking, the theoretical expression $g = b \times ROE$ holds exactly only when ROE is calculated using beginning of period shareholders' equity. That assumption is necessary for mathematical simplicity, but assumes that reinvested earnings are not available until the end of the period. Practically ROE is calculated using average stockholders' equity or sometimes ending stockholders' equity in financial databases and is preferred for financial analysis.

EXAMPLE 26

ROA, Financial Policies, and the Dividend Growth Rate

Baggai Enterprises has an ROA of 10 percent, retains 30 percent of earnings, and has an equity multiplier of 1.25. Mondale Enterprises also has an ROA of 10 percent, but it retains two-thirds of earnings and has an equity multiplier of 2.00. What dividend growth rates should these two companies have?

Baggai's dividend growth rate should be
$$g = 0.30 \times 10\% \times 1.25 = 3.75\%$$
Mondale's dividend growth rate should be
$$g = (2/3) \times 10\% \times 2.00 = 13.33\%$$

Because Mondale has the higher retention rate and higher financial leverage, its dividend growth rate is much higher.

If we are forecasting growth for the next five years, we should use our expectations of the four factors driving growth over this five-year period. If we are forecasting growth into perpetuity, we should use our very long-term forecasts for these variables.

To illustrate the calculation and implications of the sustainable growth rate using the expression for ROE given by the DuPont formula, assume the growth rate is $g = b \times \text{ROE} = 0.60 (15\%) = 9\%$. The ROE of 15 percent was based on a profit margin of 5 percent, an asset turnover of 2.0, and an equity multiplier of 1.5. Given fixed ratios of sales-to-assets and assets-to-equity, sales, assets, and debt will also be growing at 9 percent. Because dividends are fixed at 40 percent of income, dividends will grow at the same rate as income, or 9 percent. If the company increases dividends faster than 9 percent, this growth rate would not be sustainable using internally generated funds. Earning retentions would be reduced, and the company would not be able to finance the assets required for sales growth without external financing.

The analyst should be careful in projecting historical financial ratios into the future in using this analysis. Although a company may have grown at 20 percent a year for the last five years, this rate of growth is probably not sustainable indefinitely. Abnormally high ROEs, which may have driven that growth, are unlikely to persist for long periods of time because of competitive forces.

6.3 Financial Models and Dividends

Analysts can also forecast dividends by building more-complex models of the company's total operating and financial environment. Because there can be so many aspects to such a model, a spreadsheet is used to build pro forma income statements and balance sheets. The company's ability to pay dividends in the future can be predicted using one of these models. The example below shows the dividends that a highly profitable and rapidly growing company can pay when its growth rates and profit margins decline because of increasing competition over time.

EXAMPLE 27

Forecasting Growth with the PRAT Formula

Dell Corporation (NYSE: DELL) is not currently paying a dividend. An analysis of its ROE for the past five years is shown in Table 13.

TABLE 13   Dell Corporation

Year	ROE (%)	Profit Margin (%)	Asset Turnover	Financial Leverage
2000	39.87 =	6.83	× 2.56	× 2.28
1999	43.74 =	6.60	× 2.75	× 2.41
1998	80.57 =	8.00	× 3.27	× 3.08
1997	90.11 =	7.66	× 3.40	× 3.46
1996	58.50 =	6.68	× 3.02	× 2.90

DELL's ROEs have been very high during this period. Because it is retaining all earnings, the company has grown accordingly. It is unlikely that DELL will sustain these levels indefinitely. Their strong business model and market position, however, are expected by an analyst to maintain above-average performance (relative to the market) during the next five years. Nonetheless, the analyst believes the performance cannot realistically be expected to match prior levels. Further, the analyst assumes that the company will continue to retain all earnings for the next 10 years. The analyst's forecast for profit margin, turnover, and leverage over the next 10 years are:

Profit margin	5%
Asset turnover	2.50
Leverage	2.00

With a retention rate of 100 percent, the PRAT formula yields Short-term growth = $0.05 \times 1.00 \times 2.50 \times 2.00 = 25\%$.

Although DELL may be able to sustain this level of growth for 10 years, the analyst believes that market conditions may intervene. For example, weak demand for personal computers may result in lower growth. Accordingly, the analyst may elect to lower this growth estimate subjectively.

Assume that the analyst forecasts that after Year 10, DELL will begin to pay out 15 percent of its earnings as dividends (typical for mature technology companies). Additionally, long-term sustainable estimates for profit margin, asset turnover and leverage are:

Profit margin	4.5% (reflects declining margins in the industry)
Asset turnover	1.50 (closer to industry efficiency)
Leverage	2.00 (modest reduction from recent levels)

With a retention rate of 85 percent, the PRAT formula yields Long-term sustainable growth = $0.045 \times 0.85 \times 1.50 \times 2.00 = 11.48\%$.

Because there are no dividends for the first 10 years, the analyst would use a two-stage DDM with these growth inputs. For the trailing 12 months, DELL has earnings per share excluding non-recurring items of $0.76. Using a risk-free rate of 5.0 percent, an equity risk premium of 5.7 percent, and a beta of 1.45 results in a required rate of return of 13.3 percent. Forecasting earnings in Year 10 at 25 percent annual growth results in E_{10} of $7.08 = 0.76×1.25^{10}. The following year's earnings would be forecasted to grow at 11.48 percent to $7.89. D_{11} would be $7.89 \times 0.15 = $1.18. V_{10} would be $1.18/(0.133 - 0.1148)$ or $64.84. Discounting back to V_0 at 13.3 percent yields a current price of $18.60.

This example illustrates the use of a DDM for valuing a non-dividend-paying stock. As noted in Section 2.2, analysts often select other DCF models in such cases. We will discuss alternative DCF models in later readings.

EXAMPLE 28

A Spreadsheet Model for Forecasting Dividends

An analyst is preparing a forecast of dividends for Hoshino Distributors for the next five years. He uses a spreadsheet model with the following assumptions:

► Sales are $100 million in Year 1. They grow by 20 percent in Year 2, 15 percent in Year 3, and 10 percent in Years 4 and 5.

► Operating profits (EBIT 5 earnings before interest and taxes) are 20 percent of sales in Years 1 and 2, 18 percent of sales in Year 3, and 16 percent of sales in Years 4 and 5.

► Interest expenses are 10 percent of total debt for the current year.

► The income tax rate is 40 percent.

► Hoshino pays out 20 percent of earnings in Years 1 and 2, 30 percent in Year 3, 40 percent in Year 4, and 50 percent in Year 5.

► Retained earnings are added to equity in the next year.

► Total assets are 80 percent of the current year's sales in all years.

► In Year 1, debt is $40 million and shareholders' equity is $40 million. Debt equals total assets minus shareholders' equity. Shareholders' equity will equal the previous year's shareholders' equity plus the addition to retained earnings from the previous year.

► Hoshino has 4 million shares outstanding.

► The discount rate is 15 percent, and the value of the company at the end of Year 5 will be 10.0 times earnings.

The analyst wishes to estimate the current value per share of Hoshino. Table 14 adheres to the modeling assumptions above. Total dividends and earnings are found at the bottom of the income statement.

TABLE 14 Hoshino Distributors Pro Forma Financial Statements (in millions)

	Year 1	Year 2	Year 3	Year 4	Year 5
Income statement					
Sales	$100.00	$120.00	$138.00	$151.80	$166.98
EBIT	$20.00	$24.00	$24.84	$24.29	$26.72
Interest	$4.00	$4.83	$5.35	$5.64	$6.18
EBT	$16.00	$19.17	$19.49	$18.65	$20.54
Taxes	$6.40	$7.67	$7.80	$7.46	$8.22
Net income	$9.60	$11.50	$11.69	$11.19	$12.32
Dividends	$1.92	$2.30	$3.51	$4.48	$6.16
Balance sheet					
Total assets	$80.00	$96.00	$110.40	$121.44	$133.58
Total debt	$40.00	$48.32	$53.52	$56.38	$61.81
Equity	$40.00	$47.68	$56.88	$65.06	$71.77

Dividing the total dividends by the number of outstanding shares gives the dividend per share for each year shown below. The present value of each dividend, discounted at 15 percent, is also shown.

	Year 1	Year 2	Year 3	Year 4	Year 5
DPS	$0.480	$0.575	$0.877	$1.120	$1.540
PV	$0.417	$0.435	$0.577	$0.640	$0.766

The earnings per share in Year 5 are $12.32 million divided by 4 million shares, or $3.08 per share. Given a P/E of 10, the market price in Year 5 is predicted to be $30.80. Discounted at 15 percent (the required rate of return noted above), the present value of this price is $15.31. Adding the present values of the five dividends, which sum to $2.84, gives a total stock value today of $18.15 per share.

6.4 Investment Management and DDMs

Investment management does not involve isolated or occasional valuations of a common stock. An analyst will usually have to do valuations of a number of stocks, and these valuations will be updated regularly or whenever changing circumstances warrant an update. Teams of analysts also have to work together to evaluate the stocks in their investment universe. A competitive environment requires rapid incorporation of the best information, consistent application of valuation principles, and clear communication of investment recommendations (and their justifications).

Investment managers have used DCF models, including dividend discount models, as part of a systematic approach to security selection and portfolio formation. The portfolio formation process has a *planning step*, an *execution step*, and a *feedback step*. Although this reading has focused on the use of DDM in the execution step, we must put the reading in the context of the planning step.

In the planning step, risk and return objectives are set. Consider a U.S. domestic core equity portfolio manager with the S&P 500 as a benchmark (the comparison portfolio used to evaluate performance).[36] This investment manager may choose a risk objective in terms of tracking risk relative to the S&P 500. **Tracking risk** is the standard deviation of the differences between the portfolio's and the benchmark's returns. Hypothetically, a tracking risk objective might be set at 5 percent. (For a portfolio with this investment approach, tracking risk would commonly fall in the range of 2 percent to 6 percent.) For this manager, the return objective might be to beat the S&P 500 by 200 basis points. Planning also involves the selection of an investment strategy. DCF models are used in active investment strategies. Active managers hold securities in different-from-benchmark weights in an attempt to produce positive risk-adjusted returns or alphas.

In the execution step, the portfolio manager selects the portfolio, and the trading desk implements the portfolio decisions. Managers use DCF models to identify (select) undervalued securities. If the manager simply chose the most undervalued securities without any risk discipline, his selections might concentrate on a particular (or a few) risk factor. He might often fail to meet his risk objective. A risk-control discipline must be used. Our hypothetical manager might choose sector neutrality with respect to his benchmark as that discipline, defining his investment universe as the S&P 500. A portfolio is **sector neutral** to a benchmark if sectors are represented in the portfolio in the same proportions as in the benchmark, according to market-value weights. (Economic sector membership explains a substantial portion of risk; however, this is an illustration, not a recommendation of a particular risk-control approach.) Then the process continues as follows:

▶ *Sort stocks into groups according to the risk-control methodology.* In our example, the manager sorts the stocks into groups according to sector membership. As another example, if the manager uses a CAPM risk-control methodology, the sorting is into portfolios of similar beta risk.

▶ *Rank stocks by expected return within each group using a DCF methodology.* There are several techniques to implement this ranking. The manager may use an expression for r in terms of fundamentals and current market price, using a DCF model. This value of r is an estimate of expected return if price fully reflects value, or if price and value differ but do not converge. As explained earlier, when price (P_0) and intrinsic value (V_0) differ, expected return will have an additional component if the two come together. Then the manager's estimate of expected return is the sum of r and the return from convergence. In practice, convergence assumptions range from nonconvergence to gradual convergence over five years. At the end of this step, in our example, the manager has ranked stocks from highest to lowest expected return within sector grouping, or whatever grouping approach is used.

---

[36] This illustration is drawn from a composite of several actual investment managers.

► *Select a portfolio from the highest expected return stocks consistent with the risk control methodology.* This selection is implemented in various ways. As an illustration, the investment manager might preset the number of issues in the portfolio at 80. If the energy sector at the time has a 10 percent weight in the S&P 500, the 8 energy issues (10 percent of 80) in the S&P 500 with the highest expected return enter the portfolio with equal weights. All selected securities are equally weighted, but more-important sectors have a larger number of securities; the result is approximate sector neutrality.

As part of this process, careful investment managers will stress test the expected return inputs with respect to assumptions. Consistency of the assumptions underlying the valuations of different companies is important. For example, if different industry growth forecasts underlie different analysts' earnings projections, then relative valuation differences among stocks may simply reflect different industry forecasts rather than mispricing. As with all active investment strategies, investment results depend on the quality of the inputs. For an active strategy to consistently add value, the manager's expectations (about earnings growth, for example), must differ from consensus expectations and be, on average, correct as well.

Effective and appropriate use of DDMs, as well as the valuation models in the following readings, is essential for investment management, whether by an individual or by a team of analysts. Analysts can use DDMs to systematically select securities for inclusion in portfolios.

SUMMARY

This reading provided an overview of DCF models of valuation, discussed the estimation of a stock's required rate of return, and presented in detail the dividend discount model.

▶ In DCF models, the value of any asset is the present value of its (expected) future cash flows

$$V_0 = \sum_{t=1}^{\infty} \frac{CF_t}{(1+r)^t}$$

where V_0 is the value of the asset as of $t = 0$ (today), CF_t is the (expected) cash flow at time t, and r is the discount rate or required rate of return.

▶ Several alternative streams of expected cash flows can be used to value equities, including dividends, free cash flow, and residual income. A discounted dividend approach is most suitable for dividend-paying stocks, where the company has a discernible dividend policy that has an understandable relationship to the company's profitability, and the investor has a non-control (minority ownership) perspective.

▶ The free cash flow approach (FCFF or FCFE) might be appropriate when the company does not pay dividends, dividends differ substantially from FCFE, free cash flows align with profitability, or the investor takes a control (majority ownership) perspective.

▶ The residual income approach can be useful when the company does not pay dividends (as an alternative to a FCF approach), or free cash flow is negative.

▶ The required rate of return is the minimum rate of return that an investor would anticipate receiving in order to invest in an asset. The two major approaches to determining the cost of equity are an equilibrium method (CAPM or APT) and the bond yield plus risk premium method.

▶ The equity risk premium for use in the CAPM approach can be based on historical return data or based explicitly on expectational data.

▶ The DDM with a single holding period gives stock value as

$$V_0 = \frac{D_1}{(1+r)^1} + \frac{P_1}{(1+r)^1} = \frac{D_1 + P_1}{(1+r)^1}$$

where D_t is the expected dividend at time t (here $t = 1$) and V_t is the stock's (expected) value at time t. Assuming that V_0 is equal to today's market price, P_0, the expected holding-period return is

$$r = \frac{D_1 + P_1}{P_0} - 1 = \frac{D_1}{P_0} + \frac{P_1 - P_0}{P_0}$$

▶ Expected holding-period returns differ from required rates of return when price does not exactly reflect value. When price does not equal value, there will generally be an additional component to the expected holding-period return reflecting the convergence of price to value.

▶ The expression for the DDM for any given finite holding period n and the general expression for the DDM are, respectively,

$$V_0 = \sum_{t=1}^{n} \frac{D_t}{(1+r)^t} + \frac{P_n}{(1+r)^n} \text{ and } V_0 = \sum_{t=1}^{\infty} \frac{D_t}{(1+r)^t}$$

▶ There are two main approaches to the problem of forecasting dividends: First, we can assign the entire stream of expected future dividends to one of several stylized growth patterns. Second, we can forecast a finite number of dividends individually up to a terminal point, valuing the remaining dividends by assigning them to a stylized growth pattern, or forecasting share price as of the terminal point of our dividend forecasts. The first forecasting approach leads to the Gordon growth model and multistage dividend discount models, the second forecasting approach lends itself to spreadsheet modeling.

▶ The Gordon growth model assumes that dividends grow at a constant rate g forever, so that $D_t = D_{t-1}(1 + g)$. The dividend stream in the Gordon growth model has a value of

$$V_0 = \frac{D_0(1 + g)}{r - g}, \text{ or } V_0 = \frac{D_1}{r - g}$$

where $r > g$.

▶ The value of fixed rate perpetual preferred stock is $V_0 = D/r$, where D is the stock's (constant) annual dividend.

▶ Assuming that price equals value, the Gordon growth model estimate of a stock's expected rate of return is

$$r = \frac{D_0(1 + g)}{P_0} + g = \frac{D_1}{P_0} + g$$

▶ Given an estimate of the next-period dividend and the stock's required rate of return, we can use the Gordon growth model to estimate the dividend growth rate implied by the current market price (making a constant growth rate assumption).

▶ The present value of growth opportunities (PVGO) is the part of a stock's total value, V_0, that comes from profitable future growth opportunities in contrast to the value associated with assets already in place. The relationship is $V_0 = E/r + \text{PVGO}$, where E/r is defined as the no-growth value per share.

▶ We can express the leading price–earnings ratio (P_0/E_1) and the trailing price–earnings ratio (P_0/E_0) in terms of the Gordon growth model as, respectively,

$$\frac{P_0}{E_1} = \frac{D_1/E_1}{r - g} = \frac{1 - b}{r - g} \text{ and } \frac{P_0}{E_0} = \frac{D_0(1 + g)/E_0}{r - g} = \frac{(1 - b)(1 + g)}{r - g}$$

The above expressions give a stock's justified price–earnings ratio based on forecasts of fundamentals (given that the Gordon growth model is appropriate).

▶ The Gordon growth model may be useful for valuing broad-based equity indexes and the stock of businesses with earnings that we expect to grow at a stable rate comparable to or lower than the nominal growth rate of the economy.

▶ Gordon growth model values are very sensitive to the assumed growth rate and required rate of return.

▶ For many companies, growth falls into phases. In the growth phase, a company enjoys an abnormally high growth rate in earnings per share, called supernormal growth. In the **transition phase**, earnings growth slows. In the mature phase, the company reaches an equilibrium in which factors such as earnings growth and the return on equity stabilize at levels that can be sustained long term. Analysts often apply multistage DCF models to value the stock of a firm with multistage growth prospects.

▶ The two-stage dividend discount model assumes different growth rates in Stage 1 and Stage 2

$$V_0 = \sum_{t=1}^{n} \frac{D_0(1 + g_S)^t}{(1 + r)^t} + \frac{D_0(1 + g_S)^n(1 + g_L)}{(1 + r)^n(r - g_L)}$$

where g_S is the expected dividend growth rate in the first period and g_L is the expected growth rate in the second period.

▶ The terminal stock value, V_n, is sometimes found with the Gordon growth model or with some other method, such as applying a P/E multiplier to forecasted EPS as of the terminal date.

▶ The H-model assumes that the dividend growth rate declines linearly from a high supernormal rate to the normal growth rate during Stage 1, and then grows at a constant normal growth rate thereafter:

$$V_0 = \frac{D_0(1 + g_L)}{r - g_L} + \frac{D_0 H(g_S - g_L)}{r - g_L} = \frac{D_0(1 + g_L) + D_0 H(g_S - g_L)}{r - g_L}$$

▶ There are two basic three-stage models. In one version, the growth rate is constant in each of the three stages. In the second version, the growth rate is constant in Stage 1, declines linearly in Stage 2, and becomes constant and normal in Stage 3.

▶ Spreadsheet models are very flexible, providing the analyst with the ability to value any pattern of expected dividends.

▶ In addition to valuing equities, DDMs are used to find expected rates of return. For simpler models (like the one-period model, the Gordon growth model, and the H-model), well-known formulas may be used to calculate these rates of return. For many dividend streams, however, the rate of return must be found by trial and error, producing a discount rate that equates the present value of the forecasted dividend stream to the current market price. Adjustments to the expected return estimates may be needed to reflect the convergence of price to value.

▶ Multistage DDM models can accommodate a wide variety of patterns of expected dividends. Even though such models may use stylized assumptions about growth, they can provide useful approximations.

▶ Values from multistage DDMs are generally sensitive to assumptions. The usefulness of such values reflects the quality of the inputs.

▶ Dividend growth rates can be obtained from analyst forecasts, from statistical forecasting models, or from company fundamentals. The sustainable growth rate depends on the ROE and the earnings retention rate, b: $g = b \times$ ROE. This expression can be expanded further, using the DuPont formula, as

$$g = \frac{\text{Net income} - \text{Dividends}}{\text{Net income}} \times \frac{\text{Net income}}{\text{Sales}} \times \frac{\text{Sales}}{\text{Assets}}$$
$$\times \frac{\text{Assets}}{\text{Shareholders' equity}}$$

▶ Dividend discount models can be used as a discipline for portfolio construction. Potential investments can be screened or selected based on their estimated rates of return, along with other portfolio requirements. Often, the discipline involves three steps: sorting stocks into groups according to a risk-control methodology, ranking stocks by expected return within each group, and selecting a portfolio from the highest expected return stocks consistent with the risk-control methodology.

PRACTICE PROBLEMS FOR READING 46

1. The estimated betas for AOL Time Warner (NYSE: AOL), J.P. Morgan Chase & Company (NYSE: JPM), and The Boeing Company (NYSE: BA) are 2.50, 1.50, and 0.80, respectively. The risk-free rate of return is 4.35 percent, and the market risk premium is 8.04 percent. Calculate the required rates of return for these three stocks using the CAPM.

2. The estimated factor sensitivities of Terra Energy to the five macroeconomic factors in the Burmeister, Roll, and Ross (1994) article are given in the table below. The table also gives the market risk premiums to each of these same factors.

	Factor Sensitivity	Risk Premium (%)
Confidence risk	0.25	2.59
Time horizon risk	0.30	−0.66
Inflation risk	−0.45	−4.32
Business-cycle risk	1.60	1.49
Market-timing risk	0.80	3.61

Use the 5-factor BIRR APT model to calculate the required rate of return for Terra Energy using these estimates. The Treasury bill rate is 4.1 percent.

3. Newmont Mining (NYSE: NEM) has an estimated beta of −0.2. The risk-free rate of return is 4.5 percent, and the equity risk premium is estimated to be 7.5 percent. Using the CAPM, calculate the required rate of return for investors in NEM.

4. The expression for the value of a stock given a single-period investment horizon has four variables: V_0, D_1, P_1, and r. Solve for the value of the missing variable for each of the four stocks in the table below.

Stock	Estimated Value (V_0)	Expected Dividend (D_1)	Expected Price (P_1)	Required Rate of Return (r)
1	19.36	$0.30	$21.00	10.0%
2	$30.00		32.00	10.0
3	92.00	2.70		12.0
4	16.00	0.30	17.90	

5. General Motors (NYSE: GM) sells for $66.00 per share. The expected dividend for next year is $2.40. Use the single-period DDM to predict GM's stock price one year from today. The risk-free rate of return is 5.3 percent, the market risk premium is 6.0 percent, and GM's beta is 0.90.

6. BP PLC (NYSE: BP) has a current stock price of $50 and current dividend of $1.50. The dividend is expected to grow at 5 percent annually. BP's beta is 0.85. The risk-free interest rate is 4.5 percent, and the market risk premium is 6.0 percent.

Reading 46 • Discounted Dividend Valuation

A. What is next year's projected dividend?

B. What is BP's required rate of return based on the CAPM?

C. Using the Gordon growth model, what is the value of BP?

D. Assuming the Gordon growth model is valid, what dividend growth rate would result in a model value of BP equal to its market price?

7. The current market prices of three stocks are given below. The current dividends, dividend growth rates, and required rates of return are also given. The dividend growth rates are perpetual.

Stock	Current Price	Current Dividend ($t = 0$)	Dividend Growth Rate	Required Rate of Return
Que Corp.	$25.00	$0.50	7.0%	10.0%
SHS Company	$40.00	$1.20	6.5	10.5
True Corp.	$20.00	$0.88	5.0	10.0

A. Find the value of each stock with the Gordon growth model.

B. Which stock's current market price has the smallest premium or largest discount relative to its DDM valuation?

8. For five utility stocks, the table below provides the expected dividend for next year, the current market price, the expected dividend growth rate, and the beta. The risk-free rate is currently 5.3 percent, and the market risk premium is 6.0 percent.

5.3 + 0.6(6)

Stock	Dividend (D_1)	Price (P_0)	Dividend Growth Rate (g)	Beta (β)
American Electric (NYSE: AEP)	2.40	46.17	5.0%	0.60
Consolidated Edison (NYSE: ED)	2.20	39.80	5.0	0.60
Exelon Corp. (NYSE: EXC)	1.69	64.12	7.0	0.80
Southern Co. (NYSE: SO)	1.34	23.25	5.5	0.65
Dominion Resources (NYSE: D)	2.58	60.13	5.5	0.65

8.9

A. Calculate the expected rate of return for each stock using the Gordon growth model.

B. Calculate the required rate of return for each stock using the CAPM.

9. Vicente Garcia is a buy-side analyst for a large pension fund. He frequently uses dividend discount models such as the Gordon growth model for the consumer non-cyclical stocks that he covers. The current dividend for Procter & Gamble Co. (NYSE: PG) is $1.46, and the dividend eight years ago was $0.585. The current stock price is $80.00.

www.cfainstitute.org/toolkit—Your online preparation resource

A. What is the historical dividend growth rate for Procter & Gamble?

B. Garcia assumes that the future dividend growth rate will be exactly half of the historical rate. What is Procter & Gamble's expected rate of return using the GGM?

C. Garcia uses a beta of 0.53 (computed versus the S&P 500 index) for Procter & Gamble. The risk-free rate of return is 5.56 percent and the equity risk premium is 3.71 percent. If Garcia continues to assume that the future dividend growth rate will be exactly half of the historical rate, what is the value of the stock with the Gordon growth model?

10. NiSource Preferred B (NYSE: NI-B) is a fixed-rate perpetual preferred stock paying a $3.88 annual dividend. If the required rate of return is 7.88 percent, what is the value of one share? If the price of this preferred stock were $46.00, what would be the yield?

11. R. A. Nixon put out a "strong buy" on DuPoTex (DPT). This company has a current stock price of $88.00 per share. The company has sales of $210 million, net income of $3 million, and 300 million outstanding shares. DPT is not paying a dividend. Dorothy Josephson has argued with Nixon that DPT's valuation is excessive relative to its sales, profits, and any reasonable assumptions about future possible dividends. Josephson also asserts that DPT has a market value equal to that of many large blue-chip companies, which it does not deserve. Nixon feels that Josephson's concerns reflect an archaic attitude about equity valuation and a lack of understanding about DPT's industry.

A. What is the total market value of DPT's outstanding shares? What are the price-to-earnings and price-to-sales ratios?

B. Nixon and Josephson have agreed on a scenario for future earnings and dividends for DPT. Their assumptions are that sales grow at 60 percent annually for four years, and then at 7 percent annually thereafter. In Year 5 and thereafter, earnings will be 10 percent of sales. No dividends will be paid for four years, but in Year 5 and after, dividends will be 40 percent of earnings. Dividends should be discounted at a 12 percent rate. What is the value of a share of DPT using the discounted dividend approach to valuation?

C. Nixon and Josephson explore another scenario for future earnings and dividends for DPT. They assume that sales will grow at 7 percent in Year 5 and thereafter. Earnings will be 10 percent of sales, and dividends will be 40 percent of earnings. Dividends will be initiated in Year 5, and dividends should be discounted at 12 percent. What level of sales is required in Year 4 to achieve a discounted dividend valuation equal to the current stock price?

12. Dole Food (NYSE: DOL) has a current dividend of $0.40, which is expected to grow at 7 percent forever. Felipe Rodriguez has estimated the required rate of return for Dole using three methods. The methods and the estimates are as follows:

Bond yield plus risk premium method	$r = 9.6\%$
CAPM method	$r = 11.2\%$
APT method	$r = 10.4\%$

Using the assumed dividend pattern, what is the value of Dole Food using each of the three estimated required rates of return?

13. The CFO of B-to-C Inc., a retailer of miscellaneous consumer products, recently announced the objective of paying its first (annual) cash dividend of $0.50 in four years. Thereafter, the dividend is expected to increase by 7 percent per year for the foreseeable future. The company's required rate of return is 15 percent.

A. Assuming that you have confidence in the CFO's dividend target, what is the value of the stock of B-to-C today?

B. Suppose that you think that the CFO's outlook is too optimistic. Instead, you believe that the first dividend of $0.50 will not be received until six years from now. What is the value of the stock?

14. FPR is expected to pay a $0.60 dividend next year. The dividend is expected to grow at a 50 percent annual rate for Years 2 and 3, at 20 percent annually for Years 4 and 5, and at 5 percent annually for Year 6 and thereafter. If the required rate of return is 12 percent, what is the value per share?

15. EB Systems is selling for $11.40 and is expected to pay a $0.40 dividend next year. The dividend is expected to grow at 15 percent for the following four years, and then at 7 percent annually after Year 5. If purchased at its current price, what is the expected rate of return on EB Systems? Assume price equals value.

16. Hanson PLC (LSE: HNS) is selling for GBP 472. Hansen has a beta of 0.83 against the FTSE 100 index, and the current dividend is GBP 13.80. The risk-free rate of return is 4.66 percent, and the equity risk premium is 4.92 percent. An analyst covering this stock expects the Hanson dividend to grow initially at 14 percent but to decline linearly to 5 percent over a 10-year period. After that, the analyst expects the dividend to grow at 5 percent.

A. Compute the value of the Hanson dividend stream using the H-model. According to the H-model valuation, is Hanson overpriced or underpriced?

B. Assume that Hanson's dividends follow the H-model pattern the analyst predicts. If an investor pays the current GBP 472 price for the stock, what will be the rate of return?

17. [**Adapted from the 1995 CFA Level II Examination**] Your supervisor has asked you to evaluate the relative attractiveness of the stocks of two very similar chemical companies: Litchfield Chemical Corp. (LCC) and Aminochem Company (AOC). AOC and LCC have June 30 fiscal year ends. You have compiled the data in Exhibit P-1 for this purpose. Use a one-year time horizon and assume the following:

EXHIBIT P-1	Selected Data for Litchfield and Aminochem	
	Litchfield Chemical (LCC)	Aminochem (AOC)
Current stock price	$50	$30
Shares outstanding (millions)	10	20
Projected earnings per share (FY 1996)	$4.00	$3.20
Projected dividend per share (FY 1996)	$0.90	$1.60
Projected dividend growth rate	8%	7%
Stock beta	1.2	1.4
Investors' required rate of return	10%	11%
Balance sheet data (millions)		
Long-term debt	$100	$130
Stockholders' equity	$300	$320

▶ Real gross domestic product is expected to rise 5 percent.

▶ S&P 500 expected total return of 20 percent.

▶ U.S. Treasury bills yield 5 percent.

▶ 30-year U.S. Treasury bonds yield 8 percent.

A. Calculate the value of the common stock of LCC and AOC using the constant-growth DDM. Show your work.

B. Calculate the expected return over the next year of the common stock of LCC and AOC using the CAPM. Show your work.

C. Calculate the internal (implied, normalized, or sustainable) growth rate of LCC and AOC. Show your work.

D. Recommend LCC *or* AOC for investment. Justify your choice using your answers to A, B, and C and the information in Exhibit P-1.

18. [**Adapted from the 1999 CFA Level II Examination**] Scott Kelly is reviewing MasterToy's financial statements in order to estimate its sustainable growth rate. Using the information presented in Exhibit P-2,

A. i. Identify the three components of the DuPont formula.

ii. Calculate the ROE for 1999 using the three components of the DuPont formula.

iii. Calculate the sustainable growth rate for 1999.

Kelly has calculated actual and sustainable growth for each of the past four years and finds in each year that its calculated sustainable growth rate substantially exceeds its actual growth rate.

B. Cite one course of action (other than ignoring the problem) Kelly should encourage MasterToy to take, assuming the calculated sustainable growth rate continues to exceed the actual growth rate.

EXHIBIT P-2	Master Toy Inc. Actual 1998 and Estimated 1999 Financial Statements for FY Ending December 31 ($ millions, except per-share data)		
Income Statement	**1998**	**1999e**	**Change (%)**
Revenue	$4,750	$5,140	8.2
Cost of goods sold	$2,400	$2,540	
Selling, general, and administrative	1,400	$1,550	
Depreciation	180	210	
Goodwill amortization	10	10	
Operating income	$760	$830	9.2
Interest expense	20	25	
Income before taxes	$740	$805	
Income taxes	265	295	
Net income	$475	$510	
Earnings per share	$1.79	$1.96	9.5
Average shares outstanding (millions)	265	260	

(Exhibit continued on next page . . .)

EXHIBIT P-2	(continued)		

Balance Sheet	1998	1999e	Change (%)
Cash	$400	$400	
Accounts receivable	680	700	
Inventories	570	600	
Net property, plant, and equipment	800	870	
Intangibles	500	530	
Total assets	$2,950	$3,100	
Current liabilities	$550	$600	
Long-term debt	300	300	
Total liabilities	$850	$900	
Stockholders' equity	2,100	2,200	
Total liabilities and equity	$2,950	$3,100	
Book value per share	$7.92	$8.46	
Annual dividend per share	$0.55	$0.60	

19. **[Adapted from the 2000 CFA Level II Examination]** The management of Telluride, an international diversified conglomerate based in the United States, believes that the recent strong performance of its wholly owned medical supply subsidiary, Sundanci, has gone unnoticed. In order to realize Sundanci's full value, Telluride has announced that it will divest Sundanci in a tax-free spin-off.

Sue Carroll, CFA, is Director of Research at Kesson and Associates. In developing an investment recommendation for Sundanci, Carroll has directed four of her analysts to determine a valuation of Sundanci using various valuation disciplines. To assist her analysts, Carroll has gathered the information shown in Exhibits P-3 and P-4 below.

EXHIBIT P-3	Sundanci Actual 1999 and 2000 Financial Statements for FY Ending May 31 ($ millions, except per-share data)

Income Statement	1999	2000
Revenue	$474	$598
Depreciation	20	23
Other operating costs	368	460
Income before taxes	86	115
Taxes	26	35
Net income	60	80
Dividends	18	24
Earnings per share	$0.714	$0.952
Dividends per share	$0.214	$0.286
Common shares outstanding (millions)	84.0	84.0

(Exhibit continued on next page . . .)

EXHIBIT P-3	(continued)	

Balance Sheet	1999	2000
Current assets	$201	$326
Net property, plant and equipment	474	489
Total assets	675	815
Current liabilities	57	141
Long-term debt	0	0
Total liabilities	57	141
Shareholders' equity	618	674
Total liabilities and equity	675	815
Capital expenditures	34	38

EXHIBIT P-4	Selected Financial Information

Required rate of return on equity	14%
Growth rate of industry	13%
Industry P/E	26

Prior to determining Sundanci's valuation, Carroll analyzes Sundanci's return on equity (ROE) and sustainable growth.

A.　**i.** Calculate the *three* components of ROE in the DuPont formula for the year 2000.

　　ii. Calculate ROE for the year 2000.

　　iii. Calculate the sustainable rate of growth. Show your work.

Carroll learns that Sundanci's Board of Directors is considering the following policy changes that will affect Sundanci's sustainable growth rate:

► Director A proposes an increase in the quarterly dividend by $0.15 per share.

► Director B proposes a bond issue of $25 million, the proceeds of which will be used to increase production capacity.

► Director C proposes a 2-for-1 stock split.

B. Indicate the effect of each of these proposals on Sundanci's sustainable rate of growth, given that the other factors remain unchanged. Identify which components of the sustainable growth model, if any, are directly affected by each proposal.

Helen Morgan, CFA, has been asked by Carroll to determine the potential valuation for Sundanci using the DDM. Morgan anticipates that Sundanci's earnings and dividends will grow at 32 percent for two years and 13 percent thereafter.

C. Calculate the current value of a share of Sundanci stock using a two-stage dividend discount model and the data from Exhibits P-3 and P-4. Show your work.

20. **[Adapted from the 2001 CFA Level II Examination]** Peninsular Research is initiating coverage of a mature manufacturing industry. John Jones, CFA, head of the research department, gathers the information given in Exhibit P-5 to help in his analysis.

EXHIBIT P-5	Fundamental Industry and Market Data
Forecasted industry earnings retention rate	40%
Forecasted industry return on equity	25%
Industry beta	1.2
Government bond yield	6%
Equity risk premium	5%

A. Compute the price to earnings (P_0/E_1) ratio for the industry based on the fundamental data in Exhibit P-5. Show your work.

Jones wants to analyze how fundamental P/Es might differ among countries. He gathers the data given in Exhibit P-6:

EXHIBIT P-6	Economic and Market Data	
Fundamental Factors	**Country A**	**Country B**
Forecasted growth in real gross domestic product	5%	2%
Government bond yield	10%	6%
Equity risk premium	5%	4%

B. Determine whether each of the fundamental factors in Exhibit P-6 would cause P/Es to be generally higher for Country A or higher for Country B. Justify each of your conclusions with one reason. *Note*: Consider each fundamental factor in isolation, with all else remaining equal.

21. **[Adapted from the 1998 CFA Level II Examination]** Janet Ludlow's company requires all its analysts to use a two-stage DDM and the CAPM to value stocks. Using these models, Ludlow has valued QuickBrush Company at $63 per share. She now must value SmileWhite Corporation.

A. Calculate the required rate of return for SmileWhite using the information in Exhibit P-7 and the CAPM. Show your work.

Ludlow estimates the following EPS and dividend growth rates for SmileWhite:

First three years	12% per year
Years thereafter	9% per year

The 1997 dividend per share is $1.72.

B. Estimate the intrinsic value of SmileWhite using the data above and the two-stage DDM. Show your work.

EXHIBIT P-7	Valuation Information: December 1997	
	QuickBrush	**SmileWhite**
Beta	1.35	1.15
Market price	$45.00	$30.00
Intrinsic value	$63.00	?
Notes:		
Risk-free rate	4.50%	
Expected market return	14.50%	

C. Recommend QuickBrush or SmileWhite stock for purchase by comparing each company's intrinsic value with its current market price. Show your work.

D. Describe one strength of the two-stage DDM in comparison with the constant-growth DDM. Describe one weakness inherent in all DDMs.

FREE CASH FLOW VALUATION

by John D. Stowe, Thomas R. Robinson, Jerald E. Pinto, and
Dennis W. McLeavey

LEARNING OUTCOMES

The candidate should be able to:

a. define and interpret free cash flow to the firm (FCFF) and free cash flow to equity (FCFE);

b. describe the FCFF and FCFE approaches to valuation, and contrast the appropriate discount rates for each model and explain the strengths and limitations of the FCFE model;

c. contrast the ownership perspective implicit in the FCFE approach to the ownership perspective implicit in the dividend discount approach;

d. discuss the appropriate adjustments to net income, earnings before interest and taxes (EBIT), earnings before interest, taxes, depreciation, and amortization (EBITDA), or cash flow from operations (CFO) to calculate FCFF and FCFE;

e. calculate FCFF and FCFE given a company's financial statements prepared according to U.S. GAAP or International Accounting Standards;

f. discuss approaches for forecasting FCFF and FCFE;

g. contrast the recognition of value in the FCFE model to the recognition of value in dividend discount models;

h. explain how dividends, share repurchases, share issues, and changes in leverage may affect FCFF and FCFE;

i. critique the use of net income and EBITDA as proxies for cash flow in valuation;

j. discuss the single-stage (stable-growth), two-stage, and three-stage FCFF and FCFE models (including assumptions), and explain the company characteristics that would justify the use of each model;

k. calculate the value of a company using the single-stage, two-stage, and three-stage FCFF and FCFE models;

l. explain how sensitivity analysis can be used in FCFF and FCFE valuations;

m. discuss the approaches for calculating the terminal value in a multi-stage valuation model;

n. describe the characteristics of companies for which the FCFF model is preferred to the FCFE model.

Analysis of Equity Investments: Valuation, by John D. Stowe, Thomas R. Robinson, Jerald E. Pinto, and Dennis W. McLeavey. Copyright © 2002 by AIMR. Reprinted with permission.

347

1   INTRODUCTION TO FREE CASH FLOWS

Discounted cash flow (DCF) valuation views the intrinsic value of a security as the present value of its expected future cash flows. When applied to dividends, the DCF model is the discounted dividend approach or dividend discount model (DDM). This reading extends DCF analysis to value a company and its equity securities by valuing free cash flow to the firm (FCFF) and free cash flow to equity (FCFE). Although dividends are the cash flows actually paid to stockholders, the free cash flow models are based on the cash flows *available* for distribution.

Unlike dividends, FCFF and FCFE are not published and readily available data. Analysts need to compute these quantities from available financial information, which requires a clear understanding of free cash flows as well as the ability to interpret and use the information correctly. Forecasting future free cash flows is also challenging. The analyst's understanding of a company's financial statements, its operations and financing, and its industry and role in the economy can pay real "dividends" as he or she studies a stock. Finding current cash flows and forecasting future cash flows is a rich and challenging exercise. Because of this richness, it is not surprising that many analysts consider free cash flow models to be more useful than dividend discount models.

Analysts like to use free cash flow as return (either FCFF or FCFE) whenever one or more of the following conditions is present:

► the company is not dividend paying;
► the company is dividend paying but dividends differ significantly from the company's capacity to pay dividends;
► free cash flows align with profitability within a reasonable forecast period with which the analyst is comfortable; or
► the investor takes a control perspective.

If an investor can take control of the company (or expects another investor to do so), dividends can be changed substantially, possibly coming closer to the company's capacity to pay dividends. Free cash flows can provide an economically sound basis for valuation.

Common equity can be valued directly using FCFE or indirectly by first computing the value of the firm using a FCFF model and then subtracting the value of non-common-stock capital (usually debt)[1] from FCFF to arrive at the value of equity. The purpose of this reading is to develop the background required to use the FCFF or FCFE approaches to valuing a company's equity. To the extent that

---

[1] A company's suppliers of capital include stockholders, bondholders, and (sometimes) preferred stockholders.

free cash flows are more meaningful than dividends and that analysts have a sound economic basis for their free cash flow estimates, free cash flow models have much potential in practical application.

Section 2 defines the concepts of free cash flow to the firm and free cash flow to equity, and then presents the two valuation models based on discounting of FCFF and FCFE. We also explore the **constant growth models** for valuing FCFF and FCFE, special cases of the general models, in this section. After reviewing the FCFF and FCFE valuation process in Section 2, in Section 3 we turn to the vital task of calculating and forecasting FCFF and FCFE. Section 4 provides more-complicated valuation models and discusses some of the issues associated with their application. Analysts usually value operating assets and nonoperating assets separately and then combine them to find the total value of the firm, an approach described in Section 5.

FCFF AND FCFE VALUATION APPROACHES   2

The purpose of this section is to provide a conceptual understanding of free cash flows and the valuation models based on them. A more detailed accounting treatment of free cash flows and more-complicated valuation models will follow in subsequent sections.

2.1 Defining Free Cash Flow

Free cash flow to the firm is the cash flow available to the company's suppliers of capital after all operating expenses (including taxes) have been paid and necessary investments in working capital (e.g., inventory) and fixed capital (e.g., equipment) have been made. FCFF is the cash flow from operations minus capital expenditures. To calculate FCFF, analysts may use different equations depending on the accounting information available. As mentioned the company's suppliers of capital include common stockholders, bondholders and, sometimes, preferred stockholders.

Free cash flow to equity is the cash flow available to the company's common equity holders after all operating expenses, interest, and principal payments have been paid and necessary investments in working and fixed capital have been made. FCFE is the cash flow from operations minus capital expenditures minus payments to (and plus receipts from) debtholders.

How is free cash flow related to a company's net income, cash flow from operations, and measures such as EBITDA (earnings before interest, taxes, depreciation, and amortization)? This question is important: The analyst must understand the relationship between a company's reported accounting data and free cash flow in order to forecast free cash flow and its expected growth. Although a company reports cash flow from operations (CFO) on the statement of cash flows, CFO is *not* free cash flow. Net income and CFO data can be used, however, in determining a company's free cash flow.

The advantage of FCFF and FCFE is that they can be used in a discounted cash flow framework to value the firm or to value equity. Other earnings measures such as net income, EBIT, EBITDA, or CFO do not have this property because they either double-count or omit cash flows in some way. For example, EBIT and EBITDA are before-tax measures, and the cash flows available to investors (in the firm or in equity of the firm) must be after tax. From the stockholders' perspective, these measures do not account for differing capital structures (the after-tax interest expenses or preferred dividends) or for the funds that bondholders supply to finance investments in operating assets. Moreover, these measures do not account for the reinvestment of cash flows that the company makes in capital assets and working capital to maintain or maximize the long-run value of the firm.

Dealing with free cash flow is more challenging than dealing with dividends because the analyst must integrate the cash flows from the company's operations with those from its investing and financing activities. Because FCFF is the after-tax cash flow going to all investors in the firm, the value of the firm is found by discounting FCFF at the weighted-average cost of capital (WACC). The value of equity is then found by subtracting the value of debt from the value of the firm. On the other hand, FCFE is the cash flow going to common stockholders, so the appropriate risk-adjusted discount rate for FCFE is the required rate of return on equity. This section presents the general form of these two valuation models, the FCFF valuation model and the FCFE valuation model.

Depending on the company being analyzed, an analyst may have reasons to prefer using FCFF or FCFE. If the company's capital structure is relatively stable, FCFE is more direct and simpler to use than FCFF. In the case of a levered company with negative FCFE, however, working with FCFF to value stock may be easier. The analyst would discount FCFF to find the present value of operating assets, add cash and marketable securities to get total firm value, and then subtract the market value of debt to find the intrinsic value of equity. If a company has had a history of leverage changes in the past, a growth rate in FCFF may be more meaningful than an ever-changing growth pattern in FCFE.[2]

2.2 Present Value of Free Cash Flow

The two distinct approaches to valuation using free cash flow are the FCFF valuation approach and the FCFE valuation approach. The general expression for these valuation models is similar to the expression for the general dividend discount model. In that model, the value of a share of stock equals the present value of the dividends from Time 1 through infinity, discounted at the required rate of return for equity.

2.2.1 Present Value of FCFF

The FCFF valuation approach estimates the value of the firm as the present value of future FCFF discounted at the weighted average cost of capital (WACC):

$$\text{Firm value} = \sum_{t=1}^{\infty} \frac{\text{FCFF}_t}{(1 + \text{WACC})^t} \tag{47-1}$$

---

[2] If a company is projected to change its leverage significantly in the future, the analyst may use the **adjusted present value** (APV) approach to valuing the company. In the APV approach, firm value is the sum of the value of the company assuming no use of debt (unlevered firm value), and the net present value of any effects of debt on firm value (such as any tax benefits of using debt and any costs of financial distress). In this approach, we can estimate unlevered company value by discounting FCFF (assuming no debt) at the unlevered cost of equity (the cost of equity assuming no debt). For more details, see Ross, Westerfield, and Jaffe (2002), who explain APV in a capital budgeting context.

Because FCFF is the cash flow available to all suppliers of capital, discounting FCFF using WACC gives the total value of all of the company's capital. The value of equity is the value of the firm minus the market value of its debt:

$$\text{Equity value} = \text{Firm value} - \text{Market value of debt} \qquad \textbf{(47-2)}$$

Dividing the total value of equity by the number of outstanding shares gives the value per share.

The cost of capital is the required rate of return that investors should demand for a cash flow stream like that generated by the company. WACC depends on the risk of these cash flows. The cost of capital is often considered the opportunity cost of the suppliers of capital: If they can invest elsewhere in investments of similar risk, they will not voluntarily invest in a company unless its rate of return can replicate this opportunity cost.

The most common way to estimate the required rate of return for a company's suppliers of capital is to calculate WACC—a weighted average of required rates of return. If the suppliers of capital are creditors and stockholders, the required rates of return for debt and equity are the after-tax required rates of return for this company under current market conditions. The weights used are the proportions of the firm's total market value from each source, debt and equity. The WACC formula is

$$\text{WACC} = \frac{\text{MV(Debt)}}{\text{MV(Debt)} + \text{MV(Equity)}} r_d (1 - \text{Tax rate}) \qquad \textbf{(47-3)}$$
$$+ \frac{\text{MV(Equity)}}{\text{MV(Debt)} + \text{MV(Equity)}} r$$

MV(Debt) and MV(Equity) are the current market values of debt and equity, not their book or accounting values. Dividing MV(Debt) or MV(Equity) by the total market value of the firm, which is MV(Debt) + MV(Equity), gives the proportions of the firm's total capital from debt or equity, respectively. These weights will sum to 1.0.

Because the company's capital structure (the proportions of debt and equity financing) can change over time, WACC may also change over time. In addition, the company's current capital structure may also differ substantially from what it will be in future years. For these reasons, analysts often use *target* weights instead of the current weights when calculating WACC. These target weights incorporate both the analyst's and investors' expectations about the target capital structure that the company will tend to use over time. Target weights provide a good approximation of the WACC for cases in which the current weights misrepresent the company's normal capital structure. Target weights also offer an alternative to using annually changing weights for those companies whose capital structure changes frequently.

The before-tax required return on debt, r_d, is the expected yield to maturity based on the current market value of the company's debt. Multiplying by $(1 - \text{Tax rate})$ gives an after-tax required return on debt. Analysts can choose from several methods to estimate the required return on equity, r, including the capital asset pricing model (CAPM), arbitrage pricing theory, the Gordon growth model, and a build-up method such as the bond yield plus risk premium approach. Because payments to stockholders are usually not tax deductible, no tax adjustment is appropriate for the cost of equity.[3]

---

[3] Beginning with Modigliani and Miller (1958), capital structure and the cost of capital have been extensively researched. In addition to the amount of leverage, corporate tax rates, personal tax rates, information asymmetries, agency problems, and signaling issues affect the cost of capital. See a modern corporate finance textbook, such as Brealey and Myers (2000), for a review of capital structure theory.

2.2.2 Present Value of FCFE

The value of equity can also be found by discounting FCFE at the required rate of return on equity (r):

$$\text{Equity value} = \sum_{t=1}^{\infty} \frac{\text{FCFE}_t}{(1 + r)^t} \qquad \text{(47-4)}$$

Because FCFE is the cash flow remaining for equity holders after all other claims have been satisfied, discounting FCFE by r (the required rate of return on equity) gives the value of the firm's equity. Dividing the total value of equity by the number of outstanding shares gives the value per share.

2.3 Single-Stage FCFF and FCFE Growth Models

In the DDM approach, the Gordon (constant or stable growth) model makes the assumption that dividends grow at a constant rate. Assuming that free cash flows grow at a constant rate results in the single-stage (stable growth) FCFF and FCFE models.

2.3.1 Constant-Growth FCFF Valuation Model

Assume that FCFF grows at a constant rate g, such that FCFF in any period is equal to FCFF in the previous period multiplied by $(1 + g)$:

$$\text{FCFF}_t = \text{FCFF}_{t-1} \times (1 + g)$$

If FCFF grows at a constant rate,

$$\text{Firm value} = \frac{\text{FCFF}_1}{\text{WACC} - g} = \frac{\text{FCFF}_0(1 + g)}{\text{WACC} - g} \qquad \text{(47-5)}$$

Subtracting the market value of debt from the firm value gives the value of equity.

EXAMPLE 1

Using the Constant-Growth FCFF Valuation Model

Cagiati Enterprises has FCFF of 700 million Swiss francs (CHF) and FCFE of CHF620 million. Cagiati's before-tax cost of debt is 5.7 percent and its required rate of return for equity is 11.8 percent. The company expects a target capital structure consisting of 20 percent debt financing and 80 percent equity financing. The tax rate is 33.33 percent, and FCFF is expected to grow forever at 5.0 percent. Cagiati Enterprises has debt outstanding with a market value of CHF2.2 billion and has 200 million outstanding common shares.

What is Cagiati's weighted average cost of capital? What is the total value of Cagiati's equity using the FCFF valuation approach? What is the value per share using this approach?

Solutions: Using Equation 47-3, WACC is

$$\text{WACC} = 0.20(5.7\%)(1 - 0.3333) + 0.80(11.8\%) = 10.2\%$$

The firm value of Cagiati Enterprises is the present value of FCFF discounted using WACC. For FCFF growing at a constant 5 percent rate, the result is

$$\text{Firm value} = \frac{\text{FCFF}_1}{\text{WACC} - g} = \frac{\mathit{FCFF}_0(1 + g)}{\text{WACC} - g} = \frac{700(1.05)}{0.102 - 0.05}$$

$$= \frac{735}{0.052} = \text{CHF}14{,}134.6 \text{ million}$$

The market value of equity is the value of the firm minus the value of debt:

$$\text{Equity value} = \text{CHF}14{,}134.6 \text{ million} - \text{CHF}2{,}200 \text{ million}$$
$$= \text{CHF}11{,}934.6 \text{ million}$$

Dividing by the number of outstanding shares gives the value per share:

$$V_0 = \text{CHF}11{,}934.6 \text{ million}/200 \text{ million shares} = \text{CHF}59.67 \text{ per share}$$

2.3.2 Constant-Growth FCFE Valuation Model

The constant-growth FCFE valuation model assumes that FCFE grows at a constant rate g. FCFE in any period is equal to FCFE in the preceding period multiplied by $(1 + g)$:

$$\text{FCFE}_t = \text{FCFE}_{t-1} \times (1 + g)$$

The value of equity if FCFE is growing at a constant rate is

$$\text{Equity value} = \frac{\text{FCFE}_1}{r - g} = \frac{\text{FCFE}_0(1 + g)}{r - g} \qquad \textbf{(47-6)}$$

The discount rate is r, the required rate of return on equity. Note that the growth rate of FCFF and the growth rate of FCFE are frequently not the same.

FORECASTING FREE CASH FLOW   3

Estimating FCFF or FCFE requires a complete understanding of the company and the financial statements from which those cash flows can be drawn. In order to provide a context for the estimation of FCFF and FCFE, we will first use an extensive example to show the relation between free cash flow and accounting measures of income.

For most of Section 3, we will assume that the company has two sources of capital, debt and common stock. In Section 3.7, we will incorporate preferred stock as a third source of capital. Once the concepts of FCFF and FCFE are understood for a company financed using only debt and common stock, it is easy to incorporate preferred stock for the relatively small number of companies that actually use it.

3.1 Computing FCFF from Net Income

FCFF is the cash flow available to the company's suppliers of capital after all operating expenses (including taxes) have been paid and operating investments have been made. The company's suppliers of capital include bondholders and common stockholders (and occasionally preferred stockholders, which we ignore until later). Understanding that a noncash charge is a charge or expense that does not involve the outlay of cash, the expression for FCFF is as follows:

> FCFF = Net income available to common shareholders
> Plus: Net noncash charges
> Plus: Interest expense × (1 − Tax rate)
> Less: Investment in fixed capital[4]
> Less: Investment in working capital

This equation can be written more compactly as

$$\text{FCFF} = \text{NI} + \text{NCC} + \text{Int}(1 - \text{Tax rate}) - \text{FCInv} - \text{WCInv} \qquad \textbf{(47-4)}$$

Consider each component of FCFF. The starting point in Equation 47-4 is net income available to common shareholders—the bottom line in an income statement. It represents income after depreciation, amortization, interest expense, income taxes, and the payment of dividends to preferred shareholders (but not payment of dividends to common shareholders).

Net noncash charges represent an adjustment for noncash decreases and increases in net income. This adjustment is the first of several that analysts generally perform on a net basis. If noncash decreases in net income exceed the increases, as is usually the case, the adjustment is positive. If noncash increases exceed noncash decreases, the adjustment is negative. The most common noncash charge is depreciation expense. When a company purchases fixed capital such as equipment, the balance sheet reflects a cash outflow at the time of purchase. In subsequent periods, the company records depreciation expense as the asset is used. The depreciation expense reduces net income but is not a cash outflow. Depreciation expense is thus one (the most common) noncash charge that must be added back in computing FCFF. In the case of intangible assets, there is a similar noncash charge, amortization expense, that must also be added back. Other noncash charges vary from company to company and will be discussed in Section 3.3.

After-tax interest expense must be added back to net income to arrive at FCFF. This step is required because interest expense net of the related tax savings was deducted in arriving at net income, and because interest is a cash flow available to one of the company's capital providers. In the United States and

---

[4] In this reading, when we refer to "investment in fixed capital" or "investment in working capital," we are referring to the investments made in the specific period for which the free cash flow is calculated.

many other countries, interest is tax deductible (reduces taxes) for the company and taxable for the recipient. As we shall see later, when we discount FCFF, we do so using an after-tax cost of capital. For consistency, we thus compute FCFF using the after-tax interest paid.[5]

Similar to after-tax interest expense, if a company has preferred stock, dividends on that preferred stock are deducted in arriving at net income available to common shareholders. Because preferred stock dividends are also a cash flow available to one of the company's capital providers, this item is added back to arrive at FCFF. Further discussion of the effects of preferred stock appears in Section 3.7.

Investments in fixed capital represent the outflow of cash necessary to support the company's current and future operations. These investments are capital expenditures for long-term assets such as property, plant, and equipment (PP&E) necessary to support the company. Necessary capital expenditures can also include intangible assets such as trademarks. In the case of cash acquisition of another company in place of a direct acquisition of PP&E, this cash purchase amount can also be treated as a capital expenditure that reduces the company's free cash flow (note that this is the conservative treatment in that it reduces FCFF). In the case of large acquisitions (and all noncash acquisitions), analysts must take care in evaluating the impact on future free cash flow. If a company receives cash in disposing of any of its fixed capital, the analyst must deduct this cash in arriving at investments in fixed capital. For example, suppose we had a sale of equipment for $100,000. This cash inflow reduces the company's cash outflows for investments in fixed capital.

The company's cash flow statement is an excellent source of information on capital expenditures as well as sales of fixed capital. Analysts should be aware that some companies acquire fixed capital without using cash—for example, through an exchange for stock or debt. Such acquisitions do not appear on a company's cash flow statement but, if material, must be disclosed in the footnotes. Although noncash exchanges do not impact historical FCFF, if the capital expenditures are necessary and may be made in cash in the future, the analyst should use this information in forecasting future FCFF.

Last is an important adjustment for net increases in working capital. As noted in our earlier example, this adjustment represents the net investment in current assets, such as accounts receivable, less current liabilities such as accounts payable. Analysts can find this information by examining either the company's balance sheet or the cash flow statement.

Although working capital is often defined as current assets minus current liabilities, working capital for cash flow and valuation purposes is defined to exclude cash and short-term debt (which includes notes payable and the current portion of long-term debt). When finding the net increase in working capital for the purpose of calculating free cash flow, we define working capital to exclude cash and cash equivalents, as well as notes payable and the current portion of long-term debt. Cash and **cash equivalents** are excluded because a change in cash is what we are trying to explain. Notes payable and the current portion of long-term debt are excluded because they are liabilities with explicit interest costs that make them financing, rather than operating, items.

Example 2 shows all of the adjustments to net income required to find FCFF.

---

[5] Note that we could compute WACC on a pretax basis and compute FCFF by adding back interest paid with no tax adjustment. It is critical, however, that analysts be consistent in their measures of FCFF and WACC.

EXAMPLE 2

Calculating FCFF from Net Income

Cane Distribution, Inc., is a distribution company incorporated on 31 December 2000 with initial capital infusions of $224,000 of debt and $336,000 of common stock. This initial capital was immediately invested in fixed capital of $500,000 and working capital of $60,000. Working capital initially consists solely of inventory. The fixed capital consists of nondepreciable property of $50,000 and depreciable property of $450,000. The latter has a 10-year useful life with no salvage value. Tables 1, 2, and 3 provide Cane's financial statements for the three years following incorporation. Starting with net income, calculate Cane's FCFF for each year.

TABLE 1   Cane Distribution, Inc., Income Statement (in thousands)

Years Ending 31 December	2001	2002	2003
Earnings before interest, taxes, depreciation and amortization (EBITDA)	$200.00	$220.00	$242.00
Depreciation expense	45.00	49.50	54.45
Operating income	155.00	170.50	187.55
Interest expense	15.68	17.25	18.97
Income before taxes	139.32	153.25	168.58
Income taxes (at 30%)	41.80	45.97	50.58
Net income	$ 97.52	$107.28	$118.00

TABLE 2   Cane Distribution, Inc., Balance Sheet (in thousands)

Years Ending 31 December	2000	2001	2002	2003
Cash	$ 0.00	$108.92	$228.74	$ 360.54
Accounts receivable	0.00	100.00	110.00	121.00
Inventory	60.00	66.00	72.60	79.86
Current assets	60.00	274.92	411.34	561.40
Fixed assets	500.00	500.00	550.00	605.00
Less: Accumulated depreciation	0.00	45.00	94.50	148.95
Total assets	$560.00	$729.92	$866.84	$1,017.45
Accounts payable	$ 0.00	$ 50.00	$ 55.00	$ 60.50
Current portion of long-term debt	0.00	0.00	0.00	0.00
Current liabilities	0.00	50.00	55.00	60.50
Long-term debt	224.00	246.40	271.04	298.14
Common stock	336.00	336.00	336.00	336.00
Retained earnings	0.00	97.52	204.80	322.80
Total liabilities and equity	$560.00	$729.92	$866.84	$1,017.45

TABLE 3	Cane Distribution, Inc., Working Capital (in thousands)			
Years Ending 31 December	2000	2001	2002	2003
Current assets excluding cash				
Accounts receivable	$ 0.00	$ 100.00	$110.00	$121.00
Inventory	60.00	66.00	72.60	79.86
Total current assets excluding cash	60.00	166.00	182.60	200.86
Current liabilities excluding short-term debt				
Accounts payable	0.00	50.00	55.00	60.50
Working capital	$60.00	$116.00	$127.60	$140.36
Increase in working capital		$56.00	$11.60	$12.76

Solution: Following the logic in Equation 47-7, we calculate FCFF from net income as follows:

Years Ending 31 December	2001	2002	2003
Net income	$97.52	$107.28	$118.00
Plus: Depreciation and amortization	45.00	49.50	54.45
Plus: Interest expense $\times$ (1 − Tax rate)	10.98	12.08	13.28
Less: Investment in fixed capital	0.00	(50.00)	(55.00)
Less: Investment in working capital	(56.00)	(11.60)	(12.76)
Free cash flow to the firm	$97.50	$107.26	$117.97

3.2 Computing FCFF from the Statement of Cash Flows

FCFF is cash flow available to all capital providers (debt and equity). Analysts frequently use cash flow from operations, taken from the statement of cash flows, as a starting point to compute free cash flow because CFO incorporates adjustments for noncash expenses (such as depreciation and amortization) as well as for net investments in working capital.

In a statement of cash flows, cash flows are separated into three components: cash flow from operating activities (or cash flows from operations), cash flows from investing activities, and cash flows from financing activities. Cash flow from operations, which we abbreviate CFO, is the net amount of cash provided from operating activities. The operating section of the cash flow statement shows cash flows related to operating activities, such as cash received from customers and cash paid to suppliers. Investing activities relate to the company's investments in

EXHIBIT 1	U.S. GAAP versus IAS Treatment of Interest and Dividends	
	U.S. GAAP	**IAS**
Interest received	Operating	Operating or Investing
Interest paid	Operating	Operating or Financing
Dividends received	Operating	Operating or Investing
Dividends paid	Financing	Operating or Financing

(or sales of) long-term assets, particularly PP&E and long-term investments in other companies. Financing activities relate to the raising or repayment of the company's capital. Interestingly, under U.S. GAAP, interest expense paid to debt capital providers must be classified as part of cash flow from operations (as is interest income), although payment of dividends to equity capital providers is classified as a financing activity. International Accounting Standards (IAS), on the other hand, allow the company to classify interest paid as either an operating or financing activity. Further, IAS allow dividends paid to be classified as either an operating or financing activity. Exhibit 1 summarizes U.S. GAAP and IAS treatment of interest and dividends:

To estimate FCFF by starting with CFO, we must recognize the treatment of interest paid. If, as with U.S. GAAP, the after-tax interest expense was taken out of net income and out of CFO, after-tax interest expense must be added back in order to get FCFF. In the U.S. case, FCFF can be estimated as follows:

Free cash flow to the firm = Cash flow from operations
Plus: Interest expense $\times$ (1 − Tax rate)
Less: Investment in fixed capital

or

$$FCFF = CFO + Int(1 - \text{Tax rate}) - FCInv \qquad (47\text{-}8)$$

The after-tax interest expense is added back because it was previously taken out of net income. The investment in working capital does not appear in Equation 47-8 because CFO already includes investment in working capital. The following example illustrates the calculation of FCFF using CFO.

EXAMPLE 3

Calculating FCFF from CFO

Use the information from the statement of cash flows given in Table 4 to calculate FCFF for the three years.

TABLE 4 Cane Distribution, Inc., Statement of Cash Flows (in thousands) Indirect Method

Years Ending 31 December	2001	2002	2003
Cash flow from operations			
Net income	$ 97.52	$107.28	$118.00
Plus: Depreciation	45.00	49.50	54.45
Increase in accounts receivable	(100.00)	(10.00)	(11.00)
Increase in inventory	(6.00)	(6.60)	(7.26)
Increase in accounts payable	50.00	5.00	5.50
Cash flow from operations	86.52	145.18	159.69
Cash flow from investing activities			
Purchases of PP&E	0.00	(50.00)	(55.00)
Cash flow from financing activities			
Borrowing (repayment)	22.40	24.64	27.10
Total cash flow	108.92	119.82	131.80
Beginning cash	0.00	108.92	228.74
Ending cash	$108.92	$228.74	$360.54

Notes:
Cash paid for interest	($15.68)	($17.25)	($18.97)
Cash paid for taxes	($41.80)	($45.98)	($50.57)

Solution: As shown in Equation 47-8, FCFF equals CFO plus after-tax interest minus the investment in fixed capital.

Years Ending 31 December	2001	2002	2003
Cash flow from operations	86.52	145.18	159.69
Plus: Interest expense $\times$ (1 − Tax rate)	10.98	12.08	13.28
Less: Investment in fixed capital	0.00	(50.00)	(55.00)
Free cash flow to the firm	97.50	107.26	117.97

3.3 Noncash Charges

The best place to find historical noncash charges is in the company's statement of cash flows. If an analyst wants to use an add-back method, as in FCFF = NI + NCC + Int(1 − Tax rate) − FCInv − WCInv, the analyst should verify the noncash charges to ensure that the FCFF estimate provides a reasonable basis for forecasting. As one example, restructuring charges can involve cash expenditures and noncash charges. For example, severance pay for laid-off employees could be a cash restructuring charge. On the other hand, a write-down in the value of assets as part of a restructuring charge is a noncash item.

EXAMPLE 4

An Examination of Noncash Charges

An analyst is attempting to verify Motorola, Inc.'s historical FCFF as a basis for forecasting. Excerpts from the operating section of Motorola's 1999 statement of cash flow are given in Exhibit 2:

EXHIBIT 2	Statement of Cash Flows for Motorola (in millions)		
Years Ending 31 December	**1997**	**1998**	**1999**
Net income (loss)	$1,180	$(962)	$817
Adjustments to reconcile net income (loss) to net cash provided by operating activities:			
Restructuring and other charges	327	1,980	(226)
Iridium charges	178	360	2,119
Depreciation	2,329	2,197	2,182
Deferred income taxes	(98)	(933)	(415)
Amortization of debt discount and issue costs	10	11	11
Gain on disposition of investments and businesses, net of acquisition charges	(116)	(146)	(1,034)
Change in assets and liabilities, net of effects of acquisitions and dispositions:			
Accounts receivable	(812)	(238)	15
Inventories	(880)	254	(661)
Other current assets	(114)	31	(30)
Accounts payable and accrued liabilities	698	(753)	270
Other assets and liabilities	(106)	(780)	(1,120)
Net cash provided by operating activities	$2,596	$1,021	$1,928

Note that in arriving at cash provided by operating activities, Motorola added back "restructuring and other charges" in 1997 and 1998. This item represents the noncash portion of such charges deducted in arriving at net income for those years. In calculating historical FCFF beginning with net income, the analyst would add back the full amount of this item because the item represents noncash charges. For example, for 1998, the full amount of $1,980 million restructuring and other charges should be added back in computing historical FCFF for that year. Asset impairments and losses on asset sales represented the majority of restructuring and other charges for 1998, according to Motorola's financial statements. Motorola's financial statements also disclosed that about $658 million of the $1,980 million restructuring and other charges for 1998 represented an accrual of future employee separation costs.[6]

In contrast to asset impairments and losses on asset sales, which do not represent cash outflows in the current or future years, the $658 million accrual relates to cash outflows in subsequent years. As employees separate from employment with Motorola in subsequent years, Motorola would realize these cash separation expenses, which would result in lower CFO and FCFF in those years. From the perspective of 1998, if the analyst were to use the level of historical FCFF for 1998 to forecast subsequent FCFF, his FCFF forecasts might be biased upward because some of the accrual of separation expenses added back when computing 1998 FCFF would be realized as cash expenses in 1999 and beyond. From the perspective of 1998, the analyst's FCFF forecasts should reflect his expectations concerning the future realization of cash separation expenses.

As noted in Footnote 6, noncash restructuring charges can also cause an increase in net income in some circumstances. Gains and losses are another noncash item that can either increase or decrease net noncash charges. If a company sells a piece of equipment with a book value of $60,000 for $100,000, it reports the $40,000 gain as part of net income. The $40,000 gain is not a cash flow, however, and must be subtracted in arriving at FCFF. Note that the $100,000 is a cash flow and is part of the company's net investment in fixed capital. A loss reduces net income and thus must be added back in arriving at FCFF. Aside from depreciation gains and losses are the most commonly seen noncash charges that require an adjustment to net income. Analysts should examine the company's cash flow statement to identify items particular to a company and to determine what analyst adjustments might be needed to make the accounting numbers useful for forecasting purposes.

Table 5 summarizes the common noncash charges that impact net income and indicates for each item whether to add it to or subtract it from net income in arriving at FCFF.

TABLE 5   Noncash Items and FCFF

Noncash Item	Adjustment to NI to Arrive at FCFF
Depreciation	Added back
Amortization of intangibles	Added back
Restructuring charges (expense)	Added back
Restructuring charges (income resulting from reversal)	Subtracted
Losses	Added back
Gains	Subtracted
Amortization of long-term bond discounts	Added back
Amortization of long-term bond premiums	Subtracted
Deferred taxes	Added back but warrants special attention

[6] In 1999 Motorola reversed $226 million of the $1,980 million accrual of restructuring and other charges, increasing reported net income by that amount; as a noncash addition to net income, the amount of $226 million must be subtracted to arrive at historical CFO and FCFF for 1999. In 1999, therefore, we see $226 million as a deduction from net income to arrive at CFO, in Motorola's statement of cash flows.

The case of deferred taxes requires special attention. Deferred taxes result from differences in the timing of reporting income and expenses on the company's financial statements and the company's tax return. The income tax expense deducted in arriving at net income for financial reporting purposes is not the same as the amount of cash taxes paid. Over time, these differences between book and taxable income should offset each other and have no impact on aggregate cash flows. If the analyst's purpose is forecasting and he seeks to identify the persistent components of FCFF, then it is not appropriate to add back deferred tax changes that are expected to reverse in the near future. In some circumstances, however, a company may be able to consistently defer taxes until a much later date. If a company is growing and has the ability to indefinitely defer tax liability, an analyst adjustment (add-back) to net income is warranted. An acquirer must be aware, however, that these taxes may be payable at some time in the future.

Conversely, companies often record expenses for financial reporting purposes (e.g., restructuring charges) that are not deductible for tax purposes. In this instance, current tax payments are higher than reported on the income statement, resulting in a deferred tax asset and a subtraction from net income to arrive at cash flow on the cash flow statement. If the deferred tax asset is expected to reverse (e.g., through tax depreciation deductions) in the near future, the analyst would not want to subtract the deferred tax asset in his cash flow forecast to avoid underestimating future cash flows. On the other hand, if the company is expected to have these charges on a continual basis, a subtraction is warranted to lower the forecast of future cash flows.

Employee stock options provide another challenge. Current accounting standards do not require that an expense be recorded in arriving at net income for options provided to employees. Employee options also do not create any operating cash outflow because no cash changes hands when they are granted. When the employee exercises the option, however, the company receives some cash for the **strike price**. This cash flow is considered a financing cash flow. Also, in some cases, a company may receive a tax benefit from issuing options that increases operating cash flow but not net income[7]. If these cash flows are not expected to persist in the future, analysts should not include them in their forecast of cash flows. An analyst should consider the impact of stock options on the number of shares outstanding. When computing equity value, the analyst may want to use the number of shares expected to be outstanding based on the exercise of employee stock options rather than use currently outstanding shares.

EXAMPLE 5

A Further Examination of Noncash Charges

Consider the following cash flow statement of Dell Computer (Nasdaq NMS: DELL) in order to forecast Dell's future cash flows. The special charges relate to restructuring charges and purchased research and development expenses.

---

[7] For a more detailed discussion of the tax versus accounting treatment of employee stock option plans, see Phillips, Munter, and Robinson (2002).

Years Ending	29 Jan 1999	28 Jan 2000	2 Feb 2001
Cash flows from operating activities:			
Net income	$1,460	$1,666	$2,177
Adjustments to reconcile net income to net cash provided by operating activities:			
Depreciation and amortization	103	156	240
Tax benefits of employee stock plans	444	1,040	929
Special charges	—	194	105
Gain on sale of investments	(9)	(80)	(307)
Other	20	56	109
Changes in:			
Operating working capital	367	812	671
Non-current assets and liabilities	51	82	271
Net cash provided by operating activities	$2,436	$3,926	$4,195

How would you use the tax benefits of employee stock option plans, special charges, and the gain on sale of investments as noncash charges when using the add-back method to calculate free cash flows starting from net income?

Solution: You should make a positive adjustment (add back) to net income for depreciation and amortization, and for special charges. The gain on sale of investments should be subtracted because this gain is included in net income but does not generate operating cash flow. The tax benefits of employee stock plans resulted from the company's ability to deduct the value of options, which were considered taxable to employees. During this three-year period, Dell's stock price rose dramatically, which made employee exercise attractive. In the future, after February 2001, it is unlikely that Dell will continue to achieve this unusual operating cash flow. An analyst would probably not make this last adjustment to net income in forecasting free cash flow.

3.4 Computing FCFE from FCFF

FCFE is cash flow available to equity holders only. It is thus necessary to reduce FCFF by interest paid to debtholders and to add any net increase in borrowing[8] (subtract any net decrease in borrowing).

Free cash flow to equity = Free cash flow to the firm
Less: Interest Expense × (1 − Tax rate)
Plus: Net Borrowing

[8] Net borrowing is **net debt** issued less debt repayments over the period for which we are calculating free cash flow.

or

$$\text{FCFE} = \text{FCFF} - \text{Int}(1 - \text{Tax rate}) + \text{Net borrowing} \qquad \textbf{(47-9)}$$

As Equation 47-9 shows, FCFE is found by starting from FCFF and subtracting after-tax interest expenses and adding net new borrowing. Conversely, the analyst can also find FCFF from FCFE by making the opposite adjustments—by adding after-tax interest expenses and subtracting net borrowing: FCFF = FCFE + Int(1 − Tax rate) − Net borrowing.

Table 6 shows the calculation of FCFE starting with FCFF. For the Cane Distribution Company in Example 3, FCFE is as follows:

TABLE 6 Calculating FCFE from FCFF			
Years Ending 31 December	**2001**	**2002**	**2003**
Free cash flow to the firm	97.50	107.26	117.97
Less: Interest paid × (1 − Tax rate)	(10.98)	(12.08)	(13.28)
Plus: New debt borrowing	22.40	24.64	27.10
Less: Debt repayment	0	0	0
Free cash flow to equity	108.92	119.82	131.79

As stated earlier, FCFE is the cash flow available to common stockholders—the remaining cash flow after all operating expenses (including taxes) have been paid, capital investments have been made, and other transactions with other suppliers of capital have been made. The company's other capital suppliers include creditors, such as bondholders, and preferred stockholders. The cash flows (net of taxes) that have been transacted with creditors and preferred stockholders are deducted from FCFF to arrive at FCFE.

FCFE is the amount that the company can afford to pay out as dividends. In actuality, companies often pay out substantially more or substantially less than FCFE for many reasons, so FCFE often differs from dividends paid. One reason for this difference is that the dividend decision is a discretionary decision of the board of directors. Most corporations "manage" their dividends, preferring to raise them gradually over time, in part because they are very reluctant to cut dividends. Consequently, earnings are much more volatile than dividends. Companies often raise dividends slowly even when their earnings are increasing rapidly, and companies often maintain their current dividends even when their profitability has declined.

In Equations 47-7 and 47-8 above, we showed the calculation of FCFF starting with net income and cash flow from operations, respectively. As Equation 47-9 shows, FCFE = FCFF − Int(1 − Tax rate) + Net borrowing. By subtracting after-tax interest expense and adding net borrowing to Equations 47-7 and 47-8, we then have equations to calculate FCFE starting with net income or CFO, respectively:

$$\text{FCFE} = \text{NI} + \text{NCC} - \text{FCInv} - \text{WCInv} + \text{Net borrowing} \qquad \textbf{(47-10)}$$

$$\text{FCFE} = \text{CFO} - \text{FCInv} + \text{Net borrowing} \qquad \textbf{(47-11)}$$

EXAMPLE 6

Adjusting Net Income or CFO to Find FCFF and FCFE

The balance sheet, income statement, and statement of cash flows for the Pitts Corporation are shown in Table 7. The Pitts Corporation has net income of $240 million in 2003. Show the calculations required to do each of the following:

1. Calculate FCFF starting with the net income figure.
2. Calculate FCFE starting from the FCFF calculated in Part 1.
3. Calculate FCFE starting with the net income figure.
4. Calculate FCFF starting with CFO.
5. Calculate FCFE starting with CFO.

TABLE 7 Financial Statements for Pitts Corporation (in millions, except for per-share data)

Balance Sheet Year Ended	31 December 2002	2003
Assets		
Current assets		
Cash and equivalents	$ 190	$ 200
Accounts receivable	560	600
Inventory	410	440
Total current assets	1,160	1,240
Gross fixed assets	2,200	2,600
Accumulated depreciation	(900)	(1,200)
Net fixed assets	1,300	1,400
Total assets	$2,460	$2,640
Liabilities and shareholders' equity		
Current liabilities		
Accounts payable	$ 285	$ 300
Notes payable	200	250
Accrued taxes and expenses	140	150
Total current liabilities	625	700
Long-term debt	865	890
Common stock	100	100
Additional paid-in capital	200	200
Retained earnings	670	750
Total shareholders' equity	970	1,050
Total liabilities and shareholders' equity	$2,460	$2,640

(Table continued on next page . . .)

TABLE 7   (continued)

Statement of Income

Year Ended	31 December 2003
Total revenues	$3,000
Operating costs and expenses	2,200
EBITDA	800
Depreciation	300
Operating income (EBIT)	500
Interest expense	100
Income before tax	400
Taxes (at 40 percent)	160
Net income	240
Dividends	160
Change in retained earnings	80
Earnings per share	$ 0.48
Dividends per share	$ 0.32

Statement of Cash Flows

Year Ended	31 December 2003
Operating activities	
Net income	$240
Adjustments	
Depreciation	300
Changes in working capital	
Accounts receivable	(40)
Inventories	(30)
Accounts payable	15
Accrued taxes and expenses	10
Cash provided by operating activities	$495
Investing activities	
Purchases of fixed assets	400
Cash used for investing activities	$400
Financing activities	
Notes payable	(50)
Long-term financing issuances	(25)
Common stock dividends	160
Cash used for financing activities	$85
Cash and equivalents increase (decrease)	10
Cash and equivalents at beginning of year	190
Cash and equivalents at end of year	$200
Supplemental cash flow disclosures	
Interest paid	$100
Income taxes paid	$160

Solution to 1: The analyst can use Equation 47-7 to find FCFF from net income.

Net income available to common shareholders	$240
Plus: Net noncash charges	+300
Plus: Interest expense × (1 − Tax rate)	+60
Less: Investment in fixed capital	−400
Less: Investment in working capital	−45
Free cash flow to the firm	$155

This equation can also be written as

$$FCFF = NI + NCC + Int(1 - Tax\ rate) - FCInv - WCInv$$
$$FCFF = \$240 + 300 + 60 - 400 - 45 = \$155\ million$$

Some of these items need explanation. Capital spending is $400 million, which is the increase in gross fixed assets shown on the balance sheet as well as capital expenditures shown as an investing activity on the statement of cash flows. The increase in working capital is $45 million, which is the increase in accounts receivable of $40 million ($600 million − $560 million) plus the increase in inventories of $30 million ($440 million − $410 million) minus the increase in accounts payable of $15 million ($300 million − $285 million) minus the increase in accrued taxes and expenses of $10 million ($140 million − $130 million). When finding the increase in working capital, we ignore cash because the change in cash is what we are calculating. Furthermore, we also ignore short-term debt, such as notes payable, because it is part of the capital provided to the company and is not considered an operating item. The after-tax interest cost is the interest expense times (1 − Tax rate), or $100 million × (1 − 0.40) = $60 million. The values of the remaining items in Equation 47-7 can be taken directly from the financial statements.

Solution to 2: Finding FCFE from FCFF can be done with Equation 47-9:

Free cash flow to the firm	$155
Less: Interest expense × (1 − Tax rate)	−60
Plus: Net borrowing	+75
Free cash flow to equity	$170

Or, using

$$FCFE = FCFF - Int(1 - Tax\ rate) + Net\ borrowing$$
$$FCFE = 155 - 60 + 75 = \$170\ million$$

Solution to 3: The analyst can use Equation 47-10 to find FCFE from NI.

Net income available to common shareholders	$240
Plus: Net noncash charges	+300
Less: Investment in fixed capital	−400
Less: Investment in working capital	−45
Plus: Net borrowing	+75
Free cash flow to equity	$170

Or, using the equation

$$FCFE = NI + NCC - FCInv - WCInv + Net\ borrowing$$
$$FCFE = 240 + 300 - 400 - 45 + 75 = \$170\ million$$

Because notes payable increased by 50 (250 − 200) and long-term debt increased by 25 (890 − 865), net borrowing is 75

Solution to 4: Equation 47-8 can be used to find FCFF from CFO.

Cash flow from operations	$495
Plus: Interest expense × (1 − Tax rate)	+ 60
Less: Investment in fixed capital	−400
Free cash flow to the firm	$155

or

$$FCFF = CFO + Int(1 - Tax\ rate) - FCInv$$
$$FCFF = 495 + 60 - 400 = \$155\ million$$

Solution to 5: Equation 47-11 can be used to find FCFE from CFO.

Cash flow from operations	$495
Less: Investment in fixed capital	−400
Plus: Net borrowing	75
Free cash flow to equity	$170

or

$$FCFF = CFO - FCInv + Net\ borrowing$$
$$FCFF = 495 - 400 + 75 = \$170\ million$$

FCFE is usually less than FCFF; in this example, however, FCFE ($170 million) exceeds FCFF ($155 million) because external borrowing was large during this year.

3.5 Finding FCFF and FCFE from EBIT or EBITDA

FCFF and FCFE are most frequently calculated from a starting basis of net income or CFO (as shown above in Sections 3.1 and 3.2). Two other starting points are EBIT or EBITDA from the income statement.

To show the relationship between EBIT and FCFF, we start with Equation 47-7 and assume that the only noncash charge (NCC) is depreciation (Dep):

$$FCFF = NI + Dep + Int(1 - Tax\ rate) - FCInv - WCInv$$

Net income (NI) can be expressed as

$$NI = (EBIT - Int)(1 - Tax\ rate) = EBIT(1 - Tax\ rate) - Int(1 - Tax\ rate)$$

Substituting this equation for NI in Equation 47-7, we have

$$FCFF = EBIT(1 - \text{Tax rate}) + Dep - FCInv - WCInv \qquad \textbf{(47-12)}$$

To get FCFF from EBIT, we multiply EBIT by $(1 - \text{Tax rate})$, add back depreciation, and then subtract the investments in fixed capital and working capital.

It is also easy to show the relation between FCFF from EBITDA. Net income can be expressed as

$$NI = (EBITDA - Dep - Int)(1 - \text{Tax rate}) = EBITDA(1 - \text{Tax rate}) - Dep(1 - \text{Tax rate}) - Int(1 - \text{Tax rate})$$

Substituting this equation for NI in Equation 47-7 results in

$$FCFF = EBITDA(1 - \text{Tax rate}) + Dep(\text{Tax rate}) - FCInv - WCInv \qquad \textbf{(47-13)}$$

FCFF equals EBITDA times $(1 - \text{Tax rate})$ plus depreciation times the tax rate minus the investments in fixed capital and working capital. In comparing Equations 47-12 and 47-13, note the difference in the handling of depreciation.

Many noncash charge adjustments required to calculate FCFF based on net income are not required when starting from EBIT or EBITDA. In the calculation of net income, many noncash charges are made after computing EBIT or EBITDA, so they do not need to be added back when calculating FCFF based on EBIT or EBITDA. Another important consideration is that some noncash charges, such as depreciation, are tax deductible. A noncash charge that affects taxes must be accounted for. In summary, whether an adjustment for a noncash charge is needed depends on where in the income statement it has been deducted and whether the noncash charge is a tax-deductible expense.

It is also possible to calculate FCFE (instead of FCFF) from EBIT or EBITDA. An easy way to obtain FCFE from EBIT or EBITDA is to derive FCFF using Equation 47-12 or 47-13, and then subtract $Int(1 - \text{Tax rate})$ and add net borrowing to end up with FCFE:[9]

$$FCFE = FCFF - Int(1 - \text{Tax rate}) + \text{Net borrowing}$$

Example 7 uses the Pitts Corporation financial statements to find FCFF and FCFE from EBIT and EBITDA.

---

[9] It is also possible to derive equations for FCFE as a function of EBIT or EBITDA. To do so, start with the equation for FCFE as a function of NI (Equation 47-10), again making the assumption that the only noncash charge is depreciation: FCFE = NI + Dep − FCInv − WCInv + Net borrowing. Substituting NI = EBIT(1 − Tax rate) − Int(1 − Tax rate) and NI = EBITDA(1 − Tax rate) − Dep(1 − Tax rate) − Int(1 − Tax rate) into Equation 47-10 yields two equations for FCFE as a function of EBIT or EBITDA, respectively:

FCFE = EBIT(1 − Tax rate) − Int(1 − Tax rate) + Dep − FCInv − WCInv + Net borrowing

FCFE = EBITDA(1 − Tax rate) + Dep(Tax rate) − Int(1 − Tax rate) − FCInv − WCInv + Net borrowing

---

EXAMPLE 7

Adjusting EBIT and EBITDA to Find FCFF and FCFE

The Pitts Corporation (financial statements provided in Example 6) has EBIT of \$500 million and EBITDA of \$800 million. Show the adjustments that would be required to find FCFF and FCFE:

1. starting from EBIT, and

2. starting from EBITDA.

Solution to 1: To get FCFF from EBIT using Equation 47-12:

EBIT(1 − Tax rate) = 500(1 − 0.40)	\$300
Plus: Net noncash charges	300
Less: Net investment in fixed capital	−400
Less: Net increase in working capital	−45
Free cash flow to the firm	\$155

or

$$\text{FCFF} = \text{EBIT}(1 - \text{Tax rate}) + \text{Dep} - \text{FCInv} - \text{WCInv}$$
$$\text{FCFF} = 500(1 - 0.40) + 300 - 400 - 45 = \$155 \text{ million}$$

To obtain FCFE, make the appropriate adjustments to FCFF:

$$\text{FCFE} = \text{FCFF} - \text{Int}(1 - \text{Tax rate}) + \text{Net borrowing}$$
$$\text{FCFE} = 155 - 100(1 - 0.40) + 75 = \$170 \text{ million}$$

Solution to 2: To obtain FCFF from EBITDA using Equation 47-13:

EBITDA(1 − Tax rate) = 800(1 − 0.40)	\$480
Plus: Depreciation(Tax rate) = 300(0.40)	120
Less: Net investment in fixed capital	−400
Less: Net increase in working capital	−45
Free cash flow to the firm	\$155

or

$$\text{FCFF} = \text{EBITDA}(1 - \text{Tax rate}) + \text{Dep}(\text{Tax rate}) - \text{FCInv} - \text{WCInv}$$
$$\text{FCFF} = 800(1 - 0.40) + 300(0.40) - 400 - 45 = \$155 \text{ million}$$

Again, to obtain FCFE, make the appropriate adjustments to FCFF:

$$\text{FCFE} = \text{FCFF} - \text{Int}(1 - \text{Tax rate}) + \text{Net borrowing}$$
$$\text{FCFE} = 155 - 100(1 - 0.40) + 75 = \$170 \text{ million}$$

3.6 Forecasting FCFF and FCFE

Computing FCFF and FCFE based on historical accounting data is relatively straightforward. Often, these data are then used directly in a single-stage DCF valuation model. On other occasions, an analyst may desire to forecast future FCFF or FCFE directly. In this case, the analyst must forecast the individual components of free cash flow. This section extends our previous presentation on computing FCFF and FCFE to the more complex task of forecasting FCFF and FCFE. We present FCFF and FCFE valuation models in the next section. Given the variety of ways to derive free cash flow on a historical basis, it should come as no surprise that several methods exist for forecasting free cash flow. One approach is to calculate historical free cash flow and apply some constant growth rate. This approach would be appropriate if a company's free cash flow tended to grow at a constant rate and if historical relationships between free cash flow and fundamental factors were expected to be maintained.

EXAMPLE 8

Constant Growth in FCFF

Use Pitts Corporation data to compute its FCFF for the next three years. Assume growth in FCFF remains at historical levels of 15 percent a year.

	2003A	2004E	2004E	2005E
FCFF	155.00	178.25	204.99	235.74

A more complex approach is to forecast the components of free cash flow. This approach can better capture the complex relationships among the components. For example, one popular method[10] is to forecast the individual components of free cash flow—EBIT(1 − Tax rate), net noncash charges, investment in fixed capital, and investment in working capital. EBIT can be forecasted directly or by forecasting sales and the company's EBIT margin based on an analysis of historical data and the current and expected economic environment. Similarly, analysts can examine the historical relationship between increases in sales and investments in fixed and working capital.

In the case of investments in fixed capital, a popular shortcut method is to combine net noncash charges and investments in fixed capital. This approach works well when the only noncash charge to be added back is depreciation expense. In this approach, FCFF is calculated by forecasting EBIT(1 − Tax rate) and subtracting incremental fixed capital expenditures and incremental working capital expenditures.[11] In order to estimate FCInv and WCInv, we multiply their past proportion to sales' increases by the forecasted sales' increases. Incremental fixed capital expenditures as a proportion of sales increases are computed as follows:

$$\frac{\text{Capital expenditures} - \text{Depreciation expense}}{\text{Increase in sales}}$$

---

[10] See Rappaport (1997) for a variation of this model.
[11] See Rappaport (1997).

Similarly, incremental working capital expenditures as a proportion of sales increases are

$$\frac{\text{Increase in working capital}}{\text{Increase in sales}}$$

When depreciation is the only significant net noncash charge, this method yields the same results as the previous equations for estimating FCFF or FCFE. Rather than adding back all depreciation and subtracting all capital expenditures when starting with EBIT(1 − Tax rate), this approach simply subtracts the **net capital expenditures** in excess of depreciation.

Although it may not be obvious, this approach recognizes that capital expenditures have two components: those expenditures necessary to maintain existing capacity (fixed capital replacement) and those incremental expenditures necessary for growth. In forecasting, the former are likely to be related to the current level of sales and the latter are likely related to the forecast of sales growth.

When forecasting FCFE, analysts often make an assumption that there is a target ratio of debt financing. They often assume that a specified percentage of the net new investment in fixed capital (new fixed capital minus depreciation) and of the increase in working capital is financed with a target ratio of debt. This leads to a simplification of FCFE calculations. Recalling Equation 47-10 and assuming that depreciation is the only noncash charge, Equation 47-10, FCFE = NI + NCC − FCInv − WCInv + Net borrowing, becomes

$$\text{FCFE} = \text{NI} - (\text{FCInv} - \text{Dep}) - \text{WCInv} + \text{Net borrowing}$$

Note that FCInv − Dep represents the incremental fixed capital expenditure net of depreciation. By assuming a target debt ratio (DR), we eliminate the need to forecast net borrowing and can use the expression

$$\text{Net borrowing} = \text{DR}\,(\text{FCInv} - \text{Dep}) + \text{DR} \times \text{WCInv}$$

Using this expression, we do not need to forecast debt issuance and repayment on an annual basis to estimate net borrowing. Equation 47-10 then becomes

$$\text{FCFE} = \text{NI} - (\text{FCInv} - \text{Dep}) - \text{WCInv} + (\text{DR})(\text{FCInv} - \text{Dep}) + (\text{DR})(\text{WCInv})$$

or

$$\text{FCFE} = \text{NI} - (1 - \text{DR})(\text{FCInv} - \text{Dep}) - (1 - \text{DR})(\text{WCInv}) \quad \textbf{(47-14)}$$

We again assume that the only noncash charge is depreciation.

EXAMPLE 9

Free Cash Flow Tied to Sales

At the end of 2003, Carla Espinosa is an analyst following Pitts Corporation. Assume from Example 6 that the company's sales for 2003 are $3,000 million. Espinosa expects Pitts Corporation's sales to increase by

10 percent a year thereafter. Furthermore, Pitts is a stable company in many respects, and Espinosa expects it to maintain its historical EBIT margin and proportions of incremental investments in fixed and working capital. Sales in the previous year grew by $300 million. Pitts Corporation's EBIT for 2003 is $500 million; its EBIT margin is 16.67 percent (500/3000), and its tax rate is 40 percent.

Incremental fixed capital investment in the previous year was

(Capital expenditures − Depreciation expense)/(Increase in sales)

or

(400 − 300)/(300) = 33.33%

Incremental working capital investment in the past year was

(Increase in working capital)/(Increase in sales)

45/300 = 15%

So for every $100 increase in sales, Pitts Corporation invests $33.33 in new equipment in addition to replacement of depreciated equipment and $15 in working capital. Espinosa forecasts FCFF for 2004 as shown below:

Sales	$3,300	Up 10%
EBIT	550	16.67% of sales
EBIT(1 − Tax rate)	330	Adjusted for 40% tax rate
Incremental FC	(100)	33.33% of sales increase
Incremental WC	(45)	15% of sales increase
FCFF	$ 185	

This model can be used to forecast multiple periods and is flexible enough to allow varying sales growth rates, EBIT margins, tax rates, and incremental capital increase rates.

EXAMPLE 10

Free Cash Flow Growth Tied to Sales Growth

Continuing her work, Espinosa wants to forecast FCFF for the next five years. Espinosa is concerned that Pitts will not be able to maintain its historical EBIT margin and that the EBIT margin will decline from the current 16.67 percent to 14.5 percent in the next five years. Table 8 summarizes her forecasts.

TABLE 8   Free Cash Flow Growth for Pitts Corporation

	Year 1	Year 2	Year 3	Year 4	Year 5
Sales growth	10.00%	10.00%	10.00%	10.00%	10.00%
EBIT margin	16.67%	16.00%	15.50%	15.00%	14.50%
Tax rate	40.00%	40.00%	40.00%	40.00%	40.00%
Incremental FC investment	33.33%	33.33%	33.33%	33.33%	33.33%
Incremental WC investment	15.00%	15.00%	15.00%	15.00%	15.00%
Prior year sales	3,000.00				
Sales forecast	3,300.00	3,630.00	3,993.00	4,392.30	4,831.53
EBIT forecast	550.00	580.80	618.92	658.85	700.57
EBIT(1 − Tax rate)	330.00	348.48	371.35	395.31	420.34
Incremental FC	(100.00)	(110.00)	(121.00)	(133.10)	(146.41)
Incremental WC	(45.00)	(49.50)	(54.45)	(59.90)	(65.88)
FCFF	185.00	188.98	195.90	202.31	208.05

The model need not begin with sales; it could start with net income, cash flow from operations, or EBITDA.

A similar model can be designed for FCFE. In the case of FCFE, the analyst can begin with net income and must also forecast any net new borrowing or net preferred stock issue.

EXAMPLE 11

Finding FCFE

Espinosa decides to forecast FCFE for the year 2004. She uses the same expectations derived in the example above. Additionally, she expects

▶ the profit margin to remain at 8 percent (= 240/3000), and
▶ the company to finance incremental fixed and working capital investments with 50 percent debt—the target debt ratio.

Sales	$3,300	Up 10%
NI	264	8.0% of sales
Incremental FC	(100)	33.33% of sales increase
Incremental WC	(45)	15% of sales increase
Net borrowing	72.50	(100 FCInv + 45 WCInv) × 50%
FCFE	$191.50	

When the company has significant noncash charges other than depreciation expense, the approach just illustrated will result in a less accurate estimate of FCFE than one obtained by forecasting all the individual components.

In some cases, the analyst will have specific forecasts of planned components, such as capital expenditures. In other cases, the analyst studies historical relationships, such as previous capital expenditures and sales levels, to develop a forecast.

3.7 Other Issues with Free Cash Flow Analysis

3.7.1 Analyst Adjustments to CFO

Although corporate financial statements are often straightforward, frequently they are not transparent. Sometimes, difficulties in analysis arise because the companies and their transactions are simply more complicated than the example provided by the Pitts Corporation (above).

For instance, in many corporate financial statements, the changes in balance sheet items (the increase in an asset or the decrease in a liability) differ from those reported on the statement of cash flows. Likewise, depreciation in the statement of cash flows may differ from depreciation expense in the income statement. How do such problems arise?

Two factors can cause discrepancies between changes in balance sheet accounts and the changes reported in the statement of cash flows: acquisitions and divestitures, and foreign subsidiaries. For example, an increase in an inventory account can result from purchases from suppliers (which is an operating activity) or from an acquisition or merger with another company that has inventory on its balance sheet (which is an investing activity). Discrepancies can also occur from currency translations of foreign subsidiaries.

As discussed in Section 3.2, the CFO figure from the statement of cash flows may be contaminated by cash flows arising from financing and/or investing activities. As a consequence, when analysts use CFO in a valuation context, ideally they should remove such contaminations and produce an analyst-adjusted CFO before using it as a starting point for free cash flow calculations.

3.7.2 Free Cash Flow versus Dividends and Other Earnings Components

Many analysts have a strong preference for free cash flow valuation models over dividend discount models (DDMs). Although perhaps no theoretical advantage exists for one type of model over another, legitimate reasons to prefer one model can arise in the process of applying free cash flow models versus DDMs. First, many corporations pay no, or very low, cash dividends. Using dividend discount models to value these companies puts the analyst in an awkward situation, forcing her to speculate about when dividends will be initiated and established at a material level. Second, dividend payments are at the discretion of the corporation's board of directors. As such, they may imperfectly signal the company's long-run profitability. Some corporations clearly pay dividends that are substantially less than their free cash flow, and others pay dividends that are substantially more. Finally, as mentioned in Section 1, dividends are the cash flow going to shareholders and free cash flow to equity is the cash flow available to shareholders if they controlled the company. If a company is being analyzed as a takeover target, free cash flow is the appropriate cash flow measure; once the company is taken over, the new owners will have discretion over free cash flow.

We have defined FCFF and FCFE and presented alternative (equivalent) ways to calculate both of them. So you should have a good feel for what is included in FCFF or FCFE. You may wonder why some cash flows are not included. Specifically, what role do dividends, share repurchases, share issuance, or leverage changes have on FCFF and FCFE? The simple answer is: not much. Recall two formulas for FCFF and FCFE:

$$FCFF = NI + NCC + Int(1 - Tax\ rate) - FCInv - WCInv$$
$$FCFE = NI + NCC - FCInv - WCInv + Net\ borrowing$$

Notice that dividends and these other transactions are absent from the formulas. The reason is that FCFF and FCFE are the cash flows *available* to investors or to stockholders; dividends and share repurchases are *uses* of these cash flows. So the simple answer is that transactions between the company and its shareholders (through cash dividends, share repurchases and share issuances) do not affect free cash flow. Leverage changes, such as using more debt financing, would have some impact because they would increase the interest tax shield (reduce corporate taxes because of the tax deductibility of interest) and reduce the cash flow available to equity. In the long run, however, investing and financing decisions made today will affect future cash flows.

If all inputs were known and mutually consistent, a dividend discount model and a FCFE model would result in identical valuations for a stock. One possibility is that FCFE, from Equation 47-10 above, equals cash dividends each year. Both cash flow streams are discounted at the required return for equity and would thus have the same present value. Generally, FCFE and dividends will differ. FCFE recognizes value as the cash flow available to stockholders (NI + NCC − FCInv − WCInv + Net borrowing) even if it is not paid out in dividends. The company's board of directors, because of its discretion over dividends, can choose to pay dividends that are lower or higher than FCFE. Generally, however, the same economic forces that lead to low (high) dividends lead to low (high) FCFE. For example, a rapidly growing company with superior investment opportunities will retain a high proportion of earnings and pay low dividends. This same company would have high investments in fixed capital and working capital (in Equation 47-10, for example) and have a low FCFE. Conversely, a mature company that is investing relatively little might have high dividends and high FCFE. In spite of this tendency, however, FCFE and dividends will usually differ.

FCFF and FCFE, as defined in this reading, are measures of cash flow designed for valuation of the firm or its equity. Other definitions of "free cash flow" frequently appear in textbooks, articles, and vendor-supplied databases of financial information on public companies. In many cases, these other definitions of free cash flow are not designed for valuation purposes and thus should not be used for valuation. Using numbers supplied by others without knowing exactly how they are defined increases the likelihood of making errors in valuation. As consumers and producers of research, analysts are well advised to clarify the definition of free cash flow being used because so many versions exist.

Because free cash flow analysis requires considerable care and understanding in its use, some practitioners erroneously use earnings components such as NI, EBIT, EBITDA, or CFO in a discounted cash flow valuation. Such mistakes may lead the analyst to systematically overstate or understate the value of a stock. Shortcuts can be costly.

One common shortcut is to use EBITDA as a proxy for the cash flow to the firm. Equation 47-13 clearly showed the differences between EBITDA and FCFF:

$$FCFF = EBITDA(1 - Tax\ rate) + Dep(Tax\ rate) - FCInv - WCInv$$

Depreciation charges as a percentage of EBITDA vary substantially for different companies and industries, as does the depreciation tax shield (the depreciation charge times the tax rate). Although FCFF captures this difference, EBITDA does not. EBITDA also does not account for the investments a company makes in fixed capital or working capital. Hence, EBITDA is a very poor measure of the cash flow available to the company's investors. Using EBITDA in a discounted cash flow model (instead of an actual cash flow) has another important aspect as well: EBITDA is a before-tax measure, so the discount rate applied to EBITDA would need to be a before-tax rate. The WACC used to discount FCFF is an after-tax rate.

EBITDA is a poor proxy for FCFF because it does not account for the depreciation tax shield and the investment in fixed capital and working capital, but it is an even poorer proxy for free cash flow to equity. From a stockholder's perspective, additional defects of EBITDA include its failure to account for the after-tax interest costs or cash flows from new borrowing or debt repayments. Example 12 shows the mistakes sometimes made in discussions of cash flows.

EXAMPLE 12

The Mistake of Using Net Income for FCFE and EBITDA for FCFF

A recent job applicant made some interesting comments about FCFE and FCFF: "I don't like the definitions for FCFE and FCFF because they are unnecessarily complicated and confusing. The best measure of FCFE, the funds available to pay dividends, is simply net income. You take the net income number straight off the income statement and don't need to make any further adjustments. Likewise, the best measure of FCFF, the funds available to the company's suppliers of capital, is EBITDA. You can take EBITDA straight off the income statement and don't need to consider using anything else."

How would you respond to the job applicant's definition of (1) FCFE and (2) FCFF?

Solution to 1: The FCFE is the cash generated by the business's operations less the amounts it must reinvest in additional assets plus the amounts it is borrowing. Equation 47-10, which starts with net income to find FCFE, shows these items:

Free cash flow to equity = Net income available to common shareholders
                 Plus: Net noncash charges
                 Less: Investment in fixed capital
                 Less: Investment in working capital
                 Plus: Net borrowing

Net income does not include several cash flows. Investments in fixed or working capital reduce the cash available to stockholders, as do loan repayments. New borrowing increases the cash available. FCFE includes the cash generated from operating the business and also accounts for the investing and financing activities of the company. So, net income tells only part of the overall story. Of course, a special case exists in which net income and FCFE are the same. This case occurs when new investments exactly equal depreciation and the company is not investing in working capital or engaging in any net borrowing.

Solution to 2: Assuming that EBITDA equals FCFF introduces several possible mistakes. Equation 47-10 highlights these mistakes:

$$
\begin{aligned}
\text{Free cash flow to the firm} = \ &\text{EBITDA}(1 - \text{Tax rate}) \\
&\text{Plus: Depreciation}(\text{Tax rate}) \\
&\text{Less: Investment in fixed capital} \\
&\text{Less: Investment in working capital}
\end{aligned}
$$

The job applicant is ignoring taxes, which obviously reduce the cash available to the company's suppliers of capital.

3.7.3 Free Cash Flow and More-Complicated Capital Structures

For the most part, the discussion of FCFF and FCFE above assumes a simple capital structure in which the company has two sources of capital, debt and equity. Including preferred stock as a third source of capital would cause the analyst to add terms to the equations for FCFF and FCFE for the dividends paid on preferred stock and for the issuance or repurchase of preferred shares. Instead of including those terms in all of the equations, we chose to leave preferred stock out because only a minority of corporations use preferred stock. For companies that do have preferred stock, however, its effects can be incorporated where appropriate. For example, in Equation 47-7, which calculates FCFF starting with net income available to common shareholders, preferred dividends paid would have to be added to the cash flows to obtain FCFF. In Equation 47-10, which calculates FCFE starting with net income available to common shareholders, if preferred dividends were already subtracted when arriving at net income available to common, no further adjustment for preferred dividends would be required. Issuing (redeeming) preferred stock increases (decreases) the cash flow available to common stockholders, however, so this term must be added in. In many respects, the existence of preferred stock in the capital structure has many of the same effects as the existence of debt, except that unlike interest payments on debt, preferred stock dividends paid are not tax deductible.

EXAMPLE 13

FCFF Valuation with Preferred Stock in the Capital Structure

Welch Corporation uses bond, preferred stock, and common stock financing. The market value of each of these sources of financing and the before-tax required rates of return for each are given below:

	Market Value	Required Return
Bonds	$400,000,000	8.0%
Preferred stock	$100,000,000	8.0%
Common stock	$500,000,000	12.0%
Total	$1,000,000,000	

Other financial information:

► net income available to common shareholders = $110,000,000
► interest expenses = $32,000,000
► preferred dividends = $8,000,000
► depreciation = $40,000,000
► investment in fixed capital = $70,000,000
► investment in working capital = $20,000,000
► net borrowing = $25,000,000
► tax rate = 30 percent
► stable growth rate of FCFF = 4.0 percent
► stable growth rate of FCFE = 5.0 percent

1. Calculate Welch Corporation's WACC.
2. Calculate the current value of FCFF.
3. Based on forecasted FCFF, what is the total value of the firm and the value of equity?
4. Calculate the current value of FCFE.
5. Based on forecasted FCFE, what is the value of equity?

Solution to 1: Based on the weights and after-tax costs of each source of capital, the WACC is

$$\text{WACC} = \frac{400}{1,000}8\%(1 - 0.30) + \frac{100}{1,000}8\% + \frac{500}{1,000}12\% = 9.04\%$$

Solution to 2: If the company did not issue preferred stock, FCFF would be

$$\text{FCFF} = \text{NI} + \text{NCC} + \text{Int}(1 - \text{Tax rate}) - \text{FCInv} - \text{WCInv}$$

If preferred stock dividends have been paid (and net income is income available to common), the preferred dividends must be added back just as after-tax interest expenses are above. The modified equation (including preferred dividends) for FCFF would be

$$\text{FCFF} = \text{NI} + \text{NCC} + \text{Int}(1 - \text{Tax rate}) + \text{Preferred dividends} - \text{FCInv} - \text{WCInv}$$

For Welch Corporation, FCFF is

$$\text{FCFF} = 110 + 40 + 32(1 - 0.30) + 8 - 70 - 20 = \$90.4 \text{ million}$$

Solution to 3: The total value of the firm is

$$\text{Firm} = \frac{\text{FCFF}_1}{\text{WACC} - g} = \frac{90.4(1.04)}{0.0904 - 0.04} = \frac{94.016}{0.0504} = \$1,865.40 \text{ million}$$

The value of equity is the total value of the company minus the value of debt and preferred stock:

$$\text{Equity} = 1,865.40 - 400 - 100 = \$1,365.40 \text{ million}$$

Solution to 4: With no preferred stock, FCFE is

$$\text{FCFE} = \text{NI} + \text{NCC} - \text{FCInv} - \text{WCInv} + \text{Net borrowing}$$

If the company has preferred stock, the FCFE equation is essentially the same. Net borrowing would be the total of new debt borrowing and net issuances of new preferred stock. For Welch Corporation, FCFE is

$$\text{FCFE} = 110 + 40 - 70 - 20 + 25 = \$85 \text{ million}$$

Solution to 5: Valuing FCFE, which is growing at 5.0 percent, we have a value of equity of

$$\text{Equity} = \frac{\text{FCFE}_1}{r - g} = \frac{85(1.05)}{0.12 - 0.05} = \frac{89.25}{0.07} = \$1,275.00 \text{ million}$$

Paying cash dividends on common stock does not affect FCFF or FCFE, the amounts of cash *available* to all investors or to common stockholders. It is simply a use of the available cash. Share repurchases of common stock also do not affect FCFF or FCFE. Share repurchases, in many respects, are substitutes for cash dividends. Similarly, issuing shares of common stock does not affect FCFF or FCFE. On the other hand, changing leverage (changing the amount of debt financing in the company's capital structure) does have some effects. An increase in leverage will not affect FCFF (although it might affect the calculations you use to arrive at FCFF). An increase in leverage affects FCFE in two ways. In the year the debt is issued, it increases the FCFE by the amount of debt issued. After the debt is issued, FCFE is then reduced by the after-tax interest expense.

Section 3 has discussed the concepts of FCFF and FCFE and their estimation. The next section presents additional valuation models using forecasts of FCFF or FCFE to value the firm or its equity. These DCF models are similar to the dividend discount models discussed in the previous reading, although the analyst must face the reality that estimating free cash flows is a more time-consuming exercise than estimating dividends.

FREE CASH FLOW MODEL VARIATIONS

Section 4 presents several extensions of the FCF models presented earlier. In many cases, especially when inflation rates are volatile, analysts will value real cash flows instead of **nominal values**. As with dividend discount models, free cash flow models are very sensitive to the data inputs, and analysts routinely perform sensitivity analyses on their valuations. Previously, in Section 2, we presented single-stage free cash flow models, which have a constant growth rate. This section presents two-stage and three-stage free cash flow valuation models.

4.1 An International Application of the Single-Stage Model

Valuation using real values instead of nominal values has much appeal when inflation rates are high and volatile. Many analysts use this adaptation for both domestic and foreign stocks, but the use of **real values** is especially helpful for valuing international stocks. Special challenges to valuing equities from multiple countries include incorporating economic factors such as interest rate, inflation rate, and growth rate differences across countries as well as dealing with variable accounting standards. Furthermore, performing analyses in multiple countries challenges the analyst, and most particularly a team of analysts, to use consistent assumptions for all countries.

Several securities firms have adapted the single-stage FCFE model to address some of these challenges of international valuation. They choose to analyze companies using real cash flows and real discount rates instead of using nominal values. To estimate real discount rates, they use a modification of the build-up method. Starting with a "country return", which is a real required rate of return for stocks from a particular country, they then make adjustments to the country return for the stock's industry, size, and leverage:

Country return (real)	x.xx%
+/− Industry adjustment	x.xx%
+/− Size adjustment	x.xx%
+/− Leverage adjustment	x.xx%
Required rate of return (real)	x.xx%

The adjustments in the model should have sound economic justification. They should reflect factors expected to impact the relative risk and return associated with an investment.

The growth rate of FCFE also is predicted in real terms. These securities firms supply all analysts with estimates of the real growth rates for each country. The analyst then chooses a real growth rate for the stock benchmarked against the real country growth rate. This approach is particularly useful for countries with high or variable inflation rates. The value of the stock is found with an equation essentially like Equation 47-6 except that all terms in the equation are in real terms. If $FCFE_0$ is for the current year, say 2002, then the value of the stock will be in 2002 currency.

$$V_0 = \frac{FCFE_0(1 + g_{real})}{r_{real} - g_{real}}$$

Whenever real discount rates and real growth rates can be estimated more reliably than nominal discount rates and nominal growth rates, this method is worth using. Example 14 shows how this procedure can be applied.

EXAMPLE 14

Using Real Cash Flows and Discount Rates for International Stocks

YPF Sociedad Anonima (NYSE: YPF) is an integrated oil and gas company headquartered in Buenos Aires, Argentina. Although cash flows have been volatile, an analyst has estimated a normalized FCFE of 1.05 Argentine pesos (ARS) per share for the year just ended. The real country return for Argentina is 7.30 percent; adjustments to the country return for YPF S.A. are an industry adjustment of +0.80 percent, a size adjustment of −0.33 percent, and a leverage adjustment of −0.12 percent. The long-term real growth rate for Argentina is estimated to be 3.0 percent, and the real growth rate of YPF S.A. is expected to be about 0.5 percent below the country rate. The real required rate of return for YPF S.A. is:

Country return (real)	7.30%
Industry adjustment	+0.80%
Size adjustment	−0.33%
Leverage adjustment	−0.12%
Required rate of return	7.65%

The real growth rate of FCFE is expected to be 2.5 percent (3.0% − 0.5%), so the value of one share is

$$V_0 = \frac{FCFE_0(1 + g_{real})}{r_{real} - g_{real}} = \frac{1.05(1.025)}{0.0765 - 0.025} = \frac{1.07625}{0.0515} = ARS20.90$$

4.2 Sensitivity Analysis of FCFF and FCFE Valuations

In large measure, growth in FCFF and in FCFE depend on a company's future profitability. Sales growth and changes in net profit margins dictate future net profits. Sales growth and profit margins depend on the growth phase of the company and the profitability of the industry. A highly profitable company in a growing industry can enjoy years of profit growth. Eventually, its profit margins are likely to be eroded by increased competition, and sales growth is likely to abate as well because of fewer opportunities for expansion of market size and market share. Growth rates and the duration of growth are difficult to forecast.

The base-year values for the FCFF or FCFE growth models are also critical. Given the same required rates of return and growth rates, the value of the firm or the value of equity will increase or decrease proportionately with the initial value of FCFF or FCFE employed.

Valuing a company involves forecasts of the company's future cash flows as well as estimates of the opportunity cost of funds that should be used to find the present value of the future cash flows. Analysts can perform a sensitivity analysis, which shows how sensitive the final valuation is to changes in each of a valuation model's input variables. Some input variables have a much larger impact on stock valuation than others. Example 15 shows the sensitivity of the valuation of Anheuser-Busch Companies to five input variables.

EXAMPLE 15

Sensitivity Analysis of a FCFE Valuation

Steve Bono has valued Anheuser-Busch Companies (NYSE: BUD) using the FCFE constant-growth approach. His best estimates of the input values for the analysis are that $FCFE_0$ is \$1.64 per share, the FCFE growth rate is 5.20 percent forever, the risk-free return is 5.5 percent, the equity risk premium is also 5.5 percent, and the company's beta is 0.60. The required rate of return for BUD is

$$r = E(R_i) = R_F + \beta_i[E(R_M) - R_F] = 5.5\% + 0.60(5.5\%) = 8.80\%$$

The value per share is

$$\text{Value} = \frac{FCFE_0(1 + g)}{r - g} = \frac{1.64(1.052)}{0.088 - 0.052} = \frac{1.7253}{0.036} = \$47.92$$

Bono has also collected other reasonable estimates for the variables. Bono's original estimates are given in the table as the "base case" estimates, and the highest and lowest of the alternative estimates are shown in Table 9 as the high and low estimates. The column "Valuation with Low Estimate" gives the estimated value of BUD using the low estimate for the variable on the same row of the first column and the base case estimates for the remaining four variables. "Valuation with High Estimate" performs a similar exercise using the high estimate for the variable at issue.

TABLE 9 Sensitivity Analysis for Anheuser-Busch Valuation

Variable	Base Case Estimate	Low Estimate	High Estimate	Valuation with Low Estimate	Valuation with High Estimate
Free cash flow to equity	\$1.64	\$1.55	\$1.75	\$45.29	\$51.14
Beta	0.60	0.40	0.70	\$69.01	\$41.57
Risk-free rate of return	5.5%	5.3%	5.7%	\$50.74	\$45.40
Equity risk premium	5.5%	4.5%	6.0%	\$57.51	\$44.23
FCFE growth rate	5.2%	3.8%	6.0%	\$34.05	\$62.09

As the table shows, the value of Anheuser-Busch is very sensitive to the inputs. Of the five variables in the valuation model, the stock valuation was least sensitive to the range of estimates of FCFE and of the risk-free rate. The range of estimates for the risk-free rate of return and for FCFE gave the smallest ranges of stock values (from \$50.74 to \$45.40 for the risk-free rate and from \$45.29 to \$51.14 for FCFE). The stock value was most sensitive to the extreme values for beta and for the FCFE growth rate. These ranges were roughly \$28 (from \$69.01 to \$41.57 for beta and from \$34.05 to \$62.09 for the FCFE growth rate).

> Of course, the variables to which the stock price is most sensitive vary from case to case. A sensitivity analysis gives the analyst a guide as to which variables are most critical to the final valuation.

4.3 Two-Stage Free Cash Flow Models

Several two-stage and multistage models exist for valuing FCF streams, just as several such models are available for valuing dividend streams. The free cash flow models are much more complex than the discounted dividend models because the analyst usually incorporates sales, profitability, investments, financing costs, and new financing to find FCFF or FCFE.

In two-stage FCF models, the growth rate in the second stage is a long-run sustainable growth rate. For a declining industry, the second-stage growth rate could be slightly below the GDP growth rate. For an industry that will grow in the future relative to the overall economy, the second-stage growth rate could be slightly greater than the GDP growth rate.

The two most popular versions of the two-stage FCFF and FCFE models are distinguished by the pattern of the growth rates in Stage 1. In one version, the growth rate is constant in Stage 1 before dropping to the long-run sustainable rate in Stage 2. In the other version, the growth rates decline in Stage 1, reaching the sustainable rate at the beginning of Stage 2. The latter model is like the H-model for dividend valuation in Reading 46, in which dividend growth rates decline in Stage 1 and are constant in Stage 2.

The growth rates can be applied to different variables. The growth rate could be the growth rate for FCFF or FCFE, or the growth rate for income (such as net income), or the growth rate for sales. If the growth rate were for net income, the changes in FCFF or FCFE would also depend on investments in operating assets and financing of these investments. When the growth rate in income declines, such as between Stage 1 and Stage 2, investments in operating assets will probably decline at the same time. If the growth rate is for sales, changes in net profit margins as well as investments in operating assets and financing policies will determine FCFF and FCFE.

A general expression for the two-stage FCFF valuation model is

$$\text{Firm value} = \sum_{t=1}^{n} \frac{\text{FCFF}_t}{(1 + \text{WACC})^t} + \frac{\text{FCFF}_{n+1}}{(\text{WACC} - g)} \frac{1}{(1 + \text{WACC})^n} \qquad \textbf{(47-15)}$$

The summation gives the present value of the first n years of FCFF. The terminal value of the FCFF from Year $n + 1$ onward is $\text{FCFF}_{n+1}/(\text{WACC} - g)$, which is discounted at the WACC for n periods to obtain its present value. Subtracting the value of outstanding debt gives the value of equity. The value per share is then found by dividing the total value of equity by the number of outstanding shares.

The general expression for the two-stage FCFE valuation model is

$$\text{Equity} = \sum_{t=1}^{n} \frac{\text{FCFE}_t}{(1 + r)^t} + \frac{\text{FCFE}_{n+1}}{r - g} \frac{1}{(1 + r)^n} \qquad \textbf{(47-16)}$$

The summation is the present value of the first n years of FCFE, and the terminal value of $\text{FCFE}_{n+1}/(r-g)$ is discounted at the required rate of return on equity for n years. The value per share is found by dividing the total value of equity by the number of outstanding shares.

In Equation 47-16, the terminal value of the stock at $t = n$ is found using the constant-growth model. In this case, $\text{TV}_n = \text{FCFE}_{n+1}/(r-g)$. Of course, the analyst might choose to estimate the terminal value, TV_n, another way, such as using a P/E multiplied by the company's forecasted EPS. The terminal value estimation is critical for a simple reason—the present value of the terminal value often represents a substantial portion of the total value of the stock. For example, in Equation 47-16 above, when calculating the total present value of the first n cash flows (FCFE) and the present value of the terminal value, the latter is often substantial. In the examples that follow, the terminal value is usually very important. The same is true in practice.

4.3.1 Fixed Growth Rates in Stage 1 and Stage 2

The simplest two-stage FCFF or FCFE growth model has a constant growth rate in each stage. Example 16 finds the value of a firm that has a 20 percent sales growth rate in Stage 1 and a 6 percent sales growth rate in Stage 2.

EXAMPLE 16

A Two-Stage FCFE Valuation Model with a Constant Growth Rate in Each Stage

Uwe Henschel is doing a valuation of TechnoSchaft using the following information:

- Year 0 sales per share = €25.
- sales growth rate = 20 percent annually for three years and 6 percent annually thereafter.
- net profit margin = 10 percent forever.
- net investment in fixed capital (net of depreciation) = 50 percent of the sales increase.
- annual increase in working capital = 20 percent of the sales increase.
- debt financing = 40 percent of the net investments in capital equipment and working capital.
- TechnoSchaft beta = 1.20, risk-free rate of return = 7 percent, equity risk premium = 4.5 percent.

The required rate of return for equity is

$$r = E(R_i) = R_F + \beta_i[E(R_M) - R_F] = 7\% + 1.2(4.5\%) = 12.4\%$$

Table 10 shows the calculations for FCFE.

TABLE 10	FCFE Estimates for TechnoSchaft					
Year	**1**	**2**	**3**	**4**	**5**	**6**
Sales growth rate	20%	20%	20%	6%	6%	6%
Sales per share	30.000	36.000	43.200	45.792	48.540	51.452
Net profit margin	10%	10%	10%	10%	10%	10%
Earnings per share	3.000	3.600	4.320	4.579	4.854	5.145
Net FCInv per share	2.500	3.000	3.600	1.296	1.374	1.456
WCInv per share	1.000	1.200	1.440	0.518	0.550	0.582
Debt financing per share	1.400	1.680	2.016	0.726	0.769	0.815
FCFE per share	0.900	1.080	1.296	3.491	3.700	3.922
Growth rate of FCFE		20%	20%	169%	6%	6%

In the table, sales grow at 20 percent annually for the first three years and then at 6 percent thereafter. Profits, which are 10 percent of sales, grow at the same rates. The net investments in fixed capital and working capital are 50 percent of the increase in sales and 20 percent of the increase in sales, respectively. New debt financing equals 40 percent of the total increase in net fixed capital and working capital. FCFE is EPS minus the net investment in fixed capital per share minus the investment in working capital per share plus the debt financing per share.

Notice that FCFE grows by 20 percent annually for the first three years. Then, between Year 3 and Year 4, when the sales growth rate drops from 20 percent to 6 percent, FCFE increases substantially. In fact, FCFE increases by 169 percent from Year 3 to Year 4. This large increase in FCFE occurs because profits grow at 6 percent but the investments in capital equipment and working capital (and the increase in debt financing) drop substantially from the previous year. In Years 5 and 6 in the table, sales, profit, investments, financing, and FCFE all grow at 6 percent.

The stock value is the present value of the first three years' FCFE plus the present value of the terminal value of the FCFE from Years 4 and later. The terminal value is

$$TV_3 = FCFE_4 / (r - g) = 3.491 / (0.124 - 0.06) = 54.55.$$

The present values are

$$V_0 = \frac{0.900}{1.124} + \frac{1.080}{(1.124)^2} + \frac{1.296}{(1.124)^3} + \frac{54.55}{(1.124)^3}$$
$$= 0.801 + 0.855 + 0.913 + 38.415 = €40.98.$$

The estimated value of this stock is €40.98 per share.

As mentioned previously, the terminal value may account for a large fraction of the value of a stock. For this case, the present value of the terminal value is €38.415 out of a total value of €40.98. The present value of the terminal value is almost 94 percent of the total value of TechnoSchaft stock.

4.3.2 Declining Growth Rates in Stage 1 and Constant Growth in Stage 2

Growth rates usually do not drop precipitously from one rate to another as they do between the stages in the two-stage model above, but growth rates can decline over time for many reasons. Sometimes, a small company has a high growth rate that is not sustainable as its market share increases. A highly profitable company also can attract competition that makes it harder for the company to sustain its high profit margins.

In this section, we present two examples of the two-stage model with declining growth rates in Stage 1. In the first example, the growth rate of EPS declines during Stage 1. As a company's profitability declines and the company is no longer generating very high returns, the company will usually reduce its net new investment in operating assets. The debt financing accompanying the new investments will also decline. It is not unusual for highly profitable, growing companies to have negative or low cash flows. Later, when growth in profits slows, investments will tend to slow and the company will experience positive cash flows. Of course, the negative cash flows incurred in the high-growth stage help determine the cash flows that occur in future years.

Example 17 below models FCFE per share as a function of EPS, which declines constantly during Stage 1. Because of declining earnings growth rates, the company in the example reduces its new investments over time as well. The value of the company depends on these free cash flows, which are substantial after the high-growth (and high-profitability) period has largely elapsed.

EXAMPLE 17

A Two-Stage FCFE Valuation Model with Declining Net Income Growth in Stage 1

Vishal Noronha needs to prepare a valuation of Sindhuh Enterprises. Noronha has assembled the following information for his analysis. It is now the first day of 2003.

► EPS for 2002 is $2.40.

► For the next five years, the growth rate in EPS is given below. After 2007, the growth rate will be 7 percent.

Year	2003	2004	2005	2006	2007
Growth rate for EPS	30%	18%	12%	9%	7%

► Net investment in fixed capital (net of depreciation) for the next five years are given below. After 2007, capital expenditures are expected to grow at 7 percent annually.

Year	2003	2004	2005	2006	2007
Net capital expenditure per share	3.000	2.500	2.000	1.500	1.000

► The investment in working capital each year will equal 50 percent of the net investment in capital items.

- ▶ Thirty percent of the net investment in fixed capital and investment in working capital will be financed with new debt financing.
- ▶ Current market conditions dictate a risk-free rate of 6.0 percent, an equity risk premium of 4.0 percent, and a beta of 1.10 for Sindhuh Enterprises.

1. What is the per-share value of Sindhuh Enterprises on the first day of 2003?

2. What should be the trailing P/E on the first day of 2003 and the first day of 2007?

Solution to 1: The required return for Sindhuh should be

$$r = E(R_i) = R_F + \beta_i[E(R_M) - R_F] = 6\% + 1.1(4\%) = 10.4\%$$

The FCFEs for the company for years 2003 through 2007 are given in Table 11 below.

TABLE 11   FCFE Estimates for Sindhuh Enterprises

Year	2003	2004	2005	2006	2007
Growth rate for EPS	30%	18%	12%	9%	7%
Earnings per share	$3.120	$3.682	$4.123	$4.494	$4.809
Net FCInv per share	3.000	2.500	2.000	1.500	1.000
WCInv per share	1.500	1.250	1.000	0.750	0.500
Debt financing per share[a]	1.350	1.125	0.900	0.675	0.450
FCFE per share[b]	−0.030	1.057	2.023	2.919	3.759
PV of FCFE discounted at 10.4%	−0.027	0.867	1.504	1.965	

[a] 30 percent of (Net FCInv + WCInv).
[b] EPS 2 Net FCInv per share − WCInv per share + Debt financing per share.

Earnings are $2.40 in 2002. Earnings increase each year by the growth rate given in the table. Net capital expenditures (capital expenditures minus depreciation) are the amounts that Noronha assumed. The increase in working capital each year is 50 percent of the increase in net capital expenditures. Debt financing is 30 percent of the total outlays for net capital expenditures and working capital each year. The FCFE each year is net income minus net capital expenditures minus increase in working capital plus new debt financing. Finally, for years 2003 through 2006, the present value of FCFE is found by discounting FCFE by the 10.4 percent required rate of return for equity.

After 2006, FCFE will grow by a constant 7 percent annually, so the constant growth FCFE valuation model can be used to value this cash flow stream. At the end of 2006, the value of the future FCFE is

$$V_{2006} = \frac{FCFE_{2007}}{r-g} = \frac{3.759}{0.104 - 0.07} = \$110.56$$

To find the present value of V_{2006} as of the end of 2002, V_{2002}, we discount V_{2006} at 10.4 percent for four years:

$$PV = 110.56/(1.104)^4 = \$74.425$$

The total present value of the company is the present value of the first four years' FCFE plus the present value of the terminal value, or

$$V_{2002} = -0.027 + 0.867 + 1.504 + 1.965 + 74.42 = \$78.73$$

Solution to 2: Using the estimated $78.73 stock value, the trailing P/E at the beginning of 2003 would be

$$P/E = 78.73/2.40 = 32.8$$

At the beginning of 2007, the expected stock value is $110.56 and the previous year's earnings per share is $4.494, so the trailing P/E at this time would be

$$P/E = 110.56/4.494 = 24.6$$

After its high-growth phase has ended, the P/E for the company declines substantially.

FCFE in this example was based on forecasts of future earnings per share. Analysts often model a company by forecasting future sales and then estimating the profits, investments, and financing associated with those sales levels. For large companies, analysts may estimate the sales, profitability, investments, and financing for each division or large subsidiary. The free cash flows for all of the divisions or subsidiaries are aggregated to get the free cash flow for the company as a whole.

Example 18 below is a two-stage FCFE model with declining sales growth rates in Stage 1, with profits, investments, and financing keyed to sales. In Stage 1, the growth rate of sales and the profit margin on sales both decline as the company matures and faces more competition and lower growth.

EXAMPLE 18

A Two-Stage FCFE Valuation Model with Declining Sales Growth Rates

Medina Werks has a competitive advantage that will probably deteriorate over time. Flavio Torino expects this deterioration to be reflected in declining sales growth rates as well as declining profit margins. To value the company, Torino has accumulated the following information:

► Current sales are $600 million. Over the next six years, the annual sales growth rate and the net profit margin are projected to be as follows:

Year	1	2	3	4	5	6
Sales growth rate	20%	16%	12%	10%	8%	7%
Net profit margin	14%	13%	12%	11%	10.50%	10%

► Beginning in Year 6, the 7 percent sales growth rate and 10 percent net profit margin should persist indefinitely.
► Capital expenditures (net of depreciation) in the amount of 60 percent of the sales increase will be required each year.
► Investments in working capital equal to 25 percent of the sales increase will also be required each year.
► Debt financing will be used to fund 40 percent of the investments in net capital items and working capital.
► The beta for Medina Werks is 1.10. The risk-free rate of return is 6.0 percent and the equity risk premium is 4.5 percent.
► There are 70 million outstanding shares.

What is the estimated total market value of equity and the value per share?

The required return for Medina is

$$r = E(R_i) = R_F + \beta_i[E(R_M) - R_F] = 6\% + 1.10(4.5\%) = 10.95\%$$

The annual sales and net profit can be found readily as shown in Table 12 below.

TABLE 12   FCFE Estimates for Medina Werks

Year	1	2	3	4	5	6
Sales growth rate	20%	16%	12%	10%	8%	7%
Net profit margin	14%	13%	12%	11%	10.50%	10%
Sales	720.000	835.200	935.424	1028.966	1111.284	1189.074
Net profit	100.800	108.576	112.251	113.186	116.685	118.907
Net FCInv	72.000	69.120	60.134	56.125	49.390	46.674
WCInv	30.000	28.800	25.056	23.386	20.579	19.447
Debt financing	40.800	39.168	34.076	31.804	27.988	26.449
FCFE	39.600	49.824	61.137	65.480	74.703	79.235
PV of FCFE at 10.95%	35.692	40.475	44.763	43.211	44.433	

Sales increase each year by the sales growth rate in Table 12. Net profit each year is the year's net profit margin times the year's sales. Capital investment (net of depreciation) equals 60 percent of the sales increase from the previous year. The investment in working capital is 25 percent of the sales increase from the previous year. The debt financing each year is equal to 40 percent of the total net investment in capital items and working capital for that year. FCFE is net income minus the net capital investment minus the working capital investment plus the debt financing. The present value of each year's FCFE is found by discounting FCFE at the required rate of return for equity, 10.95 percent.

In Year 6 and beyond, sales will increase at 7 percent annually. Net income will be 10 percent of sales, so net profit will also grow at a 7 percent annual rate. Because they are pegged to the 7 percent sales increase, the investments in capital items and working capital and debt financing will also grow at the same 7 percent rate. The amounts in Year 6 for net income, investment in capital items, investment in working capital, debt financing, and FCFE will grow at 7 percent.

The terminal value of FCFE in Year 6 and beyond is

$$TV_5 = \frac{FCFE_6}{r - g} = \frac{79.235}{0.1095 - 0.07} = 2{,}005.95 \text{ million}$$

The present value of this amount is

$$PV = 2{,}005.95/(1.1095)^5 = 1{,}193.12 \text{ million}$$

The estimated total market value of the firm is the present value of FCFE for Years 1 through 5 plus the present value of the terminal value: Market value = 35.692 + 40.475 + 44.763 + 43.211 + 44.433 + 1,193.12 = \$1,401.69 million. Dividing by the 70 million outstanding shares gives the estimated value per share of \$20.02.

4.4 Three-Stage Growth Models

Three-stage models are a straightforward extension of the two-stage models. One common version of a three-stage model is to assume a constant growth rate in each of the three stages. The growth rates could be for sales, and profits, investments in fixed and working capital, and external financing could be a function of the level of sales or changes in sales. A more simplistic model would apply the growth rate to FCFF or FCFE.

A second common model is a three-stage model with constant growth rates in Stages 1 and 3 and a declining growth rate in Stage 2. Again, the growth rates could be applied to sales or to FCFF or FCFE. Although it is unlikely that future FCFF and FCFE will follow the assumptions of either of these three-stage growth models, analysts often consider such models to provide useful approximations.

Example 19 is a three-stage FCFF valuation model with declining growth rates in Stage 2. The model is directly forecasting FCFF instead of deriving FCFF from a more complicated model that estimates cash flow from operations and investments in fixed capital and working capital. Because Marathon Oil spun off substantial assets in 2001, the analyst is unsure how much value remains in the company. Hence, he is updating his valuation of the firm with a new model and estimated parameters.

EXAMPLE 19

**A Three-Stage FCFF Valuation Model
with Declining Growth in Stage 2**

Charles Jones is evaluating Marathon Oil Company (NYSE: MRO) using a
three-stage growth model. He has accumulated the following information:

▶ current FCFF = $745 million

▶ outstanding shares = 309.39 million

▶ equity beta = 0.90, risk-free rate = 5.04 percent, and equity risk
  premium = 5.5 percent

▶ cost of debt = 7.1 percent

▶ marginal tax rate = 34 percent

▶ capital structure = 20 percent debt, 80 percent equity

▶ long-term debt = $1.518 billion

▶ growth rate of FCFF =

  ▶ 8.8 percent annually in Stage 1, Years 1–4

  ▶ 7.4 percent in Year 5, 6.0 percent in Year 6, 4.6 percent in Year 7

  ▶ 3.2 percent in Year 8 and thereafter

Using the information that Jones has accumulated, estimate the following:

1. WACC

2. Total value of the firm

3. Total value of equity

4. Value per share

Solution to 1: The required return for equity is

$$r = E(R_i) = R_F + \beta_i[E(R_M) - R_F] = 5.04\% + 0.9(5.5\%) = 9.99\%$$

WACC is

$$\text{WACC} = 0.20(7.1\%)(1 - 0.34) + 0.80(9.99\%) = 8.93\%$$

Solution to 2: Table 13 displays the projected FCFF over the next eight
years and the present values of each, discounted at 8.93 percent:

TABLE 13   Forecasted FCFF for Marathon Oil

Year	1	2	3	4	5	6	7	8
Growth rate	8.80%	8.80%	8.80%	8.80%	7.40%	6.00%	4.60%	3.20%
FCFF	811	882	959	1,044	1,121	1,188	1,243	1,283
PV at 8.93%	744	743	742	741	731	711	683	

The terminal value at the end of Year 7 is

$$TV_7 = FCFF_8/(WACC - g) = 1,283/(0.0893 - 0.032)$$
$$= \$22,391 \text{ million.}$$

The present value of this amount, discounted at 8.93 percent for seven years, is

$$\text{PV of } TV_7 = 22,391/(1.0893)^7 = \$12,304 \text{ million}$$

The total present value of the first seven years' FCFE is $5,097 million. The total value of the firm is $12,304 million + $5,097 million = $17,401 million.

Solution to 3: The value of equity is the value of the firm minus the market value of debt: $17,401 million − $1,518 million = $15,883 million.

Solution to 4: Dividing the equity value by the number of shares yields the value per share: $15,883 million/309.39 million = $51.33.

NON OPERATING ASSETS AND FIRM VALUE

If a company has significant nonoperating assets such as excess cash, excess marketable securities, or land held for investment, then analysts often calculate the value of the firm as the value of its operating assets plus the value of its nonoperating assets:

$$\text{Value of firm} = \text{Value of operating assets}$$
$$+ \text{Value of nonoperating assets} \qquad \textbf{(47-17)}$$

Recall that when calculating FCFF or FCFE, investments in working capital do not include any investments in cash and marketable securities. The value of cash and marketable securities should be added to the value of the company's operating assets to find the total firm value. Some companies have substantial noncurrent investments in stocks and bonds that are not operating subsidiaries but financial investments. These investments should be reflected at their current market value. Those securities reported at book values based on accounting conventions, should be revalued to market values.

SUMMARY

Discounted cash flow models are used widely by analysts to value companies.

▶ Free cash flow to the firm (FCFF) and free cash flow to equity (FCFE) are the cash flows available to all of the investors in the company and to common stockholders, respectively.

▶ Analysts like to use free cash flow as return (either FCFF or FCFF):
  ▶ if the company is not dividend paying;
  ▶ if the company is dividend paying but dividends differ significantly from the company's capacity to pay dividends;
  ▶ if free cash flows align with profitability within a reasonable forecast period with which the analyst is comfortable; or
  ▶ if the investor takes a control perspective.

▶ The FCFF valuation approach estimates the value of the firm as the present value of future FCFF discounted at the weighted average cost of capital (WACC):

$$\text{Firm value} = \sum_{t=1}^{\infty} \frac{\text{FCFF}_t}{(1 + \text{WACC})^t}$$

The value of equity is the value of the firm minus the value of the firm's debt:

$$\text{Equity value} = \text{Firm value} - \text{Market value of debt}$$

Dividing the total value of equity by the number of outstanding shares gives the value per share.
The WACC formula is

$$\text{WACC} = \frac{\text{MV(Debt)}}{\text{MV(Debt)} + \text{MV(Equity)}} \, r_d(1 - \text{Tax rate}) + \frac{\text{MV(Equity)}}{\text{MV(Debt)} + \text{MV(Equity)}} \, r$$

▶ The value of the firm if FCFF is growing at a constant rate is

$$\text{Firm value} = \frac{\text{FCFF}_1}{\text{WACC} - g} = \frac{\text{FCFF}_0(1 + g)}{\text{WACC} - g}$$

▶ With the FCFE valuation approach, the value of equity can be found by discounting FCFE at the required rate of return on equity (r):

$$\text{Equity value} = \sum_{t=1}^{\infty} \frac{\text{FCFE}_t}{(1 + r)^t}$$

Dividing the total value of equity by the number of outstanding shares gives the value per share.

▶ The value of equity if FCFE is growing at a constant rate is

$$\text{Equity value} = \frac{\text{FCFE}_1}{r - g} = \frac{\text{FCFE}_0(1 + g)}{r - g}$$

▶ FCFF and FCFE are frequently calculated starting with net income:

$$FCFF = NI + NCC + Int(1 - Tax\ rate) - FCInv - WCInv$$
$$FCFE = NI + NCC - FCInv - WCInv + Net\ borrowing$$

▶ FCFF and FCFE are related to each other as follows:

$$FCFE = FCFF - Int(1 - Tax\ rate) + Net\ borrowing$$

▶ FCFF and FCFE can be calculated starting from cash flow from operations:

$$FCFF = CFO + Int(1 - Tax\ rate) - FCInv$$
$$FCFE = CFO - FCInv + Net\ borrowing$$

▶ FCFF can also be calculated from EBIT or EBITDA:

$$FCFF = EBIT(1 - Tax\ rate) + Dep - FCInv - WCInv$$
$$FCFF = EBITDA(1 - Tax\ rate) + Dep(Tax\ rate) - FCInv - WCInv$$

FCFE can then be found by using $FCFE = FCFF - Int(1 - Tax\ rate) +$ Net borrowing.

▶ Finding CFO, FCFF, and FCFE can require careful interpretation of corporate financial statements. In some cases, the needed information may not be transparent.

▶ Earnings components such as net income, EBIT, EBITDA, and CFO should not be used as cash flow measures to value a firm. These earnings components either double-count or ignore parts of the cash flow stream.

▶ More-complicated capital structures, such as those with preferred stock, are easily adapted to find FCFF or FCFE.

▶ A general expression for the two-stage FCFF valuation model is

$$Firm\ value = \sum_{t=1}^{n} \frac{FCFF_t}{(1 + WACC)^t} + \frac{FCFF_{n+1}}{(WACC - g)} \frac{1}{(1 + WACC)^n}$$

▶ A general expression for the two-stage FCFE valuation model is

$$Equity\ value = \sum_{t=1}^{n} \frac{FCFE_t}{(1 + r)^t} + \frac{FCFE_{n+1}}{r - g} \frac{1}{(1 + r)^n}$$

▶ One common two-stage model assumes a constant growth rate in each stage, and a second common model assumes declining growth in Stage 1 followed by a long-run sustainable growth rate in Stage 2.

▶ To forecast FCFF and FCFE, analysts build a variety of models of varying complexity. A common approach is to forecast sales, with profitability, investments, and financing derived from changes in sales.

▶ Three-stage models are often considered to be good approximations for cash flow streams that, in reality, fluctuate from year to year.

▶ Nonoperating assets such as excess cash and marketable securities, noncurrent investment securities, and nonperforming assets are usually segregated from the company's operating assets. They are valued separately and then added to the value of the company's operating assets to find total firm value.

PRACTICE PROBLEMS FOR READING 47

1. Indicate the effect on this period's FCFF and FCFE of a change in each of the items listed below. Assume a $100 increase in each case and a 40 percent tax rate.
   A. Net income
   B. Cash operating expenses
   C. Depreciation
   D. Interest expense
   E. EBIT
   F. Accounts receivable
   G. Accounts payable
   H. Property, plant, and equipment
   I. Notes payable
   J. Cash dividends paid
   K. Proceeds from issuing new common shares
   L. Common stock share repurchases

2. LaForge Systems, Inc., has net income of $285 million for the year 2003. Using information from the company's financial statements below, show the adjustments to net income that would be required to find:
   A. FCFF
   B. FCFE
   C. In addition, show the adjustments to FCFF that would result in FCFE.

LaForge Systems, Inc.
Balance Sheet

(in millions)	31 December 2002	2003
Assets		
Current assets		
Cash and equivalents	$ 210	$ 248
Accounts receivable	474	513
Inventory	520	564
Total current assets	1,204	1,325
Gross fixed assets	2,501	2,850
Accumulated depreciation	(604)	(784)
Net fixed assets	1,897	2,066
Total assets	$3,101	$3,391
Liabilities and shareholders' equity		
Current liabilities		
Accounts payable	$ 295	$ 317
Notes payable	300	310
Accrued taxes and expenses	76	99
Total current liabilities	671	726

Long-term debt	1,010	1,050
Common stock	50	50
Additional paid-in capital	300	300
Retained earnings	1,070	1,265
Total shareholders' equity	**1,420**	**1,615**
Total liabilities and shareholders' equity	**$3,101**	**$3,391**

Statement of Income
(in millions, except per share data)   31 December 2003

Total revenues	$2,215
Operating costs and expenses	1,430
EBITDA	785
Depreciation	180
EBIT	605
Interest expense	130
Income before tax	475
Taxes (at 40 percent)	190
Net income	285
Dividends	90
Addition to retained earnings	195

Net Borrows [handwritten]

Statement of Cash Flows
(in millions)   31 December 2003

Operating activities

Net income	$285
Adjustments	
Depreciation	180
Changes in working capital	
Accounts receivable	(39)
Inventories	(44)
Accounts payable	22
Accrued taxes and expenses	23
Cash provided by operating activities	$427

Investing activities

Purchases of fixed assets	349
Cash used for investing activities	$349

Financing activities

Notes payable	(10)
Long-term financing issuances	(40)
Common stock dividends	90
Cash used for financing activities	$40

Notes Payable + Long-term financing issues [handwritten]

(continued on next page . . .)

Statement of Cash Flows (in millions)	31 December 2003
Cash and equivalents increase (decrease)	38
Cash and equivalents at beginning of year	210
Cash and equivalents at end of year	$248
Supplemental cash flow disclosures	
Interest paid	$130
Income taxes paid	$190

3. For LaForge Systems, whose financial statements are given in Problem 2 above, show the adjustments from the current levels of CFO (which is 427), EBIT (605), and EBITDA (785) to find

  A. FCFF

  B. FCFE

4. The term "free cash flow" is frequently applied to cash flows that differ from the definition for FCFF that should be used to value a firm. Two such definitions of "free cash flow" are given below. Compare the definitions given for FCF to FCFF.

  A. FCF = Net income + Depreciation and amortization − Cash dividends − Capital expenditures.

  B. FCF = Cash flow from operations (from the statement of cash flows) − Capital expenditures.

5. Proust Company has FCFF of $1.7 billion and FCFE of $1.3 billion. Proust's WACC is 11 percent and its required rate of return for equity is 13 percent. FCFF is expected to grow forever at 7 percent and FCFE is expected to grow forever at 7.5 percent. Proust has debt outstanding of $15 billion.

  A. What is the total value of Proust's equity using the FCFF valuation approach?

  B. What is the total value of Proust's equity using the FCFE valuation approach?

6. Quinton Johnston is evaluating Taiwan Semiconductor Manufacturing Co., Ltd., (NYSE: TSM) headquartered in Hsinchu, Taiwan. In 2001, when Johnston is performing his analysis, the company—and indeed, the whole industry—is unprofitable. Furthermore, TSM pays no dividends on its common shares. Johnston decides to value TSM using his forecasts of FCFE and makes the following assumptions:

  ▶ The company has 17.0 billion outstanding shares.

  ▶ Sales will be $5.5 billion in 2002, increasing at 28 percent annually for the next four years (through 2006).

  ▶ Net income will be 32 percent of sales.

  ▶ Investment in fixed assets will be 35 percent of sales, investment in working capital will be 6 percent of sales, and depreciation will be 9 percent of sales.

  ▶ 20 percent of the investment in assets will be financed with debt.

  ▶ Interest expenses will be only 2 percent of sales.

  ▶ The tax rate will be 10 percent.

  ▶ TSM's beta is 2.1, the risk-free government bond rate is 6.4 percent, and the equity risk premium is 5.0 percent.

▶ At the end of 2006, Johnston projects TSM will sell for 18 times earnings. What is the value of one ordinary share of Taiwan Semiconductor Manufacturing Co., Ltd.?

7. Do Pham is evaluating Phaneuf Accelerateur using the FCFF and FCFE valuation approaches. Pham has collected the following information (currently in euro):

▶ Phaneuf has net income of 250 million, depreciation of 90 million, capital expenditures of 170 million, and an increase in working capital of 40 million.

▶ Phaneuf will finance 40 percent of the increase in net fixed assets (capital expenditures less depreciation) and 40 percent of the increase in working capital with debt financing.

▶ Interest expenses are 150 million. The current market value of Phaneuf's outstanding debt is 1,800 million.

▶ FCFF is expected to grow at 6.0 percent indefinitely, and FCFE is expected to grow at 7.0 percent.

▶ The tax rate is 30 percent.

▶ Phaneuf is financed with 40 percent debt and 60 percent equity. The before-tax cost of debt is 9 percent and the before-tax cost of equity is 13 percent.

▶ Phaneuf has 10 million outstanding shares.

    A. Using the FCFF valuation approach, estimate the total value of the firm, the total market value of equity, and the value per share.

    B. Using the FCFE valuation approach, estimate the total market value of equity and the value per share.

8. PHB Company currently sells for $32.50 per share. In an attempt to determine if PHB is fairly priced, an analyst has assembled the following information:

▶ The before-tax required rates of return on PHB debt, preferred stock, and common stock are 7.0 percent, 6.8 percent, and 11.0 percent, respectively.

▶ The company's target capital structure is 30 percent debt, 15 percent preferred stock, and 55 percent common stock.

▶ The market value of the company's debt is $145 million, and its preferred stock is valued at $65 million.

▶ PHB's FCFF for the year just ended is $28 million. FCFF is expected to grow at a constant rate of 4 percent for the foreseeable future.

▶ The tax rate is 35 percent.

▶ PHB has 8 million outstanding common shares.

What is PHB's estimated value per share? Is PHB's stock underpriced?

9. Watson Dunn is planning to value BHP Billiton Ltd. (NYSE: BHP) using a single-stage FCFF approach. BHP Billiton, headquartered in Melbourne, Australia, provides a variety of industrial metals and minerals. The financial information Dunn has assembled for his valuation is as follows:

▶ The company has 1,852 million shares outstanding.

▶ Market value of debt is $3.192 billion.

▶ FCFF is currently $1.1559 billion.

▶ Equity beta is 0.90, the equity risk premium is 5.5 percent, and the risk-free rate is 5.5 percent.

▶ The before-tax cost of debt is 7.0 percent.

▶ The tax rate is 40 percent.

▶ To calculate WACC, assume the company is financed 25 percent with debt.

▶ FCFF growth rate is 4 percent.

Using Dunn's information, calculate the following:

A. WACC

B. Value of the firm

C. Total market value of equity

D. Value per share

10. Kenneth McCoin is valuing McDonald's Corporation and performing a sensitivity analysis on his valuation. He uses a single-stage FCFE growth model. The "base case" values for each of the parameters in the model are given in the table below, along with possible "low" and "high" estimates for each variable.

Variable	Base Case Value	Low Estimate	High Estimate
Normalized $FCFE_0$	$0.88	$0.70	$1.14
Risk-free rate	5.08%	5.00%	5.20%
Equity risk premium	5.50%	4.50%	6.50%
Beta	0.70	0.60	0.80
FCFE perpetual growth rate	6.40%	4.00%	7.00%

A. Use the base case values to estimate the current value of McDonald's Corporation.

B. Calculate the range of stock prices that would occur if the base case value for $FCFE_0$ were replaced by the low and high estimate for $FCFE_0$. Similarly, using the base case values for all other variables, calculate the range of stock prices caused by the using the low and high values for beta, the risk-free rate, the equity risk premium, and the growth rate. Rank the sensitivity of the stock price to each of the five variables based on these ranges.

11. An aggressive financial planner who claims to have a superior method for picking undervalued stocks is courting one of your clients. The planner claims that the best way to find the value of a stock is to divide EBITDA by the risk-free bond rate. The planner is urging your client to invest in Alcan, Inc. (NYSE: AL). Alcan is the parent of a group of companies engaged in all aspects of the aluminum business. The planner says that Alcan's EBITDA of $1,580 million divided by the long-term government bond rate of 7 percent gives a total value of $22,571 million. With 318 million outstanding shares, Alcan's value per share using this method is $70.98. Shares of Alcan currently trade for $36.50, and the planner wants your client to make a large investment in Alcan through him.

A. Provide your client with an alternative valuation of Alcan based on a two-stage FCFE valuation approach. Use the following assumptions:

▶ Net income is currently $600 million. Net income will grow by 20 percent annually for the next three years.

▶ The net investment in operating assets (capital expenditures less depreciation plus investment in working capital) will be $1,150 million next year and grow at 15 percent for the following two years.

▶ Forty percent of the net investment in operating assets will be financed with net new debt financing.

▶ Alcan's beta is 1.3, the risk-free bond rate is 7 percent, and the equity risk premium is 4 percent.

▶ After three years, the growth rate of net income will be 8 percent and the net investment in operating assets (capital expenditures minus depreciation plus increase in working capital) each year will drop to 30 percent of net income.

▶ Debt is, and will continue to be, 40 percent of total assets.

▶ Alcan has 318 million outstanding shares.

Find the value per share of Alcan.

B. Criticize the valuation approach that the aggressive financial planner used.

12. Bron has earnings per share of $3.00 in 2002 and expects earnings per share to increase by 21 percent in 2003. Earnings per share are expected to grow at a decreasing rate for the following five years, as shown in the table below. In 2008, the growth rate will be 6 percent and is expected to stay at that rate thereafter. Net capital expenditures (capital expenditures minus depreciation) will be $5.00 per share in 2002 and then follow the pattern predicted in the table. In 2008, net capital expenditures are expected to be $1.50 and will then grow at 6 percent annually. The investment in working capital parallels the increase in net capital expenditures and is predicted to equal 25 percent of net capital expenditures each year. In 2008, investment in working capital will be $0.375 and is predicted to grow at 6 percent thereafter. Bron will use debt financing to fund 40 percent of net capital expenditures and 40 percent of the investment in working capital.

Year	2003	2004	2005	2006	2007	2008
Growth rate for earnings per share	21%	18%	15%	12%	9%	6%
Net capital expenditure per share	$5.00	$5.00	$4.50	$4.00	$3.50	$1.50

The required rate of return for Bron is 12 percent. Find the value per share using a two-stage FCFE valuation approach.

13. **[Adapted from the 2000 CFA Level II Examination]** The management of Telluride, an international diversified conglomerate based in the United States, believes that the recent strong performance of its wholly owned medical supply subsidiary, Sundanci, has gone unnoticed. To realize Sundanci's full value, Telluride announced that it will divest Sundanci in a tax-free spinoff.

Sue Carroll, CFA, is Director of Research at Kesson and Associates. In developing an investment recommendation for Sundanci, Carroll has gathered the information shown in Exhibits P-1 and P-2 below.

| EXHIBIT P-1 | Sundanci Actual 1999 and 2000 Financial Statements for Fiscal Years Ending 31 May (in millions, except per-share data) |

Income Statement	1999	2000
Revenue	$474	$598
Depreciation	20	23
Other operating costs	368	460
Income before taxes	86	115
Taxes	26	35
Net income	60	80
Dividends	18	24
Earnings per share	$0.714	$0.952
Dividends per share	$0.214	$0.286
Common shares outstanding	84.0	84.0

Balance Sheet	1999	2000
Current assets (includes $5 cash in 1999 and in 2000)	$201	$326
Net property, plant, and equipment	474	489
Total assets	675	815
Current liabilities (all non-interest bearing)	57	141
Long-term debt	0	0
Total liabilities		
Shareholders' equity	618	674
Total liabilities and equity	675	815
Capital expenditures	34	38

| EXHIBIT P-2 | Selected Financial Information |

Required rate of return on equity	14%
Growth rate of industry	13%
Industry P/E	26

Abbey Naylor, CFA, has been directed by Carroll to determine the value of Sundanci's stock using the FCFE model. Naylor believes that Sundanci's FCFE will grow at 27 percent for two years, and 13 percent thereafter. Capital expenditures, depreciation, and working capital are all expected to increase proportionately with FCFE.

A. Calculate the amount of FCFE per share for 2000 using the data from Exhibit P-1. Show your work.

B. Calculate the current value of a share of Sundanci stock based on the two-stage FCFE model. Show your work.

C. Describe limitations that the two-stage DDM and FCFE models have in common.

14. **[Adapted from the 2001 CFA Level II Examination]** John Jones, CFA, is head of the research department of Peninsular Research. One of the companies he is researching, Mackinac, Inc., is a U.S.-based manufacturing company. Mackinac has released its June 2001 financial statements, shown in Exhibits P-3, P-4, and P-5.

EXHIBIT P-3	Mackinac, Inc., Annual Income Statement 30 June 2001 (in thousands, except per-share data)

Sales	$250,000
Cost of goods sold	125,000
Gross operating profit	125,000
Selling, general, and administrative expenses	50,000
EBITDA	75,000
Depreciation and amortization	10,500
EBIT	64,500
Interest expense	11,000
Pretax income	53,500
Income taxes	16,050
Net income	$37,450
Shares outstanding	13,000
EPS	$2.88

EXHIBIT P-4	Mackinac, Inc., Balance Sheet, 30 June 2001 (in thousands)

Current assets

Cash and equivalents	$20,000	
Receivables	40,000	
Inventories	29,000	
Other current assets	23,000	
Total current assets		$112,000

(Exhibit continued on next page . . .)

EXHIBIT P-4	**(continued)**	

Noncurrent assets

Property, plant, and equipment	$145,000	
Less: Accumulated depreciation	(43,000)	
Net property, plant, and equipment	102,000	
Investments	70,000	
Other noncurrent assets	36,000	
Total noncurrent assets		208,000
Total assets		$320,000

Current liabilities

Accounts payable	$41,000	
Short-term debt	12,000	
Other current liabilities	17,000	
Total current liabilities		$70,000

Noncurrent liabilities

Long-term debt	100,000	
Total noncurrent liabilities		100,000
Total liabilities		170,000

Shareholders' equity

Common equity	40,000	
Retained earnings	110,000	
Total equity		150,000
Total liabilities and equity		$320,000

EXHIBIT P-5	**Mackinac, Inc., Cash Flow Statement 30 June 2001 (in thousands)**

Cash flow from operating activities

Net income		$37,450
Depreciation and amortization		10,500

Change in working capital

(Increase) Decrease in receivables	($5,000)	
(Increase) Decrease in inventories	(8,000)	
Increase (Decrease) in payables	6,000	
Increase (Decrease) in other current liabilities	1,500	
Net change in working capital		(5,500)
Net cash from operating activities		$42,450

(Exhibit continued on next page…)

EXHIBIT P-5	(continued)

Cash Flow from investing activities

| Purchase of property, plant, and equipment | ($15,000) | |
| Net cash from investing activities | | ($15,000) |

Cash flow from financing activities

Change in debt outstanding	$4,000	
Payment of cash dividends	(22,470)	
Net cash from financing activities		(18,470)

Net change in cash and cash equivalents		$8,980
Cash at beginning of period		11,020
Cash at end of period		$20,000

Mackinac has announced that it has finalized an agreement to handle North American production of a successful product currently marketed by a foreign company. Jones decides to value Mackinac using the dividend discount model (DDM) and the free cash flow-to-equity (FCFE) model. After reviewing Mackinac's financial statements above and forecasts related to the new production agreement, Jones concludes the following:

▶ Mackinac's earnings and FCFE are expected to grow 17 percent a year over the next three years before stabilizing at an annual growth rate of 9 percent.

▶ Mackinac will maintain the current payout ratio.

▶ Mackinac's beta is 1.25.

▶ The government bond yield is 6 percent, and the market equity risk premium is 5 percent.

A. Calculate the value of a share of Mackinac's common stock using the two-stage DDM. Show your calculations.

B. Calculate the value of a share of Mackinac's common stock using the two-stage FCFE model. Show your calculations.

C. Jones is discussing with a corporate client the possibility of that client acquiring a 70 percent interest in Mackinac. Discuss whether the DDM or FCFE model is more appropriate for this client's valuation purposes.

15. SK Telecom Co. is a cellular telephone paging and computer communication services company in Seoul, South Korea. The company is traded on the Korea, New York, and London stock exchanges (NYSE: SKM). Sol Kim has estimated the normalized FCFE for SK Telecom to be 1,300 Korean won (per share) for the year just ended. The real country return for South Korea is 6.50 percent. To estimate the required return for SK Telecom, the adjustments to the real country return are an industry adjustment of +0.60 percent, a size adjustment of −0.10 percent, and a leverage adjustment of +0.25 percent. The long-term real growth rate for South Korea is estimated at 3.5 percent, and Kim expects the real growth rate of SK Telecom to track the country rate.

A. What is the real required rate of return for SK Telecom?

   B. Using the single-stage FCFE valuation model and real values for the dis-
          count rate and FCFE growth rate, estimate the value of one share of SK
          Telecom.

16. Lawrence McKibben is preparing a valuation of Tele Norte Leste Participa-
     coes SA (NYSE: TNE), a telecom services company headquartered in Rio de
     Janeiro, Brazil. McKibben has decided to use a three-stage FCFE valuation
     model and the following estimates. The FCFE per share for the current year
     is $0.75. FCFE is expected to grow at 10 percent for next year, then at 26
     percent annually for the following three years, and then grow at 6 percent
     in Year 5 and thereafter. TNE's estimated beta is 2.00, and McKibben feels
     that current market conditions dictate a 4.5 percent risk-free rate of return
     and a 5.0 percent equity risk premium. Given McKibben's assumptions and
     approach, what is the value of Tele Norte Leste Participacoes?

17. Clay Cooperman has valued the operating assets of Johnson Extrusion at
     $720 million. The company also has short-term cash and securities with a
     market value of $60 million. The noncurrent investments have a book value
     of $30 million and a market value of $45 million. The company also has an
     overfunded pension plan, with plan assets of $210 million and plan liabili-
     ties of $170 million. Johnson Extrusion has $215 million of notes and bonds
     outstanding and 100 million outstanding shares. What is the value per
     share?

$$
\begin{array}{r}
60 \\
+\,45 \\
+\,40 \quad (210-170) \\
\hline
145
\end{array}
$$

$$
\frac{720 + 145 - 215}{100}
$$

$$
= 6.50 \quad \text{Per Share}
$$

Questions 18–23 relate to Gabriela Cervera

Gabriela Cervera is a new equity analyst at Mita Asset Management (MAM). Cervera's supervisor has asked her to prepare valuations of two companies— Geo, Inc. and Raylord Corporation—to present at an upcoming investment policy committee meeting. The supervisor states that MAM would like to assess the value that a prospective acquirer would pay to take control of the companies. He asks Cervera to consider the following models and advise the committee as to which model is most appropriate for Geo:

► free cash flow model

► Gordon growth model

► residual income model

► two-stage dividend discount model

Geo pays a constant dividend of $2.00 and is expected to do so for the foreseeable future regardless of the growth in earnings or cash flow. Cervera expects Geo's free cash flow to equity to grow at 8 percent per year for the next five years and 4 percent per year thereafter. Geo's financial statements reveal that the clean surplus relation does not hold.

Cervera estimates that Raylord's dividends will grow at an initial rate of 12 percent with the growth rate declining linearly over a 4-year period to a final and perpetual growth rate of 5 percent. Raylord's free cash flow to equity is expected to grow at 11 percent for the next three years and 4 percent thereafter. Financial data for Raylord are presented in Exhibit 1.

EXHIBIT 1	Financial Data for Raylord Corporation
Current free cash flow to equity (in millions)	$850
Capital expenditures (in millions)	$150
Current dividend per share	$1.50
Required return for equity	12.5%
Percentage of equity	100%
Percentage of debt	0%
Current price per share	$67

Cervera prepares analyses based on the dividend discount model and the discounted free cash flow model for Raylord.

In preparation for the meeting with the investment policy committee, Cervera writes a note on the application of free cash flow models, part of which is reproduced in Exhibit 2.

EXHIBIT 2	Free Cash Flow Valuation Note

The computation of a company's current-year free cash flow to equity is not affected by:

a. paying cash dividends in that year

b. new debt issuances in that year

A year later, Geo announces a change in dividend policy from a constant dollar dividend to a constant payout ratio. Cervera decides to perform a computation of sustainable growth to determine whether the current growth rate assumptions are appropriate. Cervera creates a long-term forecast for Geo as presented in Exhibit 3.

EXHIBIT 3	Long-term Forecast Information for Geo, Inc.
Net profit margin	5%
Asset turnover	1.25
Financial leverage (asset/equity)	2.00
Dividend payout ratio	40%
Income tax rate	30%

18. Given Geo's initial circumstances, which model is most appropriate for valuing Geo's equity?

  A. Free cash flow model.

  B. Gordon growth model.

  C. Residual income model.

  D. Two-stage dividend discount model.

19. Using the H-model version of the discounted dividend approach, Raylord's equity value per share is *closest* to

  A. $21.00.

  B. $22.24.

  C. $23.80.

  D. $25.48.

20. Compared with free cash flow to equity (FCFE), Raylord's free cash flow to the firm (FCFF) and cash flow from operating activities (CFO), respectively, are *most likely* to be

	FCFF	CFO
A.	higher	lower
B.	higher	higher
C.	the same	lower
D.	the same	higher

21. Using a free cash flow to equity model, the total value of Raylord's equity (in millions) is *closest* to

  A. $ 9,990.

  B. $11,360.

  C. $12,470.

  D. $13,150.

22. Regarding the effect of cash dividends and new debt issuances, respectively, on free cash flow to equity, Cervera's note (Exhibit 2) is

2006 exam

	Cash Dividends	New Debt Issuances
A.	Correct	Correct
B.	Correct	Incorrect
C.	Incorrect	Correct
D.	Incorrect	Incorrect

23. Based on Exhibit 3, the *best* estimate of the sustainable growth rate for Geo is

   A. 5.00%.

   B. 5.25%.

   C. 6.00%.

   D. 7.50%.

CFA
2006 exam

(handwritten notes:) D. Pont

$(1-0.4)$?? result

$5\% + 1.25 \times 2$

$= 12.5 \times 0.6$

$= 7.5$

$4\frac{7}{8}$ 4

$5\frac{1}{2}$ $5\frac{1}{2}$ $-$ $\frac{3}{8}$

$5\frac{1}{2}$ $21\frac{3}{16}$ $-$ $\frac{1}{16}$

$20\frac{5}{8}$ $21\frac{3}{16}$ $-$ $\frac{7}{8}$

$17\frac{3}{8}$ $18\frac{1}{8}$ $+$

$15\frac{1}{2}$ $6\frac{1}{2}$ $6\frac{1}{2}$ $-$ $\frac{1}{2}$

$7\frac{1}{4}$ $6\frac{1}{2}$ $31\frac{1}{32}$ $-$

$\frac{15}{16}$

1 $\frac{9}{16}$

$\frac{9}{16}$ $\frac{9}{16}$

$13\frac{1}{32}$

$7\frac{13}{16}$ $7\frac{15}{16}$

$7\frac{15}{16}$ $7\frac{13}{16}$ $7\frac{15}{16}$

$2\frac{5}{8}$ $2\frac{11}{32}$ $2\frac{1}{2}$ $+$

$2\frac{3}{4}$ $2\frac{1}{4}$ $2\frac{1}{4}$

$6\frac{1}{2}$ $12\frac{1}{16}$ $11\frac{3}{8}$ $11\frac{3}{4}$ $+$

87 $33\frac{3}{4}$ 33 $33\frac{1}{8}$ $-$

502 $25\frac{5}{8}$ $24\frac{9}{16}$ $25\frac{3}{8}$ $+$

833 12 $11\frac{5}{8}$ $11\frac{7}{8}$ $+$

16 $10\frac{1}{2}$ $10\frac{1}{2}$ $10\frac{1}{2}$ $-$

78 $15\frac{7}{8}$ $15\frac{13}{16}$ $15\frac{7}{8}$

4508 $9\frac{1}{16}$ $8\frac{1}{4}$ $8\frac{1}{8}$

430 $11\frac{1}{4}$ $10\frac{1}{8}$ $10\frac{1}{8}$

$4\frac{7}{8}$

MARKET-BASED VALUATION: PRICE MULTIPLES

by John D. Stowe, Thomas R. Robinson, Jerald E. Pinto, and Dennis W. McLeavey

LEARNING OUTCOMES

The candidate should be able to:

a. distinguish between the method of comparables and the method based on forecasted fundamentals as approaches to using price multiples in valuation, and discuss the economic rationales for each approach;

b. define a justified price multiple;

c. discuss rationales for using each price multiple and dividend yield in valuation, discuss possible drawbacks to the use of each price multiple and dividend yield, and calculate each price multiple and dividend yield;

d. calculate underlying earnings given earnings per share (EPS) and nonrecurring items in the income statement and discuss the methods of normalizing EPS, and calculate normalized EPS by each method;

e. explain and justify the use of earnings yield (E/P);

f. discuss the fundamental factors that influence each price multiple and dividend yield;

g. calculate the justified price-to-earnings ratio (P/E), price-to-book ratio (P/B), and price-to-sales ratio (P/S) for a stock, based on forecasted fundamentals;

h. calculate a predicted P/E, given a cross-sectional regression on fundamentals, and explain limitations to the cross-sectional regression methodology;

i. define the benchmark value of a multiple;

j. evaluate a stock by the method of comparables using each of the price multiples and explain the importance of fundamentals in using the method of comparables;

k. calculate the P/E-to-growth ratio (PEG), and explain its use in relative valuation;

l. calculate and explain the use of price multiples in determining terminal value in a multi-stage discounted cash flow (DCF) model;

m. discuss alternative definitions of cash flow used in price multiples, and explain the limitations of each definition;

n. discuss the sources of differences in cross-border valuation comparisons;

o. describe the main types of momentum indicators and their use in valuation.

Analysis of Equity Investments: Valuation, by John D. Stowe, Thomas R. Robinson, Jerald E. Pinto, and Dennis W. McLeavey. Copyright © 2002 by AIMR. Reprinted with permission.

411

INTRODUCTION

Among the most familiar and widely used valuation tools are price multiples. **Price multiples** are ratios of a stock's market price to some measure of value per share. The intuition behind price multiples is that we cannot evaluate a stock's price—judge whether it is fairly valued, overvalued, or undervalued—without knowing what a share buys in terms of assets, earnings, or some other measure of value. As valuation indicators (measures or indicators of value), price multiples have the appealing qualities of simplicity in use and ease in communication. A price multiple summarizes in a single number the valuation relationship between a stock's price and a familiar quantity such as earnings, sales, or book value per share. Among the questions we will study in this reading that will help us use price multiples professionally are the following:

▶ What accounting issues affect particular price multiples, and how can analysts address them?
▶ How do price multiples relate to fundamentals, such as earnings growth rates, and how can analysts use this information when making valuation comparisons among stocks?
▶ For which types of valuation problems is a particular price multiple appropriate or inappropriate?
▶ What challenges arise in applying price multiples internationally?

According to surveys of professional practice, **momentum indicators** are popular. These relate either price or a fundamental (such as earnings) to the time series of its own past values, or in some cases to its expected value. The logic behind the use of momentum indicators is the proposition that such indicators may provide information on future patterns of returns over some time horizon. Because the purpose of valuation is to help select rewarding investments, momentum indicators are also a class of valuation indicators, with a focus different from and complementary to that of price multiples.

The reading is organized as follows: In Section 2, we put the use of price multiples in its economic context and present certain themes common to the use of any price multiple. We then begin a treatment of individual ratios: Section 3 presents price-to-earnings multiples (P/Es), Section 4 presents price-to-book multiples (P/Bs), Section 5 presents price-to-sales multiples (P/Ss), and Section 6 presents price-to-cash flow multiples.

Enterprise value is the total market value of all sources of financing including common stock (a more technical definition will follow); EBITDA (earnings before interest, tax, depreciation, and amortization) is an accounting concept related to cash flow from operations. We present valuation using the ratio of enterprise value to EBITDA in Section 7. Dividends in relation to price have been used as a valuation indicator. Because the ratio of price to dividends is not defined for stocks that do not pay dividends, we discuss valuation in terms of dividend yield (D/P) in Section 8. Section 9 presents issues in using price multiples internationally. In Section 10, we turn to a discussion of momentum valuation indicators. We present some practical aspects of using valuation indicators in investment management in Section 11, and we conclude with a summary of the reading.

PRICE MULTIPLES IN VALUATION

In practice, analysts use price multiples in two ways: the method of comparables and the method based on forecasted fundamentals. Each of these methods relates to a definite economic rationale. In this section, we introduce the two methods and their associated economic rationales.

The idea behind price multiples is that we need to evaluate a stock's price in relation to what it buys in terms of earnings, assets, or some other measure of value. Obtained by dividing price by a measure of value per share, a price multiple gives the price to purchase one unit of value, however value is measured. For example, a price-to-sales ratio of 2 means that it takes two units of currency (for example, €2) to buy one unit of sales (for example, €1 of sales).

This scaling of price per share by value per share also makes comparisons possible among different stocks. For example, an investor pays more for a unit of sales for a stock with a P/S of 2.5 than for another stock with a P/S of 2. If the securities are otherwise closely similar (if they have similar risk, profit margins, and growth prospects, for example), the investor might conclude that the second security is undervalued relative to the first.

So, price multiples are price scaled by a measure of value, which provides the basis for the method of comparables. The **method of comparables** involves using a price multiple to evaluate whether an asset is relatively fairly valued, relatively undervalued, or relatively overvalued when compared to a benchmark value of the multiple. The word *relatively* is necessary. An asset may be undervalued relative to a comparison asset or group of assets, and an analyst may expect the asset to outperform the comparison asset or assets on a relative basis. If the comparison asset or assets themselves are not efficiently priced, however, the stock may not be undervalued—it could be fairly valued or even overvalued (on an absolute basis).

Many choices for the benchmark value of a multiple have appeared in stock valuation, including the multiple of a closely matched individual stock as well as the average or median value of the multiple for the stock's company or industry peer group. The economic rationale underlying the method of comparables is the law of one price—the economic principle that two identical assets should sell at the same price.[1] The method of comparables is perhaps the most widely used approach for analysts reporting valuation judgments on the basis of price multiples.

Because cash flows are related to fundamentals, we can also relate multiples to company fundamentals through a discounted cash flow (DCF) model. Expressions for price multiples in terms of fundamentals permit analysts to examine how valuation differences across stocks relate to different expectations concerning fundamentals such as earnings growth rates.

---

[1] In practice, analysts can at best only approximately match characteristics across companies. To keep our classification simple, we treat comparisons with a market index and with historical values of a stock's multiple under the rubric of the method of comparables. Nevertheless, the law of one price is the idea driving the method of comparables.

Recall that DCF models view the intrinsic value of stock as the present value of all its expected future returns or cash flows. Fundamentals—characteristics of a business related to profitability or financial strength—drive cash flows. Price multiples are calculated with respect to a single value of a fundamental, such as earnings per share (EPS). For example, we calculate what we will later discuss as a leading price–earnings multiple (P/E) on the basis of a forecast of EPS for the next year. Despite being stated with respect to only a single value of a fundamental, we can relate any price multiple to the entire future stream of expected cash flows through its DCF value. We do this by first taking the present value of the stream of expected future cash flows; we then divide that present value by the fundamental (e.g., forecasted EPS).

For example, if the DCF value of a U.K. stock is GBP10.20 and forecasted EPS is GBP1.2, the P/E consistent with the DCF value is GBP10.20/GBP1.2 = 8.5. We can do this exercise using any DCF model (defining cash flows as dividends, free cash flow, or residual income) and any definition of price multiple. We illustrated this concept in Reading 46, where we explained P/E in terms of perhaps the simplest DCF model, the Gordon growth dividend discount model, in an expression that includes the expected dividend growth rate (among other variables). We call the approach relating a price multiple to fundamentals through a DCF model the **method based on forecasted fundamentals**.[2] DCF valuation, because it incorporates forecasts of all future returns or cash flows, is the most basic valuation approach in theory. That characteristic of DCF models and the possibility of relating price multiples to DCF models provide the economic rationale for the method based on forecasted fundamentals.

We can also usefully incorporate the insights from the method based on forecasted fundamentals in explaining valuation differences based on comparables, because we seldom find other than approximate comparables. In the sections covering each multiple, we will present the method based on forecasted fundamentals first so we can refer to it when using the method of comparables.

In summary, we can approach valuation using multiples from two perspectives. First, we can use the method of comparables, which involves comparing a stock's multiple to a standard of comparison. Similar assets should sell at similar prices. Second, we can use the method based on forecasted fundamentals, which involves forecasting the stock's fundamentals rather than making comparisons with other stocks. The price multiple of an asset should be related to the prospective cash flows from holding it.

Using either method, how can an analyst express his view of the value of a stock? Of course the analyst can offer just the qualitative judgment that the stock appears to be fairly valued, overvalued, or undervalued (and offer definite reasons for the view). The analyst may also be more precise, communicating a **justified price multiple** for the stock: the estimated fair value of that multiple.[3] An analyst can justify a multiple based on the method of comparables or the method based on forecasted fundamentals.

For example, suppose that we are using the price-to-book multiple (P/B) in a valuation and that the mean P/B for the company's peer group, the standard of comparison, is 2.3. The stock's justified P/B, based on the method of comparables, is 2.3 (without making possible adjustments for differences in fundamentals). We can compare the justified with the actual P/B based on market price to form an opinion on value. If the justified P/B is larger (smaller) than the actual

---

[2] For brevity, we sometimes use the phrase "based on fundamentals" in describing multiples calculated according to this approach.

[3] The justified price multiple is also called the warranted price multiple or the intrinsic price multiple.

P/B, the stock may be undervalued (overvalued). We can also translate the justified P/B based on comparables into an estimate of absolute fair value of the
stock, on the assumption that the comparison assets are fairly priced. If the current book value per share is $23, then the fair value of the stock is 2.3 × $23 =
$52.90, which can be compared with its market price.

On the other hand, suppose that on the basis of a residual income model
valuation, the DCF value of the stock is $46. Then the justified P/B based on
forecasted fundamentals is $46/$23 = 2.0, which we can again compare with the
actual value of the stock's ratio. We can also state our estimate of the stock's
absolute fair value as 2 × $23 = $46. (Note that the analyst could report valuation judgments related to a DCF model in terms of the DCF value directly; however, price multiples are a familiar form in which to state valuations.)

In the next section, we begin our discussion of specific implementations of
the price multiple approach to valuation.

PRICE TO EARNINGS   3

In the first edition of *Security Analysis*, Benjamin Graham and David L. Dodd
(1934, p. 351) described common stock valuation based on P/Es as the standard
method of that era, and the price-to-earnings ratio is doubtless still the most
familiar valuation measure today.

We begin our discussion of the P/E with rationales offered by analysts for its
use, as well as possible drawbacks. We then define the two chief variations of the
P/E: the trailing P/E and the leading P/E. The multiple's numerator, market
price, is (as in other multiples) definitely determinable; it presents no special
problems of interpretation. But the denominator, EPS, is based on the complex
rules of accrual accounting and presents important interpretation issues. We
discuss those issues and the adjustments analysts can make to obtain more-
meaningful P/Es. Finally, we conclude the section by examining how analysts use
P/Es to value a stock using the method of forecasted fundamentals and the
method of comparables. As mentioned earlier, we discuss fundamentals first so
that we can draw from that discussion's insights when using comparables.

Analysts have offered several rationales for using P/Es:

▶ Earnings power is a chief driver of investment value, and EPS, the denominator of the P/E ratio, is perhaps the chief focus of security analysts' attention. In Block's 1999 survey of AIMR members, earnings ranked first among
   four variables—earnings, cash flow, book value, and dividends—as an input
   in valuation.

▶ The P/E ratio is widely recognized and used by investors.

▶ Differences in P/Es may be related to differences in long-run average
   returns, according to empirical research.[4]

Drawbacks to using P/Es derive from the characteristics of EPS:

▶ EPS can be negative, and the P/E ratio does not make economic sense with
   a negative denominator.

---

[4] Block (1999) documented a belief among AIMR members that low-P/E stocks tend to outperform
the market. See Bodie, Kane, and Marcus (2001) for a brief summary of the related academic
research, which has wide ramifications and is the subject of continuing active debate.

▶ The ongoing or recurring components of earnings are the most important in determining intrinsic value. Earnings often have volatile, transient components, however, making the analyst's task difficult.

▶ Management can exercise its discretion within allowable accounting practices to distort EPS as an accurate reflection of economic performance. Distortions can affect the comparability of P/Es across companies.

Analysts have developed methods to attempt to address these potential drawbacks, and we will discuss these methods later. In the next section, we discuss the definition and calculation of EPS for use in P/Es.

3.1 Determining Earnings

In calculating a P/E, the current price for publicly traded companies is generally easily obtained and unambiguous. Determining the earnings figure to be used in the denominator, however, is not as straightforward. The following two issues must be considered:

▶ the time horizon over which earnings are measured, which results in two chief alternative definitions of the P/E; and

▶ adjustments to accounting earnings that the analyst may make, so that P/Es can be compared across companies.

The two chief alternative definitions of P/E are trailing P/E and leading P/E. A stock's **trailing P/E** (sometimes referred to as a **current P/E**) is its current market price divided by the most recent four quarters' EPS. In such calculations, EPS is sometimes referred to as trailing 12 months (TTM) EPS. Trailing P/E is the P/E published in financial newspapers' stock listings. The **leading P/E** (also called the **forward P/E** or **prospective P/E**) is a stock's current price divided by next year's expected earnings. Other names and time horizon definitions also exist: First Call/Thomson Financial reports as the "current P/E" a stock's market price divided by the last reported annual EPS; Value Line reports as the "P/E" a stock's market price divided by the sum of the preceding two quarters' trailing earnings and the next two quarters' expected earnings.

In using the P/E, the same definition should be applied to all companies and time periods under examination. Otherwise the P/Es are not comparable, either for a given company over time or for different companies at a specific point in time. The differences in P/E calculated using different methods could be systematic (as opposed to random). For example, for companies with rising earnings, the leading P/E will be smaller than the trailing P/E because the denominator in the leading P/E calculation will be larger.

Logic sometimes indicates that a particular definition of the P/E is not relevant. For example, a major acquisition or divestiture may change the nature of a business so that the trailing P/E based on past EPS is not informative about the future and thus not relevant to a valuation. In such a case, the leading P/E is the appropriate measure. Valuation is a forward-looking process and the analyst, when she has earnings forecasts, usually features the leading P/E in analyses. If a company's future earnings are not readily predictable, however, then a trailing P/E (or alternative valuation metric) may be more appropriate. In the following sections, we address issues that arise in calculating trailing and leading P/Es.

3.1.1 Calculating the Trailing P/E

When calculating a P/E using trailing earnings, care must be taken in determining the EPS used in the denominator. An analyst must consider the following:

▶ transitory, nonrecurring components of earnings that are company specific;

▶ transitory components of earnings due to cyclicality (business or industry cyclicality);

▶ differences in accounting methods; and

▶ potential dilution of EPS.

Example 1 illustrates the first bullet point. Items in earnings that are not expected to recur in the future (nonrecurring earnings) are generally removed by analysts. Such items are not expected to reappear in future earnings, and valuation looks to the future as concerns cash flows. The analyst's focus is on estimating **underlying earnings**: earnings excluding nonrecurring components.[5] An increase in underlying earnings reflects an increase in earnings that the analyst expects to persist into the future.

EXAMPLE 1

Adjusting EPS for Nonrecurring Items

You are calculating a trailing P/E for American Electric Power (NYSE: AEP) as of 9 November 2001, when the share price closed at $44.50. In its fiscal year ended 31 December 2000, AEP recorded EPS of $0.83 that included an extraordinary loss of $0.11. Additionally, AEP took an expense of $203 million for merger costs during that calendar year, which are not expected to recur, and had unusual deficits in two out of four quarters. As of November 2001, the trailing twelve months' EPS was $2.16, including three quarters in 2001 and one quarter in 2000. The fourth quarter of calendar year 2000 had $0.69 per share in nonrecurring expenses. Without making an adjustment for nonrecurring items, the trailing P/E was $44.50/$2.16 = 20.6. Adjusting for these items, you arrive at a figure for trailing EPS of $2.85 using an underlying earnings concept, and a trailing P/E of $44.50/$2.85 = 15.6. This number is the P/E an analyst would use in valuation, being consistent in the treatment of earnings for all stocks under review. In the course of this reading, we will illustrate adjustments to earnings in many examples.

The identification of nonrecurring items often requires detailed work, in particular the examination of the income statement, the footnotes to the income statement, and management's discussion and analysis. The analyst cannot rely only on income statement classifications in identifying the nonrecurring components of earnings. Nonrecurring items (for example, gains and losses from the

---

[5] Other names for underlying earnings include **persistent earnings**, **continuing earnings**, and **core earnings**.

sale of assets, asset write-downs, provisions for future losses, and changes in accounting estimates) often appear in the income from continuing operations portion of a business's income statement.[6] An analyst taking the income statement classification at face value could draw incorrect conclusions in a valuation.

Besides company-specific effects such as restructuring costs, transitory effects on earnings can come from business-cycle or industry-cycle influences, as stated in the second bullet point above. These effects are somewhat different in nature. Because business cycles repeat, such effects (although transitory) can be expected to recur over subsequent cycles.

Because of cyclic effects, the most recent four quarters of earnings may not accurately reflect the average or long-term earnings power of the business, particularly for **cyclical businesses**—businesses with high sensitivity to business- or industry-cycle influences. Trailing EPS for such stocks are often depressed or negative at the bottom of the cycle and unusually high at the top of the cycle. Empirically, P/Es for cyclical companies are often highly volatile over a cycle without any change in business prospects: high P/Es on depressed EPS at the bottom of the cycle and low P/Es on unusually high EPS at the top of the cycle, a countercyclical property of P/Es known as the **Molodovsky effect**.[7] Analysts address this problem by normalizing EPS—that is, calculating the level of EPS that the business could achieve currently under mid-cyclical conditions (**normalized earnings per share** or **normal earnings per share**).[8] Two of several available methods to calculate normal EPS are as follows:

▶ *The method of historical average EPS.* Normal EPS is calculated as average EPS over the most recent full cycle.

▶ *The method of average return on equity.* Normal EPS is calculated as the average return on equity (ROE) from the most recent full cycle, multiplied by current book value per share.

The first method is one of several possible statistical approaches to the problem of cyclical earnings; however, this method does not account for changes in the business's size. The second alternative, by using recent book value per share, reflects more accurately the effect on EPS of growth or shrinkage in the company's size. For that reason, the method of average ROE is sometimes preferred.[9] When reported current book value does not adequately reflect company size in relation to past values (because of items such as large write-downs), the analyst can make the appropriate accounting adjustment. The analyst can also estimate normalized earnings by multiplying total assets by an estimate of the long-run return on total assets.[10]

---

[6] An asset **write-down** is a reduction in the value of an asset as stated in the balance sheet. The timing and amount of write-downs often are at least in part discretionary. **Accounting estimates** include the useful lives of assets (depreciable lives), warranty costs, and the amount of uncollectible receivables.

[7] Named after Nicholas Molodovsky, who wrote on this subject in the 1950s. We can state the Molodovsky effect another way: P/Es may be negatively related to the recent earnings growth rate but positively related to the anticipated future growth rate, because of expected rebounds in earnings.

[8] The wording is based on a definition in Kisor and Whitbeck (1963, p. 57). Some writers describe the removal of any one-time or nonrecurring items from earnings as normalizing earnings as well.

[9] This approach has appeared in valuation research, as in Michaud (1999), who calculated a normalized earnings yield rather than a normalized P/E. (Earnings yield is earnings per share divided by price.)

[10] An example of the application of this method is Lee, Myers, and Swaminathan (1999), who used 6 percent of total assets as an estimate of normal earnings levels when current earnings for a company were negative, in their study of the intrinsic value of the Dow Jones Industrial Average, a U.S. equity index. According to the authors, the long-run return on total assets in the United States is approximately 6 percent.

EXAMPLE 2

Normalizing EPS for Business-Cycle Effects

You are researching the valuation of Koninklijke Philips Electronics N.V.
(NYSE: PHG), Europe's largest electronics company, as of the beginning
of November 2001. On 8 November 2001, PHG stock closed at $25.72.
PHG experienced a severe cyclical contraction in its Consumer Electronics division in 2001, resulting in a loss of $1.94 per share; you thus
decide to normalize earnings. You believe the 1995–2000 period (which
excludes 2001) reasonably captures average profitability over a business
cycle. Table 1 supplies data on EPS, book value per share (BVPS), and
return on equity (ROE).[11]

TABLE 1	Koninklijke Philips (EPS and BVPS in U.S. dollars)						
	2001	**2000**	**1999**	**1998**	**1997**	**1996**	**1995**
EPS	(1.94)	2.11	1.15	0.87	1.16	0.55	1.14
BVPS	13.87	16.62	9.97	11.68	6.57	6.43	6.32
ROE	NM	0.129	0.104	0.072	0.168	0.083	0.179

NM = not meaningful.
Sources: www.philips.com for 2001 data; *The Value Line Investment Survey* for other data.

Using the data in Table 1,

1. Calculate a normal EPS for PHG based on the method of historical
   average EPS, and then calculate the P/E based on that estimate of
   normal EPS.

2. Calculate a normal EPS for PHG based on the method of average
   ROE and the P/E based on that estimate of normal EPS.

3. Explain the source of the differences in the normal EPS calculated
   by the two methods, and contrast the impact on the estimate of a
   normal P/E.

Solution to 1: Averaging EPS over the 1995–2000 period, we find that
($1.14 + $0.55 + $1.16 + $0.87 + $1.15 + $2.11)/6 = $1.16. Accord-
ing to the method of historical average EPS, PHG's normal EPS is
$1.16. The P/E based on this estimate is $25.72/1.16 = 22.2.

Solution to 2: Averaging ROE over the 1995–2000 period, we find that
(0.179 + 0.083 + 0.168 + 0.072 + 0.104 + 0.129)/6 = 0.1225, or
12.25%. For current BVPS, we use the 2001 value of $13.87. According to
the method of average ROE, we have 0.1225 × $13.87 = $1.70 as normal
EPS. The P/E based on this estimate is $25.72/$1.70 = 15.1.

---

[11] EPS and BVPS are based on EUR/USD translation rates for 2001 and 2000 and on Dutch
guilder/USD translation rates for earlier years, as given by Value Line.

Solution to 3: From 1995 to 2001, BVPS increased from $6.32 to $13.87, an increase of about 219 percent. The estimate of $1.70 from the average ROE method compared with $1.16 from the historical average EPS method reflects the use of information on the current size of the company. Because of that difference, PHG appears more conservatively valued (as indicated by a lower P/E) using the method based on average ROE.

We also need to adjust EPS for differences in accounting methods between the company and its standard of comparison or benchmark, so that the P/Es are comparable.

EXAMPLE 3

Adjusting for Differences in Accounting Methods

In late October 1999, Coachmen Industries (NYSE: COA) was trading at a price of $16 per share and had trailing twelve months EPS of $1.99. COA's P/E was thus 8.04. At the same time, Winnebago Industries (NYSE: WGO) was trading at a price of $17 per share and had trailing twelve months EPS of $1.99 for a P/E of 8.54. COA uses the first-in, first-out (FIFO) method of accounting for its inventory. WGO uses the last-in, first-out (LIFO) method of accounting for its inventory. Adjusting WGO's results for differences between the LIFO and FIFO methods produces an adjusted EPS of $2.02 and an adjusted P/E of 8.42. Adjusting EPS for WGO for consistency with COA's inventory accounting method narrows the difference between the two companies' P/Es.

In addition to adjustments for nonrecurring items and accounting methods, the analyst should consider the impact of potential dilution on EPS.[12] Companies are required to present both basic EPS and diluted EPS. **Basic earnings per share** reflects total earnings divided by the weighted-average number of shares actually outstanding during the period. **Diluted earnings per share** reflects division by the number of shares that would be outstanding if holders of securities such as executive stock options, equity warrants, and **convertible bonds** exercised their options to obtain common stock.

---

[12] Dilution refers to the reduction in the proportional ownership interests as a result of the issuance of new shares.

EXAMPLE 4

Basic versus Diluted Earnings per Share

For the fiscal year ended 31 June 2001, Microsoft (Nasdaq NMS: MSFT) had basic EPS of \$1.38 and diluted EPS of \$1.32. Based on a stock price of \$60 shortly after the release of the annual report, Microsoft's trailing P/E is 43.5 using basic EPS and 45.5 using diluted EPS.

Two issues concerning P/Es that relate to their use in investment management and research are (1) negative earnings and (2) look-ahead bias in calculating trailing P/Es. (**Look-ahead bias** is the use of information that is not contemporaneously available in computing a quantity.)

Stock selection disciplines that use P/Es or other price multiples often involve ranking stocks from highest value of the multiple to lowest value of the multiple. The security with the lowest positive P/E has the lowest purchase cost per currency unit of earnings among the securities ranked. Negative earnings, however, result in a negative P/E. A negative-P/E security will rank below the lowest positive-P/E security but, because earnings are negative, the negative-P/E security is actually the most costly in terms of earnings purchased.[13]

Negative P/Es are not meaningful. In some cases, an analyst might handle negative EPS by using normal EPS in its place. Also, when trailing EPS is negative, year-ahead EPS and thus the leading P/E may be positive. If the analyst is interested in a ranking, an available solution (applicable to any ratio involving a quantity that can be negative or zero) is to restate the ratio with price in the denominator, because price is never negative.[14] In the case of the P/E, the associated ratio is E/P, the **earnings yield** ratio. Ranked by earnings yields from highest to lowest, the securities are correctly ranked from cheapest to most costly in terms of the amount of earnings one unit of currency buys.

Table 2 illustrates the above points for a group of personal computer manufacturers, three of which have negative EPS. When reporting a P/E based on negative earnings, analysts should report such P/Es as NM (not meaningful).

Investment analysts often research investment strategies involving P/Es and other price multiples using historical data. When doing so, analysts must be aware that time lags in the reporting of financial results create the potential for look-ahead bias in the research. For example, as of early January 2003, most companies have not reported EPS for the last quarter of 2002, so a trailing P/E would be based on EPS for first, second, and third quarters of 2002 and the last quarter of 2001. An investment strategy based on a trailing P/E calculated using actual EPS for the last quarter of 2002 could be examined with hindsight, but because the portfolio manager could not implement the strategy in practice, it would involve look-ahead bias. The correction is to calculate the trailing P/E based on four quarters of EPS, lagged by a sufficient amount of time relative to the time at

[13] Some research indicates that stocks with negative P/Es have special risk-return characteristics (see Fama and French 1992), so care should be exercised in interpreting such rankings.
[14] Earnings yield can be based on normal EPS and expected next-year EPS as well as on trailing EPS. In these cases too, earnings yield provides a consistent ranking.

TABLE 2   P/E and E/P for Four Personal Computer Manufacturers (as of 13 November 2001; in U.S. dollars)

	Current Price	Trailing EPS	Trailing P/E	E/P
Dell Computer Corporation (Nasdaq NMS: DELL)	26.00	0.49	53.06	1.9%
Apple Computer (Nasdaq NMS: AAPL)	19.20	−0.11	NM	−0.6%
Compaq Computer Corporation (NYSE: CPQ)	8.59	−0.40	NM	−4.7%
Gateway (NYSE: GTW)	8.07	−3.15	NM	−39.0%

Source: Morningstar, Inc.

which stock price is observed, so that the EPS information would be contemporaneously available. The same principle applies to other multiples calculated on a trailing basis.

3.1.2 Calculating a Leading P/E

In the definition of leading P/E, analysts have interpreted "next year's expected earnings" as:

► expected EPS for the next four quarters; or

► expected EPS for the next fiscal year.

We can take the first definition, which is closest to how cash flows are dated in our discussion of DCF valuation, as what we understand by leading P/E, unless stated otherwise.[15] To illustrate the calculation, suppose the current market price of a stock is $15 as of 1 March 2003, and the most recently reported quarterly EPS (for the quarter ended 31 December 2002) is $0.22. Your forecasts of EPS are as follows:

► $0.15 for the quarter ending 31 March 2003

► $0.18 for the quarter ending 30 June 2003

► $0.18 for the quarter ending 30 September 2003

► $0.24 for the quarter ending 31 December 2003

The sum of the forecasts for the next four quarters to report is $0.15 + $0.18 + $0.18 + $0.24 = $0.75, and the leading P/E for this stock is $15/$0.75 = 20.0.

For examples of the fiscal year concept, First Call/Thomson Financial reports a stock's "forward P/E" (leading P/E) in two ways: first, based on the

---

[15] Analysts have developed DCF expressions incorporating fractional time periods. In practice, uncertainty in forecasts is the more limiting factor to accuracy in estimating justified P/Es.

EXAMPLE 5

Calculating a Leading P/E Ratio (1)

A market price for the common stock of American Electric Power (NYSE: AEP) in mid-November 2001 was $44.55. AEP's fiscal year coincides with the calendar year. According to Zacks Investment Research, the consensus EPS forecast for 2001 (FY1 as of November 2001) was $3.87. The consensus EPS forecast for 2002 (FY2 as of November 2001) was $3.69.

1. Calculate AEP's leading P/E based on a fiscal year definition and FY1 consensus forecasted EPS.
2. Calculate AEP's leading P/E based on a fiscal year definition and FY2 consensus forecasted EPS.

Solution to 1: AEP's leading P/E is $44.55/$3.87 = 11.5 based on FY1 forecasted EPS. Note that this EPS number involves the forecast of only one quarter as of November 2001.

Solution to 2: AEP's leading P/E is $44.55/$3.69 = 12.1 based on FY2 forecasted EPS.

mean of analysts' current fiscal year (FY1 = Fiscal Year 1) forecasts, in which analysts may have actual EPS in hand for some quarters; and second, based on analysts' following fiscal year (FY2 = Fiscal Year 2) forecasts, which must be based entirely on forecasts. For First Call, "forward P/E" contrasts with "current P/E", which is based on the last reported annual EPS, as mentioned earlier. Clearly, analysts must be consistent in the definition of leading P/E when comparing stocks.

In Example 5, the business's EPS was expected to be relatively stable, and the leading P/Es based on the two different EPS specifications presented did not vary substantially from each other. Example 6 presents the calculation of leading P/Es for the company examined in Example 2, Koninklijke Philips. Valuations according to leading P/E can vary dramatically depending on the definition of earnings for businesses with volatile earnings. The analyst was probably justified in normalizing EPS in Example 2.

EXAMPLE 6

Calculating a Leading P/E Ratio (2)

In Example 2, we calculated a normalized EPS for Koninklijke Philips (NYSE: PHG) and a P/E based on normalized EPS. In this example, we compute leading P/Es for PHG using alternative definitions. Table 3 presents PHG's actual and forecasted EPS, which reflect a severe downturn in its Consumer Electronics division.

> **TABLE 3   Quarterly EPS for PHG (in U.S. dollars, excluding nonrecurring items)**
>
> | | 31 March | 30 June | 30 September | 31 December |
> |-------|----------|---------|--------------|-------------|
> | 2001 | 0.08 | (0.34) | (0.27) | E0.00 |
> | 2002 | E(0.05) | E0.10 | E0.15 | E0.30 |
>
> *Source: The Value Line Investment Survey.*

On 8 November 2001, PHG stock closed at $25.72. PHG's fiscal year ends on 31 December. As of 8 November 2001, solve the following problems using the information in Table 3:

1. Calculate PHG's leading P/E based on the next four quarters of forecasted EPS.
2. Calculate PHG's leading P/E based on a fiscal year definition and current fiscal year (2001) forecasted EPS.
3. Calculate PHG's leading P/E based on a fiscal year definition and next fiscal year (2002) forecasted EPS.

Solution to 1: We sum forecasted EPS as follows:

4Q:2001 EPS (estimate)	$0.00
1Q:2002 EPS (estimate)	($0.05)
2Q:2002 EPS (estimate)	$0.10
3Q:2002 EPS (estimate)	$0.15
Sum	$0.20

The leading P/E by this definition is $25.72/$0.20 = 128.6.

Solution to 2: We sum EPS as follows:

1Q:2001 EPS (actual)	$0.08
2Q:2001 EPS (actual)	($0.34)
3Q:2001 EPS (actual)	($0.27)
4Q:2001 EPS (estimate)	$0.00
Sum	($0.53)

The leading P/E is $25.72/($0.53) = −48.5 or not meaningful (NM).

Solution to 3: We sum EPS as follows:

1Q:2002 EPS (estimate)	($0.05)
2Q:2002 EPS (estimate)	$0.10
3Q:2002 EPS (estimate)	$0.15
4Q:2002 EPS (estimate)	$0.30
Sum	$0.50

The leading P/E by this definition is $25.72/$0.50 = 51.4.

Having explored the issues involved in calculating P/Es, we turn to using them in valuation.

3.2 Valuation Based on Forecasted Fundamentals

The analyst who understands DCF valuation models can use them not only in developing an estimate of the justified P/E for a stock but also to gain insight into possible sources of valuation differences using the method of comparables. The simplest of all DCF models is the Gordon growth form of the dividend discount model. In Reading 46, we related the P/E to the Gordon growth model value of the stock through the expressions

$$\frac{P_0}{E_1} = \frac{D_1/E_1}{r - g} = \frac{1 - b}{r - g}$$

which was Equation 46-21 for the leading P/E, and

$$\frac{P_0}{E_0} = \frac{D_0(1 + g)/E_0}{r - g} = \frac{(1 - b)(1 + g)}{r - g}$$

which was Equation 46-22 for the trailing P/E. Note that both expressions state P/E as a function of two fundamentals: the stock's required rate of return, r, reflecting its risk, and the expected (stable) dividend growth rate, g. The dividend payout ratio, $1 - b$, also enters into the expression. A particular value of the P/E is associated with a set of forecasts of the fundamentals (and dividend payout ratio). This value is the stock's justified P/E based on forecasted fundamentals (that is, the P/E justified by fundamentals). The higher the expected dividend growth rate or the lower the stock's required rate of return, the higher the stock's intrinsic value and the higher its justified P/E, all else equal. This intuition carries over to more-complex DCF models. Using any DCF model, all else equal, justified P/E is:

▶ inversely related to the stock's required rate of return; and

▶ positively related to the growth rate(s) of future expected cash flows, however defined.

We illustrate the calculation of a justified leading P/E in Example 7.

EXAMPLE 7

Leading P/E Based on Fundamental Forecasts (1)

FPL Group (NYSE: FPL) is a southeastern U.S. utility. Jan Unger, a utility analyst, forecasts a long-term earnings retention rate (b) of 50 percent and a long-term growth rate of 5 percent. Unger also calculates a required rate of return of 9 percent. Based on Unger's forecasts of fundamentals and the equation above, FPL's justified leading P/E is

$$\frac{P_0}{E_1} = \frac{1 - b}{r - g} = \frac{1 - 0.50}{0.09 - 0.05} = 12.5$$

When assuming a complex DCF model for valuing the stock, we may not be able to express the P/E as a function of fundamental variables. Nevertheless, we can still calculate a justified P/E by dividing the DCF value by the fundamental used in the multiple, as illustrated in Example 8.

EXAMPLE 8

Leading P/E Based on Fundamental Forecasts (2)

Hyundai Motor Company Ltd (KSE: 05380.KS) manufactures and sells cars, trucks, and commercial vehicles. As of the beginning of February 2002, you are valuing Hyundai stock (which closed at Korean won 29,300 on that day). Using a spreadsheet free-cash-flow-to-equity model in which you have forecasted FCFE individually for 2002 and 2003, and valuing the final piece using a P/E, you obtain a FCFE value for the stock of KRW31,500. For ease of communication, you want to express your valuation in terms of a leading P/E based on forecasted year 2002 EPS of KRW4,446.

1. What is Hyundai's justified P/E based on forecasted fundamentals?
2. State whether the stock appears to be fairly valued, overvalued, or undervalued, based on your answer to Problem 1.

Solution to 1: KRW31,500/KRW4,446 = 7.1 is the justified leading P/E.

Solution to 2: The justified P/E of 7.1 is slightly larger than the leading P/E based on market price, KRW29,300/KRW4,446 = 6.6. Consequently, the stock appears to be slightly undervalued.

Although related to a justified P/E, a predicted P/E can be estimated from cross-sectional regressions of P/E on the fundamentals believed to drive security valuation. Kisor and Whitbeck (1963) and Malkiel and Cragg (1970) pioneered this approach. The P/Es, and the stock and company characteristics thought to determine P/E, are measured as of a given year for a group of stocks. The P/Es are regressed against the stock and company characteristics. The estimated equation shows the relationships in the data set between P/E and the characteristics for that group of stocks and for that time period. The Kisor and Whitbeck study included the historical growth rate in earnings, the dividend payout ratio, and the standard deviation of EPS changes as explanatory (independent) variables. Malkiel and Cragg (1970) introduced explanatory variables based on expectations (alongside regressions on historical values). The analyst can in fact conduct such cross-sectional regressions using any set of variables he believes determines investment value. Other DCF models besides the dividend discount model (DDM) can provide ideas for such variables.

The cross-sectional regression method summarizes a large amount of data in a single equation and can provide a useful additional perspective on a valuation.

EXAMPLE 9

Predicted P/E Based on a Cross-Sectional Regression

You are valuing a food company with a beta of 0.9, a dividend payout ratio of 0.45, and an earnings growth rate of 0.08. The estimated regression for a group of other stocks in the same industry is

$$\text{Predicted P/E} = 12.12 + (2.25 \times \text{DPR}) - (0.20 \times \text{beta}) + (14.43 \times \text{EGR})$$

where

DPR = the dividend payout ratio
beta = the stock's beta
EGR = the five-year earnings growth rate

1. What is the predicted P/E for the food company based on the above cross-sectional regression?
2. If the stock's actual trailing P/E is 18, is the stock fairly valued, overvalued, or undervalued?

Solution to 1: Predicted P/E = $12.12 + (2.25 \times 0.45) - (0.20 \times 0.9) + (14.43 \times 0.08) = 14.1$. The predicted P/E is 14.1.

Solution to 2: Because the predicted P/E of 14.1 is less than the actual P/E of 18, the stock appears to be overvalued (selling at a higher multiple than is justified by its fundamentals).

It is infrequently used as a main tool, however, because it is subject to at least three limitations:

▶ The method captures valuation relationships for a specific time period and sample of stocks. The predictive power of the regression for a different stock and different time period is not known.

▶ The regression coefficients and explanatory power of the regressions tend to change substantially over a number of years. The relationships between P/E and fundamentals may thus change over time.

▶ Because regressions using this method are prone to the problem of multicollinearity (correlation within linear combinations of the independent variables), interpreting individual regression coefficients is difficult.

3.3 Valuation Using Comparables

The most common application of the P/E approach to valuation is to compare a stock's price multiple with a benchmark value of the multiple. This section explores these comparisons for P/Es. To apply the method of comparables using any multiple, an analyst must follow these steps:

► Select and calculate the price multiple that will be used in the comparison.

► Select the comparison asset or assets.

► Calculate the value of the multiple for the comparison asset. For a group of comparison assets, calculate a mean or median value of the multiple for the assets. The result in either case is the **benchmark value of the multiple**.

► Compare the subject stock's actual multiple with the benchmark value.

► When feasible, assess whether differences between the actual and benchmark values of the multiple are explained by differences in the fundamental determinants of the price multiple and modify conclusions about relative valuation accordingly.

The above bullet points provide the structure for this reading's presentation of the method of comparables. Some practitioners will take the benchmark value of the multiple, possibly subjectively adjusted for differences in fundamentals, as the basis for a point estimate of value. This variation is illustrated in Example 11, Problem 2. We can apply this discussion to P/Es. Choices for the P/E benchmark value that have appeared in practice include:

► the P/E of the most closely matched individual stock;

► the average or median value of the P/E for the company's peer group of companies within an industry;

► the average or median value of the P/E for the company's industry or sector;

► the P/E for a representative equity index; and

► an average past value of the P/E for the stock.

Because of averaging, valuation errors are probably less likely to occur when we use an equity index or a group of stocks than when we use a single stock. Hence, the focus of the following discussion will be the last four methods (we will illustrate a comparison with a closely matched individual stock in the section on price to cash flow).

Economists and investment analysts have long attempted to group companies by similarities and differences in their business operations. A country's economy overall is grouped most broadly into **economic sectors** or large industry groupings. These groupings can change over time. As one example, Standard & Poor's once divided the U.S. economy into 11 sectors, shown in Table 4 (beginning with Basic Materials).[16]

Companies in an economic sector share some characteristics that distinguish them from companies in other sectors; however, a given sector usually contains businesses with very distinct business operations. Analysts thus further

---

[16] Standard & Poor's has since revised its sector classifications to the following 10 sectors: Consumer Discretionary, Consumer Staples, Energy, Financials, Health Care, Industrials, Information Technology, Materials, Telecommunication, and Utilities. Consumer Discretionary, Industrials, and Information Technology largely correspond to the old sectors Consumer Cyclicals, Capital Goods, and Technology, respectively; the former Transportation sector has been folded into the new Industrial sector. Within the sectors, Standard & Poor's has also made revisions to its industry classifications. For more information, visit www.spglobal.com/gics.html.

TABLE 4 Valuation of U.S. Sectors: P/E (as of 31 May 2001)

	2000	2001E	Long-Term Average
S&P 1500	22.4	23.5	26.5
S&P 500	25.1	23.8	17.8
Mid-Cap 400	22.6	20.4	23.8
Small-Cap 600	21.9	18.8	23.8
Basic Materials	24.7	26.4	26.3
Capital Goods	28.6	24.1	33.1
Communications Services	22.7	31.0	26.9
Consumer Cyclicals	24.2	22.5	21.3
Consumer Staples	31.7	28.9	28.7
Energy	14.7	14.3	21.6
Financial	19.4	16.7	13.0
Health Care	37.7	28.5	24.9
Technology	30.6	43.1	28.8
Transportation	18.3	16.3	20.7
Utilities	28.6	16.5	13.4

Source: Standard & Poor's *Industry Surveys: Monthly Investment Review* (June 2001).

sort companies into industries within a sector. Many different government and investment industry classification schemes exist. According to Standard & Poor's, however, Consumer Cyclicals contains 23 industries, including Textiles with a P/E of 17.9 and Leisure Time Products with a P/E of 46.6.[17] Within Textiles, there is a subgroup—Textiles (Apparel). Within Textiles (Apparel), Standard & Poor's distinguishes peer groups of companies, or companies that are most similar within an industry. For example, one Standard & Poor's peer group in Textiles (Apparel) is Hosiery/Intimate/Bridal Apparel, composed of nine companies that manufacture and sell apparel in these categories.

An analyst could form even more-narrowly defined peer groups within the S&P peer group. One tool for identifying similarities and differences among businesses being used as comparables is financial ratio analysis. Financial ratios can point to contrasts in:

► a company's ability to meet short-term financial obligations (liquidity ratios);
► the efficiency with which assets are being used to generate sales (asset turnover ratios);
► the use of debt in financing the business (leverage ratios);
► the degree to which fixed charges such as interest on debt are met by earnings or cash flow (coverage ratios); and
► profitability (profitability ratios).

[17] According to the June 2001 issue of the *Industry Surveys: Monthly Investment Review*.

With this understanding of terms in hand, we turn to presenting the method of comparables, beginning with industry peer groups and moving to comparison assets that are progressively less closely matched to the stock. We then turn to using historical P/Es in comparisons. Finally, we sketch how both fundamentals- and comparables-driven models for P/Es can be used to calculate a value for the mature phase in a multistage DCF valuation.

3.3.1 Peer Company Multiples

A business's peer group of companies is frequently used for comparison assets. The advantage to using a peer group is that the constituent companies are typically similar in their business mix. This approach is consistent with the idea underlying the method of comparables—that similar assets should sell at similar prices. The subject stock's P/E is then compared to the mean or median P/E for the peer group to arrive at a relative valuation. Multiplying the justified P/E by EPS, we can also arrive at an absolute value that can be compared with the stock's market price. The absolute value represents an estimate of intrinsic value if the comparison assets were efficiently (fairly) priced.

EXAMPLE 10

A Simple Peer Group Comparison

As a housing industry analyst at a brokerage firm, you are valuing Lennar Corporation (NYSE: LEN), a U.S. builder of moderately priced homes with nationwide operations. The valuation metric that you have selected is the trailing P/E. You are evaluating the P/E using the median trailing P/E of peer group companies as the benchmark value. LEN is in the homebuilding industry, and its peer group is Homebuilders-National. Table 5 presents the relevant data.

TABLE 5 Trailing P/Es of U.S. National Homebuilders (as of 9 November 2001)	
Company	**Trailing P/E**
Beazer Homes USA (NYSE: BZH)	6.83
Centex Corporation (NYSE: CTX)	7.36
D.R. Horton (NYSE: DHI)	7.99
Lennar Corporation (NYSE: LEN)	7.20
MDC Holdings (NYSE: MDC)	4.91
Pulte Homes (NYSE: PHM)	5.94
Ryland Group (NYSE: RYL)	6.70
Toll Brothers (NYSE: TOL)	6.29
Mean	6.65
Median (midway between 6.70 and 6.83)	6.77

Source: Morningstar, Inc.

> Based on the data in Table 5, answer the following questions:
>
> **1.** Given the definition of the benchmark stated above, state the benchmark value of the P/E for LEN.
>
> **2.** State whether LEN is relatively fairly valued, relatively overvalued, or relatively undervalued, assuming no differences in fundamentals among the peer group companies. Justify your answer.
>
> **3.** Which stocks in the Homebuilders-National group appear to be relatively undervalued using the mean trailing P/E as a benchmark? What further analysis may be appropriate to confirm your answer?
>
> **Solution to 1:** The median trailing P/E for the group is 6.77, so 6.77 represents the benchmark value of the multiple (the analyst chose to use the median rather than the mean).
>
> **Solution to 2:** LEN appears to be overvalued because its P/E is greater than the median P/E of 6.77.
>
> **Solution to 3:** MDC, PHM, and TOL appear to be undervalued relative to their peers because their trailing P/Es are lower than the mean P/E of 6.65. The apparent differences in valuation may be explained by differences in risk and expected growth rates compared with their peers. In addition, financial ratio analysis may help analysts determine the precise dimensions along which businesses may differ by risk and expected return.

In actual practice, analysts often find that the stock being valued has some significant differences from the median or mean fundamental characteristics of the comparison assets. In applying the method of comparables, analysts usually attempt to judge whether differences from the benchmark value of the multiple can be explained by differences in the fundamental factors believed to influence the multiple. The following relationships for P/E hold, all else equal:

► If the subject stock has higher-than-average (or median) expected earnings growth, a higher P/E than the benchmark P/E is justified.

► If the subject stock has higher-than-average (or median) risk (operating or financial), a lower P/E than the benchmark P/E is justified.

Another perspective on the above two points is that for a group of stocks with comparable relative valuations, the stock with the greatest expected growth rate (or the lowest risk) is the most attractively valued, all else equal. Example 11, Problem 1, illustrates this principle.

One metric that appears to address the impact of earnings growth on P/E is the P/E-to-growth (**PEG**) ratio. PEG is calculated as the stock's P/E divided by the expected earnings growth rate. The ratio in effect calculates a stock's P/E per unit of expected growth. Stocks with lower PEGs are more attractive than stocks with higher PEGs, all else equal. PEG is useful but must be used with care for several reasons:

► PEG assumes a linear relationship between P/Es and growth. The model for P/E in terms of DDM shows that in theory the relationship is not linear.

► PEG does not factor in differences in risk, a very important component of P/Es.

► PEG does not account for differences in the duration of growth. For example, dividing P/Es by short-term (five-year) growth forecasts may not capture differences in growth in long-term growth prospects.

The way in which fundamentals can add insight to comparables is illustrated in Example 11.

EXAMPLE 11

A Peer Group Comparison Modified by Fundamentals

Continuing with the valuation of homebuilders, you gather information on fundamentals related to risk (beta[18]), profitability (five-year earnings growth forecast), and valuation (trailing and leading P/E). These data are reported in Table 6, which lists companies in order of descending earnings growth forecasts. The use of leading P/Es recognizes that differences in trailing P/Es could be the result of transitory effects on earnings.

TABLE 6   Valuation Data for U.S. National Homebuilders (as of 9 November 2001)

	Trailing P/E	Leading P/E	Five-Year EPS Growth Forecast	Leading PEG	Beta
TOL	6.29	6.43	14.60%	0.44	1.05
DHI	7.99	7.37	14.20%	0.52	1.40
LEN	7.20	7.12	14.00%	0.51	1.45
BZH	6.83	7.29	14.00%	0.52	1.00
CTX	7.36	7.63	13.30%	0.57	1.20
MDC	4.91	5.93	13.30%	0.45	1.05
RYL	6.70	7.76	11.80%	0.66	1.20
PHM	5.94	6.08	11.70%	0.52	1.05
Mean	6.65	6.95	13.36%	0.52	1.18
Median	6.77	7.21	13.65%	0.52	1.13

Source: Morningstar, Inc.

---

[18] In comparables work, analysts may also use other measures of risk, for example financial leverage.

Based on the data in Table 6, answer the following questions:

1. In Example 10, Problem 3, MDC, PHM, and TOL were identified as possibly relatively undervalued compared with the peer group as whole. Using information relating to profitability and risk, which of the three stocks appears to be the relatively *most* undervalued? Justify your answer with three reasons.

2. TOL has a consensus year-ahead EPS forecast of $5.48. Suppose that the median P/E of 7.21 for the peer group is subjectively adjusted upward to 7.5 for the justified P/E for TOL, reflecting TOL's lower risk and superior fundamentals. Estimate TOL's intrinsic value.

3. TOL's current market price is $35.25. State whether TOL appears to be fairly valued, overvalued, or undervalued on an absolute basis, given your answer to Problem 2 above.

Solution to 1: Among MDC, PHM, and TOL, TOL appears to represent the greatest undervaluation, according to the data in Table 6. Of the three stocks, TOL has:

► the highest five-year consensus earnings growth forecast;
► the lowest PEG based on leading P/E; and
► the same level of risk as measured by beta.

Solution to 2: $5.48 × 7.50 = $41.10 is an estimate of intrinsic value. Because the adjustment is subjective, we might prefer to say that TOL should trade at a premium to $5.48 × 7.21 = $39.51.

Solution to 3: Because $41.10 is greater than $35.25, TOL appears to be undervalued on an absolute basis.

Analysts frequently compare a stock's multiple with the median or mean value of the multiple for larger sets of assets than a company's peer group. As one example, Value Line reports a relative P/E that is calculated as the stock's current P/E divided by the median P/E under Value Line review. The less closely matched the stock is to the comparison assets, the more dissimilarities are likely to be present to complicate the interpretation. Arguably, however, the larger the number of assets, the more likely it is that mispricings of individual assets cancel out. For example, during the 1998–2000 Internet boom, valuation relative to the overall market was more likely to point to the possibility of a crash in 2000–2001 than valuation relative to other Internet stocks alone. The next sections examine these larger groups.

3.3.2 Industry and Sector Multiples

Mean or median industry P/Es, as well as economic sector P/Es, are frequently used in relative valuation. The median is insensitive to outliers. Many databases, however, report only mean values of multiples for industries. The mechanics of using industry multiples are identical to the case of **peer group comparisons**. We make a comparison of a stock's multiple to the mean or median multiple for the company's industry, taking account of relevant fundamental information.

The analyst may want to explore whether the comparison assets themselves are efficiently priced. This will give insight into whether the relative valuation (justified P/E based on comparables) accurately reflects absolute intrinsic value.

EXAMPLE 12

Relative Industry Valuation

In general, the U.S. pharmaceutical industry traded at a substantial premium to the market (S&P 500) in the years 1951 to 1993.[19] In the early 1990s, the industry's relative valuation was at its lowest level and priced at a discount to the market. Had the U.S. pharmaceutical industry prospects changed?

To some extent, the industry outlook had changed due to the prospect of U.S. health care reform and secular changes in the industry in the early 1990s. Nevertheless, stocks in this sector continued to rise dramatically through the year 2000. Recent S&P industry data indicate that as of 31 May 2001, the U.S. pharmaceutical industry was trading at an average P/E of 33.7 compared to an S&P 500 P/E of 25.1—once again, at a premium to the market.

3.3.3 Overall Market Multiple

Although the logic of the comparables approach points to industry and peer companies as comparison assets, equity market indexes also have been used as comparison assets. The mechanics of using the method of comparables are not changed, although the user should be cognizant of any size differences between the subject stock and the stocks in the selected index. The question of whether the overall market is fairly priced has captured analyst interest over the entire history of investments. We mentioned one approach to market valuation (using a DDM) in Reading 53. We end the discussion of using an equity market index as a comparison asset with two topical developments in market valuation.

EXAMPLE 13

Valuation Relative to the Market

You are analyzing three large-cap European stock issues with approximately equal earnings growth prospects and risk. As one step in your analysis, you have decided to check valuations relative to the Financial Times Stock Exchange (FTSE) Eurotop 300, an index of Europe's 300 largest companies. Table 7 provides the data.

TABLE 7	Comparison with an Index Multiple (prices and EPS in €)			
As of 28 February 2002	Stock A	Stock B	Stock C	FTSE Eurotop 300
Current price	23	50	260	1229
P/E 2003E	20	25.5	20	23.2
Five-year average P/E (as a percent of Eurotop 300 P/E)	80	110	105	

Source: Bank Leu *Stock Guide* (March 2002) for FTSE Eurotop 300 data.

---

[19] The example draws on information in Haley (1993).

Based only on the data in Table 7, answer the following questions:

1. Which stock appears relatively undervalued against the FTSE Euro-top 300?

2. State the assumption underlying the five-year average P/E comparisons.

Solution to 1: Stock C appears to be undervalued against the FTSE Euro-top 300. Stock A and Stock C both are trading at a P/E of 20 relative to 2003 estimated earnings, versus a P/E of 23.2 for the market. But Stock A has historically traded at P/E reflecting a 20 percent discount to the market (which would equal a P/E of $0.8 \times 23.2 = 18.6$). In contrast, Stock C has usually traded at a premium to the market P/E but now trades at a discount to it. Stock B trades at a high P/E, in line with its historical relationship to the market P/E ($1.1 \times 23.2 = 25.5$).

Solution to 2: Using historical relative valuation information in investment decisions relies on an assumption of stable underlying economic relationships (that the past is relevant for the future).

Because many equity indexes are market capitalization weighted, most vendors report the average market P/E with the individual P/Es weighted by the company's market capitalization. As a consequence, the largest constituent stocks heavily influence the calculated P/E. To the extent there are systematic differences in the P/Es by market capitalization, differences from the index's multiple may be explained by such effects. For stocks in middle capitalization ranges in particular, the analyst should favor using the median P/E for the index as the benchmark value of the multiple.[20]

As with other comparison assets, the analyst may be interested in whether the equity index itself is efficiently priced. A common comparison is the index's P/E in relation to historical values. For example, the current P/E of 27.83 for the Dow Jones Industrial Average as of 31 October 2001 was well above the 10-year average P/E of 17.4 reported by Value Line through 2000. Using a broader index of stocks over the 1871–1996 period, Siegel (1998) computed a long-term median P/E for U.S. stocks of 13.70. Two potential justifications for a higher P/E are lower interest rates and higher expected growth rates. An alternative hypothesis is that the market as a whole is currently overvalued or, alternatively, that earnings are abnormally low. The use of past data relies on the key assumption that the past (sometimes the distant past) is relevant for the future.

Other methods of examining market valuation have been used as well. Reading 53 mentioned the use of DCF models. Examples 14 and 15 illustrate other approaches.

---

[20] The differences can be substantial. For example, as of 31 October 2001, including only stocks with positive earnings, the market-cap-weighted mean P/E for the S&P 500 was 25.8 but the median P/E was 22.

EXAMPLE 14

The Fed Model

One of the main drivers of P/E for the market as a whole is the level of interest rates. The inverse relationship between value and interest rates can be seen from the expression of P/E in terms of fundamentals, because the risk-free rate is one component of the required rate of return that is inversely related to value. The U.S. Federal Reserve Board of Governors uses one such valuation model that relates the inverse of the S&P 500 P/E, the earnings yield, to the yield to maturity on 10-year Treasury bonds. As already defined in Section 3.1.1, Earnings yield = E/P, where the Fed uses expected earnings for the next 12 months in calculating this ratio.

The model asserts that the market is overvalued when the stock market's current earnings yield is less than the 10-year Treasury bond yield. The intuition is that when Treasury bonds yield more than the earnings yield on the stock market, which is riskier than bonds, stocks are an unattractive investment. Figure 1 shows the historical indications of market overvaluation by performance of this model.

FIGURE 1   The Fed Stock Valuation Model

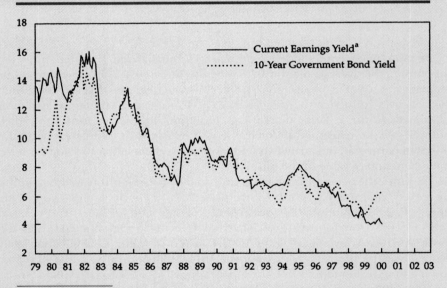

[a] I/B.E.S consensus estimates of earnings over the coming 12 months divided by S&P 500 Index. Reprinted with permission of Dr. Edward Yardeni.

Figure 1 shows that, in general, the earnings yield has tracked the 10-year Treasury bond yield quite closely. Interestingly, the model indicated that the S&P 500 was overvalued at the beginning of 2000, a year in which the S&P 500 returned −9.1 percent. According to the model, the justified or fair-value P/E for the S&P 500 is the reciprocal of the 10-year T-bond yield. As of 1 March 2002, with a 10-year T-bond yielding 4.975 percent, the justified P/E on the S&P 500 was 1/0.04975 = 20.1, according to the model. The leading P/E for the S&P 500 as of same date based on the consensus 2002 EPS from First Call/Thomson Financial was 29.6.

Earlier, we presented an expression for the justified P/E in terms of the Gordon growth model. That expression indicates that the expected growth rate in dividends or earnings is a variable entering into the intrinsic value of a stock (or an index of stocks). That variable is lacking in the Fed model.[21] Example 15 presents a model that takes a step toward addressing these concerns.

EXAMPLE 15

The Yardeni Model

Yardeni (2000) developed a model that incorporates the expected growth rate in earnings—a variable that is missing in the Fed model.[22] Yardeni's model is

$$CEY = CBY - b \times LTEG + Residual$$

CEY is the current earnings yield on the market index, CBY is the current Moody's A rated corporate bond yield, and LTEG is the consensus five-year earnings growth rate forecast for the market index. The coefficient b measures the weight the market gives to five-year earnings projections (recall that the expression for P/E in terms of the Gordon growth model is based on the long-term sustainable growth rate and that five-year forecasts of growth may not be sustainable). Note that although CBY incorporates a **default risk premium** relative to T-bonds, it does not incorporate an equity risk premium per se (for example, in the bond yield plus risk premium model for the cost of equity, presented in Reading 53, we added 300 to 400 basis points to a corporate bond yield).

Yardeni has found that the historical coefficient b has averaged 0.10. Noting that CEY is E/P and taking the inverse of both sides of this equation, Yardeni obtains the following expression for the justified P/E on the market:

$$\frac{P}{E} = \frac{1}{(CBY - b \times LTEG)}$$

Consistent with valuation theory, in Yardeni's model, higher current corporate bond yields imply a lower justified P/E, and higher expected long-term growth results in a higher justified P/E. Yardeni's model uses a five-year growth forecast as a proxy for longer-term growth. Figure 2 illustrates the fair value predictions of the Yardeni model for the S&P 500. Figure 2 shows that in the years 1997 through 1999, the S&P 500 appeared to be overvalued using the historical weighting of 0.10 on growth; at the end of 1999, the model required a 0.25 weighting on growth to justify the market valuation, possibly indicating too much optimism was built into prices. As of 1 March 2002, with 10-year A rated

---

[21] The earnings yield is in fact the expected rate of return on a no-growth stock (under the assumption that price equals value). See Equation 46-20 in Reading 46, setting price equal to value: $P_0 = E/r$ + PVGO. Setting the present value of growth opportunities equal to zero and rearranging, $r = E/P_0$.

[22] This model is presented as one example of more-complex models than the Fed model. Economic analysts at most investment companies have their own models that incorporate growth and historical relationships of market indices and government bonds.

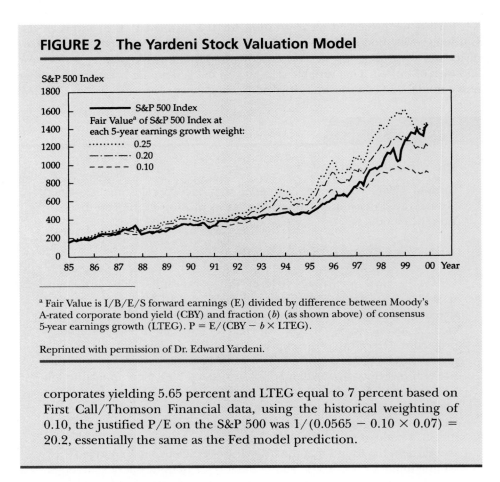

FIGURE 2   The Yardeni Stock Valuation Model

ª Fair Value is I/B/E/S forward earnings (E) divided by difference between Moody's A-rated corporate bond yield (CBY) and fraction (*b*) (as shown above) of consensus 5-year earnings growth (LTEG). P = E/(CBY − *b* × LTEG).

Reprinted with permission of Dr. Edward Yardeni.

corporates yielding 5.65 percent and LTEG equal to 7 percent based on First Call/Thomson Financial data, using the historical weighting of 0.10, the justified P/E on the S&P 500 was 1/(0.0565 − 0.10 × 0.07) = 20.2, essentially the same as the Fed model prediction.

3.3.4 Own Historical P/E Comparisons

As an alternative to comparing a stock's valuation with that of other stocks, another tradition uses past values of a stock's own P/E as a basis for comparison. Underlying this use is the idea that a stock's P/E may regress to historical average levels. A benchmark value can be obtained in a variety of ways with this approach. Value Line reports as a "P/E median" a rounded average of four middle values of a stock's average annual P/E for the previous 10 years. The five-year average trailing P/E is another reasonable alternative. In general, trailing P/Es are more commonly used than leading P/Es in such computations. Besides "higher" and "lower" comparisons with this benchmark, justified price based on this approach may be calculated as follows:

$$\text{Justified price} = (\text{Benchmark value of own historical P/Es}) \times (\text{Most recent EPS}) \quad \textbf{(48-1)}$$

Normalized EPS replaces most recent EPS in Equation 48-1 when EPS is negative and as otherwise appropriate (see Section 3.1.1).

Changes in the interest rate environment and economic fundamentals over different time periods are a limitation to using an average past value of P/E for a

EXAMPLE 16

Valuation Relative to Own Historical P/Es

As of the beginning of 2001, you are valuing the Bank of Nova Scotia (TSE: BNS.TO), Canada's fourth-largest bank in terms of assets. You are investigating the method of comparables using BNS.TO's five-year average P/E as the benchmark value of the multiple. Table 8 presents the data.

TABLE 8   Historical P/Es for BNS.TO

	2000	1999	1998	1997	1996	Overall Mean
Average annual P/E	9.7	11.1	12.8	11.0	8.0	10.5

Source: The Value Line Investment Survey.

1. State a benchmark value for BNS.TO's P/E.
2. Given 2000 EPS of CAD3.55, calculate a justified price for BNS.

Solution to 1: From Table 8, this benchmark value is 10.5.

Solution to 2: The calculation is 10.5 × CAD3.55 = CAD37.28.

stock as a benchmark. One specific caution is that inflation can distort the economic meaning of reported earnings. Consequently, comparisons of own P/E with average P/E, calculated with respect to a period with a different inflationary environment, can be misleading.[23] Further, analysts should be alert to the impact of changes in a company's business mix over time on valuation levels. If the company's business has changed substantially over the time period examined, the method based on own past P/Es is prone to error.

3.3.5 Using P/Es to Obtain Terminal Value in Multistage Dividend Discount Models

In valuing a stock using a DDM, whether using a multistage model or modeling within a spreadsheet (forecasting cash flows individually up to some horizon), the accurate estimation of the terminal value of the stock is important. The key condition that must be satisfied is that terminal value reflects earnings growth

[23] In the presence of inflation, reported earnings can overstate the real economic value of earnings that investors in principle are concerned about. Investors may value a given amount of reported earnings less during inflationary periods, tending to lower observed P/Es during such periods. For more details, see Bodie, Kane, and Marcus (2001).

that the company can sustain in the long run. Analysts frequently use price multiples to estimate terminal value, in particular P/Es and P/Bs. We can call such multiples **terminal price multiples**. Some choices available to the analyst in the multiples approach (where n is the point in time at which the final stage begins) include the following:

Terminal Price Multiple Based on Fundamentals

Analysts may restate the Gordon growth model value as a multiple by dividing it by B_n or E_n (for a trailing terminal price multiple) or by B_{n+1} or E_{n+1} (for a leading terminal price multiple). Of course, multiplying by the same value of the fundamental gives estimated terminal value. Because of their familiarity, multiples may be a useful way to communicate an estimate of terminal value.

Terminal Price Multiple Based on Comparables

The expression for terminal value (using P/E as an example) is

$$V_n = \text{Benchmark value of trailing P/E} \times E_n$$

or

$$V_n = \text{Benchmark value of leading P/E} \times E_{n+1}$$

Analysts have used various choices for the benchmark value, including:

▶ median industry P/E;

▶ average industry P/E; and

▶ average of own past P/Es.

The use of a comparables approach has the strength that it is entirely grounded in market data. In contrast, the Gordon growth model calls for specific estimates (the required rate of return, the dividend payout ratio, and the expected mature growth rate) and is very sensitive to perturbations in those estimates. A possible disadvantage to the comparables approach, however, is that when the benchmark value reflects mispricing (over- or undervaluation), so will the estimate of terminal value.

EXAMPLE 17

Valuing the Mature Growth Phase Using P/Es

As an energy analyst, you are valuing the stock of an oil exploration company. You have projected earnings and dividends three years out (to $t = 3$), and you have gathered the following data and estimates:

▶ required rate of return = 0.10

▶ average dividend payout rate for mature companies in the market = 0.45

▶ industry average ROE = 0.13

▶ E_3 = \$3.00

▶ industry average P/E = 14.3

On the basis of the above information, answer the following questions:

1. Calculate terminal value based on comparables.
2. Contrast your answer in Problem 1 to an estimate of terminal value using the Gordon growth model.

Solution to 1: V_n = Benchmark value of P/E $\times E_n$ = 14.3 $\times$ \$3.00
= \$42.90

Solution to 2: In the sustainable growth rate expression, $g = b \times$ ROE, we can use $(1 - 0.45) = 0.55 = b$, and ROE = 0.13 (the industry average), obtaining $g = b \times$ ROE = 0.55 $\times$ 0.13 = 0.0715. Given the required rate of return of 0.10, we obtain the estimate \$3.00 $(0.45)(1.0715)/(0.10 - 0.0715)$ = \$50.76. In this case, the Gordon growth model estimate of terminal value is $(\$50.76 - \$42.90)/\$42.90$ = 0.1832, or 18.3 percent higher than the estimate based on multiples.

PRICE TO BOOK VALUE
4

The ratio of market price per share to book value per share (P/B), like P/E, has a long history of use in valuation practice (as discussed in Graham and Dodd 1934). In Block's 1999 survey of AIMR members, book value ranked distinctly behind earnings and cash flow, but ahead of dividends, of the four factors surveyed.[24] According to the *Merrill Lynch Institutional Factor Survey*, in the years 1989 to 2001, P/B has been only slightly less popular than P/E as a factor consistently used among institutional investors.[25]

In the P/E ratio, the measure of value (EPS) in the denominator is a flow variable relating to the income statement. In contrast, the measure of value in the P/B's denominator (book value per share) is a stock or level variable coming from the balance sheet. Intuitively, book value per share attempts to represent the investment that common shareholders have made in the company, on a per-share basis. (*Book* refers to the fact that the measurement of value comes from accounting records or books, in contrast to market value.) To define book value per share more precisely, we first find **shareholders' equity** (total assets minus total liabilities). Because our purpose is to value common stock, we subtract from shareholders' equity any value attributable to preferred stock; we thus obtain common shareholders' equity or the **book value of equity** (often called simply **book value**).[26] Dividing book value by the number of common stock shares outstanding, we obtain book value per share, the denominator in the P/B.

In the balance of this section, we present the reasons analysts have offered for using P/B as well as possible drawbacks to its use. We then illustrate the

---

[24] Earnings received a ranking of 1.55, cash flow a ranking of 1.65, book value a ranking of 3.29, and dividends a ranking of 3.51, where 1, 2, 3, and 4 were assigned to inputs ranked first, second, third, and last in importance in averaging responses.

[25] From 1989 to 2001, an average of 37.3 percent of respondents reported consistently using P/B in valuation, compared with 40.4 percent for earnings yield (the reciprocal of P/E rather than P/E was the actual variable surveyed by Merrill Lynch).

[26] If we were to value a company as a whole, rather than just the common stock, we would not exclude the value of preferred stock from the computation.

calculation of P/B and discuss the fundamental factors that drive P/B. We end the section by showing the use of P/B based on the method of comparables. Analysts have offered several rationales for the use of the P/B:

► Because book value is a cumulative balance sheet amount, book value is generally positive even when EPS is negative. We can generally use P/B when EPS is negative, whereas P/E based on a negative EPS is not meaningful.

► Because book value per share is more stable than EPS, P/B may be more meaningful than P/E when EPS is abnormally high or low, or is highly variable.

► As a measure of net asset value per share, book value per share has been viewed as appropriate for valuing companies composed chiefly of **liquid assets**, such as finance, investment, insurance, and banking institutions (Wild, Bernstein, and Subramanyam 2001, p. 233). For such companies, book values of assets may approximate market values.

► Book value has also been used in the valuation of companies that are not expected to continue as a going concern (Martin 1998, p. 22).

► Differences in P/Bs may be related to differences in long-run average returns, according to empirical research.[27]

Possible drawbacks of P/Bs in practice include the following:

► Other assets besides those recognized in accounting may be critical operating factors. For example, in many service companies, **human capital**—the value of skills and knowledge possessed by the workforce—is more important than physical capital as an operating factor.

► P/B can be misleading as a valuation indicator when significant differences exist among the level of assets used by the companies under examination. Such differences may reflect differences in business models, for example.

► Accounting effects on book value may compromise book value as a measure of shareholders' investment in the company. As one example, book value can understate shareholders' investment as a result of the expensing of investment in research and development (R&D). Such expenditures often positively affect income over many periods and in principle create assets. Accounting effects such as these can impair the comparability of P/B across companies and countries.[28]

► In the accounting of most countries, including the United States, book value largely reflects the historical purchase costs of assets, as well as accumulated accounting depreciation expenses. Inflation as well as technological change eventually drive a wedge between the book value and the market value of assets. As a result, book value per share often poorly reflects the value of shareholders' investments. Such effects can impair the comparability of P/Bs across companies, for example when significant differences exist in the average age of assets among companies being compared.

Example 18 illustrates one possible disadvantage to using P/B in valuation.

---

[27] See Bodie, Kane, and Marcus (2001) for a brief summary of the empirical research.
[28] For example, in some countries the values of brand name assets created by advertising are recognized on the balance sheet; in the United States, they are not.

EXAMPLE 18

Differences in Business Models Reflected in Differences in P/Bs

Dell Computer Corporation (Nasdaq NMS: DELL), Apple Computer (Nasdaq NMS: AAPL), Gateway (NYSE: GTW), and Compaq Computer Corporation (NYSE: CPQ) compete with each other in the personal computer industry. Table 9 gives valuation data for these companies according to P/B, as of the end of 2001.

TABLE 9	P/Bs for Four Peer Companies
Company	**P/B**
Dell	14.42
Apple	1.76
Gateway	1.83
Compaq	1.23

Source: Morningstar, Inc.

Dell is an assembler rather than a manufacturer, uses a just-in-time inventory system for parts needed in assembly, and sells built-to-order computers directly to the end consumer. Just-in-time inventory systems attempt to minimize the amount of time that parts needed for building computers are held in inventory. How can these practices explain the much higher P/B of Dell compared with the P/Bs of peer group stocks?

Because Dell assembles parts manufactured elsewhere, it requires smaller investments in fixed assets than it would if it were a manufacturer; this translates into a smaller book value per share. The just-in-time inventory system reduces Dell's required investment in working capital. Because Dell does not need to respond to the inventory needs of large resellers, its need to invest in working capital is reduced. The overall effect of this business model is that Dell generates its sales on a comparatively small base of assets. As a result, Dell's P/B is not comparable with those of its peer group, and the question of relative valuation is not resolved by the comparison in Table 9. Using P/B as a valuation indicator effectively penalizes Dell's efficient business model.[29]

4.1 Determining Book Value

In this section, we illustrate the calculation of book value and how analysts may adjust book value to improve the comparability of P/B ratios across companies. To compute book value per share, we need to refer to the business's balance

---

[29] There is a second reason for Dell's relatively high P/B; Dell's substantial share repurchases have reduced its book value per share in the years preceding this data.

sheet, which has a shareholders' (or stockholders') equity section. The computation of book value is as follows:

▶ (Shareholders' equity) − (Total value of equity claims that are senior to common stock) = Common shareholders' equity

▶ (Common shareholders' equity)/(Number of common stock shares outstanding) = Book value per share

EXAMPLE 19

Computing Book Value per Share

Ennis Business Forms (NYSE: EBF), a wholesale manufacturer of custom business forms and other printed business products, reported the balance sheet given in Table 10 for its fiscal year ending 28 February 2001.

TABLE 10 Ennis Business Forms Balance Sheet (in thousands, except per-share amounts)

	28 Feb 2001
Assets	
Current assets	
Cash and cash equivalents	$ 8,964
Short term investments	980
Net receivables	29,957
Inventory	13,088
Unbilled contract revenue	364
Other current assets	4,910
Total Current Assets	58,263
Noncurrent assets	
Investment securities	2,170
Net property, plant, and equipment	57,781
Goodwill	23,615
Other assets	1,025
Total Assets	**$ 142,854**
Liabilities and Shareholders' Equity	
Current liabilities	
Current installments of long-term debt	$ 4,176
Accounts payable	6,067
Accrued expenses	7,665
Total Current Liabilities	17,908
Noncurrent liabilities	
Long-term debt	23,555
Deferred credits	9,851
Total Liabilities	51,314

(Table continued on next page . . .)

TABLE 10 (continued)

	28 Feb 2001
Shareholders' equity	
Common stock	
($2.50 par value. Authorized 40,000,000;	
issued 21,249,860)	53,125
Additional paid-in capital	1,040
Retained earnings	127,817
Treasury stock	
(cost of 4,979,095 shares repurchased in 2001)	(90,442)
Total Shareholders' Equity	91,540
Total Liabilities and Shareholders' Equity	**$ 142,854**

The entries in the balance sheet should be familiar. Treasury stock results from share repurchases (or buybacks) and is a deduction (recorded at cost above) to reach shareholders' equity. For the number of shares to be used in the divisor, we take 21,249,860 shares issued (under Common stock) and subtract 4,979,095 shares repurchased in 2001 to get 16,270,765 shares outstanding.

1. Using the data in Table 10, calculate book value per share as of 28 February 2001.

2. Given a closing price per share for EBF of $8.42 as of 4 June 2001, and your answer to Problem 1, calculate EBF's P/B as of 4 June 2001.

Solution to 1: (Common shareholders' equity)/(Number of common stock shares outstanding) = $91,540,000/16,270,765 = $5.63.

Solution to 2: P/B = $8.42/$5.63 = 1.5.

Possible senior claims to common stock include the value of preferred stock and dividends in arrears on preferred stock.[30] Example 19 illustrates the calculation.

Example 19 illustrated the calculation of book value per share without any adjustments. Adjusting P/B has two purposes: (1) to make P/B more accurately reflect the value of shareholders' investment and (2) to make P/B more useful for comparisons among different stocks.

► Some services and analysts report a **tangible book value per share**. Computing tangible book value per share involves subtracting reported intangible assets from the balance sheet from common shareholders' equity. The analyst should be familiar with the calculation. However, from the viewpoint of

---

[30] Some preferred stock issues have the right to premiums (liquidation premiums) if they are liquidated. If present, these premiums should be deducted as well.

financial theory, the general exclusion of all intangibles may not be warranted. In the case of individual intangible assets such as patents, which can be separated from the entity and sold, exclusion may not be justified. Exclusion may be appropriate, however, for goodwill from acquisitions. **Goodwill** represents the excess of the purchase price of an acquisition over the net asset value of tangible assets and specifically identifiable intangibles. Many analysts feel that goodwill does not represent an asset, because it is not separable and may reflect overpayment for an acquisition.

▶ For book value per share to most accurately reflect current values, the balance sheet should be adjusted for significant off-balance-sheet assets and liabilities and for differences in the fair value of these assets/liabilities from recorded accounting amounts.[31] Internationally, accounting methods currently report some assets/liabilities at historical cost (with some adjustments) and others at fair value.[32] For example, assets such as land or equipment are reported at their historical acquisitions cost, and in the case of equipment are being depreciated over their useful lives. These assets may have appreciated over time, or they may have declined in value more than is reflected in the depreciation computation. Other assets such as investments in marketable securities are reported at fair market value. Reporting assets at fair value would make P/B more relevant for valuation (including comparisons among companies).

▶ Certain adjustments may be appropriate for comparability. For example, one company may use FIFO and a peer company may use LIFO, which in an inflationary environment will generally understate inventory values. To more accurately assess the relative valuation of the two companies, the analyst should restate the book value of the company using LIFO to what it would be on a FIFO basis. Example 20 illustrates this and other adjustments to book value.[33]

Regarding the second bullet point, over the last few years, there has been a trend among accounting standard setters toward a fair value model—more assets/liabilities are stated at fair value. If this trend continues, the need for adjustments will be reduced (but not eliminated).

EXAMPLE 20

Adjusting Book Value

Edward Stavros is a junior analyst at a major U.S. pension fund. Stavros is researching Harley Davidson (NYSE: HDI) for the fund's Consumer Cyclical portfolio. Stavros is particularly interested in determining Harley Davidson's relative P/B. He obtains the condensed balance sheet for Harley Davidson from Edgar Online (a computerized database of U.S. SEC filings); his data are shown in Table 11.

[31] An example of an off-balance sheet liability is a guarantee to pay a debt of another company in the event of that company's default. See Chapter 11 of White, Sondhi, and Fried (1998).

[32] **Fair value** has been defined as the price at which an asset or liability would change hands between a willing buyer and a willing seller when the former is not under any compulsion to buy and the latter is not under any compulsion to sell.

[33] For a complete discussion of balance sheet adjustments, see "Analysis of Financial Statements: A Synthesis," in White, Sondhi, and Fried (1998).

TABLE 11 Harley Davidson Condensed Consolidated Balance Sheet (in thousands)

	31 Dec 2000
Assets	
Current assets	
Cash and cash equivalents	$ 419,736
Accounts receivable, net	98,311
Finance receivables, net	530,859
Inventories	191,931
Other current assets	56,427
Total Current Assets	1,297,264
Noncurrent assets	
Finance receivables, net	234,091
Property, plant, and equipment, net	754,115
Goodwill	54,331
Other assets	96,603
Total Assets	**$ 2,436,404**
Liabilities and Shareholders' Equity	
Current liabilities	
Accounts payable	$ 169,844
Accrued and other liabilities	238,390
Current portion of finance debt	89,509
Total Current Liabilities	497,743
Noncurrent liabilities	
Finance debt	355,000
Other long-term liabilities	97,340
Postretirement health care benefits	80,666
Contingencies	
Shareholders' equity	1,405,655
Total Liabilities and Shareholders' Equity	**$ 2,436,404**

Stavros computes book value per share initially by dividing total shareholders' equity ($1,405,655,000) by the number of shares outstanding at 31 December 2000 (302,070,745). The resulting book value per share is $4.65. Stavros then realizes that he must examine the full set of financial statements to assess the impact of accounting methods on balance sheet data. Harley Davidson's footnotes indicate that the company uses the LIFO inventory method. Inventories on a FIFO basis are presented in the company's footnotes at $210,756,000. Additionally, an examination of Harley's pension footnotes indicates that the pension plan is currently overfunded but that accounting rules require the recognition of a net liability of $21,705,000. This overstatement of a liability is somewhat offset by an underfunded post-retirement health care plan that understates liabilities by $15,400,000.

> Stavros makes the following adjustments on an after-tax basis (HDI's **average tax rate** is 37 percent) to his book value computation (in dollars):
>
> | | |
> |---|---|
> | Total shareholders equity | $1,405,655,000 |
> | Plus inventory adjustment | 18,825,000 × 0.63 = 11,859,750 |
> | Plus pension adjustment | 21,705,000 × 0.63 = 13,674,150 |
> | Less post-retirement adjustment | 15,400,000 × 0.63 = (9,702,000) |
> | Adjusted book value | $1,421,486,900 |
> | Adjusted book value per share | $4.71 |
>
> In the above calculations, the after-tax amount is found by multiplying the pretax amount by $(1 - 0.37) = 0.63$. Stavros is putting all the company's inventory valuation on a FIFO basis for comparability. Using after-tax amounts is necessary because if Harley Davidson were to change its inventory method to FIFO, the change would result in higher taxes as HDI liquidates old inventory. Although inventory on the balance sheet would increase by $18,825,000, taxes payable would also increase (or cash would decrease). As a result, the net effect on book value equals the change in inventory less the associated tax increase.
>
> In conclusion, adjusted book value per share is $4.71.[34] Based on a price of $42.00 shortly after year-end, HDI has a P/B (adjusted basis) of $42/$4.71 = 8.9. Outstanding stock options could dilute both book value per share figures by $0.07, which would have a small impact on these ratios.

4.2 Valuation Based on Forecasted Fundamentals

We can use fundamental forecasts to estimate a stock's justified P/B. For example, assuming the Gordon growth model and using the expression $g = b \times ROE$ for the sustainable growth rate, the expression for the justified P/B based on the most recent book value (B_0) is[35]

$$\frac{P_0}{B_0} = \frac{ROE - g}{r - g} \tag{48-2}$$

For example, if a business's ROE is 12 percent, its required rate of return is 10 percent, and its expected growth rate is 7 percent, then its justified P/B based on fundamentals is $(0.12 - 0.07)/(0.10 - 0.07) = 1.7$.

---

[34] The calculation of tangible book value per share (adjusted basis for inventory accounting method) is as follows:

Adjusted book value	$1,421,486,900
Less goodwill	(54,331,000)
Tangible adjusted book value	$1,367,155,900
Tangible adjusted book value per share	$4.53

and price to tangible book value is 9.3.

[35] According to the Gordon growth model, $V_0 = E_1 \times (1 - b)/(r - g)$. Defining ROE $= E_1/B_0$, so $E_1 = B_0 \times ROE$, and substituting for E_1 into the prior expression, we have $V_0 = B_0 \times ROE \times (1 - b)/(r - g)$, giving $V_0/B_0 = ROE \times (1 - b)/(r - g)$. The sustainable growth rate expression is $g = b \times ROE$. Substituting $b = g/ROE$ into the expression just given for V_0/B_0, we have $V_0/B_0 = (ROE - g)/(r - g)$. Because justified price is intrinsic value, V_0, we obtain Equation 48-2.

Equation 48-2 states that the justified P/B is an increasing function of ROE, all else equal. Because the numerator and denominator are differences of ROE and r, respectively, from the same quantity, g, what determines the justified P/B in Equation 48-2 is ROE in relation to the required rate of return, r. The larger ROE is in relation to r, the higher the justified P/B based on fundamentals.[36]

A practical insight from Equation 48-2 is that we cannot evaluate whether a particular value of the P/B reflects undervaluation without taking into account the business's profitability. Equation 48-2 suggests as well that given two stocks with the same P/B, the one with the higher ROE is relatively undervalued, all else equal. These relationships have been confirmed using cross-sectional regression analysis.[37]

Further insight into the P/B comes from the residual income model, which was mentioned in Reading 46. The expression for the justified P/B based on the residual income valuation is[38]

$$\frac{P_0}{B_0} = 1 + \frac{\textit{Present value of expected future residual earnings}}{B_0} \qquad \textbf{(48-3)}$$

Equation 48-3, which makes no special assumptions about growth, states the following:

► If the present value of expected future residual earnings is zero—for example, if the business just earns its required return on investment in every period—the justified P/B is 1.

► If the present value of expected future residual earnings is positive (negative), the justified P/B is greater than (less than) 1.

4.3 Valuation Using Comparables

To use the method of comparables for valuing stocks using a P/B, we follow the same steps given in Section 3.3, illustrated there with P/Es. In contrast to EPS, however, analysts' forecasts of book value are not aggregated and widely disseminated by vendors such as First Call/Thomson Financial and Zacks; in practice, most analysts use trailing book value in calculating P/Bs.[39] Evaluation of relative P/Bs should consider differences in return on invested capital (as measured by ROE in this context), risk, and expected earnings growth.

---

[36] This relationship can be seen clearly if we set $g = 0$ (the no-growth case): $P_0/B_0 = \text{ROE}/r$.

[37] Harris and Marston (1994) perform a regression of B/MV (book to market, the inverse of the P/B) against variables for growth (mean analyst forecasts) and risk (beta) for a large sample of companies over the period July 1982 to December 1989. The estimated regression was

B/MV = $1.172 - 4.15 \times$ Growth $+ 0.093 \times$ Risk ($R^2 = 22.9\%$)

The coefficient of -4.15 indicates that expected growth was negatively related to B/MV, and, as a consequence, positively related to P/B. Risk was positively related to B/MV and thus negatively related to P/B. Both variables were statistically significant with growth having the greatest impact. Fairfield (1994) also found that P/Bs are related to future expectations of ROE in the predicted fashion.

[38] Noting that $(\text{ROE} - r) \times B_0$ would define a level residual income stream, we can show that Equation 48-2 is consistent with Equation 48-3 (a general expression) as follows. In $P_0/B_0 = (\text{ROE} - g)/(r - g)$, we can successively rewrite the numerator $(\text{ROE} - g) + r - r = (r - g) + (\text{ROE} - r)$, so $P_0/B_0 = [(r - g) + (\text{ROE} - r)]/(r - g) = 1 + (\text{ROE} - r)/(r - g)$, which can be written $P_0/B_0 = 1 + [(\text{ROE} - r)/(r - g)] \times B_0/B_0 = 1 + [(\text{ROE} - r) \times B_0/(r - g)]/B_0$; the second term in the final expression is the present value of residual income divided by B_0 as in Equation 48-3.

[39] Because equity in successive balance sheets is linked by net income from the income statement, however, the analyst could, given dividend forecasts, translate EPS forecasts into corresponding book value forecasts, taking account of any anticipated ownership transactions.

EXAMPLE 21

P/B Comparables Approach

Todd Fisher, CFA, is a portfolio manager with Midland Value, a mid-cap value mutual fund. Recently, a property and casualty company owned by the fund was acquired by a large-cap insurance company. Todd is seeking a mid-cap replacement for this position. Given the fund's value orientation, Todd is particularly interested in mid-cap property and casualty companies selling at a reasonable multiple to book value. Todd's initial research has resulted in a short list of four candidates: Allmerica Financial Corporation (NYSE: AFC), American Financial Group (NYSE: AFG), Safeco Corporation (Nasdaq NMS: SAFC), and Old Republic International Corporation (NYSE: ORI). Table 12 presents information on these companies.[40]

TABLE 12 P/B Comparables Approach

| | Price to Book Value | | | | | | | | |
Year	1996	1997	1998	1999	2000	Five-Year Average	Current	Forecasted ROE	Beta
AFC	1.0	1.1	1.4	1.4	1.6	1.3	0.8	9.5%	1.10
AFG	1.5	1.5	1.6	1.2	1.0	1.4	1.0	13.5%	0.95
SAFC	1.2	1.2	1.1	0.8	0.9	1.0	1.1	10%	1.05
ORI	1.4	1.6	1.4	0.6	1.6	1.3	1.2	11%	0.90
Property/ casualty industry (mean value)							2.2	11%	

Sources: Morningstar and *The Value Line Investment Survey* for ROE forecasts.

Based only on the information in Table 12, answer the following questions:

1. Discuss the valuation of ORI relative to the industry.
2. Discuss the valuation of AFG relative to the industry and peer companies.

Solution to 1: ORI is selling at a P/B that is only 55 percent of the industry mean, although its forecasted ROE equals the mean forecasted ROE for the industry, 11 percent. ORI appears to be relatively undervalued based on an industry benchmark.

Solution to 2: AFG is selling at a P/B that is only 45 percent of the industry mean P/B. At the same time, its expected ROE is distinctly higher than the industry's. On the basis of the data given, AFG appears to be undervalued relative to the industry benchmark. AFG also

---

[40] Forecasted ROE refers to forecasts for 2004 to 2006.

appears to be undervalued with respect to SAFC and probably AFC and ORI as well, based on the data given:

- ▶ AFG zhas a lower P/B, a higher expected ROE, and a lower beta than SAFC.
- ▶ Although the P/B of AFG is 25 percent higher than that of AFC, its expected ROE is 42 percent higher than AFC, with lower risk as judged by beta.
- ▶ With a P/B that is about 17 percent smaller than ORI's, a higher expected ROE, and only a 0.05 difference in beta, AFG also may be relatively undervalued with respect to ORI.

PRICE TO SALES   5

Certain types of privately held companies, including investment management companies and companies in partnership form, have long been valued as a multiple of annual revenues. In recent decades, the ratio of price to sales has become well known as a valuation indicator for publicly traded companies as well. According to the *Merrill Lynch Institutional Factor Survey*, from 1989 to 2001, on average, slightly more than one-quarter of respondents consistently used the P/S in their investment process.

Analysts have offered the following rationales for using P/S:

- ▶ Sales are generally less subject to distortion or manipulation than are other fundamentals, such as EPS or book value. Through discretionary accounting decisions concerning expenses, for example, management can distort EPS as a reflection of economic performance. In contrast, total sales, as the top line in the income statement, is prior to any expenses.
- ▶ Sales are positive even when EPS is negative. Therefore, analysts can use P/S when EPS is negative, whereas the P/E based on a negative EPS is not meaningful.
- ▶ Because sales are generally more stable than EPS, which reflects operating and financial leverage, P/S is generally more stable than P/E. P/S may be more meaningful than P/E when EPS is abnormally high or low.
- ▶ P/S has been viewed as appropriate for valuing the stock of mature, cyclical, and zero-income companies (Martin 1998).
- ▶ Differences in P/Ss may be related to differences in long-run average returns, according to empirical research.[41]

Possible drawbacks of using P/S in practice include the following:

- ▶ A business may show high growth in sales even when it is not operating profitably as judged by earnings and cash flow from operations. To have value as a going concern, a business must ultimately generate earnings and cash.
- ▶ P/S does not reflect differences in cost structures among different companies.
- ▶ Although relatively robust with respect to manipulation, revenue recognition practices offer the potential to distort P/S.

---

[41] See Nathan, Sivakumar, and Vijayakumar (2001), O'Shaughnessy (1997), and Senchack and Martin (1987).

5.1 Determining Sales

P/S is calculated as price per share divided by annual net sales per share (net sales is total sales less returns and customer discounts). Analysts usually use annual sales from the company's most recent fiscal year in the calculation, as illustrated in Example 22. Because valuation is forward-looking in principle, the analyst may also develop and use P/Ss based on forecasts of next year's sales.

EXAMPLE 22

Calculating P/S

In 2001, Abitibi-Consolidated (Toronto Stock Exchange: A.TO), a manufacturer of newsprint and groundwood papers, reported 2001 net sales of CAD6,032,000,000 with 440 million shares outstanding. Calculate the P/S for Abitibi based on a closing price of CAD13.38 on 14 February 2002.

Sales per share = CAD6,032,000,000/440,000,000 = CAD13.71

So, P/S = CAD13.38/CAD13.71 = 0.9759 or 1.0.

Although the determination of sales is more straightforward than the determination of earnings, the analyst should evaluate a company's revenue recognition practices, in particular those tending to speed up the recognition of revenues. An analyst using a P/S approach who does not also assess the quality of accounting for sales may be led to place too high a value on such companies' shares. Example 23 illustrates the problem.

EXAMPLE 23

Revenue Recognition Practices (1)

Analysts label stock markets as *bubbles* when market prices appear to lose contact with intrinsic value. The run-up of the prices of Internet stocks in U.S. markets in the 1998–2000 period, in the view of many, represented a bubble. During this period, many analysts adopted P/S as a metric for valuing Internet stocks with negative earnings and cash flow. Perhaps at least partly as a result of this practice, some Internet companies engaged in questionable revenue recognition practices to justify their high valuations. In order to increase sales, some companies engaged in activities such as bartering website advertising with other Internet companies. For example, Internet Revenue.com might barter $1,000,000 worth of banner advertising with RevenueIsUs.com. Each would show $1,000,000 of revenue and $1,000,000 of expense. Although neither had any net income or cash flow, each company's revenue growth and market valuation was enhanced (at least temporarily). The value placed on the advertising was also questionable. As a result of these and other questionable activities, the U.S. SEC issued a stern warning to companies. International accounting standard setters have begun a study to define revenue recognition principles. The analyst should review footnote disclosures to assess whether the company may be recognizing revenue prematurely or otherwise aggressively.

Example 24 illustrates another instance in which an analyst would need to look behind the accounting numbers.

EXAMPLE 24

Revenue Recognition Practices (2)

Sales on a **bill-and-hold basis** involve selling products but not delivering those products until a later date.[42] Sales on this basis have the effect of accelerating sales into an earlier reporting period. The following is a case in point. In its Form 10K filed 6 March 1998, for fiscal year ended 28 December 1997, Sunbeam Corporation listed the following footnote:

1. *Operations and significant accounting policies revenue recognition.* The company recognizes revenues from product sales principally at the time of shipment to customers. In limited circumstances, at the customer's request the company may sell seasonal product on a bill and hold basis provided that the goods are completed, packaged and ready for shipment, such goods are segregated and the risks of ownership and legal title have passed to the customer. The amount of such bill and hold sales at 29 December 1997 was approximately 3 percent of consolidated revenues. Net sales are comprised of gross sales less provisions for expected customer returns, discounts, promotional allowances and cooperative advertising.

After internal and SEC investigations, the company restated its financial results, including a restated revenue recognition policy:

Revenue recognition. The company recognizes sales and related cost of goods sold from product sales when title passes to the customers which is generally at the time of shipment. Net sales is comprised of gross sales less provisions for estimated customer returns, discounts, promotional allowances, cooperative advertising allowances and costs incurred by the company to ship product to customers. Reserves for estimated returns are established by the company concurrently with the recognition of revenue. Reserves are established based on a variety of factors, including historical return rates, estimates of customer inventory levels, the market for the product and projected economic conditions. The company monitors these reserves and makes adjustment to them when management believes that actual returns or costs to be incurred differ from amounts recorded. In some situations, the company has shipped product with the right of return where the company is unable to reasonably estimate the level of returns and/or the sale is contingent upon the resale of the product. In these situations, the company does not recognize revenue upon product shipment, but rather when it is reasonably expected the product will not be returned.

---

[42] For companies whose reports must conform to U.S. SEC accounting regulations, revenue from bill-and-hold sales cannot be reported unless the risk of loss on the products transfers to the buyer and additional criteria are met (see SEC Staff Accounting Bulletin 101 for criteria).

> The company had originally reported revenue of $1,168,182,000 for the fiscal year ended 31 December 1997. After restatement, the company reported revenue of $1,073,000,000 for the same period—a more than 8 percent reduction in revenue. The analyst reading the footnote in the original report would have noted the bill-and-hold practices and reduced revenue by 3 percent. This company engaged in other accounting practices tending to inflate revenue, which did not come to light until the investigation.

Sometimes, as in Example 24, it is not possible to determine precisely by how much sales may be overstated. If a company is engaged in questionable revenue recognition practices of an unknown amount, the analyst may well suggest avoiding that security. At the very least, the analyst should be skeptical and assess a higher risk premium, which would result in a lower justified P/S.

5.2 Valuation Based on Forecasted Fundamentals

Like other multiples, P/S can be linked to DCF models. In terms of the Gordon growth model, we can state P/S as[43]

$$\frac{P_0}{S_0} = \frac{(E_0/S_0)\,(1-b)\,(1+g)}{r-g} \qquad \text{(48-4)}$$

where E_0/S_0 is the business's profit margin PM_0. Although the profit margin is stated in terms of trailing sales and earnings, the analyst may use a long-term forecasted profit margin in Equation 48-4. Equation 48-4 states that the justified P/S is an increasing function of its profit margin and earnings growth rate, and the intuition generalizes to more complex DCF models. Profit margin is a determinant of the justified P/S not only directly, but also through its effect on g. We can illustrate this concept by restating Equation 46-33 from Reading 46 for the sustainable growth rate, g:

$$g = b \times PM_0 \times \frac{\text{Sales}}{\text{Assets}} \times \frac{\text{Assets}}{\text{Shareholders' equity}}$$

where the last three terms come from the DuPont analysis of ROE. An increase (decrease) in the profit margin produces a higher (lower) sustainable growth rate, so long as sales do not decrease (increase) proportionately.[44]

5.3 Valuation Using Comparables

Using the method of comparables for valuing stocks using P/S follows the steps given in Section 3.3, which we earlier illustrated using P/E and P/B. As men-

---

[43] The Gordon growth model is $P_0 = D_0(1+g)/(r-g)$. Substituting $D_0 = E_0(1-b)$ into the previous equation produces $P_0 = E_0(1-b)(1+g)/(r-g)$. Dividing both sides by S_0 gives $P_0/S_0 = (E_0/S_0)(1-b)(1+g)/(r-g)$.

[44] That is, it is possible that an increase (decrease) in the profit margin could be offset by a decrease (increase) in total asset turnover (Sales/Assets).

EXAMPLE 25

Justified P/S Based on Forecasted Fundamentals

As an automobile analyst, you are valuing the stocks of three automobile manufacturers including General Motors (NYSE: GM) as of the end of 2001. You estimate that GM's required rate of return is 11 percent based on an average of a capital asset pricing model (CAPM) estimate and a bond yield plus risk premium estimate. Your other forecasts are as follows:

- ▶ long-term profit margin = 3.5 percent;
- ▶ dividend payout ratio = 30 percent; and
- ▶ earnings growth rate = 5 percent.

Although you forecast that GM's profit margin for 2001 will be 1 percent, you recognize that 2001 was a year of economic contraction. A profit margin of 3.5 percent is close to GM's long-term average, and an earnings growth rate of 5 percent is close to the median analyst forecast, according to First Call/Thomson Financial. As a first estimate of GM's justified P/S based on forecasted fundamentals, you decide to use Equation 48-4.

1. Based on the above data, calculate GM's justified P/S.

2. Given an estimate of GM's sales per share for 2001 of $295, what is the intrinsic value of GM stock?

3. Given a market price for GM of $53 as of 6 December 2001, and your answer to Problem 2, state whether GM stock appears to be fairly valued, overvalued, or undervalued.

Solution to 1: Using Equation 48-4, we calculate GM's justified P/S as follows:

$$\frac{P_0}{S_0} = \frac{0.035 \times 0.30 \times 1.05}{0.11 - 0.05} = 0.1838$$

Solution to 2: An estimate of intrinsic value is 0.1838 × $295 = $54.22. Rounding P/S to two decimal places, we can calculate intrinsic value as 0.18 × $295 = $53.10.

Solution to 3: GM stock appears to be approximately fairly valued, or slightly undervalued.

---

tioned earlier, P/Ss are usually reported based on trailing sales. The analyst may also base a relative valuation on P/Ss calculated on forecasted sales, given that the analyst has developed models for forecasting sales.[45] In valuing stocks using the method of comparables, analysts should also gather information on profit margin, expected earnings growth, and risk. As always, the quality of accounting merits investigation as well.

---

[45] Unlike EPS forecasts, analysts' sales forecasts are not generally gathered and disseminated.

EXAMPLE 26

P/S Comparables Approach

Continuing with the valuation project, you have compiled the information on GM and peer companies Ford Motor Corporation (NYSE: F) and DaimlerChrysler (NYSE: DCX) given in Table 13.

TABLE 13   P/S Comparables (as of 6 December 2001)

| | **Price to Sales** | | | | | | |
	Current Close	YTD High	YTD Low	2000 Profit Margin	Forecast Profit Margin	Median Analyst Long-Term EPS Growth Forecast	Beta
General Motors (GM)	0.16	0.21	0.12	3.0%	2.5%	5.0%	1.11
Ford (F)	0.19	0.29	0.16	2.8%	3.0%	5.0%	0.99
DaimlerChrysler (DCX)	0.32	0.37	0.18	2.2%	2.6%	7.0%	1.23

Sources: Bloomberg LLC, *The Value Line Investment Survey* for profit margin and ROE forecasts, and First Call/Thomson Financial for EPS growth forecasts.

Answer the following questions using the data in Table 13:

1. Based on the P/S (using the current close) and referencing no other information, does GM appear to be relatively undervalued?

2. State whether GM or DCX is most closely comparable to Ford. Justify your answer.

3. As of the end of 2001, the S&P 500 had a weighted average P/S of 2.5 and a median P/S of 1.27. GM, F, and DCX have traded at P/Ss that represent discounts of as much as 90 percent from the weighted average P/S for the S&P 500. Can you conclude from this fact alone that, as a group, the three automobile makers were undervalued in absolute terms? Explain your answer.

Solution to 1: Because the P/S for GM, 0.16, is the lowest of the three P/Ss, GM appears to be relatively undervalued, referencing no other information.

Solution to 2: Ford appears to be more closely matched to GM than to DaimlerChrysler on the basis of the information given. The profit margin, the growth rate g, and risk are key fundamentals in the P/S approach. Ford closely matches GM along the dimension of expected growth. The risk of Ford stock as measured by beta is closer to GM than to DaimlerChrysler. The comparison of profit margins, reflecting cost structure, is less conclusive but does not contradict the general conclusion. The current profit margin of Ford is close to that of General Motors (2.8%/3% = 0.933 or 93% of GM's) but well above that of DaimlerChrysler (2.8%/2.2% = 1.27 or 127% of DCX's). The forecast is for Ford to take the lead in profit margin over GM and DCX by about an equal amount.

An interesting point arises here. DCX's actual net profit margin per the unadjusted numbers in its Form 20-F Annual Report filing with the U.S. SEC was 4.86%, and some vendors report that number. Using 4.86%, the analyst might conclude that DCX had the lowest cost structure among the three companies, rather than the highest, in 2000. This percentage, however, includes gains from the sales of business units in 2000, which are nonrecurring. The comparisons in Table 13 better reflect underlying earnings.

Solution to 3: No, such a conclusion would not be warranted. Before concluding that the automakers as a group were undervalued in absolute terms, the analyst would need to establish that:

▶ the automakers were relatively undervalued given differences in profit margin, earnings growth prospects, and risk, in relation to the S&P 500; and

▶ the S&P 500 itself was fairly valued at a weighted average P/S of 2.5.

PRICE TO CASH FLOW   6

Price to cash flow is a widely reported valuation indicator. In Block's 1999 survey of AIMR members, cash flow ranked behind only earnings in importance. According to the *Merrill Lynch Institutional Factor Survey*, price to cash flow on average saw wider use in investment practice than P/E, P/B, P/S, or dividend yield in the 1989–2001 period, among the institutional investors surveyed.[46]

In this section, we present price to cash flow based on alternative major cash flow concepts. With the wide variety of cash flow concepts in use, the analyst should be especially careful that she understands (and communicates, as a writer) the exact definition of *cash flow* that is the basis for the analysis.

Analysts have offered the following rationales for the use of price to cash flow:

▶ Cash flow is less subject to manipulation by management than earnings.[47]

▶ Because cash flow is generally more stable than earnings, price to cash flow is generally more stable than P/E.

▶ Using price to cash flow rather than P/E addresses the issue of differences in accounting conservatism between companies (differences in the quality of earnings).

▶ Differences in price to cash flow may be related to differences in long-run average returns, according to empirical research.[48]

Possible drawbacks to the use of price to cash flow include the following:

---

[46] On average, 46.1 percent of respondents reported consistently using price to cash flow over this period. In one year (2001), price to cash flow ranked first among the 23 factors surveyed.

[47] Cash flow from operations, precisely defined, can be manipulated only through "real" activities, such as the sale of receivables.

[48] See for example O'Shaughnessy (1997), who examined price to cash flow, and Hackel, Livnat, and Rai (1994) and Hackel and Livnat (1991), who examined price to average free cash flow.

Accounting Methods and Cash Flow

One approximation of cash flow in practical use is EPS plus depreciation, amortization, and depletion. Even this simple approximation can point to issues of interest to the analyst in valuation, as this stylized illustration shows. Hypothetical companies A and B have constant cash revenues and cash expenses (as well as a constant number of shares outstanding) in 2000, 2001, and 2002. Company A incurs total depreciation of $15.00 per share during the three-year period, which it spreads out evenly (straight-line depreciation, SLD). Because revenues, expenses, and depreciation are constant over the period, EPS for Business A is also constant, say at $10, as given in Column 1 in Table 14. Business B is identical to Business A except that it uses accelerated depreciation: Depreciation is 150 percent of SLD in 2000, declining to 50 percent of SLD in 2002, as given in Column 5. (We assume both A and B use the same depreciation method for tax purposes.)

TABLE 14 Earning Growth Rates and Cash Flow (all amounts per share)

Year	Company A Earnings (1)	Depreciation (2)	Cash Flow (3)	Company B Earnings (4)	Depreciation (5)	Cash Flow (6)
2000	$10.00	$5.00	$15.00	$7.50	$7.50	$15.00
2001	$10.00	$5.00	$15.00	$10.00	$5.00	$15.00
2002	$10.00	$5.00	$15.00	$12.50	$2.50	$15.00
	Sum	$15.00		Sum	$15.00	

Because of different choices in how Company A and B depreciate for financial reporting purposes, Company A's EPS is flat at $10.00 (Column 1) whereas Company B's shows 29 percent compound growth, $(\$12.50/\$7.50)^{1/2} - 1.00 = 0.29$ (Column 4). Company B shows apparent positive earnings momentum. As analysts comparing Companies A and B, we might be misled using EPS numbers as reported (without putting EPS on a comparable basis). For both companies, however, cash flow per share is level at $15. Depreciation may be the simplest noncash charge to understand; write-offs and other noncash charges may offer more latitude for the management of earnings. Hawkins (1998) summarizes many corporate accounting issues for analysts, including how accounting choices can create the effect of **earnings momentum**.

► When the EPS plus noncash charges approximation to cash flow from operations is used, items affecting actual cash flow from operations, such as noncash revenue and net changes in working capital, are ignored.[49]

---

[49] For example, aggressive recognition (front-end loading) of revenue would not be captured in the earnings-plus-noncash-charges definition.

▶ Theory views free cash flow to equity (FCFE) rather than cash flow as the appropriate variable for valuation. We can use P/FCFE ratios but FCFE does have the possible drawback of being more volatile compared to cash flow, for many businesses. FCFE is also more frequently negative than cash flow.

6.1 Determining Cash Flow

In practice, analysts and data vendors often use simple approximations to cash flow from operations in calculating cash flow in price to cash flow. For many companies, depreciation and amortization are the major noncash charges regularly added to net income in the process of calculating cash flow from operations by the add-back method. A representative approximation specifies cash flow per share as EPS plus per-share depreciation, amortization, and depletion.[50] We call this estimation the earnings-plus-noncash-charges definition and use the symbol CF for it, understanding that this definition is one common usage in calculating price to cash flow rather than a technically accurate definition from an accounting perspective. We will also introduce more technically accurate cash flow concepts: cash flow from operations (CFO), free cash flow to equity (FCFE), and EBITDA, an estimate of pre-interest, pre-tax operating cash flow.[51]

EXAMPLE 28

Calculating Earnings-Plus-Noncash Charges (CF)

In 2000, Koninklijke Philips Electronics N.V. reported net income of €9,602 million, equal to basic EPS of €7.31, as well as depreciation and amortization of €2,320 million or €1.75 per share. Koninklijke Philips trades both on the New York Stock Exchange (NYSE: PHG) and Euronext Amsterdam (AEX: PHIA). An AEX price for Koninklijke Philips as of early March 2001 was €30. Calculate the P/CF ratio for PHIA.

EPS plus per-share depreciation, amortization, and depletion is €7.31 + €1.75 = €9.06 per share. Thus P/CF = €30/€9.06 = 3.31, or 3.3.

Most frequently, trailing price to cash flow are reported. A trailing price to cash flow is calculated as the current market price divided by the sum of the most recent four quarters' cash flow per share. A fiscal year definition is also possible, just as in the case of EPS.

Rather than use an approximate EPS-plus-noncash charges concept of cash flow, analysts can use cash flow from operations (CFO) in a price multiple. CFO is found in the statement of cash flows. Careful analysts often adjust CFO as reported to remove the effects of any items related to financing or investing activities. For example, when CFO includes cash outflows for interest expense and cash inflows for interest income, as in U.S. GAAP accounting, one common adjustment is to add back to CFO the quantity (Net cash interest outflow) ×

---

[50] This representation is, for example, the definition in Value Line (2001). Value Line states its definition of cash flow in terms of "net income minus preferred dividends (if any)," which is net income to common shareholders, to which it adds the above three noncash charges. The resulting sum is then divided by the number of shares outstanding. Note that depletion is an expense only for natural resource companies.

[51] See Grant and Parker (2001). Grant and Parker point out that EBITDA as a cash flow approximation assumes that changes in working capital accounts are immaterial. The EPS-plus-noncash-charges definition makes the same assumption (it is essentially earnings before depreciation and amortization).

$(1 - \text{Tax rate}).$[52] Analysts also adjust CFO for components not expected to persist into future time periods.

In addition, the analyst can relate price to FCFE, the cash flow concept with the strongest link to valuation theory. Because the amount of capital expenditures as a fraction of CFO will generally differ among companies being compared, the analyst may find that rankings by P/CFO (as well as P/CF) will differ from rankings by P/FCFE. Because period-by-period FCFE can be more volatile than CFO (or CF), however, a trailing P/FCFE is not necessarily more informative in a valuation. As an example, consider two similar businesses with the same CFO and capital expenditures over a two-year period. If the first company times the expenditures towards the beginning of the period and the second times the expenditures towards the end, the P/FCFE ratios for the two stocks may differ sharply without pointing to a meaningful economic difference between them.[53] This concern can be addressed at least in part by using price to average free cash flow, as in Hackel, Livnat, and Rai (1994).

Another ratio sometimes reported is P/EBITDA.[54] EBITDA is earnings before interest, taxes, depreciation, and amortization. To calculate EBITDA, as discussed in Reading 47, analysts usually start with earnings from continuing operations excluding nonrecurring items. To that earnings number, interest, taxes, depreciation, and amortization are added. When per-share price is in the numerator, per-share EBITDA is used in the denominator. EBITDA, as already mentioned, is a pre-tax and pre-interest number. Because EBITDA is pre-interest, it is a flow to both debt and equity. As a result, with EBITDA in the denominator of a ratio, total company value (debt plus equity) is more appropriate than common stock value in the numerator. In Section 7, we present a multiple, enterprise value to EBITDA, that is consistent with this observation.

EXAMPLE 29

Alternative Price to Cash Flow Concepts

In Example 18, we concluded that the P/B was inappropriate for valuing Dell Computer (Nasdaq NMS: DELL) relative to peer companies. In particular, Dell's relatively efficient use of assets penalizes it in P/B comparisons. Because Dell's business model results in relatively strong cash flow, we might compare Dell with its peers on the basis of one or more cash flow measures or related concepts:

- ► EPS-plus-noncash charges (CF);
- ► CFO;
- ► FCFE; and/or
- ► EBITDA.

In this example, we illustrate the calculation of price multiples based on these concepts from actual financials. The two financial statements needed to calculate any of these concepts are the income statement and the statement of cash flows, given in Tables 15(A) and 15(B).

---

[52] Under International Accounting Standards (IAS), interest income and interest expense may or may not be in CFO. Therefore, an adjustment may be necessary to match U.S. GAAP and IAS. Consistency in treatment is important.
[53] The analyst could appropriately use the FCFE discounted cash flow model value, which incorporates all expected future free cash flows to equity, however.
[54] Another concept that has become popular is **cash earnings**, which has been defined in various ways, such as earnings plus amortization of intangibles or EBITDA less net financial expenses.

Other information for Dell is as follows:

► In the last three years, Dell has had a cash flow "tax benefits of employee stock plans," which it has classified as an operating cash flow. This item, amounting to $929 million in 2001, relates to tax benefits from the exercise of employee stock options during a period of rising stock prices. The amount of such benefits in the future is related to continuing rising stock prices for Dell.

► Net investment income of $531 million included $47 million in interest expense. Actual cash interest paid for the year was $49 million. Cash flow from operations as reported incorporates such financing effects. The effective tax rate per the income statement was 30 percent.

► Dell stock closed at $27.11 on 16 April 2001.

TABLE 15(A) **Dell Computer Corporation Consolidated Statement of Income (in millions, except per-share amounts)**

	2 Feb 2001
Net revenue	$ 31,888
Cost of revenue	25,445
Gross margin	6,443
Operating expenses	
Selling, general, and administrative	3,193
Research, development, and engineering	482
Special charges	105
Total operating expenses	3,780
Operating income	2,663
Investment and other income, net	531
Income before income taxes and cumulative effect of change in accounting principle	3,194
Provision for income taxes	(958)
Cumulative effect of change in accounting principle, net	(59)
Net income	$ 2,177
Earnings per common share:	
Before cumulative effect of change in accounting principle:	
Basic	$ 0.87
Diluted	$ 0.81
After cumulative effect of change in accounting principle:	
Basic	$ 0.84
Diluted	$ 0.79
Weighted average shares outstanding:	
Basic	2,582
Diluted	2,746

TABLE 15(B) Dell Computer Corporation Consolidated Statement of Cash Flows (in millions)

	2 Feb 2001
Cash flows from operating activities:	
Net income	$ 2,177
Adjustments to reconcile net income to net cash provided by operating activities	
Depreciation and amortization	240
Tax benefits of employee stock plans	929
Special charges	105
Gain on sale of investments	(307)
Other	109
Changes in	
Operating working capital	671
Non-current assets and liabilities	271
Net cash provided by operating activities	4,195
Cash flows from investing activities:	
Investments	
Purchases	(2,606)
Maturities and sales	2,331
Capital expenditures	(482)
Net cash used in investing activities	(757)
Cash flows from financing activities	
Purchase of common stock	(2,700)
Issuance of common stock under employee plans	404
Proceeds from issuance of long-term debt, net of issuance costs	—
Other	(9)
Net cash used in financing activities	(2,305)
Effect of exchange rate changes on cash	(32)
Net increase in cash	1,101
Cash and cash equivalents at beginning of period	3,809
Cash and cash equivalents at end of period	$4,910

Based on the above data, answer the following questions:

1. Calculate P/CF.
2. Calculate P/CFO, adjusting CFO for the "tax benefits of employee stock plans" and for financing effects.
3. Calculate P/FCFE consistent with your work in Problem 2.
4. Calculate P/EBITDA.

Solution to 1: Net income = $2,177 million; depreciation and amortization = $240 million; so CF = 2,177 + 240 = $2,417 million. There are 2,582 million shares outstanding. Thus CF = 2,417/2,582 = 0.94 and P/CF = 27.11/0.94 = 28.8.

Solution to 2: Cash flow from operations is $4,195 million. Excluding $929 million associated with tax benefits of employee stock plans gives 4,195 − 929 = $3,266. To further adjust CFO for the effect of actual cash interest paid, we have 3,266 + 49(1 − 0.30) = $3,266 + $34.3 = $3,300.3. So $3,300.3/2,582 = $1.28. So P/CFO based on adjusted per-share CFO of $1.28 equals $27.11/$1.28 = 21.2.[55] The logic of excluding the $929 million is that because such tax benefits depend on stock price performance, they may not persist into the future.

Solution to 3: Recall that FCFE is cash flow from operations less net investment in fixed capital plus net borrowing. Net cash used in fixed capital (reported above as capital expenditures) was $482 million and net borrowing was zero. Because FCFE is a flow to equity, we must subtract the add-back of $34.3 million that we made in Problem 2. So FCFE is $3,300.3 − $482 − $34.3 = $2,784. Per share we have $2,784/2,582 = $1.08. P/FCFE = $27.11/$1.08 = 25.1.

Solution to 4: Net income = $2,177 million, Interest expense = $47 million, Depreciation and amortization = $240 million, Taxes = $958 million. EBITDA = $2,177 + $47 + $240 million + $958 = $3,422. Per share EBITDA = $3,422/2,582 = $1.32. P/EBITDA = $27.11/$1.32 = 20.5.

In summary, this exercise produced multiples ranging from 20.5 for P/EBITDA to 28.8 for P/CF. Consistency in definition is important. Furthermore, if the analyst were featuring diluted EPS in her analysis, she would report cash flow multiples based on 2,746 million diluted shares.

6.2 Valuation Based on Forecasted Fundamentals

The relationship between the justified price to cash flow and fundamentals follows from the familiar mathematics of the present value model. The justified price to cash flow is inversely related to the stock's required rate of return and positively related to the growth rate(s) of expected future cash flows (however defined), all else equal. We can find a justified price to cash flow based on fundamentals by finding the value of a stock using the most suitable DCF model and dividing that number by cash flow, using our chosen definition of cash flow. Example 30 illustrates the process.

---

[55] Although 30 percent was the effective tax rate per the income statement, interestingly Dell actually paid no taxes for the year because of the effect of the employee stock options. The adjustment we just illustrated would be appropriate for use in forecasting; adding back the full $49 million (reflecting no taxes) would better reflect actual cash flow for the year purged of financing items.

EXAMPLE 30

Justified Price to Cash Flow Based on Forecasted Fundamentals

As a technology analyst, you are working on the valuation of Dell Computer (Nasdaq NMS: DELL). You have calculated per-share FCFE for DELL of 1.39. As a first estimate of value, you are applying a FCFE model under the assumption of a stable long-term growth rate in FCFE:

$$V_0 = \frac{(1 + g)\,\mathrm{FCFE}_0}{r - g}$$

where g is the expected growth rate of FCFE. You estimate trailing FCFE at $1.39 per share and trailing CF (based on the earnings plus noncash charges definition) at $0.75. Your other estimates are a 14.5 percent required rate of return and an 8.5 percent expected growth rate of FCFE.

1. What is the intrinsic value of DELL, according to a constant-growth FCFE model?

2. What is the justified P/CF, based on forecasted fundamentals?

3. What is the justified P/FCFE, based on forecasted fundamentals?

Solution to 1: Calculate intrinsic value as (1.085 × $1.39)/(0.145 − 0.085) = $25.14.

Solution to 2: Calculate a justified P/CF based on forecasted fundamentals as $25.14/$0.75 = 33.5.

Solution to 3: The justified P/FCFE ratio is $25.14/$1.39 = 18.1.

6.3 Valuation Using Comparables

Using the method of comparables for valuing stocks based on price to cash flow follows the steps given in Section 3.3, which we earlier illustrated using P/E, P/B, and P/S.

EXAMPLE 31

Price to Cash Flow and Comparables

As a technology analyst, you have been asked to compare the valuation of Compaq Computer Corporation (NYSE: CPQ) with Gateway, Inc. (NYSE: GTW).[56] One valuation metric you are considering is P/CF. Table 16 gives information on P/CF, P/FCFE, and selected fundamentals as of 16 April 2001.

---

[56] In 2002, Compaq Computer Corporation merged with Hewlett-Packard Corporation.

TABLE 16 A Comparison between Two Companies (all amounts per share)

	Current Price	Trailing CF per Share	P/CF	Trailing FCFE per Share	P/FCFE	Consensus Five-Year Growth Forecast	Beta
CPQ	$17.98	$1.84	9.8	$0.29	62	13.4%	1.50
GTW	$15.65	$1.37	11.4	−$1.99	NM	10.6%	1.45

Source: The Value Line Investment Survey.

Using the information in Table 16, compare the valuations of CPQ and GTW using the P/CF multiple, assuming that the two stocks have approximately equal risk.

CPQ is selling at a P/CF (9.8) approximately 14 percent smaller than the P/CF of GTW (11.4). We would expect on that basis that, all else equal, investors anticipate a higher growth rate for GTW. In fact, the consensus five-year earnings growth forecast for CPQ is 280 basis points higher than for GTW. As of the date of the comparison, CPQ appears to be relatively undervalued compared with GTW, as judged by P/CF. The information in Table 16 on FCFE supports the proposition that CPQ may be relatively undervalued. Positive FCFE for CPQ suggests that growth was funded internally; negative FCFE for GTW suggests the need for external funding of growth.

ENTERPRISE VALUE TO EBITDA   7

In Section 6, when presenting the P/EBITDA multiple, we stated that because EBITDA is a flow to both debt and equity, a multiple using total company value in the numerator was logically more appropriate. Enterprise value to EBITDA responds to this need. **Enterprise value (EV)** is total company value (the market value of debt, common equity, and preferred equity) minus the value of cash and investments. Because the numerator is enterprise value, EV/EBITDA is a valuation indicator for the overall company rather than common stock. If the analyst can assume that the business's debt and preferred stock (if any) are efficiently priced, the analyst can also draw an inference about the valuation of common equity. Such an assumption is often reasonable.

Analysts have offered the following rationales for using EV/EBITDA:

▶ EV/EBITDA may be more appropriate than P/E for comparing companies with different financial leverage (debt), because EBITDA is a pre-interest earnings figure, in contrast to EPS, which is post-interest.

▶ By adding back depreciation and amortization, EBITDA controls for differences in depreciation and amortization across businesses. For this reason, EV/EBITDA is frequently used in the valuation of capital-intensive businesses (for example, cable companies and steel companies). Such businesses typically have substantial depreciation and amortization expenses.

▶ EBITDA is frequently positive when EPS is negative.

Possible drawbacks to EV/EBITDA include the following:

▶ EBITDA will overestimate cash flow from operations if working capital is growing. EBITDA also ignores the effects of differences in revenue recognition policy on cash flow from operations.[57]

▶ Free cash flow to the firm (FCFF), which directly reflects the amount of required capital expenditures, has a stronger link to valuation theory than does EBITDA. Only if depreciation expenses match capital expenditures do we expect EBITDA to reflect differences in businesses' capital programs. This qualification to EBITDA comparisons can be meaningful for the capital-intensive businesses to which EV/EBITDA is often applied.

7.1 Determining EBITDA

We illustrated the calculation of EBITDA in Reading 47 as well as in Section 6 of this reading. As discussed above, analysts commonly define enterprise value as follows:

	Market value of common equity
	(Number of shares outstanding × Price per share)
Plus:	Market value of preferred stock (if any)
Plus:	Market value of debt
Less:	Cash and investments
Equals:	Enterprise value

Cash and investments (sometimes termed nonearning assets) are subtracted because EV is designed to measure the price an acquirer would pay for a company as a whole. The acquirer must buy out current equity and debt providers but then gets access to the cash and investments, which lower the net cost of the acquisition. The same logic explains the use of market values: In repurchasing debt, an acquirer would have to pay market prices. Some debt, however, may be private and not trade, or be publicly traded but trade infrequently. When the analyst does not have market values, he uses book values (values as given in the balance sheet). Example 32 illustrates the calculation of EV/EBITDA.

EXAMPLE 32

Calculating EV/EBITDA

Comcast Corporation is principally engaged in the development, management, and operation of hybrid fiber-coaxial broadband cable networks, cellular and personal communications systems, and the provision of content. Table 17 gives excerpts from the consolidated balance sheet (as of 31 December 2000).

---

[57] See Moody's Investors Service (2000) and Grant and Parker (2001) for additional issues and concerns.

TABLE 17	Comcast Corporation Liabilities and Shareholders' Equity (in millions, except per share)
	31 Dec 2000
Liabilities and Shareholders' Equity	
Current liabilities	
Accounts payable and accrued expenses	$2,852.9
Accrued interest	105.5
Deferred income taxes	789.9
Current portion of long-term debt	293.9
Total Current Liabilities	4,042.2
Noncurrent liabilities	
Long-term debt, less current portion	10,517.4
Deferred income taxes	5,786.7
Minority interest and other commitments and contingencies	1,257.2
Common equity **put options**	54.6
Total Noncurrent Liabilities	17,615.9
Shareholders' equity	
Preferred Stock: Authorized, 20,000,000 shares 5.25%	
Series B mandatorily redeemable convertible, $1,000 par value; issued, 59,450 at redemption value	59.5
Class A special common stock, $1 par value: Authorized, 2,500,000,000 shares; issued, 931,340,103; outstanding, 908,015,192	908.0
Class A common stock, $1 par value: Authorized, 200,000,000 shares; issued and outstanding, 21,832,250	21.8
Class B common stock, $1 par value: Authorized, 50,000,000 shares; issued and outstanding, 9,444,375	9.4
Additional capital	11,598.8
Retained earnings (accumulated deficit)	1,056.5
Accumulated other comprehensive income	432.4
Total shareholders' equity	14,086.4
Total Liabilities and Shareholders' Equity	$35,744.5

An unusual item in the balance sheet is "common equity put options," which were issued as part of a share repurchase program. Because the value of these puts should be reflected in the price of the common stock, the $54.6 million should not be included in calculating EV. The balance sheet shows that Comcast has three classes of common stock:

► Class A Special Common Stock (NASDAQ NMS: CMCSK) is generally nonvoting. This issue is a component of the S&P 500;

► Class A (NASDAQ NMS: CMCSA) is entitled to one vote; and

► Class B is entitled to 15 votes and is convertible, share for share, into Class A or Class A Special Common Stock. This issue is not publicly traded.

Closing share prices as of 7 March 2001 were $45.875 for CMCSK and $45.25 for CMCSA. "Minority interest and other" is to be viewed as an equity item.[58]

The asset side of the balance sheet (as of 31 December 2000) gave the following items (in millions):

Cash and cash equivalents	$651.5
Investments	$3,059.7

The income statement for the year ending 31 December 2000 gave the following items (in millions):

Net income	$2,021.5
Net income for common stockholders	$1,998.0
Interest expense	$691.4
Taxes	$1,441.3
Depreciation	$837.3
Amortization	$1,794.0

Based on the above information, calculate EV/EBITDA.

Solution: We first calculate EBITDA. We always select net income (which is net income available to both preferred and common equity) in the EBITDA calculation:

	2000
Net income	$2,021.5
Interest	$691.4
Taxes	$1,441.3
Depreciation	$837.3
Amortization	+$1,794.0
EBITDA	$6,785.5

We calculate the value of all equity, adding to it "minority interest and other."

	Millions
CMCSK issue ($45.875 × 908.015192 million shares)	41,655.20
CMCSA issue ($45.25 × 21.83225 million shares)	987.91
Class B stock (per books)	9.4
Common equity value	42,652.51
Preferred equity (per books)	59.5
Total equity	42,712.01
Minority interest and other	1,257.2
Common equity plus minority interest	43,969.21

---

[58] Minority interest represents the proportionate stake of minority shareholders in a company's consolidated, majority-owned subsidiary.

The value of long-term debt (per the books) is \$10,517.4 million. The sum of cash and cash equivalents plus investments is \$651.5 million + \$3,059.7 million = \$3,711.2 million.

So, EV = \$43,969.21 million + \$10,517.4 million − \$3,711.2 million = \$50,775.41 million. We conclude that EV/EBITDA = (\$50,775.41 million)/(\$6,785.5 million) = 7.5.

7.2 Valuation Based on Forecasted Fundamentals

As with other multiples, intuition concerning the fundamental drivers of enterprise value to EBITDA can help when applying the method of comparables. All else equal, the justified EV/EBITDA based on fundamentals should be positively related to expected growth rate in FCFF and negatively related to the business's weighted-average cost of capital. The analyst should review the statement of cash flows to get a better picture of the relationship of EBITDA to the company's underlying cash flow from operations.

7.3 Valuation Using Comparables

A recent equity research report on the cable industry, excerpted in Table 18, illustrates a format for the presentation of relative valuations using EV/EBITDA, which is informally called a "cash flow multiple" in the report. All else equal, a lower EV/EBITDA value relative to peers indicates relative undervaluation. The analyst's recommendations are clearly not completely determined by relative EV/EBITDA, however; from the analyst's perspective, EV/EBITDA is simply one piece of information to consider.

DIVIDEND YIELD   8

Total return has a capital appreciation component and a dividend yield component. Dividend yield is frequently reported to supply the investor with an estimate of the dividend yield component of total return. Dividend yield is also used as a valuation indicator. According to the *Merrill Lynch Institutional Factor Survey*, from 1989 to 2001, on average slightly less than one-quarter of respondents reported using dividend yield as a factor in the investment process.

Analysts have offered the following rationales for using dividend yields in valuation:

▶ Dividend yield is a component of total return.

▶ Dividends are a less risky component of total return than capital appreciation.

Possible drawbacks of dividend yield include the following:

▶ Dividend yield is only one component of total return; not using all information related to expected return is suboptimal.

▶ Dividends paid now displace earnings in all future periods (a concept known as the **dividend displacement of earnings**). Investors trade off future earnings growth to receive higher current dividends.

TABLE 18 EV/EBITDA Multiples Are Well Below Recent Averages. Calendar 2002E Cash Flow Multiples (in millions, except per share)

	CMCSK[c]	CHTR[d]	COX	ADLAC[e]	CVC	MCCC[f]	ICCI[g]	Average
Rating	Strong Buy	Strong Buy	Buy	Strong Buy	Buy	Buy	Buy	
Size ranking	3	4	5	6	7	8		
Price	$33.98	$17.62	$39.65	$28.97	$40.00	$16.10	$20.25	
Times . . . Diluted shares outstanding[a]	964	657	620	173	178	119.9	61.3	
Equals . . . Equity market capitalization	$32,754	$11,583	$24,576	$5,016	$7,104	$1,930	$1,242	
Plus . . . Debt at 12/02	$10,852	$17,618	$8,988	$13,936	$6,147	$3,059	$1,055	
Plus . . . Preferred	$0	$0	$281	$148	$2,630	$0	$0	
Less . . . Nonearning assets at 12/02	$15,726	$144	$5,792	($139)	$3,885	$7	$19	
Less . . . Options exercise	$507	$0	$80	$0	$481	$0	$21	
Equals . . . Enterprise value	$27,373	$29,057	$27,973	$19,239	$11,514	$4,982	$2,257	
Adjusted Cable EBITDA[b]	$2,455	$2,134	$1,822	$1,616	$1,012	$387	$185	
Equals . . .								
Cable Cash Flow Multiple	**11.1×**	**13.6×**	**15.4×**	**11.9×**	**11.4×**	**12.9×**	**12.2×**	**12.6×**
Pro forma subscribers at 12/02	8,475	7,130	6,402	5,858	3,059	1,593	592	
Pro forma homes passed at 12/02	13,610	12,161	10,016	9,503	4,417	2,595	1,035	
Enterprise value per subscriber	**$3,230**	**$4,075**	**$4,369**	**$3,284**	**$3,764**	**$3,127**	**$3,809**	**$3,665**
Enterprise value per homes passed	**$2,011**	**$2,389**	**$2,793**	**$2,024**	**$2,607**	**$1,920**	**$2,181**	
Percent of plant > 550 MHz at 12/02	98%	95%	96%	96%	95%	86%	95%	

[a] Includes primary shares plus in-the-money employee/management options and convertible instruments.

[b] Adjusted Cable EBITDA includes allocated corporate overhead.

[c] Pro forma the AT&T and Adelphia system swaps and AT&T system acquisitions as if all were completed prior to January 1, 2001.

[d] Pro forma the Kalamazoo and AT&T systems acquisitions as if they occurred January 1, 2000.

[e] Pro forma the Century, Frontier, Harron, Coaxial, Benchmark, Cablevision (Cleveland), Prestige, and GS Communications acquisitions as if they took place on January 1, 2000.

[f] Pro forma the AT&T acquisition as if it occurred before January 1, 2000.

[g] All numbers proportional of Insight's 50% stake in the Insight Midwest JV. Pro forma the JV rollup as if it occurred before January 1, 2000.

Source: Shapiro, Savner, and Toohig (2001).

▶ The argument about the relative safety of dividends presupposes that the market prices reflect in a biased way differnces in the relative risk of the components of return.

8.1 Calculation of Dividend Yield

This reading thus far has presented multiples with market price in the numerator. Price to dividend (P/D) ratios have occasionally appeared in valuation, particularly with respect to indexes. Many stocks, however, do not pay dividends, and the P/D ratio is undefined with zero in the denominator; for such stocks, dividend yield is defined. For practical purposes, dividend yield is the preferred way to present this variable. **Trailing dividend yield** is generally calculated as four times the most recent quarterly per-share dividend divided by the current market price per share. (The most recent quarterly dividend times four is known as the **dividend rate**.) The **leading dividend yield** is calculated as forecasted dividends per share over the next year divided by the current market price per share.

EXAMPLE 33

Calculating Dividend Yield

Table 19 gives dividend data for Ford Motor Company (NYSE: F).

TABLE 19 Dividend Data for Ford Motor Company

	Dividends per share
1Q:2002	$0.10
4Q:2001	$0.15
3Q:2001	$0.30
2Q:2001	$0.30
Total	$0.85

Source: Standard & Poor's Stock Reports.

Given a price per share of $14.62, calculate the trailing dividend yield of Ford.

The dividend rate is $0.10 × 4 = $0.40. The dividend yield is $0.40/$14.62 = 0.0274 or 2.7%. This percentage is the yield reported by Standard & Poor's in a stock report on Ford Motor Company dated 16 February 2002.

8.2 Valuation Based on Forecasted Fundamentals

The relationship of dividend yield to fundamentals can be illustrated in the context of the Gordon growth model. From that model we obtain the expression

$$\frac{D_0}{P_0} = \frac{r - g}{1 + g} \tag{48-5}$$

Equation 48-5 shows that dividend yield is negatively related to the expected rate of growth in dividends and positively related to the stock's required rate of return. The first point implies that the selection of stocks with relatively high dividend yields is consistent with an orientation to a value rather than growth investment style.

8.3 Valuation Using Comparables

Using dividend yield with comparables is similar to the process that has been illustrated for other multiples. An analyst compares a company with its peers to determine whether it is attractively priced considering its dividend yield and risk. The analyst should examine whether differences in expected growth explain difference in dividend yield. Another consideration used by some investors is the security of the dividend (the probability that it will be cut).

EXAMPLE 34

Dividend Yield Comparables

William Leiderman is a portfolio manager for a U.S. pension fund's domestic equity portfolio. The portfolio is exempt from taxes, so any differences in the taxation of dividends and capital gains are not relevant. Leiderman's client has a high current income requirement. Leiderman is considering the purchase of utility stocks for the fund as of early April 2002. He has narrowed down his selection to three large-cap utilities serving the southeastern United States, given in Table 20.

TABLE 20   Using Dividend Yield to Compare Stocks

Company	Consensus Forecast Growth	Beta	Dividend Yield
Florida Power and Light (NYSE: FPL)	6.95%	0.13	3.7%
Progress Energy (NYSE: PGN)	6.79%	0.09	4.4%
Southern Company (NYSE: SO)	5.44%	−0.06	4.7%

Source: First Call/Thomson Financial.

All of the securities exhibit similar and low market risk. Although Southern Company has the highest dividend yield, it also has the lowest expected growth rate. Leiderman determines that Progress Energy provides the greatest combination of dividend yield and growth, amounting to 11.19 percent.

INTERNATIONAL VALUATION CONSIDERATIONS

9

Clearly, to perform a relative value analysis, an analyst must use comparable companies and underlying financial data prepared using comparable methods. Using relative valuation methods in an international setting is thus difficult. Comparing companies across borders frequently involves accounting method differences, cultural differences, economic differences, and resulting differences in risk and growth opportunities. P/Es for individual companies in the same industry across borders have been found to vary widely.[59] Furthermore, national market P/Es often vary substantially at any single point in time. As of 30 November 1998, P/Es in 10 markets around the world ranged from a low of 18.1 in Hong Kong to a high of 191.0 in Japan.[60]

Although international accounting standards are beginning to converge, significant differences across borders still exist, making comparisons difficult. Even if harmonization of accounting principles is achieved, the need to adjust accounting data for comparability will always remain. As we have seen in earlier sections, even within a single country's accounting standards, differences between companies result from management's accounting choices (e.g., FIFO versus LIFO). The U.S. SEC requires that foreign companies whose securities trade in U.S. markets provide a reconciliation of their earnings from home country accounting principles to U.S. GAAP. This requirement not only assists the analyst in making necessary adjustments but also provides some insight into appropriate adjustments for other companies not required to provide this data. Table 21 presents a reconciliation from International Accounting Standards to U.S. GAAP for Nokia Corporation (NYSE: NOK).

In a study of companies filing such reconciliations to U.S. GAAP, Harris and Muller (1999) classify common differences into seven categories.

| | Mean Adjustment Direction | |
Category	Earnings	Equity
Differences in the treatment of goodwill	Minus	Plus
Deferred income taxes	Plus	Plus
Foreign exchange adjustments	Plus	Minus
Research and development costs	Minus	Minus
Pension expense	Minus	Plus
Tangible asset revaluations	Plus	Minus
Other	Minus	Minus

Although the mean adjustments are presented above, adjustments for individual companies can vary considerably. This list, however, provides the analyst with common adjustments that should be made.

International accounting differences affect the comparability of all price multiples. Of the price multiples examined in this reading, P/CFO and P/FCFE will generally be least affected by accounting differences. P/Bs and P/Es will

---

[59] Copeland, Koller, and Murrin (1994, p. 375) provide an interesting example.
[60] See Schieneman (2000).

TABLE 21 Principal Differences between IAS and U.S. GAAP for Nokia Corporation (years ended 31 December; in millions)

	1999	1998
Reconciliation of net income		
Net income reported under IAS	€2,577	€1,750
U.S. GAAP adjustments		
Deferred income taxes	0	−70
Pension expense	9	16
Development costs	−47	−18
Marketable securities	−15	29
Sale-leaseback transaction	4	1
Deferred tax effect of U.S. GAAP adjustments	14	−19
Net income under U.S. GAAP	€2,542	€1,689
Reconciliation of shareholders' equity		
Total shareholders' equity reported under IAS	€7,378	€5,109
U.S. GAAP adjustments		
Pension expense	54	45
Development costs	−186	−138
Marketable securities	142	89
Sale-leaseback transaction	0	−4
Deferred tax effect of U.S. GAAP adjustments	−4	1
Total shareholders' equity under U.S. GAAP	€7,384	€5,102

Source: Nokia Corporation Annual Report, 1999.

generally be more severely affected, as will multiples based on concepts such as EBITDA, which start from accounting earnings.

10   MOMENTUM VALUATION INDICATORS

The valuation indicators we call momentum indicators relate either price or a fundamental such as earnings to the time series of their own past values, or in some cases to the fundamental's expected value. One style of **growth investing** uses positive momentum in various senses as a selection criterion, and practitioners sometimes refer to such strategies as growth/momentum investment strategies. Momentum indicators based on price, such as the relative strength indicator discussed below, have also been referred to as **technical indicators**. According to the *Merrill Lynch Institutional Factor Survey*, momentum indicators were among the most popular valuation indicators over 1989 to 2001.[61] In this

---

[61] During the time period, the percentage of respondents who indicated that they used EPS surprise (surprise relative to consensus forecasts), EPS momentum (defined as 12-month trailing EPS divided by year-ago 12-month trailing EPS), and relative strength (defined as the difference between 3-month and 12-month price performance) was 51.5 percent, 46.3 percent, and 39.1 percent, respectively. EPS surprise was the most popular factor of the 23 surveyed over the entire time period.

section, we review three representative momentum group indicators: earnings surprise, standardized unexpected earnings, and relative strength.

To define standardized unexpected earnings, we define **unexpected earnings** (also called **earnings surprise**) as the difference between reported earnings and expected earnings,

$$UE_t = EPS_t - E(EPS_t)$$

where UE_t is the unexpected earnings for quarter t, EPS_t is the reported EPS for quarter t, and $E(EPS_t)$ is the expected EPS for the quarter. For example, a stock with reported quarterly earnings of \$1.05 and expected earnings of \$1.00 would have a positive earnings surprise of \$0.05. Often the percent earnings surprise, earnings surprise divided by expected EPS, is reported; in this example, percent earning surprise would be \$0.05/\$1.00 = 0.05 or 5%. When used directly as a valuation indicator, earnings surprise is generally scaled by a measure reflecting the variability or range in analysts' EPS estimates. The principle is that a given size EPS forecast error in relation to the mean is more meaningful the less the disagreement among analysts' forecasts. A way to accomplish such scaling is to divide unexpected earnings by the standard deviation of analysts' earnings forecasts, which we can call **scaled earnings surprise**.

EXAMPLE 35

Calculating Scaled Earnings Surprise Using Analyst Forecasts

As of the end of November, the mean December 2001 quarterly consensus earnings forecast for International Business Machines (NYSE: IBM) was \$1.32. For the 18 analysts covering the stock, the low forecast is \$1.22 and the high is \$1.37, and the standard deviation of the forecasts is \$0.03. If reported earnings come in \$0.04 above the mean forecast, what is the earnings surprise for IBM, scaled to reflect the dispersion in analysts' forecasts?

In this case, scaled earnings surprise is \$0.04/\$0.03 = 1.33.

The rationale behind using earnings surprises is the thesis that positive surprises may be associated with persistent positive abnormal returns, or alpha. The same rationale lies behind a momentum indicator that is closely related to earnings surprise but more highly researched: **standardized unexpected earnings** (SUE). SUE is defined as

$$SUE_t = \frac{EPS_t - E(EPS_t)}{\sigma[EPS_t - E(EPS_t)]}$$

where the numerator is the unexpected earnings for t and the denominator, $\sigma[EPS_t - E(EPS_t)]$, is the standard deviation of past unexpected earnings over some period prior to time t—for example, the 20 quarters prior to t as in Latané and Jones (1979), the article that introduced the SUE concept. In SUE, the magnitude of unexpected earnings is scaled by a measure of the size of historical forecast errors or surprises. The principle is that a given size EPS forecast error is more (less) meaningful the smaller (the larger) the historical size of forecast errors.

Suppose that for a stock that had a \$0.05 earnings surprise, the standard deviation of past surprises is \$0.20. The \$0.05 surprise is relatively small compared to past forecast errors, reflected in a SUE of $0.05/$0.20 = 0.25. If the standard error of past surprises were smaller, say $0.07, the SUE would be $0.05/$0.07 = 0.71. SUE has been the subject of a number of studies.[62]

Another set of indicators, **relative strength (RSTR) indicators**, compare a stock's performance during a particular period either to its own past performance[63] or to the performance of some group of stocks. The simplest relative strength indicator of the first type is the stock's compound rate of return over some specified time horizon, such as six months or one year.[64] Despite its simplicity, this measure has appeared in numerous recent studies including Chan, Jegadeesh, and Lakonishok (1999) and Lee and Swaminathan (2000). The rationale behind its use is the thesis that patterns of persistence or reversal exist in stock returns, which may depend empirically on the investor's time horizon (Lee and Swaminathan 2000).

A simple relative strength indicator of the second type is the stock's performance divided by the performance of an equity index. If the value of this ratio increases, the stock price increases relative to the index and displays positive relative

EXAMPLE 36

Relative Strength in Relation to an Equity Index

Table 22 shows the values of the utility and the finance components of the NYSE Common Stock Indexes for the end of each of 12 months from November 2000 through October 2001. Values for the NYSE Composite Index are also given.

TABLE 22	NYSE Indexes		
	Utility	**Finance**	**Composite**
November	434.95	592.35	629.78
December	440.54	646.95	656.87
January	442.51	641.37	663.64
February	406.01	603.76	626.94
March	394.69	585.48	595.66
April	421.41	604.65	634.83
May	406.49	625.11	641.67
June	376.61	626.65	621.76
July	370.92	616.58	616.94
August	346.92	585.54	597.84
September	340.74	549.41	543.84
October	323.46	543.16	546.34

---

[62] See Reilly and Brown (2000) and Sharpe, Alexander, and Bailey (1999) for a summary.

[63] Other definitions relate a stock's return over a recent period to its return over a longer period that includes the more recent period.

[64] This concept has also been referred to as **price momentum** in the academic literature.

To produce the information for Table 23, we divide each industry index value by the NYSE Composite value for the same month and then scale those results so that relative strength for November 2001 equals 1.0.

TABLE 23 Relative Strength Indicators		
	RSTR Utility	**RSTR Finance**
November	1.000	1.000
December	0.971	1.047
January	0.965	1.028
February	0.938	1.024
March	0.959	1.045
April	0.961	1.013
May	0.917	1.036
June	0.877	1.072
July	0.871	1.063
August	0.840	1.041
September	0.907	1.074
October	0.857	1.057

On the basis of Tables 22 and 23, answer the following questions:

1. State the relative strength of utilities and finance over the entire time period November 2000 through October 2001. Interpret the relative strength for each sector over that period.

2. Discuss the relative performance of utilities and finance in the month of April 2001.

Solution to 1: The relative strength of utilities was 0.857. This number represents $1 - 0.857 = 0.143$ or 14.3% underperformance relative to the NYSE Composite over the time period. The relative strength of finance was 1.057. This number represents $1.057 - 1.000 = 0.057$ or 5.7% outperformance relative to the NYSE Composite over the time period.

Solution to 2: April 2001 utilities' RSTR at 0.961 was higher than in the prior month, but finance's RSTR at 1.013 was lower than in the prior month. In contrast to performance for the entire period, utilities outperformed finance in April.

strength. Often the relative strength indicator may be scaled to 1.0 at the beginning of the study period. If the stock goes up at a higher (lower) rate than the index, for example, then relative strength will be above (below) 1.0. Relative strength in this sense is often calculated for industries as well as for individual stocks.

Momentum group indicators have substantial followings among professional investors. The rigorous study of the use of such indicators is a subject of current active research both in industry and business schools.

VALUATION INDICATORS AND INVESTMENT MANAGEMENT

All the valuation indicators discussed in this reading are quantitative aids, but not necessarily solutions, to the problem of security selection. Because each carefully selected and calculated price multiple, momentum indicator, or fundamental may supply some piece of the puzzle of stock valuation, many investors use more than one valuation indicator (in addition to other criteria) in stock selection.[65] The application of a set of criteria to reduce an investment universe to a

---

EXAMPLE 37

Using Screens to Find Stocks for a Portfolio

Janet Larsen manages an institutional portfolio and is currently looking for new stocks to add to the portfolio. Larsen has a commercial database with information on 7,532 U.S. stocks. She has designed several screens to select stocks with low P/E, P/CF, and Enterprise Value/EBITDA multiples. She also wants stocks that are currently paying a cash dividend and have positive earnings, and stocks with a total market capitalization between $1 billion and $5 billion. Table 24 shows the number of stocks that meet each of six screens reflecting these desires, as well as the number of stocks meeting all screens simultaneously, as of January 2002.

TABLE 24   A Stock Screen

	Stocks Meeting Screen	
Screen	**Number**	**Percent**
P/E < 20.0	2,549	33.8%
P/CF < 12.0	4,209	55.9%
Enterprise value/EBITDA < 10.0	4,393	58.3%
Dividends > 0	2,411	32.0%
EPS > 0	4,116	54.6%
Market capitalization from 1 billion to 5 billion	1,009	13.4%
All six screens simultaneously	117	1.6%

---

[65] According to the *Merrill Lynch Institutional Factor Survey* for 2001, from 1989 to 2001 responding institutional investors on average used about 8 factors (of the 23 surveyed) in selecting stocks. The survey factors include not only price multiples, momentum indicators, and DDM, but the fundamentals ROE, debt to equity, projected five-year EPS growth, EPS variability, EPS estimate dispersion, size, beta, foreign exposure, low price, and neglect.

► The product of the fractions of stocks passing each screen individually is $0.338 \times 0.559 \times 0.583 \times 0.32 \times 0.546 \times 0.134 = 0.0026$, or 0.26%.

► The P/E of the S&P 500 was 24.4, the P/E of S&P 500/BARRA Growth Index was 32.4, and the P/E of the S&P 500/BARRA Value Index was 19.2 as of January 2002, excluding companies with negative earnings from the calculation of P/E.

Answer the following questions using the information supplied above:

1. What type of valuation indicators does Larsen not include in her stock screen?

2. Characterize the overall orientation of Larsen as to investment style.

3. Why is the fraction of stocks passing all six screens simultaneously, 1.6 percent, larger than the product of the fraction of stocks passing each screen individually, 0.26 percent?

4. State two limitations of Larsen's stock screen.

Solution to 1: Larsen has not included momentum indicators in the screen.

Solution to 2: Larsen can be characterized as a mid-cap value investor. Her screen does not include explicit growth rate criteria or include momentum indicators, such as positive earnings surprise, usually associated with a growth orientation. Larsen also specifies a cutoff for P/E that is consistent with the S&P 500/BARRA Value Index. Note that her multiples criteria are all "less than" criteria.[66]

Solution to 3: The fraction of stocks passing all screens simultaneously is greater than 0.26 percent because the criteria are not all independent. For example, we expect that some stocks that pass the P/CF criterion also will pass the P/E criteria because cash flow is positively correlated with earnings, on average.

Solution to 4: Larsen does not include any fundamental criteria. This is a limitation because a stock's expected low growth rate or high risk may explain its low P/E. A second limitation of her screen is that the computations of the value indicators in a commercial database may not reflect the appropriate adjustments to inputs. The absence of qualitative criteria is also a possible limitation.

smaller set of investments is called **screening**. Stock screens often include not only criteria based on the valuation measures discussed in this reading but fundamental criteria that may explain differences in such measures. Computerized stock screening is an efficient way to narrow a search for investments and is a part of many stock-selection disciplines. The limitations to such screens usually relate to the lack of control over the calculation of important inputs (such as EPS)

[66] In using multiples such as P/E or P/B in this widely used fashion to characterize a portfolio, an analyst should be aware of the limitations. A high-P/E stock is usually labeled as a growth stock but may actually be an overpriced low-growth stock in the sense of future earnings growth.

when using many commercial databases and screening tools; the absence of qualitative factors in most databases is another important limitation.

Investors also apply all the metrics that we have illustrated in terms of individual stocks to industries and economic sectors. For example, average price multiples and momentum indicators can be used in sector rotation strategies to determine relatively under- or overvalued sectors.[67] (A **sector rotation strategy** is an investment strategy that over-weights economic sectors that are anticipated to outperform or lead the overall market.)

---

[67] See Salsman (1997) for an example.

SUMMARY

In this reading, we have defined and explained the most important valuation indicators in professional use and illustrated their application to a variety of valuation problems.

▶ Price multiples are ratios of a stock's price to some measure of value per share.

▶ Momentum indicators relate either price or a fundamental to the time series of their own past values (or in some cases to their expected value).

▶ Price multiples are most frequently applied to valuation using the method of comparables. This method involves using a price multiple to evaluate whether an asset is relatively undervalued, fairly valued, or overvalued in relation to a benchmark value of the multiple.

▶ The benchmark value of the multiple may be the multiple of a similar company or the median or average value of the multiple for a peer group of companies, an industry, an economic sector, an equity index, or the median or average own past values of the multiple.

▶ The economic rationale for the method of comparables is the law of one price.

▶ Price multiples may also be applied to valuation using the method based on forecasted fundamentals. Discounted cash flow models provide the basis and rationale for this method. Fundamentals also interest analysts who use the method of comparables, because differences between a price multiple and its benchmark value may be explained by differences in fundamentals.

▶ The key idea behind the use of P/Es is that earning power is a chief driver of investment value and EPS is probably the primary focus of security analysts' attention. EPS, however, is frequently subject to distortion, often volatile, and sometimes negative.

▶ The two alternative definitions of P/E are trailing P/E, based on the most recent four quarters of EPS, and leading P/E, based on next year's expected earnings.

▶ Analysts address the problem of cyclicality by normalizing EPS—that is, calculating the level of EPS that the business could achieve currently under mid-cyclical conditions (normal EPS).

▶ Two methods to normalize EPS are the method of historical average EPS (over the most recent full cycle) and the method of average ROE (average ROE multiplied by current book value per share).

▶ Earnings yield (E/P) is the reciprocal of the P/E. When stocks have negative EPS, a ranking by earnings yield is meaningful whereas a ranking by P/E is not.

▶ Historical trailing P/Es should be calculated with EPS lagged a sufficient amount of time to avoid look-ahead bias. The same principle applies to other multiples calculated on a trailing basis.

▶ The fundamental drivers of P/E are expected earnings growth rate(s) and the required rate of return. The justified P/E based on fundamentals bears a positive relationship to the first factor and an inverse relationship to the second factor.

▶ PEG (P/E to growth) is a tool to incorporate the impact of earnings growth on P/E. PEG is calculated as the ratio of the P/E to the consensus growth forecast. Stocks with lower PEGs are more attractive than stocks with higher PEGs, all else equal.

► We can estimate terminal value in multistage DCF models using price multiples based on comparables. The expression for terminal value is (using P/E as an example)

$$V_n = \text{Benchmark value of trailing P/E} \times E_n$$

or

$$V_n = \text{Benchmark value of leading P/E} \times E_{n+1}$$

► Book value per share attempts to represent the investment that common shareholders have made in the company, on a per-share basis. Inflation, technological change, and accounting distortions, however, can impair book value for this purpose.

► Book value is calculated as common shareholders' equity divided by the number of shares outstanding. Analysts adjust book value to more accurately reflect the value of shareholders' investment and to make P/B more useful for comparing different stocks.

► The fundamental drivers of P/B are ROE and the required rate of return. The justified P/B based on fundamentals bears a positive relationship to the first factor and an inverse relationship to the second factor.

► An important rationale for the price-to-sales ratio (P/S) is that sales, as the top line in an income statement, are generally less subject to distortion or manipulation than other fundamentals such as EPS or book value. Sales are also more stable than earnings and never negative.

► P/S fails to take into account differences in cost structure between businesses, may not properly reflect the situation of companies losing money, and can be subject to manipulation through revenue recognition practices.

► The fundamental drivers of P/S are profit margin, growth rate, and the required rate of return. The justified P/S based on fundamentals bears a positive relationship to the first two factors and an inverse relationship to the third factor.

► A key idea behind the use of price-to-cash-flow ratios is that cash flow is less subject to manipulation than are earnings. Price to cash flow are often more stable than P/E. Some common approximations to cash flow from operations have limitations, however, because they ignore items that may be subject to manipulation.

► The major cash flow and related concepts used in multiples are earnings-plus-noncash charges (CF), cash flow from operations (CFO), free cash flow to equity (FCFE), and earnings before interest, taxes, depreciation, and amortization (EBITDA).

► In calculating price to cash flow, the earnings-plus-noncash charges concept is traditionally used, although the FCFE has the strongest link to financial theory.

► CF and EBITDA are not strictly cash flow numbers because they do not account for noncash revenue and net changes in working capital.

► The fundamental drivers of price to cash flow, however defined, are the expected growth rates of future cash flows and the required rate of return. The justified price to cash flow based on fundamentals bears a positive relationship to the first factor and an inverse relationship to the second.

► Enterprise value (EV) is total company value (the market value of debt, common equity, and preferred equity) minus the value of cash and investments.

▶ EV/EBITDA is preferred to P/EBITDA because EBITDA as a pre-interest number is a flow to all providers of capital.

▶ EV/EBITDA may be more appropriate than P/E for comparing companies with different amounts of financial leverage (debt).

▶ EV/EBITDA is frequently used in the valuation of capital-intensive businesses.

▶ The fundamental drivers of EV/EBITDA are the expected growth rate in free cash flow to the firm and the weighted-average cost of capital. The justified EV/EBITDA based on fundamentals bears a positive relationship to the first factor and an inverse relationship to the second.

▶ Dividend yield has been used as a valuation indicator because it is a component of total return, and is less risky than capital appreciation. However, investors trade off future earnings growth to receive higher current dividends.

▶ Trailing dividend yield is calculated as four times the most recent quarterly per-share dividend divided by the current market price.

▶ The fundamental drivers of dividend yield are the expected growth rate in dividends and the required rate of return.

▶ Comparing companies across borders frequently involves accounting method differences, cultural differences, economic differences, and resulting differences in risk and growth opportunities.

▶ Momentum valuation indicators include earnings surprise, standardized unexpected earnings, and relative strength.

▶ Unexpected earnings (or earnings surprise) equals the difference between reported earnings and expected earnings.

▶ Standardized unexpected earnings (SUE) is unexpected earnings divided by the standard deviation in past unexpected earnings.

▶ Relative-strength indicators compare a stock's performance during a period either with its own past performance (first type) or with the performance of some group of stocks (second type). The rationale behind using relative strength is the thesis of patterns of persistence or reversal in returns.

▶ Screening is the application of a set of criteria to reduce an investment universe to a smaller set of investments and is a part of many stock selection disciplines. In general, limitations of such screens include the lack of control over the calculation of important inputs and the absence of qualitative factors.

PRACTICE PROBLEMS FOR READING 48

1. As of February 2002, you are researching Smith International (NYSE: SII), an oil field services company subject to cyclical demand for its services. You believe the 1997–2000 period reasonably captures average profitability. SII closed at $57.98 on 2 February 2002.

	2001	2000	1999	1998	1997
EPS	E$3.03	$1.45	$0.23	$2.13	$2.55
BVPS	E19.20	16.21	14.52	13.17	11.84
ROE	E16%	8.9%	1.6%	16.3%	21.8%

Source: The Value Line Investment Survey.

   A. Define normal EPS.

   B. Calculate a normal EPS for SII based on the method of historical average EPS, and then calculate the P/E based on that estimate of normal EPS.

   C. Calculate a normal EPS for SII based on the method of average ROE and the P/E based on that estimate of normal EPS.

2. An analyst plans to use P/E and the method of comparables as a basis for recommending one of two peer group companies in the personal digital assistant business. Data on the companies' prices, trailing EPS, and expected growth rates in sales (five-year compounded rate) are given in the table below. Neither business has been profitable to date, and neither is anticipated to have positive EPS over the next year.

	Price	Trailing EPS	P/E	Expected Growth (Sales)
Hand	$22	−$2.20	NM	45%
Somersault	$10	−$1.25	NM	40%

   Unfortunately, because the earnings for both companies were negative, the P/Es were not meaningful. On the basis of the above information, answer the following questions.

   A. State how the analyst might make a relative valuation in this case.

   B. Which stock should the analyst recommend?

3. May Stewart, CFA, a retail analyst, is performing a P/E-based comparison of two jewelry stores as of early 2001. She has the following data for Hallwhite Stores (HS) and Ruffany (RUF).

   ▶ HS is priced at $44. RUF is priced at $22.50.

   ▶ HS has a simple capital structure, earned $2.00 per share in 2000, and is expected to earn $2.20 in 2001.

   ▶ RUF has a complex capital structure as a result of its outstanding stock options. Moreover, it had several unusual items that reduced its basic EPS in 2000 to $0.50 (versus the $0.75 that it earned in 1999).

▶ For 2001, Stewart expects RUF to achieve net income of $30 million. RUF has 30 million shares outstanding and options outstanding for an additional 3,333,333 shares.

A. Which P/E (trailing or leading) should Stewart use to compare the two companies' valuation?

B. Which of the two stocks is relatively more attractively valued on the basis of P/Es (assuming that all other factors are approximately the same for both stock)?

4. You are researching the valuation of the stock of a company in the food processing industry. Suppose you intend to use the mean value of the leading P/Es for the food processing industry stocks as the benchmark value of the multiple. That mean P/E is 18.0. The leading or expected EPS for the next year for the stock you are studying is $2.00. You calculate 18.0 × $2.00 = $36, which you take to be the intrinsic value of the stock based only on the information given above. Comparing $36 with the stock's current market price of $30, you conclude the stock is undervalued.

A. Give two reasons why your conclusion that the stock is undervalued may be in error.

B. What additional information about the stock and the peer group would support your original conclusion?

5. A. Identify two significant differences between Yardeni's model of stock market valuation and the Fed model.

B. Suppose an analyst uses an equity index as a comparison asset in valuing a stock. Which price multiple(s) would cause concern about the impact of potential overvaluation of the equity index on a decision to recommend purchase of an individual stock?

6. [Adapted from the 2000 CFA Level II Examination] Christie Johnson, CFA, has been assigned to analyze Sundanci. Johnson assumes that Sundanci's earnings and dividends will grow at a constant rate of 13 percent. Exhibits P-1 and P-2 provide financial statements and other information for Sundanci.

A. Calculate a justified P/E based on information in Exhibits P-1 and P-2 and on Johnson's assumptions for Sundanci. Show your work.

B. Identify, within the context of the constant dividend growth model, how *each* of the fundamental factors shown below would affect the P/E.

 i. The risk (beta) of Sundanci increases substantially.

 ii. The estimated growth rate of Sundanci's earnings and dividends increases.

 iii. The market risk premium increases.

 Note: A change in a fundamental factor is assumed to happen in isolation; interactive effects between factors are ignored. Every other item of the company is unchanged.

7. At a meeting of your company's investment policy committee, Bill Yu presents a recommendation based on a P/E analysis. He presents the case for Connie's Sporting Goods (CSG), a small chain of retail stores that receives almost no coverage by analysts. Yu begins by noting that CSG appeared to be fairly valued compared with its peers on a P/E basis. CSG's 10-Q filing revealed, however, that an initiative at CSG to offer sports instruction (e.g., golf lessons) along with equipment should immediately raise the earnings growth rate at the company from 5 percent to 6 percent. Yu thus expects the company's trailing P/E to rise from 10.5 to 13.25, a 26 percent increase,

EXHIBIT P-1	Sundanci Actual 1999 and 2000 Financial Statements For Fiscal Years Ending 31 May (in millions, except per-share data)	

Income Statement	1999	2000
Revenue	$474	$598
Depreciation	20	23
Other operating costs	368	460
Income before taxes	86	115
Taxes	26	35
Net income	60	80
Dividends	18	24
Earnings per share	$0.714	$0.952
Dividends per share	$0.214	$0.286
Common shares outstanding	84.0	84.0

Balance Sheet	1999	2000
Current assets	$201	$326
Net property, plant, and equipment	474	489
Total assets	675	815
Current liabilities	57	141
Long-term debt	0	0
Total liabilities		
Shareholders' equity	618	674
Total liabilities and equity	675	815
Capital expenditures	34	38

EXHIBIT P-2	Selected Financial Information

Required rate of return on equity	14%
Growth rate of industry	13%
Industry P/E	26

as soon as the investment community recognizes this development. The computations supporting his analysis follow.

Currently the justified P/E based on fundamentals is

$$\frac{P_0}{E_0} = \frac{(1 - b)(1 + g)}{r - g} = \frac{(1 - 0.5)(1.05)}{0.10 - 0.05} = 10.5$$

He points out that when g rises to 0.06, the trailing P/E should increase to 13.25, providing investors with appreciation in excess of 20 percent. When asked if he expects CSG's ROE to improve with the initiative, Yu indicated that it would likely be flat for the first several years. A colleague argues that because of the flat ROE, CSG's justified P/E will not increase to 13.25 because *b* must increase to be consistent with the sustainable growth rate expression for *g*. Only companies with at least 20 percent near-term appreciation potential are candidates for inclusion on your company's focus list of stocks.

A. How would you expect the new initiative to affect the trailing P/E accorded to CSG's stock, assuming Yu's assumptions are correct? (Growth will increase as indicated above and ROE will be steady.)

B. Is CSG a good candidate for your company's focus list?

8. Tom Smithfield is valuing the stock of a food processing business. He has projected earnings and dividends to four years (to $t = 4$). Other information and estimates are:

▶ Required rate of return = 0.09

▶ Average dividend payout rate for mature companies in the market = 0.45

▶ Industry average ROE = 0.10

▶ E_3 = $3.00

▶ Industry average P/E = 12

On the basis of the above, answer the following questions:

A. Compute terminal value based on comparables.

B. Contrast your answer in Part A to an estimate of terminal value using the Gordon growth model.

9. Discuss three types of stocks or investment problems for which an analyst could appropriately use P/B in valuation.

10. Avtech is a multinational distributor of semiconductor chips and related products to businesses. Its leading competitor around the world is Target Electronics. Avtech has a current market price of $10, 20 million shares outstanding, annual sales of $1 billion, and a 5 percent profit margin. Target has a market price of $20, 30 million shares outstanding, annual sales of $1.6 billion, and a profit margin of 4.9 percent. Based on the information given, answer the following questions.

A. Which of the two companies has a more attractive valuation based on P/S?

B. Identify and explain one advantage of P/S over P/E as a valuation tool.

11. Wilhelm Müller, CFA, has organized the selected data on four food companies that appear below (TTM stands for trailing 12 months):

	Hormel Foods	Tyson Foods	IBP Corp	Smithfield Foods
Stock price	$25.70	$11.77	$23.65	$24.61
Shares out (1,000s)	138,923	220,662	108,170	103,803
Market cap ($ mil)	3,570	2,597	2,558	2,523
Sales ($ mil)	4,124	10,751	17,388	6,354
Net income ($ mil)	182	88	122	252
TTM EPS	$1.30	$0.40	$1.14	$2.31
Return on equity	19.20%	4.10%	6.40%	23.00%
Net profit margin	4.41%	0.82%	0.70%	3.99%

On the basis of the data given, answer the following questions.

A. Calculate the trailing P/E and P/S for each company.

B. Explain on the basis of fundamentals why these stocks have different P/Ss.

12. **[Adapted from the 2001 CFA Level II Examination]** John Jones, CFA, is head of the research department at Peninsular Research. Peninsular has a client who has inquired about the valuation method best suited for comparison of companies in an industry with the following characteristics:

▶ Principal competitors within the industry are located in the United States, France, Japan, and Brazil.

▶ The industry is currently operating at a cyclical low, with many companies reporting losses.

Jones recommends that the client consider the following valuation ratios:

1. P/E
2. P/B
3. P/S

Determine which *one* of the three valuation ratios is most appropriate for comparing companies in this industry. Support your answer with one reason that makes that ratio superior to either of the other two ratios in this case.

13. General Electric (NYSE: GE) is currently selling for $38.50, with trailing 12-month earnings and dividends of $1.36 and $0.64, respectively. P/E is 28.3, P/B is 7.1, and P/S is 2.9. The return on equity is 27.0 percent, and the profit margin on sales is 10.9 percent. The Treasury bond rate is 4.9 percent, the equity risk premium is 5.5 percent, and GE's beta is 1.2.

A. What is GE's required rate of return, based on the capital asset pricing model?

B. Assume that the dividend and earnings growth rates are 9 percent. What P/Es, P/Bs, and P/Ss would be justified given the required rate of return in Part A and current values of the dividend payout ratio, ROE, and profit margin?

C. Given that the assumptions and constant growth model are appropriate, state whether GE appears to be fairly valued, overvalued, or undervalued based on fundamentals.

14. Jorge Zaldys, CFA, is researching the relative valuation of two companies in the aerospace/defense industry, NCI Heavy Industries (NCI) and Relay Group International (RGI). He has gathered relevant information on the companies in the table on the next page.

Using the information in the table, answer the following questions:

A. Calculate P/EBITDA for NCI and RGI.

B. Calculate EV/EBITDA for NCI and RGI.

C. Select NCI or RGI for recommendation as relatively undervalued. Justify your selection.

EBITDA Comparisons (in € millions except for per share)		
Company	**RGI**	**NCI**
Price per share	150	100
Shares outstanding	5 million	2 million
Market value of debt	50	100
Book value of debt	52	112
Cash and investments	5	2
Net income	49.5	12
Net income from continuing operations	49.5	8
Interest expense	3	5
Depreciation and amortization	8	4
Taxes	2	3

15. Define the major alternative cash flow concepts, and state one limitation of each.

16. Data for two hypothetical companies in the pharmaceutical industry, DriveMed and MAT Technology, are given in the table below. For both companies, expenditures in fixed capital and working capital during the previous year reflected anticipated average expenditures over the foreseeable horizon.

	DriveMed	**MAT Tech.**
Current price	$46.00	$78.00
Trailing CF per share	$3.60	$6.00
P/CF	12.8	13.0
Trailing FCFE per share	$1.00	$5.00
P/FCFE	46.0	15.6
Consensus five-year growth forecast	15%	20%
Beta	1.25	1.25

On the basis of the information supplied, discuss the valuation of MAT Technology relative to DriveMed. Justify your conclusion.

17. Your value-oriented investment management company recently hired a new analyst, Bob Westard, because of his expertise in the life sciences and biotechnology areas. At the company's weekly meeting, during which each analyst proposes a stock idea for inclusion on the company's approved list, Westard recommends Human Cloning International (HCI). He bases his recommendation to the Investment Committee on two considerations. First, HCI has pending patent applications but a P/E that he judges to be low given the potential earnings from the patented products.

Second, HCI has had high relative strength versus the S&P 500 over the past month.

A. Explain the difference between price multiples and relative strength approaches.

B. State which, if any, of the bases for Westard's recommendation is consistent with the investment orientation of your company.

18. Kirstin Kruse, a portfolio manager, has an important client who wants to alter the composition of her equity portfolio, which is currently a diversified portfolio of 60 global common stocks. The client wants a portfolio that meets the following criteria:

► Stocks must be in the Dow Jones Industrial Average, Transportation Average, or Utilities Average.
► Stocks must have a dividend yield of at least 5.0 percent.
► Stocks must have a P/E no greater than 20.
► Stocks must have a total market capitalization of at least $2.0 billion.

The table below shows how many stocks satisfied each screen, which was run in November 2001.

Screen	Number Satisfying
In Dow Jones Industrial Average, Transportation Average, or Utilities Average	65
Dividend yield of at least 5.0%	10
P/E less than 20	27
Total market cap of at least $2.0 billion	52
Satisfies all four screens	6

Other facts are:

► In total, there are 65 stocks in these three indexes (30 in the Industrial Average, 20 in the Transportation Average, and 15 in the Utilities Average).
► The stocks meeting all four screens were Southern Co. (utility), TXU Corporation (utility), Eastman Kodak Co. (consumer goods), Public Service Enterprise Group (utility), Reliant Energy (utility), and Consolidated Edison (utility).

A. Which valuation indicator or fundamental in Kruse's screen is most restrictive?

B. Critique the construction of the screen.

C. Do these screens identify an appropriate replacement portfolio for the client?

Questions 19–24 relate to Cecilia Tan and are based on Readings 40 and 48

Cecilia Tan is an equity analyst who is preparing an analysis of two securities for presentation at an upcoming meeting of her firm's portfolio managers.

The first security is the common stock of Diamondback Industries, a manufacturer of household products. Tan decides to use the method of comparables to value Diamondback by comparing Diamondback's price multiples with those of comparable peer companies. Tan collects fundamental data, including price multiples, on Diamondback and the peer companies, which are presented in Exhibit 1. Tan selects the price-to-earnings ratio (P/E) as her primary price multiple for evaluating Diamondback. She also evaluates Diamondback's P/E relative to growth (PEG) and compares it with the PEGs of four peer companies. Diamondback has a required rate of return of 11 percent and a long-term expected return on equity (ROE) of 13 percent.

EXHIBIT 1	Fundamental Data for Diamondback Industries and Peer Companies			
Company	Price per Share ($)	Last Four Quarters Cumulative Earnings per Share ($)	Estimate of Next Four Quarters Cumulative Earnings per Share ($)	Expected Five-Year Annual Growth Rate in Earnings (%)
Diamondback	20	1.00	1.10	10
Peer 1	30	1.60	1.70	10
Peer 2	26	1.35	1.50	16
Peer 3	70	3.75	4.00	9
Peer 4	18	0.95	1.15	15

The second security is the common stock of Indigo Corporation, a manufacturer of industrial equipment whose sales are strongly tied to the overall economic cycle. Tan plans to evaluate the current P/E of Indigo compared with its P/E over the recent business cycle. For overall valuation purposes, Tan will compute normalized earnings per share. Tan believes that the 2005 results are abnormal and that the period from 2000 to 2004 captures average profitability over a business cycle. Historical data for Indigo are presented in Exhibit 2. Because Indigo has cyclical earnings, Tan also decides to compute a justified price-to-sales ratio (P/S). Tan estimates a long-term profit margin of 6 percent, a long-term dividend payout ratio of 40 percent, an earnings growth rate of 6 percent, and a required rate of return of 10 percent.

EXHIBIT 2	Historical Data for Indigo Corporation		
Year	Earnings per Share ($)	Book Value per Share at End of Period ($)	Return on Equity (%)
2005	0.40	13.50	2.90
2004	1.40	13.50	10.77
2003	1.00	12.50	8.20
2002	0.50	11.90	4.22
2001	0.95	11.80	8.25
2000	1.76	11.25	16.40
Average 2000–2004	1.12	12.19	9.57
Average 2000–2005	1.00	12.41	8.46

Tan examines the impact of inflation on P/Es. She prepares an example to demonstrate intrinsic P/E values for a hypothetical company that has no growth in real earnings and has a real required rate of return of 6 percent. She assumes the company can only pass 60 percent of inflation through its earnings (a flow-through rate of 60 percent). She computes an intrinsic P/E for an inflation rate of 4 percent.

19. The most appropriate rationale for Tan's decision to use the method of comparables to value Diamondback is

    A. the law of one price.

    B. that intrinsic value is the present value of expected cash flows.

    C. that forecasted fundamentals determine justified price multiples.

    D. the relationship of price multiples to discounted cash flow models.

20. What is the *most* appropriate justification for Tan's selection of the P/E as her primary price multiple for Diamondback?

    A. Earnings can be negative.

    B. Earnings can have volatile, transient components.

    C. Earnings power is a chief driver of investment value.

    D. Management has discretion over the determination of earnings.

21. Based on a leading P/E, which peer company appears to have the lowest relative valuation according to the PEG ratio?

    A. Peer 1.

    B. Peer 2.

    C. Peer 3.

    D. Peer 4.

22. Indigo's 2005 normalized earnings per share under the method of average ROE is *closest* to

   A. $1.12.
   B. $1.14.
   C. $1.19.
   D. $1.29.

23. The year-end 2005 justified trailing P/S ratio for Indigo is *closest* to

   A. 0.600.
   B. 0.636.
   C. 0.900.
   D. 0.954.

24. For an expected inflation rate of 4 percent, what is the prospective (leading) intrinsic P/E of Tan's hypothetical company?

   A. 10.00.
   B. 13.16.
   C. 16.67.
   D. 25.00.

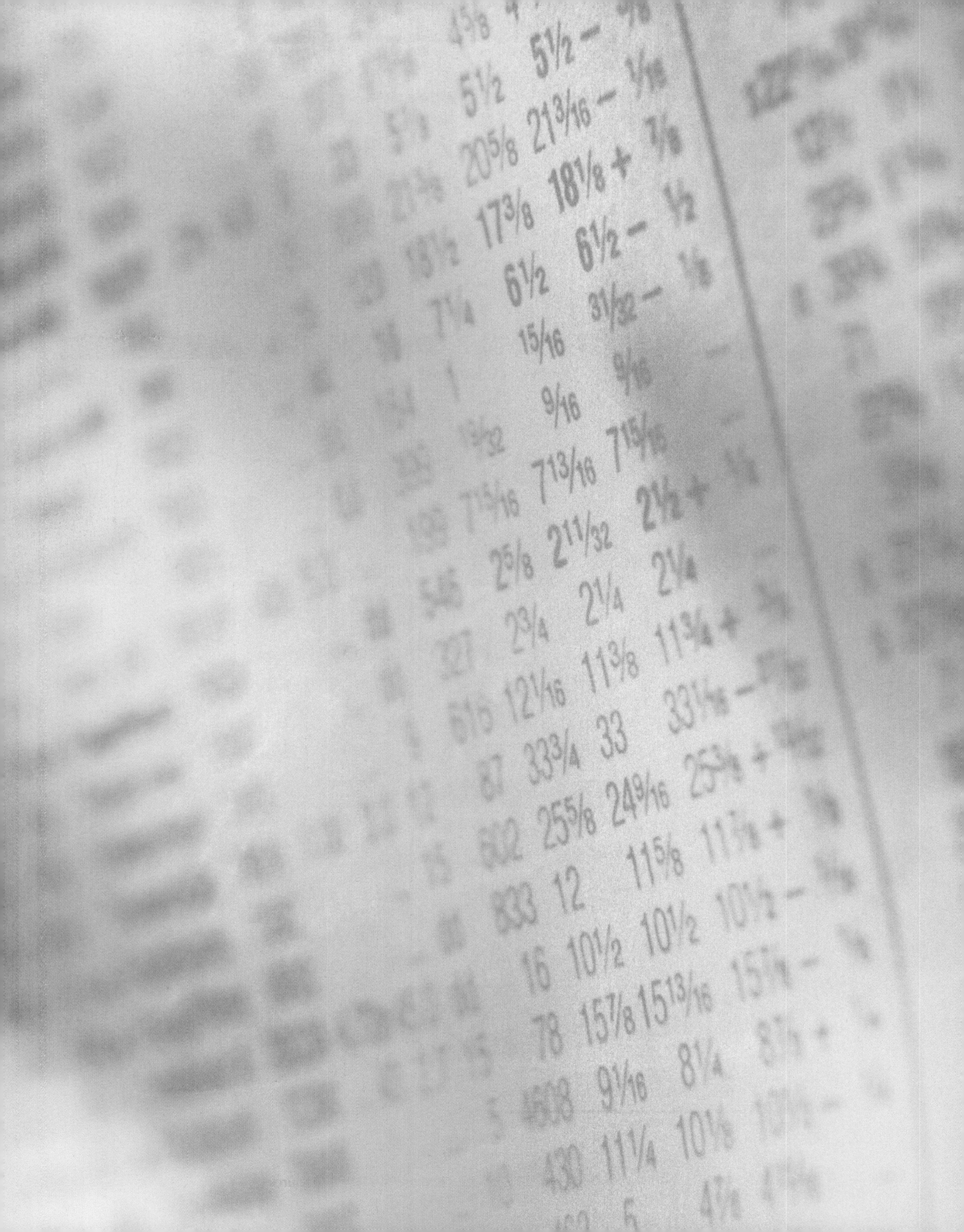

4⅝ 4...
5½ 5½ − ⅛
5½ 21³⁄₁₆ − ⅜
20⅝ 21³⁄₁₆ − ⅜
17⅜ 18⅛ + ⅜
6½ 6½ − ½
7¼ 31³⁄₃₂ −
15⁄₁₆
9⁄₁₆ 9⁄₁₆
7¹⁵⁄₁₆ 7¹³⁄₁₆ 7¹⁵⁄₁₆
2⅝ 2¹¹⁄₃₂ 2½ +
2¾ 2¼ 2¼
12¹⁄₁₆ 11⅜ 11¾ +
33¾ 33 33¹⁄₁₆ −
25⅝ 24⁹⁄₁₆ 25⅜ +
12 11⅝ 11⁷⁄₁₆ +
10½ 10½ 10½ −
15⅝ 15¹³⁄₁₆ 15¼ −
9⁄₁₆ 8¼ 8⅞ +
11¼ 10⅛
4⅞

STUDY SESSION 13
EQUITY INVESTMENTS:
Residual Income and Alternative Investments

This study session presents a final widely used equity valuation approach (residual income analysis) and two of the major categories of alternative investments. Residual income models (including economic value added models) can be a useful alternative to other valuation models (such as DDMs, FCF models, or price multiples) to evaluate performance and value equities. Real estate and hedge funds have become two of the major alternative investments asset categories. The two real estate readings apply traditional valuation models to commercial real estate. Finally, we address the unique challenges in evaluating hedge funds.

READING ASSIGNMENTS

Reading 49   Residual Income Valuation
Reading 50   Security Analysis Using Value-Based Metrics
Reading 51   Investment Analysis
Reading 52   Income Property Analysis and Appraisal
Reading 53   Evaluating the Performance of Your Hedge Funds
Reading 54   Buyers Beware: Evaluating and Managing the Many Facets of the Risks of Hedge Funds

LEARNING OUTCOMES

Reading 49: Residual Income Valuation
The candidate should be able to:

a. calculate and interpret residual income and describe and calculate alternative measures of residual earnings (i.e., economic value added, market value added);

b. discuss the uses of residual income models;

c. calculate future values of residual income, given current book value, consensus earnings growth estimates, and an assumed dividend payout ratio, and calculate the intrinsic value of a share of common stock using the residual income model;

d. contrast the recognition of value in the residual income model to value recognition in other present value models, discuss the strengths and weaknesses of the residual income model, and justify the choice of the residual income model for equity valuation, given characteristics of the company being valued;

495

e. discuss the fundamental determinants or drivers of residual income;

f. explain the relationship between residual income valuation and the justified price-to-book ratio based on forecasted fundamentals;

g. explain the relationship of the residual income model to the dividend discount model and the free cash flow to equity model;

h. discuss the major accounting issues in applying residual income models;

i. calculate an implied growth rate in residual income, given the market price-to-book ratio and an estimate of the required rate of return on equity;

j. define continuing residual income and list the common assumptions regarding continuing residual income;

k. justify an estimate of continuing residual income at the earnings forecast horizon, given company and industry prospects;

l. calculate and interpret the intrinsic value of a share of common stock using a single-stage residual income model;

m. calculate and interpret the intrinsic value of a share of common stock using a multi-stage residual income model, given the required rate of return, forecasted earnings per share over a finite horizon, and forecasted continuing residual earnings.

Reading 50: Security Analysis Using Value-Based Metrics
The candidate should be able to:

a. calculate and interpret economic value added (EVA®) as in the reading above, differentiate between accounting profitability as measured by ROE and economic profitability as measured by EVA, and explain the significance of a positive or negative EVA;

b. describe methods for increasing EVA;

c. describe the process for determining cash flow return on investment (CFROI);

d. explain why the spread between CFROI and weighted average cost of capital is similar to the concept of EVA spread;

e. describe how value-based metrics can be used in stock selection.

Reading 51: Investment Analysis
The candidate should be able to:

a. illustrate, for a particular type of real property investment: its main value determinants, investment characteristics, principal risks, and its most likely investor;

b. evaluate a real estate investment using net present value (NPV) and internal rate of return (IRR) analysis from the perspective of an equity investor;

c. calculate the after-tax cash flow and the after-tax equity reversion from real estate properties;

d. explain the potential problems in using IRR as a measurement tool in real estate investments.

Reading 52: Income Property Analysis and Appraisal
The candidate should be able to:

a. explain the relationship between a real estate capitalization rate and discount rate;

b. determine the capitalization rate by the market-extraction method, band-of-investment method, and built-up method and justify the use of each technique in capitalization rate determination;

c. estimate the market value of a real estate investment using the direct income capitalization approach and the gross income multiplier technique;

d. contrast the limitations of the direct capitalization approach to those of the gross income multiplier technique.

Reading 53: Evaluating the Performance of Your Hedge Funds

The candidate should be able to:

a. discuss how the characteristics of hedge funds affect traditional methods of performance measurements;

b. compare and contrast the use of market indexes, hedge fund indexes, and positive risk-free rates as means to evaluating hedge fund performance.

Reading 54: Buyers Beware: Evaluating and Managing the Many Facets of the Risks of Hedge Funds

The candidate should be able to:

a. discuss common types of investment risks for hedge funds;

b. evaluate the use of maximum drawdown and value-at-risk as tools for measuring risks of hedge funds.

4⅝ 4
5½ 5½ — ⅝
5⅜
20⅝ 21³/₁₆ — ⅜
17³/₈ 18⅛ +
16½ 6½ 6½ — ½
7¼ 31³/₃₂ —
15/₁₆
9/₁₆ 9/₁₆
1
19/₃₂ 7¹⁵/₁₆
7¹⁵/₁₆ 7¹³/₁₆ 7¹⁵/₁₆
2⅝ 2¹¹/₃₂ 2½ +
2¾ 2¼ 2¼
61 12¹/₁₆ 11⅜ 11¾ +
87 33¾ 33 33¹/₁₆ —
802 25⅝ 24⁹/₁₆ 25⅜ +
833 12 11⅝ 11⅞ +
16 10½ 10½ 10½ —
78 15⅝ 15¹³/₁₆ 15⅞ —
608 9¹/₁₆ 8¼ 8⅞
430 11¼ 10⅛ 10⅛ —
5 4⅞ 4

RESIDUAL INCOME VALUATION

by John D. Stowe, Thomas R. Robinson, Jerald E. Pinto,
and Dennis W. McLeavey

LEARNING OUTCOMES

The candidate should be able to:

a. calculate and interpret residual income and describe and calculate alternative measures of residual earnings (i.e., economic value added, market value added);

b. discuss the uses of residual income models;

c. calculate future values of residual income, given current book value, consensus earnings growth estimates, and an assumed dividend payout ratio and calculate the intrinsic value of a share of common stock using the residual income model;

d. contrast the recognition of value in the residual income model to value recognition in other present value models, discuss the strengths and weaknesses of the residual income model, and justify the choice of the residual income model for equity valuation, given characteristics of the company being valued;

e. discuss the fundamental determinants or drivers of residual income;

f. explain the relationship between residual income valuation and the justified price-to-book ratio based on forecasted fundamentals;

g. explain the relationship of the residual income model to the dividend discount model and the free cash flow to equity model;

h. discuss the major accounting issues in applying residual income models;

i. calculate an implied growth rate in residual income, given the market price-to-book ratio and an estimate of the required rate of return on equity;

j. define continuing residual income and list the common assumptions regarding continuing residual income;

k. justify an estimate of continuing residual income at the earnings forecast horizon, given company and industry prospects;

l. calculate and interpret the intrinsic value of a share of common stock using a single-stage residual income model;

m. calculate and interpret the intrinsic value of a share of common stock using a multi-stage residual income model, given the required rate of return, forecasted earnings per share over a finite horizon, and forecasted continuing residual earnings.

Analysis of Equity Investments: Valuation, by John D. Stowe, Thomas R. Robinson, Jerald E. Pinto, and Dennis W. McLeavey. Copyright © 2002 by AIMR. Reprinted with permission.

499

| 1 |

INTRODUCTION

Residual income models of equity value have become widely recognized tools in both investment practice and research. Conceptually, residual income is net income less a charge (deduction) for common shareholders' opportunity cost in generating net income. As an economic concept, residual income has a long history. As far back as the 1920s, General Motors employed the concept in evaluating business segments.[1] More recently, residual income has received renewed attention and interest, sometimes under names such as economic profit, abnormal earnings, or economic value added.

The appeal of residual income models stems from a shortcoming of traditional accounting. Specifically, although a company's income statement includes a charge for the cost of debt capital in the form of interest expense, it does not include a charge for the cost of equity capital. A company can have positive net income but may still not be adding value for shareholders if it does not earn more than the cost of equity capital. Residual income concepts have been used in a variety of contexts, including the measurement of internal corporate performance. This reading, however, will focus on the residual income model for estimating the intrinsic value of common stock. Among the questions we will study to help us use residual income models professionally are the following:

► How is residual income measured, and how can an analyst use residual income in valuation?
► How does residual income relate to fundamentals, such as return on equity and earnings growth rates?
► How is residual income linked to other valuation methods, such as a price-multiple approach?
► What challenges arise in applying residual income valuation internationally?

The reading is organized as follows: In Section 2, we develop the concept of residual income and present alternative measures used in practice. In Section 3, we derive the residual income valuation model and illustrate its use in valuing common stock. Section 4 addresses accounting and international issues in the use of residual income valuation. In subsequent sections, we present practical applications of residual income models: Section 5 presents the single-stage (constant-growth) residual income model, and Section 6 presents multistage residual income models. We summarize the reading in the final section.

---

[1] See, for example, Young (1999) and Lo and Lys (2000).

RESIDUAL INCOME   2

Traditional financial statements, particularly the income statement, are prepared to reflect earnings available to owners. As a result, net income includes an expense to represent the cost of debt capital in the form of interest expense. Dividends or other charges for equity capital, however, are not deducted. Traditional accounting lets the owners decide whether earnings cover their opportunity costs. The economic concept of residual income, on the other hand, explicitly deducts the estimated cost of equity capital, the finance concept that measures shareholders' opportunity costs. Residual income models have been used to value both individual stocks[2] and the Dow Jones Industrial Average[3] and have been proposed as a solution to measuring goodwill impairment by accounting standard setters.[4] Residual income models have been found more useful than some other major present value models of equity value in explaining stock prices (American Accounting Association, 2001). Example 1 illustrates, in a stylized setting, the calculation and interpretation of residual income.[5]

EXAMPLE 1

The Calculation of Residual Income

Axis Manufacturing Company, Inc. (AXCI), a very small company in terms of market capitalization, has total assets of €2,000,000 financed 50 percent with debt and 50 percent with equity capital. The cost of debt capital is 7 percent before taxes (4.9 percent after taxes) and the cost of equity capital is 12 percent.[6] The company has **earnings before interest and taxes (EBIT)** of €200,000 and a tax rate of 30 percent. Net income for AXCI can be determined as follows:

EBIT	€200,000
Less: Interest expense	70,000
Pretax income	€130,000
Less: Income tax expense	39,000
Net income	€91,000

With earnings of €91,000, AXCI is clearly profitable in an accounting sense. But was the company profitable enough to satisfy its owners? Unfortunately, it was not. To incorporate the cost of equity capital, we compute

---

[2] See Fleck, Craig, Bodenstab, Harris, and Huh (2001).

[3] See Lee and Swaminathan (1999) and Lee, Myers, and Swaminathan (1999).

[4] See American Accounting Association Financial Accounting Standards Committee (2001). **Impairment** in an accounting context means downward adjustment. **Goodwill**, in this context, is an intangible asset that may appear on a company's balance sheet as a result of its purchase of another company.

[5] To simplify the following introduction, we assume here that net income accurately reflects *clean surplus accounting*, which we will explain later in this reading. Our discussions in this reading assume that companies' financing consists of common equity and debt only. In the case of a company that also has preferred stock financing, the calculation of residual income would reflect the deduction of preferred stock dividends from net income.

[6] See Reading 46 for a discussion of estimating required rates of return for equity.

residual income. One approach to calculating residual income is to deduct an **equity charge** (the estimated cost of equity capital in money terms) from net income. We compute the equity charge as follows:

Equity charge = Equity capital × Cost of equity capital in percent
= €1,000,000 × 12% = €120,000.

As stated, residual income is equal to net income minus the equity charge:

Net income	€91,000
Equity charge	120,000
Residual income	€(29,000)

AXCI did not earn enough to cover the cost of equity capital. As a result, it has negative residual income. Although AXCI is profitable in an accounting sense, it is not profitable in an economic sense.

In Example 1, we calculated residual income based on net income and a charge for the cost of equity capital. Analysts will also encounter another approach to calculating residual income that yields the same results. In this second approach, which takes the perspective of all providers of capital (both debt and equity), we subtract a **capital charge** (the company's total cost of capital in money terms) from the company's after-tax operating profit. In the case of AXCI in Example 1, net operating profit after taxes (NOPAT) is €140,000 (€200,000 less 30 percent taxes). AXCI's after-tax weighted-average cost of capital (WACC) is 8.45 percent, computed as 50 percent (capital structure weight of equity) times the cost of equity of 12 percent plus 50 percent (capital structure weight of debt) times the after-tax cost of debt, 4.9 percent.[7] The capital charge is €169,000 (= 8.45% × €2,000,000), which is higher than its after-tax operating profit of €140,000 by €29,000, the same figure obtained in Example 1. That the company is not profitable in an economic sense can also be seen by comparing the company's WACC, 8.45 percent, with after-tax operating profits as a percent of total assets (the after-tax net operating return on total assets or capital). The after-tax net operating return on total assets is €140,000/€2,000,000 = 7 percent, which is less than WACC by 1.45 percentage points.[8]

We can illustrate the impact of residual income on equity valuation using the case of AXCI presented in Example 1. Assume the following:

► Initially, AXCI equity is selling for book value or €1,000,000, with 100,000 shares outstanding. Thus, AXCI's book value per share and initial share price are both €10.

► Earnings per share (EPS) are €91,000/100,000 = €0.91.

► Earnings will continue at the current level indefinitely.

► All net income is distributed as dividends.

---

[7] This example of the weighted-average cost of capital assumes that interest is tax deductible. In countries where corporate interest is not tax deductible, the after-tax cost of debt would equal the pretax cost of debt. In the rest of the reading, we will refer to *after-tax cost of capital or after-tax WACC as cost of capital and WACC*, respectively, for brevity.

[8] After-tax net operating profits as a percent of total assets or capital has been called **return on invested capital (ROIC)**. Residual income can also be calculated as (ROIC − WACC) × (Beginning capital).

Because AXCI is not earning its cost of equity, as shown in Example 1, the company's share price should fall. In Reading 46, we explained that for a no-growth company, as here, the earnings yield (E/P) is an estimate of the expected rate of return. Therefore, when price reaches the point at which E/P equals the required rate of return on equity, an investment in the stock is expected to just cover the stock's required rate of return. With EPS of €0.91, the earnings yield is exactly 12 percent (AXCI's cost of equity) when share price is €7.58333. At a share price of €7.58333, the total market value of AXCI equity is €758,333. At this level, the equity charge is €91,000 (€758,333 × 12%) and residual income is zero. When a company has negative residual income, we expect shares to sell at a discount to book value. In this example, AXCI's price-to-book ratio (P/B) would be 0.7583. Conversely, if we changed the data in Example 1 so that AXCI earned positive residual income, we would conclude that its shares would sell at a premium to book value. In summary, we expect higher residual income to be associated with higher market prices (and higher P/Bs), all else equal.

Residual income and residual income valuation models have been referred to by a variety of names. Residual income has sometimes been called **economic profit** because it represents the economic profit of the company after deducting the cost of all capital, debt, and equity. In forecasting future residual income, the term **abnormal earnings** is also used. Assuming that in the long term the company is expected to earn its cost of capital (from all sources), any earnings in excess of the cost of capital can be termed abnormal earnings. The residual income valuation model has also been called the discounted abnormal earnings model (DAE model) and the Edwards-Bell-Ohlson model (EBO model) after the names of researchers in the field.[9] This reading focuses on a presentation of a general residual income valuation model that can be used by analysts using publicly available data and nonproprietary accounting adjustments. A number of commercial implementations of the approach are also very well known, however. Before returning to the general residual income valuation model in Section 3, we briefly discuss one such commercial implementation.

2.1 Commercial Implementations

One example of several competing commercial implementations of the residual income concept is **economic value added** (EVA®), trademarked by Stern Stewart & Company.[10] In the previous section, we illustrated the calculation of residual income starting from net operating profit after taxes, and EVA takes the same broad approach. Specifically, EVA is computed as

$$EVA = NOPAT - (C\% \times TC) \qquad \text{(49-1)}$$

where NOPAT is the company's net operating profit after taxes, C% is the cost of capital and TC is total capital. In this model, both NOPAT and TC determined under generally accepted accounting principles are adjusted for a number of items.[11] Some of the more common adjustments follow:

▶ Research and development expenses are capitalized and amortized rather than expensed (R&D expense is added back to earnings to compute NOPAT).

[9] More information on the background of the model is given later.
[10] For a complete discussion, see Stern (1991) and Peterson and Peterson (1996).
[11] See, for example, Ehrbar (1998).

▶ In the case of strategic investments that are not expected to generate a return immediately, a charge for capital is suspended until a later date.

▶ Goodwill is capitalized and not amortized (amortization expense is added back in arriving at NOPAT, and accumulated amortization is added back to capital).

▶ Deferred taxes are eliminated such that only cash taxes are treated as an expense.

▶ Any inventory LIFO reserve is added back to capital and any increase in the LIFO reserve is added in arriving at NOPAT.

▶ Operating leases are treated as capital leases, and nonrecurring items are adjusted.

Because of the adjustments made under EVA, a different numerical result will be obtained, in general, than that resulting from the use of the simple computation presented in Example 1. In practice, general (nonbranded) residual income (RI) valuation also considers the impact of accounting methods on reported results. However, analysts' adjustments to reported accounting results in estimating residual income will generally reflect some differences from the set specified for EVA. Section 4 of this reading will explore accounting considerations in more detail.

Over time, a company must generate EVA in order for its market value to increase. A related concept is market value added (MVA):

$$\text{MVA} = \text{Market value of the company} - \text{Total capital} \qquad \textbf{(49-2)}$$

A company that generates positive EVA should have a market value in excess of the accounting book value of its capital.

Research on the ability of value-added concepts to explain equity value and stock returns has reached mixed conclusions. Peterson and Peterson (1996) found that value-added measures are slightly more highly correlated with stock returns than traditional measures such as return on assets and return on equity. Bernstein and Pigler (1997) and Bernstein, Bayer, and Pigler (1998) found that value-added measures are no better at predicting stock performance than are measures such as earnings growth.

A variety of commercial models related to the residual income concept have been marketed by other major accounting and consulting firms. Interestingly, the application focus of these models is not, in general, equity valuation. Rather, these implementations of the residual income concept are marketed primarily for measuring internal corporate performance and determining executive compensation.

3   THE RESIDUAL INCOME VALUATION MODEL

In Section 2, we discussed the concept of residual income and briefly introduced the relationship of residual income to equity value. In the long term, companies that earn more than the cost of capital should sell for more than book value and companies that earn less than the cost of capital should sell for less than book value. The **residual income model** (RIM) of valuation analyzes the intrinsic value of equity into two components:

▶ the current book value of equity; plus

▶ the present value of expected future residual income.

Note that when we turn from valuing total shareholders' equity to directly valuing an individual common share, we work with earnings per share rather than net income. According to the residual income model, the intrinsic value of common stock can be expressed as follows:

$$V_0 = B_0 + \sum_{t=1}^{\infty} \frac{RI_t}{(1+r)^t} = B_0 + \sum_{t=1}^{\infty} \frac{E_t - rB_{t-1}}{(1+r)^t}$$ **(49-3)**

where

V_0 = value of a share of stock today ($t = 0$)
B_0 = current per − share book value of equity
B_t = expected per − share book value of equity at any time t
r = required rate of return on equity (cost of equity)
E_t = expected EPS for period t
RI_t = expected per − share residual income, equal to $E_t - rB_{t-1}$

The per-share residual income in period t, RI_t, is the EPS for the period, E_t, minus the per-share equity charge for the period, which is the required rate of return on equity times the book value per share at the beginning of the period, or rB_{t-1}. Whenever earnings per share exceed the per-share cost of equity, per-share residual income is positive; and whenever earnings are less, per-share residual income is negative. Example 2 illustrates the calculation of per-share residual income.

EXAMPLE 2

Per-Share Residual Income Forecasts

David Smith is evaluating the expected residual income for Scottish-Power (London Stock Exchange: SPW). Smith determines that SPW has a required rate of return of 8 percent. He obtains the following data from Thomson Financial as of 4 March 2002:

Current market price	GBP4.00
Book value per share	GBP3.41
Consensus annual earnings estimates	
March 2002	GBP0.33
March 2003	GBP0.39
Annualized dividend per share:	GBP0.26

What is the forecast residual income for fiscal years ended March 2002 and March 2003?

Solution:

TABLE 1

Year	2002	2003
Beginning book value (BV₀)	3.41	3.48
Earnings per share forecast (E)	0.33	0.39
Dividend forecast (D)	0.26	0.26
Forecast book value per share (BV$_0$ + E − D)	3.48	3.61
Per-share equity charge (BV$_0$ × r)	0.27	0.28
Per-share residual income (EPS forecast − Equity charge)	0.06	0.11

We illustrate the use of Equation 49-3, the expression for the estimated intrinsic value of common stock, in Example 3.

EXAMPLE 3

Using the Residual Income Model (1)

Bugg Properties' expected EPS is $2.00, $2.50, and $4.00 for the next three years, respectively. Analysts expect that Bugg will pay dividends of $1.00, $1.25, and $12.25 for the three years. The last dividend is anticipated to be a liquidating dividend; analysts expect Bugg will cease operations after Year 3. Bugg's current book value is $6.00 per share, and its required rate of return on equity is 10 percent.

1. Calculate per-share book value and residual income for the next three years.
2. Estimate the stock's value using the residual income model given in Equation 49-3:

$$V_0 = B_0 + \sum_{t=1}^{\infty} \frac{E_t - rB_{t-1}}{(1 + r)^t}$$

Solution to 1: The book values and residual incomes for the next three years are as follows:

TABLE 2

Year	1	2	3
Beginning book value per share	6.00	7.00	8.25
Retained earnings ($E - D$)	1.00	1.25	−8.25
Ending book value	7.00	8.25	0
Net income	2.00	2.50	4.00
Less equity charge ($r \times$ Beginning BV)	0.60	0.70	0.825
Residual income	1.40	1.80	3.175

Solution to 2: The value using the residual income model is

$$V_0 = 6.00 + \frac{1.40}{(1.10)} + \frac{1.80}{(1.10)^2} + \frac{3.175}{(1.10)^3}$$

$$= 6.00 + 1.2727 + 1.4876 + 2.3854$$

$$= \$11.15$$

Example 4 illustrates an important point that the recognition of value in residual income models typically occurs earlier than in dividend discount models.

EXAMPLE 4

Valuing a Perpetuity with the Residual Income Model

Assume the following data:

▶ A company will earn $1.00 per share forever.
▶ The company pays out all earnings as dividends.
▶ Book value per share is $6.00.
▶ The required rate of return on equity (or the percent cost of equity) is 10 percent.

1. Calculate the value of this stock using the dividend discount model (DDM).
2. Calculate the level amount of per-share residual income that will be earned each year.
3. Calculate the value of the stock using a residual income valuation model.
4. Create a table summarizing the recognition of value in the dividend discount model and the residual income model.

Solution to 1: Because the dividend is a perpetuity, $V_0 = D/r = 1.00/0.10 = \$10.00$ per share.

Solution to 2: Because each year all net income is paid out as dividends, book value per share will be constant at $6.00. Therefore, with a required rate of return on equity of 10 percent, for all future years per share residual income will be as follows:

$$\text{RI}_t = E_t - rB_{t-1} = 1.00 - 0.10(6.00) = 1.00 - 0.60 = \$0.40$$

Solution to 3: Using a residual income model, the estimated value equals the current book value per share plus the present value of future expected residual income (which here can be valued as a perpetuity):

$$
\begin{aligned}
V_0 &= \text{Book value} + \text{PV of expected future per-share residual income} \\
&= 6.00 + 0.40/0.10 \\
&= 6.00 + 4.00 = \$10.00
\end{aligned}
$$

Solution to 4: Table 3 on the following page summarizes when values are recognized in the DDM and the RI valuation models.

TABLE 3   Value Recognition in DDM and RIM Valuation

Year	Dividend Discount Model		Residual Income Model	
	D_t	PV of D_t	B_0 or RI_t	PV of B_0 or RI_t
0			6.00	6.000
1	1.00	0.909	0.40	0.364
2	1.00	0.826	0.40	0.331
3	1.00	0.751	0.40	0.301
4	1.00	0.683	0.40	0.273
5	1.00	0.621	0.40	0.248
6	1.00	0.564	0.40	0.226
7	1.00	0.513	0.40	0.205
8	1.00	0.467	0.40	0.187
⋮	⋮	⋮	⋮	⋮
Total		$10.00		$10.00

Table 3 shows that in the residual income valuation, current book value of $6.00 represents 60 percent of the stock's total present value of $10. Most of the total value is recognized now (today) for this stock. The DDM valuation also estimates the value of the stock as $10. As an exercise, suppose we add up the present values of the first five years' dividends. This sum of $3.79 ($0.909 + $0.826 + $0.751 + $0.683 + $0.621) represents approximately 38 percent of the total present value of $10. In the DDM, value is recognized with the receipt of dividends; typically the recognition of value occurs earlier in a residual income model than in a dividend discount model.

As illustrated in Example 4, the dividend discount and residual income models are in theory mutually consistent. Because of the real-world uncertainty in forecasting distant cash flows, however, we may find that the earlier recognition of value in a residual income approach relative to other present value approaches is a practical advantage. In the dividend discount and free cash flow models (discussed in Readings 46 and 47, respectively), we often model a stock's value as the sum of the present values of individually forecasted dividends or free cash flows up to some terminal point plus the present value of the expected terminal value of the stock. In practice, analysts often find that a large fraction of a stock's total present value, using either the dividend discount or free cash flow to equity model, is represented by the present value of the expected terminal value. However, substantial uncertainty often surrounds the terminal value. In contrast, residual income valuations typically are relatively less sensitive to terminal value estimates. (In some residual income valuation contexts the terminal value may actually be set equal to zero, as we will discuss in a later section.) The early recognition of value is one reason residual income valuation can be a useful analytical tool.

Before we discuss the implementation of the residual income model in detail, it is helpful to have an overview of the strengths and weaknesses of the residual income approach. The strengths of the residual income models include the following:

▶ Terminal values do not make up a large portion of the total present value, relative to other models.

▶ The RI models use readily available accounting data.

▶ The models can be readily applied to companies that do not pay dividends or to companies that do not have positive expected near-term free cash flows.

▶ The models can be used when cash flows are unpredictable.

▶ The models have an appealing focus on economic profitability.

The potential weaknesses of residual income models include the following:

▶ The models are based on accounting data that can be subject to manipulation by management.

▶ Accounting data used as inputs may require significant adjustments.

▶ The models require that the clean surplus relation holds, or that the analyst makes appropriate adjustments when the clean surplus relation does not hold. In the next section we will present the clean surplus relation (or clean surplus accounting), previously mentioned in Reading 46.

The above list of potential weaknesses helps explain the reading's focus in Section 4 on accounting considerations. In light of its strengths and weaknesses, we state the following broad guidelines for using a residual income model in common stock valuation. A residual income model is most appropriate when:

▶ a company does not pay dividends, or its dividends are not predictable;

▶ a company's expected free cash flows are negative within the analyst's comfortable forecast horizon; or

▶ there is great uncertainty in forecasting terminal values using an alternative present value approach.

Residual income models are least appropriate when:

▶ there are significant departures from clean surplus accounting; or

▶ significant determinants of residual income, such as book value and ROE, are not predictable.

The balance of Section 3 develops the most familiar general expression for the residual income model and illustrates the model's application.

3.1 The General Residual Income Model

The residual income model is conceptually sound and hence will have a clear relationship to other sound models, such as the dividend discount model. In fact, the residual income model given in Equation 49-3 can be derived from the dividend discount model. The general expression for the dividend discount model is

$$V_0 = \frac{D_1}{(1+r)^1} + \frac{D_2}{(1+r)^2} + \frac{D_3}{(1+r)^3} + \cdots$$

The **clean surplus relation** states the relationship among earnings, dividends, and book value as follows:

$$B_t = B_{t-1} + E_t - D_t$$

In other terms, the ending book value of equity equals the beginning book value plus earnings less dividends, apart from ownership transactions. The condition that income (earnings) reflect all changes in the book value of equity other than ownership transactions is known as clean surplus accounting. Rearranging the clean surplus relation, the dividend for each period can be viewed as the net income minus the earnings retained for the period, or net income minus the increase in book value:

$$D_t = E_t - (B_t - B_{t-1}) = E_t + B_{t-1} - B_t$$

Substituting $E_t + B_{t-1} - B_t$ for D_t in the expression for V_0 results in

$$V_0 = \frac{E_1 + B_0 - B_1}{(1+r)^1} + \frac{E_2 + B_1 - B_2}{(1+r)^2} + \frac{E_3 + B_2 - B_3}{(1+r)^3} + \cdots$$

This equation can be re-written as follows:

$$V_0 = B_0 + \frac{E_1 - rB_0}{(1+r)^1} + \frac{E_2 - rB_1}{(1+r)^2} + \frac{E_3 - rB_2}{(1+r)^3} + \cdots$$

Expressed with summation notation, the following equation restates the residual income model that we gave in Equation 49-3:

$$V_0 = B_0 + \sum_{t=1}^{\infty} \frac{RI_t}{(1+r)^t} = B_0 + \sum_{t=1}^{\infty} \frac{E_t - rB_{t-1}}{(1+r)^t}$$

According to the above expression, the value of a stock equals its book value per share plus the present value of expected future per-share residual income. Note that when the present value of expected future per-share residual income is positive (negative), intrinsic value V_0 is greater (smaller) than book value per share, B_0.

The residual income model used in practice today has largely developed from the recent academic work of Ohlson (1995) and Feltham and Ohlson (1995) and the earlier work of Edwards and Bell (1961), although in the United States this method has been used to value small businesses in tax cases since the 1920s.[12] The general expression for the residual income model based on this work[13] can also be stated as

$$V_0 = B_0 + \sum_{t=1}^{\infty} \frac{(ROE_t - r) \times B_{t-1}}{(1+r)^t} \qquad \textbf{(49-4)}$$

Equation 49-4 is equivalent to the expressions for V_0 given earlier because in any year t, $RI_t = (ROE_t - r) \times B_{t-1}$. Other than the required rate of return on common stock, the inputs to the residual income model come from accounting data. Example 5 illustrates the estimation of value using Equation 49-4.

---

[12] In tax valuation, the method is known as the excess earnings method. For example, see Hawkins and Paschall (2001) and U.S. IRS Revenue Ruling 68-609.

[13] See, for example, Hirst and Hopkins (2000).

EXAMPLE 5

Using the Residual Income Model (2)

To recap the data from Example 3, Bugg Properties has expected earnings per share of $2.00, $2.50, and $4.00, and expected dividends per share of $1.00, $1.25, and $12.25 over next three years. Analysts expect that the last dividend will be a liquidating dividend and that Bugg will cease operating after Year 3. Bugg's current book value per share is $6.00, and its estimated required rate of return on equity is 10 percent.

Using the above data, estimate the value of Bugg Properties stock using a residual income model of the form

$$V^0 = B_0 + \sum_{t=1}^{\infty} \frac{(ROE_t - r) \times B_{t-1}}{(1 + r)^t}$$

Solution: To value the stock, we need to forecast residual income. Table 4 illustrates the calculation of residual income. (Note that Table 4 arrives at the same estimates of residual income as did Table 2 in Example 3.)

TABLE 4

Year	1	2	3
Earnings per share	2.00	2.50	4.00
Beginning book value per share	6.00	7.00	8.25
ROE	0.3333	0.3571	0.4848
Abnormal rate of return (ROE − r)	0.2333	0.2571	0.3848
Residual income (ROE − r) × Beginning BV	1.40	1.80	3.175

We estimate the stock value as follows:

$$V_0 = 6.00 + \frac{1.40}{(1.10)} + \frac{1.80}{(1.10)^2} + \frac{3.175}{(1.10)^3}$$
$$= 6.00 + 1.2727 + 1.4876 + 2.3854$$
$$= \$11.15$$

Note that the value is identical to the estimate obtained using Equation 49-3, as illustrated in Example 3, because the assumptions are the same and Equations 49-3 and 49-4 are equivalent expressions.

Example 5 showed that residual income value can be estimated using current book value, forecasts of earnings, forecasts of book value, and an estimate of the required rate of return on equity. The forecasts of earnings and book value translate into ROE forecasts.

EXAMPLE 6

Valuing a Company Using the General Residual Income Model

Robert Sumargo, an equity analyst, is considering the valuation of Dell Computer (NYSE: DELL), which closed on 19 April 2002 at $27.34. Sumargo notes that DELL has had very high ROE in the past 10 years and that consensus analyst forecasts for EPS for fiscal years ending in January 2003 and 2004 reflect expected ROEs of 50 percent and 48 percent, respectively. Sumargo expects that high ROEs may not be sustainable in the future. Sumargo often takes a present value approach to valuation. As of the date of the valuation, DELL does not pay dividends; although a discounted dividend valuation is possible, Sumargo does not feel confident about predicting the date of dividend initiation. He decides to apply the residual income model to value DELL, using the following data and assumptions:

▶ According to the capital asset pricing model (CAPM), DELL has a required rate of return of 14 percent.

▶ DELL's book value per share at 1 February 2002 was $1.78.

▶ ROE is expected to be 50 percent for fiscal year-end January 2003. Because of competitive pressures, Sumargo expects ROE to decline by 2 percent each year thereafter until it reaches the CAPM required rate of return.

▶ DELL does not currently pay a dividend. Sumargo does not expect one to be paid in the foreseeable future, so that all earnings will be reinvested.

1. Compute the value of DELL using the residual income model (Equation 49-4).

2. After reviewing Sumargo's valuation, a colleague points out that DELL has been issuing stock options to employees, which are not recorded as an expense, and repurchasing shares on the market to offset the dilutive impact of the stock options. These activities have resulted in a large decline in book value per share in recent years. At the same time, the colleague expects that the diminution of book value per share from the use of employee stock options will continue into the future. Discuss the potential impact on Sumargo's estimate of value if the colleague is correct.

Solution to 1: Book value per share is initially $1.78. Based on a ROE forecast of 50 percent in the first year, the forecast EPS would be $0.89. Because no dividends are paid and the clean surplus relation is assumed to hold, book value at the end of the period is forecast at $2.67. For 2003, residual income is measured as the beginning book value per share times the difference between ROE and r or $0.64. The present value of $0.64 at 14 percent for one year is $0.56. This process is continued year by year as presented in Table 5. The value of DELL under this residual income model would be the present value of each year's residual income plus the current book value per share. Because residual income is zero starting in 2021, no forecast is required beyond that period. The estimated value under this model is $27.01, as shown in Table 5.

TABLE 5	Valuation of DELL Using the Residual Income Model							
FYE January	Book Value per Share (beginning)	Forecast EPS	Forecast DPS	Forecast ROE (on beg. BV, %)	Required Return (%)	ROE − r (%)	(ROE − r) × BV	PV of (ROE − r) × BV
2003	1.78	0.89	0	50	14	36	0.64	0.56
2004	2.67	1.28	0	48	14	34	0.91	0.70
2005	3.95	1.82	0	46	14	32	1.26	0.85
2006	5.77	2.54	0	44	14	30	1.73	1.02
2007	8.31	3.49	0	42	14	28	2.33	1.21
2008	11.80	4.72	0	40	14	26	3.07	1.40
2009	16.52	6.28	0	38	14	24	3.96	1.58
2010	22.79	8.21	0	36	14	22	5.01	1.76
2011	31.00	10.54	0	34	14	20	6.20	1.91
2012	41.54	13.29	0	32	14	18	7.48	2.02
2013	54.83	16.45	0	30	14	16	8.77	2.08
2014	71.28	19.96	0	28	14	14	9.98	2.07
2015	91.23	23.72	0	26	14	12	10.95	1.99
2016	114.95	27.59	0	24	14	10	11.50	1.84
2017	142.54	31.36	0	22	14	8	11.40	1.60
2018	173.90	34.78	0	20	14	6	10.43	1.28
2019	208.68	37.56	0	18	14	4	8.35	0.90
2020	246.25	39.40	0	16	14	2	4.92	0.47
2021	285.65	39.99	0	14	14	0	0.00	0.00
						Total PV		25.23
						Initial Book value		1.78
						Total value		27.01

Solution to 2: Unless the inputs are corrected to reflect clean surplus accounting, the residual income valuation will probably overstate intrinsic value because forecasted book value growth will not be realized. The clean surplus relation assumes that all changes to book value other than ownership transactions flow through earnings. If that relation is violated, estimated share value can be overstated (or understated). In the case of DELL, in recent years (relative to the date of Sumargo's analysis) many transactions have affected book value per share without flowing through the income statement. DELL has made wide use of employee stock options, which have not been recorded as an expense on the income statement. DELL has issued shares under these stock option plans and has aggressively repurchased shares to manage the resulting dilution of employee stock options. These transactions have greatly reduced book value per share in recent years. If this trend continues, DELL is not likely to see the increases in book value forecast in the model above, and the residual income model will likely overstate the value of DELL.

Example 6, Part 2, touched on the issue of violations of clean surplus accounting. The residual income model, as stated earlier, assumes clean surplus accounting. **Comprehensive income** is income under clean surplus accounting; as such, comprehensive income reflects all changes in equity other than contributions by, and distributions to, owners. Comprehensive income often includes several items that bypass the current income statement such as the impact of changes in the market value of certain securities.[14] Strictly speaking, in using residual income models we are concerned with comprehensive income (income under clean surplus accounting); analysts thus adjust net income for material differences from clean surplus accounting. Section 4.1 explores violations of the clean surplus accounting in more detail.

3.2 Fundamental Determinants of Residual Income

The residual income model in general makes no assumptions about future earnings and dividend growth. If we assume constant earnings and dividend growth (at g), we can derive a version of the residual income model that is useful for illustrating the fundamental drivers of residual income. In Reading 48, we developed the following expression for justified P/B based on forecasted fundamentals, assuming the Gordon (constant growth) DDM and the sustainable growth rate equation, $g = b \times \text{ROE}$:[15]

$$\frac{P_0}{B_0} = \frac{ROE - g}{r - g}$$

which is mathematically equivalent to

$$\frac{P_0}{B_0} = 1 + \frac{ROE - r}{r - g}$$

The justified price is the stock's intrinsic value ($P_0 = V_0$). Therefore, using the previous equation, we can express a stock's intrinsic value under the residual income model, assuming constant growth, as

$$V_0 = B_0 + \frac{ROE - r}{r - g}B_0 \qquad \textbf{(49-5)}$$

Under this model, the estimated value of a share is thus the book value per share (B_0) plus the present value of the expected level stream of residual income, $(\text{ROE} - r) \times B_0$. In the case of a company for which ROE exactly equals the cost of equity, the intrinsic value should equal the book value per share. We call Equation 49-5 the single-stage (or constant-growth) residual income model.

In an ideal world, where the book value of equity represents the fair value of net assets and clean surplus accounting prevails, the term B_0 reflects the value of assets owned by the company less its liabilities. The second term, $(\text{ROE} - r) \times B_0/(r - g)$, represents additional value expected because of the company's ability to generate returns in excess of its cost of equity; the second term is the present value of the company's expected economic profits. Unfortunately, both U.S.

---

[14] In U.S. financial statements, items that bypass the income statement (**dirty surplus items**) are entered into **other comprehensive income**. The relationship is Comprehensive income = Net income + Other comprehensive income.

[15] Interestingly, the sustainable growth rate formula itself can be derived from the clean surplus relation.

and international accounting rules enable companies to exclude some liabilities from their balance sheets, and neither set of rules reflects the fair value of many corporate assets. There is, however, a move internationally toward fair value accounting, particularly for financial assets. Controversies, such as the failure of Enron Corporation in the United States, have highlighted the importance of identifying off-balance-sheet financing techniques.

The single-stage residual income model also assumes that the company's positive residual income continues indefinitely and that book value grows at a constant rate. More likely, a company's ROE will revert to a mean value of ROE over time and at some point, the company's residual income will be zero. In light of these considerations, the residual income model has been adapted in practice to handle declining residual income and deficiencies in the current accounting model. For example, Lee and Swaminathan (1999) and Lee, Myers, and Swaminathan (1999) used a residual income model to value the Dow 30 assuming that ROE fades (reverts) to the industry mean over time. Lee and Swaminathan found that the residual income model had more ability to predict future returns than traditional price multiples. Bauman (1999) demonstrated how accounting data could be useful in equity valuation using a residual income model.

3.3 Residual Income Valuation in Relation to Other Approaches

Before proceeding to the next section, which addresses both domestic and international issues in using accounting data in the residual income model, we should briefly summarize the relationships of the residual income model to other valuation models.

Valuation models based on discounting dividends or on discounting free cash flow to equity (FCFE) are theoretically sound models, as is the residual income model. Unlike the residual income model, however, DDM and FCFE models forecast future cash flows and find the value of stock by discounting them back to the present using the required return on equity. The RI model approaches this process differently. It starts with a value based on the balance sheet, the book value of equity, and adjusts this value by adding the present values of expected future residual income. Thus, the recognition of value is different, but the total present value, whether using expected dividends, expected free cash flow, or book value plus expected residual income, should be consistent, in theory.[16]

In fact, because each model can be derived from the same underlying theoretical model, when fully consistent assumptions are used to forecast earnings, cash flow, dividends, book value, and residual income through a full set of pro forma (projected) financial statements, and the same required rate of return on equity is used as the discount rate, the same estimate of value should result using each model. Practically speaking, however, it may not be possible to forecast each of these items with the same degree of certainty.[17] For example, if a company has near-term negative free cash flow and forecasts for the terminal value are uncertain, a residual income model may be more appropriate. On the other hand, a company with positive, predictable cash flow that does not pay a dividend would be well suited for a discounted free cash flow valuation.

---

[16] See, for example, Shrieves and Wachowicz (2001).

[17] For a lively debate on this issue, see Penman and Sougiannis (1998), Penman (2001), Lundholm and O'Keefe (2001a), and Lundholm and O'Keefe (2001b).

A residual income model can also be used in conjunction with other models to assess the consistency of results. If a wide variation of estimates is found and the models appear appropriate, the inconsistency may lie with the assumptions used in the models. The analyst would need to perform additional work to determine whether the assumptions are mutually consistent and which model is most appropriate for the subject company. Residual income models, just like the DDM and FCFE models, can also be used to establish justified market multiples, such as P/E or P/B. For example, the value can be determined using a residual income model and divided by earnings to arrive at a justified P/E in conjunction with a relative valuation approach. The residual income model is most closely related to the P/B ratio. A stock's justified P/B ratio is directly related to expected future residual income. Another closely related concept is **Tobin's *q***, the ratio of the market value of debt and equity to the replacement cost of total assets:[18]

$$\text{Tobin's } q = \frac{\text{Market value of debt and equity}}{\text{Replacement cost of total assets}}$$

Although similar to P/B, Tobin's *q* also has some obvious differences: The numerator includes the market value of total capital (debt as well as equity). The denominator uses total assets rather than equity. Further, assets are valued at replacement cost rather than a historical accounting cost; replacement costs take account of the effects of inflation. All else equal, we expect Tobin's *q* to be higher, the greater the productivity of a company's assets.[19] One difficulty in computing Tobin's *q* is the lack of information on assets' replacement costs. If available, market values of assets or replacement costs can be more useful in a valuation than historical costs.

4   ACCOUNTING AND INTERNATIONAL CONSIDERATIONS

In practice, to most accurately apply the residual income model, the analyst needs to adjust book value of common equity for off-balance-sheet items and adjust reported net income to obtain comprehensive income. In this section, we will discuss issues relating to these tasks.

Bauman (1999) has noted that the strength of the residual income valuation model is that the two components (book value and future earnings) of the model have a balancing effect on each other, provided that the clean surplus relationship is followed:

> All other things held constant, companies making aggressive (conservative) accounting choices will report higher (lower) book values and lower (higher) future earnings. In the model, the present value of differences in future income is exactly offset by the initial differences in book value (Baumann 1999, page 31).

Unfortunately, this argument has several problems in practice. The clean surplus relationship does not prevail, and analysts often use past earnings to predict future earnings. International Accounting Standards (IAS) and U.S. GAAP permit a variety of items to bypass the income statement and be reported directly in stockholders' equity. Further, companies have managed to keep some liabilities off the balance sheet and to obscure financial results with nonoperating and

---

[18] See Tobin (1969) or more recent work such as Landsman and Shapiro (1995).

[19] Tobin theorized that *q* would average to 1 over all companies, as the **economic rents** or profits earned by assets would average to zero.

nonrecurring items. The analyst must thus watch for such practices in evaluating the book value of equity and return on equity to be used as inputs into a residual income model.

With regard to the contention that aggressive accounting choices will lead to lower reported future earnings, take an example in which a company chooses to capitalize an expenditure in the current year rather than to expense it. Doing so overstates current-year earnings as well as current book value. If an analyst uses current earnings (or ROE) naively in predicting future residual earnings, the residual income model will overestimate the value of the company. Take, for example, a company with $1,000,000 of book value and $200,000 of earnings before taxes, after expensing an expenditure of $50,000. Ignoring taxes, this company has a ROE of 20 percent. If the company capitalized the expenditure rather than expensing it immediately, it would have a ROE of 23.81 percent ($250,000/$1,050,000).

Although at some time in the future this capitalized item will likely be amortized or written off, thus reducing realized future earnings, analysts' expectations often rely on historical data. If capitalization persists over time for a stable company, ROE can decline because net income will normalize over the long term, but book value will be overstated. For a growing company, for which the expenditure in question is increasing, ROE can continue at high levels over time. We suggest that because the residual income model uses primarily accounting data as inputs, the model can be sensitive to accounting choices and aggressive accounting methods (e.g., accelerating revenues or deferring expenses) can result in errors in valuation. The analyst must be particularly careful, therefore, in analyzing a company's reported data for use in a residual income model.

As we have seen, two principal drivers of residual earnings are ROE and book value. The analyst must understand how to use historical reported accounting data for these items to the extent he uses historical data in forecasting future ROE and book value. Reading 46 explained the DuPont analysis of ROE, which can be used as a tool in forecasting. Reading 48 discussed the calculation of book value. We extend these previous discussions below with specific application to residual income valuation, particularly in addressing the following accounting considerations:

▶ violations of the clean surplus relationship;

▶ balance sheet adjustments for fair value;

▶ intangible assets;

▶ nonrecurring items;

▶ aggressive accounting practices; and

▶ international considerations.

In any valuation, we must pay close attention to the accounting practices of the company being valued. In the following sections, we address the above issues as they particularly affect residual income valuation.

4.1 Violations of the Clean Surplus Relationship

One potential accounting issue in applying a residual income model is a violation of clean surplus accounting. Violations may occur when accounting standards permit charges directly to stockholders' equity, bypassing the income statement. An example is the case of changes in the market value of long-term investments. IAS provide that the change in market value can be reported in current profits or can bypass the income statement and be reported in shareholders' equity. Under U.S. GAAP, the balance sheet includes, at market value, investments considered to be "available for sale"; however, any change in their market value is reflected in stockholders' equity as other comprehensive income rather than as income on the income statement.

Earlier, we defined comprehensive income as all changes in equity other than contributions by and distributions to owners. Comprehensive income includes net income reported on the income statement. *Other comprehensive income* (also previously defined) is the result of other events and transactions that result in a change to equity but are not reported on the income statement. Items that commonly bypass the income statement include:[20]

► foreign currency translation adjustments;

► certain pension adjustments; and

► fair value changes of some financial instruments.

EXAMPLE 7

Evaluating Clean Surplus Violations

The statement of changes in stockholders' equity for Nokia Corporation (NYSE: NOK), prepared under IAS as of 31 December 1999, is partially replicated below.

TABLE 6   Nokia Corporation Statement of Changes in Stockholders' Equity (€ millions)

	Share Capital	Share Issue Premium	Treasury Share	Translation Differences	Retained Earnings	Total
Balance at 31 December 1998	255	909	(110)	182	3,873	5,109
Share issue	3	191				194
Bonus issue	36	(36)				0
Cancellation of Treasury shares	(15)	15	110		(110)	0
Acquisition of Treasury shares			(24)		24	0
Dividend					(586)	(586)
Dividend on Treasury shares					31	31
Translation differences				61		61
Other increase/ decrease, net					(8)	(8)
Net profit					2,577	2,577
Balance at 31 December 1999	279	1,079	(24)	243	5,801	7,378

---

[20] See Frankel and Lee (1999).

> The column "Translation Differences" reflects the cumulative amount of translation adjustments on equity that have bypassed the income statement. Because there is a positive adjustment to stockholders' equity, this item would have increased income if it had been reported on the income statement. Because the balance is accumulating, it does not appear to be reversing (netting to zero) in the long term. If the analyst expects this trend to continue, an increase in expected ROE might be warranted. It is possible, however, that future exchange rates will reverse this impact. Additionally, the decision to forgo making an adjustment to ROE would result in a conservative valuation in this case.

In all of these cases, the book value of equity is stated accurately, but net income is not from the perspective of residual income valuation. The analyst should be most concerned with the impact of these items on forecasts of net income and ROE (which has net income in the numerator), and hence also residual income.[21] Because some items (including those listed above) bypass the income statement, they are excluded from historical ROE data. As noted by Frankel and Lee (1999), bias will be introduced into the valuation only if the present expected value of the clean surplus violations do not net to zero. In other words, reductions in income from some periods may be offset by increases from other periods. The analyst must examine the equity section of the balance sheet and the related statements of shareholders' equity and comprehensive income carefully for items that have bypassed the income statement; the analyst can then assess whether amounts are likely to be offsetting and can assess the impact on future ROE.

4.2 Balance Sheet Adjustments for Fair Value

In order to have a reliable measure of book value of equity, an analyst must identify and scrutinize significant off-balance-sheet assets and liabilities. Additionally, reported assets and liabilities should be adjusted to fair value when possible. Off-balance-sheet assets and liabilities may become apparent by an examination of the financial statement footnotes. Examples include pension liabilities, the use of operating leases, and the use of special purpose entities to remove both debt and assets from the balance sheet. Some items such as the pension liability often result in an understatement of liabilities and overstatement of equity. Others, such as leases, may not affect the amount of equity (for example, off-balance-sheet assets offset off-balance-sheet liabilities) but can impact an assessment of future earnings for the residual income component of value. Other assets and liabilities may be stated at other than fair value. For example, inventory may be stated at LIFO and require adjustment to restate to current value. Presented below are some common items to review for balance sheet adjustments. Note, however, that this list is not all-inclusive:[22]

▶ inventory;
▶ deferred tax assets and liabilities;

---

[21] The analyst should most precisely calculate historical ROE at the aggregate level (e.g., as net income divided by shareholders' equity) rather than as earnings per share divided by book value per share, because actions such as share issuance and share repurchases can distort ROE calculated on a per-share basis.

[22] See also Chapter 17 of White, Sondhi, and Fried (1998).

▶ pension plan assets and liabilities;

▶ operating leases;

▶ special-purpose entities;

▶ reserves and allowances (for example, bad debts); and

▶ intangible assets.

Additionally, the analyst should examine the financial statements and footnotes for items unique to the subject company.

4.3 Intangible Assets

Intangible assets can have a significant impact on book value. In the case of specifically identifiable intangibles that can be separated from the entity (e.g., sold), it is appropriate to include these in the determination of book value of equity. If these assets are wasting (declining in value over time), they will be amortized over time as an expense. Goodwill, on the other hand, requires special consideration, particularly in light of recent changes in accounting for goodwill. Goodwill represents the excess of the purchase price of an acquisition over the value of the net assets acquired. Goodwill is generally not recognized as an asset unless it results from an acquisition (most international accounting standards do not allow the recognition of internally generated goodwill on the balance sheet). To demonstrate this, consider two companies, Alpha and Beta, with the following summary financial information (all amounts in thousands, except per-share data).

	Alpha	Beta
Cash	€1,600	€100
Property, plant, and equipment	€3,400	€900
Total assets	€5,000	€1,000
Equity	€5,000	€1,000
Net income	€600	€150

Each company pays out all net income as dividends (no growth), and the clean surplus relation holds. Alpha has a 12 percent ROE and Beta has a 15 percent ROE, both expected to continue indefinitely. Each has a 10 percent required rate of return. The fair market value of each company's property, plant, and equipment is the same as its book value. What is the value of each company in a residual income framework?

Using total book value rather than per-share data, the value of Alpha would be €6,000, determined as follows:[23]

$$V_0 = B_0 + \frac{\text{ROE} - r}{r - g}B_0 = 5{,}000 + \frac{0.12 - 0.10}{0.10 - 0.00}5{,}000 = 6{,}000$$

---

[23] Results would be the same if done on a per-share basis.

Similarly, the value of Beta would be €1,500:

$$V_0 = B_0 + \frac{\text{ROE} - r}{r - g}B_0 = 1{,}000 + \frac{0.15 - 0.10}{0.10 - 0.00}1{,}000 = 1{,}500$$

The value of the companies on a combined basis would be €7,500. Note that both companies are valued more highly than the book value of equity because they have ROEs in excess of the required rate of return. Absent an acquisition transaction, the financial statements of Alpha and Beta do not reflect this value. If either is acquired, however, goodwill would appear as an asset and result in higher book value of equity. For instance, suppose Alpha acquires Beta by paying Beta's former shareholders €1,500 in cash. Alpha has just paid €500 in excess of the value of Beta's total assets (€1,000), which is recorded as goodwill. The balance sheet of Alpha immediately after the acquisition would be[24]

	Alpha
Cash	€200
Property, plant, and equipment	€4,300
Goodwill	€500
Total assets	€5,000
Equity	€5,000

Note that the total book value of equity did not change, because cash was used in the transaction. Assuming that goodwill is amortized over a 10-year period, the combined company's expected net income would be €700 (€600 + €150 − €50 amortization). Expected ROE would be 14 percent. Under a residual income model with no adjustment for goodwill amortization, the value of the combined company would be

$$V_0 = B_0 + \frac{\text{ROE} - r}{r - g}B_0 = 5{,}000 + \frac{0.14 - 0.10}{0.10 - 0.00}5{,}000 = 7{,}000$$

Why should the combined company be worth less than the two separate companies? Assuming that a fair price was paid to the former shareholders, the combined value should not be lower. The lower value results from a reduction in ROE due to the amortization of goodwill. If goodwill were not amortized (or we added back the amortization expense before computing ROE), net income would be €750 and ROE would be 15 percent. The value of the combined entity would be

$$V_0 = B_0 + \frac{\text{ROE} - r}{r - g}B_0 = 5{,}000 + \frac{0.15 - 0.10}{0.10 - 0.00}5{,}000 = 7{,}500$$

This amount is the same as the sum of the values of the companies on a separate basis.

---

[24] For example, cash at €200 is calculated as €1,600 (cash of Alpha) + €100 (cash of Beta) − €1,500 (purchase price of Beta).

Recently, U.S. GAAP has altered the treatment of goodwill amortization. Goodwill is still listed as an asset when purchased but is no longer amortized.[25] Under IAS, goodwill is currently required to be amortized over a period not to exceed 20 years. To ensure international comparability and to avoid the adverse impact of amortization noted above, we recommend adjusting earnings to remove any amortization of goodwill.

Would the answer be different if the acquiring company used newly issued stock rather than cash in the acquisition? The form of currency used to pay for the transaction should not impact the total value. If Alpha used €1,500 of newly issued stock to acquire Beta, its balance sheet would be

	Alpha
Cash	€1,700
Property, plant, and equipment	€4,300
Goodwill	€500
Total assets	€6,500
Equity	€6,500

Projected earnings, excluding the amortization of goodwill, would be €750, and projected ROE would be 11.538 percent. Value under the residual income model would be

$$V_0 = B_0 + \frac{\text{ROE} - r}{r - g}B_0 = 6{,}500 + \frac{0.11538 - 0.10}{0.10 - 0.00}6{,}500 = 7{,}500$$

The overall value remains unchanged. The book value of equity is higher but offset by the impact on ROE. Once again, this assumes that the buyer paid a fair value for the acquisition. If an acquirer overpays for an acquisition, this should become evident in a reduction in future residual income and write-off of previously recorded goodwill.

Research and development costs provide another example of an intangible asset that must be given careful consideration. Under U.S. GAAP, R&D is expensed to the income statement directly. Under IAS, some R&D costs can be capitalized and amortized over time. R&D expenditures are reflected in a company's ROE, and hence residual income, over time. If a company engages in unproductive R&D expenditures, these will lower residual income through the expenditures made. If a company engages in productive R&D expenditures, these should result in higher revenues to offset the expenditures over time. In summary, on an ongoing basis for a mature company, ROE should reflect the productivity of R&D expenditures.

Bauman (1999) applied a residual income model to Cisco Systems, Inc. by capitalizing and amortizing purchased in-process R&D that was expensed under U.S. GAAP rather than becoming part of goodwill. He found that when purchased in-process R&D is capitalized and then amortized over a short period, there is no impact on overall value compared with immediate expensing of R&D in a residual income framework. White, Sondhi, and Fried (1998), however, noted that expensing of R&D in the long term results in higher ROEs over the

[25] If goodwill is later deemed to be impaired, a write-off or loss is taken.

long term. The analyst should carefully consider the company's R&D expenditures and their impact on long-term ROE.

4.4 Nonrecurring Items

In applying a residual income model, it is important to develop a forecast of future residual income based on recurring items. Often, companies report nonrecurring charges as part of earnings or classify nonoperating income (e.g., sale of assets) as part of operating income. These misclassifications can lead to overestimates and underestimates of future residual earnings if no adjustments are made. No adjustments to book value are necessary for these items, however, because nonrecurring gains and losses are reflected in the value of assets in place. Hirst and Hopkins (2000) noted that nonrecurring items sometimes result from accounting rules and at other times result from "strategic" management decisions. Regardless, they highlighted the importance of examining the financial statement notes and other sources for items that may warrant adjustment in determining recurring earnings, such as:

► unusual items;

► extraordinary items;

► restructuring charges;

► discontinued operations; and

► accounting changes.

In some cases, management may record restructuring or unusual charges in every period. In these cases, the item may be considered an ordinary operating expense and may not require adjustment.

Companies sometimes inappropriately classify nonoperating gains as a reduction in operating expenses (such as selling, general, and administrative expenses). If material, this inappropriate classification can usually be uncovered by a careful reading of financial statement footnotes and press releases. Analysts should consider whether these items are likely to continue and contribute to residual income over time. More likely, they should be removed from operating earnings when forecasting residual income.

4.5 Other Aggressive Accounting Practices

Companies may engage in accounting practices that result in the overstatement of assets (book value) and/or overstatement of earnings. We discussed many of these practices in the preceding sections.[26] Other activities that a company may engage in include accelerating revenues to the current period or deferring expenses to a later period.[27] Both activities simultaneously increase earnings and book value. For example, a company might ship unordered goods to customers at year-end, recording revenues and a receivable. Conversely, a company could capitalize rather than expense a cash payment, resulting in lower expenses and an increase in assets. The analyst must evaluate a company's accounting policies carefully and consider the integrity of management in assessing the inputs in a residual income model. Companies have also been criticized recently for the use of "cookie jar" reserves (reserves saved for future use), in which excess losses or

---

[26] Also see Reading 37.

[27] See, for example, Schilit (1993).

expenses are recorded in an earlier period (for example, in conjunction with an acquisition or restructuring) and then used to reduce expense and increase income in future periods. The analyst should carefully examine the use of reserves when assessing residual earnings.

4.6 International Considerations

Accounting standards differ internationally. These differences result in different measures of book value and earnings internationally and suggest that valuation models based on accrual accounting data might not perform as well as other pres-ent value models in international contexts. It is interesting to note, however, that Frankel and Lee (1999) found that the residual income model works well in valuing companies on an international basis. Using a simple residual income model without any of the adjustments discussed in this reading, they found that their residual income valuation model accounted for 70 percent of the cross-sectional variation of stock prices across 20 countries. Table 7 shows the model's explanatory power by country.

Germany had the lowest explanatory power. Japan had low explanatory power for companies reporting only parent company results; the explanatory power for Japanese companies reporting on a consolidated basis was considerably higher. Explanatory power was highest in France, the United Kingdom, and the United States. Frankel and Lee concluded that there are three primary considerations in applying a residual income model internationally:

► the availability of reliable earnings forecasts;

► systematic violations of the clean surplus assumption; and

► "poor quality" accounting rules that result in delayed recognition of value changes.

Analysts should expect the model to work best in situations in which earnings forecasts are available, clean surplus violations are limited, and accounting rules do not result in delayed recognition. Because Frankel and Lee found good explanatory power for a residual income model using unadjusted accounting data, it should be expected that if adjustments are made to the reported data to

TABLE 7   International Application of Residual Income Models

Explanatory Power	Country
40–50 percent	Germany
	Japan (parent company reporting)
60–70 percent	Australia
	Canada
	Japan (consolidated reporting)
	United Kingdom
More than 70 percent	France
	United States

Source: Frankel and Lee (1999).

correct for clean surplus and other violations, international comparisons should result in comparable valuations. For circumstances in which clean surplus violations exist, accounting choices result in delayed recognition, or accounting disclosures do not permit adjustment, the residual income model would not be appropriate and the analyst should consider a model less dependent on accounting data, such as a FCFE model.

SINGLE-STAGE RESIDUAL INCOME VALUATION   5

The single-stage (constant-growth) residual income model assumes that a company has a constant return on equity and constant earnings growth rate over time. This model was given in Equation 49-5, repeated below:

$$V_0 = B_0 + \frac{\text{ROE} - r}{r - g} B_0$$

EXAMPLE 8

Single-Stage Residual Income Model (1)

Joseph Yoh is evaluating a purchase of Canon, Inc. (NYSE: CAJ). Current book value per share is $12.90, and the current price per share is $32.41 (from Value Line, 8 February 2002). Yoh expects long-term ROE to be 10 percent and long-term growth to be 8 percent. Assuming a cost of equity of 9 percent, what is the intrinsic value of Canon stock using a residual income model?

$$V_0 = 12.90 + \frac{0.10 - 0.09}{0.09 - 0.08} 12.90 = \$25.80$$

Similar to the Gordon growth DDM, the single-stage residual income model can be used to assess the market expectations of residual income growth by inputting the current price into the model and solving for g.

EXAMPLE 9

Single-Stage Residual Income Model (2)

Joseph Yoh is curious about the market-perceived growth rate, given that he is comfortable with his other inputs. Using the current price per share of $32.41 for Canon, Yoh solves for g:

$$32.41 = 12.90 + \frac{0.10 - 0.09}{0.09 - g} 12.90$$

He finds an implied growth rate of 8.34 percent.

In the above example, the company was valued at twice its book value because its ROE exceeded its cost of equity. If ROE were equal to the cost of equity, the company would be valued at book value. If ROE were lower than the cost of equity, the company would have negative residual income and be valued at less than book value. In the case in which a company cannot cover its cost of capital, a liquidation of the company and redeployment of assets may be appropriate. Assuming the market appropriately values the company below book value, this case may also be an opportunity for an acquisition or other restructuring in which new management may be able to improve residual income and add value to the company.

In many applications, a drawback to the single-stage model is that it assumes the excess ROE above the cost of equity will persist indefinitely. Evidence suggests that ROE is mean reverting over time, which should not be surprising. If a company or industry has an abnormally high ROE, other companies will enter the marketplace, increasing competition and lowering returns for all companies. Similarly, if an industry has a low ROE, companies will exit the industry (through bankruptcy or otherwise) and ROEs will tend to rise over time. As with the single-stage DDM, the single-stage residual income model assumes a constant growth rate over time. Fortunately, other models are available that enable us to relax these assumptions.

6   MULTISTAGE RESIDUAL INCOME VALUATION

As with the DDM and DCF approaches, a multistage approach can be used when residual income is forecast for a certain time horizon and a terminal value based on continuing residual income is estimated at the end of the time horizon. **Continuing residual income** is residual income after the forecast horizon. As with other valuation models, the forecast horizon for the initial stage should based on the ability to explicitly forecast inputs into the model. Unlike in other models, the terminal value is not a major driver of value in a residual income approach. Frequently, in DCF approaches, the value of early cash flows makes up a small portion of total value, whereas the present value of the terminal value is a significant portion of that value. In a residual income approach, the current book value often captures a large portion of total value. Because ROEs have been found to revert to mean levels over time and may decline to the cost of equity in a competitive environment, the terminal value may not be a large component of total value, particularly as ROE approaches the cost of equity. A ROE equal to the cost of equity would result in residual income of zero.

Analysts make a variety of assumptions concerning continuing residual income. Frequently, one of the following assumptions is made:

► residual income continues indefinitely at a positive level;

► residual income is zero from the terminal year forward;

► residual income declines to zero as ROE reverts to the cost of equity over time; or

► residual income reflects the reversion of ROE to some mean level.

We illustrate several of these approaches below.

One finite-horizon model of residual income valuation assumes that at the end of time horizon T, there is a certain premium over book value $(P_T - B_T)$ for the company; in this case, current value equals the following:[28]

$$V_0 = B_0 + \sum_{t=1}^{T} \frac{(E_t - rB_{t-1})}{(1 + r)^t} + \frac{P_T - B_T}{(1 + r)^T}$$

(49-6)

Alternatively,

$$V_0 = B_0 + \sum_{t=1}^{T} \frac{(\text{ROE}_t - r) \times B_{t-1}}{(1 + r)^t} + \frac{P_T - B_T}{(1 + r)^T}$$

(49-7)

The last component in both specifications represents the premium over book value at the end of the forecast horizon. The longer the forecast period, the greater the chance that the company's residual income will converge to zero. For long forecast periods, this last term may thus be treated as zero. For shorter forecast periods, a forecast of the premium must be calculated.

EXAMPLE 10

Multistage Residual Income Model (1)

Diana Rosato, CFA, is considering an investment in Taiwan Semiconductor Manufacturing Ltd., a manufacturer and marketer of integrated circuits. Listed on the Taiwan Stock Exchange (2330), the company's stock is also traded on the New York Stock Exchange (NYSE: TSM). Rosato obtained the following information from Bloomberg and Value Line as of 21 February 2002:

► Current price = TWD81.

► Cost of equity = 14.33 percent.

► Taiwan Semiconductor's ROEs have ranged from 18.3 percent to 26.2 percent over the last four years.

► Five-year forecast of growth in book value = 22 percent a year.

► TSM does not pay dividends.

Additionally, Rosato reviews annual financial statements for 2000 and quarterly financial statements for 2001. The fourth-quarter financial statements indicate a book value per share of TWD16.47. In 2001, ROE declined to 5.5 percent, but Rosato and other analysts expect a rebound in ROE for the years 2002 and 2003. Analyst EPS forecasts (from Multex Global Estimates) are 2.07 for 2002 and 4.81 for 2003.

Rosato expects Taiwan Semiconductor's ROE after 2003 to stabilize at 25 percent until 2011 and then decline to 20 percent until 2021. Rosato assumes that after that date, residual income will be zero and the terminal premium over book value would thus be zero. Rosato's residual income model is as follows:

---

[28] See Bauman (1999).

TABLE 8   Taiwan Semiconductor

Year	Projected Income	Ending Book Value	Forecast ROE (beg. equity, %)	Cost of Equity (%)	Cost of Equity (TWD)	Residual Income	PV of RI	Total PV of RI
		16.47					16.47	59.18
2002	2.07	18.54	12.57	14.33	2.36	−0.29	(0.25)	
2003	4.81	23.35	25.94	14.33	2.66	2.15	1.65	
2004	5.84	29.19	25.00	14.33	3.35	2.49	1.67	
2005	7.30	36.48	25.00	14.33	4.18	3.11	1.82	
2006	9.12	45.61	25.00	14.33	5.23	3.89	1.99	
2007	11.40	57.01	25.00	14.33	6.54	4.87	2.18	
2008	14.25	71.26	25.00	14.33	8.17	6.08	2.38	
2009	17.81	89.07	25.00	14.33	10.21	7.60	2.60	
2010	22.27	111.34	25.00	14.33	12.76	9.50	2.85	
2011	27.84	139.18	25.00	14.33	15.96	11.88	3.11	
2012	27.84	167.01	20.00	14.33	19.94	7.89	1.81	
2013	33.40	200.41	20.00	14.33	23.93	9.47	1.90	
2014	40.08	240.50	20.00	14.33	28.72	11.36	1.99	
2015	48.10	288.60	20.00	14.33	34.46	13.64	2.09	
2016	57.72	346.32	20.00	14.33	41.36	16.36	2.20	
2017	69.26	415.58	20.00	14.33	49.63	19.64	2.30	
2018	83.12	498.70	20.00	14.33	59.55	23.56	2.42	
2019	99.74	598.43	20.00	14.33	71.46	28.28	2.54	
2020	119.69	718.12	20.00	14.33	85.76	33.93	2.66	
2021	143.62	861.75	20.00	14.33	102.91	40.72	2.80	

Terminal premium = 0.00.

The market price of TWD81 exceeds the estimated value of TWD59.18. Rosato concludes that the company is overvalued in the current marketplace.

Lee and Swaminathan (1999) and Lee, Myers, and Swaminathan (1999) have presented a residual income model based on explicit forecasts of residual income for three years. Thereafter, ROE is forecast to fade to the industry mean value of ROE. The terminal value at the end of the forecast horizon (*T*) is estimated as the terminal-year residual income discounted as a perpetuity. Lee and Swaminathan stated that this assumes that any growth in earnings after *T* is value neutral. Table 8 presents some recent industry ROE data from Baseline. In forecasting a fading ROE, the analyst should also consider any trends in industry ROE.

TABLE 9   U.S. Industry ROEs, 2000

Industry	ROE	Industry	ROE
Advertising	32.00%	Insurance–Multiline	14.00%
Aerospace/Defense	18.00	Insurance–Prop/Casualty	10.00
Agricultural Product	5.00	IT Consulting & Svc	20.00
Air Freight & Couriers	14.00	Internet Software & Svc	4.00
Aluminum	18.00	Leisure Facilities	9.00
Apparel & Accessory	17.00	Leisure Products	9.00
Application Software	19.00	Machinery Industrial	19.00
Airlines	13.00	Meat Poultry & Fish	11.00
Auto Parts & Equip	20.00	Broadcasting & Cable	2.00
Automobile Mfrs	23.00	Diverse Metal/Mining	6.00
Banks	34.00	Motorcycle Mfrs	27.00
Soft Drinks	30.00	Multi–Utilities	12.00
Biotechnology	24.00	Networking Equipment	21.00
Building Products	18.00	Office Electronics	20.00
Brewers	37.00	Services–Office/Supp	37.00
Chemicals–Commodity	45.00	Oil & Gas–Drilling	6.00
Consumer Electronics	15.00	Oil & Gas–Equip/Svc	7.00
Computer Hardware	29.00	Oil & Gas–Explor/Prod	27.00
Industrial Conglomerates	28.00	Oil & Gas–Integrated	30.00
Construction Materials	16.00	Oil & Gas–Refng/Mktg	21.00
Contain Metal/Glass	9.00	Services–Environmental	18.00
Casinos & Gaming	12.00	Integrated Telecom Svc	24.00
Personal Products	53.00	Photographic Prods	38.00
Chemicals–Diverse	17.00	Packaged Foods	55.00
Services–Div/Comm'l	29.00	Paper Packaging	12.00
Computer Storage/Peripherals	27.00	Paper Products	7.00
Distributors	18.00	Precious Metal & Mineral	19.00
Diverse Financial Svc	24.00	Commercial Printing	22.00
Services–Data Proc	24.00	Publishing & Printing	18.00
Pharmaceuticals	34.00	Railroads	8.00
Distiller & Vintners	22.00	Reinsurance	8.00
Electrical Component	18.00	Restaurants	24.00
Electronic Equip/Inst	17.00	Retail–Apparel	36.00
Construction & Engineer	5.00	Retail–Catalog	18.00
Movies & Entertainment	11.00	Retail–Comp/Electronic	21.00
Electric Utilities	15.00	Department Stores	12.00
Chemicals–Agri/Fertilizer	11.00	Retail–Drugs	19.00
Consumer Finance	25.00	General Merchandise	23.00

(Table continued on next page . . .)

TABLE 9 (continued)

Industry	ROE	Industry	ROE
Food Distributors	27.00	Retail–Home Improve	18.00
Retail–Food	23.00	Specialty Stores	19.00
Forest Products	11.00	Chemicals–Specialty	15.00
Gold	6.00	Semiconductors	27.00
Gas Utilities	14.00	Semiconductor Equip	32.00
Healthcare–Dist/Svc	14.00	Marine	12.00
Healthcare–Equipment	27.00	Footwear	18.00
Healthcare–Facility	6.00	Services–Employment	29.00
Healthcare–Managed Care	17.00	Steel	10.00
Healthcare–Supplies	7.00	Systems Software	37.00
Homebuilding	23.00	Tobacco	55.00
Home Furnishings	15.00	Telecom Equipment	11.00
Hotels	16.00	Tires & Rubber	3.00
Household Appliances	36.00	Wireless Telecom Svc	5.00
Household Products	36.00	Trade Cos & Distr	15.00
Housewares & Specs	16.00	Machinery Const/Farm	16.00
Industrial Gases	9.00	Trucking	9.00
Insurance–Brokers	21.00	Textiles	5.00
Insurance–Life/Health	12.00	Water Utilities	10.00

Source: Baseline.

EXAMPLE 11

Multistage Residual Income Model (2)

Rosato's supervisor questions her assumption that Taiwan Semiconductor will have no premium at the end of her forecast period. Rosato amends her model to use a terminal value based on a perpetuity of Year 2021 residual income. She computes the following terminal value:

TV = 40.72/0.1433 = 284.16

The present value of this terminal value is as follows:

PV = 284.16/(1.1433)^{20} = 19.51

Adding this number to the previous value of 58.91 (for which the terminal value was zero) yields a total value of TWD78.69. Because the current market price of TWD81 is greater than TWD78.69, Rosato concludes that market participants expect a positive continuing residual income after her forecast period.

Another multistage model assumes that ROE fades over time to the cost of equity. In this approach, ROE can be explicitly forecast each period until reaching the cost of equity. The forecast would then end and the terminal value would be zero. Example 6 presented such a model using Dell Computer Corporation.

Dechow, Hutton, and Sloan (1998) presented an analysis of a residual income model in which residual income fades over time:[29]

$$V_0 = B_0 + \sum_{t=1}^{T-1} \frac{(E_t - rB_{t-1})}{(1+r)^t} + \frac{E_T - rB_{T-1}}{(1+r-\omega)(1+r)^{T-1}}$$ **(49-8)**

This model adds a persistence factor, ω, which is between 0 and 1. A persistence factor of 1.0 implies that residual income will continue indefinitely (a perpetuity). A persistence factor of 0 implies that residual income will not continue after the initial forecast horizon. The higher the value of the persistence factor, the higher the valuation. Dechow et al. found that in a large sample of company data from 1976 to 1995, the persistence factor equaled 0.62. This persistence factor considers the long-run mean-reverting nature of ROE, assuming that over time ROE regresses toward r and that resulting residual income fades toward zero. Bauman (1999) noted that the above results imply that residual income decays at a rate of 38 percent a year on average. Bauman uses the Dechow et al. model to demonstrate residual income valuation for Cisco. Bauman uses a persistence factor of 0.80 for Cisco, stating that Cisco's market leadership implies a lower rate of decay (20 percent). Clearly, the persistence factor varies from company to company. Dechow et al. provided insight into some characteristics that can indicate a lower or higher level of persistence, listed in Table 10.

TABLE 10 Final-Stage Residual Income Persistence

Lower Residual Income Persistence	Higher Residual Income Persistence
Extreme accounting rates of return (ROE)	Low dividend payout
Extreme levels of special items (e.g., nonrecurring items)	High historical persistence in the industry
Extreme levels of accounting accruals	

EXAMPLE 12

Multistage Residual Income Model (3)

Rosato extends her analysis to consider the possibility that ROE will slowly decay after 2022 toward r, rather than using a perpetuity of Year

---

[29] See Dechow, Hutton, and Sloan (1998) and Bauman (1999).

2021 residual income. Rosato estimates a persistence parameter of 0.60. The present value of the terminal value is determined as

$$\frac{E_T - rB_{T-1}}{(1 + r - \omega)(1 + r)^{T-1}}$$

with $T = 21$ and 2022 residual income equal to $40.72 \times 1.20 = 48.86$.

$$\frac{48.86}{(1 + 0.1433 - 0.60)(1.1433)^{20}} = 6.18$$

Total value is TWD65.36 calculated by adding 6.18 to 59.18. Rosato concludes that if Taiwan Semiconductor's residual income does not persist at a stable level past 2022 and deteriorates over time, the shares are overvalued.

Example 12 illustrates the assumption that continuing residual income will decline to zero as ROE approaches the required rate of return on equity.

SUMMARY

This reading has discussed the use of residual income models in valuation. Residual income is an appealing economic concept because it attempts to measure economic profit: profits after accounting for all opportunity costs of capital.

▶ Residual income is calculated as net income minus a deduction for the cost of equity capital. The deduction is called the equity charge, and is equal to equity capital multiplied by the required rate of return on equity (the cost of equity capital in percent).

▶ Economic value added (EVA) is a commercial implementation of the residual income concept. EVA = NOPAT − (C% × TC), where NOPAT is net operating profit after taxes, C% is the percent cost of equity capital, and TC equals total capital.

▶ Residual income models (including commercial implementations) are used not only for equity valuation but also to measure internal corporate performance and for determining executive compensation.

▶ We can forecast per-share residual income as forecasted earnings per share minus the required rate of return on equity multiplied by beginning book value per share. Alternatively, we can forecast per-share residual income as beginning book value per share multiplied by the difference between forecasted ROE and the required rate of return on equity.

▶ According to the residual income model, the intrinsic value of a share of common stock is the sum of book value per share and the present value of expected future per-share residual income. According to the residual income model, equivalent mathematical expressions for intrinsic value of a common stock are

$$V_0 = B_0 + \sum_{t=1}^{\infty} \frac{\text{RI}_t}{(1+r)^t} = B_0 + \sum_{t=1}^{\infty} \frac{E_t - rB_{t-1}}{(1+r)^t}$$

$$= B_0 + \sum_{t=1}^{\infty} \frac{(\text{ROE}_t - r) \times B_{t-1}}{(1+r)^t}$$

where

V_0 = value of a share of stock today ($t = 0$)
B_0 = current per-share book value of equity
B_t = expected per-share book value of equity at any time t
r = required rate of return on equity (cost of equity)
E_t = expected earnings per share for period t
RI_t = expected per-share residual income, equal to $E_t - rB_{t-1}$
  or to $(\text{ROE} - r) \times B_{t-1}$

▶ In most cases, value is recognized earlier in the residual income model compared with other present value models of stock value such as the dividend discount model.

▶ Strengths of the residual income model include the following:

  ▶ Terminal values do not make up a large portion of the value relative to other models.

  ▶ The models use readily available accounting data.

- ▶ The models can be used in the absence of dividends and near-term positive free cash flows.
- ▶ The models can be used when cash flows are unpredictable.
- ▶ Weaknesses of the residual income model include the following:
  - ▶ These models are based on accounting data that can be subject to manipulation by management.
  - ▶ Accounting data used as inputs may require significant adjustments.
  - ▶ The models require that the clean surplus relation holds, or that the analyst makes appropriate adjustments when the clean surplus relation does not hold.
- ▶ The residual income model is most appropriate in the following cases:
  - ▶ A company is not paying dividends or if it exhibits an unpredictable dividend pattern.
  - ▶ A company has negative free cash flow many years out but is expected to generate positive cash flow at some point in the future.
  - ▶ There is a great deal of uncertainty in forecasting terminal values.
- ▶ The fundamental determinants or drivers of residual income are book value of equity and return on equity.
- ▶ Residual income valuation is most closely related to P/B. When the present value of expected future residual income is positive (negative), the justified P/B based on fundamentals is greater than (less than) 1.
- ▶ When fully consistent assumptions are used to forecast earnings, cash flow, dividends, book value, and residual income through a full set of pro forma (projected) financial statements, and the same required rate of return on equity is used as the discount rate, the same estimate of value should result from a residual income, dividend discount, or free cash flow valuation. In practice, however, analysts may find one model much easier to apply and possibly arrive at different valuations using the different models.
- ▶ The residual income model assumes the clean surplus relation $B_t = B_{t-1} + E_t - D_t$. In other terms, the ending book value of equity equals the beginning book value plus earnings less dividends, apart from ownership transactions.
- ▶ In practice, to apply the residual income model most accurately, the analyst needs to:
  - ▶ adjust book value of common equity for off-balance-sheet items; and
  - ▶ adjust reported net income to reflect clean surplus accounting, where necessary.
- ▶ Continuing residual income is residual income after the forecast horizon. Frequently, one of the following assumptions concerning continuing residual income is made:
  - ▶ Residual income continues indefinitely at a positive level.
  - ▶ Residual income is zero from the terminal year forward.
  - ▶ Residual income declines to zero as ROE reverts to the cost of equity over time.
  - ▶ Residual income declines to some mean level.

1. Based on the following information, determine whether Vertically Integrated Manufacturing (VIM) earned any residual income for its shareholders in 2001:

▶ VIM had total assets of $3,000,000, financed with twice as much debt capital as equity capital.

▶ VIM's pretax cost of debt is 6 percent and cost of equity capital is 10 percent.

▶ VIM had EBIT of $300,000 and was taxed at a rate of 40 percent.

2. Using the following information, estimate the intrinsic value of VIM's common stock using the residual income model:

▶ VIM had total assets of $3,000,000, financed with twice as much debt capital as equity capital.

▶ VIM's pretax cost of debt is 6 percent and cost of equity capital is 10 percent.

▶ VIM had EBIT of $300,000 and was taxed at a rate of 40 percent. EBIT is expected to continue at $300,000 indefinitely.

▶ VIM's book value per share is $20.

▶ VIM has 50,000 shares of common stock outstanding.

3. Palmetto Steel, Inc. (PSI) maintains a dividend payout ratio of 80 percent because of its limited opportunities for expansion. Its return on equity is 15 percent. The required rate of return on PSI equity is 12 percent, and its long-term growth rate is 3 percent. Compute the justified P/B based on forecasted fundamentals, consistent with the residual income model and a constant growth rate assumption.

4. Because NewMarket Products (NMP) markets consumer staples, it is able to make use of considerable debt in its capital structure; specifically, 90 percent of the company's total assets of $450,000,000 are financed with debt capital. Its cost of debt is 8 percent before taxes, and its cost of equity capital is 12 percent. NMP achieved a pretax income of $5.1 million in 2001 and had a tax rate of 40 percent. What was NMP's residual income for 2001?

5. In 2002, Smithson-Williams Investments (SWI) achieved an operating profit after taxes of €10 million on total assets of €100 million. Half of its assets were financed with debt with a pretax cost of 9 percent. Its cost of equity capital is 12 percent, and its tax rate is 40 percent. Did SWI achieve a positive residual income?

6. Calculate the economic value added (EVA) or residual income, as requested, for each of the following:

A. NOPAT = $100

Beginning book value of debt = $200

Beginning book value of equity = $300

WACC = 11 percent

Calculate EVA.

B. Net income = €5.00

Dividends = €1.00

Beginning book value of equity = €30.00

Required rate of return on equity = 11 percent

Calculate residual income.

C. Return on equity = 18 percent

Required rate of return on equity = 12 percent

Beginning book value of equity = €30.00

Calculate residual income.

7. [Adapted from the 2000 CFA Level II Examination] Jim Martin is using economic value added (EVA) and market value added (MVA) to measure the performance of Sundanci. Martin uses the fiscal 2000 information below for his analysis.

▶ Adjusted net operating profit after tax (NOPAT) is $100 million.

▶ Total capital is $700 million (no debt).

▶ Closing stock price is $26.

▶ Sundanci has 84 million shares outstanding.

▶ The cost of equity is 14 percent.

Calculate the following for Sundanci. Show your work.

A. EVA for fiscal 2000

B. MVA as of fiscal year-end 2000

8. Protected Steel Corporation (PSC) has a book value of $6 per share. PSC is expected to earn $0.60 per share forever and pays out all of its earnings as dividends. The required rate of return on PSC's equity is 12 percent. Calculate the value of the stock using the following:

A. Dividend discount model

B. Residual income model

9. Notable Books (NB) is a family-controlled company that dominates the retail book market. NB has book value of $10 per share, is expected to earn $2.00 forever, and pays out all of its earnings as dividends. Its required return on equity is 12.5 percent. Place a value on the stock of NB using the following:

A. Dividend discount model

B. Residual income model

10. Simonson Investment Trust International (SITI) is expected to earn $4.00, $5.00, and $8.00 for the next three years. SITI will pay annual dividends of $2.00, $2.50, and $20.50 in each of these years. The last dividend includes the liquidating payment to shareholders at the end of Year 3 when the trust terminates. SITI's book value is $8 per share and its required return on equity is 10 percent.

A. What is the current value per share of SITI according to the dividend discount model?

B. Calculate per-share book value and residual income for SITI for each of the next 3 years and use those results to find the stock's value using the residual income model.

C. Calculate return on equity and use it as an input to the residual income model to calculate SITI's value.

11. Foodsco Incorporated (FI), a leading distributor of food products and materials to restaurants and other institutions, has a remarkably steady track record in terms of both return on equity and growth. At year-end 2000, FI had a book value of $30 per share. For the foreseeable future, you expect the company to achieve a ROE of 15 percent (on trailing book value) and to pay out one-third of its earnings in dividends. Your required return is 12 percent. Forecast FI's residual income for the year ending 31 December 2005.

12. Lendex Electronics (LE) has had a great deal of turnover of top management for several years and was not followed by analysts during this period of turmoil. Because the company's performance has been improving steadily for the past three years, technology analyst Steve Kent recently reinitiated coverage of LE. A meeting with management confirmed Kent's positive impression of LE's operations and strategic plan. Kent decides LE merits further analysis.

    Careful examination of LE's financial statements revealed that the company had negative other comprehensive income from changes in the value of available-for-sale securities in each of the past five years. How, if at all, should this observation about LE's other comprehensive income affect the figures that Kent uses for the company's ROE and book value for those years?

13. Retail fund manager Seymour Simms is considering the purchase of shares in upstart retailer Hot Topic Stores (HTS). The current book value of HTS is $20 per share, and its market price is $35. Simms expects long-term ROE to be 18 percent, long-term growth to be 10 percent, and cost of equity to be 14 percent. What conclusion would you expect Simms to arrive at if he uses a single-stage residual income model to value these shares?

14. Dayton Manufactured Homes (DMH) builds prefabricated homes and mobile homes. Both favorable demographics and the likelihood of slow, steady increases in market share should enable DMH to maintain its ROE of 15 percent and growth rate of 10 percent over time. DMH has a book value of $30 per share and the required rate of return on its equity is 12 percent. Compute the value of its equity using the single-stage residual income model.

15. Use the following inputs and the finite horizon form of the residual income model to compute the value of Southern Trust Bank (STB) shares as of 31 December 2001:

    ▶ ROE will continue at 15 percent for the next five years (and 10 percent thereafter) with all earnings reinvested (no dividends paid).
    ▶ Cost of Equity = 10 percent.
    ▶ B_0 = $10 per share (at year-end 2001).
    ▶ Premium over book value at the end of five years will be 20 percent.

For Problems 16 and 17, use the following data for Taiwan Semiconductor Manufacturing Ltd. (TSM). Refer to Equation 49-8 in the reading.

    ▶ Current price = TWD81.
    ▶ Cost of equity = 14.33 percent.
    ▶ Five-year forecast of growth in book value = 22 percent.
    ▶ Book value per share = TWD16.47.
    ▶ Analyst EPS forecasts are TWD2.07 for 2002 and TWD4.81 for 2003.
    ▶ Analysts expect ROE to stabilize at 25 percent from 2002 through 2011, and then decline to 20 percent through 2022 in Problem 16 and 2023 in Problem 17.
    ▶ As of the beginning of 2002, an analyst estimates the intrinsic value using the residual income model as TWD59.18 with the zero premium shown in Example 10.

16. In the above analysis, the analyst uses the multistage residual income model and assumes that TSM's ROE will fade toward the cost of equity capital after 2022. How would her conclusion about TSM's valuation change if she believed that the persistence parameter for this company should be 0.90 (rather than 0.60) because of patent protection for some of TSM's technology?

17. Having completed the revised analysis, which gives TSM greater credit for its patented technology, the analyst realizes that the changes warrant an additional adjustment. Although she generally employs a 20-year time frame when implementing the multistage residual income model, she believes that the TSM's ROE will remain at 20 percent through 2023 before fading toward the cost of equity capital. (Recall she is now using a persistence parameter of 0.90.) How does this extension of the period with above-normal ROE alter her valuation of TSM?

18. Shunichi Kobayashi is valuing United Parcel Service (NYSE: UPS). Kobayashi has made the following assumptions:

  ▶ Book value per share is estimated at $9.62 on 31 December 2001.

  ▶ EPS will be 22 percent of the beginning book value per share for the next eight years.

  ▶ Cash dividends paid will be 30 percent of EPS.

  ▶ At the end of the eight-year period, the market price per share will be three times the book value per share.

  ▶ The beta for UPS is 0.60, the risk-free rate is 5.00 percent, and the equity risk premium is 5.50 percent.

    The current market price of UPS is $59.38, which indicates a current P/B of 6.2.

  A. Prepare a table showing the beginning and ending book values, net income, and cash dividends annually for the eight-year period.

  B. Estimate the residual income and the present value of residual income for the eight years.

  C. Estimate the value per share of UPS stock using the residual income model.

  D. Estimate the value per share of UPS stock using the dividend discount model. How does this value compare with the estimate from the residual income model?

19. Boeing Company (NYSE: BA) has a current stock price of $49.86. It also has a P/B of 3.57 and book value per share of $13.97. Assume that the single-stage growth model is appropriate for valuing BA. Boeing's beta is 0.80, the risk-free rate is 5.00 percent, and the equity risk premium is 5.50 percent.

  A. If the growth rate is 6 percent and the ROE is 20 percent, what is the justified P/B for Boeing?

  B. If the growth rate is 6 percent, what ROE is required to yield Boeing's current P/B?

  C. If the ROE is 20 percent, what growth rate is required for Boeing to have its current P/B?

SECURITY ANALYSIS USING VALUE-BASED METRICS

by James A. Abate and James L. Grant

LEARNING OUTCOMES

The candidate should be able to:

a. calculate and interpret economic value added (EVA®), differentiate between accounting profitability as measured by ROE and economic profitability as measured by EVA, and explain the significance of a positive or negative EVA;

b. describe methods for increasing EVA;

c. describe the process for determining cash flow return on investment (CFROI);

d. explain why the spread between CFROI and weighted average cost of capital is similar to the concept of EVA spread;

e. describe how value-based metrics can be used in stock selection.

INTRODUCTION · 1

The world of security analysis is undergoing a revolution of sorts with increased focus on "value-based" metrics that are designed to give shareholders their due. Chief among these measures of corporate financial success is a metric called *economic value added* (EVA[1]). EVA and related value-based measures such as *cash flow return on investment* (CFROI[2]) are now making significant inroads into the realm of security analysis and equity portfolio management. These metrics are also paving the way for a "modern" school of equity fundamental analysis that

---

[1] EVA® is a registered trademark of Stern Stewart & Co. For a discussion and application of their value-based (economic profit) measure in a corporate finance setting, see G. Bennett Stewart III, *The Quest for Value* (New York: Harper Collins, 1991), and Al Ehrbar, *EVA: The Real Key to Creating Wealth* (New York: John Wiley & Sons, 1998).

[2] CFROI® is a value-based metric of HOLT Value Associates, L.P. For a discussion of the CFROI approach to measuring economic profit, see Bartley J. Madden, *CFROI Valuation: A Total Systems Approach to Valuing the Firm* (Woburn, MA: Butterworth-Heinemann, 1999).

539

departs from the traditional method, with its prior focus on accounting measures such as earnings per share and return on equity.

Perhaps the best-known value-based metric among today's corporate and investment players is EVA. Introduced in 1982 by Joel Stern and G. Bennett Stewart, this economic profit measure gained early acceptance among the corporate financial community because of its innovative way of looking at profitability net of the dollar weighted cost of debt *and* equity capital. Indeed, many firms—including corporate giants like AT&T, Coca-Cola, Diageo, Guidant, and SPX—have used an EVA platform to design incentive pay schemes that lead managers to make wealth-enhancing investment decisions for the shareholders. EVA is also gaining popularity in the investment community. For example, Goldman Sachs U.S. Research, and C.S. First Boston use EVA to evaluate the performance potential of many sectors of the economy. Also, Global Asset Management and Oppenheimer Capital have successfully used economic profit principles to actively manage investment portfolios from a "bottom-up" fundamental perspective.

We'll begin the reading with a look at how to estimate EVA in a basic setting. This will allow us to see the benefits of a value-based framework without getting tangled up in a plethora of value-based accounting adjustments. We'll then look at standard accounting adjustments that are necessary to estimate economic profit in practice. This entails a closer look at how to estimate a company's net operating profit after tax (NOPAT) as well as the dollar weighted average cost of capital, $WACC. Next, we'll examine the basic link between EVA and its close associate, CFROI. We'll then explain how a multi-factor EVA risk model can be used to obtain improved estimates of the required return on common stock (equivalently, the cost of equity capital). This risk measurement innovation is important in light of the empirical limitations of CAPM. Finally, we'll see how value-based metrics such as EVA can be used to evaluate companies in a stock selection context.

2   A WORD ON LEVERED AND UNLEVERED FIRMS

Central to the basic economic profit calculation is the distinction between a *levered* firm and an *unlevered* firm. A levered firm, like most real-world companies, is one that is financed with both debt and equity sources of capital. In contrast, an equivalent business-risk unlevered firm is one that, in principle, is 100% equity financed. This firm-type classification is helpful to understanding the economic profit calculation because EVA is measured by subtracting a company's dollar cost of invested capital—a reflection of its weighted average cost of debt and equity capital—from its unlevered net operating profit after tax (noted as NOPAT, versus LNOPAT for levered net operating profit). With this distinction, the firm's EVA is generally defined as:

EVA = NOPAT − $WACC

NOPAT is used in the EVA formulation for two reasons. First, an economic profit emphasis on this term serves as a modern-day reminder that a company largely receives profits from the desirability, or lack thereof, of its overall products and services. Along this line, the risk or uncertainty of NOPAT is a reflection of the firm's inherent business risk. Second, since most firms have some form of business debt outstanding, they receive a yearly interest tax subsidy—measured by the corporate tax rate *times* a company's interest expense—that is already reflected in the dollar cost of capital, $WACC.

As we'll see shortly, an incorrect focus by managers or investors on the levered firm's net operating profit after tax, LNOPAT, rather than its unlevered net operating profit, NOPAT, would lead to an *upward* bias in the company's reported economic profit. By recognizing the possible "double counting" of a firm's debt-interest tax subsidies (on both debt and debt equivalents such as operating leases), the manager or investor avoids imparting a *positive* bias in the firm's EVA, and, ultimately, its enterprise value and stock price.

THE BASIC EVA FORMULATION   3

Before getting immersed in a sea of value-based accounting adjustments, we'll look at the key features of economic profit measurement in a *basic* setting. In this context, we'll unfold EVA into its two basic ingredients—namely, NOPAT, which represents a company's unlevered net operating profit after tax, and $WACC, which represents a firm's dollar cost of invested capital. We'll first look at NOPAT.

In the absence of any EVA accounting adjustments, the firm's NOPAT can be expressed in terms of its tax-adjusted earnings before interest and taxes, EBIT, according to:[3]

$$\text{NOPAT} = \text{EBIT} \times (1 - t) = [\text{S} - \text{COGS} - \text{SG\&A} - D] \times (1 - t)$$

In this expression, $\text{EBIT} \times (1 - t)$ is the unlevered firm's net operating profit after tax. This basic EVA term is a reflection of the firm's earnings before interest and taxes, EBIT, less *unlevered* business taxes—measured by EBIT less t times EBIT. Likewise, the terms, S, COGS, and SG&A in the NOPAT specification refer to the firm's sales, cost of goods sold, and selling, general and administrative expenses, respectively. In principle, the depreciation term, D, should be a charge that reflects the *economic* obsolescence of the firm's assets. In this context, using an estimate of economic depreciation rather than accounting depreciation when the NOPAT differences are meaningful.[4]

In turn, the firm's dollar cost of capital, $WACC, can be expressed as:

$$\$\text{WACC} = \text{WACC} \times C$$

In this expression, WACC is the weighted-average cost of debt *and* equity capital (expressed as a required rate in decimal form), and C is the firm's invested capital. In turn, the weighted average cost of capital, WACC, is given by:

$$\text{WACC} = \text{After-tax Debt Cost} \times \text{Debt Weight} + \text{Equity Cost} \times \text{Equity Weight}$$

---

[3] We'll provide an overview of the conventional accounting adjustments to estimating EVA later. For an exhaustive discussion of EVA accounting adjustments, see Stewart, *The Quest for Value.*

[4] See, Stephen F. O'Byrne, "Does Value-Based Management Discourage Investment in Intangibles?" Chapter 5 in Frank J. Fabozzi and James L. Grant (eds.), *Value-Based Metrics: Foundations and Practice* (New Hope, PA: Frank J. Fabozzi Associates, 2000).

Taken together, these financial developments show that the firm's EVA can be expressed in basic terms as:

$$EVA = NOPAT - \$WACC$$
$$= EBIT \times (1 - t) - WACC \times C$$
$$= (S - COGS - SG\&A - D) \times (1 - t) - WACC \times C$$

In the next section, we'll look at a simple income statement and balance sheet to show how to measure a firm's "EVA," absent value-based accounting adjustments that will be explained later.

4

"OK BEVERAGE COMPANY"

In an attempt to reinforce the concept of value-based measurement, we'll now apply the basic EVA formulation to a hypothetical firm called "OK Beverage Company." Exhibits 1 and 2 show the standard income statement and balance sheets for the beverage producer at an established point in time.

Looking at OK Beverage Company's financial statements from a traditional accounting perspective, it seems that the firm is a profitable beverage producer. Based on the income statement shown in Exhibit 1, the firm reports *positive* net income and earnings per share, at $8,213 and $1.31, respectively. In addition, with Stockholders' Equity at $96,600 the beverage producer's rate of return on equity (ROE) is positive, at 8.5% (8,213/96,600 × 100). Moreover, this accounting ROE results from multiplying OK-B's positive return on assets (ROA), at 5.4%, by its equity-leverage multiplier (Assets/Equity) of 1.57.

OK-B's Economic Profit

To see if OK Beverage Company is truly a profitable company—that is, a wealth creator with (discounted) positive EVA—we'll first estimate the firm's *unlevered* net operating profit after tax, NOPAT. Upon substituting the beverage pro-

EXHIBIT 1	OK Beverage Company Income Statement
	Status Quo Position
Sales	$125,000
COGS	86,000
SG&A	22,000
Interest expense	3,312
Pretax profit	13,688
Taxes (at 40%)	5,475
Net income	$8,213
Shares outstanding	6,250
EPS	$1.31

EXHIBIT 2	OK Beverage Company Balance Sheet		
Cash	750	Accounts payable	10,000
U.S. govt. securities	1,250	Wages payable	2,000
Accounts receivable	17,000	Tax accruals	2,000
Inventory	63,000	Current liabilities	14,000
Current assets	82,000	(*non*-interest bearing)	
Property (land)	4,000	Long-term debt	41,400
Net plant	15,000	(8% coupon)	
Net equipment	51,000		
Net fixed assets	70,000	Common stock at par	625
		Add'l. paid in capital	14,375
		Retained earnings	81,600
		Stockholders' equity	96,600
		Liabilities and	
Total assets	152,000	stockholders' equity	152,000

ducer's sales; cost of goods sold; selling, general, and administrative expenses, and tax rate figures into the NOPAT formulation, we obtain:[5]

$$\text{NOPAT} = (S - \text{COGS} - \text{SG\&A}) \times (1 - t)$$
$$= (125{,}000 - 86{,}000 - 22{,}000) \times (1 - 0.4) = \$10{,}200$$

In order to calculate OK-B's projected *dollar* cost of capital, the manager or investor needs to know something about (1) the after-tax cost of debt, (2) the estimated cost of equity capital, and (3) the "target" debt weight, *if any*,[6] in the firm's capital structure, and (4) the amount of invested capital employed in the beverage business. With respect to the first requirement, OK-B's after-tax cost of debt can be estimated according to:

$$\text{After-tax Debt Cost} = \text{Pre-tax Debt Cost} \times (1 - t)$$
$$= 0.08 \times (1 - 0.4) = 0.048 \text{ or } 4.8\%$$

In this expression, the pre-tax debt cost, at 8%, is taken as the firm's average coupon rate on the balance sheet (for simplicity, we assume that the firm's bonds are trading at par value). In this context, OK-B's pre-tax borrowing cost of 8% can also be obtained by dividing the firm's interest expense, $3,312, by the face amount of its long term debt, at $41,400.

In turn, we'll use the Capital Asset Pricing Model (CAPM)[7] to estimate OK-B's cost of equity capital despite its limitations. With a risk-free interest rate of 6.5%, a

---

[5] For convenience, we assume that depreciation is included in selling, general, and administrative expense account of OK Beverage.

[6] The "optimal" mix (if any) of debt and equity capital on a firm's balance sheet is a controversial issue in the study of corporate finance. An economic profit interpretation of the Miller-Modigliani hypothesis on capital structure is explained in Frank J. Fabozzi and James L. Grant, "Value-Based Metrics in Financial Theory," Chapter 2 in *Value-Based Metrics: Foundations and Practice*.

[7] William F. Sharpe, "Capital Asset Prices: A Theory of Market Equilibrium under Conditions of Risk," *Journal of Finance* (September 1964), pp. 425–442.

market-driven equity risk premium of 6%, and a common stock beta of 1.0, the firm's CAPM-based cost of equity capital becomes:

Expected return = Risk-free rate + Market risk premium × Beta
= 0.065 + 0.06 × 1.0 = 0.125 or 12.5%

Moreover, if we assume that OK-B's "target" debt-to-capital ratio is, say, 30%, the firm's weighted average cost of capital can be measured according to:

WACC = After-tax debt cost × Debt weight + Equity cost × Equity weight
= 0.048 × (0.3) + 0.125 × (0.7) = 0.102 or 10.2%

Repackaging the Balance Sheet

With knowledge of OK-B's operating capital it is possible to calculate the dollar cost of invested capital, \$WACC.[8] In this context, it is helpful to recognize that the firm's balance sheet can be "repackaged" in a way that shows the *equivalency* of the firm's operating and financial capital. Exhibit 3 illustrates this result.

Exhibit 3 shows that OK-B's operating *and* financing capital is \$138,000. The operating capital (left hand side of balance sheet) is equal to net working capital plus net plant, property, and equipment. Likewise, in the absence of EVA accounting adjustments, the financing capital is just long-term debt plus stock-holders' equity. Hence, the firm's overall dollar-cost of capital can be calculated by applying the weighted average cost of capital, at 10.2%, to either the firm's tangible operating capital or its equivalent financing source of invested capital. Whatever side of the EVA balance sheet is chosen, OK-B's *dollar* cost of capital is \$14,076:

$$\$WACC = WACC \times C = 0.102 \times 138,000 = \$14,076$$

EXHIBIT 3	OK Beverage Company Operating and Financial Capital (Aggregate Results)		
Operating Capital		**Financing Capital**	
Net working captial			
Current assets	82,000		
Current liabilities (*non*-interest bearing)	(14,000)		
	68,000	Long-term debt	41,400
Net fixed assets	70,000	Stockholders' equity	96,600
Totals	138,000		138,000

[8] In this basic EVA application, we use the terms operating capital and invested capital interchangeably. In practice, operating capital is generally viewed as invested capital less goodwill arising from premiums paid in acquisitions. For an insightful discussion of the difference between these capital measures, see Tom Copeland, Tim Koller, and Jack Murrin, *Valuation: Measuring and Managing the Value of Companies* (New York: John Wiley & Sons, 1996).

Most importantly, since OK-B's dollar cost of financing, $WACC, is higher than its unlevered net operating profit after tax, NOPAT, the firm has *negative* economic profit:

$$\text{EVA} = \text{NOPAT} - \$\text{WACC} = 10{,}200 - 14{,}076 = -\$3{,}876$$

While OK-B *looks* like a profitable beverage producer from a traditional accounting perspective, the EVA insight reveals that the firm is a (potential[9]) wealth destroyer. This happens because the firm's net operating profitability is not sufficient enough to cover the weighted average cost of debt *and* equity capital.

OK-B's Residual Return on Capital (RROC)

We can also show that OK-B has negative EVA because its underlying "residual (or surplus) return on capital," RROC, is negative. This wealth-wasting situation occurs when a firm's after-tax return on invested capital, ROC, falls short of the weighted average capital cost, WACC. To illustrate this, simply define RROC as the firm's EVA-to-Capital ratio. At -2.8%, one sees that OK-B's adverse *surplus* return on invested capital is caused by its negative economic profit:

$$\text{RROC} = \text{EVA}/\text{Capital} = -3{,}876/138{,}000 = -0.028 \text{ or } -2.8\%$$

Likewise, since EVA can be expressed as the firm's invested capital, C, times the residual return on capital, RROC, this same result is obtained by focusing on the *spread* (also referred to as the "EVA spread") between the firm's after-tax return on invested capital, ROC, and its weighted average cost of debt and equity capital, WACC:

$$\begin{aligned}\text{RROC} = \text{EVA}/C &= (\text{ROC} - \text{WACC}) \\ &= (0.074 - 0.102) = -0.028 \text{ or } -2.8\%\end{aligned}$$

In this expression, ROC, at 7.4%, results from dividing NOPAT, $10,200, by the firm's invested capital, $138,000. The WACC is the familiar cost of capital percentage of 10.2%.

OK-B's Interest Tax Subsidy

As we noted before, when looking at a firm's economic profit, it is important to use unlevered net operating profit after tax, NOPAT, in the first step of the EVA calculation. This is important because the dollar cost of invested capital (step two in the EVA calculation) already reflects the interest tax subsidy (if any) received on the firm's outstanding debt obligations. By double counting this debt-induced tax subsidy, the manager or investor would not only overestimate the firm's operating profit, but one would also impart a positive bias in the firm's enterprise value and its stock price.

To show leverage-induced bias, it is helpful to note that the levered firm's net operating profit after tax, LNOPAT, can be expressed in terms of the equivalent

---

[9] Wealth destruction occurs when persistently adverse EVA leads to negative net present value. This of course results in a decline in a company's enterprise value and its stock price.

business-risk unlevered firm's net operating profit, NOPAT, *plus* a yearly interest tax subsidy. Looking at OK-B in this levered (with debt) and unlevered (without debt) fashion yields:

$$\text{LNOPAT} = \text{NOPAT} + t \times \text{Interest}$$
$$= \$10,200 + 0.4 \times \$3,312 = \$11,525$$

In this expression, $t \times$ Interest (at \$1,325) is the yearly interest tax subsidy that OK-B receives as a levered firm, as opposed to a debt-free company. However, this *same* interest tax benefit is already reflected in the firm's dollar cost of capital through the reduced cost of corporate debt financing.

To show this, recall that OK-B's after tax cost of debt was previously expressed as:

$$\text{After-tax debt cost} = \text{Pre-tax debt cost} \times (1 - t)$$
$$= 0.08 \times (1 - 0.4) = 0.048 \text{ or } 4.8\%$$

In this formulation, the firm's pre-tax cost of debt, 8%, is reduced by 320 basis points due to the tax benefit that OK-B receives from deductibility of its debt interest expense. Expressing this leverage-induced reduction in the firm's dollar cost of capital yields the same yearly interest tax benefit that is already reflected in the beverage company's levered operating profit:

$$\$\text{WACC tax subsidy} = t \times (\text{Pre-tax debt cost}) \times \text{Debt}$$
$$= 0.4 \times (3,312/41,400) \times 41,400 = \$1,325$$

Thus, to avoid imparting leverage-induced bias, OK-B's economic profit must be calculated by *first* estimating what its net operating profit after tax, NOPAT, would be as an equivalent business-risk unlevered firm—namely, an "OK-B like" company with no business debt—and *then* subtracting the overall dollar cost of debt and equity capital from this unlevered net operating profit figure.

OK-B's EVA on a Pre-Tax Basis

If the manager or investor were inclined to calculate OK Beverage Company's EVA on a pretax basis, then the beverage producer's unlevered net operating profit before taxes, at \$17,000, would be used in conjunction with the *pre*-tax dollar cost of capital. The only complication here is that the after-tax cost of equity capital needs to be "grossed up" by one *minus* the business tax rate to convert it to a pre-tax financing rate.[10] To see how this works, note that OK-B's weighted average cost of capital can be expressed on a before tax basis as:

Pre-tax WACC
= Debt Weight × Pre-tax Debt Cost + Equity Weight × Pre-tax Equity Cost
= 0.3 × 0.08 + 0.7 × 0.125/(1 − 0.4) = 0.17 or 17%

---

[10] The pre-tax approach to estimating a firm's economic profit is helpful because the manager or investor focuses *directly* on the unlevered firm's cash operating profit without getting tangled up with tax issues arising from depreciation and other accounting complexities. However, tax considerations *do* arise when converting the after-tax cost of equity capital (CAPM or otherwise) to a pre-tax required rate of return.

In this formulation, the firm's *pre-tax* cost of equity capital is 20.8%, and its pre-tax cost of invested capital is 17%. With this development, OK-B's *pre-tax* EVA is:

$$\text{Pre-tax EVA} = \text{Pre-tax net operating profit} - \text{Pre-tax \$WACC}$$
$$= \text{EBIT} - \text{Pre-tax WACC} \times C$$
$$= \$17{,}000 - 0.17 \times \$138{,}000 = -\$6{,}460$$

Likewise, the firm's pre-tax EVA is equal to its after-tax EVA "grossed up" by one *minus* the business tax rate, t:

$$\text{Pre-tax EVA} = \text{After-tax EVA}/(1 - t)$$
$$= (-\$3{,}876)/(1 - 0.4) = -\$6{,}460$$

OK-B's Growth Opportunities

Given that OK Beverage Company has negative economic profit, the firm has a clear incentive to find a *positive* growth opportunity. In this context, let's suppose that the firm's managers discover that they can invest $20,000 in a new product distribution system that will increase yearly sales by $40,000. In turn, suppose that OK-B's cost of goods sold and selling, general, and administrative expenses will rise by $25,000 and $5,000 per annum, respectively. With these assumptions, the firm's estimated annual NOPAT will go up by $6,000:

$$\Delta\text{NOPAT} = \Delta(S - \text{COGS} - \text{SG\&A}) \times (1 - t)$$
$$= (40{,}000 - 25{,}000 - 5{,}000) \times (1 - 0.4) = \$6{,}000$$

Since the beverage producer's operating capital rises by $20,000 to support the higher sales forecast, OK-B's estimated (annual) capital costs rise by $2,040:

$$\Delta\text{\$WACC} = \text{WACC} \times \Delta C = 0.102 \times 20{,}000 = \$2{,}040$$

If sustainable, the changes in NOPAT and $WACC reveal that OK-B's growth opportunity is a desirable investment for its shareholders.[11] With these figures, OK-B's EVA rises by $3,960:

$$\Delta\text{EVA} = \Delta\text{NOPAT} - \Delta\text{\$WACC} = \$6{,}000 - \$2{,}040 = \$3{,}960$$

As a result of OK Beverage Company's investment opportunity, it is interesting to see that the firm has moved from a wealth-destroyer to a wealth-neutral position. That is, at $84 (-3,876 + $3,960), *total* EVA now exceeds zero. Among other things, this implies that the firm's revised return on invested capital, 10.3% (16,200/158,000), is now close to the overall cost of capital, 10.2%. Likewise, in this wealth neutral situation, the firm's residual return on capital, RROC, is nearly zero. Of course, with further growth opportunities, OK-B has the *potential* to become a wealth creator with *discounted* positive economic profit. In the next section, we'll look at the valuation consequences of OK-B's growth opportunity, including a basic estimate of the firm's enterprise value.

[11] In other words, the investment opportunity has discounted positive EVA (equivalently, positive NPV).

Valuation Considerations

Up to this point, we used the income and balance sheets for "OK Beverage Company" to calculate economic profit (EVA) in a basic setting. However, nothing was said about the market value of OK-B as an ongoing company. Without getting into detailed valuation considerations,[12] some simple pricing insights are obtained by assuming that investors pay an NPV (net present value) multiple of, say, *10-times* the estimated EVA[13] of "OK-B-like" companies. In the ensuing pricing application, we'll express the firm's enterprise value, V_F, as the sum of (1) the total operating capital employed in the business, C, *plus*, (2) the net present value (NPV=MVA[14]) derived from the firm's existing assets and future growth opportunity:

$$V_F = C + \text{NPV}$$

With an EVA multiplier of *10-times* OK-B's aggregate EVA of $84 (recall, $-3,876 + 3,960$), the firm's market value added is $840. Upon adding this NPV figure to its revised operating capital (with the $20,000 growth opportunity), we obtain:

$$V_F = C + \text{NPV} = 158,000 + \$840 = \$158,840$$

Summarizing these basic valuation findings: With the positive EVA growth opportunity, OK-B has moved from a wealth-waster to a wealth-neutral position. The firm's zero-expected *total* EVA is generated by a return on invested capital, ROC, that now approximately equals the weighted average cost of capital—even though ROC is higher than the firm's pre- and post-tax cost of corporate debt financing. Because of OK-B's wealth-neutral position, the firm's enterprise value-to-capital (or, in more popular terms, the "price-book" ratio) is near unity. At this point, OK-B's profitability index ratio (ROC/WACC) is also close to one. Moreover, with further EVA growth opportunities, the firm has the potential to become a wealth creator and thus witness a noticeably sharp improvement in its enterprise value and stock price. Managers and investors should take note of such positive EVA growth opportunities!

5   WAYS TO INCREASE EVA

We see that basic EVA is helpful for managers and investors because it provides a transparent look at the key features of economic profit measurement. In this context, basic EVA reveals that a company is not economically profitable until it covers its usual operating expenses and all of its financial capital costs—namely, the dollar cost of debt *and* equity capital. In this fundamental sense, EVA is superior to traditional accounting profit measures such as net income, earnings per share and

---

[12] For an explanation of the economic profit approach to enterprise and stock valuation, see James L. Grant and James A. Abate, *Focus on Value: A Corporate and Investor Guide to Wealth Creation* (New York: John Wiley & Sons, 2001).

[13] In practice, we would *first* need to make the necessary value-based accounting adjustments that we explain in an upcoming section before attempting to measure the firm's NPV, enterprise value, and of course its stock price.

   From a valuation perspective, it is worth noting that multiplying a firm's EVA by a NPV multiple of "10" is tantamount to discounting its EVA perpetuity at a rate of 10%.

[14] MVA, for market value added, is the popular equivalent of NPV. These value-added terms are used interchangeably in the EVA literature.

return on equity. Additionally, we can use basic EVA to gain some strategic insight on the steps that managers must take to permanently improve the economic profit outlook and, thereby, shareholder wealth. Active investors can also benefit by earning abnormal returns ("alpha") to the extent that a company's successful effort to improve the EVA outlook is not already impounded in stock price.[15]

There are several meaningful ways that a company can improve its economic profit outlook.[16] In this context, the basic EVA formulation suggests that wealth conscious managers should take steps to:

► increase revenue

► reduce operating expenses where prudent

► use less capital to produce the same amount of goods and services

► use more capital in the presence of *positive* growth opportunities

► reduce WACC

Expanding a firm's market share is of course captured by rising sales levels in the basic EVA formula. All other things being the same (operating expenses and capital costs), higher revenue means higher margins and thus economic profit. It should also be no surprise that reducing a company's operating expenses via cost cutting and/or achieving tax efficiency enhances economic profit because the SG&A and tax accounts go down. However, when using cost cutting as a tool to improve the EVA outlook, managers (and investors) must be cautioned that too much cost cutting, "cuts" the fabric of a company's future economic profit—and in so doing, reduces the enterprise value of the firm and its stock price.

Also, if EVA is to be taken seriously as an improvement over traditional accounting profit measures, then it must do more than just show that increasing revenue and/or reducing operating expenses will improve the firm's enterprise value and its stock price. Fortunately, this is where economic profit and traditional accounting measures depart since EVA fully "accounts" for the dollar cost of capital in terms of both the amount of operating capital employed in a business and the opportunity cost of that invested capital.

EVA emphasizes the role of invested capital as shown in the basic EVA formulation. Clearly, anything that managers can do to (1) improve inventory and net PP&E (plant, property, and equipment) turnover ratios on the balance sheet, and (2) reduce business uncertainty (as reflected in a decline in NOPAT volatility) will have beneficial dollar cost of capital implications via the impact on C and WACC, respectively. Moreover, we used the basic EVA formula to show that investing more capital in *positive* economic profit growth opportunities is really what shareholder value creation is all about.

On balance, EVA links the income statement and balance sheets with a value-based focus on net operating profit (NOPAT, from adjusted income statement) and invested capital (C, from adjusted balance sheet). Unlike accounting profit, EVA measures the dollar cost of capital by multiplying the amount of invested capital by the *overall* cost of capital. Hence, EVA measures economic profit in the classical economists notion of "profit" because the business owners' normal return on invested capital is "fully reflected" in the profit calculation. Since accounting profit accounts only for the dollar cost of debt financings, via interest expense, it completely misses the dollar cost of equity capital. This cost of

---

[15] We'll look at company (or stock) selection using value-based principles in a later section.

[16] The first four ways to improve economic profit are consistent with those emphasized in Shawn Tully, "The Real Key to Creating Wealth," *Fortune*, September 20, 1993.

financing omission is particularly important for companies that typically finance their growth opportunities with mostly equity capital—such as firms in the technology and health care fields.

6 EVA MEASUREMENT CHALLENGES

The basic EVA formulation is helpful in showing how a *value-based* metric like EVA differs from a traditional accounting measure of profit such as net income. However, the basic EVA illustration belies the *complexity* of the economic profit calculation in practice. In this context, C.S. First Boston, Goldman Sachs U.S. Equity Research, and Stern Stewart & Co. point out that there are some 160 accounting adjustments that can be made to a firm's financial statements (income and balance sheets) to convert them to a *value-based* format emphasizing cash operating profit and asset replacement cost considerations.[17] Many of the potential accounting adjustments can have a material impact on a manager or investor's estimate of a company's after-tax return on capital through their *joint* impact on NOPAT and invested capital. Additionally, there are significant empirical anomalies and academic issues that embroil the weighted average cost of capital, WACC—primarily, the cost of equity, which we touch on later.

As mentioned before, the firm's after-tax return on capital is calculated by dividing its *unlevered* net operating profit after tax, NOPAT, by the amount of invested capital employed in the business. In practice, however, there are numerous accounting items that *jointly* impact the numerator and the denominator of the ROC ratio. These potential distortions arise from the accounting-versus-economic treatment of depreciation, intangibles (including research and development and goodwill arising from corporate acquisitions), deferred income taxes, inventory costing (LIFO versus FIFO), and other equity reserve adjustments. Such EVA measurement issues are important because they impact the analyst's estimate of cash operating profit in the numerator of the after-tax return on capital (e.g., profit impact of accounting depreciation *versus* economic obsolescence) and the invested capital estimate used in the denominator of the ROC ratio (e.g., impact of net fixed assets on the balance sheet *versus* economic replacement cost of assets).[18]

7 NOPAT ADJUSTMENTS

To help reduce the complexity of the EVA calculation, Bennett Stewart offers a practical guide to estimating a firm's net operating profit after tax (NOPAT) and its invested capital.[19] In this context, he shows equivalent "bottom-up and top-down" approaches to estimating a company's net operating profit after taxes along with equivalent "asset and financing" approaches to estimating invested capital. Exhibit 4 shows some of the key accounting adjustments in the equiva-

---

[17] For example, see Steven G. Einhorn, Gabrielle Napolitano, and Abby Joseph Cohen, "EVA: A Primer," *U.S. Research* (Goldman Sachs, September 10, 1997).

[18] However, managers and investors must be careful not to get overly caught up in value-based accounting adjustments and, in so doing, miss the "big picture" perspective of economic profit measurement and valuation.

[19] See Stewart, *The Quest for Value*. Also, for a recent application of EVA with accounting adjustments, see Pamela Peterson, "Value-Based Measures of Performance," Chapter 4 in *Value-Based Metrics: Foundations and Practice.*

EXHIBIT 4	Calculation of NOPAT from Financial Statement Data

A. *Bottom-Up Approach*

Begin:

    Operating profit after depreciation and amortization

Add:

    Implied interest expense on operating leases
    Increase in LIFO reserve
    Increase in capitalized research and development
    Increase in accumulated goodwill amortization
    Increase in cumulative write-offs of special items[a]

Equals:

    Adjusted operating profit before taxes

Subtract:

    Cash operating taxes

Equals:

    NOPAT

B. *Top-Down Approach*

Begin:

    Sales

Subtract:

    Cost of goods sold
    Selling, general, and administrative expenses
    Depreciation

Add:

    Implied interest expense on operating leases
    Increase in equity reserve accounts (see above listing)
    Other operating income

Equals:

    Adjusted operating profit before taxes

Subtract:

    Cash operating taxes

Equals:

    NOPAT

---

[a] To the extent that write-offs are included in operating results rather than an extraordinary or unusual item.

Note: Exhibit based on information in G. Bennett Stewart III, *The Quest for Value* (New York: Harper Collins, 1991).

---

lent NOPAT approaches recommended by Stewart, while Exhibit 5 shows the companion accounting adjustments that must be made when estimating a company's invested capital in practice.

    In the "bottom-up" approach to estimating NOPAT (Exhibit 4), the manager or investor begins with operating profit after depreciation and amortization. This is just the familiar earnings before interest and taxes (EBIT) figure on a

EXHIBIT 5	Calculation of Capital Using Accounting Financial Statements

A. Asset Approach

Begin:

  Net short term operating assets

Add:

  Net plant and equipment
  Other assets
  LIFO reserve
  Capitalized research and development
  Accumulated goodwill amortization
  Cummulative write-offs of special items
  Present value of operating leases

Equals:

  Capital

B. Sources of Financing Approach

Begin:

  Book value of common equity

Add equity equivalents:

  Preferred stock
  Minority interest
  Deferred income tax
  Equity reserve accounts (see above listing)

Add debt and debt equivalents:

  Interest-bearing short-term debt
  Long-term debt
  Present value of operating leases

Equals:

  Capital

Note: Exhibit based on information in G. Bennett Stewart III, *The Quest for Value* (New York: Harper Collins, 1991).

---

company's income statement. To this amount, several value-based accounting adjustments are made to arrive at a closer approximation of the firm's pre-tax cash operating profit. For examples, the rise in the LIFO reserve account is added back to operating profit to adjust for the overstatement of cost of goods sold—due to an overstatement of product costing—in a period of rising prices, while the net increase in research and development expenditure is added back to operating profit to recognize that R&D investment generates a *future* stream of benefits.[20]

---

[20] In a value-based framework, R&D expenditures are generally capitalized and amortized over a useful time period such as five years—rather than expensed in the current year as if these expenditures have no future cash flow benefits.

Likewise, the change in accumulated goodwill amortization is added back to pre-tax operating profit to reflect the fact that goodwill is a form of capital investment that needs to earn a cost of capital return just like expenditures on physical capital. In a value-based (economic profit) context, annual corporate restructuring write-offs (a "special item") get added back since they are viewed as a form of restructuring "investment." Also, the implied interest expense on operating leases is added back to pre-tax operating profit to recognize that leasing is a form of debt financing. In other words, the implied interest expense on operating leases should be reflected in the firm's cost of debt financing, rather than showing up in its *unlevered* net operating profit. However, in industries where operating leases are common and similar in financial magnitude, such as in certain segments of retail for example, the manager or investor should use judgment to decide whether the leasing adjustment will materially enhance the accuracy of the economic profit calculation for company comparisons.

From an EVA tax perspective, the rise in a company's deferred tax account (obtained from the balance sheet) should be subtracted from reported income taxes to adjust for the overstatement of actual cash taxes. Also, the tax subsidies received on debt financings (including debt equivalents such as operating leases) should be added back to reported income taxes to arrive at a more accurate representation of the cash taxes paid by an *unlevered* firm. As we explained before, tax subsidies received by a company from debt financings show up in the after-tax cost of debt and must therefore be excluded in the estimation of NOPAT. Upon making the "bottom-up" accounting adjustments, Exhibit 4 shows that the manager or investor arrives at a company's NOPAT by subtracting cash operating taxes from adjusted operating profit before taxes.

Exhibit 4 also shows the "top-down" approach to estimating NOPAT. In this approach, the manager or investor begins with sales or revenue. Usual income statement items such as cost of goods sold, selling, general and administrative expenses, and depreciation[21] are then subtracted from this figure. Next, the EVA items that we mentioned before—including the rise in "equity reserve" accounts (e.g., increase in LIFO reserve and accumulated goodwill amortization) as well as the implied interest expense on operating leases—are added to the EVA income statement to obtain a more accurate measure of the firm's pre-tax cash operating profit. As with the bottom-up approach, cash operating taxes are then subtracted from adjusted operating profit before taxes to arrive at a company's net operating profit after tax (NOPAT).

Invested Capital

A look at Exhibit 5 reveals the companion EVA accounting adjustments that must be made to arrive at invested capital. Based on the "assets" approach, the manager or investor begins with net short-term operating capital. This reflects moneys tied up in current asset accounts like accounts receivables and inventories as well as a *normal* amount of cash needed for operations.[22] Current liability accounts such as accounts payable, accrued expenses, and taxes payable are netted from the short-term operating asset accounts. Notes payable are excluded from net short-term operating capital because they represent a source of debt financing. Also, their interest cost is reflected in the calculation of a company's dollar cost of capital.

---

[21] In principle, an estimate of economic depreciation should be used on EVA financial statements.

[22] Research estimates on a normal range of cash required for operations vary by industry—such as 0.5% to 2% of net sales. See Copeland, Koller, and Murrin, *Valuation: Measuring and Managing the Value of Companies*.

Net plant, property, and equipment is then added to capital along with other assets and several equity-based reserve accounts. Some managers or investors may choose to adjust property, plant, and equipment to a *gross* basis by adding back accumulated depreciation in an effort to eliminate differing depreciation policies and to approximate replacement cost of assets. Obviously, the accumulated depreciation adjustment would be made in both asset and financing approaches to calculating capital along with an appropriate annual depreciation add back to arrive at NOPAT.

As shown in Exhibit 5, the equity reserve adjustments to arrive at invested capital include (but are not limited to) the add back of LIFO reserve, accumulated goodwill amortization, capitalized research and development, and cumulative write-off of special items like restructuring and re-engineering costs. Unfortunately, some companies view a write-off of restructuring costs that result in a reduction of capital as an immediate boost to return on invested capital and then profess progress in operations. However, unless there is an outright asset disposal, with proceeds received in the sale or liquidation, then this latter adjustment is critical for objective company benchmarking and analysis. Additionally, the present value of operating leases, if any, would be added to the EVA balance sheet to arrive at a company's overall invested capital.

In the sources of "financing" approach (again, see Exhibit 5), the analyst begins with the book value of common equity. To this, he or she adds several "equity equivalent" accounts including preferred stock, minority interest, deferred income tax reserve, and the equity reserve accounts that were listed in the "assets" approach to invested capital. Debt and debt equivalents are then added to arrive at a value-based figure for invested capital. These debt-related accounts include interest bearing short-term debt, long-term debt, and (as before) the present value of operating leases. Either way—the assets or financing approach—we arrive at invested capital for use in calculation of a firm's economic profit.

Caveats

Having introduced the "conventional"[23] accounting adjustments to estimate NOPAT and invested capital, it is important to realize that we have only provided a means to estimate the after-tax return on a company's *existing* assets. This is simply NOPAT divided by invested capital. Estimates of capital returns on future growth assets will of course require similar EVA-based accounting adjustments, but just as importantly, the forecasts themselves can be highly sensitive to unforeseen industry and macroeconomic developments. In other words, an undue focus on all the value-based accounting adjustments that might be made when estimating current economic profit components (such as NOPAT) may cause the manager or investor to miss key valuation and economic profit effects from future growth assets. Moreover, since EVA is NOPAT *less* the dollar cost of capital, the manager or investor needs to consider key economic profit issues that impact the cost of invested capital. We'll highlight some WACC concerns in the context of using CAPM to estimate the cost of equity.[24]

---

[23] There are even EVA refinements that can be made to standard accounting adjustments that we cite in the text. For example, the concept of positive *and* negative economic depreciation can be used to improve economic profit estimates—especially the concept of negative depreciation for strategic investments like corporate acquisitions and R&D investments. For further discussion of these "EVA on EVA" refinements, see O'Byrne, "Does Value-Based Management Discourage Investment in Intangibles?"

[24] Further insight on economic profit and the cost of capital can be found in Fabozzi and Grant, "Value-Based Metrics in Financial Theory."

EVA MULTI-FACTOR RISK MODEL 　　　　　8

In our calculation of basic EVA, we used the CAPM to estimate the cost of equity; which in turn, is a central component of the overall weighted average cost of capital, WACC. While CAPM is a widely used formula for the pricing of investment risk, it does not fully capture risks found to systematically impact the return on stocks. This pricing omission has led to the use of multi-factor risk models that include common factors in addition to market risk (the only risk considered by the CAPM). However, currently the common factors used are based on traditional accounting measures rather than on value-based metrics.

As with the CAPM, a multi-factor risk model's output is the expected return for the stock and can therefore be used to estimate the expected return on equity in the cost of capital formula. Here we describe the common factors in addition to beta used in an EVA-based factor model approach employed by Global Asset Management to estimate the required return on common stock (cost of equity). They are size (equity capitalization), NPV-to-Capital ratio, and the standard deviation of economic profit (EVA). The inclusion of the first common factor, namely size, has considerable empirical support and is also found in the fundamental multi-factor risk models.

The second common factor, NPV-to-Capital ratio, captures the risk associated with troubled firms.[25] The NPV-to-Capital ratio is a measure of a company's ability (or lack thereof) to invest in wealth creating projects. It is therefore a measure of company *strength* or resilience. In this context, wealth creators have a high NPV-to-Capital ratio, while wealth destroyers have a low to negative NPV-to-Capital ratio. For troubled or distressed companies, NPV is low or negative due to their fundamental inability to invest in projects that have an after-tax return on invested capital (ROC) that exceeds the WACC. Consequently, it can be argued that investors require high-expected return for investing in the stocks of troubled firms—companies with low to negative NPV–while comparatively low expected return for investing in the stocks of stable and robust firms—namely, companies with attractive NPV. There is empirical support for the inclusion of this factor.[26]

The standard deviation of economic profit is included as a common factor to account for the market-adjusted volatility in a company's economic profit. In practice, the EVA-based factor model estimate of the required return on equity is combined with the after-tax cost of debt to obtain the weighted average cost of capital, WACC. At Global Asset Management, the cost of capital is viewed as a critical input in the estimation and analysis of a company's economic profit and its stock price. Moreover, we believe that EVA factors such as the NPV-to-Capital ratio and the standard deviation of economic profit are important considerations in portfolio construction, risk control, and performance measurement.

CASH FLOW RETURN ON INVESTMENT 　　　　　9

There are of course other prominent value-based metrics beyond EVA. In this context, we'll provide some basic insight on another well-known and widely used VBM—namely, Cash Flow Return on Investment (CFROI). While in theory, EVA

---

[25] We employ the NPV-to-Capital ratio rather than price-to-book value ratio typically used in multi-factor risk models for two reasons: (1) the price/book ratio is plagued by accounting problems due to book value, and, most importantly, (2) NPV is a *direct* measure of wealth creation.

[26] See, James L. Grant, *Foundations of Economic Value Added* (New Hope, PA: Frank J. Fabozzi Associates, 1997) and Ken C. Yook and George M. McCabe, "An Examination of MVA in the Cross-Section of Expected Stock Returns," *Journal of Portfolio Management* (Spring 2001), pp. 75–87.

and CFROI can be used to derive the same result for a company's economic profit, the two VBMs differ in practice in several important ways. Specifically, EVA is a dollar-based measure of economic profit while CFROI is an internal rate of return-type metric that measures the expected rate of return over the average life of a company's existing assets. Unlike EVA, CFROI uses gross cash flow and gross capital investment measures and the resulting IRR is measured in real terms as opposed to nominal terms.

Without getting into all the details, the following *five* steps can be used to estimate a company's CFROI:[27]

- ▶ compute the average life of a company's existing assets
- ▶ compute the gross cash flow
- ▶ compute the gross investment
- ▶ compute the sum of *non*-depreciating assets
- ▶ solve for the CFROI (or internal rate of return)

In the first step, the average life of a company's existing assets can be measured by dividing gross depreciable assets by depreciation expense. Next, gross cash flow is equal to net income adjusted for financing expenses—such as interest expense and operating rental payments—and *non*-cash operating expenses including depreciation and amortization. Gross cash flow also includes the changes in LIFO reserve, deferred income taxes, and other equity reserve accounts.

In turn, **gross investment** includes *gross* plant and equipment and the EVA capital adjustments that we looked at before—including LIFO reserve, capitalized research and development, accumulated goodwill amortization, restructuring charges, and the present value of operating leases (among others). Also, in the CFROI calculation, *non*-depreciating assets include net short-term operating assets (current assets *less* non-interest bearing current liabilities), land, and other *non*-depreciating assets. Following the above-mentioned procedure, managers and investors can estimate a company's (nominal[28]) cash flow return on investment. The resulting CFROI or IRR-based percentage is then compared to the (percentage) cost of capital to determine whether a company's has positive or negative economic profit. Equivalently, a manager or investor, to decide whether a company is a wealth creator or a wealth destroyer, can use the "spread" between CFROI and WACC, just like we explained before using the "EVA spread."

CFROI Application

Before moving on, we'll look at the IRR (internal rate of return) nature of cash flow return on investment. We'll explain this relationship in terms of "OK Beverage Company." Suppose that after making all the necessary accounting adjustments (equity reserve accounts and other adjustments *not* shown for sake of brevity) to estimate CFROI, we obtain the *gross* cash flow and *gross* investment information for the beverage producer shown in Exhibit 6. The IRR "keystrokes" are indicated within parentheses.

Based on the five-step procedure to estimate CFROI, we see that OK Beverage Company's CFROI is 10.08%. This figure is equivalent to the estimated after-tax

[27] For rigorous explanation and application of CFROI, see Madden, *CFROI Valuation: A Total Systems Approach to Valuing the Firm.*

[28] For simplicity, we'll look at nominal as opposed to real CFROI.

EXHIBIT 6	OK Beverage Company CFROI	
Gross investment[a] (present value)		$150,000
Gross cash flow[b] (payment)		$20,000
Non-depreciating assets[c] (future value)		$72,000
Average asset life (n)		10 years
Nominal CFROI (IRR)		10.08%

[a] Sum of gross plant and equipment, cumulative equity reserve accounts, present value of operating leases.
[b] Sum of net income, changes in equity reserve, interest and rental expense.
[c] Sum of net working capital and land.

internal rate of return (IRR) earned on the company's existing assets over a useful life of 10 years. Since OK Beverage Company's estimated CFROI just meets the firm's cost of invested capital, at 10.2% (calculated before), the firm remains in a position of wealth neutrality. Clearly, OK Beverage still needs a positive growth opportunity (as defined by CFROI *greater than* WACC) so that it can (1) (finally) become a wealth creator, and (2) experience a noticeable improvement in its enterprise value and stock price.

COMPANY SELECTION USING VBM   10

Now that we have explained the accounting and economic issues that surround value-based metrics such as EVA and CFROI, we'll demonstrate that an economic profit approach to company or security analysis has real world practical merit. In this context, we'll provide an overview of the economic profit (or value-based) approach to company analysis that has been developed by the authors and expanded upon elsewhere.[29] In this context, Exhibit 7 shows the "Excess Return on Invested Capital" versus the "Market Value of Invested Capital-to-Replacement Cost of Invested Capital"[30] for a universe of U.S. companies that we track at Global Asset Management.

In Exhibit 7, the excess return on invested capital is simply the after-tax return on invested capital (ROC, including the value-based accounting adjustments that we spoke of before) *less* the weighted average cost of capital (WACC). In this exhibit, we show the market value of invested capital (equivalently, the "enterprise value") measured relative to replacement cost of invested capital for consistency with the conventional method of evaluating companies in profitability versus "price-to book" context. There is *no* slippage of EVA focus here because

---

[29] For additional insight on security analysis using EVA, see Grant and Abate, *Focus on Value: A Corporate and Investor Guide to Wealth Creation.*

[30] Note that the "excess return on invested capital" is equivalent to the economic profit-to-capital ratio or the residual return on capital that we spoke of before. This is also referred to as the "EVA spread." Moreover, the use of market value-to-replacement cost of invested capital is really just a scaling of the NPV-to-invested capital ratio.

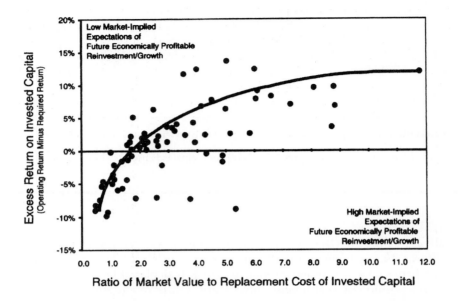

| EXHIBIT 7 | Excess Return Relative to Valuation |

Source: James L. Grant and James A. Abate, *Focus on Value: A Corporate and Investor Guide to Wealth Creation* (New York: John Wiley & Sons, 2001).

it can be shown that the market value of invested capital-to-replacement cost of invested capital is *directly* related to a company's NPV-to-invested capital.[31]

Exhibit 7 shows a scatter plot of companies measured relative to a curve of "best fit" through the data points. The data points that lie above the curve represent potentially undervalued companies (or stocks), while those data points that fall below the curve represent potentially overvalued companies. For companies that plot above the curve, Exhibit 7 suggests that at such excess return on invested capital positions, the companies should command a higher market valuation. If correct, this upward revaluation would be reflected in a rise in the market value of invested capital-to-replacement cost of invested capital ratio. In a more fundamental sense, internal or "warranted" expectation of economic profit growth for companies that plot above the curve is higher than the market implied growth rate of economic profit imbedded in current stock price.

Specifically, while the capital market at large is expecting compression in future economic profit down to the curve for any given market value-to-replacement cost of invested capital ratio, actual internal expectations of economically profitable reinvestment for combinations above the curve imply a noticeably higher valuation for any company's stock. Astute investors can expect to earn potentially positive abnormal return (alpha) on stocks that plot above the curve because of the fortuitously positive (and presumed consistent) economic profit positions of these companies.

---

[31] In principle, the enterprise value-to-invested capital ratio can be written as:

$$V/C = 1 + NPV/C$$

In this expression, V refers to enterprise value (or market value of invested capital) and C is an EVA measure of invested capital. Hence, V/C is greater than one when NPV is positive, while V/C is less than one when NPV is negative. The market value of invested capital-to-replacement cost of invested capital is also a measure of "Tobin's Q."

Conversely, for companies that plot below the curve, Exhibit 7 implies that these firms should command a lower stock market valuation. In this case, internal expectation of economic profit growth is lower than the market implied growth (rate) imbedded in current share price. Here, the capital market incorrectly expects an upward revision in economic profit to the curve for any given market value of invested capital-to-replacement cost of invested capital ratio. However, consistently low to negative expectations of economically profitable reinvestment for companies that fall below the curve implies a lower stock valuation. Active-minded investors should thus look elsewhere if they are restricted to a "long only" position in common stocks. Taken together, we see that the stocks of companies that plot above the curve are potential buy opportunities, while stocks that plot below the curve are potential sell (or short sell) candidates. On a more sophisticated note, the "longs" and "shorts" can be combined into an economic profit approach to long-short investing.

PRACTICE PROBLEMS FOR READING 50

Questions 1-6 relate to Robert Davenport and are based on Readings 40, 49, and 50

Robert Davenport, CFA, is preparing a new investment report on Master Appliance for 2006. Master Appliance is a U.S. company operating in the home appliance industry.

Condensed data from the 31 December 2004 and 2005 balance sheets and from the 2005 income statement are shown in Exhibits 1 and 2. For these financial statements, Davenport has determined that assets and liabilities are at fair value and the clean surplus relation holds.

EXHIBIT 1	Master Appliance Condensed Balance Sheets at 31 December (US$ millions)	
	2005	**2004**
Total current assets	8,920	8,665
Fixed assets, net	4,901	4,584
Total assets	13,821	13,249
Current liabilities (non-interest-bearing)	2,016	1,936
Long-term debt	3,192	3,188
Shareholders' equity	8,613	8,125
Total liabilities and shareholders' equity	13,821	13,249

EXHIBIT 2	Master Appliance Condensed Income Statement Year Ended 31 December 2005 (US$ millions except for share data)	
Operating income (EBIT)	1,633
Interest expense	240
Income before taxes	1,393
Income tax (30%)	418
Net income	975
Dividends per share	$0.60
Number of shares outstanding (millions)	812

Master Appliance's share price was $10.00 per share on 31 December 2005. The cost of equity capital (r) is 12.0 percent and the after-tax weighted average cost of capital (WACC) is 10.1 percent.

Davenport will focus on value-based metrics and residual income valuation. Before preparing his report, Davenport collects the following information on Master Appliance:

▶ Davenport forecasts a negative $50 million residual income for Master Appliance for each of the years 2006, 2007, and 2008, and zero residual income thereafter.

▶ Master Appliance has already announced several new projects that will greatly increase the size of the company. Davenport expects that shareholder value for Master Appliance will decrease despite the new projects and larger company size.

Davenport turns his attention to the valuation of Harker Electric, a Master Appliance competitor. Davenport prepares a basic scenario for Harker Electric, shown in Exhibit 3. He then values Harker Electric's equity using the value-based metrics approach and the franchise value approach.

EXHIBIT 3	Harker Electric Valuation Data
Return on equity[a]	14%
Growth rate of earnings[a]	7%
Cost of equity capital	12.5%
Pre-tax WACC	11.3%
After-tax WACC	10.6%
Book value per share	$12.00
Market value per share	$14.00

[a] Assumed to remain constant indefinitely.

Davenport is concerned that any of the following changes may cause Harker Electric's franchise P/E value to fall:

▶ A new tax that reduces the ROE without affecting the cost of equity capital.
▶ The cost of equity capital decreases.
▶ The market value per share of the company decreases.
▶ The company lowers its earnings retention ratio.

1. Master Appliance's residual income in 2005 was *closest* to
   A. –$ 59.
   B. $0.
   C. $154.
   D. $168.

2. Davenport's *best* estimate of the expected ratio of the intrinsic value of Master Appliance equity to its book value as of the end of 2005 is
   A. less than zero.
   B. greater than zero but less than one.
   C. equal to one.
   D. greater than one.

2006 exam

3. Which of the following results from value-based metrics would best support Davenport's belief about the effect of new projects and larger company size on Master Appliance's shareholder value?

A. Economic Value Added (EVA®) spread > 0.

B. Cash flow return on investment (CFROI) > 0.

C. Dollar WACC > Net operating profit after taxes.

D. Return on equity (ROE) > Cost of equity capital (r).

2006 exam

4. Given the basic scenario, Harker Electric's intrinsic value per share, using the residual income valuation model, is *closest* to

A. $12.00.

B. $15.27.

C. $19.53.

D. $23.33.

2006 exam

5. Given the basic scenario, Harker Electric's franchise P/E value is closest to

A. 1.09.

B. 2.00.

C. 8.00.

D. 9.09.

2006 exam

6. The change that *least* justifies Davenport's concern that the franchise P/E value of Harker Electric might fall relates to the

A. new tax.

B. cost of equity capital.

C. market value per share.

D. earnings retention ratio.

INVESTMENT ANALYSIS
by James D. Shilling

LEARNING OUTCOMES

The candidate should be able to:

a. illustrate, for a particular type of real property investment: its main value determinants, investment characteristics, principal risks, and its most likely investor;

b. evaluate a real estate investment using net present value (NPV) and internal rate of return (IRR) analysis from the perspective of an equity investor;

c. calculate the after-tax cash flow and the after-tax equity reversion from real estate properties;

d. explain the potential problems in using IRR as a measurement tool in real estate investments.

Buy land. They ain't making any more of the stuff.

—*Will Rogers, American humorist*

OPTIONAL SEGMENT BEGINS

Investors have varying goals depending on their available resources (mainly money), age, and decision-making horizon. A recent college graduate with $5,000 to invest differs from an established family with investment experience and $100,000 to invest. An elderly person with $500,000 looking for an investment opportunity would be in still another class.

Some investors may want the comfort and convenience of owning a personal residence free-and-clear of any debt. Others may seek to own real estate as protection against inflation. Still others may enter real estate as a way of building prestige and maximizing wealth.

Real Estate, Thirteenth Edition, by James D. Shilling. Copyright © 2002 by Thomson South-Western. Reprinted with permission of South-Western, a division of Thomson Learning.

563

Investors also operate subject to constraints or limitations. Age, analytical ability, executive ability, energy level, work preferences, and time availability all act as constraints on an investor. A young person can afford a longer time horizon than can an elderly person. A person with limited time or energy is probably best advised to invest in a medium requiring little effort. Likewise, a person with limited ability to analyze and administer investments is better off avoiding active investments, meaning most real estate investments. Locational preferences as personal constraints are self-explanatory.

Note that we make simple, everyday decisions about what to eat or wear or do, about whom to see or where to go, by feel, habit, hunch, or intuition. Actions generally flow out of the decisions in a very natural manner. As situations become more complex, it becomes worthwhile to devote more time to identifying alternatives and their implications prior to making a decision and taking action. It also becomes worthwhile to devote more time to administering or implementing the decision. The benefits of a good decision or the costs of a bad decision become great enough at some point to warrant spending extra time, money, and effort to reach the best choice.

Real estate decisions clearly warrant spending extra time, money, and effort to reach the best choice. On a long-term basis, the investment must be reviewed periodically to determine if past choices and actions are working out. Often this means comparing the risks and rates of return from stocks and bonds with the risks and rates of return from real estate; it is a portfolio management concern. Additional or larger real estate investments may eventually be desirable. Investment in different types of properties may also become advantageous.

In this reading we devote considerable attention to identifying real estate investment opportunities and making investment decisions. Here we will assume that the property to be acquired is 100 percent equity-financed, meaning that the property is purchased for all cash.

1   WHY INVEST IN REAL ESTATE?

Many of the advantages of real estate as an investment are in its surrounding traditions and institutions.

Leverage   *Leverage* is the use of borrowed money to increase the rate of return earned from an equity real estate investment. Traditionally, real estate investors have been able to borrow up to 90 percent of the value of any property owned or acquired. Nowadays, because of the tightening of the credit markets for any new development, even the best financiers of real estate are rarely able to borrow more than 60 to 75 percent of the value of the property acquired. Nonetheless, leverage can be advantageous when the investment earns a higher rate of return than the interest on the borrowed money.

Leverage also enables an investor to control more property with a given amount of money. An investor can leverage by stretching out the repayment schedule or by refinancing. By maintaining high leverage, an investor may pyramid investments more quickly. **Pyramiding** is controlling additional property through reinvestment, refinancing, and exchanging. The objective is to control the maximum value in property with the least resources. Needless to say, pyramiding carries a high risk of a total wipe-out during a recession.

Tax Shelter   Tax depreciation, installment sales, and tax-deferred exchanges all enable a real estate investor to minimize or defer income taxes.

Purchasing Power Protection   Real estate usually offers protection against inflation. Whereas most capital assets tend to lose value in terms of purchasing power or constant dollars in inflationary periods, adequately improved realty, especially apartments, shopping centers, and selected commercial properties, tend to gain value as measured in constant dollars. In the absence of rent and **price controls**, real property, like a ship upon ocean waters, floats above its purchasing power-constant dollar line irrespective of depth or rise in the level of prices. For this real-value holding power to be true of a specific parcel of income real estate, the property must be well located, have rentals that can be adjusted periodically, and not be subject to sudden sharp increases in operating costs.

Pride of Ownership   Many real estate investors gain identity by being "in the game" or by being "shrewd operators." Some investors also realize great satisfaction from owning something tangible that can be touched, felt, and shown to friends and relatives.

Control   The immediate and direct control of an owner over realty enables the owner or an agent to make continuing decisions about the property as a financial asset and as a productive property. This control enables the investor to manage property to meet personal goals, whether they are to maintain the property as a showpiece for pride of ownership or to operate the property for maximum rate of return. Many owners experience a great sense of power and independence in this control.

Entrepreneurial Profit   A last important advantage is that added value may be realized by building or rehabilitating a property, and the added value is immediately invested in the property without being taxed. Thus, many investors also develop property. Other investors combine real estate investing with brokerage or property management.

RATIONAL INVESTOR VERSUS ECONOMIC-BEING ASSUMPTION

2

The person making the real estate investment decision is assumed to be a rational investor. The assumptions about this rational investor are generally consistent with the *economic person* theory commonly found in economics. Each acts in self-interest. Each is strongly influenced by the institutional environment. But there are differences.

An economic person is defined in economic literature as a primary decision-maker motivated to maximize his or her economic return. The economic person has an uncanny knowledge of the alternatives and of what to expect under varying production, cost, and pricing strategies. In this sense, the economic person looks at the use of land resources from the viewpoint of the typical investor.

A *rational investor* operates under slightly different assumptions than does the economic person. Knowledge is less than total, which means that risk and uncertainty are present. Also, institutional considerations (laws and taxes, mainly) affect investors individually and specifically. These differences are the major reasons why the viewpoint of an individual, rational investor is preferred in making decisions about real estate as a financial asset.

The goal of maximizing self-interest (wealth) is an important assumption for our rational investor. The concept of a rational investor was developed shortly after World War II by Herbert Simon, who won a Nobel Prize for his work in economic and decision theory in 1978. Acting in self-interest, a rational investor always selects the choice or alternative within his or her range of knowledge that gives the greatest personal advantage. A rational investor will also anticipate the future and incorporate any expected changes into the current market price of real estate.

Note that self-interest is neither good nor bad, desirable nor undesirable, per se. In a sense, self-interest is to people as gravity is to the earth. Gravity may keep us from flying at will and require us to exert energy to conquer distance or elevation, but gravity also works to our advantage. It causes rain to fall and rivers to flow downhill. We turn gravity to our advantage in our work and play when we irrigate gardens, ski, skydive, or play ball.

Self-interest is a force or motivation that causes us to try to maximize our satisfactions in life. We seek leisure, self-expression, travel, company of loved ones, thrills from skydiving, or social changes out of self-interest. Most of us seek money only as an intermediate goal. In our complex society, an investor seeking profits may be making a contribution to society as great as or even greater than a doctor seeking fees or a politician seeking power.

Self-interest acts to push real estate to its highest-and-best use. *Highest-and-best use* is that legal and possible land use that gives it its greatest present value while preserving its utility. A *land use* is that activity by which a parcel of real estate is made productive—that is, it generates services of value—as a residential, commercial, or industrial property.

Highest-and-best use of a parcel to one investor in the market may well differ from the highest-and-best use of another investor because of differences in what each is seeking to maximize. This difference is the major reason why a financial approach rather than an economic approach to real estate investment is needed. Using a financial approach provides us with a highly useful model for numerous investment decisions about real estate as an asset.

3   HOW DO DIFFERENT PROPERTY TYPES STACK UP?

Differing property types offer distinct advantages to specific investors. Figure 1 summarizes these comments.

Vacant or Raw Land

Land is only one of several alternatives open to an investor. Supply is limited; demand is growing; therefore, investing in land is a sure thing. While generally valid, this argument is also limited.

The return from land must be realized through value appreciation, which depends on supply and demand. The supply of land is limited. But the supply of urban land may be increased simply by extending roads, water and sewer lines, and electrical services.

Demand for land depends on expansion of demand in the specific community. Location relative to local road and travel patterns goes far to determine the demand for a specific parcel of realty. Finally, planning, zoning, and probable highest-and-best use greatly determine chances for value enhancement.

Land is passive and illiquid as an investment medium. Low loan-to-value ratios make it difficult to leverage land highly. Owning land gives no tax depreciation, and carrying costs must be capitalized. In that land earns little or no income, an investor must pay carrying costs from other income. Such an investment is sometimes called an "alligator" because it has to be fed. If the owner suffers reduced income, a distress sale may be necessary. The rate and amount of value appreciation likely to occur over a period adds additional uncertainty to investment in land.

The most likely investors in land are speculators for short-term gains and developers for long-term operating needs. Estates and others seeking a store of value and an easily managed hedge against inflation are also likely investor types for land.

Apartments

The number of households and income levels are the primary determinants of value for residential real estate. Some apartment buildings also realize value based on prestige considerations. Location, convenience, and environment also greatly influence value.

Apartments require moderately active attention as an investment. Apartments are more liquid than most realty investments because investors are more knowledgeable about residential properties than other types of property. Thus, with more investors, the market is broader. Also, high leverage is possible; up to 90 percent, and sometimes higher, loan-to-value ratios are possible. The rate of return may be enhanced both by periodic receipt of income and increase in value.

Apartments offer a good inflation hedge because apartment leases are adjusted annually (compared to three-to-ten-year terms common on other property types). Apartment performance has been less volatile than most other property types. Occupancy levels over the long term have rarely dropped below 90 percent. The commodity nature of apartments tends to produce a more efficient market.

The major risks in apartment investment are during the start-up period of new properties and in obtaining or providing quality management on a continuing basis. For large complexes, professional management is almost a must because of the considerable know-how required and the need to avoid harassment from tenants and others. Smaller properties, roughly 12 units or less, may be managed and maintained by an owner with adequate time. Personal management gives the owner closer control, in addition to "psychological payment" for the services rendered.

The competition from single family homes as an alternative to renting is often cited as a main deterrent to apartment investment. Apartment construction has declined steadily since 1985. Multifamily starts peaked in 1985 at 576,000 units. Multifamily starts dropped to a 35-year low of 138,000 units in 1991 (see Figure 2). In many communities, current construction has not kept pace with demolition and conversion.

FIGURE 1   Generalized Characteristics of Real Property Investment Types

Property Type	Main Value Determinants	Investment Characteristics	Principal Risks	Most Likely Investor Type
Vacant or raw land	Expansion of demand Convenient location Travel patterns Planning/zoning/highest-and-best use	Passive Illiquid Limited leverage Rate of return by value appreciation No tax depreciation Capital gains taxation Expenses capitalized	Carrying costs: "alligator" Value appreciation uncertain	Speculator Developer Estate as store of value
Residential rentals (apartments)	Expanding population Rising incomes Location: convenience, favorable exposure Prestige, sometimes important	Moderately liquid High leverage (loan-to-value ratio) Rate of return by periodic income and value appreciation Tax depreciation Ordinary and capital gains taxation	Start up when new Management: probably necessary to hire professional for larger projects	High income: benefiting from tax shelter Suitable for anyone but must be able to put up equity investment
Office buildings	Expanding local economy Location linkages Prestige/status sometimes important Tenant mix compatibility	Active, unless leased to one firm Moderately liquid Rate of return by periodic income and value appreciation Tax depreciation Ordinary and capital gains taxation	Start up when new Management: high level of service provided Competitive facilities Obsolescence Shift in location of business activity	High income: needing tax shelter Suitable for anyone if professional management hired and able to put up initial equity investment
Warehouses	Commercial/industrial activity	Most passive: often on long-term lease	Obsolescence due to changes in material handling equipment and technology	Retired: desiring both cash flow and limited management

Property Type	Main Value Determinants	Investment Characteristics	Principal Risks	Most Likely Investor Type
	Location for ease of movement Structural design to endure change	Moderately liquid Moderate leverage Rate of return mainly by periodic income Tax depreciation Ordinary and capital gains taxation		Anyone desiring tax shelter who has adequate initial equity capital
Neighborhood shopping centers	Community growth Effective demand: population and income Convenient location relative to competition Adequate parking Tenant mix relative to spending patterns Effective lease negotiation	Moderately active Liquidity limited Moderate leverage Rate of return by periodic income and value appreciation Tax depreciation Ordinary and capital gains taxation	Start up: getting proper tenant mix Management: need to provide adequate level of service Vacancies Competitive facilities Obsolescence	Reasonably wealthy: need to make large equity investment Anyone able to use tax shelter plus other benefits
Hotels/motels	Location: linkages and convenience Demand: conference, tourist, resort, business Mix of facilities and services	Active Moderately liquid Moderate to poor leverage Rate of return periodic income and value appreciation Tax depreciation Ordinary and capital gains taxation	Management: high tenant turnover (professional management almost a necessity) Competing facilities	Anyone able to use tax shelter and with adequate initial equity capital Smaller properties suitable for investors also willing to manage and maintain

FIGURE 2   Multifamily Housing

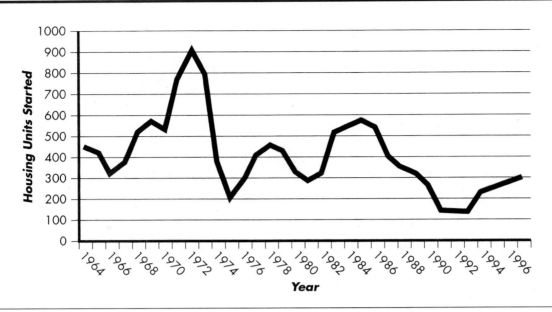

Source: www.census.gov/ftp/pub/const/www/c20index.html.

Development of multifamily units tends to be somewhat difficult. Land zoned for multifamily use in most communities is scarce. Moreover, government regulations for new apartment development are becoming more stringent, increasing the cost of new construction. In-fill properties in strong markets where single family alternatives are relatively expensive are where you can often find monopolistic opportunities.

The assisted living rental housing market is one of the fastest growing markets in the United States today. Assisted living residences are housing environments that provide individualized health and personal care assistance in a home-like setting. The level of care provided is between that provided in congregate housing (housing with meal services) and a skilled nursing home. Most assisted living residences are targeted toward individuals needing help preparing meals, bathing, and dressing. Assisted living residences also are targeted toward individuals requiring some health care assistance or monitoring, or individuals needing transportation to doctors, shopping, and personal business. Demand for assisted living housing is extraordinary. Supply is somewhat limited, however. Most attempts to build assisted living facilities divide nearby residents and advocates of affordable housing for the elderly.

Office Buildings

The value of office buildings depends heavily on the business health of the area. A convenient location, a compatible tenant mix, and a prestigious image also add to value. Office buildings generally require active participation of an owner unless leased to a single party, because tenant demands must be dealt with. Liquidity and leverage are generally moderate. The rate of return is produced both by periodic receipt of income and value appreciation.

The main risks with an office property are during start-up, maintaining high-quality management, and obsolescence, most of which are within the control of the owner. Shifts in location of business activity and development of competitive facilities are risks outside the direct influence of the owner.

Likely owners of large office buildings are wealthy or high-income investors who are likely to have the high initial equity investment required, as is implied by the moderate leverage. Public and private business organizations are often formed to own office buildings, thereby opening the investment opportunity to persons of more moderate means.

For most office buildings, it is difficult to say which comes first, the building or the lease. Lenders normally want leases first. They want these leases to provide security for their loans. Leases with AAA tenants provide better collateral than leases to local tenants.

New York City has the highest rents per square foot in downtown office markets in the United States, while Shreveport, Louisiana has the lowest. Not only does New York City lead the way in terms of rents per square feet in a downtown office market, it also has the highest expenses (including cleaning expenses, repairs/maintenance, utilities, roads/grounds, security, and administration).

Lease terms in most office buildings are staggered—not all tenants can move at the same time. Moreover, a long-term tenant may want room to expand in the future, therefore planning that his or her immediate neighbors will be given short-term leases. Having long-term office leases that run for five or 10 years and carry options to renew for 10 or 20 years more means that it will normally take a few years to obtain a rent structure that will be quite close to the final stable one. In a recovering office market, then, increases in net operating income will tend to lag behind increases in asking rents.

Vacancies have a big impact on office rents. Office vacancy rates currently are as low as they have been since the early 1980s. The consequence has been steadily rising office rents and prices, often at a double-digit pace (see Figure 3). Of course, whether this trend continues is the most significant long-term risk to

FIGURE 3 Prices and Rents per Square Foot of Office Space

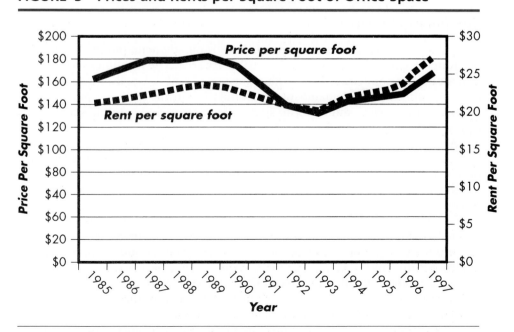

Source: National Real Estate Index, National CBD Office Market.

the office market. If the supply of new office space once again were to outstrip the absorption of new space, vacancy rates would rise, and rents and prices could easily fall.

Warehouses

Warehouses obviously depend heavily on the level of commercial and industrial activity for value. To maintain value, warehouses must be designed and built to accommodate changes in the methods of handling materials. Ceilings too low and aisles too narrow to accommodate forklift trucks caused many warehouses to become obsolete in the 1950s and 1960s, for example. Warehouse value also depends on a location that allows easy movement through a community.

A warehouse on long-term lease to one firm tends to be a passive investment. Leverage and liquidity are moderate. Cash flow tends to be somewhat higher as a proportion of value than with some other improved properties because less value appreciation is expected. In turn, people desiring high cash flow and limited management requirements find warehouses an excellent investment. In most other respects, warehouses are similar to apartment and office buildings.

REITs and institutional investors tend to favor larger and more modern facilities. For these properties, debt financing is readily available. The most active industrial warehouse markets appear to be the Southeast. Industrial warehouse space is relatively inexpensive to build, which makes the warehouse market prone to conditions of oversupply.

Another advantage of an industrial warehouse building is its low lease rollover cost. When one tenant moves out and another tenant moves in, there is very little that an industrial warehouse landlord needs to do with that space in order to make it reuseable. It also is an area that can grow on its own, especially given the shift that is taking place in the United States from an economy dealing with hard goods to an economy dealing with information, entertainment, and communications.

Shopping Centers

The value of shopping centers depends heavily on adequate purchasing power, meaning people and incomes, in their tributary area. The location must be convenient for the population and parking must be plentiful. Finally, the tenant mix must be suited to the demands of the population in the tributary area. Supermarkets, small variety and discount stores, restaurants, and gasoline stations are typical tenants.

Active management is required to establish and maintain a center. Effective lease negotiation is important. Liquidity is limited because few investors have the broad knowledge needed to manage a center; also, leverage is moderate. The tax treatment of shopping center investment is similar to that of other commercial properties. Vacancies and lease negotiation, obsolescence, and development of competitive facilities are the main risks of center ownership. Also, as with office buildings, a reasonably large equity investment is required. In other respects, any investor seeking periodic income and capital gains would find shopping center investment inviting.

Figure 4 shows the number of centers in six size categories, together with the average gross leaseable area for each category and the average sales per square foot for each category. As can be seen, most shopping centers are fairly small, less than 100,001 square feet. Total annual sales in shopping centers are around $980 billion, representing 55 percent of all non-automotive retail sales in the nation.

FIGURE 4   Shopping Center Census

Average Center Size (in square feet)	Number of Centers	Percent of Total	Total Sales (in billion $)	Average Gross Leaseable Area per Center	Sales per Square Foot
Less than 100,001	26,928	62.69%	$285	48,951	215.9
100,001–200,000	10,400	24.21%	$249	137,594	173.98
200,001–400,000	3,595	8.37%	$150	266,902	155.99
400,001–800,000	1,324	3.08%	$127	556,178	172.39
800,001–1,000,000	316	0.74%	$62	901,206	219.38
More than 1,000,000	390	0.91%	$107	1,281,277	214.90
Total	42,953	100.00%	$980	121,749	187.4

One drawback of shopping centers is that most anchor tenants require substantial inducement to become part of the center. These inducements have included: free land for the store site, with the anchor tenant erecting its own store, or tenancy in a store custom built to the anchor tenant's requirements at a rental rate that produces no economic return to the developer. In some cases, major tenants also are able to negotiate large signing bonuses—dollars that tenants have used to buy inventory with. To offset these low rental tenancies and inducements, it is necessary for shopping center developers to include in the center a large amount of space rented to small chains and independent retailers paying a high rental rate. These stores are often relegated to inferior locations in the center. They also tend to be higher risk tenants.

Financing for a shopping center generally cannot be obtained until leases with the anchor tenants are finalized. Shopping center financing also tends to be contingent on receiving a minimum or base rental. Without this minimum or base rental, most permanent lenders are unwilling to make a mortgage on a shopping center.

Hotels and Motels

Hotels and motels depend primarily on tourist and business travelers for their demand. In recent years it has been in vogue to hold business conferences in large hotels. Having a location and the facilities to satisfy this demand with ease is a large determinant of value.

Hotels and motels are active investments with limited liquidity and offer moderate-to-poor leverage. They receive tax treatment as business property.

Major risks in hotel and motel investment are maintaining adequate size and competent management. Economies of scale apply. And high tenant turnover means that management must be effective. Obsolescence and the development of more adequate competing facilities are also major risks.

Large hotels and motels require considerable equity investment and, therefore, are limited to REITs and wealthy investors. Smaller properties are suitable for less affluent investors who are also willing to manage and maintain the property.

There are three types of hotels: limited service hotels, mid-priced limited service hotels, and traditional full service hotels. Limited service hotels offer guests the amenities that they need while omitting those amenities not wanted. Mid-priced

FIGURE 5   Hotel Room Occupancy and Room Rental Rates

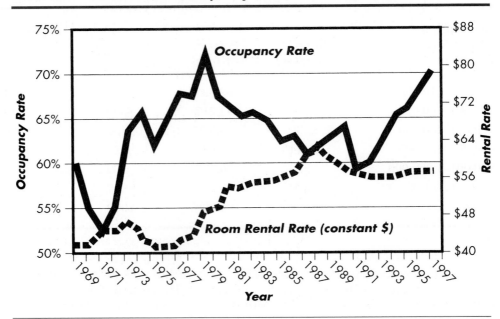

Source: William C. Wheaton and Lawrence Rossoff, "The Cyclic Behavior of the U.S. Lodging Industry," *Real Estate Economics,* 26: 1988, 67–82.

limited service hotels provide guests with a slightly higher level of amenities at a higher price. Traditional full service hotels offer a full range of guest services.

Demand for hotel night stays—the measure of lodging demand—moves very closely with the level of economic activity. This is because most overnight stays are business related. The desire to maximize profits leads most hotels to not fully book up space with (low-rate) plan-in-advance business travel. Most hotels, instead, prefer to hold some inventory for the more variable (high-rate) walk-in traveler.

Hotel room occupancy rates and room rental rates (constant dollars) are shown in Figure 5. As can be seen, occupancy rates can be quite cyclic. One reason for the cycles seems to be the slow adjustment of room rates and the long delivery lags with supply. Part of the long delivery lags with supply reflects considerable planning and/or site assembly times.

4   HOW SPECIFIC INVESTMENTS ARE ANALYZED

Why are buildings like the Bank of America building in San Francisco or New York's Rockefeller Center eagerly sought by investors? The answer seems clear: they are the best in their markets. They are the most attractive, rentable, and efficient. Also, they generally yield a handsome rate of return.

By way of contrast, why are no-frills older buildings, with mixed or low tenant prestige, poor design, inferior locations, and below-average workmanship and materials often sought by investors? The answer: even the worst properties in a market can yield an attractive rate of return if priced appropriately.

The point to note is that, after all things are considered, most decisions to invest in real estate are undertaken to earn a profit. One widely used criterion for measuring whether a specific project is likely to earn a profit over and above a normal required rate of return is known as the *net present value rule.*

Let us look more closely at the net present value (*NPV*) criterion. Net present value is simply the difference between the present value of benefits and the market value or cost of the investment. If we define $ATCF_t$ as the expected *after-tax cash flow* generated by the property in period t and $ATER$ as the *after-tax equity reversion* due on sale, we may write:

$$NPV = \text{Present worth of cash flows} - \text{Equity investment}$$

$$NPV = \frac{ACTF_1}{(1 + r_a)^1} + \frac{ACTF_2}{(1 + r_a)^2} + \cdots + \frac{ACTF_n}{(1 + r_a)^n} + \frac{ATER}{(1 + r_a)^n} - I$$

where r_a denotes the required after-tax rate of return on the property and I is the equity cost of the investment.[1]

The *NPV* formula tells us if *NPV* > 0 or if *NPV* = 0, then buy. The rationale is as follows: a positive *NPV* means that the present worth of the property is greater than the equity cost of the investment; hence, the position of the equity investor is improved by undertaking the investment. A zero *NPV* means that the wealth of the equity investor is unaffected. Projects with zero *NPV* are a matter of indifference and, consequently, should be undertaken. In either of these circumstances, the buyer's investment goals will be realized or exceeded.

If *NPV* < 0, then don't invest. A negative *NPV* means that the investment is worth less than it costs. In this situation, the investor would not invest since the investment is not expected to earn the required rate of return if purchased at the market value.

NET PRESENT VALUE ANALYSIS FOR DOUGLAS MANOR APARTMENTS—AN EXAMPLE

5

Our case property, Douglas Manor Apartments, will be used to illustrate the elements and techniques of *NPV* analysis, with cash flows on an after-tax basis. The viewpoint is that of the equity investor.

The data or information needed to determine investment value, plus any additional assumptions or inputs for Douglas Manor Apartments, are stated here in summary form for easy reference. Figure 6 provides a summary of projected cash flows and market value levels for the Douglas Manor Apartments. What follows is summary data:

1. Net operating income is $64,000.

2. The purchase price of Douglas Manor Apartments is taken to be $525,000 (rounded).

3. Improvements are assumed to make up 85.9 percent of the $525,000 purchase price, or $451,000. Using a 27.5-year life, with straight-line cost recovery as required by the Tax Reform Act of 1986, gives $16,399 per year of tax depreciation.

4. Equity contribution: $131,250.

---

[1] For ease of exposition, we have assumed that the project's discount rate, r_a, is a constant across all periods. It is a simple matter, however, to allow r_a to vary from period to period.

FIGURE 6   Douglas Manor Apartments: Projected Cash Flows and Market Value Levels

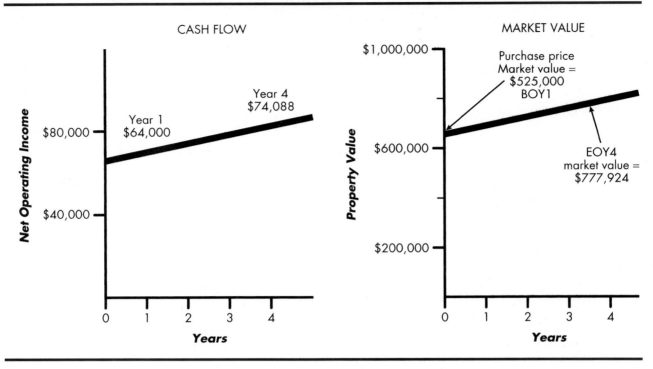

5. Debt contribution: a fixed-rate mortgage is obtained for $393,750 at 8 percent per annum (compounded monthly) for 30 years. The monthly payment to amortize this loan is $2,889.20. The loan-to-value ratio is 75 percent.

6. The investors are assumed to have a 36 percent marginal income tax rate. The investor's capital gains tax rate is 20 percent. Recaptured depreciation will be taxed at the rate of 25 percent.

7. The investors have a minimum of 12 percent per year after-tax required rate of return on any equity investment.

8. The property is assumed to be held for only four years, during which time its net operating income is expected to increase at 5 percent per year. The end-of-year 4 market value, which is also the disposition price, is expected to be $777,924. Disposition or selling costs at the end of year 4 are assumed to be 7 percent of the sales price. The outstanding loan balance at the end of year 4 is $xxxxxx (rounded).

9. Annual compounding is used for the equity time-value-of-money calculations.

We begin by calculating the investment value of Douglas Manor Apartments. Investment value equals the present value of the cash flow from operations, plus the present value of the reversion upon sale at the end of the holding period, discounted at the investor's required rate of return.

Note that with circumstances unique to an individual investor, such as being in a favorable tax position or having access to available financing at a below-market interest rate, the investment value of the property can conceivably exceed the market value of the property. This can also happen when individual investors are motivated by reasons other than wealth maximization for investing in a specific real estate project. In many instances real estate investors are willing to accept a lower rate of return on their investment in return for certain other intangible or subjective benefits, which are often difficult to quantify.

PROCESS USED TO DETERMINE AFTER-TAX CASH FLOW AND AFTER-TAX EQUITY REVERSION

6

The process used to calculate the after-tax cash flow (*ATCF*) from operations and the after-tax equity reversion (*ATER*) is illustrated below and in Figure 7.

Step 1: Determining Tax Payable

Generally speaking, taxable income from real estate equals net operating income less the depreciation expense and less interest paid on money borrowed to finance the property.

Depreciation expense, you may recall, is a tax-deductible allowance to account for the decline in value or useful life of the real estate resulting from wear, tear, obsolescence, or actions of the elements. Depreciation expense can be taken regardless of whether the equity investor is leveraged. Interest expense, on the other hand, can be taken only if you borrow money to finance the purchase. Annual interest expense can be calculated as the year's total debt service payments less the change in principal balance over this same period. Multiplying the taxable income by the marginal income tax rate gives the tax payable on income from the property.

Figures 8 and 9 give a detailed cash-flow projection for the Douglas Manor Apartments, including the calculation of the income tax payable by an owner in a 36 percent tax bracket.

FIGURE 7 Process for Calculating Tax Payable and After-Tax Cash Flow

Calculation of Tax Payable		Calculation of After-Tax Cash Flow	
Potential gross income	$		
Less: Vacancy and collection losses	_____		
Effective gross income	$		
Less: Operating expenses	_____		
Net operating income	$	Net operating income	$ _____
Less: Tax depreciation		Less: Annual debt service	_____
Less: Interest on loan	_____		
Taxable income	$	Before-tax cash flow	$
Multiplied by tax rate		Less: Tax payable	_____
Tax payable	$ _____	After-tax cash flow	$ _____

FIGURE 8   Douglas Manor Apartments: Calculation of Annual Tax on Income for an Equity Owner in 36 Percent Tax Bracket

	Year			
	1	2	3	4
Net operating income	$64,000	$67,200	$70,560	$74,088
Less: Straight-line tax depreciation	−16,399	−16,399	−16,399	−16,399
Less: Interest paid	−31,381	−31,108	−30,812	−30,492
Taxable income	$16,220	$19,693	$23,349	$27,197
Times: Tax rate	×36%	×36%	×36%	×36%
Income tax payable	$5,839	$7,089	$8,406	$9,791

For year 1, taxable income is $16,220 and income tax payable is $5,839:

Net operating income	$64,000
Less: Depreciation	$16,399
Less: Interest paid	$31,381
Taxable income	$16,220
Times: Income tax rate	× 0.36
Income tax payable (tax savings)	$5,839

By year 4 in Figure 8, *NOI* has increased so that the Douglas Manor Apartments has taxes payable of $9,791.

Step 2: Determining After-Tax Cash Flow

The next step in the analysis is to determine *ATCF* from the property for each year of ownership. Generally speaking, *before-tax cash flow* (*BTCF*) equals *NOI* less annual debt service. Subtracting the tax payable on income from operations yields the *ATCF* that can be pocketed.

Having financed 75 percent of the purchase price with debt, the *BTCF* will equal *NOI* less the required annual debt service payment to the lender.

FIGURE 9   Douglas Manor Apartments: Calculation of After-Tax Cash Flows from Operations

	Year			
	1	2	3	4
Net operating income	$64,000	$67,200	$70,560	$74,088
Less: Annual debt service	−34,670	−34,670	−34,670	−34,670
Before-tax cash flow	$29,330	$32,530	$35,890	$39,418
Less: Tax payable	($5,839)	($7,089)	($8,406)	($9,791)
After-tax cash flow	$23,491	$25,441	$27,484	$29,627

For year 1, annual debt service payments of $34,670 are deducted from a *NOI* of $64,000 resulting in a *BTCF*-to-equity of $29,330. Deducting the income tax payable from *BTCF* gives an *ATCF* of $23,491:

Net operating income	$64,000
Less: Annual debt service	$34,670
Before-tax cash flow	$29,330
Less: Income tax payable	$5,839
After-tax cash flow	$23,491

By year 4, *ATCF* has increased to $29,627.

Step 3: After-Tax Equity Reversion

After-tax equity reversion equals sale price less disposition costs, less the amortized mortgage balance, if any, and less capital gains taxes.

Let us look now at the projected disposition or sale of Douglas Manor Apartments. The calculations are summarized in Figure 10. Douglas Manor Apartments is projected to have increased in value by more than 48 percent, so a disposition sale price of $777,924 is realized. This figure is arrived at by taking the expected *NOI* for year 5, $77,792, and dividing by a 10 percent overall capitalization rate.

FIGURE 10   Douglas Manor Apartments: Calculation of End of Year 4 Taxes Due on Sale and After Tax Equity Reversion

Sales price, end-of-year 4		$777,924
Less: Selling expenses @ 7.0%		54,455
Net sales price		$723,469
Less: Adjusted basis		
Purchase price	$525,000	
Less: Accumulated depreciation	65,596	$459,404
Gain realized on sale		$264,065
Gain realized on sale		$264,065
Less: Depreciation recaptured		$65,596
Gain recognized on sale		$198,469
Tax on depreciation recapture	$65,596 × 25% =	$16,399
Tax on capital gain	$198,469 × 20% =	39,694
Taxes due on sale		$56,093
Sales price, end-of-year 4		$777,924
Less: Selling expenses @ 7.0%		54,455
Net sales price		$723,469
Less: Mortgage balance outstanding		378,862
Before-tax equity reversion		$344,607
Less: Taxes due on sale		56,093
After-tax equity reversion		$288,514

The mortgage balance at the end of four years is $378,862. The long-term capital gain realized on the sale is $264,065. Of this gain, $65,596 is subject to depreciation recapture and the remaining $198,469 is a long-term capital gain. Total taxes payable are $56,093. Total payments deducted from the sales price amount to $110,548 (selling expense of $54,455 plus taxes payable of $56,093), which leaves a net after-tax equity reversion of $288,514.

7 NET PRESENT VALUE

At a 12 percent required rate of return, the net present value of Douglas Manor Apartments is $131,752:

$$NPV = \frac{\$23,491}{(1+.12)^1} + \frac{\$25,441}{(1+.12)^2} + \frac{\$27,484}{(1+.12)^3}$$
$$+ \frac{\$29,627}{(1+.12)^4} + \frac{\$288,514}{(1+.12)^4} - \$131,250 = \$131,752$$

For decision purposes, the rule is that *NPV* must be zero or positive for a go decision to invest. Thus, in this case, the decision rule says invest.

At a 38 percent required rate of return, we get a present value for the cash flows of $128,560. In turn, *NPV* of the investment is a negative $2,690:

$$NPV = \frac{\$23,491}{(1+.38)^1} + \frac{\$25,441}{(1+.38)^2} + \frac{\$27,484}{(1+.38)^3} + \frac{\$29,627}{(1+.38)^4}$$
$$+ \frac{\$288,514}{(1+.38)^4} - \$131,250 = (\$2,690)$$

In this case, the decision rule says "do not invest."

8 INTERNAL RATE OF RETURN

The internal rate of return is sometimes used as an alternative to *NPV* in making financial decisions. The *internal rate of return* (*IRR*) is that rate of return that discounts future cash flows to the exact amount of the investment. Stated another way, if used in *NPV* analysis, *IRR* would result in a *NPV* of zero.

Let us calculate *IRR* for Douglas Manor Apartments. We already have enough information to approximate it. The present value of the cash flows at 12 percent is $263,002, and at 38 percent it is $128,560. The equity investment cash outlay is $131,250; therefore, *NPV* of the cash flows at 12 percent is $131,752, and it is ($2,690) at 38 percent. Thus, we know that *IRR* is somewhere between 12 and 38 percent. By trial and error, we find that *IRR* is:

$$NPV = \frac{\$23,491}{(1+.3714)^1} + \frac{\$25,441}{(1+.3714)^2} + \frac{\$27,484}{(1+.3714)^3}$$
$$+ \frac{\$29,627}{(1+.3714)^4} + \frac{\$288,514}{(1+.3714)^4} - \$131,250 = 0$$

or 37.14 percent after tax. The same result could be obtained either through the use of a financial calculator or by interpolation.[2]

The decision rule for *IRR* is that if *IRR* is greater than or equal to the required rate of return, the investment should be made. Since the *IRR* of 37.14 percent exceeds 12 percent, the investment should be made.

NEGOTIATION AND RATE OF RETURN   9

What options are available when *IRR* is less than the investor's required rate of return? The decision rule for *IRR* would say "do not invest." Possible alternatives are to renegotiate a lower purchase price or shift some of the risk.

Frequent negotiation between the buyer and seller is likely when the *IRR* is less than the investor's required rate of return. It is a fair assumption that the owner will want to sell for as much as possible and is unlikely to accept less than market value. In turn, the investor will want to buy for as little as possible.

Successful negotiating involves the following four steps:

1. An investor must understand his or her personal goals and negotiating style. What are the relative priorities of the goals? What negotiating style best achieves the goals?

2. The property must be understood. What is its highest investment value to me as a buyer-investor? What is the lowest price at which as an owner, I will sell (market value, unless in distress)? What influence will terms have on these prices?

3. The investor must know the opponent and his or her goals. When buying, look in the public records to find out how much the seller paid for the property and how long it has been owned. Is the owner's tax depreciation about used up? Also, estimate the owner's mortgage balance and terms, if not included in the listing. Are there other liens against the property? Under how much pressure to sell is the owner?

4. Don't buy real estate, buy a set of financial assumptions. Some real estate locations are better than other locations. Likewise, some buildings are more attractive than other buildings. Yet, no matter how good the site or attractive the building, unless you are able to earn a suitable return on investment, you should not invest in real estate. This statement is true regardless of whether this is your first investment in real estate or your twentieth

---

[2] The target *NPV* value equals $131,752 at 12 percent and ($2,690) at 38 percent. By interpolation, then, the approximate *IRR* is calculated as follows: the difference between *NPV* at 12 percent and 38 percent is:

Difference between *NPV* @ 12% and 38% = $131,752 − ($2,690) = $134,442

Likewise, the difference between *NPV* at 12 percent and IRR% (by definition) is

Difference between *NPV* @ 12% and *IRR*% = $131,752 − 0 = $131,752

This implies an approximate *IRR* of:

Approximate *IRR*% = 12% + (38% − 12%)$\frac{\$131,752}{\$134,442}$ = 37.48%

By calculator, the *IRR* is 37.14% after tax.

investment in real estate, or whether you are investing U.S. capital in the United States, French capital in France, or German capital in Germany, or some combination thereof. You never should buy real estate unless the property has a return that is higher than the cost of debt, and has a high or a higher value to you than it does to the seller. Also recognize that a lot of assumptions go into forecasting the value of a property, and that it is unrealistic to expect every one of these forecasts to be achieved. Thus, if you cannot buy the assumptions as presented, you cannot afford the real estate about which those assumptions were made. Of course, once a bargain is struck, you should look for ways in which to improve upon the exchange by modifying terms. Cooperative negotiations are better for both parties in the long run.

Clearly, undue pressure on a buyer or seller, differences in negotiating ability, or lack of adequate information might result in an agreed price being above or below market value.

10 A CAUTION ABOUT BEING TOO OPTIMISTIC

Being overly optimistic in your forecasts can lead to artificially inflated *NPV*s. Thus, when in doubt, always look first to the marketplace for objective information about market rents and expenses, and a market-derived discount rate. A positive *NPV* may simply be an indication that either something has been left out of normal operating expenses, like reserves and replacements for a new roof or new fixtures, or market rents have been overstated. Of course, a positive *NPV* may be indicative of monopoly profits, but don't expect these monopoly profits to last forever. Whenever there are positive excess profits to be made, supply will usually increase, thereby exerting downward pressure on market rents and profit levels.

If your development project is large enough, you will also have to worry about how the increased supply of new space will affect market rents. In such circumstances it will not be good enough simply to look at market rents in forecasting expected revenues; instead, one must estimate *ex post market rents*—that is, market rents after the new supply has been added to the market. Only in instances where you are reasonably protected by local zoning, or in the case of a regional shopping center, by a natural monopoly, do you not have to worry about increased competition exerting downward pressure on rents and profit levels.

11 A CAUTION ABOUT RELYING TOO HEAVILY ON INTERNAL RATE OF RETURN ANALYSIS

IRR analysis is fraught with potential problems when the cash flows from investment start out positive and then become negative. In this case *IRR* may have multiple roots—one positive and one negative. *IRR* analysis may also be misleading when comparing investments of different size or varying durations. Some examples follow.

Multiple Solutions

Most real estate projects will have a unique rate of return, which implies the *NPV* function crosses the horizontal axis once, and only once. To illustrate, consider the following real estate project:

Project A: $2 Million Office Building

Year	ATCF ($000's)	ATER ($000's)
0	($2,000)	
1	$400	
2	$400	$2,000

If the required rate of return is 10 percent after tax, what is *NPV*? The calculation of *NPV* is:

$$NPV = \frac{\$400,000}{(1 + .10)} + \frac{\$400,000}{(1 + .10)^2} + \frac{\$2,000,000}{(1 + .10)^2} - \$2,000,000 = \$347,000$$

If you plot a graph like Figure 11, you will find that *NPV* decreases as the discount rate increases. You can also see in Figure 11 that *IRR* is 20 percent after tax.

FIGURE 11   Relationship between *NPV* and Required Rate of Return for $2 Million Office Building

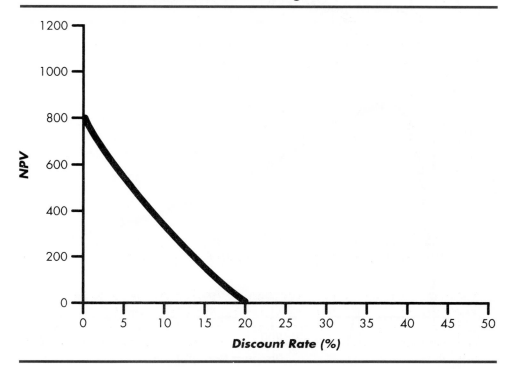

Now compare this investment to a $2 million coal mine, with the following cash flows:

Project B: $2 Million Coal Mine		
Year	ATCF ($000's)	ATER ($000's)
0	($2,000)	
1	$12,000	
2	$0	($11,000)

This project has an *IRR* of both 13 and 387 percent (see Figure 12). The two *IRR*s come about because the project generates $12 million in year 1 and then requires the investor to pay out $11 million in year 2.

Different Scales of Investment

NPV and *IRR* analysis will rank mutually exclusive projects differently when the scale of investment is different. To illustrate, consider the following mutually exclusive real estate investments:

FIGURE 12   Relationship between *NPV* and Required Rate of Return for $2 Million Coal Mine

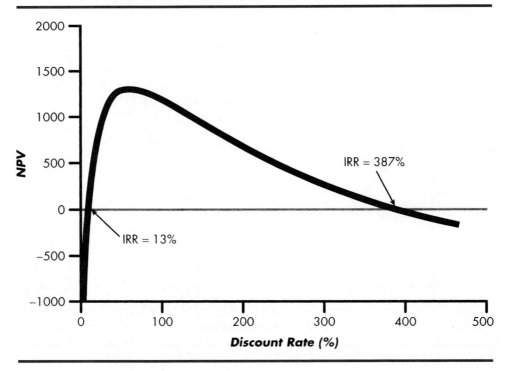

Two Mutually Exclusive Real Estate Projects with Different Scales of Investment

Year	Garden Apartments ATCF ($000's)	Garden Apartments ATER ($000's)	Office Building ATCF ($000's)	Office Building ATER ($000's)
0	($1,000)		($11,000)	
1	$505		$5,000	
2	$505		$5,000	
3	$505	$0	$5,000	$0
IRR	24%		17%	
NPV @ 10%	$256		$1,434	

Here the *IRR* decision rule ranks the $1 million garden apartments (the smaller project) higher; its *IRR* is 24 percent, while the *IRR* for the $11 million office building is 17 percent. In comparison, the *NPV* decision rule favors the $11 million office building (the larger project); its *NPV* is $1.434 million, while the *NPV* for the garden apartments is $0.256 million.

Given this conflict, which project should be accepted? Is it better to go with the garden apartments or the office building? Clearly, the answer depends on how much money the investor has. The answer also depends on the investor's discount rate.

Let us assume that the equity investor has sufficient cash to undertake either investment. We shall also assume that the investor's required rate of return on both projects is 10 percent after tax. Next, to show why the office building investment (the larger project) should be accepted, let us look at the differential cash flows between the two projects.

Differential Cash Flows between Garden Apartments and Office Building

Year	Office Building less Garden Apartments Cash Flows ($000's)
0	($10,000)
1	$4,495
2	$4,495
3	$4,495
IRR	16.58%
NPV @ 10%	$1,178

This hypothetical investment has a cost of $10 million (the added cost of undertaking the office building). The *NPV* on this incremental investment is $1.178 million and generates your required 10 percent after-tax return; therefore, you should prefer the office building to the garden apartments.

Timing of Cash Flows Is Different

Even if the initial cash outlays are the same, the *NPV* and *IRR* ranking may vary if the cash flow patterns are very different.

Two Mutually Exclusive Retail Shopping Centers with Different Timing of the Cash Flows

	Center A		Center B	
Year	ATCF ($000's)	ATER ($000's)	ATCF ($000's)	ATER ($000's)
0	($100)		($100)	
1	$20		$100	
3	$20	$100	$0	$31.25
IRR	20%		25%	
NPV @ 10%	$17.3		$16.7	

As can be seen, center A has a higher *NPV*, but center B has a higher *IRR*. Again, there is a conflict between *NPV* and *IRR*.

So which project should be selected? To answer this question, we start with the differential cash flows between the two projects.

Differential Cash Flows for Retail Shopping Center

Year	Center A less Center B ($000's)
0	$0
1	($80)
2	$88.75
NPV @ 10%	$0.62

The *NPV* of the incremental cash flows is $620,000; therefore, you should undertake center A rather than center B.

On a long-term basis, the investment must be reviewed periodically to determine if the past choices and actions are working out. This means comparing risks and rates of return from stocks and bonds with the risks and rates of return from real estate which is a portfolio-management strategy concern.

SUMMARY

Investment analysis attempts to ascertain the *NPV* of a property to a specific investor, based on available financing, desired rate of return, tax position, and other assumptions unique to the investor. *NPV* is the difference between the equity cost of an investment and the present value of the cash flows from the investment, discounted at the investor's required rate of return:

$$NPV = \frac{ATCF_1}{(1 + r_a)^1} + \frac{ATCF_2}{(1 + r_a)^2} + \cdots + \frac{ATCF_n}{(1 + r_a)^n} + \frac{ATER}{(1 + r_a)^n} - I$$

The decision rule is that *NPV* must be zero or positive in order for the investment to be undertaken; otherwise, the investment should be rejected.

IRR is sometimes used as an alternative to *NPV* analysis. The *IRR* of an investment is that rate of return that discounts future cash flows to the exact amount of the investment or, stated another way, it is the return on the property. The decision rule for *IRR* is that if *IRR* is greater than or equal to the required rate of return, the investment should be made; otherwise, the investment should be rejected.

INCOME PROPERTY ANALYSIS AND APPRAISAL

by James D. Shilling

LEARNING OUTCOMES

The candidate should be able to:

a. explain the relationship between a real estate capitalization rate and discount rate;

b. determine the capitalization rate by the market-extraction method, band-of-investment method, and built-up method and justify the use of each technique in capitalization rate determination;

c. estimate the market value of a real estate investment using the direct income capitalization approach and the gross income multiplier technique;

d. contrast the limitations of the direct capitalization approach to those of the gross income multiplier technique.

There are few sorrows, however poignant, in which a good income is of no avail.

—*Logan Pearsall Smith*

In this reading, our attention is directed to the estimation of market value for income-producing property. Income-producing real estate is generally owned as an investment. In turn, the value of any income property is a direct result of the quality, amount, and duration of the income it generates. That is, the higher the earning power of a property, the greater its value.

Valuing income properties involves estimating both market value and investment value. *Investment value* is the value to a specific investor and is akin to subjective value, or value in use. Market value is the most probable selling price and is equivalent to objective value or value in exchange. Market value is based on impersonal, detached, market-oriented data and assumptions;

Real Estate, Thirteenth Edition, by James D. Shilling. Copyright © 2002 by Thomson South-Western. Reprinted with permission of South-Western, a division of Thomson Learning.

investment value, on the other hand, depends on data and assumptions that are personal and subjective. Market and investment value may coincide if the data and assumptions of the specific investor are the same as those of the typical investor in the market.

Market value is clearly the focal point of almost any real estate decision. Whether buying, selling, investing, developing, lending, exchanging, renting, assessing, or acquiring property for public use, market value needs to be known for the decision and action to be sound.

1   HOW INCOME PROPERTIES ARE VALUED

The market value of an income-producing property is the present value of an expected cash flow stream. This is usually written as:

$$MV_0 = \sum_{t=1}^{n} \frac{NOI_t}{(1 + r)^t} + \frac{MV_n}{(1 + r)^n}$$

where MV_0 is the current market value of the property, NOI_t is the property's net operating income at time t, MV_n is the expected sales price of the property at the end of n period, and n is some finite holding period. Here we ignore the effects of selling expenses on the net sales proceeds at disposition. The term Σ is a shorthand notation for the word *summation*. Therefore, the equation above could also be written as:

$$MV_0 = \frac{NOI_1}{(1 + r)^1} + \frac{NOI_2}{(1 + r)^2} + \cdots + \frac{NOI_n}{(1 + r)^n} + \frac{MV_n}{(1 + r)^n}$$

Notice that if this price formula holds, then investors n periods from now will also determine MV_n by looking at the property's net operating income and its expected sales proceeds over the m-period holding period from $t = n + 1$ to $t = n + m$. This means that we can express MV_n in terms of NOI_t and $MV_n + {}_m$

$$MV_n = \sum_{t=n+1}^{n+m} \frac{NOI_t}{(1 + r)^{t-n}} + \frac{MV_{n+m}}{(1 + r)^m}$$

The same is true for the value of the property when it is resold at time $n + m$

$$MV_{n+m} = \sum_{t=n+m+1}^{n+m+k} \frac{NOI_t}{(1 + r)^{t-n-k}} + \frac{MV_{n+m+k}}{(1 + r)^k}$$

In this case we assume that the property will be held for k periods; that is, from time $n + m + 1$ to time $n + m + k$.

In principle, with an infinite horizon and an infinite chain of investors succeeding each other, the market value of the property is:

$$MV_0 = \sum_{t=1}^{\infty} \frac{NOI_t}{(1 + r)^t}$$

where the sign ∞ is used to indicate infinity.

FIGURE 1   Steps in the Direct Capitalization Approach to Estimating Market Value

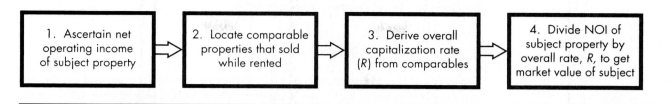

This discounted cash flow formula for the market value of real estate reduces to:

$$MV_0 = \frac{NOI}{r - g} = \frac{NOI}{R_0}$$

assuming *NOI* is growing at a constant rate, *g*, and $g < r$. In valuation terminology, the above expression is known as the *direct income capitalization approach* and $R_0 = r - g$ is known as the *capitalization rate* or *going-in rate*. The idea of direct income capitalization is to convert a stream of expected future income payments into a lump sum, or capital, value. See Figure 1 for the steps involved.

RELATIONSHIP BETWEEN DISCOUNT RATES AND CAPITALIZATION RATES

2

It is extremely important to distinguish between discount rates and capitalization rates. Discount rates represent the required rate of return, or yield, on real estate. For a retail shopping center, for example, pretax yields might range from 11 to 15 percent, depending on the risk involved. On a high-rise suburban office building pretax yields might range from 12 to 17 percent.

Capitalization rates, on the other hand, are net of value appreciation or depreciation. In times of rapid inflation, a very low capitalization rate is likely. Also, experience has shown that capitalization rates vary over time with the fluctuation in interest rates. To illustrate, consider the recent acquisition of South Hills Village Mall, one of Pittsburgh's oldest enclosed malls, by the New York-based O'Connor Group. The O'Connor Group purchased the 24-year-old mall on behalf of Shopping Center Associates, an investment group, and an unidentified investor.

Suppose the O'Connor Group expects to earn an 11 percent pretax return on the investment. Further suppose that South Hills Village Mall is expected to appreciate by 3.5 percent per annum. This means:

$$R_0 = r - g$$
$$= 11\% - 3.5\% = 7.5\%$$

The R_0 in this example is 7.5 percent. But the expected pretax rate of return on investment is 11 percent. The lower R_0 gives a higher value, reflecting favorable future income and/or capital gains expectations.

Notice that we could have just as easily dealt with the situation in which South Hills Village Mall was expected to depreciate by 3.5 percent per annum. In this case the overall capitalization rate is:

$$R_0 = r - g$$
$$= 11\% - (-3.5\%) = 14.5\%$$

The effect of this assumption is to raise, rather than lower, the overall capitalization rate and to lower appraised value for a given NOI. The negative 3.5 percent premium in this case represents a **recapture premium**—that is, an amortization of the building component. This is as it should be; absent inflation, NOI must also provide for a return *of* the invested capital. Otherwise there would be no mechanism by which investors could recapture the building's future depreciation.

There is also the possibility that with a 25-year remaining economic life, South Hills Village Mall could depreciate in real terms by 1.5 percent per annum, while appreciating in nominal terms by 3.5 percent per annum. The net (of depreciation) recapture rate in this case is 2 percent and the overall capitalization rate applicable to the building is:

$$R_0 = r - g$$
$$= 11\% - 2\% = 9\%$$

Appropriate capitalization rates are clearly influenced by the conditions under which the particular investment is being operated. Capitalization rates are also affected by prevailing interest rates, availability of funds, and risk.

3 DERIVING THE CAPITALIZATION RATE

Market-Extraction Method

Direct income capitalization is most meaningful when the capitalization rate is derived from the market. This is called the *market-extraction method.*

Assuming comparable income properties can be found, the only information required about each property is its net operating income and its sale price. Dividing the sale price into the net operating income yields:

$$R_0 = r - g = \frac{NOI}{MV_0}$$

This is really only a reversal of the process of estimating MV_0. With three comparable office buildings, the calculations might be as follows:

For comparable 1 $R_0 = \dfrac{\$594,000}{\$6,000,000} = 0.0990$, or 9.9%

For comparable 2 $R_0 = \dfrac{\$748,000}{\$7,400,000} = 0.1011$, or 10.01%

For comparable 3 $R_0 = \dfrac{\$465,000}{\$4,680,000} = 0.0994$, or 9.94%

On the basis of these three ratios, an overall capitalization rate of 10 percent would seem to be a reasonable reflection of what the market is actually doing.

Given an estimate of R_0, finding the indicated market value of an income-producing property is straightforward. The NOI of the subject property is divided by the market-derived overall capitalization rate, R_0.

The proper calculation is:

$$MV_0 = \frac{NOI}{.1000} = \frac{\$780{,}000}{.1000} = \$7{,}800{,}000$$

assuming that NOI in a stabilized year of operation for the subject property is $780,000. With R_0 equal to 10 percent, we obtain an indicated market value of $7,800,000.

Band-of-Investment Method

Under the **band-of-investment method**, individual rates of interest applicable to properties that use both debt and equity financing are weighted to arrive at the market rate of capitalization. To illustrate: assuming that first mortgage loans are made for up to 65 percent of property value at 8 percent interest for 20 years (monthly compounding), and that the equity balance requires a return of 12 percent—after provision for appreciation or depreciation—to be financially attractive to owners or investors, then the market rate would be as follows:

1. We know that the lender will require an 8 percent return on all funds advanced. We also know that the lender requires that the first mortgage loan be amortized over 20 years, with monthly compounding. Thus, we must set aside an annuity each month to pay off the mortgage at the end of 20 years. The amount of the annuity at 8 percent interest for 20 years is:

$$\text{Return of capital to lender} = \frac{i}{(1+i)^n - 1}$$
$$= \frac{.08/12}{(1 + .08/12)^{240} - 1}$$
$$= .0017 \text{ per month}$$
$$= .0017 \times 12 = .0204 \text{ per annum}$$

This fraction is known as a **sinking fund factor**—that is, it is the amount that must be set aside each period to have $1 at the end of 20 years if we are paying an 8 percent rate. This fraction can also be computed using a financial calculator. Simply enter $1 for future value, $8\% \div 12$ for interest rate, $20 \times 12 = 240$ for the number of periods, and solve for the annuity payment. Then multiply by 12 to convert to an annual interest rate factor.

The total required payment to the lender is thus:

$$\text{Mortgage constant} = \text{return on funds} + \text{return of capital to lender}$$
$$= .08 + .0204$$
$$= 10.04\%$$

2. We know that the equity investor requires a return of 12 percent after provision for appreciation or depreciation. Thus, the weighted average rate is:

Split Interest	Percent of Value		Split Rate	Weighted Rate
First mortgage	65%	×	10.04%	= 6.53%
Equity	35%	×	12.00%	= 4.20%
Total	1.00			10.73%

If the net income of a property were $800,000 per annum, then the capitalized value of that income at 10.73 percent would be $800,000 divided by .1073, or $7,455,732. The income of $800,000 would be distributed as follows:

Split Interest	Value		Rate of Earning	Dollar Earnings
First mortgage	$4,846,226	×	10.04%	= $487,000
Equity	$2,609,506	×	12.00%	= $313,000
Total	$7,455,732			$800,000

It is to be emphasized that the weighted average rate (10.73 percent in this example) represents an *overall capitalization rate* for the property. It applies to any property that is 65 percent debt-financed that is priced to yield a total required payment to the lender of 10.04 percent and a cash-on-cash return to the equity investor of 12 percent. This 12 percent cash-on-cash return to the equity investor is known as the **equity dividend rate**.

Built-Up Method

Under the *built-up method,* the rate of capitalization would be a composite of the following: (1) pure interest, e.g., interest that can be secured on government bonds (adjusted for the tax savings associated with real estate); (2) rate for nonliquidity, e.g., rate necessary to compensate for relative inability to cash in the investment; (3) a recapture premium, e.g., a return of investment or an adjustment for appreciation; and (4) rate of risk. The risk rate varies with the type of investment.

To illustrate, the rate applicable to an equity property may be composed as follows:

Pure interest	6.50 percent
Nonliquidity	1.00 percent
Recapture premium	2.00 percent
Risk (of loss)	2.00 percent
Total	11.50 percent

The recapture premium in this case provides for a 2 percent return of investment, net of appreciation. This adjustment to the pure interest rate accounts for the fact that improvements have limited lives. It also supposedly accounts for the value of the land 10, 30, 50, or more years in the future, when its availability, free from present structural improvements, may be counted on, and it also accounts for any appreciation or depreciation in the value of the improvements.

Here is a simple example: we will make the following assumptions to demonstrate the application of the built-up method of capitalization.

Net operating income	$130,000
Anticipated economic life of structure	50 years
Pure interest rate	6.50%
Nonliquidity premium	2.00%
Recapture premium	2.00%
Risk premium	1.50%

The built-up rate is thus:

$$R_0 = 6.50\% + 2.00\% + 2.00\% + 1.50\% = 12.00\%$$

which provides for an amortization rate of 2 percent per year (under the assumption that the property is expected to last fifty years).

The capitalized value of net income is:

$$MV = \frac{NOI}{R_0}$$
$$= \frac{\$130,000}{.12}$$
$$= \$1,083,333$$

The higher the built-up rate of capitalization when applied to a given income, the lower the restaurant value. To illustrate, suppose the built-up rate of capitalization were equal to 18 percent. With no change in net income, the capitalized value would be:

$$MV = \frac{NOI}{R_0}$$
$$= \frac{\$130,000}{.18}$$
$$= \$722,222$$

To be conservative, therefore, many appraisers use a high built-up rate for capitalization of net income.

LIMITATIONS OF DIRECT CAPITALIZATION   **4**

The chief difficulty in the direct capitalization approach to value lies in the selection of a capitalization rate. In order to make the maximum use of the capitalization approach, the capitalization rate must accurately reflect the behavior of investors in the marketplace. This difficulty might explain why appraisers typically regard the capitalization rate as a ratio that is derived from the market. Recall that the ratio of net operating income to value is a direct measure of the capitalization rate on a specific property. Where such data are available and of sufficient quality, viewing the capitalization rate as a ratio provides the most compelling evidence of the equity yields necessary to attract potential investors. Where the data on net operating income or value are lacking, or are not clear, as frequently happens, the appraiser must select a capitalization rate by considering the equity yield rates and financing conditions available, plus the possibility of increased rentals and capital appreciation. In selecting a capitalization rate, certainty of the returns, the relative case of liquidation of the investment, the relative burden of managing the investment, and the possibility of producing tax-sheltered cash flow must also be considered.

Also note that the income approach to value, as a rule, is limited to property that is used primarily for income or investment purposes. It does not provide an accurate valuation of owner-occupied homes because the benefits or amenities derived by owners are difficult to measure in terms of dollars, or even as hypothetical rental income. For apartment houses, commercial, or industrial properties, however, the income approach is applicable.

5   GROSS INCOME MULTIPLIER TECHNIQUE

The *gross income multiplier technique* is also used primarily for income-producing properties. A *gross income multiplier* (GIM) relates total annual income to market value. The basic steps in the GIM technique are: (1) ascertain the gross annual market income of the subject property, (2) derive a GIM from the market, and (3) apply the GIM to the subject property to estimate its market value. For small, one- to four-family residential properties, monthly rental is commonly used instead of gross annual market income.

Derivation of the market GIM is equivalent to extracting the market capitalization rate. That is, sales prices of comparable properties are divided by their respective gross annual incomes to get a range of GIMs. Sample calculations follow.

Suppose we collected a sample of three comparable brownstone rental dwelling units. The term *brownstone* is used as a generic word to denote small, urban, multiple dwellings (up to 10 units) that either are rented or sold as condominiums. These buildings may also be called *graystones* or *townhouses*. Dividing sales price by the gross annual market income gives a GIM. The calculations are:

$$GIM \text{ for a property } = \frac{\text{Sales price}}{\text{Gross annual income}}$$

$$GIM, \text{ comparable } 1 = \frac{\$610,000}{\$101,400} = 6.02$$

$$GIM, \text{ comparable } 2 = \frac{\$745,760}{\$124,500} = 5.99$$

$$GIM, \text{ comparable } 3 = \frac{\$680,000}{\$113,200} = 6.01$$

On the basis of these calculations, a market GIM of 6.00 seems reasonable for brownstone units in this particular neighborhood at this time.

Applying the market GIM to the gross annual income of the subject property, \$108,000, gives an indicated market value of:

$$\text{Indicated market value} = \text{Gross income} \times \text{Market-derived GIM}$$
$$= \$108,000 \times 6.00 = \$648,000$$

LIMITATIONS OF THE GIM TECHNIQUE 6

One of the major limitations of the gross income multiplier approach is that sales of some types of income properties occur infrequently; thus, the derivation of a market GIM must be based on limited information. In addition, rental data are not always available for deriving the multiplier. Another limitation is that gross rents are used instead of net operating income; if the building-to-land ratios differ, or if the buildings are different ages, the results may be distorted. Further, the GIM is subject to some distortion because adverse zoning, lack of maintenance, or heavy property taxes will negatively influence sale price with little effect on rental levels. Thus, unless the comparables are similar in all respects, a distorted GIM may be derived from the market. Finally, the technique is not useful for properties that are unique or that generate income in the form of amenities.

SUMMARY

The procedure whereby the market value of income-producing property is calculated by capitalizing the annual net income generated by the property at an overall capitalization rate is known as direct capitalization. The process can be summarized as follows:

$$MV_0 = \frac{NOI}{R_0}$$

where MV_0 is market value, NOI is annual net income, and R_0 is the capitalization rate necessary to attract investors.

The capitalization rate represents the required rate of return, or yield, on real estate, less the possibility of capital appreciation. Also considered by investors in selecting a capitalization rate are the certainty of the returns, the relative ease of liquidation of the investment, the relative burden of managing the investment, and the possibility of producing tax-sheltered cash flow. In order to make maximum use of the direct capitalization approach, the capitalization rate must accurately reflect the behavior of investors in the marketplace.

An alternative, income approach to value is the gross income multiplier (GIM) technique. The GIM approach to value relates total annual income to market value. The basic formula is:

Indicated market value = Gross income × Market-derived GIM

The GIM multiplier is derived by looking at the sales prices of comparable properties, divided by their respective gross annual incomes.

EVALUATING THE PERFORMANCE OF YOUR HEDGE FUNDS

by Vinh Q. Tran

LEARNING OUTCOMES

The candidate should be able to:

a. discuss how the characteristics of hedge funds affect traditional methods of performance measurements;

b. compare and contrast the use of market indexes, hedge fund indexes, and positive risk-free rates as means to evaluating hedge fund performance.

In assessing hedge funds' performance, not only rates of return are important, but risks, or, more accurately, changes in the risk profiles of the funds, are crucial. Among funds of funds, it is a well-known practice that sometimes a fund is terminated after a period of generating extraordinarily large gains. In traditional investing, such results would be lauded as exceptional talent. In contrast, a fund of funds manager might look at such instances as signs that the hedge fund managers were taking exceptional risks.

As a result of the evaluation of performance and reassessment of the risk profiles, the underperforming funds would be shed. At this time, the cash raised from redemptions from poorly performing funds may be reinvested in new funds, or simply new investments need to be made. Accordingly, new managers need to be identified and selected and portfolio construction issues arise regarding the risk and return to be expected from the newly reconfigured portfolio. For investors who are active in hedge fund investing, the three-step process of manager evaluation, portfolio construction, and monitoring are continuous, overlapping, and integral.

1   HOW WELL IS YOUR HEDGE FUND PORTFOLIO?

Most individual investors who invest in stocks and bonds would be happy if their investment advisers produce a 20 percent return when the stock market goes up by, say, 25 percent, and they would be content even if their accounts increase somewhat less. In other words, these investors are mostly content if their investments increase in value. They would be happy to have the bragging right of seeing their portfolios outperforming the market; but usually this is not how they view the performance of their managers. On the other hand, they become very concerned if their investments lose value, even if their losses are less than those of the market. Furthermore, they are reluctant to fire the managers who incur losses worse than the return of the market, hoping to recoup when the market recovers. At this time, they may contemplate redeeming from the managers if the underperformance continues.

Thus, individual investors are inclined to achieve some sort of absolute returns from their managers. Institutional investors, by contrast, are mostly interested in relative performances. If the market is up by 25 percent, as desirable as this return might be as viewed in the context of the market's historical averages, they would still prefer to see their investment managers go up by more, even if the managers take on unusual risks to achieve these returns. Not only that, they would reward those managers who exceed the market as well as most of their peers with rewards in the form of allocating more money to these managers. They still would reward these managers, or at least not punish them by termination, if these managers lose less than the market and most of their peer groups.

Thus, in contrast to individuals who are apt to seek absolute returns, institutions prefer to evaluate their managers relative to the market.

Unfortunately, whereas in traditional investing the "market" is commonly equated with the S&P 500, Russell 3000, or similar indexes, "market" is a more elusive concept in hedge funds. Hence, a market benchmark for hedge funds is more difficult to define.

The lack of an objective measurement benchmark for hedge funds is further complicated by the tendency of institutional investors to continue to be influenced by the return of stock market indexes like the S&P 500; that is, "The market rose 28 percent last year and my fund gained only 15 percent!" They often forget that hedge fund investing is about achieving an absolute and positive rate of return regardless of the condition of the market, up or down. For the uncommitted investors who entered into hedge funds because of concerns due to the prolonged bear market, periods of strong market returns coupled with lower returns by hedge funds may have an influence on how hedge funds are evaluated.

Hedge funds themselves hardly help the matter due to high portfolio turnover and the lack of transparency in their investment strategies and processes as well as changes thereof. They also are apt to cite their positive returns when the market indexes go down as proof of their talent, or alpha. In the absence of relevant information and mixed signals from their hedge funds, investors often resort to the convenience of market benchmarks to judge their managers.

2   BASIC CONCEPTS OF PERFORMANCE MEASUREMENT

The fundamental approach to measuring a funds performance is to adjust its return for the risk it incurs. Modern portfolio theory defines risk as the fund's total risk measured by its standard deviation. This gives rise to the familiar

Sharpe ratio. The higher the Sharpe ratio, the better the fund. In the hedge fund world, the Sharpe ratio has become the standard for performance measurement of risk-adjusted returns.[1]

The advance of the capital asset pricing model, which relates the return of a risky asset to the market by a factor called beta, led to another method of measuring risk-adjusted performance by using beta as the measure of risk. To the extent that a fund's return exceeds the return of a market benchmark after adjusting for beta, the excess return or alpha, represented by the familiar Greek letter α, measures the outperformance of the fund. This relationship is expressed in the familiar equation:

$$\overline{R}_i = \alpha + [r_f + \beta_i(\overline{F}_j - r_f)]$$

In this equation, a hedge fund's excess return over the Treasury bill rate in a time period t can be explained by some factor F_j (and there can be more than one factor) in the same period, adjusted by a coefficient beta. Accordingly, the methodology is to regress the fund's excess return over the one-month Treasury bill rate onto a single factor such as a stock market index, or a set of multiple return-generating factors. The fund's performance is then evaluated on the basis of the significance of the term α. Its risk would be judged to be low if beta is small or close to zero. Once a fund's beta takes on values in excess of 0.5, it is considered long-biased.

It is obvious that the most crucial issue in evaluating hedge fund performance is the definition of the F_j term. In long-only equity investing, the term is often equated with the S&P 500. Though approximate, this index is not as applicable to a fund trading in, as an example, small-cap stocks as to a large-cap stock fund. It is of course far less relevant to a hedge fund. Furthermore, the equation assumes that the term beta would stay constant. This is not an unreasonable assumption as it applies to traditional long-only portfolios, whose managers normally stay invested in their respective markets—say, large-market capitalization stocks—whether their markets go up or down.

The assumption, however, is not realistic with regard to hedge fund managers who are apt to adjust their strategies to cope with the changing market conditions by reducing or increasing risks from exposures to different market factors. Finally, the significance of alpha would vary with the time period, for example, one quarter, one year, or five years. As discussed previously, research has shown that alpha has a tendency to degenerate over time (after an initial rise) and older funds tend to do worse than young funds.

ISSUES DIRECTLY RELATED TO HEDGE FUNDS   3

Hedge funds follow certain styles. They just do not go long on the market, whatever the market is. They also short the market, sometimes by as much as the long position. Thus long/short equity funds go long certain stocks and short others, whereas equity market neutral have equal long and short positions. Similarly, fixed income arbitrage funds buy and sell securities in the fixed income markets. However, they may change their strategies in a number of different ways, all of which have great bearing on their investment results as well as risks.

---

[1] In long-only investing, an alternative risk-adjusted measure is the Treynor ratio, which uses beta as the denominator instead of the standard deviation. It thus expresses the price per unit of systemic risk, instead of per unit of total risk as in the Sharpe ratio. Since beta is supposed to be small, except for predominantly directional strategies, total risk is a more relevant risk measure for hedge funds.

Changes in Leverage

A fund may increase the amount of leverage. Fixed income arb funds typically use greater leverage than equity-oriented funds. It is not unusual for such funds to have leverage 20 times or more of their capital bases, although Long-Term Capital Management was a very unusual case. These leverages can change not only during the year, but as often as during any monthly period. For fixed income funds, such as fixed income or convertible arbitrage, shifts in the amounts of leverages can occur not only with greater frequency, but also by greater amounts.

The use of leverage clearly has a great impact on the return and risk of a fund. Suppose it is a diversified stock fund, and its performance is assessed against the S&P 500. If such a fund is leveraged by 50 percent, should its return not be compared to 1.5 times the return of the S&P 500? Yet, it is a common practice that the leverage amount is not explicitly factored into the performance assessment.

Changes in Hedging Techniques

An equity market neutral fund is supposed to be zero-beta or long and short stocks by equal amounts. The short side can be accomplished by short selling the stocks such that if the short stocks decline by 1 percent, the overall short position will gain 1 percent times the amount of the short position. But short selling can also be accomplished by using derivatives such as put options. The return/risk relationships of options are much different from a long or short stock position. If you buy a put option, you have to pay a premium, which is only a fraction of the price of the stock. If the stock goes down, the gain depends on the so-called delta, which is the extent to which the value of the option responds to the changes in the stock's price. However, if the stock keeps on increasing in value, the maximum loss would be the premium. A long/short equity or an equity market neutral fund that buys put options in lieu of direct short selling of securities would participate in a rising overall stock market to a greater extent than those managers who directly short sell securities. But also the risks of such funds are much different: In a down market a put option would provide less protection than outright short positions; a deep out-of-the-money put has little protection.

Style Drifts

Style drifts are a common problem both in long-only traditional managers as well as in hedge funds. Managers who specialize in certain sectors of the markets, such as large-cap stocks, may start buying small-cap or mid-cap stocks when they perceive that large-cap stocks begin to lag the others, or vice versa. Mortgage-backed securities traders may likewise begin to dabble in nonconforming mortgages to increase yields and leverage. Thus, when strategies drift, the original factors F_i are no longer appropriate to measure manager performance.

Portfolio Turnover

This is also a common change seen in both traditional and hedge fund managers. In fact, during the 2000–2002 bear market and as the stock market recovers, traditional managers have sharply increased their portfolio turnovers to unprecedented levels.[2] For hedge funds, rapid-fire trading in periods of market

---

[2] Ian McDonald, "Funds Adjust to Volatile Markets," *Wall Street Journal*, February 2, 2004, p. R1.

instability is not an unusual activity. In fact, they take advantage of such volatility in order to generate excess returns.

Once a hedge fund begins to change its strategy, its risk factors and sources of alpha also change. To the extent that a hedge fund is hired because of the manager's expertise in that particular strategy, any changes will have an effect on the fund's risk/return profile. Thus, any excess return generated from the new strategies may be a random event, perhaps due to luck. At the same time, market conditions do change and the ability of a hedge fund to tactically modify its trading strategies, perhaps by shortening the holding periods of its positions, which would cause higher portfolio turnover, may be a sign of strength.

MARKET AND HEDGE FUND INDEXES

4

Although market indexes may not be entirely depended upon to judge hedge fund performances, they are not wholly irrelevant, either. We will examine these benchmarks in some detail.

Market Indexes

To assess hedge fund performance, the relevance of market indexes is limited. Some of the reasons were discussed earlier. Also, hedge funds have low correlation to market indexes. Table 1 examines the correlations of several CSFB/Tremont strategies against major market indexes.

TABLE 1 Correlation of Select Hedge Funds with Major Market Indexes

Market Index	CSFB/Tremont Hedge Fund Index		
	Fixed Income Arbitrage	Distressed Securities	Convertible Arbitrage
Lehman Aggregate Bond Index	0.176	0.068	0.144
S&P 500	0.029	0.546	0.126
Russell 3000	0.041	0.571	0.147
Merrill Lynch High Yield	0.296	0.640	0.401

Market Index	CSFB/Tremont Hedge Index			
	Long/Short Equity	Equity Market Neutral	Global Macro	Emerging Markets
S&P 500	0.583	0.400	0.231	0.480
Russell 3000	0.649	0.398	0.238	0.510

Source: CSFB/Tremont, Standard & Poor's, PerTrac.

Hedge funds that navigate the bond markets by using fixed income or convertible arbitrage or trading distressed securities might be presumed to be more correlated to the bond market than to equities. As it turns out, the correlations of these CSFB/Tremont strategies have significantly higher correlation with the market when the market is defined as the Merrill Lynch High Yield Index than with either the Lehman Aggregate Bond Index or the S&P 500. In fact, the Merrill index explained 64 percent of the returns of Distressed Securities, 40 percent of Convertible Arbitrage, and 30 percent of Fixed Income Arb. These correlations are higher than when the S&P 500 was the market proxy and indicate a significantly greater dependence by these hedge funds on their markets to generate returns.

In the equity space, Long/Short Equity is shown to have greater correlation with the Russell 3000 than with the S&P 500, reflecting the fact that these funds extensively troll the market of less-researched small-capitalization stocks in their search for alpha. However, the Russell 3000 does not explain the performance of Equity Market Neutral and Global Macro any better than the S&P 500 does.

From this limited evidence, it appears that if market indexes are used in evaluating hedge funds, broad-based indexes such as the Merrill Lynch High Yield Master for fixed income funds or Russell 3000 for equity-oriented funds can better capture the performance of hedge funds. More likely, a combination of indexes would have higher correlations with hedge funds than any individual index. In this respect, academic research on mutual funds has shown that multifactor models do a better job than any single index at explaining the returns of mutual funds.[3]

Furthermore, while market indexes cannot entirely explain the returns of hedge funds, market returns demarcate the boundaries of the returns that can be expected from hedge funds. A hedge fund that produces return streams outside of these boundaries may demonstrate manager talent, unusual risk taking by the manager, or simply a mere random event that is not repeatable. In any case, such outlier returns may be indicative of the need to investigate the sources of the unusual returns, positive or negative.

Hedge Fund Indexes

Obviously hedge fund indexes such as the CSFB/Tremont Hedge Fund Index and its components are more reflective of hedge funds than market indexes are. This is more so since correlations among managers have been shown to be fairly high.[4] If the hedge fund index is a category index like Fixed Income Arbitrage or Long/Short Equity, it has a basis for performing peer analysis.

However, even in this situation, there still are significant differences between a hedge fund's strategy versus the strategies embedded in the category index. One example is the mortgage-backed securities strategy, which is only one of a variety of fixed income strategies underlying the CSFB/Tremont Fixed Income Arbitrage index. Thus, comparing the performance of a mortgage-backed securities manager against the index does not even allow a comparison between the fund and its peers. And it certainly does not give any clue as to how well it does in terms of the exact strategy that it employs to generate the returns.

---

[3] See for example, Martin J. Gruber, "Another Puzzle: The Growth in Actively Managed Mutual Funds," *Journal of Finance* 51, No. 3, July 1996, pp. 783–810.

[4] See Greg Jensen and Jason Rotenberg, "Hedge Funds Selling Beta as Alpha," Bridgewater Associates Daily Observations, June 17, 2003.

TABLE 2 Hedge Fund Index Data

Data shortcomings:

- ▶ Fund listing is up to individual hedge fund managers.
- ▶ Indexes include many small funds and miss some large funds.
- ▶ Data from hedge funds are not verified by index publishers.

Questionable statistics:

- ▶ Funds in index are subject to turnover.
- ▶ Survivor and backfill biases may overestimate returns.
- ▶ Presence of large funds that are closed to new investors creates under/over-estimates bias.
- ▶ Autocorrelation may significantly underestimate volatility.
- ▶ Track records are still relatively short.

Furthermore, there are also aspects relating to the construction of the hedge fund indexes that require caution in using them for performance evaluation. Some of these are listed in Table 2. For these reasons, hedge fund indexes would be useful to the extent that they set the boundaries of returns, helping to detect potentially unusual activities at a hedge fund that generates exceptional returns outside of these boundaries. Yet, these indexes can be misleading as a basis for evaluating a hedge fund's alpha or ability to generate excess returns.

Positive Risk-Free Rate

The risk-free rate has been recommended by consultants and used by many institutional investors as a benchmark for hedge fund performance. A variation of this measure is to add a margin from 300 to 600 basis points.

It has been argued that the risk-free rate indicates investors' requirement for positive return, independent from the market. Also, arbitrage strategies have short positions that earn a "short" rebate linked to the risk-free rate.

The justification for using the risk-free rate is the notion that arbitrage strategies are supposed to be neutral to the market. Therefore, the expected return from such strategies should be the risk-free rate. Adding a few percentage points to this rate reflects the expectation that hedge fund managers have skills to generate excess return and they are well compensated for it. And this expectation should be built into the benchmark for performance measurement. Exactly what this margin is depends on the institutions.

The hedge fund strategy that comes closest to pure risk-free arbitrage is equity market neutral. However, as discussed previously, market neutral does not mean risk free. A dollar-neutral strategy is certainly not market neutral even though it has equal amounts in long and short positions. A **zero-beta portfolio** may not be market neutral, either, because we don't know what the "market" is. Even if the "market" is known, the portfolio's weighted beta shifts in the interim reporting periods. Thus, the portfolio is never truly zero-beta. And it is certainly not risk free. If the portfolio is not well diversified, the company-specific risks of the stocks in the portfolio are not diversified away, leaving a residual risk in the portfolio.

If the readers are inclined to accept the risk-free rate plus a margin as a practical and acceptable approximation of a true benchmark for equity market neutral, other strategies hardly qualify as risk-free arbitrage. Fixed income arbitrage takes advantage of the differences in the yields of two fixed income securities. On the long side, the security is one that has a higher yield, and the short side is one that has lower yield. The net difference is the spread. Typically, spreads are relatively small, such as spreads between U.S. Treasury securities and investment grade corporate bonds. But spreads can be several hundred basis points in cases of Treasuries versus high-yield or junk bonds. Against mortgage-backed securities, spreads above Treasuries average about 100 basis points. In order to achieve high-single-digit or double-digit rates of return, fixed income arbitrage managers engage in leverage. Leverages of 20 times the base capital are not unusual.

Thus the risks of fixed income arbitrage funds come from the leverage as well as the potential widening of the spreads. In times of unusual market volatility, the combination is explosive, as in July 2003 when it contributed to the collapse of Beacon Hill as well as unusual losses at other fixed income arb firms. Risk free plus a safety margin hardly qualifies as a measurement benchmark for the return of fixed income arb hedge funds.

5   KNOW YOUR HEDGE FUND MANAGERS OR KEY DRIVERS OF RETURNS

Underlying the preceding discussion is the fact that hedge fund strategies are vastly different, even among funds with similar styles. Application of some universal benchmark, no matter how well constructed, is unlikely to capture the essence of all hedge funds' performances. Evaluation of hedge fund performance therefore requires an intimate understanding of how returns are generated by individual funds, from the amount of leverage to trading style and proclivity to take risks by the lead portfolio managers. Such individual variations cannot be captured by just looking at a benchmark index of some kind. Furthermore, hedge fund investing is about capturing an absolute positive rate of return even when the market, whatever it means, goes down. As the market experiences periods of unusual volatility, different management styles will produce different results. Understanding these styles would greatly enhance the ability to judge the performance of hedge fund managers. In the following, we discuss what can be expected from different investment styles and strategies.

Equity-Oriented Hedge Funds

There are three principal hedge fund equity strategies: long/short, market neutral, and short bias. In terms of dollar amounts, long/short is net long, short bias is net short, and market neutral has close to equal amounts. Using dollar amounts as measures of the equity market exposures most certainly would misestimate the amount of market risk, leaving aside the nonsystematic risks specific to the underlying securities.

A better measure of the market risk is the weighted average beta of the individual securities. This is the sum of the securities' beta multiplied by the percentage weightings of the securities. This sum is then divided by the number of securities. The result is not the same as the *ex post* return of the portfolio, which is correlated to the market's return to arrive at a calculated beta.

A portfolio's weighted average beta of individual securities would then be correlated to the return of the market to arrive at its expected return. An equity hedge fund's expected return calculated from weighted average beta would then be compared with its actual return. A fund's excess return or alpha is the difference between its actual return and its weighted average beta return. The use of weighted average beta in performance and risk analyses will be discussed in greater detail in Reading 54.

Fixed Income Funds

For fixed income funds, the amounts of leverage are the key to their return and risk profiles. When credit spreads narrow, fund managers tend to increase leverage in order to generate returns. However, increasing leverage would increase the funds' risks.

Thus, in evaluating fund performance, it is essential to assess the attendant risks due to the use of leverage. A simple way to gauge leverage is to add the long positions to the short side to find the total face value of all positions. In normal market conditions, these nominal amounts need to be adjusted for their exposures to interest rates in terms of duration and implied options. However, in times of market dislocations, these adjustments can lead to underestimation of the interest rate risk.

One approximate method of estimating the expected return of a fixed income arbitrage fund is to multiply the amount of credit spread by the amount of leverage.

A more elaborate method of estimating the return of a fixed income arb fund as suggested by Hsieh and Fung (2002)[5] is to use changes in the credit spread during a given period. Thus, for the 1990 to 1997 period, this methodology would yield the following formulas for estimating the return of the HFR Fixed Income Arbitrage strategy:

$$\text{HFR Fixed Income Arb return} = 0.0096 - 5.37 * [\text{Change in credit spread}]$$
$$(10.0) \quad (6.6)$$
$$R^2 = 0.32$$

If this relationship holds true in any period, the estimated return can be compared to the actual performance of a fixed income arbitrage hedge fund's returns, and inferences can be made as to whether the fund generates any excess return, or it simply follows the market, which is the credit spread.

HEDGE FUND BENCHMARKS IN PRACTICE   6

To incorporate the ideas that hedge funds seek market neutrality or at least protection against market downturns while at the same time being exposed to market factor risks, some combination of the risk-free rate and market indexes have been used by leading institutional investors as benchmarks for their hedge fund investments. Some of these benchmarks are:

▶ Related market index: Russell 3000 plus a margin.

▶ Hedge fund index: Return on a pool of hedge funds of different or same styles.

---

[5] David A. Hsieh and William Fung, "The Risk in Fixed Income Hedge Fund Styles," August 2002 (http://faculty.fuqua.duke.edu/~dah7/Fixedinc.pdf); *Journal of Fixed Income*, forthcoming.

> ► Market-linked absolute return.
>> ► Risk-free rate plus a spread:
>>> 30-day Treasury bills + 5%
>>>
>>> 60% of Salomon Global Equity Index + 20% of J. P. Morgan Global Bonds + 20% of (LIBOR + 5%)
>> ► Minimum return plus some market upside:
>>> 60% Wilshire 5000 + 40% Treasury bills + 3%
> ► Others have suggested an absolute target such as 10 percent or a target that is linked to the inflation rate, such as the consumer price index plus a margin.

Clearly any absolute target may be unachievable in the short term, while it may be too lenient at other times depending on the market conditions, such as the inflation rate and the general level of interest rates. Furthermore, a performance benchmark should be one that can be used to judge the performance of the hedge fund. A benchmark that is applied to all hedge funds in a portfolio is not as much a performance benchmark as the investment objective of the investors. A hedge fund that fails to meet the objective of such a benchmark may not necessarily fall short because the fund is a poor performer given its strategy, although it may justifiably be eliminated from the portfolio because the fund and its strategy are no longer suitable for the portfolio.

7   EVALUATING PERFORMANCE: A HEURISTIC PROCESS

In evaluating hedge fund performances, it is useful to keep in mind that hedge fund managers operate within the constraints of the capital markets. Though they have specialized skills to discover and profit from anomalies in certain segments of the broad stock and bond markets, such opportunities must exist for them to exploit. When the conditions in these market niches are favorable, these hedge fund managers are well positioned to earn excess returns. If they take additional risks by leveraging in multiples of the capital base, the excess return would be extraordinary. In times of sudden shifts in the direction of the broad markets, it is likely that these market niches would experience dislocations. Only the most talented managers are positioned to cope with these inflection points in the markets. The average manager, however, would likely record excess negative returns, as the hedge fund indexes have shown. Less risk-averse managers, those who put on additional leverage to maintain returns as the opportunities in their market niches dwindle, such as when credit spreads have narrowed to historical lows, would likely endure unmitigated losses.

Therefore, it is most critical to understand the market niches that the hedge fund managers operate in: the conditions, opportunities, and potential risks in these markets; the strategies that are employed to achieve returns; and the managers' predisposition to take risks. Some managers are more prone to take higher risks to take advantage of small opportunities, especially when they are falling behind in their return targets. Other managers are less willing to increase their risk exposures even when they believe that risk taking is warranted and would be handsomely rewarded by unusual opportunities.

Only when equipped with this understanding of the hedge funds' strategies can an investor properly evaluate their performances.

Shortcut approaches such as hedge fund indexes or peer groups can point out potential problem managers by identifying outlier performers. In such instances, more intense reviews of the managers' trades and strategies would reveal more information on the causes of these outlier returns. However, even when the hedge funds' returns are within some normal bounds, they may be extraordinary nevertheless if the risks taken to achieve them are relatively low. Conversely, normal returns may mask potential problems.

Hedge funds should generate positive returns in all market conditions. However, in cases of extreme market dislocations, a small amount of loss should not be considered poor performance. In this instance, a relevant index should provide a ready comparison. A strong performance relative to the peer group suggests the managers are still in top form.

Lagging behind a rising stock market is not necessarily a sin, especially if the market's rally is very substantial, as in 2003. However, if the fund manager gained only a few percentage points or incurred losses following prior periods of mediocre results, in 2001 and 2003 for example, it might be a signal that the manager was losing his touch. In this case, a focused review of the manager's strategy and investments would be in order. Another aspect of the use of a market benchmark is that in times of high volatility a fund may choose to reduce the exposure. Its return, though good, may as a result show underperformance relative to the benchmark index if the index registers strong results.

When a hedge fund navigates in multiple markets, it has the opportunity to take advantage of different market conditions to generate returns that are not available to funds that are focused on single markets or types of trades. The hurdle of expectations for these funds may be higher as a result. As such, a single absolute target or one-factor benchmark would not truly reflect the opportunities and risks available to them. Accordingly, a complex multifactor model of expected return and risk would more likely capture these funds' potential performance. Though the multifactor approach has weaknesses, mainly in the construction and identification of the relevant factors that drive returns, it captures more fully the range of possible returns and risks of multistrategy funds.

Strategy Review

Underlying the evaluation of the performance of a hedge fund is the need to assess the strategy it employs to achieve the reported rate of return. Therefore, the entire investment strategy and process of the hedge fund needs to be reviewed as part of the performance evaluation.

Funds of funds and large institutional investors typically follow monthly reports of investment results from their hedge funds with conference calls with the managers of these funds. They discuss a review of the market conditions, what accounts for the gains or losses, the good trades that generated the gains, and the adverse developments in the markets that led to disappointments in the results. Often only the most glaring mistakes are revealed by the hedge funds and the market usually is blamed for the losses. However, investors use this opportunity to glean from the conversations indications of any changes in strategies or any unusual trades that may exacerbate the gains or losses. On balance, it is in the interest of the hedge funds to attribute positive returns to talent, and losses to adverse conditions in the market. Typically, whether or not relevant, returns that exceed a hedge fund index would be seized upon as evidence of special skills. On the investors' part, a month with good returns, especially when the competition fares poorly, often dulls any urgent sense of need to delve into the behind-the-scenes trades that account for the good results.

Review of Investment Suitability

Whether a hedge fund is a star or an underperformer is not the only objective of performance review. An additional question is whether it continues to be suitable to contribute to the investor's investment objective. Not all hedge fund strategies perform equally well in all market environments. Furthermore, in times of high volatility in the capital markets or economic expansion, hedge funds may not add value, as suggested in Kat and Miffre (2002).[6] Also, a fund that seeks low volatility by investing in strategies such as fixed income arb may in fact find this leads to high volatility. This is because of the left tail risks inherent in fixed income arbitrage.

In such situations, the investor may be well advised to redeem from a fund that is performing well. Funds of funds often face this type of decision as the capital markets evolve, creating new profitable opportunities that funds of funds wish to take advantage of.

8   CONCLUSION

Evaluating hedge fund performance is a far more complex issue than simply comparing a fund's return with an index, whether the return is adjusted for volatility or for tracking errors vis-à-vis a market index. The difficulty lies in the fact that hedge funds navigate in a multitude of markets while often making strategy shifts and adjusting risks with leverage. Thus, hedge fund returns are not readily assessable against a market benchmark like the S&P 500, or an aggregation of different hedge fund strategies like the CSFB/Tremont Hedge Fund Index. Nevertheless, market and peer group indexes can serve as the boundaries of returns or indicators of the ranges of average results. If a hedge fund's return falls in the tail ends of the distribution, either negative or positive, it might be a signal for review, to analyze and evaluate the circumstances whereby such returns are generated: Are new strategies being employed? Have unusual risks been undertaken? Or is it mere luck?

To improve on the relevance of an index to a hedge fund's particular strategy, special indexes can be constructed. Discussed in this reading is an index relating fixed income arbitrage returns to credit spreads and a methodology using weighted average beta to evaluate equity market neutral and long/short equity funds.

However, no matter how well a performance evaluation benchmark is constructed, it cannot substitute for an intimate understanding of a hedge fund's strategy to generate the returns and risks. We have discussed evaluating returns in this reading. We now turn to evaluating hedge fund risks in Reading 54.

---

[6] Harry M. Kat and Joelle Miffre, "Performance Evaluation and Conditioning Information: The Case of Hedge Funds," Working Paper #0006, August 23, 2002.

BUYERS BEWARE: EVALUATING AND MANAGING THE MANY FACETS OF THE RISKS OF HEDGE FUNDS

by Vinh Q. Tran

LEARNING OUTCOMES

The candidate should be able to:

a. discuss common types of investment risks for hedge funds;

b. evaluate the use of maximum drawdown and value-at-risk as tools for measuring risks of hedge funds.

Long-Term Capital Management (LTCM) has been etched into the collective memory of investors and the history of Wall Street as the ultimate folly of hedge funds. Formed in 1993 by the former star trader John Meriwether of the now-defunct Salomon Brothers, and populated by celebrity Harvard professors and Nobel Prize winners, it made a big splash by raising $1.25 billion at the start, only to require a multibillion-dollar bailout organized by the Federal Reserve following its near collapse in September 1998. Postmortem analyses abound as to what and whom to blame for the disaster.[1] Yet it is an irony that the types of strategies that led to the LTCM disaster are now being employed every day at hedge funds, often successfully and profitably for their clients. LTCM itself has been reincarnated to become JWM Capital Management with close to $1 billion of assets under management.

LTCM engaged in a variety of fixed income arbitrage trades. Among the basic ones employed by the firm were going long off-the-run Treasuries and going short on-the-run Treasury bonds. Because the former have higher yields due to

---

[1] Roger Lowenstein, *When Genius Failed: The Rise and Fall of Long-Term Capital Management,* New York: Random House, 2000; Kevin Dowd, "Too Big to Fail?: Long-Term Capital Management and the Federal Reserve," *CATO Institute Briefing Paper No. 52,* September 23, 1999; and Philippe Jorion, "Risk Management Lessons from Long-Term Capital Management," *European Financial Management,* September 2000, pp. 277–300.

their relative lack of liquidity, the trade yielded a small price advantage of a few hundredths of 1 percent. In order to generate returns in the low teens, say 10 to 12 percent, leverages of 20 to 30 times and higher had to be used.

Two things went wrong. First, as success piled up, the firm ventured into trades that were drastic departures from the initial strategies. It began to arbitrage between dissimilar securities such as Italian bonds and German **Bund** futures or Danish mortgage securities. In 1997, according to newspaper accounts, the firm went into trading equity index options and stocks involved in takeover positions—that is, merger arbitrage.

Second, the firm took on huge amounts of leverage. At the beginning of 1998, LTCM had capital of $4.8 billion but a portfolio of $200 billion in securities, many of them liquid, plus derivatives of $1.2 trillion in notional value. As arbitrage trades, many of these positions offset one another such that when market conditions returned to equilibrium, the price differences between these securities would return to normal, allowing LTCM to book large profits from its hugely leveraged trades. But the market did not return to normal. The price differences on LTCM arbitrage positions widened further, partly because of the flight to quality that was precipitated by the Russian crisis, and also because other market participants had taken positions opposite to LTCM, reportedly to take advantage of its overexposures. But it was the huge leverages that caused the losses that precipitated the firm's collapse. One of the trades that it had on its books was long/short on off-the-run against on-the-run Treasuries. At the end of September 1998, the spread between these two securities had widened from 5 basis points (0.05 percent) to 15 basis points. It was a big move, but not fatal on an unleveraged portfolio of $4.8 billion. The loss would have been a mere $4.8 million, or 0.1 percent. But multiplied by 100 times, the loss would be gargantuan. On August 21, LTCM reportedly lost $550 million. By September 21, the firm was said to have lost an additional $500 million.

The LTCM fiasco highlighted the need for understanding the risks of hedge funds before investments are made and for postinvestment monitoring and managing these risks. And certainly high returns should not lull investors into complacency. After all, in the first full year of operation, 1995, LTCM produced an eye-popping 43 percent after all fees and expenses. In the following year, it recorded profits of 41 percent. In fact, in its first two or three years of operation, LTCM would have passed with flying colors any of the standard tests of performance evaluation such as the Sharpe ratio.

However, alert and dispassionate investors might have noticed the low-returning nature of the markets LTCM was navigating, and the extraordinary results it generated, both of which should have served as warning signs of the kind of risks that LTCM had been taking with its investors' money. This lesson has been memorized by some experienced investors: Several fund of funds managers in my sample said that one of the reasons they redeem from a hedge fund is that it generates very unusually high returns. They believe such returns not only will not be repeatable in the future, but also are indicative of the unusual risks taken by these hedge funds.

However, extraordinary investment risks such as those taken at LTCM are not the only causes of hedge funds' collapses. In fact, according to Capital Markets Company, operations problems, including mispricing of securities, have been found to contribute to more than a third of hedge fund failures.[2]

Overall, having made the investments in hedge funds, investors would need to monitor closely the strategies and operations of their funds. Hedge fund investors are interested in making sure that their investments will perform in the future in the way they were led to believe they would prior to making the investments. They certainly would not want their money to be stolen or spent on the fund managers' personal habits. Furthermore, any individual hedge funds will see their investment performances vary over time. The market niches that have in the past produced superior returns may become crowded and opportunities to earn excess return may evaporate. Or the competition may become fierce, and the hedge fund managers may become complacent or their skills become less attuned to the new conditions in those market niches. "Further, the attractiveness of a particular strategy or manager is likely to vary over time, since a) many hedge fund strategies rely on niche areas of market imperfections, which may disappear over time, and as money seeks to exploit them, b) particular managers may lose their motivation over time, and their skills may become less applicable as market conditions change. For these reasons, [hedge funds] may be limited in the amount of money they can accommodate, and require close attention and monitoring."[3]

In this reading we discuss the types of risks that necessitate close monitoring and the steps investors can take to minimize those risks.

THE MANY FACETS OF HEDGE FUNDS' RISKS   1

Risks of hedge funds come in many facets, not just in the volatility of returns. We distinguish three broad categories of risk that face hedge fund investors: fraud, operations risks, and investment risks.

Frauds

Newspaper accounts abound with stories about frauds in the hedge fund industry. Regulatory authorities also have taken punitive actions against those who claimed

---

[2] Stuart Feffer and Christopher Kundro, "Understanding and Mitigating Operational Risk in Hedge Fund Investing," Capco White Paper, The Capital Markets Company, March 2003.

[3] George Crawford, "Must Prudent Investors Understand Hedge Fund Strategies," Fiduciary Foundation, July 2002 (www.fifo.org/Hedge_Fund.pdf).

to manage hedge funds, but in fact used these vehicles to steal investors' money. The misdeeds usually included misrepresentation of managers' backgrounds, investment track records, assets under management, and circumstances that were designed to inflate the attractiveness of the investments. The end game was usually to misappropriate investors' funds for personal use and other purposes.

Such was the case in a complaint filed by the Securities and Exchange Commission (SEC) against Ashbury Capital Partners and its 23-year-old president and portfolio manager Mark Yagala whereby Yagala was charged with misappropriating for personal use a substantial portion of the millions he had raised from 20 investors.[4] Or the case against Burton G. Friedlander whereby the SEC accused him of misrepresenting the value of investor assets in a fund and spending over $2 million of investors' money to pay for his company's operations and for his personal expenses, including country club dues.[5] The common thread in these fraudulent cases is that the perpetrators falsely represented their backgrounds and qualifications, and their investment track records. To detect these fraudulent activities, experienced practitioners insist on due diligence whereby a thorough investigation of the hedge fund managers and their operations is conducted. These investigations would include, as a minimum, verification of employment history, reference checks, and search of court records.

Sometimes the frauds arise from attempts to conceal losses and to attract new investors. That was the case against Michael T. Higgins of San Francisco, California, wherein the SEC charged in civil and criminal actions that he claimed to have produced returns of 54 percent in 1998 when in fact he had losses.[6] Sometimes the misdeed would be comic were it not for the losses that investors suffered as a result. Ryan J. Fontaine was a 22-year-old college student living with his parents who claimed to have $250 million under management and to have produced an annualized return of 39.5 percent for 13 years, including an average of over 21 percent for two years during the bear market.[7]

When investment results are extraordinary, whether or not these outsized returns are real, investors need to investigate how these returns were generated. In fraudulent cases, the returns are often claimed to have been generated in the context of some obscure investment strategies. Or the strategies are relatively straightforward, like trading S&P 500 index futures, but the returns are so great that investors might do well to recall the old saying "too good to be true." This is especially so when the portfolio managers are unknown to the investors.

But frauds can be committed by hedge fund managers whose backgrounds are beyond reproach, at least on the surface, and whose investment strategies are sound. In *SEC v. Beacon Hill Asset Management, L.L.C.* (November 15, 2002), the Securities and Exchange Commission charged Beacon Hill Asset Management with deliberate falsification of its investment results to investors.[8] For the month of September 2002, Beacon Hill reported to its investors that two of its mortgage-backed securities hedge funds suffered losses of 25 percent. Nine days later, the firm restated the losses to be 54 percent, including losses that had not been reported during prior periods.

---

[4] U.S. Securities and Exchange Commission, *SEC v. Ashbury Capital Partners L.P.*, Litigation Release No. 16770, October 17, 2000.

[5] U.S. Securities and Exchange Commission, *SEC v. Burton G. Friedlander*, Litigation Release No. 18426, October 2003.

[6] U.S. Securities and Exchange Commission, *SEC v. Higgins*, Litigation Release No. 17841, November 15, 2002.

[7] U.S. Securities and Exchange Commission, *SEC v. Ryan J. Fontaine and Simpleton Holdings a/k/a Signature Investments Hedge Fund*, Litigation Release No. 17864, November 26, 2002 (www.sec.gov/litigation/litreleases/lr17864.htm).

[8] *SEC v. Beacon Hill Asset Management, L.L.C.* (November 15, 2002), as described in "Beacon Hill Principals Charged with Fraud, Case Expanded (Infovest21)," *Altnews*, June 17, 2004.

In the complaint, the SEC charged Beacon Hill with fraud and named as defendants the firm's four principals: John Barry, the president; Tom Daniels, the chief investment officer; John Irwin, senior portfolio manager; and Mark Miszkiewicz, chief financial officer. The SEC alleged that the four principals of Beacon Hill together implemented a fraudulent scheme resulting in losses of more than $300 million to investors. The allegations were that from at least the beginning of 2002 through October 2002, Beacon Hill and its principals defrauded and made material misrepresentations to investors by way of methodology Beacon Hill used for calculating the net asset values (NAVs) of the hedge funds it managed, the hedging and trading strategy for the purportedly market neutral funds, and the value and the performance of the funds.

The SEC also alleged that central to Beacon Hill's fraud was its method of valuing securities in the hedge funds to show steady and positive returns: that Beacon Hill manipulated its valuation procedures and thus allowed it to report steady growth and hide losses in its master fund, which was the core hedge fund that held and traded securities in its three feeder hedge funds.

According to the complaint, as the value of these Beacon Hill hedge funds decreased over the summer of 2002, the firm continued to report positive returns by inflating the prices of the securities in the master fund to maintain the appearance of positive returns. At the same time, contrary to what it was telling investors, Beacon Hill made an increasing and ultimately unsuccessful bet in the hope of profiting from interest rates rising in an attempt to cover its hidden losses. Additionally, Beacon Hill was alleged to have entered into a series of trades between the master fund and other accounts it managed for two institutional clients at prices that defrauded the master fund and allowed the managed accounts, whose performance had also declined, to reap substantial profits. The SEC argued that Beacon Hill was able to hide the losses resulting from these fraudulent trades by inflating the value of the securities in the master fund to an even greater extent.

As their situation started to unravel, in September 2002 three of the four principals liquidated an account in which they were the only investors by selling the securities in their account to the master fund without disclosure to investors. In early October 2002, when Beacon Hill's prime broker challenged the valuation of the master fund and they were forced to admit it had sustained losses, the principals misrepresented the magnitude of the actual losses in an attempt to save Beacon Hill's operations and make the losses appear to be the result of market conditions.

On October 17, 2002, Beacon Hill finally announced the full extent of investor losses, admitting that as of September 30, the NAVs of its hedge funds had declined 54 percent from the previously reported August 31, 2002, levels, and further acknowledged that it had mispriced securities in the funds prior to August. Clearly, this acknowledgment did not reveal the extent of the machinations alleged by the SEC that Beacon Hill and its principals had undertaken to defraud investors.

One thing that was different between Beacon Hill and LTCM was that LTCM did not hide its losses; everyone in the marketplace knew about them. However, both firms employed strategies that involved a high level of leverage, and these strategies traded illiquid securities and market sectors that were susceptible to stresses during market dislocations. Once the losses became substantial, Beacon Hill, as it was alleged, engaged in deception.

Operational Risks

Operational risks may be rooted in insufficiencies in resources, infrastructures, and technologies. They may result from lax supervision in trading that leads to unauthorized trading or violation of trading guidelines. Operational risks are also manifested in ways that often result in inflated valuation of securities, even with the possible absence of the intention to deceive. In the absence of fraudulent intentions, inflated valuations—inflated because there has never been any known case whereby a hedge fund or any investment fund gets into trouble due to *under*reporting of investment results—often originate with derivatives and illiquid securities that are traded in the dealer market, as opposed to the exchange-listed markets.

Exchange-listed securities, even if they are thinly traded, always have closing prices and tradable bids and offers that serve as verifiable bases for securities' valuation. However, securities that are traded in the dealer market, such as bonds and foreign exchange contracts among and between banks and their customers, are those that rely on quotes for bids and offers from dealers. Exactly the same securities, even those that are traded in large volumes by numerous dealers such as U.S. Treasury notes and bonds, can get different quotes from different dealers. Differences in quotes on U.S. Treasury securities, however, are usually no more than a few ticks or 32nds. (Bonds are quoted in 32nds. This means a dealer may quote a bid, that is, to buy, for a 30-year Treasury bond at $100^{25}\!/_{32}$ while another may quote the same bond at $100^{15}\!/_{16}$.) Quote differences among illiquid lowerrated securities are often much larger. In times of market turmoil, quote differences usually increase. Sometimes there are no dealer quotes at all. During the crisis of 1998, some dealers reportedly did not even pick up the phones to answer calls from longtime customers.

Many complex securities, such as derivatives, require dealers to make mathematical calculations involving different markets and different securities to arrive at fair prices. These calculations by necessity are based on assumptions that may be theoretically reasonable but are not realistic in the then-prevailing market conditions.

Often certain derivatives were constructed by one dealer for a particular client. To obtain a price, the client must go back to the same dealer. In this type of situation, it is very difficult to arrive at the fair market value for these securities. One example is a three-year note denominated in U.S. dollars, which would be pegged to the relationship between two currencies such as the British pound and the Japanese yen, and have a leverage of multiples of the face value of the note. One advantage of such securities is that it does not show up in the calculation of the leverage of the fund. In times when trading volume is low, such as in summer, or even in normal market conditions, the differences between bid and ask prices can be quite significant even from the same dealer. Under these circumstances, "put these natural, inherent difficulties in pricing complex or illiquid investments together with a powerful financial incentive to show strong (or hide weak) performance, and then situate these factors in an environment with minimal regulatory oversight, or without strict discipline and internal controls (still far too typical in the hedge fund industry), and there is potential for trouble."[9]

This was the situation that apparently happened at the big hedge fund Clinton Group. In November 2003, a senior portfolio manager resigned from the firm saying he disagreed with management about the way certain mortgage-backed securities were valued. This triggered a cascade of redemptions from investors, causing Clinton's assets under management to tumble from a high of $10 billion to $4.5 billion in December, then $2.2 billion as of January 2004.

Many securities are also subject to counterparty risks. This is the failure of any trading counterparty in a chain of intermediaries prior to settlement. This is

---

[9] Stuart Feffer and Christopher Kundro, "Valuation Issues and Operational Risk in Hedge Funds," A Capco White Paper, The Capital Markets Company, December 2003.

prevalent in any transaction that is not exchange traded, such as derivatives, foreign exchange, and bonds. This issue has come to the fore after the collapse of Enron, which was of course a onetime dominant player in the energy market. A less serious risk, though one that nevertheless can be costly, is the transaction risk whereby a transaction fails to settle on the specified date. It has been estimated that 8 to 20 percent of cross-border trades involving non-U.S. stocks, bonds, and foreign currencies fail to settle on time.[10] While the impact of settlement failures is not as crippling as counterpartly risk, when a hedge fund is involved in exotic emerging markets with a high level of leverage and use of derivatives, settlement failures may have snowballing effects on the entire fund.

Investment Risks: Ongoing Focus

Investors should want to make sure that the investment returns did not result from any unusually substantial risks that the managers were taking. As in the case of LTCM, its first two years' returns of more than 40 percent in each year partly stemmed from the extraordinary leverage that it piled onto its capital base.

Investment risks refer to the risks embedded in the strategies used by the hedge funds under consideration, their trading styles, the markets they operate in (stocks or bonds, U.S. or foreign, developed or emerging markets), and the kinds of securities they trade (small-cap or large-cap stocks, U.S. Treasury securities or mortgage-backed securities, high-yield bonds, foreign bonds).

Traditional long-only investment managers strive to stay within their stated strategies and styles. Hedge funds have much greater flexibility, especially with regard to broad-based strategies such as multistrategy, global macro, and fixed income arb. Multistrategy and global macro managers trade in all manners of markets and all kinds of securities. Fixed income arb managers navigate in a wide spectrum of the fixed income market. Even managers of seemingly narrowly defined strategies such as convertible arb can have distinctly different styles. Some rely on hedging by short selling stocks while others emphasize credit analysis to generate returns.

In Reading 53 we discussed the difficulties in measuring and evaluating hedge fund performance. The opposite side of the evaluation issue is the measuring and evaluating of hedge fund risks.

Short History of Hedge Funds

As in performance measurement, the issue is the lack of a benchmark for comparison. Additionally, when it comes to risks, the short history of hedge funds further complicates the measurement and management of risks. Even though the concept and strategy of hedge fund investing have been in existence for some 50 years, organized collection and presentation of hedge fund data have begun fairly recently. The CSFB/Tremont database of hedge funds has historical data going back only to 1994. Of the approximately 7,000 hedge funds, this database contains only a few hundred. Most of the HFRI indexes began in 1990, although a few include data since 1987.

Analyses of hedge funds and their risks thus rely on information that date no earlier than the late 1980s. This period happens to be relatively stable from the viewpoint of the long-term history of the financial markets, in spite of the sharp rise in interest rates in 1994, the Asian crisis in 1997, the Russian debt default in 1998, and the burst of the equity market bubble in 2000. As an example,

---

[10] Adam Bryan, "The Many Faces of Risk," *Journal of Financial Transformation* 5, August 2002.

although the equity bear market lasted for three years, Black Monday in October 1987 was far more traumatic in its shock effect. In the fixed income market, July 2003 was most unpleasant for fixed income arbitrage managers as interest rates rose and credit spreads widened, causing large losses at these funds. Even funds of funds that were supposed to be well diversified suffered losses as a result. The problems at the Clinton Group originated from this period. The July 2003 interest rate moves, however, were relatively small compared to late 1979 when the Federal Reserve Board under Chairman Paul Volcker shifted its policy to money supply targeting instead of setting interest rates at specific levels.

How would hedge funds perform and handle risks under those circumstances? To have a glimpse, and this is no more than a glimpse, at the risks of fixed income arbitrage hedge funds in times of stress, Hsieh and Fung (2002)[11] attempted to analyze the factors that determine the performance and risk of fixed income funds. They first reported that the biggest risks to these funds are credit spreads, which are the differences between U.S. Treasury securities and other types of bonds. They also examined the history of credit spreads dating back to the 1920s and found that in terms of credit spreads the 1990s was a friendly period to fixed income funds as compared to earlier periods such as the 1920s and the 1960s through the mid-1980s.

In the summer of 1998, between June and October, credit spreads widened by 110 basis points. Based on the authors' model for estimating the impact of credit spreads, fixed income arbitrage funds would have lost 4.95 percent in those months. It is interesting to note that the CSFB Fixed Income Arb index recorded actual losses of −11.32 percent during this period, or more than twice the model's estimate. In April 1932, credit spreads widened by 187 basis points, implying a loss of −9.08 percent for fixed income arbitrage funds if they had been in existence then. One can only wonder how much higher the actual losses to such funds would have been. In this connection, it is worthwhile to note that the model would estimate the loss suffered by LTCM to be −15.85 percent in July–August 1998. Its actual loss was −44.8 percent. Thus, it is only prudent to expect that in times of systemic stress, losses can be substantially much larger than anticipated.

Credit Spreads

Also, historically, widening of credit spreads can last for prolonged periods. During these times, just as in stocks, there have been movements lasting for months or several years whereby credit spreads widened very sharply to be followed by short-lived calmer periods, only to be interrupted by sharp increases of spreads. One such period started in late 1963 from about 50 basis points only to keep widening to over 400 basis points in late 1974, punctuated in the meantime by shorter-term contractions of 100 to 180 basis points. By comparison, between 1984 and 1995, credit spreads widened by about 100 basis points, with relatively little fluctuations in the interim. How would fixed income arbitrage funds perform in periods of high volatility, which have been unseen in the past 10 to 15 years? How many funds would survive such an onslaught?

Fixed Income Arb Funds and Equity Risks

Another aspect of the risk of fixed income arbitrage funds that is not well recognized is its correlation with the movements of the stock market. The CSFB

[11] David A. Hsieh and William Fung, "The Risk in Fixed Income Hedge Fund Styles," August 2002 (http://faculty.fuqua.duke.edu/~dah7/Fixedinc.pdf); *Journal of Fixed Income*, forthcoming.

Fixed Income Arbitrage Index showed virtually zero correlation with the S&P 500, NASDAQ, Dow Jones Industrial Average, and the MSCI World Index. This suggests that fixed income arbitrage funds can perform well even when stocks performed poorly. And indeed these funds did produce on average high-single-digit rates of return during the three-year bear market of stocks. However, in their study, Hsieh and Fung (2002)[12] found that there was a significant correlation between the S&P 500 and credit spreads such that if the S&P 500 dropped by 10 percent, fixed income arbitrage funds would lose 1.5 percent. This implies that "there exists cyclical exposure to risk factors inherent in most fixed income arbitrage funds that may be masked by the short existence of the funds themselves."[13]

How can fixed income strategies lose if the stock market declines? Isn't it true that when stocks decline, signifying economic weakness, interest rates would be cut, benefiting fixed income securities? Such would be the case if the hedge fund managers are long high-credit-quality bonds such as U.S. Treasuries. But in arbitrage trades, in one form or another, managers go short Treasuries and go long lower-credit bonds. In times of economic weakness, lower-credit bonds experience declines in yields and higher prices, just as in Treasuries and high-credit securities, but by smaller amounts. In other words, credit spreads widen. Arbitrage managers owning such credit spread positions would suffer losses from their short side that are larger than the gains coming from the long side, which consists of lower-credit bonds. Some of the lower-credit bonds may in fact lose principal even when the overall level of interest rate declines. This happens when the corporations issuing the bonds suffer profit declines or losses, or even bankruptcies. Arbitrage managers holding such securities would suffer a double hit: losses from the short Treasury position and losses from the bonds that receive credit downgrades or go into default.

Stock Market Risks and Equity Funds

Switching to equity-oriented funds, a study by Capital Market Risk Advisors indicated that merger arbitrage funds take on more equity market risk exposure than the strategy may imply.[14] This explains why these funds produced greater returns than a pure merger arbitrage strategy. During the bubble period, defined as between 1998 and March 2000, merger arbitrage funds had a correlation of 0.55 with the S&P 500 compared with 0.46 by the pure strategy. After the bubble burst, merger arbitrage funds continued to be correlated with the stock market, though the correlation ratio had declined to 0.37. This correlation with the equity market brought returns on merger arbitrage funds down from 13.1 percent during the bubble to 3.8 percent, compared to 8.9 percent net from the pure strategy.

In the study by Asness, Krail, and Liew (2001)[15] previously discussed, it was found that hedge funds had greater exposure to equity risks than commonly assumed. A look at recent correlation data shows that the exposure to the equity market risk continues to be more significant than standard deviation statistics imply. For example, the CSFB/Tremont Long/Short Equity index had a standard deviation of 11 percent during 1994–2003. Equity Market Neutral showed a

---

[12] Ibid.

[13] Ibid., p. 25.

[14] Richard Horwitz and Luis Rodriguez, "Merger Arbitrage Funds: Do They Deliver What They Promise?," Capital Market Risk Advisors.

[15] Clifford Asness, Robert Krail, and John Liew, "Do Hedge Funds Hedge?," *Journal of Portfolio Management,* Fall 2001 (www.aqrcapital.com).

volatility of 3.07 percent during the period, while Risk Arbitrage's volatility was a bit higher at 4.4 percent. The two strategies' standard deviations are similar or lower than the standard deviation of Fixed Income Arbitrage, and much lower than Long/Short Equity's. From these standard deviations, one would conclude that Long/Short Equity has much greater risk than the other two. The following correlation data, however, clearly indicate that Risk Arbitrage and Equity Market Neutral are significantly exposed to equity market risks, though less so than Long/Short Equity.

	Dow	MSCI World	S&P 500	NASDAQ
Risk arbitrage	0.44	0.45	0.44	0.39
Long/short equity	0.45	0.61	0.58	0.76
Equity market neutral	0.39	0.36	0.39	0.29

Stock Market Risk Exposure

The equity market exposure underlying those strategies that are seemingly neutral to equity market risks is an issue that needs to be understood by hedge fund investors. In some strategies, the equity market risk is in fact asymmetric to the detriment of investors. For example, Lo (2002)[16] found that strategies involving emerging market equities have an up-market beta of 0.16, seemingly market neutral, but a down-market beta of 1.49. Thus, these funds would decline more than their markets in downturns, but significantly lag behind in upturns. In funds that use relative value option arbitrage, betas for up and down markets are actually of the opposite signs: −0.78 in up markets and 0.33 in down markets. Since these funds would follow the S&P 500 on the way down and produce losses when the stock market was up, theirs is hardly a strategy that is market neutral. Additionally, they exhibit the undesirable characteristics of "poor" correlations.

Thus, there are reasons to believe that hedge fund arbitrage strategies, whether equity or fixed income oriented, actually have greater exposures to equity and interest rate risks than they may purport to have. Because of the existence of these common risk exposures, in times of market dislocations seemingly uncorrelated strategies such as long/short equity and fixed income arbitrage can move in the same direction. This occurred in August to October 1998 when both strategies had significant losses in the aftermath of the Russian debt default. The CSFB Long/Short Equity index recorded a loss for only one month, in August at −11.43 percent. The CSFB Fixed Income Arbitrage index had a loss totaling −11.75 percent, but it was spread out over three months, August through October. These losses were in addition to very lackluster performance since the beginning of the year.

Style Drifts

From an investment point of view, money managers for both traditional investments and hedge funds often get into trouble because they depart from their core competencies.

In favorable market conditions, taking risks by venturing into unfamiliar investment spaces or strategies may be rewarded in the short term. The additional

---

[16] Andrew Lo, "Risk Management for Hedge Funds: Introduction and Overview," *Financial Analysts Journal 57*, No. 6, November 2002, p. 16.

risks thus are masked by results that are above historical norms. However, careful analysis of the risk/return trade-offs would indicate inferior risk-adjusted rewards for the risks these funds have taken on. When market dislocations disrupt normal relationships in prices across securities and asset classes, often precipitated by liquidity drains in low-credit sectors and illiquid securities and flight to quality and near-cash safe havens, the lack of expertise in these strategies invariably leads to above-normal and sometimes catastrophic losses.

Increases in Risk Taking

Hedge fund strategies differ in their use of leverage to boost returns. In a survey by HBV in June 2002,[17] the leverages used at the time by major hedge fund strategies range as follows:

Fixed income arbitrage	20 to 30 times capital base
Convertible arbitrage	2 to 10 times
Risk arbitrage	2 to 5 times
Equity market neutral	1 to 5 times
Long/short equity	1 to 2 times
Distressed securities	1 to 2 times

Thus, historically fixed income arb funds employ the highest amount of leverage. Typically, these funds' goals are to exploit credit spreads that are normally less than 100 basis points (i.e., less than 1 percent). To achieve rates of return in the double-digit range, they would have to leverage their funds 10 times or more. When credit spreads contract, the temptation to increase leverage rises in order to obtain high returns. If LTCM had adhered to a leverage limit of 30 times, the one-day loss on the spread widening would have $150 million, or 3 percent, a severe blow but not systemically crippling. But its return would have been a fraction of what it reported in its first full-year results of 40 percent in 1995.

EVALUATING THE RISKS OF YOUR HEDGE FUNDS

2

It is now clear that risks of hedge funds go beyond such measures as standard deviation or beta. In order to have a successful hedge fund investment program, investors need to put a process in place to monitor and assess the risks.

To pick the right hedge fund managers, the principle is "know your managers." The same principle is applied in monitoring your hedge fund risks: Continue to know your managers. It is only common sense that the job of evaluating hedge funds does not stop after the managers are selected and allocations of funds to them are made.

In a nutshell, risk management seeks to detect the yellow flags or the warning signs that signal potential trouble ahead. A best-practices risk management system would include an ongoing ability to (1) assess worst possible losses; (2) detect significant deviations from stated strategies; (3) evaluate the target versus potential

---

[17] Pascal Lambert and Peter Rose, "Risk Management for Hedge Funds—A Prime Broker's Perspective" (www.eubfn.com/arts/760_bearstearns.htm).

risk/return profiles; (4) identify sources and causes of risks: manager skills, strategy changes, style drifts, or market dislocations.

Worst-Case Scenarios

Most investors can tolerate some degree of loss in the normal course of investing. But few investors can accept total or huge losses due to fraudulent practices, business failures, or catastrophic events in the market. It is therefore important for investors to realize the extent of worst-case loss potential of any investment. If the worst possible losses are beyond the ability or willingness of the investors to tolerate, such investments probably are not suitable. Investors unwilling or unable to accept losses more than 10 to 15 percent from any manager should not invest in strategies such as emerging markets or global macro.

Frauds and Operational Risks

Huge or total losses are usually the consequences of frauds or operational failures. For such risks, a thorough preinvestment due diligence is the first defense. Postinvestment due diligence will include monitoring for any changes in the circumstances surrounding the personal and business operations of the hedge fund managers that may point to potential risk areas.

Some fund of funds managers believe changes in the personal lifestyles of hedge fund managers are an issue that needs to be monitored. As is often the case, undue personal stress caused by events such as changes in marital status, extravagant personal spending, or financial or legal difficulties may create conditions for abnormal risk taking or business failure. They may even be the telltale signs of potential trouble that may have been missed during preinvestment due diligence. To achieve this awareness, fund of funds managers develop a network of personal and business contacts to pick up on information that is not otherwise available.

One obvious change that should be further investigated is any change in key personnel such as the chief financial officer, who has direct responsibility and supervisory authority over the compilation, collection, and dissemination of fund returns. In the non–hedge fund world, a change of the chief financial officer, especially at large public companies, is a significant event. In hedge funds it is more so, as it might signal irregularities in financial and accounting matters as well as distracting disagreements among key managers on business strategies.

The one person who is critical to the success or failure of a fund is the portfolio manager responsible for its actual day-to-day investment management. In hedge funds, the portfolio manager, the chief executive officer, and the owner are sometimes one person. However, portfolio managers should not play a direct role in determining the prices of securities in the portfolios they manage. This responsibility should reside with the chief financial officer, who should have the authority to make the final determination of the fair values of the securities. At hedge funds where this separation of authority is not in place, investors are denied a safeguard for accurate accounting and investor protection, and therefore face a greater risk of erroneous reporting of investment returns.

Sometimes changes of key personnel may be well justified. This appeared to be the case of the resignation of the portfolio manager of two funds at Stamford, Connecticut–based Andor Capital after the two funds that he managed, the Diversified Growth Fund with $1.5 billion of assets and the $250 million Diversified Growth Perennial Fund, suffered large losses in 2003. Even then, investors had already lost 17.5 percent in the Diversified Growth Fund and 21.5 percent in the Perennial Fund, which would be liquidated.[18] Nevertheless, facing such losses, a fair question that should be asked by investors is: Why should the hedge fund be retained? A review of the circumstances of the investment losses, how such lapses can be prevented in the future, and the specific changes to be made are topics that investors should discuss with the firm.

At other times, a key resignation is a sign of impending trouble. The resignation of a senior portfolio manager at the Clinton Group was a classic case. Upon leaving the firm, the portfolio manager stated that his resignation was caused by his disagreement with management over the ways in which the securities in the portfolio he managed were valued. Those investors who redeemed their investments from the Clinton Group could congratulate themselves for taking timely action.

Audited Reports

Audited reports of returns and financial conditions, including the amounts of assets under management, are crucial to both pre- and postinvestment monitoring of hedge fund risks. While financial statement audits are naturally expected in public companies, not all hedge funds are audited. According to one study of hedge fund audits in 2000,[19] as much as 40 percent of hedge funds did not have auditors, or were not audited. And the audited funds reported distinctly more accurate return data than nonaudited funds; the data quality difference amounted to an average of 1.8 percent a year. Not surprisingly, defunct funds were more often not audited than live funds, and larger funds tended to be audited while small funds were less so. Also, the Big Four auditing firms produced fewer errors than smaller auditors. Thus, as common sense and evidence suggest, investors should demand that hedge funds supply audited reports, and the auditors should be reputable firms.

Deviations from Stated Strategies

It is not possible to understand and monitor the risk of a hedge fund without knowing what its investment strategy is. As with evaluating its performance, risk management needs to identify how the fund generates returns. But the focus of risk management is different: First, it seeks to anticipate the potential losses that this strategy can generate; and second, it seeks to recognize if the managers change the investment strategy.

Deviations from stated strategies invariably are manifested in a number of indicators. First are changes in the amount of leverage. Second, there are a number of statistics to detect changes in the investment styles of hedge fund managers. The variations among different managers in these figures indicate differences in styles. Here are the commonly used indicators.

Security and Sector Concentration

Expressed as percentages of the portfolio's holdings in individual securities and in different sectors of the broad market, these indicators measure the degree of portfolio concentration in these securities and sectors. The idea is that more

[18] Amanda Cantrell, "Andor Replaces Manager of Poorly Performing Hedge Funds," *HedgeWorld*, December 17, 2003.

[19] Bing Liang, "Hedge Fund Returns: Auditing and Accuracy," forthcoming in *Journal of Portfolio Management* (www.sec.gov/spotlight/hedgefunds/hedge-liang.htm).

concentrated portfolios are subject to greater risks. Thus, portfolios with 10 or 15 securities are supposed to be riskier than those with 50 or more stocks. Likewise, portfolios concentrated in one or two sectors, say, technology or biotech, are thought to be subject to greater risk than those invested in the broad market. At the same time, concentrated portfolios are more common in hedge funds than in traditional portfolios. Some very successful hedge funds with billions of dollars of assets have been known to hold only 20 to 30 stocks.

Price-Earnings Multiples

The idea behind price-earnings (P/E) ratios as a risk indicator is that presumably stocks with high P/E multiples are riskier than those with low multiples. They also indicate if the managers are value or growth oriented because high-P/E multiples are associated with growth styles.

For fixed income–oriented funds, there are similar measures of sector concentration, such as holdings in mortgage-backed securities, investment grade corporate bonds, high yield bonds, foreign bonds, and so on. The distinctions are also made in terms of the credit ratings, such as BBB or lower. A host of other measures related to portfolio duration are also used to assess market neutrality or lack thereof.

These indicators are then monitored over time to detect shifts in strategies. Their values by necessity will vary from period to period. As long as they remain within relatively small ranges, the shifts should not be deemed significant enough to suggest changes. However, if the variations are large and frequent, clearly style drifts become an issue for consideration and for review.

These indicators have been made popular to investors and fund managers in the context of traditional long-only investments. In hedge fund investing, where returns are supposed to be uncorrelated to markets and investments vary across time frames, securities, and sectors, fund of funds managers and other experienced investors tend to place much less reliance on these indicators in the assessment of their portfolios' risks. Part of the reason is that hedge funds' mission is to search for alpha wherever it exists. But also, not all hedge funds are willing to provide such detailed statistics to their investors, either directly to the investors or indirectly to a third-party risk assessment firm.

As a result of these limiting practicalities, experienced hedge fund investors place particular emphasis on frequent contact with their hedge fund managers, in telephone conferences, and, less frequently, in on-site visits. As discussed previously, these meetings are supposed to provide investors with insight as to the thinking of the hedge fund managers and their thoughts on changes in market conditions, shifts in trading strategies, where alpha can be found, areas of potential risks, expectations of prospective returns, and market rumors. These meetings are expected to provide a more insightful understanding of the hedge funds' strategies, risks, and any changes thereof than any available statistics.

Factor Risks

Unable to rely entirely on risks data specific to individual hedge funds, active hedge fund investors such as funds of funds look to macroeconomic and market information to guide their assessment of the potential risks, and potential rewards, of their investments. They hope to benefit from these analyses to make decisions in retaining or redeeming from their existing managers, as well as in hiring new managers whose specialties are in areas of attractive future rewards. In this respect, these funds of funds are supported by evidence presented in this book and elsewhere that in order to generate returns, hedge funds are dependent to a significant extent on market factors such as the broad equity market, credit spreads, interest rate directions, merger activity, and so on. They are more beta dependent than one might assume from correlation and standard deviation statistics. The ability to unearth the emerging promising trends in any of these markets would allow funds of funds to invest with hedge funds that are strong in these areas.

In fixed income, traditional long-only funds are exposed to the risk of interest rates rising. The extent of the impact depends on the duration of the funds. Additionally, they are subject to changes in the credit upgrades or deterioration of the underlying securities. These credit risks may result in lesser increases in the prices of the bonds if interest rates decline, as compared to U.S. Treasuries. However, those bonds that receive credit upgrades may experience higher prices even if the overall interest rates increase.

Generally, fixed income arbitrage funds have little duration risk, and therefore are little impacted by shifts in interest rates, although they are still affected by yield curve shifts due to rate movements. The key risks inherent in these funds stem from credit spreads. To estimate the effects of changes in credit spreads, in terms of both risks and potential returns, Hsieh and Fung (2002)[20] formulated, as cited previously, the following relationship for the HFR Fixed Income Arbitrage strategy:

$$\text{HFR FI Arb} = 0.0096 - 5.37 * (\text{Changes in Credit Spread})$$
$$(10.0) \quad (6.6)$$
$$R^2 = 0.32$$

This relationship can be updated and fine-tuned for more specific fixed income markets.

A similar approach can be used to estimate the impact of the stock market on equity-oriented funds. As can be readily recalled, one feature of hedge fund strategies is low correlation to markets or market neutrality. Thus, fund managers often cite low portfolio beta as evidence of low correlation. Beta that is used in this citation comes from the familiar equation:

$$\bar{R}_{Fa} = r_f + \beta_F(\bar{R}_M - r_f)$$

In this equation, β_F is the result of two time series; one is the *ex post* returns of the F hedge fund, and the other is the actual returns of the market factor. It thus shows the effect of portfolio strategies, not the sources and causes of portfolio returns. To understand the causes of portfolio returns—that is, to determine the extent to which the portfolio's return is generated by the market—a more insightful measure is the weighted average betas of the individual securities in the portfolio.

$$\bar{R}_{Fe} = r_f + wa\beta_i(\bar{R}_M - r_f)$$

where $wa\beta_i$ is the weighted average of the individual securities in the portfolio F. It can be calculated by multiplying each security's beta by its weighting in the portfolio, summing them up, then dividing the sum by the number of securities in the portfolio. Mathematically,

$$wa\beta_i = \sum_{i=1}^{N} X_i\beta_i$$

---

[20] Hsieh and Fung, "Risk in Fixed Income Hedge Fund Styles."

Given the actual return of the market factor and the weighted average beta, the preceding equation would produce the *expected* return of the hedge fund, and it can be compared to the fund's *actual* return.

An equity market neutral fund is supposed to have zero beta because it generates returns independently of the market's moves. The portfolio's weighted average beta may tell a different story, however. In terms of weighted average beta, if it is long beta as the market rises, short beta as the market declines, and low beta in flat markets, it is not market neutral, although it may have a very low or zero portfolio β_F. Thus, changes in $wa\beta_i$ point to the fund riding on the market to generate returns. Unfortunately, due to the lack of transparency, these moves of shifting $wa\beta_i$ may not be detected by investors as the only data made available would be β_F.

Over time, changes in a fund's $wa\beta_i$ can be tracked to analyze the sources of returns generated by its portfolio, as well as to assess its risk profile. Thus, a fund's $wa\beta_i$ can be correlated to market returns. If correlation is high, it would indicate that the fund may have generated returns from taking market risks. It does not necessarily mean that the fund manager lacks stock-picking or market-timing skills. The opposite can be true if the returns are good. A positive excess return—that is, $\bar{R}_{Fa}$ is greater than $\bar{R}_{Fe}$—coupled with $wa\beta_i$'s high correlation with the market would suggest that the fund manager generates excess return by being exposed to the market at the right time. As such, since target $wa\beta_i$ can be compared to actual $wa\beta_i$, using $wa\beta_i$ can assess more accurately the amount of actual market exposure of a fund. Compared to β_F, $wa\beta_i$ is also a more revealing measure of the degree to which the portfolio is exposed to the market in its position taking. Further attribution analysis can then be used to assess the extent to which a fund manager relies on stock selection or beta risk taking to generate excess return. This information can be useful to determine the veracity of a fund manager's claim as a stock picker or a **market timer**, and the fund's strategy shifts over time.

3   "LEFT TAIL" RISKS AND OTHER QUANTITIES

Standard deviation measures the overall volatility around the average of a stream of returns. It does not differentiate between positive and negative deviations from the mean; any deviation from the average is treated as risk. Left tail risks, however, reflect greater concerns about the potential losses or the left tail of the normal distribution. When the return distribution is skewed to the left because of large losses and below-average gains, the distribution is said to have a fat left tail. In evaluating potential losses, investors should look at the left tail risk in addition to the standard deviation or volatility of returns of a hedge fund. There are a number of ways to measure the left tail risks. One is the maximum drawdown.

Maximum Drawdown

A drawdown is a loss. It is defined as the retrenchment in percentages from an equity peak to an equity valley. A drawdown is in effect from the time a retrenchment starts until a new equity high is reached (i.e., in terms of time, a drawdown encompasses both the period from equity peak to equity valley (length) and the time from the equity valley to a new equity high (recovery). Maximum drawdown is simply the largest percentage drawdown that has occurred in any stream of returns. Thus, the larger a fund's maximum drawdown is, the higher is its left tail risk.

A shortcoming of this maximum drawdown measure is that it does not give a sense as to the context and probability of such large losses. For perspective, between the near total loss of the Dow Jones Industrial Average in 1929 and the huge decline in the NASDAQ following the 2000 bubble burst, there was a time gap of 70 years of profits, sometimes extraordinary. However, most investors would shun any hedge funds that have experienced drawdowns approaching anywhere near such magnitude, and rightly so.

Value at Risk

Value at risk (VaR) is similar to maximum drawdown in that it is an indication of the largest possible loss, except that it is a probabilistic estimate based on past experience. The value-at-risk concept, pioneered at J. P. Morgan, seeks to estimate the maximum amount of losses with the highest possible level of confidence. Thus, the VaR estimate can be expressed as, "There is a 95 percent confidence that fund A will not lose more than X percent over the next year."

Although frequently touted, VaR is not widely used in hedge funds and funds of funds. For the latter, portfolio turnover or strategy changes in their hedge funds substantially reduce the quality of the value-at-risk measure. By itself, VaR is a statistical measure based on historical data; without additional information, it is hardly a reliable estimate for the future. Witness the data on the catastrophic losses of the stock market in the 1929 and 2000 bear markets. Also, from a technical standpoint, hedge fund returns are not normally distributed, a key prerequisite for the value at risk to be meaningful. Furthermore, some methodologies to calculate value at risk assume risks are either additive or reductive when in fact they may be multiplicative, such as the currency risk in foreign currency investments.

Nevertheless, risks of hedge funds tend to persist. From a practical viewpoint, it is fair to assume that hedge funds with large maximum drawdowns or high VaR in their records will remain risky. Investors with low tolerance for such risk levels might be better off looking elsewhere. Post investment, if any of the portfolio's hedge funds exhibit deterioration in these risk measures, it is probable that things have gone wrong at the fund. Perhaps the degenerating statistics may have been foretold by events such as the resignation of a key analyst. If so, it would be time for a detailed investigation and critical review of the fund's strategies and operations.

While drawdowns and VaR focus on the tail end of the left tail, the following statistics analyze the entire left side of the distribution. (For convenience, the definitions used here are from PerTrac.com. See http://support.pertrac2000.com/statistics2000.asp.) However, they all focus on the returns below a number, be it the average of the returns or a required minimum.

Loss Standard Deviation

While standard deviation analyzes both positive and negative deviations from the average, loss standard deviation focuses solely on the losses. However, the methodologies of both statistics are similar. Loss standard deviation calculates an average return for only the periods with a *loss* and then measures the variation of only the *losing* periods around this loss mean. As such, this statistic measures the volatility of downside performance.

N_L = number of periods that $R_i < 0$

$$\text{Loss Mean, } M_L = \left(\sum_{i=1}^{N} L_i \right) \div N_L$$

$$\text{Loss Deviation} = \left[\sum_{i=1}^{N} (LL_i)^2 \div (N_L - 1) \right]^{1/2}$$

where

N = number of periods
R_i = return for period i
M_L = loss mean
L_i = R_i (if $R_i < 0$) or 0 (if $R_i \geq 0$)
LL_i = $R_i - M_L$ (if $R_i < 0$) or 0 (if $R_i \geq 0$)

Downside Deviation

This statistic is similar to loss standard deviation, except for the introduction of a minimum acceptable return (MAR). MAR is usually a positive number. Thus, the downside deviation considers only returns that fall below a MAR rather than the arithmetic mean of the losses, which is always a negative number, as in loss standard deviation. For example, if MAR is assumed to be 10 percent, the downside deviation would measure the variation of each period that falls below 10 percent.

$$\text{Downside Deviation} = [\Sigma (L_i)^2 \div N]^{1/2}$$

where

R_i = return for period i
N = number of periods
R_{MAR} = period minimum acceptable return
L_i = $R_i - R_{\text{MAR}}$ (if $R_i - R_{\text{MAR}} < 0$) or 0 (if $R_i - R_{\text{MAR}} \geq 0$)

Sortino Ratio

This risk statistic is similar to the Sharpe ratio, except that it places emphasis on a required minimum rate. The numerator is defined as the incremental compound average period return over a minimum acceptable return (MAR). In the Sharpe ratio, the numerator is the return in excess of the risk-free rate. If MAR is equal to the risk-free rate, the numerator in both ratios would be equivalent.

Risk (denominator) is defined as the downside deviation below a minimum acceptable return (MAR). MAR can be (1) a user-defined value, (2) the risk-free rate, or (3) zero. In the Sharpe ratio, the denominator is simply the standard deviation of returns.

$$\text{Sortino Ratio} = (\text{Compound Period Return} - R_{\text{MAR}}) \div DD_{\text{MAR}}$$

where

R_i = return for period i
N = number of periods
R_{MAR} = period minimum acceptable return
DD_{MAR} = downside deviation
L_i = $R_i - R_{\text{MAR}}$ (if $R_i - R_{\text{MAR}} < 0$) or 0 (if $R_i - R_{\text{MAR}} \geq 0$)
DD_{MAR} = $[\Sigma (L_i)^2 \div N]^{1/2}$

Obviously these downside risk measures focus on the concern for losses or returns below some required minimum. Investors who have lower tolerance for losses or require a minimum rate of return would find these statistics useful but at the expense of downgrading funds with higher average returns.

ONGOING RISK MANAGEMENT: RISK AND PERFORMANCE MATRIX   4

Overall, evaluating a hedge fund's strategy and performance postinvestment is the same as before the investment is made, except that most likely greater insight has been gained from more in-depth and frequent contacts with the manager. Nevertheless, hedge fund evaluation is an ongoing process whereas key factors need to be continuously reviewed. Changes in these factors should be rescored and the viability of the hedge fund should be reassessed. The resignation of a key portfolio manager of the management team may or may not affect the fund's performance, but its prospects need to be reevaluated in the light of this event. Or when the chief financial officer is terminated, or there is high turnover in the back-office operation, or there is an unusual delay in the issuance of monthly returns and audit reports, questions should be raised about the fund's risk controls and security and portfolio valuation issues. If the fund has an unusually large return, positive or negative, the scoring for the style drift/discipline factor of the matrix may be downgraded if there is evidence of unusual risk taking.

CONCLUSION   5

Of the key issues confronting investors in hedge funds, risks and risk management are most important in determining the success of a hedge fund investment program. Management of hedge funds' risks requires not only a thorough understanding of the risks of the strategies, what they are, how they are generated, and if and how the managers manage them, but also the strategies themselves and how these strategies are executed over time. If "know your managers" is the key to selecting good hedge funds, "continue to know your managers" is the key to having a successful hedge fund portfolio.

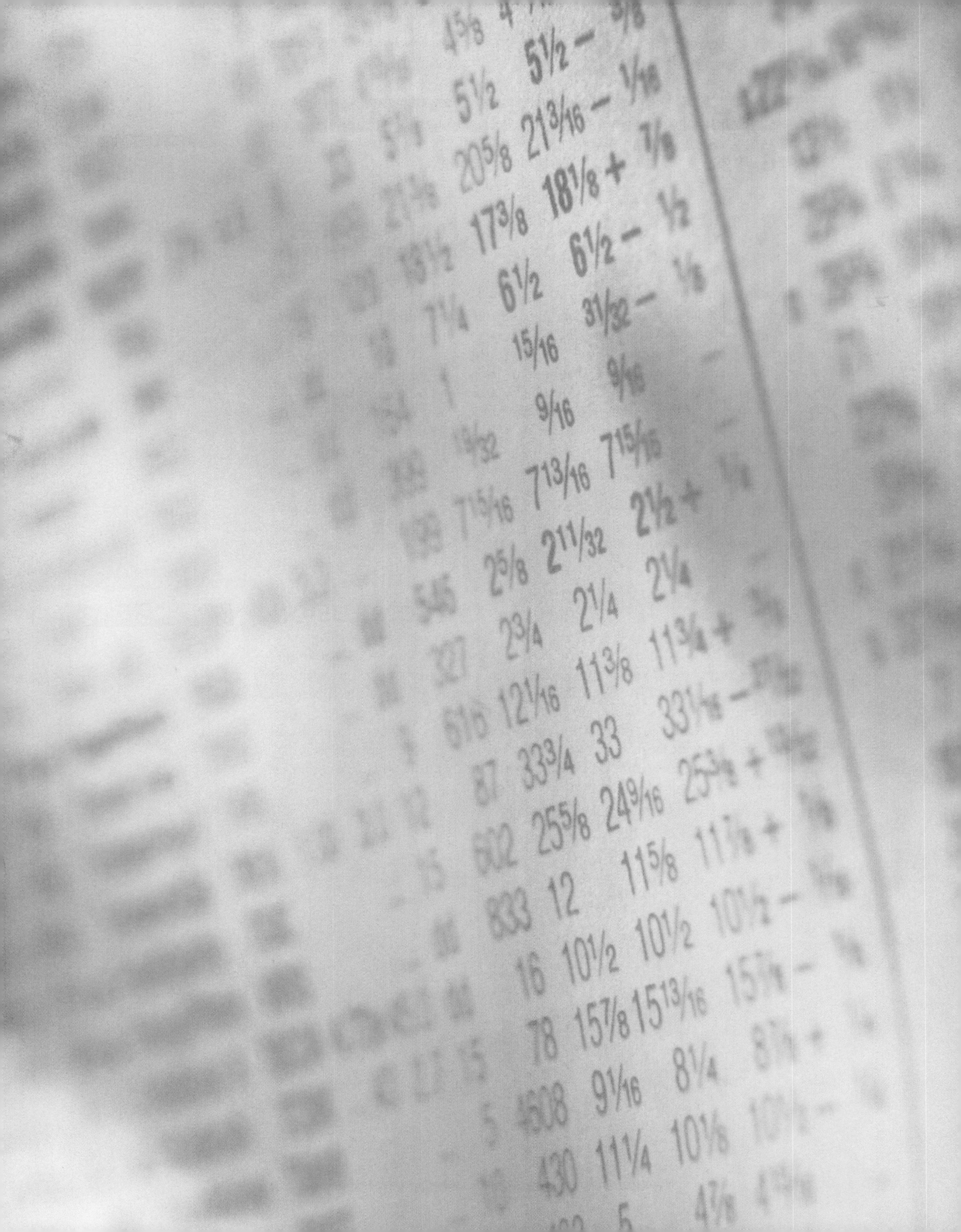

4⅝ 4... ⅝
5½ 5½ — ⅝
5½ 21³⁄₁₆ — ⅛
20⅝ 18⅛ + ⅞
17⅜
6½ 6½ — ½
7¼ 6½
15⁄₁₆ 3¹⁄₃₂ — ⅛
9⁄₁₆ 9⁄₁₆
9⁄₁₆
7¹⁵⁄₁₆
7⁵⁄₁₆ 7¹³⁄₁₆ 7¹⁵⁄₁₆
2⅝ 2¹¹⁄₃₂ 2½ +
2¾ 2¼ 2¼
6⅛ 12¹⁄₁₆ 11⅜ 11¾ +
33¾ 33 33¹⁄₈ —
25⅝ 24⁹⁄₁₆ 25¾ +
12 11⅝ 11⅞ +
10½ 10½ 10½ —
15⅞ 15¹³⁄₁₆ 15⅞
9¹⁄₁₆ 8¼ 8
11¼ 10⅛

APPENDIX A

Appendix A Solutions to End-of-Reading Problems

SOLUTIONS FOR READING 37

1. A. A satisfactory answer includes any four of the following uses of valuation models: (1) stock selection, (2) inferring market expectations (about variables such as future growth), (3) evaluating corporate events, (4) fairness opinions, (5) evaluating business strategies and models, (6) communication with analysts and shareholders, or (7) appraisal of private businesses.

B. A portfolio manager's most important use of valuation models is stock selection.

C. A corporate officer would be most directly concerned with using valuation concepts and models to evaluate corporate events, evaluate business strategies and models, and communicate with analysts and shareholders. To the extent that the corporate officer's company had a program of acquisitions, the use of valuation models in fairness opinions would also be relevant.

2. A. If Cornell had used a higher discount rate, the revenue growth rate consistent with a price of $61.50 would have been higher than 20 percent a year.

B. In any present value model, present value is inversely related to the discount rate applied to expected future cash flows. The higher the discount rate applied, the greater the future cash flows needed to equal a given value such as $61.50. To obtain the higher future revenue estimates needed to obtain a present value of $61.50 assuming a higher discount rate, a higher revenue growth rate assumption must be made. Therefore, if Cornell had assumed a higher discount rate, he would have concluded that the market expected Intel's revenue growth rate to be even higher than 20 percent.

3. A. As part of the planning step (after specification of investment objectives), the investor will generally elaborate on his approach to investment analysis and security selection. An active investor may specify in substantial detail the valuation models and/or criteria that he plans to use.

B. In the execution step, investment strategies are integrated with expectations to select a portfolio. In selecting a portfolio, the investor is continually put to the test to make accurate valuations of securities. Therefore, skill in valuation plays a key role in this step of the portfolio management process.

4. An investor trying to replicate a stock index does not need to make valuation judgments about securities. For example, the manager of an account indexed to the S&P 500, a type of passive investment strategy, seeks only to replicate the returns on the S&P 500, whether or not the index is fairly valued. In contrast, active investors attempt to identify mispriced securities—in particular, securities expected to earn a positive excess risk-adjusted return.

5. A. The *ex ante* alpha is the expected return minus the required return for a stock. Because the analysts feel their stocks are undervalued, the expected returns should exceed the required rates of return and the *ex ante* alphas should be positive (greater than zero).

B. The *ex post* alpha is the actual return minus the contemporaneous required return.

For KMG, the *ex post* alphas are as follows:

1998: $-34.0\% - 26.6\% = -60.6\%$
1999: $65.4\% - 19.6\% = 45.8\%$
2000: $20.9\% - (-8.5\%) = 29.4\%$
2001: $-12.9\% - (-11.0\%) = -1.9\%$

For NUE, the *ex post* alphas are as follows:

1998: $-8.5\% - 29.2\% = -37.7\%$
1999: $29.4\% - 21.5\% = 7.9\%$
2000: $-25.3\% - (-9.3\%) = -16.0\%$
2001: $37.3\% - (-12.1\%) = 49.4\%$

6. A. Wal-Mart's expected return consists of the following:

Price correction = 56.00 − 53.12 =	$2.88
Additional price appreciation	4.87
Cash dividends	0.28
Total return	$8.03

The expected rate of return is the expected dollar return divided by the price, or $8.03/53.12 = 15.1$ percent.

B. *Ex ante* alpha = Expected holding-period return − Required return
Ex ante alpha = $15.1 - 9.2 = 5.9$ percent

C. *Ex post* alpha = Actual holding-period return − Contemporaneous required return
Ex post alpha = $8.9 - (-10.4) = 19.3$ percent

7. A. *Ex ante* alpha is the expected holding-period return on a security minus the security's required return. An asset with a positive (negative) expected alpha is undervalued (overvalued).

B. Alpha of Security 1 = $0.20 - 0.21 = -0.01$ or -1 percent
Alpha of Security 2 = $0.18 - 0.08 = 0.10$ or 10 percent
Alpha of Security 3 = $0.11 - 0.10 - 0.01$ or 1 percent
The ranking is:

Security 2, alpha = 10% (most attractive)
Security 3, alpha = 1%
Security 1, alpha = -1% (least attractive)

C. According to Part B, Security 2 and Security 3 offer positive expected alphas. We might thus decide to invest in Security 2 and Security 3. The risks in such a decision include the following:

▶ We may have made an incorrect or incomplete adjustment for risk. We may not have accounted for all sources of risk reflected in the prices of the securities.

▶ Our own expectations may be biased or otherwise flawed.

▶ Even if our expectations are more accurate than the expectations reflected in the prices of the securities, there is no assurance that the mispricing will be corrected during our investment horizon, if at all.

It is also possible to enumerate other risks.

8. A. The analyst collects, organizes, analyzes, and communicates corporate information to investors and then recommends appropriate investment actions based on his analysis. When an analyst does his work well, clients are helped in reaching their investment objectives.

B. When well executed, the work of analysts promotes informed buy and sell decisions. Such informed decisions make asset prices better reflections of underlying value, with the result that capital flows to its highest-valued uses. By monitoring managers' actions, investment analysts can also help prevent managers from exploiting corporate resources for their own benefit.

9. We need to know (1) the time horizon for the price target and (2) the required rate of return on MBFG.MI. The price target of €9.20 represents a rate of return to investing in the stock calculated as $(€9.20 + 0.05)/€7.73 - 1.0 = 0.197$, or 20 percent. Without a time frame, we cannot evaluate how attractive that rate is. Suppose that the time horizon is one year. To further interpret a 20 percent expected one-year rate of return, we need to adjust it for risk. Subtracting the required rate of return from 20 percent would give the share's expected alpha. This number would allow us to conclude whether the stock was fairly valued.

Another acceptable answer is that we would need to know the analyst's current estimate of intrinsic value for MBFG.MI. This may or may not be the target price of €9.20.

10. A. XMI's expensing policies with respect to acquisitions inflate its earnings per share growth rate. By pushing down pre-acquisition EPS to an artificially low number, XMI can show unusual post-acquisition earnings growth rates.

B. Based on both expensing and revenue recognition policies, earnings clearly do not accurately reflect underlying economics. As noted in Part A, XMI attempts to manipulate the expensing policy of acquisitions to benefit its own earnings growth rate. In speeding up the recognition of revenue in its telecommunications subsidiary, XMI's revenue recognition policy is aggressive. In summary, the quality of XMI earnings is poor. (Note that the quality of XMI's disclosures is also poor, but disclosure was treated under the rubric of accounting risk factors in the text.)

C. The statement is a comparison of value, based on XMI's P/E relative to the P/Es of similar stocks. The underlying model is a relative valuation model (or the method of comparables).

D. Risk factors might include:

▶ Possible negative regulatory and legal developments. When and if XMI's accounting and business practices become known, XMI may be subject to legal and regulatory action.

▶ Risks in the forecasts. Because of the poor quality of XMI's earnings and the poor quality of its accounting disclosures, there is great uncertainty in any forecasts in a valuation of XMI.

▶ Other risks. A downward revision to the market price of XMI could occur if the extent of its quality of earnings issues and management's policies were to become known.

SOLUTIONS FOR READING 38

1. The central electronic limit order book is the hub of those automated markets that are order-driven (not price-driven). Statement III, therefore, is not correct.

2. A. The market order will be executed against the best matching order(s). Accordingly, Vincent Jacquet will buy 500 shares at €146 each, 500 shares at €147 each, and the remaining 500 shares at €149 each.

  B. Again, the market order will be executed against the best matching order(s). Accordingly, Vincent Jacquet will sell 500 shares at €145 each and 500 shares at €143 each.

3. On the Paris Bourse, the investor who placed the limit order at €24 stands to lose. Informed market participants can sell the share to this investor at €24, although the share is truly worth only €21. In contrast, the dealer is exposed to lose on Nasdaq. The dealer quote is $23.90–24.45, which is equivalent to €24.90–25.47 at the prevailing exchange rate. Informed market participants can sell the share to the Nasdaq dealer at the bid price of $23.90, although the share is truly worth only €21 or $20.16.

4. Small orders are generally market orders (buy or sell at the best price available in the market). In an order-driven system without developed market making, the automated limit order book generally shows a huge spread between the lowest ask and the highest bid of the orders currently in the system. When a new market order reaches the system, it is unlikely that a matching opposing market order will reach the system at exactly the same time. So, the market order will be executed against the limit order book. Given the wide spread, this will generally imply a transaction at a price that is very different from that of the previous transaction. To avoid this problem, one could have a periodic auction system in which all small orders are stored for a while and an auction takes place infrequently. Another alternative is the "trading halt" used in Tokyo.

   Very large orders (such as block trades—trades of 10,000 shares or more) run a serious risk of being "picked off" on an order-driven system. A large limit order is likely to remain posted for a long time on the computer system. The client is exposed to the risk that someone gets some news about the company or the market before the client is able to revise the posted limit price on the order. Buyers or sellers of large blocks of shares do not wish to be exposed to such a risk. Hence, special procedures have been put into place. Generally, block trades take place off the automated system and are reported only after some accepted delay.

5. Each of the three statements about ECNs is true.

6. A. There are not enough buy orders to meet the minimum fill requirement of Participant C, and his order would not be fulfilled. Participant A would buy 50,000 shares at €37 each, and Participant B would sell 50,000 shares at €37 each. Half of participant A's order would remain unfulfilled. Because the prevailing price is €37, Participant D's order to buy at €36 would remain unfulfilled. All unfulfilled orders of Participants A, C, and D would be resubmitted to the next crossing session because they are all GFD orders.

   B. Taking into account the trading activity in the first crossing session and the new orders submitted to the next session, the following orders would be there for the next session:
- ► Participant A: a market order to buy 50,000 shares
- ► Participant C: a market order to sell 150,000 shares, with a minimum fill of 125,000 shares
- ► Participant D: an order to buy 20,000 shares at €36
- ► Participant E: a market order to buy 150,000 shares
- ► Participant F: a market order to sell 50,000 shares

   In this session, the orders of participants A, C, E, and F would be completely filled. Participants A and E would buy 50,000 and 150,000 shares, respectively. Participants C and F would sell 150,000 and 50,000 shares, respectively. All the transactions would be at €38 per share. Participant D's order would still not be executed and would be resubmitted to the next crossing session later that day.

7. B is correct. Unlike U.S. banks, it is common for European banks to own shares of their client banks.

8. Because there are no cross-holdings by either Beta or Gamma in Alpha, IWF for Alpha = 100%. For Beta, IWF = 100 − 5 − 15 = 80%. For Gamma, IWF = 100 − 5 = 95%.

9. The apparent market capitalization of these four companies taken together is 50 million × 4 = 200 million. But because of their cross-holdings, there is some double counting. The usual free-float adjustment would be to retain only the portion that is not owned by other companies within the group.

   A. The adjusted market capitalization is as follows:
- ► Company A: 50 × (1 − 0.10) = $45 million (because 10% of Company A is held by Company C).
- ► Company B: 50 × (1 − 0.20 − 0.10) = $35 million (because 20% of Company B is held by Company A and 10% of Company B is held by Company C).
- ► Company C: 50 × (1 − 0.10 − 0.15) = $37.5 million (because 10% of Company C is held by Company A and 15% of Company C is held by Company B).
- ► Company D: 50 × (1 − 0.05) = $47.5 million (because 5% of Company D is held by Company C).

   B. From (a) above, the total adjusted market capitalization = 45 + 35 + 37.5 + 47.5 = $165 million. Because the unadjusted market capitalization of each company is the same, the total adjusted market cap can also be computed by subtracting the total cross-holdings from 200 million. The total cross-holdings are 50 × (0.20 + 0.10 + 0.15 + 0.10 + 0.10 + 0.05) = $35 million. Thus, the total adjusted market cap = 200 − 35 = $165 million.

10. A. Net dividend in euros, after deducting withholding tax = €0.50 per share × 1,000 shares × (1 − 0.15) = €425. So, the net dividend in dollars = €425 × $0.9810/€ = $416.93.

   B. The investor bought the shares for €56.91 per share × 1,000 shares = €56,910, or €56,910 × $0.9795/€ = $55,743.35.

      The investor sold the shares for €61.10 per share × 1,000 shares = €61,100, or €61,100 × $0.9810/€ = $59,939.1.

      Thus, capital gains = 59,939.1 − 55,743.35 = $4,195.75.

C. The investor would need to declare the total dividends, that is, without deducting the withholding tax, as dividend income. So, the dividend income to be declared is €0.50 per share × 1,000 shares × $0.9810/€ = $490.50.

Note that because of the tax treaty between the U.S. and Germany, however, the investor can deduct from income tax a tax credit for the dividends withheld in Germany; the tax credit is 490.50 − 416.93 = $73.57. (The tax credit can be computed alternatively as €0.50 per share × 1,000 shares × 0.15 × $0.9810/€ = $73.57.)

11. A. Initial investment = 41 × 100 = $4,100

Gross dividend = 2 × 100 = $200

Selling value = 51 × 100 = $5,100

Gross return in dollars = (5,100 + 200 − 4,100)/4,100 = 0.2927, or 29.27 percent

B. Initial investment = $4,100 × Skr9.4188/$ = Skr 38,617.08

Gross dividend = $200 × Skr9.8710/$ = Skr 1,974.20

Selling value = $5,100 × Skr9.8710/$ = Skr 50,342.10

Gross return in kroners = (50,342.10 + 1,974.20 − 38,617.08)/38,617.08 = 0.3547, or 35.47 percent

C. Capital gains = Selling value − Initial investment = 50,342.10 − 38,617.08 = Skr 11,725.02

Capital gains tax = 0.15 × 11,725.02 = Skr 1,758.75

Though 15% of the dividend was withheld in the United States, income tax in Sweden would be levied on the gross dividend of Skr 1,974.20. So, income tax = 0.50 × 1,974.20 = Skr 987.10. The effect of the dividends withheld in the U.S. is exactly offset by the withholding tax credit. So, we could use the gross dividend (net of Swedish income taxes) in computing the net return. Accordingly, rate of return, in kroners, net of taxes = (Capital gains + Gross dividend − Capital gains tax − Income tax)/Initial investment = (11,725.02 + 1,974.20 − 1,758.75 − 987.10)/38,617.08 = 0.2836, or 28.36 percent.

12. C is correct. Investors in non-domestic common stock normally avoid double taxation on dividend income by receiving a tax credit for taxes paid to the country where the investment is made.

13. Cost in U.S. dollars per share = $24.37 × 4 = $97.48 (because one Lafarge ADR is equivalent to one-fourth of a Lafarge share.) Therefore,

Cost in U.S. dollars for 10,000 shares = $974,800
Cost of purchasing in London = £67.17 × $1.4580/£ × 10,000
= $979,338.60
Cost of purchasing in Paris = €100.30 × $0.9695/€ × 10,000
= $972,408.50

Thus, it is the cheapest to buy the shares in Paris.

14. The German firm is considering a Level III ADR program. Accordingly, it must satisfy the requirements of both the NYSE and the U.S. Securities and Exchange Commission (SEC). This could impose substantial dual-listing costs on the German firm. The SEC will require the German firm to file a Form 20-F annually. On this form, the firm will have to provide a reconciliation of earnings and shareholder equity under German and U.S. GAAP. This implies that the company will have to supply all information necessary to comply with U.S. GAAP. Furthermore, the NYSE will require timely disclosure of various information, including quarterly accounting statements.

Overall, the disclosure requirements may cause considerable concern, as German and U.S. accounting practices differ substantially. Also, German firms are not accustomed to disclosing as much information in Germany as is required in the United States. They are also not used to producing frequent reports in English. The firm may face another hurdle if it is accustomed to smoothening reported earnings by using various hidden reserves. Another concern that the German firm may have is that cross-listing may increase the volatility of its share prices. It may feel that the U.S. investors may be quicker in selling their shares of the German firm in response to bad news than would the German investors.

15. The cost in British pounds, including commission and transaction tax, would be £3.60/share × 10,000 shares × (1 + 0.0010 + 0.0050) = £36,216. So, the cost in dollars would be £36,216 × $1.5010£ = $54,360.22.

16. The receipt in TW$, after excluding commission and transaction tax, would be TW$150.35/share × 20,000 shares × (1 − 0.0010 − 0.0030) = TW$2,994,972. So, the receipt in euros would be TW$2,994,972/ TW$32.88/€ = €91,087.96.

17. Each of the three statements is true.

18. The creation of WEBS for a country creates an additional option for an investor seeking to invest in equities in that country. Having an additional method by which to participate in a foreign market is likely to cause the premium on an existing closed-end country fund to narrow if the fund is trading at a premium. Or, if the existing closed-end country fund is trading at a discount, the launching of WEBS for that country is likely to make it even less attractive, leading to a widening of the discount.

19. The announcement of foreign investment restrictions increases the importance of closed-end country funds for U.S. investors who want exposure to that country in their investment portfolios. Therefore, all other things constant, these restrictions are likely to increase the premium or decrease the discount on the country-fund's shares. That is, the price–net asset value ratio is likely to increase.

20. The cost of 20,000 shares in the United States is $43.65 per share × 20,000 shares = $873,000. The cost in Germany in euros, including a 0.10% commission, would be €44.95 × 20,000 shares × 1.0010 = €899,899. So, the cost in dollars is €899,899 × $/€0.9710 = $873,801.93. Thus, it is better to buy the shares traded on the NYSE, saving 873,801.93 − 873,000.00 = $801.93.

21. During the six-hour time period when London is trading but the United States is not, the NAV of the fund in British pounds would be fluctuating in accordance with how the prices of the stocks in the index are changing. Because the U.S. market is closed, the most recent reported dollar price of the fund in the United States would not have changed. Then the U.S. market opens, and the fund's shares in the United States would open at a price based on the NAV in the United Kingdom at that time and the prevailing dollar-to-pound exchange rate. During the two-hour overlapping time period when both markets are open, the NAV in pounds would continue to change. The price of the fund in dollars would also be changing consistent with the changes in NAV and exchange rate. During the subsequent 4.5-hour time period when the New York market is open but the London market is not, the most recent reported NAV in pounds would remain the same. However, the price of the fund in the United States could change as the exchange rate changes and as new information comes in that affects investors' expectations about future stock prices in the United Kingdom. Then, the U.S. market closes, and during the time period when both markets are closed, the most recent reported U.S. prices and NAV in pounds also stay the same.

SOLUTIONS FOR READING 40

1. The book value represents mostly the historical value of the firm. Most assets and liabilities are carried at their historical cost, allowing for possible depreciation. The stock market price reflects the future earning power of the firm. If rapid growth in earnings is expected, the stock price could be well above the book value.

2. General provisions ("hidden reserves") appear as a liability, although they are in fact equity reserves. These provisions are "hidden" as a liability to allow the firm to use it in the future to smoothen earnings. Accordingly, the true book value is greater than the reported book value by the amount of these reserves. Thus, the practice of allowing corporations to build general provisions leads to an understatement of the reported book value, and an overstatement of the ratio of market price to book value.

3. Some of the reasons why German earnings are understated compared with U.S. earnings are as follows:

   ▶ German firms take provisions quite generously, and they are deducted from the reported earnings when initially taken.

   ▶ Reported earnings are tax earnings that are subject to many actions taken to reduce taxation.

   ▶ Many German firms tend to publish separately the nonconsolidated financial statements of the various companies belonging to the same group.

4. **A.** Without expensing the options, the firm's pretax earnings per share are $2,000,000/500,000 = $4 per share.

   B. The expense due to the options is $20,000 \times \$4 = \$80,000$. The pretax income per share would be ($2,000,000 - $80,000)/500,000 = $3.84 per share.

   C. The expense due to the options based on the different valuation is $20,000 \times \$5.25 = \$105,000$. The pretax income per share would be ($2,000,000 - $105,000)/500,000 = $3.79 per share.

5. **A.** Consolidated earnings are as follows:

   Company A: 10 million + 10% of 30 million =   13 million
   Company B: 30 million + 20% of 10 million =   32 million

   B. The P/E ratios are as follows:

	Company A	Company B
Nonconsolidated	200/10 = 20	450/30 = 15
Consolidated	200/13 = 15.4	450/32 = 14.1

   Due to nonconsolidation, the earnings are understated. Thus, the P/E ratios are overstated due to nonconsolidation. As seen here, the consolidation of earnings adjusts the P/E ratios downward.

International Investments, Fifth Edition, by Bruno Solnik and Dennis McLeavey. Copyright © 2004 by Pearson Education. Reprinted with permission of Pearson Education, publishing as Pearson Addison Wesley.

6. Under the assumption that the total worldwide revenue of all firms in this industry was $250 billion, the market shares of the top five corporations are the following:

> AOL Time Warner: $38 billion/$250 billion = 15.2%
>
> Walt Disney: 25/250 = 10.0%
>
> Vivendi Universal: 25/250 = 10.0%
>
> Viacom: 23/250 = 9.2%
>
> News Corporation: 13/250 = 5.2%

A. The three-firm concentration ratio is the combined market share of the largest three firms in the industry = 15.2 + 10 + 10 = 35.2%.

The five-firm concentration ratio is the combined market share of the largest five firms in the industry = 15.2 + 10 + 10 + 9.2 + 5.2 = 49.6%.

B. The three-firm Herfindahl index is the sum of the squared market shares of the largest three firms in the industry = $0.152^2 + 0.10^2 + 0.10^2$ = 0.043, or 430 percent squared. The five-firm Herfindahl index is the sum of the squared market shares of the largest five firms in the industry = $0.152^2 + 0.10^2 + 0.10^2 + 0.092^2 + 0.052^2 = 0.054$.

C. The combined market share of the top five firms, as computed in part (a), is 49.6 percent. Therefore, the combined market share of the 40 other firms is 100 − 49.6 = 50.4%. Assuming that each of them has the same share, the share of each is 50.4/40 = 1.26%. So, the Herfindahl index for the industry, which is the sum of the squared market shares of all the firms in the industry, is $0.152^2 + 0.10^2 + 0.10^2 + 0.092^2 + 0.052^2 + 0.0126^2 + \ldots + 0.0126^2 = 0.054 + 40 \times 0.0126^2 = 0.0603$.

D. The combined market share of the 10 other firms is 100 − 49.6 = 50.4%. Assuming that each of them has the same share, the share of each is 50.4/10 = 5.04%. So, the Herfindahl index for the industry, which is the sum of the squared market shares of all the firms in the industry, is $0.152^2 + 0.10^2 + 0.10^2 + 0.092^2 + 0.052^2 + 0.0504^2 + \ldots + 0.0504^2 = 0.054 + 10 \times 0.0504^2 = 0.0794$.

E. There is greater competition in the scenario in Part C than in Part D. The Herfindahl index in Part C is smaller than that in Part D, reflecting a more competitive industry structure in Part C. Also, the reciprocal of the Herfindahl index is 16.6 in Part C and 12.6 in Part D. Thus, the market structure in Part C is equivalent to having 16.6 firms of the same size, and the market structure in Part D is equivalent to having 12.6 firms of the same size. This reflects that the market structure in Part D is relatively more oligopolistic, or less competitive, than in Part C.

7. A. Though News Corporation is based in Australia, it is really a global conglomerate, and a majority of its businesses are outside of Australia. About 77 percent of its revenues are in the United States, 15 percent in Europe, and only 8 percent in Australia and Asia together. Its major competitors include firms headquartered in the United States and Vivendi Universal, a firm headquartered in France. In view of the global characteristics of News Corporation, its valuation should be done primarily relative to the global industry.

B. Due to differences in accounting standards and practices among countries, the analyst would be concerned if he were comparing ratios of News Corporation, computed as per Australian GAAP, with those of Vivendi Universal, computed as per French GAAP. However, both firms trade in the United States as registered ADRs and prepare statements as per U.S. GAAP. Therefore, the analyst could simply compare ratios computed based on these statements.

8. A. ROE = NI/Equity. So,

ROE for Walt Disney = 1,300/20,975 = 0.062
ROE for News Corporation = 719/16,374 = 0.044

Clearly, Walt Disney did better than News Corporation in terms of ROE.

B. One version of the DuPont model breaks down ROE into three contributing elements, as follows:

ROE = Net profit margin $\times$ Asset turnover $\times$ Leverage

where

Net profit margin = NI/Sales
Asset turnover = Sales/Assets
Leverage = Assets/Equity

The three contributing elements for both the companies are computed based on the data given in the problem, and are given in the following table:

	Walt Disney	News Corp.
Net profit margin	0.056	0.050
Asset turnover	0.536	0.403
Leverage	2.082	2.179

The numbers in the table indicate that the main reason Walt Disney did better than News Corporation is that it had a better asset turnover. That is, it utilized its assets more efficiently than did News Corporation. Walt Disney also had a higher net profit margin than did News Corporation. The only contributing element that is higher for News Corporation is leverage, implying that News Corporation levered its operating results using more debt than did Walt Disney.

To analyze why the net profit margin for Walt Disney is a little higher than that for News Corporation, the net profit margin is broken down as follows:

Net profit margin = NI/EBT $\times$ EBT/EBIT $\times$ EBIT/Sales

The breakdown of net profit margin is given in the following table:

	Walt Disney	News Corp.
NI/EBT	0.562	0.593
EBT/EBIT	0.762	0.666
EBIT/Sales	0.130	0.126

The data in the table suggest that the net profit margin for Walt Disney was higher than that for News Corporation because of a higher EBT/EBIT ratio (i.e., a lower debt burden, because a higher value of EBT/EBIT implies a lower debt burden.) This is not unexpected, because we saw in the breakdown earlier that Walt Disney had a lower leverage than did News Corporation.

9. In an efficient market, all available information is already incorporated in current stock prices. The fact that economic growth is currently higher in Country A than in Country B implies that current stock prices are already "higher" in A than in B. Only unanticipated news about future growth rates should affect future stock prices. Current growth rates can explain past performance of stock prices, but only differences in future growth rates from their current anticipated levels should guide your country selection. Hence, you should decide whether your own economic growth forecasts differ from those implicit in current stock prices.

10. The intrinsic value is given by:

$$P_0 = \frac{D_1}{r - g} = \frac{E_1(1 - b)}{r - g}$$

where

E_1 is next year's earnings = 4 per share
$1 - b$ is the earnings payout ratio = 0.70
r is the required rate of return on the stock = 0.12
g is the growth rate of earnings = $1.25 \times 2.8\%$ = 3.5% or 0.035

So,

$P_0 = 4 \times 0.70/(0.12 - 0.035) = $ €32.94 per share
$P_0/E_1 = 0.70/(0.12 - 0.035) = 8.24$

11. **A.** Intrinsic P/E ratio $= \dfrac{P_0}{E_1} = \dfrac{1}{r}\left[1 + \dfrac{b(\mathrm{ROE} - r)}{r - \mathrm{ROE} \times b}\right]$. In this case, $b = 0$, because the company pays out all its earnings. So, $P_0/E_1 = 1/r = 1/0.13 = 7.69$.

B. Again, $P_0/E_1 = 1/r = 1/0.13 = 7.69$.

C. It is clear from the expression in part (a) that if $b = 0$, the intrinsic P/E value is independent of ROE. To further explore this, realize that the intrinsic P/E value can also be expressed as $P_0/E_1 = (1/r) + \mathrm{FF} \times \mathrm{G}$, where the franchise factor is $\mathrm{FF} = (\mathrm{ROE} - r)/(\mathrm{ROE} \times r)$ or $1/r - 1/\mathrm{ROE}$, and the growth factor is $\mathrm{G} = g/(r - g)$. If $b = 0$, then $g = 0$, and therefore, the growth factor $\mathrm{G} = 0$. Thus, regardless of how big the ROE—and consequently the franchise factor FF—is, the franchise value, $\mathrm{FF} \times \mathrm{G}$, is zero, and the intrinsic P/E value is simply $1/r$.

D. Again, $P_0/E_1 = 1/r = 1/0.13 = 7.69$.

E. In part (d), ROE $= r = 13\%$. It is clear from the expression in part (a) that if ROE $= r$, the intrinsic P/E value is independent of the retention ratio, b. To further explore this, let us again look at the expression for intrinsic P/E value discussed in part (c). If ROE $= r$, then the franchise factor FF $= 0$. Thus, regardless of how large the retention ratio—and consequently the growth factor G—is, the franchise value, $\mathrm{FF} \times \mathrm{G}$, is zero, and the intrinsic P/E value is simply $1/r$.

12. **i.** Franchise factor $= 1/r - 1/\text{ROE} = 1/0.10 - 1/0.12 = 1.67$.

ii. Growth factor $= g/(r - g) = (b \times \text{ROE})/(r - b \times \text{ROE}) = (0.70 \times 0.12)/(0.10 - 0.70 \times 0.12) = 5.25$.

iii. Franchise P/E value $=$ Franchise factor $\times$ Growth factor $= 1.67 \times 5.25 = 8.77$.

iv. Tangible P/E value $= 1/r = 1/0.10 = 10$.

v. Intrinsic P/E value $=$ Franchise P/E value $+$ Tangible P/E value $= 8.77 = 10 = 18.77$. We can also verify that intrinsic P/E value $(1 - b)/(r - g) + (1 - 0.70)/(0.10 - 0.70 \times 0.12) = 18.75$ (the slight difference is due to rounding).

13. The P/E is equal to

$$P_0/E_1 = \frac{1}{\rho + (1 - \lambda)I}$$

where

$I =$ rate of inflation $= 3\%$
$\rho =$ *real required rate of return* $= 8\% - 3\% = 5\%$

i. $\lambda = 1$: $P_0/E_1 = 1/\rho = 1/0.05 = 20$.

ii. $\lambda = 0.4$: $P_0/E_1 = 1/(0.05 + 0.60 \times 0.03) = 1/0.068 = 14.71$.

iii. $\lambda = 0$: $P_0/E_1 = 1/(\rho + I) = 1/0.08 = 12.50$.

We observe that the higher the inflation flow-through rate, the higher the P/E ratio. In other words, the less a firm is able to pass inflation through its earnings, the more it is penalized.

14. For both Company B and Company U, $\lambda = 0.60$, or $1 - \lambda = 0.40$. Also, $\rho = 0.08$ for both.

$$P_0/E_1 \text{ for Company } B = \frac{1}{\rho + (1 - \lambda)I} = 1/(0.08 + 0.40 \times 0.09) = 8.62$$

$$P_0/E_1 \text{ for Company } U = \frac{1}{\rho + (1 - \lambda)I} = 1/(0.08 + 0.40 \times 0.025)$$
$$= 11.11$$

P/E for Company B, which is subject to a higher inflation rate, is smaller than that for Company U. Thus, if full inflation pass-through cannot be achieved, then the higher the inflation rate, the more negative the influence on the stock price.

15. **A.** If the company can completely pass inflation through its earnings, $P/E = 1/\rho = 1/0.07 = 14.29$ in each of the years. Inflation has no effect on the P/E ratio, because the firm can completely pass inflation through its earnings.

B. $P/E = \dfrac{1}{\rho + (1 - \lambda)I} = 1/(0.07 + 0.50 \times I)$

Year	Inflation (%)	P/E
1995	22.0	5.56
1996	9.1	8.66
1997	4.3	10.93
1998	2.5	12.12
1999	8.4	8.93

C. As mentioned in part (a), inflation has no effect on the P/E ratio if the firm can completely pass inflation through its earnings. However, if the firm cannot completely pass inflation through its earnings as in part (b), then the higher the inflation rate (e.g., in the year 1995), the more severe the influence on the stock price.

16. Due to the appreciation of the euro relative to the dollar, the French goods will become more expensive in terms of the dollar. If the French company is able to completely pass through this increase to its U.S.-based customers, its P/E ratio will not suffer. Regardless of the extent of the appreciation of the euro, the company's P/E ratio will be unaffected if it is able to completely pass the appreciation through to its customers. However, if the company is able to only partially pass the euro appreciation through to its U.S.-based customers, the P/E ratio will go down. The higher the euro appreciation, the more severe will be the decline in the P/E ratio.

17. A. Because the portfolio is equally invested in the two stocks, the factor exposures of the portfolio would be equally weighted averages of the factor exposures of the two stocks. So, the factor exposures of the portfolio would be as follows:

	Portfolio
Confidence	0.4
Time horizon	0.7
Inflation	−0.3
Business cycle	3.0
Market timing	0.85

B. The stocks have a positive exposure to business cycle and a negative exposure to inflation. Also, you expect strong economic growth and an increase in inflation. Therefore, you should overweigh the stock with a greater exposure to business cycle and a smaller exposure (in absolute terms) to inflation. Stock A satisfies both, and accordingly you should overweigh stock A.

18. It is clear by looking at the table that in each of the three size categories, the low price-to-book value stock (P/BV) outperforms the high P/BV stock. Thus, there seems to be a *value effect*, as the value firms seem to outperform the growth firms. That is, the value factor seems to be significant.

   To clearly see the *size effect*, we rearrange the stocks in the two P/BV categories, as follows:

Stock	Size	P/BV	Return (%)
A	Huge	High	4
C	Medium	High	9
E	Small	High	13
B	Huge	Low	6
D	Medium	Low	12
F	Small	Low	15

In both P/BV categories, smaller firms outperform bigger firms. Thus, there seems to be a *size effect,* and the size factor seems to be significant.

19. We first compute the changes in the two factors and the returns on each stock. The following table has the numbers. Because we are computing the changes, we lose one observation.

Period	Change in Interest Rate	Change in Approval	Return on Stock		
			A	B	C
2	−2.1	5	−0.12	−0.49	−0.45
3	0.3	−1	−0.22	0.39	0.39
4	1.7	−2	0.40	0.42	0.21
5	−1.8	19	−0.33	−0.33	−0.19
6	−0.2	−19	−0.16	−0.30	−0.22
7	2.3	23	1.10	1.14	0.96
8	0.1	−27	0.01	0.14	−0.25
9	−2.3	2	−0.50	−0.48	−0.23
10	−0.2	20	−0.14	−0.15	−0.24

We now estimate the following factor model for each of the three stocks, using the respective nine observations from the preceding table.

$$R_i = \alpha_i + \beta_{1i}f_1 + \beta_{2i}f_2 + \varepsilon_i$$

where

R_i is the rate of return on stock i

α_i is a constant

f_1 and f_2 are the two factors common to the three stocks (f_1 is the change in interest rate, and f_2 is the change in approval rating)

β_{1i} and β_{2i} are the risk exposures of stock i to each of the two factors

ε_i is a random term specific to stock i

The results of the estimation are as follows:

	Stock A	Stock B	Stock C
α	0.05	0.10	0.03
(*t*-statistic)	(0.56)	(1.31)	(0.36)
β_1	0.25[a]	0.31[a]	0.22[a]
(*t*-statistic)	(4.32)	(6.20)	(3.89)
β_2	0.01	0.01	0.01
(*t*-statistic)	(1.27)	(1.18)	(1.66)

[a] Statistically significant at the 99% level.

The values of β_1 are highly statistically significant, with a p-value of less than 0.01, for each of the three stocks. In contrast, none of the values of β_2 are statistically significant (each of the p-values is greater than 0.10). The magnitudes of β_1 are several times bigger than the magnitudes of β_2. Clearly, the first factor (change in interest rate) influences stock returns in this country, while the second factor (change in approval) does not.

20. A. $R_f = 4\%$, $RP_w = 5\%$, and $RP_{SFr} = 1\%$. So,

$$E(R_i) = 4\% + \beta_1 \times 5\% + \beta_2 \times 1\%$$

Accordingly,

$$E(R_A) = 4\% + 1 \times 5\% + 1 \times 1\% = 10\%$$
$$E(R_B) = 4\% + 1 \times 5\% + 0 \times 1\% = 9\%$$
$$E(R_C) = 4\% + 1.2 \times 5\% + 0.5 \times 1\% = 10.5\%$$
$$E(R_D) = 4\% + 1.4 \times 5\% - 0.5 \times 1\% = 10.5\%$$

B. Stocks that should be purchased are those with a forecasted return, higher than their theoretical expected return, given the stock's risk exposures. Because the forecasted returns given in the problem are the returns in Swiss francs, we need to convert them to dollar returns first. We expect the Swiss franc to appreciate relative to the dollar by 2 percent. Therefore, using a linear approximation, the dollar return is the return in Swiss francs + 2%. The following table summarizes the forecasted returns in francs and in dollars, and the theoretical expected returns in dollars (computed in Part A).

	Stock A	Stock B	Stock C	Stock D
Forecasted return (in francs)	8%	9%	11%	7%
Forecasted return (in dollars)	10%	11%	13%	9%
Theoretical expected return (in dollars)	10%	9%	10.5%	10.5%

Looking at this table, we find that the broker forecasts superior returns for stocks B and C. Therefore, they should be bought. Conversely, stock D should be sold.

SOLUTIONS FOR READING 41

1. D is correct. The Swiss watch industry is in the mature life cycle phase, with growth in sales corresponding to the economic growth of its three largest distribution (primary export) regions. In terms of the business cycle, cyclical industries are those whose earnings track the cycle. The profits of the Swiss watch industry "benefit from economic upturns, but suffer in a downturn. The earnings movement is exaggerated." Therefore, JQC is a cyclical business.

2. D is correct. Duvalier states that high barriers to entry are the primary determinant of industry profitability. Industry economic and technical characteristics that are important determinants of high entry barriers are:

   ► Economies of scale
   ► Proprietary product differences
   ► Brand identity
   ► Switching costs
   ► Capital requirements
   ► Access to distribution
   ► Absolute cost advantages: proprietary learning curve, access to necessary inputs, proprietary low-cost product design
   ► Government policy
   ► Expected retaliation

   Supplier concentration is not a determinant of entry barriers, but it is a determinant of the bargaining power of suppliers.

3. D is correct. "The crucial question in determining profitability is whether firms can capture the value they create for buyers, or whether this value is competed away to others. Industry structure determines who captures the value. The threat of entry determines the likelihood that new firms will enter an industry and compete away the value, either passing it on to buyers in the form of lower prices or dissipating it by raising the costs of competing." In this case, the barriers to entry are high and, therefore, the threat of entry is low. Thus, the value that Swiss watchmakers create for buyers is kept by companies in the industry in the form of higher prices. This conclusion is supported by the fact that 80 percent of the watches sold worldwide are manufactured in Hong Kong and Japan, but more than half of the value is generated by the Swiss watch industry.

4. A is correct. "The long-term supply/demand balance is strongly influenced by the industry structure as are the consequences of a supply/demand imbalance for profitability. . . . The height of entry barriers underpins the likelihood that new entrants will enter an industry and bid down prices." Because entry barriers are high in the Swiss watchmaking industry, new entrants are unlikely to enter the industry and bid down prices. Capacity expansion and price wars are often fueled by competitive rivalry, whereas exit barriers influence whether existing competitors will leave.

5. A is correct. The sustainability of a generic strategy requires that a company possess some barriers that make imitation of the strategy difficult. One risk of a differentiation strategy is that cost proximity or parity relative to competitors is lost. "A differentiator cannot ignore its cost position, because its premium prices will be nullified by a markedly inferior cost position. A differentiator thus aims at a cost parity or proximity relative to its competitors, by reducing costs in all areas that do not affect differentiation."

6. A is correct. "New regulations, or changes to old laws can impact an industry's sales and earnings." In this case, the Swiss Government passed a law in 1992 regulating the use of the name "Swiss" for watches. . . . In addition, the Swiss watch industry has been able to effectively segment its product offerings by reputation, i.e., "the 'Swiss made' designation enjoys a solid reputation throughout the world and globalization of the trade has done nothing to diminish its importance." The Swiss watchmaking industry does not face obsolescence from competing technologies. The level of industry concentration is not given so its impact cannot be determined.

SOLUTIONS FOR READING 46

1. For AOL Time Warner, the required return is

$$r = R_F + \beta[E(R_M) - R_F] = 4.35\% + 2.50(8.04\%) = 4.35\% + 20.10\%$$
$$= 24.45\%$$

For JP Morgan Chase, the required return is

$$r = R_F + \beta[E(R_M) - R_F] = 4.35\% + 1.50(8.04\%) = 4.35\% + 12.06\%$$
$$= 16.41\%$$

For Boeing, the required return is

$$r = R_F + \beta[E(R_M) - R_F] = 4.35\% + 0.80(8.04\%) = 4.35\% + 6.43\%$$
$$= 10.78\%$$

2. The five-factor APT model is of the form

$$E(R_i) = \text{T-bill rate} + (\text{Sensitivity to confidence risk} \times 2.59\%)$$
$$- (\text{Sensitivity to time horizon risk} \times 0.66\%)$$
$$- (\text{Sensitivity to inflation risk} \times 4.32\%)$$
$$+ (\text{Sensitivity to business-cycle risk} \times 1.49\%)$$
$$+ (\text{Sensitivity to market-timing risk} \times 3.61\%)$$

For Terra Energy, the required return is

$$r = 4.1\% + (0.25 \times 2.59\%) - (0.30 \times 0.66\%) - (-0.45 \times 4.32\%)$$
$$+ (1.60 \times 1.49\%) + (0.80 \times 3.61\%)$$
$$= 4.10\% + 0.65\% - 0.20\% + 1.94\% + 2.38\% + 2.89\% = 11.76\%$$

3. The required return is given by

$$r = R_F + \beta[E(R_M) - R_F] = 0.045 + (-0.2)(0.075) = 4.5\% - 1.5\% = 3.0\%$$

Newmont Mining has a required return of 3 percent. When beta is negative, an asset has a CAPM required rate of return that is below the risk-free rate.

4. The equation for the single-period DDM is $V_0 = \dfrac{D_1 + P_1}{1 + r}$

$$\textit{For Stock 1, } V_0 = \frac{0.30 + 21.00}{1.10} = \$19.36$$

$$\textit{For Stock 2, } 30.00 = \frac{D_1 + 32.00}{1.10}, D_1 = 1.10(30.00) - 32.00 = \$1.00$$

$$\textit{For Stock 3, } 92.00 = \frac{2.70 + P_1}{1.12}, P_1 = 92.00(1.12) - 2.70 = \$100.34$$

$$\textit{For Stock 4, } 16.00 = \frac{0.30 + 17.90}{1 + r}, r = \frac{0.30 + 17.90}{16.00} - 1 = 0.1375$$
$$= 13.75\%$$

5. Using the CAPM, GM's required rate of return is

$$r = R_F + \beta[E(R_M) - R_F] = 5.3\% + 0.90(6.00\%) = 5.3\% + 5.4\% = 10.7\%$$

Substituting the values into the single-period DDM, we obtain

$$V_0 = \frac{D_1 + P_1}{(1 + r)^1}, \text{ or } 66.00 = \frac{2.40 + P_1}{(1.107)^1}$$

The expected price is $P_1 = 66.00(1.107) - 2.40 = 73.06 - 2.40 = \$70.66$.

6. A. The projected dividend is $D_1 = D_0(1 + g) = 1.50(1.05) = \$1.575$.

   B. $r = R_F + \beta[E(R_M) - R_F] = 4.5\% + 0.85(6.0\%) = 4.5\% + 5.1\% = 9.6\%$

   C. $V_0 = D_1/(r - g) = 1.575/(0.096 - 0.05) = 1.575/0.046 = \$34.24$

   D. The stock price predicted by the Gordon growth model (\$34.24) is below the market price of \$50. A $g > 5$ percent is required for the value estimated with the model to be \$50. To find the g that would yield a \$50 price, we solve

$$50 = \frac{1.50(1 + g)}{0.096 - g}, \text{ which simplifies to}$$

$$4.8 - 50g = 1.5 + 1.5g$$
$$51.5g = 3.3$$
$$g = 0.06408, \text{ or } g = 6.408\%$$

To verify that this growth rate results in a value of \$50, substitute $g = 6.408$ percent into the Gordon growth model equation:

$$V_0 = \frac{D_0(1 + g)}{r - g} = \frac{1.50(1.06408)}{0.096 - 0.06408} = \frac{1.59612}{0.03192} = \$50.00$$

7. A. The value of each stock using the Gordon growth model is

$$V_{Que} = \frac{0.50(1.07)}{0.10 - 0.07} = \frac{0.535}{0.03} = \$17.83$$

$$V_{SHS} = \frac{1.20(1.065)}{0.105 - 0.065} = \frac{1.278}{0.04} = \$31.95$$

$$V_{True} = \frac{0.88(1.05)}{0.10 - 0.05} = \frac{0.924}{0.05} = \$18.48$$

   B. All three stocks are selling at a premium above their DDM estimated values. The percentage premiums are

$$\text{Premium (Que)} = (25 - 17.83)/17.83 = 7.17/17.83 = 40.2\%$$
$$\text{Premium (SHS)} = (40 - 31.95)/31.95 = 8.05/31.95 = 25.2\%$$
$$\text{Premium (True)} = (20 - 18.48)/18.48 = 1.52/18.48 = 8.2\%$$

True Corporation is selling for the smallest relative premium over its estimated value found with the Gordon growth model.

8. A. In the Gordon growth model, the expected rate of return is
$r = D_1/P_0 + g.$

AEP	$r = 2.40/46.17 + 5.0\% = 5.20\% + 5.0\% = 10.2\%$
Consolidated Edison	$r = 2.20/39.80 + 5.0\% = 5.53\% + 5.0\% = 10.53\%$
Exelon	$r = 1.69/64.12 + 7.0\% = 2.64\% + 7.0\% = 9.64\%$
Southern Co.	$r = 1.34/23.25 + 5.5\% = 5.76\% + 5.5\% = 11.26\%$
Dominion Resources	$r = 2.58/60.13 + 5.5\% = 4.29\% + 5.5\% = 9.79\%$

B. With the capital asset pricing model, the required return is

$r = R_F + \beta[E(R_M) - R_F]$:

AEP	$r = 5.3\% + 0.60(6.0\%) = 5.3\% + 3.6\% = 8.9\%$
Consolidated Edison	$r = 5.3\% + 0.60(6.0\%) = 5.3\% + 3.6\% = 8.9\%$
Exelon	$r = 5.3\% + 0.80(6.0\%) = 5.3\% + 4.8\% = 10.1\%$
Southern Co.	$r = 5.3\% + 0.65(6.0\%) = 5.3\% + 3.9\% = 9.2\%$
Dominion Resources	$r = 5.3\% + 0.65(6.0\%) = 5.3\% + 3.9\% = 9.2\%$

9. A. Compounded for eight years, $0.585(1 + g)^8 = 1.46$. Solving for g, we get $g = 12.11\%$.

B. For the future dividend growth rate, use $g = 12.11\%/2 = 6.06\%$. The expected rate of return is

$$r = \frac{D_1}{P_0} + g = \frac{1.46(1.0606)}{80.00} + 0.0606 = 0.0800 = 8.00\%$$

C. The required rate of return for PG is using the CAPM

$$r = R_F + \beta[E(R_M) - R_F] = 5.56\% + 0.53(3.71\%) = 7.53\%$$

$$V_0 = \frac{D_1}{r - g} = \frac{1.46(1.0606)}{0.0753 - 0.0606} = \$105.34$$

10. The value of one share of NiSource Preferred B is $V_0 = D/r = 3.88/0.0788 = \$49.24$.

If the price is \$46.00, the yield is $r = D/P_0 = 3.88/46.00 = 0.0843 = 8.43\%$.

11. A. Total market value = (Price/share) × (Number of shares) = $88.00(300,000,000) = \$26.4$ billion.

Earnings per share = EPS = $\$3,000,000/300,000,000$ shares = $\$0.01$ per share

$P/E = 88.00/0.01 = 8,800$

Sales per share = $\$210,000,000/300,000,000$ shares = $\$0.70$

Price/Sales = $88.00/0.70 = 125.7$

B. Sales in Year 0 (the current year) are \$210 million.

Sales in Year 4 = $Sales_4 = 210$ million × $(1.60)^4 = \$1,376.26$ million.

Sales in Year 5 = $Sales_5 = Sales_4 \times (1.07) = 1,376.26$ million $(1.07) = \$1,472.59$ million.

Earnings in Year 5 = $10\% \times Sales_5 = 0.10\,(1,472.59) = \$147.26$ million.

Finally, dividends in Year 5 = 0.40×147.26 million = \$58.90 million.

The dividend per share is 58.90 million/300 million = \$0.1963 per share.

Using the Gordon growth model, the value of one share at the end of Year 4 would be $V_4 = D_5/(r - g) = 0.1963/(0.12 - 0.07) = \$3.93$ per share.

V_0, the present value of V_4, is $V_0 = 3.93/(1.12)^4 = \$2.50$, which is far less than the current market value of \$88.00 per share.

C. We solve this problem by finding the sales and dividend per share in Year 4 that would be required to produce the current \$88.00 price. Then we multiply this sales per share figure by the number of outstanding shares to get the total sales figure.

$$88.00 = \frac{1}{(1.12)^4}V_4 = \frac{1}{(1.12)^4}\left(\frac{D_5}{0.12 - 0.07}\right)$$

Solving this expression, we find that $D_5 = \$6.92$. Because dividends are growing at 7 percent, $D_4 = 6.92/1.07 = \$6.47$. Because dividends are 40 percent of earnings, $EPS_4 = 6.47/0.40 = \$16.175$. Because earnings are 10 percent of sales, Sales per share $= 16.175/0.10 = \$161.75$.

Finally, the total sales of the company is $\$161.75 \times 300$ million $= \$48.53$ billion. In this scenario, the current valuation of the stock is justified if sales can increase from $210 million to $48.53 billion in four years!

12. In the Gordon (constant dividend growth) model, $V_0 = D_0(1 + g)/(r - g)$. With the bond yield plus risk premium method, with $r = 9.6\%$, the value of Dole is

$$V_0 = 0.40(1 + 0.07)/(0.096 - 0.07) = 0.428/0.026 = \$16.46.$$

With the CAPM method, $r = 11.2\%$ and the value of Dole is

$$V_0 = 0.40(1 + 0.07)/(0.112 - 0.07) = 0.428/0.042 = \$10.19.$$

With the APT, $r = 10.4\%$ and the value of Dole is

$$V_0 = 0.40(1 + 0.07)/(0.104 - 0.07) = 0.428/0.034 = \$12.59.$$

13. A. An analyst accepting the CFO's dividend target would compute the value as follows:

$$V_3 = D_4/(r - g)$$
$$V_3 = 0.50/(0.15 - 0.07) = \$6.25$$
$$V_0 = V_3/(1 + r)^3$$
$$V_0 = \$6.25/(1.15)^3 = \$4.11$$

B. An analyst extending the dividend target would compute the value as follows:

$$V_5 = D_6/(r - g)$$
$$V_5 = 0.50/(0.15 - 0.07) = \$6.25$$
$$V_0 = V_5/(1 + r)^5$$
$$V_0 = \$6.25/(1.15)^5 = \$3.11$$

14. The table below calculates the first five dividends and also finds their present values discounted at 12 percent. The value of the dividends for Year 6 and after is found using the Gordon growth model, where the value at time $t = 5$ depends on the dividend at $t = 6$. D_6 is found by growing the D_1 dividend at 50 percent for two years, at 20 percent for two more years, and at 5 percent for one year.

$$D_6 = 0.60(1.50)^2(1.20)^2(1.05) = \$2.0412$$

V_5 is

$$V_5 = \frac{D_6}{r - g} = \frac{2.0412}{0.12 - 0.05} = \frac{2.0412}{0.07} = \$29.16$$

The present values of V_5 and the dividends for $t = 1$ through $t = 5$ are in the far right column of the table.

Time	Value	Calculation	D_t or V_t	Present Values $D_t/(1.12)^t$ or $V_t/(1.12)^t$
1	D_1	0.60	0.60	0.536
2	D_2	0.60(1.50)	0.90	0.717
3	D_3	$0.60(1.50)^2$	1.35	0.961
4	D_4	$0.60(1.50)^2(1.20)$	1.62	1.030
5	D_5	$0.60(1.50)^2(1.20)^2$	1.944	1.103
5	V_5	$0.60(1.50)^2(1.20)^2(1.05)/(0.12 - 0.05)$	29.16	16.546
Total				20.893

The dividend for FPR grows at different rates for three time periods. The total present value of the stock's dividends is $20.89.

15. EB Systems dividends are expected to grow in two stages, and the two-stage DDM is used to value the stock. The expected rate of return is the discount rate that causes the present value of the future dividend stream to equal the current price of $11.40. If EB Systems' dividend stream were growing at 7 percent (like the Gordon growth model), the rate of return would be $r = D_1/P_0 + g = 0.40/11.40 + 7\% = 3.51\% + 7\% = 10.51\%$. Because the dividend is growing more rapidly during Years 1 through 5, the rate of return will exceed 10.51 percent.

In the table below, we illustrate using trial and error to find the discount rate. The second column shows the dividends for Years 1 through 5. The following columns calculate the present value of these five dividends discounted at 11 percent, 11.5 percent, and 12 percent, respectively. The value of the dividends after Year 5 is $V_5 = D_6/(r - g)$, which is $V_5 = 0.7486/(r - 0.07)$. Notice that r changes, so the terminal values for $r = 11\%$, 11.5%, and 12% also change, as shown in the table. The present value of V_5 is calculated and added to the present value of the first five dividends in the bottom row of the table.

Year	Dividend	PV at 11%	PV at 11.5%	PV at 12%	PV at 11.563%
1	0.400	0.360	0.359	0.357	0.359
2	0.460	0.373	0.370	0.367	0.370
3	0.529	0.387	0.382	0.377	0.381
4	0.608	0.401	0.394	0.387	0.393
5	0.700	0.415	0.406	0.397	0.405
Total PV of Dividends		1.936	1.910	1.884	1.907
Terminal price (V_5)		18.714	16.635	14.971	16.405
PV of terminal price		11.106	9.653	8.495	9.493
Total PV of Div and V_5		13.042	11.563	10.379	11.399

The current stock price of $11.40 occurs with a discount rate between 11.5 percent and 12 percent. Further trial and error reveals the discount rate to be 11.563 percent, which gives a total present value of the dividend stream close to $11.40, as shown in the last column of the table.

16. A. The required rate of return for Hanson is $r = R_F + \beta[E(R_M) - R_F] = 4.66\% + 0.83(4.92\%) = 8.74\%$. Using the H-model, the value of Hanson PLC is

$$V_0 = \frac{D_0(1 + g_L)}{r - g_L} + \frac{D_0 H(g_S - g_L)}{r - g_L} = \frac{13.80(1 + 0.05)}{0.0874 - 0.05}$$

$$+ \frac{13.80(5)(0.14 - 0.05)}{0.0874 - 0.05}$$

$$V_0 = \frac{14.49}{0.0374} + \frac{6.21}{0.0374} = 387.43 + 166.04 = \text{GBP } 553.47$$

The market price of GBP 472 is below the H-model price of GBP 553.47, so Hanson seems to be underpriced at this time.

B. For the H-model the expected rate of return can be derived as

$$r = \left(\frac{D_0}{P_0}\right)\left[(1 + g_L) + H(g_S - g_L)\right] + g_L$$

$$r = \left(\frac{13.80}{472}\right)\left[(1 + 0.05) + 5(0.14 - 0.05)\right] + 0.05$$

$$= 0.0439 + 0.05 = 0.0939 = 9.39\%$$

Hanson will return 9.39 percent to the investor if all of these assumptions hold.

17. A. Using the constant-growth dividend discount model, $V_0 = D_1/(r - g)$

For LCC: $V_0 = \$0.90/(0.10 - 0.08) = \$45.00$

For AOC: $V_0 = \$1.60/(0.11 - 0.07) = \$40.00$

B. Using the CAPM, the expected return $r = R_F + \beta[E(R_M) - R_F]$

For LCC: $r = 8\% + 1.2(20\% - 8\%) = 22.4\%$

For AOC: $r = 8\% + 1.4(20\% - 8\%) = 24.8\%$

Alternatively, using CAPM and using the Treasury bill rate as the risk-free rate

For LCC: $r = 5\% + 1.2(20\% - 5\%) = 23\%$

For AOC: $r = 5\% + 1.4(20\% - 5\%) = 26\%$

C. The internal growth rate is $g = b \times \text{ROE} = [(E - D)/E] \times (E/BV)$

For LCC: $BV = \$300/10 = \$30$

$$g = [(\$4.00 - \$0.90)/\$4.00] \times (\$4.00/\$30) = 0.775 \times 13.33\%$$
$$= 10.33\%$$

For AOC: $BV = \$320/20 = \$16$

$$g = [(\$3.20 - \$1.60)/\$3.20] \times (\$3.20/\$16) = 0.50 \times 20\% = 10.00\%$$

D. *Recommendation*: Aminochem (AOC) is a more attractive investment than Litch-field (LCC) based on the answers to parts A, B, and C and the information provided in Exhibit P-1.

Justification: Using the constant-growth dividend discount model (DDM), the stock price of AOC is more attractive, at a price of $30 (well below its DDM value of $40), than that of LCC. LCC's internal growth rate (computed in part C) is higher than that of AOC, but LCC's higher P/E of 12.5 ($50/$4) versus 9.4 ($30/$3.20) for AOC is not justified by the small difference in growth rates.

18. A. **i.** Return on equity (ROE) = Profit margin × Asset turnover
× Financial leverage
ROE = (Net income/Revenue) × (Revenue/Assets) × (Assets/Equity)

ii. ROE = (510/5,140) × (5,140/3,100) × (3,100/2,200) = 23.18%
This calculation used end-of-year (1999e) values. Slightly different and acceptable values would be obtained if balance sheet averages were used for assets and equity or if the beginning value for equity were used.

iii. Sustainable growth rate = ROE × Retention rate
The retention rate = 1 − Dividend payout ratio
Dividend payout ratio = 0.60/1.96 = 0.306
Retention rate = 1 − 0.306 = 0.694
Sustainable growth rate = 23.18% × 0.694 = 16.09%

B. The sustainable growth rate (of 16.09 percent) exceeds MasterToy's actual growth rate. If the problem were temporary, management could simply accumulate resources in anticipation of future growth. Assuming this trend continues longer term (as the question states), however, management has at least two alternative courses of action when actual growth is below sustainable growth:

▶ Return money to shareholders by increasing the dividend or the dividend payout ratio.

▶ Return money to shareholders by buying back stock.

19. A. **i.** Return on equity is the product of three components: profitability (net profit margin), asset turnover ratio (sales/assets), and financial leverage or equity multiplier (asset-to-equity ratio).
Net profit margin = Net income/Sales = 80/598 = 13.378%
Total asset turnover = Sales/Assets = 598/815 = 0.7337
Financial leverage = Assets/Equity = 815/674 = 1.2092

ii. Return on equity = Net income/Equity = 80/674 = 11.87%
or, ROE = 13.378% × 0.7337 × 1.2092 = 11.87%.

iii. If the company maintains the current capital structure and a stable dividend payout rate, the sustainable rate of growth is defined by the product of ROE, which was calculated above, and the retention rate (1 minus the dividend payout rate), which can be determined from Exhibit 19-1. Sustainable growth rate = ROE × Retention rate = 11.87% × (1 − 24/80) = 8.31%.

B.

Proposal	Effect on Sustainable Growth Rate	Component Directly Affected (if any)
Increase in quarterly dividend	Decrease	Retention rate. An increase in the dividend payout rate lowers the retention rate and thus decreases the sustainable growth rate.
Bond issue	Increase	Financial leverage or equity multiplier. An increase in the debt ratio raises financial leverage or the equity multiplier and thus increases sustainable growth.
Stock split	No effect	None. A stock split affects none of the components and thus does not affect the sustainable growth rate.

C. Using a two-stage dividend discount model, the current value of a share of Sundanci is calculated as follows:

Year 1 dividend per share (D_1) = \$0.286 (1.32) = \$0.37752
Year 2 dividend per share (D_2) = \$0.286 (1.32)^2 = \$0.49833
Year 3 dividend per share (D_3) = \$0.286 (1.32)^2 (1.13) = \$0.56311
Terminal value (V_2) = $D_3/(r - g)$ = 0.56311/(0.14 - 0.13) = \$56.311

The value of one share is the present value of the first two dividends plus the present value of the terminal share value:

$$V_0 = \frac{0.37752}{1.14} + \frac{0.49833}{(1.14)^2} + \frac{56.311}{(1.14)^2}$$

$$= 0.331 + 0.383 + 43.329 = \$44.04$$

20. A. The industry's estimated P/E can be computed using the following model:

$$P_0/E_1 = \text{Payout ratio}/(r - g)$$

Because r and g are not explicitly given, however, they must be computed. The growth rate is

$$g = \text{ROE} \times \text{Retention rate} = 0.25 \times 0.40 = 0.10$$

The required rate of return is

$$r = R_F + \beta[E(R_M) - R_F] = 0.06 + 1.2(0.05)$$
$$= 0.06 + 0.06 = 0.12$$
$$P_0/E_1 = 0.60/(0.12 - 0.10) = 30.0$$

B.

Fundamental Factor	P/Es Higher for Country A or Country B?	Justification
Forecasted growth in real gross domestic product (GDP)	P/E should be higher for Country A.	Higher expected growth in GDP implies higher earnings growth and a higher P/E.
Government bond yield	P/E should be higher for Country B.	A lower government bond yield implies a lower risk-free rate and a higher P/E.
Equity risk premium	P/E should be higher for Country B.	A lower equity risk premium implies a lower required return and a higher P/E.

21. A. The required rate of return is the risk-free rate + beta × (expected market rate of return − risk-free rate):

$$r = R_F + \beta[E(R_M) - R_F] = 0.045 + 1.15(0.145 - 0.045) = 16.0\%$$

B. The formula for the two-stage DDM is

$$V_0 = \sum_{t=1}^{3} \frac{D_t}{(1+r)^t} + \frac{V_3}{(1+r)^3}$$

The estimated future dividends are

$$D_1 = 1.72 \times 1.12 = 1.93$$
$$D_2 = 1.93 \times 1.12 = 2.16$$
$$D_3 = 2.16 \times 1.12 = 2.42$$
$$D_4 = 2.42 \times 1.09 = 2.64$$

The terminal stock price at $t = 3$ is

$$V_3 = D_4/(r-g) = 2.64/(0.16 - 0.09) = 37.71$$

The present values of the first three dividends and the terminal value are

$$1.93 \times 1/(1.16)^1 = 1.66$$
$$2.16 \times 1/(1.16)^2 = 1.61$$
$$2.42 \times 1/(1.16)^3 = 1.55$$
$$37.71 \times 1/(1.16)^3 = 24.16$$
$$\text{Total present value} = 28.98$$

C. *Recommendation:* Janet Ludlow should recommend QuickBrush for purchase because it is selling below Ludlow's intrinsic value estimate, whereas SmileWhite is selling above Ludlow's intrinsic value estimate. QuickBrush should have an expected return above its required rate of return, whereas SmileWhite should have an expected return below its required return.

QuickBrush has an intrinsic value of $63.00 versus a current market price of $45.00, or an intrinsic value of 40% above the market price. SmileWhite has an intrinsic value of $28.98 versus a current market price of $30.00, an intrinsic value of 3.40% below the market price.

D. *Strengths of the two-stage DDM in comparison with the constant-growth DDM.* The DDM is extremely sensitive to the estimated growth rate, g. The two-stage model allows for a separate valuation of two distinct periods in a company's future. As a result, a company such as QuickBrush can be evaluated in light of an anticipated change in sustainable growth. Industries have distinct life cycles in which they typically move from a period of rapid growth to a period of normal growth and then to declining growth. The two-stage model has many of the same problems as the constant-growth model, but it is probably a more realistic approach than assuming a constant growth rate for all time. The use of a two-stage model is a key valuation tool, in that analysts with superior insight into a potential shift in a company's growth rate at a future date can use that expectation to assess the proper valuation at each stage.

Weaknesses inherent in all DDMs. All dividend discount models are extremely sensitive to input values. For example, small changes in the growth rate estimates, g, and/or the required rate of return, r, lead to large changes in a stock's estimated value. These inputs are difficult to estimate and may be based on unrealistic assumptions.

SOLUTIONS FOR READING 47

1.

$100 Increase In	Change in FCFF	Change in FCFE
A. Net income	1100	1100
B. Cash operating expenses	−60	−60
C. Depreciation	+40	+40
D. Interest expense	0	−60
E. EBIT	+60	+60
F. Accounts receivable	−100	−100
G. Accounts payable	+100	+100
H. Property, plant, and equipment	−100	−100
I. Notes payable	0	+100
J. Cash dividends paid	0	0
K. Shares issued	0	0
L. Share repurchases	0	0

[Handwritten margin note: "Non Cash" with bracket pointing to rows]

2. A. Free cash flow to the firm, found with Equation 47-7, is

$$FCFF = NI + NCC + Int(1 - Tax\ rate) - FCInv - WCInv$$
$$- 349 - (39 + 44 - 22 - 23)$$
$$FCFF = 285 + 180 + 130(1 - 0.40)$$
$$FCFF = 285 + 180 + 78 - 349 - 38 = \$156\ million$$

B. Free cash flow to equity, found with Equation 47-10, is

$$FCFE = NI + NCC - FCInv - WCInv + Net\ borrowing$$
$$FCFE = 285 + 180 - 349 - (39 + 44 - 22 - 23) + (10 + 40)$$
$$FCFE = 285 + 180 - 349 - 38 + 50 = \$128\ million$$

C. To find FCFE from FCFF, use the relationship in Equation 47-9:

$$FCFE = FCFF - Int(1 - Tax\ rate) + Net\ borrowing$$
$$FCFE = 156 - 130(1 - 0.40) + (10 + 40)$$
$$FCFE = 156 - 78 + 50 = \$128\ million$$

3. A. To find FCFF from CFO, EBIT, or EBITDA, the analyst can use Equations 47-8, 47-12, and 47-13.
To get FCFF from CFO:

$$FCFF = CFO + Int(1 - Tax\ rate) - FCInv$$
$$FCFF = 427 + 130(1 - 0.40) - 349 = 427$$
$$+ 78 - 349 = \$156\ million$$

To get FCFF from EBIT:

$$FCFF = EBIT(1 - \text{Tax rate}) + Dep - FCInv - WCInv$$
$$FCFF = 605(1 - 0.40) + 180 - 349 - 38$$
$$FCFF = 363 + 180 - 349 - 38 = \$156 \text{ million}$$

Finally, to obtain FCFF from EBITDA:

$$FCFF = EBITDA(1 - \text{Tax rate}) + Dep(\text{Tax rate}) - FCInv - WCInv$$
$$FCFF = 785(1 - 0.40) + 180(0.40) - 349 - 38$$
$$FCFF = 471 + 72 - 349 - 38 = \$156 \text{ million}$$

B. The simplest approach is to calculate FCFF from CFO, EBIT, or EBITDA as was done in Part A above, and then to find FCFE by making the appropriate adjustments to FCFF:

$$FCFE = FCFF - Int(1 - \text{Tax rate}) + \text{Net borrowing.}$$
$$FCFE = 156 - 130(1 - 0.40) + 50 = 156$$
$$- 78 + 50 = \$128 \text{ million}$$

You can also find FCFE using CFO, EBIT, or EBITDA directly. Starting with CFO, using Equation 47-11, FCFE is

$$FCFE = CFO - FCInv + \text{Net borrowing}$$
$$FCFE = 427 - 349 + 50 = \$128 \text{ million}$$

Starting with EBIT, FCFE (found with an equation derived in Footnote 9) is

$$FCFE = EBIT(1 - \text{Tax rate}) + Dep - Int(1 - \text{Tax rate})$$
$$- FCInv - WCInv + \text{Net borrowing}$$
$$FCFE = 605(1 - 0.40) + 180 - 130(1 - 0.40) - 349 - 38 + 50$$
$$FCFE = 363 + 180 - 78 - 349 - 38 + 50 = \$128 \text{ million}$$

Finally, starting with EBITDA, FCFE (found with an equation derived in Footnote 9) is

$$FCFE = EBITDA(1 - \text{Tax rate}) + Dep(\text{Tax rate})$$
$$- Int(1 - \text{Tax rate}) - FCInv - WCInv + \text{Net borrowing}$$
$$FCFE = 785(1 - 0.40) + 180(0.40) - 130(1 - 0.40)$$
$$- 349 - 38 + 50$$
$$FCFE = 471 + 72 - 78 - 349 - 38 + 50 = \$128 \text{ million}$$

4. A. FCF = Net income + Depreciation and amortization − Cash dividends − Capital expenditures. This definition of FCF is sometimes used to determine how much "discretionary" cash flow management has at its disposal. Management discretion concerning dividends is limited by investor expectations that dividends will be maintained. Comparing this definition with Equation 47-7,

$$FCFF = NI + NCC + Int(1 - \text{Tax rate}) - FCInv - WCInv$$

FCFF includes a reduction for investments in working capital and the addition of after-tax interest expense. Common stock dividends are not subtracted from FCFF because doing so represents a distribution of the cash *available* to investors. (If a company pays preferred dividends, they are added back in Equation 47-7 to include them in FCFF if they had previously been taken out when calculating net income available to common.)

B. FCF = Cash flow from operations (from the statement of cash flows) − Capital expenditures. Comparing this definition of FCF with Equation 47-8 can highlight the relation to FCFF:

$$FCFF = CFO + Int(1 - Tax\ rate) - FCInv$$

The primary difference is that after-tax interest is added back in order to arrive at the cash flow available to investors. If preferred dividends had been subtracted to obtain net income (in CFO), they would also have to be added back in. This definition is commonly used to approximate FCFF, and it generally understates the actual FCFF by the amount of after-tax interest expense.

5. A. The firm value is the present value of FCFF discounted at the weighted-average cost of capital (WACC), or

$$Firm = \frac{FCFF_1}{WACC - g} = \frac{FCFF_0(1 + g)}{WACC - g} = \frac{1.7(1.07)}{0.11 - 0.07} = \frac{1.819}{0.04} = 45.475$$

The market value of equity is the value of the firm minus the value of debt:

$$Equity = 45.475 - 15 = \$30.475\ billion$$

B. Using the FCFE valuation approach, the present value of FCFE, discounted at the required rate of return on equity, is

$$PV = \frac{FCFE_1}{r - g} = \frac{FCFE_0(1 + g)}{r - g} = \frac{1.3(1.075)}{0.13 - 0.075} = \frac{1.3975}{0.055} = 25.409$$

The value of equity using this approach is \$25.409 billion.

6. The required rate of return found with the CAPM is

$$r = E(R_i) = R_F + \beta_i[E(R_M) - R_F] = 6.4\% + 2.1\ (5.0\%) = 16.9\%$$

The table on the next page shows the values of Sales, Net income, Capital expenditures less depreciation, and Investments in working capital. FCFE equals net income less the investments financed with equity:

$$FCFE = Net\ income - (1 - DR)(Capital\ expenditures$$
$$- Depreciation) - (1 - DR)(Investment\ in\ working\ capital)$$

Because 20 percent of new investments are financed with debt, 80 percent of the investments are financed with equity, reducing FCFE by 80 percent of (Capital expenditures − Depreciation) and 80 percent of the investment in working capital.

All Data in $ Billions	2002	2003	2004	2005	2006
Sales (growing at 28%)	5.500	7.040	9.011	11.534	14.764
Net Income = 32% of sales	1.760	2.253	2.884	3.691	4.724
FCInv − Dep = (35% − 9%) × Sales	1.430	1.830	2.343	2.999	3.839
WCInv = (6% of Sales)	0.330	0.422	0.541	0.692	0.886
0.80 × (FCInv − Dep + WCInv)	1.408	1.802	2.307	2.953	3.780
FCFE = NI − 0.80 × (FCInv − Dep + WCInv)	0.352	0.451	0.577	0.738	0.945
PV of FCFE discounted at 16.9%	0.301	0.330	0.361	0.395	0.433
Terminal stock value		85.032			
PV of Terminal value discounted at 16.9%		38.950			
Total PV of FCFE		1.820			
Total value of firm		40.770			

The terminal stock value is 18.0 times the earnings in 2006, or $18 \times 4.724 = \$85.03$ billion. The present value of the terminal value ($38.95 billion) plus the present value of the first five years' FCFE ($1.82 billion) is $40.77 billion. Because there are 17 billion outstanding shares, the value per ordinary share is $2.398.

(Taiwan Semiconductor Manufacturing Co. has ADRs trading on the New York Stock Exchange, where one ADR equals five ordinary shares. So the ADR price would be $5(2.398) = \$11.99$ per ADR.)

7. A. The free cash flow to the firm is

$$FCFF = NI + NCC + Int(1 - \text{Tax rate}) - FCInv - WCInv$$
$$FCFF = 250 + 90 + 150(1 - 0.30) - 170 - 40$$
$$FCFF = 250 + 90 + 105 - 170 - 40 = 235 \text{ million}$$

The weighted-average cost of capital is

$$WACC = 9\%(1 - 0.30)(0.40) + 13\%(0.60) = 10.32\%$$

The value of the firm is

$$\text{Firm value} = \frac{FCFF_1}{WACC - g} = \frac{FCFF_0(1 + g)}{WACC - g} = \frac{235(1.06)}{0.1032 - 0.06}$$
$$= \frac{249.1}{0.0432} = 5,766.20$$

The total value of equity is the total firm value minus the value of debt, Equity = 5,766.20 million − 1,800 million = 3,966.20 million. Dividing by the number of shares gives the per share estimate of $V_0 =$ 3,966.20 million/10 million = 396.62 per share.

B. The free cash flow to equity is

$$FCFE = NI + NCC - FCInv - WCInv + \text{Net borrowing}$$
$$FCFE = 250 + 90 - 170 - 40 + 0.40(170 - 90 + 40)$$
$$FCFE = 250 + 90 - 170 - 40 + 48 = 178$$

Because the company is borrowing 40 percent of the increase in net capital expenditures $(170 - 90)$ and working capital (40), net borrowing is 48.

The total value of equity is the FCFE discounted at the required rate of return of equity,

$$\text{Equity value} = \frac{FCFE_1}{r - g} = \frac{FCFE_0(1 + g)}{r - g} = \frac{178(1.07)}{0.13 - 0.07}$$
$$= \frac{190.46}{0.06} = 3{,}174.33$$

The value per share is $V_0 = 3{,}174.33$ million$/10$ million $= 317.43$ per share.

8. The weighted-average cost of capital for PHB Company is

$$\text{WACC} = 0.30(7.0\%)(1 - 0.35) + 0.15(6.8\%) + 0.55\,(11.0\%) = 8.435\%$$

The firm value is

Firm value $= FCFF_0(1 + g)/(\text{WACC} - g)$
Firm value $= 28(1.04)/(0.08435 - 0.04) = 29.12/0.04435$
$\qquad = \$656.60$ million

The value of equity is the firm value minus the value of debt minus the value of preferred stock: Equity $= 656.60 - 145 - 65 = \$446.60$ million. Dividing this by the number of shares gives the estimated value per share of $\$446.60$ million$/8$ million shares $= \$55.82$. The estimated value for the stock is greater than the market price of $\$32.50$, so the stock appears to be undervalued.

9. **A.** The required return on equity is

$$r = E(R_i) = R_F + \beta_i[E(R_M) - R_F] = 5.5\% + 0.90(5.5\%) = 10.45\%$$

The weighted-average cost of capital is

$$\text{WACC} = 0.25(7.0\%)(1 - 0.40) + 0.75(10.45\%) = 8.89\%$$

B. Firm value $= FCFF_0(1 + g)/(\text{WACC} - g)$
Firm value $= 1.1559(1.04)/(0.0889 - 0.04) = \$24.583$ billion

C. Equity value $=$ Firm value $-$ Market value of debt
Equity value $= 24.583 - 3.192 = \$21.391$ billion

D. Value per share $=$ Equity value$/$Number of shares
Value per share $= 21.391/1.852 = \$11.55$

10. **A.** The required rate of return for McDonald's found with the CAPM is

$$r = E(R_i) = R_F + \beta_i[E(R_M) - R_F] = 5.08\% + 0.70(5.50\%) = 8.93\%$$

The value per share is

$$V_0 = \frac{FCFE_0(1 + g)}{r - g} = \frac{0.88(1.064)}{0.0893 - 0.064} = \$37.01$$

B. The table below shows the calculated price for McDonald's using the base case values for all values except for the variable being changed from the base case value.

Variable	Estimated Price with Low Value	Estimated Price with High Value	Range (Rank)
Normalized $FCFE_0$	$29.44	$47.94	$18.50(3)
Risk-free rate	$38.22	$35.33	$ 2.89(5)
Equity risk premium	$51.17	$28.99	$22.18(2)
Beta	$47.29	$30.40	$16.89(4)
FCFE perpetual growth rate	$18.56	$48.79	$30.23(1)

As the table shows, the value of McDonald's is most sensitive to the changes in the FCFE growth rate, with the price moving over a very wide range. McDonald's stock price is least sensitive to alternative values of the risk-free rate. Alternative values of beta, the equity risk premium, or the initial FCFE value also have a large impact on the value of the stock, although the impacts of these variables are smaller than that of the growth rate.

11. A. Using the CAPM, the required rate of return for Alcan is

$$r = E(R_i) = R_F + \beta_i[E(R_M) - R_F] = 7\% + 1.3(4\%) = 12.2\%$$

To estimate FCFE, use Equation 47-14:

$$\text{FCFE} = \text{Net income} - (1 - \text{DR})(\text{FCINV} - \text{Depreciation}) - (1 - \text{DR}) - (\text{WCINV})$$

where DR is the debt ratio—that is, new debt financing as a percentage of the net new investments in fixed capital and the increase in working capital. The table below shows net income, which grows at 20 percent annually for Years 1, 2, and 3, and then at 8 percent for Year 4. Investment (Capital expenditures − Depreciation + Investment in WC) are 1,150 in Year 1 and grow at 15 percent annually for Years 2 and 3. Debt financing is 40 percent of this investment. FCFE is NI − investments + financing. Finally, the present value of FCFE for Years 1, 2, and 3 is found by discounting at 12.2 percent.

Year	1	2	3	4
Net income	$720.00	$864.00	$1,036.80	$1,119.74
Investment in operating assets	1,150.00	1,322.50	1,520.88	335.92
New debt financing	460.00	529.00	608.35	134.37
Free cash flow to equity	30.00	70.50	124.27	918.19
PV of FCFE discounted at 12.2%	26.74	56.00	87.98	

In Year 4, net income is 8 percent larger than in Year 3. In Year 4, the investment in operating assets is 30 percent of net income, and debt financing is 40 percent of this investment. The FCFE in Year 4 is $918.19 million. The value of FCFE after Year 3 is found using the constant-growth model:

$$V_3 = \frac{FCFE_4}{r - g} = \frac{918.19}{0.122 - 0.08} = \$21,861.67 \text{ million.}$$

The present value of V_3 discounted at 12.2 percent is $15,477.64 million. The total value of equity, the present value of the first three years' FCFE plus the present value of V_3, is $15,648.36 million. Dividing this by the number of outstanding shares (318 million) gives a value per share of $49.21. For the first three years, Alcan has a small FCFE because of the large investments it is making during the high-growth phase. In the normal-growth phase, FCFE is much larger because the investments required are much smaller.

B. The planner's estimate of the share value of $70.98 is much higher than the FCFE model estimate of $49.21 for several reasons. First, taxes and interest expenses, have a prior claim to the company's cash flow and should be taken out because these cash flows are not available to equity holders. The planner did not do this.

Second, EBITDA does not account for the company's reinvestments in operating assets. So, EBITDA overstates the funds available to stockholders if reinvestment needs exceed depreciation charges, which is the case for growing companies such as Alcan.

Third, EBITDA does not account for the company's capital structure. Using EBITDA to represent a benefit to stockholders (as opposed to stockholders and bondholders combined) is a mistake.

Finally, dividing EBITDA by the bond rate commits major errors as well. The risk-free bond rate is an inappropriate discount rate for risky equity cash flows; the proper measure is the required rate of return on the company's equity. Dividing by a fixed rate also assumes erroneously that the cash flow stream is a fixed perpetuity. EBITDA cannot be a perpetual stream because, if it were distributed, the stream would eventually decline to zero (lacking capital investments). Alcan is actually a growing company, so assuming it to be a nongrowing perpetuity is a mistake.

12. The table below develops the information to calculate FCFE.

Year	2003	2004	2005	2006	2007	2008
Growth rate for EPS	21%	18%	15%	12%	9%	6%
EPS	3.630	4.283	4.926	5.517	6.014	6.374
Capital expenditure per share	5.000	5.000	4.500	4.000	3.500	1.500
Investment in WC per share	1.250	1.250	1.125	1.000	0.875	0.375
New debt financing = 40% of (Capital expenditure + WCInv)	2.500	2.500	2.250	2.000	1.750	0.750
FCFE = NI − Capital expenditure − WCInv + New debt financing	−0.120	0.533	1.551	2.517	3.389	5.249
PV of FCFE discounted at 12%	−0.107	0.425	1.104	1.600	1.923	

Earnings for 2002 are $3.00, and the EPS estimates for 2003 through 2008 in the table are found by increasing the previous year's earnings per share by that year's growth rate. The net capital expenditures each year were specified by the analyst. The increase in working capital per share is equal to 25 percent of net capital expenditures. Finally, debt financing is 40 percent of that year's total net capital expenditures and investment in working capital. For example, in 2003, net capital expenditures plus investment in working capital is $5.00 plus $1.25 = $6.25. Debt financing is 40 percent of $6.25, or $2.50. Debt financing for 2004 through 2008 is found in the same way.

FCFE equals net income minus net capital expenditures minus investment in working capital plus new debt financing. Notice that FCFE is initially negative in 2003 because of large capital investments and investments in working capital. As these investments decline relative to net income, FCFE becomes very substantial and positive.

The present values of FCFE from 2003 through 2007 are given in the bottom row of the table. These five present values sum to $4.944. Because the FCFE from 2008 onward will grow at a constant 6 percent, the constant-growth model can be used to value these cash flows.

$$V_{2007} = \frac{FCFE_{2008}}{r-g} = \frac{5.249}{0.12-0.06} = \$87.483$$

The present value of this stream is $87.483/(1.12)^5 = \$49.640$. The value per share is the value of the first five FCFE (2003 through 2007) plus the present value of the FCFE after 2007, or $4.944 + $49.640 = $54.58.

13. A. FCFE is defined as the cash flow remaining after the company meets all financial obligations, including debt payment, and covers all capital expenditure and working capital needs. FCFE measures how much a company can afford to pay out as dividends, but in a given year, FCFE may be more or less than the amount actually paid out.

Sundanci's FCFE for the year 2000 is calculated as follows:

Net income	= $80 million
Plus: Depreciation expense	= 23
Less: Capital expenditures	= 38
Less: Investment in IWC	= 41
Equals: FCFE	= 24 million
Number of shares	= 84 million
FCFE per share	= $0.286

At the given dividend payout ratio, Sundanci's FCFE equals the dividends paid.

B. The FCFE model requires forecasts of FCFE for the high-growth years (2001 and 2002) plus a forecast for the first year of stable growth (2003) to allow for an estimate of the terminal value in 2002 based on perpetual growth. Because all of the components of FCFE are expected to grow at the same rate, the values can be obtained by projecting the FCFE at the common rate. (Alternatively, the components of FCFE can be projected and aggregated for each year.)

The following template shows the process for estimating Sundanci's current value on a per share basis.

Free Cash Flow to Equity

Base Assumptions

Shares outstanding (millions)	84
Required return on equity (r)	14%

	Total	Per share	Actual 2000	Projected 2001	Projected 2002	Projected 2003
Growth rate (g)				27%	27%	13%
Earnings after tax	$80	$0.952		$1.2090	$ 1.5355	$1.7351
Plus: Depreciation expense	$23	$0.274		$0.3480	$ 0.4419	$0.4994
Less: Capital expenditures	$38	$0.452		$0.5740	$ 0.7290	$0.8238
Less: Increase in net working capital	$41	$0.488		$0.6198	$ 0.7871	$0.8894
Equals: FCFE	$24	$0.286		$0.3632	$ 0.4613	$0.5213
Terminal value[a]					$52.1300	
Total cash flows to equity[b]				$0.3632	$52.5913	
Discounted value[c]				$0.3186	$40.4673	
Current value per share[d]		$40.7859				

[a] Projected 2002 terminal value = Projected 2003 FCFE/$(r - g)$.

[b] Projected 2002 total cash flows to equity = Projected 2002 FCFE plus Projected 2002 Terminal value.

[c] Discounted values obtained using $r = 14$ percent.

[d] Current value per share = Discounted value 2001 plus Discounted value 2002.

C. The following limitations of the DDM *are* addressed by the FCFE model: The DDM uses a strict definition of cash flows to equity; that is, the expected dividends on the common stock. The FCFE model expands the definition of cash flows to include the balance of residual cash flows after all financial obligations and investment needs have been met. Thus the FCFE model explicitly recognizes the company's investment and financing policies as well as its dividend policy. In instances of a change of corporate control, and thus the possibility of changing dividend policy, the FCFE model provides a better estimate of value.

Both two-stage valuation models allow for two distinct phases of growth, an initial finite period where the growth is abnormal, followed by a stable growth period that is expected to last forever. These two-stage models share the same limitations with respect to the growth assumptions.

First, there is the difficulty of defining the duration of the extraordinary growth period. For example, a longer period of high growth will lead to a higher valuation, and analysts may be tempted to assume an unrealistically long period of extraordinary growth.

Second, an assumption of a sudden shift from high growth to lower, stable growth is unrealistic. The transformation more likely will occur gradually over a period of time.

Third, because value is quite sensitive to the steady-state growth assumption, overestimating or underestimating this rate can lead to large errors in value. The two models share other limitations as well, notably difficulties in accurately estimating required rates of return.

14. A. Using a two-stage dividend discount model, the value of a share of Mackinac is calculated as follows:

$$DPS_0 = \text{Cash dividends/Shares outstanding} = \$22,470/13,000$$
$$= \$1.7285$$
$$DPS_1 = DPS_0 \times 1.17 = \$2.0223$$
$$DPS_2 = DPS_0 \times 1.17^2 = \$2.3661$$
$$DPS_3 = DPS_0 \times 1.17^3 = \$2.7683$$
$$DPS_4 = DPS_0 \times 1.17^3 \times 1.09 = \$3.0175$$

Using the CAPM, the required return on equity is

$$\text{Cost of Equity } (r) = \text{Government bond rate} + (\text{Beta} \times \text{Equity risk premium})$$
$$= 0.06 + (1.25 \times 0.05) = 0.1225 \text{ or } 12.25 \text{ percent}$$
$$\text{Value per share} = DPS_1/(1+r) + DPS_2/(1+r)^2 + DPS_3/(1+r)^3$$
$$+ [DPS_4/(r - g_{stable})]/(1+r)^3$$
$$\text{Value per share} = \$2.0223/1.1225 + \$2.3661/1.1225^2$$
$$+ \$2.7683/1.1225^3$$
$$+ [\$3.0175/(0.1225 - 0.09)]/1.1225^3$$
$$= \$1.8016 + \$1.8778 + \$1.9573$$
$$+ \$65.6450 = \$71.28$$

B. Using the two-stage FCFE model, the value of a share of Mackinac is calculated as follows:

Net income = \$37,450
Depreciation = \$10,500
Capital expenditures = \$15,000
Change in working capital = \$5,500
New debt issuance − Principal repayments =
Change in debt outstanding = \$4,000
$$FCFE_0 = \text{Net income} + \text{Depreciation} - \text{Capital expenditures} -$$
Change in working Capital − Principal repayments + New debt issues
$$FCFE_0 = \$37,450 + \$10,500 - \$15,000 - \$5,500 + \$4,000 = \$31,450$$
$$FCFE_0 \text{ per share} = \$31,450/13,000 = \$2.4192$$
$$FCFE_1 = FCFE_0 \times 1.17 = \$2.8305$$
$$FCFE_2 = FCFE_0 \times 1.17_2 = \$3.3117$$
$$FCFE_3 = FCFE_0 \times 1.17_3 = \$3.8747$$
$$FCFE_4 = FCFE_0 \times 1.17_3 \times 1.09 = \$4.2234$$
$$\text{Cost of equity } (r) = \text{Government bond rate} + (\text{Beta} \times \text{Equity risk premium})$$
$$= 0.06 + (1.25 \times 0.05) = 0.1225 \text{ or } 12.25 \text{ percent}$$
$$\text{Value per share} = FCFE_1(1+r) + FCFE_2/(1+r) + FCFE_3/(1+r)^3$$
$$+ [FCFE_4/(r - g_{stable})]/(1+r)^3$$

$$\begin{aligned}
\text{Value per share} &= \$2.8305/1.1225 + \$3.3117/1.1225^2 \\
&\quad + \$3.8747/1.1225^3 + [\$4.2234/(0.1225 - \\
&\quad 0.09)]/1.1225^3 \\
&= \$2.5216 + \$2.6283 + \$2.7395 + \$91.8798 \\
&= \$99.77
\end{aligned}$$

C. The FCFE model is best for valuing firms for takeovers or in situations that have a reasonable chance for a change in corporate control. Because controlling stockholders can change the dividend policy, they are interested in estimating the maximum residual cash flow after meeting all financial obligations and investment needs. The dividend discount model is based on the premise that the only cash flows received by stockholders are dividends. FCFE uses a more expansive definition to measure what a company can afford to pay out as dividends.

15. A. The real required rate of return for SK Telecom Co. is

Country return (real)	6.50%
Industry adjustment	+ 0.60%
Size adjustment	− 0.10%
Leverage adjustment	+0.25%
Required rate of return	7.25%

B. The real growth rate of FCFE is expected to be the same as the country rate of 3.5 percent. The value of one share is

$$V_0 = \frac{FCFE_0(1 + g_{real})}{r_{real} - g_{real}} = \frac{1,300(1.035)}{0.0725 - 0.035} = 35,880 \text{ Korean Won.}$$

16. The required return for TNE, found with the CAPM, is $r = E(R_i) = R_F + \beta_i[E(R_M) - R_F] = 4.5\% + 2.0(5.0\%) = 14.5\%$. The estimated future values of FCFE are given in the table below.

Year t	Variable	Calculation	Value in Year t	Present Value at 14.5%
1	$FCFE_1$	0.75(1.10)	0.825	0.721
2	$FCFE_2$	0.75(1.10)(1.26)	1.040	0.793
3	$FCFE_3$	0.75(1.10)(1.26)^2	1.310	0.873
4	$FCFE_4$	0.75(1.10)(1.26)^3	1.650	0.960
4	TV_4	$FCFE_5/(r-g)$	20.580	11.974
		$= 0.75(1.10)(1.26)^3(1.06)/(0.145 - 0.085)$		
		$= 1.749/0.085$		
0		Total value = PV of FCFE for Years 1−4 + PV of Terminal value		15.32

The FCFE grows at 10 percent for Year 1 and then at 26 percent for Years 2–4. These calculated values for FCFE are shown in the table. The present values of the FCFE for the first four years discounted at the required rate of return are given in the last column of the table. After Year 4, FCFE will grow at 6 percent forever, so the constant-growth FCFE model is used to find the terminal value at Time 4, which is $TV_4 = FCFE_5/(r - g)$. TV_4 is discounted at the required return for four periods to find its present value, as shown in the table. Finally, the total value of the stock, \$15.32, is the sum of the present values of the first four years' FCFE plus the present value of the terminal value.

17. The total value of non operating assets is

        \$ 60 million short-term securities
        \$ 45 million market value of noncurrent assets
        <u>\$ 40 million pension fund surplus</u>
        \$145 million non operating assets

    The total value of the firm is the value of the operating assets plus the value of the non operating assets, or \$720 million plus \$145 million = \$865 million. The equity value is the value of the firm minus the value of debt, or \$865 million − \$215 million = \$650 million. The value per share is \$650 million/100 million shares = \$6.50 per share.

18. A is correct. The company's free cash flow is aligned with profitability and the investor is taking a control perspective. Furthermore, while the company is dividend paying, in the long run the dividend will fall short of free cash flow.

19. C is correct. The value under the H-model is:

$$V_0 = \frac{D_0(1 + g_L)}{r - g_L} + \frac{D_0H(g_s - g_L)}{r - g_L}$$

$$V_0 = \frac{1.5 \times 1.05}{0.125 - 0.05} + \frac{1.5 \times 2 \times (0.12 - 0.05)}{0.125 - 0.05}$$

$$V_0 = \frac{1.575}{0.075} + \frac{0.21}{0.075}$$

$$V_0 = \$23.80$$

20. D is correct. Because Raylord has no debt, FCFE = FCFF. Furthermore, FCFE is equal to CFO − FCInv when there is no debt, so CFO = FCFE + FCInv and CFO is higher than FCFE.

21. C is correct. FCFE would grow at 11% for 3 years and 4% thereafter. In a two-stage model, the calculation is as follows.

	Current	Year 1	Year 2	Year 3
Growth	NA	11%	11%	11%
FCFE	850	943.50	1047.28	1162.49
Present Value at 12.5%	NA	838.67	827.48	816.45

FCFE in Year 4 = 1,162.49 × 1.04 = 1,208.99
Terminal Value = 1,208.99/ (0.125 − 0.04) = \$14,223.36
Present Value of Terminal Value = 9,989.52 (discounted at 12.5% for three years)

$$PV = \frac{943.50}{1.125} + \frac{1047.28}{1.125^2} + \frac{1162.49}{1.125^3} + \frac{1162.49(1.04)/(0.125 - 0.04)}{1.125^3}$$

PV = 838.67 + 827.48 + 816.45 + 9,989.52 = \$12,472.15

22. B is correct. Changing leverage (new debt issuances) affects free cash flow to equity, but paying dividends does not, as indicated in the FCFE equation:

$$FCFE = NI + NCC - FCInv - WCInv + Net\ borrowing$$

23. D is correct. The sustainable growth rate is:

$g = b \times ROE$ and $ROE = $ Profit Margin $\times$ Asset Turnover
    $\times$ Financial Leverage
$ROE = 5\% \times 1.25 \times 2.00 = 12.5\%$
$b = 1 - $ dividend payout $= 0.60$
$g = 0.60 \times 12.5\% = 7.5\%$

SOLUTIONS FOR READING 48

1. **A.** Normal EPS is the level of earnings per share that the company could currently achieve under mid-cyclical conditions.

   B. Averaging EPS over the 1997–2000 period, we find that ($2.55 + $2.13 + $0.23 + $1.45)/4 = $1.59. According to the method of historical average EPS, SII's normal EPS is $1.59. The P/E based on this estimate is $57.98/1.59 = 36.5.

   C. Averaging ROE over the 1997–2000 period, we find that (0.218 + 0.163 + 0.016 + 0.089)/4 = 0.1215. For current BVPS, we use the estimated value of $19.20. According to the method of average ROE, we have 0.1215 × $19.20 = $2.33 as normal EPS. The P/E based on this estimate is $57.98/$2.33 = 24.9.

2. **A.** The analyst can rank the two stocks by earnings yield (E/P). Whether EPS is positive or negative, a lower E/P reflects a richer valuation and a ranking from high to low E/P has a meaningful interpretation.

      In some cases, an analyst might handle negative EPS by using normal EPS in its place. Neither business, however, has a history of profitability. When year-ahead EPS is expected to be positive, leading P/E is positive. Thus the use of leading P/Es sometimes addresses the problem of trailing negative EPS. Leading P/E is not meaningful in this case, however, because next year's earnings are expected to be negative.

   B. Hand has an E/P of −0.100, and Somersault has an E/P of −0.125. A higher earnings yield has a similar interpretation to a lower P/E, and Hand appears to be relatively undervalued. The difference in earnings yield cannot be explained by differences in sales growth forecasts. In fact, Hand has a higher expected sales growth rate than Somersault. Therefore, the analyst should recommend Hand.

3. **A.** Because investing looks to the future, analysts often feature leading P/E when earnings forecasts are available, as they are here. But a specific reason to use leading P/Es based on the facts given is that RUF had some unusual items affecting EPS for 2000. The data to make appropriate adjustments to RUF's 2000 EPS are not given. In summary, Stewart should use leading P/Es.

   B. Because RUF has a complex capital structure, the P/Es of the two companies must be compared on the basis of diluted EPS.

      For HS: leading P/E = $44/2.20 = 20
      For RUF: leading P/E per diluted share = $22.50/(30,000,000/33,333,333) = 25

      Therefore, HS has the more attractive valuation at present. The problem illustrates some of the considerations that should be taken into account in using the P/Es and the method of comparables.

4. **A.** Your conclusion may be in error because of the following:

   ▶ The peer group stocks themselves may be overvalued. Stated another way, the mean P/E of 18 may be too high in terms of intrinsic value. If that is the case, using 18 as a multiplier of the stock's expected EPS will lead to an estimate of stock value in excess of intrinsic value.

   ▶ The stock's fundamentals may differ from those of the mean food processing industry stock. For example, if the stock's expected growth

Solutions to 1–18 taken from *Analysis of Equity Investments: Valuation,* by John D. Stowe, Thomas R. Robinson, Jerald E. Pinto, and Dennis W. McLeavey. Copyright © 2002 by AIMR. Reprinted with permission. All other solutions copyright © 2006 by CFA Institute.

rate is lower than the mean industry growth rate and its risk is higher than the mean, the stock may deserve a lower P/E than the mean.

In addition, mean P/E may be influenced by outliers.

B. The following evidence supports the original conclusion:

    ▶ Evidence that stocks in the industry are at least on average fairly valued (that stock prices reflect fundamentals).

    ▶ Evidence that no significant differences exist in the fundamental drivers of P/E for comparing the stock with the average industry stock.

5. A. Yardeni's model uses corporate, rather than U.S. government, bond yields and incorporates an estimate of earnings growth to arrive at an estimate of the fair value of stock market.

B. In principle, the use of any of this readings price multiples for valuation is vulnerable to this problem in comparing a company's characteristics to the overall market. If the stock market is overvalued, an asset that appears to be comparably valued may also be overvalued.

6. A. The formula for calculating P/E for a stable-growth company is the payout ratio divided by the difference between the required rate of return and the growth rate of dividends. If the P/E is being calculated on trailing earnings (Year 0), the payout ratio is increased by the growth rate.

P/E based on trailing earnings:
$$P/E = [\text{Payout ratio } (1 + g)]/(r - g)$$
$$= (0.30\ 3\times 1.13)/(0.14 - 0.13) = 33.9$$
P/E based on next year's earnings:
$$P/E = \text{Payout ratio}/(r - g)$$
$$= 0.30/(0.14 - 0.13) = 30$$

B.

Fundamental Factor	Effect on P/E	Explanation (not required in question)
The risk (beta) of Sundanci increases substantially.	Decrease	P/E is a decreasing function of risk—as risk increases, the P/E decreases. Increases in the risk of Sundanci stock would be expected to lower the P/E.
The estimated growth rate of Sundanci's earnings and dividends increases.	Increase	P/E is an increasing function of the growth rate of the company—the higher the expected growth the higher the P/E. Sundanci would command a higher P/E if analysts increase the expected growth rate.
The market risk premium increases.	Decrease	P/E is a decreasing function of the market risk premium. An increased market risk premium would increase the required rate of return, lowering the price of a stock relative to its earnings. A higher market risk premium would be expected to lower Sundanci's P/E.

7. A. We would expect the trailing P/E accorded to CSG to increase to 13.25 as anticipated by Yu. The colleague is referring to the sustainable growth rate expression $g = b \times \text{ROE}$. The colleague's argument is that if ROE is level over the next several years, b will need to increase (dividend payout will need to decrease) to support a higher (6 percent) growth rate. The idea is that if b increases when growth becomes 6 percent, the P/E does not increase to 13.25. The argument concerning a change in dividend payout is incorrect. Any of the following arguments may be made:

- ▶ Although ROE is expected to be flat only for several years, long-term ROE is the proper value to use in the sustainable growth rate expression.
- ▶ If b actually increases, g will increase above 6 percent, offsetting the effect of b.
- ▶ The sustainable growth rate expression assumes no external equity financing and keeping the capital structure constant. CSG can borrow, either short term while ROE is flat or even long term (possibly increasing debt's weight in the capital structure) to fund this growth. The company can also issue new stock. The sustainable growth rate formula cannot realistically serve as a basis to predict a cut in dividends.
- ▶ Dividend payout, which is a discretionary decision of the board of directors, is not an economic fundamental. Investors look to the underlying cash flow of the business in valuation.

B. Because Yu is correct, CSG should be added to the focus list.

8. A. $V_n =$ Benchmark value of $\text{P/E} \times E_n = 12 \times \$3.00 = \$36.0$

B. In the sustainable growth rate expression $g = b \times \text{ROE}$, we can use $(1 - 0.45) = 0.55 = b$, and $\text{ROE} = 0.10$ (the industry average), obtaining $0.55 \times 0.10 = 0.055$. Given the required rate of return of 0.09, we obtain the estimate $\$3.00(0.45)(1.055)/(0.09 - 0.055) = \$40.69$. In this case the Gordon growth model estimate of terminal value is higher than the estimate based on multiples. The two estimates may differ for a number of reasons, including the sensitivity of the Gordon growth model to the values of inputs.

9. Although the measurement of book value has a number of widely recognized shortcomings, it can still be applied fruitfully in several categories of circumstances:

- ▶ The company is not expected to continue as a going concern. When a company is likely to be liquidated (so that ongoing earnings and cash flow are not relevant) the value of its assets less its liabilities is of utmost importance. Naturally, the analyst must establish the fair value of these assets.
- ▶ The company is composed mainly of liquid assets, such as finance, investment, insurance, and banking institutions.
- ▶ The company's EPS is highly variable or negative.

10. A. Avtech: $\text{P/S} = (\$10 \text{ price per share})/[(\$1 \text{ billion sales})/(20 \text{ million shares})] = \$10/(\$1,000,000,000/20,000,000) = 0.2$

Target: $\text{P/S} = (\$20 \text{ price per share})/[(\$1.6 \text{ billion sales})/(30 \text{ million shares})] = 20/(\$1,600,000,000/\$30,000,000) = 0.375$

Avtech has a more attractive valuation based on its lower P/S but comparable profit margins.

B. One advantage of P/S over P/E is that companies' accounting decisions can have a much greater impact on reported earnings than they are likely to have on reported sales. Although companies are able to make a number of legitimate business and accounting decisions that affect earnings, their discretion over reported sales (revenue recognition) is more limited.

11. A. The P/Es are

Hormel	25.70/1.30 = 19.8
Tyson	11.77/0.40 = 29.4
IBP	23.65/1.14 = 20.7
Smithfield	24.61/2.31 = 10.7

Sales per share are found by dividing sales by shares outstanding. Dividing this into the share price gives the P/Ss:

Hormel	25.70/(4,124/138.923) = 25.70/29.69 = 0.866
Tyson	11.77/(10,751/220.662) = 11.77/48.72 = 0.242
IBP	23.65/(17,388/108.170) = 23.65/160.75 = 0.147
Smithfield	24.61/(6,354/103.803) = 24.61/61.21 = 0.402

B. If we rank the stocks by P/S from highest to lowest, we have

	P/S	Profit Margin
Hormel	0.866	4.41%
Smithfield	0.402	3.99%
Tyson	0.242	0.82%
IBP	0.147	0.70%

The differences in P/S appear to be explained, at least in part, by differences in cost structure as measured by profit margin.

12. For companies in the industry described, P/S would be superior to either of the other two ratios. Among other considerations, P/S is:

▶ More useful in valuing companies with negative earnings.

▶ Better able to compare companies in different countries that are likely to use different accounting standards (a consequence of the multinational nature of the industry).

▶ Less subject to manipulation (i.e., managing earnings by management, a frequent consequence when companies are in a cyclical low and likely to report losses).

▶ Not as volatile as P/E multiples and hence may be more reliable for use in valuation.

13. A. Using the CAPM, the required rate of return is 4.9% + 1.2 × 5.5% = 11.5%.

B. The dividend payout ratio is $0.64/$1.36 = 0.47. The justified values for the three valuation ratios should be

$$\frac{P_0}{E_0} = \frac{(1-b) \times (1+g)}{r-g} = \frac{0.47 \times 1.09}{0.115 - 0.09} = \frac{0.5123}{0.025} = 20.5$$

$$\frac{P_0}{B_0} = \frac{ROE - g}{r-g} = \frac{0.27 - 0.09}{0.115 - 0.09} = \frac{0.18}{0.025} = 7.2$$

$$\frac{P_0}{S_0} = \frac{PM \times (1-b) \times (1+g)}{r-g} = \frac{0.109 \times 0.47 \times 1.09}{0.115 - 0.09}$$
$$= \frac{0.05584}{0.025} = 2.2$$

C. The justified P/E is lower than the trailing P/E (20.5 versus 28.3), the justified P/B is higher than actual P/B (7.2 versus 7.1), and the justified P/S is lower than the actual P/S (2.2 versus 2.9). Therefore, based on P/E and P/S, GE appears to be over-valued but, based on P/B, appears to be slightly undervalued.

14. A. EBITDA = Net income (from continuing operations) + Interest expense + Taxes + Depreciation + Amortization

> EBITDA for RGI = €49.5 million + €3 million + €2 million + €8 million = €62.5 million
> Per-share EBITDA = (€62.5 million)/(5 million shares) = €12.5
> P/EBITDA for RGI = €150/€12.5 = 12
> EBITDA for NCI = €8 million + €5 million + €3 million + €4 million = €20 million
> Per-share EBITDA = (€20 million)/(2 million shares) = €10
> P/EBITDA for NCI = €100/€10 = 10

B. Market value of equity for RGI = €150 × 5 million = €750 million

> Market value of debt for RGI = €50
> Total market value of RGI = €750 million + €50 = €800 million
> Enterprise value (EV) = €800 million − €5 million (cash and investments) = €795 million

Now we divide EV by total (as opposed to per-share) EBITDA:

▶ EV/EBITDA for RGI = (€795 million)/(€62.5 million) = 12.72

> Market value of equity for NCI = €100 × 2 million = €200 million
> Market value of debt for NCI = €100
> Total market value of NCI = €200 million + €100 = €300 million
> Enterprise value (EV) = €300 million − €2 million (cash and investments) = €298 million

Now we divide EV by total (as opposed to per-share) EBITDA:

▶ EV/EBITDA for NCI = (€298 million)/(€20 million) = 14.9

C. Zaldys should select RGI as relatively undervalued.

First, it is correct that NCI *appears* to be relatively undervalued based on P/EBITDA, because NCI has a lower P/EBITDA multiple:

▶ P/EBITDA = €150/€12.5 = 12 for RGI

▶ P/EBITDA = €100/€10 = 10 for NCI

RGI is relatively undervalued based on EV/EBITDA, however, because RGI has the lower EV/EBITDA multiple:

▶ EV/EBITDA = (€795 million)/(€62.5 million) = 12.72 for RGI

▶ EV/EBITDA = (€298 million)/(€20 million) = 14.9 for NCI

EBITDA is a pre-interest flow; therefore, it is a flow to both debt and equity and the EV/EBITDA multiple is more appropriate than the P/EBITDA multiple. Zaldys would rely on EV/EBITDA to reach his decision when the two ratios conflicted. Note that P/EBITDA does not take into account differences in the use of financial leverage. Substantial differences in leverage exist in this case (NCI uses much more debt), so the preference for EV/EBITDA over P/EBITDA is increased.

15. The major concepts are as follows:

▶ EPS plus per-share depreciation, amortization, and depletion (CF)

Limitation: Ignores changes in working capital and noncash revenue. Not a free cash flow concept.

▶ Cash flow from operations (CFO)

Limitation: Not a free cash flow concept, so not directly linked to theory.

▶ Free cash flow to equity (FCFE)

Limitation: Often more variable and more frequently negative than other cash flow concepts.

▶ Earnings before interest, taxes, depreciation, and amortization (EBITDA)

Limitation: Ignores changes in working capital and noncash revenue. Not a free cash flow concept. Relative to its use in P/EBITDA, EBITDA is mismatched with the numerator because it is a pre-interest concept.

16. MAT Technology is relatively undervalued compared with DriveMed based on a P/FCFE multiple that is 34 percent the size of DriveMed's FCFE multiple (15.6/46 = 0.34, or 34%). The only comparison slightly in DriveMed's favor, or approximately equal, is that based on P/CF (12.8 for DriveMed versus 13.0 for MAT Technology). However, FCFE is more strongly grounded in valuation theory than P/CF. Because DriveMed and MAT Technology's expenditures in fixed capital and working capital during the previous year reflected anticipated average expenditures over the foreseeable horizon, we have additional confidence with the P/FCFE comparison.

17. A. Relative strength is based strictly on price movement (a technical indicator). As used by Westard, the comparison is between the returns on HCI and the returns on the S&P 500. In contrast, the price-multiple approaches are based on the relationship of current price not to past prices but to some measure of value such as EPS, book value, sales, or cash flow.

B. Only the reference to the P/E in relationship to the pending patent applications in Westard's recommendation is consistent with the company's value orientation, because it addresses HCI's P/E in relationship to expected future earnings.

18. A. The most restrictive criterion as judged by the number of stocks meeting it is the dividend yield criterion, which results in only 10 eligible investments. The screen strongly emphasizes dividend yield as a valuation indicator.

B. The screen may be too narrowly focused on dividend yield. It did not include variables related to expected growth, required rate of return or risk, or financial strength.

C. The screen results in a very concentrated portfolio. Except for Eastman Kodak, the companies are all utilities, which typically pay high dividends. They belong to a very small segment of the investment universe and would constitute a narrowly focused and non-diversified portfolio.

19. A is correct. Tan has selected the method of comparables rather than the method based on forecasted fundamentals within a price multiple approach.

20. C is correct. This is one of the rationales for using the P/E multiple.

21. D is correct. Peer 4 has the lowest leading PEG:

	Price	Next 4 Quarters EPS	Leading PE	Expected Growth	Leading PEG
Peer 1	$30	1.70	17.65	10	1.765
Peer 2	$26	1.50	17.33	16	1.08
Peer 3	$70	4.00	17.50	9	1.94
Peer 4	$18	1.15	15.65	15	1.04

22. D is correct. The average ROE over 2000–2004 is:

$(10.77\% + 8.20\% + 4.22\% + 8.25\% + 16.4\%)/5 = 9.568\%$

Normalized EPS = Average ROE $\times$ Current book value

Normalized EPS = $9.568\% \times \$13.50 = \$1.29$

23. B is correct. The justified P/S ratio is

$$\frac{P_0}{S_0} = \frac{(E_0/S_0)(1-b)(1+g)}{r-g} = \frac{(0.06)(0.40)(1.06)}{0.10 - 0.06} = 0.636$$

24. B is correct. The formula for the prospective (leading) intrinsic P_0/E_1 is $P/E = 1/[\rho + (1-\lambda)I]$ where I is inflation, λ is the inflation passthrough rate, and ρ is the real required rate of return. Therefore,

$P0/E_1 = 1/[0.06 + (1 - 0.60)0.04] = 13.16$

The P/E for a firm with 0% passthrough (real earnings declining) would be $1/0.10 = 10\times$. The P/E for a firm with a 100% passthrough (real earnings constant) would be $1/0.06 = 16.67\times$. The correct answer of 13.16 is the only choice between 10 and 16.67.

SOLUTIONS FOR READING 49

1. Yes, VIM earned a positive residual income:

EBIT	300,000	
Interest	120,000	$(2,000,000 \times 6\%)$
Pretax income	180,000	
Tax expense	72,000	
Net income	108,000	

$$\begin{aligned} \text{Equity charge} &= \text{Equity capital} \times \text{Required return on equity} \\ &= (1/3)(3,000,000) \times 0.10 \\ &= 1,000,000 \times 0.10 = 100,000 \end{aligned}$$

$$\begin{aligned} \text{Residual income} &= \text{Net income} - \text{Equity charge} \\ &= 108,000 - 100,000 = 8,000 \end{aligned}$$

2. According to the residual income model, intrinsic value for a share of common stock equals book value per share plus the present value of expected future per-share residual income. Book value per share was given as $20. Noting that debt is $(2/3)(\$3,000,000) = \$2,000,000$ so that interest is $\$2,000,000 \times 6\% = \$120,000$, we find that VIM has residual income of $8,000 calculated (as in Problem 1) as follows:

$$\begin{aligned} \text{Residual income} &= \text{Net income} - \text{Equity charge} \\ &= [(\text{EBIT} - \text{Interest})(1 - \text{Tax rate})] \\ &\quad - [(\text{Equity capital})(\text{Required return on equity})] \\ &= [(\$300,000 - \$120,000)(1 - 0.40)] \\ &\quad - [(\$1,000,000)(0.10)] \\ &= \$108,000 - \$100,000 \\ &= \$8,000 \end{aligned}$$

Therefore, residual income per share is $8,000/50,000 shares = $0.16 per share. Because EBIT is expected to continue at the current level indefinitely, we treat the expected per-share residual income of $0.16 as a perpetuity. With a required return on equity of 10 percent, we have

Intrinsic value = $20 + $0.16/0.10 = $20 + $1.60 = $21.60

3. With $g = b \times \text{ROE} = (1 - 0.80)(0.15) = (0.20)(0.15) = 0.03$,

$$\begin{aligned} P/B &= (ROE - g)/(r - g) \\ &= (0.15 - 0.03)/(0.12 - 0.03) \\ &= 0.12/0.09 = 1.33 \end{aligned}$$

or

$$\begin{aligned} P/B &= 1 + (ROE - r)/(r - g) \\ &= 1 + (0.15 - 0.12)/(0.12 - 0.03) \\ &= 1.33 \end{aligned}$$

4. In this problem, interest expense has already been deducted in arriving at NMP's pretax income of $5.1 million. Therefore,

$$\text{Net income} = \text{Pretax income} \times (1 - \text{Tax rate})$$
$$= \$5.1 \text{ million} \times (1 - 0.4)$$
$$= \$5.1 \times 0.6 = \$3.06 \text{ million}$$

Equity charge: Total equity $\times$ Cost of equity capital
$$= (0.1 \times \$450 \text{ million}) \times 12\%$$
$$= \$45 \text{ million} \times 0.12 = \$5,400,000$$

Residual income = Net income $-$ Equity charge
$$= \$3,060,000 - \$5,400,000 = -\$2,340,000$$

NMP had negative residual income of $-\$2,340,000$ in 2001.

5. To achieve a positive residual income, a company's net operating profit after taxes as a percentage of its total assets can be compared with the weighted-average cost of its capital. For SWI:

$$\text{NOPAT/Assets} = 10 \text{ million}/100 \text{ million} = 10 \text{ percent}$$
$$\text{WACC} = (0.5)(\text{After-tax cost of debt})$$
$$+ (0.5)(\textit{Cost of equity})$$
$$= (0.5)(0.09)(0.6) + (0.5)(0.12)$$
$$= (0.5)(0.054) + (0.5)(0.12) = 0.027 + 0.06$$
$$= 0.087 = 8.7\%$$

Therefore, SWI's residual income was positive. Specifically, residual income equals $(0.10 - 0.087) \times €100 \text{ million} = €1.3 \text{ million}$.

6. A. EVA = NOPAT $-$ WACC $\times$ (Beginning book value of assets)
$$= 100 - (11\%) \times (200 + 300) = 100 - (11\%)(500) = \$45$$

B. $\text{RI}_t = E_t - rB_{t-1}$
$$= 5.00 - (11\%)(30.00) = 5.00 - 3.30 = 1.70$$

C. $\text{RI}_t = (\text{ROE}_t - r) \times B_{t-1}$
$$= (18\% - 12\%) \times (30) = 1.80$$

7. A. Economic value added = Net operating profit after taxes $-$ (Cost of capital $\times$ Total capital) = \$100 million $-$ (14% $\times$ \$700 million) = \$2 million. In the absence of information that would be required to calculate the weighted average cost of debt and equity, and given that Sundanci has no long-term debt, the only capital cost used is the required rate of return on equity of 14 percent.

B. Market value added = Market value of capital $-$ Total capital

\$26 stock price $\times$ 84 million shares $-$ \$700 million = \$1.48 billion

8. A. Because the dividend is a perpetuity, the no-growth form of the DDM is applied as follows:

$$V_0 = D/r$$
$$= \$0.60/0.12 = \$5 \text{ per share}$$

B. According to the residual income model, V_0 = Book value per-share + Present value of expected future per-share residual income.

$$RI_t = E - rB_{t-1}$$
$$= 0.60 - (0.12)(6) = -\$0.12$$

Present value of perpetual stream of residual income equals

$$RI_t/r = -\$0.12/0.12 = -\$1.00$$
$$V_0 = \$6.00 - \$1.00 = \$5.00 \text{ per share}$$

9. A. According to the DDM, $V_0 = D/r$ for a no-growth company.

$$V_0 = \$2.00/0.125 = \$16 \text{ per share}$$

B. Under the residual income model, $V_0 = B_0 +$ Present value of expected future pershare residual income:

$$RI_t = E - rB_{t-1}$$
$$= \$2 - (0.125)(\$10) = \$0.75$$

Present value of stream of residual income $= RI_t/r$

$$= 0.75/0.125 = \$6$$
$$V_0 = \$10 + \$6 = \$16 \text{ per share}$$

10. A. $V_0 =$ Present value of the future dividends
$$= 2/1.10 + 2.50/(1.1)^2 + 20.50/(1.1)^3$$
$$= \$1.818 + \$2.066 + \$15.402 = \$19.286$$

B. The book values and residual incomes for the next three years are:

Year	1	2	3
Beginning book value	8.00	10.00	12.50
Retained earnings (Net income − Dividends)	2.00	2.50	(12.50)
Ending book value	10.00	12.50	0.00
Net income	4.00	5.00	8.00
Less equity charge ($r \times$ Book value)	0.80	1.00	1.25
Residual income	3.20	4.00	6.75

$$V_0 = 8.00 + 3.20/1.1 + 4.00/(1.1)^2 + 6.75/(1.1)^3$$
$$V_0 = 8.00 + 2.909 + 3.306 + 5.071 = \$19.286$$

C.

Year	1	2	3
Net income	4.00	5.00	8.00
Beginning book value	8.00	10.00	12.50
Return on equity (ROE)	50%	50%	64%
ROE − r	40%	40%	54%
Residual income (ROE − r) $\times$ Book value	3.20	4.00	6.75

$$V_0 = 8.00 + 3.20/1.1 + 4.00/(1.1)^2 + 6.75/(1.1)^3$$
$$V_0 = 8.00 + 2.909 + 3.306 + 5.071 = \$19.286$$

Note: Because the residual incomes for each year are necessarily the same in Parts B and C, the results for stock valuation are identical.

11.

Year	2001	2002	2005
Beginning book value	30.00	33.00	43.92
Net income = ROE × Book value	4.50	4.95	6.59
Dividends	1.50	1.65	2.20
Equity charge (r × Book value)	3.60	3.96	5.27
Residual income	0.90	0.99	1.32
Ending book value	33.00	36.30	48.32

The table shows that residual income in Year 2001 is $0.90, which equals Book value (beginning of year) × (ROE − r) = $30 × (0.15 − 0.12) = $0.90. By examining the Year 2002 column, one can see that residual income grew by 10 percent to $0.99, which follows from the fact that growth in residual income relates directly to the growth in net income as this company is configured. When both net income and dividends are a function of book value and return on equity is constant, then growth can be predicted from g = (ROE)(1 − Dividend payout ratio). In this case, g = 0.15 × (1 − 0.333) = 0.10 or 10 percent. Net income and residual income will grow by 10 percent annually.

Therefore, residual income in Year 2005 = (Residual income in Year 2001) × $(1.1)^4$. Residual income in Year 2005 = 0.90 × 1.4641 = $1.32.

12. When items such as changes in the value of available-for-sale securities bypass the income statement, they are generally assumed to be nonoperating items that will fluctuate from year to year, although averaging to zero over a period of years. The evidence suggests, however, that changes in the value of available-for-sale securities are not averaging to zero but are persistently negative. Furthermore, these losses are bypassing the income statement. It appears that the company is either making an inaccurate assumption or misleading investors in one way or another. Accordingly, Kent might adjust LE's income downward by the amount of loss for other comprehensive income for each of those years. ROE would then decline commensurately. LE's book value would *not* be misstated because the decline in the value of these securities was already recognized.

13. $V_0 = B_0 + [(ROE − r)/(r − g)] × B_0$
= $20 + [(0.18 − 0.14)/(0.14 − 0.10)] × $20
= $20 + 1.0 ($20) = $40

Simms will probably conclude that the shares are somewhat undervalued.

14. $V_0 = B_0 + (ROE − r) × B_0/(r − g)$
= 30 + (0.15 − 0.12) × 30/(0.12 − 0.10)
= 30 + 45 = $75 *per share*

15.

Year	Net Income (Projected)	Ending Book Value	ROE (%)	Equity Charge (in currency)	Residual Income	PV of RI
2001		10.00				
2002	1.50	11.50	15	1.00	0.50	0.45
2003	1.73	13.23	15	1.15	0.58	0.48
2004	1.99	15.22	15	1.32	0.67	0.50
2005	2.29	17.51	15	1.52	0.77	0.53
2006	2.63	20.14	15	1.75	0.88	0.55
						2.51

Using the finite horizon form of residual income valuation,

$$V_0 = B_0 + \text{Sum of discounted RIs} + \text{Premium (also discounted to present)}$$
$$= \$10 + \$2.51 + (0.20)(20.14)/(1.10)^5$$
$$= \$10 + \$2.51 + \$2.50 = \$15.01$$

16. The present value of the terminal value would then be

$$\text{RI}_T/(1 + r - \omega)(1 + r)^{T-1} = 48.86/(1 + 0.1433 - 0.90)(1.1433)^{20}$$
$$= 13.79$$

Total value is $59.18 + 13.79 = \text{TWD}72.97$. The analyst would again conclude that TSM's shares are overvalued.

17. The value of TSM for the forecast period would be

Year	Net Income (Projected)	Book Value	Forecast ROE (beg. equity, %)	Cost of Equity (%)	Equity Charge TWD	Residual Income	PV of RI	Total
2001		16.47					16.47	62.11
2002	2.07	18.54	12.57	14.33	2.36	−0.29	(0.25)	
2003	4.81	23.35	25.94	14.33	2.66	2.15	1.65	
2004	5.84	29.19	25.00	14.33	3.35	2.49	1.67	
2005	7.30	36.48	25.00	14.33	4.18	3.11	1.82	
2006	9.12	45.61	25.00	14.33	5.23	3.89	1.99	
2007	11.40	57.01	25.00	14.33	6.54	4.87	2.18	
2008	14.25	71.26	25.00	14.33	8.17	6.08	2.38	
2009	17.81	89.07	25.00	14.33	10.21	7.60	2.60	
2010	22.27	111.34	25.00	14.33	12.76	9.50	2.85	
2011	27.84	139.18	25.00	14.33	15.96	11.88	3.11	
2012	27.84	167.01	20.00	14.33	19.94	7.89	1.81	
2013	33.40	200.41	20.00	14.33	23.93	9.47	1.90	
2014	40.08	240.50	20.00	14.33	28.72	11.36	1.99	
2015	48.10	288.60	20.00	14.33	34.46	13.64	2.09	
2016	57.72	346.32	20.00	14.33	41.36	16.36	2.20	
2017	69.26	415.58	20.00	14.33	49.63	19.64	2.30	
2018	83.12	498.70	20.00	14.33	59.55	23.56	2.42	
2019	99.74	598.43	20.00	14.33	71.46	28.28	2.54	
2020	119.69	718.12	20.00	14.33	85.76	33.93	2.66	
2021	143.62	861.75	20.00	14.33	102.91	40.72	2.80	
2022	172.35	1034.10	20.00	14.33	123.49	48.86	2.93	
2023	206.82	1240.91	20.00	14.33	148.19	58.63		

The present value of the terminal value would then be

$$\text{RI}_T/(1 + r - \omega)(1 + r)^{T-1} = 58.63/(1 + 0.1433 - 0.90)(1.1433)^{21}$$
$$= 14.47$$

Total value is $62.11 + 14.47 = \text{TWD}76.58$. The analyst would again conclude that TSM's shares are overvalued.

18. A. The table below shows calculations for book values, net income, and dividends.

Year	Beginning Book Value	Net Income	Dividends	Ending Book Value	Residual Income	PV of RI
1	9.620	2.116	0.635	11.101	1.318	1.217
2	11.101	2.442	0.733	12.811	1.521	1.297
3	12.811	2.818	0.846	14.784	1.755	1.382
4	14.784	3.252	0.976	17.061	2.025	1.472
5	17.061	3.753	1.126	19.688	2.337	1.569
6	19.688	4.331	1.299	22.720	2.697	1.672
7	22.720	4.998	1.500	26.219	3.113	1.781
8	26.219	5.768	1.730	30.257	3.592	1.898

For each year above, net income is 22 percent of beginning book value. Dividends are 30 percent of net income. The ending book value is the beginning book value plus net income minus dividends.

B. Residual income is Net income − Cost of equity (%) × Beginning book value. To find the cost of equity,

$$r = R_F + \beta_i[E(R_M) - R_F] = 5\% + (0.60)(5.5\%) = 8.30\%$$

For Year 1 in the table above,

$$\text{Residual income} = 2.116 - (8.30\%)(9.62) = 2.116 - 0.798 = \$1.318$$

This same calculation is repeated for Years 2 through 8. The final column of the table gives the present value of the calculated residual income, discounted at 8.30 percent.

C. To find the stock value with the residual income method, we use the equation

$$V_0 = B_0 + \sum_{t=1}^{T} \frac{(E_t - rB_{t-1})}{(1 + r)^t} + \frac{P_T - B_T}{(1 + r)^T}$$

In this equation, B_0 is the current book value per share of $9.62. The sum of the present values of the eight years' residual income is the sum of the present values of the residual incomes in the table above, $12.288. We need to estimate the final term, the present value of the excess of the terminal stock price over the terminal book value. The terminal stock price is assumed to be 3.0 times the terminal book value, or $P_T = 3.0(30.257) = \$90.771$. $P_T - B_T$ is 90.771 − 30.257 = \$60.514. The present value of this amount discounted at 8.30 percent for eight years is $31.976. Adding these terms together gives a stock price of $V_0 = 9.62 + 12.288 + 31.976 = \$53.884$.

D. The appropriate DDM expression is

$$V_0 = \sum_{t=1}^{T} \frac{D_t}{(1 + r)^t} + \frac{P_T}{(1 + r)^T}$$

We have calculated the dividends and terminal stock price above. Discounting them at 8.30 percent would give the value of the stock:

Year	Dividend	PV of Dividend
1	0.635	0.586
2	0.733	0.625
3	0.846	0.666
4	0.976	0.709
5	1.126	0.756
6	1.299	0.805
7	1.500	0.858
8	1.730	0.914
All		5.919

The present value of the eight dividends is $5.92. The terminal stock price is assumed to be $90.771, which is worth $47.964 discounted at 8.30 percent for eight years. The value for the stock, the present value of the dividends plus the present value of the terminal stock price, is $V_0 = 5.92 + 47.964 = \$53.884$. The stock values estimated with the residual income model and the dividend discount model are identical. Because they are based on similar financial assumptions, this equivalency is expected. Even though the recognition of income differs between the two models, their final results are the same.

19. **A.** The justified P/B can be found with the following formula:

$$\frac{P_0}{B_0} = 1 + \frac{ROE - r}{r - g}$$

ROE is 20%, g is 6%, and $r = R_F + \beta_i[E(R_M) - R_F] = 5\% + (0.80)(5.5\%) = 9.4\%$. Substituting in the values gives a justified P/B of

$$\frac{P_0}{B_0} = 1 + \frac{0.20 - 0.094}{0.094 - 0.06} = 4.12$$

The assumed parameters give a justified P/B of 4.12, slightly above the current value of 3.57.

B. To find the ROE that would result in a P/B of 3.57, we substitute 3.57, r, and g into the following equation:

$$\frac{P_0}{B_0} = 1 + \frac{ROE - r}{r - g}$$

This yields

$$3.57 = 1 + \frac{ROE - 0.094}{0.094 - 0.06}$$

Solving for ROE, after several steps we finally derive ROE of 0.18138 or 18.1 percent. This value of ROE is consistent with a P/B of 3.57.

C. To find the growth rate that would result in a P/B of 3.57, we use the expression given in Part B, solving for *g* instead of ROE:

$$\frac{P_0}{B_0} = 1 + \frac{ROE - r}{r - g}$$

Substituting in the values, we have

$$3.57 = 1 + \frac{0.20 - 0.094}{0.094 - g}$$

Solving for *g*, after several steps we obtain a growth rate of 0.05275 or 5.3 percent. Assuming that the single-stage growth model is applicable to Boeing, the current P/B and current market price can be justified with values for ROE or *g* that are not much different from our starting values of 20 percent and 6 percent, respectively.

SOLUTIONS FOR READING 50

1. B is correct.

$$\begin{aligned}\text{Residual income} &= \text{Net income in 2005} - (\text{Cost of equity capital} \\ &\qquad \times \text{Equity capital as of 31 December 2004}) \\ &= 975 - (0.12 \times 8{,}125) \\ &= 0\end{aligned}$$

2. B is correct. The intrinsic value of the equity is equal to its book value plus the present value (PV) of the residual incomes (RIs). If the residual incomes are negative, their present value will be also. [The PV of the negative RI (PV of $50 for 3 years) is also less than the book value ($8,613).] Hence, the intrinsic value of the equity will be less than its book value and the intrinsic-to-book ratio will be less than 1.0 and more than 0.

3. C is correct. $\text{EVA}^{\circledR} = \text{NOPAT} - \$\text{WACC}$ so that when $\$\text{WACC} > \text{NOPAT}$, $\text{EVA}^{\circledR} < 0$.

4. B is correct. Intrinsic value $= BV_0 + \dfrac{ROE - r}{r - g} \times BV_0$ (with constant growth)

$$\begin{aligned}&= 12 + \frac{0.14 - 0.125}{0.125 - 0.07} \times 12 \\ &= \$15.27.\end{aligned}$$

5. A is correct. The franchise P/E value of the firm:

$$\begin{aligned}&= \text{Franchise factor} \times \text{Growth factor} \\ &= \left(\frac{1}{r} - \frac{1}{ROE}\right) \times \frac{g}{r - g} \\ &= \left(\frac{1}{0.125} - \frac{1}{0.14}\right) \times \frac{0.07}{0.125 - 0.07} \\ &= 1.09\end{aligned}$$

The second way to estimate the franchise P/E value is:

$$\begin{aligned}\text{Intrinsic P/E} &= \text{Tangible P/E} + \text{Franchise P/E} \\ \text{Intrinsic P/E} &= \frac{(1 - b)}{r - b} = \frac{0.5}{0.125 - 0.07} = 9.0909 \\ \text{Tangible P/E} &= \frac{1}{r} = \frac{1}{0.125} = 8.0 \\ \text{Franchise P/E} &= 9.0909 - 8.0 = 1.0909\end{aligned}$$

6. B is correct. A reduction in the cost of capital will increase the excess of the return on equity over the cost of capital, which increases the franchise value.

GLOSSARY

Abandonment option The ability to terminate a project at some future time if the financial results are disappointing.

Abnormal earnings See *Residual income.*

Abnormal rate of return The amount by which a security's actual return differs from its expected rate of return which is based on the market's rate of return and the security's relationship with the market.

Abnormal return Return on a stock beyond what would be predicted by market movements alone. Cumulative abnormal return (CAR) is the total abnormal return for the period surrounding an announcement or the release of information.

Absolute dispersion The amount of variability present without comparison to any reference point or benchmark.

Absolute frequency The number of observations in a given interval (for grouped data).

Absolute priority rule The hierarchy whereby claims are satisfied in corporate liquidation.

Absolute valuation model A model that specifies an asset's intrinsic value.

Accounting A detailed report to the trust beneficiaries by a trustee of his stewardship, also used to discharge the trustee.

Accounting earnings Earnings of a firm as reported on its income statement.

Accounting estimates Estimates of items such as the useful lives of assets, warranty costs, and the amount of uncollectible receivables.

Accounting profit Total revenues minus total explicit costs.

Accounting risk The risk associated with accounting standards that vary from country to country or with any uncertainty about how certain transactions should be recorded.

Accounting Standards Board (ASB) The Accounting Standards Board issues Financial Reporting Standards (FRSs) for the United Kingdom. It took over the task of setting accounting standards from the Accounting Standards Committee in 1990.

Accounts payable A liability that results from the purchase of goods or services on open account, that is, without a signed note payable.

Accounts receivable Amounts owed to a company by customers as a result of delivering goods or services and extending credit in the ordinary course of business. Also referred to as *trade receivables.*

Accrual accounting The system of recording financial transactions as they come into existence as a legally enforceable claim, rather than when they settle.

Accrued interest Interest earned but not yet paid.

Accumulate Wall Street expression for buying on a large scale over time, typically by an institution. "Accumulation" of a stock is said to occur if a number of institutions are gradually adding to their holdings.

Accumulated other comprehensive income Cumulative gains or losses reported in shareholders' equity that arise from changes in the fair value of available-for-sale securities, from the effects of changes in foreign-currency exchange rates on consolidated foreign-currency financial statements, from certain gains and losses on financial derivatives and from adjustments for underfunded pension plans.

Acquiring company or acquirer The company in a merger or acquisition that is acquiring the target.

Acquisition The purchase of some portion of one company by another; the purchase may be for assets, a definable segment of another entity, or the purchase of an entire company.

Active factor risk The contribution to active risk squared resulting from the portfolio's different-than-benchmark exposures relative to factors specified in the risk model.

Active investment managers Managers who hold portfolios that differ from their benchmark portfolio in an attempt to produce positive risk-adjusted returns.

Active management Attempts to achieve portfolio returns more than commensurate with risk, either by forecasting broad market trends or by identifying particular mispriced sectors of a market or securities in a market.

Active portfolio In the context of the Treynor-Black model, the portfolio formed by mixing analyzed stocks of perceived nonzero alpha values. This portfolio is ultimately mixed with the passive market index portfolio.

Active return The return on a portfolio minus the return on the portfolio's benchmark.

Active risk The standard deviation of active returns.

Active risk squared The variance of active returns; active risk raised to the second power.

Active specific risk or asset selection risk The contribution to active risk squared resulting from the portfolio's active weights on individual assets as those weights interact with assets' residual risk.

G-1

Addition rule for probabilities A principle stating that the probability that *A* or *B* occurs (both occur) equals the probability that *A* occurs, plus the probability that *B* occurs, minus the probability that both *A* and *B* occur.

Additional information Information that is required or recommended under the GIPS standards and is not considered as "supplemental information" for the purposes of compliance.

Additions Assets transferred to a trust after the initial funding.

Add-on interest A procedure for determining the interest on a bond or loan in which the interest is added onto the face value of a contract.

Adjustable-rate mortgage A mortgage whose interest rate varies according to some specified measure of the current market interest rate.

Adjusted beta Historical beta adjusted to reflect the tendency of beta to be mean reverting.

Adjusted present value (APV) As an approach to valuing a company, the sum of the value of the company, assuming no use of debt, and the net present value of any effects of debt on company value.

Adjusted R^2 A measure of goodness-of-fit of a regression that is adjusted for degrees of freedom and hence does not automatically increase when another independent variable is added to a regression.

Administrative fees All fees other than the trading expenses and the investment management fee. Administrative fees include custody fees, accounting fees, consulting fees, legal fees, performance measurement fees, or other related fees. These administrative fees are typically outside the control of the investment management firm and are not included in either the gross-of-fees return or the net-of-fees return. However, there are some markets and investment vehicles where administrative fees are controlled by the firm.

After-tax cash flow (ATCF) Net operating income less debt service and less taxes payable on income from operations.

Agency costs Agency costs are the incremental costs arising from conflicts of interest when an agent makes decisions for a principal. In the context of a corporation, agency costs arise from conflicts of interest between managers, shareholders, and bondholders.

Agency problem or principal-agent problem or agency conflict A conflict of interest that arises when the agent in an agency relationship has goals and incentives that differ from those of the principal.

Agency relationships An arrangement whereby someone, an agent, acts on behalf of another person, the principal.

Agency trade A trade in which a broker acts as an agent only, not taking a position on the opposite side of the trade.

Aggregate demand (1) The relationship between the quantity of real GDP demanded and the price level. (2) The total of all planned expenditures for the entire economy.

Aggregate production function The relationship between the quantity of real GDP supplied and the quantities of labor and capital and the state of technology.

Aggressive With respect to equity valuation, the term implies a concentrated portfolio holding smaller capitalization stocks than the general market, often with higher price/earnings and lower yields, together with low reserves. Often implies unusual volatility.

AICPA The American Institute of Certified Public Accountants. The AICPA is the national association of CPAs in the United States.

AIMR Performance presentation standards (AIMR-PPS®) A comprehensive set of reporting guidelines created by the Association for Investment Management and Research (AIMR) (now CFA Institute) in 1993 that converged to the Global Investment Performance Standards on 1 January 2006.

Allocative efficiency A situation in which we cannot produce more of any good without giving up some of another good that we value more highly.

Alpha (or abnormal return) The return on an asset in excess of the asset's required rate of return; the risk-adjusted excess return.

Alternative hypothesis The hypothesis accepted when the null hypothesis is rejected.

Alternative investments Hedge funds, venture capital pools, options and other derivatives, real estate, and other non-stock or -bond market assets.

American Depositary Receipt (ADR) A certificate of ownership issued by a U.S. bank to promote local trading in a foreign stock. The U.S. bank holds the foreign shares and issues ADRs against them.

American option An option contract that can be exercised at any time until its expiration date.

American terms With reference to U.S. dollar exchange rate quotations, the U.S. dollar price of a unit of another currency.

Amortizing or accreting swaps A swap in which the notional principal changes according to a formula related to changes in the underlying.

Analysis of variance (ANOVA) The analysis of the total variability of a dataset (such as observations on the dependent variable in a regression) into components representing different sources of variation; with reference to regression, ANOVA provides the inputs for an *F*-test of the significance of the regression as a whole.

Annual percentage rate The cost of borrowing expressed as a yearly rate.

Annuity A finite set of level sequential cash flows.

Annuity due An annuity having a first cash flow that is paid immediately.

Anomalies (1) Security price relationships that appear to contradict a well-regarded hypothesis; in this case, the efficient market hypothesis. (2) Patterns of returns that seem to contradict the efficient market hypothesis.

Antitrust legislation or antitrust laws Laws that restrict the formation of monopolies and regulate certain anticompetitive business practices.

A priori probability A probability based on logical analysis rather than on observation or personal judgment.

Appraisal ratio The ratio of alpha to residual standard deviation.

Appreciation An increase in the exchange value of one nation's currency in terms of the currency of another nation.

Arbitrage The simultaneous purchase of an undervalued asset or portfolio and sale of an overvalued but equivalent asset or portfolio, in order to obtain a riskless profit on the price differential.

Arbitrage opportunity An opportunity to conduct an arbitrage; an opportunity to earn an expected positive net profit without risk and with no net investment of money.

Arbitrage portfolio The portfolio that exploits an arbitrage opportunity.

Arbitrage pricing theory (APT) An asset pricing theory that is derived from a factor model, using diversification and arbitrage arguments. The theory describes the relationship between expected returns on securities, given that there are no opportunities to create wealth through risk-free arbitrage investments.

Arithmetic mean The sum of the observations divided by the number of observations.

Arrears swap A type of interest rate swap in which the floating payment is set at the end of the period and the interest is paid at that same time.

Asian call option A European-style option with a value at maturity equal to the difference between the stock price at maturity and the average stock price during the life of the option, or $0, whichever is greater.

Ask price The price at which a market maker is willing to sell a security (also called *offer price*).

Asset allocation Dividing of investment funds among several asset classes to achieve diversification.

Asset allocation decision Choosing among broad asset classes such as stocks versus bonds.

Asset beta The unlevered beta; reflects the business risk of the assets; the asset's systematic risk.

Asset class Securities that have similar characteristics, attributes, and risk/return relationships.

Asset purchase An acquisition in which the acquirer purchases the target company's assets and payment is made directly to the target company.

Asset turnover (ATO) The annual sales generated by each dollar of assets (sales/assets).

Asset-based valuation An approach to valuing natural resource companies that estimates company value on the basis of the market value of the natural resources the company controls.

Assets under management (AUM) The total market value of the assets managed by an investment firm.

Assets Amounts owned; all items to which a business or household holds legal claim.

Asymmetric information Possession of information by one party in a financial transaction but not by the other party.

At the money option An option for which the underlying's market price equals the option's exercise price.

Auction market A market in which the orders of multiple buyers compete for execution.

Autocorrelation The correlation of a time series with its own past values.

Autoregressive (AR) model A time series regressed on its own past values, in which the independent variable is a lagged value of the dependent variable.

Available-for-sale security A default classification for an investment in a debt or equity security that is not classified as either a held-to-maturity security or a trading security.

Average tax rate The total tax payment divided by total income. It is the proportion of total income paid in taxes.

Backward integration A merger involving the purchase of a target ahead of the acquirer in the value or production chain; for example, to acquire a supplier.

Backwardation Condition in which spot price of commodity exceeds the futures price (cf. *contango*).

Balance of payments A system of accounts that measures transactions of goods, services, income, and financial assets between domestic households, businesses, and governments and residents of the rest of the world during a specific time period.

Balance of payments accounts   A country's record of international trading, borrowing, and lending.

Balance sheet   A financial statement that shows what assets the firm controls at a fixed point in time and how it has financed these assets.

Balanced budget   A government budget in which tax revenues and expenditures are equal.

Balanced fund   A mutual fund with, generally, a three-part investment objective: (1) to conserve the investor's principal, (2) to pay current income, and (3) to increase both principal and income. The fund aims to achieve this by owning a mixture of bonds, preferred stocks, and common stocks.

Balloon payment   Large final payment (e.g., when a loan is repaid in installments).

Band-of-investment method   A widely used approach to estimate an overall capitalization rate. It is based on the premise that debt and equity financing is typically involved in a real estate transaction.

Bank discount basis   A quoting convention that annualizes, on a 360-day year, the discount as a percentage of face value.

Barriers to entry   Legal or natural constraints that protect a firm from potential competitors.

Barter   The direct exchange of goods and services for other goods and services without the use of money.

Base year   The year that is chosen as the point of reference for comparison of prices in other years.

Basic earnings per share   Total earnings divided by the weighted average number of shares actually outstanding during the period.

Basis point   A hundredth of a percent; thus 75 basis points equals three-quarters of 1 percentage point.

Basis point value (BPV)   Also called *present value of a basis point* or *price value of a basis point* (PVBP), the change in the bond price for a 1 basis point change in yield.

Basis swap   A swap in which both parties pay a floating rate.

Bayes' formula   A method for updating probabilities based on new information.

Bear hug   A tactic used by acquirers to circumvent target management's objections to a proposed merger by submitting the proposal directly to the target company's board of directors.

Bear market   Widespread decline in security prices (cf. *bull market*).

Bear spread   An option strategy that involves selling a put with a lower exercise price and buying a put with a higher exercise price. It can also be executed with calls.

Before-tax cash flow   A measure of the expected annual cash flow from the operation of a real estate investment after all expenses but before taxes.

Behavioral finance   (1) The analysis of various psychological traits of individuals and how these traits affect how they act as investors, analysts, and portfolio managers. (2) Branch of finance that stresses aspects of investor irrationality.

Benchmark   A comparison portfolio used to evaluate performance; a point of reference or comparison.

Benchmark bond   A bond representative of current market conditions and used for performance comparison.

Benchmark value of the multiple   In using the method of comparables, the value of a price multiple for the comparison asset; when we have comparison assets (a group), the mean or median value of the multiple for the group of assets.

Bernoulli random variable   A random variable having the outcomes 0 and 1.

Bernoulli trial   An experiment that can produce one of two outcomes.

Beta   A measure of an asset's systematic risk based upon an asset's covariance with the market portfolio.

Bid price   The price at which a dealer is willing to purchase a security.

Bid-ask spread (or bid-asked spread)   The difference between the quoted ask and the bid prices.

Bidder   The acquiring firm.

Bilateral arbitrage   With reference to currencies, an arbitrage involving two currencies only.

Bill-and-hold basis   Sales on a bill-and-hold basis involve selling products but not delivering those products until a later date.

Binomial model   A model for pricing options in which the underlying price can move to only one of two possible new prices in each specified time interval.

Binomial random variable   The number of successes in n Bernoulli trials for which the probability of success is constant for all trials and the trials are independent.

Binomial tree   The graphical representation of a model of asset price dynamics in which, at each period, the asset moves up with probability p or down with probability $(1 - p)$.

Black-Scholes or Black-Scholes-Merton option pricing model (formula)   An equation to value a call option based on five variables: the price of the underlying, the exercise price, the risk-free interest rate, the time to maturity, and the standard deviation of the underlying's return.

Block   Orders to buy or sell that are too large for the liquidity ordinarily available in dealer networks or stock exchanges.

Blue chip   A large, stable, well-known, widely held, seasoned company with a strong financial position, usually paying a reasonable dividend.

Boilerplate   Standard terms and conditions, e.g., in a debt contract.

Bond   A security issued by a borrower that obligates the issuer to make specified payments to the holder over a specific period. A *coupon bond* obligates the issuer to make interest payments called coupon payments over the life of the bond, then to repay the *face value* at maturity.

Bond-equivalent yield   The yield to maturity on a basis that ignores compounding.

Bond indenture   A legal contract specifying the terms of a bond issue.

Bond option   An option in which the underlying is a bond; primarily traded in over-the-counter markets.

Bond rating   Rating of the likelihood of bond's default.

Bond yield plus risk premium method   A method of determining the required rate of return on equity (cost of equity) for a company as the sum of the yield to maturity on the company's long-term debt plus a risk premium.

Bonding costs   Costs borne by management to assure owners that they are working in the owners' best interest (e.g., implicit cost of non-compete agreements).

Book entry   Registered ownership of stock without issue of stock certificate.

Book value of equity (or book value)   Shareholders' equity (total assets minus total liabilities) minus the value of preferred stock; common shareholders' equity; book value per share is book value of equity divided by the number of common shares outstanding.

Books   In accounting, a shorthand reference to shareholder as opposed to income tax financial information.

Bootstrapping earnings   An increase in a company's earnings that results as a consequence of the idiosyncrasies of a merger transaction itself rather than because of resulting economic benefits of the combination.

Bottom-up forecasting approach   A forecasting approach that involves aggregating the individual company forecasts of analysts into industry forecasts, and finally into macroeconomic forecasts.

Bottom-up or bottom-up investing   An approach to investing that focuses on the individual characteristics of securities rather than on macroeconomic or overall market forecasts.

Bourse   A French term often used to refer to a stock market.

Box spread   An option strategy that combines a bull spread and a bear spread having two different exercise prices, which produces a risk-free payoff of the difference in the exercise prices.

Breakeven point   The number of units produced and sold at which the company's net income is zero (revenues = total costs).

Breakup value (or private market value)   The value that can be achieved if a company's assets are divided and sold separately.

Breusch–Pagan test   A test for conditional heteroskedasticity in the error term of a regression.

Broker   An agent who executes orders to buy or sell securities on behalf of a client in exchange for a commission.

Brokerage   The business of acting as agents for buyers or sellers, usually in return for commissions.

Brokered market   A market where an intermediary (a broker) offers search services to buyers and sellers.

Budget constraint   All of the possible combinations of goods that can be purchased (at fixed prices) with a specific budget.

Budget deficit   The amount by which government spending exceeds government revenues.

Build-up method   A method for determining the required rate of return on equity as the sum of risk premiums, in which one or more of the risk premiums is typically subjective rather than grounded in a formal equilibrium model.

Bull market   Widespread rise in security prices (cf. *bear market*).

Bull spread   An option strategy that involves buying a call with a lower exercise price and selling a call with a higher exercise price. It can also be executed with puts.

Bullet payment   Single final payment, e.g., of a loan (in contrast to payment in installments).

Bund   Long-term German government *bond.*

Business cycle   The periodic but irregular up-and-down movement in production.

Business risk   The risk associated with operating earnings; risk that is related to the uncertainty of revenues.

Butterfly spread   An option strategy that combines two bull or bear spreads and has three exercise prices.

Buy-and-hold strategy   A passive portfolio management strategy in which securities (bonds or stocks) are bought and held to maturity.

Buyback   Repurchase agreement.

Buy-side analysts   Analysts who work for investment management firms, trusts, and bank trust departments, and similar institutions.

Call   An option that gives the holder the right to buy an underlying asset from another party at a fixed price over a specific period of time.

Callable bond   A bond that the issuer may repurchase at a given price in some specified period.

Call auction   See *fixing*.

Call option   A contract that gives its holder the right to buy an asset, typically a financial instrument, at a specified price through a specified date.

Call provision   Provision that allows an issuer to buy back the *bond* issue at a stated price.

Cannibalization   Cannibalization occurs when an investment takes customers and sales away from another part of the company.

Cap agreement (or cap)   A contract that on each settlement date pays the holder the greater of the difference between the reference rate and the cap rate or zero; it is equivalent to a series of call options at the reference rate.

Capital   The tools, equipment, buildings, and other constructions that businesses now use to produce goods and services.

Capital account   Foreign investment in a country minus its investment abroad.

Capital accumulation   The growth of capital resources.

Capital allocation decision   Allocation of invested funds between risk-free assets versus the risky portfolio.

Capital allocation line (CAL)   A graph line that describes the combinations of expected return and standard deviation of return available to an investor from combining the optimal portfolio of risky assets with the risk-free asset.

Capital appreciation   A return objective in which the investor seeks to increase the portfolio value, primarily through capital gains, over time to meet a future need rather than dividend yield.

Capital asset pricing model (CAPM)   An equation describing the expected return on any asset (or portfolio) as a linear function of its beta.

Capital budget   List of planned investment projects, usually prepared annually.

Capital budgeting   The allocation of funds to relatively long-range projects or investments.

Capital charge   The company's total cost of capital in money terms.

Capital consumption   The decrease in the capital stock that results from wear and tear and obsolescence.

Capital Employed (Real Estate)   The denominator of the return expressions, defined as the "weighted-average equity" (weighted-average capital) during the measurement period. Capital employed should not include any income or capital return accrued *during* the measurement period. Beginning capital is adjusted by weighting the cash flows (contributions and distributions) that occurred during the period. Cash flows are typically weighted based on the actual days the flows are in or out of the portfolio. Other weighting methods are acceptable; however, once a methodology is chosen, it should be consistently applied.

Capital expenditures   Expenditures made in the purchase of long-term productive assets, such as property, plant, and equipment, whose cost is amortized against income in future periods.

Capital gain   The amount by which the sale price of an asset exceeds the purchase price. If a share of stock is bought for $5 and then sold for $15, the capital gain is $10.

Capital goods   Producer durables; nonconsumable goods that firms use to make other goods.

Capital lease   A lease that transfers, in an economic sense, the risks and rewards of ownership to the lessee without transferring title. Lease payments made are comprised of interest and principal. Property held under a capital-lease agreement is accounted for as an asset. This cost is amortized over the relevant useful life.

Capital loss   The amount by which the sale price of an asset is less than the purchase price. If a share of stock is bought for $15 and then sold for $5, the capital loss is $10.

Capital market   Financial market (particularly the market for long-term securities).

Capital market instruments   Fixed-income or equity investments that trade in the secondary market.

Capital market line (CML)   The line with an intercept point equal to the risk-free rate that is tangent to the efficient frontier of risky assets; represents the efficient frontier when a risk-free asset is available for investment.

Capital rationing   Shortage of funds that forces a company to choose between worthwhile projects.

Capital stock   The total quantity of plant, equipment, buildings, and inventories.

Capital structure   The mix of debt and equity that a company uses to finance its business.

Capitalization   Long-term debt plus preferred stock plus net worth.

Capitalization rate   The divisor in the expression for the value of a perpetuity.

Capitalized interest   Interest incurred during the construction period on monies invested in assets under construction that is added to the cost of the assets.

Caplet Each component call option in a cap.

CAPM Capital asset pricing model.

Capped swap A swap in which the floating payments have an upper limit.

Capture hypothesis A theory of regulatory behavior that predicts that the regulators will eventually be captured by the special interests of the industry being regulated.

Capture theory A theory of regulation that states that the regulations are supplied to satisfy the demand of producers to maximize producer surplus.

Cash Currency, coin, and funds on deposit that are available for immediate withdrawal without restriction. Money orders, certified checks, cashier's checks, personal checks, and bank drafts are also considered cash.

Cash and carry Purchase of a security and simultaneous sale of a *future,* with the balance being financed with a loan or *repo.*

Cash earnings Cash revenue minus cash expenses.

Cash equivalents Short-term and highly liquid investments readily convertible into known amounts of cash and close enough to maturity that there is insignificant risk of changes in value from interest rate movements.

Cash flow A flow based on cash receipts and cash disbursements; may refer to either total cash flow or, more commonly, operating cash flow.

Cash flow additivity principle The principle that dollar amounts indexed at the same point in time are additive.

Cash flow analysis The search for the fundamental drivers that underlie a company's cash flow stream and affect its sustainability.

Cash flow at risk (CFAR) A variation of VAR that reflects the risk of a company's cash flow instead of its market value.

Cash flow from operations A term used on the cash flow analysis statement that consists of cash flow available for debt service less total interest paid. The term also is used to refer to cash provided or used by operating activities and operating cash flow as those terms are defined by generally accepted accounting principles.

Cash offering A merger or acquisition that is to be paid for with cash; the cash for the merger might come from the acquiring company's existing assets or from a debt issue.

Cash operating expense A Uniform Credit Analysis®–defined cash flow amount that consists of cash paid for sales and marketing, general and administrative, and research and development expenditures. The term is defined the same way on the cash flow analysis statement.

Cash price or spot price The price for immediate purchase of the underlying asset.

Cash settlement A procedure used in certain derivative transactions that specifies that the long and short parties engage in the equivalent cash value of a delivery transaction.

Catalyst An event or piece of information that causes the marketplace to re-evaluate the prospects of a company.

Caution One of the three components of the standard of prudence governing trustees; avoidance of undue risk and attentiveness to the protection of trust property.

Central bank A bank's bank and a public authority that regulates a nation's depository institutions and controls the quantity of money.

Central limit theorem A result in statistics that states that the sample mean computed from large samples of size n from a population with finite variance will follow an approximate normal distribution with a mean equal to the population mean and a variance equal to the population variance divided by n.

Centralized risk management or companywide risk management When a company has a single risk management group that monitors and controls all of the risk-taking activities of the organization. Centralization permits economies of scale and allows a company to use some of its risks to offset other risks. See also *enterprise risk management.*

CEO Chief executive officer.

Certificate of deposit (CD) An unsecured evidence of indebtedness of a bank, which may be sold to others. Usually with a face value of $100,000 or more and bearing interest below the prime rate.

Ceteris paribus Other things being equal—all other relevant things remaining the same.

CFO Chief financial officer.

CFTC Commodity Futures Trading Commission.

Chaebol A Korean conglomerate.

Chain rule of forecasting A forecasting process in which the next period's value as predicted by the forecasting equation is substituted into the right-hand side of the equation to give a predicted value two periods ahead.

Chapter 11 A U.S. bankruptcy procedure designed to reorganize and rehabilitate defaulting firm.

Chapter 7 A U.S. bankruptcy procedure whereby a debtor's assets are sold and the proceeds are used to repay creditors.

Cheapest to deliver A bond in which the amount received for delivering the bond is largest compared with the amount paid in the market for the bond.

Cherry-picking When a bankrupt company is allowed to enforce contracts that are favorable to it while walking away from contracts that are unfavorable to it.

CHIPS Clearinghouse Interbank Payments System.

Classical growth theory A theory of economic growth based on the view that real GDP growth is temporary and that when real GDP per person increases above subsistence level, a population explosion brings real GDP back to subsistence level.

Clayton Act A federal antitrust law passed in 1914. Section 7, which is most relevant to mergers and acquisitions, prohibits the acquisition of stock and assets of a company when the effect is to lessen competition.

Clean surplus accounting Accounting that satisfies the condition that all changes in the book value of equity other than transactions with owners are reflected in income.

Clean surplus relation The relationship between earnings, dividends, and book value in which ending book value is equal to the beginning book value plus earnings less dividends, apart from ownership transactions.

Clearinghouse An entity associated with a futures market that acts as middleman between the contracting parties and guarantees to each party the performance of the other.

Clientele effect The preference some investors have for shares that exhibit certain characteristics.

Closed-end fund An investment company with a fixed number of shares. New shares cannot be issued and the old shares cannot be redeemed. Shares are traded in the marketplace, and their value may differ from the underlying net asset value of the fund.

Closeout netting Netting the market values of *all* derivative contracts between two parties to determine one overall value owed by one party to another in the event of bankruptcy.

CMOs Collateralized mortgage obligations.

Coefficient of variation (CV) The ratio of a set of observations' standard deviation to the observations' mean value.

Cointegrated Describes two time series that have a long-term financial or economic relationship such that they do not diverge from each other without bound in the long run.

Collar An option strategy involving the purchase of a put and sale of a call in which the holder of an asset gains protection below a certain level, the exercise price of the put, and pays for it by giving up gains above a certain level, the exercise price of the call. Collars also can be used to provide protection against rising interest rates on a floating-rate loan by giving up gains from lower interest rates.

Collateral A specific asset pledged against possible default on a bond. Mortgage bonds are backed by claims on property. Collateral trust bonds are backed by claims on other securities. Equipment obligation bonds are backed by claims on equipment.

Collateralized mortgage obligation (CMO) A mortgage pass-through security that partitions cash flows from underlying mortgages into classes called tranches that receive principal payments according to stipulated rules.

Combination A listing in which the order of the listed items does not matter.

Commercial bank A firm that is licensed by the Comptroller of the Currency in the U.S. Treasury or by a state agency to receive deposits and make loans.

Commercial paper Unsecured short-term corporate debt that is characterized by a single payment at maturity.

Commingled fund Typically, an investment pool run by a bank, in which participation is represented by accounting units rather than shares.

Commission recapture Credit for brokerage generated is then applied to such services as custody and appraisal.

Commodity forward A contract in which the underlying asset is oil, a precious metal, or some other commodity.

Commodity futures Futures contracts in which the underlying is a traditional agricultural, metal, or petroleum product.

Commodity option An option in which the asset underlying the futures is a commodity, such as oil, gold, wheat, or soybeans.

Commodity swap A swap in which the underlying is a commodity such as oil, gold, or an agricultural product.

Common size statements Financial statements in which all elements (accounts) are stated as a percentage of a key figure such as revenue for an income statement or total assets for a balance sheet.

Common stock Equities, or equity securities, issued as ownership shares in a publicly held corporation. Shareholders have voting rights and may receive dividends based on their proportionate ownership.

Company fundamental factors Factors related to the company's internal performance, such as factors relating to earnings growth, earnings variability, earnings momentum, and financial leverage.

Company share-related factors Valuation measures and other factors related to share price or the trading characteristics of the shares, such as earnings yield, dividend yield, and book-to-market value.

Comparative advantage A person or country has a comparative advantage in an activity if that person or country can perform the activity at a lower opportunity cost than anyone else or any other country.

Competitive environment The level of intensity of competition among firms in an industry, determined by an examination of five competitive forces.

Competitive market A market that has many buyers and many sellers, so no single buyer or seller can influence the price.

Competitive strategy The search by a firm for a favorable competitive position within an industry within the known competitive environment.

Complement With reference to an event S, the event that S does not occur.

Complete portfolio The entire portfolio, including risky and risk-free assets.

Composite A universe of portfolios with similar investment objectives.

Composition Voluntary agreement to reduce payments on a firm's debt.

Compound interest Reinvestment of each interest payment on money invested to earn more interest (cf. *simple interest*).

Compounding The process of accumulating interest on interest.

Comprehensive income All changes in equity other than contributions by, and distributions to, owners; income under clean surplus accounting.

Concentration ratio The percentage of all sales contributed by the leading four or leading eight firms in an industry; sometimes called the *industry concentration ratio*.

Conditional expected value The expected value of a stated event given that another event has occurred.

Conditional heteroskedasticity Heteroskedasticity in the error variance that is correlated with the values of the independent variable(s) in the regression.

Conditional probability The probability of an event given (conditioned on) another event.

Conditional variances The variance of one variable, given the outcome of another.

Confidence interval A range that has a given probability that it will contain the population parameter it is intended to estimate.

Conglomerate A combination of unrelated firms.

Conglomerate merger A merger involving companies that are in unrelated businesses.

Consistency A desirable property of estimators; a consistent estimator is one for which the probability of estimates close to the value of the population parameter increases as sample size increases.

Consistent With reference to estimators, describes an estimator for which the probability of estimates close to the value of the population parameter increases as sample size increases.

Consolidation A merger in which both companies terminate their previous legal existence and become part of a newly formed company.

Constant growth model A form of the dividend discount model that assumes dividends will grow at a constant rate.

Constant maturity swap or CMT swap A swap in which the floating rate is the rate on a security known as a constant maturity treasury or CMT security.

Constant maturity treasury or CMT A hypothetical U.S. Treasury note with a constant maturity. A CMT exists for various years in the range of 2 to 10.

Consumer Price Index (CPI) An index that measures the average of the prices paid by urban consumers for a fixed "basket" of the consumer goods and services.

Consumption The use of goods and services for personal satisfaction. Can also be viewed as spending on new goods and services out of a household's current income. Whatever is not consumed is saved. Consumption includes such things as buying food and going to a concert.

Consumption expenditure The total payment for consumer goods and services.

Consumption goods Goods bought by households to use up, such as food and movies.

Contango A situation in a futures market where the current futures price is greater than the current spot price for the underlying asset.

Contestable market A market in which firms can enter and leave so easily that firms in the market face competition from potential entrants.

Contingent claims Derivatives in which the payoffs occur if a specific event occurs; generally referred to as options.

Continuing residual income Residual income after the forecast horizon.

Continuous compounding Interest compounded continuously rather than at fixed intervals.

Continuous random variable A random variable for which the range of possible outcomes is the real line (all real numbers between $-\infty$ and $+\infty$) or some subset of the real line.

Continuous time Time thought of as advancing in extremely small increments.

Continuously compounded return The natural logarithm of 1 plus the holding period return, or equivalently, the natural logarithm of the ending price over the beginning price.

Contract price The transaction price specified in a forward or futures contract.

Contraction A business fluctuation during which the pace of national economic activity is slowing down.

Contribution margin The amount available for fixed costs and profit after paying variable costs; revenue minus variable costs.

Control premium An increment or premium to value associated with a controlling ownership interest in a company.

Controller Officer responsible for budgeting, accounting, and auditing in a firm (cf. *treasurer*).

Convenience yield The nonmonetary return offered by an asset when the asset is in short supply, often associated with assets with seasonal production processes.

Conventional cash flow A conventional cash flow pattern is one with an initial outflow followed by a series of inflows.

Conversion factor An adjustment used to facilitate delivery on bond futures contracts in which any of a number of bonds with different characteristics are eligible for delivery.

Conversion parity price The price at which common stock can be obtained by surrendering the convertible instrument at par value.

Conversion premium The excess of the market value of the convertible security over its equity value if immediately converted into common stock. Typically expressed as a percentage of the equity value.

Conversion ratio The number of shares of common stock for which a convertible security may be exchanged.

Conversion value The value of the convertible security if converted into common stock at the stock's current market price.

Convertible A bond or preferred stock that offers the investor the right to convert his holding into common stock under set terms.

Convertible bond A bond with an option allowing the bondholder to exchange the bond for a specified number of shares of common stock in the firm. A *conversion ratio* specifies the number of shares. The *market conversion price* is the current value of the shares for which the bond may be exchanged. The *conversion premium* is the excess of the bond's value over the conversion price.

Convexity A measure of the degree to which a bond's price-yield curve departs from a straight line. This characteristic affects estimates of a bond's price volatility for a given change in yields.

Corporate bonds Long-term debt issued by private corporations typically paying semiannual coupons and returning the face value of the bond at maturity.

Corporate governance The system of principles, policies, procedures, and clearly defined responsibilities and accountabilities used by stakeholders to overcome the conflicts of interest inherent in the corporate form.

Corporate raider A person or organization seeking to profit by acquiring a company and reselling it, or seeking to profit from the takeover attempt itself (e.g. greenmail).

Corporate trustee A bank or trust company having federal or state authority to serve as a trustee.

Corporation A legal entity that may conduct business in its own name just as an individual does; the owners of a corporation, called shareholders, own shares of the firm's profits and enjoy the protection of limited liability.

Correlation analysis The analysis of the strength of the linear relationship between two data series.

Correlation or correlation coefficient A number between -1 and $+1$ that measures the co-movement (linear association) between two random variables.

Cost averaging The periodic investment of a fixed amount of money.

Cost leadership The competitive strategy of being the lowest cost producer while offering products comparable to those of other firms, so that products can be priced at or near the industry average.

Cost of capital Opportunity cost of capital.

Cost of carry The cost associated with holding some asset, including financing, storage, and insurance costs. Any yield received on the asset is treated as a negative carrying cost.

Cost of carry model A model for pricing futures contracts in which the futures price is determined by adding the cost of carry to the spot price.

Cost of equity The required rate of return on common stock.

Cost-of-service regulation Regulation based on allowing prices to reflect only the actual cost of production and no monopoly profits.

Cost structure The mix of a company's variable costs and fixed costs.

Counterparty Party on the other side of a *derivative* contract.

Coupon The interest rate on a bond, expressed as a percentage of its face (not market) value. At one time bonds (and indeed stocks) contained coupons resembling postage stamps, which one "clipped" or cut periodically and presented for payment of interest (or dividends).

Coupon rate   A bond's interest payments per dollar of par value.

Covariance   A measure of the co-movement (linear association) between two random variables.

Covariance matrix   A matrix or square array whose entries are covariances; also known as a variance-covariance matrix.

Covariance stationary   Describes a time series when its expected value and variance are constant and finite in all periods and when its covariance with itself for a fixed number of periods in the past or future is constant and finite in all periods.

Covenant   Clause in a loan agreement.

Covered call   An option strategy involving the holding of an asset and sale of a call on the asset.

Covered interest arbitrage   A transaction executed in the foreign exchange market in which a currency is purchased (sold) and a forward contract is sold (purchased) to lock in the exchange rate for future delivery of the currency. This transaction should earn the risk-free rate of the investor's home country.

Covered option   *Option* position with an offsetting position in the underlying asset.

Creative response   Behavior on the part of a firm that allows it to comply with the letter of the law but violates the spirit, significantly lessening the law's effects.

Credit analysis   An active bond portfolio management strategy designed to identify bonds that are expected to experience changes in rating. This strategy is critical when investing in high-yield bonds.

Credit derivatives   A contract in which one party has the right to claim a payment from another party in the event that a specific credit event occurs over the life of the contract.

Credit enhancement   Contract for *hedging* against loan default or changes in credit risk (see *default swap*).

Credit-linked notes   Fixed-income securities in which the holder of the security has the right to withhold payment of the full amount due at maturity if a credit event occurs.

Credit risk or default risk   The risk of loss due to nonpayment by a counterparty.

Credit scoring   A procedure for assigning scores to borrowers on the basis of the risk of default.

Credit spread option   An option on the yield spread on a bond.

Credit swap   A type of swap transaction used as a credit derivative in which one party makes periodic payments to the other and receives the promise of a payoff if a third party defaults.

Credit VAR, Default VAR, or Credit at Risk   A variation of VAR that reflects credit risk.

Creditor nation   A country that during its entire history has invested more in the rest of the world than other countries have invested in it.

Cross-product netting   Netting the market values of all contracts, not just derivatives, between parties.

Cross-rate   The exchange rate between two currencies, derived from their exchange rates with a third currency.

Cross-sectional data   Observations over individual units at a point in time, as opposed to time-series data.

Cum dividend   With dividend.

Cumulative distribution function   A function giving the probability that a random variable is less than or equal to a specified value.

Cumulative relative frequency   For data grouped into intervals, the fraction of total observations that are less than the value of the upper limit of a stated interval.

Currency   The bills and coins that we use today.

Currency appreciation   The rise in the value of one currency in terms of another currency.

Currency depreciation   The fall in the value of one currency in terms of another currency.

Currency exposure   The sensitivity of the asset return, measured in the investor's domestic currency, to a movement in the exchange rate.

Currency forward   A forward contract in which the underlying is a foreign currency.

Currency option   An option that allows the holder to buy (if a call) or sell (if a put) an underlying currency at a fixed exercise rate, expressed as an exchange rate.

Currency swap   A contract to exchange streams of fixed cash flows denominated in two different currencies.

Current account   A record of the payments for imports of goods and services, receipts from exports of goods and services, the interest income, and net transfers.

Current asset   Asset that will normally be turned into cash within a year.

Current credit risk   The risk associated with the possibility that a payment currently due will not be made.

Current income   A return objective in which the investor seeks to generate income rather than capital gains; generally a goal of an investor who wants to supplement earnings with income to meet living expenses.

Current liability   Liability that will normally be repaid within a year.

Current ratio   A ratio representing the ability of the firm to pay off its current liabilities by liquidating current assets (current assets/current liabilities).

Current yield   A bond's annual coupon payment divided by its price. Differs from yield to maturity.

Custodians   Agents who hold property in safekeeping for others, usually without inherent investment management responsibility.

Customer acquisition costs   Initial direct costs incurred in adding to a company's customer base, including direct-response advertising, commissions, and related administrative costs. When capitalized, prospective customer-related revenues must be expected to exceed amounts capitalized. Depending on the industry, such costs may have other names, including subscriber acquisition costs and policy acquisition costs.

Cyclical businesses or cyclical companies   Businesses with high sensitivity to business- or industry-cycle influences.

Cyclical industries   Industries with above-average sensitivity to the state of the economy.

Cyclical stock   A stock with a high beta; its gains typically exceed those of a rising market and its losses typically exceed those of a falling market.

Cyclicals   Some industries are perennially subject to the vagaries of the business cycle: mining, steel, construction, automobiles, chemicals, machine tools, and the like. It is impossible to get away from the cyclical effect in business, just as there is always alternation between good and bad weather, so a cyclical company will have an irregular earnings pattern, and usually an irregular stock price pattern too.

Daily settlement   See *marking to market*.

Data mining   The practice of determining a model by extensive searching through a dataset for statistically significant patterns.

Day trader   A trader holding a position open somewhat longer than a scalper but closing all positions at the end of the day.

DCF   Discounted cash flow.

DDM   Dividend discount model.

Dead-hand provision   A poison pill provision that allows for the redemption or cancellation of a poison pill provision only by a vote of continuing directors (generally directors who were on the target company's board prior to the takeover attempt).

Dealer   An agent that buys and sells securities as a principal (for its own account) rather than as a broker for clients. A dealer may function, at different times, as a broker or as a dealer. Sometimes called a *market maker*.

Debenture   Unsecured bond.

Debt ratings   An objective measure of the quality and safety of a company's debt based upon an analysis of the company's ability to pay the promised cash flows, as well as an analysis of any indentures.

Debtor nation   A country that during its entire history has borrowed more from the rest of the world than it has lent to it.

Decentralized risk management   A system that allows individual units within an organization to manage risk. Decentralization results in duplication of effort but has the advantage of having people closer to the risk be more directly involved in its management.

Deciles   Quantiles that divide a distribution into 10 equal parts.

Decision rule   With respect to hypothesis testing, the rule according to which the null hypothesis will be rejected or not rejected; involves the comparison of the test statistic to rejection point(s).

Decision tree   Method of representing alternative sequential decisions and the possible outcomes from these decisions.

Declaration date   The day that the corporation issues a statement declaring a specific dividend.

Deep in the money   Said of call options for which the market price of the underlying is far above the exercise price or of put options for which the market price of the underlying is far below the exercise price.

Deep out of the money   Said of call options for which the market price of the underlying is far below the exercise price or of put options for which the market price of the underlying is far above the exercise price.

Default risk   The risk that an issuer will be unable to make interest and principal payments on time.

Default risk premium   A differential in promised return relative to default-free debt that compensates investors for the possibility that the borrower will fail to make a promised payment at the contracted time and in the contracted amount.

Default swap   *Credit derivative* in which one party makes fixed payments while the payments by the other party depend on the occurrence of a loan default.

Defeasance   Practice whereby the borrower sets aside cash or *bonds* sufficient to service the borrower's debt. Both the borrower's debt and the offsetting cash or bonds are removed from the balance sheet.

Defensive industries Industries with little sensitivity to the state of the economy.

Deferred tax assets Future tax benefits that result from (1) the origination of a deductible temporary difference, that is, a tax deduction that can be used in a future period, or (2) a loss or tax-credit carryover. These future tax benefits are realized upon the reversal of deductible temporary differences. In addition, realization can occur by the offsetting of a loss carryforward against taxable income or a tax credit carryforward against taxes currently payable.

Deferred tax liabilities Future tax obligations that result from the origination of taxable temporary differences. Upon origination, these temporary difference cause pretax financial income to exceed taxable income. These future tax obligations are paid later when temporary differences reverse, now causing taxable income to exceed pretax book income.

Defined benefit pension plan or defined benefit plan A pension plan to which the company contributes a certain amount each year and promises to pay employees a specified income after they retire. The benefit size is based on factors such as workers' salary and time of employment.

Defined contribution pension plan or defined contribution plan A pension plan in which worker benefits are determined by the size of employees' contributions to the plan and the returns earned on the fund's investments.

Definitive merger agreement A contract signed by both parties to a merger that clarifies the details of the transaction, including the terms, warranties, conditions, termination details, and the rights of all parties.

Deflation The situation in which the average of all prices of goods and services in an economy is falling.

Degree of confidence The probability that a confidence interval includes the unknown population parameter.

Degree of financial leverage (DFL) The ratio of the percentage change in net income to the percentage change in operating income; the sensitivity of the cash flows available to owners when operating income changes.

Degree of operating leverage (DOL) The ratio of the percentage change in operating income to the percentage change in units sold; the sensitivity of operating income to changes in units sold.

Degree of total leverage The ratio of the percentage change in net income to the percentage change in units sold; the sensitivity of the cash flows to owners to changes in the number of units produced and sold.

Degrees of freedom (df) The number of independent observations used.

Delivery A process used in a deliverable forward contract in which the long pays the agreed-upon price to the short, which in turn delivers the underlying asset to the long.

Delivery option The feature of a futures contract giving the short the right to make decisions about what, when, and where to deliver.

Delta The relationship between the option price and the underlying price, which reflects the sensitivity of the price of the option to changes in the price of the underlying.

Delta hedge An option strategy in which a position in an asset is converted to a risk-free position with a position in a specific number of options. The number of options per unit of the underlying changes through time, and the position must be revised to maintain the hedge.

Delta-normal method A measure of VAR equivalent to the analytical method but that refers to the use of delta to estimate the option's price sensitivity.

Demand The relationship between the quantity of a good that consumers plan to buy and the price of the good when all other influences on buyers' plans remain the same. It is described by a demand schedule and illustrated by a demand curve.

Demand curve A curve that shows the relationship between the quantity demanded of a good and its price when all other influences on consumers' planned purchases remain the same.

Demand for labor The relationship between the quantity of labor demanded and the real wage rate when all other influences on a firm's hiring plans remain the same.

Dependent With reference to events, the property that the probability of one event occurring depends on (is related to) the occurrence of another event.

Dependent variable The variable whose variation about its mean is to be explained by the regression; the left-hand-side variable in a regression equation.

Depreciation Reduction in the value of capital goods over a one-year period due to physical wear and tear and also to obsolescence; also called *capital consumption allowance.* Can also be viewed as a decrease in the exchange value of one nation's currency in terms of the currency of another nation.

Depression An extremely severe recession.

Deregulation The elimination or phasing out of regulations on economic activity.

Derivative A financial instrument that offers a return based on the return of an underlying asset.

Derivatives dealers The commercial and investment banks that make markets in derivatives. Also referred to as market makers.

Descriptive statistics The study of how data can be summarized effectively.

Devaluation Deliberate downward adjustment of a currency against its fixed parity.

Differential expectations Expectations that differ from consensus expectations.

Differential swap or diff swap or diff A swap in which the payments are based on the difference between interest rates in two countries but payments are made in only a single currency.

Differentiation The competitive strategy of offering unique products or services along some dimensions that are widely valued by buyers so that the firm can command premium prices.

Diffuse prior The assumption of equal prior probabilities.

Diluted earnings per share Total earnings divided by the number of shares that would be outstanding if holders of securities such as executive stock options and convertible bonds exercised their options to obtain common stock.

Dilution Reduction in shareholders' equity per share or earnings per share that arises from some changes among shareholders' proportionate interests.

Diminishing marginal returns The tendency for the marginal product of an additional unit of a factor of production to be less than the marginal product of the previous unit of the factor.

Direct exchange rate The amount of local or domestic currency required to purchase one unit of foreign currency.

Direct income capitalization approach Division of net operating income by an overall capitalization rate to arrive at market value.

Direct Investments (Private Equity) An investment made directly in venture capital or private equity assets (i.e., not via a partnership or fund).

Direct quote For foreign exchange, the number of U.S. dollars needed to buy one unit of a foreign currency (cf. *indirect quote*).

Directed brokerage A manager is asked to direct business to a specified broker, usually to pay for services.

Dirty surplus items Items that affect comprehensive income but which bypass the income statement.

Discontinued operations Net income and the gain or loss on disposal of a discontinued business segment or separately measured business unit.

Discount To reduce the value of a future payment in allowance for how far away it is in time; to calculate the present value of some future amount. Also, the amount by which an instrument is priced below its face value.

Discount factor *Present value* of $1 received at a stated future date.

Discount interest A procedure for determining the interest on a loan or bond in which the interest is deducted from the face value in advance.

Discount rate (1) Rate used to calculate the present value of future cash flows. (2) The interest rate at which the U.S. Federal Reserve System stands ready to lend reserves to depository institutions.

Discounted cash flow (DCF) Future cash flows multiplied by discount factors to obtain present value.

Discounted cash flow analysis Analysis of value in terms of the present value of expected future cash flows.

Discounting The conversion of a future amount of money to its present value.

Discrete random variable A random variable that can take on at most a countable number of possible values.

Discrete time Time thought of as advancing in distinct finite increments.

Discretionary account An account of a customer who gives a broker the authority to make buy and sell decisions on the customer's behalf.

Discriminant analysis A multivariate classification technique used to discriminate between groups, such as companies that either will or will not become bankrupt during some time frame.

Dispersion The variability around the central tendency.

Diversifiable risk Risk attributable to firm-specific risk, or nonmarket risk. *Nondiversifiable* risk refers to systematic or market risk.

Diversification (1) Spreading a portfolio over many investments to avoid excessive exposure to any one source of risk. (2) In mergers and acquisitions, a term that refers to buying companies or assets outside the companies' current lines of business.

Divestiture The sale, liquidation, or spin-off of some major component of a business.

Dividend Payment by a company to its stockholders.

Dividend discount model (DDM) A present value model of stock value that views the intrinsic value of a stock as present value of the stock's expected future dividends.

Dividend displacement of earnings The concept that dividends paid now displace earnings in all future periods.

Dividend payout policy The strategy a company follows with regard to the amount and timing of dividend payments.

Dividend payout ratio Percentage of earnings paid out as dividends.

Dividend rate The most recent quarterly dividend multiplied by four.

Dividend reinvestment plan (DRIP) Plan that allows shareholders to reinvest dividends automatically.

Dividend yield Annual dividend divided by share price.

Dividends paid A term used on the cash flow analysis statement that refers to cash disbursements for dividends on common and preferred stock.

Double taxation With reference to certain tax jurisdictions, the practice of taxing corporate earnings twice. First, corporate earnings are taxed regardless of whether they will be distributed as dividends or retained at the corporate level, and second, dividends are taxed again at the individual shareholder level.

Dow Jones Industrial Average (DJI or DJIA) A price-weighted average of thirty industrial companies.

Down transition probability The probability that an asset's value moves down in a model of asset price dynamics.

Due diligence Investigation and analysis in support of a recommendation; the failure to exercise due diligence may sometimes result in liability according to various securities laws.

Dummy variable A type of qualitative variable that takes on a value of 1 if a particular condition is true and 0 if that condition is false.

Dumping The sale by a foreign firm of exports at a lower price that the cost of production.

Duration A measure of an option-free bond's average maturity. Specifically, the weighted average maturity of all future cash flows paid by a security, in which the weights are the present value of these cash flows as a fraction of the bond's price. A measure of a bond's price sensitivity to interest rate movements.

Dutch Book Theorem A result in probability theory stating that inconsistent probabilities create profit opportunities.

Dynamic hedging Hedging that involves making frequent adjustments to the quantity of the instrument used for hedging in relation to the instrument being hedged.

Early stage With reference to venture capital financing, the stage associated with moving into operation and before commercial manufacturing and sales have occurred. Includes the start-up and first stages.

Earnings at risk (EAR) A variation of VAR that reflects the risk of a company's earnings instead of its market value.

Earnings before interest and taxes (EBIT) Net income measured before interest expense and before income tax expense. EBIT has a long history of being used as a basis for measuring fixed-charge coverage.

Earnings before interest, taxes, depreciation, and amortization (EBITDA) An earnings-based measure that often serves as a surrogate for cash flow. The measure actually represents working capital provided by operations before interest and taxes.

Earnings management The practice of using flexibility in accounting rules to improve the apparent profitability of the firm.

Earnings momentum A strategy in which portfolios are constructed of stocks of firms with rising earnings.

Earnings retention ratio Plowback ratio.

Earnings surprise A company announcement of earnings that differs from analysts' prevailing expectations.

Earnings yield Earnings per share divided by price; the reciprocal of the P/E ratio.

EBIT Earnings before interest and taxes.

EBITDA Earnings before interest, taxes, depreciation, and amortization.

Economic depreciation The change in the market value of capital over a given period.

Economic efficiency A situation that occurs when the firm produces a given output at the least cost.

Economic exposure Risk that arises from changes in real exchange rates (cf. *transaction exposure, translation exposure*).

Economic growth (1) Increases in per capita real GDP measured by its rate of change per year. (2) The expansion of production possibilities that results from capital accumulation and technological change.

Economic growth rate The percentage change in the quantity of goods and services produced from one year to the next.

Economic income Cash flow plus change in *present value*.

Economic model A description of some aspect of the economic world that includes only those features of the world that are needed for the purpose at hand.

Economic profit Total revenue minus total opportunity costs of all inputs used, or the total of all implicit and explicit costs; a firm's after-tax net operating profit minus its opportunity cost of capital.

Economic rent A payment for the use of any resource over and above its opportunity cost.

Economic risk As used in currency risk management, the risk that arises when the foreign currency value of a foreign investment reacts systematically to an exchange rate movement.

Economic sectors Large industry groupings.

Economic theory A generalization that summarizes what we think we understand about the economic choices that people make and the performance of industries and entire economies.

Economic value added (EVA®) The spread between ROA and cost of capital multiplied by the capital invested in the firm. It measures the dollar value of the firm's return in excess of its opportunity cost.

Economic welfare A comprehensive measure of the general state of economic well-being.

Economics The social science that studies the choices that individuals, businesses, governments, and entire societies make and how they cope with scarcity and the incentives that influence and reconcile those choices.

Economies of scale The reduction of a company's average costs due to increasing output and spreading out fixed costs over higher output levels; the savings achieved through the consolidation of operations and elimination of duplicate resources.

Economies of scope The ability of a firm to utilize one set of inputs to provide a broader range of outputs or services.

Effective annual rate The amount by which a unit of currency will grow in a year with interest on interest included.

Effective annual yield (EAY) An annualized return that accounts for the effect of interest on interest; EAY is computed by compounding 1 plus the holding period yield forward to one year, then subtracting 1.

Effective tax rate The income tax provision divided by income before the income tax provision.

Efficiency In statistics, a desirable property of estimators; an efficient estimator is the unbiased estimator with the smallest variance among unbiased estimators of the same parameter.

Efficient capital market A market in which security prices rapidly reflect all information about securities.

Efficient diversification The organizing principle of modern portfolio theory, which maintains that any risk-averse investor will search for the highest expected return for any level of portfolio risk.

Efficient frontier The portion of the minimum-variance frontier beginning with the global minimum-variance portfolio and continuing above it; the graph of the set of portfolios offering the maximum expected return for their level of variance of return.

Efficient market A market in which any relevant information is immediately impounded in asset prices.

Efficient portfolio A portfolio offering the highest expected return for a given level of risk as measured by variance or standard deviation of return.

Elasticity A measure of sensitivity; the incremental change in one variable with respect to an incremental change in another variable.

Electronic crossing networks Order-driven trading systems in which market orders are anonymously matched at prespecified times at prices determined in the primary market for the system.

Emerging Issues Task Force (EITF) The EITF assists the Financial Accounting Standards Board through the timely identification, discussion, and resolution of financial accounting issues based on existing authoritative literature.

Emerging markets Often, countries so defined by the International Finance Corporation (IFC), based on their per capita income.

Empirical Relying on real-world data in evaluating the usefulness of a model.

Empirical duration Measures directly the interest rate sensitivity of an asset by examining the percentage price change for an asset in response to a change in yield during a specified period of time.

Employee Retirement Income Security Act (ERISA) Governs most private pension and benefit plans.

Endogenous growth theory A theory of economic growth that does not assume that the marginal productivity of capital declines as capital is added.

Endowment funds Organizations chartered to invest money for specific purposes.

Endowments The various resources in an economy, including both physical resources and such human resources as ingenuity and management skills.

Enhanced derivatives products companies (EDPC) or special purpose vehicles (SPVs) A type of subsidiary engaged in derivatives transactions that is separated from the parent company in order to have a higher credit rating than the parent company.

Enterprise risk management A form of *centralized risk management* that typically encompasses the management of a broad variety of risks, including insurance risk.

Enterprise value (EV) Total company value (the market value of debt, common equity, and preferred equity) minus the value of cash and investments.

EPS Earnings per share.

Equilibrium The condition in which supply equals demand.

Equilibrium price The price at which the quantity demanded equals the quantity supplied.

Equities Another name for shares. The capitalization of a company consists of "equity"—or ownership—represented by common or preferred shares (stock), and debt, represented by bonds, notes, and the like. (In England, "corporation stock" means municipal bonds, incidentally.)

Equitizing cash A strategy used to replicate an index. It is also used to take a given amount of cash and turn it into an equity position while maintaining the liquidity provided by the cash.

Equity (1) *Common stock* and *preferred stock*. Often used to refer to common stock only. (2) *Net worth*.

Equity carve-out A form of restructuring that involves the creation of a new legal entity and the sale of equity in it to outsiders.

Equity charge The estimated cost of equity capital in money terms.

Equity dividend rate Income rate that reflects the relationship between equity income and equity capital.

Equity forward A contract calling for the purchase of an individual stock, a stock portfolio, or a stock index at a later date at an agreed-upon price.

Equity options Options on individual stocks; also known as stock options.

Equity risk premium The expected return on equities minus the risk-free rate.

Equity security An ownership interest in an enterprise, including preferred and common stock.

Equity swap A swap transaction in which at least one cash flow is tied to the return to an equity portfolio position, often an index.

Error autocorrelation The autocorrelation of the error term.

Error term The portion of the dependent variable that is not explained by the independent variable(s) in the regression.

Estimate The particular value calculated from sample observations using an estimator.

Estimated (or fitted) parameters With reference to regression analysis, the estimated values of the population intercept and population slope coefficient(s) in a regression.

Estimated rate of return The rate of return an investor anticipates earning from a specific investment over a particular future holding period.

Estimation With reference to statistical inference, the subdivision dealing with estimating the value of a population parameter.

Estimator An estimation formula; the formula used to compute the sample mean and other sample statistics are examples of estimators.

Euribor Interbank offer rate for short-term deposits in euros. Euribor is determined by an association of European banks.

Eurobond A bond underwritten by a multinational syndicate of banks and placed mainly in countries other than the country of the issuer; sometimes called an *international bond*.

Eurodollar A dollar deposited outside the United States.

Eurodollar deposit Dollar deposit with a bank outside the United States.

Eurodollar market The U.S. dollar segment of the Eurocurrency market.

European option An option that can be exercised only at expiration.

European terms With reference to U.S. dollar exchange rate quotations, the price of a U.S. dollar in terms of another currency.

European Union (EU) A formal association of European countries founded by the Treaty of Rome in 1957. Formerly known as the EEC.

EVA Economic value added.

Event Any outcome or specified set of outcomes of a random variable.

Excess kurtosis Degree of peakedness (fatness of tails) in excess of the peakedness of the normal distribution.

Excess return Rate of return in excess of the risk-free rate.

Exchange for physicals (EFP) A permissible delivery procedure used by futures market participants, in which the long and short arrange a delivery procedure other than the normal procedures stipulated by the futures exchange.

Exchange of assets Acquisition of another company by purchase of its assets in exchange for cash or shares.

Exchange rate Price of a unit of one country's currency in terms of another country's currency.

Exchange rate risk Uncertainty due to the denomination of an investment in a currency other than that of the investor's own country.

Exchange ratio The number of shares that target stockholders are to receive in exchange for each of their shares in the target company.

Exchanges National or regional auction markets providing a facility for members to trade securities. A seat is a membership on an exchange.

Exchange-traded funds (ETFs) A type of mutual fund traded like other shares on a stock market, having special characteristics particularly related to redemption, and generally designed to closely track the performance of a specified stock market index.

Ex-dividend date The first date that a share trades without (i.e. "ex") the right to a declared dividend.

Executor The legal representative of a person who dies with a will.

Exercise or exercising the option The process of using an option to buy or sell the underlying.

Exercise price (striking price) Price at which a call option or put option may be exercised.

Exercise rate or strike rate The fixed rate at which the holder of an interest rate option can buy or sell the underlying.

Exhaustive Covering or containing all possible outcomes.

Expansion A business cycle phase between a trough and a peak—phase in which real GDP increases.

Expectational arbitrage Investing on the basis of differential expectations.

Expectations theory Theory that forward interest rate (forward exchange rate) equals expected spot rate.

Expected holding-period return The expected total return on an asset over a stated holding period; for stocks, the sum of the expected dividend yield and the expected price appreciation over the holding period.

Expected return or expected rate of return Average of possible returns weighted by their probabilities.

Expected return–beta relationship Implication of the CAPM that security risk premiums (expected excess returns) will be proportional to beta.

Expected utility The average utility arising from all possible outcomes.

Expected value The probability-weighted average of the possible outcomes of a random variable.

Expiration date The date on which a derivative contract expires.

Exports The goods and services that we sell to people in other countries.

Ex-Post After the fact.

External financing A term used on the cash flow analysis statement that consists of net debt and equity capital raised from external sources.

External growth Company growth in output or sales that is achieved by buying the necessary resources externally (i.e., achieved through mergers and acquisitions).

Externality A consequence of an economic activity that spills over to affect third parties; a situation in which the costs (or benefits) of an action are not fully borne (or gained) by the two parties engaged in exchange or by an individual engaging in a scarce-resource-using activity.

Extra dividend *Dividend* that may or may not be repeated (cf. *regular dividend*).

Extraordinary item Gain or loss that is unusual and infrequent in occurrence.

Face value The promised payment at maturity separate from any coupon payment. Sometimes referred to as *par value.*

Factor A common or underlying element with which several variables are correlated.

Factor beta Sensitivity of security returns to changes in a systematic factor. Alternatively, factor loading; factor sensitivity.

Factor loading See *factor beta.*

Factor model A way of decomposing the factors that influence a security's rate of return into common and firm-specific influences.

Factor portfolio A well-diversified portfolio constructed to have a beta of 1.0 on one factor and a beta of zero on any other factor.

Factor risk premium (or factor price) The expected return in excess of the risk-free rate for a portfolio with a sensitivity of 1 to one factor and a sensitivity of 0 to all other factors.

Factor sensitivity (also factor betas or factor loadings) An asset's sensitivity to a particular factor (holding all other factors constant).

Factors of production The productive resources that businesses use to produce goods and services.

Fair value (1) The amount at which an asset could be acquired or sold in a current transaction between willing parties in which the parties each acted knowledgeably, prudently, and without compulsion. (2) The theoretical value of a security based on current market conditions. The fair value is the value such that no arbitrage opportunities exist.

FASB Financial Accounting Standards Board.

Federal Deposit Insurance Corporation (FDIC) A government agency that insures the deposits held in banks and most other depository institutions; all U.S. banks are insured this way.

Federal funds Non-interest-bearing deposits by banks at the Federal Reserve. Excess reserves are lent by banks to each other.

Federal funds rate The interest rate that depository institutions pay to borrow reserves in the interbank federal funds market.

Fictitious revenue Revenue recognized on a nonexistent sale or service transaction.

Fiduciary A person who supervises or oversees the investment portfolio of a third party, such as in a trust account, and makes investment decisions in accordance with the owner's wishes.

Fiduciary call A combination of a European call and a risk-free bond that matures on the option expiration day and has a face value equal to the exercise price of the call.

Fiduciary relationship An arrangement under which a person (the fiduciary) has a duty to act for another's benefit (the beneficiary).

FIFO The first-in first-out accounting method of inventory valuation.

Financial account A component of the balance of payments covering investments by residents abroad and investments by nonresidents in the home country. Examples include direct investment made by companies, portfolio investments in equity and bonds, and other investments and liabilities.

Financial Accounting Standards Board (FASB) The principal standard-setting body in the United States. Its primary standards are Statements of Financial Accounting Standards (SFASs).

Financial assets Financial assets such as stocks and bonds are claims to the income generated by real assets or claims on income from the government.

Financial capital Funds used to purchase physical capital goods such as buildings and equipment.

Financial distress Heightened uncertainty regarding a company's ability to meet its various obligations because of lower or negative earnings.

Financial engineering Combining or dividing existing instruments to create new financial products.

Financial futures Futures contracts in which the underlying is a stock, bond, or currency.

Financial innovation The development of new financial products—new ways of borrowing and lending.

Financial intermediaries Institutions that transfer funds between ultimate lenders (savers) and ultimate borrowers.

Financial lease (capital lease, full-payout lease) Long-term, noncancelable lease (cf. *operating lease*).

Financial risk The variability of future income arising from the firm's fixed financing costs, for example, interest payments. The effect of fixed financial costs is to magnify the effect of changes in operating profit on net income or earnings per share.

Firm (1) An economic unit that hires factors of production and organizes those factors to produce and sell goods and services. (2) For purposes of the GIPS standards, the term "firm" refers to the entity defined for compliance with the GIPS standards.

Firm-specific risk See *diversifiable risk.*

First-differencing A transformation that subtracts the value of the time series in period $t - 1$ from its value in period t.

First-order serial correlation Correlation between adjacent observations in a time series.

Fiscal policy The government's attempt to achieve macroeconomic objectives such as full employment, sustained economic growth, and price level stability by setting and changing taxes, making transfer payments, and purchasing goods and services.

Fixed costs Costs that remain at the same level regardless of a company's level of production and sales.

Fixed investment Purchases by businesses of newly produced producer durables, or capital goods, such as production machinery and office equipment.

Fixed-income forward A forward contract in which the underlying is a bond.

Fixed-income security A security such as a bond that pays a specified cash flow over a specific period.

Fixed-rate perpetual preferred stock Stock with a specified dividend rate that has a claim on earnings senior to the claim of common stock, and no maturity date.

Fixing A method for determining the market price of a security by finding the price that balances buyers and sellers. A fixing takes place periodically each day at defined times. Sometimes called a *call auction.*

Flexible exchange rates Exchange rates that are allowed to fluctuate in the open market in response to changes in supply and demand. Sometimes called *floating exchange rates.*

Flexible exchange rate system A system in which exchange rates are determined by supply and demand.

Flip-in pill A poison pill takeover defense that dilutes an acquirer's ownership in a target by giving other existing target company shareholders the right to buy additional target company shares at a discount.

Flip-over pill A poison pill takeover defense that gives target company shareholders the right to purchase shares of the acquirer at a significant discount to the market price, which has the effect of causing dilution to all existing acquiring company shareholders.

Floating-rate bond A bond whose interest rate is reset periodically according to a specified market rate.

Floating-rate loan A loan in which the interest rate is reset at least once after the starting date.

Floating-rate note (FRN) Short- to intermediate-term bonds with regularly scheduled coupon payments linked to a variable interest rate, most often LIBOR.

Floor A combination of interest rate put options designed to hedge a lender against lower rates on a floating-rate loan.

Floor agreement A contract that on each settlement date pays the holder the greater of the difference between the floor rate and the reference rate or zero; it is equivalent to a series of put options on the reference rate.

Floor traders or locals Market makers that buy and sell by quoting a bid and an ask price. They are the primary providers of liquidity to the market.

Floored swap A swap in which the floating payments have a lower limit.

Floorlet Each component put option in a floor.

Flotation cost Fees charged to companies by investment bankers and other costs associated with raising new capital.

Flow A quantity measured per unit of time; something that occurs over time, such as the income you make per week or per year or the number of individuals who are fired every month.

Focus The competitive strategy of seeking a competitive advantage within a target segment or segments of the industry, either on the basis of cost leadership (cost focus) or differentiation (differentiation focus).

Foreign bond A bond issued on the domestic capital market of another country.

Foreign currency risk premium The expected movement in the (direct) exchange rate minus the interest rate differential (domestic risk-free rate minus foreign risk-free rate).

Foreign direct investment The acquisition of more than 10 percent of the shares of ownership in a company in another nation.

Foreign exchange The purchase (sale) of a currency against the sale (purchase) of another.

Foreign exchange expectation A relation that states that the forward exchange rate, quoted at time 0 for delivery at time 1, is equal to the expected value of the spot exchange rate at time 1. When stated relative to the current spot exchange rate, the relation states that the forward discount (premium) is equal to the expected exchange rate movement.

Foreign exchange market The market in which the currency of one country is exchanged for the currency of another.

Foreign exchange rate The price at which one currency exchanges for another.

Forex Foreign exchange.

Forward contract An agreement between two parties in which one party, the buyer, agrees to buy from the other party, the seller, an underlying asset at a later date for a price established at the start of the contract.

Forward discount or premium Refers to the percentage difference between the forward exchange rate and the spot exchange rate (premium if positive, discount if negative).

Forward exchange rate Exchange rate fixed today for exchanging currency at some future date (cf. *spot exchange rate*).

Forward integration A merger involving the purchase of a target that is farther along the value or production chain; for example, to acquire a distributor.

Forward interest rate (1) Interest rate fixed today on a loan to be made at some future date (cf. *spot interest rate*). (2) Rate of interest for a future period that would equate the total return of a long-term bond with that of a strategy of rolling over shorter-term bonds. The forward rate is inferred from the term structure.

Forward premium A situation where, from the perspective of the domestic country, the spot exchange rate is larger than the forward exchange rate with a foreign country.

Forward price or forward rate The fixed price or rate at which the transaction scheduled to occur at the expiration of a forward contract will take place. This price is agreed on at the initiation date of the contract. With respect to the yield curve, a short-term yield for a future holding period implied by the spot rates of two securities with different maturities.

Forward rate agreement (FRA) A forward contract calling for one party to make a fixed interest payment and the other to make an interest payment at a rate to be determined at the contract expiration.

Forward swap A forward contract to enter into a swap.

Franchise factor A firm's unique competitive advantage that makes it possible for a firm to earn excess returns (rates of return above a firm's cost of capital) on its capital projects. In turn, these excess returns and the franchise factor cause the firm's stock price to have a P/E ratio above its base P/E ratio that is equal to $1/k$.

Franchise value In P/E ratio analysis, the present value of growth opportunities divided by next year's expected earnings.

Free cash flow The actual cash that would be available to the company's investors after making all investments necessary to maintain the company as an ongoing enterprise (also referred to as free cash flow to the firm); the internally generated funds that can be distributed to the company's investors (e.g., shareholders and bondholders) without impairing the value of the company.

Free cash flow hypothesis The hypothesis that higher debt levels discipline managers by forcing them to make fixed debt service payments and by reducing the company's free cash flow.

Free cash flow to equity The cash flow available to a company's common shareholders after all operating expenses, interest, and principal payments have been made, and necessary investments in working and fixed capital have been made.

Free cash flow to equity model A model of stock valuation that views a stock's intrinsic value as the present value of expected future free cash flows to equity.

Free cash flow to the firm The cash flow available to the company's suppliers of capital after all operating expenses (including taxes) have been paid and necessary investments in working and fixed capital have been made.

Free cash flow to the firm model A model of stock valuation that views the value of a firm as the present value of expected future free cash flows to the firm.

Frequency distribution A tabular display of data summarized into a relatively small number of intervals.

Frequency polygon A graph of a frequency distribution obtained by drawing straight lines joining successive points representing the class frequencies.

Friendly transaction A potential business combination that is endorsed by the managers of both companies.

Full price (or dirty price) The total price of a bond, including accrued interest.

Fundamental beta A beta that is based at least in part on fundamental data for a company.

Fundamental factor models A multifactor model in which the factors are attributes of stocks or companies that are important in explaining cross-sectional differences in stock prices.

Fundamentals Economic characteristics of a business such as profitability, financial strength, and risk.

Funded debt Debt maturing after more than one year (cf. *unfunded debt*).

Funds Traditionally defined as working capital, that is, the excess of current assets over current liabilities.

Funds from operations (FFO) A term used by real estate investment trusts (REITs) and defined as net income or loss excluding gains or losses from debt restructuring and sales of property, plus depreciation and amortization of real estate assets.

Future value (FV) The amount to which a payment or series of payments will grow by a stated future date.

Futures commission merchants (FCMs) Individuals or companies that execute futures transactions for other parties off the exchange.

Futures contract A standardized contract to buy (sell) an asset at a specified date and a specified price (futures price). The contract is traded on an organized exchange, and the potential gain/loss is realized each day (marking to market).

Futures exchange An exchange on which futures contracts are traded.

Futures option The right to enter a specified futures contract at a futures price equal to the stipulated exercise price.

Futures price The price at which a futures trader commits to make or take delivery of the underlying asset.

GAAP See generally accepted accounting principles.

Game theory A tool that economists use to analyze strategic behavior—behavior that takes into account the expected behavior of others and the mutual recognition of independence.

Gamma A numerical measure of how sensitive an option's delta is to a change in the underlying.

GDP deflator One measure of the price level, which is the average of current-year prices as a percentage of base-year prices.

Gearing Financial leverage.

General Agreement on Tariffs and Trade An international agreement signed in 1947 to reduce tariffs on international trade.

General Partner (Private Equity) (GP) A class of partner in a partnership. The GP retains liability for the actions of the partnership. In the PRIVATE EQUITY world, the GP is the fund manager and the LIMITED PARTNERS (LPs) are the institutional and high-net-worth investors in the partnership. The GP earns a management fee and a percentage of profits.

Generalized least squares A regression estimation technique that addresses heteroskedasticity of the error term.

Generally accepted accounting principles (GAAP) A common set of standards and procedures for the preparation of general-purpose financial statements that either have been established by an authoritative accounting rule-making body, such as the Financial Accounting Standards Board (FASB), or have over time become common accepted practice.

Generic See *plain-vanilla*.

Geometric mean A measure of central tendency computed by taking the *n*th root of the product of *n* non-negative values.

Global Of a fund or portfolio, invested both in the United States and abroad.

Global Investment Performance Standards™ (GIPS®) A global industry standard for the ethical presentation of investment performance results promulgated by CFA Institute.

Globalization Tendency toward a worldwide investment environment, and the integration of national capital markets.

Going-concern assumption The assumption that the business will maintain its business activities into the foreseeable future.

Going-concern value A business's value under a going-concern assumption.

Gold standard An international monetary system in which the parity of a currency is fixed in terms of its gold content.

Golden parachute Employment contract of upper management that provides a larger payout upon the occurrence of certain control transactions, such as a certain percentage share purchase by an outside entity or when there is a tender offer for a certain percentage of the company's shares.

Goods All things from which individuals derive satisfaction or happiness.

Goods and services The objects that people value and produce to satisfy their wants.

Goodwill An intangible asset that represents the excess of the purchase price of an acquisition over the value of the net assets acquired.

Governance The oversight of a firm's management.

Government debt The total amount of borrowing that the government has borrowed. It equals the sum of past budget deficits minus budget surpluses.

Government sector surplus or deficit An amount equal to net taxes minus government purchases of goods and services.

Great Depression A decade (1929-1939) of high unemployment and stagnant production throughout the world economy.

Greenmail The purchase of the accumulated shares of a hostile investor by a company that is targeted for takeover by that investor, usually at a substantial premium over market price.

Gross domestic product A money measure of the goods and services produced within a country's borders over a stated time period.

Gross investment The total amount spent on purchases of new capital and on replacing depreciated capital.

Gross margin Revenue minus cost of goods sold. Also referred to as *gross profit*.

Gross national product (GNP) Total value of a country's output produced by residents both within the country's physical borders and abroad.

Growth accounting A method of calculating how much real GDP growth results from growth of labor and capital and how much is attributable to technological change.

Growth company A company that consistently has the opportunities and ability to invest in projects that provide rates of return that exceed the firm's cost of capital. Because of these investment opportunities, it retains a high proportion of earnings, and its earnings grow faster than those of average firms.

Growth investing Emphasizes the future over apparent immediate undervaluation. Thus, usually implies buying companies with higher than average price-earnings ratios and lower dividend yields.

Growth option or expansion option The ability to make additional investments in a project at some future time if the financial results are strong.

Growth phase A stage of growth in which a company typically enjoys rapidly expanding markets, high profit margins, and an abnormally high growth rate in earnings per share.

Growth stock A stock issue that generates a higher rate of return than other stocks in the market with similar risk characteristics.

Harmonic mean A type of weighted mean computed by averaging the reciprocals of the observations, then taking the reciprocal of that average.

Hedge fund An investment vehicle designed to manage a private, unregistered portfolio of assets according to any of several strategies. The investment strategy often employs arbitrage trading and significant financial leverage (e.g., short selling, borrowing, derivatives) while the compensation arrangement for the manager typically specifies considerable profit participation.

Hedge ratio The relationship of the quantity of an asset being hedged to the quantity of the derivative used for hedging.

Hedging A general strategy usually thought of as reducing, if not eliminating, risk.

Herfindahl Index or Herfindahl–Hirschman Index A measure of market concentration that is calculated by summing the squared market shares for competing companies in an industry; high HHI readings or mergers that would result in large HHI increases are more likely to result in regulatory challenges.

Heteroskedastic With reference to the error term of a regression, having a variance that differs across observations.

Heteroskedasticity The property of having a nonconstant variance; refers to an error term with the property that its variance differs across observations.

Heteroskedasticity-consistent standard errors Standard errors of the estimated parameters of a regression that correct for the presence of heteroskedasticity in the regression's error term.

High-yield bond A bond rated below investment grade. Also referred to as *speculative-grade bonds* or *junk bonds.*

Histogram A bar chart of data that have been grouped into a frequency distribution.

Historical method A method of estimating VAR that uses data from the returns of the portfolio over a recent past period and compiles this data in the form of a histogram.

Historical simulation (or back simulation) method Another term for the historical method of estimating VAR. This method involves not a simulation of the past but rather what actually happened in the past, sometimes adjusted to reflect the fact that a different portfolio may have existed in the past than is planned for the future.

Holder-of-record date The date that a shareholder listed on the corporation's books will be deemed to have ownership of the shares for purposes of receiving an upcoming dividend; two business days after the ex-dividend date.

Holding company A company that owns the stock of other corporations. A holding company may not engage in actual operations of its own but merely manages various operating units that it owns an interest in.

Holding period return The return that an investor earns during a specified holding period; a synonym for total return.

Homogenization Creating a contract with standard and generally accepted terms, which makes it more acceptable to a broader group of participants.

Homoskedasticity The property of having a constant variance; refers to an error term that is constant across observations.

Horizontal merger A merger involving companies in the same line of business, usually as competitors.

Hostile transaction An attempt to acquire a company against the wishes of the target's managers.

Hot issue A newly issued stock that is in strong demand; often it will go to a premium over its original issue price.

Human capital The value of skills and knowledge possessed by the workforce.

Hurdle rate The rate of return that must be offered for a project to be accepted.

Hypothesis With reference to statistical inference, a statement about one or more populations.

Hypothesis testing With reference to statistical inference, the subdivision dealing with the testing of hypotheses about one or more populations.

Impairment As used in accounting, a downward adjustment.

Impairment of capital rule A legal restriction that dividends cannot exceed retained earnings.

Implicit costs Expenses that managers do not have to pay out of pocket and hence do not normally explicitly calculate, such as the opportunity cost of factors of production that are owned; examples are owner-provided capital and owner-provided labor.

Implied repo rate The rate of return from a cash-and-carry transaction implied by the futures price relative to the spot price.

Implied volatility The volatility of an asset that is implicit in the current market price of an option on that asset and a particular option-pricing model (e.g., the Black-Scholes-Merton formula).

Imports The goods and services that we buy from people in other countries.

Imputation In reference to corporate taxes, a system that imputes, or attributes, taxes at only one level of taxation. For countries using an imputation tax system, taxes on dividends are effectively levied only at the shareholder rate. Taxes are paid at the corporate level but they are attributed to the shareholder. Shareholders deduct from their tax bill their portion of taxes paid by the company.

Imputation tax system Arrangement by which investors who receive a *dividend* also receive a tax credit for corporate taxes that the firm has paid.

In the money An option that has positive intrinsic value.

Incentive A reward that encourages or a penalty that discourages an action.

Incentive system A method of organizing production that uses a market-like mechanism inside the firm.

Income approach Measuring national income by adding up all components of national income, including wages, interest, rent, and profits.

Income beneficiary A person entitled to all or a share of the income of a trust.

Income effect The effect of a change in income on consumption, other things remaining the same.

Income from continuing operations After-tax net income before discontinued operations, extraordinary items, and the cumulative effect of changes in accounting principle.

Income fund A mutual fund providing for liberal current income from investments.

Income statement A financial statement showing a firm's revenues and expenses during a specified period.

Income stock *Common stock* with high *dividend yield* and few profitable investment opportunities (cf. *growth stock*).

Incremental cash flow The changes or increments to cash flow resulting from a decision or action; the cash flow with a decision minus the cash flow without that decision.

Indenture The legal agreement that lists the obligations of the issuer of a bond to the bondholder, including payment schedules, call provisions, and sinking funds.

Independent With reference to events, the property that the occurrence of one event does not affect the probability of another event occurring.

Independent and identically distributed (IID) With respect to random variables, the property of random variables that are independent of each other but follow the identical probability distribution.

Independent projects Independent projects are projects whose cash flows are independent of each other.

Independent variable A variable used to explain the dependent variable in a regression; a right-hand-side variable in a regression equation.

Index amortizing swap An interest rate swap in which the notional principal is indexed to the level of interest rates and declines with the level of interest rates according to a predefined scheduled. This type of swap is frequently used to hedge securities that are prepaid as interest rates decline, such as mortgage-backed securities.

Index fund A portfolio designed to replicate the performance of an index.

Index model A model of stock returns using a market index such as the SP 500 to represent common or systematic risk factors.

Index option An option in which the underlying is a stock index.

Indexing An investment strategy in which an investor constructs a portfolio to mirror the performance of a specified index.

Indirect exchange rate The amount of foreign currency required to purchase one unit of domestic currency.

Indirect quote For foreign exchange, the number of units of a foreign currency needed to buy one U.S. dollar (cf. *direct quote*).

Industry life cycle Stages through which firms typically pass as they mature.

Industry structure An industry's underlying economic and technical characteristics.

Infant-industry argument The argument that it is necessary to protect a new industry to enable it to grow into a mature industry that can compete in world markets.

Inflation The rate at which the general level of prices for goods and services is rising.

Inflation-adjusted return A rate of return that is measured in terms of real goods and services; that is, after the effects of inflation have been factored out.

Inflation premium An extra return that compensates investors for expected inflation.

Inflation rate The percentage change in the price level from one year to the next.

Information An attribute of a good market that includes providing buyers and sellers with timely, accurate information on the volume and prices of past transactions and on all currently outstanding bids and offers.

Information ratio (IR) Mean active return divided by active risk.

Initial margin The amount that an investor must deposit to open a position in futures and some other derivatives; also used to refer to the initial equity required when a stock is purchased using borrowed money.

Initial margin requirement The margin requirement on the first day of a transaction as well as on any day in which additional margin funds must be deposited.

Initial public offering (IPO) The initial issuance of common stock registered for public trading by a formerly private corporation.

Innovation Transforming an invention into something that is useful to humans.

Input list List of parameters such as expected returns, variances, and covariances necessary to determine the optimal risky portfolio.

In-sample forecast errors The residuals from a fitted time-series model within the sample period used to fit the model.

Inside information Nonpublic knowledge about a corporation possessed by corporate officers, major owners, or other individuals with privileged access to information about a firm.

Insider trading Trading by officers, directors, major stockholders, or others who hold private inside information allowing them to benefit from buying or selling stock.

Instability in the minimum-variance frontier The characteristic of minimum-variance frontiers that they are sensitive to small changes in inputs.

Institution A retirement fund, bank, investment company, investment advisor, insurance company, or other large pool of investment buying power.

Intangible asset Nonmaterial asset, such as technical expertise, a trademark, or a patent (cf. *tangible asset*).

Interest The payment for current rather than future command over resources; the cost of obtaining credit. Also, the return paid to owners of capital.

Interest rate A rate of return that reflects the relationship between differently dated cash flows; a discount rate.

Interest rate call An option in which the holder has the right to make a known interest payment and receive an unknown interest payment.

Interest rate cap, or cap A series of call options on an interest rate, with each option expiring at the date on which the floating loan rate will be reset, and with each option having the same exercise rate. A cap in general can have an underlying other than an interest rate.

Interest rate collar A combination of a long cap and a short floor, or a short cap and a long floor.

Interest rate floor, or floor A series of put options on an interest rate, with each option expiring at the date on which the floating loan rate will be reset, and with each option having the same exercise rate. A floor in general can have an underlying other than the interest rate.

Interest rate forward (See *forward rate agreement*).

Interest rate option An option in which the underlying is an interest rate.

Interest rate parity A formula that expresses the equivalence or parity of spot and forward rates, after adjusting for differences in the interest rates.

Interest rate put An option in which the holder has the right to make an unknown interest payment and receive a known interest payment.

Interest rate risk The uncertainty of returns on an investment due to possible changes in interest rates over time.

Interest rate swap An agreement calling for the periodic exchange of cash flows, one based on an interest rate that remains fixed for the life of the contract and the other that is linked to a variable-rate index.

Intergenerational data mining A form of data mining that applies information developed by previous researchers using a dataset to guide current research using the same or a related dataset.

Intermediate Of bonds, usually five to seven years' maturity.

Intermediate goods Goods used up entirely in the production of final goods.

Internal rate of return (IRR) The discount rate that makes net present value equal 0; the discount rate that makes the present value of an investment's costs (outflows) equal to the present value of the investment's benefits (inflows).

International Accounting Standard (IAS) An accounting standard issued by the International Accounting Standards Committee. This committee has been replaced by the International Accounting Standards Board (IASB). IAS standards have been adopted by the IASB.

International Accounting Standards Board (IASB) An international standard setting body. Its principal standard-setting products are International Financial Reporting Standards (IFRSs). The IASB assumed its duties from the International Accounting Standards Committee (IASC). Existing International Accounting Standards issued by the IASC were adopted by the IASB.

International CAPM An equilibrium theory that relates the expected return of an asset to its world market and foreign exchange risks.

International Financial Reporting Standard (IFRS) A financial reporting standard issued by the International Accounting Standards Board.

International Fisher relation The assertion that the interest rate differential between two countries should equal the expected inflation rate differential over the term of the interest rates.

International monetary market (IMM) The financial futures market within the Chicago Mercantile Exchange.

International Swaps and Derivatives Association (ISDA) An association of swap dealers formed in 1985 to promote uniform practices in the writing, trading, and settlement procedures of swaps and other derivatives.

Interquartile range The difference between the third and first quartiles of a dataset.

Interval With reference to grouped data, a set of values within which an observation falls.

Interval scale A measurement scale that not only ranks data but also gives assurance that the differences between scale values are equal.

In-the-money Options that, if exercised, would result in the value received being worth more than the payment required to exercise.

Intrinsic value The value of the asset given a hypothetically complete understanding of the asset's investment characteristics; for options, the greater of zero and the amount of money realized if the option were to be exercised.

Inventory investment Changes in the stocks of finished goods and goods in process, as well as changes in the raw materials that businesses keep on hand. Whenever inventories are decreasing, inventory investment is negative; whenever they are increasing, inventory investment is positive.

Inverse floater   A floating-rate note or bond in which the coupon is adjusted to move opposite to a benchmark interest rate.

Inverse relationship   A relationship between variables that move in opposite directions.

Invested Capital (Private Equity)   The amount of paid-in capital that has been invested in portfolio companies.

Investing   Buying an asset, such as a bond, corporate stock, rental property, or farm, with reasonably determinable underlying earnings.

Investment   (1) Any use of today's resources to expand tomorrow's production or consumption. Can also be viewed as spending by businesses on things such as machines and buildings, which can be used to produce goods and services in the future. The investment part of total output is the portion that will be used in the process of producing goods in the future. (2) The current commitment of dollars for a period of time in order to derive future payments that will compensate the investor for the time the funds are committed, the expected rate of inflation, and the uncertainty of future payments.

Investment Advisor (Private Equity)   Any individual or institution that supplies investment advice to clients on a per fee basis. The investment advisor inherently has no role in the management of the underlying portfolio companies of a partnership/fund.

Investment bankers   Firms specializing in the sale of new securities to the public, typically by underwriting the issue.

Investment company   A firm that issues (sells) shares, and uses the proceeds to invest in various financial instruments or other assets.

Investment Company Act of 1940   One of several pieces of federal legislation passed after the October 1929 stock market crash and the Great Depression. This law regulated the activities and reporting requirements of investment companies, which are firms whose principal business is the trading and management of securities.

Investment constraints   Internal or external limitations on investments.

Investment decision process   Estimation of intrinsic value for comparison with market price to determine whether or not to invest.

Investment grade   Bonds rated AAA to BBB.

Investment horizon   The time period used for planning and forecasting purposes or the future time at which the investor requires the invested funds.

Investment management company   A company separate from the investment company that manages the portfolio and performs administrative functions.

Investment Management Fee   The fee payable to the investment management firm for the ongoing management of a portfolio. Investment management fees are typically asset based (percentage of assets), performance based (based on performance relative to a benchmark), or a combination of the two but may take different forms as well.

Investment objectives   Desired investment outcomes; includes risk objectives and return objectives.

Investment portfolio   Set of securities chosen by an investor.

Investment strategy   An approach to investment analysis and security selection.

IPO   Initial public offering.

IRR   Internal rate of return.

Joint probability   The probability of the joint occurrence of stated events.

Joint probability function   A function giving the probability of joint occurrences of values of stated random variables.

Joint venture   When companies jointly pursue a certain business activity.

Junior debt   Subordinated debt.

Justified (fundamental) P/E   The price-to-earnings ratio that is fair, warranted, or justified on the basis of forecasted fundamentals.

Justified price multiple (or warranted price multiple or intrinsic price multiple)   The estimated fair value of the price multiple, usually based on forecasted fundamentals or comparables.

Just-in-time   System of inventory management that requires minimum inventories of materials and very frequent deliveries by suppliers.

Keiretsu   A network of Japanese companies organized around a major bank.

Keynesian   An economist who believes that left alone, the economy would rarely operate at full employment and that to achieve full employment, active help from fiscal policy and monetary policy is required.

kth Order autocorrelation   The correlation between observations in a time series separated by k periods.

Kurtosis   The statistical measure that indicates the peakedness of a distribution.

Labor   The work time and work effort that people devote to producing goods and services.

Labor force   Individuals aged 16 years or older who either have jobs or are looking and available for jobs; the number of employed plus the number of unemployed.

Labor productivity Total real domestic output (real GDP) divided by the number of workers (output per worker).

Labor unions Worker organizations that seek to secure economic improvements for their members; they also seek to improve the safety, health, and other benefits (such as job security) of their members.

Land The natural resources that are available from nature. Land as a resource includes location, original fertility and mineral deposits, topography, climate, water, and vegetation.

Law of demand The observation that there is a negative, or inverse, relationship between the price of any good or service and the quantity demanded, holding other factors constant.

Law of diminishing returns As a firm uses more of a variable input, with a given quantity of other inputs (fixed inputs), the marginal product of the variable input eventually diminishes.

Law of one price The rule stipulating that equivalent securities or bundles of securities must sell at equal prices to preclude arbitrage opportunities.

Leading dividend yield Forecasted dividends per share over the next year divided by current stock price.

Leading P/E (or forward P/E or prospective P/E) A stock's current price divided by next year's expected earnings.

Lease Long-term rental agreement.

Lease receivables Amounts due from customers on long-term sales-type lease agreements.

Legal risk The risk that the legal system will not enforce a contract in case of dispute or fraud; the risk that failures by company managers to effectively manage a company's risk exposures will lead to lawsuits and other judicial remedies, resulting in potentially catastrophic losses for the company.

Legislative and regulatory risk The risk that governmental laws and regulations directly or indirectly affecting a company's operations will change with potentially severe adverse effects on the company's continued profitability and even its long-term sustainability.

Leptokurtic Describes a distribution that is more peaked than a normal distribution.

Lessee User of a leased asset (cf. *lessor*).

Lessor Owner of a leased asset (cf. *lessee*).

Letter of credit Letter from a bank stating that it has established a credit in the company's favor.

Level of significance The probability of a Type I error in testing a hypothesis.

Leverage In the context of corporate finance, leverage refers to the use of fixed costs within a company's cost structure. Fixed costs that are operating costs (such as depreciation or rent) create operating leverage. Fixed costs that are financial costs (such as interest expense) create financial leverage.

Leverage ratio Ratio of debt to total capitalization of a firm.

Leveraged buyout (LBO) A transaction whereby the target company management team converts the target to a privately held company by using heavy borrowing to finance the purchase of the target company's outstanding shares.

Leveraged floating-rate note or leveraged floater A floating-rate note or bond in which the coupon is adjusted at a multiple of a benchmark interest rate.

Leveraged recapitalization A post-offer takeover defense mechanism that involves the assumption of a large amount of debt that is then used to finance share repurchases; the effect is to dramatically change the company's capital structure while attempting to deliver a value to target shareholders in excess of a hostile bid.

Liabilities Amounts owed; the legal claims against a business or household by nonowners.

LIFO The last-in first-out accounting method of valuing inventories.

LIFO liquidation A reduction in the physical quantity of an inventory that is accounted for using the LIFO method. A LIFO liquidation usually produces a nonrecurring increase in earnings because the older costs associated with the liquidated units are lower than current inventory costs.

Likelihood The probability of an observation, given a particular set of conditions.

Limit down A limit move in the futures market in which the price at which a transaction would be made is at or below the lower limit.

Limit move A condition in the futures markets in which the price at which a transaction would be made is at or beyond the price limits.

Limit order An order to buy or sell a security at a specific price or better (lower for a buy order and higher for a sell order).

Limit up A limit move in the futures market in which the price at which a transaction would be made is at or above the upper limit.

Limited liability A legal concept whereby the responsibility, or liability, of the owners of a corporation is limited to the value of the shares in the firm that they own.

Limited partnership *Partnership* in which some partners have *limited liability* and general partners have unlimited liability.

Linear association A straight-line relationship, as opposed to a relationship that cannot be graphed as a straight line.

Linear interpolation   The estimation of an unknown value on the basis of two known values that bracket it, using a straight line between the two known values.

Linear regression   Regression that models the straight-line relationship between the dependent and independent variable(s).

Linear trend   A trend in which the dependent variable changes at a constant rate with time.

Liquid   Term used to describe an asset that can be quickly converted to cash at a price close to fair market value.

Liquid asset   Asset that is easily and cheaply turned into cash—notably cash itself and short-term securities.

Liquidating dividend   *Dividend* that represents a return of capital.

Liquidation   To sell the assets of a company, division, or subsidiary piecemeal, typically because of bankruptcy; the form of bankruptcy that allows for the orderly satisfaction of creditors' claims after which the company ceases to exist.

Liquidation value   The value of a company if the company were dissolved and its assets sold individually.

Liquidity   With reference to an entity, the ability to satisfy short-term obligations using assets that are most readily converted into cash; with reference to an asset, the degree to which the asset can be acquired or disposed of quickly without loss relative to its fair value.

Liquidity discount   A reduction or discount to value that reflects the lack of depth of trading or liquidity in that asset's market.

Liquidity preference theory   Theory that the forward rate exceeds expected future interest rates.

Liquidity premium   An extra return that compensates investors for the risk of loss relative to an investment's fair value if the investment needs to be converted to cash quickly.

Liquidity risk   The risk that a financial instrument cannot be purchased or sold without a significant concession in price due to the size of the market.

Locked limit   A condition in the futures markets in which a transaction cannot take place because the price would be beyond the limits.

Logit model   A qualitative-dependent-variable multiple regression model based on the logistic probability distribution.

Log-linear model   With reference to time-series models, a model in which the growth rate of the time series as a function of time is constant.

Log-log regression model   A regression that expresses the dependent and independent variables as natural logarithms.

London Interbank Offer Rate (LIBOR)   The Eurodollar rate at which London banks lend dollars to other London banks; considered to be the best representative rate on a dollar borrowed by a private, high-quality borrower.

Long   The buyer of an asset or derivative contract. Also refers to the position of owning an asset or derivative contract.

Longitudinal data   Observations on characteristic(s) of the same observational unit through time.

Long position   The buyer of a commodity or security or, for a forward contract, the counterparty who will be the eventual buyer of the underlying asset.

Long run   (1) The time period during which all factors of production can be varied. (2) A period of time in which the quantities of all resources can be varied.

Long-run average cost curve   The locus of points representing the minimum unit cost of producing any given rate of output, given current technology and resource prices.

Long-term equity anticipatory securities (LEAPS)   Options originally created with expirations of several years.

Look-ahead bias   Bias that may result from the use of information that was not available on the test date.

Lower bound   The lowest possible value.

LP   Linear programming.

Macaulay duration   The duration without dividing by 1 plus the bond's yield to maturity. The term, named for one of the economists who first derived it, is used to distinguish the calculation from modified duration. See also *modified duration*.

Macroeconomic factor   A factor related to the economy, such as the inflation rate, industrial production, or economic sector membership.

Macroeconomic factor model   A multifactor model in which the factors are surprises in macroeconomic variables that significantly explain equity returns.

Macroeconomics   The study of the behavior of the economy as a whole, including such economywide phenomena as changes in unemployment, the general price level, and national income.

MACRS   Modified accelerated cost recovery system.

Maintenance margin   The minimum margin that an investor must keep on deposit in a margin account at all times.

Maintenance margin requirement   The margin requirement on any day other than the first day of a transaction.

Management buyout (MBO)   A corporate transaction in which management repurchases all outstanding common stock, usually using the proceeds of debt issuance; a leveraged buyout (LBO) led by management.

Management fee   The compensation an investment company pays to the investment management company for its services. The average annual fee is about 0.5 percent of fund assets.

Managerialism theories   Theories that posit that corporate executives are motivated to engage in mergers to maximize the size of their company rather than shareholder value.

Margin or margin deposit   The amount of money that a trader deposits in a margin account. The term is derived from the stock market practice in which an investor borrows a portion of the money required to purchase a certain amount of stock. In futures markets, there is no borrowing so the margin is more of a down payment or performance bond.

Margin account   The collateral posted with the futures exchange clearinghouse by an outside counterparty to insure its eventual performance; the *initial* margin is the deposit required at contract origination while the *maintenance* margin is the minimum collateral necessary at all times.

Margin call   A request by an investor's broker for additional capital for a security bought on margin if the investor's equity value declines below the required maintenance margin.

Marginal benefit   The benefit that a person receives from consuming one more unit of a good or service. It is measured as the maximum amount that a person is willing to pay for one more unit of the good or service.

Marginal cost   The opportunity cost of producing one more unit of a good or service; the change in total cost due to a one-unit increase in production.

Marginal cost pricing   A system of pricing in which the price charged is equal to the opportunity cost to society of producing one more unit of the good or service in question. The opportunity cost is the marginal cost to society.

Marginal product   The increase in total product that results from a one-unit increase in the variable input, with all other inputs remaining the same. It is calculated as the increase in total product divided by the increase in the variable input employed, when the quantities of all other inputs are constant.

Marginal revenue   The change in total revenue that results from a one-unit increase in the quantity sold. It is calculated as the change in total revenue divided by the change in quantity sold.

Marginal tax rate   The part of each additional dollar in income that is paid as tax.

Market   All of the arrangements that individuals have for exchanging with one another. Thus, for example, we can speak of the labor market, the automobile market, and the credit market.

Market analysis   With respect to investing, the analysis of a the current conditions of a financial market.

Market capitalization (market cap)   The number of shares a company has outstanding times the price per share.

Market demand   The demand of all consumers in the marketplace for a particular good or service. The summation at each price of the quantity demanded by each individual.

Market efficiency   The subject dealing with the relationship of price to intrinsic value. The traditional efficient markets formulation asserts that an asset's price is the best available estimate of its intrinsic value. The rational efficient markets formulation asserts that investors should expect to be rewarded for the costs of information gathering and analysis by higher gross returns.

Market failure   A state in which the market does not allocate resources efficiently.

Market impact   With reference to execution costs, the difference between the actual execution price and the market price that would have prevailed had the manager not sought to trade the security.

Market maker   An institution or individual quoting firm bid and ask prices for a security and standing ready to buy or sell the security at those quoted prices. Also called a *dealer*.

Market model   (1) Model suggesting a linear relationship between actual returns on a stock and on the market portfolio. (2) A method that is used in event studies. Regression analysis is used to compute the return that is attributable to market forces. It is used to compute "excess returns" that may be attributable to the occurrence of an event.

Market order   An order to buy or sell a security immediately at the best price available.

Market portfolio   The portfolio that includes all risky assets with relative weights equal to their proportional market values.

Market power   The ability to influence the market, and in particular the market price, by influencing the total quantity offered for sale.

Market price of risk   The slope of the capital market line, indicating the market risk premium for each unit of market risk.

Market return   The standard (typically the SP 500) against which stock portfolio performance can be measured.

Market risk (systematic risk)   Risk that cannot be diversified away. In risk management, *market risk* refers to the risk associated with interest rates, exchange rates, and equity prices.

Market risk premium The expected excess return on the market over the risk-free rate.

Market share test The percentage of a market that a particular firm supplies, used as the primary measure of monopoly power.

Market timer An investor who speculates on broad market moves rather than on specific securities.

Market timing Trying to catch short-term market movements. Extremely difficult.

Market Value The current listed price at which investors buy or sell securities at a given time.

Market value added (MVA) External management performance measure to compare the market value of the company's debt and equity with the total capital invested in the firm.

Marketability discount A reduction or discount to value for shares that are not publicly traded.

Marking to market or mark to market The settlement process used to adjust the margin account of a futures contract for (traditionally) daily gains or losses. Also known as the *daily settlement* although some futures contracts are now marked to market more frequently than daily.

Markowitz decision rule A decision rule for choosing between two investments based on their means and variances.

Mature growth rate The earnings growth rate in a company's mature phase; an earnings growth rate that can be sustained long term.

Mature phase A stage of growth in which the company reaches an equilibrium in which investment opportunities on average just earn their opportunity cost of capital.

Maturity premium An extra return that compensates investors for the increased sensitivity of the market value of debt to a change in market interest rates as maturity is extended.

Maturity strategy A portfolio management strategy employed to reduce the interest rate risk of a bond portfolio by matching the maturity of the portfolio with its investment horizon. For example, if the investment horizon is 10 years, the portfolio manager would construct a portfolio that will mature in 10 years.

MBO Management buyout.

MDA Multiple-discriminant analysis.

Mean The sum of all values in a distribution or dataset, divided by the number of values summed; a synonym of arithmetic mean.

Mean absolute deviation With reference to a sample, the mean of the absolute values of deviations from the sample mean.

Mean excess return The average rate of return in excess of the risk-free rate.

Mean reversion The tendency of a time series to fall when its level is above its mean and rise when its level is below its mean; a mean-reverting time series tends to return to its long-term mean.

Mean–variance analysis An approach to portfolio analysis using expected means, variances, and covariances of asset returns.

Means of payment A method of settling a debt.

Measure of central tendency A quantitative measure that specifies where data are centered.

Measure of location A quantitative measure that describes the location or distribution of data; includes not only measures of central tendency but also other measures such as percentiles.

Measurement error Errors in measuring an explanatory variable in a regression that leads to biases in estimated parameters.

Measurement scales A scheme of measuring differences. The four types of measurement scales are nominal, ordinal, interval, and ratio.

Median The value of the middle item of a set of items that has been sorted into ascending or descending order; the 50th percentile.

Merger The absorption of one company by another; that is, two companies become one entity and one or both of the pre-merger companies ceases to exist as a separate entity.

Mesokurtic Describes a distribution with kurtosis identical to that of the normal distribution.

Method based on forecasted fundamentals An approach to using price multiples that relates a price multiple to forecasts of fundamentals through a discounted cash flow model.

Method of comparables An approach to valuation that involves using a price multiple to evaluate whether an asset is relatively fairly valued, relatively undervalued, or relatively overvalued when compared to a benchmark value of the multiple.

Microcap Refers to companies with a market capitalization in the $100 million to $300 million range.

Microeconomics The study of the choices that individuals and businesses make, the way those choices interact, and the influence governments exert on them.

Midcap Companies with a market capitalization in the $3 billion to $4 billion range.

Minimum-variance frontier The graph of the set of portfolios that have minimum variance for their level of expected return.

Minimum-variance portfolio The portfolio with the minimum variance for each given level of expected return.

Mispricing Any departure of the market price of an asset from the asset's estimated intrinsic value.

Mixed factor models Factor models that combine features of more than one type of factor model.

Mixed offering A merger or acquisition that is to be paid for with cash, securities, or some combination of the two.

Modal interval With reference to grouped data, the most frequently occurring interval.

Mode The most frequently occurring value in a set of observations.

Model risk The use of an inaccurate pricing model for a particular investment, or the improper use of the right model.

Model specification With reference to regression, the set of variables included in the regression and the regression equation's functional form.

Modern portfolio theory (MPT) Principles underlying analysis and evaluation of rational portfolio choices based on risk-return trade-offs and efficient diversification.

Modified accelerated cost recovery system (MACRS) Schedule of *depreciation* deductions allowed for tax purposes.

Modified duration Measure of a bond's price sensitivity to interest rate movements. Equal to the duration of a bond divided by one plus its yield to maturity.

Molodovsky effect The observation that P/Es tend to be high on depressed EPS at the bottom of a business cycle, and tend to be low on unusually high EPS at the top of a business cycle.

Momentum indicators Valuation indicators that relate either price or a fundamental (such as earnings) to the time series of their own past values (or in some cases to their expected value).

Monetarists Macroeconomists who believe that inflation in the long run is always caused by excessive monetary growth and that changes in the money supply affect aggregate demand both directly and indirectly.

Monetary policy The Fed conducts the nation's monetary policy by changing interest rates and adjusting the quantity of money.

Money Any medium that is universally accepted in an economy both by sellers of goods and services as payment for those goods and services and by creditors as payment for debts.

Money illusion Reacting to changes in money prices rather than relative prices. If a worker whose wages double when the price level also doubles thinks he or she is better off, that worker is suffering from money illusion.

Money market The market for short-term debt instruments (one-year maturity or less).

Money market yield (or CD equivalent yield) A yield on a basis comparable to the quoted yield on an interest-bearing money market instrument that pays interest on a 360-day basis; the annualized holding period yield, assuming a 360-day year.

Money supply The amount of money in circulation.

Moneyness The relationship between the price of the underlying and an option's exercise price.

Money-weighted rate of return The internal rate of return on a portfolio, taking account of all cash flows.

Monitoring costs Costs borne by owners to monitor the management of the company (e.g., board of director expenses).

Monopolist The single supplier of a good or service for which there is no close substitute. The monopolist therefore constitutes its entire industry.

Monopolization The possession of monopoly power in the relevant market and the willful acquisition or maintenance of that power, as distinguished from growth or development as a consequence of a superior product, business acumen, or historical accident.

Monopoly A market structure in which there is one firm, which produces a good or service that has no close substitute and in which the firm is protected from competition by a barrier preventing the entry of new firms.

Monte Carlo simulation method A methodology using a computer to generate random outcomes according to specified probability models to find approximate solutions to complex problems.

Mortgage-backed security Ownership claim in a pool of mortgages or an obligation that is secured by such a pool. Also called a *pass-through,* because payments are passed along from the mortgage originator to the purchaser of the mortgage-backed security.

Moving average The continually recalculating average of security prices for a period, often 200 days, to serve as an indication of the general trend of prices and also as a benchmark price.

Multicollinearity A regression assumption violation that occurs when two or more independent variables (or combinations of independent variables) are highly but not perfectly correlated with each other.

Multifactor model Model of security returns positing that returns respond to multiple systematic factors.

Multiple Short for price-earnings multiple.

Multiple linear regression   Linear regression involving two or more independent variables.

Multiple linear regression model   A linear regression model with two or more independent variables.

Multiple *R*   The correlation between the actual and forecasted values of the dependent variable in a regression.

Multiplication rule for probabilities   The rule that the joint probability of events *A* and *B* equals the probability of *A* given *B* times the probability of *B*.

Multiplier   The amount by which a change in autonomous expenditure is magnified or multiplied to determine the change in equilibrium expenditure and real GDP.

Multivariate distribution   A probability distribution that specifies the probabilities for a group of related random variables.

Multivariate normal distribution   A probability distribution for a group of random variables that is completely defined by the means and variances of the variables plus all the correlations between pairs of the variables.

Municipal bonds   Tax-exempt bonds issued by state and local governments, generally to finance capital improvement projects. General obligation bonds are backed by the general taxing power of the issuer. Revenue bonds are backed by the proceeds from the project or agency they are issued to finance.

Mutual fund   An investment company that pools money from shareholders and invests in a variety of securities, including stocks, bonds, and money market securities. A mutual fund ordinarily stands ready to buy back (redeem) its shares at their current net asset value, which depends on the market value of the fund's portfolio of securities at the time. Mutual funds generally continuously offer new shares to investors.

Mutually exclusive events   Events such that only one can occur at a time.

Mutually exclusive projects   Mutually exclusive projects compete directly with each other. For example, if Projects A and B are mutually exclusive, you can choose A or B, but you cannot choose both.

***n* Factorial**   For a positive integer *n*, the product of the first *n* positive integers; 0 factorial equals 1 by definition. *n* factorial is written as *n*!.

NASDAQ   National Association of Securities Dealers Automated Quotations. It is the trading system for the over-the-counter market.

Nash equilibrium   The outcome of a game that occurs when player A takes the best possible action given the action of player B and player B takes the best possible action given the action of player A.

National income (NI)   The total of all factor payments to resource owners.

Natural monopoly   A monopoly that arises from the peculiar production characteristics in an industry. It usually arises when there are large economies of scale relative to the industry's demand such that one firm can produce at a lower average cost than can be achieved by multiple firms.

Negative relationship   A relationship between variables that move in opposite directions.

Negative serial correlation   Serial correlation in which a positive error for one observation increases the chance of a negative error for another observation, and vice versa.

Neoclassical growth theory   A theory of economic growth that proposes that real GDP grows because technological change induces a level of saving and investment that makes capital per hour of labor grow.

Net asset value (NAV)   (1) The market value of the assets owned by a fund. (2) The value of each share expressed as assets minus liabilities on a per-share basis.

Net borrower   A country that is borrowing more from the rest of the world than it is lending to it.

Net capital expenditures   Gross capital expenditures minus proceeds from the disposal of productive assets.

Net debt   Total debt minus cash on hand.

Net exports   The value of exports minus the value of imports.

Net income plus depreciation   Often referred to as traditional cash flow, its calculation removes an important noncash expense from net income.

Net investment   Net increase in the capital stock-gross investment minus depreciation.

Net lender   A country that is lending more to the rest of the world than it is borrowing from it.

Net operating profit less adjusted taxes (NOPLAT)   A company's operating profit with adjustments to normalize the effects of capital structure.

Net present value (NPV)   The present value of an investment's cash inflows (benefits) minus the present value of its cash outflows (costs).

Net public debt   Gross public debt minus all government interagency borrowing.

Netting   When parties agree to exchange only the net amount owed from one party to the other.

Network effect   A situation in which a consumer's willingness to purchase a good or service is influenced by how many others also buy the item.

Net working capital   Current assets minus current liabilities.

Net worth　(1) The difference between assets and liabilities. (2) Book value of a company's *common stock*, surplus, and *retained earnings*.

New growth theory　A theory of economic growth based on the idea that real GDP per person grows because of the choices that people make in the pursuit of ever greater profit and that growth can persist indefinitely.

New issue　Common stocks or bonds offered by companies for public sale.

Node　Each value on a binomial tree from which successive moves or outcomes branch.

No-growth company　A company without positive expected net present value projects.

No-growth value per share　The value per share of a no-growth company, equal to the expected level amount of earnings divided by the stock's required rate of return.

Nominal GDP　The value of the final goods and services produced in a given year valued at the prices that prevailed in that same year. It is a more precise name for GDP.

Nominal interest rate　The interest rate in terms of nominal (not adjusted for purchasing power) dollars.

Nominal risk-free interest rate　The sum of the real risk-free interest rate and the inflation premium.

Nominal scale　A measurement scale that categorizes data but does not rank them.

Nominal values　The values of variables such as GDP and investment expressed in current dollars, also called money values; measurement in terms of the actual market prices at which goods and services are sold.

Nominal yield　A bond's yield as measured by its coupon rate.

Noncontrolling interest　Generally, minority interest. However, the term is used to reflect a minority shareholder interest when the definition of control is extended beyond a simple majority share ownership interest. Any interest in an entity besides that of a controlling shareholder.

Nonconventional cash flow　In a nonconventional cash flow pattern, the initial outflow is not followed by inflows only, but the cash flows can flip from positive (inflows) to negative (outflows) again (or even change signs several times).

Nondeliverable forwards (NDFs)　Cash-settled forward contracts, used predominately with respect to foreign exchange forwards.

Nondiversifiable risk　See *systematic risk*.

Nonlinear relation　An association or relationship between variables that cannot be graphed as a straight line.

Nonparametric test　A test that is not concerned with a parameter, or that makes minimal assumptions about the population from which a sample comes.

Nonrecurring cash flow　Operating cash flow that appears infrequently or that may appear with some regularity but is very irregular in amount. In addition, even though included in operating cash flow, nonrecurring cash flow often is not closely tied to the core operating activities of the firm.

Nonstationarity　With reference to a random variable, the property of having characteristics such as mean and variance that are not constant through time.

Nonsystematic risk　Nonmarket or firm-specific risk factors that can be eliminated by diversification. Also called *unique risk* or *diversifiable risk*. Systematic risk refers to risk factors common to the entire economy.

Nontariff barrier　Any action other than a tariff that restricts international trade.

Normal backwardation　The condition in futures markets in which futures prices are lower than expected spot prices.

Normal contango　The condition in futures markets in which futures prices are higher than expected spot prices.

Normal distribution　A continuous, symmetric probability distribution that is completely described by its mean and its variance.

Normal rate of return　The amount that must be paid to an investor to induce investment in a business; also known as the *opportunity cost of capital*.

Normalized (or normal) earnings per share　The earnings per share that a business could achieve currently under mid-cyclical conditions.

North American Free Trade Agreement　An agreement, which became effective on January 1, 1994, to eliminate all barriers to international trade between the United States, Canada, and Mexico after a 15-year phasing in period.

Note　Unsecured debt with a maturity of up to 10 years.

Notes payable　Promissory notes that are evidence of a debt and state the terms of interest and principal payment.

Notional principal　(1) Principal amount used to calculate swap payments. (2) The principal value of a swap transaction, which is not exchanged but is used as a scale factor to translate interest rate differentials into cash settlement payments.

***n*-Period moving average**　The average of the current and immediately prior $n-1$ values of a time series.

NPV　Net present value.

NPV rule　An investment decision rule that states that an investment should be undertaken if its NPV is positive but not undertaken if its NPV is negative.

Null hypothesis   The hypothesis to be tested.

NYSE   New York Stock Exchange.

Objective probabilities   Probabilities that generally do not vary from person to person; includes a priori and objective probabilities.

Objectives   In investments, the investor's goals expressed in terms of risk and return and included in the policy statement.

Off-balance-sheet financing   Financing that is not shown as a liability in a company's balance sheet.

Offer price   The price at which a market maker is willing to sell a security (also called *ask price*).

Official reserves   The amount of reserves owned by the central bank of a government in the form of gold, Special Drawing Rights, and foreign cash or marketable securities.

Official settlements account   A record of the change in a country's official reserves.

Off-market forward rate agreement (off-market FRA)   A contract in which the initial value is intentionally set at a value other than zero and therefore requires a cash payment at the start from one party to the other.

Offsetting   A transaction in exchange-listed derivative markets in which a party re-enters the market to close out a position.

One third rule   The rule that, with no change in technology, a 1 percent increase in capital per hour of labor brings, on the average, a one third of 1 percent increase in real GDP per hour of labor.

One-sided hypothesis test (or one-tailed hypothesis test)   A test in which the null hypothesis is rejected only if the evidence indicates that the population parameter is greater than (smaller than) θ_0. The alternative hypothesis also has one side.

Open-end fund   An investment company that continuously offers to sell new shares, or redeem them, at prices based on the market value of the assets owned by the fund (net asset value).

Operating breakeven   The number of units produced and sold at which the company's operating profit is zero (revenues = operating costs).

Operating cash flow   Cash flow from operating activities computed in accordance with generally accepted accounting principles.

Operating earnings   An earnings measure that excludes selected items of nonrecurring gain, revenue, loss, and expense. This is not a GAAP measure, and its determination may vary widely among different companies.

Operating income   See *operating profit.*

Operating lease   A lease that does not transfer the risks and rewards of ownership to the lessee.

Operating lease payments are expensed as incurred.

Operating profit   Core pretax profit from central operations calculated as revenue minus cost of goods sold, selling, general and administrative expense, and research and development expense.

Operating risk   The risk attributed to the operating cost structure, in particular the use of fixed costs in operations; the risk arising from the mix of fixed and variable costs; the risk that a company's operations may be severely affected by environmental, social, and governance risk factors.

Operating working capital   Current assets, including operating receivables, inventory, and prepaid expenses, that are used in operations minus current liabilities, including operating payables and accrued expenses payable that are incurred in operations.

Operations risk or operational risk   The risk of loss from failures in a company's systems and procedures (for example, due to computer failures or human failures) or events completely outside of the control of organizations (which would include "acts of God" and terrorist actions).

Opportunity cost   The alternative return that investors forgo by choosing a particular course of action; the value of something in its best alternative use.

Opportunity cost of capital   The normal rate of return, or the available return on the next-best alternative investment. Economists consider this a cost of production, and it is included in our cost examples.

Opportunity set   The set of assets available for investment.

Optimal capital structure   The capital structure at which the value of the company is maximized.

Optimal portfolio   The portfolio on the efficient frontier that has the highest utility for a given investor. It lies at the point of tangency between the efficient frontier and the curve with the investor's highest possible utility.

Optimal risky portfolio   An investor's best combination of risky assets to be mixed with safe assets to form the complete portfolio.

Optimizer   A specialized computer program or a spreadsheet that solves for the portfolio weights that will result in the lowest risk for a specified level of expected return.

Option   A financial instrument that gives one party the right, but not the obligation, to buy (for a call option) or sell (for a put option) an underlying asset from or to another party at a fixed price over a specific period of time.

Option-adjusted spread A type of yield spread that considers changes in the term structure and alternative estimates of the volatility of interest rates. It is spread after adjusting for embedded options.

Option contract An agreement that grants the owner the right, but not the obligation, to make a future transaction in an underlying commodity or security at a fixed price and within a predetermined time in the future.

Option delta Hedge ratio.

Option price, option premium, or premium The amount of money a buyer pays and seller receives to engage in an option transaction.

Options Clearing Corporation (OCC) A company designed to guarantee, monitor margin accounts, and settle exchange-traded option transactions.

Order-driven market A market without active market makers in which buy-and-sell orders directly confront each other; an auction market.

Ordinal scale A measurement scale that sorts data into categories that are ordered (ranked) with respect to some characteristic.

Ordinary annuity An annuity with a first cash flow that is paid one period from the present.

Ordinary least squares (OLS) An estimation method based on the criterion of minimizing the sum of the squared residuals of a regression.

Organic growth Company growth in output or sales that is achieved by making investments internally (i.e., excludes growth achieved through mergers and acquisitions).

Origin The intersection of the *y* axis and the *x* axis in a graph.

Orthogonal Uncorrelated; at a right angle.

OTC Over-the-counter.

Other comprehensive income Changes to equity that bypass (are not reported in) the income statement; the difference between comprehensive income and net income.

Outcome A possible value of a random variable.

Outliers Small numbers of observations at either extreme (small or large) of a sample.

Out-of-sample forecast errors The differences between actual and predicted value of time series outside the sample period used to fit the model.

Out-of-sample test A test of a strategy or model using a sample outside the time period on which the strategy or model was developed.

Out-of-the-money Said of options that, if exercised, would require the payment of more money than the value received and therefore would not be currently exercised.

Overnight A deal from today to the next business day.

Overnight index swap (OIS) A swap in which the floating rate is the cumulative value of a single unit of currency invested at an overnight rate during the settlement period.

Over-the-counter (OTC) Informal market that does not involve a securities exchange. Specifically used to refer to the Nasdaq dealer market for *common stocks*.

Overweighted A condition in which a portfolio, for whatever reason, includes more of a class of securities than the relative market value alone would justify.

P/E ratio Share price divided by earnings per share.

Paid-In Capital (Private Equity) The amount of committed capital a limited partner has actually transferred to a venture fund. Also known as the *cumulative drawdown amount*.

Paired comparisons test A statistical test for differences based on paired observations drawn from samples that are dependent on each other.

Paired observations Observations that are dependent on each other.

Pairs arbitrage trade A trade in two closely related stocks that involves buying the relatively undervalued stock and selling short the relatively overvalued stock.

Panel data Observations through time on a single characteristic of multiple observational units.

Par value (1) The principal amount repaid at maturity of a bond. Also called *face value*. (2) The officially determined value of a currency.

Par yield curve The yield curve drawn for government coupon bonds of different maturities that trade at, or around, par.

Parameter A descriptive measure computed from or used to describe a population of data, conventionally represented by Greek letters.

Parameter instability The problem or issue of population regression parameters that have changed over time.

Parametric test Any test (or procedure) concerned with parameters or whose validity depends on assumptions concerning the population generating the sample.

Partial regression coefficients or partial slope coefficients The slope coefficients in a multiple regression.

Partnership A business owned by two or more joint owners, or partners, who share the responsibilities and the profits of the firm and are individually liable for all the debts of the partnership.

Passive investment strategy See *passive management*.

Passive management Buying a well-diversified portfolio to represent a broad-based market index without attempting to search out mispriced securities.

Passive portfolio   A market index portfolio.

Passive strategy   See *passive management*.

Pass-through securities   *Notes* or *bonds* backed by a package of assets such as home mortgage loans.

Patent   A government-sanctioned exclusive right granted to the inventor of a good, service, or productive process to produce, use, and sell the invention for a given number of years.

Payables   Accounts payable.

Payback   The time required for the added income from the convertible security relative to the stock to offset the conversion premium.

Payer swaption   A swaption that allows the holder to enter into a swap as the fixed-rate payer and floating-rate receiver.

Payment date   The day that the company actually mails out (or electronically transfers) a dividend payment.

Payment netting   A means of settling payments in which the amount owed by the first party to the second is netted with the amount owed by the second party to the first; only the net difference is paid.

Payoff   The value of an option at expiration.

Payout ratio   The percentage of total earnings paid out in dividends in any given year (in per-share terms, DPS/EPS).

Peak   The point at which a business cycle turns from expansion into recession.

Pecking order theory   The theory that managers take into account how their actions might be interpreted by outsiders and thus order their preferences for various forms of corporate financing. Forms of financing that are least visible to outsiders (e.g., internally generated funds) are most preferable to managers and those that are most visible (e.g., equity) are least preferable.

Peer group comparison   A method of measuring portfolio performance by collecting the returns produced by a representative universe of investors over a specific period of time.

PEG   The P/E-to-growth ratio, calculated as the stock's P/E divided by the expected earnings growth rate.

Per capita   Latin, meaning "by the head." Distributing to "issue per capita" means to distribute trust property to persons who take, in their own right, an equal portion of the property.

Per unit contribution margin   The amount that each unit sold contributes to covering fixed costs—that is, the difference between the price per unit and the variable cost per unit.

Percentiles   Quantiles that divide a distribution into 100 equal parts.

Perfect collinearity   The existence of an exact linear relation between two or more independent variables or combinations of independent variables.

Perfect competition   An industry structure characterized by certain conditions, including many buyers and sellers, homogeneous products, perfect information, easy entry and exit, and no barriers to entry. The existence of these conditions implies that each seller is a price taker.

Performance appraisal   The evaluation of risk-adjusted performance; the evaluation of investment skill.

Performance attribution   The attribution of investment performance to specific investment decisions (such as asset allocation and country weighting).

Performance guarantee   A guarantee from the clearinghouse that if one party makes money on a transaction, the clearinghouse ensures it will be paid.

Performance measurement   The calculation of returns in a logical and consistent manner.

Periodic rate   The quoted interest rate per period; the stated annual interest rate divided by the number of compounding periods per year.

Permutation   An ordered listing.

Perpetuity   A perpetual annuity, or a set of never-ending level sequential cash flows, with the first cash flow occurring one period from now; a stream of level payments extending to infinity.

Personal income (PI)   The amount of income that households actually receive before they pay personal income taxes.

Personal trust   An amount of money set aside by a grantor and often managed by a third party, the trustee. Often constructed so one party receives income from the trust's investments and another party receives the residual value of the trust after the income beneficiaries' death.

Pet projects   Projects in which influential managers want the corporation to invest. Often, unfortunately, pet projects are selected without undergoing normal capital budgeting analysis.

Physical capital   All manufactured resources, including buildings, equipment, machines, and improvements to land that is used for production.

PIK   Pay-in-kind bond.

Plain-vanilla   Refers to a security, especially a bond or a swap, issued with standard features. Sometimes called *generic*.

Plain vanilla swap   An interest rate swap in which one party pays a fixed rate and the other pays a floating rate, with both sets of payments in the same currency.

Platykurtic Describes a distribution that is less peaked than the normal distribution.

Point One percent (1%).

Point estimate A single numerical estimate of an unknown quantity, such as a population parameter.

Poison pill A pre-offer takeover defense mechanism that makes it prohibitively costly for an acquirer to take control of a target without the prior approval of the target's board of directors.

Poison puts A pre-offer takeover defense mechanism that gives target company bondholders the right to sell their bonds back to the target at a pre-specified redemption price, typically at or above par value; this defense increases the need for cash and raises the cost of the acquisition.

Policy statement A statement in which the investor specifies investment goals, constraints, and risk preferences.

Political risk Possibility of the expropriation of assets, changes in tax policy, restrictions on the exchange of foreign currency for domestic currency, or other changes in the business climate of a country.

Pooling of interest Method of accounting for *mergers* (no longer available in the US). The consolidated balance sheet of the merged firm is obtained by combining the balance sheets of the separate firms (cf. *purchase accounting*).

Population All members of a specified group.

Population mean The arithmetic mean value of a population; the arithmetic mean of all the observations or values in the population.

Population standard deviation A measure of dispersion relating to a population in the same unit of measurement as the observations, calculated as the positive square root of the population variance.

Population variance A measure of dispersion relating to a population, calculated as the mean of the squared deviations around the population mean.

Portfolio A group of investments. Ideally, the investments should have different patterns of returns over time.

Portfolio implementation problem The part of the execution step of the portfolio management process that involves the implementation of portfolio decisions by trading desks.

Portfolio investment The purchase of less than 10 percent of the shares of ownership in a company in another nation.

Portfolio management Process of combining securities in a portfolio tailored to the investor's prefer-

ences and needs, monitoring that portfolio, and evaluating its performance.

Portfolio performance attribution The analysis of portfolio performance in terms of the contributions from various sources of risk.

Portfolio possibilities curve A graphical representation of the expected return and risk of all portfolios that can be formed using two assets.

Portfolio selection/composition problem The part of the execution step of the portfolio management process in which investment strategies are integrated with expectations to select a portfolio of assets.

Position trader A trader who typically holds positions open overnight.

Positive market feedback A tendency for a good or service to come into favor with additional consumers because other consumers have chosen to buy the item.

Positive relationship A relationship between two variables that move in the same direction.

Positive serial correlation Serial correlation in which a positive error for one observation increases the chance of a positive error for another observation, and a negative error for one observation increases the chance of a negative error for another observation.

Posterior probability An updated probability that reflects or comes after new information.

Potential credit risk The risk associated with the possibility that a payment due at a later date will not be made.

Power of a test The probability of correctly rejecting the null—that is, rejecting the null hypothesis when it is false.

Preferences A description of a person's likes and dislikes.

Preferred habitat theory Holds that investors prefer specific maturity ranges but can be induced to switch if risk premiums are sufficient.

Preferred stock A class of stock with priority rights, both as to dividends and in liquidation, over the common stock of the same company. Corporations pay a much lower income tax on dividends from their investments in other corporations (where it has already been taxed) than on direct business earnings. Preferred stock is usually priced at the level that makes it attractive to a corporation, taking account of this tax exemption, and as a result is rarely tax-efficient for individuals.

Pre-investing The strategy of using futures contracts to enter the market without an immediate outlay of cash.

Premium   (1) A bond selling at a price above par value due to capital market conditions. (2) The purchase price of an option.

Present value (PV)   The current (discounted) value of a future cash flow or flows.

Present (price) value of a basis point (PVBP)   The change in the bond price for a 1 basis point change in yield. Also called *basis point value* (BPV).

Present value model or discounted cash flow model   A model of intrinsic value that views the value of an asset as the present value of the asset's expected future cash flows.

Present value of growth opportunities (or value of growth)   The difference between the actual value per share and the no-growth value per share.

Price controls   Government-mandated minimum or maximum prices that may be charged for goods and services.

Price discovery   A feature of futures markets in which futures prices provide valuable information about the price of the underlying asset.

Price discrimination   Selling a given product at more than one price, with the price difference being unrelated to differences in cost.

Price-driven market   A market in which dealers (market makers) adjust their quotes continuously to reflect supply and demand; also known as a *dealer market*.

Price–earnings multiple   See *price–earnings ratio.*

Price–earnings ratio   The ratio of a stock's price to its earnings per share. Also referred to as the *P/E multiple.*

Price effect   The effect of a change in the price on the quantity of a good consumed, other things remaining the same.

Price level   The average level of prices as measured by a price index.

Price limits   Limits imposed by a futures exchange on the price change that can occur from one day to the next.

Price momentum   A valuation indicator based on past price movement.

Price multiple   The ratio of a stock's market price to some measure of value per share.

Price relative   A ratio of an ending price over a beginning price; it is equal to 1 plus the holding period return on the asset.

Price risk   The component of interest rate risk due to the uncertainty of the market price of a bond caused by changes in market interest rates.

Price-setting option   The operational flexibility to adjust prices when demand varies from forecast. For example, when demand exceeds capacity, the company could benefit from the excess demand by increasing prices.

Price war   A pricing campaign designed to capture additional market share by repeatedly cutting prices.

Priced risk   Risk that investors require an additional return for bearing.

Primary market   The market in which newly issued securities are sold by their issuers, who receive the proceeds.

Prime rate   Benchmark lending rate set by U.S. banks.

Principal   The amount of funds originally invested in a project or instrument; the face value to be paid at maturity.

Principal-agent problem   The problem of devising compensation rules that induce an agent to act in the best interest of a principal.

Principal trade   A trade through a broker who guarantees full execution at specified discount/premium to the prevailing price.

Prior probabilities   Probabilities reflecting beliefs prior to the arrival of new information.

Private equity   *Equity* that is not publicly traded and that is used to finance business start-ups, *leveraged buy-outs,* etc.

Private placement   A new issue sold directly to a small group of investors, usually institutions.

Private sector surplus or deficit   An amount equal to saving minus investment.

Private trusts   A term used to identify trusts created by individuals for individuals, either during life or under will.

Pro forma   Projected.

Probability   A number between 0 and 1 describing the chance that a stated event will occur.

Probability density function   A function with non-negative values such that probability can be described by areas under the curve graphing the function.

Probability distribution   A distribution that specifies the probabilities of a random variable's possible outcomes.

Probability function   A function that specifies the probability that the random variable takes on a specific value.

Probit model   A qualitative-dependent-variable multiple regression model based on the normal distribution.

Producer Price Index (PPI)   A statistical measure of a weighted average of prices of goods and services that firms produce and sell.

Product differentiation   The distinguishing of products by brand name, color, and other minor attributes. Product differentiation occurs in other than perfectly competitive markets in which products are, in theory, homogeneous, such as wheat or corn.

Production   Any activity that results in the conversion of resources into products that can be used in consumption.

Production-flexibility   The operational flexibility to alter production when demand varies from forecast. For example, if demand is strong, a company may profit from employees working overtime or from adding additional shifts.

Productivity curve   A relationship that shows how real GDP per hour of labor changes as the amount of capital per hour of labor changes with a given state of technology.

Productivity growth slowdown   A slowdown in the growth rate of output per person.

Profit   The income earned by business.

Profit margin or Net profit margin   Net income divided by sales.

Profitability index   Ratio of a project's *NPV* to the initial investment.

Pro-forma earnings   A measure of earnings performance that selectively excludes nonrecurring as well as some noncash items.

Program trading   Coordinated buy orders and sell orders of entire portfolios, usually with the aid of computers, often to achieve index arbitrage objectives.

Project sequencing   To defer the decision to invest in a future project until the outcome of some or all of a current project is known. Projects are sequenced through time, so that investing in a project creates the option to invest in future projects.

Property rights   Social arrangements that govern the ownership, use, and disposal of resources or factors of production, goods, and services that are enforceable in the courts.

Proprietorship   A business owned by one individual who makes the business decisions, receives all the profits, and is legally responsible for the debts of the firm.

Prospectus   Summary of the *registration* statement providing information on an issue of securities.

Protective put   An option strategy in which a long position in an asset is combined with a long position in a put.

Proxy   An instrument empowering an agent to vote in the name of the shareholder.

Proxy fight or proxy contest   An attempt to take control of a company through a shareholder vote.

Proxy statement   A public document that provides the material facts concerning matters on which shareholders will vote.

Proxy vote   Vote cast by one person on behalf of another.

Prudent investor rule   An investment manager must act in accord with the actions of a hypothetical prudent investor.

Pseudo-random numbers   Numbers produced by random number generators.

Public good   A good or service that is both nonrival and nonexcludable—it can be consumed simultaneously by everyone and from which no one can be excluded.

Purchase accounting   Method of accounting for *mergers*. The assets of the acquired firm are shown at market value on the balance sheet of the acquirer (cf. *pooling of interest*).

Purchased in-process research and development costs   Costs of research and development in progress at an acquired company; often, part of the purchase price of an acquired company is allocated to such costs.

Purchasing power   The value of money for buying goods and services. If your money income stays the same but the price of one good that you are buying goes up, your effective purchasing power falls, and vice versa.

Purchasing power parity (PPP)   A theory stating that the exchange rate between two currencies will exactly reflect the purchasing power of the two currencies.

Pure discount instruments   Instruments that pay interest as the difference between the amount borrowed and the amount paid back.

Pure factor portfolio   A portfolio with sensitivity of 1 to the factor in question and a sensitivity of 0 to all other factors.

Put   An option that gives the holder the right to sell an underlying asset to another party at a fixed price over a specific period of time.

Put–call parity   An equation expressing the equivalence (parity) of a portfolio of a call and a bond with a portfolio of a put and the underlying, which leads to the relationship between put and call prices.

Put–call–forward parity   The relationship among puts, calls, and forward contracts.

Put option   A contract that gives its holder the right to sell an asset, typically a financial instrument, at a specified price through a specified date.

***p*-Value**   The smallest level of significance at which the null hypothesis can be rejected; also called the marginal significance level.

Pyramiding   Controlling additional property through reinvestment, refinancing, and exchanging.

q   Ratio of the market value of an asset to its replacement cost.

Qualified Institutional buyers (QIBs)   Institutions that are allowed to trade unregistered stock among themselves.

Qualitative dependent variables Dummy variables used as dependent variables rather than as independent variables.

Quality of earnings The realism and conservatism of the earnings number and the extent to which we might expect the reported level of earnings to be sustained.

Quality of earnings analysis The investigation of issues relating to the accuracy of reported accounting results as reflections of economic performance; quality of earnings analysis is broadly understood to include not only earnings management, but also balance sheet management.

Quantile (or fractile) A value at or below which a stated fraction of the data lies.

Quartiles Quantiles that divide a distribution into four equal parts.

Quick ratio A measure of liquidity similar to the current ratio except for exclusion of inventories (cash plus receivables divided by current liabilities).

Quintiles Quantiles that divide a distribution into five equal parts.

Quota A quantitative restriction on the import of a particular good, which specifies the maximum amount that can be imported in a given time period.

Random number An observation drawn from a uniform distribution.

Random number generator An algorithm that produces uniformly distributed random numbers between 0 and 1.

Random variable A quantity whose future outcomes are uncertain.

Random walk A time series in which the value of the series in one period is the value of the series in the previous period plus an unpredictable random error.

Range The difference between the maximum and minimum values in a dataset.

Rate of return The future financial benefit to making a current investment.

Ratio scales A measurement scale that has all the characteristics of interval measurement scales as well as a true zero point as the origin.

Ratio spread An option strategy in which a long position in a certain number of options is offset by a short position in a certain number of other options on the same underlying, resulting in a risk-free position.

Rational efficient markets formulation See "Market efficiency."

Rational expectation The most accurate forecast possible, a forecast that uses all the available information, including knowledge of the relevant eco-

nomic forces that influence the variable being forecasted.

Real assets Tangible assets and intangible assets used to carry on business (cf. financial assets).

Real Estate Traditionally, land and any structures permanently attached to the land.

Real exchange rate The exchange rate adjusted by the inflation differential between the two countries.

Real foreign currency risk The risk that real prices of consumption goods might not be identical in different countries. Also known as *real exchange rate risk*, or *purchasing power risk*.

Real gross domestic product (real GDP) The value of final goods and services produced in a given year when valued at constant prices.

Real income A household's income expressed as a quantity of goods that the household can afford to buy.

Real interest rate The nominal interest rate adjusted for inflation; the nominal interest rate minus the inflation rate.

Real options Options embedded in a firm's real assets that give managers valuable decision-making flexibility, such as the right to undertake, abandon, modify or postpone an investment project.

Real rate of interest The nominal rate of interest minus the anticipated rate of inflation.

Real risk-free interest rate The single-period interest rate for a completely risk-free security if no inflation were expected.

Real values Measurement of economic values after adjustments have been made for changes in the average of prices between years.

Real wage rate The quantity of goods and services that an hour's work can buy. It is equal to the money wage rate divided by the price level.

Realized capital gains Capital gains that result when an appreciated asset is sold; realized capital gains are taxable.

Rebalancing Realigning the proportions of assets in a portfolio as needed.

Recapture premium Provision for a return of investment, net of value appreciation.

Receivables Accounts receivable.

Receiver A bankruptcy practitioner appointed by secured creditors in the United Kingdom to oversee the repayment of debts.

Receiver swaption A swaption that allows the holder to enter into a swap as the fixed-rate receiver and floating-rate payer.

Recession There are two common definitions of recession. They are: (1) A business cycle phase in which real GDP decreases for at least two successive quarters. (2) A significant decline in activity spread across the economy, lasting for more than a few months, visible in industrial production, employment, real income, and wholesale-retail trade.

Reclassification adjustment An adjustment to reported operating cash flow that moves a cash flow item from one classification to another, such as from operating cash flow to investing cash flow or from financing cash flow to operating cash flow. An example would be the reclassification of a tax benefit from stock options from operating cash flow to financing cash flow. The goal of these reclassifications is to produce a more sustainable measure of operating cash flow.

Record date Date set by directors when making dividend payment. *Dividends* are sent to stockholders who are registered on the record date.

Recycling The reuse of raw materials derived from manufactured products.

Regime With reference to a time series, the underlying model generating the times series.

Registration Process of obtaining *SEC* approval for a public issue of securities.

Registration statement Required to be filed with the SEC to describe the issue of a new security.

Regression analysis In statistics, a technique for finding the line of best fit.

Regression coefficients The intercept and slope coefficient(s) of a regression.

Regression equation An equation that describes the average relatinship between a dependent variable and a set of explanatory variables.

Regular dividend *Dividend* that the company expects to maintain in the future.

Regulation Rules administrated by a government agency to influence economic activity by determining prices, product standards and types, and conditions under which new firms may enter an industry.

Regulatory risk The risk associated with the uncertainty of how derivative transactions will be regulated or with changes in regulations.

Reinvestment Profits (or depreciation reserves) used to purchase new capital equipment.

Rejection point (or critical value) A value against which a computed test statistic is compared to decide whether to reject or not reject the null hypothesis.

Relative dispersion The amount of dispersion relative to a reference value or benchmark.

Relative frequency With reference to an interval of grouped data, the number of observations in the interval divided by the total number of observations in the sample.

Relative price The ratio of the price of one good or service to the price of another good or service. A relative price is an opportunity cost.

Relative return A portfolio's return compared with its benchmark.

Relative strength (RSTR) indicators Valuation indicators that compare a stock's performance during a period either to its own past performance or to the performance of some group of stocks.

Relative valuation models A model that specifies an asset's value relative to the value of another asset.

Remainder The trust corpus existing at the termination of the life beneficiary's interest.

Rent seeking Any attempt to capture a consumer surplus, a producer surplus, or an economic profit.

Reorganization Agreements made by a company in bankruptcy under which a company's capital structure is altered and/or alternative arrangements are made for debt repayment; U.S. Chapter 11 bankruptcy. The company emerges from bankruptcy as a going concern.

Replacement cost Cost to replace a firm's assets. "Reproduction" cost.

Replacement value With reference to swaps, the market value of a swap.

Repo See *repurchase agreement.*

Reported operating cash flow Cash flow from operating activities computed in accordance with generally accepted accounting principles. Also see *operating cash flow.*

Repurchase agreement (RP, repo, buy-back) Purchase of Treasury securities from a securities dealer with an agreement that the dealer will repurchase them at a specified price.

Reputational risk The risk that a company will suffer an extended diminution in market value relative to other companies in the same industry due to a demonstrated lack of concern for environmental, social, and governance risk factors.

Required rate of return The minimum rate of return required by an investor to invest in an asset, given the asset's riskiness.

Reserves (1) Cash in a bank's vault plus the bank's deposits at Federal Reserve banks. (2) The fixed-income component of a portfolio, notably shorter-term highly liquid instruments.

Residual autocorrelations The sample autocorrelations of the residuals.

Residual claim Refers to the fact that shareholders are at the bottom of the list of claimants to assets of a corporation in the event of failure or bankruptcy.

Residual dividend approach A dividend payout policy under earnings in excess of the funds necessary to finance the equity portion of company's capital budget are paid out in dividends.

Residual income (or abnormal earnings) Earnings for a given time period, minus a deduction for common shareholders' opportunity cost in generating the earnings.

Residual income model (RIM) A model of stock valuation that views intrinsic value of stock as the sum of book value per share plus the present value of the stock's expected future residual income per share.

Residual loss Agency costs that are incurred despite adequate monitoring and bonding of management.

Residual risk The specific risk contained in a security, as distinct from the general market risk.

Residual Value (Private Equity) The remaining equity that a limited partner has in the fund. (The value of the investments within the fund.) Also can be referred to as *ending market value* or *net asset value.*

Residuals Parts of stock returns not explained by the explanatory variable (the market-index return). They measure the impact of firm-specific events during a particular period.

Resources Things used to produce other things to satisfy people's wants.

Restatement of the Law Third, Trusts A book of rules and principles promulgated by the American Law Institute, concerning the conduct of a trustee in the management of a trust. It serves as a guide for lawyers, trustees, and investment advisors.

Restructuring charge(s) Costs associated with restructuring activities, including the consolidation and/or relocation of operations or the disposition or abandonment of operations or productive assets. Such charges may be incurred in connection with a business combination, a change in an enterprise's strategic plan, or a managerial response to declines in demand, increasing costs, or other environmental factors.

Retained earnings Earnings that a corporation saves, or retains, for investment in other productive activities; earnings that are not distributed to stockholders.

Return on assets (ROA) A profitability ratio; earnings before interest and taxes dividend by total assets.

Return on equity (ROE) (1) An accounting ratio of net profits divided by equity. (2) An excellent definition is profit margin $\times$ turnover $\times$ leverage, where profit margin is sales $\div$ profits, turnover is sales $\div$ assets, and leverage is assets $\div$ equity. It is

extremely high in industries with high RD that is expensed rather than capitalized and added to equity, such as pharmaceuticals.

Return on invested capital (ROIC) The after-tax net operating profits as a percent of total assets or capital.

Return on investment (ROI) Generally, book income as a proportion of net book value.

Return on sales (ROS) See *profit margin.*

Revenue bond A bond that is serviced by the income generated from specific revenue-producing projects of the municipality such as toll roads or athletic stadiums.

Reverse stock split A reduction in the number of shares outstanding with a corresponding increase in share price, but no change to the company's underlying fundamentals.

Revolving credit Legally assured *line of credit* with a bank.

Reward-to-variability ratio Ratio of a portfolio's risk premium to its standard deviation.

Rho The sensitivity of the option price to the risk-free rate.

Risk A situation in which more than one outcome might occur and the probability of each possible outcome can be estimated.

Risk aversion Describes the fact that investors want to minimize risk for the same level of expected return. To take more risk, they require compensation by a risk premium.

Risk budgeting The establishment of risk objectives for individuals, groups, or divisions of an organization that takes into account the allocation of an acceptable level of risk.

Risk-free asset An asset with a certain rate of return; often taken to be short-term T-bills.

Risk-free rate The interest rate that can be earned with certainty.

Risk governance The setting of overall policies and standards in risk management

Risk management The process of identifying the level of risk an entity wants, measuring the level of risk the entity currently has, taking actions that bring the actual level of risk to the desired level of risk, and monitoring the new actual level of risk so that it continues to be aligned with the desired level of risk.

Risk premium The expected return on an investment minus the risk-free rate.

Risk-neutral See *risk-averse.*

Risk-neutral probabilities Weights that are used to compute a binomial option price. They are the probabilities that would apply if a risk-neutral investor valued an option.

Risk-neutral valuation   The process by which options and other derivatives are priced by treating investors as though they were risk neutral.

Risky asset   An asset with uncertain future returns.

Rival   A good or service or a resource is rival if its use by one person decreases the quantity available for someone else.

Robust   The quality of being relatively unaffected by a violation of assumptions.

Robust standard errors   Standard errors of the estimated parameters of a regression that correct for the presence of heteroskedasticity in the regression's error term.

Root mean squared error (RMSE)   The square root of the average squared forecast error; used to compare the out-of-sample forecasting performance of forecasting models.

Roy's safety first criterion   A criterion asserting that the optimal portfolio is the one that minimizes the probability that portfolio return falls below a threshold level.

Rule 144a   *SEC* rule allowing *qualified institutional buyers* to buy and trade unregistered securities.

Rule of 72   The principle that the approximate number of years necessary for an investment to double is 72 divided by the stated interest rate.

Russell 1000 Index   The 1000 largest companies in the Russell 3000 index.

Russell 2000 Index   The 2000 smallest companies in the Russell 3000 index.

Russell 3000 Index   The 3000 largest U.S. companies, capital-weighted, which represent about 98 percent of the investible equity market.

Safe harbor   Practices that satisfy such requirements as the Prudent Investor Rule.

Safety-first rules   Rules for portfolio selection that focus on the risk that portfolio value will fall below some minimum acceptable level over some time horizon.

Sales risk   Uncertainty with respect to the quantity of goods and services that a company is able to sell and the price it is able to achieve.

Salvage value   Scrap value of plant and equipment.

Sample   A subset of a population.

Sample excess kurtosis   A sample measure of the degree of a distribution's peakedness in excess of the normal distribution's peakedness.

Sample kurtosis   A sample measure of the degree of a distribution's peakedness.

Sample mean   The sum of the sample observations, divided by the sample size.

Sample selection bias   Bias introduced by systematically excluding some members of the population according to a particular attribute—for example, the bias introduced when data availability leads to certain observations being excluded from the analysis.

Sample skewness   A sample measure of degree of asymmetry of a distribution.

Sample standard deviation   The positive square root of the sample variance.

Sample statistic or statistic   A quantity computed from or used to describe a sample.

Sample variance   A sample measure of the degree of dispersion of a distribution, calculated by dividing the sum of the squared deviations from the sample mean by the sample size (n) minus 1.

Sampling   The process of obtaining a sample.

Sampling distribution   The distribution of all distinct possible values that a statistic can assume when computed from samples of the same size randomly drawn from the same population.

Sampling error   The difference between the observed value of a statistic and the quantity it is intended to estimate.

Sandwich spread   An option strategy that is equivalent to a short butterfly spread.

Sarbanes-Oxley Act   An act of the U.S. Congress signed into law on 30 July 2002 that tightened the oversight of firms that audit public companies, added criminal penalties for earnings management activities, and took steps generally to improve company internal controls and corporate governance.

Saving   The act of not consuming all of one's current income. Whatever is not consumed out of spendable income is, by definition, saved. Saving is an action measured over time (a flow), whereas savings are a stock, an accumulation resulting from the act of saving in the past.

Scaled earnings surprise   Unexpected earnings divided by the standard deviation of analysts' earnings forecasts.

Scalper   A trader who offers to buy or sell futures contracts, holding the position for only a brief period of time. Scalpers attempt to profit by buying at the bid price and selling at the higher ask price.

Scatter plot or scatter diagram   A two-dimensional plot of pairs of observations on two data series.

Scenario analysis   A risk management technique involving the examination of the performance of a portfolio under specified situations. Closely related to *stress testing*.

Screening   The application of a set of criteria to reduce an investment universe to a smaller set of investments.

Seasoned issue   Issue of a security for which there is an existing market (cf. *unseasoned issue*).

Seats   Memberships in a derivatives exchange.

SEC Securities and Exchange Commission.

Secondary issue (1) Procedure for selling blocks of *seasoned issues* of stock; (2) more generally, sale of already issued stock.

Secondary market The market in which outstanding securities are bought and sold by owners other than the issuers. Purpose is to provide liquidity for investors.

Sector neutral Said of a portfolio for which economic sectors are represented in the same proportions as in the benchmark, using market-value weights.

Sector rotation An investment strategy which entails shifting the portfolio into industry sectors that are forecast to outperform others based on macroeconomic forecasts.

Sector rotation strategy A type of top-down investing approach that involves emphasizing different economic sectors based on considerations such as macroeconomic forecasts.

Securities Exchange Act of 1934 The federal law that established the Securities and Exchange Commission. It also added further regulations for securities markets. The law has been amended several times since its initial passage. One of the amendments that is relevant to mergers is the Williams Act of 1968.

Securities Stocks and bonds.

Securities offering A merger or acquisition in which target shareholders are to receive shares of the acquirer's common stock as compensation.

Securitization Substitution of tradable securities for privately negotiated instruments.

Security analysis Determining correct value of a security in the marketplace.

Security market line (SML) The graph of the capital asset pricing model.

Self-interest The choices that you think are the best for you.

Sell-side analysts Analysts who work at brokerages.

Semideviation The positive square root of semivariance (sometimes called semistandard deviation).

Semilogarithmic Describes a scale constructed so that equal intervals on the vertical scale represent equal rates of change, and equal intervals on the horizontal scale represent equal amounts of change.

Semivariance The average squared deviation below the mean.

Senior debt Debt that, in the event of bankruptcy, must be repaid before *subordinated debt* receives any payment.

Sensitivity analysis Analysis of the effect on project profitability of possible changes in sales, costs, and so on.

Serially correlated With reference to regression errors, errors that are correlated across observations.

Services Mental or physical labor or help purchased by consumers. Examples are the assistance of physicians, lawyers, dentists, repair personnel, housecleaners, educators, retailers, and wholesalers; things purchased or used by consumers that do not have physical characteristics.

Settlement date or payment date With reference to swaps, the date on which the parties to a swap make payments.

Settlement period The time between settlement dates.

Settlement price The official price, designated by the clearinghouse, from which daily gains and losses will be determined and marked to market.

Settlement risk When settling a contract, the risk that one party could be in the process of paying the counterparty while the counterparty is declaring bankruptcy.

Settlor The creator of an inter vivos trust; also same as *grantor, trustor,* or *creator.*

Share of stock A legal claim to a share of a corporation's future profits; if it is common stock, it incorporates certain voting rights regarding major policy decisions of the corporation; if it is preferred stock, its owners are accorded preferential treatment in the payment of dividends.

Share repurchase A transaction in which a company buys back its own shares. Unlike stock dividends and stock splits, share repurchases use corporate cash.

Shareholders' equity Total assets minus total liabilities.

Share-the-gains, share-the-pains theory A theory of regulatory behavior in which the regulators must take account of the demands of three groups: legislators, who established and who oversee the regulatory agency; members of the regulated industry; and consumers of the regulated industry's products or services.

Shark repellents A pre-offer takeover defense mechanism involving the corporate charter (e.g., staggered boards of directors and supermajority provisions).

Sharpe ratio or Sharpe measure The average return in excess of the risk-free rate divided by the standard deviation of return; a measure of the average excess return earned per unit of standard deviation of return.

Short The seller of a derivative contract. Also refers to the position of being short a derivative.

Short interest rate A one-period interest rate.

Short position   The seller of a commodity or security or, for a forward contract, the counterparty who will be the eventual seller of the underlying asset.

Short run   The short run in microeconomics has two meanings. (1) For the firm, it is the period of time in which the quantity of at least one input is fixed and the quantities of the other inputs can be varied. The fixed input is usually capital—that is, the firm has a given plant size. (2) For the industry, the short run is the period of time in which each firm has a given plant size and the number of firms in the industry is fixed.

Short sale   The sale of shares not owned by the investor but borrowed through a broker and later repurchased to replace the loan. Profit is earned if the initial sale is at a higher price than the repurchase price.

Shortage   A situation in which quantity demanded is greater than quantity supplied at a price below the market clearing price.

Shortfall risk   The risk that portfolio value will fall below some minimum acceptable level over some time horizon.

Should   Encouraged (recommended) to follow the recommendation of the GIPS standards but not required.

Signal   (1) Action that demonstrates an individual's unobservable characteristics (because it would be unduly costly for someone without those characteristics to take the action). (2) An action taken by an informed person (or firm) to send a message to uninformed people or an action taken outside a market that conveys information that can be used by that market.

Simple interest   The interest earned each period on the original investment; interest calculated on the principal only.

Simple random sample   A subset of a larger population created in such a way that each element of the population has an equal probability of being selected to the subset.

Simulation   Monte Carlo simulation.

Simulation trial   A complete pass through the steps of a simulation.

Single-factor model   A model of security returns that acknowledges only one common factor. See *factor model*.

Single-payment loan   A loan in which the borrower receives a sum of money at the start and pays back the entire amount with interest in a single payment at maturity.

Sinking fund   Bond provision that requires the issuer to redeem some or all of the bond systematically over the term of the bond rather than in full at maturity.

Sinking fund factor   Amount that must be set aside each period to have $1 at some future point in time.

Skewed   Not symmetrical.

Skewness   A quantitative measure of skew (lack of symmetry); a synonym of skew.

Skill   One of the three components of the standard of prudence governing trustees; familiarity with business matters.

Slope   The change in the value of the variable measured on the y-axis divided by the change in the value of the variable measured on the x-axis.

Soft dollars   The value of research services that brokerage houses supply to investment managers "free of charge" in exchange for the investment managers' business.

Sole proprietorship   A business owned and operated by a single person.

Sovereign risk   The risk that a government may default on its debt.

Spearman rank correlation coefficient   A measure of correlation applied to ranked data.

Special purpose entity (SPE)   A non-operating entity created to carry out a specified purpose, such as leasing assets or securitizing receivables. Also known as a special purpose vehicle (SPV).

Specialist   A trader who makes a market in the shares of one or more firms and who maintains a "fair and orderly market" by dealing personally in the stock.

Specialization   The division of productive activities among persons and regions so that no one individual or one area is totally self-sufficient. An individual may specialize, for example, in law or medicine. A nation may specialize in the production of coffee, computers, or cameras.

Speculation   Undertaking a risky investment with the objective of earning a greater profit than an investment in a risk-free alternative (a risk premium).

Speculative stock   A stock that appears to be highly overpriced compared to its intrinsic valuation.

Spin-off   A form of restructuring in which a corporation separates off and separately capitalizes a component business, which is then transferred to the corporation's common stockholders; shareholders end up owning stock in two different companies where there used to be one.

Split   When a stock reaches a high price, the management of the company will split it two for one, three for two, or whatever, to create a lower price per share and thus facilitate trading. The dividend may be raised at the same time.

In a "reverse split," a low-priced stock, often of a failing company, is consolidated to bring the price per share up to a reasonable level. On the Canadian exchanges such stocks are thereafter called "Consolidated Gold Bug" (or whatever).

Split-off   A form of restructuring in which shareholders of the parent company are given shares in a newly created entity in exchange for their shares of the parent company.

Split-rate   In reference to corporate taxes, a split-rate system taxes earnings to be distributed as dividends at a different rate than earnings to be retained. Corporate profits distributed as dividends are taxed at a lower rate than those retained in the business.

Spot exchange rate   Exchange rate on currency for immediate delivery (cf. *forward exchange rate*).

Spot price   Price of asset for immediate delivery (in contrast to forward or futures price).

Spot rate   The required yield for a cash flow to be received at some specific date in the future-for example, the spot rate for a flow to be received in one year, for a cash flow in two years, and so on.

Spread   With reference to options strategies, a strategy involving the purchase of one option and sale of another option that is identical to the first in all respects except either exercise price or expiration.

Spreadsheet modeling   As used in this book, the use of a spreadsheet in executing a dividend discount model valuation, or other present value model valuation.

Spurious correlation   A correlation that misleadingly points towards associations between variables.

Squeeze   The possibility that enough long positions hold their contracts to maturity that supplies of the commodity are not adequate to cover all contracts. A *short squeeze* describes the reverse: short positions threaten to deliver an expensive-to-store commodity.

Staggered board   Also called a *classified board*. This is an antitakeover measure in which the election of directors is split in separate periods so that only a percentage of the total number of directors come up for election in a given year. It is designed to make taking control of the board of directors more difficult.

Stakeholder   Any entity that is affected by the actions of a company, which may include shareholders, management, workers, communities, consumers, and so on.

Standard deviation   The positive square root of the variance; a measure of dispersion in the same units as the original data.

Standard error   In statistics, a measure of the possible error in an estimate.

Standard normal distribution (or unit normal distribution)   The normal density with mean (μ) equal to 0 and standard deviation (σ) equal to 1.

Standardized beta   With reference to fundamental factor models, the value of the attribute for an asset minus the average value of the attribute across all stocks, divided by the standard deviation of the attribute across all stocks.

Standardized unexpected earnings (SUE)   Unexpected earnings per share divided by the standard deviation of unexpected earnings per share over a specified prior time period.

Standardizing   A transformation that involves subtracting the mean and dividing the result by the standard deviation.

Standstill agreement   An agreement that a potential hostile bidder enters into with the target corporation whereby the bidder agrees, in exchange for some consideration, not to purchase more than an agreed-upon number of shares.

Start-up stage   The opening period in a company's life cycle during which operating losses often are reported and operating cash flow is consumed.

Stated annual interest rate or quoted interest rate   A quoted interest rate that does not account for compounding within the year.

Statement of cash flows   A financial statement showing a firm's cash receipts and cash payments during a specified period.

Static trade-off theory of capital structure   A theory pertaining to a company's optimal capital structure; the optimal level of debt is found at the point where additional debt would cause the costs of financial distress to increase by a greater amount than the benefit of the additional tax shield.

Statistic   A quantity computed from or used to describe a sample of data.

Statistical factor models   A multifactor model in which statistical methods are applied to a set of historical returns to determine portfolios that best explain either historical return covariances or variances.

Statistical inference   Making forecasts, estimates, or judgments about a larger group from a smaller group actually observed; using a sample statistic to infer the value of an unknown population parameter.

Statistically significant   A result indicating that the null hypothesis can be rejected; with reference to an estimated regression coefficient, frequently understood to mean a result indicating that the corresponding population regression coefficient is different from 0.

Statistics The science of describing, analyzing, and drawing conclusions from data; also, a collection of numerical data.

Statutory merger A merger in which one company ceases to exist as an identifiable entity and all its assets and liabilities become part of a purchasing company.

Stock The quantity of something, measured at a given point in time—for example, an inventory of goods or a bank account. Stocks are defined independently of time, although they are assessed at a point in time.

Stock dividend *Dividend* in the form of stock rather than cash.

Stock exchanges Secondary markets where already-issued securities are bought and sold by members.

Stock option A contract that gives its holder the right to buy (call option) or sell (put option) an interest in stock at a specified price through a specified date.

Stock purchase An acquisition in which the acquirer gives the target company's shareholders some combination of cash and securities in exchange for shares of the target company's stock.

Stock selection An active portfolio management technique that focuses on advantageous selection of particular stocks rather than on broad asset allocation choices.

Stock split Issue by a corporation of a given number of shares in exchange for the current number of shares held by stockholders. Splits may go in either direction, either increasing or decreasing the number of shares outstanding. A *reverse split* decreases the number outstanding.

Storage costs or carrying costs The costs of holding an asset, generally a function of the physical characteristics of the underlying asset.

Straddle An option strategy involving the purchase of a put and a call with the same exercise price. A straddle is based on the expectation of high volatility of the underlying.

Straight-line depreciation An equal dollar amount of *depreciation* in each period.

Strangle A variation of a straddle in which the put and call have different exercise prices.

Strap An option strategy involving the purchase of two calls and one put.

Strategic alliance A more flexible alternative to a joint venture whereby certain companies agree to pursue certain common activities and interests.

Strategic asset allocation The allocation to the major investment asset classes that is determined to be appropriate, given the investor's long-run investment objectives and constraints.

Strategy Any rule that is used to make a choice, such as "Always pick heads."

Stratified random sampling A procedure by which a population is divided into subpopulations (strata) based on one or more classification criteria. Simple random samples are then drawn from each stratum in sizes proportional to the relative size of each stratum in the population. These samples are then pooled.

Stress testing A risk management technique in which the risk manager examines the performance of the portfolio under market conditions involving high risk and usually high correlations across markets. Closely related to *scenario analysis*.

Strike price Price at which an option can be exercised (same as *exercise price*).

Strip An option strategy involving the purchase of two puts and one call.

Structural change Economic trend occurring when the economy is undergoing a major change in organization or in how it functions.

Structured note A debt security with an embedded derivative designed to create a payoff distribution that satisfies the needs of a specific investor clientele.

Style analysis An attempt to explain the variability in the observed returns to a security portfolio in terms of the movements in the returns to a series of benchmark portfolios designed to capture the essence of a particular security characteristic such as size, value, and growth.

Subjective probability A probability drawing on personal or subjective judgment.

Subordinated debt (junior debt) Debt over which *senior debt* takes priority. In the event of bankruptcy, subordinated debtholders receive payment only after senior debt is paid off in full.

Subsidiary merger A merger in which the company being purchased becomes a subsidiary of the purchaser.

Subsidy A payment that the government makes to a producer.

Subsistence real wage rate The minimum real wage rate needed to maintain life.

Substitute A good that can be used in place of another good.

Sunk cost A cost that has already been incurred and cannot be reversed.

Supermajority Provision in a company's charter requiring a majority of, say, 80 percent of shareholders to approve certain changes, such as a *merger*.

Supernormal growth   Above average or abnormally high growth rate in earnings per share.

Supplemental Information   Any performance-related information included as part of a compliant performance presentation that supplements or enhances the required and/or recommended disclosure and presentation provisions of the GIPS standards.

Supply   A schedule showing the relationship between price and quantity supplied for a specified period of time, other things being equal.

Supply curve   The graphical representation of the supply schedule; a line (curve) showing the supply schedule, which generally slopes upward (has a positive slope), other things being equal.

Supply shock   An event that influences production capacity and costs in the economy.

Supply-side economics   The notion that creating incentives for individuals and firms to increase productivity will cause the aggregate supply curve to shift outward.

Surplus   A situation in which quantity supplied is greater than quantity demanded at a price above the market clearing price.

Surprise   The actual value of a variable minus its predicted (or expected) value.

Survivorship bias   The bias resulting from a test design that fails to account for companies that have gone bankrupt, merged, or are otherwise no longer reported in a database.

Sustainable growth rate   The rate of dividend (and earnings) growth that can be sustained for a given level of return on equity, keeping the capital structure constant over time and without issuing additional common stock.

Swap   A contract whereby two parties agree to a periodic exchange of cash flows. In certain types of swaps, only the net difference between the amounts owed is exchanged on each payment date.

Swap spread   The difference between the fixed rate on an interest rate swap and the rate on a Treasury note with equivalent maturity; it reflects the general level of credit risk in the market.

Swaption   An option to enter into a swap.

Synergy   2 1 2 5 5; a combination of businesses in which the combined entity is more valuable than the sum of the parts.

Synthetic call   The combination of puts, the underlying, and risk-free bonds that replicates a call option.

Synthetic forward contract   The combination of the underlying, puts, calls, and risk-free bonds that replicates a forward contract.

Synthetic index fund   An index fund position created by combining risk-free bonds and futures on the desired index.

Synthetic put   The combination of calls, the underlying, and risk-free bonds that replicates a put option.

Systematic factors   Factors that affect the average returns of a large number of different assets.

Systematic risk   (1) The variability of returns that is due to macroeconomic factors that affect all risky assets. Because it affects all risky assets, it cannot be eliminated by diversification. (2) Market risk.

Systematic sampling   A procedure of selecting every kth member until reaching a sample of the desired size. The sample that results from this procedure should be approximately random.

Tactical asset allocation   Short-term adjustments to the long-term asset allocation to reflect views on the current relative attractiveness of asset classes.

Takeover   A merger; the term may be applied to any transaction, but is often used in reference to hostile transactions.

Takeover premium   The amount by which the takeover price for each share of stock must exceed the current stock price in order to entice shareholders to relinquish control of the company to an acquirer.

Tangible asset   Physical asset, such as plant, machinery, and offices (cf. *intangible assets*).

Tangible book value per share   Common shareholders' equity minus intangible assets from the balance sheet, divided by the number of shares outstanding.

Target capital structure   A company's chosen proportions of debt and equity.

Target company, or target   The company in a merger or acquisition that is being acquired.

Target payout ratio   A strategic corporate goal representing the long-term proportion of earnings that the company intends to distribute to shareholders as dividends.

Target semideviation   The positive square root of target semivariance.

Target semivariance   The average squared deviation below a target value.

Tariffs   Taxes on imported goods.

Tax adjustments   Restatements of nonrecurring items of operating cash flow to place them on an after-tax basis. For example, an outsized tax-deductible pension contribution of $50 million would be reduced to an after-tax amount of $30 million if a combined federal and state marginal tax rate of 40 percent is assumed: $50 million $\times$ (1 $-$ 40 percent) $=$ $30 million.

Tax bracket   A specified interval of income to which a specific and unique marginal tax rate is applied.

Tax credits A direct dollar-for-dollar reduction in taxes payable.

Tax risk The uncertainty associated with tax laws.

T-bill Treasury bill.

***t*-Distribution** A symmetrical distribution defined by a single parameter, degrees of freedom, that is largely used to make inferences concerning the mean of a normal distribution whose variance is unknown.

Technical indicators Momentum indicators based on price.

Technological change The development of new goods and better ways of producing goods and services.

Technology (1) Any method of producing a good or service. (2) Society's pool of applied knowledge concerning how goods and services can be produced.

TED spread Difference between *LIBOR* and U.S. *Treasury bill* rate.

Temporary difference A difference between the book and tax basis of both assets and liabilities. Alternatively, a temporary difference is a difference between book and tax return earnings that will reverse at some future point in time. Temporary differences give rise to deferred tax assets and liabilities.

Tender offer A public offer whereby the acquirer invites target shareholders to submit ("tender") their shares in return for the proposed payment.

Tenor The original time to maturity on a swap or loan.

Term bond A bond that has a single maturity date.

Term structure See *yield curve.*

Term structure of interest rates The relationship between term to maturity and yield to maturity for a sample of comparable bonds at a given time. Popularly known as the *yield curve.*

Term to maturity Specifies the date or the number of years before a bond matures or expires.

Terminal price multiple The price multiple for a stock assumed to hold at a stated future time.

Terminal share price The share price at a particular point in the future.

Terminal value of the stock (or continuing value of the stock) The analyst's estimate of a stock's value at a particular point in the future.

Termination date The date of the final payment on a swap; also, the swap's expiration date.

Terms of trade The quantity of goods and services that a country exports to pay for its imports of goods and services.

Test statistic A quantity, calculated based on a sample, whose value is the basis for deciding whether or not to reject the null hypothesis.

Testamentary trust A trust created by will.

The Fed The Federal Reserve System; the central bank of the United States.

Theory of contestable markets A hypothesis concerning pricing behavior that holds that even though there are only a few firms in an industry, they are forced to price their products more or less competitively because of the ease of entry by outsiders. The key aspect of a contestable market is relatively costless entry into and exit from the industry.

Theta The rate at which an option's time value decays.

Third parties Parties who are not directly involved in a given activity or transaction.

Thrift institutions Financial institutions that receive most of their funds from the savings of the public; they include mutual savings banks, savings and loan associations, and credit unions.

Tick Minimum amount the price of a security may change.

Time deposit A deposit in a financial institution that requires notice of intent to withdraw or must be left for an agreed period. Withdrawal of funds prior to the end of the agreed period may result in a penalty.

Time-period bias The possibility that when we use a time-series sample, our statistical conclusion may be sensitive to the starting and ending dates of the sample.

Time series A set of observations on a variable's outcomes in different time periods.

Time-series data Observations of a variable over time.

Time to expiration The time remaining in the life of a derivative, typically expressed in years.

Time value (of an option) The part of the value of an option that is due to its positive time to expiration. Not to be confused with present value or the time value of money.

Time value decay The loss in the value of an option resulting from movement of the option price toward its payoff value as the expiration day approaches.

Time value of money The principles governing equivalence relationships between cash flows with different dates.

Time value or speculative value The difference between the market price of the option and its intrinsic value, determined by the uncertainty of the underlying over the remaining life of the option.

Time-weighted rate of return The compound rate of growth of one unit of currency invested in a portfolio during a stated measurement period; a measure of investment performance that is not sensitive to the timing and amount of withdrawals or additions to the portfolio.

Tobin's q The ratio of the market value of debt and equity to the replacement cost of total assets.

Top-down With respect to investment approaches, the allocation of money first to categories such as asset classes, countries, or industry followed by the selection of individual securities within category.

Top-down forecasting approach A forecasting approach that involves moving from international and national macroeconomic forecasts to industry forecasts and then to individual company and asset forecasts.

Top-down investing An approach to investing that typically begins with macroeconomic forecasts.

Total cash flow The change in reported cash and cash equivalents during a reporting period.

Total cost The cost of all the productive resources that a firm uses; the sum of total fixed cost and total variable cost.

Total fixed cost The cost of the firm's fixed inputs.

Total income The yearly amount earned by the nation's resources (factors of production). Total income therefore includes wages, rent, interest payments, and profits that are received, respectively, by workers, landowners, capital owners, and entrepreneurs.

Total interest paid A term used on the cash flow analysis statement that consists of cash payments for interest on debt and capital leases, including capitalized interest.

Total probability rule A rule explaining the unconditional probability of an event in terms of probabilities of the event conditional on mutually exclusive and exhaustive scenarios.

Total return A return objective in which the investor wants to increase the portfolio value to meet a future need by both capital gains and current income reinvestment.

Total return swap A swap in which one party agrees to pay the total return on a security. Often used as a credit derivative, in which the underlying is a bond.

Total revenue The value of a firm's sales.

Total Value (Private Equity) Residual value of the portfolio plus distributed capital.

Tracking error A synonym for tracking risk; also, the condition in which the performance of a portfolio does not match the performance of an index that serves as the portfolio's benchmark.

Tracking portfolio A portfolio having factor sensitivities that are matched to those of a benchmark or other portfolio.

Tracking risk or tracking error or tracking error volatility or active risk The standard deviation of the differences between a portfolio's returns and its benchmark's returns; a synonym of active risk.

Trade balance The balance of a country's exports and imports; part of the current account.

Trade credit Accounts receivable.

Tradeoff An exchange—giving up one thing to get something else.

Trading turnover The percentage of outstanding shares traded during a period of time.

Traditional efficient markets formulation See *Market efficiency.*

Trailing dividend yield Current market price divided by the most recent quarterly per-share dividend multiplied by four.

Trailing P/E (or current P/E) A stock's current market price divided by the most recent four quarters of earnings per share.

Tranche Refers to a portion of an issue that is designed for a specific category of investors. French for "slice."

Transaction cost (1) The cost of executing a trade. Low costs characterize an operationally efficient market. (2) All of the costs associated with exchanging, including the informational costs of finding out price and quality, service record, and durability of a product, plus the cost of contracting and enforcing that contract. Can also be viewed as all costs associated with making, reaching, and enforcing agreements.

Transaction exposure The risk associated with a foreign exchange rate on a specific business transaction such as a purchase or sale.

Transfer payments Money payments made by governments to individuals for which in return no services or goods are concurrently rendered. Examples are welfare, Social Security, and unemployment insurance benefits.

Transition phase The stage of growth between the growth phase and the mature phase of a company in which earnings growth typically slows.

Translation exposure The risk associated with the conversion of foreign financial statements into domestic currency.

Treasurer Principal financial manager (cf. *controller*).

Treasury bill Short-term, highly liquid government securities issued at a discount from the face value and returning the face amount at maturity.

Treasury bond A U.S. government security with a maturity of more than 10 years that pays interest periodically.

Treasury note A U.S. government security with maturities of 1 to 10 years that pays interest periodically.

Treasury shares Shares that were issued and subsequently repurchased by the company.

Treasury stock A corporation's issued stock that has subsequently been repurchased by the company and not retired.

Tree diagram A diagram with branches emanating from nodes representing either mutually exclusive chance events or mutually exclusive decisions.

Trend A long-term pattern of movement in a particular direction.

Triangular arbitrage With respect to currencies, an arbitrage involving three currencies only.

Trimmed mean A mean computed after excluding a stated small percentage of the lowest and highest observations.

Trough The transition point between recession and recovery.

Trust agreement or trust indenture or trust instrument The document that creates an inter vivos trust, between a grantor and a trustee, for the benefit of the beneficiaries.

t-Test A hypothesis test using a statistic (t-statistic) that follows a t-distribution.

Turnover The ratio of the trading activity of a portfolio to the assets of the portfolio.

Two-sided hypothesis test (or two-tailed hypothesis test) A test in which the null hypothesis is rejected in favor of the alternative hypothesis if the evidence indicates that the population parameter is either smaller or larger than a hypothesized value.

Type I error The error of rejecting a true null hypothesis.

Type II error The error of not rejecting a false null hypothesis.

U.S. interest rate differential A gap equal to the U.S. interest rate minus the foreign interest rate.

U.S. Official reserves The government's holdings of foreign currency.

Unanticipated inflation Inflation at a rate that comes as a surprise, either higher or lower than the rate anticipated.

Unbiasedness Lack of bias. A desirable property of estimators, an unbiased estimator is one whose expected value (the mean of its sampling distribution) equals the parameter it is intended to estimate.

Uncertainty A situation in which more than one event might occur but it is not known which one.

Unconditional heteroskedasticity Heteroskedasticity of the error term that is not correlated with the values of the independent variable(s) in the regression.

Unconditional probability (or marginal probability) The probability of an event *not* conditioned on another event.

Uncovered interest rate parity The assertion that expected currency depreciation should offset the interest differential between two countries over the term of the interest rate.

Underlying With reference to derivatives, the asset on which a derivative contract is written.

Underlying earnings (or persistent, continuing, or core earnings) Earnings excluding nonrecurring components.

Underweighted A condition in which a portfolio, for whatever reason, includes less of a class of securities than the relative market value alone would justify.

Underwriter Firm that buys an issue of securities from a company and resells it to investors.

Unemployment The total number of adults (aged 16 years or older) who are willing and able to work and who are actively looking for work but have not found a job.

Unemployment rate The percentage of the people in the labor force who are unemployed.

Unexpected earnings (also earnings surprise) The difference between reported earnings per share and expected earnings per share.

Unit root A time series that is not covariance stationary is said to have a unit root.

Univariate distribution A distribution that specifies the probabilities for a single random variable.

Unlimited funds An unlimited funds environment assumes that the company can raise the funds it wants for all profitable projects simply by paying the required rate of return.

Unlimited liability A legal concept whereby the personal assets of the owner of a firm can be seized to pay off the firm's debts.

Unsystematic risk Risk that is unique to an asset, derived from its particular characteristics. It can be eliminated in a diversified portfolio.

Unwind The negotiated termination of a forward or futures position before contract maturity.

Valuation The process of determining the value of an asset or service on the basis of variables perceived to be related to future investment returns, or on the basis of comparisons with closely similar assets.

Valuation analysis An active bond portfolio management strategy designed to capitalize on expected price increases in temporarily undervalued issues.

Valuation process Part of the investment decision process in which you estimate the value of a security.

Value The amount for which one can sell something, or the amount one must pay to acquire something.

Value at risk (VAR) A money measure of the minimum value of losses expected during a specified time period at a given level of probability.

Value chain The set of transformations to move from raw material to product or service delivery.

Value stocks Stocks that appear to be undervalued for reasons besides earnings growth potential. These stocks are usually identified based on high dividend yields, low *P/E* ratios, or low price-to-book ratios.

Value-weighted index An index calculated as the total market value of the securities in the sample. Market value is equal to the number of shares or bonds outstanding times the market price of the security.

Variable costs Costs that fluctuate with the level of production and sales.

Variance The expected value (the probability-weighted average) of squared deviations from a random variable's expected value.

Variation margin Additional margin that must be deposited in an amount sufficient to bring the balance up to the initial margin requirement.

Vega The relationship between option price and volatility.

Vendor financing Amounts owed vendors for purchased goods or services, reported as accounts payable.

Venture capital Capital to finance a new firm.

Vertical merger A merger involving companies at different positions of the same production chain; for example, a supplier or a distributor.

Visibility The extent to which a company's operations are predictable with substantial confidence.

Volatility As used in option pricing, the standard deviation of the continuously compounded returns on the underlying asset.

Volatility risk The risk in the value of options portfolios due to unpredictable changes in the volatility of the underlying asset.

Voluntary export restraint An agreement between two governments in which the government of the exporting country agrees to restrain the volume of its own exports.

Wages The income that labor earns.

Warrant An instrument that allows the holder to purchase a specified number of shares of the firm's common stock from the firm at a specified price for a given period of time.

Wealth The stock of assets owned by a person, household, firm, or nation. For a household, wealth can consist of a house, cars, personal belongings, stocks, bonds, bank accounts, and cash.

Weighted-average cost of capital (WACC) A weighted average of the after-tax required rates of return on a company's common stock, preferred stock, and long-term debt, where the weights are the fraction of each source of financing in the company's target capital structure.

Weighted mean An average in which each observation is weighted by an index of its relative importance.

Well-diversified portfolio A portfolio spread out over many securities in such a way that the weight in any security is close to zero.

White-corrected standard errors A synonym for robust standard errors.

White knight A third party that is sought out by the target company's board to purchase the target in lieu of a hostile bidder.

White squire A third party that is sought out by the target company's board to purchase a substantial minority stake in the target-enough to block a hostile takeover without selling the entire company.

Wholesale Price Index (WPI) A price index defined on a basket of goods produced.

Window dressing Toward the end of a reporting period, particularly at year end, mutual funds and banks will sometimes round up their holdings to even thousands, or sell positions that have gone down and thus constitute an eyesore.

Winner's curse The tendency for the winner in certain competitive bidding situations to overpay, whether because of overestimation of intrinsic value, emotion, or information asymmetries.

Winsorized mean A mean computed after assigning a stated percent of the lowest values equal to one specified low value, and a stated percent of the highest values equal to one specified high value.

Withholding tax A tax levied by the country of source on income paid.

Working capital Current assets minus current liabilities.

Working capital management The management of a company's short-term assets (such as inventory) and short-term liabilities (such as money owed to suppliers).

Workout period Realignment period of a temporary misaligned yield relationship.

World Bank A supranational organization of several institutions designed to assist developing countries. The International Bank for Reconstruction and Development (IBRD) and the International Finance Corporation (IFC) are the more important members of the World Bank group.

World Trade Organization An international organization that places greater obligations on its member countries to observe the GATT rules.

Write-down A reduction in the value of an asset as stated in the balance sheet.

Writer of an option A term used for the person or institution selling an option and therefore granting the right to exercise it to the buyer of the option.

x axis The horizontal axis in a graph.

y axis The vertical axis in a graph.

Yield The promised rate of return on an investment under certain assumptions.

Yield beta A measure of the sensitivity of a bond's yield to a general measure of bond yields in the market that is used to refine the hedge ratio.

Yield curve A curve showing the relationship between yield (interest rate) and maturity for a set of similar securities. For example, the yield curve can be drawn for U.S. Treasuries or for LIBOR. Typically, different yield curves are drawn for zero-coupon bonds (zero-coupon yield curve) and for coupon bonds quoted at par (par yield curve).

Yield spread The difference between the yield on a bond and the yield on a default-free security, usually a government note, of the same maturity. The yield spread is primarily determined by the market's perception of the credit risk on the bond.

Yield to maturity The total yield on a bond obtained by equating the bond's current market value to the discounted cash flows promised by the bond. Also called *actuarial yield*.

Zero-beta portfolio The minimum-variance portfolio uncorrelated with a chosen efficient portfolio.

Zero-cost collar A transaction in which a position in the underlying is protected by buying a put and selling a call with the premium from the sale of the call offsetting the premium from the purchase of the put. It can also be used to protect a floating-rate borrower against interest rate increases with the premium on a long cap offsetting the premium on a short floor.

Zero-coupon bond A bond that pays its par value at maturity but no periodic interest payments. Its yield is determined by the difference between its par value and its discounted purchase price. Also called *original issue discount (OID)*.

Z-score Measure of the likelihood of bankruptcy.

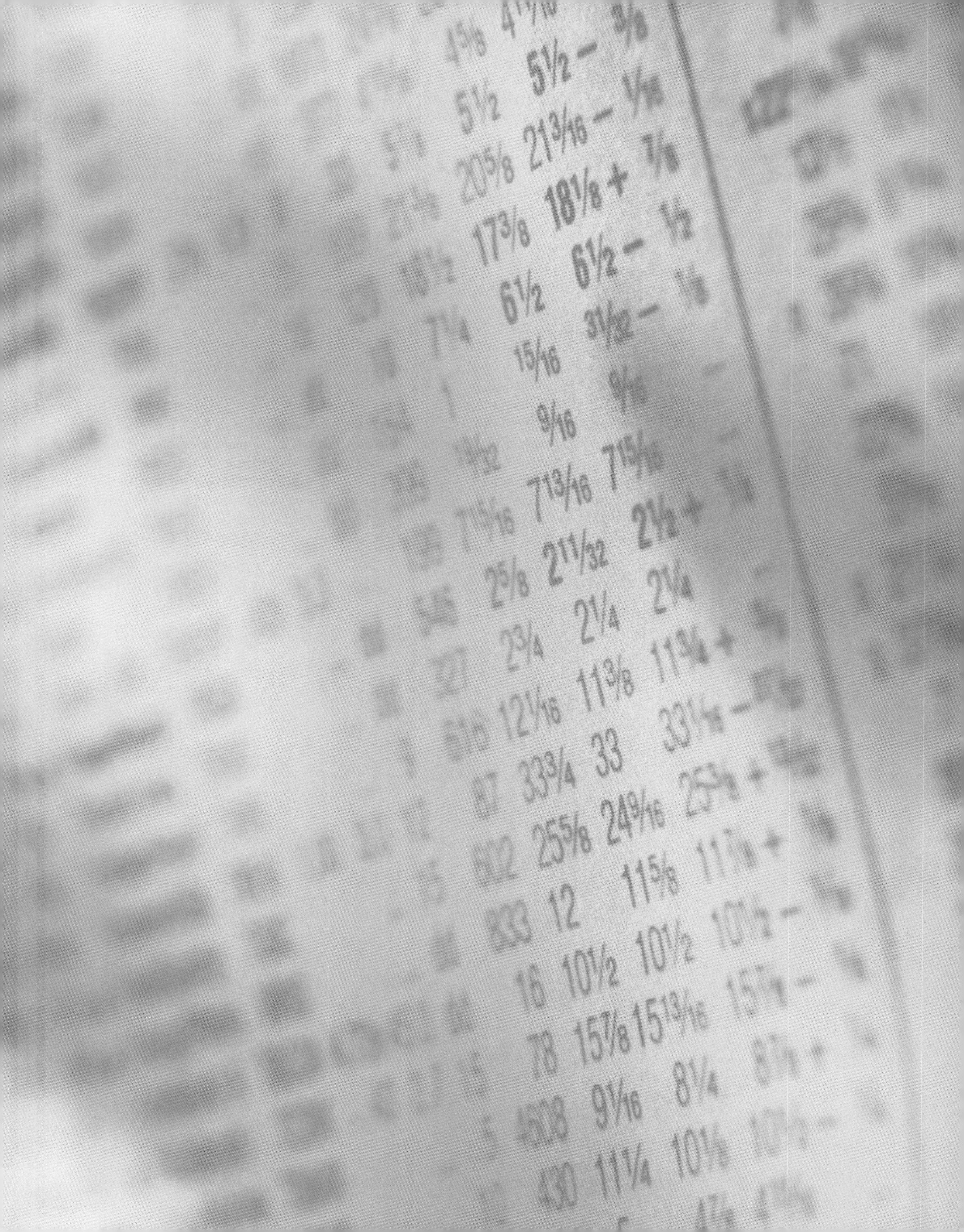

Page numbers followed by n refer to footnotes.

cap rates, V6: 306
caps: available funds caps, V5: 249
capture hypothesis, V1: 458
care, duty of. *See* loyalty, prudence, and care (duty of)
Carleton, Willard, V5: 76
carrying costs: futures contract pricing, V6: 85–86
carrying value
  equity method, V2: 27
  security classification/reporting, V2: 13–15
case studies
  Preston Partners, V1: 165–169
  Soft Dollar Standards (CFA Institute), V1: 133–140
  Super Selection, V1: 171–176
cash and carry
  defined, V6: 288
  futures contracts, V6: 96, 96n36
cash and marketable securities: balance sheet analysis for, V2: 259
cash collateralized debt obligations (CDO), V5: 262–267
cash dividends. *See also* dividends
  share repurchase, V3: 150, 171–172
  stock dividends, V3: 147–148
cash flow. *See also* tranches
  absolute valuation models, V4: 27
  accounting methods, V4: 458
  analysis of, V2: 249, 280–284; V5: 14
  auto loan-backed securities, V5: 255, 256
  average life, V5: 203–204
  Black-Scholes-Merton model, V6: 187
  capacity to pay analysis, V5: 14–17
  capital budgeting
    accelerated depreciation, V3: 34–37
    as basic principle, V3: 10–12
    corporate restructuring, V3: 291
    defined, V3: 10
    discounted payback period, V3: 17
    equation format for organizing, V3: 32–34
    inflation effects on analysis, V3: 41
    NPV/IRR ranking conflicts, V3: 21–25
    project analysis, V3: 61
    replacement projects, V3: 37–39
    spreadsheet modeling, V3: 39–41
    straight-line depreciation, V3: 34–37
    table format by type, V3: 30
    table format by year, V3: 30–31
  CDOs, V5: 263, 266
  CMOs, V5: 178–182
  collateral securitization, V5: 241
  component analysis, V2: 281–283

consolidated vs. equity method, V2: 35
credit card receivable-backed securities, V5: 260
DDM, V4: 280–285
defined, V4: 282
determination of, V4: 459–463
disclosures, V2: 249
duration, V5: 302–304
floating-rate bonds, V6: 304
foreign currency exchange, V2: 183–186
free cash flow (FCF), V2: 283–284
growth rates, V4: 148–153
interest rates, V5: 285–293
international comparisons, V2: 284
measures of, V5: 15–16, 16n16
Monte Carlo simulation, V5: 285–289
monthly prepayment rate, V5: 169–173
mortgage passthrough securities, V5: 163–164
myths about, V2: 216
from operations, V5: 15–16
in PV models, V4: 277–278
ratios, V5: 16–17
reporting quality, V2: 225
segment data on, V2: 53
SLABS, V5: 258
stress and payment structure, V5: 32
from swaptions, V6: 260–262
tests/requirements: covenant analysis, V5: 18
timing, V4: 586
uncertainty in residential mortgage loans, V5: 162
underlying
  asset in option prices, V6: 166–167
  futures contracts pricing, V6: 86–87
cash flow from operations (CFO), V1: 225–226
  analysis of, V2: 281, 284
  analyst adjustments to, V4: 375
  defined, V4: 282
  free cash flows, V4: 349, 357–359, 364–368
  price to cash flow (P/CF), V4: 459–460
cash flow multiple, V4: 469
cash flow return on investment (CFROI), V4: 539, 555–557
cash flow statements
  foreign currency disclosure, V2: 192
  manipulation of, V2: 215–222
  operating cash flows, V2: 216–217
  payables: stretching and financing, V2: 216–218

receivables: securitization, V2: 218–219
stock buybacks to offset dilution, V2: 221–222
stock option tax benefits, V2: 219–221
cash flow yield
  analysis of, V5: 282–285
  defined, V5: 282
  MBS/ABS valuation, V5: 282–284
  measurement limitations, V5: 283–284
  nominal spreads, V5: 284
cash from financing (CFF), V2: 281
cash market instruments in interest rate swap package, V6: 303–305
cash markets, V4: 47–48
cash offers, V3: 259
cash reserve funds, V5: 243
cash settlement
  contracts, V6: 282
  as controversial, V6: 67n13
  credit events, V6: 314
  forward contracts, V6: 6
  futures contracts, V6: 66–68
  stock index future contracts, V6: 107n47
catalyst, V4: 25n18
Caterpillar Tractor Company, Inc., V4: 176, 179
causation: economic measures, V1: 217
cause and effect: growth theories, V1: 437
CBOT. *See* Chicago Board of Trade (CBOT)
CD. *See* certificate of deposit (CD)
CDOs. *See* collateralized debt obligations (CDOs)
CDS. *See* credit default swaps (CDS); CRIF Decision Solutions (CDS)
ceiling on interest rates, V6: 305
Celler-Kefauver Act (1950), V3: 269
central limit theorem, V1: 234n27
Centre for Financial Market Integrity, V1: 10
CEO. *See* chief executive officer (CEO)
certificate of deposit (CD), V6: 284
Certified Financial Analyst Institute (CFA Institute). *See also* Chartered Financial Analyst® (CFA®)
  Code of Ethics, V1: 4–11, 20–21; V6: 510
  Corporate Governance of Listed Companies, The: A Manual for Investors, V3: 202–203
  goals of, V1: 6
  membership in, V1: 101–107
  ROS (*see* Research Objectivity Standards (CFA Institute))

foreign currency (FC)
asset pricing theory (APT),
V6: 437–438
debt ratings, V5: 37
exchange rates, V1: 525–527
local, currency exposure, V6: 452
risk of
efficient markets, V6: 434
ICAPM, V6: 445–446, 498, 506
risk premiums for
expected returns, V6: 450
ICAPM, V6: 442–446
speculation, V1: 475–479
translating
accounting basics, V2: 162–163
cumulative translation adjustment
(CTA), V2: 172–175
disclosure analysis, V2: 186–192
exchange rate gains and losses,
V2: 166
functional currency role,
V2: 164n3, 165–166
reporting regulations, V2: 164n2
SFAS No. 52, V2: 163–170
foreign entities: IASC on, V2: 200–201
foreign exchange (FX). *See also*
currency exchange, rates of
arbitrage, V1: 528–536
asset market approach, V6: 438–439
asset turnover ratios, V2: 181–182
bid-ask quotes, V1: 526–536
cash flow, V2: 183–186
debt to equity ratio, V2: 181
defined, V1: 524; V6: 226n2
demand, V1: 508–510
exports and, V1: 509
Forex market quotations,
V1: 524–525
forward quotes in, V1: 536–542
GDP effect, V1: 605
imports and, V1: 512
interest rates (*see under* interest and
interest rates)
local currency (LC) and,
V2: 182–183
markets, V1: 507–508
rate-return correlations, V1: 220–222
rates, V1: 507, 528–536; V2: 163, 166
for mortgages, V5: 255n15–16
risk
capital mobility, V6: 459
disclosures, V2: 251
supply, V1: 510–513
swap, V6: 226n2
foreign exchange markets,
V1: 507–508
foreign influences: as external factor,
V4: 198, 202, 203
foreign setting. *See* international
setting

foreign shares
American depository receipts
(ADRs), V4: 71–75
exchange-traded funds (ETFs),
V4: 78–80
multiple listing, V4: 71–72
foreign tax credit, V4: 58
Forex markets, quotation conventions,
V1: 524–525
Form DEF 14A, V3: 204
Form 20-F, SEC, V4: 73, 123
Form 10-K, SEC, V4: 15n8, 123
forward discount, V1: 475–479
forward exchange rates, V1: 536–537
forward integration, V3: 249
forward-looking information: FASB
disclosure categories, V2: 242
forward market and contracts, V6: 5–6.
See also prices, forward contracts;
valuation, forward contracts
bonds, V6: 13–14
contract value, V6: 23
credit risk, V6: 7, 44–45
currency, V6: 17–18, 38–44
default risk, V6: 6–7
defined, V6: 5, 283–284
delivery, V6: 6
equity, V6: 26–31
equity forwards, V6: 9–13
dividend effects on, V6: 12–13
fixed-income, V6: 31–34
formulas for, V6: 30
futures contracts vs., V6: 283–284
global, structure of, V6: 8–9
individual stocks, V6: 11
interest rate, V6: 14–17
role of, V6: 45–46
settlement, V6: 6
stock exchange, V4: 47–48
on stock indices/portfolios,
V6: 11–12
swaps, V6: 239, 302–303
termination of, V6: 7–8
types of, V6: 9–18
forward premiums, V1: 536–542
forward price, V6: 19
forward price to earnings (P/E),
V4: 416
forward quotes
foreign exchange, V1: 536–537
interest rate parity (IRP),
V1: 538–542
forward rate agreements (FRAs)
defined, V6: 14, 303n8
descriptive notation, V6: 17
Eurodollar futures, V6: 74–75
formulas for, V6: 37
as interest rate forward contract,
V6: 14–17
interest rate swaps, V6: 299n8

off-market, V6: 22
pricing, V6: 34–38
swap as series of, V6: 246
top three dealers, V6: 10
valuation, V6: 34–38
forward rates
arbitrage-free value, V5: 96
defined, V6: 19
expectation theories, V5: 70–75
LIBOR curve, V5: 67
forward swaps, V6: 264
fourth quarter surprises: improper
accounting of, as red flag, V2: 232
France
consolidated reporting, V2: 46
exchange rate quotes, V1: 527–528
historical view: stock exchanges,
V4: 46–47
securities reporting in, V2: 16–17
stock market size, V4: 54
taxes, V4: 58
trading in, V6: 60n6
franchise: fair dealing standard, V1: 59
franchise factor (FF)
equity analysis, V4: 149–151
P/E, V4: 247–248
franchise value: equity analysis,
V4: 148–153
FRAs. *See* forward rate agreements
(FRAs)
fraud: hedge fund risks, V4: 613–615,
622–623
Freddie Mac. *See* Federal Home Loan
and Mortgage Corporation
(FHLMC, Freddie Mac)
Freddie Mac PC, V5: 164n1
free cash flow (FCF), V4: 348–349;
V5: 16n16
absolute valuation models, V4: 27
analysis of, V2: 283–284
credit analysis, V5: 16
in discounted cash flow analysis,
V3: 274–279
defined of, V4: 349–350
dividends/other earnings
components vs., V4: 375–380
forecasting, V4: 353–380
hypothesis of, and agency costs,
V3: 125
international application,
V4: 381–382
model variations, V4: 381–393
more-complicated capital structures,
V4: 378–380
present value (PV), V4: 350–352
as returns, V4: 282, 284
sales/sales growth, V4: 372–375
sensitivity analysis, V4: 382–384
single-stage FCFF/FCFE growth
models, V4: 352–353

G

GAAP. *See* Generally Accepted Accounting Principles (GAAP)
gains
    capital gains, V3: 157n4, 159
    foreign currency translation, V2: 163, 166
    holding gain/loss, V2: 160–162
    from international trade, V1: 475–483
    on investment income, V2: 14, 16
    MNC exchange rates, V2: 160–162
    quality of earnings indicators, V4: 20
    realized capital gains, V2: 272
    share-the-gains-share-the-pains theory, V1: 458–459
    timing of, V2: 19–20
game theory, V4: 215
gamma
    price sensitivity, V6: 167
    underlying, options, V6: 193–194
GAO. *See* General Accounting Office (GAO)
GARCH. *See* generalized autoregressive conditional heteroskedasticity (GARCH)
gasoline: normal market price of, V1: 466
Gateway, Inc., V4: 443, 464–465
GATT. *See* General Agreement on Tariffs and Trade (GATT)
GDRs. *See* Global Depository Receipts (GDRs)
GE Capital, V2: 217
General Accounting Office (GAO): disclosures, V2: 243–244
General Agreement on Tariffs and Trade (GATT), V1: 483
General Electric Co., V2: 217; V6: 231–233
    capital structure, V3: 149, 163
    corporate governance, V3: 216–228, 249
generalized autoregressive conditional heteroskedasticity (GARCH), V1: 398
generalized least squares, V1: 299
Generally Accepted Accounting Principles (GAAP)
    accounting standards, V4: 112
    American depository receipts (ADRs), V4: 73
    APB No. 18, V2: 24, 28–29
    balance sheet analysis, V2: 257, 258
    business combinations, V2: 65, 100
    on business combinations, V2: 65
    cash flow analysis, V2: 284
    company information, V4: 63
    consolidated reporting, V2: 46

disclosures, V2: 245
employee stock options, V4: 119–120
equity method, V2: 24
FCFF and statement of cash flow, V4: 358
geographic segment report, V2: 53
goodwill amortization, V2: 272
IAS GAAP, V4: 115–116
    balance sheets, V2: 268, 269
    cash flow analysis, V2: 284
    consolidated reporting, V2: 44
    goodwill amortization, V2: 272
    U.S. Accounting Standards, V2: 14–17, 16–17
intangible assets, V4: 522
international information, V4: 123
international valuation, V4: 473–474
M&A accounting, V2: 65
nonpension benefits, V2: 136–137
price to cash flow (P/CF), V4: 459–460
proportionate consolidation, V2: 43–44
reporting quality, V2: 224, 225
residual income model (RIM), V4: 516–518
on segment reporting, V2: 53
General Mills, V4: 313–314
General Motors, V2: 222; V3: 130; V4: 144–146, 182, 455–456, 500
general partner: FASB on control, V2: 32
general residual income model, V4: 512–513
generation of ideas: capital budgeting process, V3: 8
generic interest rate: swap curve, V5: 64
geographic segment reporting, V2: 48, 52–53
geography
    boundaries in relevant markets, V1: 467
    international trade patterns, V1: 475
geometric mean returns
    calculating, V4: 288n13
    ERP, V4: 288
Georgia State University, V3: 231
Germany
    consolidated reporting, V2: 46
    Lucky Strikes currency benchmark, V4: 99–100
    residential mortgage-backed securities (RMBS), V5: 232
    stock market size, V4: 54
    trading procedures, V4: 50
GGM. *See* Gordon growth model (GGM)
gifts: standard for, V1: 22

GIM. *See* gross income multiplier (GIM)
Ginnie Mae. *See* Government National Mortgage Association (GNMA, Ginnie Mae)
Ginnie Mae MBS, V5: 164n1
GIPS. *See* Global Investment Performance Standards (GIPS)
GlaxoSmithKline PLC, V3: 157
Global Depository Receipts (GDRs), V4: 73
global economics/economy. *See* international setting
Global Equity Indexes, V3: 164–165
global financial ratio analysis, V4: 143–148
global industry analysis. *See also* international setting
    country analysis, V4: 124–129
    equity concepts/techniques, V4: 124–141
    example, V4: 138–141
    return expectation elements, V4: 129–133
    risk elements, V4: 134–138
Global Industry Classification Standard (GICS), V4: 142
Global Investment Performance Standards (GIPS), V6: 500
globalization, V2: 160
global market line, V6: 450
global markets
    forward, V6: 8–9
    options, V6: 134–138
    swap structure, V6: 224–226
global warming. *See* climate change
GMAC-RFC, V5: 228
GMI. *See* Governance Metrics International (GMI)
GNI. *See* gross national income (GNI)
GNMA. *See* Government National Mortgage Association (GNMA, Ginnie Mae)
GNP. *See* gross national product (GNP)
going-concern value, V4: 26–27
golden parachutes, V3: 265
Goldman, David P., V4: 89
Goldman Sachs Group, Inc., V6: 8
    S&P 500 valuation study, V4: 253–269
    Super-Value portfolio, V4: 254–269
gold mining: commodity swaps, V6: 237
Golub, Bennett, V5: 306
goodness of fit, V1: 287–288
goodwill
    accounting for, V4: 522
    accounting standards, V4: 112, 118
    amortization, income statement adjustment, V2: 272

long-term equity anticipatory
    securities (LEAPS), V6: 135–137
long-term growth and GDP,
    V1: 426–429
long-term interest rate futures
    contracts, V6: 75–77, 101–106
long-term sustainable growth,
    V4: 124–125
long-term yield maturity, V5: 58, 58n1
look-ahead bias, V4: 421
loopholes, V2: 225
losses
    deferred taxes, V2: 30
    equity method, V2: 25n21, 30
    foreign currency translation,
        V2: 163, 166
    holding gain/loss, V2: 160–162
    on investment income, V2: 14, 16
    MNC exchange rates, V2: 160–162
    overcollateralization, V5: 243–244
    quality of earnings indicators, V4: 20
    realized: income statement
        adjustment, V2: 272
    residual loss of agency costs, V3: 125
    standard deviation and hedge
        funds, V4: 627–628
    writedown, V2: 25n21
lower bounds
    option prices, V6: 152–157, 165–166
    volatility, V6: 202
lower of cost or market (LOCOM)
    securities, V2: 11, 12–13
    U.S. Accounting Standards,
        V2: 16–17
loyalty, prudence, and care (duty of).
    See also prudence, duty of
    application, V1: 51–53
    compliance, V1: 50–51
    Standards of Professional Conduct,
        V1: 12, 48–53
    Uniform Prudent Investor Act
        (1994), V1: 190, 193
loyalty to employers
    application, V1: 71–74
    independent practice, V1: 70
    leaving an employer, V1: 70–71
    nature of employment, V1: 71
    Standards of Professional Conduct,
        V1: 13, 69–74
    whistleblowing, V1: 71
LTCM. *See* Long-Term Capital
    Management (LTCM)
LTV ratio. *See* loan-to-value (LTV)
    ratio
Lucas, Robert, V4: 90
Lucent Technologies, V2: 49–52
Lucky Strikes currency benchmark,
    V4: 99–100

M
MA. *See* moving average (MA)
M&A. *See* mergers and acquisitions
    (M&A)
macroeconomic factors, V6: 398
macroeconomics
    arbitrage pricing theory (APT),
        V4: 291
    capital structure, V3: 134
    economic forecasting, V4: 17
    factor models of, V6: 378, 381n54
    inflation as indicator, V3: 134
    international capital structure,
        V3: 132, 135
    multifactor models of
        current practice, V6: 390–395
        fundamental factor models vs.,
            V6: 389, 396–398
        for returns, V6: 379–382
    risk, V4: 156–157
MACRS. *See* modified accelerated cost
    recovery system (MACRS)
maintenance margins: requirements
    for, V6: 61, 62, 62n11, 283
maintenance tests, V5: 18
make-whole charge, V5: 208
Malthus, Thomas Robert, V1: 438
Malthusian theory, V1: 410
management
    FASB disclosure categories, V2: 242
    hedge fund performance,
        V4: 606–607
    investing styles, V4: 111
    quality, and corporation character,
        V5: 9, 19–26
    restrictions, CDOs, V5: 266–267
management buyouts (MBOs)
    defined, V4: 11n3
    equity valuation, V4: 11
management companies: priority of
    transactions, V1: 98
management discussion and analysis
    (MD&A), V2: 49, 53
management fees, V1: 53–54
managerialism, V3: 254
manager-shareholder conflicts,
    V3: 197–200
mandate, V6: 505
Mannesmann, V3: 248
manufactured housing-backed
    securities, V5: 252
many-asset cases: portfolio theory,
    V6: 346–353, 357–358
Marco Polo, V1: 473
margin accounts, V6: 60
marginal benefits, V2: 55
marginal cost pricing, V1: 454
marginal products, V4: 127

marginal returns, diminishing, in
    growth theory, V4: 127
marginal revenues (MR), V1: 454
margin deposits, V6: 73
margins
    defined, V6: 60
    futures contracts, V6: 60–66
    requirements for, V6: 61–62, 283
    as term, V6: 61
marked to market
    cost investment provision,
        V2: 75–76
    marking to market, V2: 21–23
    return, V2: 21–23
marketability discounts: valuation
    models, V4: 31
marketable securities
    intercorporate investments,
        V2: 17–24
    investment performance analysis,
        V2: 19–24
    operating vs. investment
        performance, V2: 17–18
    performance analysis, V2: 19–23
    security classification/reporting,
        V2: 18–19
    segregation of operating vs.
        investment performance,
        V2: 17–18, 24
    SFAS 115, V2: 18–19
market analysis, V6: 468
market-based valuation. *See* price
    multiples
market capitalization
    bid-ask spread, V1: 273
    price to earnings (P/E), V4: 435
market competition, V4: 135
market consensus: forward rates,
    V5: 74–75
market conventions: yield calculation,
    V5: 283
market conversion price,
    V5: 132–133
market-cycle factor, V4: 157
market development: European whole
    loan trading, V5: 224–225
market efficiency. *See also* efficient
    markets
    equity analysis, V4: 144–148
    intrinsic value, V4: 26
market equilibrium
    domestic CAPM, V6: 434–439
    exchange rates, V1: 513
market evolution: credit derivatives,
    V6: 314–319
market expectations
    equity valuation, V4: 11–12
    inference, V4: 12–13

market exposure: CAPM, V6: 436
market-extraction method,
    V4: 592–593
market failures, V4: 93–94
market feedback in natural
    monopolies, V1: 454
market growth: credit derivatives,
    V6: 316
market impact
    of execution costs, V4: 64–65
    of stock markets, V4: 46
market imperfections: cross-border
    M&A, V3: 255
market manipulation: Standards of
    Professional Conduct, V1: 12,
    45–48
market maturity, V4: 131
market method, accounting
    defined, V2: 12
    hybrid of cost method, V2: 13–14
    level of involvement, V2: 71–77
    securities, 12; V2: 11, 13
market models: estimates, mean-
    variance analysis, V6: 369–373
market multiple: comparables for
    valuation, V4: 434–435
market organization: historical
    differences, V4: 47–48
market participants: credit derivatives,
    V6: 316–317
market power
    M&A, V3: 252
    market manipulation prohibition
        Standard, V1: 45
market prices, V1: 607–608
    CDOs, V5: 267
    in equity valuation, V4: 11
market-related asset value: pension
    expenses, V2: 132
market risk
    asset pricing, V6: 436
    capital budgeting analysis,
        V3: 452–455
    CAPM, V6: 436
    price of, V6: 362
market risk analysis, V3: 52–55
market risk premium
    CAPM, V6: 436
    defined, V4: 286
    emerging markets, V4: 28
markets
    contestable, V1: 462
    economic growth preconditions,
        V1: 429–430
    size of, V4: 54–56
market segmentation expectations
    theory, V5: 67–68
market share test, V1: 466–467

market timing
    active portfolio management,
        V6: 470–474
    imperfect forecasting, V6: 473–474
    mean-variance analysis, V6: 472
    performance evaluation, V6: 500
    valuing as an option, V6: 472–483
market-timing factor, V4: 157
market timing risk, V6: 391
    cost of equity, V4: 291
market-to-book ratio, V1: 320n66
market to market: reporting, V2: 14
market valuation adjustment (MVA),
    V2: 22–23
market value added (MVA)
    capital budgeting, V3: 67
    residual income (RI), V4: 504
market value (MV). *See also* valuation
    CDOs, V5: 263
    collateral, V5: 236n1
    and cost method, V2: 10n3
    economic depreciation vs.,
        V3: 63n15
    estimating income property analysis,
        V4: 590–591
    fair dealing standard, V1: 55
    stock splits, V3: 148
Markowitz, Harry
    decision rule, V6: 364
    on market efficiency, V6: 425–429
    portfolio selection model, V6: 469
    portfolio theory, V6: 332
mark-to-market
    credit risk in swaps, V6: 266–267
    defined, V6: 45, 59
    forward contracts, V6: 284
    futures contracts, V6: 62, 63
    interest rate futures, V6: 283
Marlborough Stirling Mortgage
    Service Ltd., V5: 232
Marriott Corporation, V2: 218–219
MAS. *See* Monetary Authority of
    Singapore (MAS)
material adverse change clause, V5: 10
material nonpublic information
    application, V1: 42–45
    compliance, V1: 39–42
    mosaic theory, V1: 38–39
    Standards of Professional Conduct,
        V1: 12, 36–45
mature phase
    company life cycle, V4: 312, 440
    industry life cycle, V4: 130, 193–194,
        197
maturity
    Australia, V5: 254
    balloon, V5: 209
    collateral cash flows, V5: 241

liquidity preference expectations
    theory, V5: 67–68
pure expectations theory-based
    strategy, V5: 70
United Kingdom, V5: 253
weighted average maturity (WAM),
    V5: 163
yield curves, V5: 58–59, 76
zero-volatility spread, V5: 284
maximum drawdowns, V4: 626–627
maximum value of options, V6:
    151–152
MBIAC. *See* Municipal Bond Investors
    Assurance Corporation (MBIAC)
MBOs. *See* management buyouts
    (MBOs)
MBS. *See* mortgage-backed securities
    (MBS)
McColl, Hugh, Jr., V4: 91
*McKenzie Walker Investment
    Management, Inc. and Richard
    McKenzie, Jr.* case, V1: 177–179
McKinsey & Company, V5: 23
MDA. *See* multiple discriminant
    analysis (MDA)
MD&A. *See* management discussion
    and analysis (MD&A)
m-day T-bill, V6: 93n32
mean
    market model estimates: mean-
        variance analysis, V6: 368–369
    mean regression sum of squares,
        V1: 286
    portfolio valuation, V4: 260
    reversion: AR models, V1: 367
    S&P 500 monthly returns,
        V1: 388n33
mean return, V4: 288
means of payment: income statement
    adjustment, V2: 276
mean squared error (MSE), V1: 286,
    293
mean-variance analysis
    adding investment to existing
        portfolio, V6: 365–366
    adjusted beta, V6: 372–373
    asset allocation, V6: 366–367
    beta, V6: 369–373
    capital allocation line (CAL),
        V6: 353–361
    capital market line (CML),
        V6: 361–362
    CAPM, V6: 362–363
    defined, V6: 333
    diversification, V6: 349–353
    existing portfolio decisions,
        V6: 364–366
    historical beta, V6: 369–372

mixed use
    analysis of, V1: 132
    Soft Dollar Standards, V1: 125
MM propositions. *See* Modigliani and
    Miller (MM) propositions
Mobil, V3: 248
Mochiai, V4: 55
Model Act. *See* Uniform Prudent
    Investor Act (1994)
modeling risk, V5: 292–293
Model Prudent Man Investment
    Statute, V1: 185
model specification
    correct functional form in,
        V1: 309–310
    data transformation, V1: 312–315
    defined, V1: 308
    multiple linear regression analysis
        and models, V1: 308–309
    principles of, V1: 308–309
    time-series misspecification in,
        V1: 317–322
    variable omission in, V1: 310–312
    variable scaling in, V1: 316–318
modern portfolio theory (MPT)
    CAPM, V6: 434–435
    defined, V6: 494
modified accelerated cost recovery
    system (MACRS), V3: 35–37
modified duration, V5: 120
modified options:
        American/Bermuda/Atlantic,
        V6: 293
Modigliani, Franco, V3: 118–123
Modigliani and Miller (MM)
        propositions
    capital structure, V3: 118–123
    dividends, V3: 176
    dividend valuations, V3: 178–179
    Proposition II without taxes,
        V3: 119–120
    Proposition I without taxes,
        V3: 118–119
Molodovsky effect, V4: 418
momentum effect, V4: 156
momentum indicators, V4: 412
momentum valuation indicators,
    V4: 474–478
monetary assets
    SFAS 52, V2: 165n5
    temporal vs. all current methods
        accounting, V2: 165–167
Monetary Authority of Singapore
    (MAS), V3: 223–224
monetary exchange: economic growth
    preconditions, V1: 429–430
monetary policy
    currency exposure of bonds,
        V6: 457
    hedge funds, V4: 618

swap-based benchmarks, V4: 98
money demand model, V6: 457
money illusion, V6: 438
money managers, V6: 492–493
moneyness of options, V6: 133–134
money supply: inflation correlation,
    V1: 227
monitoring
    agency costs, V3: 125
    capital budgeting process, V3: 9
    costs of
        agency problem, V5: 20–21
        defined, V5: 20
    function in portfolio management,
        V4: 13
    portfolio management, V6: 499–500
monoline insurers, V5: 242
monopolies
    industry analysis, V4: 213
    natural monopolies, V1: 452–454
    power, and relevant market,
        V1: 466–467
    regulation, V1: 55, 453–454, 461
monopolist, V1: 452
monopolization, V1: 466
Monte Carlo simulation
    of capital investments, V3: 52–55
    cash flow, V5: 285–289
    defined, V5: 282
    FAS 123(R), V2: 148
    interest and interest rates,
        V5: 285–293
    mean-variance analysis, V6: 367
    mortgage-backed securities (MBS)
        valuation, V5: 285–300
    present value (PV), V5: 289–291
    risk analysis, V3: 48–52
    theoretical value determination,
        V5: 290
    vs. zero-volatility spread, V5: 306–307
monthly cash flow: prepayment rate,
    V5: 169–173
monthly payment rates (MPR): credit
    card receivable-backed securities,
    V5: 261
month-of-the-year effects and returns,
    V1: 289–291
Moody's Investors Service
    capacity to pay, V5: 9–10
    credit ratings, V5: 6
    debt ratings, V3: 129–130
    default risk ratings, V5: 8
    management quality, V5: 19
    option pricing theory, V5: 41
    sovereign bonds, V5: 37
J. P. Morgan. *See* JPMorgan
JP Morgan Chase. *See* JPMorgan Chase
    & Co.
Morgan Stanley, V6: 234
Morrison Knudsen, V2: 44

mortality rates: monthly prepayment,
    V5: 166–167, 166n2
mortgage-backed securities (MBS),
    V5: 158–159
    agency, V5: 158–159
    cash flow yield analysis, V5: 282–284
    collateralized mortgage obligations
        (CMOs), V5: 178–201
    commercial, V5: 206–209
    market efficiency, V4: 89–93
    Monte Carlo simulation,
        V5: 285–300
    mortgage passthrough securities,
        V5: 162–178
    nonagency residential, V5: 204–205
    option-adjusted spreads (OAS),
        V5: 285–300
    residential, V5: 159–162, 204–205
    valuation, V5: 281–306
    zero-volatility spread, V5: 284–285
mortgage indemnity guarantee (MIG),
    V5: 253
mortgage insurance, V5: 159
mortgage passthrough securities
    average life, V5: 173
    cash flow, V5: 163–164
    defined, V5: 162
    home equity loans (HELs), V5: 249
    interest rates, V5: 285–290
    mortgage-backed bond market
        sector, V5: 162–178
    prepayment rate measures,
        V5: 165–173
    trading and settlement procedures,
        V5: 164–165
    types of, V5: 164
    values, theoretical, V5: 290
mortgage rate, V5: 159
mortgages. *See also* residential
        mortgage loans
    defined, V5: 159
    design of, V5: 159, 160
    European whole loan trading,
        V5: 223–232
    MBS/ABS sectors, V5: 158
mortgage strips, V5: 201–204
mosaic theory, V1: 38–39
most distant futures contract, V6: 282
motels/hotels: investment in, V4: 569,
    573–574
Motorola, Inc., V4: 360–361, 361n6
moving average (MA)
    autoregressive moving-average
        models (ARMA), V1: 394–395
    forecasting, moving-average time
        series models, V1: 387–389
    moving-average forecasting,
        V1: 387–389
    n-period, V1: 385–386
    simple, V1: 385–386, 387n22

nonagency securities, V5: 204, 205
non-amortizing collateral, ABS, V5: 240
noncash charges: free cash flow, V4: 354, 359–363
noncash costs in stock index futures, V6: 107n46
non-compete agreements, loyalty standard, V1: 71
nonconforming mortgage, V5: 164
noncontrolling interest, V2: 32, 35
nonconventional cash flow, V3: 11–12
non-covariance-stationary time series, V1: 363
nondeliverable forwards (NDFs), V6: 6
nondiversifiable risk, V4: 137
non-dividend-paying company, V4: 316
nonhomogeneous subsidiaries, V2: 36–39, 46
nonlinearity
 among variables, V1: 215–218
 parameters, V1: 234n26
nonmonetary assets, V2: 165–167, 165n5
nonmonetary benefits, V6: 87–88
nonoperating assets: firm value, V4: 393
nonparallel yield curves shifts, V5: 59–60
non-pay-related benefit plans, V2: 119
nonpension benefits, V2: 136
non-profit-making activities: allowance of, V1: 602
non-public companies: FAS 123(R), V2: 151–152
nonpublic information. *See* material nonpublic information
nonrecourse loans, V5: 206
nonrecurring items
 accounting for, V4: 523
 cash flow analysis, V2: 283
 income statement adjustment/analysis, V2: 273–275
nonstationarity
 defined, V1: 323
 time series, V1: 400n41
 unit root test of, V1: 380–384
nontariff barriers, V1: 487
NOPAT. *See* net operating profit after taxes (NOPAT)
NOPLAT. *See* net operating profit less adjusted taxes (NOPLAT)
normal backwardation, V6: 92
normal contango, V6: 92
normal earnings per share, V4: 418
normalization of earnings
 defined, V2: 269–270
 in economic cycle, V2: 275
 income statement adjustment/analysis, V2: 269–275, 275

normalized earnings per share (EPS), V4: 418–420
normal market price of gasoline, V1: 466
normal probability distribution: Black-Scholes-Merton model, V6: 188–190
normal yield curves, V5: 57
Nortel Networks, V3: 154, 174
North American Free Trade Association (NAFTA), V1: 473, 484, 494
notation
 options, V6: 146
 T-bill futures, V6: 93
 time-series data, V1: 231n18
notational amounts, V5: 64, 189, 268
notational IO, V5: 189
notch, rating, V5: 8n6
notes payable: "off-balance sheet" red flags, V2: 97
notice day, V6: 292
notional amount, V6: 299
notional coupon, V6: 285
notional principal
 cap/floor agreements, V6: 306
 derivative instruments, V6: 299
 interest rate options, V6: 141
not meaningful (NM), V4: 421
Novartis, V3: 163; V6: 437–438, 452, 454
n-period moving average, V1: 385–386
NPM. *See* net profit margin (NPM)
NPV. *See* net present value (NPV)
NPV to capital ratio, V4: 555
null hypothesis, V1: 226–227, 277–279
NYSE. *See* New York Stock Exchange (NYSE)

O
Oakwood Homeloans Ltd., V5: 232
OAS. *See* option-adjusted spread (OAS)
objectives
 client
  duties to client, V1: 49
  suitability standard, V1: 62
 corporate governance, V3: 193
 investment portfolio management, V6: 501–506
objectivity. *See* independence and objectivity
OCC. *See* Options Clearing Corporation (OCC)
Occidental Petroleum Corporation, V4: 281–282
Occupational Safety and Health Administration (OSHA), V1: 455, 456
OECD. *See* Organization for Economic Cooperation and Development (OECD)

OECD Principles of Corporate Governance, V3: 164
off-balance-sheet assets/liabilities
 accounting standards, V4: 118
 book value, V4: 446
 free cash flow, V4: 515, 519
"off-balance sheet" red flags, V2: 96–97. *See also* special purpose entities (SPEs)
offer price, V1: 526; V4: 48
offers
 M&A, V3: 259–260, 286–289
 post-offer defense mechanisms, V3: 265–269
 pre-offer defense mechanisms, V3: 263–265
 quotes and spreads in, V1: 526–528
 tender offers, V3: 153, 262, 262n6
office building: investment in, V4: 568, 570–572
official settlement accounts, V1: 501
off-market forward contracts, V6: 239
off-market FRA, V6: 22
offsetting
 defined-benefit standard, V2: 130
 futures contracts, V6: 60
off the run instrument, V6: 16
off-the-run Treasury issues, V5: 61, 63
OIS. *See* overnight index swap (OIS)
Old Rule (Prudent Man Rule), V1: 184–187
OLS. *See* ordinary least squares (OLS)
omitted variable bias, V1: 310–312
180-day LIBOR, V6: 15–16
one-factor model, embedded-option bonds valuation, V5: 97
"one" option, V6: 135
one-period ahead forecast, V1: 367–368
one-period binomial model, V6: 168–173
one-tailed test, V1: 286n23
one third rule, V1: 466–467
one-year cap, V6: 210n41
on-the-run Treasury issues, V5: 61, 63, 286, 292
on-the-run yield curve, V5: 106, 107, 114
open-end funds, V4: 77
open-end HELs, V5: 247
open market, V3: 153
open outcry (*criée*) system, V4: 48
open-skies laws, V4: 137
operating breakeven, V3: 112–115
operating cash flow
 analytical procedure summary, V2: 24
 credit analysis, V5: 16
operating cycles: credit analysis, V5: 12
operating income, V3: 101–107
operating leverage, degree of, V3: 105

oversight committee on the board of directors, V3: 208–209
overspending, V3: 61
over-the-counter (OTC) markets
   American depository receipts (ADRs), V4: 72
   bid-ask quotes, V1: 526
   commodity options, V6: 144
   options, V6: 134–135
   swaps, V6: 223
over-the-counter (OTC) options
   defined, V6: 131–132
   exchange traded options, V6: 296
   interest rate, V6: 298–299
overweighted economic sectors, V6: 500
Owens Corning Corporation, V3: 116
owner-of-record date, V3: 155
ownership
   accounting methods, V2: 10
   real estate, V4: 565
   reporting changes in, V2: 37–38

P
PAC. *See* planned amortization class (PAC)
Pacific Stock Exchange, V6: 133
package
   of cash market instruments, V6: 303–305
   of forward contracts, V6: 302–303
   of futures contracts, V6: 302–303
   of interest rate options, V6: 307–308
"Pac-Man," V3: 267
paid-in capital: FASB on control, V2: 33
pairs arbitrage, V4: 29n22
panel data and analysis, V1: 231n17
parallel yield curves shifts, V5: 59, 60
parameters
   consistency, V1: 293–294
   instability, V1: 255
   linear regression, V1: 231
   nonlinearity, V1: 234n26
par coupon curves, V5: 63
Parental Loans for Undergraduate Students (PLUS), V5: 258
parent company support agreements, V5: 10
parent currency, V2: 162–163
"parent-only" financial statements, V2: 31, 45–46
Paris Bourse, V4: 47
parity, V4: 175–176
parity value of convertible security, V5: 132
Parmalat, V3: 199
Parmalat Finanziaria SpA, V2: 216
parsimonious modeling, V1: 309
partial duration, V5: 76

partial regression coefficients, V1: 277–278
partial slope coefficients, V1: 278
participation certificate (PC), V5: 164n1
parties to securitization, V5: 235–237
partnerships, V3: 194, 195
par value, V5: 165
   stock splits, V3: 148
par yield curves, V5: 70–73
passive investment strategy, V6: 448–449, 497
passive management, V1: 281; V6: 378
passive portfolios, V4: 71. *See also* active portfolios
   construction, V6: 475
   management, V6: 378
   as strategy, V6: 467–469
pass-through security, V4: 90
passthrough structures, V5: 260. *See also* mortgage passthrough securities
past values, smoothing, V1: 385–386
patents, V4: 137
patterns in international trade, V1: 474–475
Paxon Communication Corp., V4: 200
payable date, V3: 155
payables: stretching and financing, V2: 216–218
payback period
   capital budgeting, V3: 15–17, 28
   discounted, V3: 17
payer options, V6: 320
payer swaption, V6: 259, 263
payment
   dates for
      dividends, V3: 154, 155–156
      for swaps, V6: 223
   M&A, V3: 259–260
   restrictions for dividends, V3: 160
   stock vs. asset purchase, V3: 258
   structure of
      credit card receivable-backed securities, V5: 260
      home equity loans (HEL), V5: 249–251
payment chronology of dividends, V3: 154–156
payment-in-kind (PIK) bonds
   high-yield corporate debt, V5: 27, 28
payoffs
   defined, V6: 146
   swaptions, V6: 260–262
payoff values
   options, V6: 146–151, 202
   synthetic forward contract, V6: 206
payout ratio
   defined, V3: 168

dividends and taxes, V3: 179
   target, V3: 168–170
pay-related benefit plans, V2: 119
PBO. *See* projected benefit obligations (PBO)
P/BV. *See* price to book value (P/BV)
PC. *See* participation certificate (PC)
PCP. *See* Professional Conduct Program (PCP) (CFA Institute)
PE. *See* price to earnings (P/E) ratio
pecking order theory, V3: 126
peer company multiples
   comparables for valuation, V4: 430–433
   P/E ratio, V4: 430–433
PEG. *See* price/earnings to growth (PEG) ratio
peg date, V5: 18
penalties, prepayment, V5: 162
penalty periods for mortgage prepayment, V5: 162
pension accounting: accounting standards, V4: 119
pension fund performance: factors explaining, V1: 271–273
pension fund RANVA: predicting, V1: 279–281
pension liability, V4: 519
pension plans, V6: 493
pensions. *See also* retirement benefit accounting
   costs/expenses: defined-benefit standard, V2: 130–131, 130n8
   defined, V2: 119
   liability/obligation, V2: 121n5, 123
PepsiCo Mexico, V2: 188–189, 190–191, 192
P/E ratio. *See* price to earnings (P/E) ratio
percentage ownership, V2: 10n1
percents of bond/collateral call, V5: 246
perfect association, V1: 216n4
perfect capital market, V3: 118, 118n13
perfect collinearity, V1: 279n15, 304
perfect market timing, V6: 470
performance
   analysis and disclosures, V2: 247–249
   ANOVA, V1: 250–252
   appraisal of, V6: 500
   attributions, V6: 500
   company, V4: 14, 17–22
   economic forecasting, V4: 17
   FAS 123(R), V2: 149, 154, 156–157
   financial forecasting, V4: 14, 17–22
   forecast AR models, V1: 371–373
   guarantee of futures exchange, V6: 58–59

LOCOM method, V2: 11, 12–13
market method, 12; V2: 11, 13
U.S. Accounting Standards,
    V2: 13–17
Securities Act (1933), V2: 252
*Securities and Exchange Commission,
    Dirks v.,* V1: 39
Securities and Exchange Commission
    (SEC). *See also* corporate
    governance
accounting standards, V4: 118
American depository receipts
    (ADRs), V4: 72–73
brokerage deregulation, V1: 461
*Dirks v. Securities and Exchange
    Commission,* V1: 39
disclosures and accounting scandal,
    V2: 241–242
exchange-listed options, V6: 143–144
FAS 123(R), V2: 147–148
Form DEF 14A, V3: 204
Form 20-F, V4: 73
Form 10-K, V4: 15n8, 123
hedge fund fraud, V4: 614
on hyperinflationary economies,
    V2: 193
international dividend forms,
    V3: 154
international information and
    GAAP, V4: 123
international valuation, V4: 473–474
margin requirements, V6: 61
Mitchell Hutchins case study,
    V1: 181–182
regulation, V1: 456
restatements and reporting quality,
    V2: 228, 230
SAB 107, V2: 149, 150
safe harbor protections, V1: 120n2
SPEs, V2: 93–94
trade allocation practices,
    V1: 177–179
Securities and Futures Authority,
    V6: 59
Securities Exchange Act (1934),
    V3: 273
disclosure, V2: 252
safe harbor protections, V1: 120,
    120n1
securities firms, V6: 300
securities laws, V3: 273
securities offerings, V3: 259
securitization
ABS process, V5: 234–247
basic transactions, V5: 234–235
bonds, V5: 237–239
call provisions, V5: 246
collateral classifications, V5: 239–241
credit analysis, V5: 33–34

credit enhancements, V5: 241–245,
    241–246
defined, V5: 233
Europe: whole loan trading, vs.,
    V5: 225
parties to, V5: 235–237
transaction structure classifications,
    V5: 239–241
security analysis
defined, V3: 8
Treynor-Black model, V6: 474–482
Security Analysis (Graham and Dodd),
    V4: 10, 415
security market line (SML)
capital budgeting, V3: 53–55
CAPM, V6: 436
defined, V3: 53; V6: 362
security returns: global risk factors in,
    V4: 154–158
security/sector concentration: hedge
    fund risks, V4: 623–624
security selection, V6: 474–482, 500
*SEC v. Beacon Hill Asset Management,
    L.L.C.,* V4: 614
segmentation of markets
efficient markets, V6: 433
ICAPM, V6: 459
segment reporting
data analysis, intercorporate
    investments, V2: 46–56
disclosure, V2: 47–49
in earnings and risk estimates,
    V2: 52–54
geographic, V2: 52–53
history of, V2: 46–47
industry segment illustration,
    V2: 49–52
management discussion and
    analysis, V2: 53
use and limitations of, V2: 53–54
segregation
of capital expenditures, V2: 281–283
of operating vs. investment
    performance, V2: 24
self-assessment of board of directors,
    V3: 206–207, 220
self-dealing: loyalty standard, V1: 70–71
self-interest, V4: 566
sellers
options, V6: 293, 298
parties to securitization, V5: 236
quality, credit analysis, V5: 31–32
sell orders, V4: 51
sell-side analysts, V4: 32n26; V6: 494
semiactive approach, V6: 498
Sengupta, Partha, V5: 23–24
senior bonds classes, V5: 238–239
senior debt: high-yield corporate debt,
    V5: 27, 28

senior prepayment percentage, V5: 245
senior-subordinate security
    class/structure, V5: 27–28,
    238–239, 244–245
senior tranche, V6: 318
sensitivity
CAPM, V6: 436
option prices, V6: 167
sensitivity analysis
FCFF/FCFE valuations, V4: 382–384
international frequency of use,
    V3: 28
risk analysis, V3: 47
Separate Trading of Registered
    Interest and Principal Securities
    (STRIPS)
coupon strips, V5: 61–62
mortgage strips, V5: 201–204
PO strips, V5: 201–204
stripped mortgage-backed
    securities, V5: 201–204
separation theorem
CAPM, V6: 435
ICAPM, V6: 443–444
sequential-pay tranches, V5: 178–183
serial correlation, V5: 83n25
consequences of, V1: 300–301
correcting for, V1: 303–304
error detection in AR models,
    V1: 363–367
multiple linear regression analysis
    and models, V1: 300–304,
    307–308
testing for, V1: 293–295
service, levels of, and fair dealing
    standard, V1: 58
service cost
as nonpension expense, V2: 136
as pension expense, V2: 130, 131
servicers
parties to securitization, V5: 236
quality, V5: 31–32
services: capital budgeting of, V3: 10
servicing
ABS loans, V5: 235
European whole loan trading,
    V5: 232
fee, residential mortgages, V5: 162
spread, V5: 162
settlement
cap/floor agreements, V6: 306
credit events, V6: 314
date for, V6: 223, 282
forward contracts, V6: 6
futures contracts, V6: 59, 62, 65,
    239n15
mark-to-market, V6: 66
mortgage passthrough securities,
    V5: 164–165

sovereign bonds, V5: 37–38
sovereign risk premium, V4: 240–241
SOX. *See* Sarbanes-Oxley Act of 2002
   (SAO or SOX)
SPC. *See* Standards of Practice Council
   (SPC) (CFA Institute)
special effects, V5: 63n6
special event risk: capacity to pay,
   V5: 10
special (extra) dividends, V3: 227–228
specialization, V1: 430
special purpose entities (SPEs)
   accounting standards, V4: 117
   company evaluation and "red flags,"
      V2: 96–97
   defined, V4: 20n14
   EITF on, V2: 93–94
   FASB on, V2: 104
   improper accounting, as red flag,
      V2: 232
   joint ventures, V2: 40
   variable interest entity (VIE),
      V2: 104–110
special purpose vehicles (SPVs). *See also*
   special purpose entities (SPEs)
   guarantees, V5: 242n4
   issuance, V5: 235
   as issuer, V5: 32
specific risk, V6: 436
speculation
   in currency, V1: 538–542
   M&A activity, V3: 285n29
speculative value, V6: 147
speed of prepayment. *See* Public
   Securities Association (PSA)
speedup in productivity, V1: 435–436
Spentzos, George, V6: 323–324
SPEs. *See* special purpose entities
   (SPEs)
spin-offs, V3: 291
   defined, V4: 11n3
   in equity valuation, V4: 11
split-offs, V3: 291
split-rate taxation of dividends,
   V3: 157, 158
sponsored ADRs, V4: 72
spot exchange, V1: 536–537
spot price
   defined, V6: 19
   futures prices, V6: 91–92
spot rate curve
   benchmark interest rates, V5: 101
   embedded-option bond valuation,
      V5: 100
   LIBOR, V5: 67
spot rates, V1: 536
   arbitrage-free value, V5: 96
   maturities, key, V5: 76–79
   relative value of securities, V5: 101

U.S. Treasury curve, V5: 61–63
   zero-volatility spreads, V5: 284
spread determinants on new high-
   yield bonds, V1: 291–293
spreads. *See also* option-adjusted
   spread (OAS)
   defined, V6: 226n2
   issuer-specific benchmarks,
      V5: 103–104
   relative value of securities,
      V5: 100–101
   swap, V6: 233
   swap spread, V5: 65–66
spreadsheet modeling
   capital budgeting, V3: 39–41
   dividend discount model (DDM),
      V4: 298, 321–322
   dividend forecasting, V4: 330–331
Sprint, V4: 96
spurious correlation, V1: 218
spurious regression, V1: 400n41
SPVs. *See* special purpose vehicles
   (SPVs)
squeeze on profits, V4: 136
stability
   dividend policies, V3: 168
   protectionism, V1: 491
stabilization stage, industry life cycle,
   V4: 131
Staff Accounting Bulletin (SAB):
   No. 107, V2: 149, 150
staggered board, V3: 264
stakeholders
   corporate governance, V5: 21–22
   defined, V5: 21
   equitable treatment, V3: 226–227
   rights of, and Corporate
      Governance Score, V5: 25
   role of, V3: 227
stand-alone risk analysis
   capital budgeting, V3: 46–52
   scenario risk analysis, V3: 48
   sensitivity analysis, V3: 47
   simulation (Monte Carlo) analysis,
      V3: 48–52
standard absorption rate (SAR)
   FAS 123(R), V2: 154
   stock-based compensation
      standards, V2: 157
standard capital asset pricing model
   (CAPM), V6: 434–439
standard deviation
   defined, V1: 214; V6: 502
   embedded-option bonds valuation,
      V5: 97
   hedge funds, V4: 625–628
   many-asset cases: portfolio theory,
      V6: 346–353
   market timing, V6: 471–472

risk-free assets: portfolio theory,
   V6: 353–362
risky assets: portfolio theory,
   V6: 342–353
three-asset cases: portfolio theory,
   V6: 343–346
two-asset cases: portfolio theory,
   V6: 334–342
variance reduction techniques,
   V5: 290n2
yield volatility, V5: 81–85, 83–85
standard error of estimate
   computing, V1: 237–238
   linear regression, V1: 236–238
standardized beta, V6: 389
standardized credit scoring, V5: 226
standardized unexpected earnings
   (SUE), V4: 475
standard of living, V1: 609
Standard Oil (New Jersey), V1: 464
Standard & Poor's (S&P)
   cash flow analysis, V5: 14, 16–17
   Corporate Governance Score, V5: 25
   credit ratings, V5: 6
   debt ratings, V3: 129–130, 161–162
   *Directory of Registered Investment
      Advisors*, V6: 492
   funds from operations, V5: 15–16
   global indexes, V4: 61–62
   industry group dividend yield,
      V3: 161–162
   returns and regression, V1: 281–283
   sector classification, V4: 428–492,
      428n16
   securitization transactions, V5: 33–34
   sovereign bonds, V5: 37–38
   S&P 500/BARRA, V1: 281–283,
      306–307
   S&P 500 Index, V4: 61, 253–269,
      603–604, 619; V6: 13, 77
   equity swaps, V6: 234
   S&P Midcap 400 futures contracts,
      V6: 78
   S&P 500 monthly returns,
      V1: 388–389
   S&P 500 Small Cap 600 Index,
      V6: 237
Standards of Practice Council (SPC)
   (CFA Institute), V1: 7, 10–11
Standards of Practice Handbook
   AIMR, V4: 38
   CFA Institute
      Code of Ethics, V1: 8
      revisions to, V1: 6–8
      trade allocation practice, V1: 178
Standards of Professional Conduct
   (CFA Institute), V5: 22–23; V6:
   510. *See also* Research Objectivity
   Standards (CFA Institute)

effects of omitting, V1: 310–312
linear combination of, V1: 288n25
linear relations, V1: 213–215
nonlinear relations, V1: 215–218
scaling, V1: 316–318
variance
defined, V1: 214
many-asset cases: portfolio theory,
V6: 346–353
market model estimates, mean-
variance analysis, V6: 368–369
mean-variance analysis, V6: 333
prediction intervals, V1: 252–254
of random variable, V6: 502
risk-free assets: portfolio theory,
V6: 353–362
three-asset cases: portfolio theory,
V6: 343–346
variance reduction techniques,
V5: 290n2
variation, coefficient of. *See* coefficient
of variation (R^2)
variation margin, V6: 63, 283
VAT. *See* value-added tax (VAT)
VBM. *See* value-based metrics (VBM)
VBO. *See* vested benefit obligation
(VBO)
vega
option volatility, V6: 196–198,
200–202
price sensitivity, V6: 167
vendors: payables, stretching and
financing, V2: 216–218
VER. *See* voluntary export restraint
(VER)
Vertex, V5: 232
vertical integration
defined, V3: 252
value chain, V4: 130
vertical mergers, V3: 249
vested benefit obligation (VBO),
V2: 125–127
vesting: FAS 123(R), V2: 149, 150, 153,
155
Veterans Administration (VA)
manufactured housing-backed
securities, V5: 252
mortgage insurance, V5: 159
VIE. *See* variable interest entity (VIE)
violations
knowledge of law standards,
V1: 16–17
of regression assumptions,
V1: 293–308
supervisors, responsibilities of, V1: 78
Virt-x, V4: 52
visibility of company operations,
V4: 298
VIX Index, V4: 96

Vodafone, V3: 248
volatility
arbitrage pricing theory (APT),
V6: 382–384
binomial interest rate tree,
V5: 107–109
Black-Scholes-Merton model,
V6: 187, 196–198, 200–202
callable bonds, V5: 117–118
closed-end country funds, V4: 77
forecasting, V5: 85–88
historical view, V5: 80–85
historical vs. implied, V5: 85
implied volatility, V6: 200–202
leverage, V4: 94–95
Monte Carlo simulation, V5: 286
option price effects, V6: 167
price volatility in futures contracts,
V4: 70
risk objectives, V6: 502
of yields, V5: 80–88
Volcker, Paul, V4: 618
volume
of international trade, V1: 475
trading, future contracts, V6: 69–70
of transactions, V4: 56–57
volume-weighted average price
(VWAP)
execution costs, V4: 65, 66–67
voluntary disclosure. *See* disclosure
voluntary export restraint (VER),
V1: 487–488
voting, V1: 50
proxy votes of shareholders,
V3: 215–216
takeover defenses, V3: 265
VWAP. *See* volume-weighted average
price (VWAP)

W
WAC. *See* weighted average coupon
rate (WAC)
WACC. *See* weighted average cost of
capital (WACC)
wage rates
classical growth theory, V1: 438–439
international, V1: 473–474
Walgreens, V4: 250–252
Wall Street Journal
extra dividends, V3: 146n1
futures contracts, V6: 70, 71–72
Wal-Mart, V1: 466; V2: 247; V3: 106,
163; V4: 182, 190, 248
Walt Disney Company, V2: 107–108
WAM. *See* weighted average maturity
(WAM)
warehouses: investment in,
V4: 568–569, 572
warranted price multiple, V4: 414n3

waste disposal firms, V4: 190
Waste Management, V2: 247
weakly stationary, V1: 362n10
wealth
suitability standard, V1: 61
transferring with share repurchase,
V3: 150–151
weather
forward contracts, V6: 18
options, V6: 145
swaps, V6: 23
Webvan.com, V3: 117
weighted average: binomial model
price, V6: 175n24
weighted average cost of capital
(WACC)
capital budgeting, V3: 55
capital structure, V3: 117, 119–120
company value, V1: 245
defined, V3: 117; V4: 286
discounted cash flow (DCF)
analysis, V3: 278–279
economic value added (EVA),
V4: 541–542
emerging markets, V4: 224–231, 240
formula, V3: 117
franchise factor, V4: 247
free cash flows, V4: 350–352
prediction intervals, V1: 253–254
Proposition II without taxes,
V3: 119–120
residual dividend approach, V3: 166
weighted average coupon rate (WAC)
CMOs, V5: 179
credit card receivable-backed
securities, V5: 261
Monte Carlo simulation, V5: 291
mortgage passthrough securities,
V5: 163, 165
prepayments, V5: 169–172
weighted average life, V5: 173, 241
weighted average maturity (WAM)
CMOs, V5: 179
collateral cash flows, V5: 241
mortgage passthrough securities,
V5: 163
prepayments, V5: 168–172, 169
well-diversified portfolios, CAPM,
V6: 436–437
West Point Pepperell, V5: 29
whistleblowing, V1: 71
White-corrected standard errors,
V1: 299n44
white knight, V3: 267–268
white squire, V3: 268
whole-loan sales, V5: 205. *See also*
European whole loan sales
wild card option, V6: 292
Williams, John Burr, V4: 7, 276, 297